REVIEWING Investor Protection, Insider Trading, and Corporate Governance

Dale Emerson served as the chief financial officer for Reliant Electric Company, a distributor of electricity serving portions of Montana and North Dakota. Reliant was in the final stages of planning a takeover of Dakota Gasworks, Inc., a natural gas distributor that operated solely within North Dakota. Emerson went on a weekend fishing trip with his uncle, Ernest Wallace. Emerson mentioned to Wallace that he had been putting in a lot of extra hours at the office planning a takeover of Dakota Gasworks. On returning from the fishing trip, Wallace met with a broker from Chambers Investments and purchased $20,000 of Reliant stock. Three weeks later, Reliant made a tender offer to Dakota Gasworks stockholders and purchased 57 percent of Dakota Gasworks stock. Over the next two weeks, the price of Reliant stock rose 72 percent before leveling out. Wallace then sold his Reliant stock for a gross profit of $14,400. Using the information presented in the chapter, answer the following questions.

1 Would registration with the SEC be required for Dakota Gasworks securities? Why or why not?

2 Did Emerson violate Section 10(b) of the Securities Exchange Act of 1934 and SEC Rule 10b-5? Why or why not?

3 What theory or theories might a court use to hold Wallace liable for insider trading?

4 Under the Sarbanes-Oxley Act of 2002, who would be required to certify the accuracy of financial statements filed with the SEC?

THE INTERNET: Exercises, Enrichment, and Support

ON THE WEB

These margin features give specific Uniform Resource Locators (URLs), or Internet addresses, concerning topics discussed in the text. You will find over one hundred such references throughout this text. Two examples are shown here.

> **ON THE WEB**
>
> An excellent Web site for information on employee benefits—including the full text of relevant statutes, such as the FMLA and COBRA, as well as case law and current articles—is BenefitsLink. Go to www.benefitslink.com/index.shtml.

> **ON THE WEB**
>
> The U.S. Department of Justice offers an impressive collection of statistics on crime, including cyber crime, at the following Web site: www.ojp.usdoj.gov/bjs.

ONLINE ACTIVITIES

Included at the end of every chapter are at least two Internet exercises that students can perform to learn more about topics covered in the chapter. These exercises, as well as interactive quiz questions, are available on the *Business Law Today: The Essentials,* Eighth Edition, Web site at:

academic.cengage.com/blaw/blt

Cengage Advantage Books
The Essentials
Text & Summarized Cases · E-Commerce · Legal · Ethical · International Environment

BUSINESS LAW TODAY

MILLER / JENTZ

Eighth Edition

For this edition of *Business Law Today: The Essentials,* we have redesigned and streamlined the text's Web site so that users can easily locate the resources they seek.

Business Law Today:
The Essentials

8TH Edition

TEXT & SUMMARIZED CASES
E-Commerce, Legal, Ethical, and International Environment

Roger LeRoy Miller
Institute for University Studies
Arlington, Texas

Gaylord A. Jentz
Herbert D. Kelleher
Emeritus Professor in Business Law
MSIS Department
University of Texas at Austin

SOUTH-WESTERN
CENGAGE Learning

Australia • Brazil • Japan • Korea • Mexico • Singapore • Spain • United Kingdom • United States

SOUTH-WESTERN
CENGAGE Learning

8ᵀᴴ Edition

Business Law Today:
The Essentials

TEXT & SUMMARIZED CASES
E-Commerce, Legal, Ethical, and International Environment

Roger LeRoy Miller   Gaylord A. Jentz

COPYRIGHT © 2008
South-Western, a part of Cengage Learning.

Printed in the United States of America
3 4 5   09 08

ISBN-13: 978–0–324–65454–7
ISBN-10: 0–324–65454–5

Library of Congress Control Number: 2007935133

For more information, contact:

South-Western Cengage Learning
5191 Natorp Boulevard
Mason, Ohio, 45040
USA

Or you can visit our Internet site at **academic.cengage.com/blaw**.

Vice President and Editorial Director
Jack Calhoun

Publisher, Business Law, and Accounting
Rob Dewey

Acquisition Editor
Steve Silverstein

Senior Developmental Editor
Jan Lamar

Executive Marketing Manager
Lisa L. Lysne

Marketing Manager
Jenny Garamy

Production Manager
Bill Stryker

Technology Project Manager
Rob Ellington

Manufacturing Buyer
Kevin Kluck

Compositor
Parkwood Composition
New Richmond, WI

Printer
Quebecor World Versailles

Senior Art Director
Michelle Kunkler

Internal Designer
Bill Stryker

Cover Designer
Diane Gliebe/Design Matters

Web site Coordinator
Brian Courter

Cover Images
© Getty Images, Inc.

INTERNATIONAL LOCATIONS

ASIA (including India)
Cengage Learning
www.cengageasia.com
tel: (65) 6410 1200

AUSTRALIA/NEW ZEALAND
Cengage Learning
www.cengage.com.au
tel: (61) 3 9685 4111

LATIN AMERICA
Cengage Learning
www.cengage.com.mx
tel: +52 (55) 1500 6000

Represented in Canada by Nelson
Education, Ltd.
www.nelson.com
tel: (416) 752 9100 / (800) 668 0671

UK/EUROPE/MIDDLE
EAST/AFRICA
Cengage Learning
www.cengage.co.uk
tel: (44) 207 067 2500

SPAIN (includes Portugal)
Cengage Learning
http://www.paraninfo.es

Contents in Brief

Contents*

*Consult the inside front and back covers of this book for easy reference to the many special features in this textbook.

Preface to the Instructor

We have always felt that business law and the legal environment should be an exciting, contemporary, and interesting course. We believe that *Business Law Today: The Essentials*, Eighth Edition, imparts this excitement to your students. We have spent a great deal of effort in giving this book a visual appeal that will encourage students to learn the law. We have also worked hard to make sure that *Business Law Today: The Essentials* continues its established tradition of being the most up-to-date text on the market. The law presented in the Eighth Edition of *Business Law Today: The Essentials* includes new statutes, regulations, and cases, as well as the most recent developments in cyberlaw.

You will find that coverage of traditional business law has not been sacrificed in the process of creating this text. Additionally, *Business Law Today: The Essentials* explicitly addresses the American Assembly of Collegiate Schools of Business's (AACSB's) broad array of curriculum requirements. For example, many of the features and special pedagogical devices in this text focus on the global, political, ethical, social, environmental, technological, and cultural contexts of business law. In addition, critical-thinking skills are reinforced throughout.

WHAT'S NEW TO THE EIGHTH EDITION

Instructors have come to rely on the coverage, accuracy, and applicability of *Business Law Today: The Essentials*. For this edition, we have added a number of features to make the text more practical for today's business environment and to promote critical-thinking skills.

Practical Elements in Every Chapter

For the Eighth Edition of *Business Law Today: The Essentials*, we have added a **special new feature entitled** *Preventing Legal Disputes* in each chapter. These brief features offer practical guidance on steps that businesspersons can take in their daily transactions to avoid legal disputes and litigation. These features are integrated throughout the text as appropriate to the topics being discussed.

In addition, every chapter in the Eighth Edition concludes with an *Application* **feature** that focuses on practical considerations related to the chapter's contents and concludes with a checklist of tips for the businessperson. Many of these features are new or have been substantially revised for this edition. For example, some of the new *Application* features include:

- How Can You Create an Ethical Workplace? (Chapter 2).
- How Can You Protect against Identity Theft? (Chapter 6).
- Establishing an Electronic Communications Policy (Chapter 10).

We have also revised the Internet exercises that conclude each chapter to focus on the practical aspects of doing business in today's global legal environment.

Critical Thinking and Legal Reasoning

Today's business leaders are often required to think "outside the box" when making business decisions. For this reason, **we have added a number of critical-thinking elements for the Eighth Edition** that are designed to challenge students' understanding of the materials beyond simple retention. Your students' critical-thinking and legal-reasoning skills will be increased as they work through the numerous pedagogical devices within the book. Nearly every feature and every case presented in the text conclude with some type of critical-thinking question. These questions include *For Critical Analysis, What If the Facts Were Different? Why Is This Case Important?* and *Why Is This Case Important to Businesspersons?*

In addition, we have also added an entirely new section to the chapter-ending *Questions and Case Problems* that focuses on critical thinking and writing. Questions in that section include *Critical Legal Thinking, Critical Thinking and Writing Assignment for Business,* and *Video Questions,* each of which will be described shortly.

Reviewing Features Added to Every Chapter

For the Eighth Edition of *Business Law Today: The Essentials,* we have added a special new feature at the end of every chapter that helps solidify students' understanding of the chapter materials. Each of these *Reviewing . . .* features presents a hypothetical scenario and then asks a series of questions that require students to identify the issues and apply the legal concepts discussed in the chapter. An instructor can use these features as the basis for a lively in-class discussion or can encourage students to use them for self-study and assessment prior to completing homework assignments. **Suggested answers to the** *Reviewing* **features' questions are available in the** *Instructor's Manual* **and the** *Answers Manual* **that accompany this text.**

New Hypothetical Questions with Sample Answers in Appendix F

In response to those instructors who would like students to have sample answers available for some of the *Questions and Case Problems,* for this edition we have added a special question in each chapter entitled *Hypothetical Question with Sample Answer.* In addition to each chapter providing one *Case Problem with Sample Answer* that is based on an actual case and answered on the text's Web site, students can now also access a sample answer to one hypothetical question per chapter by going to Appendix F at the end of the text. The answers to these questions are also posted on the text's Web site (located at **academic.cengage.com/blaw/blt**). Students can compare their own answers to the answers provided to determine whether they have applied the law correctly and to learn what needs to be included when answering the end-of-chapter *Questions and Case Problems.*

New Streamlined Organization for the Chapter-Ending *Questions and Case Problems*

For the Eighth Edition of *Business Law Today: The Essentials,* we have completely reorganized and streamlined the *Questions and Case Problems* that conclude each chapter. To facilitate assessment, the problems are now divided by subheadings into the following three categories:

1 Hypothetical Scenarios—We begin with a section of *Hypothetical Scenarios,* which present simple situations and ask students to apply the legal concepts from the chapter.

Included in this group of questions is the new *Hypothetical Question with Sample Answer*, discussed previously (for which a sample answer is available in Appendix F of the text and on the Web site).

2 Case Problems—Next are the *Case Problems*, which present the facts of recent cases and ask students to analyze how the law applies. These problems include a *Case Problem with Sample Answer* (that is provided on the text's Web site) and *A Question of Ethics*, the majority of which are new to this edition and based on 2007 cases.

3 Critical Thinking and Writing Assignments—The third subsection consists of the *Critical Thinking and Writing Assignments*, which are designed to enhance critical-thinking skills and include several types of questions that are new to this edition.

- Every chapter includes a *Critical Legal Thinking* question that requires students to think critically about some aspect of the law discussed in the chapter.

- Selected chapters include a *Critical Thinking and Writing Assignment for Business* question that focuses on critical thinking in a business-oriented context.

- Many chapters also include a special *Video Question* under this subheading that directs students to the text's Web site (at **academic.cengage.com/blaw/blt**) to access a video relevant to a topic covered in the chapter (a passcode is required—see the discussion of the Business Law Digital Video Library later in this preface). The students view the video clip, some of which are from Hollywood movies, and then answer a series of questions on how the law applies to the situation depicted in the video.

New Appendix on the Sarbanes-Oxley Act of 2002

In a number of places in this text, we refer to the Sarbanes-Oxley Act of 2002 and the corporate scandals that led to the passage of that legislation. For example, Chapter 2 mentions how the requirements of the Sarbanes-Oxley Act were intended to deter unethical corporate conduct and make certain corporate acts illegal. In Chapter 21, we discuss this act in the context of securities law and corporate governance and present an exhibit (Exhibit 21–4) containing some of the key provisions of the act relating to corporate accountability in securities transactions. In Chapter 25, we discuss whether this act can be applied extraterritorially.

Because the Sarbanes-Oxley Act is a topic of significant concern in today's business climate, for the Eighth Edition, we have added **excerpts and explanatory comments on the Sarbanes-Oxley Act of 2002 as Appendix D.** Students and instructors alike will find it useful to have the provisions of the act immediately available for reference and explained in plain language.

New Bankruptcy Reform Act of 2005 Incorporated

Chapter 16 has been significantly revamped due to the passage of the 2005 bankruptcy reform legislation. Bankruptcy reform has been a topic of major debate for many years. Now that the reform act has been enacted, we have overhauled the content of this chapter to reflect fully the changes. We also include a *Landmark in the Law* feature discussing the 2005 act.

Impact of This Case on Today's Law

Many students are unclear about how some of the older cases presented in this text affect today's courts. We have therefore added a special section for this edition entitled *Impact of This Case on Today's Law.* These sections appear at the end of all *Landmark and Classic Cases* to clarify the relevance of the particular case to modern law.

BUSINESS LAW TODAY: THE ESSENTIALS ON THE WEB

For this edition of *Business Law Today: The Essentials*, we have redesigned and stream-lined the text's Web site so that users can easily locate the resources they seek. When you visit our Web site at **academic.cengage.com/blaw/blt**, you will find a broad array of teaching/learning resources, including the following:

- *Relevant Web Sites* for all of the *Landmark in the Law* features and *Landmark and Classic Cases* that are presented in this text.
- *Sample Answers* to the *Case Problem with Sample Answer*, which appears at the end of every chapter, are posted on the student companion Web site. This problem-answer set is designed to help your students learn how to answer case problems by acquaint-ing them with model answers to selected problems. In addition, we post the answers to the *Hypothetical Questions with Sample Answers* on the Web site as well as in the text (Appendix F).
- *Videos* referenced in the *Video Questions* that appear at the ends of selected chapters of *Business Law Today: The Essentials*, Eighth Edition (available only with a passcode).
- *Practical Internet Exercises* for every chapter in the text (at least two per chapter). The Internet exercises have been refocused to provide more practical information to business law students on topics covered in the chapters and to acquaint students with the legal resources that are available online.
- *Interactive Quizzes* for every chapter in this text that include a number of questions related to each chapter's contents.
- *Key Terms* for every chapter in the text.
- *Flashcards* that provide students with an optional study tool to review the key terms in every chapter.
- *Appendix A: How to Brief Cases and Analyze Case Problems* is featured in the book and is also posted on the Web site.
- *PowerPoint slides* for this edition.
- *Legal Reference Materials* that include a "Statutes" page that offers links to the full text of selected statutes referenced in the text, a Spanish glossary, the text of the appen-dices that were removed for the Eighth Edition, and links to other important legal resources available for free on the Web.
- *Online Legal Research Guide* that offers complete yet brief guidance to using the Internet and evaluating information obtained from the Internet. As an online resource, it now includes hyperlinks to the Web sites discussed for click-through convenience.
- *Court Case Updates* that present summaries of new cases from various West legal publications, all specifically keyed to chapters in this text.

Business Law Digital Video Library

For this edition of *Business Law Today: The Essentials*, we have included special *Video Questions* at the end of selected chapters. Each of these questions directs students to the text's Web site (at **academic.cengage.com/blaw/blt**) to view a video relevant to a topic covered in the chapter. This instruction is followed by a series of questions based on the video. The questions are repeated on the Web site, when the student accesses the video. An access code for the videos can be packaged with each new copy of this textbook for no additional charge. If the Business Law Digital Video Library access did not come packaged with your textbook, it can be purchased online at **digitalvideolibrary.westbuslaw.com**.

These videos can be used as homework assignments, discussion starters, or classroom demonstrations and are useful for generating student interest. Some of the videos are clips from actual movies, such as *The Money Pit* and *Bowfinger*. By watching a video and answering the questions, students will gain an understanding of how the legal concepts they have studied in the chapter apply to the real-life situation portrayed in the video. **Suggested answers for all of the *Video Questions* are given in both the *Instructor's Manual* and the *Answers Manual* that accompany this text.** The videos are part of the *Business Law Digital Video Library*, a compendium of more than sixty-five video scenarios and explanations.

SPECIAL FEATURES AND PEDAGOGY

In addition to the components of the *Business Law Today: The Essentials* teaching/learning package described above, the Eighth Edition offers a number of special features and pedagogical devices, including those described here.

Adapting the Law to the Online Environment

Nearly every chapter in the Eighth Edition contains one of these special features, which examine cutting-edge cyberlaw issues coming before today's courts. Here are some examples of these features:

- Google China (Chapter 2).
- Legal Issues Facing Bloggers and Podcasters (Chapter 5).
- Are Online Fantasy Sports Just Another Form of Real-Life Gambling? (Chapter 8).
- Digital Funds Provide New Opportunities for Money Laundering (Chapter 15).
- New Issues in Online Privacy and Employment Discrimination (Chapter 18).

Each feature concludes with a *For Critical Analysis* section that asks the student to think critically about some facet of the issues discussed in the feature. **Suggested answers to these questions are included in both the *Instructor's Manual* and the *Answers Manual* that accompany this text.**

Landmark in the Law

This feature, which appears in most of the chapters in this edition, discusses a landmark case, statute, or other legal development that has had a significant effect on business law. Each of these features has a section titled **Application to Today's World**, which indicates how the law discussed in the feature affects the legal landscape of today's world. In addition, a **Relevant Web Sites** section is included that directs students to the book's companion Web site for links to additional information available online.

Application

In the Eighth Edition, every chapter has an *Application* feature, which presents the student with some practical advice on how to apply the law discussed in the chapter to real-world business problems. Each *Application* ends with a **Checklist** for the future businessperson on how to avoid legal problems.

Preventing Legal Disputes

As already discussed, these features provide practical information to future businesspersons on how to avoid legal problems. Every chapter includes at least one **Preventing Legal Disputes** feature, integrated as appropriate with the topics being discussed.

Beyond Our Borders

These features give students an awareness of the global legal environment by indicating how international laws or the laws of other nations deal with specific legal concepts or topics being discussed in the chapter. Each of these features concludes with a *For Critical Analysis* question. **Suggested answers to these questions are included in both the *Instructor's Manual* and the *Answers Manual* that accompany this text.**

Ethical Issues

In addition to a chapter on ethics, chapter-ending ethical questions, and the **Ethical Considerations** following selected cases presented in this text, we have included special features called **Ethical Issues**. These features, which are closely integrated with the text, open with a question addressing an ethical dimension of the topic being discussed. Each *Ethical Issue* has been given a number so that it can be easily located for review or discussion.

Reviewing Hypothetical Features

As discussed previously, the **Reviewing** features present a hypothetical scenario and ask a series of questions that require students to identify the issues and apply the legal concepts discussed in the chapter. Each chapter concludes with one of these features, which are intended to help students review the chapter materials in a simple and interesting way.

Case Presentation and Format

For this edition, we have carefully selected recent cases for each chapter that not only provide on-point illustrations of the legal principles discussed in the chapter but also are of high interest to students. The cases are numbered sequentially for easy referencing in class discussions, homework assignments, and examinations. The vast majority of cases in this text are new to the Eighth Edition.

Each case is presented in a special format, which begins with the case title and citation (including parallel citations). Whenever possible, we also include a URL, just below the case citation, that can be used to access the case online (a footnote to the URL explains how to find the specific case at that Web site). We then briefly outline the facts of the dispute, the legal issue presented, and the court's decision. To enhance student understanding, we paraphrase the reason for the court's decision.

Each case concludes with one of the following:

■ *For Critical Analysis* These questions require students to think about the court's holding from a variety of different perspectives. For instance, a student might be asked to consider the economic or social ramifications of a particular ruling. **Suggested answers to these questions are included in both the *Instructor's Manual* and the *Answers Manual* that accompany this text.**

■ *What If the Facts Were Different?* These questions ask the student to decide whether a specified change in the facts of the case would alter the outcome of the case and how. **Suggested answers to these questions are included in both the *Instructor's Manual* and the *Answers Manual* that accompany this text.**

■ *Why Is This Case Important?* and *Why Is This Case Important to Businesspersons?* These questions, which are answered in the text, clearly set forth the importance of the court's decision in the specific case in the legal environment. Some of these questions specifically focus on why businesspersons today should heed the court's ruling in a particular case.

■ *Impact of This Case on Today's Law* As mentioned earlier, for *Landmark and Classic Cases*, we have added these sections to clarify the relevance of the case to modern law. We also have a section titled *Relevant Web Sites* at the conclusion of each *Landmark and Classic Case* that directs students to the Web site for additional online resources.

Other Pedagogical Devices within Each Chapter

■ *Learning Objectives* (a series of brief questions at the beginning of each chapter designed to provide a framework for the student as he or she reads through the chapter).

■ *Chapter Outline* (an outline of the chapter's first-level headings).

■ *Margin definitions.*

■ *Margin "On the Web" features* directing students to relevant Web sites where they will find online articles, statutes, or other legal or information sources concerning a topic being discussed in the text.

■ *Highlighted and numbered examples illustrating legal principles* (we have added more for this edition to better clarify legal concepts).

■ *URLs for cases*—Whenever possible, we have included URLs that can be used to access the cases presented in the text of *Business Law Today: The Essentials*. When a URL is available, it appears just below the case citation.

■ *Quotations.*

■ *Exhibits and forms.*

■ *Concept Summaries*—Whenever key areas of law need additional emphasis, we provide a concept summary to add clarity.

■ *Photographs (with critical-thinking questions).*

Chapter-Ending Pedagogy

■ *Key Terms* (with appropriate page references).

■ *Chapter Summary* (in graphic format with page references).

■ *For Review* (the questions set forth in the chapter-opening *Learning Objectives* section are again presented to aid the student in reviewing the chapter. Answers to the even-numbered questions for each chapter are provided in Appendix E).

■ *Questions and Case Problems* (including three new subsections—*Hypothetical Scenarios*, *Case Problems*, and *Critical Thinking and Writing Assignments*).

■ *Hypothetical Question with Sample Answer* (as discussed earlier, each chapter contains one hypothetical factual situation, and we provide a sample answer for students in Appendix F of the text and on the Web site).

■ *Case Problem with Sample Answer* (as discussed earlier, each chapter contains one of these case problems, for which the answer has been provided on the text's Web site at **academic.cengage.com/blaw/blt**).

■ *A Question of Ethics.*

■ *Critical Legal Thinking.*

■ *Critical Thinking and Writing Assignment for Business* (in selected chapters).

■ *Video Question* (in selected chapters).

■ *Online Activities* (including *Practical Internet Exercises* and *Interactive Quizzes* for each chapter).

Appendices

To help students learn how to find and analyze case law, we have included a special appendix at the end of Chapter 1. There, your students will find information, including an exhibit, on how to read case citations, how to locate cases in case reporters, and what the different components of URLs (Internet addresses) mean. *The appendix to Chapter 1 also presents an annotated sample court case to help your students understand how to read and understand the cases presented within this text.*

We have included at the end of the book the following set of appendices (Appendices D and F are new to the Eighth Edition):

A How to Brief Cases and Analyze Case Problems (also now available on the Web site)

B The Constitution of the United States

C Articles 2 and 2A of the Uniform Commercial Code

D The Sarbanes-Oxley Act of 2002 (Excerpts and Explanatory Comments)

E Answers to Even-Numbered *For Review* Questions

F Sample Answers for End-of-Chapter *Hypothetical Questions with Sample Answer* (also available on the Web site)

Those appendices from the Seventh Edition that we did not include in this edition are now posted on the text's Web site (located at **academic.cengage.com/blaw/blt**).

SUPPLEMENTAL TEACHING MATERIALS

This edition of *Business Law Today: The Essentials* is accompanied by an expansive number of teaching and learning supplements. Individually and in conjunction with a number of our colleagues, we have developed supplementary teaching materials that we believe are the best available today. Each component of the supplements package is listed below.

Printed Supplements

- *Instructor's Manual* (Includes **additional cases on point** with at least one such case summary per chapter, answers to all *For Critical Analysis* questions in the features, and answers for the *Video Questions* at the end of selected chapters. Also available on the *Instructor's Resource CD-ROM*, or IRCD, described below.)
- *Study Guide.*
- A comprehensive *Test Bank* (also available on the IRCD).
- *Answers Manual* (Includes answers to the *Questions and Case Problems*, answers to the *For Critical Analysis* questions in the features, answers for the *Video Questions* that conclude selected chapters, and alternate problem sets with answers. Also available on the IRCD.)

Software, Video, and Multimedia Supplements

- *Instructor's Resource CD-ROM (IRCD)*—The IRCD includes the following supplements: *Instructor's Manual, Answers Manual, Test Bank,* Case-Problem Cases, Course Planning Guide, Case Printouts, ExamView, PowerPoint slides, Lecture Outline System, Transparencies, *Instructor's Manual* for the *Drama of the Law* video series, *Handbook of Landmark Cases and Statutes in Business Law and the Legal Environment, Handbook on Critical Thinking and Writing in Business Law and the Legal Environment, A Guide to Personal Law,* and the *Online Legal Research Guide.*

- **ExamView Testing Software** (available only on the IRCD).
- **WebTutor**—Features chat, discussion groups, testing, student progress tracking, and business law course materials.
- **PowerPoint Slides**—Many of which have been revised for the Eighth Edition.
- **Case-Problem Cases** (available only on the IRCD).
- **Transparency Acetates** (available only on the IRCD).
- **Business Law Digital Video Library**—Provides access to more than sixty-five videos, including the *Drama of the Law* videos and video clips from actual Hollywood movies. Access to Business Law Digital Video Library is available in an optional package with a new text at no additional cost. If Business Law Digital Video Library access did not come packaged with your textbook, it can be purchased online at **digitalvideolibrary.westbuslaw.com**.
- **Videos**—Qualified adopters using this text have access to the entire library of Business Law videos, a vast selection covering most business law issues. For more information about the videos, visit **video.westbuslaw.com**.

FOR USERS OF THE SEVENTH EDITION

We thought that those of you who have been using *Business Law Today: The Essentials* would like to know some of the major changes that have been made for the Eighth Edition.

New Features and Special Pedagogy

We have added the following entirely new elements for the Eighth Edition:

- *Preventing Legal Disputes.*
- *Beyond Our Borders.*
- A *What If the Facts Were Different?* section concluding selected cases.
- A *Reviewing [Chapter topic]* feature for self-study and assessment available in every chapter.
- Reorganized and streamlined chapter-ending *Questions and Case Problems* with labels for different categories and more focus on critical thinking and legal reasoning.
- *Hypothetical Question with Sample Answer* (in the *Questions and Case Problems* section).
- *Critical Thinking and Writing Assignment for Business* in selected chapters.

Significantly Revised Chapters

Every chapter of the Eighth Edition has been revised as necessary to incorporate new developments in the law or to streamline the presentations. A number of new trends in business law are also addressed in the cases and special features of the Eighth Edition. Other major changes and additions made for this edition include the following:

- Chapter 1 (The Historical and Constitutional Foundations)—The chapter has been thoroughly revised and updated to incorporate recent Supreme Court decisions, such as the case on Internet wine shipments and the dormant commerce clause. The chapter includes discussions of the USA Patriot Act's effect on constitutional rights and recent decisions on unprotected speech, freedom of religion, and privacy rights.
- Chapter 2 (Ethics and Business Decision Making)—We have supplemented our ethics coverage with even more practical elements throughout and have included a

section that deals with corporate social responsibility and profit maximization. Recent case examples are provided, and new features address the problems faced by Google China and international human rights audits.

■ Chapter 3 (Courts and Alternative Dispute Resolution)—The section on electronic evidence and discovery issues has been updated to include the new federal rules (effective in 2006). To provide greater clarity on important foundational issues, many parts of this chapter were reworked, including the discussions of personal jurisdiction, Internet jurisdiction, standing to sue, and appellate review. A chart was added to illustrate the differences among various methods of alternative dispute resolution, and the discussion of electronic filing systems and online dispute resolution was updated. Features were added to discuss the use of private judges and judicial review in other nations.

■ Chapter 4 (Torts and Cyber Torts)—The discussion of damages was expanded and enhanced, and the subsections on defamation and privacy were thoroughly updated. The negligence coverage has been simplified for clarity. New cases were added for this edition on topics that pique students' interest such as Internet dating and the risks associated with watching a soccer game. The section on cyber torts in this chapter now includes a feature discussing cross-border spam and the U.S. Safe Web Act, which was enacted in 2006 to address the problem.

■ Chapter 5 (Intellectual Property and Internet Law)—The materials on intellectual property rights in the online environment have been thoroughly revised and updated with a feature included on the legal issues facing bloggers and podcasters. Several recent Supreme Court cases are discussed. The section on patents was expanded and new examples were added. The discussion of file-sharing was updated, and a 2007 case is presented in which Sony Corporation brought a successful suit for copyright infringement against an individual who had downloaded eight songs.

■ Chapters 7 through 10—Throughout these chapters on contracts, we have added more examples to clarify and enhance our already superb contract law coverage. We have also included more up-to-date information and new features on topics likely to gain student interest, such as on online gambling (see Chapter 8).

■ Chapters 11 through 13—We have streamlined and simplified our coverage of the Uniform Commercial Code. We have added numerous new numbered examples throughout the chapters to increase student comprehension. Because no state has adopted the 2003 amendments to Articles 2 and 2A, we eliminated the references to these amendments throughout the chapters. We have included a new *Concept Summary* to clarify the major differences between contract law and sales law and have added several new features, such as the one discussing international commercial terms (Incoterms) in Chapter 11.

■ Chapter 14 (Negotiable Instruments) and Chapter 15 (Checks and Banking in the Digital Age)—We have updated these chapters throughout to accommodate the reality of digital banking and funds transfers. We have added features exploring the negotiability of checks in other nations and a new *Landmark in the Law* feature on Check Clearing in the Twenty-First Century (Check 21). Additional numbered examples, exhibits, and a *Concept Summary* help to improve the comprehensibility of the materials.

■ Chapter 16 (Creditors' Rights and Bankruptcy)—This chapter has been completely revamped in light of the passage of bankruptcy reform legislation. It now includes a *Landmark in the Law* feature on the Bankruptcy Reform Act of 2005 and a feature exploring the ethical implications of that act. We have included updated dollar amounts stated in various provisions of the Bankruptcy Code.

■ Chapter 18 (Employment Law)—This chapter covering employment law has been thoroughly updated to include discussions of legal issues facing employers today. It now includes the latest developments and United States Supreme Court decisions, such as one decision that applied Title VII of the Civil Rights Act of 1964 to an employer with fewer than fifteen employees and another that set the standard of proof for retaliation claims. The text discussion of burden of proof in unintentional discrimination cases has been revised and clarified. A feature examines new issues that have arisen in online privacy and employment discrimination.

■ Chapter 20 (Corporations)—This chapter provides an updated and streamlined presentation of issues surrounding corporation formation and termination. Because many corporations today are formed through mergers and consolidations, we have logically incorporated that material into this chapter as well. We have included several new and updated examples and additional key terms. Corporate financing is included, but the preincorporation materials have been significantly revised to reflect modern practices. A new feature discusses jurisdiction over offshore holding companies.

■ Chapter 21 (Investor Protection, Insider Trading, and Corporate Governance)—This chapter now includes more discussion of insider trading, a revised section on registration statements, and new numbered examples. The requirement of an intent to deceive (*scienter*) is explored in the text, in an *Ethical Issue*, and in a case that involved criminal allegations against Martha Stewart. An entirely new section on corporate governance has been added, with references to the Sarbanes-Oxley Act and a feature on corporate governance in other nations. We have updated the material on online securities offerings and fraud as well, and have included a feature on whether the Securities and Exchange Commission's fair disclosure rule should extend to Internet postings and blogs.

■ Chapter 22 (Promoting Competition in a Global Context)—The chapter now focuses on antitrust law in the global market and includes new examples and updated materials. A feature outlines the problems Realtor® associations face with online advertisements, and another feature discusses how antitrust lawsuits are becoming popular in the United Kingdom.

New Cases and Case Problems

In addition to the changes noted above, you will find that most of the cases in this text are new to this edition. Nearly every chapter has two new cases, and some chapters have three new cases. We have selected these cases with care, choosing topics that are engaging for today's students. Every chapter presents at least one case from 2006 or 2007. We have also added numerous new *Case Problems* and *Questions of Ethics* based on recent cases. Virtually every chapter in this edition now has at least one problem based on a case decided in 2006 or 2007 and often more than one.

ACKNOWLEDGMENTS

Numerous careful and conscientious users of *Business Law Today: The Essentials* were kind enough to help us revise the book. In addition, the staff at South-Western Cengage Learning went out of its way to make sure that this edition came out early and in accurate form. In particular, we wish to thank Rob Dewey and Steve Silverstein for their countless new ideas, many of which have been incorporated into the Eighth Edition. We also extend special thanks to Jan Lamar, our longtime developmental editor, for her many useful suggestions and for her efforts in coordinating reviews and ensuring the timely and accurate publication of all supplemental materials. We are particularly indebted to Jennifer Garamy, the book's marketing manager, for her excellent advice; to Lisa Lysne for her marketing support; and to Brian Courter and Rob Ellington for their skills in managing the Web site.

Our production manager and designer, Bill Stryker, made sure that we came out with an error-free, visually attractive edition. We will always be in his debt. We are also indebted to the staff at Parkwood Composition, our compositor. Their ability to generate the pages for this text quickly and accurately made it possible for us to meet our ambitious printing schedule.

We must especially thank Katherine Marie Silsbee for her management of the project, as well as for the application of her superb research and editorial skills. We also wish to thank Lavina Leed Miller for her significant contributions to this project, and William Eric Hollowell, coauthor of the *Instructor's Manual, Study Guide, Test Bank,* and *Online Legal Research Guide,* for his excellent research efforts. The copyediting services of Lorretta Palagi were invaluable, and the proofreading by Judy Kiviat and Pat Lewis will not go unnoticed. We also thank Vickie Reierson and Roxanna Lee for their proofreading and other assistance, which helped to ensure an error-free text. Finally, our appreciation goes to Suzanne Jasin for her many special efforts on the projects.

Acknowledgments for Previous Editions

John J. Balek
Morton College, Illinois

Lorraine K. Bannai
Western Washington University

Marlene E. Barken
Ithaca College, New York

Daryl Barton
Eastern Michigan University

Merlin Bauer
Mid State Technical College, Wisconsin

Donna E. Becker
Frederick Community College, Maryland

Brad Botz
Garden City Community College, Kansas

Teresa Brady
Holy Family College, Philadelphia

Lee B. Burgunder
*California Polytechnic University—
San Luis Obispo*

Bradley D. Childs
Belmont University, Tennessee

Dale Clark
Corning Community College, New York

Sandra J. Defebaugh
Eastern Michigan University

Patricia L. DeFrain
Glendale College, California

Julia G. Derrick
Brevard Community College, Florida

Joe D. Dillsaver
Northeastern State University, Oklahoma

Claude W. Dotson
Northwest College, Wyoming

Larry R. Edwards
*Tarrant County Junior College,
South Campus, Texas*

Jacolin Eichelberger
Hillsborough Commnity College, Florida

George E. Eigsti
Kansas City, Kansas, Community College

Florence E. Elliott-Howard
Stephen F. Austin State University, Texas

Tony Enerva
Lakeland Community College, Ohio

Benjamin C. Fassberg
*Prince George's Community College,
Maryland*

Jerry Furniss
University of Montana

Elizabeth J. Guerriero
Northeast Louisiana University

Phil Harmeson
University of South Dakota

Nancy L. Hart
Midland College, Texas

Janine S. Hiller
*Virginia Polytechnic Institute & State
University*

Karen A. Holmes
*Hudson Valley Community College,
New York*

Fred Ittner
College of Alameda, California

Susan S. Jarvis
University of Texas, Pan American

Jack E. Karns
*East Carolina University,
North Carolina*

Sarah Weiner Keidan
Oakland Community College, Michigan

Richard N. Kleeberg
Solano Community College, California

Bradley T. Lutz
*Hillsborough Community College,
Florida*

Darlene Mallick
*Anne Arundel Community College,
Maryland*

John D. Mallonee
Manatee Community College, Florida

Joseph D. Marcus
*Prince George's Community College,
Maryland*

Woodrow J. Maxwell
*Hudson Valley Community College,
New York*

Beverly McCormick
Morehead State University, Kentucky

William J. McDevitt
Saint Joseph's University, Pennsylvania

John W. McGee
Aims Community College, Colorado

James K. Miersma
*Milwaukee Area Technical Institute,
Wisconsin*

Susan J. Mitchell
Des Moines Area Community College, Iowa

Jim Lee Morgan
West Los Angeles College, California

Jack K. Morton
University of Montana

Solange North
Fox Valley Technical Institute, Wisconsin

Jamie L. O'Brien
South Dakota State University

Robert H. Orr
Florida Community College at Jacksonville

George Otto
Truman College, Illinois

Thomas L. Palmer
Northern Arizona University

David W. Pan
University of Tulsa, Oklahoma

Donald L. Petote
Genessee Community College, New York

Francis D. Polk
Ocean County College, New Jersey

Gregory Rabb
*Jamestown Community College,
New York*

Hugh Rode
Utah Valley State College

William M. Rutledge
Macomb Community College, Michigan

Martha Wright Sartoris
*North Hennepin Community College,
Minnesota*

Anne W. Schacherl
*Madison Area Technical College,
Wisconsin*

Edward F. Shafer
Rochester Community College, Minnesota

Lou Ann Simpson
Drake University, Iowa

Denise Smith
Missouri Western State College

Hugh M. Spall
Central Washington University

Maurice Tonissi
*Quinsigamond Community College,
Massachusetts*

James D. Van Tassel
Mission College, California

Frederick J. Walsh
Franklin Pierce College, New Hampshire

James E. Walsh, Jr.
Tidewater Community College, Virginia

Randy Waterman
Richland College, Texas

Jerry Wegman
University of Idaho

Edward L. Welsh, Jr.
Phoenix College, Arizona

Clark W. Wheeler
Santa Fe Community College, Florida

Lori Whisenant
University of Houston, Texas

Kay O. Wilburn
The University of Alabama at Birmingham

James L. Wittenbach
University of Notre Dame, Indiana

Joseph Zavaglia, Jr.
Brookdale Community College, New Jersey

Acknowledgments for the Eighth Edition

Jay Ballantine
University of Colorado, Boulder

Richard J. Bennett
Three Rivers Community College, Connecticut

Harriet Caplan
Fort Hays State University, Kansas

Tammy Cowart
University of Texas at Tyler

Stanley J. Dabrowski
Hudson County Community College, New Jersey

Karen A. Holmes
Hudson Valley Community College, New York

Susan Mitchell
Des Moines Area Community College, Iowa

Susan Morley
University of Colorado, Boulder

Brad Reid
Abilene Christian University, Texas

Donald A. Roark
University of West Florida

We know that we are not perfect. If you or your students find something you don't like or want us to change, write to us or let us know via e-mail, using the "Talk to Us" feature on this text's Web site. That is how we can make *Business Law Today: The Essentials* an even better book in the future.

Roger LeRoy Miller
Gaylord A. Jentz

Dedication

CHAPTER 1
The Historical and Constitutional Foundations

CHAPTER OUTLINE

- SOURCES OF AMERICAN LAW
- THE COMMON LAW TRADITION
- CLASSIFICATIONS OF LAW
- THE CONSTITUTIONAL POWERS OF GOVERNMENT
- BUSINESS AND THE BILL OF RIGHTS
- DUE PROCESS AND EQUAL PROTECTION
- PRIVACY RIGHTS

LEARNING OBJECTIVES

AFTER READING THIS CHAPTER, YOU SHOULD BE ABLE TO ANSWER THE FOLLOWING QUESTIONS:

1 What is the common law tradition?

2 What is a precedent? When might a court depart from precedent?

3 What is the difference between remedies at law and remedies in equity?

4 What constitutional clause gives the federal government the power to regulate commercial activities among the various states?

5 What is the Bill of Rights? What freedoms does the First Amendment guarantee?

> **❝** The law is of as much interest to the layman as it is to the lawyer. **❞**
>
> Lord Balfour, 1848–1930
> (British prime minister, 1902–1905)

Lord Balfour's assertion in the chapter-opening quotation emphasizes the underlying theme of every page in this book—that law is of interest to all persons, not just to lawyers. Those entering the world of business will find themselves subject to numerous laws and government regulations. A basic knowledge of these laws and regulations is beneficial—if not essential—to anyone contemplating a successful career in today's business world.

There have been and will continue to be different definitions of law. Although the definitions vary in their particulars, they all are based on the general observation that, at a minimum, **law** consists of *enforceable rules governing relationships among individuals and between individuals and their society.* These "enforceable rules" may consist of unwritten principles of behavior established by a nomadic tribe. They may be set forth in an ancient or a contemporary law code. They may consist of written laws and court decisions created by modern legislative and judicial bodies, as in the United States. Regardless of how such rules are created, they all have one thing in common: they establish rights, duties, and privileges that are consistent with the values and beliefs of their society or its ruling group. In the study of law, often referred to as **jurisprudence,** these broad statements provide a point of departure for all legal scholars and philosophers.

In this introductory chapter, we first look at the basic structures of American law, the common law tradition, and some general classifications of law. We then examine some important constitutional concepts and clauses and their significance for business. The chapter concludes with a discussion of how fundamental freedoms guaranteed by the U.S. Constitution affect businesspersons and the workplace.

LAW
A body of enforceable rules governing relationships among individuals and between individuals and their society.

JURISPRUDENCE
The science or philosophy of law.

Young students view the U.S. Constitution on display in Washington, D.C. Can a law be in violation of the Constitution and still be enforced? Why or why not?
(Michael Evans/Zuma Press)

PRIMARY SOURCE OF LAW
A document that establishes the law on a particular issue, such as a constitution, a statute, an administrative rule, or a court decision.

SECONDARY SOURCE OF LAW
A publication that summarizes or interprets the law, such as a legal encyclopedia, a legal treatise, or an article in a law review.

CONSTITUTIONAL LAW
The body of law derived from the U.S. Constitution and the constitutions of the various states.

STATUTORY LAW
The body of law enacted by legislative bodies (as opposed to constitutional law, administrative law, or case law).

CITATION
A reference to a publication in which a legal authority—such as a statute or a court decision—or other source can be found.

ORDINANCE
A regulation enacted by a city or county legislative body that becomes part of that state's statutory law.

SOURCES OF AMERICAN LAW

There are numerous sources of American law. **Primary sources of law,** or sources that establish the law, include the following:

1 The U.S. Constitution and the constitutions of the various states.

2 Statutes, or laws, passed by Congress and by state legislatures.

3 Regulations created by administrative agencies, such as the federal Food and Drug Administration.

4 Case law (court decisions).

We describe each of these important primary sources of law in the following pages. (See the appendix at the end of this chapter for a discussion of how to find statutes, regulations, and case law.)

Secondary sources of law are books and articles that summarize and clarify the primary sources of law. Legal encyclopedias, compilations (such as *Restatements of the Law,* which summarize court decisions on a particular topic), official comments to statutes, treatises, articles in law reviews published by law schools, and articles in other legal journals are examples of secondary sources of law. Courts often refer to secondary sources of law for guidance in interpreting and applying the primary sources of law discussed here.

Constitutional Law

The federal government and the states have separate written constitutions that set forth the general organization, powers, and limits of their respective governments. **Constitutional law** is the law as expressed in these constitutions.

The U.S. Constitution is the supreme law of the land. As such, it is the basis of all law in the United States. A law in violation of the Constitution, if challenged, will be declared unconstitutional and will not be enforced no matter what its source. Because of its paramount importance in the American legal system, we present the complete text of the U.S. Constitution in Appendix B.

The Tenth Amendment to the U.S. Constitution reserves to the states all powers not granted to the federal government. Each state in the union has its own constitution. Unless it conflicts with the U.S. Constitution or a federal law, a state constitution is supreme within the state's borders.

Statutory Law

Laws enacted by legislative bodies at any level of government, such as the statutes passed by Congress or by state legislatures, make up the body of law generally referred to as **statutory law.** When a legislature passes a statute, that statute ultimately is included in the federal code of laws or the relevant state code of laws. Whenever a particular statute is mentioned in this text, we usually provide a footnote showing its **citation** (a reference to a publication in which a legal authority—such as a statute or a court decision—or other source can be found). In the appendix following this chapter, we explain how you can use these citations to find statutory law.

Statutory law also includes local **ordinances**—statutes (laws, rules, or orders) passed by municipal or county governing units to govern matters not covered by federal or state law. Ordinances commonly have to do with city or county land use (zoning ordinances), building and safety codes, and other matters affecting the local governing unit.

A federal statute, of course, applies to all states. A state statute, in contrast, applies only within the state's borders. State laws thus may vary from state to state. No federal statute may violate the U.S. Constitution, and no state statute or local ordinance may violate the U.S. Constitution or the relevant state constitution.

Uniform Laws During the 1800s, the differences among state laws frequently created difficulties for businesspersons conducting trade and commerce among the states. To counter these problems, a group of legal scholars and lawyers formed the National Conference of Commissioners on Uniform State Laws (NCCUSL) in 1892 to draft **uniform laws** ("model statutes") for the states to consider adopting. The NCCUSL still exists today and continues to issue uniform laws.

Each state has the option of adopting or rejecting a uniform law. *Only if a state legislature adopts a uniform law does that law become part of the statutory law of that state.* Note that a state legislature may adopt all or part of a uniform law as it is written, or the legislature may rewrite the law however the legislature wishes. Hence, even though many states may have adopted a uniform law, those states' laws may not be entirely "uniform."

The earliest uniform law, the Uniform Negotiable Instruments Law, was completed by 1896 and was adopted in every state by the early 1920s (although not all states used exactly the same wording). Over the following decades, other acts were drawn up in a similar manner. In all, the NCCUSL has issued more than two hundred uniform acts since its inception. The most ambitious uniform act of all, however, was the Uniform Commercial Code.

The Uniform Commercial Code (UCC) The Uniform Commercial Code (UCC), which was created through the joint efforts of the NCCUSL and the American Law Institute,[1] was first issued in 1952. The UCC has been adopted in all fifty states,[2] the District of Columbia, and the Virgin Islands. The UCC facilitates commerce among the states by providing a uniform, yet flexible, set of rules governing commercial transactions. The UCC assures businesspersons that their contracts, if validly entered into, normally will be enforced.

As you will read in later chapters, from time to time the NCCUSL revises the articles contained in the UCC and submits the revised versions to the states for adoption. During the 1990s, for example, four articles (Articles 3, 4, 5, and 9) were revised, and two new articles (Articles 2A and 4A) were added. Because of its importance in the area of commercial law, we cite the UCC frequently in this text. We also present excerpts of the UCC in Appendix C. (For a discussion of the creation of the UCC, see the *Landmark in the Law* feature in Chapter 11.)

Administrative Law

Another important source of American law is **administrative law,** which consists of the rules, orders, and decisions of administrative agencies. An **administrative agency** is a federal, state, or local government agency established to perform a specific function. Rules issued by various administrative agencies now affect virtually every aspect of a business's operations, including the firm's capital structure and financing, its hiring and firing procedures, its relations with employees and unions, and the way it manufactures and markets its products.

Federal Agencies At the national level, numerous **executive agencies** exist within the cabinet departments of the executive branch. For example, the Food and Drug Administration is within the U.S. Department of Health and Human Services. Executive agencies are subject to the authority of the president, who has the power to appoint and remove officers of federal agencies. There are also major **independent regulatory agencies**

---

1. This institute was formed in the 1920s and consists of practicing attorneys, legal scholars, and judges.
2. Louisiana has adopted only Articles 1, 3, 4, 5, 7, 8, and 9.

ON THE WEB

To find state compilations (codes) of statutory laws, go to

findlaw.com/casecode/state.html.

UNIFORM LAW
A model law created by the National Conference of Commissioners on Uniform State Laws and/or the American Law Institute for the states to consider adopting. If the state adopts the law, it becomes statutory law in that state. Each state has the option of adopting or rejecting all or part of a uniform law.

ADMINISTRATIVE LAW
The body of law created by administrative agencies (in the form of rules, regulations, orders, and decisions) in order to carry out their duties and responsibilities.

ADMINISTRATIVE AGENCY
A federal or state government agency established to perform a specific function. Administrative agencies are authorized by legislative acts to make and enforce rules in order to administer and enforce the acts.

EXECUTIVE AGENCY
An administrative agency within the executive branch of government. At the federal level, executive agencies are those within the cabinet departments.

INDEPENDENT REGULATORY AGENCY
An administrative agency that is not considered part of the government's executive branch and is not subject to the authority of the president. Independent agency officials cannot be removed without cause.

at the federal level, including the Federal Trade Commission, the Securities and Exchange Commission, and the Federal Communications Commission. The president's power is less pronounced in regard to independent agencies, whose officers serve for fixed terms and cannot be removed without just cause.

State and Local Agencies   There are administrative agencies at the state and local levels as well. Commonly, a state agency (such as a state pollution-control agency) is created as a parallel to a federal agency (such as the Environmental Protection Agency). Just as federal statutes take precedence over conflicting state statutes, so do federal agency regulations take precedence over conflicting state regulations. Because the rules of state and local agencies vary widely, we focus here exclusively on federal administrative law.

Agency Creation   Because Congress cannot possibly oversee the actual implementation of all the laws it enacts, it must delegate such tasks to others, especially when the legislation involves highly technical matters, such as air and water pollution. Congress creates an administrative agency by enacting **enabling legislation,** which specifies the name, composition, purpose, and powers of the agency being created.

■ EXAMPLE 1.1   The Federal Trade Commission (FTC) was created in 1914 by the Federal Trade Commission Act.[3] This act prohibits unfair and deceptive trade practices. It also describes the procedures the agency must follow to charge persons or organizations with violations of the act, and it provides for judicial review (review by the courts) of agency orders. Other portions of the act grant the agency powers to "make rules and regulations for the purpose of carrying out the Act," to conduct investigations of business practices, to obtain reports from interstate corporations concerning their business practices, to investigate possible violations of the act, to publish findings of its investigations, and to recommend new legislation. The act also empowers the FTC to hold trial-like hearings and to **adjudicate** (resolve judicially) certain kinds of disputes that involve FTC regulations. ■

Note that the powers granted to the FTC incorporate functions associated with the legislative branch of government (rulemaking), the executive branch (investigation and enforcement), and the judicial branch (adjudication). Taken together, these functions constitute **administrative process,** which is the administration of law by administrative agencies.

Rulemaking   One of the major functions of an administrative agency is **rulemaking**—creating or modifying rules, or regulations, pursuant to its enabling legislation. The Administrative Procedure Act of 1946[4] imposes strict procedural requirements that agencies must follow in their rulemaking and other functions.

The most common rulemaking procedure involves three steps. First, the agency must give public notice of the proposed rulemaking proceedings, where and when the proceedings will be held, the agency's legal authority for the proceedings, and the terms or subject matter of the proposed rule. The notice must be published in the *Federal Register,* a daily publication of the U.S. government. Second, following this notice, the agency must allow ample time for interested parties to comment in writing on the proposed rule. After the comments have been received and reviewed, the agency takes them into consideration when drafting the final version of the regulation. The third and last step is the drafting of the final rule and its publication in the *Federal Register.* (See the appendix at the end of this chapter for an explanation of how to find agency regulations.)

ENABLING LEGISLATION
A statute enacted by Congress that authorizes the creation of an administrative agency and specifies the name, composition, purpose, and powers of the agency being created.

ADJUDICATE
To render a judicial decision. In the administrative process, adjudication is the trial-like proceeding in which an administrative law judge hears and decides issues that arise when an administrative agency charges a person or a firm with violating a law or regulation enforced by the agency.

ADMINISTRATIVE PROCESS
The procedure used by administrative agencies in the administration of law.

RULEMAKING
The process undertaken by an administrative agency when formally adopting a new regulation or amending an old one. Rulemaking involves notifying the public of a proposed rule or change and receiving and considering the public's comments.

ON THE WEB

You can find proposed and final rules issued by administrative agencies by accessing the *Federal Register* online at

www.gpoaccess.gov/fr/index.html.

---

3. 15 U.S.C. Sections 45–58.
4. 5 U.S.C. Sections 551–706.

Investigation and Enforcement   Agencies have both investigatory and prosecutorial powers. An agency can request that individuals or organizations hand over specified books, papers, electronic records, or other documents. In addition, agencies may conduct on-site inspections, although a search warrant is normally required for such inspections. Sometimes, a search of a home, an office, or a factory is the only means of obtaining evidence needed to prove a regulatory violation. Agencies investigate a wide range of activities, including coal mining, automobile manufacturing, and the industrial discharge of pollutants into the environment.

After conducting its own investigation of a suspected rule violation, an agency may decide to take action against an individual or a business. Most administrative actions are resolved through negotiated settlement at their initial stages without the need for formal adjudication. If a settlement cannot be reached, though, the agency may issue a formal complaint and proceed to adjudication.

Adjudication   Agency adjudication involves a trial-like hearing before an **administrative law judge (ALJ)**. Hearing procedures vary widely from agency to agency. After the hearing, the ALJ renders a decision in the case. The ALJ can compel the charged party to pay a fine or can prohibit the party from carrying on some specified activity. Either side may appeal the ALJ's decision to the commission or board that governs the agency. If the party fails to get relief there, appeal can be made to a federal court. If no party appeals the case, the ALJ's decision becomes final.

ADMINISTRATIVE LAW JUDGE (ALJ)
One who presides over an administrative agency hearing and has the power to administer oaths, take testimony, rule on questions of evidence, and make determinations of fact.

Case Law and Common Law Doctrines

The rules of law announced in court decisions constitute another basic source of American law. These rules of law include interpretations of constitutional provisions, of statutes enacted by legislatures, and of regulations created by administrative agencies. Today, this body of judge-made law is referred to as **case law**. Case law—the doctrines and principles announced in cases—governs all areas not covered by statutory law or administrative law and is part of our common law tradition. We look at the origins and characteristics of the common law tradition in some detail in the pages that follow.

CASE LAW
The rules of law announced in court decisions. Case law includes the aggregate of reported cases that interpret judicial precedents, statutes, regulations, and constitutional provisions.

THE COMMON LAW TRADITION

Because of our colonial heritage, much of American law is based on the English legal system. A knowledge of this tradition is crucial to understanding our legal system today because judges in the United States still apply common law principles when deciding cases.

Early English Courts

After the Normans conquered England in 1066, William the Conqueror and his successors began the process of unifying the country under their rule. One of the means they used to do this was the establishment of the king's courts, or *curiae regis*. Before the Norman Conquest, disputes had been settled according to the local legal customs and traditions in various regions of the country. The king's courts sought to establish a uniform set of rules for the country as a whole. What evolved in these courts was the beginning of the **common law**—a body of general rules that applied throughout the entire English realm. Eventually, the common law tradition became part of the heritage of all nations that were once British colonies, including the United States.

Courts developed the common law rules from the principles underlying judges' decisions in actual legal controversies. Judges attempted to be consistent, and whenever possible, they based their decisions on the principles suggested by earlier cases. They sought to

COMMON LAW
The body of law developed from custom or judicial decisions in English and U.S. courts, not attributable to a legislature.

PRECEDENT
A court decision that furnishes an example or authority for deciding subsequent cases involving identical or similar facts.

decide similar cases in a similar way and considered new cases with care, because they knew that their decisions would make new law. Each interpretation became part of the law on the subject and served as a legal **precedent**—that is, a decision that furnished an example or authority for deciding subsequent cases involving similar legal principles or facts.

In the early years of the common law, there was no single place or publication where court opinions, or written decisions, could be found. Beginning in the late thirteenth and early fourteenth centuries, however, each year portions of significant decisions of that year were gathered together and recorded in *Year Books*. The *Year Books* were useful references for lawyers and judges. In the sixteenth century, the *Year Books* were discontinued, and other reports of cases became available. (See the appendix to this chapter for a discussion of how cases are reported, or published, in the United States today.)

Stare Decisis

The practice of deciding new cases with reference to former decisions, or precedents, eventually became a cornerstone of the English and U.S. judicial systems. The practice forms a doctrine called *stare decisis*[5] ("to stand on decided cases").

STARE DECISIS
A common law doctrine under which judges are obligated to follow the precedents established in prior decisions.

The Importance of Precedents in Judicial Decision Making Under the doctrine of *stare decisis*, once a court has set forth a principle of law as being applicable to a certain set of facts, that court and courts of lower rank must adhere to that principle and apply it in future cases involving similar fact patterns. *Stare decisis* has two aspects: first, that decisions made by a higher court are binding on lower courts; and second, that a court should not overturn its own precedents unless there is a strong reason to do so.

Controlling precedents in a *jurisdiction* (an area in which a court or courts have the power to apply the law—see Chapter 3) are referred to as binding authorities. A **binding authority** is any source of law that a court must follow when deciding a case. Binding authorities include constitutions, statutes, and regulations that govern the issue being decided, as well as court decisions that are controlling precedents within the jurisdiction. United States Supreme Court case decisions, no matter how old, remain controlling until they are overruled by a subsequent decision of the Supreme Court, by a constitutional amendment, or by congressional legislation.

BINDING AUTHORITY
Any source of law that a court must follow when deciding a case. Binding authorities include constitutions, statutes, and regulations that govern the issue being decided, as well as court decisions that are controlling precedents within the jurisdiction.

Stare Decisis and Legal Stability The doctrine of *stare decisis* helps the courts to be more efficient because if other courts have carefully reasoned through a similar case, their legal reasoning and opinions can serve as guides. *Stare decisis* also makes the law more stable and predictable. If the law on a given subject is well settled, someone bringing a case to court can usually rely on the court to make a decision based on what the law has been.

Departures from Precedent Although courts are obligated to follow precedents, sometimes a court will depart from the rule of precedent if it decides that a given precedent should no longer be followed. If a court decides that a precedent is simply incorrect or that technological or social changes have rendered the precedent inapplicable, the court might rule contrary to the precedent. Cases that overturn precedent often receive a great deal of publicity.

■**EXAMPLE 1.2**] In *Brown v. Board of Education of Topeka*,[6] the United States Supreme Court expressly overturned precedent when it concluded that separate educational facil-

In a 1954 photo, a woman sits on the steps of the United States Supreme Court building with her daughter after the Court's ruling on **Brown v. Board of Education of Topeka.** (Library of Congress, Prints & Photographs Division/*U.S. News & World Report* Magazine Collection)

---

5. Pronounced *stahr*-ee dih-*si*-sis.
6. 347 U.S. 483, 74 S.Ct. 686, 98 L.Ed. 873 (1954). See the appendix at the end of this chapter for an explanation of how to read legal citations.

ities for whites and blacks, which had been upheld as constitutional in numerous previous cases,[7] were inherently unequal. The Supreme Court's departure from precedent in *Brown* received a tremendous amount of publicity as people began to realize the ramifications of this change in the law. ▣

When There Is No Precedent   At times, a court hears a case for which there are no precedents within its jurisdiction on which to base its decision. When hearing such cases, called "cases of first impression," courts often look at precedents established in other jurisdictions for guidance. Precedents from other jurisdictions, because they are not binding on the court, are referred to as **persuasive authorities.** A court may also consider various other factors, including legal principles and policies underlying previous court decisions or existing statutes, fairness, social values and customs, public policy, and data and concepts drawn from the social sciences.

Can a court consider unpublished decisions as persuasive precedent? See this chapter's *Adapting the Law to the Online Environment* feature on pages 8 and 9 for a discussion of this issue.

Equitable Remedies and Courts of Equity

A **remedy** is the means given to a party to enforce a right or to compensate for the violation of a right. ▣**EXAMPLE 1.3** Suppose that Shem is injured because of Rowan's wrongdoing. A court may order Rowan to compensate Shem for the harm by paying Shem a certain amount. ▣

In the early king's courts of England, the kinds of remedies that could be granted were severely restricted. If one person wronged another, the king's courts could award as compensation either money or property, including land. These courts became known as *courts of law*, and the remedies were called *remedies at law*. Even though this system introduced uniformity in the settling of disputes, when plaintiffs wanted a remedy other than economic compensation, the courts of law could do nothing, so "no remedy, no right."

Remedies in Equity   *Equity* refers to a branch of the law, founded in justice and fair dealing, that seeks to supply a fair and adequate remedy when no remedy is available at law. In medieval England, when individuals could not obtain an adequate remedy in a court of law, they petitioned the king for relief. Most of these petitions were decided by an adviser to the king called the *chancellor*. The chancellor was said to be the "keeper of the king's conscience." When the chancellor thought that the claim was a fair one, new and unique remedies were granted. In this way, a new body of rules and remedies came into being, and eventually formal *chancery courts*, or *courts of equity*, were established. The remedies granted by these courts were called *remedies in equity*. Thus, two distinct court systems were created, each having its own set of judges and its own set of remedies.

Plaintiffs (those bringing lawsuits) had to specify whether they were bringing an "action at law" or an "action in equity," and they chose their courts accordingly. ▣**EXAMPLE 1.4** A plaintiff might ask a court of equity to order a **defendant** (a person against whom a lawsuit is brought) to perform within the terms of a contract. A court of law could not issue such an order because its remedies were limited to payment of money or property as compensation for damages. A court of equity, however, could issue a decree for *specific performance*—an order to perform what was promised. A court of equity could also issue an *injunction*, directing a party to do or refrain from doing a particular act. In certain cases, a court of equity could allow for the *rescission* (cancellation) of the contract,

ON THE WEB

To learn how the Supreme Court justified its departure from precedent in the 1954 *Brown* decision, you can access the Court's opinion online by going to **findlaw.com/casecode/supreme.html**, entering "347" and "483" in the boxes below the "Citation Search" heading, and clicking on "get it."

PERSUASIVE AUTHORITY
Any legal authority or source of law that a court may look to for guidance but on which it need not rely in making its decision. Persuasive authorities include cases from other jurisdictions and secondary sources of law.

REMEDY
The relief given to an innocent party to enforce a right or compensate for the violation of a right.

PLAINTIFF
One who initiates a lawsuit.

DEFENDANT
One against whom a lawsuit is brought; the accused person in a criminal proceeding.

---

7. See *Plessy v. Ferguson*, 163 U.S. 537, 16 S.Ct. 1138, 41 L.Ed. 256 (1896).

ADAPTING THE LAW TO THE ONLINE ENVIRONMENT

How the Internet Is Expanding Precedent

The notion that courts should rely on precedents to decide the outcome of similar cases has long been a cornerstone of U.S. law. But what precisely is *precedent*? Today, the availability of "unpublished opinions" over the Internet is changing what the law considers to be precedent. An *unpublished opinion* is a decision issued by an appellate court that is not intended for publication in a reporter (the bound books that contain court opinions).[a] Courts traditionally have not considered unpublished opinions to be "precedents," binding or persuasive, and often have not allowed attorneys to refer to these decisions in their arguments.

Even though certain decisions are not intended for publication, they are posted ("published") almost immediately on online legal databases, such as Westlaw and Lexis. Moreover, with the proliferation of free legal databases and court Web sites, the general public also has almost instant access to the unpublished decisions of most courts. This has caused considerable debate during the last few years over whether unpublished opinions should be given the same precedential effect as published opinions. Some have even argued that categorizing some decisions as not establishing precedent is unconstitutional.[b]

What Is the Difference between Published and Unpublished Opinions?

In recent years, the number of court decisions not published in printed books has risen dramatically, causing many to wonder why some opinions are published and therefore precedential, whereas others are not. Commentators have suggested a number of reasons why so many decisions are not designated for publication. Some say it is because the courts are overloaded and judges do not have time to write detailed opinions in every case. Others say that because the cost of publishing is so high, judges must determine which decisions are significant enough to appear in official books; the unpublished cases are the ones that courts deem to be less important. Still others say judges refrain from publishing the decisions in difficult cases and deem them nonprecedential because they do not wish to set a bad precedent.

Whatever the reason, most decisions made by today's courts are not printed in the case reporters. By some estimates, nearly 80 percent of the decisions issued by federal

a. Recently decided cases that are not yet published are also sometimes called *unpublished opinions,* but because these decisions will eventually be printed in reporters, we do not include them here.

b. See, for example, *Anastasoff v. United States,* 235 F.3d 1054 (2001), in which the U.S. Court of Appeals for the Eighth Circuit vacated its prior ruling that denying precedential effect to unpublished opinions was unconstitutional.

---

thereby returning the parties to the positions that they held prior to the contract's formation. ■ Equitable remedies will be discussed in greater detail in Chapter 9.

REMEMBER Even though, in most states, courts of law and equity have merged, the principles of equity still apply.

The Merging of Law and Equity   Today, in most states the courts of law and equity have merged, and thus the distinction between the two courts has largely disappeared. A plaintiff may now request both legal and equitable remedies in the same action, and the trial court judge may grant either form—or both forms—of relief. The merging of law and equity, however, does not diminish the importance of distinguishing legal remedies from equitable remedies. To request the proper remedy, a businessperson (or her or his attorney) must know what remedies are available for the specific kinds of harms suffered. Today, as a rule, courts will grant an equitable remedy only when the remedy at law (money damages) is inadequate. Exhibit 1–1 summarizes the procedural differences (applicable in most states) between an action at law and an action in equity.

EQUITABLE PRINCIPLES AND MAXIMS
General propositions or principles of law that have to do with fairness (equity).

Equitable Principles and Maxims   Over time, the courts have developed a number of **equitable principles and maxims** that provide guidance in deciding whether plaintiffs should be granted equitable relief. Because of their importance, both historically and in our judicial system today, these principles and maxims are set forth in this chapter's *Landmark in the Law* feature on page 10.

appellate courts are unpublished. The number is equally high in some state court systems. California's intermediate appellate courts, for example, publish only about 7 percent of their decisions. Given the situation, why should the courts not be able to consider prior rulings in unpublished decisions?

Should Unpublished Decisions Establish Precedent?

Prior to the Internet, one might have been able to justify not considering unpublished decisions as precedent on the grounds of fairness. How could lawyers know about unpublished decisions if they were not printed in the case reporters? Because only the wealthiest clients could afford to pay their attorneys to research unpublished decisions, treating them as precedent would have led to inequality in justice. Now that opinions are available with the click of a mouse, however, this justification is no longer valid.

A more significant argument against allowing unpublished decisions to be precedent has to do with who authors these opinions. Staff attorneys and law clerks frequently write unpublished opinions so that judges can spend more time shaping and editing the opinions intended for publication. Consequently, allowing unpublished decisions to establish precedent could result in bad precedents because the reasoning in these unpublished decisions may not be up to par. Others counter that if the decision is considered merely as persuasive precedent, judges who disagree with the reasoning are free to reject the conclusion.

The United States Supreme Court Changes Federal Rules on Unpublished Opinions after 2007

In spite of objections from several hundred judges and lawyers, the United States Supreme Court made history in 2006 when it announced that it would allow lawyers to refer to (cite) unpublished decisions in all federal courts. The new rule, Rule 32.1 of the Federal Rules of Appellate Procedure, states that federal courts may not prohibit or restrict the citation of federal judicial opinions that have been designated as "not for publication," "nonprecedential," or "not precedent." The rule applies only to federal courts and only to unpublished opinions issued after January 1, 2007. It does not specify what weight a court must give to its own unpublished opinions or to those from another court. Basically, Rule 32.1 simply establishes a uniform rule for all of the federal courts that allows attorneys to cite—and judges to consider as persuasive precedent—unpublished decisions as of 2007.

The impact of this new rule remains to be seen. At present, the majority of the states do not allow their state courts to consider unpublished cases as persuasive precedent, and this rule does not affect the states. The Supreme Court's decision, however, provides an example of how technology—the availability of unpublished opinions over the Internet—has affected the law.

FOR CRITICAL ANALYSIS *Now that the Supreme Court is allowing unpublished decisions to be used as persuasive precedent in federal courts, should state courts follow? Why or why not?*

EXHIBIT 1–1 Procedural Differences between an Action at Law and an Action in Equity		
PROCEDURE	ACTION AT LAW	ACTION IN EQUITY
Initiation of lawsuit	By filing a complaint	By filing a petition
Decision	By jury or judge	By judge (no jury)
Result	Judgment	Decree
Remedy	Monetary damages	Injunction, specific performance, or rescission

CLASSIFICATIONS OF LAW

The huge body of the law may be broken down according to several classification systems. For example, one classification system divides law into **substantive law** (all laws that define, describe, regulate, and create legal rights and obligations) and **procedural law** (all laws that establish the methods of enforcing the rights established by substantive law). Other classification systems divide law into federal law and state law or private law (dealing with

SUBSTANTIVE LAW
Law that defines, describes, regulates, and creates legal rights and obligations.

PROCEDURAL LAW
Law that establishes the methods of enforcing the rights established by substantive law.

LANDMARK IN THE LAW | Equitable Principles and Maxims

In medieval England, courts of equity had the responsibility of using discretion in supplementing the common law. Even today, when the same court can award both legal and equitable remedies, it must exercise discretion. Courts often invoke equitable principles and maxims when making their decisions. Here are some of the most significant equitable principles and maxims:

1 *Whoever seeks equity must do equity.* (Anyone who wishes to be treated fairly must treat others fairly.)
2 *Where there is equal equity, the law must prevail.* (The law will determine the outcome of a controversy in which the merits of both sides are equal.)
3 *One seeking the aid of an equity court must come to the court with clean hands.* (Plaintiffs must have acted fairly and honestly.)
4 *Equity will not suffer a wrong to be without a remedy.* (Equitable relief will be awarded when there is a right to relief and there is no adequate remedy at law.)
5 *Equity regards substance rather than form.* (Equity is more concerned with fairness and justice than with legal technicalities.)
6 *Equity aids the vigilant, not those who rest on their rights.* (Equity will not help those who neglect their rights for an unreasonable period of time.)

The last maxim has become known as the *equitable doctrine of laches.* The doctrine arose to encourage people to bring lawsuits while the evidence was fresh; if they failed to do so, they would not be allowed to bring a lawsuit. What constitutes a reasonable time, of course, varies according to the circumstances of the case. Time periods for different types of cases are now usually fixed by **statutes of limitations.** After the time allowed under a statute of limitations has expired, no action can be brought, no matter how strong the case was originally.

APPLICATION TO TODAY'S WORLD *The equitable maxims listed above underlie many of the legal rules and principles that are commonly applied by the courts today— and that you will read about in this book. For example, in Chapter 7 you will read about the doctrine of promissory estoppel. Under this doctrine, a person who has reasonably and substantially relied on the promise of another may be able to obtain some measure of recovery, even though no enforceable contract, or agreement, exists. The court will estop (bar, or impede) the one making the promise from asserting the lack of a valid contract as a defense. The rationale underlying the doctrine of promissory estoppel is similar to that expressed in the fourth and fifth maxims above.*

RELEVANT WEB SITES *To locate information on the Web concerning equitable principles and maxims, go to this text's Web site at* **academic.cengage.com/blaw/blt***, select "Chapter 1," and click on "URLs for Landmarks."*

STATUTE OF LIMITATIONS
A federal or state statute setting the maximum time period during which a certain action can be brought or certain rights enforced.

relationships between persons) and public law (addressing the relationship between persons and their governments).

Frequently, people use the term **cyberlaw** to refer to the emerging body of law that governs transactions conducted via the Internet. Cyberlaw is not really a classification of law, nor is it a new *type* of law. Rather, it is an informal term used to describe traditional legal principles that have been modified and adapted to fit situations that are unique to the online world. Of course, in some areas new statutes have been enacted, at both the federal and the state levels, to cover specific types of problems stemming from online communications. Throughout this book, you will read how the law in a given area is evolving to govern specific legal issues that arise in the online context.

Civil Law and Criminal Law

Civil law spells out the rights and duties that exist between persons and between persons and their governments, and the relief available when a person's rights are violated. Typically, in a civil case, a private party sues another private party (although the government can also sue a party for a civil law violation) to make that other party comply with a duty or pay for the damage caused by the failure to comply with a duty. If you find yourself a party to a lawsuit, this chapter's *Application* feature discusses how to choose a lawyer.

Much of the law that we discuss in this text is civil law. Contract law, for example, which we discuss in Chapters 7 through 10, is civil law. The whole body of tort law (see Chapter 4) is civil law. Note that *civil law* is not the same as a *civil law system*. As you will read shortly, a **civil law system** is a legal system based on a written code of laws.

Criminal law has to do with wrongs committed against society for which society demands redress. Criminal acts are proscribed by local, state, or federal government statutes. Thus, criminal defendants are prosecuted by public officials, such as a district attorney (D.A.), on behalf of the state, not by their victims or other private parties. Whereas in a civil case the object is to obtain remedies (such as money damages) to compensate the injured party, in a criminal case the object is to punish the wrongdoer in an attempt to deter others from similar actions. Penalties for violations of criminal statutes consist of fines and/or imprisonment—and, in some cases, death. We will discuss the differences between civil and criminal law in greater detail in Chapter 6.

National and International Law

The law of a particular nation, such as the United States or Sweden, is **national law.** National law, of course, varies from country to country because each country's law reflects the interests, customs, activities, and values that are unique to that nation's culture. Even though the laws and legal systems of various countries differ substantially, broad similarities do exist, as discussed in this chapter's *Beyond Our Borders* feature on pages 12 and 13.

International Law In contrast to national law, international law applies to more than one nation. **International law** can be defined as a body of written and unwritten laws observed by independent nations and governing the acts of individuals as well as governments. International law is an intermingling of rules and constraints derived from a variety of sources, including the laws of individual nations, the customs that have evolved among nations in their relations with one another, and treaties and international organizations. In essence, international law is the result of centuries-old attempts to reconcile the traditional need of each nation to be the final authority over its own affairs with the desire of nations to benefit economically from trade and harmonious relations with one another.

CYBERLAW
An informal term used to refer to all laws governing electronic communications and transactions, particularly those conducted via the Internet.

CIVIL LAW
The branch of law dealing with the definition and enforcement of all private or public rights, as opposed to criminal matters.

CIVIL LAW SYSTEM
A system of law derived from that of the Roman Empire and based on a code rather than case law; the predominant system of law in the nations of continental Europe and the nations that were once their colonies. In the United States, Louisiana, because of its historical ties to France, has, in part, a civil law system.

CRIMINAL LAW
Law that defines and governs actions that constitute crimes. Generally, criminal law has to do with wrongful actions committed against society for which society demands redress.

NATIONAL LAW
Law that pertains to a particular nation (as opposed to international law).

INTERNATIONAL LAW
The law that governs relations among nations. National laws, customs, treaties, and international conferences and organizations are generally considered to be the most important sources of international law.

BEYOND OUR BORDERS   National Law Systems

Despite their varying cultures and customs, virtually all countries have laws governing torts, contracts, employment, and other areas, just as the United States does. In part, this is because two types of legal systems predominate around the globe today. One is the common law system of England and the United States, which we have discussed elsewhere. The other system is based on Roman civil law, or "code law." The term *civil law,* as used here, refers not to civil as opposed to criminal law but to codified law—an ordered grouping of legal principles enacted into law by a legislature or governing body. In a *civil law system,* the primary source of law is a statutory code, and case precedents are not judicially binding, as they normally are in a common law system. Although judges in a civil law system commonly refer to previous decisions as sources of legal guidance, they are not bound by precedent; in other words, the doctrine of *stare decisis* does not apply.

A third, less prevalent, legal system is common in Islamic countries, where the law is often influenced by *sharia,* the religious law of Islam. *Sharia* is a comprehensive code of principles that governs both the public and private lives of Islamic persons, directing many aspects of day-to-day life, including politics, economics, banking, business law, contract law, and social issues. Although *sharia* affects the legal codes of many Muslim countries, the extent of its impact and its interpretation vary widely. In some Middle Eastern nations, aspects of *sharia* have been codified in modern legal codes and are enforced by national judicial systems.

The accompanying exhibit lists some countries that today follow either the common law system or the civil law system. Generally, those countries that were once colonies of Great Britain retained their English common law heritage after they achieved independence. Similarly, the civil law system, which is followed in most continental European nations, was retained in the Latin American, African, and Asian countries that were once colonies of those nations. Japan and South Africa also have civil law systems.

The key difference between national law and international law is that government authorities can enforce national law. If a nation violates an international law, however, the most that other countries or international organizations can do (if persuasive tactics fail) is to resort to coercive actions against the violating nation. Coercive actions range from the severance of diplomatic relations and boycotts to, as a last resort, war. We examine the laws governing international business transactions in later chapters (including parts of Chapters 11 through 13, which cover contracts for the sale of goods, and all of Chapter 25).

THE CONSTITUTIONAL POWERS OF GOVERNMENT

Laws that govern business in the United States have their origin in the lawmaking authority granted by the U.S. Constitution, which is the supreme law in this country. As mentioned earlier in this chapter, neither Congress nor any state can enact a law that is in conflict with the Constitution.

FEDERAL FORM OF GOVERNMENT
A system of government in which the states form a union and the sovereign power is divided between the central government and the member states.

The U.S. Constitution created a **federal form of government** in which the national government and the states *share* sovereign power. The Constitution sets forth specific powers that can be exercised by the national government and provides that the national government has the implied power to undertake actions necessary to carry out its expressly designated powers. All other powers are "reserved" to the states. The broad language of the Constitution, though, has left much room for debate over the specific nature

In the United States, the state of Louisiana, because of its historical ties to France, has, in part, a civil law system. The legal systems of Puerto Rico, Québec, and Scotland are similarly characterized as having elements of the civil law system.

Realize that although national law systems share many commonalities, they also have distinct differences. Even when the basic principles are fundamentally similar (as they are in contract law, for example), significant variations exist in the practical application and effect of these laws across countries. Therefore, those persons who plan to do business in another nation would be wise to become familiar with the laws of that nation.

 FOR CRITICAL ANALYSIS *Does the civil law system offer any advantages over the common law system, or vice versa? Explain.*

THE LEGAL SYSTEMS OF SELECTED NATIONS			
CIVIL LAW		**COMMON LAW**	
Argentina	Indonesia	Australia	Nigeria
Austria	Iran	Bangladesh	Singapore
Brazil	Italy	Canada	United Kingdom
Chile	Japan	Ghana	United States
China	Mexico	India	Zambia
Egypt	Poland	Israel	
Finland	South Korea	Jamaica	
France	Sweden	Kenya	
Germany	Tunisia	Malaysia	
Greece	Venezuela	New Zealand	

ON THE WEB

The Library of Congress offers extensive information on national and international law at www.loc.gov.

and scope of these powers. Generally, it has been the task of the courts to determine where the boundary line between state and national powers should lie—and that line changes over time.

The Commerce Clause

To prevent states from establishing laws and regulations that would interfere with trade and commerce among the states, the Constitution expressly delegated to the national government the power to regulate interstate commerce. Article I, Section 8, of the U.S. Constitution expressly permits Congress "[t]o regulate Commerce with foreign Nations, and among the several States, and with the Indian Tribes." This clause, referred to as the **commerce clause,** has had a greater impact on business than any other provision in the Constitution.

Initially, the commerce power was interpreted as being limited to *interstate* commerce (commerce among the states) and not applicable to *intrastate* commerce (commerce within a state). In 1824, however, in *Gibbons v. Ogden*,[8] the United States Supreme Court held that commerce within a state could also be regulated by the national government as long as the commerce *substantially affected* commerce involving more than one state.

COMMERCE CLAUSE
The provision in Article I, Section 8, of the U.S. Constitution that gives Congress the power to regulate interstate commerce.

---

8. 22 U.S. (9 Wheat.) 1, 6 L.Ed. 23 (1824).

The Commerce Clause and the Expansion of National Powers As the nation grew and faced new kinds of problems, the commerce clause became a vehicle for the additional expansion of the national government's regulatory powers. Even activities that seemed purely local came under the regulatory reach of the national government if those activities were deemed to substantially affect interstate commerce. ■EXAMPLE 1.5 In 1942, in *Wickard v. Filburn*,[9] the Supreme Court held that wheat production by an individual farmer intended wholly for consumption on his own farm was subject to federal regulation. The Court reasoned that the home consumption of wheat reduced the market demand for wheat and thus could have a substantial effect on interstate commerce. ■

The following landmark case involved a challenge to the scope of the national government's constitutional authority to regulate local activities.

---

9. 317 U.S. 111, 63 S.Ct. 82, 87 L.Ed. 122 (1942).

CASE 1.1   Heart of Atlanta Motel v. United States

LANDMARK AND CLASSIC CASES

Supreme Court of the United States, 379 U.S. 241, 85 S.Ct. 348, 13 L.Ed.2d 258 (1964).
supct.law.cornell.edu/supct/cases/name.htm[a]

HISTORICAL AND SOCIAL SETTING In the first half of the twentieth century, state governments sanctioned segregation on the basis of race. In 1954, the United States Supreme Court decided that racially segregated school systems violated the Constitution. In the following decade, the Court ordered an end to racial segregation imposed by the states in other public facilities, such as beaches, golf courses, buses, parks, auditoriums, and courtroom seating. Privately owned facilities that excluded or segregated African Americans and others on the basis of race were not subject to the same constitutional restrictions, however. Congress passed the Civil Rights Act of 1964 to prohibit racial discrimination in "establishments affecting interstate commerce." These facilities included "places of public accommodation."

FACTS The owner of the Heart of Atlanta Motel, in violation of the Civil Rights Act of 1964, refused to rent rooms to African Americans. The motel owner brought an action in a federal district court to have the Civil Rights Act declared unconstitutional, alleging that Congress had exceeded its constitutional authority to regulate commerce by enacting the act. The owner argued that his motel was not engaged in interstate commerce but was "of a purely local character."

a. This is the "Historic Supreme Court Decisions—by Party Name" page within the "Supreme Court" collection that is available at the Web site of the Legal Information Institute. Click on the "H" link, or scroll down the list of cases to the entry for the *Heart of Atlanta* case. Click on the case name, and select the format in which you would like to view the case.

The motel, however, was accessible to state and interstate highways. The owner advertised nationally, maintained billboards throughout the state, and accepted convention trade from outside the state (75 percent of the guests were residents of other states). The court ruled that the act did not violate the Constitution and enjoined (prohibited) the owner from discriminating on the basis of race. The owner appealed. The case ultimately went to the United States Supreme Court.

ISSUE Did Congress exceed its constitutional power to regulate interstate commerce by enacting the Civil Rights Act of 1964?

DECISION No. The United States Supreme Court upheld the constitutionality of the act.

REASON The Court noted that the act was passed to correct "the deprivation of personal dignity" accompanying the denial of equal access to "public establishments." Testimony before Congress leading to the passage of the act indicated that African Americans in particular experienced substantial discrimination in attempting to secure lodging while traveling. This discrimination impeded interstate travel and thus impeded interstate commerce. As for the owner's argument that his motel was "of a purely local character," the Court said that even if this was true, the motel affected interstate commerce. According to the Court, "if it is interstate commerce that feels the pinch, it does not matter how local the operation that applies the squeeze." Therefore, under the

CASE 1.1–Continued

commerce clause, "the power of Congress to promote interstate commerce also includes the power to regulate the local incidents thereof, including local activities."

IMPACT OF THIS CASE ON TODAY'S LAW *If the United States Supreme Court had invalidated the Civil Rights Act of 1964, the legal landscape of the United States would be much different today. The act prohibits discrimination based on race, color, national origin, religion, or gender in all "public accommodations," including hotels and restaurants. The act*

also prohibits discrimination in employment based on these criteria. Although state laws now prohibit many of these forms of discrimination as well, the protections available vary from state to state—and it is not certain when (and if) such laws would have been passed had the 1964 federal Civil Rights Act been deemed unconstitutional.

RELEVANT WEB SITES *To locate information on the Web concerning the Heart of Atlanta Motel decision, go to this text's Web site at* **academic.cengage.com/blaw/blt**, *select "Chapter 1," and click on "URLs for Landmarks."*

The Commerce Power Today   At least theoretically, the power over commerce authorizes the national government to regulate every commercial enterprise in the United States. Today, federal (national) legislation governs virtually every major activity conducted by businesses—from hiring and firing decisions to workplace safety, competitive practices, and financing. In the last decade, however, the Supreme Court has begun to curb somewhat the national government's regulatory authority under the commerce clause. In 1995, the Court held—for the first time in sixty years—that Congress had exceeded its regulatory authority under the commerce clause. The Court struck down an act that banned the possession of guns within one thousand feet of any school because the act attempted to regulate an area that had "nothing to do with commerce."[10] Subsequently, the Court invalidated key portions of two other federal acts on the ground that they exceeded Congress's commerce clause authority.[11]

The Regulatory Powers of the States   As part of their inherent sovereignty, state governments have the authority to regulate affairs within their borders. This authority stems in part from the Tenth Amendment to the Constitution, which reserves to the states all powers not delegated to the national government. State regulatory powers are often referred to as **police powers.** The term encompasses not only the enforcement of criminal law but also the right of state governments to regulate private activities to protect or promote the public order, health, safety, morals, and general welfare. Fire and building codes, antidiscrimination laws, parking regulations, zoning restrictions, licensing requirements, and thousands of other state statutes covering virtually every aspect of life have been enacted pursuant to a state's police powers. Local governments, including cities, also exercise police powers.[12] Generally, state laws enacted pursuant to a state's police powers carry a strong presumption of validity.

POLICE POWERS
Powers possessed by the states as part of their inherent sovereignty. These powers may be exercised to protect or promote the public order, health, safety, morals, and general welfare.

The "Dormant" Commerce Clause   The United States Supreme Court has interpreted the commerce clause to mean that the national government has the *exclusive* authority to regulate commerce that substantially affects trade and commerce among the

---

10. The United States Supreme Court held the Gun-Free School Zones Act of 1990 to be unconstitutional in *United States v. Lopez*, 514 U.S. 549, 115 S.Ct. 1624, 131 L.Ed.2d 626 (1995).

11. See, for example, *Printz v. United States*, 521 U.S. 898, 117 S.Ct. 2365, 138 L.Ed.2d 914 (1997), involving the Brady Handgun Violence Prevention Act of 1993; and *United States v. Morrison*, 529 U.S. 598, 120 S.Ct. 1740, 146 L.Ed.2d 658 (2000), concerning the federal Violence Against Women Act of 1994.

12. Local governments derive their authority to regulate their communities from the state because they are creatures of the state. In other words, they cannot come into existence unless authorized by the state to do so.

Congress attempted to create gun-free zones around schools. But those who believe in states' rights contend that only states and municipalities should create and use such police powers. Ultimately, the United States Supreme Court ruled that creating gun-free zones within one thousand feet of schools had "nothing to do with commerce" and certainly not interstate commerce. Can state and local jurisdictions still create such zones if they wish? (AP Photo/Matt York)

states. This express grant of authority to the national government, which is often referred to as the "positive" aspect of the commerce clause, implies a negative aspect—that the states do *not* have the authority to regulate interstate commerce. This negative aspect of the commerce clause is often referred to as the "dormant" (implied) commerce clause.

The dormant commerce clause comes into play when state regulations affect interstate commerce. In this situation, the courts normally weigh the state's interest in regulating a certain matter against the burden that the state's regulation places on interstate commerce. Because courts balance the interests involved, it can be extremely difficult to predict the outcome in a particular case.

At one time, many states regulated the sale of alcoholic beverages, including wine, through a "three-tier" system. This system required separate licenses for producers, wholesalers, and retailers, subject to a complex set of overlapping regulations that effectively banned direct sales to consumers from out-of-state wineries. In-state wineries, by contrast, could obtain a license for direct sales to consumers. Did these laws violate the dormant commerce clause? That was the question in the following case.

CASE 1.2   **Granholm v. Heald**

Supreme Court of the United States, 544 U.S. 460, 125 S.Ct. 1885, 161 L.Ed.2d 796 (2005).
www.findlaw.com/casecode/supreme.html[a]

FACTS In 2005, consumer spending on direct wine shipments accounted for more than 3 percent of all wine sales. Because it was not economical for every wholesaler to carry every winery's products, many small wineries relied on direct shipping to reach consumers. Domaine Alfred, a small

winery in California, received requests for its wine from Michigan consumers but could not fill the orders because of that state's direct-shipment ban. The Swedenburg Estate Vineyard, a small winery in Virginia, was unable to fill orders from New York because of that state's laws. Domaine and others filed a suit in a federal district court against Michigan and others, contending that its laws violated the commerce clause. The court upheld the laws, but on appeal, the U.S. Court of Appeals for the Sixth Circuit reversed this ruling. Swedenburg and others filed a suit in a different federal

---

a. In the "Browsing" section, click on "2005 Decisions." In the result, click on the name of the case to access the opinion. FindLaw is part of West Group, the foremost provider of e-information and solutions to the U.S. legal market.

CASE 1.2–Continued

district court against New York and others, arguing that its laws violated the commerce clause. The court issued a judgment in the plaintiffs' favor, but on appeal, the U.S. Court of Appeals for the Second Circuit reversed this judgment. Both cases were appealed to the United States Supreme Court.

ISSUE Do state restrictions on out-of-state wineries' direct shipments to consumers violate the dormant commerce clause?

DECISION Yes. The United States Supreme Court concluded that "New York, like Michigan, discriminates against interstate commerce through its direct-shipping laws." The Court affirmed the judgment of the U.S. Court of Appeals for the Sixth Circuit, which invalidated the Michigan laws, and reversed the judgment of the U.S. Court of Appeals for the Second Circuit, which upheld the New York laws.

REASON The Supreme Court held that "state laws violate the Commerce Clause if they mandate differential treatment of in-state and out-of-state economic interests that benefits the former and burdens the latter." The laws of Michigan and New York at issue in this case benefited in-state wineries. The Michigan statute banned out-of-state shipments altogether. New York's regulations required an out-of-state winery to set up a distribution system in the state, subject to a licensing scheme. These laws "deprive citizens of their right to have access to the markets of other States on equal terms. * * * Allowing States to discriminate against out-of-state wine invites a multiplication of preferential trade areas destructive of the very purpose of the Commerce Clause." The Court stated that it viewed "with particular suspicion state statutes requiring business operations to be performed in the home State that could more efficiently be performed elsewhere. New York's in-state presence requirement runs contrary to our admonition that States cannot require an out-of-state firm to become a resident in order to compete on equal terms."

 WHAT IF THE FACTS WERE DIFFERENT?
Suppose that the states had only required the out-of-state wineries to obtain a special license that was readily available. How might this have affected the result in this case? Explain.

The Supremacy Clause

Article VI of the Constitution provides that the Constitution, laws, and treaties of the United States are "the supreme Law of the Land." This article, commonly referred to as the **supremacy clause,** is important in the ordering of state and federal relationships. When there is a direct conflict between a federal law and a state law, the state law is rendered invalid. Because some powers are *concurrent* (shared by the federal government and the states), however, it is necessary to determine which law governs in a particular circumstance.

Preemption occurs when Congress chooses to act exclusively in a concurrent area. In this circumstance, a valid federal statute or regulation will take precedence over a conflicting state or local law or regulation on the same general subject. Often, it is not clear whether Congress, in passing a law, intended to preempt an entire subject area against state regulation. In these situations, it is left to the courts to determine whether Congress intended to exercise exclusive power over a given area. No single factor is decisive as to whether a court will find preemption. Generally, congressional intent to preempt will be found if a federal law regulating an activity is so pervasive, comprehensive, or detailed that the states have little or no room to regulate in that area. Also, when a federal statute creates an agency—such as the National Labor Relations Board—to enforce the law, matters that may come within the agency's jurisdiction will likely preempt state laws.

EXAMPLE 1.6 In September 2006, the governor of California, Arnold Schwarzenegger, signed into law the first state statute that attempts to limit the amount of greenhouse gas emissions from automobiles within the state.[13] Under federal law, the U.S. Environmental Protection Agency (EPA) is the agency that regulates and sets standards for air pollution and tailpipe emissions across the country (see Chapter 24). Normally, because EPA regulations are comprehensive and detailed, they preempt state statutes attempting to regulate

SUPREMACY CLAUSE
The provision in Article VI of the Constitution that provides that the Constitution, laws, and treaties of the United States are "the supreme Law of the Land." Under this clause, state and local laws that directly conflict with federal law will be rendered invalid.

PREEMPTION
A doctrine under which certain federal laws preempt, or take precedence over, conflicting state or local laws.

---

13. The law amends California Health & Safety Code Section 43018.5.

the same area. Therefore, although Californians might want to enact more stringent standards for greenhouse gas emissions due to the number of vehicles operated within the state, it is likely that a court will find that the federal standards preempt this legislation. ■

BUSINESS AND THE BILL OF RIGHTS

The importance of having a written declaration of the rights of individuals eventually caused the first Congress of the United States to enact twelve amendments to the U.S. Constitution and submit them to the states for approval. The first ten of these amendments, commonly known as the **Bill of Rights,** were adopted in 1791 and embody a series of protections for the individual against various types of interference by the federal government.[14] Some constitutional protections apply to business entities as well. For example, corporations exist as separate legal entities, or legal persons, and enjoy many of the same rights and privileges as natural persons do. Summarized here are the protections guaranteed by these ten amendments (see the U.S. Constitution in Appendix B for the complete text of each amendment):

BILL OF RIGHTS
The first ten amendments to the U.S. Constitution.

BE CAREFUL Although most of these rights apply to actions of the states, some of them apply only to actions of the federal government.

1 The First Amendment guarantees the freedoms of religion, speech, and the press and the rights to assemble peaceably and to petition the government.
2 The Second Amendment guarantees the right to keep and bear arms.
3 The Third Amendment prohibits, in peacetime, the lodging of soldiers in any house without the owner's consent.
4 The Fourth Amendment prohibits unreasonable searches and seizures of persons or property.
5 The Fifth Amendment guarantees the rights to *indictment* (formal accusation—see Chapter 6) by grand jury, to due process of law, and to fair payment when private property is taken for public use. The Fifth Amendment also prohibits compulsory self-incrimination and double jeopardy (trial for the same crime twice).
6 The Sixth Amendment guarantees the accused in a criminal case the right to a speedy and public trial by an impartial jury and with counsel. The accused has the right to cross-examine witnesses against him or her and to solicit testimony from witnesses in his or her favor.
7 The Seventh Amendment guarantees the right to a trial by jury in a civil (noncriminal) case involving at least twenty dollars.[15]
8 The Eighth Amendment prohibits excessive bail and fines, as well as cruel and unusual punishment.
9 The Ninth Amendment establishes that the people have rights in addition to those specified in the Constitution.
10 The Tenth Amendment establishes that those powers neither delegated to the federal government nor denied to the states are reserved for the states.

As originally intended, the Bill of Rights limited only the powers of the national government. Over time, however, the Supreme Court "incorporated" most of these rights into the protections against state actions afforded by the Fourteenth Amendment to the Constitution. That amendment, passed in 1868 after the Civil War, provides in part that

---

14. One of these proposed amendments was ratified 203 years later (in 1992) and became the Twenty-seventh Amendment to the U.S. Constitution. See Appendix B.
15. Twenty dollars was forty days' pay for the average person when the Bill of Rights was written.

"[n]o State shall . . . deprive any person of life, liberty, or property, without due process of law." Starting in 1925, the Supreme Court began to define various rights and liberties guaranteed in the national Constitution as constituting "due process of law," which was required of state governments under the Fourteenth Amendment. Today, most of the rights and liberties set forth in the Bill of Rights apply to state governments as well as the national government.

We will look closely at several of the amendments in the above list in Chapter 6, in the context of criminal law and procedures. Here, we examine two important guarantees of the First Amendment—freedom of speech and freedom of religion. These and other First Amendment freedoms (of the press, assembly, and petition) have all been applied to the states through the due process clause of the Fourteenth Amendment. As you read through the following pages, keep in mind that none of these (or other) constitutional freedoms confers an absolute right. Ultimately, it is the United States Supreme Court, as the final interpreter of the U.S. Constitution, that gives meaning to these rights and determines their boundaries.

The First Amendment—Freedom of Speech

Freedom of speech is the most prized freedom that Americans have. Indeed, it is essential to our democratic form of government, which could not exist if people were not allowed to express their political opinions freely and criticize government actions or policies. Because of its importance, the courts traditionally have protected this right to the fullest extent possible.

REMEMBER The First Amendment guarantee of freedom of speech applies only to *government* restrictions on speech.

Speech often includes not only what we say, but also what we do to express our political, social, and religious views. The courts generally protect **symbolic speech**—gestures, movements, articles of clothing, and other forms of nonverbal expressive conduct. **■EXAMPLE 1.7** In 1989, the Supreme Court held that the burning of the American flag to protest government policies is a constitutionally protected form of expression.[16] Similarly, participating in a hunger strike or wearing a black armband would be protected as symbolic speech. ■

SYMBOLIC SPEECH
Nonverbal expressions of beliefs. Symbolic speech, which includes gestures, movements, and articles of clothing, is given substantial protection by the courts.

Expression—oral, written, or symbolized by conduct—is subject to reasonable restrictions. For example, on the campus of a public high school, certain rights may be circumscribed or denied, in part to protect minors from predatory adults and to protect adults and others from predatory minors. A balance must be struck, however, between a government's obligation to protect its citizens and those citizens' exercise of their rights.

Corporate Political Speech   Political speech by corporations also falls within the protection of the First Amendment. **■EXAMPLE 1.8** National banking associations and business corporations sought United States Supreme Court review of a Massachusetts statute that prohibited corporations from making political contributions or expenditures that individuals were permitted to make. The Court ruled that the Massachusetts law was unconstitutional because it violated the right of corporations to freedom of speech.[17] ■ The Court has also held that a law prohibiting a corporation from using bill inserts to express its views on controversial issues violated the First Amendment.[18] Although a more conservative Supreme Court subsequently reversed this trend somewhat,[19] corporate political speech continues to be given significant protection under the First Amendment.

---

16. See *Texas v. Johnson*, 491 U.S. 397, 109 S.Ct. 2533, 105 L.Ed.2d 342 (1989).

17. *First National Bank of Boston v. Bellotti*, 435 U.S. 765, 98 S.Ct. 1407, 55 L.Ed.2d 707 (1978).

18. *Consolidated Edison Co. v. Public Service Commission*, 447 U.S. 530, 100 S.Ct. 2326, 65 L.Ed.2d 319 (1980).

19. See *Austin v. Michigan Chamber of Commerce*, 494 U.S. 652, 110 S.Ct. 1391, 108 L.Ed.2d 652 (1990), in which the Court upheld a state law prohibiting corporations from using general corporate funds for independent expenditures in state political campaigns.

Commercial Speech The courts also give substantial protection to "commercial" speech, which consists of communications—primarily advertising and marketing—made by business firms that involve only their commercial interests. The protection given to commercial speech under the First Amendment is not as extensive as that afforded to noncommercial speech, however. A state may restrict certain kinds of advertising, for example, in the interest of protecting consumers from being misled by the advertising practices. States also have a legitimate interest in the beautification of roadsides, and this interest allows states to place restraints on billboard advertising. **■EXAMPLE 1.9** Café Erotica, a nude dancing establishment, sued the state after being denied a permit to erect a billboard along an interstate highway in Florida. The state appellate court decided that because the law directly advanced a substantial government interest in highway beautification and safety, it was not an unconstitutional restraint on commercial speech.[20] ■

Generally, a restriction on commercial speech will be considered valid as long as it meets three criteria: (1) it must seek to implement a substantial government interest, (2) it must directly advance that interest, and (3) it must go no further than necessary to accomplish its objective. **■EXAMPLE 1.10** The South Carolina Supreme Court held that a state statute banning ads for video gambling violated the First Amendment because the statute did not directly advance a substantial government interest. Although the court acknowledged that the state had a substantial interest in minimizing gambling, there was no evidence that a reduction in video gambling ads would result in a reduction in gambling.[21] ■

Unprotected Speech The United States Supreme Court has made it clear that certain types of speech will not be given any protection under the First Amendment. Speech that harms the good reputation of another, or defamatory speech (see Chapter 4), will not be protected. Speech that violates criminal laws (such as threatening speech) is not constitutionally protected. Other unprotected speech includes "fighting words," or words that are likely to incite others to respond violently.

The First Amendment, as interpreted by the United States Supreme Court, also does not protect obscene speech. Establishing an objective definition of obscene speech has proved difficult, however, and the Court has grappled from time to time with this problem. In a 1973 case, *Miller v. California*,[22] the Court created a test for legal obscenity, which involved a set of requirements that must be met for material to be legally obscene. Under this test, material is obscene if (1) the average person finds that it violates contemporary community standards; (2) the work taken as a whole appeals to a prurient (arousing or obsessive) interest in sex; (3) the work shows patently offensive sexual conduct; and (4) the work lacks serious redeeming literary, artistic, political, or scientific merit.

Because community standards vary widely, the *Miller* test has had inconsistent application, and obscenity remains a constitutionally unsettled issue. Numerous state and federal statutes make it a crime to disseminate obscene materials, however, and the Supreme Court has often upheld such laws, including laws prohibiting the sale and possession of child pornography.[23]

The First Amendment also does not protect statements that assert facts. Unlike an opinion, a statement of purported fact can be verified and may require proof in a suit based on a claim that the statement is defamatory. In the following case, the issue was whether or not a certain statement was an unprotected factual assertion.

20. *Café Erotica v. Florida Department of Transportation,* 830 So.2d 181 (Fla.App. 1 Dist. 2002); review denied, *Café Erotica/We Dare to Bare v. Florida Department of Transportation,* 845 So.2d 888 (Fla. 2003).
21. *Evans v. State,* 344 S.C. 60, 543 S.E.2d 547 (2001).
22. 413 U.S. 15, 93 S.Ct. 2607, 37 L.Ed.2d 419 (1973).
23. For example, see *Osborne v. Ohio,* 495 U.S. 103, 110 S.Ct. 1691, 109 L.Ed.2d 98 (1990).

CASE 1.3   Lott v. Levitt

United States District Court, Northern District of Illinois, Eastern Division, 469 F.Supp.2d 575 (2007).

FACTS In 2005, economist Steven Levitt and journalist Stephen Dubner co-authored the best-selling book *Freakonomics.* Levitt and Dubner discuss in a single paragraph a theory of fellow economist John Lott, Jr.:

*   *   * [T]here is an *   *   * argument—that we need more guns on the street, but in the hands of the right people *   *   * . The economist John R. Lott Jr. is the main champion of this idea. His calling card is the book *More Guns, Less Crime,* in which he argues that violent crime has decreased in areas where law-abiding citizens are allowed to carry concealed weapons. His theory might be surprising, but it is sensible. If a criminal thinks his potential victim may be armed, he may be deterred from committing the crime. Handgun opponents call Lott a pro-gun ideologue *   *   * . [T]here was the troubling allegation that Lott actually invented some of the survey data that support his more-guns/less-crime theory. Regardless of whether the data were faked, Lott's admittedly intriguing hypothesis doesn't seem to be true. When other scholars have tried to replicate his results, they found that right-to-carry laws simply don't bring down crime.

Economist John McCall sent Levitt an e-mail regarding this paragraph. McCall cited an issue of *The Journal of Law and Economics,* in which other scholars claimed to "replicate" Lott's research. Levitt responded, "It was not a peer refereed edition of the *Journal.* For $15,000 he was able to buy an issue and put in only work that supported him. My best friend was the editor and was outraged the press let Lott do this." Based in part on this e-mail, Lott filed a suit in a federal district court against Levitt and others, claiming, among other things, defamation. Levitt filed a motion to dismiss this claim.

ISSUE Did Levitt's e-mail constitute speech that was protected under the First Amendment?

DECISION No. The court denied the motion to dismiss Lott's complaint. Levitt's e-mail was "a string of defamatory assertions *   *   * that—no matter how rash or short-sighted Levitt was when he made them—cannot be reasonably interpreted as innocent or mere opinion." The court encouraged the parties to attempt to settle their dispute before proceeding to trial.

REASON The court explained that the test for whether a statement is factual is "whether the statement is precise, readily understood, and susceptible of being verified as true or false." Language that is "loose, figurative, or hyperbolic" most likely expresses an opinion. Statements that are subjective, theoretical, or conjectural likewise comprise opinions. Expressions of opinion are protected under the First Amendment. But the statement of a speaker or writer who claims to possess "objectively verifiable facts" may be actionable. Here, Levitt's e-mail met the test. "First, it would be unreasonable to interpret Levitt's unqualified statement that the journal edition was not 'peer refereed' as Levitt merely giving his opinion on the 'peers' *   *   * . Second, a reasonable reader would not interpret Levitt's assertion that 'For $15,000 he was able to buy an issue and put in only work that supported him' as simply a statement of Levitt's opinion." Finally, the assertion that the editor of the *Journal* was "outraged" could be verified by the editor, who might also be able to attest to the truth or falsity of the other statements.

 FOR CRITICAL ANALYSIS–Social Consideration
Did the statements about Lott in Freakonomics *constitute unprotected speech? Explain.*

Online Obscenity Congress first attempted to protect minors from pornographic materials on the Internet by passing the Communications Decency Act (CDA) of 1996. The CDA declared it a crime to make available to minors online any "obscene or indecent" message that "depicts or describes, in terms patently offensive as measured by contemporary community standards, sexual or excretory activities or organs."[24] The act was challenged as an unconstitutional restraint on speech, and ultimately the United States Supreme Court ruled that portions of the act were unconstitutional. The Court held that

24. 47 U.S.C. Section 223(a)(1)(B)(ii).

the terms *indecent* and *patently offensive* covered large amounts of nonpornographic material with serious educational or other value.[25]

A second attempt to protect children from online obscenity, the Child Online Protection Act (COPA) of 1998,[26] met with a similar fate. Although the COPA was more narrowly tailored than its predecessor, the CDA, it still used "contemporary community standards" to define which material was obscene and harmful to minors. Ultimately, in 2004 the United States Supreme Court prevented enforcement of the COPA, concluding that it was likely that the act violated the right to free speech.[27]

In 2000, Congress enacted the Children's Internet Protection Act (CIPA),[28] which requires public schools and libraries to install **filtering software** to block online access to adult content by children. Such software is designed to prevent persons from viewing certain Web sites by responding to a site's Internet address or its key words. In 2003, the United States Supreme Court held that the act did not violate the First Amendment.[29]

The First Amendment–Freedom of Religion

The First Amendment states that the government may neither establish any religion nor prohibit the free exercise of religious practices. The first part of this constitutional provision is referred to as the **establishment clause,** and the second part is known as the **free exercise clause.** Government action, both federal and state, must be consistent with this constitutional mandate.

The Establishment Clause   The establishment clause prohibits the government from establishing a state-sponsored religion, as well as from passing laws that promote (aid or endorse) religion or that show a preference for one religion over another. The establishment clause does not require a complete separation of church and state, though. On the contrary, it requires the government to accommodate religions.[30]

The establishment clause covers all conflicts about such matters as the legality of state and local government support for a particular religion, government aid to religious organizations and schools, the government's allowing or requiring school prayers, and the teaching of evolution versus fundamentalist theories of creation. The United States Supreme Court has held that for a government law or policy to be constitutional, it must be secular in aim, must not have the primary effect of advancing or inhibiting religion, and must not create "an excessive government entanglement with religion."[31] Generally, federal or state regulation that does not promote religion or place a significant burden on religion is constitutional even if it has some impact on religion.

Religious displays on public property have often been challenged as violating the establishment clause, and the United States Supreme Court has ruled on a number of such cases. Generally, the Court has focused on the proximity of the religious display to nonreligious symbols, such as reindeers and candy canes, or to symbols from different religions, such as a menorah (a nine-branched candelabrum used in celebrating Hanukkah).[32] In 2005, however, the Supreme Court took a slightly different approach. The dispute involved

FILTERING SOFTWARE
A computer program that is designed to block access to certain Web sites based on their content. The software prevents the retrieval of a site whose URL or key words are on a list within the program.

ESTABLISHMENT CLAUSE
The provision in the First Amendment to the U.S. Constitution that prohibits the government from establishing any state-sponsored religion or enacting any law that promotes religion or favors one religion over another.

FREE EXERCISE CLAUSE
The provision in the First Amendment to the U.S. Constitution that prohibits the government from interfering with people's religious practices or forms of worship.

25. *Reno v. American Civil Liberties Union,* 521 U.S. 844, 117 S.Ct. 2329, 138 L.Ed.2d 874 (1997).
26. 47 U.S.C. Section 231.
27. *American Civil Liberties Union v. Ashcroft,* 542 U.S. 656, 124 S.Ct. 2783, 159 L.Ed.2d 690 (2004). See also *Ashcroft v. American Civil Liberties Union,* 535 U.S. 564, 122 S.Ct. 1700, 152 L.Ed.2d 771 (2002); and *American Civil Liberties Union v. Ashcroft,* 322 F.3d 240 (3d Cir. 2003).
28. 17 U.S.C. Sections 1701–1741.
29. *United States v. American Library Association,* 539 U.S. 194, 123 S.Ct. 2297, 156 L.Ed.2d 221 (2003).
30. *Zorach v. Clauson,* 343 U.S. 306, 72 S.Ct. 679, 96 L.Ed. 954 (1952).
31. *Lemon v. Kurtzman,* 403 U.S. 602, 91 S.Ct. 2105, 29 L.Ed.2d 745 (1971).
32. See, for example, *Lynch v. Donnelly,* 465 U.S. 668, 104 S.Ct. 1355, 79 L.Ed.2d 604 (1984); and *County of Allegheny v. American Civil Liberties Union,* 492 U.S. 573, 109 S.Ct. 3086, 106 L.Ed.2d 472 (1989).

a six-foot-tall monument of the Ten Commandments on the Texas state capitol grounds. The Court held that the monument did not violate the establishment clause because the Ten Commandments had historical as well as religious significance.[33]

The Free Exercise Clause   The free exercise clause guarantees that a person can hold any religious belief that she or he wants; or a person can have no religious belief. When religious *practices* work against public policy and the public welfare, however, the government can act. For example, regardless of a child's or parent's religious beliefs, the government can require certain types of vaccinations. Similarly, although children of Jehovah's Witnesses are not required to say the Pledge of Allegiance at school, their parents cannot prevent them from accepting medical treatment (such as blood transfusions) if their lives are in danger. Additionally, public school students can be required to study from textbooks chosen by school authorities.

For business firms, an important issue involves the accommodation that businesses must make for the religious beliefs of their employees. For example, if an employee's religion prohibits him or her from working on a certain day of the week or at a certain type of job, the employer must make a reasonable attempt to accommodate these religious requirements. Employers must reasonably accommodate an employee's religious beliefs even if the beliefs are not based on the tenets or dogma of a particular church, sect, or denomination. The only requirement is that the belief be religious in nature and sincerely held by the employee. (We will look further at this issue in Chapter 18, in the context of employment discrimination.)

ETHICAL ISSUE 1.1

Does the free exercise clause protect illegal drug use? According to the United States Supreme Court in 2006, the First Amendment does protect the use of a controlled substance in the practice of a sincerely held religious belief. The case involved a religious sect in New Mexico that follows the practices of a Brazil-based church. Its members ingest hoasca tea as part of a ritual to connect with and better understand God. Hoasca tea, which is brewed from plants native to the Amazon rain forest, contains an illegal hallucinogenic drug, dimethyltryptamine (DMT), that is regulated by the Controlled Substances Act. Federal drug agents had confiscated the church's shipment of hoasca tea as it entered the country. The church members filed a suit, claiming that the confiscation violated their right to freely exercise their religion. Ultimately, the Court agreed, ruling that the government had failed to demonstrate a sufficiently compelling interest in barring the sect's sacramental use of hoasca. Chief Justice Roberts wrote the decision, relying on the Religious Freedom Restoration Act of 1993[34] and on earlier decisions allowing the sacramental use of peyote (a cactus that contains mescaline, another hallucinogenic drug). In short, the Court will allow the use of illegal hallucinogenic drugs as a religious practice but will not allow the use of marijuana for medical purposes.[35] Is this fair?

◼

DUE PROCESS AND EQUAL PROTECTION

Two other constitutional guarantees of great significance to Americans are mandated by the due process clauses of the Fifth and Fourteenth Amendments and the equal protection clause of the Fourteenth Amendment.

---

33. *Van Orden v. Perry,* 545 U.S. 677, 125 S.Ct. 2854, 162 L.Ed.2d 607 (2005).

34. 42 U.S.C. Sections 2000bb *et seq.*

35. *Gonzales v. O Centro Espirita Beneficente Uniao Do Vegetal,* 546 U.S. 418, 126 S.Ct. 1211, 163 L.Ed.2d 1017 (2006).

Due Process

Both the Fifth and the Fourteenth Amendments provide that no person shall be deprived "of life, liberty, or property, without due process of law." The **due process clause** of each of these constitutional amendments has two aspects—procedural and substantive. Note that the due process clause applies to "legal persons," such as corporations, as well as to individuals.

Procedural Due Process   Procedural due process requires that any government decision to take life, liberty, or property must be made fairly. For example, fair procedures must be used in determining whether a person will be subjected to punishment or have some burden imposed on him or her. Fair procedure has been interpreted as requiring that the person have at least an opportunity to object to a proposed action before a fair, neutral decision maker (which need not be a judge). Thus, for example, if a driver's license is construed as a property interest, the state must provide some sort of opportunity for the driver to object before suspending or terminating the license.

Many of the constitutional protections discussed in this chapter have become part of our culture in the United States. Due process, especially procedural due process, has become synonymous with what Americans consider "fair." For this reason, businesspersons seeking to avoid legal disputes should consider giving due process to anyone who might object to some business decision or action, whether that person is an employee, a partner, an affiliate, or a customer. For instance, giving ample notice of new policies to all affected persons is a prudent move, as is giving them at least an opportunity to express their opinions on the matter. Providing an opportunity to be heard is often the ideal way to make people feel that they are being treated fairly. If people believe that a businessperson or firm is fair and listens to both sides of an issue, they are less likely to sue that businessperson or firm.

◼

Substantive Due Process   Substantive due process focuses on the content, or substance, of legislation. If a law or other governmental action limits a *fundamental right*, it will be held to violate substantive due process unless it promotes a compelling or overriding state interest. Fundamental rights include interstate travel, privacy, voting, and all First Amendment rights. Compelling state interests could include, for example, the public's safety. **◼EXAMPLE 1.11** Laws setting speed limits may be upheld even though they affect interstate travel, if they are shown to reduce highway fatalities. The courts uphold these laws because the state has a compelling interest in protecting the lives of its citizens. ◼

In situations not involving fundamental rights, a law or action does not violate substantive due process if it rationally relates to any legitimate governmental end. It is almost impossible for a law or action to fail the "rationality" test. Under this test, virtually any business regulation will be upheld as reasonable. The United States Supreme Court has sustained insurance regulations, price and wage controls, banking limitations, and restrictions on unfair competition and trade practices against substantive due process challenges.

◼EXAMPLE 1.12 If a state legislature enacted a law imposing a fifteen-year term of imprisonment without a trial on all businesspersons who appeared in their own television commercials, the law would be unconstitutional on both substantive and procedural grounds. Substantive review would invalidate the legislation because it infringes on freedom of speech. Procedurally, the law is unfair because it imposes the penalty without giving the accused a chance to defend her or his actions. ◼ Lack of procedural due process will cause a court to invalidate any statute or prior court decision. Similarly, the courts will overrule any state or federal law that violates the U.S. Constitution by denying substantive due process.

Equal Protection

Under the Fourteenth Amendment, a state may not "deny to any person within its jurisdiction the equal protection of the laws." The United States Supreme Court has used the due process clause of the Fifth Amendment to make the **equal protection clause** applicable to the federal government as well. Equal protection means that the government must treat similarly situated individuals in a similar manner.

Both substantive due process and equal protection require review of the substance of the law or other governmental action rather than review of the procedures used. When a law or action limits the liberty of all persons to do something, it may violate substantive due process; when a law or action limits the liberty of some persons but not others, it may violate the equal protection clause. **■EXAMPLE 1.13** If a law prohibits all persons from buying contraceptive devices, it raises a substantive due process question. If a law prohibits only unmarried persons from buying the same devices, it raises an equal protection issue. ■

Basically, in determining whether a law or action violates the equal protection clause, a court will consider questions similar to those previously noted as applicable in a substantive due process review. Under an equal protection inquiry, when a law or action distinguishes between or among individuals, the basis for the distinction—that is, the classification—is examined. Depending on the classification, the courts apply different levels of scrutiny, or "tests," to determine whether the law or action violates the equal protection clause.

1 *Minimal Scrutiny—The "Rational Basis" Test.* Generally, laws regulating economic and social matters are presumed to be valid and are subject to only minimal scrutiny. A classification will be considered valid if there is any conceivable "rational basis" on which the classification might relate to a *legitimate government interest*. It is almost impossible for a law or action to fail the rational basis test.

2 *Intermediate Scrutiny.* A harder standard to meet, that of "intermediate scrutiny," is applied in cases involving discrimination based on gender or legitimacy. Laws using these classifications must be substantially related to *important government objectives*.

3 *Strict Scrutiny.* The most difficult standard to meet is that of "strict scrutiny." Very few cases survive strict-scrutiny analysis. Strict scrutiny is applied when a law or action inhibits some persons' exercise of a fundamental right or is based on a suspect trait (such as race, national origin, or citizenship status). Strict scrutiny means that the court will examine very closely the law or action involved and will allow it to stand only if the law or action is necessary to promote a *compelling government interest*.

PRIVACY RIGHTS

In the past, privacy issues typically related to personal information that government agencies, including the Federal Bureau of Investigation, might obtain and keep about an individual. Since the 1990s, one of the major concerns of individuals has been how to protect privacy rights in cyberspace and to safeguard private information that may be revealed online (including credit-card numbers and financial information).

EQUAL PROTECTION CLAUSE
The provision in the Fourteenth Amendment to the Constitution that guarantees that no state will "deny to any person within its jurisdiction the equal protection of the laws." This clause mandates that the state governments must treat similarly situated individuals in a similar manner.

The USA Patriot Act allows authorities to review library records without any proof that the patron is suspected of having committed a crime. In this photo, Connecticut librarians speak out against the Federal Bureau of Investigation's ability to demand patrons' records without obtaining a warrant from a court. What aspect of privacy rights might be violated in such situations?
(AP Photo/Shiho Fukada)

Today, individuals face additional concerns about government intrusions into their privacy. The USA Patriot Act, which was passed by Congress in the wake of the terrorist attacks of September 11, 2001, has given increased authority to government officials to monitor Internet activities (such as e-mail and Web site visits) and to gain access to personal financial data and student information.[36] Using technology, law enforcement officials can track the telephone and e-mail conversations of one party to find out the identity of the other party or parties. The government must certify that the information likely to be obtained is relevant to an ongoing criminal investigation, but it does not need to provide proof of any wrongdoing to gain access to this information. Privacy advocates argue that this law has adversely affected the constitutional rights of all Americans, and it has been widely criticized in the media, fueling the public debate over how to secure privacy rights in an electronic age.

In this section, we look at the protection of privacy rights under the U.S. Constitution and various federal statutes. Note that state constitutions and statutes also protect individuals' privacy rights, often to a significant degree. Privacy rights are also protected under tort law (see Chapter 4). Additionally, the Federal Trade Commission has played an active role in protecting the privacy rights of online consumers (see Chapter 13). The protection of employees' privacy rights, particularly with respect to electronic monitoring practices, is another area of growing concern (see Chapter 18).

ETHICAL ISSUE 1.2

Does the threat of terrorism justify the U.S. government's invasion of its citizens' privacy?
Since the USA Patriot Act was enacted, the National Security Agency (NSA) has engaged in domestic surveillance and monitoring activities that have been highly controversial. Critics claim that these activities endanger numerous constitutionally protected freedoms, such as the right to privacy and the right to be free from unreasonable searches (under the Fourth Amendment). In December 2005, government sources leaked that President George W. Bush had authorized the NSA to secretly intercept phone calls between U.S. citizens and suspected terrorists abroad—without first obtaining a warrant as would be required even under the Patriot Act. Although eavesdropping on phone calls and monitoring e-mails are certainly powerful tools for tracking down terrorists, they are also the kinds of activities that the framers of the U.S. Constitution sought to curtail.

Some claim that the government's intrusion into our private communications is warranted because the government is looking only for those "bad" people who interact with terrorists. If the government can monitor what any person views or searches for on the Internet, however, are anyone's Internet activities really private? To illustrate, consider what happened in August 2006, when America Online (AOL) released randomly selected user search log data from 658,000 subscribers. AOL thought it was doing a good deed by providing this database to researchers at universities and small businesses that normally would not have access to this type of data. To protect subscribers' privacy, the data identified users by numbers rather than by names.

As it turned out, though, an individual's identity could be tracked down using various bits of information. All search engines compile this type of user data, which can be valuable for marketing purposes. Such data can also be invaluable to government law enforcement. For example, searches like "how to make homemade bombs" or "torture methods" *might* indicate a propensity for terrorist activities. But what happens if government monitors find that a person has searched for "underground kiddy porn pictures" or "how to make meth"? Can we assume that law enforcement officials will ignore information found online about illegal activities unrelated to terrorism? Do we have a right to keep private searches or communications on personal topics, such as "homosexuality" or "can you adopt after a suicide attempt"?

■

---

36. Uniting and Strengthening America by Providing Appropriate Tools Required to Intercept and Obstruct Terrorism Act of 2001, also known as the USA Patriot Act, was enacted as Pub. L. No. 107-56 (2001) and extended in early 2006 by Pub. L. No. 109-173.

Constitutional Protection of Privacy Rights

The U.S. Constitution does not explicitly mention a general right to privacy, and only relatively recently have the courts regarded the right to privacy as a constitutional right. In a landmark 1965 case, *Griswold v. Connecticut*,[37] the United States Supreme Court invalidated a Connecticut law that effectively prohibited the use of contraceptives. The Court held that the law violated the right to privacy. Justice William O. Douglas formulated a unique way of reading this right into the Bill of Rights. He claimed that "emanations" from the rights guaranteed by the First, Third, Fourth, Fifth, and Ninth Amendments formed and gave "life and substance" to "penumbras" (partial shadows) around these guaranteed rights. These penumbras included an implied constitutional right to privacy.

When we read these amendments, we can see the foundation for Justice Douglas's reasoning. Consider the Fourth Amendment. By prohibiting unreasonable searches and seizures, the amendment effectively protects individuals' privacy. Consider also the words of the Ninth Amendment: "The enumeration in the Constitution of certain rights, shall not be construed to deny or disparage others retained by the people." In other words, although neither the Constitution nor its amendments mention the right to privacy, this right does exist.

Federal Statutes Protecting Privacy Rights

In the last several decades, Congress has enacted a number of statutes that protect the privacy of individuals in various areas of concern. In the 1960s, Americans were sufficiently alarmed by the accumulation of personal information in government files that they pressured Congress to pass laws permitting individuals to access their files. Congress responded in 1966 with the Freedom of Information Act, which allows any person to request copies of any information on her or him contained in federal government files. In 1974, Congress passed the Privacy Act, which also gives persons the right to access such information. These and other major federal laws protecting privacy rights are listed and described in Exhibit 1–2 on the next page.

Responding to the growing need to protect the privacy of individuals' health records—particularly computerized records—Congress passed the Health Insurance Portability and Accountability Act (HIPAA) of 1996.[38] This act, which took effect on April 14, 2003, defines and limits the circumstances in which an individual's "protected health information" may be used or disclosed.

---

37. 381 U.S. 479, 85 S.Ct. 1678, 14 L.Ed.2d 510 (1965).
38. HIPAA was enacted as Pub. L. No. 104-191 (1996) and is codified in 29 U.S.C.A. Sections 1181 *et seq.*

REVIEWING **Constitutional Law**

A state legislature enacted a statute that required any motorcycle operator or passenger on the state's highways to wear a protective helmet. Jim Alderman, a licensed motorcycle operator, sued the state to block enforcement of the law. Alderman asserted that the statute violated the equal protection clause because it placed requirements on motorcyclists that were not imposed on other motorists. Using the information presented in the chapter, answer the following questions.

1 Why does this statute raise equal protection issues instead of substantive due process concerns?

2 What are the three levels of scrutiny that the courts use in determining whether a law violates the equal protection clause?

3 Which standard, or test, of scrutiny would apply to this situation? Why?

4 Applying this standard, or test, is the helmet statute constitutional? Why or why not?

EXHIBIT 1–2 Federal Legislation Relating to Privacy	
TITLE	**PROVISIONS CONCERNING PRIVACY**
Freedom of Information Act (1966)	Provides that individuals have a right to obtain access to information about them collected in government files.
Family and Educational Rights and Privacy Act (1974)	Limits access to computer-stored records of education-related evaluations and grades in private and public colleges and universities.
Privacy Act (1974)	Protects the privacy of individuals about whom the federal government has information. Under this act, agencies that use or disclose personal information must make sure that the information is reliable and guard against its misuse. Individuals must be able to find out what data concerning them the agency is compiling and how the data will be used. In addition, the agency must give individuals a means to correct inaccurate data and must obtain their consent before using the data for any other purpose.
Tax Reform Act (1976)	Preserves the privacy of personal financial information.
Right to Financial Privacy Act (1978)	Prohibits financial institutions from providing the federal government with access to customers' records unless a customer authorizes the disclosure.
Electronic Communications Privacy Act (1986)	Prohibits the interception of information communicated by electronic means.
Driver's Privacy Protection Act (1994)	Prevents states from disclosing or selling a driver's personal information without the driver's consent.
Health Insurance Portability and Accountability Act (1996)	Prohibits the use of a consumer's medical information for any purpose other than that for which such information was provided, unless the consumer expressly consents to the use. Final rules became effective on April 14, 2003.
Financial Services Modernization Act (Gramm-Leach-Bliley Act) (1999)	Prohibits the disclosure of nonpublic personal information about a consumer to an unaffiliated third party unless strict disclosure and opt-out requirements are met. Final rules became mandatory on July 1, 2001.

APPLICATION   How Can You Choose and Use a Lawyer?

I f you are contemplating a career in the business world, sooner or later you will probably face the question, "Do I need a lawyer?" The answer will likely be "Yes," at least at some time during your career. Today, it is virtually impossible for nonexperts to keep up with the myriad rules and regulations that govern the conduct of business in the United States. It is also increasingly possible for businesspersons to incur penalties for violating laws or regulations of which they are totally unaware.

Although lawyers may seem expensive—anywhere from $100 to $500 or more per hour—cautious businesspersons will make sure that they are not "penny wise and pound foolish." The consultation fee paid to an attorney can be insignificant compared with the potential liability facing a businessperson. Obtaining competent legal advice *before* a dispute arises may enable a businessperson to avoid potentially costly mistakes. Also, keep in mind that sometimes higher-priced attorneys from larger firms may be worth the extra expense because they may have more clout in the local legal community to wield on your behalf.

Selecting an Attorney

In selecting an attorney, you can ask friends, relatives, or business associates to recommend someone. Alternatively, you can call the local or state bar association to obtain the names of several lawyers or check the Yellow Pages in your local telephone directory for listings. West Group has an online database containing biographies of attorneys throughout the country, listed by area of specialty and by state. You can find attorneys in your area by accessing West's Legal Directory online at **directory.findlaw.com**. You might also investigate legal clinics and prepaid legal service plans.

For your initial meeting with an attorney you are considering hiring, prepare a written list of your questions and a brief summary of the problem for which you need legal advice. Also, bring copies of any relevant documents that the lawyer might need to see. While at the meeting, ask about legal fees, discuss the legal problem you are facing (or anticipate facing), and clarify the scope of what you want the lawyer to do for you. Remember that virtually everything you say at this meeting is protected by the attorney-client privilege of confidentiality.

Evaluating Your Attorney

Before hiring the attorney, ask yourself the following questions after your first meeting: Did the attorney seem knowl-

edgeable about what is needed to address your concerns? Did he or she seem willing to investigate the law and the facts further to ensure an accurate understanding of your legal situation? Did you communicate well with each other? Did the attorney perceive what issues were of foremost concern to you and address those issues to your satisfaction? Did the attorney "speak your language" when explaining the legal implications of those issues?

Even after you hire the attorney, continue to evaluate the relationship over time. For many businesspersons, relationships with attorneys last for decades. Make sure that your relationship with your attorney will be a fruitful one.

CHECKLIST FOR CHOOSING AND USING A LAWYER

1 If you ever think that you need legal advice, you probably do.
2 When choosing an attorney, try to get recommendations from friends, relatives, or business associates who have had long-standing relationships with their attorneys. If that fails, check with your local or state bar association, West Group's online directory, or the Yellow Pages.
3 When you initially consult with an attorney, bring a written list of questions to which you want answers, perhaps a summary of your problem, and copies of relevant documents.
4 Do not hesitate to ask about the legal fees that your attorney will charge, and be sure to clarify the scope of the work to be undertaken by the attorney. Ask any and all questions that you feel are necessary to ensure that you understand your legal options.

KEY TERMS

adjudicate 4
administrative agency 3
administrative law 3
administrative law judge (ALJ) 5
administrative process 4
Bill of Rights 18
binding authority 6
case law 5
citation 2
civil law 11
civil law system 11

commerce clause 13
common law 5
constitutional law 2
criminal law 11
cyberlaw 11
defendant 7
due process clause 24
enabling legislation 4
equal protection clause 25
equitable principles
  and maxims 8

establishment clause 22
executive agency 3
federal form of government 12
filtering software 22
free exercise clause 22
independent regulatory agency 3
international law 11
jurisprudence 1
law 1
national law 11
ordinance 2

CHAPTER SUMMARY The Historical and Constitutional Foundations

Sources of American Law (See pages 2–5.)	1. *Constitutional law*—The law as expressed in the U.S. Constitution and the various state constitutions. The U.S. Constitution is the supreme law of the land. State constitutions are supreme within state borders to the extent that they do not violate the U.S. Constitution or a federal law. 2. *Statutory law*—Laws or ordinances created by federal, state, and local legislatures and governing bodies. None of these laws can violate the U.S. Constitution or the relevant state constitutions. Uniform laws, when adopted by a state legislature, become statutory law in that state. 3. *Administrative law*—The rules, orders, and decisions of federal or state government administrative agencies. Federal administrative agencies are created by enabling legislation enacted by the U.S. Congress. Agency functions include rulemaking, investigation and enforcement, and adjudication. 4. *Case law and common law doctrines*—Judge-made law, including interpretations of constitutional provisions, of statutes enacted by legislatures, and of regulations created by administrative agencies. The common law—the doctrines and principles embodied in case law—governs all areas not covered by statutory law (or agency regulations issued to implement various statutes).

The Common Law Tradition (See pages 5–9.)	1. *Common law*—Law that originated in medieval England with the creation of the king's courts, or *curiae regis,* and the development of a body of rules that were common to (or applied throughout) the land.
	
	2. *Stare decisis*—A doctrine under which judges "stand on decided cases"—or follow the rule of precedent—in deciding cases. *Stare decisis* is the cornerstone of the common law tradition.
	
	3. *Remedies*—
	  a. Remedies at law—Money or something else of value.
	  b. Remedies in equity—Remedies that are granted when the remedies at law are unavailable or inadequate. Equitable remedies include specific performance, an injunction, and contract rescission (cancellation).

Classifications of Law (See pages 9–12.)	The law may be broken down according to several classification systems, such as substantive or procedural law, federal or state law, and private or public law. Two broad classifications are civil and criminal law, and national and international law. Cyberlaw is not really a classification of law but a term that is applied to the growing body of case law and statutory law that applies to Internet transactions.
The Constitutional Powers of Government (See pages 12–18.)	The U.S. Constitution established a federal form of government, in which government powers are shared by the national government and the state governments. At the national level, government powers are divided among the legislative, executive, and judicial branches. 1. *The commerce clause*— a. The expansion of national powers—The commerce clause expressly permits Congress to regulate commerce. Over time, courts expansively interpreted this clause, thereby enabling the national government to wield extensive powers over the economic life of the nation.

CHAPTER SUMMARY The Historical and Constitutional Foundations–Continued

The Constitutional Powers of Government– Continued	b. The commerce power today–Today, the commerce power authorizes the national government, at least theoretically, to regulate every commercial enterprise in the United States. In recent years, the United States Supreme Court has reined in somewhat the national government's regulatory powers under the commerce clause.
	c. The regulatory powers of the states–The Tenth Amendment reserves all powers not expressly delegated to the national government to the states. Under their police powers, state governments may regulate private activities to protect or promote the public order, health, safety, morals, and general welfare.
	d. The "dormant" commerce clause–If state regulations substantially interfere with interstate commerce, they will be held to violate the "dormant" commerce clause of the U.S. Constitution. The positive aspect of the commerce clause, which gives the national government the exclusive authority to regulate interstate commerce, implies a "dormant" aspect–that the states do not have this power.
	2. *The supremacy clause*–The U.S. Constitution provides that the Constitution, laws, and treaties of the United States are "the supreme Law of the Land." Whenever a state law directly conflicts with a federal law, the state law is rendered invalid.
Business and the Bill of Rights (See pages 18–23.)	The Bill of Rights, which consists of the first ten amendments to the U.S. Constitution, was adopted in 1791 and embodies a series of protections for individuals–and, in some instances, business entities–against various types of interference by the federal government. Freedoms guaranteed by the First Amendment that affect businesses include the following:
	1. *Freedom of speech*–Speech, including symbolic speech, is given the fullest possible protection by the courts. Corporate political speech and commercial speech also receive substantial protection under the First Amendment. Certain types of speech, such as defamatory speech and lewd or obscene speech, are not protected under the First Amendment. Government attempts to regulate unprotected forms of speech in the online environment have, to date, met with numerous challenges.
	2. *Freedom of religion*–Under the First Amendment, the government may neither establish any religion (the establishment clause) nor prohibit the free exercise of religion (the free exercise clause).
Due Process and Equal Protection (See pages 23–25.)	1. *Due process*–Both the Fifth and the Fourteenth Amendments provide that no person shall be deprived of "life, liberty, or property, without due process of law." Procedural due process requires that any government decision to take life, liberty, or property must be made fairly, using fair procedures. Substantive due process focuses on the content of legislation. Generally, a law that is not compatible with the U.S. Constitution violates substantive due process unless the law promotes a compelling state interest, such as public safety.
	2. *Equal protection*–Under the Fourteenth Amendment, a state may not "deny to any person within its jurisdiction the equal protection of the laws." A law or action that limits the liberty of some persons but not others may violate the equal protection clause. Such a law may be deemed valid, however, if there is a rational basis for the discriminatory treatment of a given group or if the law substantially relates to an important government objective.
Privacy Rights (See pages 25–28.)	Americans are increasingly becoming concerned over privacy issues raised by Internet-related technology. The U.S. Constitution does not contain a specific guarantee of a right to privacy, but such a right has been derived from guarantees found in several constitutional amendments. A number of federal statutes protect privacy rights. Privacy rights are also protected by many state constitutions and statutes, as well as under tort law.

FOR REVIEW

Answers for the even-numbered questions in this **For Review** *section can be found in Appendix E at the end of this text.*

1 What is the common law tradition?

2 What is a precedent? When might a court depart from precedent?

3 What is the difference between remedies at law and remedies in equity?

4 What constitutional clause gives the federal government the power to regulate commercial activities among the various states?

5 What is the Bill of Rights? What freedoms does the First Amendment guarantee?

QUESTIONS AND CASE PROBLEMS

HYPOTHETICAL SCENARIOS

1.1 Binding versus Persuasive Authority. A county court in Illinois is deciding a case involving an issue that has never been addressed before in that state's courts. The Iowa Supreme Court, however, recently decided a case involving a very similar fact pattern. Is the Illinois court obligated to follow the Iowa Supreme Court's decision on the issue? If the United States Supreme Court had decided a similar case, would that decision be binding on the Illinois court? Explain.

1.2 Legal Systems. What are the key differences between a common law system and a civil law system? Why do some countries have common law systems and others have civil law systems?

1.3 Hypothetical Question with Sample Answer. This chapter discussed a number of sources of American law. Which source of law takes priority in each of the following situations, and why?

  1 A federal statute conflicts with the U.S. Constitution.

  2 A federal statute conflicts with a state constitution.

  3 A state statute conflicts with the common law of that state.

  4 A state constitutional amendment conflicts with the U.S. Constitution.

  5 A federal administrative regulation conflicts with a state constitution.

For a sample answer to Question 1.3, go to Appendix F at the end of this text.

1.4 Commerce Clause. Suppose that Georgia enacts a law requiring the use of contoured rear-fender mudguards on trucks and trailers operating within its state lines. The statute further makes it illegal for trucks and trailers to use straight mudguards. In thirty-five other states, straight mudguards are legal. Moreover, in the neighboring state of Florida, straight mudguards are explicitly required by law. There is some evidence suggesting that contoured mudguards might be a little safer than straight mudguards. Discuss whether this Georgia statute would violate the commerce clause of the U.S. Constitution.

1.5 Freedom of Religion. A business has a backlog of orders, and to meet its deadlines, management decides to run the firm seven days a week, eight hours a day. One of the employees, Marjorie Tollens, refuses to work on Saturday on religious grounds. Her refusal to work means that the firm may not meet its production deadlines and may therefore suffer a loss of future business. The firm fires Tollens and replaces her with an employee who is willing to work seven days a week. Tollens claims that in terminating her employment, her employer violated her constitutional right to the free exercise of her religion. Do you agree? Why or why not?

CASE PROBLEMS

1.6 Due Process. In 1994, the Board of County Commissioners of Yellowstone County, Montana, created Zoning District 17 in a rural area of the county and a planning and zoning commission for the district. The commission adopted zoning regulations, which provided, among other things, that "dwelling units" could be built only through "on-site construction." Later, county officials could not identify any health or safety concerns that the on-site construction provision addressed, and there was no indication that homes built off-site would affect property values or any other general welfare interest of the community. In December 1999, Francis and Anita Yurczyk bought two forty-acre tracts in District 17. The Yurczyks also bought a modular home and moved it onto the property the following spring. Within days, the county advised the Yurczyks that the home violated the on-site construction regulation and would have to be removed. The Yurczyks filed a suit in a Montana state court against the county, alleging in part that the regulation violated the Yurczyks' due process rights. Should the court rule in the plaintiffs' favor? Explain. [*Yurczyk v. Yellowstone County,* 2004 MT 3, 319 Mont. 169, 83 P.3d 266 (2004)]

1.7 Case Problem with Sample Answer. To protect the privacy of individuals identified in information systems maintained by federal agencies, the Privacy Act of 1974 regulates the use of the information. The statute provides for a minimum award of $1,000 for "actual damages sustained" caused by "intentional or willful actions" to the "person entitled to recovery." Buck Doe filed for certain disability benefits with an office of the U.S. Department of Labor (DOL). The application form asked for Doe's Social Security number, which the DOL used to identify his claim on documents sent to groups of claimants, their employers, and the lawyers involved in their cases. This disclosed Doe's Social Security number beyond the limits set by the Privacy Act. Doe filed a suit in a federal district court against the DOL, alleging that he was "torn * * * all to pieces" and "greatly concerned and worried" because of the disclosure of his Social Security number and its potentially "devastating" consequences. He did not offer any proof of actual injury, however. Should damages be awarded in such circumstances solely on the basis of the agency's conduct, or should proof of some actual injury be required? Why? [*Doe v. Chao,* 540 U.S. 614, 124 S.Ct. 1204, 157 L.Ed.2d 1122 (2004)]

After you have answered Problem 1.7, compare your answer with the sample answer given on the Web site that accompanies this text. Go to academic.cengage.com/blaw/blt, select "Chapter 1," and click on "Case Problem with Sample Answer."

1.8 Supremacy Clause. The Federal Communications Act of 1934 grants the right to govern all *interstate* telecommunications to the Federal Communications Commission (FCC) and the right to regulate all *intrastate* telecommunications to the states. The federal Telephone Consumer Protection Act of 1991, the Junk Fax Protection Act of 2005, and FCC rules permit a party to send unsolicited fax ads to recipients with whom they have an "established business relationship" if those ads include an "opt-out" alternative. Section 17538.43 of California's Business and Professions Code (known as "SB 833") was enacted in 2005 to provide the citizens of California with greater protection than that afforded under federal law. SB 833 omits the "established business relationship" exception and requires a sender to obtain a recipient's express consent (or "opt-in") before faxing an ad to that party. The rule applies whether the sender is located in California or outside that state. The Chamber of Commerce of the United States filed a suit against Bill Lockyer, California's state attorney general, seeking to block the enforcement of SB 833. What principles support the plaintiff's position? How should the court resolve the issue? Explain. [*Chamber of Commerce of the United States v. Lockyer,* 463 F.3d 1076 (9th Cir. 2006)]

1.9 **A Question of Ethics.** *In 1999, in an effort to reduce smoking by children, the attorney general of Massachusetts issued comprehensive regulations governing the advertising and sale of tobacco products. Among other things, the regulations banned cigarette advertisements within one thousand feet of any elementary school, secondary school, or public playground and required retailers to post any advertising in their stores at least five feet off the floor, out of the immediate sight of young children. A group of tobacco manufacturers and retailers filed suit against the state, claiming that the regulations were preempted by the federal Cigarette Labeling and Advertising Act of 1965, as amended. That act sets uniform labeling requirements and bans broadcast advertising for cigarettes. Ultimately, the case reached the United States Supreme Court, which held that the federal law on cigarette ads preempted the cigarette advertising restrictions adopted by Massachusetts. The only portion of the Massachusetts regulatory package to survive was the requirement that retailers had to place tobacco products in an area accessible only by the sales staff. In view of these facts, consider the following questions.* [Lorillard Tobacco Co. v. Reilly, 533 U.S. 525, 121 S.Ct. 2404, 69 L.Ed.2d 532 (2001)]

1 Some argue that having a national standard for tobacco regulation is more important than allowing states to set their own standards for tobacco regulation. Do you agree? Why or why not?

2 According to the Court in this case, the federal law does not restrict the ability of state and local governments to adopt general zoning restrictions that apply to cigarettes, so long as those restrictions are "on equal terms with other products." How would you argue in support of this reasoning? How would you argue against it?

CRITICAL THINKING AND WRITING ASSIGNMENTS

1.10 Critical Legal Thinking. Courts of equity tend to follow general rules or maxims rather than following common law precedents, as courts of law do. Some of these maxims were listed in this chapter's *Landmark in the Law* feature on page 10. Why do equity courts give credence to such general maxims rather than to a hard-and-fast body of law?

1.11 Critical Thinking and Writing Assignment for Business. The commerce clause, as originally interpreted by the United States Supreme Court, was thought to allow the federal government to regulate interstate commerce. Over time, however, the Supreme Court has made it clear that the commerce clause applies not only to interstate commerce, but also to commerce that is purely intrastate. Today, the federal government has the power to regulate every commercial enterprise in the United States. What does this mean for commercial businesses that operate only within the borders of one state? Does it promote or discourage intrastate commerce?

ONLINE ACTIVITIES

 PRACTICAL INTERNET EXERCISES

Go to this text's Web site at **academic.cengage.com/blaw/blt**, select "Chapter 1," and click on "Practical Internet Exercises." There you will find the following Internet research exercises that you can perform to learn more about the topics covered in this chapter.

PRACTICAL INTERNET EXERCISE 1-1 LEGAL PERSPECTIVE—Internet Sources of Law

PRACTICAL INTERNET EXERCISE 1-2 MANAGEMENT PERSPECTIVE—Privacy Rights in Cyberspace

BEFORE THE TEST

Go to this text's Web site at **academic.cengage.com/businesslaw**, select "Chapter 1," and click on "Interactive Quizzes." You will find a number of interactive questions relating to this chapter.

APPENDIX TO CHAPTER 1:
Finding and Analyzing the Law

The statutes, agency regulations, and case law referred to in this text establish the rights and duties of businesspersons engaged in various types of activities. The cases presented in the following chapters provide you with concise, real-life illustrations of how the courts interpret and apply these laws. Because of the importance of knowing how to find statutory, administrative, and case law, this appendix offers a brief introduction to how these laws are published and to the legal "shorthand" employed in referencing these legal sources.

FINDING STATUTORY AND ADMINISTRATIVE LAW

When Congress passes laws, they are collected in a publication titled *United States Statutes at Large*. When state legislatures pass laws, they are collected in similar state publications. Most frequently, however, laws are referred to in their codified form—that is, the form in which they appear in the federal and state codes. In these codes, laws are compiled by subject.

United States Code

The *United States Code* (U.S.C.) arranges all existing federal laws of a public and permanent nature by subject. Each of the fifty subjects into which the U.S.C. arranges the laws is given a title and a title number. For example, laws relating to commerce and trade are collected in "Title 15, Commerce and Trade." Titles are subdivided by sections. A citation to the U.S.C. includes title and section numbers. Thus, a reference to "15 U.S.C. Section 1" means that the statute can be found in Section 1 of Title 15. ("Section" may also be designated by the symbol §, and "Sections" by §§.)

Sometimes a citation includes the abbreviation *et seq.*—as in "15 U.S.C. Sections 1 *et seq.*" The term is an abbreviated form of *et sequitur*, which is Latin for "and the following"; when used in a citation, it refers to sections that concern the same subject as the numbered section and follow it in sequence.

Commercial publications of these laws and regulations are available and are widely used. For example, West Group publishes the *United States Code Annotated* (U.S.C.A.). The U.S.C.A. contains the complete text of laws included in the U.S.C., notes of court decisions that interpret and apply specific sections of the statutes, and the text of presidential proclamations and executive orders. The U.S.C.A. also includes research aids, such as cross-references to related statutes, historical notes, and library references. A citation to the U.S.C.A. is similar to a citation to the U.S.C.: "15 U.S.C.A. Section 1."

State Codes

State codes follow the U.S.C. pattern of arranging law by subject. The state codes may be called codes, revisions, compilations, consolidations, general statutes, or statutes, depending

ON THE WEB

You can search the *United States Code* online at
www.law.cornell.edu/uscode.

on the preferences of the states. In some codes, subjects are designated by number. In others, they are designated by name. For example, "13 Pennsylvania Consolidated Statutes Section 1101" means that the statute can be found in Title 13, Section 1101, of the Pennsylvania code. "California Commercial Code Section 1101" means the statute can be found in Section 1101 under the subject heading "Commercial Code" of the California code. Abbreviations may be used. For example, "13 Pennsylvania Consolidated Statutes Section 1101" may be abbreviated "13 Pa. C.S. § 1101," and "California Commercial Code Section 1101" may be abbreviated "Cal. Com. Code § 1101."

Administrative Rules

Rules and regulations adopted by federal administrative agencies are compiled in the *Code of Federal Regulations* (C.F.R.). Like the U.S.C., the C.F.R. is divided into fifty titles. Rules within each title are assigned section numbers. A full citation to the C.F.R. includes title and section numbers. For example, a reference to "17 C.F.R. Section 230.504" means that the rule can be found in Section 230.504 of Title 17.

FINDING CASE LAW

Before discussing the case reporting system, we need to look briefly at the court system (which will be discussed in detail in Chapter 3). There are two types of courts in the United States, federal courts and state courts. Both the federal and the state court systems consist of several levels, or tiers, of courts. *Trial courts*, in which evidence is presented and testimony given, are on the bottom tier (which also includes lower courts handling specialized issues). Decisions from a trial court can be appealed to a higher court, which commonly would be an intermediate *court of appeals*, or an *appellate court*. Decisions from these intermediate courts of appeals may be appealed to an even higher court, such as a state supreme court or the United States Supreme Court.

State Court Decisions

Most state trial court decisions are not published. Except in New York and a few other states that publish selected opinions of their trial courts, decisions from state trial courts are merely filed in the office of the clerk of the court, where the decisions are available for public inspection. (Sometimes, they can be found online as well.) Written decisions of the appellate, or reviewing, courts, however, are published and distributed. As you will note, most of the state court cases presented in this book are from state appellate courts. The reported appellate decisions are published in volumes called *reports* or *reporters*, which are numbered consecutively. State appellate court decisions are found in the state reporters of that particular state.

Additionally, state court opinions appear in regional units of the *National Reporter System*, published by West Group. Most lawyers and libraries have the West reporters because they report cases more quickly and are distributed more widely than the state-published reports. In fact, many states have eliminated their own reporters in favor of West's National Reporter System. The National Reporter System divides the states into the following geographic areas: *Atlantic* (A. or A.2d), *North Eastern* (N.E. or N.E.2d), *North Western* (N.W. or N.W.2d), *Pacific* (P., P.2d, or P.3d), *South Eastern* (S.E. or S.E.2d), *South Western* (S.W., S.W.2d, or S.W.3d), and *Southern* (So. or So.2d). (The 2d and 3d in the abbreviations refer to *Second Series* and *Third Series*, respectively.) The states included in each of these regional divisions are indicated in Exhibit 1A–1, which illustrates West's National Reporter System.

EXHIBIT 1A–1 **West's National Reporter System—Regional/Federal**

Regional Reporters	Coverage Beginning	Coverage
Atlantic Reporter (A. or A.2d)	1885	Connecticut, Delaware, District of Columbia, Maine, Maryland, New Hampshire, New Jersey, Pennsylvania, Rhode Island, and Vermont.
North Eastern Reporter (N.E. or N.E.2d)	1885	Illinois, Indiana, Massachusetts, New York, and Ohio.
North Western Reporter (N.W. or N.W.2d)	1879	Iowa, Michigan, Minnesota, Nebraska, North Dakota, South Dakota, and Wisconsin.
Pacific Reporter (P., P.2d, or P.3d)	1883	Alaska, Arizona, California, Colorado, Hawaii, Idaho, Kansas, Montana, Nevada, New Mexico, Oklahoma, Oregon, Utah, Washington, and Wyoming.
South Eastern Reporter (S.E. or S.E.2d)	1887	Georgia, North Carolina, South Carolina, Virginia, and West Virginia.
South Western Reporter (S.W., S.W.2d, or S.W.3d)	1886	Arkansas, Kentucky, Missouri, Tennessee, and Texas.
Southern Reporter (So. or So.2d)	1887	Alabama, Florida, Louisiana, and Mississippi.

Federal Reporters		
Federal Reporter (F., F.2d, or F.3d)	1880	U.S. Circuit Courts from 1880 to 1912; U.S. Commerce Court from 1911 to 1913; U.S. District Courts from 1880 to 1932; U.S. Court of Claims (now called U.S. Court of Federal Claims) from 1929 to 1932 and since 1960; U.S. Courts of Appeals since 1891; U.S. Court of Customs and Patent Appeals since 1929; U.S. Emergency Court of Appeals since 1943.
Federal Supplement (F.Supp. or F.Supp.2d)	1932	U.S. Court of Claims from 1932 to 1960; U.S. District Courts since 1932; U.S. Customs Court since 1956.
Federal Rules Decisions (F.R.D.)	1939	U.S. District Courts involving the Federal Rules of Civil Procedure since 1939 and Federal Rules of Criminal Procedure since 1946.
Supreme Court Reporter (S.Ct.)	1882	United States Supreme Court since the October term of 1882.
Bankruptcy Reporter (Bankr.)	1980	Bankruptcy decisions of U.S. Bankruptcy Courts, U.S. District Courts, U.S. Courts of Appeals, and the United States Supreme Court.
Military Justice Reporter (M.J.)	1978	U.S. Court of Military Appeals and Courts of Military Review for the Army, Navy, Air Force, and Coast Guard.

NATIONAL REPORTER SYSTEM MAP

After appellate decisions have been published, they are normally referred to (cited) by the name of the case; the volume, name, and page number of the state's official reporter (if different from West's National Reporter System); the volume, name, and page number of the *National Reporter;* and the volume, name, and page number of any other selected reporter. This information is included in the *citation.* (Citing a reporter by volume number, name, and page number, in that order, is common to all citations.) When more than one reporter is cited for the same case, each reference is called a *parallel citation.* For example, consider the following case: *Buell-Wilson v. Ford Motor Co.,* 141 Cal.App.4th 525, 46 Cal.Rptr.3d 147 (2006). We see that the opinion in this case may be found in Volume 141 of the official *California Appellate Reports, Fourth Series,* on page 525. The parallel citation is to Volume 46 of the *California Reporter, Third Series,* page 147. In presenting appellate opinions in this text, in addition to the reporter, we give the name of the court hearing the case and the year of the court's decision.

A few states—including those with intermediate appellate courts, such as California, Illinois, and New York—have more than one reporter for opinions issued by their courts. Sample citations from these courts, as well as others, are listed and explained in Exhibit 1A–2.

Federal Court Decisions

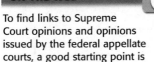

ON THE WEB

To find links to Supreme Court opinions and opinions issued by the federal appellate courts, a good starting point is FindLaw's guide at

findlaw.com/10fedgov/judicial.

Federal district court decisions are published unofficially in West's *Federal Supplement* (F. Supp. or F.Supp.2d), and opinions from the circuit courts of appeals (federal reviewing courts) are reported unofficially in West's *Federal Reporter* (F., F.2d, or F.3d). Cases concerning federal bankruptcy law are published unofficially in West's *Bankruptcy Reporter* (Bankr.). The official edition of United States Supreme Court decisions is the *United States Reports* (U.S.), which is published by the federal government. Unofficial editions of Supreme Court cases include West's *Supreme Court Reporter* (S.Ct.) and the *Lawyers' Edition of the Supreme Court Reports* (L.Ed. or L.Ed.2d). Sample citations for federal court decisions are also listed and explained in Exhibit 1A–2.

Unpublished Opinions and Old Cases

Many court opinions that are not yet published or that are not intended for publication can be accessed through Westlaw® (abbreviated in citations as "WL"), an online legal database maintained by West Group. When no citation to a published reporter is available for cases cited in this text, we give the WL citation (see Exhibit 1A–2 for an example).

On a few occasions, this text cites opinions from old, classic cases dating to the nineteenth century or earlier; some of these are from the English courts. The citations to these cases may not conform to the descriptions given above because the reporters in which they were published have since been replaced.

READING AND UNDERSTANDING CASE LAW

The cases in this text have been condensed from the full text of the courts' opinions and paraphrased by the authors. For those wishing to review court cases for future research projects or to gain additional legal information, the following sections will provide useful insights into how to read and understand case law.

Case Titles and Terminology

The title of a case, such as *Adams v. Jones,* indicates the names of the parties to the lawsuit. The *v.* in the case title stands for *versus,* which means "against." In the trial court, Adams was the plaintiff—the person who filed the suit. Jones was the defendant. If the

EXHIBIT 1A–2 **How to Read Citations**

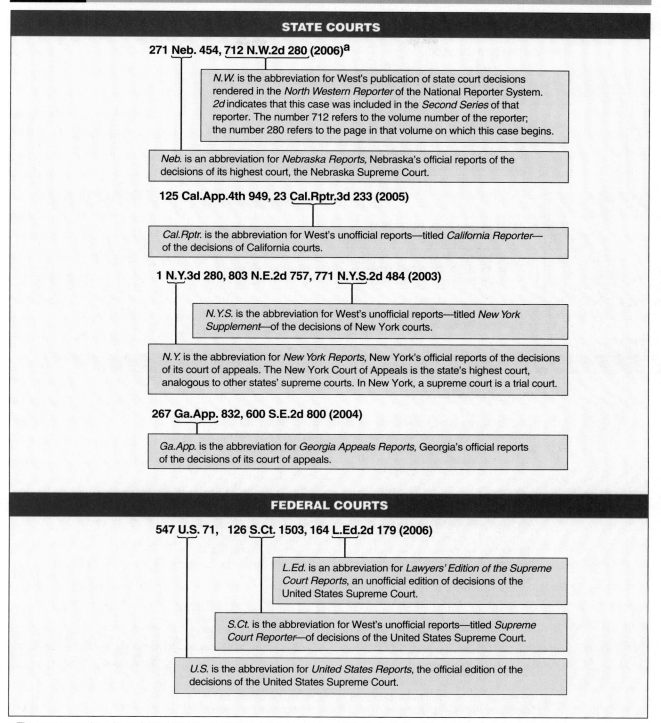

a. The case names have been deleted from these citations to emphasize the publications. It should be kept in mind, however, that the name of a case is as important as the specific page numbers in the volumes in which it is found. If a citation is incorrect, the correct citation may be found in a publication's index of case names. In addition to providing a check on errors in citations, the date of a case is important because the value of a recent case as an authority is likely to be greater than that of older cases.

(Continued)

EXHIBIT 1A–2 | **How to Read Citations—Continued**

FEDERAL COURTS (Continued)

439 F.3d 884 (8th Cir. 2006)

> *8th Cir.* is an abbreviation denoting that this case was decided in the United States Court of Appeals for the Eighth Circuit.

340 F.Supp.2d 1051 (D. S.D. 2004)

> *D. S.D.* is an abbreviation indicating that the United States District Court for the District of South Dakota decided this case.

ENGLISH COURTS

9 Exch. 341, 156 Eng.Rep. 145 (1854)

> *Eng.Rep.* is an abbreviation for *English Reports, Full Reprint,* a series of reports containing selected decisions made in English courts between 1378 and 1865.

> *Exch.* is an abbreviation for *English Exchequer Reports,* which includes the original reports of cases decided in England's Court of Exchequer.

STATUTORY AND OTHER CITATIONS

18 U.S.C. Section 1961(1)(A)

> *U.S.C.* denotes *United States Code,* the codification of *United States Statutes at Large.* The number 18 refers to the statute's U.S.C. title number and 1961 to its section number within that title. The number 1 in parentheses refers to a subsection within the section, and the letter A in parentheses to a subdivision within the subsection.

UCC 2–206(1)(b)

> *UCC* is an abbreviation for *Uniform Commercial Code.* The first number 2 is a reference to an article of the UCC, and 206 to a section within that article. The number 1 in parentheses refers to a subsection within the section, and the letter b in parentheses to a subdivision within the subsection.

Restatement (Second) of Torts, Section 568

> *Restatement (Second) of Torts* refers to the second edition of the American Law Institute's *Restatement of the Law of Torts.* The number 568 refers to a specific section.

17 C.F.R. Section 230.505

> *C.F.R.* is an abbreviation for *Code of Federal Regulations,* a compilation of federal administrative regulations. The number 17 designates the regulation's title number, and 230.505 designates a specific section within that title.

EXHIBIT 1A–2 **How to Read Citations—Continued**

WESTLAW® CITATIONS[b]

2006 WL 1193212

WL is an abbreviation for Westlaw. The number 2006 is the year of the document that can be found with this citation in the Westlaw database. The number 1193212 is a number assigned to a specific document. A higher number indicates that a document was added to the Westlaw database later in the year.

UNIFORM RESOURCE LOCATORS (URLs)

http://www.westlaw.com[c]

The suffix *com* is the top level domain (TLD) for this Web site. The TLD *com* is an abbreviation for "commercial," which usually means that a for-profit entity hosts (maintains or supports) this Web site.

westlaw is the host name—the part of the domain name selected by the organization that registered the name. In this case, West Group registered the name. This Internet site is the Westlaw database on the Web.

www is an abbreviation for "World Wide Web." The Web is a system of Internet servers that support documents formatted in *HTML* (hypertext markup language). HTML supports links to text, graphics, and audio and video files.

http://www.uscourts.gov

This is "The Federal Judiciary Home Page." The host is the Administrative Office of the U.S. Courts. The TLD *gov* is an abbreviation for "government." This Web site includes information and links from, and about, the federal courts.

http://www.law.cornell.edu/index.html

This part of a URL points to a Web page or file at a specific location within the host's domain. This page is a menu with links to documents within the domain and to other Internet resources.

This is the host name for a Web site that contains the Internet publications of the Legal Information Institute (LII), which is a part of Cornell Law School. The LII site includes a variety of legal materials and links to other legal resources on the Internet. The TLD *edu* is an abbreviation for "educational institution" (a school or a university).

http://www.ipl.org/div/news

This part of the Web site points to a static *news* page at this Web site, which provides links to online newspapers from around the world.

div is an abbreviation for "division," which is the way that the Internet Public Library tags the content on its Web site as relating to a specific topic.

ipl is an abbreviation for "Internet Public Library," which is an online service that provides reference resources and links to other information services on the Web. The IPL is supported chiefly by the School of Information at the University of Michigan. The TLD *org* is an abbreviation for "organization" (normally nonprofit).

b. Many court decisions that are not yet published or that are not intended for publication can be accessed through Westlaw, an online legal database.
c. The basic form for a URL is "service://hostname/path." The Internet service for all of the URLs in this text is *http* (hypertext transfer protocol). Because most Web browsers add this prefix automatically when a user enters a host name or a hostname/path, we have omitted the http:// from the URLs listed in this text.

case is appealed, however, the appellate court will sometimes place the name of the party appealing the decision first, so the case may be called *Jones v. Adams.* Because some reviewing courts retain the trial court order of names, it is often impossible to distinguish the plaintiff from the defendant in the title of a reported appellate court decision. You must carefully read the facts of each case to identify the parties.

The following terms and phrases are frequently encountered in court opinions and legal publications. Because it is important to understand what these terms and phrases mean, we define and discuss them here.

Plaintiffs and Defendants   As mentioned in Chapter 1, the plaintiff in a lawsuit is the party that initiates the action. The defendant is the party against which a lawsuit is brought. Lawsuits frequently involve more than one plaintiff and/or defendant.

Appellants and Appellees   The *appellant* is the party that appeals a case to another court or jurisdiction from the court or jurisdiction in which the case was originally brought. Sometimes, an appellant is referred to as the *petitioner.* The *appellee* is the party against which the appeal is taken. Sometimes, the appellee is referred to as the *respondent.*

Judges and Justices   The terms *judge* and *justice* are usually synonymous and represent two designations given to judges in various courts. All members of the United States Supreme Court, for example, are referred to as justices. And justice is the formal title usually given to judges of appellate courts, although this is not always the case. In New York, a justice is a judge of the trial court (which is called the Supreme Court), and a member of the Court of Appeals (the state's highest court) is called a judge. The term *justice* is commonly abbreviated to J., and *justices* to JJ. A Supreme Court case might refer to Justice Ginsburg as Ginsburg, J., or to Chief Justice Roberts as Roberts, C.J.

Decisions and Opinions   Most decisions reached by reviewing, or appellate, courts are explained in written *opinions.* The opinion contains the court's reasons for its decision, the rules of law that apply, and the judgment. When all judges or justices unanimously agree on an opinion, the opinion is written for the entire court and can be deemed a *unanimous opinion.* When there is not unanimous agreement, a *majority opinion* is written, outlining the views of the majority of the judges or justices deciding the case.

Often, a judge or justice who feels strongly about making or emphasizing a point that was not made or emphasized in the unanimous or majority opinion will write a *concurring opinion.* That means the judge or justice agrees (concurs) with the judgment given in the unanimous or majority opinion but for different reasons. When there is not a unanimous opinion, a *dissenting opinion* is usually written by a judge or justice who does not agree with the majority. The dissenting opinion is important because it may form the basis of the arguments used years later in overruling the precedential majority opinion. Occasionally, a court issues a *per curiam* (Latin for "of the court") opinion, which does not indicate which judge or justice authored the opinion.

A Sample Court Case

Knowing how to read and analyze a court opinion is an essential step in undertaking accurate legal research. A further step involves "briefing" the case. Legal researchers routinely brief cases by summarizing and reducing the texts of the opinions to their essential elements. (For instructions on how to brief a case, go to Appendix A at the end of this text.) The cases contained within the chapters of this text have already been analyzed and briefed by the authors, and the essential aspects of each case are presented in a convenient

*The United States Supreme Court
building in Washington, D.C. In what
reporters are Supreme Court
opinions published?* (PhotoDisc)

format consisting of four basic sections: *Facts, Issue, Decision,* and *Reason,* as shown in
Exhibit 1A–3 on pages 44 and 45, which has also been annotated to illustrate the kind of
information that is contained in each section.

Throughout this text, in addition to this basic format, we sometimes include a special
introductory section entitled *Historical and Social* [*Economic, Technological, Political,* or
other] *Setting.* In a few instances, a *Company Profile* is included in place of the introductory setting. These profiles provide background on one of the parties to the lawsuit. Each
case is followed by either a brief *For Critical Analysis* section, which, as in Exhibit 1A–3,
presents a question regarding some issue raised by the case; a *Why Is This Case Important
to Businesspersons?* section, which explains the significance of the case; or a *What If the
Facts Were Different?* question, which alters the facts slightly and asks you to consider how
this would change the outcome. A section entitled *Impact of This Case on Today's Law*
concludes the *Landmark and Classic Cases* that appear throughout the text to indicate the
significance of the case for today's legal landscape.

EXHIBIT 1A–3 **A Sample Court Case**

1

SAMPLE CASE **Nunez v. Carrabba's Italian Grill, Inc.**

Supreme Judicial Court of Massachusetts, 448 Mass. 170, 859 N.E.2d 801 (2007).

2

FACTS At about 7 P.M. on May 10, 2002, Robert Nunez, who was then eighteen years old, went to Carrabba's Italian Grill, Inc., a restaurant in Peabody, Massachusetts, where he had worked as a waiter. He ate dinner and drank six alcoholic beverages served to him by a bartender whom he knew. About 9:30 P.M., he drove home. Two hours later, he went to the Palace, a nightclub in Saugus. He had done promotional work for the club and had otherwise visited it at least thirty times, gaining entry with false identification. At the Palace, he was served one or two alcoholic beverages by a bartender whom he knew. After midnight, as he drove home, his vehicle approached an intersection with a green traffic light, and he accelerated to get through the light before it turned red. In the intersection, his car was struck by another car that failed to stop at the red light for the opposite direction. Nunez was thrown from his car and seriously injured. To recover for his injuries, he filed a suit in a Massachusetts state court against Carrabba's and the Palace, claiming, in part, that they were negligent in serving alcoholic beverages to him, an "intoxicated underage adult," and thus contributed to his injuries. The court issued a summary judgment partly in the defendants' favor. All of the parties appealed to the Supreme Judicial Court, Massachusetts's highest court.

ISSUE Does a commercial establishment licensed to sell alcohol to the public owe the same duty of care to a minor as it does to a person who is between eighteen and twenty-one years old?

DECISION Yes. The Supreme Judicial Court affirmed the lower court's judgment and remanded the case to that court for further proceedings. The duty of care that a licensed commercial establishment selling alcoholic beverages owes to an underage adult is the same as its duty to a minor.

3

REASON To persons under eighteen years of age (minors), a licensed establishment owes a duty to refrain from serving them any alcohol. In this case, the court pointed out that the Massachusetts state legislature has identified in many statutes the dangers of furnishing alcohol to underage adults (persons between eighteen and twenty-one years of age). "In light of these clear legislative concerns," the court concluded that the duty of care owed to minors applies "with equal force when the person to whom the alcohol is served is between the ages of eighteen and twenty-one years." In either circumstance, the person is under the legal drinking age. A certain statute forbids the serving of alcoholic beverages to those under the age of twenty-one years because "they are thought to be peculiarly susceptible to the effects of alcohol and less able to make decisions about what amount of alcohol they may safely consume in various situations." The court reasoned, "If the Legislature had deemed these concerns less significant for individuals between the ages of eighteen and twenty-one years, then it could have lowered the legal drinking age." Since 1984, however, the legal drinking age in Massachusetts has been twenty-one. To hold the defendants liable, the plaintiff need only show that they served him alcoholic beverages, though aware that he was under twenty-one, and that, as a consequence, he was injured.

 FOR CRITICAL ANALYSIS–Social Consideration *Should the duty applied in this case to certain commercial establishments apply with "equal force" to a social host serving alcohol to guests when one of those being served is an adult, but underage, individual? Why or why not?*

Review of Sample Court Case

1 The name of the case is *Nunez v. Carrabba's Italian Grill, Inc.* The injured underage adult at the center of this case is the plaintiff; one of the commercial establishments at which the plaintiff was served alcohol is the named defendant.

2 The court deciding this case is the Supreme Judicial Court of Massachusetts.

3 The case citation includes citations to the official *Massachusetts Reports* and to the unofficial *North Eastern Reporter, Second Series.* The case can be found in volume 448 of the *Massachusetts Reports* at page 170, and in volume 859 of the *North Eastern Reporter, Second Series,* at page 801.

4 The **FACTS** section identifies the plaintiff and the defendants, describes the events leading up to the lawsuit, and indicates what the plaintiff sought to obtain by bringing the action. Because this is a case before an appellate court, the ruling of the lower court is also included here.

5 The **ISSUE** section presents the central issue (or issues) to be decided by the court. In this case, the court is faced with an issue that has not yet been decided by any Massachusetts state court. Most cases concern more than one issue, but the authors of this textbook have edited each case to focus on just one issue.

6 The **DECISION** section, as the term indicates, contains the court's decision on the issue or issues before the court. The decision reflects the opinion of the judge, or the majority of the judges or justices, hearing the case. In this particular case, the court affirmed the lower court's judgment. Decisions by appellate courts are frequently phrased in reference to the lower court's decision—that is, the appellate court may "affirm" the lower court's ruling or "reverse" it. In either situation, the appellate court may "remand," or send back, the case for further proceedings.

7 The **REASON** section indicates what relevant laws and judicial principles were applied in forming the particular conclusion arrived at in the case at bar ("before the court"). In this case, the principle that was applied concerned the duty that a commercial establishment licensed to serve alcohol to the public owes to underage patrons. The court determined that such an establishment owes the same duty to all underage patrons, whether they are minors or adults.

8 The **FOR CRITICAL ANALYSIS—Social Consideration** section raises a question to be considered in relation to the case just presented. Here the question involves a "social" consideration. In other cases presented in this text, the "consideration" may involve a cultural, economic, environmental, ethical, international, political, or technological consideration.

CHAPTER 2
Ethics and Business Decision Making

"New occasions teach new duties."

James Russell Lowell, 1819–1891
(American editor, poet, and diplomat)

CHAPTER OUTLINE

–BUSINESS ETHICS

–SETTING THE RIGHT ETHICAL TONE

–COMPANIES THAT DEFY THE RULES

–BUSINESS ETHICS AND THE LAW

–APPROACHES TO ETHICAL REASONING

–BUSINESS ETHICS ON A GLOBAL LEVEL

LEARNING OBJECTIVES

AFTER READING THIS CHAPTER, YOU SHOULD BE ABLE TO ANSWER THE FOLLOWING QUESTIONS:

1 What is ethics? What is business ethics? Why is business ethics important?

2 How can business leaders encourage their companies to act ethically?

3 What are corporate compliance programs?

4 How do duty-based ethical standards differ from outcome-based ethical standards?

5 What types of ethical issues might arise in the context of international business transactions?

During the early part of the 2000s, the American public was shocked as one business ethics scandal after another became headline news. Each scandal involved serious consequences. Certainly, those officers and directors responsible for grossly inflating the reported profits at WorldCom, Inc., ended up not only destroying shareholder value in a great company but also facing prison terms. Those officers and directors at Enron Corporation who utilized a system of complicated off-the-books transactions to inflate current earnings saw their company go bankrupt—one of the largest bankruptcies in U.S. history. They harmed not only their employees and shareholders but also the communities in which they worked—and themselves (several of them have since received prison sentences). The officers and directors of Tyco International who used corporate funds to pay for lavish personal lifestyles also ended up in court. The shareholders of that company suffered dearly, too.

In response to the public's outrage over these scandals, Congress passed the Sarbanes-Oxley Act of 2002, which will be explained in detail in Chapter 21. In addition, excerpts and explanatory comments about this act can be found in Appendix D. This act imposed requirements on corporations that are designed to deter similar unethical and illegal business behavior in the future. Nevertheless, allegations of unethical business conduct continue to surface. As the chapter-opening quotation states, "New occasions teach new duties." Indeed, the ethics scandals in the last ten years taught businesses throughout the country that corporate governance is not to be taken lightly.

Business ethics, the focus of this chapter, is not just theory. It is practical, useful, and essential. Although a good understanding of business law and the legal environment is critical, it is not enough. Understanding how one should act in her or his business dealings is equally—if not more—important in today's business arena.

BUSINESS ETHICS

Before we look at business ethics, we need to discuss what is meant by ethics generally. **Ethics** can be defined as the study of what constitutes right or wrong behavior. It is the branch of philosophy that focuses on morality and the way in which moral principles are derived or the way in which a given set of moral principles applies to one's conduct in daily life. Ethics has to do with questions relating to the fairness, justness, rightness, or wrongness of an action. What is fair? What is just? What is the right thing to do in this situation? These are essentially ethical questions.

ETHICS
Moral principles and values applied to social behavior.

What Is Business Ethics?

Business ethics focuses on what constitutes right or wrong behavior in the business world and on how businesspersons apply moral and ethical principles to situations that arise in the workplace. Note that business ethics is not a separate *kind* of ethics. The ethical standards that guide our behavior as, say, mothers, fathers, or students apply equally well to our activities as businesspersons. Business decision makers, though, must often address more complex ethical issues and conflicts in the workplace than they face in their personal lives.

BUSINESS ETHICS
Ethics in a business context; a consensus as to what constitutes right or wrong behavior in the world of business and the application of moral principles to situations that arise in a business setting.

Why Is Business Ethics Important?

Why is business ethics important? The answer to this question is clear from this chapter's introduction. A keen and in-depth understanding of business ethics is important to the long-run viability of a corporation. A thorough knowledge of business ethics is also important to the well-being of the individual officers and directors of the corporation, as well as to the welfare of the firm's employees and various "stakeholders" in the entity's well-being. Certainly, corporate decisions and activities can significantly affect not only those who own, operate, or work for the company but also such groups as suppliers, the community, and society as a whole.

Note that questions concerning ethical and responsible behavior are not confined to the corporate context. Business ethics applies to *all* businesses, regardless of their organizational forms. In a business partnership, for example, partners owe a *fiduciary duty* (a duty of trust and loyalty) to each other and to their firm, just as corporate directors and officers owe fiduciary duties to the corporation (see Chapter 20).[1] Persons who act solely in their own interests may violate their duties to the firm or to the other partners.

President George W. Bush shakes hands with Congressman Mike Oxley (R., Ohio) during the signing ceremony for the Sarbanes-Oxley Act of 2002. The president stated, "This new law sends very clear messages that all concerned must heed. This law says to every dishonest corporate leader: you will be exposed and punished; the era of low standards and false profits is over; no boardroom in America is above or beyond the law." Has the 2002 act deterred unethical business conduct by corporate leaders? (White House Photo)

SETTING THE RIGHT ETHICAL TONE

Many unethical business decisions are made simply because they *can* be made. In other words, the decision makers not only have the opportunity to make such decisions but also are not too concerned about being seriously sanctioned for their unethical actions. Perhaps one of the most difficult challenges for business leaders today is to create the right "ethical tone" in their workplaces so as to deter unethical conduct.

---

1. For an example of the consequences that can result when business partners violate their ethical duties to one another, see *Time Warner Entertainment Co. v. Six Flags Over Georgia, L.L.C.*, 254 Ga.App. 598, 563 S.E.2d 178 (2002).

The Importance of Ethical Leadership

Talking about ethical business decision making means nothing if management does not set standards. Moreover, managers must apply those standards to themselves and to the employees in the company. The *Application* feature at the end of this chapter provides additional suggestions on how management can create an ethical workplace.

Attitude of Top Management   One of the most important factors in creating and maintaining an ethical workplace is the attitude of top management. Managers who are not totally committed to maintaining an ethical workplace will rarely succeed in creating one. Surveys of business executives indicate that management's behavior, more than anything else, sets the ethical tone of a firm. In other words, employees take their cue from management. If a firm's managers adhere to obvious ethical norms in their business dealings, employees will likely follow their example. In contrast, if managers act unethically, employees will see no reason not to do so themselves. ▣**EXAMPLE 2.1** Suppose that Kevin observes his manager cheating on her expense account. Kevin quickly understands that such behavior is acceptable. Later, when Kevin is promoted to a managerial position, he "pads" his expense account as well—knowing that he is unlikely to face sanctions for doing so. ▣

Looking the Other Way   A manager who looks the other way when he or she knows about an employee's unethical behavior also sets an example—one indicating that ethical transgressions will be accepted. Managers must show that they will not tolerate unethical business behavior. Although this may seem harsh, managers have found that discharging even one employee for ethical reasons has a tremendous impact as a deterrent to unethical behavior in the workplace. The following case illustrates what can happen when managers look the other way.

CASE 2.1   In re the *Exxon Valdez*

United States District Court, District of Alaska, 296 F.Supp.2d 1071 (2004).

FACTS Exxon Shipping Company owned the *Exxon Valdez,* an oil supertanker as long as three football fields with the capacity to hold 53 million gallons of crude oil. The captain of the *Valdez* was Joseph Hazelwood, an alcoholic, who had sought treatment in 1985 but had relapsed before the next spring. Exxon knew that Hazelwood had relapsed and that he drank while on board ship, but nevertheless allowed him to command the *Valdez*. On March 24, 1989, the *Valdez* ran aground on Bligh Reef in Prince William Sound, Alaska. About 11 million gallons of crude oil leaked from the ship and spread around the sound. Commercial fisheries closed for the rest of the year. Subsistence fishing and shore-based businesses dependent on the fishing industry were disrupted. Exxon spent $2.1 billion to clean up the spilled oil and paid $303 million to those whose livelihoods were disrupted. Thousands of claims were consolidated into a single case tried in a federal district court. The jury awarded, in part, $5 billion in punitive damages against Exxon. Exxon appealed to the U.S. Court of Appeals for

the Ninth Circuit, which remanded the case for reconsideration of this award, according to the reprehensibility [degree of wrongfulness] of the defendant's conduct and other factors. The appellate court also instructed the lower court to reduce the amount if the award was upheld.

ISSUE Did the $5 billion punitive damages award against Exxon constitute grossly excessive or arbitrary punishment?

DECISION No. The federal district court determined that Exxon's conduct was "intentionally malicious" and "highly reprehensible." Concluding that "[p]unitive damages should reflect the enormity of the defendant's offense," the court upheld the award but reduced the amount to $4.5 billion "as the means of resolving the conflict between its conclusion and the directions of the court of appeals."

REASON The court pointed out that "Exxon's conduct did not simply cause economic harm to the plaintiffs. Exxon's

CASE 2.1–Continued

decision to leave Captain Hazelwood in command of the *Exxon Valdez* demonstrated reckless disregard for a broad range of legitimate Alaska concerns: the livelihood, health, and safety of the residents of Prince William Sound, the crew of the *Exxon Valdez,* and others. Exxon's conduct targeted some financially vulnerable individuals, namely subsistence fishermen [those who barely make their living by fishing]. Plaintiffs' harm was not the result of an isolated incident but was the result of Exxon's repeated decisions, over a period of approximately three years, to allow Captain Hazelwood to remain in command despite Exxon's knowledge that he was drinking and driving again." The court compared Exxon's conduct with other cases in which punitive damages were awarded and concluded that "Exxon's conduct was many degrees of magnitude more egregious [conspicuously wrongful]. For approximately three years, Exxon management, with knowledge that Captain Hazelwood had fallen off the wagon, willfully permitted him to operate a fully loaded, crude oil tanker in and out of Prince William Sound—a body of water which Exxon knew to be highly valuable for its fisheries resources. Exxon's argument that its conduct in permitting a relapsed alcoholic to operate an oil tanker should be characterized as less reprehensible * * * suggests that Exxon, even today, has not come to grips with the opprobrium [disgrace, contempt] which society rightly attaches to drunk driving."

 WHY IS THIS CASE IMPORTANT TO BUSINESSPERSONS? *This case is a good illustration of the consequences that a business may face when it ignores a potentially significant risk that has been created by its action (or inaction). By allowing Captain Hazelwood, a relapsed alcoholic, to remain in charge of the Exxon Valdez, Exxon created serious risks to the environment and the residents of Prince William Sound. These risks led to severe harms. The consequences for Exxon—$4.5 billion in punitive damages—were also severe.*

Setting Realistic Goals Helps   Managers can reduce the probability that employees will act unethically by setting realistic production or sales goals. ▣**EXAMPLE 2.2** Suppose that a sales quota can be met only through high-pressure and unethical sales tactics. Employees trying to act "in the best interests of the firm" may think that management is implicitly asking them to behave unethically. ▣

Periodic Evaluation   Some companies require their managers to meet individually with employees and to grade them on their ethical (or unethical) behavior. ▣**EXAMPLE 2.3** One company asks its employees to fill out ethical checklists each month and return them to their supervisors. This practice serves two purposes: First, it demonstrates to employees that ethics matters. Second, employees have an opportunity to reflect on how well they have measured up in terms of ethical performance. ▣

Creating Ethical Codes of Conduct

One of the most effective ways of setting a tone of ethical behavior within an organization is to create an ethical code of conduct. A well-written code of ethics explicitly states a company's ethical priorities and demonstrates the company's commitment to ethical behavior.

Business owners wishing to avoid disputes over ethical violations must focus on creating a written ethical code that is clear and understandable (in plain English). The code should establish specific procedures that employees can follow if they have questions or complaints. It should assure employees that their jobs will be secure and that they will not face reprisals if they do file a complaint. Business owners should also explain to employees why these ethics policies are important to the company. A well-written code might include examples to clarify what the company considers to be acceptable and unacceptable conduct.

PREVENTING LEGAL DISPUTES

Costco—An Example   Exhibit 2–1 illustrates a code of ethics created by Costco Wholesale Corporation, a large warehouse-club retailer with more than 55 million "members." This code of conduct indicates Costco's commitment to legal compliance, as well as to the welfare of its members (those who purchase its goods), its employees, and its suppliers. The code also details some specific ways in which the interests and welfare of these different groups will be protected. You will also notice that Costco acknowledges that by protecting these groups' interests, it will realize its "ultimate goal"—rewarding its shareholders with maximum shareholder value.

Another Necessity—Providing Ethics Training to Employees   For an ethical code to be effective, its provisions must be clearly communicated to employees. Most large companies have implemented ethics training programs, in which managers discuss with employees on a face-to-face basis the firm's policies and the importance of ethical conduct. Some firms hold periodic ethics seminars during which employees can openly discuss any ethical problems that they may be experiencing and learn how the firm's ethical policies apply to those specific problems. Smaller firms should also offer some form of ethics training to employees because if a firm is accused of an ethics violation, the court will consider the presence or absence of such training in evaluating the firm's conduct.

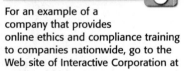

ON THE WEB

For an example of a company that provides online ethics and compliance training to companies nationwide, go to the Web site of Interactive Corporation at

www.integrity-interactive.com/ welcome.htm.

Johnson & Johnson—An Example of Web-Based Ethics Training   Creating a code of conduct and implementing it are two different activities. In many companies, codes of conduct have very little relevance to day-to-day operations. When Johnson & Johnson wanted to "do better" than other companies with respect to ethical business decision making, it created a Center for Legal and Credo Awareness. (Its code of ethical conduct is called its credo.) The center created a Web-based set of instructions designed to enhance the corporation's efforts to train employees in the importance of its code of conduct. Given that Johnson & Johnson has more than 115,000 employees in fifty-seven countries around the world, reinforcing its code of conduct and its values has not been easy, but Web-based training has helped.

The company established a Web-based legal and compliance center, which uses a set of interactive modules to train employees in areas of law and ethics. The curriculum is tailored to the individual employee based on his or her activities and job responsibilities. Moreover, employees can do the training right from their desks whenever they have the time. The company can track the employees' progress. The Web-based courses are then integrated into an ethical training program that also involves face-to-face classes. This comprehensive program helped Johnson & Johnson win an award from the *Wall Street Journal* for having the best corporate reputation in America.

Corporate Compliance Programs

In large corporations, ethical codes of conduct are usually just one part of a comprehensive corporate compliance program. Other components of such a program, some of which were already mentioned, include a corporation's ethics committee, ethical training programs, and internal audits to monitor compliance with applicable laws and the company's standards of ethical conduct.

The Sarbanes-Oxley Act and Web-Based Reporting Systems   The Sarbanes-Oxley Act of 2002[2] requires companies to set up confidential systems so that employees and others can "raise red flags" about suspected illegal or unethical auditing and accounting practices. The act required publicly traded companies to have such systems in place by April 2003.

---

2. 15 U.S.C. Sections 7201 *et seq.*

EXHIBIT 2-1 Costco's Code of Ethics

COSTCO
CODE OF ETHICS

By Jim Sinegal

OBEY THE LAW

The law is irrefutable! Absent a moral imperative to challenge a law, we must conduct our business in total compliance with the laws of every community where we do business.

- Comply with all statutes.
- Cooperate with authorities.
- Respect all public officials and their positions.
- Avoid all conflict of interest issues with public officials.
- Comply with all disclosure and reporting requirements.
- Comply with safety and security standards for all products sold.
- Exceed ecological standards required in every community where we do business.
- Comply with all applicable wage and hour laws.
- Comply with all applicable anti-trust laws.
- Protect "inside information" that has not been released to the general public.

TAKE CARE OF OUR MEMBERS

The member is our key to success. If we don't keep our members happy, little else that we do will make a difference.

- Provide top-quality products at the best prices in the market.
- Provide a safe shopping environment in our warehouses.
- Provide only products that meet applicable safety and health standards.
- Sell only products from manufacturers who comply with "truth in advertising/packaging" standards.
- Provide our members with a 100% satisfaction guaranteed warranty on every product and service we sell, including their membership fee.
- Assure our members that every product we sell is authentic in make and in representation of performance.
- Make our shopping environment a pleasant experience by making our members feel welcome as our guests.
- Provide products to our members that will be ecologically sensitive.

Our member is our reason for being. If they fail to show up, we cannot survive. Our members have extended a "trust" to Costco by virtue of paying a fee to shop with us. We can't let them down or they will simply go away. We must always operate in the following manner when dealing with our members:
Rule #1 – The member is always right.
Rule #2 – In the event that the member is ever wrong, refer to rule #1.

There are plenty of shopping alternatives for our members. We will succeed only if we do not violate the trust they have extended to us. We must be committed at every level of our company, with every ounce of energy and grain of creativity we have, to constantly strive to "bring goods to market at a lower price."

If we do these four things throughout our organization, we will realize our ultimate goal, which is to REWARD OUR SHAREHOLDERS.

TAKE CARE OF OUR EMPLOYEES

To claim "people are our most important asset" is true and an understatement. Each employee has been hired for a very important job. Jobs such as stocking the shelves, ringing members' orders, buying products, and paying our bills are jobs we would all choose to perform because of their importance. The employees hired to perform these jobs are performing as management's "alter egos." Every employee, whether they are in a Costco warehouse, or whether they work in the regional or corporate offices, is a Costco ambassador trained to give our members professional, courteous treatment.

Today we have warehouse managers who were once stockers and callers, and vice presidents who were once in clerical positions for Costco. We believe that Costco's future executive officers are currently working in our warehouses, depots, buying offices, and accounting departments, as well as in our home offices.

To that end, we are committed to these principles:

- Provide a safe work environment.
- Pay a fair wage.
- Make every job challenging, but make it fun!
- Consider the loss of any employee as a failure on the part of the company and a loss to the organization.
- Teach our people how to do their jobs and how to improve personally and professionally.
- Promote from within the company to achieve the goal of a minimum of 80% of management positions being filled by current employees.
- Create an "open door" attitude at all levels of the company that is dedicated to "fairness and listening."

RESPECT OUR VENDORS

Our vendors are our partners in business and for us to prosper as a company, they must prosper with us. It is important that our vendors understand that we will be tough negotiators, but fair in our treatment of them.

- Treat all vendors and their representatives as you would expect to be treated if visiting their places of business.
- Pay all bills within the allocated time frame.
- Honor all commitments.
- Protect all vendor property assigned to Costco as though it were our own.
- Always be thoughtful and candid in negotiations.
- Provide a careful review process with at least two levels of authorization before terminating business with an existing vendor of more than two years.
- Do not accept gratuities of any kind from a vendor.

These guidelines are exactly that – guidelines, some common sense rules for the conduct of our business. Intended to simplify our jobs, not complicate our lives, these guidelines will not answer every question or solve every problem. At the core of our philosophy as a company must be the implicit understanding that not one of us is required to lie or cheat on behalf of PriceCostco. In fact, dishonest conduct will not be tolerated. To do any less would be unfair to the overwhelming majority of our employees who support and respect Costco's commitment to ethical business conduct.

If you are ever in doubt as to what course of action to take on a business matter that is open to varying ethical interpretations, take the high road and do what is right.

If you want our help, we are always available for advice and counsel. That's our job and we welcome your questions or comments.

Our continued success depends on you. We thank each of you for your contribution to our past success and for the high standards you have insisted upon in our company.

"Truth in advertising/packaging" legal standards are part of the statutes and regulations that are discussed in Chapter 13, which deals with consumer law.

If the company did not provide products that comply with safety and health standards, it could be held liable in civil suits on legal grounds that are classified as torts (see Chapter 4).

Disclosure of "inside information" that constitutes *trade secrets* could subject an employee to civil liability or criminal prosecution (see Chapters 5 and 6).

Antitrust laws apply to illegal restraints of trade—an agreement between competitors to set prices, for example, or an attempt by one company to control an entire market. Antitrust laws are discussed in Chapter 22.

Failure to comply with "ecological" standards could be a violation of environmental laws (see Chapter 24).

Accepting "gratuities" from a vendor might be interpreted as accepting a bribe. This can be a crime (see Chapter 6). In an international context, a bribe can be a violation of the Foreign Corrupt Practices Act. This act is discussed in Chapters 2 and 25.

If the company fails to honor one of its commitments, it may be sued for breach of contract (see Chapters 9 and 12).

Failing to pay bills when they become due could subject the company to the creditors' remedies discussed in Chapter 16. The company might even be forced into involuntary bankruptcy (see Chapter 16).

Promotions and other benefits of employment cannot be granted or withheld on the basis of discrimination. This is against the law. Employment discrimination is the subject of Chapter 18.

Safety standards for the work environment are governed by the Occupational Safety and Health Act and other statutes. Laws regulating safety in the workplace are discussed in Chapter 18.

Costco Background

Costco Wholesale Corporation operates a chain of cash-and-carry membership warehouses that sell high-quality, nationally branded, and selected private-label merchandise at low prices. Its target markets include both businesses that buy goods for commercial use or resale and individuals who are employees or members of specific organizations and associations. The company tries to reach high sales volume and fast inventory turnover by offering a limited choice of merchandise in many product groups at competitive prices.

The company takes a strong position on behaving ethically in all transactions and relationships. It expects employees to behave ethically. For example, no one can accept gratuities from vendors. The company also expects employees to behave ethically, according to domestic ethical standards, in any country in which it operates.

Some companies have implemented online reporting systems. In one Web-based reporting system, employees can click on an icon on their computers that anonymously links them with Ethicspoint, an organization based in Vancouver, Washington. Through Ethicspoint, employees can report suspicious accounting practices, sexual harassment, and other possibly unethical behavior. Ethicspoint, in turn, alerts management personnel or the audit committee at the designated company to the possible problem. Those who have used the system say that it is less inhibiting than calling a company's toll-free number.

ON THE WEB

You can find articles on issues relating to corporate governance and accountability at the Corporate Governance Web site. Go to

www.corpgov.net.

Corporate Governance Principles   Implementation of the Sarbanes-Oxley Act has prompted many companies to create new rules of *corporate governance*. As you will read in Chapter 21, corporate governance refers to the internal principles establishing the rights and responsibilities of a corporation's management, its board of directors, its shareholders, and its *stakeholders* (those affected by corporate decisions, including employees, customers, suppliers, and creditors, for example). Corporate governance principles usually go beyond what is required to comply with existing laws. The goal is to set up a system of fair procedures and accurate disclosures that keeps all parties well informed and accountable to one another and provides a mechanism for the corporation to resolve any problems that arise. Ultimately, good corporate governance should attract investors and stimulate growth while discouraging unethical behavior and fraud.

Compliance Programs Must Be Integrated   To be effective, a compliance program must be integrated throughout the firm. For large corporations, such integration is essential. Ethical policies and programs need to be coordinated and monitored by a committee that is separate from various corporate departments. Otherwise, unethical behavior in one department can easily escape the attention of those in control of the corporation or the corporate officials responsible for implementing and monitoring the company's compliance program.

Conflicts and Trade-Offs

Management constantly faces ethical trade-offs, some of which may lead to legal problems. As mentioned earlier, firms have implied ethical (and legal) duties to a number of groups, including shareholders and employees.

When a company decides to reduce costs by downsizing and restructuring, the decision may benefit shareholders, but it will harm those employees who are laid off or fired. When downsizing occurs, which employees should be laid off first? Cost-cutting considerations might dictate firing the most senior employees, who generally have higher salaries, and retaining less senior employees, whose salaries are much lower. A company does not necessarily act illegally when it does so (but may face lawsuits nonetheless). Yet the decision to be made by management clearly involves an important ethical question: Which group's interests—those of the shareholders or those of employees who have been loyal to the firm for a long period of time—should take priority in this situation?

■EXAMPLE 2.4   In one case, an employer facing a dwindling market and decreasing sales decided to reduce its costs by eliminating some of its obligations to its employees. It did this by establishing a subsidiary corporation and then transferring some of its employees, and the administration of their retirement benefits, to that entity. The company expected the subsidiary to fail, and when it did, some employees and retirees who were left with no retirement benefits sued the company. The plaintiffs claimed that the company had breached a fiduciary duty under a federal law governing employer-provided pensions. Ultimately, the United States Supreme Court agreed with the plaintiffs, stating, among other things, that "[l]ying is inconsistent with the duty of loyalty owed by all fiduciaries."[3] ■

---

3. *Varity Corp. v. Howe*, 516 U.S. 489, 116 S.Ct. 1065, 134 L.Ed.2d 130 (1996).

COMPANIES THAT DEFY THE RULES

One of the best ways to learn the ethical responsibilities inherent in operating a business is to look at the mistakes made by other companies. In the following subsections, we describe some of the ethical failures of companies that have raised public awareness of corporate misconduct and highlighted the need for ethical leadership in business.

Enron's Growth and Demise in a Nutshell

The Enron Corporation was one of the first companies to benefit from the deregulated electricity market. By 1998, Enron was the largest energy trader in the market. When competition in energy trading increased, Enron diversified into water, power plants, and eventually high-speed Internet and fiber optics (the value of which soon became negligible). Because Enron's managers received bonuses based on whether they met earnings goals, they had an incentive to inflate the anticipated earnings on energy contracts, which they did. Enron included these anticipated earnings in its current earnings reports, which vastly overstated the company's actual profit. Then, to artificially maintain and even increase its reported earnings, Enron created a complex network of subsidiaries that enabled it to move losses to the subsidiaries and hide its debts.

The overall effect of these actions was to increase Enron's apparent net worth. These "off-the-books" transactions were also frequently carried out in the Cayman Islands to avoid paying federal income taxes. In addition, Enron's longtime chief executive officer (CEO) Kenneth Lay engaged in a pattern of self-dealing by doing business with companies owned by his son and daughter.[4] Enron's management was informed about these incidents of misconduct on numerous occasions, yet the company concealed the financial improprieties for several years—until Enron was bankrupt.

Deceptive accounting practices were at the heart of the Enron debacle, which led to one of the largest bankruptcies in the history of U.S. business. For years to come, the Enron scandal will remain a symbol of the cost of unethical behavior to management, employees, suppliers, shareholders, the community, society, and indeed the world. Enron's shareholders lost $62 billion of value in a very short period of time in the early 2000s as a result of management's deceptive accounting practices, conflicts of interest, and deviation from accepted ethical standards of business.

Merck & Company—A Brief History of Vioxx

In 1999, Merck & Company, Inc., the maker of Vioxx, received approval from the U.S. Food and Drug Administration (FDA) to market the drug for the treatment of acute pain in adults. The FDA gave Vioxx a six-month priority review because it was thought that Vioxx caused fewer gastrointestinal side effects, such as bleeding, than other painkillers (including ibuprofen and aspirin). Merck spent millions of dollars persuading physicians and consumers to use Vioxx for pain, especially arthritis pain, instead of less expensive alternatives, which could cause stomach bleeding. Many people who used Vioxx found that it provided more effective short-term relief for pain, particularly from athletic injuries, than any other painkiller on the market at the time. At its peak, Vioxx had more than 20 million users.

Shortly after the drug's debut, however, troubling signs began to appear. In March 2000, Merck reported the results of a study of eight thousand people who had used Vioxx over long periods. The study compared the gastrointestinal effects of Vioxx and

---

4. In 2006, Lay was found guilty of securities fraud and other charges but died before he could be sentenced. As a result of his death, his conviction was vacated. In October 2006, Jeffrey K. Skilling, who served as Enron's CEO from February to August 2001, was sentenced to more than twenty-four years in prison for corporate fraud and forced to pay back $45 million that he had obtained through his illegal conduct.

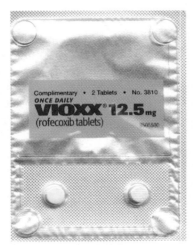

Studies found that patients who took high doses of Vioxx over long periods had significantly more heart attacks and strokes than similar patients who took other medications. Does this finding necessarily mean that the makers of Vioxx behaved unethically by continuing to market the drug? Why or why not? (Justin Griffith/Creative Commons)

naproxen, another popular painkiller. Although the study ultimately found that patients taking Vioxx had less stomach bleeding than those taking naproxen, the study also indicated that patients taking Vioxx had up to four times as many heart attacks and strokes as patients using naproxen. These results occurred even though the study had excluded patients with heart risks.

Independent studies of the drug conducted in 2001, 2002, and 2004 all suggested correlations between Vioxx and increased risk of heart attack. Finally, Merck's own study revealed that Vioxx increased cardiovascular risks after eighteen months of daily use. Shortly after that, in September 2004, Merck voluntarily removed Vioxx from the worldwide market in the largest drug recall in history.

Merck's Awareness of the Risks of Vioxx   As mentioned, the initial 2000 study on Vioxx and naproxen showed that patients taking Vioxx for an extended period had up to four times as many heart attacks and strokes as those who took naproxen. Because the drug was often prescribed on a long-term basis for arthritis patients, this was a significant finding. Merck attributed the result to naproxen's strong, protective effect on the heart. Merck never tested this theory, however, and scientists outside the company who found this explanation unlikely began to conduct independent studies of the drug.

In 2001, a cardiologist proposed to Merck a study of Vioxx in patients with severe chest pain, but Merck declined. When a 2002 study found that patients who took high doses of Vioxx had significantly more heart attacks and strokes than similar patients, Merck maintained that it still had confidence in the drug's safety. Merck maintained this stance even after receiving a warning letter from the FDA in 2001 reprimanding the company for understating the drug's potentially serious cardiovascular effects. The FDA required Merck to send letters to physicians across the country to correct false or misleading impressions and information.

Merck's Choice   Merck's top research and marketing executives met in 2000 to consider ways to defend Vioxx against allegations that it posed cardiovascular risks. One suggestion was to develop a study that would directly test whether Vioxx posed these risks. That idea was rejected. Merck's marketing executives were apparently afraid that conducting a study would send the wrong signal about the company's faith in Vioxx. The company's position over the following years stayed the same: Vioxx was safe unless proved otherwise. The company continued to maintain that stance in the face of thousands of lawsuits that were filed blaming Vioxx for patients' injuries or deaths. Merck argued that every plaintiff in those suits must prove that the drug, not something else, caused the alleged injury or death. This tactic focused attention on such factors as users' lifestyles and preexisting health issues rather than on the alleged dangers of Vioxx.

The Debate Continues   The debate over the safety of Vioxx and whether Merck's conduct was ethical poses an interesting question: At what point does a corporation have an ethical duty to act when presented with evidence that its product may be harmful? Various studies estimate that as many as 139,000 people who used Vioxx suffered injuries or death. This figure may seem large, but it is actually less than 1 percent of Vioxx's total users. Some would argue that even one death is too many and that Merck should be responsible for compensating all those who were injured. Others would counter that the use of any drug involves risks and that Merck did nothing wrong by waiting for conclusive evidence of harm before recalling Vioxx.

To date, more than 27,000 lawsuits have been filed against Merck over Vioxx, many with multiple plaintiffs. Merck has been fairly successful in litigation so far, convincing about half of the juries that other health problems (such as high cholesterol, clogged arteries, old age, and smoking) caused the harm to the plaintiffs. Nevertheless, the company has spent millions of dollars litigating these cases and has set aside approximately $970 million to cover the costs. These costs will ultimately be borne by Merck's shareholders.

Concerns over drug safety, unethical practices by pharmaceutical companies, and mass consumer advertising of new medications have prompted many to criticize the FDA and recommend an overhaul of its drug-approval system. Even if the FDA eventually adopts revised procedures, however, questions remain over what exactly a corporation must do to fulfill its ethical duties with regard to notifying the public about the potential risks of using a product.

BUSINESS ETHICS AND THE LAW

Today, legal compliance is regarded as a **moral minimum**—the minimum acceptable standard for ethical business behavior. Had Enron Corporation strictly complied with existing laws and generally accepted accounting practices, very likely the "Enron scandal" would never have happened. Simply obeying the law does not fulfill all business ethics obligations, however, as illustrated by the controversy surrounding the safety of the drug Vioxx. In the interests of preserving personal freedom, as well as for practical reasons, the law does not—and cannot—codify all ethical requirements. No law says, for example, that it is illegal to lie to one's family, but it may be unethical to do so.

It might seem that determining the legality of a given action should be simple. Either something is legal or it is not. In fact, one of the major challenges businesspersons face is that the legality of a particular action is not always clear. In part, this is because there are so many laws regulating business that it is possible to violate one of them without realizing it. The law also contains numerous "gray areas," making it difficult to predict with certainty how a court will apply a given law to a particular action.

MORAL MINIMUM
The minimum degree of ethical behavior expected of a business firm, which is usually defined as compliance with the law.

How can a business decide whether a warning is "adequate"? As an example of how it is not always clear what the law is on a particular subject, consider the laws dealing with product misuse. As you will read in Chapter 13, product liability laws require manufacturers and sellers to warn consumers of the kinds of injuries that might result from the foreseeable misuse of their products. An exception to this rule is made when a risk associated with a product is "open and obvious." Sharp knives, for example, can obviously injure their users. Sometimes, however, a business has no way of predicting how a court might rule in deciding whether a particular risk is open and obvious or whether consumers should be warned of the risk. If consumers should be warned, a further question arises: What constitutes an adequate warning? Even the courts often disagree on such matters.

ETHICAL ISSUE 2.1

In one case, for example, a company sold small aerosol cans of butane, a fuel for cigarette lighters. On each can was the warning "DO NOT BREATHE SPRAY." Nonetheless, twenty-year-old Stephen Pavlik died from *intentionally* inhaling the contents of one of the cans. In the lawsuit that followed, brought by Pavlik's father, the trial court and the appellate court came to different conclusions. The trial court reasoned that Pavlik must have been aware of the dangers of inhaling butane and that a more specific warning would not have affected his conduct. The appellate court, though, concluded that the warning gave Pavlik "no notice of the serious nature of the danger posed by inhalation, intentional or otherwise."[5] Cases such as this send a clear message to businesspersons: never assume that a risk that may seem open and obvious to you will necessarily be open and obvious to a court.

---

5. *Pavlik v. Lane Ltd./Tobacco Exporters International*, 135 F.3d 876 (3d Cir. 1998).

Laws Regulating Business

Today's business firms are subject to extensive government regulation. As mentioned in Chapter 1, virtually every action a firm undertakes—from the initial act of going into business, to hiring and firing personnel, to selling products in the marketplace—is subject to statutory law and to numerous rules and regulations issued by administrative agencies. Furthermore, these rules and regulations are changed or supplemented frequently.

Determining whether a planned action is legal thus requires that decision makers keep abreast of the law. Normally, large business firms have attorneys on their staffs to assist them in making key decisions. Small firms must also seek legal advice before making important business decisions because the consequences of just one violation of a regulatory rule may be costly. Ignorance of the law will not excuse a business owner or manager from liability for violating a statute or regulation.

"Gray Areas" in the Law

In many situations, business firms can predict with a fair amount of certainty whether a given action would be legal. For instance, firing an employee solely because of that person's race or gender would clearly violate federal laws prohibiting employment discrimination. In some situations, though, the legality of a particular action may be less clear. **EXAMPLE 2.5** Suppose that a firm decides to launch a new advertising campaign. How far can the firm go in making claims for its products or services? Federal and state laws prohibit firms from engaging in "deceptive advertising." At the federal level, the test for deceptive advertising normally used by the Federal Trade Commission is whether an advertising claim would deceive a "reasonable consumer."[6] At what point, though, would a reasonable consumer be deceived by a particular ad? ■

In short, business decision makers need to proceed with caution and evaluate an action and its consequences from an ethical perspective. Generally, if a company can demonstrate that it acted in good faith and responsibly in the circumstances, it has a better chance of successfully defending its action in court or before an administrative law judge.

The following case demonstrates that businesses and their customers may have differing expectations with respect to the standard of care required in handling personal information. The case also illustrates how the legal standards in this context may be inconsistent and vague.

---

6. See Chapter 13 for a discussion of the Federal Trade Commission's role in regulating deceptive trade practices, including misleading advertising.

CASE 2.2   **Guin v. Brazos Higher Education Service Corp.**

United States District Court, District of Minnesota, __ F.Supp.2d __ (2006).

FACTS Brazos Higher Education Service Corporation, which is based in Waco, Texas, makes and services student loans. Brazos issued a laptop computer to its employee John Wright, who works from an office in his home in Silver Spring, Maryland, analyzing loan information. Wright used the laptop to store borrowers' personal information. In September 2004,

Wright's home was burglarized and the laptop was stolen. Based on Federal Trade Commission (FTC) guidelines and California state law (which requires notice to all resident borrowers), Brazos sent a letter to all of its 550,000 customers. The letter stated that "some personal information associated with your student loan, including your name, address, Social Security number and loan balance, may have been inappropriately

CASE 2.2–Continued

accessed by [a] third party." The letter urged borrowers to place "a free 90-day security alert" on their credit bureau files and review FTC consumer assistance materials. Brazos set up a call center to answer further questions and track any reports of identity theft. Stacy Guin, a Brazos customer, filed a suit against Brazos in a federal district court, alleging negligence. Brazos filed a motion for summary judgment.

ISSUE Does a lender that complies with the legal requirements for safeguarding its customers' personal information breach a duty to those customers if the information is "inappropriately accessed by [a] third party"?

DECISION No. The court granted the defendant's motion for summary judgment and dismissed the case. Brazos may have owed Guin a duty of care, but neither Brazos nor Wright breached that duty. Wright had followed Brazos's written security procedures, which was all that the law requires.

REASON The court acknowledged that Brazos had a duty to protect the security and confidentiality of its customers' personal information. Under the Gramm-Leach-Bliley (GLB) Act, a financial institution must "[d]evelop, implement, and

maintain a comprehensive written information security program that * * * contains administrative, technical, and physical safeguards that are appropriate to * * * the sensitivity of any customer information." Guin argued that Brazos breached this duty by (1) "providing Wright with [personal information] that he did not need for the task at hand," (2) "permitting Wright to continue keeping [personal information] in an unattended, insecure personal residence," and (3) "allowing Wright to keep [personal information] on his laptop unencrypted." The court disagreed. Brazos had established written security policies and other mandated safeguards for its customers' personal information. Brazos gave Wright access to the information because Wright needed it to analyze loan portfolios. Besides, the GLB Act does not prohibit someone from working with sensitive data on a laptop computer in a home office or require that the data be encrypted.

WHAT IF THE FACTS WERE DIFFERENT? *Suppose that Wright had not been a financial analyst and that his duties for Brazos had not included reviewing confidential loan data. How might the opinion of the court have been different?*

APPROACHES TO ETHICAL REASONING

Each individual, when faced with a particular ethical dilemma, engages in **ethical reasoning**—that is, a reasoning process in which the individual examines the situation at hand in light of her or his moral convictions or ethical standards. Businesspersons do likewise when making decisions with ethical implications.

How do business decision makers decide whether a given action is the "right" one for their firms? What ethical standards should they apply? Broadly speaking, ethical reasoning relating to business traditionally has been characterized by two fundamental approaches. One approach defines ethical behavior in terms of duty, which also implies certain rights. The other approach determines what is ethical in terms of the consequences, or outcome, of any given action. We examine each of these approaches here.

In addition to the two basic ethical approaches, a few theories have been developed that specifically address the social responsibility of corporations. Because these theories also influence today's business decision makers, we conclude with a discussion of the different views of corporate social responsibility.

ETHICAL REASONING
A reasoning process in which an individual links his or her moral convictions or ethical standards to the particular situation at hand.

BE CAREFUL Ethical concepts about what is right and what is wrong can change.

Duty-Based Ethics

Duty-based ethical standards are often derived from revealed truths, such as religious precepts. They can also be derived through philosophical reasoning.

Religious Ethical Standards In the Judeo-Christian tradition, which is the dominant religious tradition in the United States, the Ten Commandments of the Old Testament establish fundamental rules for moral action. Other religions have their own sources of revealed truth. Religious rules generally are absolute with respect to the behavior of their adherents. **■EXAMPLE 2.6** The commandment "Thou shalt not steal" is an absolute mandate for a person who believes that the Ten Commandments reflect revealed truth. Even a benevolent motive for stealing (such as Robin Hood's) cannot justify the act because the act itself is inherently immoral and thus wrong. ■

Ethical standards based on religious teachings also involve an element of *compassion*. **■EXAMPLE 2.7** Even though it might be profitable for a firm to lay off a less productive employee, if that employee's family would suffer as a result, a religious person might give this potential suffering substantial weight. ■ Compassionate treatment of others is also mandated to some extent by the "Golden Rule" ("Do unto others as you would have them do unto you"), which most religions follow.

Kantian Ethics Duty-based ethical standards may also be derived solely from philosophical reasoning. The German philosopher Immanuel Kant (1724–1804), for example, identified some general guiding principles for moral behavior based on what he believed to be the fundamental nature of human beings. Kant believed that human beings are qualitatively different from other physical objects and are endowed with moral integrity and the capacity to reason and conduct their affairs rationally. Therefore, a person's thoughts and actions should be respected. When human beings are treated merely as a means to an end, they are being viewed as the equivalent of objects and are being denied their basic humanity.

A central theme in Kantian ethics is that individuals should evaluate their actions in light of the consequences that would follow if *everyone* in society acted in the same way. This **categorical imperative** can be applied to any action. **■EXAMPLE 2.8** Suppose that you are deciding whether to cheat on an examination. If you have adopted Kant's categorical imperative, you will decide not to cheat because if everyone cheated, the examination would be meaningless. ■

The Principle of Rights The principle that human beings have certain fundamental rights (to life, freedom, and the pursuit of happiness, for example) is deeply embedded in Western culture. As discussed in Chapter 1, the natural law tradition embraces the concept that certain actions (such as killing another person) are morally wrong because they are contrary to nature (the natural desire to continue living). Those who adhere to this **principle of rights,** or "rights theory," believe that a key factor in determining whether a business decision is ethical is how that decision affects the rights of others. These others include the firm's owners, its employees, the consumers of its products or services, its suppliers, the community in which it does business, and society as a whole.

A potential dilemma for those who support rights theory, however, is that they may disagree on which rights are most important. When considering all those affected by a business decision, for example, how much weight should be given to employees relative to shareholders, customers relative to the community, or employees relative to society as a whole?

In general, rights theorists believe that whichever right is stronger in a particular circumstance takes precedence. **■EXAMPLE 2.9** Suppose that a firm can shut down a plant to avoid polluting a river with contaminants that would negatively affect the health of thousands of people. Alternatively, the firm could keep the plant open (and pollute the river) but save the jobs of the twelve workers in the plant. In this situation, a rights theorist can easily choose which group to favor. (Not all choices are so clear-cut, however.) ■

Outcome-Based Ethics: Utilitarianism

"Thou shalt act so as to generate the greatest good for the greatest number." This is a paraphrase of the major premise of the utilitarian approach to ethics. **Utilitarianism** is a

CATEGORICAL IMPERATIVE
A concept developed by the philosopher Immanuel Kant as an ethical guideline for behavior. In deciding whether an action is right or wrong, or desirable or undesirable, a person should evaluate the action in terms of what would happen if everybody else in the same situation, or category, acted the same way.

PRINCIPLE OF RIGHTS
The principle that human beings have certain fundamental rights (to life, freedom, and the pursuit of happiness, for example). Those who adhere to this "rights theory" believe that a key factor in determining whether a business decision is ethical is how that decision affects the rights of various groups. These groups include the firm's owners, its employees, the consumers of its products or services, its suppliers, the community in which it does business, and society as a whole.

UTILITARIANISM
An approach to ethical reasoning that evaluates behavior in light of the consequences of that behavior for those who will be affected by it, rather than on the basis of any absolute ethical or moral values. In utilitarian reasoning, a "good" decision is one that results in the greatest good for the greatest number of people affected by the decision.

philosophical theory developed by Jeremy Bentham (1748–1832) and modified by John Stuart Mill (1806–1873)—both British philosophers. In contrast to duty-based ethics, utilitarianism is outcome oriented. It focuses on the consequences of an action, not on the nature of the action itself or on any set of preestablished moral values or religious beliefs.

Under a utilitarian model of ethics, an action is morally correct, or "right," when, among the people it affects, it produces the greatest amount of good for the greatest number. When an action affects the majority adversely, it is morally wrong. Applying the utilitarian theory thus requires (1) a determination of which individuals will be affected by the action in question; (2) a **cost-benefit analysis,** which involves an assessment of the negative and positive effects of alternative actions on these individuals; and (3) a choice among alternative actions that will produce maximum societal utility (the greatest positive net benefits for the greatest number of individuals).

The utilitarian approach to decision making commonly is employed by businesses, as well as by individuals. Weighing the consequences of a decision in terms of its costs and benefits for everyone affected by it is a useful analytical tool in the decision-making process. Utilitarianism is often criticized, however, because it tends to reduce the welfare of human beings to plus and minus signs on a cost-benefit worksheet and to "justify" human costs that many find totally unacceptable.

COST-BENEFIT ANALYSIS
A decision-making technique that involves weighing the costs of a given action against the benefits of that action.

CORPORATE SOCIAL RESPONSIBILITY
The idea that corporations can and should act ethically and be accountable to society for their actions.

Corporate Social Responsibility

For many years, groups concerned with civil rights, employee safety and welfare, consumer protection, environmental preservation, and other causes have pressured corporate America to behave in a responsible manner with respect to these causes. Thus was born the concept of **corporate social responsibility**—the idea that those who run corporations can and should act ethically and be accountable to society for their actions. Just what constitutes corporate social responsibility has been debated for some time, however, and there are a number of different theories today.

Profit Maximization Under the traditional view, the primary goal of corporations is profit maximization. Milton Friedman, the late Nobel Prize–winning economist and a proponent of the profit-maximization view, saw "one and only one" social responsibility of a corporation: "to use its resources and engage in activities designed to increase its profits, so long as it stays within the rules of the game, which is to say, engages in open and free competition without deception and fraud."[7] Those who accept this position argue that a firm can best contribute to society by generating profits.

Stakeholder Approach Another view of corporate social responsibility stresses that corporations have a duty not just to shareholders, but also to other groups affected by corporate decisions ("stakeholders"). Under this approach, a corporation would consider the impact of its decision on the firm's employees, customers, creditors, suppliers, and the community in which the corporation operates. The reasoning behind this "stakeholder view" is that in some circumstances, one or more of these other groups may have a greater stake in company decisions than the shareholders do. Although this may be true, it is often difficult to decide which group's interests should receive greater weight if the interests conflict (see the discussion of conflicts and trade-offs on page 52).

One of the vice presidents at Sun Microsystems discusses eco-responsibility at a climate protection summit. The electricity used by computers is thought to create 200 million tons of carbon dioxide emissions per year—more than all the cars in China. As part of Sun's commitment to corporate social responsibility, the company is focusing on creating computer servers that use less power (and emit less carbon dioxide). Sun also has a program that allows employees to work from home, which further reduces the amount of carbon dioxide emitted into the air. How might a company's environmentally friendly practices positively affect the ethical culture within the corporation and its standing within the community?
(Kevin Krejci/Creative Commons)

Corporate Citizenship Another theory of social responsibility argues that corporations should behave as good citizens by promoting

---

7. Milton Friedman, "Does Business Have Social Responsibility?" *Bank Administration,* April 1971, pp. 13–14.

goals that society deems worthwhile and taking positive steps toward solving social problems. The idea is that because so much of the wealth and power of this country is controlled by business, business in turn has a responsibility to society to use that wealth and power in socially beneficial ways. Under a corporate citizenship view, companies are judged on how much they donate to social causes, as well as how they conduct their operations with respect to employment discrimination, human rights, environmental concerns, and similar issues.

Maximum versus Optimum Profits Today's corporate decision makers are often torn between profitability and ethical responsibility. If they emphasize profits at the expense of perceived ethical responsibilities to other groups, they may become the target of negative media exposure and even lawsuits. If they go too far in the other direction (keep an unprofitable plant open so that the employees do not lose their jobs, invest too heavily in charitable works or social causes, and the like), their profits will suffer, and they may go out of business. Instead of maximum profits, many firms today aim for optimum profits—the maximum profits a firm can realize while staying within legal *and* ethical limits.

In the following case, a corporation's board of directors did not seem to doubt the priority of the firm's responsibilities. Focused solely on the profits delivered into the hands of the shareholders, the board failed to check the actions of the firm's chief executive officer (CEO) and, in fact, appeared to condone the CEO's misconduct. If the board had applied a different set of priorities, the shareholders might have been in a better financial position, however. A regulatory agency soon found the situation "troubling" and imposed a restriction on the firm. The board protested. The protest reminded the court of "the old saw about the child who murders his parents and then asks for mercy because he is an orphan."

CASE 2.3 **Fog Cutter Capital Group, Inc. v. Securities and Exchange Commission**

United States Court of Appeals, District of Columbia Circuit, 474 F.3d 822 (2007).

FACTS The National Association of Securities Dealers (NASD) operates the Nasdaq, an electronic securities exchange, on which Fog Cutter Capital Group was listed.[a] Andrew Wiederhorn had founded Fog Cutter in 1997 to manage a restaurant chain and make other investments. With family members, Wiederhorn controlled more than 50 percent of Fog Cutter's stock. The firm agreed that if Wiederhorn was terminated "for cause," he was entitled only to his salary through the date of termination. If terminated "without cause," he would be owed three times his $350,000 annual salary, three times his largest annual bonus from the previous three years, and any unpaid salary and bonus. "Cause" included being convicted of a felony. In 2001, Wiederhorn became the target of an investigation into the collapse of Capital Consultants, LLC. Fog Cutter then redefined "cause" in his termination agreement to cover only a felony *involving Fog Cutter*. In June 2004, Wiederhorn agreed to plead guilty to two

felonies, serve eighteen months in prison, pay a $25,000 fine, and pay $2 million to Capital Consultants. The day before he entered his plea, Fog Cutter agreed that while he was in prison, he would keep his title, responsibilities, salary, bonuses, and other benefits. It also agreed to a $2 million "leave of absence payment." In July, the NASD delisted Fog Cutter from the Nasdaq. Fog Cutter appealed this decision to the Securities and Exchange Commission (SEC), which dismissed the appeal. Fog Cutter petitioned the U.S. Court of Appeals for the District of Columbia Circuit for review.

ISSUE Was the SEC's action justified?

DECISION Yes. The U.S. Court of Appeals for the District of Columbia Circuit denied the firm's petition for review. The SEC's dismissal was not "arbitrary, capricious, or an abuse of discretion."

REASON Fog Cutter's deals with Wiederhorn indicated that, as the SEC found, he had "thorough control" over the firm. As further evidence in support of the SEC's decision, the court noted that Fog Cutter had done nothing to check Wiederhorn's

a. Securities (stocks and bonds—see Chapter 20) can be bought and sold through national exchanges. Whether a security is listed on an exchange is subject to the discretion of the agency that operates it. The Securities and Exchange Commission oversees the securities exchanges.

CASE 2.3–Continued

conduct. In fact, the board's actions only "aggravated the concerns Wiederhorn's conviction and imprisonment raised." In its petition for review of the SEC's dismissal, Fog Cutter claimed that the NASD's decision was unfair. The court pointed out, however, that the decision was in accord with the NASD's rules, which gave it "broad discretion to determine whether the public interest requires delisting securities in light of events at a company." In this case, "Fog Cutter made a deal with Wiederhorn that cost the company $4.75 million in a year in which it reported a $3.93 million net loss. We know as well that Fog Cutter handed Wiederhorn a $2 million bonus right before he went off to prison, a bonus stemming directly from

the consequences of Wiederhorn's criminal activity." Fog Cutter knew that Wiederhorn would use this "bonus" to pay Capital Consultants. In its appeal, Fog Cutter also claimed that if it fired Wiederhorn in light of his guilty plea, it would have to pay him $6 million under his termination agreement. But, the court responded, Fog Cutter amended this agreement during the investigation of Wiederhorn, "knowing full well" that it would "dramatically" increase the cost of firing him.

 FOR CRITICAL ANALYSIS–Ethical Consideration
Should more consideration have been given to the fact that Fog Cutter was not convicted of a violation of the law? Why or why not?

BUSINESS ETHICS ON A GLOBAL LEVEL

Given the various cultures and religions throughout the world, it is not surprising that conflicts in ethics frequently arise between foreign and U.S. businesspersons. **EXAMPLE 2.10** In certain countries, the consumption of alcohol and specific foods is forbidden for religious reasons. Under such circumstances, it would be thoughtless and imprudent for a U.S. businessperson to invite a local business contact out for a drink. ■ (For another example of how ethical issues can arise due to cultural differences, see this chapter's *Adapting the Law to the Online Environment* feature on pages 62 and 63.)

The role played by women in other countries may also present some difficult ethical problems for firms doing business internationally. Equal employment opportunity is a fundamental public policy in the United States, and Title VII of the Civil Rights Act of 1964 prohibits discrimination against women in the employment context (see Chapter 18). Some other countries, however, offer little protection for women against gender discrimination in the workplace, including sexual harassment.

We look here at how laws governing workers in other countries, particularly developing countries, have created some especially difficult ethical problems for U.S. sellers of goods manufactured in foreign countries. We also examine some of the ethical ramifications of laws prohibiting U.S. businesspersons from bribing foreign officials to obtain favorable business contracts.

Monitoring the Employment Practices of Foreign Suppliers

Many U.S. businesses now contract with companies in developing nations to produce goods, such as shoes and clothing, because the wage rates in those nations are significantly lower than wages in the United States. Yet what if a foreign company exploits its workers—by hiring women and children at below-minimum-wage rates, for example, or by requiring its employees to work long hours in a workplace full of health hazards? What if the company's supervisors routinely engage in workplace conduct that is offensive to women? Given today's global communications network, few companies can assume that their actions in other nations will go unnoticed by "corporate watch" groups that discover and publicize unethical corporate behavior. As a result, U.S. businesses today usually take steps to avoid such adverse publicity—either by refusing to deal with certain suppliers or

Google China

As discussed in the chapter text, doing business on a global level can sometimes involve serious ethical challenges. Consider the ethical firestorm that erupted when Google, Inc., decided to market "Google China." This version of Google's widely used search engine was especially tailored to the Chinese government's censorship requirements. To date, the Chinese government has maintained strict control over the flow of information in that country. The government's goal is to stop the flow of "harmful information." Web sites that offer pornography, government criticism, or information on sensitive topics, such as the Tiananmen Square massacre in 1989, are censored—that is, they cannot be accessed by Web users. Government agencies enforce the censorship and encourage citizens to inform on one another. Thousands of Web sites are shut down each year, and the sites' operators are subject to potential imprisonment.

Google's code of conduct opens with the company's informal motto: "Don't be evil." Yet critics question whether Google is following this motto. Human rights groups have come out strongly against Google's decision, maintaining that the company is seeking profits in a lucrative marketplace at the expense of assisting the Chinese Communist Party in suppressing free speech. In February 2006, Tom Lantos, the only Holocaust survivor serving in Congress, stated that the "sickening collaboration" of Google and three other Web companies (Cisco Systems, Microsoft Corporation, and Yahoo!, Inc.) with the Chinese government was "decapitating the voice of dissidents" in that nation.[a]

a. As cited in Tom Ziller, Jr., "Web Firms Questioned on Dealings in China," *The New York Times*, February 16, 2006.

by arranging to monitor their suppliers' workplaces to make sure that the employees are not being mistreated. (To see how far one company has gone to monitor its foreign workforce, read this chapter's *Beyond Our Borders* feature on page 64.)

The Foreign Corrupt Practices Act

Another ethical problem in international business dealings has to do with the legitimacy of certain side payments to government officials. In the United States, the majority of contracts are formed within the private sector. In many foreign countries, however, government officials make the decisions on most major construction and manufacturing

These Asian workers assemble and test fiber-optic systems for American electronics firms. Suppose that because of the health hazards involved in testing fiber optics, workers in the United States demand a much higher salary for performing this task. By hiring the Asian workers at this factory, the U.S. firm can pay substantially less in wages and will not have to comply with federal and state workplace safety regulations. Does the mere fact that it may cost less to have overseas workers perform a hazardous job make it unethical for a company to do so? (Steve Jurvetson/Creative Commons)

Google's Response

Google defends its actions by pointing out that its Chinese search engine at least lets users know which sites are being censored. Google China includes the links to censored sites, but when a user tries to access a link, the program states that it is not accessible. Google claims that its approach is essentially the "lesser of two evils": if U.S. companies did not cooperate with the Chinese government, Chinese residents would have less user-friendly Internet access. Moreover, Google asserts that providing Internet access, even if censored, is a step toward more open access in the future because technology is, in itself, a revolutionary force.

The Chinese Government's Defense

The Chinese government insists that in restricting access to certain Web sites, it is merely following the lead of other national governments, which also impose controls on information access. As an example, it cites France, which bans access to any Web sites selling or portraying Nazi paraphernalia. The

United States itself prohibits the dissemination of certain types of materials, such as child pornography, over the Internet. Furthermore, the U.S. government monitors Web sites and e-mail communications to protect against terrorist threats. How, ask Chinese officials, can other nations point their fingers at China for engaging in a common international practice?

FOR CRITICAL ANALYSIS *Do you agree with Google's assumption that, in time, technological advances and the desire of the Chinese people to embrace liberty will overcome the current limitations imposed by the Chinese government? Why or why not?*

contracts because of extensive government regulation and control over trade and industry. Side payments to government officials in exchange for favorable business contracts are not unusual in such countries, where they are not considered to be unethical. In the past, U.S. corporations doing business in these countries largely followed the dictum "When in Rome, do as the Romans do."

In the 1970s, however, the U.S. press, and government officials as well, uncovered a number of business scandals involving large side payments by U.S. corporations to foreign representatives for the purpose of securing advantageous international trade contracts. In response to this unethical behavior, in 1977 Congress passed the Foreign Corrupt Practices Act (FCPA), which prohibits U.S. businesspersons from bribing foreign officials to secure advantageous contracts.

Prohibition against the Bribery of Foreign Officials The first part of the FCPA applies to all U.S. companies and their directors, officers, shareholders, employees, and agents. This part prohibits the bribery of most officials of foreign governments if the purpose of the payment is to get the officials to act in their official capacity to provide business opportunities.

The FCPA does not prohibit payment of substantial sums to minor officials whose duties are ministerial. These payments are often referred to as "grease," or facilitating payments. They are meant to accelerate the performance of administrative services that might otherwise be carried out at a slow pace. Thus, for example, if a firm makes a payment to a minor official to speed up an import licensing process, the firm has not violated the FCPA.

Generally, the act, as amended, permits payments to foreign officials if such payments are lawful within the foreign country. The act also does not prohibit payments to private foreign companies or other third parties unless the U.S. firm knows that the payments will be passed on to a foreign government in violation of the FCPA.

Accounting Requirements In the past, bribes were often concealed in corporate financial records. Thus, the second part of the FCPA is directed toward accountants. All

BEYOND OUR BORDERS A Human Rights Audit That Sets the Standard

Many large multinational mining companies can find themselves in difficult situations. Their mines may be in countries ruled by repressive governments that take harsh measures to put down civil wars and rebellions. Freeport-McMoRan Copper and Gold, Inc., is one such multinational. It has gold and copper mines in the Indonesian province of Papua. This New Orleans–based company has been accused of allowing human rights violations against its workers and their families by various governments in Indonesia. Its most recent response was a *human rights review.*

Asking for an Outsider's Analysis Freeport hired the International Center for Corporate Accountability, Inc. (ICCA), to undertake an independent audit of the company's Papuan mining complex. The ICCA examined the entire mining operation. The resulting 133-page report set the standard for human rights reviews for all Western multinationals. Many of the findings were a shock even to Freeport's management.

Some Negative Findings Among the problems discovered by the human rights audit were the following:

1 Even though the company was putting $20 million a year into a local development fund, that fund was being mismanaged by tribal leaders. The ICCA recommended that Freeport verify how the funds were being used.
2 The high school dormitories operated by the company were being poorly run. The audit suggested that Freeport's on-site management become more actively involved in supervising the dorms.
3 Acquisition of skills by Papuan tribal members was lagging. As a result, few of them were qualified to advance into higher-level positions.

companies must keep detailed records that "accurately and fairly" reflect the company's financial activities. In addition, all companies must have an accounting system that provides "reasonable assurance" that all transactions entered into by the company are accounted for and legal. These requirements assist in detecting illegal bribes. The FCPA further prohibits any person from making false statements to accountants or false entries in any record or account.

Penalties for Violations Business firms that violate the FCPA may be fined up to $2 million. Individual officers or directors who violate the act may be fined up to $100,000 (the fine cannot be paid by the company) and may be imprisoned for up to five years.

Other Nations Denounce Bribery

For twenty years, the FCPA was the only law of its kind in the world, despite attempts by U.S. political leaders to convince other nations to pass similar legislation. That situation is now changing. In 1997, the Organization for Economic Cooperation and Development created a convention (treaty) that made the bribery of foreign public officials a serious crime. By 2008, at least thirty-six nations had adopted the convention,

4 The company was using lower-paid contract labor instead of full-time employees even though this practice was against company policy and sometimes against Indonesian labor law.

Codes of Conduct versus Third-Party Accountability Most U.S. multinationals have codes of conduct. These codes reflect the growing desire to make sure that overseas labor practices are in line with those in the United States. The problem with such codes is that it is difficult to verify that they are being enforced. When a third party undertakes an audit, though, and particularly if this third party is a nonprofit organization, the corporation gains credibility. The ICCA, for example, has impeccable credentials with respect to its independence. It is based at the City University of New York and is willing to work in the most challenging of environments. (Freeport's gold mine is located at an altitude of 14,000 feet in an area that receives 300 inches of rain a year!)

The Trend toward Nonfinancial Reporting The human rights report created for Freeport is a small part of a larger movement called *nonfinancial reporting*. Various firms throughout the world (but not many in the United States) are creating environmental and social impact overviews. Many of these reports show, for example, how companies' carbon dioxide emissions from energy use are falling. Nonfinancial reporting is an art rather than a science, however. Moreover, multinationals are free to disclose only what they wish.

 FOR CRITICAL ANALYSIS *To what extent can human rights audits and nonfinancial reporting help a multinational corporation's shareholders in the long run?*

■

which obligates them to enact legislation within their own nations in accordance with the convention. In addition, other international institutions, including the European Union, the Organization of American States, and the United Nations, have either passed or are in the process of negotiating rules against bribery in business transactions.

International Ethics Centers

The Ethics Resource Center, a nonprofit organization devoted to promoting ethics, has been instrumental in providing ethics-related training programs to business organizations across the globe. The center, which is located in Washington, D.C., helps organizations establish ethics programs, create codes of conduct and code reviews, and develop content and deliver ethics training. The center works with the private sector to address corruption and has created and is partners with four nonprofit centers in Colombia, South Africa, Turkey, and the United Arab Emirates. Another international ethics center is the Gulf Centre for Excellence in Ethics (GCEE). The goal of the GCEE is to bring organizational ethics and corporate governance programs to business and government organizations throughout the Middle East.

REVIEWING Ethics and Business Decision Making

Isabel Arnett is the chief executive officer (CEO) of Tamik, Inc., a pharmaceutical company that manufactures a vaccine called Kafluk, which supposedly provides some defense against bird flu. The company began marketing Kafluk throughout Asia. After numerous media reports that bird flu may soon become a worldwide epidemic, the demand for Kafluk increased, sales soared, and Tamik earned record profits. Tamik's CEO, Arnett, then began receiving disturbing reports from Southeast Asia that in some patients, Kafluk had caused psychiatric disturbances, including severe hallucinations, and heart and lung problems. Arnett was informed that six children in Japan had committed suicide by jumping out of windows after receiving the vaccine. To cover up the story and prevent negative publicity, Arnett instructed Tamik's partners in Asia to offer cash to the Japanese families whose children had died in exchange for their silence. Arnett also refused to authorize additional research within the company to study the potential side effects of Kafluk. Using the information presented in the chapter, answer the following questions.

1 In this scenario, it is not clear that the other corporate officers and Tamik's board of directors were aware of the actions of its CEO, Arnett. How might an integrated corporate governance system ensure that all parties were informed of Arnett's conduct?

2 Would a person who adheres to the principle of rights consider it ethical for Arnett not to disclose potential safety concerns and to refuse to perform additional research on Kafluk? Why or why not?

3 If, during this same period, Kafluk prevented one thousand Asian people who were exposed to bird flu from dying, would Arnett's conduct in this situation be ethical under a utilitarian model of ethics? Why or why not?

4 Did Tamik or Arnett violate the Foreign Corrupt Practices Act in this scenario? Why or why not?

APPLICATION   How Can You Create an Ethical Workplace?*

If you are a manager, rest assured that unless you are totally committed to the goal of creating and maintaining an ethical workplace, you will not succeed in achieving it. In addition to your attitude toward ethics and your conduct, two other factors help to create an ethical workplace environment: a written code of ethics, or policy statement, and the effective communication of the firm's ethical policies to employees. Finally, you should provide employees with a way to make anonymous complaints about unethical behavior on the part of their co-workers or supervisors.

The Role of Management

As mentioned in this chapter, management's behavior is crucial in establishing the ethical tone of a firm. Managers must make it clear, both in their words and by their conduct, that unethical behavior is not acceptable. If an employee persists in unethical behavior, you should consider discharging the employee as a clear example to other employees that you will not tolerate unethical actions. Studies have shown that employees quickly adapt to the "rules" of their workplace environments, but it is up to the company managers to let employees know what those rules are—and to enforce them.

Instruct Employees in Ethical Standards

A written ethics code or policy statement helps to make clear to employees how they are expected to relate to their supervisors or managers, to consumers, to suppliers, and to other employees. Above all, it is important to state explicitly what your firm's ethical priorities are and make sure that the firm's employees are aware of those priorities.

A good way to communicate these priorities to employees is by implementing an ethics training program, in which managers discuss with employees—face to face—the firm's policies and the importance of ethical conduct. Ethics

* This *Application* is not meant to substitute for the services of an attorney who is licensed to practice law in your state.

seminars should be held at routine intervals so that employees have an opportunity to discuss ethical problems as they arise. Another effective technique is to periodically evaluate the ethical performance of each employee.

Employees should also be instructed in how they can anonymously report unethical behavior. For publicly traded companies, federal law now requires the establishment of confidential reporting systems for this purpose. This can be accomplished through a Web-based reporting system, as described earlier in this chapter, or by using a company "hot line" installed for this purpose.

2 Create, print, and distribute an ethical code clearly stating your firm's ethical goals and priorities, as well as what behavior is expected of employees in their areas of responsibility.
3 Implement an ethics training program to communicate your firm's ethical policies to employees.
4 Devise a method, such as an ethical checklist, for evaluating the ethical performance of each individual employee.
5 Provide a mechanism through which employees can anonymously complain about unethical behavior in the workplace.

CHECKLIST FOR THE BUSINESS MANAGER

1 Make sure that management is committed to ethical behavior and sets an ethical example.

KEY TERMS

business ethics 47
categorical imperative 58
corporate social responsibility 59

cost-benefit analysis 59
ethical reasoning 57
ethics 47

moral minimum 55
principle of rights 58
utilitarianism 58

CHAPTER SUMMARY Ethics and Business Decision Making

Business Ethics (See page 47.)	Ethics can be defined as the study of what constitutes right or wrong behavior. Business ethics focuses on how moral and ethical principles are applied in the business context.
Setting the Right Ethical Tone (See pages 47–52.)	1. *Role of management*—Management's commitment and behavior are essential in creating an ethical workplace. Most large firms have ethical codes or policies and training programs to help employees determine whether certain actions are ethical.
	2. *Corporate compliance programs*—Set up by companies to monitor their own compliance with applicable laws and ethical standards. The Sarbanes-Oxley Act (which will be discussed in detail in Chapter 21) requires firms to set up confidential systems so that employees can report suspected illegal or unethical auditing or accounting practices.
	3. *Ethical trade-offs*—Management constantly faces ethical trade-offs because firms have ethical and legal duties to a number of groups, including shareholders and employees.
Companies That Defy the Rules (See pages 53–55.)	The Enron debacle—involving one of the largest bankruptcies in U.S. history—serves as an example of a culture that fostered unethical and, in part, illegal business behavior. Another example is Merck & Company, Inc., which became the target of much criticism (and many lawsuits) when it continued to market its painkiller Vioxx until 2004, despite its awareness of studies indicating that the drug significantly increased the risk of heart attacks and strokes.
Business Ethics and the Law (See pages 55–57.)	1. *The moral minimum*—Lawful behavior is a moral minimum. The law has its limits, though, and some actions may be legal but not ethical.

(Continued)

CHAPTER SUMMARY — Ethics and Business Decision Making—Continued

Business Ethics and the Law— Continued	2. *Legal uncertainties*—It may be difficult to predict with certainty whether particular actions are legal, given the numerous and frequent changes in the laws regulating business and the "gray areas" in the law.
Approaches to Ethical Reasoning (See pages 57–61.)	1. *Duty-based ethics*—Ethics based on religious beliefs; philosophical reasoning, such as that of Immanuel Kant; and the basic rights of human beings (the principle of rights). 2. *Outcome-based ethics (utilitarianism)*—Ethics based on philosophical reasoning, such as that of John Stuart Mill. 3. *Corporate social responsibility*—A number of theories based on the idea that corporations can and should act ethically and be accountable to society for their actions.
Business Ethics on a Global Level (See pages 61–65.)	Businesses must take account of the many cultural, religious, and legal differences among nations. Notable differences relate to the role of women in society, employment laws governing workplace conditions, and the practice of giving side payments to foreign officials to secure favorable contracts.

FOR REVIEW

Answers for the even-numbered questions in this **For Review** *section can be found in Appendix E at the end of this text.*

1 What is ethics? What is business ethics? Why is business ethics important?

2 How can business leaders encourage their companies to act ethically?

3 What are corporate compliance programs?

4 How do duty-based ethical standards differ from outcome-based ethical standards?

5 What types of ethical issues might arise in the context of international business transactions?

QUESTIONS AND CASE PROBLEMS

 **HYPOTHETICAL SCENARIOS**

2.1 Business Ethics. Some business ethicists maintain that whereas personal ethics has to do with right or wrong behavior, business ethics is concerned with appropriate behavior. In other words, ethical behavior in business has less to do with moral principles than with what society deems to be appropriate behavior in the business context. Do you agree with this distinction? Do personal and business ethics ever overlap? Should personal ethics play any role in business ethical decision making?

2.2 Hypothetical Question with Sample Answer. If a firm engages in "ethical" behavior solely for the purpose of gaining profits from the goodwill it generates, the "ethical" behavior is essentially a means toward a self-serving end (profits and the accumulation of wealth). In this situation, is the firm acting unethically in any way? Should motive or conduct carry greater weight on the ethical scales in this situation?

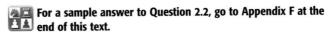 **For a sample answer to Question 2.2, go to Appendix F at the end of this text.**

2.3 Ethical Decision Making. Shokun Steel Co. owns many steel plants. One of its plants is much older than the others. Equipment at that plant is outdated and inefficient, and the costs of production at that plant are now twice as high as at any of Shokun's other plants. The company cannot raise the price of steel because of competition, both domestic and international. The plant employs more than one thousand workers and is located in Twin Firs, Pennsylvania, which has a population of about 45,000. Shokun is contemplating whether to close the plant. What factors should the firm consider in making its decision? Will the firm violate any ethical duties if it closes the plant? Analyze these questions from the two basic perspectives on ethical reasoning discussed in this chapter.

CASE PROBLEMS

2.4 Ethical Conduct. Richard Fraser was an "exclusive career insurance agent" under a contract with Nationwide Mutual Insurance Co. Fraser leased computer hardware and software from Nationwide for his business. During a dispute between Nationwide and the Nationwide Insurance Independent Contractors Association, an organization representing Fraser and other exclusive career agents, Fraser prepared a letter to Nationwide's competitors asking whether they were interested in acquiring the represented agents' policyholders. Nationwide obtained a copy of the letter and searched its electronic file server for e-mail indicating that the letter had been sent. It found a stored e-mail that Fraser had sent to a co-worker indicating that the letter had been sent to at least one competitor. The e-mail was retrieved from the co-worker's file of already received and discarded messages stored on the server. When Nationwide canceled its contract with Fraser, he filed a suit in a federal district court against the firm, alleging, among other things, violations of various federal laws that prohibit the interception of electronic communications during transmission. In whose favor should the court rule, and why? Did Nationwide act ethically in retrieving the e-mail? Explain. [*Fraser v. Nationwide Mutual Insurance Co.*, 352 F.3d. 107 (3d Cir. 2004)]

2.5 Case Problem with Sample Answer. Eden Electrical, Ltd., owned twenty-five appliance stores throughout Israel, at least some of which sold refrigerators made by Amana Co. Eden bought the appliances from Amana's Israeli distributor, Pan El A/Yesh Shem, which approached Eden about taking over the distributorship. Eden representatives met with Amana executives. The executives made assurances about Amana's good faith, its hope of having a long-term business relationship with Eden, and its willingness to have Eden become its exclusive distributor in Israel. Eden signed a distributorship agreement and paid Amana $2.4 million. Amana failed to deliver this amount in inventory to Eden, continued selling refrigerators to other entities for the Israeli market, and represented to others that it was still looking for a long-term distributor. Less than three months after signing the agreement with Eden, Amana terminated it without explanation. Eden filed a suit in a federal district court against Amana, alleging fraud. The court awarded Eden $12.1 million in damages. Is this amount warranted? Why or why not? How does this case illustrate why business ethics is important? [*Eden Electrical, Ltd. v. Amana Co.*, 370 F.3d 824 (8th Cir. 2004)]

After you have answered Problem 2.5, compare your answer with the sample answer given on the Web site that accompanies this text. Go to academic.cengage.com/blaw/blt, select "Chapter 2," and click on "Case Problem with Sample Answer."

2.6 Ethical Conduct. Unable to pay more than $1.2 billion in debt, Big Rivers Electric Corp. filed a petition to declare bankruptcy in a federal bankruptcy court in September 1996. Big Rivers' creditors included Bank of New York (BONY), Chase Manhattan Bank, Mapco Equities, and others. The court appointed J. Baxter Schilling to work as a "disinterested" (neutral) party with Big Rivers and the creditors to resolve their disputes; the court set an hourly fee as Schilling's compensation. Schilling told Chase, BONY, and Mapco that he wanted them to pay him an additional percentage fee based on the "success" he attained in finding "new value" to pay Big Rivers' debts. He said that without such a deal, he would not perform his mediation duties. Chase agreed; the others disputed the deal, but no one told the court. In October 1998, Schilling asked the court for nearly $4.5 million in compensation, including the hourly fees, which totaled about $531,000, and the percentage fees. Big Rivers and others asked the court to deny Schilling any fees on the basis that he had improperly negotiated "secret side agreements." How did Schilling violate his duties as a "disinterested" party? Should he be denied compensation? Why or why not? [*In re Big Rivers Electric Corp.*, 355 F.3d 415 (6th Cir. 2004)]

2.7 Ethical Conduct. Ernest Price suffered from sickle-cell anemia. In 1997, Price asked Dr. Ann Houston, his physician, to prescribe Oxycontin, a strong narcotic, for the pain. Over the next several years, Price saw at least ten different physicians at ten different clinics in two cities, and used seven pharmacies in three cities, to obtain and fill simultaneous prescriptions for Oxycontin. In March 2001, when Houston learned of these activities, she refused to write more prescriptions for Price. As other physicians became aware of Price's actions, they also stopped writing his prescriptions. Price filed a suit in a Mississippi state court against Purdue Pharma Co. and other producers and distributors of Oxycontin, as well as his physicians and the pharmacies that had filled the prescriptions. Price alleged negligence, among other things, claiming that Oxycontin's addictive nature caused him injury and that this was the defendants' fault. The defendants argued that Price's claim should be dismissed because it arose from his own wrongdoing. Who should be held *legally* liable? Should any of the parties be considered *ethically* responsible? Why or why not? [*Price v. Purdue Pharma Co.*, 920 So.2d 479 (Miss. 2006)]

2.8 Ethical Leadership. In 1999, Andrew Fastow, chief financial officer of Enron Corp., asked Merrill Lynch, an investment firm, to participate in a bogus sale of three barges so that Enron could record earnings of $12.5 million from the sale. Through a third entity, Fastow bought the barges back within six months and paid Merrill for its participation. Five Merrill employees were convicted of conspiracy to commit wire fraud in part on an "honest services" theory. Under this theory, an employee deprives his employer of "honest services" when the employee promotes his own interests, rather than the interests of the employer. Four of the employees appealed to the U.S. Court of Appeals for the Fifth Circuit, arguing that this charge did not apply to the conduct in which they engaged. The court agreed, reasoning that the barge deal was conducted to benefit Enron, not to enrich the Merrill employees at Enron's expense. Meanwhile, Kevin Howard, chief financial officer of Enron Broadband Services (EBS), engaged in "Project Braveheart," which enabled EBS to show earnings of $111 million in 2000 and 2001. Braveheart involved the sale of an interest in the future revenue of a video-on-demand venture to nCube, a small technology firm, which was paid for its help when EBS bought the interest back. Howard was convicted of wire fraud in part on the "honest services" theory. He filed a motion to vacate this conviction on the same basis that the Merrill employees had argued. Did Howard act unethically? Explain. Should the court grant his motion? Discuss. [*United States v. Howard*, 471 F.Supp.2d 772 (S.D.Tex. 2007)]

2.9 **A Question of Ethics.** *Steven Soderbergh is the Academy Award–winning director of Erin Brockovich, Traffic, and many other films. CleanFlicks, LLC, filed a suit in a federal district court against Soderbergh, fifteen other directors, and the Directors Guild of America. The plaintiff asked the court to rule that it had the right to sell DVDs of the defendants' films altered without the defendants' consent to delete scenes of "sex, nudity, profanity and gory violence." CleanFlicks sold or rented the edited DVDs under the slogan "It's About Choice" to consumers, sometimes indirectly through retailers. It would not sell to retailers that made unauthorized copies of the edited films. The defendants, with DreamWorks, LLC, and seven other movie studios that own the copyrights to the films, filed a counterclaim against CleanFlicks and others engaged in the same business, alleging copyright infringement. Those filing the counterclaim asked the court to enjoin (prevent) CleanFlicks and the others from making and marketing altered versions of the films. [Clean Flicks of Colorado, LLC v. Soderbergh, 433 F.Supp.2d 1236 (D.Colo. 2006)]*

1 Movie studios often edit their films to conform to content and other standards and sell the edited versions to network television and other commercial buyers. In this case, however, the studios objected when CleanFlicks edited the films and sold the altered versions directly to consumers. Similarly, CleanFlicks made unauthorized copies of the studios' DVDs to edit the films, but objected to others' making unauthorized copies of the altered versions. Is there anything unethical about these apparently contradictory positions? Why or why not?

2 CleanFlicks and its competitors asserted, in part, that they were making "fair use" of the studios' copyrighted works. They argued that by their actions "they are criticizing the objectionable content commonly found in current movies and that they are providing more socially acceptable alternatives to enable families to view the films together, without exposing children to the presumed harmful effects emanating from the objectionable content." If you were the judge, how would you view this argument? Is a court the appropriate forum for making determinations of public or social policy? Explain.

CRITICAL THINKING AND WRITING ASSIGNMENTS

2.10 Critical Legal Thinking. Human rights groups, environmental activists, and other interest groups concerned with unethical business practices have often conducted publicity campaigns against various corporations that those groups feel have engaged in unethical practices. Can a small group of well-organized activists dictate how a major corporation conducts its affairs? Discuss fully.

2.11 Critical Thinking and Writing Assignment for Business. Assume that you are a high-level manager for a shoe manufacturer. You know that your firm could increase its profit margin by producing shoes in Indonesia, where you could hire women for $100 a month to assemble them. You also know that human rights advocates recently accused a competing shoe manufacturer of engaging in exploitative labor practices because the manufacturer sold shoes made by Indonesian women for similarly low wages. You personally do not believe that paying $100 a month to Indonesian women is unethical because you know that in their country, $100 a month is a better-than-average wage rate. Assuming that the decision is yours to make, should you have the shoes manufactured in Indonesia and make higher profits for your company? Should you instead avoid the risk of negative publicity and the consequences of that publicity for the firm's reputation and subsequent profits? Are there other alternatives? Discuss fully.

2.12 **Video Question.** Go to this text's Web site at **academic.cengage.com/blaw/blt** and select "Chapter 2." Click on "Video Questions" and view the video titled *Ethics: Business Ethics an Oxymoron?* Then answer the following questions.

1 According to the instructor in the video, what is the primary reason that businesses act ethically?

2 Which of the two approaches to ethical reasoning that were discussed in the chapter seems to have had more influence on the instructor in the discussion of how business activities are related to societies? Explain your answer.

3 The instructor asserts that "[i]n the end, it is the unethical behavior that becomes costly, and conversely ethical behavior creates its own competitive advantage." Do you agree with this statement? Why or why not?

ONLINE ACTIVITIES

PRACTICAL INTERNET EXERCISES

Go to this text's Web site at **academic.cengage.com/blaw/blt**, select "Chapter 2," and click on "Practical Internet Exercises." There you will find the following Internet research exercises that you can perform to learn more about the topics covered in this chapter.

PRACTICAL INTERNET EXERCISE 2–1   LEGAL PERSPECTIVE—Ethics in Business

PRACTICAL INTERNET EXERCISE 2–2   MANAGEMENT PERSPECTIVE—Environmental Self-Audits

BEFORE THE TEST

Go to this text's Web site at **academic.cengage.com/blaw/blt**, select "Chapter 2," and click on "Interactive Quizzes." You will find a number of interactive questions relating to this chapter.

CHAPTER 3
Courts and Alternative Dispute Resolution

"The Judicial Department comes home in its effects to every man's fireside: it passes on his property, his reputation, his life, his all."

John Marshall, 1755–1835
(Chief justice of the United States Supreme Court, 1801–1835)

LEARNING OBJECTIVES

AFTER READING THIS CHAPTER, YOU SHOULD BE ABLE TO ANSWER THE FOLLOWING QUESTIONS:

1 What is judicial review? How and when was the power of judicial review established?

2 Before a court can hear a case, it must have jurisdiction. Over what must it have jurisdiction? How are the courts applying traditional jurisdictional concepts to cases involving Internet transactions?

3 What is the difference between a trial court and an appellate court?

4 In a lawsuit, what are the pleadings? What is discovery, and how does electronic discovery differ from traditional discovery? What is electronic filing?

5 How are online forums being used to resolve disputes?

As Chief Justice John Marshall remarked in the chapter-opening quotation, ultimately, we are all affected by what the courts say and do. This is particularly true in the business world—nearly every businessperson will face either a potential or an actual lawsuit at some time or another. For this reason, anyone contemplating a career in business will benefit from an understanding of court systems in the United States, including the mechanics of lawsuits.

In this chapter, after examining the judiciary's overall role in the American governmental scheme, we discuss some basic requirements that must be met before a party may bring a lawsuit before a particular court. We then look at the court systems of the United States in some detail and, to clarify judicial procedures, follow a hypothetical case through a state court system. Even though there are fifty-two court systems in the United States—one for each of the fifty states, one for the District of Columbia, plus a federal system—similarities abound. Keep in mind that the federal courts are not superior to the state courts; they are simply an independent system of courts, which derives its authority from Article III, Sections 1 and 2, of the U.S. Constitution. The chapter concludes with an overview of some alternative methods of settling disputes, including methods for settling disputes in online forums.

Note that technological developments are affecting court procedures just as they are affecting all other areas of the law. In this chapter, we will also indicate how court doctrines and procedures, as well as alternative methods of dispute settlement, are being adapted to the needs of a cyber age.

THE JUDICIARY'S ROLE IN AMERICAN GOVERNMENT

As you learned in Chapter 1, the body of American law includes the federal and state constitutions, statutes passed by legislative bodies, administrative law, and the case decisions and legal principles that form the common law. These laws would be meaningless, however, without the courts to interpret and apply them. This is the essential role of the judiciary—the courts—in the American governmental system: to interpret and apply the law.

Judicial Review

The U.S. Constitution divided the national government's powers among the three branches of government: (1) the legislative branch makes the laws, (2) the executive branch enforces the laws, and (3) the judicial branch interprets the laws. Thus, the judiciary can decide, among other things, whether the laws or actions of the other two branches are constitutional. The process for making such a determination is known as **judicial review.** The power of judicial review enables the judicial branch to act as a check on the other two branches of government, in line with the checks-and-balances system established by the U.S. Constitution. (Judicial review can also be found in other countries—see this chapter's *Beyond Our Borders* feature on the following page.)

JUDICIAL REVIEW
The process by which a court decides on the constitutionality of legislative enactments and actions of the executive branch.

The Origins of Judicial Review in the United States

The power of judicial review was not mentioned in the Constitution, but the concept was not new at the time the nation was founded. Indeed, before 1789 state courts had already overturned state legislative acts that conflicted with state constitutions. Additionally, many of the founders expected the United States Supreme Court to assume a similar role with respect to the federal Constitution. Alexander Hamilton and James Madison both emphasized the importance of judicial review in their essays urging the adoption of the new Constitution. When was the doctrine of judicial review established? See this chapter's *Landmark in the Law* feature on page 75 for the answer.

BASIC JUDICIAL REQUIREMENTS

Before a court can hear a lawsuit, certain requirements must first be met. These requirements relate to jurisdiction, venue, and standing to sue. We examine each of these important concepts here.

Jurisdiction

In Latin, *juris* means "law," and *diction* means "to speak." Thus, "the power to speak the law" is the literal meaning of the term **jurisdiction.** Before any court can hear a case, it must have jurisdiction over the person (or company) against whom the suit is brought (the defendant) or over the property involved in the suit. The court must also have jurisdiction over the subject matter.

JURISDICTION
The authority of a court to hear and decide a specific case.

Jurisdiction over Persons Generally, a court can exercise personal jurisdiction (*in personam* jurisdiction) over any person or business that resides in a certain geographic area. A state trial court, for example, normally has jurisdictional authority over residents (including businesses) in a particular area of the state, such as a county or district. A state's highest court (often called the state supreme court)[1] has jurisdiction over all residents of that state.

---

1. As will be discussed shortly, a state's highest court is frequently referred to as the state supreme court, but there are exceptions. For example, in New York, the supreme court is a trial court.

BEYOND OUR BORDERS Judicial Review in Other Nations

The concept of judicial review was pioneered by the United States. Some maintain that one of the reasons the doctrine was readily accepted in this country was that it fit well with the checks and balances designed by the founders. Today, all established constitutional democracies have some form of judicial review—the power to rule on the constitutionality of laws—but its form varies from country to country.

For example, Canada's Supreme Court can exercise judicial review but is barred from doing so if a law includes a provision explicitly prohibiting such review. In France, the Constitutional Council rules on the constitutionality of laws *before* the laws take effect. Laws can be referred to the council for prior review by the president, the prime minister, and the heads of the two chambers of parliament. Prior review is also an option in Germany and Italy, if requested by the national or a regional government. In contrast, the United States Supreme Court does not give advisory opinions; the Supreme Court will render a decision only when there is an actual dispute concerning an issue.

Members of the Constitutional Council of France. The council rules on the constitutionality of laws before the laws take effect. Does the United States have a similar system? (Photo Courtesy of the Conseil Constitutionnel)

FOR CRITICAL ANALYSIS *In any country in which a constitution sets forth the basic powers and structure of government, some governmental body has to decide whether laws enacted by the government are consistent with that constitution. Why might the courts be best suited to handle this task? What might be a better alternative?*

LONG ARM STATUTE
A state statute that permits a state to obtain personal jurisdiction over nonresident defendants. A defendant must have certain "minimum contacts" with that state for the statute to apply.

In addition, under the authority of a state **long arm statute,** a court can exercise personal jurisdiction over certain out-of-state defendants based on activities that took place within the state. Before exercising long arm jurisdiction over a nonresident, however, the court must be convinced that the defendant had sufficient contacts, or *minimum contacts*, with the state to justify the jurisdiction.[2] Generally, this means that the defendant must have enough of a connection to the state for the judge to conclude that it is fair for the state to exercise power over the defendant. **■EXAMPLE 3.1** If an out-of-state defendant caused an automobile accident or sold defective goods within the state, for instance, a court will usually find that minimum contacts exist to exercise jurisdiction over that defendant. Similarly, a state may exercise personal jurisdiction over a nonresident defendant who is sued for breaching a contract that was formed within the state. ■

In regard to corporations,[3] the minimum-contacts requirement applies if a corporation does business within the state or has an office or branch within the state. **■EXAMPLE 3.2** Suppose that a Maine corporation has a branch office or a manufacturing plant in Georgia. Does this Maine corporation have sufficient minimum contacts with the state of Georgia to allow a Georgia court to exercise jurisdiction over it? Yes, it does. If the Maine corporation advertises and sells its products in Georgia, those activities will also likely suffice to meet the minimum-contacts requirement, even if the corporate headquarters are located in a different state. ■

---

2. The minimum-contacts standard was established in *International Shoe Co. v. State of Washington*, 326 U.S. 310, 66 S.Ct. 154, 90 L.Ed. 95 (1945).

3. In the eyes of the law, corporations are "legal persons"—entities that can sue and be sued. See Chapter 20.

LANDMARK IN THE LAW *Marbury v. Madison* (1803)

The *Marbury v. Madison*[a] decision is widely viewed as a cornerstone of constitutional law. When Thomas Jefferson defeated John Adams in the presidential election of 1800, Adams feared the Jeffersonians' antipathy toward business and also toward a strong national government. Adams thus rushed to "pack" the judiciary with loyal Federalists (those who believed in a strong national government) by appointing what came to be called "midnight judges" just before Jefferson took office. All of the fifty-nine judicial appointment letters had to be certified and delivered, but Adams's secretary of state (John Marshall) was only able to deliver forty-two of them by the time Jefferson took over as president. Jefferson refused to order his secretary of state, James Madison, to deliver the remaining commissions.

Marshall's Dilemma   William Marbury and three others to whom the commissions had not been delivered sought a writ of *mandamus* (an order directing a government official to fulfill a duty) from the United States Supreme Court, as authorized by the Judiciary Act of 1789. As fate would have it, John Marshall (Adams's secretary of state) had just been appointed as chief justice of the Supreme Court. Marshall faced a dilemma: If he ordered the commissions delivered, the new secretary of state (Madison) could simply refuse to deliver them—and the Court had no way to compel action. At the same time, if Marshall simply allowed the new administration to do as it wished, the Court's power would be severely eroded.

Marshall's Decision   Marshall masterfully fashioned his decision to enlarge the power of the Supreme Court by affirming the Court's power of judicial review. He stated, "It is emphatically the province and duty of the Judicial Department to say what the law is. . . . If two laws conflict with each other, the courts must decide on the operation of each. . . . So if the law be in opposition to the Constitution . . . [t]he Court must determine which of these conflicting rules governs the case."

Marshall's decision did not require anyone to do anything. He concluded that the highest court did not have the power to issue a writ of *mandamus* in this particular case. Although the Judiciary Act of 1789 specified that the Supreme Court could issue writs of *mandamus* as part of its original jurisdiction, Article III of the U.S. Constitution, which spelled out the Court's original jurisdiction, did not mention writs of *mandamus*. Because Congress did not have the right to expand the Supreme Court's jurisdiction, this section of the Judiciary Act was unconstitutional—and thus void. The decision still stands today as a judicial and political masterpiece.

APPLICATION TO TODAY'S WORLD   *Since the* Marbury *decision, the power of judicial review has remained unchallenged and today is exercised by both federal and state courts. If the courts did not have the power of judicial review, the constitutionality of Congress's acts could not be challenged in court—a congressional statute would remain law until changed by Congress. The courts of other countries that have adopted a constitutional democracy often cite this decision as a justification for judicial review.*

RELEVANT WEB SITES   *To locate information on the Web concerning the* Marbury *decision, go to this text's Web site at* **academic.cengage.com/blaw/blt**, *select "Chapter 3," and click on "URLs for Landmarks."*

a. 5 U.S. (1 Cranch) 137, 2 L.Ed. 60 (1803).

The following case involved a lawsuit filed by a California resident against a Nevada hotel and others for failing to provide notice of an energy surcharge imposed on the guests. Although the hotel had no bank accounts or employees in California, it advertised heavily in that state and obtained a significant percentage of its business from California residents. Based on these activities, could a California state court exercise personal jurisdiction over the hotel?

CASE 3.1   **Snowney v. Harrah's Entertainment, Inc.**

California Supreme Court, 35 Cal.4th 1054, 112 P.3d 28, 29 Cal.Rptr.3d 33 (2005).

FACTS Harrah's Entertainment, Inc., owns and operates hotels in Nevada. In 2001, Frank Snowney, a California resident, reserved a room in one of Harrah's hotels by phone from his home. The reservations clerk told him that the cost was $50 per night plus the room tax. When Snowney checked out, however, the bill included a $3 energy surcharge. Snowney filed a suit in a California state court against Harrah's and other hotel owners, alleging in part fraud for levying the surcharge without notice. The defendants filed a motion to dismiss for lack of personal jurisdiction, claiming that they did not do business in California. Snowney argued in part that the hotels advertised extensively to California residents through billboards, newspapers, and radio and television stations in the state and through an interactive Web site that accepted reservations from state residents. The court granted the defendants' motion, but on Snowney's appeal, a state intermediate appellate court reversed this ruling. The hotels appealed to the California Supreme Court.

ISSUE Could a California state court exercise personal jurisdiction over out-of-state hotels, based on the hotels' in-state advertising and significant business with California residents?

DECISION Yes. The California Supreme Court affirmed the judgment of the state intermediate appellate court, holding that the Nevada defendants were subject to personal jurisdiction in California state courts.

REASON The state supreme court identified three requirements for a court's exercise of jurisdiction over a nonresident defendant: the defendant must avail itself of "forum benefits," the case must relate to the defendant's contacts with the state, and the assertion of jurisdiction must be fair. The court reasoned that through a Web site, the hotels had "availed" themselves "of forum benefits. * * * By touting the proximity of their hotels to California and providing driving directions from California to their hotels, defendants' site specifically targeted residents of California. Defendants also concede that many of their patrons come from California and that some of these patrons undoubtedly made reservations using their Web site." The hotels advertised extensively in the state through direct mail, billboards, newspapers, and radio and television stations located in the state. "Given the intensity of defendants' activities in California, we * * * have little difficulty in finding a substantial connection between the two." Finally, "defendants do not contend the exercise of jurisdiction would be unfair or unreasonable, and we see no reason to conclude otherwise."

WHAT IF THE FACTS WERE DIFFERENT? *If the Nevada hotels had not extensively advertised for California residents' business, would the outcome in this case have been the same? Why or why not?*

Jurisdiction over Property   A court can also exercise jurisdiction over property that is located within its boundaries. This kind of jurisdiction is known as *in rem* jurisdiction, or "jurisdiction over the thing." **EXAMPLE 3.3** Suppose that a dispute arises over the ownership of a boat in dry dock in Fort Lauderdale, Florida. The boat is owned by an Ohio resident, over whom a Florida court normally cannot exercise personal jurisdiction. The other party to the dispute is a resident of Nebraska. In this situation, a lawsuit concerning the boat could be brought in a Florida state court on the basis of the court's *in rem* jurisdiction. ■

Jurisdiction over Subject Matter   Jurisdiction over subject matter is a limitation on the types of cases a court can hear. In both the federal and the state court systems, there are courts of *general* (unlimited) *jurisdiction* and courts of *limited jurisdiction*. An example of a court of general jurisdiction is a state trial court or a federal district court. An example of a state court of limited jurisdiction is a probate court. **Probate courts** are state courts that handle only matters relating to the transfer of a person's assets and obligations after that person's death, including matters relating to the custody and guardianship of children. An example of a federal court of limited subject-matter jurisdiction is a bankruptcy court. **Bankruptcy courts** handle only bankruptcy proceedings, which are governed by federal bankruptcy law (discussed in Chapter 16). In contrast, a court of general jurisdiction can decide a broad array of cases.

A court's jurisdiction over subject matter is usually defined in the statute or constitution creating the court. In both the federal and the state court systems, a court's subject-matter jurisdiction can be limited not only by the subject of the lawsuit but also by the amount in controversy, by whether a case is a felony (a more serious type of crime) or a misdemeanor (a less serious type of crime), or by whether the proceeding is a trial or an appeal.

Original and Appellate Jurisdiction   The distinction between courts of original jurisdiction and courts of appellate jurisdiction normally lies in whether the case is being heard for the first time. Courts having original jurisdiction are courts of the first instance, or trial courts—that is, courts in which lawsuits begin, trials take place, and evidence is presented. In the federal court system, the *district courts* are trial courts. In the various state court systems, the trial courts are known by various names, as will be discussed shortly.

The key point here is that any court having original jurisdiction is normally known as a trial court. Courts having appellate jurisdiction act as reviewing courts, or appellate courts. In general, cases can be brought before appellate courts only on appeal from an order or a judgment of a trial court or other lower court.

Jurisdiction of the Federal Courts   Because the federal government is a government of limited powers, the jurisdiction of the federal courts is limited. Article III of the U.S. Constitution establishes the boundaries of federal judicial power. Section 2 of Article III states that "[t]he judicial Power shall extend to all Cases, in Law and Equity, arising under this Constitution, the Laws of the United States, and Treaties made, or which shall be made, under their Authority."

Whenever a plaintiff's cause of action is based, at least in part, on the U.S. Constitution, a treaty, or a federal law, then a **federal question** arises, and the case comes under the judicial power of the federal courts. Any lawsuit involving a federal question can originate in a federal court. People who claim that their rights under the U.S. Constitution have been violated can begin their suits in a federal court. Note that most cases involving a federal question do not have to be tried in a federal court. The plaintiff can file the action in either a federal court or a state trial court (because the federal and state courts have *concurrent jurisdiction* over many matters, as will be discussed shortly).

Federal district courts can also exercise original jurisdiction over cases involving **diversity of citizenship.** Such cases may arise between (1) citizens of different states, (2) a foreign country and citizens of a state or of different states, or (3) citizens of a state and citizens or subjects of a foreign country. The amount in controversy must be more than $75,000 before a federal district court can take jurisdiction in such cases. For purposes of diversity jurisdiction, a corporation is a citizen of both the state in which it is incorporated and the state in which its principal place of business is located. A case involving diversity of citizenship can

PROBATE COURT
A state court of limited jurisdiction that conducts proceedings relating to the settlement of a deceased person's estate.

BANKRUPTCY COURT
A federal court of limited jurisdiction that handles only bankruptcy proceedings, which are governed by federal bankruptcy law.

FEDERAL QUESTION
A question that pertains to the U.S. Constitution, acts of Congress, or treaties. A federal question provides a basis for federal jurisdiction.

DIVERSITY OF CITIZENSHIP
Under Article III, Section 2, of the U.S. Constitution, a basis for federal district court jurisdiction over a lawsuit between (1) citizens of different states, (2) a foreign country and citizens of a state or of different states, or (3) citizens of a state and citizens or subjects of a foreign country. The amount in controversy must be more than $75,000 before a federal district court can take jurisdiction in such cases.

be filed in the appropriate federal district court, or, if the case starts in a state court, it can sometimes be transferred to a federal court. A large percentage of the cases filed in federal courts each year are based on diversity of citizenship.

Note that in a case based on a federal question, a federal court will apply federal law. In a case based on diversity of citizenship, however, a federal court will apply the relevant state law (which is often the law of the state in which the court sits).

Exclusive versus Concurrent Jurisdiction   When both federal and state courts have the power to hear a case, as is true in suits involving diversity of citizenship, **concurrent jurisdiction** exists. When cases can be tried only in federal courts or only in state courts, **exclusive jurisdiction** exists. Federal courts have exclusive jurisdiction in cases involving federal crimes, bankruptcy, patents, and copyrights; in suits against the United States; and in some areas of admiralty law (law governing transportation on the seas and ocean waters). States also have exclusive jurisdiction over certain subject matter—for example, divorce and adoption. The concepts of exclusive and concurrent jurisdiction are illustrated in Exhibit 3–1.

When concurrent jurisdiction exists, a party has a choice of whether to bring a suit in, for example, a federal or a state court. The party's lawyer will consider several factors in counseling the party as to which choice is preferable. The lawyer may prefer to litigate the case in a state court because he or she is more familiar with the state court's procedures, or perhaps the attorney believes that the state's judge or jury would be more sympathetic to the client and the case. Alternatively, the lawyer may advise the client to sue in federal court. Perhaps the state court's **docket** (the court's schedule listing the cases to be heard) is crowded, and the case could come to trial sooner in a federal court. Perhaps some feature of federal practice or procedure could offer an advantage in the client's case. Other important considerations include the law in the particular jurisdiction, how that law has been applied in the jurisdiction's courts, and what the results in similar cases have been in that jurisdiction.

Jurisdiction in Cyberspace

The Internet's capacity to bypass political and geographic boundaries undercuts the traditional basic limitations on a court's authority to exercise jurisdiction. These limits include

---

CONCURRENT JURISDICTION
Jurisdiction that exists when two different courts have the power to hear a case. For example, some cases can be heard in a federal or a state court.

EXCLUSIVE JURISDICTION
Jurisdiction that exists when a case can be heard only in a particular court or type of court.

DOCKET
The list of cases entered on a court's calendar and thus scheduled to be heard by the court.

EXHIBIT 3–1 **Exclusive and Concurrent Jurisdiction**

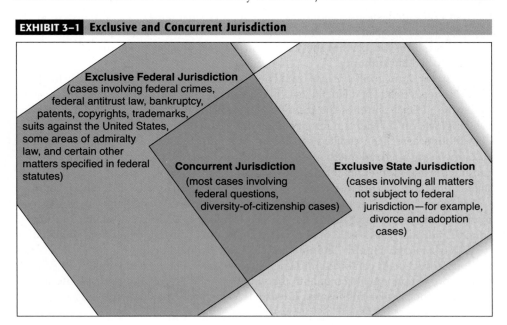

Exclusive Federal Jurisdiction
(cases involving federal crimes, federal antitrust law, bankruptcy, patents, copyrights, trademarks, suits against the United States, some areas of admiralty law, and certain other matters specified in federal statutes)

Concurrent Jurisdiction
(most cases involving federal questions, diversity-of-citizenship cases)

Exclusive State Jurisdiction
(cases involving all matters not subject to federal jurisdiction—for example, divorce and adoption cases)

a party's contacts with a court's geographic jurisdiction. As already discussed, for a court to compel a defendant to come before it, there must be at least minimum contacts—the presence of a salesperson within the state, for example. Are there sufficient minimum contacts if the defendant's only connection to a jurisdiction is an ad on the Web originating from a remote location?

The "Sliding-Scale" Standard   Gradually, the courts are developing a standard—called a "sliding-scale" standard—for determining when the exercise of jurisdiction over an out-of-state defendant is proper. In developing this standard, the courts have identified three types of Internet business contacts: (1) substantial business conducted over the Internet (with contracts and sales, for example), (2) some interactivity through a Web site, and (3) passive advertising. Jurisdiction is proper for the first category, is improper for the third, and may or may not be appropriate for the second.[4] An Internet communication is typically considered passive if people have to voluntarily access it to read the message, and active if it is sent to specific individuals.

In certain situations, even a single contact can satisfy the minimum-contacts requirement. ■**EXAMPLE 3.4** A Texas resident, Davis, sent an unsolicited e-mail message to numerous Mississippi residents advertising a pornographic Web site. Davis falsified the "from" header in the e-mail so that it appeared that Internet Doorway had sent the mail. Internet Doorway filed a lawsuit against Davis in Mississippi claiming that its reputation and goodwill in the community had been harmed. The U.S. district court in Mississippi held that Davis's single e-mail to Mississippi residents satisfied the minimum-contacts requirement for jurisdiction. The court concluded that Davis, by sending the e-mail solicitation, should reasonably have expected that she could be "haled into court in a distant jurisdiction to answer for the ramifications."[5] ■

International Jurisdictional Issues   Because the Internet is international in scope, international jurisdictional issues understandably have come to the fore. What seems to be emerging in the world's courts is a standard that echoes the "minimum-contacts" requirement applied by the U.S. courts. Most courts are indicating that minimum contacts—doing business within the jurisdiction, for example—are enough to compel a defendant to appear and that a physical presence is not necessary. The effect of this standard is that a business firm has to comply with the laws in any jurisdiction in which it targets customers for its products. This situation is complicated by the fact that many countries' laws on particular issues—free speech, for example—are very different from U.S. laws.

 ■**EXAMPLE 3.5** To understand some of the problems created by Internet commerce, consider a French court's judgment against the U.S.-based Internet company Yahoo!, Inc. Yahoo operates an online auction site on which Nazi memorabilia have been offered for sale. In France, the display of any objects representing symbols of Nazi ideology subjects the person or entity displaying such objects to both criminal and civil liability. The International League against Racism and Anti-Semitism filed a lawsuit in Paris against Yahoo for displaying Nazi memorabilia and offering them for sale via its Web site.

The French court asserted jurisdiction over Yahoo on the ground that the materials on the company's U.S.-based servers could be viewed on a Web site accessible in France. The French court ordered Yahoo to eliminate all Internet access in France to the Nazi memorabilia offered for sale through its online auctions. Yahoo then took the case to a federal district court in the United States, claiming that the French court's order violated the First Amendment. Although the federal district court ruled in favor of Yahoo, the U.S. Court of

---

4. For a leading case on this issue, see *Zippo Manufacturing Co. v. Zippo Dot Com, Inc.*, 952 F.Supp. 1119 (W.D.Pa. 1997).
5. *Internet Doorway, Inc. v. Parks*, 138 F.Supp.2d 773 (S.D.Miss. 2001).

Appeals for the Ninth Circuit reversed. According to the appellate court, U.S. courts lacked personal jurisdiction over the French groups involved. The ruling leaves open the possibility that Yahoo, and anyone else who posts anything on the Internet, could be held answerable to the laws of any country in which the message might be received.[6] ∎

Venue

Jurisdiction has to do with whether a court has authority to hear a case involving specific persons, property, or subject matter. **Venue**[7] is concerned with the most appropriate physical location for a trial. Two state courts (or two federal courts) may have the authority to exercise jurisdiction over a case, but it may be more appropriate or convenient to hear the case in one court than in the other.

Basically, the concept of venue reflects the policy that a court trying a suit should be in the geographic neighborhood (usually the county) where the incident leading to the lawsuit occurred or where the parties involved in the lawsuit reside. Venue in a civil case typically is where the defendant resides, whereas venue in a criminal case normally is where the crime occurred. Pretrial publicity or other factors, though, may require a change of venue to another community, especially in criminal cases when the defendant's right to a fair and impartial jury has been impaired. **▪EXAMPLE 3.6** A change of venue from Oklahoma City to Denver, Colorado, was ordered for the trials of Timothy McVeigh and Terry Nichols, who had been indicted in connection with the 1995 bombing of the Alfred P. Murrah Federal Building in Oklahoma City. (At trial, both McVeigh and Nichols were convicted. McVeigh received the death penalty and was put to death by lethal injection in early 2001. Nichols was sentenced to life imprisonment.) ∎

VENUE
The geographic district in which a legal action is tried and from which the jury is selected.

STANDING TO SUE
The requirement that an individual must have a sufficient stake in a controversy before he or she can bring a lawsuit. The plaintiff must demonstrate that he or she has been either injured or threatened with injury.

JUSTICIABLE CONTROVERSY
A controversy that is not hypothetical or academic but real and substantial; a requirement that must be satisfied before a court will hear a case.

Standing to Sue

Before a person can bring a lawsuit to court, the party must have **standing to sue,** or a sufficient "stake" in the matter to justify seeking relief through the court system. In other words, to have standing, a party must have a legally protected and tangible interest at stake in the litigation. The party bringing the lawsuit must have suffered a harm, or have been threatened by a harm, as a result of the action about which she or he has complained. Standing to sue also requires that the controversy at issue be a **justiciable**[8] **controversy**—a controversy that is real and substantial, as opposed to hypothetical or academic.

▪EXAMPLE 3.7 To persuade DaimlerChrysler Corporation to build a $1.2 billion Jeep assembly plant in the area, the city of Toledo, Ohio, gave the company an exemption from local property tax for ten years, as well as a state franchise tax credit. Toledo taxpayers filed a lawsuit in state court claiming that the tax breaks violated the commerce clause in the U.S. Constitution. The taxpayers alleged that the tax exemption and credit injured them because they would have to pay higher taxes to cover the shortfall in tax revenues. In 2006, the United States Supreme Court ruled that the taxpayers lacked standing to sue over the incentive program because their alleged injury was "conjectural or hypothetical" and, therefore, there was no justiciable controversy.[9] ∎

The Jeep assembly plant in Toledo, Ohio, which was built after the makers of Jeep, the DaimlerChrysler Corporation, received substantial tax breaks and tax credits from state and city governments. Ohio residents complained that the tax breaks given to DaimlerChrysler would result in a higher tax burden for individuals. What did the United States Supreme Court conclude about whether taxpayers in this situation have standing to sue? (AP Photo/J.D. Pooley)

---

6. *Yahoo!, Inc. v. La Ligue Contre le Racisme et l'Antisemitisme,* 379 F.3d 1120 (9th Cir. 2004); on rehearing, *Yahoo!, Inc. v. La Ligue Contre le Racisme et l'Antisemitisme,* 433 F.3d 1199 (9th Cir. 2006); *cert.* denied, ___ U.S. ___, 126 S.Ct. 2332, 164 L.Ed.2d 848 (2006).

7. Pronounced *ven-yoo.*

8. Pronounced jus-*tish*-uh-bul.

9. *DaimlerChrysler v. Cuno,* ___ U.S. ___, 126 S.Ct.1854, 164 L.Ed.2d 589 (2006).

Note that in some situations a person may have standing to sue on behalf of another person, such as a minor or a mentally incompetent person. ▪**EXAMPLE 3.8** Suppose that three-year-old Emma suffers serious injuries as a result of a defectively manufactured toy. Because Emma is a minor, her parent or legal guardian can bring a lawsuit on her behalf. ▪

THE STATE AND FEDERAL COURT SYSTEMS

As mentioned earlier in this chapter, each state has its own court system. Additionally, there is a system of federal courts. Although state court systems differ, Exhibit 3–2 illustrates the basic organizational structure characteristic of the court systems in many states. The exhibit also shows how the federal court system is structured. We turn now to an examination of these court systems, beginning with the state courts.

State Court Systems

Typically, a state court system will include several levels, or tiers, of courts. As indicated in Exhibit 3–2, state courts may include (1) trial courts of limited jurisdiction, (2) trial courts of general jurisdiction, (3) appellate courts, and (4) the state's highest court (often called the state supreme court). Generally, any person who is a party to a lawsuit has the opportunity to plead the case before a trial court and then, if he or she loses, before at least one level of appellate court. Finally, if the case involves a federal statute or federal constitutional issue, the decision of the state supreme court on that issue may be further appealed to the United States Supreme Court.

The states use various methods to select judges for their courts. Usually, voters elect judges, but sometimes judges are appointed. In Iowa, for example, the governor appoints judges, and then the general population decides whether to confirm their appointment in the next general election. The states usually specify the number of years that the judge will serve. In contrast, as you will read shortly, judges in the federal court system are appointed by the president of the United States and, if they are confirmed by the Senate, hold office for life—unless they engage in blatantly illegal conduct.

ON THE WEB

If you want to find information on state court systems, the National Center for State Courts (NCSC) offers links to the Web pages of all state courts at

www.ncsconline.org.

EXHIBIT 3–2 Federal and State Court Systems

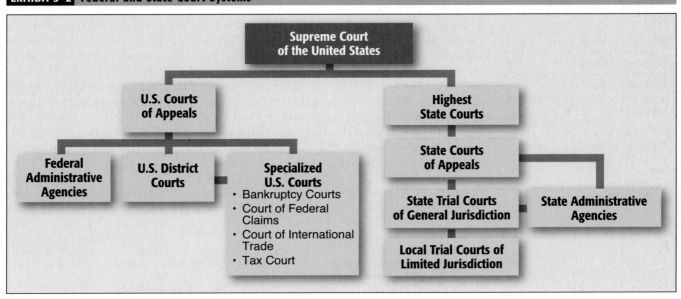

Does the use of private judges threaten our system of justice? The use of private judges has gained popularity in some states. In California, for example, a number of celebrity divorces—such as that of Brad Pitt and Jennifer Aniston—have taken place in private forums out of the public eye. Unlike a divorce mediator, a private judge (usually a retired judge who charges the parties a hefty fee) has the power to conduct trials and grant legal resolutions, such as divorce decrees.

In 2006, private judging came under fire in Ohio because private judges were conducting jury trials and using county courtrooms at the expense of taxpayers. Under an Ohio statute, parties to any civil action can have their dispute tried by a retired judge of their choosing who will make a decision in the matter.[10] Although the parties in one case had opted for a jury trial before a private judge, a public judge, Nancy Margaret Russo, refused to give up jurisdiction over the case on the ground that private judges are not authorized to conduct jury trials. Ultimately, the Ohio Supreme Court agreed with Judge Russo, holding that while the legislature had authorized private judges, they were not allowed to conduct jury trials and must reimburse the county for the use of courtrooms. As the court noted, private judging raises significant public-policy issues that the legislature needs to consider.[11] Some litigants may be willing and able to pay the extra cost to have their dispute heard by a private judge long before they would be able to set a trial date in a regular court. But is such a system fair for those who cannot afford private judges? What are the ethical implications of allowing parties to avoid the public scrutiny of a normal trial by opting to pay extra for a private judge and secret proceedings? Could allowing private judges to hear the cases of wealthier litigants lead to two different systems of justice?

Trial Courts Trial courts are exactly what their name implies—courts in which trials are held and testimony taken. State trial courts have either general or limited jurisdiction. Trial courts that have general jurisdiction as to subject matter may be called county, district, superior, or circuit courts.[12] The jurisdiction of these courts is often determined by the size of the county in which the court sits. State trial courts of general jurisdiction have jurisdiction over a wide variety of subjects, including both civil disputes and criminal prosecutions. (In some states, trial courts of general jurisdiction may hear appeals from courts of limited jurisdiction.)

Some courts of limited jurisdiction are called special inferior trial courts or minor judiciary courts. **Small claims courts** are inferior trial courts that hear only civil cases involving claims of less than a certain amount, such as $5,000 (the amount varies from state to state). Suits brought in small claims courts are generally conducted informally, and lawyers are not required (in a few states, lawyers are not even allowed). Another example of an inferior trial court is a local municipal court that hears mainly traffic cases. Decisions of small claims courts and municipal courts may sometimes be appealed to a state trial court of general jurisdiction. Other courts of limited jurisdiction as to subject matter include domestic relations courts, which handle primarily divorce actions and child-custody disputes, and probate courts, as mentioned earlier.

SMALL CLAIMS COURT
A special court in which parties may litigate small claims (such as $5,000 or less). Attorneys are not required in small claims courts and, in some states, are not allowed to represent the parties.

Appellate, or Reviewing, Courts Every state has at least one court of appeals (appellate court, or reviewing court), which may be an intermediate appellate court or the state's

---

10. See Ohio Revised Code Section 2701.10.

11. *State ex rel. Russo v. McDonnell*, 110 Ohio St.3d 144, 852 N.E.2d 145 (2006). (*Ex rel.* is Latin for *ex relatione*. The phrase refers to an action brought on behalf of the state, by the attorney general, at the instigation of an individual who has a private interest in the matter.)

12. The name in Ohio is court of common pleas; the name in New York is supreme court.

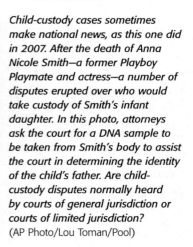

Child-custody cases sometimes make national news, as this one did in 2007. After the death of Anna Nicole Smith—a former Playboy Playmate and actress—a number of disputes erupted over who would take custody of Smith's infant daughter. In this photo, attorneys ask the court for a DNA sample to be taken from Smith's body to assist the court in determining the identity of the child's father. Are child-custody disputes normally heard by courts of general jurisdiction or courts of limited jurisdiction?
(AP Photo/Lou Toman/Pool)

highest court. About three-fourths of the states have intermediate appellate courts. Generally, courts of appeals do not conduct new trials, in which evidence is submitted to the court and witnesses are examined. Rather, an appellate court panel of three or more judges reviews the record of the case on appeal, which includes a transcript of the trial proceedings, and determines whether the trial court committed an error.

Usually, appellate courts focus on questions of law, not questions of fact. A **question of fact** deals with what really happened in regard to the dispute being tried—such as whether a party actually burned a flag. A **question of law** concerns the application or interpretation of the law—such as whether flag-burning is a form of speech protected by the First Amendment to the Constitution. Only a judge, not a jury, can rule on questions of law. Appellate courts normally defer to a trial court's findings on questions of fact because the trial court judge and jury were in a better position to evaluate testimony—by directly observing witnesses' gestures, demeanor, and nonverbal behavior during the trial. At the appellate level, the judges review the written transcript of the trial, which does not include these nonverbal elements.

An appellate court will challenge a trial court's finding of fact only when the finding is clearly erroneous (that is, when it is contrary to the evidence presented at trial) or when there is no evidence to support the finding. **EXAMPLE 3.9** Suppose that a jury concluded that a manufacturer's product harmed the plaintiff but no evidence was submitted to the court to support that conclusion. In that situation, the appellate court would hold that the trial court's decision was erroneous. The options exercised by appellate courts will be discussed in more detail later in this chapter. ■

Highest State Courts The highest appellate court in a state is usually called the supreme court but may be called by some other name. For example, in both New York and Maryland, the highest state court is called the court of appeals. The decisions of each state's highest court are final on all questions of state law. Only when issues of federal law are involved can a decision made by a state's highest court be overruled by the United States Supreme Court.

The Federal Court System

The federal court system is basically a three-tiered model consisting of (1) U.S. district courts (trial courts of general jurisdiction) and various courts of limited jurisdiction, (2) U.S. courts of appeals (intermediate courts of appeals), and (3) the United States Supreme Court. Unlike

QUESTION OF FACT
In a lawsuit, an issue that involves only disputed facts, and not what the law is on a given point. Questions of fact are decided by the jury in a jury trial (by the judge if there is no jury).

QUESTION OF LAW
In a lawsuit, an issue involving the application or interpretation of a law. Only a judge, not a jury, can rule on questions of law.

BE CAREFUL The decisions of a state's highest court are final on questions of state law.

state court judges, who are usually elected, federal court judges—including the justices of the Supreme Court—are appointed by the president of the United States and confirmed by the U.S. Senate. All federal judges receive lifetime appointments (because under Article III they "hold their offices during Good Behavior").

U.S. District Courts At the federal level, the equivalent of a state trial court of general jurisdiction is the district court. There is at least one federal district court in every state. The number of judicial districts can vary over time, primarily owing to population changes and corresponding caseloads. Currently, there are ninety-four federal judicial districts.

U.S. district courts have original jurisdiction in federal matters. Federal cases typically originate in district courts. There are other courts with original, but special (or limited), jurisdiction, such as the federal bankruptcy courts, shown in Exhibit 3–2 on page 81.

U.S. Courts of Appeals In the federal court system, there are thirteen U.S. courts of appeals—also referred to as U.S. circuit courts of appeals. The federal courts of appeals for twelve of the circuits, including the U.S. Court of Appeals for the District of Columbia Circuit, hear appeals from the federal district courts located within their respective judicial circuits. The Court of Appeals for the Thirteenth Circuit, called the Federal Circuit, has national appellate jurisdiction over certain types of cases, such as cases involving patent law and cases in which the U.S. government is a defendant.

The decisions of the circuit courts of appeals are final in most cases, but appeal to the United States Supreme Court is possible. Exhibit 3–3 shows the geographic boundaries of the U.S. circuit courts of appeals and the boundaries of the U.S. district courts within each circuit.

The United States Supreme Court The highest level of the three-tiered model of the federal court system is the United States Supreme Court. According to the language of Article III of the U.S. Constitution, there is only one national Supreme Court. All other courts in the federal system are considered "inferior." Congress is empowered to create other inferior courts as it deems necessary. The inferior courts that Congress has created include the second tier in our model—the U.S. courts of appeals—as well as the district courts and any other courts of limited, or specialized, jurisdiction.

The United States Supreme Court consists of nine justices. Although the Court has original, or trial, jurisdiction in rare instances (set forth in Article III, Section 2), most of its work is as an appeals court. The Court can review any case decided by any of the federal courts of appeals, and it also has appellate authority over some cases decided in the state courts.

Appeals to the United States Supreme Court. To bring a case before the Court, a party requests that the Court issue a writ of *certiorari.* A **writ of *certiorari***[13] is an order issued by the Court to a lower court requiring the latter to send it the record of the case for review. The Court will not issue a writ unless at least four of the nine justices approve of it. This is called the **rule of four.** Whether the Court will issue a writ of *certiorari* is entirely within its discretion. The Court is not required to issue one, and most petitions for writs are denied. (Thousands of cases are filed with the United States Supreme Court each year; yet it hears, on average, fewer than one hundred of these cases.)[14] A denial is not a decision on the merits of a case, nor does it indicate agreement with the lower court's opinion. Furthermore, a denial of the writ has no value as a precedent.

WRIT OF *CERTIORARI*
A writ from a higher court asking the lower court for the record of a case.

RULE OF FOUR
A rule of the United States Supreme Court under which the Court will not issue a writ of *certiorari* unless at least four justices approve of the decision to issue the writ.

---

13. Pronounced sur-shee-uh-*rah*-ree.
14. From the mid-1950s through the early 1990s, the United States Supreme Court reviewed more cases per year than it has in the last few years. In the Court's 1982–1983 term, for example, the Court issued opinions in 151 cases. In contrast, in its 2006–2007 term, the Court issued opinions in only 75 cases.

EXHIBIT 3–3   Boundaries of the U.S. Courts of Appeals and U.S. District Courts

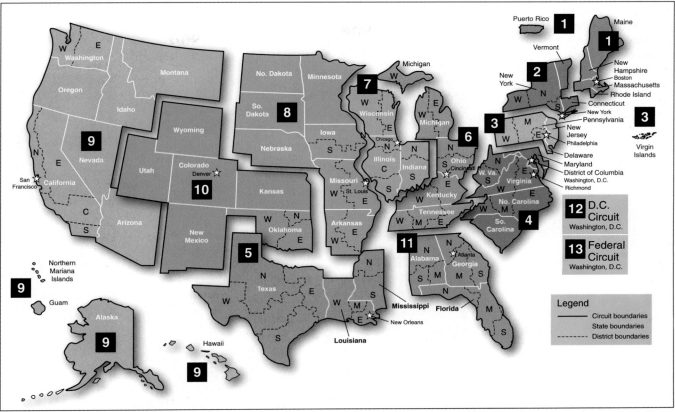

Source: Administrative Office of the United States Courts.

Petitions Granted by the Court.   Typically, the Court grants petitions when cases raise important constitutional questions or when the lower courts are issuing conflicting decisions on a significant issue. The justices, however, never explain their reasons for hearing certain cases and not others, so it is difficult to predict which type of case the Court might select.

FOLLOWING A STATE COURT CASE

To illustrate the procedures that would be followed in a civil lawsuit brought in a state court, we present a hypothetical case and follow it through the state court system. The case involves an automobile accident in which Kevin Anderson, driving a Mercedes, struck Lisa Marconi, driving a Ford Taurus. The accident occurred at the intersection of Wilshire Boulevard and Rodeo Drive in Beverly Hills, California. Marconi suffered personal injuries, incurring medical and hospital expenses as well as lost wages for four months. Anderson and Marconi are unable to agree on a settlement, and Marconi sues Anderson. Marconi is the plaintiff, and Anderson is the defendant. Both are represented by lawyers.

During each phase of the **litigation** (the process of working a lawsuit through the court system), Marconi and Anderson will have to observe strict procedural requirements. A large body of law—procedural law—establishes the rules and standards for determining disputes in courts. Procedural rules are very complex, and they vary from court to court and from state to state. There is a set of federal rules of procedure as well as various sets of rules for state courts. Additionally, the applicable procedures will depend on whether

LITIGATION
The process of resolving a dispute through the court system.

The justices of the United States Supreme Court (as of 2007). Does the fact that these justices are appointed for life have any effect on the decisions they reach in the cases they hear? Why or why not? (Photos from Collection of the Supreme Court of the United States)

the case is a civil or criminal proceeding. Generally, the Marconi-Anderson civil lawsuit will involve the procedures discussed in the following subsections. Keep in mind that attempts to settle the case may be ongoing throughout the trial.

The Pleadings

PLEADINGS
Statements made by the plaintiff and the defendant in a lawsuit that detail the facts, charges, and defenses involved in the litigation. The complaint and answer are part of the pleadings.

COMPLAINT
The pleading made by a plaintiff alleging wrongdoing on the part of the defendant; the document that, when filed with a court, initiates a lawsuit.

SUMMONS
A document informing a defendant that a legal action has been commenced against him or her and that the defendant must appear in court on a certain date to answer the plaintiff's complaint.

The complaint and answer (and the counterclaim and reply)—all of which are discussed below—taken together are called the **pleadings**. The pleadings inform each party of the other's claims and specify the issues (disputed questions) involved in the case. Because the rules of procedure vary depending on the jurisdiction of the court, the style and form of the pleadings may be quite different in different states.

The Plaintiff's Complaint Marconi's suit against Anderson commences when her lawyer files a **complaint** with the appropriate court. The complaint contains a statement alleging (asserting to the court, in a pleading) the facts necessary for the court to take jurisdiction, a brief summary of the facts necessary to show that the plaintiff is entitled to a remedy, and a statement of the remedy the plaintiff is seeking. Complaints may be lengthy or brief, depending on the complexity of the case and the rules of the jurisdiction.

After the complaint has been filed, the sheriff, a deputy of the county, or another *process server* (one who delivers a complaint and summons) serves a **summons** and a copy of the complaint on defendant Anderson. The summons notifies Anderson that he must file an answer to the complaint with both the court and the plaintiff's attorney within a specified time period (usually twenty to thirty days). The summons also informs Anderson that failure to answer may result in a **default judgment** for the plaintiff, meaning the plaintiff could be awarded the damages alleged in her complaint.

DEFAULT JUDGMENT
A judgment entered by a court against a defendant who has failed to appear in court to answer or defend against the plaintiff's claim.

Service of process is essential in our legal system. No case can proceed to a trial unless the plaintiff can prove that he or she has properly served the defendant. Did the plaintiff effect proper service of the summons and the complaint on an out-of-state corporation? That was the question in the following case.

CASE 3.2 **Cruz v. Fagor America, Inc.**

California Court of Appeal, Fourth District, Division 1, 146 Cal.App.4th 488, 52 Cal.Rptr.3d 862 (2007).

FACTS At the San Diego County Fair in California in the summer of 2001, Alan Cruz's parents bought a pressure cooker distributed by Fagor America, Inc. On September 10, sixteen-year-old Cruz tried to take the lid off of the pressure cooker and was burned on the left side of his torso and thigh. Cruz's parents e-mailed Fagor to alert the company to what had happened. Fagor denied liability. Cruz filed a suit in a California state court against Fagor, alleging negligence and product liability (see Chapters 4 and 13). Cruz mailed a summons and a copy of the complaint to Fagor by certified mail, return receipt requested. The envelope was addressed to "Patricio Barriga, Chairman of the Board, FAGOR AMERICA, INC., A Delaware Corporation, 1099 Wall Street, Lyndhurst, NJ 07071-3678." The receipt was returned with the signature of "Tina Hayes." When Fagor did not file an answer to Cruz's complaint, Cruz obtained a default judgment and was awarded damages of $259,114.50. More than nine months later, Barriga claimed that he had not been notified of the suit, and Fagor filed a motion to set aside the judgment. The court granted the motion, in part, on the ground that Cruz's service of process had not been effective. Cruz appealed to a state intermediate appellate court.

ISSUE Was Cruz's service of process effective?

DECISION Yes. The state intermediate appellate court reversed the decision of the lower court, ruling that it erred in concluding that the judgment against Fagor was void for the lack of a valid service of process.

REASON The appellate court concluded that Cruz met all of the requirements for serving an out-of-state corporation. In compliance with a California state statute, Cruz sent the summons and a copy of the complaint via first-class mail, return receipt requested. Significantly, Cruz addressed the service to Barriga, Fagor's president, not to the corporation itself. Barriga did not sign the receipt, but Hayes did. Under a state statute, service is proper when the summons and a copy of the complaint are delivered to "a person authorized by the corporation to receive service." According to a representative of the U.S. Postal Service, Hayes was a Fagor employee who regularly received mail on her employer's behalf. "The only reasonable inference from the evidence in the record is that Hayes was authorized to accept mail on behalf of Fagor's president at the time she signed the return receipt for the summons and complaint." Furthermore, reasoned the court, "By virtue of her authority to accept mail on Fagor's behalf, Hayes's notice of the action is imputed to Fagor and its officers. * * * To hold otherwise would be to ignore the realities of corporate life, in which the duty to sign for mail received often resides with a designated mailroom employee, a receptionist, a secretary, or an assistant."

FOR CRITICAL ANALYSIS–Social Consideration
Should a plaintiff be required to serve a defendant with a summons and a copy of a complaint more than once? Why or why not?

The Defendant's Answer The defendant's **answer** either admits the statements or allegations set forth in the complaint or denies them and outlines any defenses that the defendant may have. If Anderson admits to all of Marconi's allegations in his answer, the court will enter a judgment for Marconi. If Anderson denies any of Marconi's allegations, the litigation will go forward.

ANSWER
Procedurally, a defendant's response to the plaintiff's complaint.

COUNTERCLAIM
A claim made by a defendant in a civil lawsuit against the plaintiff. In effect, the defendant is suing the plaintiff.

REPLY
Procedurally, a plaintiff's response to a defendant's answer.

MOTION TO DISMISS
A pleading in which a defendant asserts that the plaintiff's claim fails to state a cause of action (that is, has no basis in law) or that there are other grounds on which a suit should be dismissed. Although the defendant normally is the party requesting a dismissal, either the plaintiff or the court can also make a motion to dismiss the case.

MOTION FOR JUDGMENT ON THE PLEADINGS
A motion by either party to a lawsuit at the close of the pleadings requesting the court to decide the issue solely on the pleadings without proceeding to trial. The motion will be granted only if no facts are in dispute.

MOTION FOR SUMMARY JUDGMENT
A motion requesting the court to enter a judgment without proceeding to trial. The motion can be based on evidence outside the pleadings and will be granted only if no facts are in dispute.

DISCOVERY
A phase in the litigation process during which the opposing parties may obtain information from each other and from third parties prior to trial.

Anderson can deny Marconi's allegations and set forth his own claim that Marconi was in fact negligent and therefore owes him compensation for the damage to his Mercedes. This is appropriately called a **counterclaim.** If Anderson files a counterclaim, Marconi will have to answer it with a pleading, normally called a **reply,** which has the same characteristics as an answer.

Anderson can also admit the truth of Marconi's complaint but raise new facts that may result in dismissal of the action. This is called raising an *affirmative defense.* For example, Anderson could assert the expiration of the time period under the relevant *statute of limitations* (a state or federal statute that sets the maximum time period during which a certain action can be brought or rights enforced) as an affirmative defense.

Motion to Dismiss A **motion to dismiss** requests the court to dismiss the case for stated reasons. Grounds for dismissal of a case include improper delivery of the complaint and summons, improper venue, and the plaintiff's failure to state a claim for which a court could grant relief (a remedy). For example, if Marconi had suffered no injuries or losses as a result of Anderson's negligence, Anderson could move to have the case dismissed because Marconi had not stated a claim for which relief could be granted.

If the judge grants the motion to dismiss, the plaintiff generally is given time to file an amended complaint. If the judge denies the motion, the suit will go forward, and the defendant must then file an answer. Note that if Marconi wishes to discontinue the suit because, for example, an out-of-court settlement has been reached, she can likewise move for dismissal. The court can also dismiss the case on its own motion.

Pretrial Motions

Either party may attempt to get the case dismissed before trial through the use of various pretrial motions. We have already mentioned the motion to dismiss. Two other important pretrial motions are the motion for judgment on the pleadings and the motion for summary judgment.

At the close of the pleadings, either party may make a **motion for judgment on the pleadings,** or on the merits of the case. The judge will grant the motion only when there is no dispute over the facts of the case and the sole issue to be resolved is a question of law. In deciding on the motion, the judge may consider only the evidence contained in the pleadings.

In contrast, in a **motion for summary judgment,** the court may consider evidence outside the pleadings, such as sworn statements (affidavits) by parties or witnesses, or other documents relating to the case. A motion for summary judgment can be made by either party. As with the motion for judgment on the pleadings, a motion for summary judgment will be granted only if there are no genuine questions of fact and the sole question is a question of law. Pretrial motions, including summary judgment motions and motions for judgment on the pleadings, are listed and described in Exhibit 3–4.

Discovery

Before a trial begins, each party can use a number of procedural devices to obtain information and gather evidence about the case from the other party or from third parties. The process of obtaining such information is known as **discovery.** Discovery includes gaining access to witnesses, documents, records, and other types of evidence.

The Federal Rules of Civil Procedure and similar rules in the states set forth the guidelines for discovery activity. The rules governing discovery are designed to make sure that a witness or a party is not unduly harassed, that privileged material (communications that need not be presented in court) is safeguarded, and that only matters relevant to the case at hand are discoverable.

EXHIBIT 3–4 Pretrial Motions

MOTION TO DISMISS

A motion normally filed by the defendant in which the defendant asks the court to dismiss the case for a specified reason, such as improper service, lack of personal jurisdiction, or the plaintiff's failure to state a claim for which relief can be granted.

MOTION TO STRIKE

A motion filed by the defendant in which the defendant asks the court to strike (delete) from the complaint certain paragraphs contained in the complaint. Motions to strike help to clarify the underlying issues that form the basis for the complaint by removing paragraphs that are redundant or irrelevant to the action.

MOTION TO MAKE MORE DEFINITE AND CERTAIN

A motion filed by the defendant to compel the plaintiff to clarify the basis of the plaintiff's cause of action. The motion is filed when the defendant believes that the complaint is too vague or ambiguous for the defendant to respond to it in a meaningful way.

MOTION FOR JUDGMENT ON THE PLEADINGS

A motion that may be filed by either party in which the party asks the court to enter a judgment in his or her favor based on information contained in the pleadings. A judgment on the pleadings will be made only if there are no facts in dispute and the only question is how the law applies to a set of undisputed facts.

MOTION TO COMPEL DISCOVERY

A motion that may be filed by either party in which the party asks the court to compel the other party to comply with a discovery request. If a party refuses to allow the opponent to inspect and copy certain documents, for example, the party requesting the documents may make a motion to compel production of those documents.

MOTION FOR SUMMARY JUDGMENT

A motion that may be filed by either party in which the party asks the court to enter judgment in her or his favor without a trial. Unlike a motion for judgment on the pleadings, a motion for summary judgment can be supported by evidence outside the pleadings, such as witnesses' affidavits, answers to interrogatories, and other evidence obtained prior to or during discovery.

Discovery prevents surprises at trial by giving parties access to evidence that might otherwise be hidden. This allows both parties to learn as much as they can about what to expect at a trial before they reach the courtroom. It also serves to narrow the issues so that trial time is spent on the main questions in the case.

Depositions and Interrogatories Discovery can involve the use of depositions or interrogatories, or both. A **deposition** is sworn testimony by a party to the lawsuit or any witness. The person being deposed (the deponent) answers questions asked by the attorneys, and the questions and answers are recorded by an authorized court official and sworn to and signed by the deponent. (Occasionally, written depositions are taken when witnesses are unable to appear in person.) The answers given to depositions will, of course, help the attorneys prepare their cases. Depositions can also be used in court to impeach (challenge the credibility

DEPOSITION
The testimony of a party to a lawsuit or a witness taken under oath before a trial.

of) a party or a witness who changes his or her testimony at the trial. In addition, the answers given in a deposition can be used as testimony if the witness is not available at trial.

Interrogatories are written questions for which written answers are prepared and then signed under oath. The main difference between interrogatories and written depositions is that interrogatories are directed to a party to the lawsuit (the plaintiff or the defendant), not to a witness, and the party can prepare answers with the aid of an attorney. The scope of interrogatories is broader because parties are obligated to answer the questions, even if that means disclosing information from their records and files.

INTERROGATORIES
A series of written questions for which written answers are prepared by a party to a lawsuit, usually with the assistance of the party's attorney, and then signed under oath.

Requests for Other Information   A party can serve a written request on the other party for an admission of the truth of matters relating to the trial. Any matter admitted under such a request is conclusively established for the trial. For example, Marconi can ask Anderson to admit that he was driving at a speed of forty-five miles an hour. A request for admission saves time at trial because the parties will not have to spend time proving facts on which they already agree.

A party can also gain access to documents and other items not in her or his possession in order to inspect and examine them. Likewise, a party can gain "entry upon land" to inspect the premises. Anderson's attorney, for example, normally can gain permission to inspect and photocopy Marconi's car repair bills.

When the physical or mental condition of one party is in question, the opposing party can ask the court to order a physical or mental examination. If the court is willing to make the order, which it will do only if the need for the information outweighs the right to privacy of the person to be examined, the opposing party can obtain the results of the examination.

E-EVIDENCE
Evidence that consists of computer-generated or electronically recorded information, including e-mail, voice mail, spreadsheets, word-processing documents, and other data.

Electronic Discovery   Any relevant material, including information stored electronically, can be the object of a discovery request. Electronic evidence, or **e-evidence,** includes all types of computer-generated or electronically recorded information, such as e-mail, voice mail, spreadsheets, word-processing documents, and other data. E-evidence is important because it can reveal significant facts that are not discoverable by other means. For example, whenever a person is working on a computer, information is being recorded on the hard drive disk without ever being saved by the user. This information includes the file's location, path, creator, date created, date last accessed, concealed notes, earlier versions, passwords, and formatting. It reveals information about how, when, and by whom a document was created, accessed, modified, and transmitted. This information can be obtained only from the file in its electronic format—not from printed-out versions.

The federal rules and most state rules (as well as court decisions) allow parties to obtain discovery of electronic data (or e-evidence). In fact, amendments to the Federal Rules of Civil Procedure that took effect in December 2006 specifically deal with the preservation, retrieval, and production of electronic data. Traditional means, such as interrogatories and depositions, are still used to find out about the e-evidence, but the parties must usually hire an expert to retrieve evidence in its electronic format. Using special software, the expert can reconstruct e-mail exchanges to establish who knew what and when they knew it. The expert can even recover files from a computer that the user thought had been deleted. Reviewing back-up copies of documents and e-mail can provide useful—and often quite damaging—information about how a particular matter progressed over several weeks or months. Data stored on back-up tapes, however, become usable only when fragmented data contained on the tapes are joined together and erased data are reconstructed.

Although electronic discovery has significant advantages over paper discovery, it is time consuming and expensive. These costs are amplified when the parties involved are large corporations with many offices. Moreover, as some businesses are finding out, failure to retain electronic data or to comply with electronic discovery requests can also be costly.

This chapter's *Adapting the Law to the Online Environment* feature on pages 92 and 93 discusses how the law pertaining to electronic discovery is evolving.

Pretrial Conference

Either party or the court can request a pretrial conference, or hearing. Usually, the hearing consists of an informal discussion between the judge and the opposing attorneys after discovery has taken place. The purpose of the hearing is to explore the possibility of a settlement without trial and, if this is not possible, to identify the matters that are in dispute and to plan the course of the trial.

Jury Selection

A trial can be held with or without a jury. The Seventh Amendment to the U.S. Constitution guarantees the right to a jury trial for cases in *federal* courts when the amount in controversy exceeds $20, but this guarantee does not apply to state courts. Most states have similar guarantees in their own constitutions (although the threshold dollar amount is higher than $20). The right to a trial by jury does not have to be exercised, and many cases are tried without a jury. In most states and in federal courts, one of the parties must request a jury in a civil case, or the right is presumed to be waived.

Before a jury trial commences, a jury must be selected. The jury selection process is known as **voir dire**.[15] During *voir dire* in most jurisdictions, attorneys for the plaintiff and the defendant ask prospective jurors oral questions to determine whether a potential jury member is biased or has any connection with a party to the action or with a prospective witness. In some jurisdictions, the judge may do all or part of the questioning based on written questions submitted by counsel for the parties.

During *voir dire*, a party may challenge a certain number of prospective jurors *peremptorily*—that is, ask that an individual not be sworn in as a juror without providing any reason. Alternatively, a party may challenge a prospective juror *for cause*—that is, provide a reason why an individual should not be sworn in as a juror. If the judge grants the challenge, the individual is asked to step down. A prospective juror may not be excluded from the jury by the use of discriminatory challenges, however, such as those based on racial criteria[16] or gender.[17]

At the Trial

At the beginning of the trial, the attorneys present their opening arguments, setting forth the facts that they expect to provide during the trial. Then the plaintiff's case is presented. In our hypothetical case, Marconi's lawyer would introduce evidence (relevant documents, exhibits, and the testimony of witnesses) to support Marconi's position. The defendant has the opportunity to challenge any evidence introduced and to cross-examine any of the plaintiff's witnesses.

At the end of the plaintiff's case, the defendant's attorney has the opportunity to ask the judge to direct a verdict for the defendant on the ground that the plaintiff has presented no evidence that would justify the granting of the plaintiff's remedy. This is called a **motion for a directed verdict** (known in federal courts as a *motion for judgment as a matter of law*). If the motion is not granted (it seldom is granted), the defendant's attorney then presents the evidence and witnesses for the defendant's case. At the conclusion of the defendant's case, the defendant's attorney has another opportunity to make a motion

---

ON THE WEB

Picking the "right" jury is often an important aspect of litigation strategy, and a number of firms now specialize in jury consulting services. You can learn more about these services by going to the Web site of the Jury Research Institute at

www.jri-inc.com.

VOIR DIRE
Old French phrase meaning "to speak the truth." In legal language, the phrase refers to the process in which the attorneys question prospective jurors to learn about their backgrounds, attitudes, biases, and other characteristics that may affect their ability to serve as impartial jurors.

TAKE NOTE A prospective juror cannot be excluded solely on the basis of his or her race or gender.

MOTION FOR A DIRECTED VERDICT
In a jury trial, a motion for the judge to take the decision out of the hands of the jury and to direct a verdict for the party who filed the motion on the ground that the other party has not produced sufficient evidence to support her or his claim.

---

15. Pronounced vwahr *deehr*.
16. *Batson v. Kentucky*, 476 U.S. 79, 106 S.Ct. 1712, 90 L.Ed.2d 69 (1986).
17. *J.E.B. v. Alabama ex rel. T.B.*, 511 U.S. 127, 114 S.Ct. 1419, 128 L.Ed.2d 89 (1994).

ADAPTING THE LAW TO THE ONLINE ENVIRONMENT — Electronic Discovery and Document Retention

Under the Federal Rules of Civil Procedure (FRCP), the party responding to a discovery request has traditionally been required to pay the expenses involved in obtaining the requested materials. Only if compliance was too burdensome or costly could a judge limit the scope of the request or shift some or all of the costs to the requesting party. Today, however, electronic discovery has dramatically increased the costs associated with complying with discovery requests. Electronic discovery typically involves hiring computer forensics experts to make "image" copies of desktop, laptop, and server hard drives. Experts are also needed to retrieve and reconstruct data from removable storage media (such as DVDs, CD-ROMs, and pen drives), back-up tapes, voice mail, cell phones, and any other devices that digitally store data. Consequently, both providing electronic data discovery and failing to preserve electronic data for discovery can prove costly for today's businesspersons.

Courts May Shift the Costs of Electronic Data Discovery

As mentioned in the text, the process of electronic data discovery is expensive and can easily run into thousands—if not millions—of dollars. In one case, for example, a court found that restoring the back-up tapes of just one of the many defen-

dants in the case would cost $9.75 million. Acquiring 200,000 e-mail messages from another defendant could cost as much as $84,000, with an additional $247,000 to have an attorney review the retrieved documents.[a]

Increasingly, the courts are shifting part of the costs of obtaining e-evidence to the party requesting it (usually the plaintiff), particularly if the electronic data are in a relatively inaccessible form, such as in back-up tapes or deleted files. If the data are in an accessible format, the usual rules of discovery apply: the responding party pays the costs of producing responsive data. Cost-shifting is appropriate only when the electronic discovery imposes an undue burden or expense on the responding party. In deciding whether to shift the costs, the courts also consider other factors, such as the availability of the information from other sources, the total cost of production compared with the amount in controversy, and each party's ability to pay the costs. Sometimes, a court may require the responding party to restore and produce representative documents from a small sample of the requested medium to verify the relevance of the data before the party incurs significant expenses.[b]

a. *Rowe Entertainment, Inc. v. William Morris Agency*, 2002 WL 975713 (S.D.N.Y. 2002).

b. See, for example, *Zubulake v. UBS Warburg, LLC*, 2003 WL 21087884 (S.D.N.Y. 2003); and *Quinby v. WestLB AG*, 2006 WL 2597900 (S.D.N.Y. 2006).

---

for a directed verdict. The plaintiff's attorney can challenge any evidence introduced and cross-examine the defendant's witnesses.

After the defense concludes its presentation, the attorneys present their closing arguments, each urging a verdict in favor of her or his client. The judge instructs the jury in the law that applies to the case (these instructions are often called *charges*), and the jury retires to the jury room to deliberate a verdict. In the Marconi-Anderson case, the jury will not only decide for the plaintiff or for the defendant but, if it finds for the plaintiff, will also decide on the amount of the **award** (the compensation to be paid to her).

Posttrial Motions

After the jury has rendered its verdict, either party may make a posttrial motion. If Marconi wins and Anderson's attorney has previously moved for a directed verdict, Anderson's attorney may make a **motion for judgment n.o.v.**, from the Latin *non obstante veredicto*, which means "notwithstanding the verdict"—called a *motion for judgment as a matter of law* in the federal courts. Such a motion will be granted only if the jury's verdict was unreasonable and erroneous. If the judge grants the motion, the jury's verdict will be set aside, and a judgment will be entered in favor of the opposite party (Anderson).

AWARD
In litigation, the amount of monetary compensation awarded to a plaintiff in a civil lawsuit as damages. In the context of alternative dispute resolution, the decision rendered by an arbitrator.

MOTION FOR JUDGMENT N.O.V.
A motion requesting the court to grant judgment in favor of the party making the motion on the ground that the jury's verdict against him or her was unreasonable and erroneous.

The Need to Preserve Electronic Data

Many companies have no written document-preservation policies and routinely delete data from servers and overwrite e-mails. Whenever there is a "reasonable anticipation of litigation," however, the law requires that all relevant documents must be preserved. In addition, newly amended Rule 26(b)(2) of the FRCP states that even though a party is not required to produce "inaccessible" data (unless the court has granted a motion to compel), the data must still be preserved. Preserving data can be a challenge, particularly for large companies that have electronic data scattered across multiple networks, servers, desktops, laptops, handheld devices, and even home computers or other off-site locations. Nevertheless, it is a necessity. Given that most documents today are in electronic form and are never printed out to hard copy, litigation success can hinge on electronic discovery.

The Consequences of Failing to Preserve or Provide E-Evidence Discovery

As an example of the serious consequences of failing to preserve electronic data, consider what happened to Morgan Stanley & Company, Inc.[c] Coleman Holdings sued Morgan Stanley (MS) for fraud in connection with a stock sale transaction that took place in 1998 and 1999. After receiving notice of the suit in 2003, MS directed its investment bankers to preserve paper documents but continued its practice of overwriting e-mails, even though Coleman had requested e-mail discovery. In April 2004, the court ordered MS to search the

back-up tapes relating to the thirty-six employees involved in the transaction. One month later, MS produced 1,300 pages of e-mails, but it did not search or disclose the existence of more than 1,700 back-up tapes at its various offices.

Six months after the discovery deadline set by the court, MS notified Coleman that it had discovered additional e-mail back-up tapes and provided an additional 8,000 pages of e-mails and attachments. The court concluded that MS had willfully ignored its discovery obligations and imposed sanctions on the firm. The court also authorized the jury to be instructed that a reasonable person could conclude that evidence of MS's discovery misconduct demonstrated its consciousness of guilt. The court reasoned that MS had a duty to preserve and maintain e-mails in readily accessible form.

In other cases, failure to preserve e-evidence or provide electronic discovery has led a firm to settle the case. For instance, Gateway's failure to preserve and produce a single damaging e-mail caused that firm to settle a dispute on the evening before trial.[d]

FOR CRITICAL ANALYSIS *Given the significant and often burdensome costs associated with electronic discovery, should courts consider cost-shifting in every case involving electronic discovery? Why or why not? How might a large corporation protect itself from allegations that it intentionally failed to preserve electronic data? What should companies do to be proactive in preserving electronic data for discovery?*

c. *Coleman (Parent) Holdings, Inc. v. Morgan Stanley & Co., Inc.,* 2005 WL 679071 (Fla.Cir.Ct. 2005).

d. *Adams v. Gateway, Inc.,* 2006 WL 2563418 (D. Utah 2006).

Alternatively, Anderson could make a **motion for a new trial,** asking the judge to set aside the adverse verdict and to hold a new trial. The motion will be granted if, after looking at all the evidence, the judge is convinced that the jury was in error but does not feel it is appropriate to grant judgment for the other side. A judge can also grant a new trial on the basis of newly discovered evidence, misconduct by the participants or the jury during the trial, or error by the judge.

MOTION FOR A NEW TRIAL
A motion asserting that the trial was so fundamentally flawed (because of error, newly discovered evidence, prejudice, or another reason) that a new trial is necessary to prevent a miscarriage of justice.

The Appeal

Assume here that any posttrial motion is denied and that Anderson appeals the case. (If Marconi wins but receives a smaller monetary award than she sought, she can appeal also.) Keep in mind, though, that a party cannot appeal a trial court's decision simply because he or she is dissatisfied with the outcome of the trial. A party must have legitimate grounds to file an appeal; that is, he or she must be able to claim that the lower court committed an error. If Anderson has grounds to appeal the case, a notice of appeal must be filed with the clerk of the trial court within a prescribed time. Anderson now becomes the appellant, or petitioner, and Marconi becomes the appellee, or respondent.

Filing the Appeal   Anderson's attorney files with the appellate court the record on appeal, which includes the pleadings, the trial transcript, the judge's rulings on motions made by the parties, and other trial-related documents. Anderson's attorney will also provide a condensation of the record, known as an *abstract*, which is filed with the reviewing court along with the brief. The **brief** is a formal legal document outlining the facts and issues of the case, the judge's rulings or jury's findings that should be reversed or modified, the applicable law, and arguments on Anderson's behalf (citing applicable statutes and relevant cases as precedents).

Marconi's attorney will file an answering brief. Anderson's attorney can file a reply to Marconi's brief, although it is not required. The reviewing court then considers the case.

Appellate Review   As mentioned earlier, a court of appeals does not hear evidence. Rather, it reviews the record for errors of law. Its decision concerning a case is based on the record on appeal, the abstracts, and the attorneys' briefs. The attorneys can present oral arguments, after which the case is taken under advisement. In general, appellate courts do not reverse findings of fact unless the findings are unsupported or contradicted by the evidence.

If the reviewing court believes that an error was committed during the trial or that the jury was improperly instructed, the judgment will be *reversed*. Sometimes, the case will be *remanded* (sent back to the court that originally heard the case) for a new trial. Even when a case is remanded to a trial court for further proceedings, however, the appellate court normally spells out how the relevant law should be interpreted and applied to the case.

A case may be remanded for several reasons. For instance, if the appellate court decides that a judge improperly granted summary judgment, the case will be remanded for a trial. If the appellate court decides that the trial judge erroneously applied the law, the case will be remanded for a new trial, with instructions to the trial court to apply the law as clarified by the appellate court. If the appellate court decides that the trial jury's award of damages was too high, the case will be remanded with instructions to reduce the damages award. In most cases, the judgment of the lower court is *affirmed*, resulting in the enforcement of the court's judgment or decree.

Appeal to a Higher Appellate Court   If the reviewing court is an intermediate appellate court, the losing party may decide to appeal to the state supreme court (the highest state court). Such a petition corresponds to a petition for a writ of *certiorari* from the United States Supreme Court. Although the losing party has a right to ask (petition) a higher court to review the case, the party does not have a right to have the case heard by the higher appellate court. Appellate courts normally have discretionary power and can accept or reject an appeal. Like the United States Supreme Court, state supreme courts generally deny most appeals. If the appeal is granted, new briefs must be filed before the state supreme court, and the attorneys may be allowed or requested to present oral arguments. Like the intermediate appellate court, the supreme court may reverse or affirm the appellate court's decision or remand the case. At this point, the case typically has reached its end (unless a federal question is at issue and one of the parties has legitimate grounds to seek review by a federal appellate court).

Enforcing the Judgment

The uncertainties of the litigation process are compounded by the lack of guarantees that any judgment will be enforceable. Even if a plaintiff wins an award of damages in court, the defendant may not have sufficient assets or insurance to cover that amount. Usually, one of the factors considered before a lawsuit is initiated is whether the defendant has sufficient assets to cover the amount of damages sought, should the plaintiff win the case. What other factors should be considered when deciding whether to initiate a lawsuit? See the *Application* feature at the end of this chapter for answers to this question.

THE COURTS ADAPT TO THE ONLINE WORLD

We have already mentioned that the courts have attempted to adapt traditional jurisdictional concepts to the online world. Not surprisingly, the Internet has also brought about changes in court procedures and practices, including new methods for filing pleadings and other documents and issuing decisions and opinions. Some jurisdictions are exploring the possibility of cyber courts, in which legal proceedings could be conducted totally online.

Electronic Filing

The federal court system first experimented with an electronic filing system in January 1996, and its Case Management/Electronic Case Files (CM/ECF) system has now been implemented in nearly all of the federal appellate courts and bankruptcy courts, as well as a majority of the district courts. The CM/ECF system allows federal courts to accept documents filed electronically in PDF format via the Internet. A few federal bankruptcy courts now even *require* some documents to be filed electronically.

Nearly half of the states have some form of electronic filing. These states include Arizona, California, Colorado, Connecticut, Delaware, Georgia, Kansas, Maryland, Michigan, New Hampshire, New Jersey, New Mexico, New York, North Carolina, North Dakota, Ohio, Pennsylvania, Texas, Utah, Virginia, Washington, and Wisconsin, as well as the District of Columbia. Some of these states, including Arizona, California, Colorado, Delaware, and New York, offer statewide e-filing systems. Generally, when electronic filing is made available, it is optional. Nonetheless, some state courts have now made e-filing mandatory in certain types of disputes, such as complex civil litigation.

The expenses associated with an appeal can be considerable, and e-filing can add substantially to the cost. In some cases, appellants who successfully appeal a judgment are entitled to be awarded their costs, including an amount for printing the copies of the record on appeal and the briefs. In other cases, the courts have refused to award e-filing costs to the successful party even though the court encouraged the parties to submit briefs and other documents in an electronic format.[18]

Courts Online

Most courts today have sites on the Web. Of course, each court decides what to make available at its site. Some courts display only the names of court personnel and office phone numbers. Others add court rules and forms. Many appellate court sites include judicial decisions, although the decisions may remain online for only a limited time period. In addition, in some states, such as California and Florida, court clerks offer docket information and other searchable databases online.

Appellate court decisions are often posted online immediately after they are rendered. Recent decisions of the U.S. courts of appeals, for example, are available online at their Web sites. The United States Supreme Court also has an official Web site and publishes its opinions there immediately after they are announced to the public. (These Web sites

ON THE WEB

For a list of the federal courts that accept electronic filing, go to the following page at a Web site maintained by the Administrative Office of the U.S. Courts:

www.uscourts.gov/cmecf/cmecf_court.html.

ON THE WEB

For links to state court rules addressing e-filing issues, go to the following site, which is provided by the American Bar Association:

www.abanet.org/tech/ltrc/research/ efiling/rules.html.

---

18. See, for example, *Phansalkar v. Andersen Weinroth & Co.*, 356 F.3d 188 (2d Cir. 2004).

are listed elsewhere in this chapter in the *On the Web* features.) In fact, even decisions that are designated as unpublished opinions by the appellate courts are often published online.

Cyber Courts and Proceedings

Someday, litigants may be able to use cyber courts, in which judicial proceedings take place only on the Internet. The parties to a case could meet online to make their arguments and present their evidence. This might be done with e-mail submissions, through video cameras, in designated "chat" rooms, at closed sites, or through the use of other Internet facilities. These courtrooms could be efficient and economical. We might also see the use of virtual lawyers, judges, and juries—and possibly the replacement of court personnel with computer software. Already the state of Michigan has passed legislation creating cyber courts that will hear cases involving technology issues and high-tech businesses. Many lawyers predict that other states will follow suit.

The courts may also use the Internet in other ways. In a groundbreaking decision in early 2001, for example, a Florida county court granted "virtual" visitation rights in a couple's divorce proceeding. Although the court granted custody of the couple's ten-year-old daughter to the father, the court also ordered each parent to buy a computer and a videoconferencing system so that the mother could "visit" with her child via the Internet at any time.[19]

ON THE WEB

To read about Michigan's cyber court legislation, go to the following Web page sponsored by Matthew R. Halpin & Associates, P.C.:

www.michigancyberlaw.com.

ETHICAL ISSUE 3.2

How will online access to courts affect privacy? In the past, trial court records, although normally available to the public, remained obscure because they were difficult to access: a person had to travel to the courthouse in person and ask to see the documents. As online access to court records increases and electronic filing becomes the norm, this "practical obscurity," as lawyers call it, may soon disappear. Electronic filing on a nationwide basis would open up all court documents to anyone with an Internet connection and a Web browser. Utilizing special "data-mining" software, anyone could go online and within just a few minutes access information—ranging from personal health records to financial reports to criminal violations—from dozens of courts. This means that serious privacy issues are at stake. Many courts are struggling with the issue of whether to restrict public access to certain types of documents and have taken a myriad of different approaches. Some courts make civil case information available but restrict Internet access to criminal case information. Other courts, such as those in Florida, have deemed certain types of documents and court proceedings confidential and no longer post this information online.[20] Still other courts, such as those in South Dakota, Vermont, and Washington, have developed policies to prevent the parties' confidential data and Social Security numbers from being released on public documents.

ALTERNATIVE DISPUTE RESOLUTION

ALTERNATIVE DISPUTE RESOLUTION (ADR)
The resolution of disputes in ways other than those involved in the traditional judicial process. Negotiation, mediation, and arbitration are forms of ADR.

Litigation is expensive. It is also time consuming. Because of the backlog of cases pending in many courts, several years may pass before a case is actually tried. For these and other reasons, more and more businesspersons are turning to **alternative dispute resolution (ADR)** as a means of settling their disputes.

The great advantage of ADR is its flexibility. Methods of ADR range from the parties sitting down together and attempting to work out their differences to multinational corporations

---

19. For a discussion of this case, see Shelley Emling, "After the Divorce, Internet Visits?" *Austin American-Statesman,* January 30, 2001, pp. A1 and A10.
20. *In re Report of Supreme Court Workgroup on Public Records,* 825 So.2d 889 (Fla. 2002). See also *Brennan v. Giles County Board of Education,* ___ S.W.3d ___ (Tenn.Ct.App. 2005).

agreeing to resolve a dispute through a formal hearing before a panel of experts. Normally, the parties themselves can control how the dispute will be settled, what procedures will be used, whether a neutral third party will be present or make a decision, and whether that decision will be legally binding or nonbinding.

Today, more than 90 percent of cases are settled before trial through some form of ADR. Indeed, most states either require or encourage parties to undertake ADR prior to trial. Many federal courts have instituted ADR programs as well. In the following pages, we examine the basic forms of ADR. Keep in mind, though, that new methods of ADR—and new combinations of existing methods—are constantly being devised and employed.

Negotiation

The simplest form of ADR is **negotiation,** a process in which the parties attempt to settle their dispute informally, with or without attorneys to represent them. Attorneys frequently advise their clients to negotiate a settlement voluntarily before they proceed to trial. Parties may even try to negotiate a settlement during a trial, or after the trial but before an appeal. Negotiation traditionally involves just the parties themselves and (typically) their attorneys. The attorneys, though, are advocates—they are obligated to put their clients' interests first.

NEGOTIATION
A process in which parties attempt to settle their dispute informally, with or without attorneys to represent them.

Mediation

In **mediation,** a neutral third party acts as a mediator and works with both sides in the dispute to facilitate a resolution. The mediator talks with the parties separately as well as jointly and emphasizes their points of agreement in an attempt to help the parties evaluate their options. Although the mediator may propose a solution (called a mediator's proposal), he or she does not make a decision resolving the matter. States that require parties to undergo ADR before trial often offer mediation as one of the ADR options or (as in Florida) the only option.

One of the biggest advantages of mediation is that it is not as adversarial as litigation. In trials, the parties "do battle" with each other in the courtroom, trying to prove one another wrong, while the judge is usually a passive observer. In mediation, the mediator takes an active role and attempts to bring the parties together so that they can come to a mutually satisfactory resolution. The mediation process tends to reduce the hostility between the disputants, allowing them to resume their former relationship without bad feelings. For this reason, mediation is often the preferred form of ADR for disputes involving business partners, employers and employees, or other parties involved in long-term relationships.

MEDIATION
A method of settling disputes outside of court by using the services of a neutral third party, who acts as a communicating agent between the parties and assists them in negotiating a settlement.

■EXAMPLE 3.10 Suppose that two business partners have a dispute over how the profits of their firm should be distributed. If the dispute is litigated, the parties will be adversaries, and their respective attorneys will emphasize how the parties' positions differ, not what they have in common. In contrast, when a dispute is mediated, the mediator emphasizes the common ground shared by the parties and helps them work toward agreement. The business partners can work out the distribution of profits without damaging their continuing relationship as partners. ■

ON THE WEB

For a collection of information and links related to alternative dispute resolution, mediation, and arbitration, go to the Web site of Hieros Gamos at

www.hg.org/adr.html.

Arbitration

A more formal method of ADR is **arbitration,** in which an arbitrator (a neutral third party or a panel of experts) hears a dispute and imposes a resolution on the parties. Arbitration is unlike other forms of ADR because the third party hearing the dispute makes a decision for the parties. Exhibit 3–5 on the next page outlines the basic differences among the three traditional forms of ADR. Usually, the parties in arbitration agree that the third party's

ARBITRATION
The settling of a dispute by submitting it to a disinterested third party (other than a court), who renders a decision that is (most often) legally binding.

EXHIBIT 3–5	Basic Differences in the Traditional Forms of ADR		
TYPE OF ADR	**DESCRIPTION**	**NEUTRAL THIRD PARTY PRESENT**	**WHO DECIDES THE RESOLUTION**
Negotiation	The parties meet informally with or without their attorneys and attempt to agree on a resolution.	No	The parties themselves reach a resolution.
Mediation	A neutral third party meets with the parties and emphasizes points of agreement to help them resolve their dispute.	Yes	The parties, but the mediator may suggest or propose a resolution.
Arbitration	The parties present their arguments and evidence before an arbitrator at a hearing, and the arbitrator renders a decision resolving the parties' dispute.	Yes	The arbitrator imposes a resolution on the parties that may be either binding or nonbinding.

ARBITRATION CLAUSE
A clause in a contract that provides that, in the event of a dispute, the parties will submit the dispute to arbitration rather than litigate the dispute in court.

Supporters of a union that represents firefighters and paramedics stage a protest during a contract dispute with the city of Philadelphia. An arbitration panel ruled in favor of the union and ordered a wage increase, and the city appealed. On what grounds can a court, on appeal, set aside the decision of an arbitration panel?
(Photo Courtesy of the Philadelphia Fire Fighters' Union—IAFF Local 22. All rights reserved.)

decision will be *legally binding,* although the parties can also agree to *nonbinding* arbitration. (Additionally, arbitration that is mandated by the courts often is not binding on the parties.) In nonbinding arbitration, the parties can go forward with a lawsuit if they do not agree with the arbitrator's decision.

In some respects, formal arbitration resembles a trial, although usually the procedural rules are much less restrictive than those governing litigation. In the typical arbitration, the parties present opening arguments and ask for specific remedies. Evidence is then presented, and witnesses may be called and examined by both sides. The arbitrator then renders a decision, which is called an *award.*

An arbitrator's award is usually the final word on the matter. Although the parties may appeal an arbitrator's decision, a court's review of the decision will be much more restricted in scope than an appellate court's review of a trial court's decision. The general view is that because the parties were free to frame the issues and set the powers of the arbitrator at the outset, they cannot complain about the results. The award will be set aside only if the arbitrator's conduct or "bad faith" substantially prejudiced the rights of one of the parties, if the award violates an established public policy, or if the arbitrator exceeded her or his powers (arbitrated issues that the parties did not agree to submit to arbitration).

Arbitration Clauses and Statutes   Virtually any commercial matter can be submitted to arbitration. Frequently, parties include an **arbitration clause** in a contract (a written agreement—see Chapter 7); the clause provides that any dispute that arises under the contract will be resolved through arbitration rather than through the court system. Parties can also agree to arbitrate a dispute after a dispute arises.

Most states have statutes (often based in part on the Uniform Arbitration Act of 1955) under which arbitration clauses will be enforced, and some state statutes compel arbitration of certain types of disputes, such as those involving public employees. At the federal level, the Federal Arbitration Act (FAA), enacted in 1925, enforces arbitration clauses in contracts involving maritime activity and interstate commerce (though its applicability to employment contracts has been controversial, as discussed in a later subsection). Because of the breadth of the commerce clause (see Chapter 1), arbitration agreements involving transactions only slightly connected to the flow of interstate commerce may fall under the FAA.

The question in the following case was whether a court or an arbitrator should consider a claim that an entire contract, including its arbitration clause, is rendered void by the alleged illegality of a separate provision in the contract.

CASE 3.3   Buckeye Check Cashing, Inc. v. Cardegna

Supreme Court of the United States, 546 U.S. 440, 126 S.Ct. 1204, 163 L.Ed.2d 1038 (2006).
www.law.cornell.edu/supct/index.html[a]

FACTS Buckeye Check Cashing, Inc., cashes personal checks for consumers in Florida. Buckeye agrees to delay submitting a check for payment in exchange for a consumer's payment of a "finance charge." For each transaction, the consumer signs a "Deferred Deposit and Disclosure Agreement," which states, "By signing this Agreement, you agree that i[f] a dispute of any kind arises out of this Agreement * * * th[e]n either you or we or third parties involved can choose to have that dispute resolved by binding arbitration." John Cardegna and others filed a suit in a Florida state court against Buckeye, alleging that the "finance charge" represented an illegally high interest rate in violation of Florida state laws, thereby rendering the agreement "criminal on its face." Buckeye filed a motion to compel arbitration. The court denied the motion. On Buckeye's appeal, a state intermediate appellate court reversed this denial, but on the plaintiffs' appeal, the Florida Supreme Court reversed the lower appellate court's decision. Buckeye appealed to the United States Supreme Court.

ISSUE Can a court consider a claim that an entire contract, including its arbitration clause, is rendered void by the alleged illegality of a separate provision in the contract?

DECISION No. The United States Supreme Court reversed the judgment of the Florida Supreme Court and remanded the case for further proceedings. The Court ruled that a challenge to the validity of a contract as a whole, and not specifically to an arbitration clause contained in the contract, must be resolved by an arbitrator.

a. In the "Supreme Court Collection" menu at the top of the page, click on "Search." When that page opens, in the "Search for:" box, type "Buckeye Check," choose "All decisions" in the accompanying list, and click on "Search." In the result, scroll to the name of the case and click on the appropriate link to access the opinion.

REASON The Court set out three propositions. "First, as a matter of substantive federal arbitration law, an arbitration provision is severable [capable of being legally separated] from the remainder of the contract. Second, unless the challenge is to the arbitration clause itself, the issue of the contract's validity is considered by the arbitrator in the first instance. Third, this arbitration law applies in state as well as federal courts." The Court concluded that here, because the plaintiffs challenged the contract's "finance charge," but not its arbitration provisions, those provisions were enforceable apart from the remainder of the contract. "The challenge should therefore be considered by an arbitrator, not a court." The plaintiffs also argued that the only arbitration agreements to which the Federal Arbitration Act (FAA) applies are those involving contracts and that the Buckeye agreement was not a contract because it was "void ab initio" (from the beginning). The FAA allows a challenge to an arbitration provision "upon such grounds as exist at law or in equity for the revocation [cancellation] of any contract." The Court reasoned that this includes contracts that later prove to be void. "Otherwise, the grounds for revocation would be limited to those that rendered a contract voidable—which would mean [implausibly] that an arbitration agreement could be challenged as voidable but not as void."

WHY IS THIS CASE IMPORTANT TO BUSINESSPERSONS? *The result illustrates the rule that the Federal Arbitration Act can be the basis for severing an arbitration clause from a contract and separately enforcing the clause. The holding in the* Buckeye *case makes this possible even if the remainder of the contract is later held to be invalid and even if a state law otherwise prohibits the enforcement of an arbitration clause in a contract that is unenforceable under state law.*

■

The Issue of Arbitrability   When a dispute arises as to whether the parties have agreed in an arbitration clause to submit a particular matter to arbitration, one party may file suit to compel arbitration. The court before which the suit is brought will decide *not* the basic controversy but rather the issue of arbitrability—that is, whether the matter is one that must be resolved through arbitration. If the court finds that the subject matter in controversy is covered by the agreement to arbitrate, then a party may be compelled to arbitrate the dispute. Even when a claim involves a violation of a statute passed to protect a certain class of people, such as employees, a court may determine that the parties must nonetheless

KEEP IN MIND Litigation—even of a dispute over whether a particular matter should be submitted to arbitration—can be time consuming and expensive.

abide by their agreement to arbitrate the dispute. Usually, a court will allow the claim to be arbitrated if the court, in interpreting the statute, can find no legislative intent to the contrary.

No party, however, will be ordered to submit a particular dispute to arbitration unless the court is convinced that the party consented to do so.[21] Additionally, the courts will not compel arbitration if it is clear that the prescribed arbitration rules and procedures are inherently unfair to one of the parties. **◼EXAMPLE 3.11** In one case, an employer asked a court to issue an order compelling a former employee to submit to arbitration in accordance with an arbitration agreement that the parties had signed. Under that agreement, the employer was to establish the procedure and the rules for the arbitration. The court held that the employee did not have to submit her claim to arbitration because "the rules were so one sided that their only possible purpose is to undermine the neutrality of the proceeding." According to the court, the biased rules created "a sham system unworthy even of the name of arbitration" in violation of the parties' agreement to arbitrate.[22] ◼

Mandatory Arbitration in the Employment Context A significant question in the last several years has concerned mandatory arbitration clauses in employment contracts. Many claim that employees' rights are not sufficiently protected when the workers are forced, as a condition of being hired, to agree to arbitrate all disputes and thus waive their rights under statutes specifically designed to protect employees. The United States Supreme Court, however, has generally held that mandatory arbitration clauses in employment contracts are enforceable.

◼EXAMPLE 3.12 In a landmark 1991 decision, *Gilmer v. Interstate/Johnson Lane Corp.*,[23] the Supreme Court held that a claim brought under a federal statute prohibiting age discrimination (see Chapter 18) could be subject to arbitration. The Court concluded that the employee had waived his right to sue when he agreed, as part of a required registration application to be a securities representative with the New York Stock Exchange, to arbitrate "any dispute, claim, or controversy" relating to his employment. ◼

The *Gilmer* decision was controversial and generated much discussion during the 1990s. By the early 2000s, some lower courts began to question whether Congress intended the FAA—which expressly excludes the employment contracts of seamen, railroad employees, or any other class of workers engaged in foreign or interstate commerce—to apply to any employment contracts. In 2001, however, the United States Supreme Court clarified that the act applies to most employment contracts, except those that involve interstate transportation workers.[24]

PREVENTING LEGAL DISPUTES

The United States Supreme Court has made it clear that arbitration clauses in employment contracts are enforceable under the FAA. Nevertheless, to prevent future disputes, business owners and managers would be wise to exercise caution when drafting such clauses and requiring employees to sign them. It is especially important to make certain that the terms of the agreement (including how the parties will split the costs of the arbitration procedure, for example) are not so one sided and unfair that a court could declare the entire agreement unenforceable.

◼

---

21. See, for example, *Wright v. Universal Maritime Service Corp.*, 525 U.S. 70, 119 S.Ct. 391, 142 L.Ed.2d 361 (1998).
22. *Hooters of America, Inc. v. Phillips*, 173 F.3d 933 (4th Cir. 1999).
23. 500 U.S. 20, 111 S.Ct. 1647, 114 L.Ed.2d 26 (1991).
24. *Circuit City Stores, Inc. v. Adams*, 532 U.S. 105, 121 S.Ct. 1302, 149 L.Ed.2d 234 (2001). See also *Circuit City Stores, Inc. v. Adams*, 279 F.3d 889 (9th Cir. 2002).

Other Types of ADR

The three forms of ADR just discussed are the oldest and traditionally the most commonly used. In recent years, a variety of new types of ADR have emerged. Some parties today are using *assisted negotiation,* in which a third party participates in the negotiation process. The third party may be an expert in the subject matter of the dispute. In *early neutral case evaluation,* the parties explain the situation to the expert, and the expert assesses the strengths and weaknesses of each party's claims. Another form of assisted negotiation is the *mini-trial,* in which the parties present arguments before the third party (usually an expert), who renders an advisory opinion on how a court would likely decide the issue. This proceeding is designed to assist the parties in determining whether they should settle or take the dispute to court.

Other types of ADR combine characteristics of mediation with those of arbitration. In *binding mediation,* for example, the parties agree that if they cannot resolve the dispute, the mediator can make a legally binding decision on the issue. In *mediation-arbitration,* or "med-arb," the parties agree to first attempt to settle their dispute through mediation. If no settlement is reached, the dispute will be arbitrated.

Today's courts are also experimenting with a variety of ADR alternatives to speed up (and reduce the cost of) justice. Numerous federal courts now hold **summary jury trials (SJTs),** in which the parties present their arguments and evidence and the jury renders a verdict. The jury's verdict is not binding, but it does act as a guide to both sides in reaching an agreement during the mandatory negotiations that immediately follow the trial. Other alternatives being employed by the courts include summary procedures for commercial litigation and the appointment of special masters to assist judges in deciding complex issues.

SUMMARY JURY TRIAL (SJT)
A method of settling disputes, used in many federal courts, in which a trial is held, but the jury's verdict is not binding. The verdict acts only as a guide to both sides in reaching an agreement during the mandatory negotiations that immediately follow the summary jury trial.

Providers of ADR Services

ADR services are provided by both government agencies and private organizations. A major provider of ADR services is the American Arbitration Association (AAA), which was founded in 1926 and now handles more than 200,000 claims a year in its numerous offices worldwide. Most of the largest U.S. law firms are members of this nonprofit association.

Cases brought before the AAA are heard by an expert or a panel of experts in the area relating to the dispute and are usually settled quickly. Generally, about half of the panel members are lawyers. To cover its costs, the AAA charges a fee, paid by the party filing the claim. In addition, each party to the dispute pays a specified amount for each hearing day, as well as a special additional fee for cases involving personal injuries or property loss. The AAA has a special team devoted to resolving large complex disputes across a wide range of industries.

Hundreds of for-profit firms around the country also provide various forms of dispute-resolution services. Typically, these firms hire retired judges to conduct arbitration hearings or otherwise assist parties in settling their disputes. The judges follow procedures similar to those of the federal courts and use similar rules. Usually, each party to the dispute pays a filing fee and a designated fee for a hearing session or conference.

ON THE WEB

To obtain information on the services offered by the American Arbitration Association (AAA), as well as forms that are used to submit a case for arbitration, go to the AAA's Web site at

www.adr.org.

ONLINE DISPUTE RESOLUTION

An increasing number of companies and organizations offer dispute-resolution services using the Internet. The settlement of disputes in these online forums is known as **online dispute resolution (ODR).** The disputes resolved in these forums have most commonly involved disagreements over the rights to domain names (Web site addresses—see Chapter 5) or over the quality of goods sold via the Internet, including goods sold through Internet auction sites.

ONLINE DISPUTE RESOLUTION (ODR)
The resolution of disputes with the assistance of organizations that offer dispute-resolution services via the Internet.

ODR may be best for resolving small- to medium-sized business liability claims, which may not be worth the expense of litigation or traditional ADR. Rules being developed in online forums, however, may ultimately become a code of conduct for everyone who does business in cyberspace. Most online forums do not automatically apply the law of any specific jurisdiction. Instead, results are often based on general, universal legal principles. As with most offline methods of dispute resolution, any party may appeal to a court at any time.

Negotiation and Mediation Services

The online negotiation of a dispute is generally simpler and more practical than litigation. Typically, one party files a complaint, and the other party is notified by e-mail. Password-protected access is possible twenty-four hours a day, seven days a week. Fees are generally low (often 2 to 4 percent, or less, of the disputed amount).

CyberSettle.com, National Arbitration and Mediation (NAM), and other Web-based firms offer online forums for negotiating monetary settlements. Even the Better Business Bureau now provides online dispute settlement (**www.bbbonline.org**). The parties to a dispute may agree to submit offers; if the offers fall within a previously agreed-on range, they will end the dispute. Special software keeps secret any offers that are not within the range. If there is no agreed-on range, typically an offer includes a deadline when the offer will expire, and the other party must respond before then. The parties can drop the negotiations at any time.

Mediation providers have also tried resolving disputes online. SquareTrade, for example, provides mediation services for the online auction site eBay as well as other parties. It has resolved more than 2 million disputes between merchants and consumers in 120 countries. SquareTrade uses Web-based software that walks participants through a five-step e-resolution process. Disputing parties first attempt to negotiate directly on a secure page within SquareTrade's Web site. There is no fee for negotiation. If the parties cannot reach an agreement, they can consult with a mediator. The entire process takes as little as ten to fourteen days.

Arbitration Programs

A number of organizations, including the American Arbitration Association, offer online arbitration programs. The Internet Corporation for Assigned Names and Numbers (ICANN), a nonprofit corporation that the federal government set up to oversee the distribution of domain names, has issued special rules for the resolution of domain name disputes.[25] ICANN has also authorized several organizations to arbitrate domain name disputes in accordance with ICANN's rules.

Resolution Forum, Inc. (RFI), a nonprofit organization associated with the Center for Legal Responsibility at South Texas College of Law, offers arbitration services through its CAN-WIN conferencing system. Using standard browser software and an RFI password, the parties to a dispute access an online conference room.

The Virtual Magistrate (VMAG) is a program provided through Chicago-Kent College of Law. VMAG offers arbitration for disputes involving online activities, including torts such as spamming and defamation (discussed in Chapter 4), wrongful messages and postings, and online contract or property disputes. VMAG attempts to resolve a dispute quickly (within seventy-two hours) and inexpensively. A VMAG arbitrator's decision is issued in a written opinion and may be appealed to a court.

ON THE WEB

To read about the policies and goals of the Virtual Magistrate program, go to

www.vmag.org.

---

25. ICANN's Rules for Uniform Domain Name Dispute Resolution Policy are online at **www.icann.org/dndr/udrp/uniform-rules.htm**. Domain names will be discussed in more detail in Chapter 5, in the context of trademark law.

REVIEWING **Courts and Alternative Dispute Resolution**

Stan Garner resides in Illinois and promotes boxing matches for SuperSports, Inc., an Illinois corporation. Garner created the promotional concept of the "Ages" fights—a series of three boxing matches pitting an older fighter (George Foreman) against a younger fighter, such as John Ruiz or Riddick Bowe. The concept included titles for each of the three fights ("Challenge of the Ages," "Battle of the Ages," and "Fight of the Ages"), as well as promotional epithets to characterize the two fighters ("the Foreman Factor"). Garner contacted George Foreman and his manager, who both reside in Texas, to sell the idea, and they arranged a meeting at Caesar's Palace in Las Vegas, Nevada. At some point in the negotiations, Foreman's manager signed a nondisclosure agreement prohibiting him from disclosing Garner's promotional concepts unless they signed a contract. Nevertheless, after negotiations between Garner and Foreman fell through,

Foreman used Garner's "Battle of the Ages" concept to promote a subsequent fight. Garner filed a lawsuit against Foreman and his manager in a federal district court located in Illinois, alleging breach of contract. Using the information presented in the chapter, answer the following questions.

1 On what basis might the federal district court in Illinois exercise jurisdiction in this case?

2 Does the federal district court have original or appellate jurisdiction?

3 Suppose that Garner had filed his action in an Illinois state court. Could an Illinois state court exercise personal jurisdiction over Foreman or his manager? Why or why not?

4 Assume that Garner had filed his action in a Nevada state court. Would that court have personal jurisdiction over Foreman or his manager? Explain.

APPLICATION **To Sue or Not to Sue?***

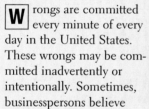

Wrongs are committed every minute of every day in the United States. These wrongs may be committed inadvertently or intentionally. Sometimes, businesspersons believe that wrongs have been committed against them by other businesspersons; by consumers; or by the local, state, or federal government. If you are deciding whether or not to sue for a wrong that has been committed against you or your business, you must consider many issues.

The Question of Cost

Competent legal advice is not inexpensive. Good commercial business law attorneys charge $100 to $600 an hour, plus expenses. It is almost always worthwhile to make an initial visit to an attorney who has skills in the area in which you are going to sue to get an estimate of the expected costs of pursuing redress for your grievance. You may be charged for the initial visit as well.

Note that less than 10 percent of all corporate lawsuits go to trial—the rest are settled beforehand. You may end up settling for far less than you think you are "owed" simply because of the length of time it will take for your case to come to trial and the cost of going to court. And then you might not win, anyway!

Basically, then, you must do a cost-benefit analysis to determine whether you should sue. Your attorney can give you an estimate of the dollar costs involved in litigating the dispute. Realize, though, that litigation also involves nondollar costs. These costs include time away from your business, stress, inconvenience, and publicity—to name but a few. You need to weigh all of these costs against the benefits. You can "guesstimate" the benefits by multiplying the probable size of the award by the probability of obtaining that award.

The Alternatives before You

Another method of settling your grievance is by alternative dispute resolution (ADR). Negotiation, mediation, arbitration, and other ADR forms are becoming increasingly attractive alternatives to court litigation (and private judges) because

* This *Application* is not meant to substitute for the services of an attorney who is licensed to practice law in your state.

(Continued)

they usually yield quick results at a comparatively low cost. Most disputes relating to business can be mediated or arbitrated through the American Arbitration Association (AAA), which can be accessed online at **www.adr.org**.

There are numerous other ADR providers as well. You can obtain information on ADR from the AAA, courthouses, chambers of commerce, law firms, state bar associations, or the American Bar Association. The Yellow Pages in large metropolitan areas usually list agencies and firms that can help you settle your dispute out of court (look under "Mediation"). You can also locate providers on the Web by using a general search engine, such as Google, and searching for arbitration providers in a specific city, such as "arbitration providers in Portland, Oregon."

Depending on the nature of the dispute and the amount of damages you seek, you might wish to contact one of the organizations that offer online dispute-resolution services, such as those discussed in this chapter.

CHECKLIST FOR DECIDING WHETHER TO SUE

1 Are you prepared to pay for going to court? Make this decision only after you have consulted an attorney to get an estimate of the costs of litigating the dispute.
2 Do you have the patience to follow a court case through the judicial system, even if it takes several years?
3 Is there a way for you to settle your grievance without going to court? Even if the settlement is less than you think you are owed—in net terms corrected for future expenses, lost time, and frustration—you may be better off settling now for the smaller figure.
4 Can you use some form of alternative dispute resolution? Before you say no, investigate these alternatives—they are usually cheaper and quicker to use than the standard judicial process.

KEY TERMS

alternative dispute
   resolution (ADR) 96
answer 87
arbitration 97
arbitration clause 98
award 92
bankruptcy court 77
brief 94
complaint 86
concurrent jurisdiction 78
counterclaim 88
default judgment 87
deposition 89
discovery 88
diversity of citizenship 77
docket 78
e-evidence 90

exclusive jurisdiction 78
federal question 77
interrogatories 90
judicial review 73
jurisdiction 73
justiciable controversy 80
litigation 85
long arm statute 74
mediation 97
motion for a directed verdict 91
motion for a new trial 93
motion for judgment *n.o.v.* 92
motion for judgment on the
   pleadings 88
motion for summary judgment 88
motion to dismiss 88
negotiation 97

online dispute
   resolution (ODR) 101
pleadings 86
probate court 77
question of fact 83
question of law 83
reply 88
rule of four 84
small claims court 82
standing to sue 80
summary jury trial (SJT) 101
summons 86
venue 80
voir dire 91
writ of *certiorari* 84

CHAPTER SUMMARY Courts and Alternative Dispute Resolution

The Judiciary's Role in American Government (See page 73.)	The role of the judiciary—the courts—in the American governmental system is to interpret and apply the law. Through the process of judicial review—determining the constitutionality of laws—the judicial branch acts as a check on the executive and legislative branches of government.
Basic Judicial Requirements (See pages 73–81.)	1. *Jurisdiction*—Before a court can hear a case, it must have jurisdiction over the person against whom the suit is brought or the property involved in the suit, as well as jurisdiction over the subject matter.

CHAPTER SUMMARY | Courts and Alternative Dispute Resolution—Continued

Basic Judicial Requirements— Continued	a. Limited versus general jurisdiction—Limited jurisdiction exists when a court is limited to a specific subject matter, such as probate or divorce. General jurisdiction exists when a court can hear any kind of case.
	b. Original versus appellate jurisdiction—Original jurisdiction exists when courts have authority to hear a case for the first time (trial courts). Appellate jurisdiction exists with courts of appeals, or reviewing courts; generally, appellate courts do not have original jurisdiction.
	c. Federal jurisdiction—Arises (1) when a federal question is involved (when the plaintiff's cause of action is based, at least in part, on the U.S. Constitution, a treaty, or a federal law) or (2) when a case involves diversity of citizenship (citizens of different states, for example) and the amount in controversy exceeds $75,000.
	d. Concurrent versus exclusive jurisdiction—Concurrent jurisdiction exists when two different courts have authority to hear the same case. Exclusive jurisdiction exists when only state courts or only federal courts have authority to hear a case.
	2. *Jurisdiction in cyberspace*—Because the Internet does not have physical boundaries, traditional jurisdictional concepts have been difficult to apply in cases involving activities conducted via the Web. Gradually, the courts are developing standards to use in determining when jurisdiction over a Web site owner or operator located in another state is proper.
	3. *Venue*—Venue has to do with the most appropriate location for a trial, which is usually the geographic area where the event leading to the dispute took place or where the parties reside.
	4. *Standing to sue*—A requirement that a party must have a legally protected and tangible interest at stake sufficient to justify seeking relief through the court system. The controversy at issue must also be a justiciable controversy—one that is real and substantial, as opposed to hypothetical or academic.
The State and Federal Court Systems (See pages 81–85.)	1. *Trial courts*—Courts of original jurisdiction, in which legal actions are initiated.
	a. State—Courts of general jurisdiction can hear any case; courts of limited jurisdiction include domestic relations courts, probate courts, traffic courts, and small claims courts.
	b. Federal—The federal district court is the equivalent of the state trial court. Federal courts of limited jurisdiction include the U.S. Tax Court, the U.S. Bankruptcy Court, and the U.S. Court of Federal Claims.
	2. *Intermediate appellate courts*—Courts of appeals, or reviewing courts; generally without original jurisdiction. Many states have an intermediate appellate court; in the federal court system, the U.S. circuit courts of appeals are the intermediate appellate courts.
	3. *Supreme (highest) courts*—Each state has a supreme court, although it may be called by some other name; appeal from the state supreme court to the United States Supreme Court is possible only if the case involves a federal question. The United States Supreme Court is the highest court in the federal court system and the final arbiter of the U.S. Constitution and federal law.
Following a State Court Case (See pages 85–95.)	Rules of procedure prescribe the way in which disputes are handled in the courts. Rules differ from court to court, and separate sets of rules exist for federal and state courts, as well as for criminal and civil cases. A sample civil court case in a state court would involve the following procedures:
	1. *The pleadings*—
	a. Complaint—Filed by the plaintiff with the court to initiate the lawsuit; served with a summons on the defendant.
	b. Answer—A response to the complaint in which the defendant admits or denies the allegations made by the plaintiff; may assert a counterclaim or an affirmative defense.

(Continued)

CHAPTER SUMMARY	Courts and Alternative Dispute Resolution—Continued

Following a State Court Case—Continued	c. Motion to dismiss—A request to the court to dismiss the case for stated reasons, such as the plaintiff's failure to state a claim for which relief can be granted.
	
	2. *Pretrial motions (in addition to the motion to dismiss)*—
	
	  a. Motion for judgment on the pleadings—May be made by either party; will be granted if the parties agree on the facts and the only question is how the law applies to the facts. The judge bases the decision solely on the pleadings.
	
	  b. Motion for summary judgment—May be made by either party; will be granted if the parties agree on the facts. The judge applies the law in rendering a judgment. The judge can consider evidence outside the pleadings when evaluating the motion.
	
	3. *Discovery*—The process of gathering evidence concerning the case. Discovery involves depositions (sworn testimony by a party to the lawsuit or any witness), interrogatories (written questions and answers to these questions made by parties to the action with the aid of their attorneys), and various requests (for admissions, documents, and medical examinations, for example). Discovery may also involve electronically recorded information, such as e-mail, voice mail, word-processing documents, and other data compilations. Although electronic discovery has significant advantages over paper discovery, it is also more time consuming and expensive and often requires the parties to hire experts.
	
	4. *Pretrial conference*—Either party or the court can request a pretrial conference to identify the matters in dispute after discovery has taken place and to plan the course of the trial.
	
	5. *Trial*—Following jury selection (*voir dire*), the trial begins with opening statements from both parties' attorneys. The following events then occur:
	
	  a. The plaintiff's introduction of evidence (including the testimony of witnesses) supporting the plaintiff's position. The defendant's attorney can challenge evidence and cross-examine witnesses.
	
	  b. The defendant's introduction of evidence (including the testimony of witnesses) supporting the defendant's position. The plaintiff's attorney can challenge evidence and cross-examine witnesses.
	
	  c. Closing arguments by the attorneys in favor of their respective clients, the judge's instructions to the jury, and the jury's verdict.
	
	6. *Posttrial motions*—
	
	  a. Motion for judgment *n.o.v.* ("notwithstanding the verdict")—Will be granted if the judge is convinced that the jury was in error.
	
	  b. Motion for a new trial—Will be granted if the judge is convinced that the jury was in error; can also be granted on the grounds of newly discovered evidence, misconduct by the participants during the trial, or error by the judge.
	
	7. *Appeal*—Either party can appeal the trial court's judgment to an appropriate court of appeals. After reviewing the record on appeal, the abstracts, and the attorneys' briefs, the appellate court holds a hearing and renders its opinion.

The Courts Adapt to the Online World (See pages 95–96.)	A number of state and federal courts now allow parties to file litigation-related documents with the courts via the Internet or other electronic means. Nearly all of the federal appellate courts and bankruptcy courts and a majority of the federal district courts have implemented electronic filing systems. Almost every court now has a Web page offering information about the court and its procedures, and increasingly courts are publishing their opinions online. In the future, we may see "cyber courts," in which all trial proceedings are conducted online.
Alternative Dispute Resolution (See pages 96–101.)	1. *Negotiation*—The parties come together, with or without attorneys to represent them, and try to reach a settlement without the involvement of a third party.

CHAPTER SUMMARY Courts and Alternative Dispute Resolution–Continued

Alternative Dispute Resolution—Continued	2. *Mediation*—The parties themselves reach an agreement with the help of a neutral third party, called a mediator, who proposes solutions. At the parties' request, a mediator may make a legally binding decision.
	3. *Arbitration*—A more formal method of ADR in which the parties submit their dispute to a neutral third party, the arbitrator, who renders a decision. The decision may or may not be legally binding, depending on the circumstances.
	4. *Other types of ADR*—These include early neutral case evaluation, mini-trials, and summary jury trials (SJTs); generally, these are forms of "assisted negotiation."
	5. *Providers of ADR services*—The leading nonprofit provider of ADR services is the American Arbitration Association. Hundreds of for-profit firms also provide ADR services.
Online Dispute Resolution (See pages 101–102.)	A number of organizations and firms are now offering negotiation, mediation, and arbitration services through online forums. To date, these forums have been a practical alternative for the resolution of domain name disputes and e-commerce disputes in which the amount in controversy is relatively small.

FOR REVIEW

Answers for the even-numbered questions in this For Review *section can be found in Appendix E at the end of this text.*

1 What is judicial review? How and when was the power of judicial review established?

2 Before a court can hear a case, it must have jurisdiction. Over what must it have jurisdiction? How are the courts applying traditional jurisdictional concepts to cases involving Internet transactions?

3 What is the difference between a trial court and an appellate court?

4 In a lawsuit, what are the pleadings? What is discovery, and how does electronic discovery differ from traditional discovery? What is electronic filing?

5 How are online forums being used to resolve disputes?

■

QUESTIONS AND CASE PROBLEMS

 **HYPOTHETICAL SCENARIOS**

3.1 Arbitration. In an arbitration proceeding, the arbitrator need not be a judge or even a lawyer. How, then, can the arbitrator's decision have the force of law and be binding on the parties involved?

3.2 Hypothetical Question with Sample Answer. Marya Callais, a citizen of Florida, was walking along a busy street in Tallahassee when a large crate flew off a passing truck and hit her, causing numerous injuries to Callais. She incurred a great deal of pain and suffering plus significant medical expenses, and she could not work for six months. She wishes to sue the trucking firm for $300,000 in damages. The firm's headquarters are in Georgia, although the company does business in Florida. In what court may Callais bring suit—a Florida state court, a Georgia state court, or a federal court? What factors might influence her decision?

 For a sample answer to Question 3.2, go to Appendix F at the end of this text.

■

CASE PROBLEMS

3.3 Standing. Blue Cross and Blue Shield insurance companies (the Blues) provide 68 million Americans with health-care financing. The Blues have paid billions of dollars for care attributable to illnesses related to tobacco use. In an attempt to recover some of this amount, the Blues filed a suit in a federal district court against tobacco companies and others, alleging fraud, among other things. The Blues claimed that beginning in 1953, the defendants conspired to addict millions of Americans, including members of Blue Cross plans, to cigarettes and other tobacco products. The conspiracy involved misrepresentation about the safety of nicotine and its addictive properties, marketing efforts targeting children, and agreements not to produce or market safer cigarettes. As a result of the defendants' efforts, many tobacco users developed lung, throat, and other cancers, as well as heart disease, stroke, emphysema, and other illnesses. The defendants asked the court to dismiss the case on the ground that the plaintiffs did not have standing to sue. Do the Blues have standing in this case? Why or why not? [*Blue Cross and Blue Shield of New Jersey, Inc. v. Philip Morris, Inc.*, 36 F.Supp.2d 560 (E.D.N.Y. 1999)]

3.4 Case Problem with Sample Answer. Ms. Thompson filed a suit in a federal district court against her employer, Altheimer & Gray, seeking damages for alleged racial discrimination in violation of federal law. During *voir dire*, the judge asked the prospective jurors whether "there is something about this kind of lawsuit for monetary damages that would start any of you leaning for or against a particular party?" Ms. Leiter, one of the prospective jurors, raised her hand and explained that she had "been an owner of a couple of businesses and am currently an owner of a business, and I feel that as an employer and owner of a business that will definitely sway my judgment in this case." She explained, "I am constantly faced with people that want various benefits or different positions in the company or better contacts or, you know, a myriad of issues that employers face on a regular basis, and I have to decide whether or not that person should get them." Asked by Thompson's lawyer whether "you believe that people file lawsuits just because they don't get something they want," Leiter answered, "I believe there are some people that do." In answer to another question, she said, "I think I bring a lot of background to this case, and I can't say that it's not going to cloud my judgment. I can try to be as fair as I can, as I do every day." Thompson filed a motion to strike Leiter for cause. Should the judge grant the motion? Explain. [*Thompson v. Altheimer & Gray*, 248 F.3d 621 (7th Cir. 2001)]

After you have answered Problem 3.4, compare your answer with the sample answer given on the Web site that accompanies this text. Go to academic.cengage.com/blaw/blt, select "Chapter 3," and click on "Case Problem with Sample Answer."

3.5 Arbitration. Alexander Little worked for Auto Stiegler, Inc., an automobile dealership in Los Angeles County, California, eventually becoming the service manager. While employed, Little signed an arbitration agreement that required all employment-related disputes to be submitted to arbitration. The agreement also provided that any award over $50,000 could be appealed to a second arbitrator. Little was later demoted and terminated. Alleging that these actions were in retaliation for investigating and reporting warranty fraud and thus were in violation of public policy, Little filed a suit in a California state court against Auto Stiegler. The defendant filed a motion with the court to compel arbitration. Little responded that the arbitration agreement should not be enforced because, among other things, the appeal provision was unfairly one sided. Is this provision enforceable? Should the court grant Auto Stiegler's motion? Why or why not? [*Little v. Auto Stiegler, Inc.*, 29 Cal.4th 1064, 63 P.3d 979, 130 Cal.Rptr.2d 892 (2003)]

3.6 Standing to Sue. Lamar Advertising of Penn, LLC, an outdoor advertising business, wanted to erect billboards of varying sizes in a multiphase operation throughout the town of Orchard Park, New York. An Orchard Park ordinance restricted the signs to certain sizes in certain areas, to advertising products and services available for sale only on the premises, and to other limits. Lamar asked Orchard Park for permission to build signs in some areas larger than the ordinance allowed in those locations (but not as large as allowed in other areas). When the town refused, Lamar filed a suit in a federal district court, claiming that the ordinance violated the First Amendment. Did Lamar have standing to challenge the ordinance? If the court could sever the provisions of the ordinance restricting a sign's content from the provisions limiting a sign's size, would your answer be the same? Explain. [*Lamar Advertising of Penn, LLC v. Town of Orchard Park, New York*, 356 F.3d 365 (2d Cir. 2004)]

3.7 Jurisdiction. Xcentric Ventures, LLC, an Arizona firm, operates RipOffReport.com and BadBusinessBureau.com. Visitors to the Web sites can buy a copy of a book titled *Do-It-Yourself Guide: How to Get Rip-Off Revenge*. The price ($21.95) includes shipping to anywhere in the United States, including Illinois, to which thirteen copies have been shipped. The sites accept donations and feature postings by individuals who claim to have been "ripped off." Some visitors posted comments about George S. May International Co., a management-consulting firm. The postings alleged fraud, larceny, possession of child pornography, and possession of controlled substances (illegal drugs). May filed a suit against Xcentric and others in a federal district court in Illinois, alleging, in part, "false descriptions and representations." The defendants filed a motion to dismiss for lack of jurisdiction. What is the standard for exercising jurisdiction over a party whose only connection to a jurisdiction is over the Web? How would that standard apply in this case? Explain. [*George S. May International Co. v. Xcentric Ventures, LLC*, 409 F.Supp.2d 1052 (N.D.Ill. 2006)]

3.8 Appellate Review. BSH Home Appliances Corp. makes appliances under the Bosch, Siemens, Thermador, and Gaggenau brands. To make and market the "Pro 27 Stainless Steel Range," a restaurant-quality range for home use, BSH gave specifications for its burner to Detroit Radiant Products Co. and requested a price for 30,000 units. Detroit quoted $28.25 per unit, offering to absorb all tooling and research and development costs. In 2001 and 2003, BSH sent Detroit two purchase orders, for 15,000 and 16,000 units, respectively. In 2004, after Detroit had shipped 12,886 units, BSH stopped scheduling deliveries. Detroit filed a suit against BSH, alleging breach of contract. BSH argued, in part, that the second purchase order had not added to the first but had replaced it. After a trial, a federal district court issued its "Findings of Fact and Conclusions of Law." The court found that the two purchase orders "required BSH to purchase 31,000 units of the burner at $28.25 per unit." The court ruled that Detroit was entitled to $418,261 for 18,114 unsold burners. BSH appealed to the U.S. Court of Appeals for the Sixth Circuit. Can an appellate court set aside a trial court's findings of fact? Can an appellate court come to its own conclusions of law? What should the court rule in this case? Explain. [*Detroit Radiant Products Co. v. BSH Home Appliances Corp.*, 473 F.3d 623 (6th Cir. 2007)]

3.9 **A Question of Ethics.** *Narnia Investments, Ltd., filed a suit in a Texas state court against several defendants, including Harvestons Securities, Inc., a securities dealer.*

(Securities *are documents evidencing the ownership of a corporation, in the form of stock, or debts owed by it, in the form of bonds.*) *Harvestons is registered with the state of Texas and thus may be served with a summons and a copy of a complaint delivered to the Texas Securities Commissioner. In this case, the return of service indicated that process was served on the commissioner "by delivering to JoAnn Kocerek, defendant, in person, a true copy of this [summons] together with the accompanying copy(ies) of the [complaint]." Harvestons did not file an answer, and Narnia obtained a default judgment against the defendant for $365,000, plus attorneys' fees and interest. Five months after this judgment, Harvestons filed a motion for a new trial, which the court denied. Harvestons appealed to a state intermediate appellate court, claiming that it had not been served in strict compliance with the rules governing service of process.* [Harvestons Securities, Inc. v. Narnia Investments, Ltd., 218 S.W.3d 126 (Tex.App. — Houston [14 Dist.] 2007)]

1 Harvestons asserted that Narnia's service was invalid in part because "the return of service states that process was delivered to 'JoAnn Kocerek'" and did not show that she "had the authority to accept process on behalf of Harvestons or the Texas Securities Commissioner." Should such a detail, if it is required, be strictly construed and applied? Should it apply in this case? Explain.

2 Whose responsibility is it to see that service of process is accomplished properly? Was it accomplished properly in this case? Why or why not?

CRITICAL THINKING AND WRITING ASSIGNMENTS

3.10 Critical Legal Thinking. Suppose that a state statute requires that all civil lawsuits involving damages of less than $50,000 be arbitrated and allows such a case to be tried in court only if a party is dissatisfied with the arbitrator's decision. Suppose further that the statute also provides that if a trial does not result in an improvement of more than 10 percent in the position of the party who demanded the trial, that party must pay the entire costs of the arbitration proceeding. Would such a statute violate litigants' rights of access to the courts and to trial by jury? Would it matter if the statute was part of a pilot program and affected only a few judicial districts in the state?

3.11 **Video Question.** Go to this text's Web site at **academic. cengage.com/blaw/blt** and select "Chapter 3." Click on "Video Questions" and view the video titled *Jurisdiction in Cyberspace.* Then answer the following questions.

1 What standard would a court apply to determine whether it has jurisdiction over the out-of-state computer firm in the video?

2 What factors is a court likely to consider in assessing whether sufficient contacts exist when the only connection to the jurisdiction is through a Web site?

3 How do you think a court would resolve the issue in this case?

PRACTICAL
INTERNET EXERCISES

Go to this text's Web site at **academic.cengage.com/blaw/blt**, select "Chapter 3," and click on "Practical Internet Exercises." There you will find the following Internet research exercises that you can perform to learn more about the topics covered in this chapter.

PRACTICAL INTERNET EXERCISE 3-1   LEGAL PERSPECTIVE—The Judiciary's Role in American Government

PRACTICAL INTERNET EXERCISE 3-2   MANAGEMENT PERSPECTIVE—Alternative Dispute Resolution

PRACTICAL INTERNET EXERCISE 3-3   SOCIAL PERSPECTIVE—Resolve a Dispute Online

BEFORE THE TEST

Go to this text's Web site at **academic.cengage.com/blaw/blt**, select "Chapter 3," and click on "Interactive Quizzes." You will find a number of interactive questions relating to this chapter.

CHAPTER 4
Torts and Cyber Torts

LEARNING OBJECTIVES

AFTER READING THIS CHAPTER, YOU SHOULD BE ABLE TO ANSWER THE FOLLOWING QUESTIONS:

1 What is a tort?

2 What is the purpose of tort law? What are two basic categories of torts?

3 What are the four elements of negligence?

4 What is meant by strict liability? In what circumstances is strict liability applied?

5 What is a cyber tort, and how are tort theories being applied in cyberspace?

> ❝ 'Tort' more or less means 'wrong' . . . . One of my friends [in law school] said that Torts is the course which proves that your mother was right.❞
>
> Scott Turow, 1949–present (American lawyer and author)

As Scott Turow's statement in the chapter-opening quotation indicates, **torts** are wrongful actions.[1] Through tort law, society compensates those who have suffered injuries as a result of the wrongful conduct of others. Although some torts, such as assault and trespass, originated in the English common law, the field of tort law continues to expand. As new ways to commit wrongs are discovered, such as the use of the Internet to commit wrongful acts, the courts are extending tort law to cover these wrongs.

As you will see in later chapters of this book, many of the lawsuits brought by or against business firms are based on the tort theories discussed in this chapter. Some of the torts examined here can occur in any context, including the business environment. Others, traditionally referred to as **business torts,** involve wrongful interference with the business rights of others. Business torts include such vague concepts as *unfair competition* and *wrongfully interfering with the business relations of another.*

THE BASIS OF TORT LAW

Two notions serve as the basis of all torts: wrongs and compensation. Tort law is designed to compensate those who have suffered a loss or injury due to another person's wrongful act. In a tort action, one person or group brings a personal suit against another person or group to obtain compensation (money **damages**) or other relief for the harm suffered.

TORT
A civil wrong not arising from a breach of contract; a breach of a legal duty that proximately causes harm or injury to another.

BUSINESS TORT
Wrongful interference with another's business rights.

DAMAGES
Money sought as a remedy for a breach of contract or a tortious action.

---

1. The word *tort* is French for "wrong."

The Purpose of Tort Law

Generally, the purpose of tort law is to provide remedies for the invasion of various *protected interests*. Society recognizes an interest in personal physical safety, and tort law provides remedies for acts that cause physical injury or interfere with physical security and freedom of movement. Society recognizes an interest in protecting real and personal property, and tort law provides remedies for acts that cause destruction or damage to property. Society also recognizes an interest in protecting certain intangible interests, such as personal privacy, family relations, reputation, and dignity, and tort law provides remedies for invasion of these protected interests.

Damages Available in Tort Actions

Because the purpose of tort law is to compensate the injured party for the damage suffered, it is important to have a basic understanding of the types of damages that plaintiffs seek in tort actions.

COMPENSATORY DAMAGES
A monetary award equivalent to the actual value of injuries or damage sustained by the aggrieved party.

Compensatory Damages **Compensatory damages** are intended to compensate or reimburse a plaintiff for actual losses—to make the plaintiff whole and put her or him in the same position that she or he would have been in had the tort not occurred. Compensatory damages awards are often broken down into special damages and general damages. *Special damages* compensate the plaintiff for quantifiable monetary losses, such as medical expenses, lost wages and benefits (now and in the future), extra costs, the loss of irreplaceable items, and the costs of repairing or replacing damaged property. *General damages* compensate individuals (not companies) for the nonmonetary aspects of the harm suffered, such as pain and suffering. A court might award general damages for physical or emotional pain and suffering, loss of companionship, loss of consortium (losing the emotional and physical benefits of a spousal relationship), disfigurement, loss of reputation, or loss or impairment of mental or physical capacity.

PUNITIVE DAMAGES
Monetary damages that may be awarded to a plaintiff to punish the defendant and deter future similar conduct.

Punitive Damages Occasionally, **punitive damages** may also be awarded in tort cases to punish the wrongdoer and deter others from similar wrongdoing. Punitive damages are appropriate only when the defendant's conduct was particularly egregious (bad) or reprehensible (unacceptable). Usually, this means that punitive damages are available mainly in intentional tort actions and only rarely in negligence lawsuits (*intentional torts* and *negligence* are explained later in the chapter). They may be awarded, however, in suits involving *gross negligence*, which can be defined as an intentional failure to perform a manifest duty in reckless disregard of the consequences of such a failure for the life or property of another.

Great judicial restraint is exercised in granting punitive damages to plaintiffs in tort actions, because punitive damages are subject to the limitations imposed by the due process clause of the U.S. Constitution (discussed in Chapter 1). In *State Farm Mutual Automobile Insurance Co. v. Campbell*,[2] the United States Supreme Court held that to the extent an award of punitive damages is grossly excessive, it furthers no legitimate purpose and violates due process requirements. Although this case dealt with intentional torts (fraud and intentional infliction of emotional distress), the Court's holding applies equally to punitive damages awards in gross negligence cases (as well as to product liability cases, which will be discussed in Chapter 13).

---

2. 538 U.S. 408, 123 S.Ct. 1513, 155 L.Ed.2d 585 (2003).

Classifications of Torts

There are two broad classifications of torts: *intentional torts* and *unintentional torts* (torts involving negligence). The classification of a particular tort depends largely on how the tort occurs (intentionally or negligently) and the surrounding circumstances. In the following pages, you will read about these two classifications of torts.

Torts committed via the Internet are sometimes referred to as **cyber torts.** We look at how the courts have applied traditional tort law to wrongful actions in the online environment in the concluding pages of this chapter.

INTENTIONAL TORTS AGAINST PERSONS

An **intentional tort,** as the term implies, requires *intent.* The **tortfeasor** (the one committing the tort) must intend to commit an act, the consequences of which interfere with the personal or business interests of another in a way not permitted by law. An evil or harmful motive is not required—in fact, the actor may even have a beneficial motive for committing what turns out to be a tortious act. In tort law, intent means only that the actor intended the consequences of his or her act or knew with substantial certainty that certain consequences would result from the act. The law generally assumes that individuals intend the *normal* consequences of their actions. Thus, forcefully pushing another—even if done in jest and without any evil motive—is an intentional tort (if injury results), because the object of a strong push can ordinarily be expected to fall down.

This section discusses intentional torts against persons, which include assault and battery, false imprisonment, infliction of emotional distress, defamation, invasion of the right to privacy, appropriation, misrepresentation, and wrongful interference.

Assault and Battery

Any intentional, unexcused act that creates in another person a reasonable apprehension of immediate harmful or offensive contact is an **assault.** Apprehension is not the same as fear. If a contact is such that a reasonable person would want to avoid it, and if there is a reasonable basis for believing that the contact will occur, then the plaintiff suffers apprehension whether or not he or she is afraid. The interest protected by tort law concerning assault is the freedom from having to expect harmful or offensive contact. The arousal of apprehension is enough to justify compensation.

The *completion* of the act that caused the apprehension, if it results in harm to the plaintiff, is a **battery,** which is defined as an unexcused and harmful or offensive physical contact *intentionally* performed. Suppose that Ivan threatens Jean with a gun, then shoots her. The pointing of the gun at Jean is an assault; the firing of the gun (if the bullet hits Jean) is a battery. The interest protected by tort law concerning battery is the right to personal security and safety. The contact can be harmful, or it can be merely offensive (such as an unwelcome kiss). Physical injury need not occur. The contact can involve any part of the body or anything attached to it—for example, a hat or other item of clothing, a purse, or a chair or an automobile in which one is sitting. Whether the contact is offensive or not is determined by the *reasonable person standard.*[3] The contact can be made by the defendant or by some force the defendant sets in motion—for example, a rock thrown, food poisoned, or a stick swung.

ON THE WEB

You can find cases and articles on torts in the tort law library at the Internet Law Library's Web site. Go to **www.lawguru.com/ilawlib.**

CYBER TORT
A tort committed in cyberspace.

INTENTIONAL TORT
A wrongful act knowingly committed.
TORTFEASOR
One who commits a tort.

ASSAULT
Any word or action intended to make another person fearful of immediate physical harm; a reasonably believable threat.

BATTERY
The unprivileged, intentional touching of another.

---

3. The reasonable person standard is an "objective" test of how a reasonable person would have acted under the same circumstances. See "The Duty of Care and Its Breach" later in this chapter.

Compensation   If the plaintiff shows that there was contact, and the jury (or judge, if there is no jury) agrees that the contact was offensive, the plaintiff has a right to compensation. There is no need to show that the defendant acted out of malice; the person could have just been joking or playing around. The underlying motive does not matter, only the intent to bring about the harmful or offensive contact to the plaintiff. In fact, proving a motive is never necessary (but is sometimes relevant). A plaintiff may be compensated for the emotional harm or loss of reputation resulting from a battery, as well as for physical harm.

Defenses to Assault and Battery   A defendant who is sued for assault, battery, or both can raise any of the following legally recognized **defenses** (reasons why plaintiffs should not obtain what they are seeking):

DEFENSE
A reason offered and alleged by a defendant in an action or suit as to why the plaintiff should not recover or establish what she or he seeks.

BE AWARE   Some of these same four defenses can be raised by a defendant who is sued for other torts.

1 *Consent.* When a person consents to the act that is allegedly tortious, this may be a complete or partial defense to liability (legal responsibility).

2 *Self-defense.* An individual who is defending her or his life or physical well-being can claim self-defense. In situations of both *real* and *apparent* danger, a person may use whatever force is *reasonably* necessary to prevent harmful contact.

3 *Defense of others.* An individual can act in a reasonable manner to protect others who are in real or apparent danger.

4 *Defense of property.* Reasonable force may be used in attempting to remove intruders from one's home, although force that is likely to cause death or great bodily injury can never be used just to protect property.

False Imprisonment

False imprisonment is the intentional confinement or restraint of another person's activities without justification. False imprisonment interferes with the freedom to move without restraint. The confinement can be accomplished through the use of physical barriers, physical restraint, or threats of physical force. Moral pressure or threats of future harm do not constitute false imprisonment. It is essential that the person being restrained would not willingly wish to be constrained.

Businesspersons are often confronted with suits for false imprisonment after they have attempted to confine a suspected shoplifter for questioning. Under the "privilege to detain" granted to merchants in some states, a merchant can use the defense of *probable cause* to justify delaying a suspected shoplifter. In this context, probable cause exists when there is sufficient evidence to support the belief that a person is guilty (as you will read in Chapter 6, *probable cause* is defined differently in the context of criminal law). Although laws pertaining to the privilege to detain vary from state to state, generally they require that any detention be conducted in a *reasonable* manner and for only a *reasonable* length of time.

Intentional Infliction of Emotional Distress

The tort of *intentional infliction of emotional distress* can be defined as an intentional act that amounts to extreme and outrageous conduct resulting in severe emotional distress to another.
⬛**EXAMPLE 4.1** A prankster telephones Jesse and says that Jesse's spouse has just been in a horrible accident. As a result, Jesse suffers intense mental pain or anxiety. The caller's behavior is deemed to be extreme and outrageous conduct that exceeds the bounds of decency accepted by society and is therefore **actionable** (capable of serving as the ground for a lawsuit). ◼

ACTIONABLE
Capable of serving as the basis of a lawsuit. An actionable claim can be pursued in a lawsuit or other court action.

Emotional distress claims pose several problems. One major problem is that such claims must be subject to some limitation, or the courts could be flooded with lawsuits alleging emotional distress. A society in which individuals are rewarded if they are unable to endure the normal emotional stresses of day-to-day living is obviously undesirable. Therefore, the law usually focuses on the nature of the acts that fall under this tort. Indignity or annoyance alone is usually not sufficient to support a lawsuit based on intentional infliction of emotional distress.

Many times, however, repeated annoyances (such as those experienced by a person who is being stalked), coupled with threats, are enough. In a business context, for example, the repeated use of extreme methods to collect an overdue debt may be actionable. Because it is difficult to prove the existence of emotional suffering, a court may require that the emotional distress be evidenced by some physical symptom or illness. Alternatively, a court might require evidence of a specific emotional disturbance that can be documented by a psychiatric consultant or other medical professional.

Defamation

As discussed in Chapter 1, the freedom of speech guaranteed by the First Amendment to the U.S. Constitution is not absolute. In interpreting the First Amendment, the courts must balance free speech rights against other strong social interests, including society's interest in preventing and redressing attacks on reputation.

Defamation of character involves wrongfully hurting a person's good reputation. The law has imposed a general duty on all persons to refrain from making *false,* defamatory *statements of fact* about others. Breaching this duty in writing or other permanent form (such as a digital recording) involves the tort of **libel.** Breaching this duty orally involves the tort of **slander.** As you will read later in this chapter, the tort of defamation can also arise when a false statement of fact is made about a person's product, business, or legal ownership rights to property.

Often at issue in defamation lawsuits is whether the defendant made a statement of fact or a *statement of opinion.* Statements of opinion are normally not actionable because they are protected under the First Amendment. In other words, making a negative statement about another person is not defamation unless the statement is false and represents something as a fact (for example, "Vladik cheats on his taxes") rather than a personal opinion (for example, "Vladik is a jerk").

DEFAMATION
Anything published or publicly spoken that causes injury to another's good name, reputation, or character.

LIBEL
Defamation in writing or other form having the quality of permanence (such as a digital recording).

SLANDER
Defamation in oral form.

The Publication Requirement The basis of the tort of defamation is the publication of a statement or statements that hold an individual up to contempt, ridicule, or hatred. *Publication* here means that the defamatory statements are communicated to persons other than the defamed party. **■EXAMPLE 4.2** If Thompson writes Andrews a private letter accusing him of embezzling funds, the action does not constitute libel. If Peters calls Gordon dishonest and incompetent when no one else is around, the action does not constitute slander. In neither instance was the message communicated to a third party. ■

The courts have generally held that even dictating a letter to a secretary constitutes publication, although the publication may be privileged (privileged communications will be discussed shortly). Moreover, if a third party overhears defamatory statements by chance, the courts usually hold that this also constitutes publication. Defamatory statements made via the Internet are also actionable, as you will read later in this chapter. Note further that any individual who republishes or repeats defamatory statements is liable even if that person reveals the source of such statements.

Damages for Libel Once a defendant's liability for libel is established, *general damages* are presumed as a matter of law. As mentioned earlier, general damages are designed to compensate the plaintiff for nonspecific harms such as disgrace or dishonor in the eyes of the community, humiliation, injured reputation, and emotional distress—harms that are difficult to measure. In other words, to recover damages in a libel case, the plaintiff need not prove that she or he was actually injured in any way as a result of the libelous statement.

Damages for Slander   In contrast to cases alleging libel, in a case alleging slander, the plaintiff must prove *special damages* to establish the defendant's liability. In other words, the plaintiff must show that the slanderous statement caused the plaintiff to suffer actual economic or monetary losses. Unless this initial hurdle of proving special damages is overcome, a plaintiff alleging slander normally cannot go forward with the suit and recover any damages. This requirement is imposed in cases involving slander because slanderous statements have a temporary quality. In contrast, a libelous (written) statement has the quality of permanence, can be circulated widely, and usually results from some degree of deliberation on the part of the author.

Exceptions to the burden of proving special damages in cases alleging slander are made for certain types of slanderous statements. If a false statement constitutes "slander *per se*," no proof of special damages is required for it to be actionable. The following four types of utterances are considered to be slander *per se*:

1 A statement that another has a loathsome disease (historically, leprosy and sexually transmitted diseases, but now also including allegations of mental illness).

2 A statement that another has committed improprieties while engaging in a business, profession, or trade.

3 A statement that another has committed or has been imprisoned for a serious crime.

4 A statement that a person (usually only an unmarried person and sometimes only a woman) is unchaste or has engaged in serious sexual misconduct.

Defenses against Defamation   Truth is normally an absolute defense against a defamation charge. In other words, if the defendant in a defamation suit can prove that his or her allegedly defamatory statements were true, normally no tort has been committed. Other defenses to defamation may exist if the statement is privileged or concerns a public figure. Note that the majority of defamation actions in the United States are filed in state courts, and the states may differ in how they define both defamation and the particular defenses they allow, such as privilege (discussed next).

Privileged Communications.   In some circumstances, a person will not be liable for defamatory statements because she or he enjoys a **privilege**, or immunity. Privileged communications are of two types: absolute and qualified.[4] Only in judicial proceedings and certain government proceedings is an *absolute* privilege granted. For example, statements made in the courtroom by attorneys and judges during a trial are absolutely privileged. So are statements made by government officials during legislative debate, even if the officials make such statements maliciously—that is, knowing them to be untrue. An absolute privilege is granted in these situations because government personnel deal with matters that are so much in the public interest that the parties involved should be able to speak out fully and freely without restriction.

In other situations, a person will not be liable for defamatory statements because he or she has a *qualified*, or conditional, privilege. An employer's statements in written evaluations of employees are an example of a qualified privilege. Generally, if the statements are made in good faith and the publication is limited to those who have a legitimate interest

PRIVILEGE
A legal right, exemption, or immunity granted to a person or a class of persons. In the context of defamation, an absolute privilege immunizes the person making the statements from a lawsuit, regardless of whether the statements were malicious.

---

4. Note that the term *privileged communication* in this context is not the same as privileged communication between a professional, such as an attorney, and his or her client.

in the communication, the statements fall within the area of qualified privilege. **■EXAMPLE 4.3** Jorge applies for membership at the local country club. After the country club's board rejects his application, Jorge sues the club's office manager for making allegedly defamatory statements to the board concerning a conversation she had with Jorge. Assuming that the office manager had simply relayed what she thought was her duty to convey to the club's board, her statements would likely be protected by qualified privilege.[5] ■

The concept of conditional privilege rests on the assumption that in some situations, the right to know or speak is paramount to the right not to be defamed. Only if the privilege is abused or the statement is knowingly false or malicious will the person be liable for damages.

Public Figures. Public officials who exercise substantial governmental power and any persons in the public limelight are considered *public figures.* In general, public figures are considered fair game, and false and defamatory statements about them that are published in the press will not constitute defamation unless the statements are made with **actual malice.**[6] To be made with actual malice, a statement must be made *with either knowledge of falsity or a reckless disregard of the truth.* Statements made about public figures, especially when the statements are made via a public medium, are usually related to matters of general interest; they are made about people who substantially affect all of us. Furthermore, public figures generally have some access to a public medium for answering disparaging (belittling, discrediting) falsehoods about themselves; private individuals do not. For these reasons, public figures have a greater burden of proof in defamation cases (they must prove actual malice) than do private individuals.

Invasion of the Right to Privacy

A person has a right to solitude and freedom from prying public eyes—in other words, to privacy. As discussed in Chapter 1, the United States Supreme Court has held that a fundamental right to privacy is also implied by various amendments to the U.S. Constitution. Some state constitutions explicitly provide for privacy rights. In addition, a number of federal and state statutes have been enacted to protect individual rights in specific areas. Tort law also safeguards these rights through the tort *invasion of privacy.* Four acts qualify as an invasion of privacy:

1 *Appropriation of identity.* Under the common law, using a person's name, picture, or other likeness for commercial purposes without permission is a tortious invasion of privacy. Most states today have also enacted statutes prohibiting appropriation (discussed further in the next subsection).

2 *Intrusion into an individual's affairs or seclusion.* For example, invading someone's home or illegally searching someone's briefcase is an invasion of privacy. The tort has been held to extend to eavesdropping by wiretap, the unauthorized scanning of a bank account, compulsory blood testing, and window peeping.

3 *False light.* Publication of information that places a person in a false light is another category of invasion of privacy. This could be a story attributing to the person ideas not held or actions not taken by the person. (Publishing such a story could involve the tort of defamation as well.)

4 *Public disclosure of private facts.* This type of invasion of privacy occurs when a person publicly discloses private facts about an individual that an ordinary person would find

ACTUAL MALICE
The deliberate intent to cause harm, which exists when a person makes a statement either knowing that it is false or showing a reckless disregard for whether it is true. In a defamation suit, a statement made about a public figure normally must be made with actual malice for the plaintiff to recover damages.

ON THE WEB
You can find information and cases relating to employee privacy rights with respect to electronic monitoring at the Web site of the American Civil Liberties Union (ACLU). Go to

www.aclu.org/privacy/workplace/index.html.

---

5. For a case involving a qualified privilege, see *Hickson Corp. v. Northern Crossarm Co.,* 357 F.3d 1256 (11th Cir. 2004).
6. *New York Times Co. v. Sullivan,* 376 U.S. 254, 84 S.Ct. 710, 11 L.Ed.2d 686 (1964).

objectionable or embarrassing. A newspaper account of a private citizen's sex life or financial affairs could be an actionable invasion of privacy, even if the information revealed is true, because it is not of public concern.

Appropriation

The use by one person of another person's name, likeness, or other identifying characteristic, without permission and for the benefit of the user, constitutes the tort of **appropriation.** Under the law, an individual's right to privacy normally includes the right to the exclusive use of her or his identity.

■EXAMPLE 4.4 Vanna White, the hostess of the popular television game show *Wheel of Fortune,* brought a case against Samsung Electronics America, Inc. Without White's permission, Samsung included in an advertisement for its videocassette recorders (VCRs) a depiction of a robot dressed in a wig, gown, and jewelry, posed in a scene that resembled the *Wheel of Fortune* set, in a stance for which White is famous. The court held in White's favor, holding that the tort of appropriation does not require the use of a celebrity's name or likeness. The court stated that Samsung's robot ad left "little doubt" as to the identity of the celebrity whom the ad was meant to depict.[7] ■

Cases of wrongful appropriation, or misappropriation, may also involve the rights of those who invest time and funds in the creation of a special system, such as a method of broadcasting sports events. Commercial misappropriation may also occur when a person takes and uses the property of another for the sole purpose of capitalizing unfairly on the goodwill or reputation of the property owner.

Fraudulent Misrepresentation

A misrepresentation leads another to believe in a condition that is different from the condition that actually exists. This is often accomplished through a false or incorrect statement. Although persons sometimes make misrepresentations accidentally because they are unaware of the existing facts, the tort of **fraudulent misrepresentation,** or fraud, involves *intentional* deceit for personal gain. The tort includes several elements:

1 The misrepresentation of facts or conditions with knowledge that they are false or with reckless disregard for the truth.

2 An intent to induce another to rely on the misrepresentation.

3 Justifiable reliance by the deceived party.

4 Damages suffered as a result of the reliance.

5 A causal connection between the misrepresentation and the injury suffered.

For fraud to occur, more than mere **puffery,** or *seller's talk,* must be involved. Fraud exists only when a person represents as a fact something she or he knows is untrue. For example, it is fraud to claim that a roof does not leak when one knows it does. Facts are objectively ascertainable, whereas seller's talk is not. "I am the best accountant in town" is seller's talk. The speaker is not trying to represent something as fact because *best* is a subjective, not an objective, term.[8]

Normally, the tort of misrepresentation or fraud occurs only when there is reliance on a *statement of fact.* Sometimes, however, reliance on a *statement of opinion* may involve

7. *White v. Samsung Electronics America, Inc.,* 971 F.2d 1395 (9th Cir. 1992).
8. In contracts for the sale of goods, Article 2 of the Uniform Commercial Code distinguishes, for warranty purposes, between statements of opinion (puffery) and statements of fact. See Chapter 13 for a further discussion of this issue.

the tort of misrepresentation if the individual making the statement of opinion has a superior knowledge of the subject matter. For example, when a lawyer makes a statement of opinion about the law in a state in which the lawyer is licensed to practice, a court would construe reliance on such a statement to be equivalent to reliance on a statement of fact. We examine fraudulent misrepresentation in further detail in Chapter 8, in the context of contract law.

Wrongful Interference

Business torts involving wrongful interference are generally divided into two categories: wrongful interference with a contractual relationship and wrongful interference with a business relationship.

Wrongful Interference with a Contractual Relationship The body of tort law relating to *intentional interference with a contractual relationship* has expanded greatly in recent years. A landmark case involved an opera singer, Joanna Wagner, who was under contract to sing for a man named Lumley for a specified period of years. A man named Gye, who knew of this contract, nonetheless "enticed" Wagner to refuse to carry out the agreement, and Wagner began to sing for Gye. Gye's action constituted a tort because it wrongfully interfered with the contractual relationship between Wagner and Lumley.[9] (Of course, Wagner's refusal to carry out the agreement also entitled Lumley to sue Wagner for breach of contract.)

REMEMBER It is the intent to do an act that is important in tort law, not the motive behind the intent.

Three elements are necessary for wrongful interference with a contractual relationship to occur:

1 A valid, enforceable contract must exist between two parties.

2 A third party must know that this contract exists.

3 The third party must *intentionally* induce a party to breach the contract.

In principle, any lawful contract can be the basis for an action of this type. The contract could be between a firm and its employees or a firm and its customers. Sometimes, a competitor of a firm draws away one of the firm's key employees. Only if the original employer can show that the competitor knew of the contract's existence and intentionally induced the breach can damages be recovered from the competitor.

■EXAMPLE 4.5 Carlin has a contract with Sutter that calls for Sutter to do gardening work on Carlin's large estate every week for fifty-two weeks at a specified price per week. Mellon, who needs gardening services and knows nothing about the Sutter-Carlin contract, contacts Sutter and offers to pay Sutter a wage that is substantially higher than that offered by Carlin. Sutter breaches his contract with Carlin so that he can work for Mellon. Carlin cannot sue Mellon because Mellon knew nothing of the Sutter-Carlin contract and was totally unaware that the higher wage he offered induced Sutter to breach that contract. ■

Wrongful Interference with a Business Relationship Businesspersons devise countless schemes to attract customers, but they are prohibited from unreasonably interfering with another's business in their attempts to gain a share of the market. There is a difference between competitive methods and **predatory behavior**—actions undertaken with the intention of unlawfully driving competitors completely out of the market. The distinction usually depends on whether a business is attempting to attract customers in general or to solicit only those customers who have shown an interest in a similar product or service of a specific competitor.

PREDATORY BEHAVIOR
Business behavior that is undertaken with the intention of unlawfully driving competitors out of the market.

---

9. *Lumley v. Gye,* 118 Eng.Rep. 749 (1853).

■EXAMPLE 4.6 A shopping mall contains two athletic shoe stores: Joe's and SneakerSprint. Joe's cannot station an employee at the entrance of SneakerSprint to divert customers to Joe's and tell them that Joe's will beat SneakerSprint's prices. This type of activity constitutes the tort of wrongful interference with a business relationship, which is commonly considered to be an unfair trade practice. If this type of activity were permitted, Joe's would reap the benefits of SneakerSprint's advertising. ■

Defenses to Wrongful Interference A person will not be liable for the tort of wrongful interference with a contractual or business relationship if it can be shown that the interference was justified, or permissible. Bona fide competitive behavior is a permissible interference even if it results in the breaking of a contract. **■EXAMPLE 4.7** If Antonio's Meats advertises so effectively that it induces Sam's Restaurant to break its contract with Burke's Meat Company, Burke's Meat Company will be unable to recover against Antonio's Meats on a wrongful interference theory. After all, the public policy that favors free competition in advertising outweighs any possible instability that such competitive activity might cause in contractual relations. ■ Although luring customers away from a competitor through aggressive marketing and advertising strategies obviously interferes with the competitor's relationship with its customers, courts typically allow such activities in the spirit of competition.

> **REMEMBER** What society and the law consider permissible often depends on the circumstances.

INTENTIONAL TORTS AGAINST PROPERTY

Intentional torts against property include trespass to land, trespass to personal property, conversion, and disparagement of property. These torts are wrongful actions that interfere with individuals' legally recognized rights with regard to their land or personal property. The law distinguishes personal property from real property (see Chapters 23 and 24, respectively). *Real property* is land and things "permanently" attached to the land. *Personal property* consists of all other items, which are basically movable. Thus, a house and lot are real property, whereas the furniture inside a house is personal property. Cash and stocks and bonds are also personal property.

Trespass to Land

> **TRESPASS TO LAND**
> The entry onto, above, or below the surface of land owned by another without the owner's permission or legal authorization.

A **trespass to land** occurs whenever a person, without permission, enters onto, above, or below the surface of land that is owned by another; causes anything to enter onto the land; remains on the land; or permits anything to remain on it. Actual harm to the land is not an essential element of this tort because the tort is designed to protect the right of an owner to exclusive possession of her or his property. Common types of trespass to land include walking or driving on someone else's land, shooting a gun over the land, throwing rocks at a building that belongs to someone else, building a dam across a river and thereby causing water to back up on someone else's land, and constructing a building so that part of it is on an adjoining landowner's property.

Trespass Criteria, Rights, and Duties Before a person can be a trespasser, the owner of the real property (or other person in actual and exclusive possession of the property) must establish that person as a trespasser. For example, "posted" trespass signs expressly establish as a trespasser a person who ignores these signs and enters onto the property. A guest in your home is not a trespasser—unless she or he has been asked to leave but refuses. Any person who enters onto your property to commit an illegal act (such as a thief entering a lumberyard at night to steal lumber) is established impliedly as a trespasser, without posted signs.

At common law, a trespasser is liable for damages caused to the property and generally cannot hold the owner liable for injuries sustained on the premises. This common law rule is being abandoned in many jurisdictions in favor of a *reasonable duty of care* rule that varies depending on the status of the parties; for example, a landowner may have a duty to post a notice that the property is patrolled by guard dogs. Also, under the *attractive nuisance* doctrine, children do not assume the risks of the premises if they are attracted to the property by some object, such as a swimming pool, an abandoned building, or a sand pile. Trespassers normally can be removed from the premises through the use of reasonable force without the owner's being liable for assault, battery, or false imprisonment.

Defenses against Trespass to Land Trespass to land involves wrongful interference with another person's real property rights. One defense to this claim is to show that the trespass was warranted—for example, that the trespasser entered the property to assist someone in danger. Another defense exists when the trespasser can show that he or she had a license to come onto the land. A *licensee* is one who is invited (or allowed to enter) onto the property of another for the licensee's benefit. A person who enters another's property to read an electric meter, for example, is a licensee. When you purchase a ticket to attend a movie or sporting event, you are licensed to go onto the property of another to view that movie or event. Note that licenses to enter onto another's property are *revocable* by the property owner. If a property owner asks a meter reader to leave and the meter reader refuses to do so, the meter reader at that point becomes a trespasser.

Trespass to Personal Property

Whenever an individual wrongfully takes or harms the personal property of another or otherwise interferes with the lawful owner's possession of personal property, **trespass to personal property** occurs (also called *trespass to chattels* or *trespass to personalty*[10]). In this context, harm means not only destruction of the property, but also anything that diminishes its value, condition, or quality. Trespass to personal property involves intentional meddling with a possessory interest, including barring an owner's access to personal property. **■EXAMPLE 4.8** If Kelly takes Ryan's business law book as a practical joke and hides it so that Ryan is unable to find it for several days prior to the final examination, Kelly has engaged in a trespass to personal property. (Kelly has also committed the tort of *conversion*—to be discussed next.) ■

If it can be shown that the trespass to personal property was warranted, then a complete defense exists. Most states, for example, allow automobile repair shops to hold a customer's car (under what is called an *artisan's lien*, discussed in Chapter 16) when the customer refuses to pay for repairs already completed.

> **TRESPASS TO PERSONAL PROPERTY**
> The unlawful taking or harming of another's personal property; interference with another's right to the exclusive possession of his or her personal property.

Conversion

Whenever a person wrongfully possesses or uses the personal property of another without permission, the tort of **conversion** occurs. Any act that deprives an owner of personal property or the use of that property without that owner's permission and without just cause can be conversion. Often, when conversion occurs, a trespass to personal property also occurs because the original taking of the personal property from the owner was a trespass, and wrongfully retaining it is conversion. Conversion is the civil side of crimes related to theft, but it is not limited to theft. Even if the rightful owner consented to the initial taking of the property, so there was no theft or trespass, a failure to return the personal property may still be conversion. **■EXAMPLE 4.9** Chen borrows Marik's iPod to use while traveling home from school for the holidays. When Chen returns to school, Marik asks for his iPod back. Chen tells Marik that she gave it to her little brother for Christmas. In

> **CONVERSION**
> Wrongfully taking or retaining possession of an individual's personal property and placing it in the service of another.

> **KEEP IN MIND** In tort law, the underlying motive for an act does not matter. What matters is the intent to do the act that results in the tort.

---

10. Pronounced *per*-sun-ul-tee.

this situation, Marik can sue Chen for conversion, and Chen will have to either return the iPod or pay damages equal to its value. ■

Even if a person mistakenly believed that she or he was entitled to the goods, the tort of conversion may occur. In other words, good intentions are not a defense against conversion; in fact, conversion can be an entirely innocent act. Someone who buys stolen goods, for example, can be liable for conversion even if he or she did not know that the goods were stolen. If the true owner brings a tort action against the buyer, the buyer must either return the property to the owner or pay the owner the full value of the property, despite having already paid the purchase price to the thief.

A successful defense against the charge of conversion is that the purported owner does not, in fact, own the property or does not have a right to possess it that is superior to the right of the holder.

Disparagement of Property

Disparagement of property occurs when economically injurious falsehoods are made about another's product or property, not about another's reputation. Disparagement of property is a general term for torts that can be more specifically referred to as *slander of quality* or *slander of title*.

Slander of Quality   Publication of false information about another's product, alleging that it is not what its seller claims, constitutes the tort of **slander of quality**, or **trade libel**. The plaintiff must prove that actual damages proximately resulted from the slander of quality. In other words, the plaintiff must show not only that a third person refrained from dealing with the plaintiff because of the improper publication but also that there were associated damages. The economic calculation of such damages—they are, after all, conjectural—is often extremely difficult.

An improper publication may be both a slander of quality and defamation of character. For example, a statement that disparages the quality of a product may also, by implication, disparage the character of the person who would sell such a product.

Slander of Title   When a publication denies or casts doubt on another's legal ownership of any property, and this results in financial loss to that property's owner, the tort of **slander of title** may exist. Usually, this is an intentional tort in which someone knowingly publishes an untrue statement about property with the intent of discouraging a third person from dealing with the person slandered. For example, it would be difficult for a car dealer to attract customers after competitors published a notice that the dealer's stock consisted of stolen autos.

UNINTENTIONAL TORTS (NEGLIGENCE)

The tort of **negligence** occurs when someone suffers injury because of another's failure to live up to a required *duty of care*. In contrast to intentional torts, in torts involving negligence, the tortfeasor neither wishes to bring about the consequences of the act nor believes that they will occur. The actor's conduct merely creates a *risk* of such consequences. If no risk is created, there is no negligence. Moreover, the risk must be foreseeable—that is, it must be such that a reasonable person engaging in the same activity would anticipate the risk and guard against it. In determining what is reasonable conduct, courts consider the nature of the possible harm.

Many of the actions discussed earlier in the chapter in the section on intentional torts constitute negligence if the element of intent is missing. **■EXAMPLE 4.10** Suppose that Juarez walks up to Natsuyo and intentionally shoves her. Natsuyo falls and breaks an arm as a result. In this situation, Juarez has committed an intentional tort (assault and battery). If Juarez carelessly bumps into Natsuyo, however, and she falls and breaks an arm as a result, Juarez's action will constitute negligence. In either situation, Juarez has committed a tort. ■

To succeed in a negligence action, the plaintiff must prove each of the following:

1 That the defendant owed a duty of care to the plaintiff.
2 That the defendant breached that duty.
3 That the plaintiff suffered a legally recognizable injury.
4 That the defendant's breach caused the plaintiff's injury.

Next, we discuss each of these four elements of negligence and the defenses against negligence.

The Duty of Care and Its Breach

Central to the tort of negligence is the concept of a **duty of care.** The idea is that if we are to live in society with other people, some actions can be tolerated and some cannot; some actions are right and some are wrong; and some actions are reasonable and some are not. The basic principle underlying the duty of care is that people are free to act as they please so long as their actions do not infringe on the interests of others.

When someone fails to comply with the duty to exercise reasonable care, a potentially tortious act may have been committed. Failure to live up to a standard of care may be an act (setting fire to a building) or an omission (neglecting to put out a campfire). It may be a careless act or a carefully performed but nevertheless dangerous act that results in injury. Courts consider the nature of the act (whether it is outrageous or commonplace), the manner in which the act is performed (cautiously versus heedlessly), and the nature of the injury (whether it is serious or slight) in determining whether the duty of care has been breached.

The Reasonable Person Standard Tort law measures duty by the **reasonable person standard.** In determining whether a duty of care has been breached, the courts ask how a reasonable person would have acted in the same circumstances. The reasonable person standard is said to be (though in an absolute sense it cannot be) objective. It is not necessarily how a particular person would act. It is society's judgment on how people *should* act. If the so-called reasonable person existed, he or she would be careful, conscientious, even tempered, and honest. The courts frequently use this hypothetical reasonable person in decisions relating to other areas of law as well. That individuals are required to exercise a reasonable standard of care in their activities is a pervasive concept in business law, and many of the issues discussed in subsequent chapters of this text have to do with this duty.

In negligence cases, the degree of care to be exercised varies, depending on the defendant's occupation or profession, her or his relationship with the plaintiff, and other factors. Generally, whether an action constitutes a breach of the duty of care is determined on a case-by-case basis. The outcome depends on how the judge (or jury, if it is a jury trial) decides a reasonable person in the position of the defendant would act in the particular circumstances of the case.

DUTY OF CARE
The duty of all persons, as established by tort law, to exercise a reasonable amount of care in their dealings with others. Failure to exercise due care, which is normally determined by the reasonable person standard, constitutes the tort of negligence.

REASONABLE PERSON STANDARD
The standard of behavior expected of a hypothetical "reasonable person"; the standard against which negligence is measured and that must be observed to avoid liability for negligence.

ETHICAL ISSUE 4.1

Does a person's duty of care include a duty to come to the aid of a stranger in peril?
Suppose that you are walking down a city street and notice that a pedestrian is about to step directly in front of an oncoming bus. Do you have a legal duty to warn that individual? No. Although most people would probably concede that the observer has an *ethical* or moral duty to warn the other in this situation, tort law does not impose a general duty to rescue others in peril. People involved in special relationships, however, have been held to have a duty to rescue other parties within the relationship. A person has a duty to rescue his or her child or spouse if either is in danger, for example. Other special relationships, such as those between teachers and students or hiking and hunting partners, may also give rise to a duty to rescue. In addition, if a person who has no duty to rescue undertakes to rescue another, then the rescuer is charged with a duty to follow through with due care in the rescue attempt.

BUSINESS INVITEE
A person, such as a customer or a client, who is invited onto business premises by the owner of those premises for business purposes.

The Duty of Landowners   Landowners are expected to exercise reasonable care to protect persons coming onto their property from harm. As mentioned earlier, in some jurisdictions, landowners are held to owe a duty to protect even trespassers against certain risks. Landowners who rent or lease premises to tenants (see Chapter 24) are expected to exercise reasonable care to ensure that the tenants and their guests are not harmed in common areas, such as stairways, entryways, and laundry rooms.

Retailers and other firms that explicitly or implicitly invite persons to come onto their premises are usually charged with a duty to exercise reasonable care to protect those persons, who are considered **business invitees.** For example, if you entered a supermarket, slipped on a wet floor, and sustained injuries as a result, the owner of the supermarket would be liable for damages if, when you slipped, there was no sign warning that the floor was wet. A court would hold that the business owner was negligent because the owner failed to exercise a reasonable degree of care in protecting the store's customers against foreseeable risks about which the owner knew or *should have known.* That a patron might slip on the wet floor and be injured as a result was a foreseeable risk, and the owner should have taken care to avoid this risk or to warn the customer of it.

The landowner also has a duty to discover and remove any hidden dangers that might injure a customer or other invitee. Store owners have a duty to protect customers from potentially slipping and injuring themselves on merchandise that has fallen off the shelves. In one case, for example, Wal-Mart was held liable because a customer was injured when he slipped on shotgun shell pellets that had fallen off a display and were on the floor.[11]

Some risks, of course, are so obvious that the owner need not warn of them. For instance, a business owner does not need to warn customers to open a door before attempting to walk through it. Other risks, however, may seem obvious to a business owner but may not be so in the eyes of another, such as a child. For example, a hardware store owner may think it is unnecessary to warn customers not to climb a stepladder leaning against the back wall of the store. It is possible, though, that a child could climb up and tip the ladder over and be hurt as a result and that the store could be held liable.

The issue in the following case was whether the obviousness of the existence of wet napkins on the floor of a nightclub obviated the owner's duty to its customers to maintain the premises in a safe condition.

A sign in a merchant's window warns business invitees about slippery floors. If a customer subsequently slips on a wet floor and is injured, can the merchant be held liable? (Debaird/Creative Commons)

---

11. *Martin v. Wal-Mart Stores, Inc.,* 183 F.3d 770 (1999).

CASE 4.1 **Izquierdo v. Gyroscope, Inc.**

District Court of Appeal of Florida, Fourth District, 946 So.2d 115 (2007).

FACTS Giorgio's Grill in Hollywood, Florida, is a restaurant that becomes a nightclub after hours. At those times, traditionally, as the manager of Giorgio's knew, the staff and customers threw paper napkins into the air as the music played. The napkins landed on the floor, but no one picked them up. If they became too deep, customers pushed them to the side. Because drinks were occasionally spilled, sometimes the napkins were wet. One night, Jane Izquierdo went to Giorgio's to meet a friend. She had been to the club five or six times and knew of the napkin-throwing tradition. She had one drink and went to the restroom. On her return, she slipped and fell, breaking her leg. After surgery, she relied on a wheelchair for three months and continued to suffer pain. She filed a suit in a Florida state court against Gyroscope, Inc., the owner of Giorgio's, alleging negligence. A jury returned a verdict in favor of the defendant, and Izquierdo filed a motion for a new trial, which the court denied. She appealed to a state intermediate appellate court.

ISSUE Does the obviousness of a risk discharge a business owner's duty to its invitees to maintain the premises in a safe condition?

DECISION No. The state intermediate appellate court reversed the lower court's decision, concluding that "the trial court abused its discretion" in denying Izquierdo's motion. The appellate court remanded the case for a new trial.

REASON The court reasoned that "the uncontroverted evidence shows at least some negligence on the part of the restaurant." The court emphasized, "[I]mportantly, the manager of the restaurant admitted that permitting the wet napkins to remain on the floor was a hazardous condition." Izquierdo testified that she slipped, fell down on a wet floor, and found napkins on her shoes. "The inference that the wet napkins on the floor caused her fall clearly was the only reasonable inference which could be drawn from the facts." Izquierdo knew of the napkin-throwing tradition, and the existence of napkins on the floor was obvious, but these circumstances "merely discharge[d] the landowner's duty to warn. It does not discharge the landowner's duty to maintain the premises in a reasonably safe condition."

 FOR CRITICAL ANALYSIS–Social Consideration
Should the result in this case have been different if, in all the years that the napkin-throwing tradition existed, no one had ever fallen on them before Izquierdo did?

It can sometimes be difficult for business owners to determine whether risks are obvious. Because the law imposes liability on business owners who fail to discover hidden dangers on the premises and protect patrons from being injured, it is advisable to post warnings of any potential risks on the property. Businesspersons should train their employees to be on the lookout for possibly dangerous conditions on the premises at all times and to notify a superior immediately if they notice something. Making the business premises as safe as possible for all persons who might be there, including children, the elderly, and individuals with disabilities, is one of the best ways to prevent potential legal disputes.

PREVENTING LEGAL DISPUTES

The Duty of Professionals If an individual has knowledge, skill, or intelligence superior to that of an ordinary person, the individual's conduct must be consistent with that status. Professionals—including physicians, dentists, architects, engineers, accountants, lawyers, and others—are required to have a standard minimum level of special knowledge and ability. Therefore, in determining whether professionals have exercised reasonable care, their training and expertise are taken into account. In other words, an accountant cannot defend against a lawsuit for negligence by stating, "But I was not familiar with that principle of accounting."

ON THE WEB

You can locate the professional standards for various organizations at **www.lib.uwaterloo.ca/society/ standards.html**.

MALPRACTICE
Professional misconduct or the lack of the requisite degree of skill as a professional. Negligence—the failure to exercise due care—on the part of a professional, such as a physician, is commonly referred to as malpractice.

If a professional violates her or his duty of care toward a client, the professional may be sued for **malpractice,** which is essentially professional negligence. For example, a patient might sue a physician for *medical malpractice.* A client might sue an attorney for *legal malpractice.*

The Injury Requirement and Damages

For a tort to have been committed, the plaintiff must have suffered a *legally recognizable* injury. To recover damages (receive compensation), the plaintiff must have suffered some loss, harm, wrong, or invasion of a protected interest. Essentially, the purpose of tort law is to compensate for legally recognized injuries resulting from wrongful acts. If no harm or injury results from a given negligent action, there is nothing to compensate—and no tort exists. **■EXAMPLE 4.11** If you carelessly bump into a passerby, who stumbles and falls as a result, you may be liable in tort if the passerby is injured in the fall. If the person is unharmed, however, there normally could be no suit for damages because no injury was suffered. Although the passerby might be angry and suffer emotional distress, few courts recognize negligently inflicted emotional distress as a tort unless it results in some physical disturbance or dysfunction. **■**

Compensatory damages are the norm in negligence cases. As noted earlier, a court will award punitive damages only if the defendant's conduct was grossly negligent, reflecting an intentional failure to perform a duty with reckless disregard of the consequences to others.

Causation

Another element necessary to a tort is *causation.* If a person fails in a duty of care and someone suffers an injury, the wrongful activity must have caused the harm for the activity to be considered a tort. In deciding whether there is causation, the court must address two questions:

CAUSATION IN FACT
An act or omission without which an event would not have occurred.

1 *Is there causation in fact?* Did the injury occur because of the defendant's act, or would it have occurred anyway? If an injury would not have occurred without the defendant's act, then there is causation in fact. **Causation in fact** can usually be determined by the use of the *but for* test: "but for" the wrongful act, the injury would not have occurred. Theoretically, causation in fact is limitless. One could claim, for example, that "but for" the creation of the world, a particular injury would not have occurred. Thus, as a practical matter, the law has to establish limits, and it does so through the concept of proximate cause.

PROXIMATE CAUSE
Legal cause; exists when the connection between an act and an injury is strong enough to justify imposing liability.

2 *Was the act the proximate cause of the injury?* **Proximate cause,** or legal cause, exists when the connection between an act and an injury is strong enough to justify imposing liability. **■EXAMPLE 4.12** Ackerman carelessly leaves a campfire burning. The fire not only burns down the forest but also sets off an explosion in a nearby chemical plant that spills chemicals into a river, killing all the fish for a hundred miles downstream and ruining the economy of a tourist resort. Should Ackerman be liable to the resort owners? To the tourists whose vacations were ruined? These are questions of proximate cause that a court must decide. **■**

Both of these questions must be answered in the affirmative for liability in tort to arise. If a defendant's action constitutes causation in fact but a court decides that the action is not the proximate cause of the plaintiff's injury, the causation requirement has not been met—and the defendant normally will not be liable to the plaintiff.

NOTE Proximate cause can be thought of as a question of social policy. Should the defendant be made to bear the loss instead of the plaintiff?

Questions of proximate cause are linked to the concept of foreseeability because it would be unfair to impose liability on a defendant unless the defendant's actions created a foreseeable risk of injury. Probably the most cited case on proximate cause is the *Palsgraf* case, discussed in this chapter's *Landmark in the Law* feature. In determining the issue of

LANDMARK IN THE LAW · *Palsgraf v. Long Island Railroad Co.* (1928)

In 1928, the New York Court of Appeals (that state's highest court) issued its decision in *Palsgraf v. Long Island Railroad Co.,*[a] a case that has become a landmark in negligence law and proximate cause.

The Facts of the Case   The plaintiff, Helen Palsgraf, was waiting for a train on a station platform. A man carrying a small package wrapped in newspaper was rushing to catch a train that had begun to move away from the platform. As the man attempted to jump aboard the moving train, he seemed unsteady and about to fall. A railroad guard on the train car reached forward to grab him, and another guard on the platform pushed him from behind to help him board the train. In the process, the man's package fell on the railroad tracks and exploded, because it contained fireworks. The repercussions of the explosion caused scales at the other end of the train platform to fall on Palsgraf, who was injured as a result. She sued the railroad company for damages in a New York state court.

The Question of Proximate Cause   At the trial, the jury found that the railroad guards were negligent in their conduct. On appeal, the question before the New York Court of Appeals was whether the conduct of the railroad guards was the proximate cause of Palsgraf's injuries. In other words, did the guards' duty of care extend to Palsgraf, who was outside the zone of danger and whose injury could not reasonably have been foreseen?

The court stated that the question of whether the guards were negligent *with respect to Palsgraf* depended on whether her injury was *reasonably foreseeable* to the railroad guards. Although the guards may have acted negligently with respect to the man boarding the train, this had no bearing on the question of their negligence with respect to Palsgraf. This was not a situation in which a person commited an act so potentially harmful (for example, firing a gun at a building) that he or she would be held responsible for any harm that resulted. The court stated that here "there was nothing in the situation to suggest to the most cautious mind that the parcel wrapped in newspaper would spread wreckage through the station." The court thus concluded that the railroad guards were not negligent with respect to Palsgraf because her injury was not reasonably foreseeable.

APPLICATION TO TODAY'S WORLD   *The* Palsgraf *case established foreseeability as the test for proximate cause. Today, the courts continue to apply this test in determining proximate cause—and thus tort liability for injuries. Generally, if the victim of a harm or the consequences of a harm done are unforeseeable, there is no proximate cause. Note, though, that in the online environment, distinctions based on physical proximity, such as the "zone of danger" cited by the court in this case, are largely inapplicable.*

RELEVANT WEB SITES   *To locate information on the Web concerning the* Palsgraf *decision, go to this text's Web site at* **academic.cengage.com/blaw/blt**, *select "Chapter 4," and click on "URLs for Landmarks."*

a. 248 N.Y. 339, 162 N.E. 99 (1928).

ASSUMPTION OF RISK
A doctrine under which a plaintiff may not recover for injuries or damage suffered from risks he or she knows of and has voluntarily assumed.

proximate cause, the court addressed the following question: Does a defendant's duty of care extend only to those who may be injured as a result of a foreseeable risk, or does it extend also to a person whose injury could not reasonably be foreseen?

Defenses to Negligence

Defendants often defend against negligence claims by asserting that the plaintiffs failed to prove the existence of one or more of the required elements for negligence. Additionally, there are three basic *affirmative* defenses in negligence cases (defenses that a defendant can use to avoid liability even if the facts are as the plaintiff states): (1) assumption of risk, (2) superseding cause, and (3) contributory and comparative negligence.

Assumption of Risk   A plaintiff who voluntarily enters into a risky situation, knowing the risk involved, will not be allowed to recover. This is the defense of **assumption of risk.** The requirements of this defense are (1) knowledge of the risk and (2) voluntary assumption of the risk. This defense is frequently asserted when the plaintiff is injured during recreational activities that involve known risk, such as skiing and parachuting.

The risk can be assumed by express agreement, or the assumption of risk can be implied by the plaintiff's knowledge of the risk and subsequent conduct. For example, a driver entering a race knows that there is a risk of being killed or injured in a crash. Of course, the plaintiff does not assume a risk different from or greater than the risk normally carried by the activity. In our example, the race driver would not assume the risk that the banking in the curves of the racetrack will give way during the race because of a construction defect.

Risks are not deemed to be assumed in situations involving emergencies. Neither are they assumed when a statute protects a class of people from harm and a member of the class is injured by the harm. For example, employees are protected by statute from harmful working conditions and therefore do not assume the risks associated with the workplace. An employee who is injured will generally be compensated regardless of fault under state workers' compensation statutes (discussed in Chapter 18).

In the following case, a ball kicked by a player practicing on a nearby field injured a man who was attending his son's soccer tournament. The question before the court was whether a bystander who was not watching a soccer match at the time of the injury had nevertheless assumed the risk of being struck by a wayward ball.

Two bungee jumpers leap from a platform. If they are injured and sue the operator of the jump for negligence, what defenses might the operator use to avoid liability?
(Mark Setchell/Creative Commons)

CASE 4.2   Sutton v. Eastern New York Youth Soccer Association, Inc.

New York Supreme Court, Appellate Division, Third Department, 8 A.D.3d 855, 779 N.Y.S.2d 149 (2004).

FACTS On May 30, 1999, James Sutton's son, a member of the Latham Circle Soccer Club, was participating in the Highland Soccer Club Tournament at Maalyck Park in Glenville, New York. Sutton attended as a spectator. After watching his son's second game from the sidelines, Sutton walked to the end of the field to a tent that his son's team had put up thirty to forty yards behind the goal line to provide shade for the players when they were not engaged on the field. Half a dozen players from the Guilderland Soccer Club were on the field warming up for the next game. In the tent, while taking a sandwich from a cooler, Sutton was struck in the chest and knocked off his feet by a ball kicked from the field by a Guilderland player, Ian Goss. Sutton filed a suit in a New York state court against the Eastern New York Youth Soccer Association and others sponsoring or participating in the tournament, as well as Goss, seeking to recover damages for injuries he sustained to his knee as a result of the accident. The court found that Sutton had assumed the risk of being struck by a soccer ball, issued a summary judgment in favor of

CASE 4.2–Continued

all of the defendants, and dismissed the complaint. Sutton appealed this order to a state intermediate appellate court.

ISSUE Does a bystander or a spectator who is not watching a soccer match assume the risk of being struck by an errant ball?

DECISION Yes. The state intermediate appellate court affirmed the order of the lower court. "The doctrine of assumption of risk can apply not only to participants of sporting events, but to spectators and bystanders who are not actively engaged in watching the event at the time of their injury."

REASON The state intermediate appellate court emphasized that "the spectator at a sporting event, no less than the participant, accepts the dangers that inhere in it so far as they are obvious and necessary." This "tournament involved hundreds of players with teams playing at various times on at least five fields and plaintiff had been at the

tournament all morning, surrounded by this activity." Sutton argued that the "defendants unreasonably enhanced the risk of injury * * * by essentially inviting him to stand at the end of the field through their placement of the team tent." The court reasoned, however, that "just as the owner of a baseball park is not responsible for the spectator who leaves his or her seat and walks through a potentially more hazardous zone to reach a bathroom or concession stand, thereby assuming the open and obvious risk of being hit by a ball, defendants here cannot be held responsible for the risk assumed by plaintiff when he, aware that players were active on the field, left the sidelines and stood in the tent positioned in the arguably more dangerous zone behind the goal line." Also, Sutton "was familiar with the game of soccer having admittedly been a frequent spectator of the game for over 14 years."

 FOR CRITICAL ANALYSIS–Cultural Consideration
What is the basis underlying the defense of assumption of risk, and how does that basis support the court's decision in the Sutton *case?*

Superseding Cause An unforeseeable intervening event may break the connection between a wrongful act and an injury to another. If so, the event acts as a *superseding cause*—that is, it relieves a defendant of liability for injuries caused by the intervening event. **■EXAMPLE 4.13** Derrick, while riding his bicycle, negligently hits Julie, who is walking on the sidewalk. As a result of the impact, Julie falls and fractures her hip. While she is waiting for help to arrive, a small aircraft crashes nearby and explodes, and some of the fiery debris hits her, causing her to sustain severe burns. Derrick will be liable for the damages caused by Julie's fractured hip because the risk was foreseeable. Normally, Derrick will not be liable for the burns caused by the plane crash—because the risk of a plane crashing nearby and injuring Julie was not foreseeable. ■

Contributory and Comparative Negligence All individuals are expected to exercise a reasonable degree of care in looking out for themselves. In the past, under the common law doctrine of **contributory negligence,** a plaintiff who was also negligent (failed to exercise a reasonable degree of care) could not recover anything from the defendant. Under this rule, no matter how insignificant the plaintiff's negligence was relative to the defendant's negligence, the plaintiff would be precluded from recovering any damages. Today, only a few jurisdictions still hold to this doctrine.

In the majority of states, the doctrine of contributory negligence has been replaced by a **comparative negligence** standard. Under the comparative negligence standard, both the plaintiff's and the defendant's negligence are computed, and the liability for damages is distributed accordingly. Some jurisdictions have adopted a "pure" form of comparative negligence that allows the plaintiff to recover, even if the extent of his or her fault is greater than that of the defendant. For example, if the plaintiff was 80 percent at fault and the defendant 20 percent at fault, the plaintiff may recover 20 percent of his or her damages. Many states' comparative negligence statutes, however, contain a "50 percent" rule under which the plaintiff recovers nothing if she or he was more than 50 percent at fault. Following this rule, a plaintiff who is 35 percent at fault could recover 65 percent of his or her damages, but a plaintiff who is 65 percent (more than 50 percent) at fault could recover nothing.

CONTRIBUTORY NEGLIGENCE
A rule in tort law that completely bars the plaintiff from recovering any damages if the damage suffered is partly the plaintiff's own fault; used in a minority of states.

COMPARATIVE NEGLIGENCE
A rule in tort law that reduces the plaintiff's recovery in proportion to the plaintiff's degree of fault, rather than barring recovery completely; used in the majority of states.

Special Negligence Doctrines and Statutes

There are a number of special doctrines and statutes relating to negligence. We examine a few of them here.

Res Ipsa Loquitur   Generally, in lawsuits involving negligence, the plaintiff has the burden of proving that the defendant was negligent. In certain situations, however, under the doctrine of ***res ipsa loquitur***[12] (meaning "the facts speak for themselves"), the courts may infer that negligence has occurred. Then the burden of proof rests on the defendant to prove she or he was *not* negligent. This doctrine is applied only when the event creating the damage or injury is one that ordinarily would occur only as a result of negligence. **■EXAMPLE 4.14** A person undergoes abdominal surgery and following the surgery has nerve damage in her spine near the area of the operation. In this situation, the person can sue the surgeon under a theory of *res ipsa loquitur*, because the injury would never have occurred in the absence of the surgeon's negligence.[13] ■

Negligence *Per Se*   Certain conduct, whether it consists of an action or a failure to act, may be treated as **negligence *per se*** (*per se* means "in or of itself"). Negligence *per se* may occur if an individual violates a statute or ordinance and thereby causes the kind of harm that the statute was intended to prevent. The injured person must prove (1) that the statute clearly sets out what standard of conduct is expected, when and where it is expected, and of whom it is expected; (2) that he or she is in the class intended to be protected by the statute; and (3) that the statute was designed to prevent the type of injury that he or she suffered. The standard of conduct required by the statute is the duty that the defendant owes to the plaintiff, and a violation of the statute is the breach of that duty.

■EXAMPLE 4.15 A statute requires a landowner to maintain a building in safe condition and to keep all electrical, plumbing, and heating installations in good working order. The statute is meant to protect tenants and those who are rightfully in the building. Irving, a landlord, violates the statute by failing to keep the lighting in his building's stairwell in working order. A tenant, Swan, falls down the stairs and is injured due to the lack of lighting. In this situation, a majority of courts will hold that the violation of the statute conclusively establishes Irving's breach of a duty of care—that is, that Irving is negligent *per se*. ■

"Danger Invites Rescue" Doctrine   Sometimes, a person who is trying to avoid harm—such as an individual who swerves to avoid colliding with an oncoming car—ends up causing harm to another as a result (the driver of the other car). In those situations, the original wrongdoer is liable to anyone who is injured, even if the injury actually resulted from another person's attempt to escape harm. The "danger invites rescue" doctrine extends the same protection to a person who is trying to rescue another from harm—the original wrongdoer is liable for injuries to an individual attempting a rescue. The idea is that the rescuer should not be held liable for any damages because he or she did not cause the danger and because danger invites rescue.

■EXAMPLE 4.16 Ludlam, while driving down a street, fails to see a stop sign because he is trying to stop a squabble between his two young children in the car's back seat. Salter, on the curb near the stop sign, realizes that Ludlam is about to hit a pedestrian and runs into the street to push the pedestrian out of the way. If Ludlam's vehicle hits Salter instead, Ludlam will be liable for Salter's injury, as well as for any injuries the other pedestrian sustained. ■ Rescuers may injure themselves, or the person rescued, or even a stranger, but the original wrongdoer will still be liable.

RES IPSA LOQUITUR
A doctrine under which negligence may be inferred simply because an event occurred, if it is the type of event that would not occur in the absence of negligence. Literally, the term means "the facts speak for themselves."

NEGLIGENCE *PER SE*
An action or failure to act in violation of a statutory requirement.

---

12. Pronounced *rehz ihp*-suh *low*-kwuh-tuhr.
13. See, for example, *Gubbins v. Hurson*, 885 A.2d 269 (D.C. 2005).

Special Negligence Statutes   A number of states have enacted statutes prescribing duties and responsibilities in certain circumstances. For example, most states now have what are called **Good Samaritan statutes.**[14] Under these statutes, someone who is aided voluntarily by another cannot turn around and sue the "Good Samaritan" for negligence. These laws were passed largely to protect physicians and medical personnel who voluntarily render services in emergency situations to those in need, such as individuals hurt in car accidents.

Many states have also passed **dram shop acts,**[15] under which a tavern owner or bartender may be held liable for injuries caused by a person who became intoxicated while drinking at the bar or who was already intoxicated when served by the bartender. Some states' statutes also impose liability on *social hosts* (persons hosting parties) for injuries caused by guests who became intoxicated at the hosts' homes. Under these statutes, it is unnecessary to prove that the tavern owner, bartender, or social host was negligent.

STRICT LIABILITY

Another category of torts is called **strict liability,** or *liability without fault.* Intentional torts and torts of negligence involve acts that depart from a reasonable standard of care and cause injuries. Under the doctrine of strict liability, liability for injury is imposed for reasons other than fault. Strict liability for damages proximately caused by an abnormally dangerous or exceptional activity is one application of this doctrine. Courts apply the doctrine of strict liability in such cases because of the extreme risk of the activity. Even if blasting with dynamite is performed with all reasonable care, there is still a risk of injury. Balancing that risk against the potential for harm, it seems reasonable to ask the person engaged in the activity to pay for injuries caused by that activity. Although there is no fault, there is still responsibility because of the dangerous nature of the undertaking.

There are other applications of the strict liability principle. Persons who keep dangerous animals, for example, are strictly liable for any harm inflicted by the animals. A significant application of strict liability is in the area of *product liability*—liability of manufacturers and sellers for harmful or defective products. Liability here is a matter of social policy and is based on two factors: (1) the manufacturer or seller can better bear the cost of injury because it can spread the cost throughout society by increasing prices of goods and services, and (2) the manufacturer or seller is making a profit from its activities and therefore should bear the cost of injury as an operating expense. We will discuss product liability in greater detail in Chapter 13.

CYBER TORTS

Torts can also be committed in the online environment. Torts committed via the Internet are often called *cyber torts.* Over the last ten years, the courts have had to decide how to apply traditional tort law to torts committed in cyberspace. Consider, for example, issues of proof. How can it be proved that an online defamatory remark was "published" (which requires that a third party see or hear it)? How can the identity of the person who made the remark be discovered? Can an Internet service provider (ISP), such as America Online, Inc. (AOL), be forced to reveal the source of an anonymous comment made by one of its subscribers? We explore some of these questions in this section, as well as some of the legal questions that have arisen with respect to bulk e-mail advertising.

An automobile struck a man who was crossing the street near a shopping mall in Columbus, Ohio. The woman in the photo was a passerby who rushed to his assistance. Suppose that the woman drags the man out of the street so that he will not be hit by another car, and in doing so, she makes his injuries worse. Can she be held liable for damages? (AP Photo/Jack Kustron)

GOOD SAMARITAN STATUTE
A state statute stipulating that persons who provide emergency services to, or rescue, someone in peril cannot be sued for negligence, unless they act recklessly, thereby causing further harm.

DRAM SHOP ACT
A state statute that imposes liability on the owners of bars and taverns, as well as those who serve alcoholic drinks to the public, for injuries resulting from accidents caused by intoxicated persons when the sellers or servers of alcoholic drinks contributed to the intoxication.

STRICT LIABILITY
Liability regardless of fault. In tort law, strict liability is imposed on a manufacturer or seller that introduces into commerce a good that is unreasonably dangerous when in a defective condition.

---

14. These laws derive their name from the Good Samaritan story in the Bible. In the story, a traveler who had been robbed and beaten lay along the roadside, ignored by those passing by. Eventually, a man from the country of Samaria (the "Good Samaritan") stopped to render assistance to the injured person.

15. Historically, a *dram* was a small unit of liquid, and spirits were sold in drams. Thus, a dram shop was a place where liquor was sold in drams.

Defamation Online

Recall from the discussion of defamation earlier in this chapter that one who repeats or otherwise republishes a defamatory statement can be subject to liability as if she or he had originally published it. Thus, publishers generally can be held liable for defamatory contents in the books and periodicals that they publish. Now consider online forums. These forums allow anyone—customers, employees, or crackpots—to complain about a firm's personnel, policies, practices, or products. Whatever the truth of the complaint is, it might have an impact on the business of the firm. One of the early questions in the online legal arena was whether the providers of such forums could be held liable, as publishers, for defamatory statements made in those forums.

Liability of Internet Service Providers Newspapers, magazines, and television and radio stations may be held liable for defamatory remarks that they disseminate, even if those remarks are prepared or created by others. Before the passage of the Communications Decency Act (CDA) of 1996, the courts grappled with the question of whether ISPs should be held liable for defamatory messages made by users of their services. The CDA resolved the issue by stating that "[n]o provider or user of an interactive computer service shall be treated as the publisher or speaker of any information provided by another information content provider."[16] The CDA has been invoked to shield ISPs from liability for defamatory postings on their bulletin boards.

    ■EXAMPLE 4.17 In a leading case on this issue, America Online, Inc. (AOL, now part of Time Warner, Inc.), was not held liable even though it did not promptly remove defamatory messages of which it had been made aware. A federal appellate court stated that the CDA "plainly immunizes computer service providers like AOL from liability for information that originates with third parties." The court explained that the purpose of the statute is "to maintain the robust nature of Internet communication and, accordingly, to keep government interference in the medium to a minimum."[17] ■ Courts have reached similar conclusions in subsequent cases[18] and have also extended the immunity to liability to online auction providers, such as eBay.[19]

    Is an Internet dating service liable for a false profile of an actual person—in this case, an actress who has appeared in *Star Trek: Deep Space Nine* and other television shows and movies—posted by an identity thief who provided the content? That was the question in the following case.

---

16. 47 U.S.C. Section 230.
17. *Zeran v. America Online, Inc.*, 129 F.3d 327 (4th Cir. 1997); *cert.* denied, 524 U.S. 937, 118 S.Ct. 2341, 141 L.Ed.2d 712 (1998).
18. See, for example, *Noah v. AOL Time Warner, Inc.*, 261 F.Supp.2d 532 (E.D.Va. 2003).
19. *Stoner v. eBay, Inc.*, 2000 WL 1705637 (Cal.Super.Ct. 2000).

CASE 4.3   Carafano v. Metrosplash.com, Inc.

United States Court of Appeals, Ninth Circuit, 339 F.3d 1119 (2003).

FACTS Matchmaker.com is a commercial Internet dating service. For a fee, members post anonymous profiles and view profiles of other members, contacting them via e-mail sent through Matchmaker. In October 1999, someone posted a profile of Christianne Carafano without her knowledge or consent. Under the stage name Chase Masterson, Carafano has appeared in films and television shows, including *Star Trek: Deep Space Nine* and *General Hospital.* Contacting the profile's e-mail address produced an automatic reply that

CASE 4.3–Continued

included Carafano's home address and phone number. She began to receive messages responding to the profile, some of which were threatening. Alarmed, she contacted the police. She felt unsafe in her home and stayed away for several months. Meanwhile, Siouxzan Perry, who handled Carafano's e-mail, learned of the false profile and demanded that Matchmaker remove it immediately. Carafano filed a suit in a California state court against Matchmaker and its owner, Metrosplash.com, Inc., alleging invasion of privacy, appropriation, defamation, and other torts. The case was moved to a federal district court, which issued a summary judgment in the defendants' favor. Carafano appealed to the U.S. Court of Appeals for the Ninth Circuit.

ISSUE Does an online dating service qualify for the same immunity as an Internet service provider (ISP) for the defamatory posting of a false profile using a celebrity's personal information?

DECISION Yes. The U.S. Court of Appeals for the Ninth Circuit affirmed the lower court's decision. The appellate court held that under the Communications Decency Act (CDA), Matchmaker was not responsible for the "underlying misinformation" that characterized the false profile of Carafano.

REASON The court reasoned that in the CDA, "Congress granted most Internet services immunity from liability for publishing false or defamatory material so long as the information was provided by another party * * * for two basic policy reasons: to promote the free exchange of information and ideas over the Internet and to encourage voluntary monitoring for offensive or obscene material." In light of these concerns, the courts have adopted "a relatively expansive definition of 'interactive computer service' and a relatively restrictive definition of 'information content provider.'" An "interactive computer service" qualifies for immunity "so long as it does not also function as an 'information content provider' for the portion of the statement or publication at issue. * * * Thus, despite the serious and utterly deplorable consequences that occurred in this case, we conclude that Congress intended that service providers such as Matchmaker be afforded immunity from suit."

WHY IS THIS CASE IMPORTANT? *The holding in this case shows that courts will go out of their way to grant immunity from liability for online defamation under the CDA—even when the consequences in a given case are "utterly deplorable."*

Piercing the Veil of Anonymity A threshold barrier to anyone who seeks to bring an action for online defamation is discovering the identity of the person who posted the defamatory message online. ISPs can disclose personal information about their customers only when ordered to do so by a court. Consequently, businesses and individuals are increasingly resorting to lawsuits against "John Does." Then, using the authority of the courts, they can obtain from the ISPs the identities of the persons responsible for the messages.

■EXAMPLE 4.18 Eric Hvide, a former chief executive of a company called Hvide Marine, sued a number of "John Does" who had posted allegedly defamatory statements about his company on various online message boards. Hvide sued the John Does for libel in a Florida court. The court ruled that Yahoo and AOL had to reveal the identities of the defendant Does.[20] ■

In some other cases, however, the rights of plaintiffs in such situations have been balanced against the defendants' rights to free speech. For example, a New Jersey court refused to compel Yahoo to disclose the identity of a person who had posted an allegedly defamatory message on Yahoo's message board. The court reasoned that more than a bare allegation of defamation is required to outweigh an individual's "competing right of anonymity in the exercise of [the] right of free speech."[21]

20. *Does v. Hvide*, 770 So.2d 1237 (Fla.App.3d 2000).
21. *Dendrite International, Inc. v. Doe No. 3*, 342 N.J.Super. 134, 775 A.2d 756 (2001).

Spam

SPAM
  Bulk, unsolicited ("junk") e-mail.

Bulk, unsolicited e-mail ("junk" e-mail) sent to all of the users on a particular e-mailing list is often called **spam**.[22] Typically, spam consists of a product ad sent to all of the users on an e-mailing list or all of the members of a newsgroup. Spam can waste user time and network bandwidth (the amount of data that can be transmitted within a certain time). It also imposes a burden on an ISP's equipment as well as on an e-mail recipient's computer system. Because of the problems associated with spam, a majority of the states now have laws regulating its transmission. In 2003, the U.S. Congress also enacted a law to regulate spam, but the volume of spam has actually increased since the law was enacted. (See this chapter's *Beyond Our Borders* feature for a discussion of another law passed by Congress in 2006 attempting to address spam originating outside the United States.)

ON THE WEB

The Center for Democracy and Technology conducted a study on spam. The report and the center's recommendations on how to avoid receiving spam are available online at

www.cdt.org/speech/spam/030319spamreport.shtml.

State Regulation of Spam   In an attempt to combat spam, thirty-six states have enacted laws that prohibit or regulate its use. Many state laws regulating spam require the senders of e-mail ads to instruct the recipients on how they can "opt out" of further e-mail ads from the same sources. For instance, in some states an unsolicited e-mail ad must include a toll-free phone number or return e-mail address through which the recipient can contact the sender to request that no more ads be e-mailed. The most stringent state law is California's antispam law, which went into effect on January 1, 2004. That law follows the "opt-in" model favored by consumer groups and antispam advocates. In other words, the law prohibits any person or business from sending e-mail ads to or from any e-mail address in California unless the recipient has expressly agreed to receive e-mails from the sender. An exemption is made for e-mail sent to consumers with whom the advertiser has a "preexisting or current business relationship."

The Federal CAN-SPAM Act   In 2003, Congress enacted the Controlling the Assault of Non-Solicited Pornography and Marketing (CAN-SPAM) Act, which took effect on January 1, 2004. The legislation applies to any "commercial electronic mail messages" that are sent to promote a commercial product or service. Significantly, the statute preempts state antispam laws except for those provisions in state laws that prohibit false and deceptive e-mailing practices.

Generally, the act permits the use of unsolicited commercial e-mail but prohibits certain types of spamming activities, including the use of a false return address and the use of false, misleading, or deceptive information when sending e-mail. The statute also prohibits the use of "dictionary attacks"—sending messages to randomly generated e-mail addresses—and the "harvesting" of e-mail addresses from Web sites through the use of specialized software. Additionally, the law requires senders of commercial e-mail to do the following:

1 Include a return address on the e-mail.

2 Include a clear notification that the message is an ad and provide a valid physical postal address.

3 Provide a mechanism that allows recipients to "opt out" of further e-mail ads from the same source.

4 Take action on a recipient's "opt-out" request within ten days.

5 Label any sexually oriented materials as such.

---

22. The term *spam* is said to come from a skit by Monty Python, a popular group of British comedians in the 1970s and 1980s, in which they sang a song with the lyrics, "Spam spam spam spam, spam spam spam spam, lovely spam, wonderful spam." Like these lyrics, spam online is often considered to be a repetition of worthless text.

BEYOND OUR BORDERS Cross-Border Spam

Spam is a serious problem in the United States, but enforcing antispam laws has been complicated by the fact that many spammers are located outside U.S. borders. After the CAN-SPAM Act of 2003 prohibited false and deceptive e-mails originating in the United States, spamming from other nations increased, and the wrongdoers generally were able to escape detection and legal sanctions.

Before 2006, the Federal Trade Commission (FTC) lacked the authority to investigate cross-border spamming activities and to communicate with foreign nations concerning spam and other deceptive practices conducted via the Internet. In 2006, however, Congress passed the U.S. Safe Web Act (also known as the Undertaking Spam, Spyware, and Fraud Enforcement with Enforcers Beyond Borders Act),[a] which increased the FTC's ability to combat spam on a global level.

The act allows the FTC to cooperate and share information with foreign agencies in investigating and prosecuting those involved in Internet fraud and deception, including spamming, spyware, and various Internet scams. Although the FTC and foreign agencies can provide investigative assistance to one another, the act exempts foreign agencies from U.S. public disclosure laws. In other words, the activities undertaken by the foreign agency (even if requested by the FTC) will be kept secret.

FOR CRITICAL ANALYSIS *A provision in the U.S. Safe Web Act provides Internet service providers with a "safe harbor" (immunity from liability) for supplying information to the FTC concerning possible unfair or deceptive conduct in foreign jurisdictions. Is this provision fair? Why or why not?*

a. Pub. L. No. 109-455, 120 Stat. 3372 (December 22, 2006), which enacted 15 U.S.C.A. Sections 57b-2a, 57b-2b, 57c-1, and 57c-2, and amended various other sections of the *United States Code.*

■

REVIEWING Torts and Cyber Torts

Two sisters, Darla and Irene, are partners in an import business located in a small town in Rhode Island. Irene is also campaigning to be the mayor of their town. Both sisters travel to other countries to purchase the goods they sell at their retail store. Irene buys Indonesian goods, and Darla buys goods from Africa. After a tsunami (tidal wave) destroys many of the cities in Indonesia to which Irene usually travels, she phones one of her contacts there and asks him to procure some items and ship them to her. He informs her that it will be impossible to buy these items now because the townspeople are being evacuated due to a water shortage. Irene is angry and tells the man that if he cannot purchase the goods, he should just take them without paying for them after

the town has been evacuated. Darla overhears her sister's instructions and is outraged. They have a falling-out, and Darla decides that she no longer wishes to be in business with her sister. Using the information presented in the chapter, answer the following questions.

1 Suppose that Darla tells several of her friends about Irene's instructing the man to take goods without paying for them from the people of Indonesia after the tsunami disaster. If Irene files a tort action against Darla alleging slander, will her suit be successful? Why or why not?

2 Now suppose that Irene wins the election and becomes the city's mayor. Darla then writes a letter to the editor of the local newspaper disclosing Irene's misconduct. If Irene accuses Darla of committing libel, what defenses could Darla assert?

(Continued)

3 If Irene accepts goods shipped from Indonesia that were wrongfully obtained, has she committed an intentional tort against property? Explain.

4 Suppose now that Darla was in the store one day with an elderly customer, Betty Green, who was looking for a unique gift for her granddaughter's graduation present. When the phone rang, Darla left the customer and walked to the counter to answer the phone. Green wandered around the store and eventually went through an open door into the stockroom area, where she fell over some boxes on the floor and fractured her hip. Green files a negligence action against the store. Did Darla breach her duty of care? Why or why not?

Although there are more claims for breach of contract than any other category of lawsuits, the dollar amount of damages awarded in tort actions is typically much higher than the awards in contract claims. Furthermore, tort claims are commonplace for businesses. Large companies (those grossing more than $1 billion per year) face an average of 556 pending tort claims and spend an average of $19.8 million on litigation each year.

Because of the potential for large damages awards for intentional and unintentional acts, businesspersons should take preventive measures to avoid tort liability as much as possible. Remember that injured persons can bring most tort actions against a business as well as against another person. In fact, if given a choice, plaintiffs often sue a business rather than an individual because the business is more likely to have "deep pockets" (the ability to pay large damages awards). Moreover, sometimes tort liability exists for businesses when it would not exist for individuals—for example, in situations involving business invitees, negligent hiring or supervision, trade libel, and often strict liability and cyber tort claims.

The Extent of Business Negligence Liability

A business can be exposed to negligence liability in a wide variety of instances. Consider just a few examples. Is a business that fails to warn invitees that its floor is slippery after a rainstorm liable to an injured customer? Is a grocery store liable when a customer slips and falls on a piece of fruit dropped by a previous customer? What about liability for injuries that occur in the parking lot in front of a business when conditions are icy due to the weather or there is a hole in the pavement? What if a patron falls and is injured due to a defect in the carpeting inside a store? The possibilities are almost endless, but nevertheless a business should try to anticipate circumstances that could lead to negligence actions and take preventive measures.

Even the hiring of employees can lead to negligence liability. For example, a business can be liable if it fails to do a criminal background check before hiring a person to supervise a child-care center when an investigation would have revealed that the person had previously been convicted of sexual assault. Failing to properly supervise or instruct employees can also lead to liability for a business.

Professionals such as doctors, lawyers, engineers, and accountants have a duty to their clients to exercise the skills, knowledge, and intelligence they profess to have or the standards expected of their profession. Providing anything less to the client or patient is a special type of negligence called malpractice.

Liability for Torts of Employees and Agents

A business can also be held liable for the negligence or intentional torts of its employees and agents. You will learn more about the law of agency and employment in later chapters of this text (especially in Chapters 17 and 18). For now, it is sufficient to realize that a business is liable for the torts committed by an employee who is acting within the scope of his or her employment or an agent who is acting with the authority of the business. Therefore, if a sales agent commits fraud while acting within the scope of her or his employment, the business will be held liable. Similarly, if a corporate executive posts defamatory messages about a competing firm on the company Web site, the corporation can be held liable.

* This *Application* is not meant to substitute for the services of an attorney who is licensed to practice law in your state.

CHECKLIST FOR MINIMIZING BUSINESS TORT LIABILITY

1 Constantly inspect the premises and look for areas where customers or employees might trip, slide, or fall. Take corrective action whenever you find a problem.

2 Make sure that employee training includes a segment on the importance of periodic safety inspections and procedures for reporting unsafe conditions.

3 Routinely maintain all business equipment (including vehicles) and make sure that the business has complied with any applicable administrative regulations.

4 Check with your liability insurance company for suggestions on improving the safety of your premises and operations. By following its advice, you may be able to lower your insurance premium and ensure that the company will continue to provide coverage.

5 Make sure that your general liability policy will adequately cover the potential exposure of the business. Reassess the amount of coverage annually, particularly if the business has expanded.

6 Carefully review the background and qualifications of individuals you are considering hiring as employees or agents, and eliminate candidates who may increase the business's exposure to tort liability.

7 Investigate and review all negligence claims promptly. Most claims can be settled at low cost without a filed lawsuit, and frequently it is good public relations to do so.

KEY TERMS

CHAPTER SUMMARY Torts and Cyber Torts

Intentional Torts against Persons
(See pages 113–120.)

1. *Assault and battery*—An assault is an unexcused and intentional act that causes another person to be apprehensive of immediate harm. A battery is an assault that results in physical contact.

2. *False imprisonment*—The intentional confinement or restraint of another person's movement without justification.

3. *Intentional infliction of emotional distress*—An intentional act that amounts to extreme and outrageous conduct resulting in severe emotional distress to another.

4. *Defamation (libel or slander)*—A false statement of fact, not made under privilege, that is communicated to a third person and that causes damage to a person's reputation. For public figures, the plaintiff must also prove actual malice.

5. *Invasion of the right to privacy*—The use of a person's name or likeness for commercial purposes without permission, wrongful intrusion into a person's private activities, publication

(Continued)

CHAPTER SUMMARY	Torts and Cyber Torts–Continued
Intentional Torts against Persons—Continued	of information that places a person in a false light, or disclosure of private facts that an ordinary person would find objectionable. 6. *Appropriation*—The use of another person's name, likeness, or other identifying characteristic, without permission and for the benefit of the user. 7. *Misrepresentation (fraud)*—A false representation made by one party, through misstatement of facts or through conduct, with the intention of deceiving another and on which the other reasonably relies to his or her detriment. 8. *Wrongful interference*—The knowing, intentional interference by a third party with an enforceable contractual relationship or an established business relationship between other parties for the purpose of advancing the economic interests of the third party.
Intentional Torts against Property (See pages 120–122.)	1. *Trespass to land*—The invasion of another's real property without consent or privilege. Specific rights and duties apply once a person is expressly or impliedly established as a trespasser. 2. *Trespass to personal property*—Unlawfully damaging or interfering with the owner's right to use, possess, or enjoy her or his personal property. 3. *Conversion*—Wrongfully taking personal property from its rightful owner or possessor and placing it in the service of another. 4. *Disparagement of property*—Any economically injurious falsehood that is made about another's product or property; an inclusive term for the torts of *slander of quality* and *slander of title*.

Unintentional Torts (Negligence) (See pages 122–131.)	1. *Negligence*—The careless performance of a legally required duty or the failure to perform a legally required act. Elements that must be proved are that a legal duty of care exists, that the defendant breached that duty, and that the breach caused damage or injury to another.
	
	2. *Defenses to negligence*—The basic affirmative defenses in negligence cases are (a) assumption of risk, (b) superseding cause, and (c) contributory or comparative negligence.
	
	3. *Special negligence doctrines and statutes*—
	
	  a. *Res ipsa loquitur*—A doctrine under which a plaintiff need not prove negligence on the part of the defendant because "the facts speak for themselves."
	
	  b. Negligence *per se*—A type of negligence that may occur if a person violates a statute or an ordinance and the violation causes another to suffer the kind of injury that the statute or ordinance was intended to prevent.
	
	  c. Special negligence statutes—State statutes that prescribe duties and responsibilities in certain circumstances. Good Samaritan statutes and dram shop acts are examples of special negligence statutes.

Strict Liability (See page 131.)	Under the doctrine of strict liability, a person may be held liable, regardless of the degree of care exercised, for damages or injuries caused by her or his product or activity. Strict liability includes liability for harms caused by abnormally dangerous activities, by dangerous animals, and by defective products (product liability).
Cyber Torts (See pages 131–135.)	General tort principles are being extended to cover cyber torts, or torts that occur in cyberspace, such as online defamation and spamming (which may constitute trespass to personal property). Federal and state statutes may also apply to certain forms of cyber torts. For example, under the federal Communications Decency Act of 1996, Internet service providers (ISPs) are not liable for defamatory messages posted by their subscribers. A majority of the states and the federal government now regulate unwanted e-mail ads (spam).

FOR REVIEW

Answers for the even-numbered questions in this **For Review** *section can be found in Appendix E at the end of this text.*

1 What is a tort?

2 What is the purpose of tort law? What are two basic categories of torts?

3 What are the four elements of negligence?

4 What is meant by strict liability? In what circumstances is strict liability applied?

5 What is a cyber tort, and how are tort theories being applied in cyberspace?

■

QUESTIONS AND CASE PROBLEMS

HYPOTHETICAL SCENARIOS

4.1 Defenses to Negligence. Corinna was riding her bike on a city street. While she was riding, she frequently looked back to verify that the books that she had fastened to the rear part of her bike were still attached. On one occasion while she was looking behind her, she failed to notice a car that was entering an intersection just as she was crossing it. The car hit her, causing her to sustain numerous injuries. Three eyewitnesses stated that the driver of the car had failed to stop at the stop sign before entering the intersection. Corinna sued the driver of the car for negligence. What defenses might the defendant driver raise in this lawsuit? Discuss fully.

4.2 Hypothetical Question with Sample Answer. In which of the following situations will the acting party be liable for the tort of negligence? Explain fully.

  1 Mary goes to the golf course on Sunday morning, eager to try out a new set of golf clubs she has just purchased. As she tees off on the first hole, the head of her club flies off and injures a nearby golfer.

  2 Mary's doctor gives her some pain medication and tells her not to drive after she takes it, because the medication

induces drowsiness. In spite of the doctor's warning, Mary decides to drive to the store while on the medication. Owing to her lack of alertness, she fails to stop at a traffic light and crashes into another vehicle, injuring a passenger.

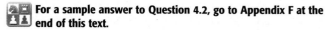

For a sample answer to Question 4.2, go to Appendix F at the end of this text.

4.3 Liability to Business Invitees. Kim went to Ling's Market to pick up a few items for dinner. It was a rainy, windy day, and the wind had blown water through the door of Ling's Market each time the door opened. As Kim entered through the door, she slipped and fell in the approximately one-half inch of rainwater that had accumulated on the floor. The manager knew of the weather conditions but had not posted any sign to warn customers of the water hazard. Kim injured her back as a result of the fall and sued Ling's for damages. Can Ling's be held liable for negligence in this situation? Discuss.

■

CASE PROBLEMS

4.4 Duty of Care. As pedestrians exited at the close of an arts and crafts show, Jason Davis, an employee of the show's producer, stood near the exit. Suddenly and without warning, Davis turned around and collided with Yvonne Esposito, an eighty-year-old woman. Esposito was knocked to the ground, fracturing her hip. After hip-replacement surgery, she was left with a permanent physical impairment. Esposito filed a suit in a fed-

eral district court against Davis and others, alleging negligence. What are the factors that indicate whether Davis owed Esposito a duty of care? What do those factors indicate in these circumstances? [*Esposito v. Davis*, 47 F.3d 164 (5th Cir. 1995)]

4.5 Invasion of Privacy. During the spring and summer of 1999, Edward and Geneva Irvine received numerous "hang up" phone calls, including three calls in the middle of the night. With the help of their local phone company, the Irvines learned that many of the calls were from the telemarketing department of the *Akron Beacon Journal* in Akron, Ohio. The *Beacon*'s sales force was equipped with an automatic dialing machine. During business hours, the dialer was used to maximize productivity by calling multiple phone numbers at once and connecting a call to a sales representative only after it was answered. After business hours, the dialer was used to dial a list of disconnected numbers to determine whether they had been reconnected. If the dialer detected a ring, it recorded the information and dropped the call. If the automated dialing system crashed, which it did frequently, it redialed the entire list. The Irvines filed a suit in an Ohio state court against the *Beacon* and others, alleging in part invasion of privacy. In whose favor should the court rule, and why? [*Irvine v. Akron Beacon Journal*, 147 Ohio App.3d 428, 770 N.E.2d 1105 (9 Dist. 2002)]

4.6 Case Problem with Sample Answer. New Hampshire International Speedway, Inc., owned the New Hampshire International Speedway, a racetrack next to Route 106 in Loudon, New Hampshire. In August 1998, on the weekend before the Winston Cup race, Speedway opened its parking facility to recreational vehicles (RVs). Speedway stationed its employee Frederick Neergaard at the entrance to the parking area at a "stop-bar" gate as a security guard. Leslie Wheeler, who was planning to attend the race, drove south in an RV on Route 106 toward Speedway. Meanwhile, Dennis Carignan was also driving south on Route 106 on a motorcycle, on which Mary Carignan was a passenger. As Wheeler approached the parking area, he saw Neergaard signaling him to turn left, which he began to do. At the same time, Carignan attempted to pass the RV on its left side, and the two vehicles collided. Mary sustained an injury to her right knee, lacerations on her ankle, and a broken hip. She filed a negligence action in a New Hampshire state court against Speedway and others. Which element of negligence is at the center of this dispute? How is a court likely to rule in this case, and why? [*Carignan v. New Hampshire International Speedway, Inc.*, 151 N.H. 409, 858 A.2d 536 (N.H. 2004)]

After you have answered Problem 4.6, compare your answer with the sample answer given on the Web site that accompanies this text. Go to academic.cengage.com/blaw/blt, select "Chapter 4," and click on "Case Problem with Sample Answer."

4.7 Defamation. Lydia Hagberg went to her bank, California Federal Bank, FSB, to cash a check made out to her by Smith Barney (SB), an investment-services firm. Nolene Showalter, a bank employee, suspected that the check was counterfeit. Showalter phoned SB and was told that the check was not valid. As she phoned the police, Gary Wood, a bank security officer, contacted SB again and was told that its earlier statement was "erroneous" and that the check was valid. Meanwhile, a police officer arrived, drew Hagberg away from the teller's window, spread her legs, patted her

down, and handcuffed her. The officer searched her purse, asked her whether she had any weapons or stolen property and whether she was driving a stolen vehicle, and arrested her. Hagberg filed a suit in a California state court against the bank and others, alleging, among other things, slander. Should the absolute privilege for communications made in judicial or other official proceedings apply to statements made when a citizen contacts the police to report suspected criminal activity? Why or why not? [*Hagberg v. California Federal Bank, FSB*, 32 Cal.4th 350, 81 P.3d 244, 7 Cal.Rptr.3d 803 (2004)]

4.8 Emotional Distress. Between 1996 and 1998, Donna Swanson received several anonymous, handwritten letters that, among other things, accused her husband, Alan, of infidelity. In 1998, John Grisham, Jr., the author of *The Firm* and many other best-selling novels, received an anonymous letter that appeared to have been written by the same person. Grisham and the Swansons suspected Katherine Almy, who soon filed a suit against them in a Virginia state court, alleging in part intentional infliction of emotional distress. According to Almy, Grisham intended to have her "really, really, suffer" for writing the letters, and the three devised a scheme to falsely accuse her. They gave David Liebman, a handwriting analyst, samples of Almy's handwriting. These included copies of confidential documents from her children's files at St. Anne's-Belfield School in Charlottesville, Virginia, where Alan taught and Grisham served on the board of directors. In Almy's view, Grisham influenced Liebman to report that Almy might have written the letters and misrepresented this report as conclusive, which led the police to confront Almy. She claimed that she then suffered severe emotional distress and depression, causing "a complete disintegration of virtually every aspect of her life" and requiring her "to undergo extensive therapy." In response, the defendants asked the court to dismiss the complaint for failure to state a claim. Should the court grant this request? Explain. [*Almy v. Grisham*, 639 S.E.2d 182 (Va. 2007)]

4.9 A Question of Ethics. *Intel Corp. has an e-mail system for its employees. Ken Hamidi, a former Intel employee, sent a series of six e-mail messages to 35,000 Intel employees over a twenty-one-month period. In the messages, Hamidi criticized the company's labor practices and urged employees to leave the company. Intel sought a court order to stop the e-mail campaign, arguing that Hamidi's actions constituted a trespass to chattels (personal property) because the e-mail significantly interfered with productivity, thereby causing economic damage. The state trial court granted Intel's motion for summary judgment and ordered Hamidi to stop sending messages. When the case reached the California Supreme Court, however, the court held that under California law, the tort of trespass to chattels required some evidence of injury to the plaintiff's personal property. Because Hamidi's e-mail had neither damaged Intel's computer system nor impaired its functioning, the court ruled that Hamidi's actions did not amount to a trespass to chattels. The court did not reject* *the idea that trespass theory could apply to cyberspace. Rather, the court simply held that to succeed in a lawsuit for trespass to chattels, a plaintiff must demonstrate that some concrete harm resulted from the unwanted e-mail. [Intel Corp. v. Hamidi, 30 Cal.4th 1342, 71 P.3d 296, 1 Cal.Rptr.3d 32 (2003)]*

1 Should a court require that spam cause actual physical damage or impairment of the computer system (by over-burdening it, for example) to establish that a spammer has committed trespass? Why or why not?

2 The content of Hamidi's messages caused much discussion among employees and managers, diverting workers' time and attention and thus interfering with productivity. Why did the court not consider this disruption to be sufficient evidence of harm? Do you agree with the court?

CRITICAL THINKING
AND WRITING ASSIGNMENTS

4.10 Critical Legal Thinking. What general principle underlies the common law doctrine that business owners have a duty of care toward their customers? Does the duty of care unfairly burden business owners? Why or why not?

4.11 **Video Question.** Go to this text's Web site at **academic. cengage.com/blaw/blt** and select "Chapter 4." Click on "Video Questions" and view the video titled *Jaws*. Then answer the following questions.

1 In the video, the mayor (Murray Hamilton) and a few other men try to persuade Chief Brody (Roy Scheider) not to close the town's beaches. If Chief Brody keeps the beaches open and a swimmer is injured or killed because

he failed to warn swimmers about the potential shark danger, has he committed a tort? If so, what kind of tort (intentional tort against persons, intentional tort against property, or negligence)? Explain your answer.

2 Can Chief Brody be held liable for any injuries or deaths to swimmers under the doctrine of strict liability? Why or why not?

3 Suppose that Chief Brody goes against the mayor's instructions and warns people to stay out of the water. Nevertheless, several swimmers do not heed his warning and are injured as a result. What defense or defenses could Chief Brody raise under these circumstances if he is sued for negligence?

ONLINE ACTIVITIES

PRACTICAL
INTERNET EXERCISES

Go to this text's Web site at **academic.cengage.com/blaw/blt**, select "Chapter 4," and click on "Practical Internet Exercises." There you will find the following Internet research exercises that you can perform to learn more about the topics covered in this chapter.

PRACTICAL INTERNET EXERCISE 4–1 LEGAL PERSPECTIVE—Online Defamation

PRACTICAL INTERNET EXERCISE 4–2 SOCIAL PERSPECTIVE—Legal and Illegal Uses of Spam

PRACTICAL INTERNET EXERCISE 4–3 MANAGEMENT PERSPECTIVE—The Duty to Warn

BEFORE THE TEST

Go to this text's Web site at **academic.cengage.com/blaw/blt**, select "Chapter 4," and click on "Interactive Quizzes." You will find a number of interactive questions relating to this chapter.

CHAPTER 5
Intellectual Property and Internet Law

INTELLECTUAL PROPERTY
Property resulting from intellectual, creative processes.

LEARNING OBJECTIVES

AFTER READING THIS CHAPTER, YOU SHOULD BE ABLE TO ANSWER THE FOLLOWING QUESTIONS:

1 What is intellectual property?

2 Why are trademarks and patents protected by the law?

3 What laws protect authors' rights in the works they generate?

4 What are trade secrets, and what laws offer protection for this form of intellectual property?

5 What steps have been taken to protect intellectual property rights in today's digital age?

O f significant concern to businesspersons today is the need to protect their rights in intellectual property. **Intellectual property** is any property resulting from intellectual, creative processes—the products of an individual's mind. Although it is an abstract term for an abstract concept, intellectual property is nonetheless familiar to almost everyone. The information contained in books and computer files is intellectual property. The software you use, the movies you see, and the music you listen to are all forms of intellectual property. In fact, in today's information age, it should come as no surprise that the value of the world's intellectual property probably now exceeds the value of physical property, such as machines and houses.

The need to protect creative works was recognized by the framers of the U.S. Constitution more than two hundred years ago: Article I, Section 8, of the Constitution authorized Congress "[t]o promote the Progress of Science and useful Arts, by securing for limited Times to Authors and Inventors the exclusive Right to their respective Writings and Discoveries." Laws protecting patents, trademarks, and copyrights are explicitly designed to protect and reward inventive and artistic creativity. Exhibit 5–1 offers a comprehensive summary of these forms of intellectual property, as well as intellectual property that consists of *trade secrets*.

An understanding of intellectual property law is important because intellectual property has taken on increasing significance, not only in the United States but globally as well. Today, the prosperity of many U.S. companies depends more on their ownership rights in intangible intellectual property than on their tangible assets. As you will read in

EXHIBIT 5-1 Forms of Intellectual Property

	DEFINITION	HOW ACQUIRED	DURATION	REMEDY FOR INFRINGEMENT
Patent	A grant from the government that gives an inventor exclusive rights to an invention.	By filing a patent application with the U.S. Patent and Trademark Office and receiving its approval.	Twenty years from the date of the application; for design patents, fourteen years.	Monetary damages, including royalties and lost profits, *plus* attorneys' fees. Damages may be tripled for intentional infringements.
Copyright	The right of an author or originator of a literary or artistic work, or other production that falls within a specified category, to have the exclusive use of that work for a given period of time.	Automatic (once the work or creation is put in tangible form). Only the *expression* of an idea (and not the idea itself) can be protected by copyright.	For authors: the life of the author plus 70 years. For publishers: 95 years after the date of publication or 120 years after creation.	Actual damages plus profits received by the party who infringed *or* statutory damages under the Copyright Act, *plus* costs and attorneys' fees in either situation.
Trademark (service mark and trade dress)	Any distinctive word, name, symbol, or device (image or appearance), or combination thereof, that an entity uses to distinguish its goods or services from those of others. The owner has the exclusive right to use that mark or trade dress.	1. At common law, ownership created by use of the mark. 2. Registration with the appropriate federal or state office gives notice and is permitted if the mark is currently in use or will be within the next six months.	Unlimited, as long as it is in use. To continue notice by registration, the owner must renew by filing between the fifth and sixth years, and thereafter, every ten years.	1. Injunction prohibiting the future use of the mark. 2. Actual damages plus profits received by the party who infringed (can be increased under the Lanham Act). 3. Destruction of articles that infringed. 4. *Plus* costs and attorneys' fees.
Trade secret	Any information that a business possesses and that gives the business an advantage over competitors (including formulas, lists, patterns, plans, processes, and programs).	Through the originality and development of the information and processes that constitute the business secret and are unknown to others.	Unlimited, so long as not revealed to others. Once revealed to others, it is no longer a trade secret.	Monetary damages for misappropriation (the Uniform Trade Secrets Act also permits punitive damages if willful), *plus* costs and attorneys' fees.

this chapter, protecting these assets in today's online world has proved particularly challenging. This is because, as indicated in the chapter-opening quotation, the Internet's capability is "profoundly different" from anything we have had in the past.

TRADEMARKS AND RELATED PROPERTY

A **trademark** is a distinctive mark, motto, device, or emblem that a manufacturer stamps, prints, or otherwise affixes to the goods it produces so that they may be identified on the market and their origins made known. At common law, the person who used a symbol or mark

TRADEMARK
A distinctive mark, motto, device, or emblem that a manufacturer stamps, prints, or otherwise affixes to the goods it produces so that they may be identified on the market and their origins made known. Once a trademark is established (under the common law or through registration), the owner is entitled to its exclusive use.

to identify a business or product was protected in the use of that trademark. Clearly, by using another's trademark, a business could lead consumers to believe that its goods were made by the other business. The law seeks to avoid this kind of confusion.

In the following classic case concerning Coca-Cola, the defendants argued that the Coca-Cola trademark was entitled to no protection under the law because the term did not accurately represent the product.

CASE 5.1 **The Coca-Cola Co. v. Koke Co. of America**

LANDMARK AND CLASSIC CASES

Supreme Court of the United States, 254 U.S. 143, 41 S.Ct. 113, 65 L.Ed. 189 (1920).
www.findlaw.com/casecode/supreme.html[a]

COMPANY PROFILE *John Pemberton, an Atlanta pharmacist, invented a caramel-colored, carbonated soft drink in 1886. His bookkeeper, Frank Robinson, named the beverage Coca-Cola after two of the ingredients, coca leaves and kola nuts. Asa Candler bought the Coca-Cola Company in 1891 and, within seven years, had made the soft drink available in all of the United States, as well as in parts of Canada and Mexico. Candler continued to sell Coke aggressively and to open up new markets, reaching Europe before 1910. In doing so, however, he attracted numerous competitors, some of whom tried to capitalize directly on the Coke name.*

FACTS The Coca-Cola Company brought an action in a federal district court to enjoin other beverage companies from using the words *Koke* and *Dope* for the defendants' products. The defendants contended that the Coca-Cola trademark was a fraudulent representation and that Coca-Cola was therefore not entitled to any help from the courts. By use of the Coca-Cola name, the defendants alleged, the Coca-Cola Company represented that the beverage contained cocaine (from coca leaves). The district court granted the injunction, but the federal appellate court reversed. The Coca-Cola Company appealed to the United States Supreme Court.

ISSUE Did the marketing of products called Koke and Dope by the Koke Company of America and other firms constitute an infringement on Coca-Cola's trademark?

DECISION Yes for Koke, but no for Dope. The United States Supreme Court enjoined the competing beverage companies from calling their products Koke but did not prevent them from calling their products Dope.

REASON The Court noted that, to be sure, prior to 1900 the Coca-Cola beverage had contained a small amount of cocaine. This ingredient had been deleted from the formula by 1906 at the latest, however, and the Coca-Cola Company had advertised to the public that no cocaine was present in its drink. Coca-Cola was a widely popular drink "to be had at almost any soda fountain." Because of the public's widespread familiarity with Coca-Cola, the retention of the name of the beverage (referring to coca leaves and kola nuts) was not misleading: "Coca-Cola probably means to most persons the plaintiff's familiar product to be had everywhere rather than a compound of particular substances." The name *Coke* was found to be so common a term for the trademarked product Coca-Cola that the defendants' use of the similar-sounding *Koke* as a name for their beverages was disallowed. The Court could find no reason to restrain the defendants from using the name *Dope*, however.

WHAT IF THE FACTS WERE DIFFERENT? *Suppose that Coca-Cola had been trying to make the public believe that its product contained cocaine. Would the result in the case likely have been different?*

IMPACT OF THIS CASE ON TODAY'S LAW *In this early case, the United States Supreme Court made it clear that trademarks and trade names (and nicknames for those marks and names, such as "Coke" for "Coca-Cola") that are in common use receive protection under the common law. This holding is significant historically because it is the predecessor to the federal statute later passed to protect trademark rights (the Lanham Act of 1946, to be discussed shortly). In many ways, that statute represented a codification of common law principles governing trademarks.*

RELEVANT WEB SITES *To locate information on the Web concerning the Coca-Cola decision, go to this text's Web site at* academic.cengage.com/blaw/blt, *select "Chapter 5," and click on "URLs for Landmarks."*

a. This is the "U.S. Supreme Court Opinions" page within the Web site of the "FindLaw Internet Legal Resources" database. This page provides several options for accessing an opinion. Because you know the citation for this case, you can go to the "Citation Search" box, type in the appropriate volume and page numbers for the *United States Reports* ("254" and "143," respectively, for the *Coca-Cola* case), and click on "Get It."

Statutory Protection of Trademarks

Statutory protection of trademarks and related property is provided at the federal level by the Lanham Act of 1946.[1] The Lanham Act was enacted in part to protect manufacturers from losing business to rival companies that used confusingly similar trademarks. The Lanham Act incorporates the common law of trademarks and provides remedies for owners of trademarks who wish to enforce their claims in federal court. Many states also have trademark statutes.

Trademark Dilution In 1995, Congress amended the Lanham Act by passing the Federal Trademark Dilution Act,[2] which extended the protection available to trademark owners by allowing them to bring a suit in federal court for trademark *dilution*. Until the passage of this amendment, federal trademark law prohibited only the unauthorized use of the same mark on competing—or on noncompeting but "related"—goods or services when such use would likely confuse consumers as to the origin of those goods and services. Trademark dilution laws protect "distinctive" or "famous" trademarks (such as Jergens, McDonald's, Dell, and Apple) from certain unauthorized uses even when the use is on noncompeting goods or is unlikely to confuse. More than half of the states have also enacted trademark dilution laws.

Use of a Similar Mark May Constitute Trademark Dilution A famous mark may be diluted not only by the use of an *identical* mark but also by the use of a *similar* mark, provided that it reduces the value of the famous mark. **■EXAMPLE 5.1** Well-known lingerie maker Victoria's Secret brought a trademark dilution action against "Victor's Little Secret," a small retail store that sold adult videos, lingerie, and other items. Although the lower courts granted Victoria's Secret an injunction prohibiting the adult store from using a similar mark, the United States Supreme Court reversed the decision. According to the Court, the *likelihood of dilution* is not enough to establish dilution. The plaintiff must present some evidence that the allegedly infringing user's mark actually reduces the value of the famous mark or lessens its capacity to identify goods and services.[3] ■

Trademark Registration

Trademarks may be registered with the state or with the federal government. To register for protection under federal trademark law, a person must file an application with the U.S. Patent and Trademark Office in Washington, D.C. Under present law, a mark can be registered (1) if it is currently in commerce or (2) if the applicant intends to put the mark into commerce within six months.

In special circumstances, the six-month period can be extended by thirty months, giving the applicant a total of three years from the date of notice of trademark approval to make use of the mark and file the required use statement. Registration is postponed until the mark is actually used. Nonetheless, during this waiting period, any applicant can legally protect his or her trademark against a third party who previously has neither used

Various billboards and neon signs in New York City's Times Square. Why are trademarks protected by the law?
(Rusty Haskell/Creative Commons)

---

1. 15 U.S.C. Sections 1051–1128.
2. 15 U.S.C. Section 1125.
3. *Moseley v. V Secret Catalogue, Inc.*, 537 U.S. 418, 123 S.Ct. 1115, 155 L.Ed.2d 1 (2003).

the mark nor filed an application for it. Registration is renewable between the fifth and sixth years after the initial registration and every ten years thereafter (every twenty years for trademarks registered before 1990).

Trademark Infringement

Registration of a trademark with the U.S. Patent and Trademark Office gives notice on a nationwide basis that the trademark belongs exclusively to the registrant. The registrant is also allowed to use the symbol ® to indicate that the mark has been registered. Whenever that trademark is copied to a substantial degree or used in its entirety by another, intentionally or unintentionally, the trademark has been *infringed* (used without authorization). When a trademark has been infringed, the owner of the mark has a cause of action against the infringer. To sue for trademark infringement, a person need not have registered the trademark, but registration does furnish proof of the date of inception of the trademark's use.

Only those trademarks that are deemed sufficiently distinctive from all competing trademarks will be protected, however. The trademarks must be sufficiently distinct to enable consumers to identify the manufacturer of the goods easily and to differentiate among competing products.

Strong Marks   Fanciful, arbitrary, or suggestive trademarks are generally considered to be the most distinctive (strongest) trademarks because they are normally taken from outside the context of the particular product and thus provide the best means of distinguishing one product from another.

EXAMPLE 5.2   Fanciful trademarks include invented words, such as "Xerox" for one manufacturer's copiers and "Kodak" for another company's photographic products. Arbitrary trademarks use common words in a fictitious or arbitrary manner to create a distinctive mark that identifies the source of the product, such as "Dutch Boy" as a name on a can of paint. Suggestive trademarks suggest something about a product without describing the product directly. For instance, "Dairy Queen" suggests an association between its products and milk, but it does not directly describe ice cream. ■

Secondary Meaning   Descriptive terms, geographic terms, and personal names are not inherently distinctive and do not receive protection under the law *until* they acquire a secondary meaning. A secondary meaning may arise when customers begin to associate a specific term or phrase, such as "London Fog," with specific trademarked items (coats with "London Fog" labels). Whether a secondary meaning becomes attached to a term or name usually depends on how extensively the product is advertised, the market for the product, the number of sales, and other factors. The United States Supreme Court has held that even a color can qualify for trademark protection.[4] Once a secondary meaning is attached to a term or name, a trademark is considered distinctive and is protected. In one recent case, a federal court ruled that trademark law protects the particular color schemes used by four state university sports teams, including Ohio State University and Louisiana State University.[5]

At issue in the following case was whether a certain mark was suggestive or descriptive.

---

4. *Qualitex Co. v. Jacobson Products Co.*, 514 U.S. 159, 115 S.Ct. 1300, 131 L.Ed.2d 248 (1995).
5. *Board of Supervisors of LA State University v. Smack Apparel Co.*, 438 F.Supp.2d 653 (2006).

CASE 5.2 **Menashe v. V Secret Catalogue, Inc.**

United States District Court, Southern District of New York, 409 F.Supp.2d 412 (2006).

FACTS In autumn 2002, Victoria's Secret Stores, Inc., and its affiliated companies, including V Secret Catalogue, Inc., began to develop a panty collection to be named "SEXY LITTLE THINGS." In spring 2004, Ronit Menashe, a publicist, and Audrey Quock, a fashion model and actress, began to plan a line of women's underwear also called "SEXY LITTLE THINGS." Menashe and Quock designed their line, negotiated for its manufacture, registered the domain name www.sexylittlethings.com, and filed an intent-to-use (ITU) application with the U.S. Patent and Trademark Office (USPTO). In July 2004, Victoria's Secret's collection appeared in its stores in Ohio, Michigan, and California and, in less than three months, was prominently displayed in all its stores, in its catalogues, and on its Web site. By mid-November, more than 13 million units of the line had been sold, accounting for 4 percent of the company's sales for the year. When the firm applied to register "SEXY LITTLE THINGS" with the USPTO, it learned of Menashe and Quock's ITU application. The firm warned the pair that their use of the phrase constituted trademark infringement. Menashe and Quock filed a suit in a federal district court against V Secret Catalogue and others, asking the court to, among other things, declare "noninfringement of the trademark."

ISSUE Is "SEXY LITTLE THINGS" a descriptive term for lingerie that had not attained secondary meaning by the time the plaintiffs filed their ITU application, or is it a suggestive mark that qualifies for trademark protection without proof of secondary meaning?

DECISION The court concluded that "SEXY LITTLE THINGS" was a suggestive mark that Victoria's Secret used in commerce prior to the time the plaintiffs filed their ITU application. For this reason, Victoria's Secret had "priority in the Mark," and Menashe and Quock were not entitled to a judgment of "noninfringement."

REASON The court explained that "to merit trademark protection, a mark must be capable of distinguishing the products it marks from those of others." A descriptive term conveys an immediate idea of the ingredients, qualities, or characteristics of the goods. In contrast, a suggestive term requires imagination, thought, and perception to reach a conclusion as to the nature of the goods. Suggestive marks are automatically protected because they are inherently distinctive; that is, their intrinsic nature serves to identify a particular source of a product. Descriptive marks are not inherently distinctive and may only be protected on a showing of secondary meaning—that is, that the purchasing public associates the mark with a particular source. In this case, the court held that the mark "SEXY LITTLE THINGS" was suggestive because it calls to mind the phrase "sexy little things" popularly used to refer to attractive young women. The court observed that because of this suggestive nature, the mark prompts the purchaser to mentally associate the lingerie with its targeted twenty- to thirty-year-old consumers. Courts have classified marks that both describe the product and evoke other associations as inherently distinctive. In addition, the court reasoned that Victoria's Secret's use of the mark does not deprive competitors of ways to describe their lingerie products. "Indeed, Victoria's Secret's own descriptions of its lingerie in its catalogues and Web site illustrate that there are numerous ways to describe provocative underwear."

 WHY IS THIS CASE IMPORTANT? *This case is notable for the court's characterization of the plaintiffs' suit as "defensive." ITU applicants may defend against other parties' claims of infringement, but they do not have the right to charge others with infringement. In this case, however, the court allowed the plaintiffs to preemptively defend themselves against Victoria's Secret's efforts to stop the use of the "SEXY LITTLE THINGS" mark.*

Generic Terms Generic terms are terms that refer to an entire class of products, such as *bicycle* and *computer*. Generic terms receive no protection, even if they acquire secondary meanings. A particularly thorny problem arises when a trademark acquires generic use. For instance, *aspirin* and *thermos* were originally trademarked products, but today the words are used generically. Other examples are *escalator*, *trampoline*, *raisin bran*, *dry ice*, *lanolin*, *linoleum*, *nylon*, and *corn flakes*.

Note that a generic term will not be protected under trademark law even if the term has acquired a secondary meaning. [■EXAMPLE 5.3] In one case, America Online, Inc. (AOL), sued AT&T Corporation, claiming that AT&T's use of "You Have Mail" on its WorldNet Service infringed AOL's trademark rights in the same phrase. The court ruled, however, that because each of the three words in the phrase was a generic term, the phrase as a whole was generic. Although the phrase had become widely associated with AOL's e-mail notification service, and thus may have acquired a secondary meaning, this issue was of no significance in this case. The court stated that it would not consider whether the mark had acquired any secondary meaning because "generic marks with secondary meaning are still not entitled to protection."[6] ■

Service, Certification, and Collective Marks

A **service mark** is essentially a trademark that is used to distinguish the *services* (rather than the products) of one person or company from those of another. For instance, each airline has a particular mark or symbol associated with its name. Titles and character names used in radio and television are frequently registered as service marks.

Other marks protected by law include certification marks and collective marks. A **certification mark** is used by one or more persons, other than the owner, to certify the region, materials, mode of manufacture, quality, or other characteristic of specific goods or services. [■EXAMPLE 5.4] Certification marks include such marks as "Good Housekeeping Seal of Approval" and "UL Tested." ■ When used by members of a cooperative, association, union, or other organization, a certification mark is referred to as a **collective mark.** [■EXAMPLE 5.5] Collective marks appear at the ends of the credits of movies to indicate the various associations and organizations that participated in making the movie. The union marks found on the tags of certain products are also collective marks. ■

Trade Names

Trademarks apply to *products.* The term **trade name** is used to indicate part or all of a business's name, whether the business is a sole proprietorship, a partnership, or a corporation. Generally, a trade name is directly related to a business and its goodwill. Trade names may be protected as trademarks if the trade name is the same as the company's trademarked product—for example, Coca-Cola. Unless also used as a trademark or service mark, a trade name cannot be registered with the federal government. Trade names are protected under the common law, however. As with trademarks, words must be unusual or fancifully used if they are to be protected as trade names. The word *Safeway,* for instance, was held by the courts to be sufficiently fanciful to obtain protection as a trade name for a grocery chain.[7]

Trade Dress

The term **trade dress** refers to the image and overall appearance of a product. Trade dress is a broad concept and can include either all or part of the total image or overall impression created by a product or its packaging. [■EXAMPLE 5.6] The distinctive decor, menu, layout, and style of service of a particular restaurant may be regarded as the restaurant's trade dress. Similarly, trade dress can include the layout and appearance of a mail-order catalogue, the use of a lighthouse as part of the design of a golf hole, the fish shape of a cracker, or the G-shaped design of a Gucci watch. ■

SERVICE MARK
A mark used in the sale or the advertising of services to distinguish the services of one person from those of others. Titles, character names, and other distinctive features of radio and television programs may be registered as service marks.

CERTIFICATION MARK
A mark used by one or more persons, other than the owner, to certify the region, materials, mode of manufacture, quality, or other characteristic of specific goods or services.

COLLECTIVE MARK
A mark used by members of a cooperative, association, union, or other organization to certify the region, materials, mode of manufacture, quality, or other characteristic of specific goods or services.

TRADE NAME
A term that is used to indicate part or all of a business's name and that is directly related to the business's reputation and goodwill. Trade names are protected under the common law (and under trademark law, if the name is the same as the firm's trademarked product).

TRADE DRESS
The image and overall appearance of a product—for example, the distinctive decor, menu, layout, and style of service of a particular restaurant. Basically, trade dress is subject to the same protection as trademarks.

---

6. *America Online, Inc. v. AT&T Corp.,* 243 F.3d 812 (4th Cir. 2001).
7. *Safeway Stores v. Suburban Foods,* 130 F.Supp. 249 (E.D.Va. 1955).

Basically, trade dress is subject to the same protection as trademarks. In cases involving trade dress infringement, as in trademark infringement cases, a major consideration is whether consumers are likely to be confused by the allegedly infringing use.

CYBER MARKS

In cyberspace, trademarks are sometimes referred to as **cyber marks.** We turn now to a discussion of trademark-related issues in cyberspace and how new laws and the courts are addressing these issues. One concern relates to the rights of a trademark's owner to use the mark as part of a domain name (Internet address). Other issues have to do with cybersquatting, meta tags, and trademark dilution on the Web. In some instances, licensing can be a way to avoid liability for infringing on another's intellectual property rights in cyberspace.

CYBER MARK
A trademark in cyberspace.

Domain Names

Conflicts over rights to domain names emerged as e-commerce expanded on a worldwide scale. By using the same, or a similar, domain name, parties have attempted to profit from the goodwill of a competitor, to sell pornography, to offer for sale another party's domain name, and to otherwise infringe on others' trademarks. A **domain name** is part of an Internet address, such as "westlaw.edu." Every domain name ends with a top level domain (TLD), which is the part to the right of the period that indicates the type of entity that operates the site (for example, "edu" is an abbreviation for "educational"). The second level domain (SLD) is the part of the name to the left of the period, which is chosen by the business entity or individual registering the domain name. Competition among firms with similar names and products preceding the *.com* TLD caused numerous disputes over domain name rights. As noted in Chapter 3, the Internet Corporation for Assigned Names and Numbers (ICANN), a nonprofit corporation, oversees the distribution of domain names. ICANN also facilitates the settlement of domain name disputes and operates an online arbitration system.

DOMAIN NAME
The last part of an Internet address, such as "westlaw.edu." The top level (the part of the name to the right of the period) indicates the type of entity that operates the site ("edu" is an abbreviation for "educational"). The second level (the part of the name to the left of the period) is chosen by the entity.

Anticybersquatting Legislation

Cybersquatting occurs when a person registers a domain name that is the same as, or confusingly similar to, the trademark of another and then offers to sell the domain name back to the trademark owner. During the 1990s, cybersquatting led to so much litigation that Congress passed the Anticybersquatting Consumer Protection Act of 1999 (ACPA), which amended the Lanham Act—the federal law protecting trademarks discussed earlier.

The ACPA makes it illegal for a person to "register, traffic in, or use" a domain name (1) if the name is identical or confusingly similar to the trademark of another and (2) if the one registering, trafficking in, or using the domain name has a "bad faith intent" to profit from that trademark. The act does not define what constitutes bad faith. Instead, it lists several factors that courts can consider in deciding whether bad faith exists. Some of these factors are whether there is an intent to divert consumers in a way that could harm the goodwill represented by the trademark, whether there is an offer to transfer or sell the domain name to the trademark owner, and whether there is an intent to use the domain name to offer goods and services.

The ACPA applies to all domain name registrations of trademarks, even domain names registered before the passage of the act. Successful plaintiffs in suits brought under the act can collect actual damages and profits or elect to receive statutory damages of $1,000 to $100,000.

CYBERSQUATTING
The act of registering a domain name that is the same as, or confusingly similar to, the trademark of another and then offering to sell that domain name back to the trademark owner.

Meta Tags

Search engines compile their results by looking through a Web site's key-word field. *Meta tags*, or key words (see Chapter 1), may be inserted into this field to increase the likelihood that a site will be included in search engine results, even though the site may have nothing to do with the inserted words. Using this same technique, one site may appropriate the key words of other sites with more frequent hits so that the appropriating site appears in the same search engine results as the more popular sites. Using another's trademark in a meta tag without the owner's permission, however, normally constitutes trademark infringement.

Some uses of another's trademark as a meta tag may be permissible if the use is reasonably necessary and does not suggest that the owner authorized or sponsored the use. **■EXAMPLE 5.7** Terri Welles, a former model who had been "Playmate of the Year" in *Playboy* magazine, established a Web site that used the terms *Playboy* and *Playmate* as meta tags. Playboy Enterprises, Inc., which publishes *Playboy*, filed suit seeking to prevent Welles from using these meta tags. The court determined that Welles's use of Playboy's meta tags to direct users to her Web site was permissible because it did not suggest sponsorship and there were no descriptive substitutes for the terms *Playboy* and *Playmate*.[8] ■

Dilution in the Online World

As discussed earlier, trademark *dilution* occurs when a trademark is used, without authorization, in a way that diminishes the distinctive quality of the mark. Unlike trademark infringement, a claim of dilution does not require proof that consumers are likely to be confused by a connection between the unauthorized use and the mark. For this reason, the products involved do not have to be similar. In the first case alleging dilution on the Web, a court precluded the use of "candyland.com" as the URL for an adult site. The suit was brought by the maker of the Candyland children's game and owner of the Candyland mark. Although consumers were not likely to connect candyland.com with the children's game, the court reasoned that the sexually explicit adult site would dilute the value of the Candyland mark.[9]

Licensing

LICENSE
In the context of intellectual property law, an agreement permitting the use of a trademark, copyright, patent, or trade secret for certain limited purposes.

One of the ways to make use of another's trademark or other form of intellectual property, while avoiding litigation, is to obtain a license to do so. A **license** in this context is essentially an agreement permitting the use of a trademark, copyright, patent, or trade secret for certain limited purposes. The party that owns the intellectual property rights and issues the license is the *licensor*, and the party obtaining the license is the *licensee*. A license grants only the rights expressly described in the license agreement. A licensor might, for example, allow the licensee to use the trademark as part of its company name, or as part of its domain name, but not otherwise use the mark on any products or services. Typically, license agreements are very detailed and should be carefully drafted. Disputes frequently arise over licensing agreements, particularly when the license involves Internet uses, such as a license allowing a trademark to be used in domain names.

■EXAMPLE 5.8 Morton and Tigrett founded the Hard Rock Café, which became a popular chain of restaurants internationally. Years later they had a falling out and split their Hard Rock Café properties throughout the world into two territories. Eventually, Tigrett sold his interests to another company, and Morton opened the Hard Rock Hotel and Casino in Las Vegas. The hotel was licensed to use some of the same trademark logos as the Hard Rock Café. When Morton later used the logos on the Web site for the hotel and on merchandise advertised on the Web site, he was sued for breaching the licensing agreement.

---

8. *Playboy Enterprises, Inc. v. Welles*, 279 F.3d 796 (9th Cir. 2002).
9. *Hasbro, Inc. v. Internet Entertainment Group, Ltd.*, 1996 WL 84858 (W.D.Wash. 1996).

The licensor claimed that Morton had exceeded the rights granted under the license because the Internet site reached beyond the territory specified in the agreement.

After several years of costly litigation, the court concluded that the licensing agreement was broad enough to allow Morton to use the logos as the Hard Rock Hotel's trademark. The court held, however, that advertising merchandise with the Hard Rock Café's logos on the hotel's Web site constituted infringement and ordered Morton to cease the advertisements. Despite the infringement, the plaintiffs were not entitled to monetary damages because they had not proved that the Web site had caused consumer confusion or that Morton had acted in bad faith or willfully deceived consumers.[10] ▣

PATENTS

A **patent** is a grant from the government that gives an inventor the exclusive right to make, use, and sell an invention for a period of twenty years from the date of filing the application for a patent. Patents for designs, as opposed to inventions, are given for a fourteen-year period. For either a regular patent or a design patent, the applicant must demonstrate to the satisfaction of the U.S. Patent and Trademark Office that the invention, discovery, process, or design is *novel, useful*, and *not obvious* in light of current technology.

In contrast to patent law in many other countries, in the United States the first person to invent a product or process gets the patent rights rather than the first person to file for a patent on that product or process. Because it is difficult to prove who invented an item first, however, the first person to file an application is often deemed the first to invent (unless the inventor has detailed research notes or other evidence). An inventor can publish the invention or offer it for sale prior to filing a patent application but must apply for a patent within one year of doing so or forfeit the patent rights. The period of patent protection begins on the date the patent application was filed, rather than when it was issued, which can sometimes be years later. After the patent period ends (either fourteen or twenty years later), the product or process enters the public domain, and anyone can make, sell, or use the invention without paying the patent holder.

PATENT
A government grant that gives an inventor the exclusive right or privilege to make, use, or sell his or her invention for a limited time period.

Searchable Patent Databases

A significant development relating to patents is the availability online of the world's patent databases. The Web site of the U.S. Patent and Trademark Office provides searchable databases covering U.S. patents granted since 1976. The Web site of the European Patent Office provides online access to 50 million patent documents in more than seventy nations through a searchable network of databases. Businesses use these searchable databases in many ways. Because patents are valuable assets, businesses may need to perform patent searches to list or inventory their assets. Patent searches may also be conducted to study trends and patterns in a specific technology or to gather information about competitors in the industry. In addition, a business might search patent databases to develop a business strategy in a particular market or to evaluate a job applicant's contributions to a technology. Although online databases are accessible to anyone, businesspersons might consider hiring a specialist to perform advanced patent searches.

ON THE WEB

You can access the European Patent Office's Web site at

www.epo.org.

What Is Patentable?

Under federal law, "[w]hoever invents or discovers any new and useful process, machine, manufacture, or composition of matter, or any new and useful improvement thereof, may obtain a patent therefor, subject to the conditions and requirements of this title."[11] At one

---

10. *Hard Rock Café International (USA), Inc. v. Morton*, 1999 WL 717995 (S.D.N.Y. 1999).
11. 35 U.S.C. 101.

time, it was difficult for developers and manufacturers of software to obtain patent protection because many software products simply automate procedures that can be performed manually. In other words, it was thought that computer programs did not meet the "novel" and "not obvious" requirements previously mentioned. Also, the basis for software is often a mathematical equation or formula, which is not patentable. In 1981, however, the United States Supreme Court held that it is possible to obtain a patent for a *process* that incorporates a computer program—providing, of course, that the process itself is patentable.[12] Subsequently, many patents have been issued for software-related inventions.

In 1998, in a landmark case, *State Street Bank & Trust Co. v. Signature Financial Group, Inc.*,[13] the U.S. Court of Appeals for the Federal Circuit ruled that business processes were patentable. After this decision, numerous technology firms applied for business process patents. Walker Digital applied for a business process patent for its "Dutch auction" system, which allowed consumers to make offers for airline tickets on the Internet and led to the creation of Priceline.com. Amazon.com obtained a business process patent for its "one-click" ordering system, a method of processing credit-card orders securely. Indeed, since the *State Street* decision, the number of Internet-related patents issued by the U.S. Patent and Trademark Office has increased dramatically.

In sum, almost anything is patentable, except (1) the laws of nature, (2) natural phenomena, and (3) abstract ideas (including algorithms). Even artistic methods, certain works of art, and the structure of storylines are patentable, provided that they are novel and not obvious. Plants that are reproduced asexually (by means other than from seed), such as hybrid or genetically engineered plants, are patentable in the United States, as are genetically engineered (or cloned) microorganisms and animals.

ETHICAL ISSUE 5.1

Is it an abuse of patent law for a company to sue farmers whose crops were accidentally contaminated by genetically modified seed? Monsanto, Inc., has been selling genetically modified (GM) seeds to farmers in the United States and throughout the world as a way to achieve higher yields using fewer pesticides. Monsanto requires farmers who buy GM seeds to sign licensing agreements promising to plant the seeds for only one crop and to pay a technology fee for each acre planted. To ensure that the farmers comply with the restrictions, Monsanto has set aside $10 million a year and a staff of seventy-five individuals to investigate and prosecute farmers who use the GM seeds illegally. If the company receives an anonymous tip about a farmer, it sends its "seed police" to investigate, take samples from the farmer's field for testing, interview neighbors, and even conduct surveillance of the farmer's family and operation.

The problem is that the patented GM seeds, like ordinary seeds, reproduce if they are scattered by the wind or transferred on farm equipment. Thus, they can contaminate neighboring fields. Consider, for example, the situation faced by a Canadian canola farmer, Percy Schmeiser. Schmeiser had not purchased any GM seeds or signed any licensing agreement, but on investigation Monsanto found that some of his crop contained evidence of a Monsanto genetic trait. Schmeiser refused to pay royalties to Monsanto because he had not planted any GM seeds. It turned out that Schmeiser's crop had been contaminated with the GM seed, likely by seed escaping from passing trucks. Nevertheless, the Canadian Supreme Court ruled that Schmeiser had committed patent infringement and ordered him to destroy the crops containing evidence of the patented seed.[14] Schmeiser's plight is not unusual. Monsanto has filed more than ninety lawsuits

---

12. *Diamond v. Diehr*, 450 U.S. 175, 101 S.Ct. 1048, 67 L.Ed.2d 155 (1981).

13. 149 F.3d 1368 (Fed. Cir. 1998).

14. *Monsanto Canada, Inc. v. Schmeiser*, 1 S.C.R. 902, 2004 SCC 34 (CanLII). Note that in contrast to most cases in the United States, the Canadian court did not award damages for the infringement and only ordered Schmeiser to stop the infringing activity.

against nearly 150 farmers in the United States and has been awarded more than $15 million in damages (not including out-of-court settlement amounts).[15] Farmers claim that Monsanto has acted unethically by intimidating them and threatening to pursue them in court for years if they refuse to settle out of court by paying royalties.

Patent Infringement

If a firm makes, uses, or sells another's patented design, product, or process without the patent owner's permission, it commits the tort of patent infringement. Patent infringement may occur even though the patent owner has not put the patented product in commerce. Patent infringement may also occur even though not all features or parts of an invention are copied. (With respect to a patented process, however, all steps or their equivalent must be copied for infringement to exist.)

Remedies for Patent Infringement

If a patent is infringed, the patent holder may sue for relief in federal court. The patent holder can seek an injunction against the infringer and can also request damages for royalties and lost profits. In some cases, the court may grant the winning party reimbursement for attorneys' fees and costs. If the court determines that the infringement was willful, the court can triple the amount of damages awarded (treble damages).

How might a farmer—like Percy Schmeiser, shown in the photo— unknowingly commit patent infringement? (Photo Courtesy of Percy Schmeiser)

In the past, permanent injunctions were routinely granted to prevent future infringement. In 2006, however, the United States Supreme Court ruled that patent holders are not automatically entitled to a permanent injunction against future infringing activities— the federal courts have discretion to decide whether equity requires it. According to the Supreme Court, a patent holder must prove that it has suffered irreparable injury and that the public interest would not be disserved by a permanent injunction.[16]

This decision gives courts discretion to decide what is equitable in the circumstances and allows them to consider what is in the public interest rather than just the interests of the parties. For example, in the first case applying this rule, a court found that although Microsoft had infringed on the patent of a small software company, the latter was not entitled to an injunction. According to the court, the small company was not irreparably harmed and could be adequately compensated by damages. Also, the public might suffer negative effects from an injunction because the infringement involved part of Microsoft's widely used Office suite software.[17]

Litigation over whether a patent has been infringed is typically expensive and often requires a team of experts to investigate and analyze the commercial, technical, and legal aspects of the case. Because of these costs, a businessperson facing patent infringement litigation—either as the patent holder or as the alleged infringer—should carefully evaluate the evidence as well as the various settlement options. If both sides appear to have good arguments as to whether the patent was infringed or whether it was valid, it may be in a firm's best interest to settle the case. This is particularly true if the firm is not certain that the court would grant an injunction. Similarly, if the patented technology is not commercially significant to one's business, it might be best to consider a

PREVENTING
LEGAL DISPUTES

---

15. See, for example, *Monsanto Co. v. Scruggs*, 459 F.3d 1328 (2006); *Monsanto Co. v. McFarling*, ___ F.Supp.2d ___ (E.D.Mo. 2005); and *Sample v. Monsanto Co.*, 283 F.Supp.2d 1088 (2003).
16. *eBay, Inc. v. MercExchange, LLC*, ___ U.S. ___ 126 S.Ct. 1837, 164 L.Ed.2d 641 (2006).
17. *Z4 Technologies, Inc. v. Microsoft Corp.*, 434 F.Supp.2d 437 (2006).

nonexclusive license as a means of resolving the dispute. This option is more important for patent holders now that injunctions may be harder to obtain. Settlement may be as simple as an agreement that one party will stop making, using, or selling the patented product or process, or it may involve monetary compensation for past activities and/or licensing for future activities.

■

COPYRIGHTS

A **copyright** is an intangible property right granted by federal statute to the author or originator of certain literary or artistic productions. Currently, copyrights are governed by the Copyright Act of 1976,[18] as amended. Works created after January 1, 1978, are automatically given statutory copyright protection for the life of the author plus 70 years. For copyrights owned by publishing houses, the copyright expires 95 years from the date of publication or 120 years from the date of creation, whichever is first. For works by more than one author, the copyright expires 70 years after the death of the last surviving author.

These time periods reflect the extensions of the length of copyright protection enacted by Congress in the Copyright Term Extension Act of 1998.[19] Critics challenged this act as overstepping the bounds of Congress's power and violating the constitutional requirement that copyrights endure for only a limited time. In 2003, however, the United States Supreme Court upheld the act in *Eldred v. Ashcroft.*[20] This ruling obviously favored copyright holders by preventing copyrighted works from the 1920s and 1930s from losing protection and falling into the public domain for an additional two decades.

Copyrights can be registered with the U.S. Copyright Office in Washington, D.C. A copyright owner no longer needs to place a © or *Copr.* or *Copyright* on the work, however, to have the work protected against infringement. Chances are that if somebody created it, somebody owns it.

What Is Protected Expression?

Works that are copyrightable include books, records, films, artworks, architectural plans, menus, music videos, product packaging, and computer software. To be protected, a work must be "fixed in a durable medium" from which it can be perceived, reproduced, or communicated. Protection is automatic. Registration is not required.

To obtain protection under the Copyright Act, a work must be original and fall into one of the following categories:

1 Literary works (including newspaper and magazine articles, computer and training manuals, catalogues, brochures, and print advertisements).
2 Musical works and accompanying words (including advertising jingles).
3 Dramatic works and accompanying music.
4 Pantomimes and choreographic works (including ballets and other forms of dance).
5 Pictorial, graphic, and sculptural works (including cartoons, maps, posters, statues, and even stuffed animals).
6 Motion pictures and other audiovisual works (including multimedia works).
7 Sound recordings.
8 Architectural works.

---

18. 17 U.S.C. Sections 101 *et seq.*
19. 17 U.S.C.A. Section 302.
20. 537 U.S. 186, 123 S.Ct. 769, 154 L.Ed.2d 683 (2003).

COPYRIGHT
The exclusive right of an author or originator of a literary or artistic production to publish, print, or sell that production for a statutory period of time. A copyright has the same monopolistic nature as a patent or trademark, but it differs in that it applies exclusively to works of art, literature, and other works of authorship (including computer programs).

ON THE WEB

For information on copyrights, go to the U.S. Copyright Office at

www.copyright/gov.

BE CAREFUL If a creative work does not fall into a certain category, it might not be copyrighted, but it may be protected by other intellectual property law.

A sign in New York City warns audience members about to attend an improv theatrical performance. Can a live performance, especially one that is improvisational in nature, be copyrighted? (Photo by W. Seltzer/ Creative Commons)

Section 102 Exclusions   Section 102 of the Copyright Act specifically excludes copyright protection for any "idea, procedure, process, system, method of operation, concept, principle, or discovery, regardless of the form in which it is described, explained, illustrated, or embodied." Note that it is not possible to copyright an *idea*. The underlying ideas embodied in a work may be freely used by others. What is copyrightable is the particular way in which an idea is *expressed*. Whenever an idea and an expression are inseparable, the expression cannot be copyrighted. Generally, anything that is not an original expression will not qualify for copyright protection. Facts widely known to the public are not copyrightable. Page numbers are not copyrightable because they follow a sequence known to everyone. Mathematical calculations are not copyrightable.

Compilations of Facts   Unlike ideas, *compilations* of facts are copyrightable. Under Section 103 of the Copyright Act, a compilation is work formed by the collection and assembling of preexisting materials or of data that are selected, coordinated, or arranged in such a way that the resulting work as a whole constitutes an original work of authorship." The key requirement for the copyrightability of a compilation is originality. **■EXAMPLE 5.9** The white pages of a telephone directory do not qualify for copyright protection when the information that makes up the directory (names, addresses, and telephone numbers) is not selected, coordinated, or arranged in an original way.[21] In one case, even the Yellow Pages of a telephone directory did not qualify for copyright protection.[22] ▣

Copyright Infringement

Whenever the form or expression of an idea is copied, an infringement of copyright occurs. The reproduction does not have to be exactly the same as the original, nor does it have to reproduce the original in its entirety. If a substantial part of the original is reproduced, there is copyright infringement.

Damages for Copyright Infringement   Those who infringe copyrights may be liable for damages or criminal penalties. These range from actual damages or statutory damages, imposed at the court's discretion, to criminal proceedings for willful violations. Actual damages are based on the harm caused to the copyright holder by the infringement, while statutory damages, not to exceed $150,000, are provided for under the Copyright Act. In addition, criminal proceedings may result in fines and/or imprisonment.

The "Fair Use" Exception   An exception to liability for copyright infringement is made under the "fair use" doctrine. In certain circumstances, a person or organization can reproduce copyrighted material without paying royalties (fees paid to the copyright holder for the privilege of reproducing the copyrighted material). Section 107 of the Copyright Act provides as follows:

> [T]he fair use of a copyrighted work, including such use by reproduction in copies or phonorecords or by any other means specified by [Section 106 of the Copyright Act,] for purposes such as criticism, comment, news reporting, teaching (including multiple copies for classroom use), scholarship, or research, is not an infringement of copyright. In determining whether the use made of a work in any particular case is a fair use the factors to be considered shall include—
>
> (1) the purpose and character of the use, including whether such use is of a commercial nature or is for nonprofit educational purposes;
> (2) the nature of the copyrighted work;

ON THE WEB

You can find a host of information on copyright law, including the Copyright Act and significant United States Supreme Court cases in the area of copyright law, at

www.law.cornell.edu/supct/cases/copyrt.htm.

---

21. *Feist Publications, Inc. v. Rural Telephone Service Co.*, 499 U.S. 340, 111 S.Ct. 1282, 113 L.Ed.2d 358 (1991).
22. *Bellsouth Advertising & Publishing Corp. v. Donnelley Information Publishing, Inc.*, 999 F.2d 1436 (11th Cir. 1993).

Legal Issues Facing Bloggers and Podcasters

C ompanies increasingly are using blogs (Web logs) and podcasts (essentially audio blogs, sometimes with video clips) internally to encourage communication among employees and externally to communicate with customers. Blogs offer many advantages, not the least of which is that setting up a blog and keeping it current (making "posts") costs next to nothing because so much easy-to-use free software is available. Podcasts, even those including video, require only a little more sophistication. Nonetheless, both blogs and podcasts also carry some legal risks for the companies that sponsor them.

Benefits of Blogs and Podcasts

Internal blogs used by a company's employees can offer a number of benefits. Blogs provide an open communications platform, potentially allowing new ways of coordinating activities among employees. For example, a team of production workers might use a blog to move a new product idea forward: the team starts a blog, one worker posts a proposal, and other team members quickly post comments in response. The blog

can be an excellent way to generate new ideas. Internal blogs also allow for team learning and encourage dialogue. When workers are spread out across the country or around the world, blogging provides a cheap means of communication that does not require sophisticated project management software.

Many companies are also creating external blogs, which are available to clients and customers. External blogs can be used to push products, obtain feedback from customers, and shape the image that the company presents to outsiders. Even some company chief executive officers (CEOs), including the CEOs of McDonald's, Boeing, and Hewlett-Packard, have started blogs.

Potential Legal Risks

Despite their many advantages, blogs and podcasts can also expose a company to a number of legal risks, including the following.

- **Tort Liability** Internal blogs and podcasts can lead to claims of defamation or sexual harassment if an employee posts racist or sexually explicit comments. At the same time, if a company monitors its employees' blogs and podcasts, it may find itself facing claims of invasion of privacy (see Chapter 18 for a discussion of similar issues involving employees' e-mail).

(3) the amount and substantiality of the portion used in relation to the copyrighted work as a whole; and

(4) the effect of the use upon the potential market for or value of the copyrighted work.

Because these guidelines are very broad, the courts determine whether a particular use is fair on a case-by-case basis. Thus, anyone reproducing copyrighted material may be committing a violation. In determining whether a use is fair, courts have often considered the fourth factor to be the most important.

Copyright Protection for Software

In 1980, Congress passed the Computer Software Copyright Act, which amended the Copyright Act of 1976 to include computer programs in the list of creative works protected by federal copyright law. The 1980 statute, which classifies computer programs as "literary works," defines a computer program as a "set of statements or instructions to be used directly or indirectly in a computer in order to bring about a certain result."

Because of the unique nature of computer programs, the courts have had many problems applying and interpreting the 1980 act. Generally, though, the courts have held that copyright protection extends not only to those parts of a computer program that can be read by humans, such as the high-level language of a source code, but also to the binary-language object code of a computer program, which is readable only by the computer.[23]

---

23. See *Stern Electronics, Inc. v. Kaufman*, 669 F.2d 852 (2d Cir. 1982); and *Apple Computer, Inc. v. Franklin Computer Corp.*, 714 F.2d 1240 (3d Cir. 1983).

- **Security of Information** Blogs may also be susceptible to security breaches. If an outsider obtains access to an internal blog, a company's trade secrets could be lost. Outsiders could also potentially gain access to blogs containing financial information.

- **Discovery Issues** As explained in Chapter 3, litigation today frequently involves electronic discovery. This can extend to blog posts and comments as well as to e-mail. Thus, a company should be aware that anything posted on its blogs can be used as evidence during litigation. A company will therefore need to preserve and retain blog postings related to any dispute likely to go to trial.

- **Compliance Issues** Many corporations are regulated by one or more agencies and required to comply with various statutes. Laws that require compliance may also apply to blog postings. For example, the Securities and Exchange Commission (SEC) has regulations establishing the information a company must disclose to potential investors and the public in connection with its stock. A company regulated by the SEC will find that these rules apply to blogs. The same is true for companies regulated under the Sarbanes-Oxley Act, which was discussed in Chapter 2 and will be discussed in Chapter 21.

- **Copyright Infringement** Blogs can also expose a company to charges of copyright infringement. Suppose, for example, that an employee posts a long passage from a magazine article on the company's blog, either internal or external, without the author's permission. Similarly, photos taken from other blogs or Web sites cannot be posted without prior permission. Note, also, that copyright infringement can occur even if the blog was created without any pecuniary (monetary) motivation. Typically, though, a blogger can claim "fair use" if she or he posts a passage from someone else's work along with an electronic link to the complete version.

External blogs carry most of the same risks as internal blogs and others as well. Not only can external blogs lead to charges of invasion of privacy, defamation, or copyright infringement related to what the company and its employees post, but they can also expose the company to liability for what visitors post. If a company's blog allows visitors to post comments and a visitor makes a defamatory statement, the company that created the blog could be held liable for publishing it. Thus, any company considering establishing blogs and podcasts, whether internal or external, should be aware of the risks and take steps to guard against them.

 FOR CRITICAL ANALYSIS *Do individuals who create blogs face the same risks as companies that use blogs? Explain.*

Additionally, such elements as the overall structure, sequence, and organization of a program have been deemed copyrightable.[24] The courts have disagreed as to whether the "look and feel"—the general appearance, command structure, video images, menus, windows, and other screen displays—of computer programs should also be protected by copyright. The courts have tended, however, not to extend copyright protection to look-and-feel aspects of computer programs.

Copyrights in Digital Information

Copyright law is probably the most important form of intellectual property protection on the Internet. This is because much of the material on the Internet consists of works of authorship (including multimedia presentations, software, and database information), which are the traditional focus of copyright law. Copyright law is also important because the nature of the Internet requires that data be "copied" to be transferred online. Copies have traditionally been a significant part of the controversies arising in this area of the law. (See this chapter's *Adapting the Law to the Online Environment* feature for a discussion of how blogs and podcasts can expose a company to legal risks including lawsuits for copyright infringement.)

The Copyright Act of 1976 When Congress drafted the principal U.S. law governing copyrights, the Copyright Act of 1976, cyberspace did not exist for most of us, and the

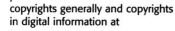

ON THE WEB

The University of Michigan provides information on copyrights generally and copyrights in digital information at www.copyright.umich.edu.

---

24. *Whelan Associates, Inc. v. Jaslow Dental Laboratory, Inc.*, 797 F.2d 1222 (3d Cir. 1986).

primary threat to copyright owners was from persons making unauthorized *tangible* copies of works. Because of the nature of cyberspace, however, one of the early controversies was determining at what point an intangible, electronic "copy" of a work has been made. The courts held that loading a file or program into a computer's random access memory, or RAM, constitutes the making of a "copy" for purposes of copyright law.[25] RAM is a portion of a computer's memory into which a file, for instance, is loaded so that it can be accessed (read or written over). Thus, a copyright is infringed when a party downloads software into RAM without owning the software or otherwise having a right to download it.[26]

Further Developments in Copyright Law   Before 1997, criminal penalties under copyright law could be imposed only if unauthorized copies were exchanged for financial gain. Yet much piracy of copyrighted materials was "altruistic" in nature; unauthorized copies were made and distributed not for financial gain but simply for reasons of generosity—to share the copies with others.

To combat altruistic piracy and for other reasons, Congress passed the No Electronic Theft (NET) Act of 1997. This act extends criminal liability for the piracy of copyrighted materials to persons who exchange unauthorized copies of copyrighted works, such as software, even though they realize no profit from the exchange. The act also imposes penalties on those who make unauthorized electronic copies of books, magazines, movies, or music for *personal* use, thus altering the traditional "fair use" doctrine. The criminal penalties for violating the act are steep; they include fines as high as $250,000 and incarceration for up to five years.

In 1998, Congress passed further legislation to protect copyright holders—the Digital Millennium Copyright Act. Because of its significance in protecting against the piracy of copyrighted materials in the online environment, this act is presented as this chapter's *Landmark in the Law* feature on pages 160 and 161.

MP3 and File-Sharing Technology

Soon after the Internet became popular, a few enterprising programmers created software to compress large data files, particularly those associated with music. The reduced file sizes make transmitting music over the Internet feasible. The most widely known compression and decompression system is MP3, which enables music fans to download songs or entire CDs onto their computers or onto a portable listening device, such as an iPod. The MP3 system also made it possible for music fans to access other music fans' files by engaging in file-sharing via the Internet.

File-sharing via the Internet is accomplished through what is called **peer-to-peer (P2P) networking.** The concept is simple. Rather than going through a central Web server, P2P involves numerous personal computers (PCs) that are connected to the Internet. Files stored on one PC can be accessed by other individuals who are members of the same network. Sometimes this is called a **distributed network.** In other words, parts of the network are distributed all over the country or the world. File-sharing offers an unlimited number of uses for distributed networks. For instance, thousands of researchers allow their home computers' computing power to be simultaneously accessed through file-sharing software so that very large mathematical problems can be solved quickly. Additionally, persons scattered throughout the country or the world can work together on the same project by using file-sharing programs.

PEER-TO-PEER (P2P) NETWORKING
The sharing of resources (such as files, hard drives, and processing styles) among multiple computers without necessarily requiring a central network server.

DISTRIBUTED NETWORK
A network that can be used by persons located (distributed) around the country or the globe to share computer files.

---

25. *MAI Systems Corp. v. Peak Computer, Inc.,* 991 F.2d 511 (9th Cir. 1993).
26. *DSC Communications Corp. v. Pulse Communications, Inc.,* 170 F.3d 1354 (Fed. Cir. 1999).

Sharing Stored Music Files   When file-sharing is used to download others' stored music files, copyright issues arise. Recording artists and their labels stand to lose large amounts of royalties and revenues if relatively few CDs are purchased and then made available on distributed networks, from which everyone can get them for free. The issue of file-sharing infringement has been the subject of an ongoing debate for some time.

■**EXAMPLE 5.10**   In the highly publicized case of *A&M Records, Inc. v. Napster, Inc.*,[27] several firms in the recording industry sued Napster, Inc., the owner of the then-popular Napster Web site. The Napster site provided registered users with free software that enabled them to transfer exact copies of the contents of MP3 files from one computer to another via the Internet. Napster also maintained centralized search indices so that users could locate specific titles or artists' recordings on the computers of other members. The firms argued that Napster should be liable for contributory and vicarious[28] (indirect) copyright infringement because it assisted others in obtaining copies of copyrighted music without the copyright owners' permission. Both the federal district court and the U.S. Court of Appeals for the Ninth Circuit agreed and held Napster liable for violating copyright laws. The court reasoned that Napster was liable for its users' infringement because the technology that Napster had used was centralized and gave it "the ability to locate infringing material listed on its search indices and the right to terminate users' access to the system." ■

After the *Napster* decision, the recording industry filed and won numerous lawsuits against companies that distribute online file-sharing software. The courts held these companies liable based on two theories: contributory infringement, which applies if the company had reason to know about a user's infringement and failed to stop it; and vicarious liability, which exists if the company was able to control the users' activities and stood to benefit financially from their infringement.

The Evolution of File-Sharing Technologies   In the wake of the *Napster* decision, other companies developed technologies that allow P2P network users to share stored music files, without paying a fee, more quickly and efficiently than ever. Software such as Morpheus, KaZaA, and LimeWire, for example, provides users with an interface that is similar to a Web browser.[29] Instead of the company's locating songs for users on other members' computers, the software automatically annotates files with descriptive information so that the music can easily be categorized and cross-referenced (by artist and title, for instance). When a user performs a search, the software is able to locate a list of peers that have the file available for downloading. Also, to expedite the P2P transfer, the software distributes the download task over the entire list of peers simultaneously. By downloading even one file, the user becomes a point of distribution for that file, which is then automatically shared with others on the network.

Because the file-sharing software was decentralized and did not use search indices, the companies had no

Will holding the companies that make file-sharing software legally responsible for the copyright infringement of their end-users stifle innovation and technology, as these demonstrators suggest?
(Beatrice Murch/Creative Commons)

27. 239 F.3d 1004 (9th Cir. 2001).

28. *Vicarious (indirect) liability* exists when one person is subject to liability for another's actions. A common example occurs in the employment context, when an employer is held vicariously liable by third parties for torts committed by employees in the course of their employment.

29. Note that in 2005, KaZaA entered a settlement agreement with four major music companies that had alleged copyright infringement. KaZaA agreed to offer only legitimate, fee-based music downloads in the future.

LANDMARK IN THE LAW   The Digital Millennium Copyright Act of 1998

The United States leads the world in the production of creative products, including books, films, videos, recordings, and software. In fact, as indicated earlier in this chapter, the creative industries are more important to the U.S. economy than the traditional product industries are. Exports of U.S. creative products, for example, surpass those of every other U.S. industry in value. Creative industries are growing at nearly three times the rate of the economy as a whole.

Steps have been taken, both nationally and internationally, to protect ownership rights in intellectual property, including copyrights. In 1996, to curb unauthorized copying of copyrighted materials, the World Intellectual Property Organization (WIPO) enacted a treaty to upgrade global standards of copyright protection, particularly for the Internet.

Implementing the WIPO Treaty   In 1998, Congress implemented the provisions of the WIPO treaty by updating U.S. copyright law. The law—the Digital Millennium Copyright Act of 1998—is a landmark step in the protection of copyright owners and, because of the leading position of the United States in the creative industries, serves as a model for other nations. Among other things, the act established civil and criminal penalties for anyone who circumvents (bypasses, or gets around—through clever maneuvering, for example) encryption software or other technological antipiracy protection. Also prohibited are the manufacture, import, sale, and distribution of devices or services for circumvention.

The act provides for exceptions to fit the needs of libraries, scientists, universities, and others. In general, the law does not restrict the "fair use" of circumvention methods for educational and other noncommercial purposes. For example, circumvention is allowed to test computer security, conduct encryption research, protect personal privacy, and enable parents to monitor their children's use of the Internet. The exceptions are to be reconsidered every three years.

Limiting the Liability of Internet Service Providers   The 1998 act also limited the liability of Internet service providers (ISPs). Under the act, an ISP is not liable for

ability to supervise or control which music (or other media files) their users exchanged. In addition, it was difficult for courts to apply the traditional doctrines of contributory and vicarious liability to these new technologies.

The Supreme Court's *Grokster* Decision In 2005, the United States Supreme Court expanded the liability of file-sharing companies in its decision in *Metro-Goldwyn-Mayer Studios, Inc. v. Grokster, Ltd.*[30] In that case, organizations in the music and film industry (the plaintiffs) sued several companies that distribute file-sharing software used in P2P networks, including Grokster, Ltd., and StreamCast Networks, Inc. (the defendants). The plaintiffs claimed that the companies were contributorily and vicariously liable for the infringement of their end users. The Supreme Court held that "one who distributes a device [software] with the object of promoting its use to infringe the copyright, as shown by clear expression or other affirmative steps taken to foster infringement, is liable for the resulting acts of infringement by third parties."

---

30. 545 U.S. 913, 125 S.Ct. 2764, 162 L.Ed.2d 781 (2005).

any copyright infringement by its customer *unless* the ISP is aware of the subscriber's violation. An ISP may be held liable only if it fails to take action to shut the subscriber down after learning of the violation. A copyright holder has to act promptly, however, by pursuing a claim in court, or the subscriber has the right to be restored to online access.

APPLICATION TO TODAY'S WORLD *The application of the Digital Millennium Copyright Act of 1998 to today's world is fairly self-evident. If Congress had not enacted this legislation, copyright owners would have a far more difficult time obtaining legal redress against those who, without authorization, decrypt and/or copy copyrighted materials. Of course, problems remain, particularly because of the global nature of the Internet. From a practical standpoint, the degree of protection afforded to copyright holders depends on the extent to which other nations that have signed the WIPO treaty actually implement its provisions and agree on the interpretation of terms, such as what constitutes an electronic copy.*

FOR CRITICAL ANALYSIS *Critics of the 1998 act claim that it has not been used as Congress originally envisioned and that it has had the unintended consequences of chilling free speech and scientific research. In one case, for example, a Russian scientist was arrested after speaking at a conference in the United States because he had worked on a software program that enabled owners of Adobe e-books to convert the files to PDF format. The scientist, who was not charged with copyright infringement, was ultimately cleared of any wrongdoing, but the incident has prompted a number of foreign scientists to refuse to attend conferences in the United States. In what other ways might the act chill free speech? Is there any way to amend the act to avoid this potential problem? Explain.*

RELEVANT WEB SITES *To locate information on the Web concerning the Digital Millennium Copyright Act of 1998, go to this text's Web site at academic.cengage.com/ blaw/blt, select "Chapter 5," and click on "URLs for Landmarks."*

Although the Supreme Court did not specify what kind of affirmative steps are necessary to establish liability, it did note that there was ample evidence that the defendants had acted with the intent to cause copyright violations. (Grokster later settled this dispute out of court and stopped distributing its software.) Essentially, this means that file-sharing companies that have taken affirmative steps to promote copyright infringement can be held secondarily liable for millions of infringing acts that their users commit daily. Because the Court did not define exactly what is necessary to impose liability, however, a substantial amount of legal uncertainty remains concerning this issue. Although some file-sharing companies have been shut down, illegal file-sharing—and lawsuits against file-sharing companies and the individuals who use them—has continued in the years since this decision.

In the following case, six recording companies filed a suit against an individual user, charging her with copyright infringement for downloading eight songs without the owners' consent.

CASE 5.3   Sony BMG Entertainment v. Villarreal

United States District Court, Middle District of Georgia, Macon Division, __ F.Supp.2d __ (2007).

FACTS Sony BMG Music Entertainment, UMG Recordings, Inc., Warner Bros. Records, Inc., Virgin Records America, Inc., Capitol Records, Inc., and BMG Music are the copyright owners or licensees of rights to certain sound recordings. In September 2006, these companies filed a suit in a federal district court against Sharon Villarreal, alleging copyright infringement. The plaintiffs complained that Villarreal "has, without the permission or consent of Plaintiffs, used (and continues to use) an online media distribution system to download Plaintiffs' copyrighted recordings, to distribute the copyrighted recordings to the public, and/or to make the copyrighted recordings available for distribution to others." The plaintiffs claimed that Villarreal had downloaded and distributed, or made available for distribution, eight of their recordings, including "Goodbye Earl" by the Dixie Chicks, "I Got a Girl" by Lou Bega, "A Long December" by the Counting Crows, "Black Balloon" by the Goo Goo Dolls, "Like a Virgin" by Madonna, "Steal My Kisses" by Ben Harper, "Another Brick in the Wall, Pt. 2" by Pink Floyd, and "I Might Get Over You" by Kenny Chesney. Villarreal was notified of the complaint but did not respond. The plaintiffs asked the court to enter a default judgment in their favor, to award damages and costs, and to issue an injunction against Villarreal.

ISSUE Were the copyright owners and licensees entitled to a judgment in their favor and the relief that they sought?

DECISION Yes. "Having considered Plaintiffs' well-pleaded allegations in this case, the Court does find a sufficient basis in the Complaint for a judgment to be entered in Plaintiffs' favor for violations of the Copyright Act."

REASON The court recognized that a defendant's failure to respond to a complaint or appear before a court should not be "treated as an absolute confession of the defendant of [her] liability and of the plaintiff's right to recover." In this case, the plaintiffs' complaint was clear, their allegations stated a claim for copyright infringement, "[a]nd, of course, by her default in this case, Defendant has admitted these allegations as true." The court determined that the plaintiffs were entitled to $6,000 in damages under the Copyright Act—the minimum statutory provision of $750 for each of the eight songs infringed—plus $490 for the costs of bringing the suit. Villarreal was also enjoined from "directly or indirectly" infringing on the plaintiffs' rights in their recordings through the use of "the Internet or any online media distribution system" and ordered to destroy all of her copies of the downloaded songs. "Defendant's past and current conduct has and will, unless enjoined, cause Plaintiffs irreparable injury that cannot be fully compensated or measured in money." Thus, "an injunction barring Defendant from infringing upon all of Plaintiffs' copyrighted recordings, and not just those eight recordings listed herein, is appropriate. For the same reasons, * * * the injunction entered in this case should likewise cover works created in the future."

FOR CRITICAL ANALYSIS–Social Consideration
What interest does the public have in upholding copyright law and granting the sort of relief that was awarded in this case? Explain.

TRADE SECRETS

TRADE SECRETS
Information or processes that give a business an advantage over competitors that do not know the information or processes.

The law of trade secrets protects some business processes and information that are not or cannot be patented, copyrighted, or trademarked against appropriation by a competitor. **Trade secrets** include customer lists, plans, research and development, pricing information, marketing techniques, production methods, and generally anything that makes an individual company unique and that would have value to a competitor.

Unlike copyright and trademark protection, protection of trade secrets extends both to ideas and to their expression. (For this reason, and because a trade secret involves no registration or filing requirements, trade secret protection may be well suited for software.) Of course, the secret formula, method, or other information must be disclosed to some persons, particularly to key employees. Businesses generally attempt to protect their trade secrets by having all employees who use the process or information agree in their contracts, or in confidentiality agreements, never to divulge it. See the *Application* feature at the end of this chapter for more advice on how a business can protect its trade secrets.

State and Federal Law on Trade Secrets

Under Section 757 of the *Restatement of Torts*, those who disclose or use another's trade secret, without authorization, are liable to that other party if (1) they discovered the secret by improper means or (2) their disclosure or use constitutes a breach of a duty owed to the other party. The theft of confidential business data by industrial espionage, as when a business taps into a competitor's computer, is a theft of trade secrets without any contractual violation and is actionable in itself.

Until nearly thirty years ago, virtually all law with respect to trade secrets was common law. In an effort to reduce the unpredictability of the common law in this area, a model act, the Uniform Trade Secrets Act, was presented to the states for adoption in 1979. Parts of this act have been adopted in more than thirty states. Typically, a state that has adopted parts of the act has adopted only those parts that encompass its own existing common law. Additionally, in 1996 Congress passed the Economic Espionage Act, which made the theft of trade secrets a federal crime. We will examine the provisions and significance of this act in Chapter 6, in the context of crimes related to business.

Trade Secrets in Cyberspace

The nature of new computer technology undercuts a business firm's ability to protect its confidential information, including trade secrets.[31] For instance, a dishonest employee could e-mail trade secrets in a company's computer to a competitor or a future employer. If e-mail is not an option, the employee might walk out with the information on a flash pen drive.

ON THE WEB

The Cyberspace Law Institute offers articles and information on such topics as trade secrets at

www.cli.org.

INTERNATIONAL PROTECTION FOR INTELLECTUAL PROPERTY

For many years, the United States has been a party to various international agreements relating to intellectual property rights. For example, the Paris Convention of 1883, to which about 169 countries are signatory, allows parties in one country to file for patent and trademark protection in any of the other member countries. Other international agreements include the Berne Convention and the Trade-Related Aspects of Intellectual Property Rights, or, more simply, TRIPS agreement. For a discussion of a treaty that allows a company to register its trademark in foreign nations with a single application, see this chapter's *Beyond Our Borders* feature on the next page.

ON THE WEB

The Web site of the American Society of International Law provides the texts of the Berne Convention and other international treaties, as well as other information and resources on international intellectual property law, at

www.asil.org/resource/index.htm.

The Berne Convention

Under the Berne Convention of 1886, an international copyright agreement, if a U.S. citizen writes a book, every country that has signed the convention must recognize the U.S. author's copyright in the book. Also, if a citizen of a country that has not signed the convention first publishes a book in one of the 162 countries that have signed, all other countries that have signed the convention must recognize that author's copyright. Copyright notice is not needed to gain protection under the Berne Convention for works published after March 1, 1989.

---

31. Note that the courts have even found that customers' e-mail addresses may constitute trade secrets. See *T-N-T Motorsports, Inc. v. Hennessey Motorsports, Inc.*, 965 S.W.2d 18 (Tex.App.—Houston [1 Dist.] 1998); rehearing overruled (1998); petition dismissed (1998).

BEYOND OUR BORDERS **The Madrid Protocol**

In the past, one of the difficulties in protecting U.S. trademarks internationally was that it was time consuming and expensive to apply for trademark registration in foreign countries. The filing fees and procedures for trademark registration vary significantly among individual countries. The Madrid Protocol, however, which President George W. Bush signed into law in the fall of 2003, may help to resolve these problems. The Madrid Protocol is an international treaty that has been signed by sixty-eight countries. Under its provisions, a U.S. company wishing to register its trademark abroad can submit a single application and designate other member countries in which it would like to register the mark. The treaty is designed to reduce the costs of obtaining international trademark protection by more than 60 percent, according to proponents.

Although the Madrid Protocol may simplify and reduce the cost of trademark registration in foreign nations, it remains to be seen whether it will provide significant benefits to trademark owners. Even with an easier registration process, the issue of whether member countries will enforce the law and protect the mark still remains.

FOR CRITICAL ANALYSIS *What are some of the pros and cons of having an international standard for trademark protection?*

Despite the Chinese government's periodic crackdowns, imitation designer goods are openly sold at the Xiangyang Fashion Market in Shanghai. What agreement has been the most significant in the effort to protect intellectual property rights internationally? (Emily Walker/ Creative Commons)

This convention and other international agreements have given some protection to intellectual property on a worldwide level. None of them, however, has been as significant and far reaching in scope as the agreement discussed next.

The TRIPS Agreement

Representatives from more than one hundred nations signed the TRIPS agreement in 1994. The agreement established, for the first time, standards for the international protection of intellectual property rights, including patents, trademarks, and copyrights for movies, computer programs, books, and music. The TRIPS agreement provides that each member country must include in its domestic laws broad intellectual property rights and effective remedies (including civil and criminal penalties) for violations of those rights.

Generally, the TRIPS agreement forbids member nations from discriminating against foreign owners of intellectual property rights (in the administration, regulation, or adjudication of such rights). In other words, a member nation cannot give its own nationals (citizens) favorable treatment without offering the same treatment to nationals of all member countries. For instance, if a U.S. software manufacturer brings a suit for the infringement of intellectual property rights under a member nation's national laws, the U.S. manufacturer is entitled to receive the same treatment as a domestic manufacturer. Each member nation must also ensure that legal procedures are available for parties who wish to bring actions for infringement of intellectual property rights. Additionally, a related document established a mechanism for settling disputes among member nations.

Particular provisions of the TRIPS agreement relate to patent, trademark, and copyright protection for intellectual property. The agreement specifically provides copyright protection for computer programs by stating that compilations of data, databases, or other materials are "intellectual creations" and that they are to be protected as copyrightable works. Other provisions relate to trade secrets and the rental of computer programs and cinematographic works.

REVIEWING Intellectual Property and Internet Law

Two computer science majors, Trent and Xavier, have an idea for a new video game, which they propose to call "Hallowed." They form a business and begin developing their idea. Several months later, Trent and Xavier run into a problem with their design and consult with a friend, Brad, who is an expert in creating computer source codes. After the software is completed but before Hallowed is marketed, a video game called Halo 2 is released for both the Xbox and Game Cube systems. Halo 2 uses source codes similar to those of Hallowed and imitates Hallowed's overall look and feel, although not all the features are alike. Using the information presented in the chapter, answer the following questions.

1 Would the name "Hallowed" receive protection as a trademark or as trade dress?

2 If Trent and Xavier had obtained a business process patent on Hallowed, would the release of Halo 2 infringe on their patent? Why or why not?

3 Based only on the facts described above, could Trent and Xavier sue the makers of Halo 2 for copyright infringement? Why or why not?

4 Suppose that Trent and Xavier discover that Brad took the idea of Hallowed and sold it to the company that produced Halo 2. Which type of intellectual property issue does this raise?

APPLICATION How Can You Protect Your Trade Secrets?*

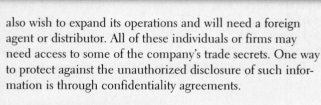

Most successful businesses have trade secrets. The law protects trade secrets indefinitely, provided that the information is not generally known, is kept secret, and has commercial value. Sometimes, of course, a business needs to disclose secret information to a party in the course of conducting business. For example, a company may need to hire a consultant to revamp a computer system, an engineer to design a manufacturing system, or a marketing firm to implement a sales program. In addition, the company may also wish to expand its operations and will need a foreign agent or distributor. All of these individuals or firms may need access to some of the company's trade secrets. One way to protect against the unauthorized disclosure of such information is through confidentiality agreements.

Confidentiality Agreements

In a confidentiality agreement, one party promises not to divulge information about the other party to anyone else or to use the other party's confidential information for his or her own benefit. Confidentiality agreements are often included in licensing and employment contracts, but they can also be

* This Application *is not meant to substitute for the services of an attorney who is licensed to practice law in your state.*

(Continued)

separate contracts. The key is to make sure that the agreement adequately protects the trade secrets and applies to any related transactions between the parties. For instance, if you execute a separate confidentiality agreement with a marketing firm, you need to make sure that it refers to any other contracts you have made with that firm prior to the confidentiality agreement. Also, subsequent contracts with the firm should either refer back to the confidentiality agreement or include a new confidentiality provision.

Defining the Scope of the Agreement

Confidentiality agreements must be reasonable. Businesspersons should consider what information needs to be protected and for how long. Make certain to define what you mean by *confidential information* in the agreement. Do you want to protect just your customer list or all financial, technical, and other business information? Think ahead, cover the bases, and be specific.

The duration of the agreement usually depends on the nature of the information. Very important secret information should remain confidential for a longer time than less important secrets. Sometimes, as with an advertising campaign, the time period for confidentiality may be self-evident (if the cam-

paign ends in six months, for example). Tailor the agreement to your needs as much as possible. If the party to whom you are disclosing information will no longer need the information after a certain date—such as when the project is completed—include a provision requiring the return of confidential information after that date. This will alleviate concerns that your confidential trade secrets might later fall into the hands of a stranger.

CHECKLIST FOR THE OWNER OF TRADE SECRETS

1 Determine what your trade secrets are and who may need access to them.
2 Make sure that confidentiality agreements define, in an all-inclusive manner, what information should be considered confidential.
3 Specify a time period that is reasonable under the circumstances.
4 Identify the agreements to which the confidentiality provisions apply.
5 Require that the confidential materials be returned to you after the project ends.

KEY TERMS

certification mark 148
collective mark 148
copyright 154
cyber mark 149
cybersquatting 149
distributed network 158

domain name 149
intellectual property 142
license 150
patent 151
peer-to-peer (P2P)
    networking 158

service mark 148
trade dress 148
trade name 148
trade secret 162
trademark 143

CHAPTER SUMMARY Intellectual Property and Internet Law

Trademarks and Related Property
(See pages 143–149.)

1. A *trademark* is a distinctive mark, motto, device, or emblem that a manufacturer stamps, prints, or otherwise affixes to the goods it produces so that they may be identified on the market and their origin vouched for.

2. The major federal statutes protecting trademarks and related property are the Lanham Act of 1946 and the Federal Trademark Dilution Act of 1995. Generally, to be protected, a trademark must be sufficiently distinctive from all competing trademarks.

3. *Trademark infringement* occurs when one uses a mark that is the same as, or confusingly similar to, the protected trademark, service mark, trade name, or trade dress of another without permission when marketing goods or services.

CHAPTER SUMMARY　Intellectual Property and Internet Law–Continued

Cyber Marks (See pages 149–151.)	A *cyber mark* is a trademark in cyberspace. Trademark infringement in cyberspace occurs when one person uses, in a domain name or in meta tags, a name that is the same as, or confusingly similar to, the protected mark of another.
Patents (See pages 151–154.)	1. A *patent* is a grant from the government that gives an inventor the exclusive right to make, use, and sell an invention for a period of twenty years (fourteen years for a design patent) from the date of filing the application for a patent. To be patentable, an invention (or a discovery, process, or design) must be genuine, novel, useful, and not obvious in light of current technology. Computer software may be patented. 2. Almost anything is patentable, except (1) the laws of nature, (2) natural phenomena, and (3) abstract ideas (including algorithms). 3. *Patent infringement* occurs when one uses or sells another's patented design, product, or process without the patent owner's permission. The patent holder can sue the infringer in federal court and request an injunction, but must prove irreparable injury to obtain a permanent injunction against the infringer. The patent holder can also request damages and attorneys' fees; if the infringement was willful, the court can grant treble damages.
Copyrights (See pages 154–162.)	1. A *copyright* is an intangible property right granted by federal statute to the author or originator of certain literary or artistic productions. Computer software may be copyrighted. 2. *Copyright infringement* occurs whenever the form or expression of an idea is copied without the permission of the copyright holder. An exception applies if the copying is deemed a "fair use." 3. Copyrights are governed by the Copyright Act of 1976, as amended. To protect copyrights in digital information, Congress passed the No Electronic Theft Act of 1997 and the Digital Millennium Copyright Act of 1998. 4. Technology that allows users to share files via the Internet on distributed networks often raises copyright infringement issues. 5. The United States Supreme Court has ruled that companies that provide file-sharing software to users can be held liable for contributory and vicarious copyright liability if they take affirmative steps to promote copyright infringement.
Trade Secrets (See pages 162–163.)	*Trade secrets* include customer lists, plans, research and development, and pricing information, for example. Trade secrets are protected under the common law and, in some states, under statutory law against misappropriation by competitors. The Economic Espionage Act of 1996 made the theft of trade secrets a federal crime (see Chapter 6).
International Protection for Intellectual Property (See pages 163–165.)	Various international agreements provide international protection for intellectual property. A landmark agreement is the 1994 agreement on Trade-Related Aspects of Intellectual Property Rights (TRIPS), which provides for enforcement procedures in all countries signatory to the agreement.

FOR REVIEW

Answers for the even-numbered questions in this **For Review** *section can be found in Appendix E at the end of this text.*

1 What is intellectual property?

2 Why are trademarks and patents protected by the law?

3 What laws protect authors' rights in the works they generate?

4 What are trade secrets, and what laws offer protection for this form of intellectual property?

5 What steps have been taken to protect intellectual property rights in today's digital age?

■

QUESTIONS AND CASE PROBLEMS

 **HYPOTHETICAL SCENARIOS**

5.1 Patent Infringement. John and Andrew Doney invented a hard-bearing device for balancing rotors. Although they registered their invention with the U.S. Patent and Trademark Office, it was never used as an automobile wheel balancer. Some time later, Exetron Corp. produced an automobile wheel balancer that used a hard-bearing device with a support plate similar to that of the Doneys. Given that the Doneys had not used their device for automobile wheel balancing, does Exetron's use of a similar hard-bearing device infringe on the Doneys' patent?

5.2 Hypothetical Question with Sample Answer. In which of the following situations would a court likely hold Maruta liable for copyright infringement?

1 At the library, Maruta photocopies ten pages from a scholarly journal relating to a topic on which she is writing a term paper.

2 Maruta makes leather handbags and sells them in her small leather shop. She advertises her handbags as "Vutton handbags," hoping that customers might mistakenly assume that they were made by Vuitton, the well-known maker of high-quality luggage and handbags.

3 Maruta owns a video store. She purchases one copy of several popular movie DVDs from various distributors. Then, using blank DVDs, she burns copies of the movies to rent or sell to her customers.

4 Maruta teaches Latin American history at a small university. She has a videocassette recorder and frequently tapes television programs relating to Latin America. She then takes the videos to her classroom so that her students can watch them.

 **For a sample answer to Question 5.2, go to Appendix F at the end of this text.**

■

CASE PROBLEMS

5.3 Trademark Infringement. Elvis Presley Enterprises, Inc. (EPE), owns all of the trademarks of the Elvis Presley estate. None of these marks is registered for use in the restaurant business. Barry Capece registered "The Velvet Elvis" as a service mark for a restaurant and tavern with the U.S. Patent and Trademark Office. Capece opened a nightclub called "The Velvet Elvis" with a menu, decor, advertising, and promotional events that evoked Elvis Presley and his music. EPE filed a suit in a federal district court against Capece and others, claiming, among other things, that "The Velvet Elvis" service mark infringed on EPE's trademarks. During the trial, witnesses testified that they thought the bar was associated with Elvis Presley. Should Capece be ordered to stop using "The Velvet Elvis" mark? Why or why not? [*Elvis Presley Enterprises, Inc. v. Capece*, 141 F.3d 188 (5th Cir. 1998)]

5.4 Trademark Infringement. A&H Sportswear, Inc., a swimsuit maker, obtained a trademark for its MIRACLESUIT in 1992. The MIRACLESUIT design makes the wearer appear slimmer. The MIRACLESUIT was widely advertised and discussed in the media. The MIRACLESUIT was also sold for a brief time in the Victoria's Secret (VS) catalogue, which is published by Victoria's Secret Catalogue, Inc. In 1993, Victoria's Secret Stores, Inc., began selling a cleavage-enhancing bra, which was named THE MIRACLE BRA and for which a trademark was obtained. The next year, THE MIRACLE BRA swimwear debuted in the VS catalogue and stores. A&H filed a suit in a federal district court against VS Stores and VS Catalogue, alleging, in part, that the miracle bra mark, when applied to swimwear, infringed on the miraclesuit mark. A&H argued that there was a "possibility of confusion" between the marks. The VS entities contended that the appropriate standard was "likelihood of confusion" and that, in this case, there was no likelihood of confusion. In whose favor will the court rule, and why? [*A&H Sportswear, Inc. v. Victoria's Secret Stores, Inc.*, 166 F.3d 197 (3d Cir. 1999)]

5.5 Patent Infringement. As a cattle rancher in Nebraska, Gerald Gohl used handheld searchlights to find and help calving animals (animals giving birth) in harsh blizzard conditions. Gohl thought that it would be more helpful to have a portable searchlight mounted on the outside of a vehicle and remotely controlled. He and Al Gebhardt developed and patented practical applications of this idea—the Golight and the wireless, remote-controlled Radio Ray, which could rotate 360 degrees—and formed Golight, Inc., to make and market these products. In 1997, Wal-Mart Stores, Inc., began selling a portable, wireless, remote-controlled searchlight that was identical to the Radio Ray except for a stop piece that prevented the light from rotating more than 351 degrees. Golight sent Wal-Mart a letter, claiming that its device infringed Golight's patent. Wal-Mart sold its remaining inventory of the devices and stopped carrying the product. Golight filed a suit in a federal district court against Wal-Mart, alleging patent infringement. How should the court rule? Explain. [*Golight, Inc. v. Wal-Mart Stores, Inc.*, 355 F.3d 1327 (Fed. Cir. 2004)]

5.6 Case Problem with Sample Answer. Gateway, Inc., sells computers, computer products, computer peripherals, and computer accessories throughout the world. By 1988, Gateway had begun its first national advertising campaign using black-and-white cows and black-and-white cow spots. By 1991, black-and-white cows and spots had become Gateway's symbol. The next year, Gateway registered a black-and-white cow-spots design in association with computers and computer peripherals as its trademark. Companion Products, Inc. (CPI), sells stuffed animals trademarked as "Stretch Pets." Stretch Pets have an animal's head and an elastic body that can wrap around the edges of computer monitors, computer cases, or televisions. CPI produces sixteen Stretch Pets, including a polar bear, a moose, several dogs, and a penguin. One of CPI's top-selling products is a black-and-white cow that CPI identifies as "Cody Cow," which was first sold in 1999. Gateway filed a suit in a federal district court against CPI, alleging trade dress infringement and related claims. What is "trade dress"? What is the major factor in cases involving trade dress infringement? Does that factor exist in this case? Explain. [*Gateway, Inc. v. Companion Products, Inc.*, 384 F.3d 503 (8th Cir. 2004)]

After you have answered Problem 5.6, compare your answer with the sample answer given on the Web site that accompanies this text. Go to academic.cengage.com/blaw/blt, select "Chapter 5," and click on "Case Problem with Sample Answer."

5.7 Trade Secrets. Briefing.com offers Internet-based analyses of investment opportunities to investors. Richard Green is the company's president. One of Briefing.com's competitors is StreetAccount, LLC (limited liability company), whose owners include Gregory Jones and Cynthia Dietzmann. Jones worked for Briefing.com for six years until he quit in March 2003, and he was a member of its board of directors until April 2003. Dietzmann worked for Briefing.com for seven years until she quit in March 2003. As Briefing.com employees, Jones and Dietzmann had access to confidential business data. For instance, Dietzmann developed a list of contacts through which Briefing.com obtained market information to display online. When Dietzmann quit, however, she did not return all of the contact information to the company. Briefing.com and Green filed a suit in a federal district court against Jones, Dietzmann, and StreetAccount, alleging that they appropriated these data and other "trade secrets" to form a competing business. What are trade secrets? Why are they protected? Under what circumstances is a party liable at common law for their appropriation? How should these principles apply in this case? [*Briefing.com v. Jones*, 2006 WY 16, 126 P.3d 928 (2006)]

5.8 Trademarks. In 1969, Jack Masquelier, a professor of pharmacology, discovered a chemical antioxidant made from the bark of a French pine tree. The substance supposedly assists in nutritional distribution and blood circulation. Horphag Research, Ltd., began to sell the product under the name Pycnogenol, which Horphag registered as a trademark in 1993. Pycnogenol became one of the fifteen best-selling herbal supplements in the United States. In 1999, through the Web site **healthierlife.com**, Larry Garcia began to sell Masquelier's Original OPCs, a supplement derived from grape pits. Claiming that this product was the "true Pycnogenol," Garcia used the mark as a meta tag and a generic term, attributing the results of research on Horphag's product to Masquelier's and altering quotes in scientific literature to substitute the name of Masquelier's product for Horphag's. Customers contacted Horphag, after buying Garcia's product, to learn that it was not Horphag's product. Others called Horphag to ask whether Garcia "was selling . . . real Pycnogenol." Horphag filed a suit in a federal district court against Garcia, alleging, in part, that he was diluting Horphag's mark. What is trademark dilution? Did it occur here? Explain. [*Horphag Research, Ltd. v. Garcia*, 475 F.3d 1029 (9th Cir. 2007)]

5.9 A Question of Ethics. *Custom Copies, Inc., in Gainesville, Florida, is a copy shop, reproducing and distributing, for profit, on request, material published and owned by others. One of the copy shop's primary activities is the preparation and sale of coursepacks, which contain compilations of readings for college courses. For a particular coursepack, a teacher selects the readings and delivers a syllabus to the copy shop, which obtains the materials from a library and copies them, and then binds and sells the copies. Blackwell Publishing, Inc., in Malden, Massachusetts, publishes books and journals in medicine and other fields and owns the copyrights to these publications. Blackwell and others filed a suit in a federal district court against Custom Copies, alleging copyright infringement for its "routine and systematic reproduction of materials from plaintiffs' publications, without seeking permission," to compile coursepacks for classes at the University of Florida. The plaintiffs asked the court to issue an injunction and award them damages, as well as the profit from the* *infringement. The defendant filed a motion to dismiss the complaint.* [*Blackwell Publishing, Inc. v. Custom Copies, Inc.,* __ *F.Supp.2d* __ *(N.D. Fla. 2007)*]

1 Custom Copies argued in part that it did not "distribute" the coursepacks. Does a copy shop violate copyright law if it only copies materials for coursepacks? Does the copying

fall under the "fair use" exception? Should the court grant the defendants' motion? Why or why not?

2 What is the potential impact if copies of a book or journal are created and sold without the permission of, and the payment of royalties or a fee to, the copyright owner? Explain.

CRITICAL THINKING AND WRITING ASSIGNMENTS

5.10 Critical Legal Thinking. In the United States, patent protection is granted to the first person to invent a given product or process, even though another person may be the first to file for a patent on the same product or process. What are the advantages of this patenting procedure? Can you think of any disadvantages? Explain.

5.11 Critical Thinking and Writing Assignment for Business. Delta Computers, Inc., makes computer-related products under the brand name "Delta," which the company registers as a trademark. Without Delta's permission, E-Product Corp. embeds the Delta mark in E-Product's Web site, in black type on a blue background. This tag causes the E-Product site to be returned at the top of the list of results on a search engine query for "Delta." Does E-Product's use of the Delta mark as a meta tag without Delta's permission constitute trademark infringement? Explain.

5.12 **Video Question.** Go to this text's Web site at **academic. cengage.com/blaw/blt** and select "Chapter 5." Click on "Video Questions" and view the video titled *The Jerk*. Then answer the following questions.

1 In the video, Navin (Steve Martin) creates a special handle for Fox's (Bill Macy's) glasses. Can Navin obtain a patent or a copyright protecting his invention? Explain your answer.

2 Suppose that after Navin legally protects his idea, Fox steals it and decides to develop it for himself, without Navin's permission. Has Fox committed infringement? If so, what kind: trademark, patent, or copyright?

3 Suppose that after Navin legally protects his idea, he realizes he doesn't have the funds to mass-produce the special handle. Navin therefore agrees to allow Fox to manufacture the product. Has Navin granted Fox a license? Explain.

4 Assume that Navin is able to manufacture his invention. What might Navin do to ensure that his product is identifiable and can be distinguished from other products on the market?

ONLINE ACTIVITIES

PRACTICAL INTERNET EXERCISES

Go to this text's Web site at **academic.cengage.com/blaw/blt**, select "Chapter 5," and click on "Practical Internet Exercises." There you will find the following Internet research exercises that you can perform to learn more about the topics covered in this chapter.

PRACTICAL INTERNET EXERCISE 5–1 LEGAL PERSPECTIVE—Unwarranted Legal Threats

PRACTICAL INTERNET EXERCISE 5–2 TECHNOLOGICAL PERSPECTIVE—File-Sharing

PRACTICAL INTERNET EXERCISE 5–3 MANAGEMENT PERSPECTIVE—Protecting Intellectual Property across Borders

BEFORE THE TEST

Go to this text's Web site at **academic.cengage.com/blaw/blt**, select "Chapter 5," and click on "Interactive Quizzes." You will find a number of interactive questions relating to this chapter.

CHAPTER 6
Criminal Law and Cyber Crimes

LEARNING OBJECTIVES

AFTER READING THIS CHAPTER, YOU SHOULD BE ABLE TO ANSWER THE FOLLOWING QUESTIONS:

1 What two elements must exist before a person can be held liable for a crime? Can a corporation commit crimes?

2 What are five broad categories of crimes? What is white-collar crime?

3 What defenses might be raised by criminal defendants to avoid liability for criminal acts?

4 What constitutional safeguards exist to protect persons accused of crimes? What are the major procedural steps in the criminal process?

5 What is cyber crime? What laws apply to crimes committed in cyberspace?

> **"**No state shall . . . deprive any person of life, liberty, or property without due process of law, nor deny to any person within its jurisdiction the equal protection of the laws.**"**
>
> Fourteenth Amendment to the U.S. Constitution, July 28, 1868

Various sanctions are used to bring about a society in which individuals engaging in business can compete and flourish. These sanctions include damages for various types of tortious conduct (as discussed in Chapter 4), damages for breach of contract (to be discussed in Chapter 9), and the equitable remedies (as discussed in Chapter 1). Additional sanctions are imposed under criminal law. Many statutes regulating business provide for criminal as well as civil sanctions. Therefore, criminal law joins civil law as an important element in the legal environment of business.

In this chapter, following a brief summary of the major differences between criminal and civil law, we look at how crimes are classified and what elements must be present for criminal liability to exist. We then examine various categories of crimes, the defenses that can be raised to avoid liability for criminal actions, and criminal procedural law. Criminal procedural law attempts to ensure that a criminal defendant's right to "due process of law" is enforced. This right is guaranteed by the Fourteenth Amendment to the U.S. Constitution, as stated in the chapter-opening quotation.

Since the advent of computer networks and, more recently, the Internet, new types of crimes or new variations of traditional crimes have been committed in cyberspace. For that reason, they are often referred to as *cyber crimes*. Generally, cyber crime refers more to the way particular crimes are committed than to a new category of crimes. We devote the concluding pages of this chapter to a discussion of this increasingly significant area of criminal activity.

CIVIL LAW AND CRIMINAL LAW

Remember from Chapter 1 that *civil law* spells out the duties that exist between persons or between persons and their governments, excluding the duty not to commit crimes. Contract law, for example, is part of civil law. The whole body of tort law, which deals with the infringement by one person on the legally recognized rights of another, is also an area of civil law.

Criminal law, in contrast, has to do with crime. A **crime** can be defined as a wrong against society proclaimed in a statute and, if committed, punishable by society through fines and/or imprisonment—and, in some cases, death. As mentioned in Chapter 1, because crimes are *offenses against society as a whole*, they are prosecuted by a public official, such as a district attorney (D.A.), not by victims. Victims often report the crime to the police, but it is ultimately the D.A.'s office that decides whether to file criminal charges and to what extent to pursue the prosecution or carry out additional investigation.

CRIME
A wrong against society proclaimed in a statute and, if committed, punishable by society through fines and/or imprisonment—and, in some cases, death.

Key Differences between Civil Law and Criminal Law

Because the state has extensive resources at its disposal when prosecuting criminal cases, there are numerous procedural safeguards to protect the rights of defendants. We look here at one of these safeguards—the higher burden of proof that applies in a criminal case—as well as the harsher sanctions for criminal acts as compared to civil wrongs. Exhibit 6–1 summarizes these and other key differences between civil law and criminal law.

Burden of Proof In a civil case, the plaintiff usually must prove his or her case by a *preponderance of the evidence*. Under this standard, the plaintiff must convince the court that, based on the evidence presented by both parties, it is more likely than not that the plaintiff's allegation is true.

In a criminal case, in contrast, the state must prove its case **beyond a reasonable doubt.** If the jury views the evidence in the case as reasonably permitting either a guilty or a not guilty verdict, then the jury's verdict must be *not* guilty. In other words, the government (prosecutor) must prove beyond a reasonable doubt that the defendant has committed every essential element of the offense with which she or he is charged. If the jurors are not convinced of the defendant's guilt beyond a reasonable doubt, they must find the defendant not guilty. Note also that in a criminal case, the jury's verdict normally must be unanimous—agreed to by all members of the jury—to convict the defendant. (In a civil trial by jury, in contrast, typically only three-fourths of the jurors need to agree.)

The higher burden of proof in criminal cases reflects a fundamental social value—the belief that it is worse to convict an innocent individual than to let a guilty person go free. We will look at other safeguards later in the chapter, in the context of criminal procedure.

BEYOND A REASONABLE DOUBT
The standard of proof used in criminal cases. If there is any reasonable doubt that a criminal defendant committed the crime with which she or he has been charged, then the verdict must be "not guilty."

EXHIBIT 6–1	Key Differences between Civil Law and Criminal Law	
ISSUE	**CIVIL LAW**	**CRIMINAL LAW**
Party who brings suit	Person who suffered harm	The state
Wrongful act	Causing harm to a person or to a person's property	Violating a statute that prohibits some type of activity
Burden of proof	Preponderance of the evidence	Beyond a reasonable doubt
Verdict	Three-fourths majority (typically)	Unanimous
Remedy	Damages to compensate for the harm or a decree to achieve an equitable result	Punishment (fine, imprisonment, or death)

Criminal Sanctions   The sanctions imposed on criminal wrongdoers are also harsher than those that are applied in civil cases. Remember from Chapter 4 that the purpose of tort law is to allow persons harmed by the wrongful acts of others to obtain compensation from the wrongdoer rather than to punish the wrongdoer. In contrast, criminal sanctions are designed to punish those who commit crimes and to deter others from committing similar acts in the future. Criminal sanctions include fines as well as the much harsher penalty of the loss of one's liberty by incarceration in a jail or prison. The harshest criminal sanction is, of course, the death penalty.

Civil Liability for Criminal Acts

Some torts, such as assault and battery, provide a basis for a criminal prosecution as well as a tort action.   ◼**EXAMPLE 6.1** Joe is walking down the street, minding his own business, when a person suddenly attacks him. In the ensuing struggle, the attacker stabs Joe several times, seriously injuring him. A police officer restrains and arrests the wrongdoer. In this situation, the attacker may be subject both to criminal prosecution by the state and to a tort lawsuit brought by Joe. ◼ Exhibit 6–2 illustrates how the same act can result in both a civil/tort action and a criminal action against the wrongdoer.

CRIMINAL LIABILITY

Two elements must exist simultaneously for a person to be convicted of a crime: (1) the performance of a prohibited act and (2) a specified state of mind or intent on the part of the actor. Additionally, to establish criminal liability, there must be a *concurrence* between the act and the intent. In other words, these two elements must occur together.

EXHIBIT 6–2   Civil/Tort Lawsuit and Criminal Prosecution for the Same Act

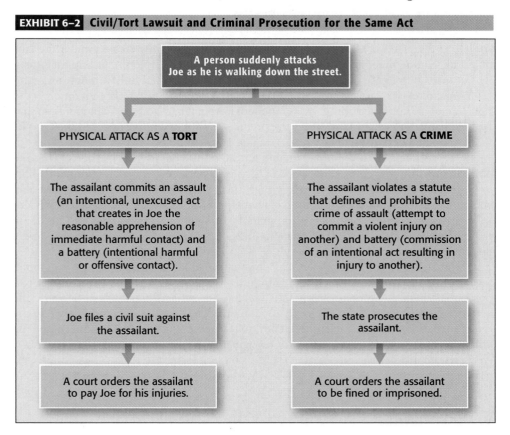

ACTUS REUS
A guilty (prohibited) act. The commission of a prohibited act is one of the two essential elements required for criminal liability, the other element being the intent to commit a crime.

MENS REA
Mental state, or intent. A wrongful mental state is as necessary as a wrongful act to establish criminal liability. What constitutes a mental state varies according to the wrongful action. Thus, for murder, the *mens rea* is the intent to take a life.

Every criminal statute prohibits certain behavior. Most crimes require an act of *commission*—that is, a person must *do* something to be accused of a crime. In criminal law, a prohibited act is referred to as the **actus reus**,[1] or guilty act. In some situations, an act of *omission* can be a crime, but only when a person has a legal duty to perform the omitted act, such as failing to file a tax return. For instance, in 2005 the federal government filed a criminal action against the former winner of the reality TV show *Survivor* for failing to report to the Internal Revenue Service more than $1 million in winnings. The *guilty act* requirement is based on one of the premises of criminal law—that a person is punished for harm done to society. For a crime to exist, the guilty act must cause some harm to a person or to property. Thinking about killing someone or about stealing a car may be wrong, but the thoughts do no harm until they are translated into action. Of course, a person can be punished for attempting murder or robbery, but normally only if he or she took substantial steps toward the criminal objective.

A wrongful mental state (**mens rea**)[2] is generally required to establish criminal liability. What constitutes such a mental state varies according to the wrongful action. For murder, the act is the taking of a life, and the mental state is the intent to take life. For theft, the guilty act is the taking of another person's property, and the mental state involves both the knowledge that the property belongs to another and the intent to deprive the owner of it. A guilty mental state can be attributed to acts of negligence or recklessness as well. *Criminal negligence* involves the mental state in which the defendant takes an unjustified, substantial, and foreseeable risk that results in harm. Under the Model Penal Code, a defendant is negligent even if she or he was not actually aware of the risk but *should have been aware* of it.[3] A defendant is criminally reckless if he or she consciously disregards a substantial and unjustifiable risk.

CORPORATE CRIMINAL LIABILITY

As will be discussed in Chapter 20, a *corporation* is a legal entity created under the laws of a state. At one time, it was thought that a corporation could not incur criminal liability because, although a corporation is a legal person, it can act only through its agents (corporate directors, officers, and employees). Therefore, the corporate entity itself could not "intend" to commit a crime. Under modern criminal law, however, a corporation may be held liable for crimes. Obviously, corporations cannot be imprisoned, but they can be fined or denied certain legal privileges (such as a license).

Today, corporations are normally liable for the crimes committed by their agents and employees within the course and scope of their employment.[4] For such criminal liability to be imposed, the prosecutor normally must show that the corporation could have prevented the act or that there was authorized consent to, or knowledge of, the act by persons in supervisory positions within the corporation. In addition, corporations can be criminally liable for failing to perform specific duties imposed by law (such as duties under environmental laws or securities laws).

Corporate directors and officers are personally liable for the crimes they commit, regardless of whether the crimes were committed for their personal benefit or on the corporation's behalf. Additionally, corporate directors and officers may be held liable for the actions of employees under their supervision. Under what has become known as the *responsible corporate officer doctrine*, a court may impose criminal liability on a corporate officer regardless of whether she or he participated in, directed, or even knew about a given criminal violation.

---

1. Pronounced *ak*-tuhs *ray*-uhs.
2. Pronounced *mehns ray*-uh.
3. Model Penal Code Section 2.02(2)(d).
4. See Model Penal Code Section 2.07.

■**EXAMPLE 6.2** In *United States v. Park,*[5] the chief executive officer of a national super-market chain was held personally liable for sanitation violations in corporate warehouses, in which the food was exposed to contamination by rodents. The United States Supreme Court upheld the imposition of personal liability on the corporate officer not because he intended the crime or even knew about it but because he was in a "responsible relationship" to the corporation and had the power to prevent the violation. ■ Since the *Park* decision, courts have applied the responsible corporate officer doctrine on a number of occasions to hold corporate officers liable for their employees' statutory violations.

TYPES OF CRIMES

The number of acts that are defined as criminal is nearly endless. Federal, state, and local laws provide for the classification and punishment of hundreds of thousands of different criminal acts. Traditionally, though, crimes have been grouped into five broad categories, or types: violent crime (crimes against persons), property crime, public order crime, white-collar crime, and organized crime. Within each of these categories, crimes may also be separated into more than one classification. *Cyber crime*—which consists of crimes committed in cyberspace with the use of computers—is, as mentioned earlier in this chapter, less a category of crime than a new way to commit crime. We will examine cyber crimes later in this chapter.

Violent Crime

Crimes against persons, because they cause others to suffer harm or death, are referred to as *violent crimes.* Murder is a violent crime. So is sexual assault, or rape. Assault and battery, which were discussed in Chapter 4 in the context of tort law, are also classified as violent crimes. **Robbery**—defined as the taking of cash, personal property, or any other article of value from a person by means of force or fear—is another violent crime. Typically, states have more severe penalties for *aggravated robbery*—robbery with the use of a deadly weapon.

Each of these violent crimes is further classified by degree, depending on the circumstances surrounding the criminal act. These circumstances include the intent of the person committing the crime, whether a weapon was used, and (in cases other than murder) the level of pain and suffering experienced by the victim.

Property Crime

The most common type of criminal activity is property crime—crimes in which the goal of the offender is some form of economic gain or the damaging of property. Robbery is a form of property crime, as well as a violent crime, because the offender seeks to gain the property of another. We look here at a number of other crimes that fall within the general category of property crime.

Burglary Traditionally, **burglary** was defined under the common law as breaking and entering the dwelling of another at night with the intent to commit a felony. Originally, the definition was aimed at protecting an individual's home and its occupants. Most state statutes have eliminated some of the requirements found in the common law definition. The time of day at which the breaking and entering occurs, for example, is usually immaterial. State statutes frequently omit the element of breaking, and some states

---
5. 421 U.S. 658, 95 S.Ct. 1903, 44 L.Ed.2d 489 (1975).

ROBBERY
The act of forcefully and unlawfully taking personal property of any value from another. Force or intimidation is usually necessary for an act of theft to be considered robbery.

BURGLARY
The unlawful entry or breaking into a building with the intent to commit a felony. (Some state statutes expand this to include the intent to commit any crime.)

ON THE WEB

Many state criminal codes are now online. To find your state's code, go to **www.findlaw.com** and select "State" under the link to "US Laws: Cases and Codes."

This is a crime scene in Brockton, Massachusetts, a few years ago. The victim, a fifteen-year-old high school student, was shot and killed on a city street. Violent crime is the type of crime about which the public is most concerned, but is it the most common kind of crime committed? (AP Photo/Craig Murray/*The Enterprise*)

do not require that the building be a dwelling. When a deadly weapon is used in a burglary, the person can be charged with *aggravated burglary* and punished more severely.

Larceny Under the common law, the crime of **larceny** involved the unlawful taking and carrying away of someone else's personal property with the intent to permanently deprive the owner of possession. Put simply, larceny is stealing or theft. Whereas robbery involves force or fear, larceny does not. Therefore, picking pockets is larceny. Similarly, taking company products and supplies home for personal use, if one is not authorized to do so, is larceny. (Note that a person who commits larceny generally can also be sued under tort law because the act of taking possession of another's property involves a trespass to personal property.)

Most states have expanded the definition of property that is subject to larceny statutes. Stealing computer programs may constitute larceny even though the "property" consists of magnetic impulses. Stealing computer time can also constitute larceny. So, too, can the theft of natural gas or Internet and television cable service. Trade secrets can be subject to larceny statutes.

The common law distinguished between grand and petit larceny depending on the value of the property taken. Many states have abolished this distinction, but in those that have not, grand larceny (or theft) is a felony and petit larceny (or theft) is a misdemeanor.

Obtaining Goods by False Pretenses It is a criminal act to obtain goods by means of false pretenses, such as buying groceries with a check knowing that one has insufficient funds to cover it or offering to sell someone a digital camera knowing that one does not actually own the camera. Statutes dealing with such illegal activities vary widely from state to state.

Receiving Stolen Goods It is a crime to receive stolen goods. The recipient of such goods need not know the true identity of the owner or the thief. All that is necessary is that the recipient knows or should have known that the goods were stolen, which implies an intent to deprive the owner of those goods.

Arson The willful and malicious burning of a building (and, in some states, personal property) owned by another is the crime of **arson**. At common law, arson traditionally applied only to burning down another person's house. The law was designed to protect human life. Today, arson statutes have been extended to cover the destruction of any building, regardless of ownership, by fire or explosion.

Every state has a special statute that covers the act of burning a building for the purpose of collecting insurance. ■**EXAMPLE 6.3** If Smith owns an insured apartment building that is falling apart and sets fire to it himself or pays someone else to do so, he is guilty not only of arson but also of defrauding the insurer, which is attempted larceny. ■ Of course, the insurer need not pay the claim when insurance fraud is proved.

Forgery The fraudulent making or altering of any writing in a way that changes the legal rights and liabilities of another is **forgery**. ■**EXAMPLE 6.4** Without authorization, Severson signs Bennett's name to the back of a check made out to Bennett and attempts to cash it. Severson has committed the crime of forgery. ■ Forgery also includes changing trademarks, falsifying public records, counterfeiting, and altering a legal document.

Public Order Crime

Historically, societies have always outlawed activities that are considered to be contrary to public values and morals. Today, the most common public order crimes include public drunkenness, prostitution, gambling, and illegal drug use. These crimes are

---

LARCENY
The wrongful taking and carrying away of another person's personal property with the intent to permanently deprive the owner of the property. Some states classify larceny as either grand or petit, depending on the property's value.

ARSON
The intentional burning of another's dwelling. Some statutes have expanded this to include any real property regardless of ownership and the destruction of property by other means—for example, by explosion.

FORGERY
The fraudulent making or altering of any writing in a way that changes the legal rights and liabilities of another.

sometimes referred to as victimless crimes because they normally harm only the offender. From a broader perspective, however, they are deemed detrimental to society as a whole because they may create an environment that gives rise to property and violent crimes.

White-Collar Crime

Crimes that typically occur only in the business context are popularly referred to as **white-collar crimes.** Although there is no official definition of white-collar crime, the term is commonly used to mean an illegal act or series of acts committed by an individual or business entity using some nonviolent means. Usually, this kind of crime is committed in the course of a legitimate occupation. Corporate crimes fall into this category. In addition, certain property crimes, such as larceny and forgery, may also be white-collar crimes if they occur within the business context.

WHITE-COLLAR CRIME
Nonviolent crime committed by individuals or corporations to obtain a personal or business advantage.

Embezzlement When a person who is entrusted with another person's property or money fraudulently appropriates it, **embezzlement** occurs. Typically, embezzlement is carried out by an employee who steals funds. Banks are particularly prone to this problem, but embezzlement can occur in any firm. In a number of businesses, corporate officers or accountants have fraudulently converted funds for their own benefit and then "jimmied" the books to cover up their crime. Embezzlement is not larceny, because the wrongdoer does not physically take the property from the possession of another, and it is not robbery, because force or fear is not used.

EMBEZZLEMENT
The fraudulent appropriation of funds or other property by a person to whom the funds or property has been entrusted.

It does not matter whether the accused takes the funds from the victim or from a third person. If the financial officer of a large corporation pockets checks from third parties that were given to her to deposit into the corporate account, she is embezzling. Frequently, an embezzler takes a relatively small amount at one time but does so repeatedly over a long period. This might be done by underreporting income or deposits and embezzling the remaining amount, for example, or by creating fictitious persons or accounts and writing checks to them from the corporate account.

Practically speaking, an embezzler who returns what has been taken might not be prosecuted because the owner is unwilling to take the time to make a complaint, cooperate with the state's investigative efforts, and appear in court. Also, the owner may not want the crime to become public knowledge. Nevertheless, the intent to return the embezzled property is not a defense to the crime of embezzlement.

To avoid potential embezzlement by corporate officers and employees, businesspersons should limit access to the firm's financial information. In addition, because embezzlement often takes place over a prolonged period of time, businesses should regularly conduct audits to discover and account for any discrepancies in the company's financial records.

PREVENTING LEGAL DISPUTES

Mail and Wire Fraud One of the most potent weapons against white-collar criminals is the Mail Fraud Act of 1990.[6] Under this act, it is a federal crime (mail fraud) to use the mails to defraud the public. Illegal use of the mails must involve (1) mailing or causing someone else to mail a writing—something written, printed, or photocopied—for the purpose of executing a scheme to defraud and (2) a contemplated or an organized scheme to defraud by false pretenses. If, for example, Johnson advertises by mail the sale of a cure

6. 18 U.S.C. Sections 1341–1342.

for cancer that he knows to be fraudulent because it has no medical validity, he can be prosecuted for fraudulent use of the mails.

Federal law also makes it a crime to use wire (for example, the telephone), radio, or television transmissions to defraud.[7] Violators may be fined up to $1,000, imprisoned for up to five years, or both. If the violation affects a financial institution, the violator may be fined up to $1 million, imprisoned for up to thirty years, or both.

The following case involved charges of mail fraud in which funds misrepresented to support charities were acquired through telemarketing. The question was whether the prosecution could offer proof of the telemarketers' commission rate when no one had lied about it.

---

7. 18 U.S.C. Section 1343.

CASE 6.1   United States v. Lyons

United States Court of Appeals, Ninth Circuit, 472 F.3d 1055 (2007).

FACTS In 1994, in California, Gabriel Sanchez formed the First Church of Life (FCL), which had no congregation, services, or place of worship. Sanchez's friend Timothy Lyons formed a fund-raising company called North American Acquisitions (NAA). Through FCL, Sanchez and Lyons set up six charities—AIDS Research Association, Children's Assistance Foundation, Cops and Sheriffs of America, Handicapped Youth Services, U.S. Firefighters, and U.S. Veterans League. NAA hired telemarketers to solicit donations on the charities' behalf. Over time, more than $6 million was raised, of which less than $5,000 was actually spent on charitable causes. The telemarketers kept 80 percent of the donated funds as commissions, and NAA took 10 percent. Most of the rest of the funds went to Sanchez, who spent it on himself. In 2002, Lyons and Sanchez were charged in a federal district court with mail fraud and other crimes. Throughout the trial, the prosecution referred to the high commissions paid to the telemarketers. The defendants were convicted, and each was sentenced to fifteen years' imprisonment. They asked the U.S. Court of Appeals for the Ninth Circuit to overturn their convictions, asserting that the prosecution had used the high cost of fund-raising as evidence of fraud even though the defendants had not lied about the cost.

ISSUE Could evidence of the commissions paid to the telemarketers be introduced when those from whom the funds were solicited were not lied to about the commissions?

DECISION Yes. The U.S. Court of Appeals for the Ninth Circuit upheld the convictions. The defendants' "undoing was not that the commissions were large but that their charitable web

was a scam. Donors were told their contributions went to specific charitable activities when, in reality, almost no money did."

REASON The court acknowledged that a failure to reveal the high cost of fund-raising to potential donors does not establish fraud. "[T]he mere fact that a telemarketer keeps [80 percent] of contributions it solicits cannot be the basis of a fraud conviction, and neither can the fact that a telemarketer fails to volunteer this information to would-be donors." But when "nondisclosure is accompanied by intentionally misleading statements designed to deceive the listener," the high cost of fund-raising may be introduced as evidence of fraud. "[T]he State may vigorously enforce its antifraud laws to prohibit professional fundraisers from obtaining money on false pretenses or by making false statements." Here, in addition to the proof of the telemarketers' commissions, the prosecution offered evidence of Lyons and Sanchez's specific misrepresentations and omissions regarding the defendants' use of the donated funds. All of this "evidence underscored the fact that virtually none of the money that ended up in the bank accounts of the six FCL charities went to any charitable activities at all, let alone the specific charitable activities mentioned in the telemarketers' calls. * * * [A]dmission of evidence regarding the fund-raising costs was essential to understanding the overall scheme and the shell game of the multiple charities."

FOR CRITICAL ANALYSIS—Ethical Consideration
It may have been legal in this case, but was it ethical for the prosecution to repeatedly emphasize the size of the telemarketers' commissions? Why or why not?

Bribery Basically, three types of bribery are considered crimes: bribery of public officials, commercial bribery, and bribery of foreign officials. The attempt to influence a public official to act in a way that serves a private interest is a crime. As an element of this crime, intent must be present and proved. The bribe can be anything the recipient considers to be valuable. Realize that *the crime of bribery occurs when the bribe is offered.* It does not matter whether the person to whom the bribe is offered accepts the bribe or agrees to perform whatever action is desired by the person offering the bribe. *Accepting a bribe* is a separate crime.

Bribing foreign officials to obtain favorable business contracts is a crime. The Foreign Corrupt Practices Act of 1977, which was discussed in Chapter 2, was passed to curb the use of bribery by U.S. businesspersons in securing foreign contracts.

Bankruptcy Fraud Federal bankruptcy law (see Chapter 16) allows individuals and businesses to be relieved of oppressive debt through bankruptcy proceedings. Numerous white-collar crimes may be committed during the many phases of a bankruptcy proceeding. A creditor, for example, may file a false claim against the debtor, which is a crime. Also, a debtor may fraudulently transfer assets to favored parties before or after the petition for bankruptcy is filed. For example, a company-owned automobile may be "sold" at a bargain price to a trusted friend or relative. Closely related to the crime of fraudulent transfer of property is the crime of fraudulent concealment of property, such as hiding gold coins.

The Theft of Trade Secrets As discussed in Chapter 5, trade secrets constitute a form of intellectual property that for many businesses can be extremely valuable. The Economic Espionage Act of 1996[8] made the theft of trade secrets a federal crime. The act also made it a federal crime to buy or possess trade secrets of another person, knowing that the trade secrets were stolen or otherwise acquired without the owner's authorization.

---

8. 18 U.S.C. Sections 1831–1839.

Mister M, an American magician, was featured on a television show during which he revealed how magic tricks are performed. As a result, some magicians in Brazil sued the Brazilian television network that aired the show. The magicians claimed that the network aided Mister M in exposing their trade secrets. They won their case. Would such a lawsuit have been successful in a U.S. court? Why or why not?
(AP Photo/Katia Tamahara)

Violations of the act can result in steep penalties. An individual who violates the act can be imprisoned for up to ten years and fined up to $500,000. If a corporation or other organization violates the act, it can be fined up to $5 million. Additionally, the law provides that any property acquired as a result of the violation, such as airplanes and automobiles, and any property used in the commission of the violation, such as computers and other electronic devices, are subject to criminal *forfeiture*—meaning that the government can take the property. A theft of trade secrets conducted via the Internet, for example, could result in the forfeiture of every computer or other device used in the commission of the crime, as well as any assets gained from the stolen trade secrets.

Insider Trading   An individual who obtains "inside information" about the plans of a publicly listed corporation can often make stock-trading profits by purchasing or selling corporate securities based on the information. *Insider trading* is a violation of securities law and will be considered more fully in Chapter 21. Generally, the rule is that a person who possesses inside information and has a duty not to disclose it to outsiders may not profit from the purchase or sale of securities based on that information until the information is made available to the public.

Organized Crime

As mentioned, white-collar crime takes place within the confines of the legitimate business world. *Organized crime*, in contrast, operates *illegitimately* by, among other things, providing illegal goods and services. For organized crime, the traditional preferred markets are gambling, prostitution, illegal narcotics, and loan sharking (lending at higher than legal interest rates), along with more recent ventures into counterfeiting and credit-card scams.

Money Laundering   The profits from organized crime and illegal activities amount to billions of dollars a year, particularly the profits from illegal drug transactions and, to a lesser extent, from racketeering, prostitution, and gambling. Under federal law, banks, savings and loan associations, and other financial institutions are required to report currency transactions involving more than $10,000. Consequently, those who engage in illegal activities face difficulties in depositing their cash profits from illegal transactions.

As an alternative to simply storing cash from illegal transactions in a safe-deposit box, wrongdoers and racketeers have invented ways to launder "dirty" money to make it "clean." This **money laundering** is done through legitimate businesses.

  ▣EXAMPLE 6.5   Matt, a successful drug dealer, becomes a partner with a restaurateur. Little by little, the restaurant shows increasing profits. As a partner in the restaurant, Matt is able to report the "profits" of the restaurant as legitimate income on which he pays federal and state taxes. He can then spend those funds without worrying that his lifestyle may exceed the level possible with his reported income. ▣

The Racketeer Influenced and Corrupt Organizations Act   In 1970, in an effort to curb the apparently increasing entry of organized crime into the legitimate business world, Congress passed the Racketeer Influenced and Corrupt Organizations Act (RICO).[9] The statute, which was enacted as part of the Organized Crime Control Act, makes it a federal crime to (1) use income obtained from racketeering activity to purchase any interest in an enterprise, (2) acquire or maintain an interest in an enterprise through racketeering activ-

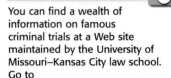

ON THE WEB
You can find a wealth of information on famous criminal trials at a Web site maintained by the University of Missouri–Kansas City law school. Go to

www.law.umkc.edu/faculty/projects/ftrials/ftrials.html.

MONEY LAUNDERING
Falsely reporting income that has been obtained through criminal activity as income obtained through a legitimate business enterprise—in effect, "laundering" the "dirty money."

---

9. 18 U.S.C. Sections 1961–1968.

ity, (3) conduct or participate in the affairs of an enterprise through racketeering activity, or (4) conspire to do any of the preceding activities.

RICO incorporates by reference twenty-six separate types of federal crimes and nine types of state felonies[10] and declares that if a person commits two of these offenses, he or she is guilty of "racketeering activity." Under the criminal provisions of RICO, any individual found guilty is subject to a fine of up to $25,000 per violation, imprisonment for up to twenty years, or both. Additionally, the statute provides that those who violate RICO may be required to forfeit (give up) any assets, in the form of property or cash, that were acquired as a result of the illegal activity or that were "involved in" or an "instrumentality of" the activity.

The broad language of RICO has allowed it to be applied in cases that have little or nothing to do with organized crime. In fact, today the statute is more often used to attack white-collar crimes than organized crime. In addition, RICO creates civil as well as criminal liability. The government can seek civil penalties, including the divestiture of a defendant's interest in a business (called forfeiture) or the dissolution of the business. Moreover, in some cases, the statute allows private individuals to sue violators and potentially recover three times their actual losses (treble damages), plus attorneys' fees, for business injuries caused by a violation of the statute. This is perhaps the most controversial aspect of RICO and one that continues to cause debate in the nation's federal courts.

ETHICAL ISSUE 6.1

Should courts allow private parties to file RICO actions against their employers based on a pattern of hiring illegal immigrants? The civil sanctions authorized by RICO have given plaintiffs a tremendous financial incentive to pursue businesses and employers for RICO violations. In one recent case, for example, a group of employees sued their employer, Mohawk Industries, Inc. The employees claimed that Mohawk had engaged in a pattern of hiring illegal immigrants willing to work for lower wages in an effort to drive down the wages of legal employees. Mohawk, the second-largest carpet manufacturer in the United States with more than 30,000 employees, allegedly conspired with recruiting agencies to hire undocumented workers and even provided illegal immigrants with transportation from the border. The plaintiffs claimed that this pattern of illegal hiring expanded Mohawk's hourly workforce and resulted in lower wages for the plaintiffs (and other legal employees). Mohawk filed a motion to dismiss for lack of evidence of racketeering activity, which the federal court denied, and the case was appealed.

The United States Supreme Court initially granted a writ of *certiorari* in this case but later dismissed the writ as "improvidently granted" and remanded the case to the U.S. Court of Appeals for the Eleventh Circuit. In September 2006, the federal appellate court ruled that the plaintiffs had presented sufficient evidence of racketeering activity to go forward with the RICO suit.[11] Although the merits of the case have not yet been resolved, the potential treble (triple) damages award against Mohawk could be substantial. In addition, the case is likely to open the door to other actions against employers that have a history of employing illegal immigrants and thereby causing injury to the economic interests of other employees.

The *Concept Summary* on the following page provides definitions and examples of the crime categories just discussed.

10. See 18 U.S.C. Section 1961(1)(A).
11. *Williams v. Mohawk Industries, Inc.*, 465 F.3d 1277 (11th Cir. 2006); *cert.* granted ___ U.S. ___, 126 S.Ct. 830, 163 L.Ed.2d 705 (2005); and *cert.* dismissed at ___ U.S. ___, 126 S.Ct. 2016, 164 L.Ed.2d 776 (2006). The holding in this case conflicts with a decision in another federal circuit; see *Baker v. IBP, Inc.*, 357 F.3d 685 (7th Cir. 2004).

CONCEPT SUMMARY	Types of Crimes
CRIME CATEGORY	**DEFINITIONS AND EXAMPLES**
Violent Crime	1. *Definition*—Crimes that cause others to suffer harm or death. 2. *Examples*—Murder, assault and battery, sexual assault (rape), and robbery.
Property Crime	1. *Definition*—Crimes in which the goal of the offender is some form of economic gain or the damaging of property; the most common form of crime. 2. *Examples*—Burglary, larceny, obtaining goods by false pretenses, receiving stolen goods, arson, and forgery.
Public Order Crime	1. *Definition*—Crimes contrary to public values and morals. 2. *Examples*—Public drunkenness, prostitution, gambling, and illegal drug use.
White-Collar Crime	1. *Definition*—An illegal act or series of acts committed by an individual or business entity using some nonviolent means to obtain a personal or business advantage; usually committed in the course of a legitimate occupation. 2. *Examples*—Embezzlement, mail and wire fraud, bribery, bankruptcy fraud, the theft of trade secrets, and insider trading.
Organized Crime	1. *Definition*—A form of crime conducted by groups operating illegitimately to satisfy the public's demand for illegal goods and services (such as gambling or illegal narcotics). 2. *Money laundering*—The establishment of legitimate enterprises through which "dirty" money (obtained through criminal activities, such as organized crime) can be "laundered" (made to appear to be legitimate income). 3. *The Racketeer Influenced and Corrupt Organizations Act (RICO) of 1970*—RICO makes it a federal crime to (a) use income obtained from racketeering activity to purchase any interest in an enterprise, (b) acquire or maintain an interest in an enterprise through racketeering activity, (c) conduct or participate in the affairs of an enterprise through racketeering activity, or (d) conspire to do any of the preceding activities. RICO provides for both civil and criminal liability.

Classification of Crimes

Depending on their degree of seriousness, crimes typically are classified as felonies or misdemeanors. **Felonies** are serious crimes punishable by death or by imprisonment for more than a year. **Misdemeanors** are less serious crimes, punishable by a fine or by confinement for up to a year. In most jurisdictions, **petty offenses** are considered to be a subset of misdemeanors. Petty offenses are minor violations, such as jaywalking or violations of building codes. Even for petty offenses, however, a guilty party can be put in jail for a few days, fined, or both, depending on state or local law.

Whether a crime is a felony or a misdemeanor can determine in which court the case is tried and, in some states, whether the defendant has a right to a jury trial. Many states also define different degrees of felony offenses (first, second, and third degree murder, for example) and vary the punishment according to the degree. Some states also have different classes (degrees) of misdemeanors.

FELONY
A crime—such as arson, murder, rape, or robbery—that carries the most severe sanctions, ranging from one year in a state or federal prison to the death penalty.

MISDEMEANOR
A lesser crime than a felony, punishable by a fine or incarceration in jail for up to one year.

PETTY OFFENSE
In criminal law, the least serious kind of criminal offense, such as a traffic or building-code violation.

DEFENSES TO CRIMINAL LIABILITY

In certain circumstances, the law may allow a person to be excused from criminal liability because she or he lacks the required mental state. Criminal defendants may also be relieved of criminal liability if they can show that their criminal actions were justified, given the circumstances. Among the most important defenses to criminal liability are infancy, intoxication, insanity, mistake, consent, duress, justifiable use of force, entrapment, and the statute of limitations. Also, in some cases, defendants are given immunity and thus relieved, at least in part, of criminal liability for crimes they committed. We look at each of these defenses here.

Note that procedural violations, such as obtaining evidence without a valid search warrant, may operate as defenses also. As you will read later in this chapter, evidence obtained in violation of a defendant's constitutional rights normally may not be admitted in court. If the evidence is suppressed, then there may be no basis for prosecuting the defendant.

Infancy

The term *infant*, as used in the law, refers to any person who has not yet reached the age of majority (see Chapter 8). In all states, certain courts handle cases involving children who are alleged to have violated the law. In some states, juvenile courts handle children's cases exclusively. In other states, however, courts that handle children's cases may also have jurisdiction over additional matters. In most states, a child may be treated as an adult and tried in a regular court if she or he is above a certain age (usually fourteen) and is charged with a felony, such as rape or murder.

Intoxication

The law recognizes two types of intoxication, whether from drugs or from alcohol: *involuntary* and *voluntary*. Involuntary intoxication occurs when a person either is physically forced to ingest or inject an intoxicating substance or is unaware that a substance contains drugs or alcohol. Involuntary intoxication is a defense to a crime if its effect was to make a person incapable of obeying the law or of understanding that the act committed was wrong. Voluntary intoxication is rarely a defense, but it may be effective in cases in which the defendant was so *extremely* intoxicated as to negate the state of mind that a crime requires.

Insanity

Just as a child is often judged to be incapable of the state of mind required to commit a crime, so also may someone suffering from a mental illness. Thus, insanity may be a defense to a criminal charge. The courts have had difficulty deciding what the test for legal insanity should be, however, and psychiatrists as well as lawyers are critical of the tests used. Almost all federal courts and some states use the relatively liberal standard set forth in the Model Penal Code:

> A person is not responsible for criminal conduct if at the time of such conduct as a result of mental disease or defect he [or she] lacks substantial capacity either to appreciate the wrongfulness of his [or her] conduct or to conform his [or her] conduct to the requirements of the law.

Some states use the *M'Naghten* test,[12] under which a criminal defendant is not responsible if, at the time of the offense, he or she did not know the nature and quality of the act or did not know that the act was wrong. Other states use the irresistible-impulse test. A person operating under an irresistible impulse may know an act is wrong but cannot refrain from doing it. Under any of these tests, proving insanity is extremely difficult. For this reason, the insanity defense is rarely used and usually is not successful.

---

12. A rule derived from *M'Naghten's Case*, 8 Eng.Rep. 718 (1843).

ON THE WEB

You can gain insights into criminal law and criminal procedures, including a number of the defenses that can be raised to avoid criminal liability, by looking at some of the famous criminal law cases included on Court TV's Web site. Go to

www.courttv.com/index.html.

These two brothers were only thirteen and fourteen years old when they killed their father with a baseball bat and then set their Florida house on fire. In court, they did not deny their wrongdoing. They were sentenced to terms of seven to eight years for third degree murder and arson. Under what circumstances should they not be held responsible for their reprehensible actions? (The Smoking Gun)

Mistake

Everyone has heard the saying "Ignorance of the law is no excuse." Ordinarily, ignorance of the law or a mistaken idea about what the law requires is not a valid defense. In some states, however, that rule has been modified. Criminal defendants who claim that they honestly did not know that they were breaking a law may have a valid defense if (1) the law was not published or reasonably made known to the public or (2) the defendant relied on an official statement of the law that was erroneous.

A *mistake of fact*, as opposed to a *mistake of law*, operates as a defense if it negates the mental state necessary to commit a crime. **EXAMPLE 6.6** If Oliver Wheaton mistakenly walks off with Julie Tyson's briefcase because he thinks it is his, there is no theft. Theft requires knowledge that the property belongs to another. ■

Consent

CONSENT
Voluntary agreement to a proposition or an act of another; a concurrence of wills.

What if a victim consents to a crime or even encourages the person intending a criminal act to commit it? Ordinarily, **consent** does not operate as a bar to criminal liability. In some rare circumstances, however, the law may allow consent to be used as a defense. In each case, the question is whether the law forbids an act that was committed against the victim's will or forbids the act without regard to the victim's wish. The law forbids murder, prostitution, and drug use regardless of whether the victim consents to it. Also, if the act causes harm to a third person who has not consented, there is no escape from criminal liability. Consent or forgiveness given after a crime has been committed is not really a defense, though it can affect the likelihood of prosecution or the severity of the sentence. Consent operates most successfully as a defense in crimes against property.

EXAMPLE 6.7 Barry gives Phong permission to stay in Barry's lakeside cabin and hunt for deer on the adjoining land. After observing Phong carrying a gun into the cabin at night, a neighbor calls the police, and an officer subsequently arrests Phong. If charged with burglary (or aggravated burglary, because he had a weapon), Phong can assert the defense of consent. He had obtained Barry's consent to enter the premises. ■

Duress

DURESS
Unlawful pressure brought to bear on a person, causing the person to perform an act that she or he would not otherwise perform.

Duress exists when the *wrongful threat* of one person induces another person to perform an act that she or he would not otherwise perform. In such a situation, duress is said to negate the mental state necessary to commit a crime. For duress to qualify as a defense, the following requirements must be met:

1 The threat must be of serious bodily harm or death.

2 The harm threatened must be greater than the harm caused by the crime.

3 The threat must be immediate and inescapable.

4 The defendant must have been involved in the situation through no fault of his or her own.

Justifiable Use of Force

SELF-DEFENSE
The legally recognized privilege to protect oneself or one's property against injury by another. The privilege of self-defense usually applies only to acts that are reasonably necessary to protect oneself, one's property, or another person.

Probably the best-known defense to criminal liability is **self-defense.** Other situations, however, also justify the use of force: the defense of one's dwelling, the defense of other property, and the prevention of a crime. In all of these situations, it is important to distinguish between deadly and nondeadly force. *Deadly force* is likely to result in death or serious bodily harm. *Nondeadly force* is force that reasonably appears necessary to prevent the imminent use of criminal force.

Generally speaking, people can use the amount of nondeadly force that seems necessary to protect themselves, their dwellings, or other property or to prevent the commission of a crime. Deadly force can be used in self-defense (1) if the defender *reasonably believes* that imminent death or grievous bodily harm will otherwise result, (2) if the attacker is using unlawful force (an example of lawful force is that exerted by a police officer), and (3) if the defender has not initiated or provoked the attack. Deadly force normally can be used to defend a dwelling only if the unlawful entry is violent and the person believes deadly force is necessary to prevent imminent death or great bodily harm or—in some jurisdictions—if the person believes deadly force is necessary to prevent the commission of a felony (such as arson) in the dwelling.

Entrapment

Entrapment is a defense designed to prevent police officers or other government agents from enticing persons to commit crimes in order to later prosecute them for criminal acts. In the typical entrapment case, an undercover agent *suggests* that a crime be committed and somehow pressures or induces an individual to commit it. The agent then arrests the individual for the crime.

For entrapment to be considered a defense, both the suggestion and the inducement must take place. The defense is intended not to prevent law enforcement agents from setting a trap for an unwary criminal but rather to prevent them from pushing the individual into it. The crucial issue is whether the person who committed a crime was predisposed to commit the illegal act or did so because the agent induced it.

ENTRAPMENT
In criminal law, a defense in which the defendant claims that he or she was induced by a public official—usually an undercover agent or police officer—to commit a crime that he or she would otherwise not have committed.

Statute of Limitations

With some exceptions, such as for the crime of murder, statutes of limitations apply to crimes just as they do to civil wrongs. In other words, the state must initiate criminal prosecution within a certain number of years. If a criminal action is brought after the statutory time period has expired, the accused person can raise the statute of limitations as a defense.

Immunity

At times, the state may wish to obtain information from a person accused of a crime. Accused persons are understandably reluctant to give information if it will be used to prosecute them, and they cannot be forced to do so. The privilege against *self-incrimination* is granted by the Fifth Amendment to the U.S. Constitution, which reads, in part, "nor shall [any person] be compelled in any criminal case to be a witness against himself." In cases in which the state wishes to obtain information from a person accused of a crime, the state can grant *immunity* from prosecution or agree to prosecute for a less serious offense in exchange for the information. Once immunity is given, the person can no longer refuse to testify on Fifth Amendment grounds because he or she now has an absolute privilege against self-incrimination.

Often, a grant of immunity from prosecution for a serious crime is part of the **plea bargaining** between the defendant and the prosecuting attorney. The defendant may be convicted of a lesser offense, while the state uses the defendant's testimony to prosecute accomplices for serious crimes carrying heavy penalties.

PLEA BARGAINING
The process by which a criminal defendant and the prosecutor in a criminal case work out a mutually satisfactory disposition of the case, subject to court approval; usually involves the defendant's pleading guilty to a lesser offense in return for a lighter sentence.

CONSTITUTIONAL SAFEGUARDS AND CRIMINAL PROCEDURES

Criminal law brings the power of the state, with all its resources, to bear against the individual. Criminal procedures are designed to protect the constitutional rights of individuals and to prevent the arbitrary use of power on the part of the government.

The U.S. Constitution provides specific safeguards for those accused of crimes. Most of these safeguards protect individuals against state government actions, as well as federal government actions, by virtue of the due process clause of the Fourteenth Amendment. These protections are set forth in the Fourth, Fifth, Sixth, and Eighth Amendments.

Fourth Amendment Protections

SEARCH WARRANT
An order granted by a public authority, such as a judge, that authorizes law enforcement personnel to search a particular premise or property.

PROBABLE CAUSE
Reasonable grounds for believing that a person should be arrested or searched.

The Fourth Amendment protects the "right of the people to be secure in their persons, houses, papers, and effects." Before searching or seizing private property, law enforcement officers must obtain a **search warrant**—an order from a judge or other public official authorizing the search or seizure. To obtain a search warrant, law enforcement officers must convince a judge that they have reasonable grounds, or **probable cause,** to believe a search will reveal a specific illegality. Probable cause requires the officers to have trustworthy evidence that would convince a reasonable person that the proposed search or seizure is more likely justified than not. Furthermore, the Fourth Amendment prohibits general warrants. It requires a particular description of what is to be searched or seized. General searches through a person's belongings are not permissible. The search cannot extend beyond what is described in the warrant. Although search warrants require specificity, if a search warrant is issued for a person's residence, items that are in that residence may be searched even if they do not belong to that individual.

■**EXAMPLE 6.8** Paycom Billing Services, Inc., facilitates payments from Internet users to its client Web sites and stores vast amounts of credit-card information in the process. Three partners at Paycom received a letter from an employee, Christopher Adjani, threatening to sell Paycom's confidential client information if the company did not pay him $3 million. Pursuant to an investigation, the Federal Bureau of Investigation (FBI) obtained a search warrant to search Adjani's person, automobile, and residence, including computer equipment. When the FBI agents served the warrant, they discovered evidence of the criminal scheme in the e-mail communications on a computer in the residence. The computer belonged to Adjani's live-in girlfriend. Adjani filed a motion to suppress this evidence, claiming that because he did not own the computer, it was beyond the scope of the warrant. Although the federal trial court granted the defendant's motion and suppressed the incriminating e-mails, the U.S. Court of Appeals for the Ninth Circuit reversed the decision in 2006. According to the appellate court, despite the novel Fourth Amendment issues raised in the case, the search of the computer was proper given the alleged involvement of computers in the crime.[13] ■

---

13. *United States v. Adjani,* 452 F.3d 1140 (9th Cir. 2006). The parties have filed a petition to have the United States Supreme Court review the case.

Passengers and their carry-on items are searched at an airport security checkpoint. Do such searches violate passengers' Fourth Amendment right? (Ralf Roletschek/Wikimedia Commons)

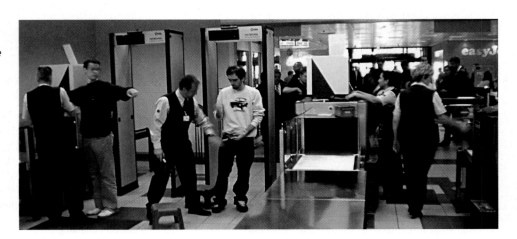

Constitutional protection against unreasonable searches and seizures also extends to businesses and professionals. As government regulation of business increased, government inspectors conducted frequent and unannounced inspections to ensure compliance with the regulations. Such inspections could be extremely disruptive. In 1978, the United States Supreme Court held that government inspectors do not have the right to enter business premises without a warrant, although the standard of probable cause is not the same as that required in nonbusiness contexts.[14] The existence of a general and neutral plan of enforcement will justify the issuance of a warrant.

Lawyers and accountants frequently possess the business records of their clients, and inspecting these documents while they are out of the hands of their true owners also requires a warrant. No warrant is required, however, for seizures of spoiled or contaminated food. Nor are warrants required for searches of businesses in such highly regulated industries as liquor, guns, and strip mining. General manufacturing is not considered to be one of these highly regulated industries, however.

The administrative search standard used for highly regulated industries is sometimes applied in other contexts as well. In the following case, the court considered whether the standard applies to airports and thus permits a suspicionless checkpoint search to screen airline passengers.

ON THE WEB

You can learn about some of the constitutional questions raised by various criminal laws and procedures by going to the Web site of the American Civil Liberties Union at

www.aclu.org.

---

14. *Marshall v. Barlow's, Inc.*, 436 U.S. 307, 98 S.Ct. 1816, 56 L.Ed.2d 305 (1978).

CASE 6.2 **United States v. Hartwell**

United States Court of Appeals, Third Circuit, 436 F.3d 174 (2006).

FACTS Christian Hartwell arrived at the Philadelphia International Airport on May 17, 2003, to catch a flight to Phoenix, Arizona. He reached the security checkpoint, placed his hand luggage on a conveyor belt to be X-rayed, and approached the metal detector. Hartwell's luggage was scanned without incident, but when he walked through the checkpoint, he set off the magnetometer. He was told to remove all items from his pockets and try again. Hartwell removed several items from his pocket but still set off the alarm. Carlos Padua, a federal Transportation Security Administration (TSA) agent, took Hartwell aside and scanned him with a handheld magnetometer. The wand revealed a solid object in Hartwell's pants pocket. Padua asked what it was, but Hartwell did not respond. Escorted to a private screening room, Hartwell refused several requests to empty his pocket. By Hartwell's account, Padua then reached into the pocket and removed two packages of crack cocaine. Hartwell was arrested and convicted on charges related to the possession of the drugs. He appealed to the U.S. Court of Appeals for the Third Circuit, arguing that the search violated the Fourth Amendment.

ISSUE Does a checkpoint search conducted in an airport to screen airline passengers violate the Fourth Amendment?

DECISION No. The U.S. Court of Appeals for the Third Circuit held that Hartwell's search was permissible under the Fourth Amendment, "even though it was initiated without individualized suspicion and was conducted without a warrant. It is permissible * * * because the State has an overwhelming interest in preserving air travel safety, and the procedure is tailored to advance that interest while proving to be only minimally invasive."

REASON Referring to the administrative search doctrine, the court balanced "the gravity of the public concerns" that have given rise to airport searches, the extent to which the searches advance the public interest, and the impact of the searches on "individual liberty." The court identified the public concern as "preventing terrorist attacks on airplanes," which "is of paramount importance." With respect to advancing the public interest, "absent a search, there is no effective means of detecting which airline passengers are reasonably likely to hijack an airplane." The court added that airport checkpoints and searches have been effective. As for any interference with liberty, the procedures in this case were "minimally intrusive. They were well tailored to protect personal privacy, escalating in invasiveness only after a lower level of screening disclosed a reason to conduct a more probing search." Besides, every airline passenger is subject to a supervised search "not far from the

CASE 6.2—Continues next page

CASE 6.2–Continued

scrutiny" of the other passengers, who—particularly since "[t]he events of September 11, 2001"—are all on notice that they will be searched, too.

WHY IS THIS CASE IMPORTANT? *In this case, the U.S. Court of Appeals for the Third Circuit applied*

the administrative search doctrine that applies to highly regulated industries. The United States Supreme Court developed this standard for analyzing suspicionless vehicle checkpoints, such as those used to determine the sobriety of randomly selected drivers. The Court has not ruled on the legality of airport screenings, however.

Fifth Amendment Protections

The Fifth Amendment offers significant protections for accused persons. One is the guarantee that no one can be deprived of "life, liberty, or property without due process of law." (See Chapter 1 for a discussion of the due process clause.) The Fifth Amendment also protects persons from **double jeopardy** (being tried twice for the same criminal offense). The prohibition against double jeopardy means that once a criminal defendant is acquitted (found not guilty) of a particular crime, the government may not retry him or her for the same crime.

Additionally, the Fifth Amendment guarantees that no person "shall be compelled in any criminal case to be a witness against himself." Thus, in any criminal proceeding, an accused person cannot be compelled to give testimony that might subject her or him to any criminal prosecution. The Fifth Amendment's guarantee against **self-incrimination** extends only to natural persons. Protection against self-incrimination does not apply to corporations or partnerships.[15]

Protections under the Sixth and Eighth Amendments

The Sixth Amendment guarantees several important rights for criminal defendants: the right to a speedy trial, the right to a jury trial, the right to a public trial, the right to confront witnesses, and the right to counsel. The Eighth Amendment prohibits excessive bail and fines, as well as cruel and unusual punishment.

The Sixth Amendment right to counsel is one of the rights of which a suspect must be advised when he or she is arrested under the *Miranda* rule (discussed later in this chapter). In many cases, a statement that a criminal suspect makes in the absence of counsel is not admissible at trial unless the suspect has knowingly and voluntarily waived this right. Is this right to counsel triggered when judicial proceedings are initiated through any preliminary step? Or is this right triggered only when a suspect is "interrogated" by the police? In the following case, the Supreme Court considered these questions.

DOUBLE JEOPARDY
A situation occurring when a person is tried twice for the same criminal offense; prohibited by the Fifth Amendment to the U.S. Constitution.

SELF-INCRIMINATION
The giving of testimony that may subject the testifier to criminal prosecution. The Fifth Amendment to the Constitution protects against self-incrimination by providing that no person "shall be compelled in any criminal case to be a witness against himself."

---

15. The privilege has been applied to some small family partnerships. See *United States v. Slutsky*, 352 F.Supp. 1105 (S.D.N.Y. 1972).

CASE 6.3 **Fellers v. United States**

Supreme Court of the United States, 540 U.S. 519, 124 S.Ct. 1019, 157 L.Ed.2d 1016 (2004).
www.law.cornell.edu/supct/index.html[a]

FACTS In February 2000, an indictment was issued charging

a. Click on "Search" in the top menu bar, and type "Fellers" in the "Search" box that appears. In the result, click on the name of the case under Supreme Court case names to access the opinion. The Legal Information Institute of Cornell Law School in Ithaca, New York, maintains this Web site.

John Fellers, a resident of Lincoln, Nebraska, with conspiracy to distribute methamphetamine. Police officers Michael Garnett and Jeff Bliemeister went to Fellers's home to arrest him. They told Fellers that the purpose of their visit was to discuss his use and distribution of methamphetamine. They said that they had

CASE 6.3–Continued

a warrant for his arrest and that the charges referred to his involvement with four individuals. Fellers responded that he knew the persons and had used methamphetamine with them. The officers took Fellers to jail and advised him for the first time of his right to counsel. He waived this right and repeated his earlier statements. Before Fellers's trial, the court ruled that his "jailhouse statements" could be admitted at his trial because he had waived his right to counsel before making them. After Fellers's conviction, he appealed to the U.S. Court of Appeals for the Eighth Circuit, arguing that the officers had elicited his incriminating "home statements" without advising him of his right to counsel and that his "jailhouse statements" should thus have been excluded from his trial as "fruits" of his earlier statements. The appellate court affirmed the lower court's judgment, holding that Fellers had not had a right to counsel at his home because he had not been subject to police "interrogation." Fellers appealed to the United States Supreme Court.

ISSUE Did Garnett and Bliemeister violate Fellers's right to counsel by deliberately eliciting information from him during their visit to his home without advising him of his right to counsel?

DECISION Yes. The United States Supreme Court reversed the lower court's decision and remanded the case for the determination of a different issue. The Court held that the Sixth Amendment bars the use at trial of a suspect's incriminating words, deliberately elicited by police after an indictment, in the absence of either counsel or a waiver of the right to counsel, regardless of whether police conduct constitutes an "interrogation."

REASON The Court explained, "The Sixth Amendment right to counsel is triggered at or after the time that judicial proceedings have been initiated * * * . [A]n accused is denied the basic protections of the Sixth Amendment when there is used against him at his trial evidence of his own incriminating words, which federal agents * * * deliberately elicited from him after he had been indicted and in the absence of his counsel." In this case, "there is no question that the officers * * * deliberately elicited information from petitioner [Fellers]. Indeed, the officers, upon arriving at petitioner's house, informed him that their purpose in coming was to discuss his involvement in the distribution of methamphetamine and his association with certain charged co-conspirators. * * * [T]he ensuing discussion took place after petitioner had been indicted [formally charged], outside the presence of counsel, and in the absence of any waiver of petitioner's Sixth Amendment rights."

 FOR CRITICAL ANALYSIS–Social Consideration
Should Fellers's "jailhouse statements" also have been excluded from his trial? Why or why not?

The Exclusionary Rule and the *Miranda* Rule

Two other procedural protections for criminal defendants are the exclusionary rule and the *Miranda* rule.

The Exclusionary Rule   Under what is known as the **exclusionary rule,** all evidence obtained in violation of the constitutional rights spelled out in the Fourth, Fifth, and Sixth Amendments, as well as all evidence derived from illegally obtained evidence, normally must be excluded from the trial. Evidence derived from illegally obtained evidence is known as the "fruit of the poisonous tree." For example, if a confession is obtained after an illegal arrest, the arrest is "the poisonous tree," and the confession, if "tainted" by the arrest, is the "fruit."

The purpose of the exclusionary rule is to deter police from conducting warrantless searches and engaging in other misconduct. The rule is sometimes criticized because it can lead to injustice. Many a defendant has "gotten off on a technicality" because law enforcement personnel failed to observe procedural requirements. Even though a defendant may be obviously guilty, if the evidence of that guilt was obtained improperly (without a valid search warrant, for example), it normally cannot be used against the defendant in court.

EXCLUSIONARY RULE
In criminal procedure, a rule under which any evidence that is obtained in violation of the accused's constitutional rights guaranteed by the Fourth, Fifth, and Sixth Amendments, as well as any evidence derived from illegally obtained evidence, will not be admissible in court.

REMEMBER Once a suspect has been informed of his or her rights, anything that person says can be used as evidence in a trial.

ON THE WEB

If you are interested in reading the United States Supreme Court's opinion in *Miranda v. Arizona*, go to **www.law.cornell.edu/ supct/cases/conlaw.htm**. Select "M" from the menu at the top of the page, and scroll down the page that opens to the *Miranda v. Arizona* case.

The *Miranda* Rule   In *Miranda v. Arizona*,[16] a case decided in 1966, the United States Supreme Court established the rule that individuals who are arrested must be informed of certain constitutional rights, including their Fifth Amendment right to remain silent and their Sixth Amendment right to counsel. If the arresting officers fail to inform a criminal suspect of these constitutional rights, any statements the suspect makes normally will not be admissible in court. Although the Supreme Court's *Miranda* decision was controversial, it has survived attempts by Congress to overrule the decision.[17]

Exceptions to the *Miranda* Rule   Over time, as part of a continuing attempt to balance the rights of accused persons against the rights of society, the United States Supreme Court has carved out numerous exceptions to the *Miranda* rule. For example, the Court has recognized a "public safety" exception, holding that certain statements—such as statements concerning the location of a weapon—are admissible even if the defendant was not given *Miranda* warnings (see Exhibit 6–3).[18] The Court has also clarified that in certain circumstances, a defendant's confession need not be excluded as evidence even if the police failed to inform the defendant of his or her *Miranda* rights.[19] If other, legally obtained evidence admitted at trial is strong enough to justify the conviction without the confession, then the fact that the confession was obtained illegally can be, in effect, ignored.[20]

The United States Supreme Court has also ruled that a suspect must unequivocally and assertively request to exercise his or her right to counsel in order to stop police questioning. Saying "Maybe I should talk to a lawyer" during an interrogation after being taken into custody is not enough. The Court held that police officers are not required to decipher the suspect's intentions in such situations.[21]

Criminal Procedures and Sentencing

As mentioned, a criminal prosecution differs significantly from a civil case in several respects. These differences reflect the desire to safeguard the rights of the individual against the state. Exhibit 6–4 summarizes the major procedural steps in processing a criminal case.

Traditionally, persons who committed the same crime might receive very different sentences, depending on the judge hearing the case, the jurisdiction in which it was heard,

---

16. 384 U.S. 436, 86 S.Ct. 1602, 16 L.Ed.2d 694 (1966).
17. *Dickerson v. United States*, 530 U.S. 428, 120 S.Ct. 2326, 147 L.Ed.2d 405 (2000).
18. *New York v. Quarles*, 467 U.S. 649, 104 S.Ct. 2626, 81 L.Ed.2d 550 (1984).
19. *Moran v. Burbine*, 475 U.S. 412, 106 S.Ct. 1135, 89 L.Ed.2d 410 (1986).
20. *Arizona v. Fulminante*, 499 U.S. 279, 111 S.Ct. 1246, 113 L.Ed.2d 302 (1991).
21. *Davis v. United States*, 512 U.S. 452, 114 S.Ct. 2350, 129 L.Ed.2d 362 (1994).

EXHIBIT 6–3 *Miranda* Warnings

1. YOU HAVE THE RIGHT TO REMAIN SILENT.
2. ANYTHING YOU SAY CAN AND WILL BE USED AGAINST YOU IN A COURT OF LAW.
3. YOU HAVE THE RIGHT TO TALK TO A LAWYER AND HAVE HIM PRESENT WITH YOU WHILE YOU ARE BEING QUESTIONED.
4. IF YOU CANNOT AFFORD TO HIRE A LAWYER, ONE WILL BE APPOINTED TO REPRESENT YOU BEFORE ANY QUESTIONING IF YOU WISH.
5. YOU CAN DECIDE AT ANY TIME TO EXERCISE THESE RIGHTS AND NOT ANSWER ANY QUESTIONS OR MAKE ANY STATEMENTS.

WAIVER

DO YOU UNDERSTAND EACH OF THESE RIGHTS I HAVE EXPLAINED TO YOU? HAVING THESE RIGHTS IN MIND, DO YOU WISH TO TALK TO US NOW?

EXHIBIT 6–4 Major Procedural Steps in a Criminal Case

ARREST

Police officer takes suspect into custody. Most arrests are made without a warrant. After the arrest, the officer searches the suspect, who is then taken to the police station.

BOOKING

At the police station, the suspect is searched again, photographed, fingerprinted, and allowed at least one telephone call. After the booking, charges are reviewed, and if they are not dropped, a complaint is filed and a magistrate (judge) reviews the case for probable cause.

INITIAL APPEARANCE

The defendant appears before the judge, who informs the defendant of the charges and of his or her rights. If the defendant requests a lawyer and cannot afford one, a lawyer is appointed. The judge sets bail (conditions under which a suspect can obtain release pending disposition of the case).

GRAND JURY

A grand jury determines if there is probable cause to believe that the defendant committed the crime. The federal government and about half of the states require grand jury indictments for at least some felonies.

PRELIMINARY HEARING

In a court proceeding, a prosecutor presents evidence, and the judge determines if there is probable cause to hold the defendant over for trial.

INDICTMENT

An *indictment* is a written document issued by the grand jury to formally charge the defendant with a crime.

INFORMATION

An *information* is a formal criminal charge made by the prosecutor.

ARRAIGNMENT

The defendant is brought before the court, informed of the charges, and asked to enter a plea.

PLEA BARGAIN

A plea bargain is a prosecutors promise to make concessions (or promise to seek concessions) in return for a defendant's guilty plea. Concessions may include a reduced charge or a lesser sentence.

GUILTY PLEA

In many jurisdictions, most cases that reach the arraignment stage do not go to trial but are resolved by a guilty plea, often as a result of a plea bargain. The judge sets the case for sentencing.

TRIAL

Trials can be either jury trials or bench trials. (In a bench trial, there is no jury, and the judge decides questions of fact as well as questions of law.) If the verdict is "guilty," the judge sets a date for the sentencing. Everyone convicted of a crime has the right to an appeal.

ADAPTING THE LAW TO THE ONLINE ENVIRONMENT — When Spamming Is a Crime

A significant issue today is whether persons who send spam (bulk unsolicited e-mail) over the Internet can be charged with a crime. As discussed in Chapter 4, spamming has become a major problem for businesses. At the time the federal CAN-SPAM Act was passed in 2003, the U.S. Senate found that spam constituted more than half of all e-mail traffic and projected that it would cost corporations more than $113 billion by 2007. By all accounts, though, the amount of spam has actually increased since the federal CAN-SPAM Act was enacted. Given that the CAN-SPAM Act has failed to reduce the amount of spam, some states have taken matters into their own hands and have now passed laws making spamming a crime.

A Few States Have Enacted Criminal Spamming Statutes

A few states, such as Maryland and Virginia, have passed groundbreaking laws that make spamming a crime.[a] Under the Virginia Computer Crimes Act (VCCA), it is a crime

a. See, for example, Maryland Code, Criminal Law, Section 3-805.1; and Virginia Criminal Code Sections 18.2–152.3:1.

against property to use a computer or computer network "with the intent to falsify or forge electronic mail transmission information or other routing information in any manner." The law further provides that attempting to send spam to more than ten thousand recipients in any twenty-four-hour period is a felony. The VCCA also includes provisions allowing authorities to seize the assets or proceeds obtained through an illegal spamming operation.

Maryland's antispamming law similarly prohibits sending commercial e-mail to recipients using false information about the identity of the sender, the origin, transmission path, or subject of the message. Under the Maryland law, however, the number of spam messages required to convict a person of the offense is much lower. Sending ten illegal messages in twenty-four hours violates the statute, and the more spam sent, the more severe the punishment will be, up to a maximum of ten years in prison and a $25,000 fine.

America's First Conviction for Felony Spamming

In the biggest case on criminal spamming to date, a Virginia appellate court in 2006 upheld the conviction of Jeremy Jaynes, a spammer who had sent more than ten thousand junk messages a day using sixteen Internet connections and a number of aliases (such as Gaven Stubberfield). Jaynes, a resident of North Carolina, had used a variety of business names

---

and many other factors. Today, however, court judges typically must follow state or federal guidelines when sentencing convicted persons.

At the federal level, the Sentencing Reform Act created the U.S. Sentencing Commission, which was charged with the task of standardizing sentences for federal crimes. The commission's guidelines, which became effective in 1987, established a range of possible penalties for each federal crime and required the judge to select a sentence from within that range. In other words, the guidelines originally established a mandatory system because judges were not allowed to deviate from the specified sentencing range. Some federal judges felt uneasy about imposing long prison sentences on certain criminal defendants, particularly first-time offenders, and in illegal substances cases involving small quantities of drugs.[22]

In 2005, the United States Supreme Court held that certain provisions of the federal sentencing guidelines were unconstitutional.[23] The case involved Freddie Booker, who was arrested with 92.5 grams of crack cocaine in his possession. During questioning by police, he signed a written statement in which he admitted to selling an additional quantity—566 grams of crack cocaine—elsewhere. The additional 566 grams of crack were not brought up at trial. Nevertheless, under the federal sentencing guidelines the judge was required to sentence Booker to twenty-two years in prison. Ultimately, the Court ruled that this sentence was unconstitutional because a jury did not find beyond a reasonable doubt that Booker had possessed the additional 566 grams of crack.

ON THE WEB

The U.S. Sentencing Guidelines can be found online at

www.ussc.gov.

---

22. See, for example, *United States v. Angelos*, 345 F.Supp.2d 1227 (D. Utah 2004).
23. *United States v. Booker*, 543 U.S. 220, 125 S.Ct. 738, 160 L.Ed.2d 621 (2005).

as fronts for his spam and had sent some of the messages through servers in Virginia.

Before his 2004 arrest, Jaynes was widely recognized as the eighth most prolific spammer in the world. He had accumulated a personal fortune of $24 million and was earning $750,000 a month spamming get-rich-quick schemes, pornography, and sham products and services. Jaynes's sister, Jessica DeGroot, was also involved in the criminal scheme, and her name was on the credit card used to purchase domain names for Jaynes's spamming operation. During the search of Jaynes's residence, police found a compact disc containing at least 176 million full e-mail addresses and more than 1.3 billion user names, as well as Zip disks containing 107 million e-mail addresses. Jaynes also had a DVD containing not only e-mail addresses, but also other personal account information for millions of individuals. All of this information had been stolen from America Online.

Jaynes was convicted of three counts of felony spamming based on the fact that he had sent more than ten thousand pieces of spam per day on three separate days, using false Internet addresses and aliases. The jury sentenced him to nine years in prison (although prosecutors had asked for a fifteen-year sentence). The trial court postponed his prison sentence, however, until after the appeal. On appeal, Jaynes argued that Virginia did not have jurisdiction over him and that the state's criminal spamming statute violated his First Amendment rights to free speech. The state appellate court

concluded that jurisdiction was proper because Jaynes had utilized servers within the state. On the First Amendment issue, the court held that the VCCA did not proscribe speech at all, because it only prohibited "intentional falsity as a machination [plot] to make massive, uncompensated use of the private property of an ISP [Internet service provider]."[b] This was the first felony conviction for spamming in the United States.

FOR CRITICAL ANALYSIS *How might criminal spamming statutes, which are likely to vary among the states, affect legitimate businesspersons who advertise on the Internet? If a business discovers that a spammer is using the business's name in connection with spam, what recourse does that business have?*

b. *Jaynes v. Commonwealth of Virginia*, 48 Va.App. 673, 634 S.E.2d 357 (2006).

The Court's ruling in 2005 essentially changed the federal sentencing guidelines from mandatory to advisory. Depending on the case's circumstances, a federal trial judge may now depart from the guidelines if he or she believes that it is reasonable to do so. Note, however, that the sentencing guidelines still exist and provide for enhanced punishment for certain types of crimes, including white-collar crimes, violations of the Sarbanes-Oxley Act (see Chapter 2), and violations of securities laws (see Chapter 21).[24]

CYBER CRIME

Some years ago, the American Bar Association defined **computer crime** as any act that is directed against computers and computer parts, that uses computers as instruments of crime, or that involves computers and constitutes abuse. Today, because much of the crime committed with the use of computers occurs in cyberspace, many computer crimes fall under the broad label of *cyber crime*. **Cyber crimes** occur online in the virtual community of the Internet, as opposed to the physical world. Here, we look at several types of activity that constitute cyber crimes against persons or property. Other cyber crimes will be discussed in later chapters as they relate to particular topics, such as banking or consumer law. For a discussion of how some states are passing laws making spamming a crime, see this chapter's *Adapting the Law to the Online Environment* feature.

COMPUTER CRIME
Any act that is directed against computers and computer parts, that uses computers as instruments of crime, or that involves computers and constitutes abuse.

CYBER CRIME
A crime that occurs online, in the virtual community of the Internet, as opposed to the physical world.

24. The sentencing guidelines were amended in 2003, as required under the Sarbanes-Oxley Act of 2002, to impose stiffer penalties for corporate securities fraud—see Chapter 21.

ON THE WEB

The U.S. Department of Justice offers an impressive collection of statistics on crime, including cyber crime, at the following Web site:

www.ojp.usdoj.gov/bjs.

IDENTITY THEFT
The act of stealing another's identifying information—such as a name, date of birth, or Social Security number—and using that information to access the victim's financial resources.

BE AWARE Technological change is one of the primary factors that lead to new types of crime.

ON THE WEB

The Computer Crime Research Center is a non-profit organization that provides up-to-date information and articles on cyber crime and cyberterrorism at

www.crime-research.org.

HACKER
A person who uses one computer to break into another. Professional computer programmers refer to such persons as "crackers."

CYBERTERRORIST
A hacker whose purpose is to exploit a target computer for a serious impact, such as corrupting a program to sabotage a business.

Computer networks also provide opportunities for employees to commit crimes that can involve serious economic losses. For example, employees of a company's accounting department can transfer funds among accounts with little effort and often with less risk than would be involved in transactions evidenced by paperwork. Generally, the dependence of businesses on computer operations has left firms vulnerable to sabotage, fraud, embezzlement, and the theft of proprietary data, such as trade secrets or other intellectual property. As noted in Chapter 5, the piracy of intellectual property via the Internet is one of the most serious legal challenges facing lawmakers and the courts today.

A form of cyber theft that has become particularly troublesome in recent years is **identity theft.** Identity theft occurs when the wrongdoer steals a form of identification—such as a name, date of birth, or Social Security number—and uses the information to access the victim's financial resources. This crime existed to a certain extent before the widespread use of the Internet. The Internet, however, has turned identity theft into perhaps the fastest-growing financial crime in the United States. See the *Application* feature at the end of this chapter for information on how to prevent identity theft.

Three federal statutes deal specifically with identity theft. The Identity Theft and Assumption Deterrence Act of 1998[25] made identity theft a federal crime and directed the U.S. Sentencing Commission to incorporate the crime into its sentencing guidelines. The Fair and Accurate Credit Transactions Act of 2003[26] gives victims of identity theft certain rights in working with creditors and credit bureaus to remove negative information from their credit reports. This act will be discussed in detail in Chapter 13 in the context of consumer law. The Identity Theft Penalty Enhancement Act of 2004[27] authorized more severe penalties in aggravated cases in which the identity theft was committed in connection with the thief's employment or with other serious crimes (such as terrorism or firearms or immigration offenses).

Hacking and Cyberterrorism

Persons who use one computer to break into another are sometimes referred to as **hackers.** Hackers who break into computers without authorization often commit cyber theft. Sometimes, however, their principal aim is to prove how smart they are by gaining access to others' password-protected computers and causing random data errors or making unpaid-for telephone calls.[28] **Cyberterrorists** are hackers who, rather than trying to gain attention, strive to remain undetected so that they can exploit computers for a serious impact. Just as "real" terrorists destroyed the World Trade Center towers and a portion of the Pentagon in September 2001, cyberterrorists might explode "logic bombs" to shut down central computers. Such activities can pose a danger to national security.

Businesses may be targeted by cyberterrorists as well as hackers. The goals of a hacking operation might include a wholesale theft of data, such as a merchant's customer files, or the monitoring of a computer to discover a business firm's plans and transactions. A cyberterrorist might also want to insert false codes or data. For example, the processing control system of a food manufacturer could be changed to alter the levels of ingredients so that consumers of the food would become ill.

A cyberterrorist attack on a major financial institution such as the New York Stock Exchange or a large bank could leave securities or money markets in flux and seriously affect the daily lives of millions of citizens. Similarly, any prolonged disruption of computer, cable, satellite, or telecommunications systems due to the actions of expert hackers

---

25. 18 U.S.C. Section 1028.
26. 15 U.S.C. Sections 1681 *et seq.*
27. 18 U.S.C. Section 1028A.
28. The total cost of crime on the Internet is estimated to be many billions of dollars annually, but two-thirds of that total is said to consist of unpaid-for toll calls.

would have serious repercussions on business operations—and national security—on a global level. Computer viruses are another tool that can be used by cyberterrorists to cripple communications networks.

Prosecuting Cyber Crimes

The "location" of cyber crime (cyberspace) has raised new issues in the investigation of crimes and the prosecution of offenders. A threshold issue is, of course, jurisdiction. A person who commits an act against a business in California, where the act is a cyber crime, might never have set foot in California but might instead reside in New York, or even in Canada, where the act may not be a crime. If the crime was committed via e-mail, the question arises as to whether the e-mail would constitute sufficient "minimum contacts" (see Chapter 3) for the victim's state to exercise jurisdiction over the perpetrator.

Identifying the wrongdoer can also be difficult. Cyber criminals do not leave physical traces, such as fingerprints or DNA samples, as evidence of their crimes. Even electronic "footprints" can be hard to find and follow. For example, e-mail may be sent through a remailer, an online service that guarantees that a message cannot be traced to its source.

For these reasons, laws written to protect physical property are difficult to apply in cyberspace. Nonetheless, governments at both the state and federal levels have taken significant steps toward controlling cyber crime, both by applying existing criminal statutes and by enacting new laws that specifically address wrongs committed in cyberspace.

Perhaps the most significant federal statute specifically addressing cyber crime is the Counterfeit Access Device and Computer Fraud and Abuse Act of 1984 (commonly known as the Computer Fraud and Abuse Act, or CFAA). This act, as amended by the National Information Infrastructure Protection Act of 1996,[29] provides, among other things, that a person who accesses a computer online, without authority, to obtain classified, restricted, or protected data, or attempts to do so, is subject to criminal prosecution. Such data could include financial and credit records, medical records, legal files, military and national security files, and other confidential information in government or private computers. The crime has two elements: accessing a computer without authority and taking the data.

This theft is a felony if it is committed for a commercial purpose or for private financial gain, or if the value of the stolen data (or computer time) exceeds $5,000. Penalties include fines and imprisonment for up to twenty years. A victim of computer theft can also bring a civil suit against the violator to obtain damages, an injunction, and other relief.

---

29. 18 U.S.C. Section 1030.

ON THE WEB

Professor Brenner at the University of Dayton Law School posts numerous articles on combating cyber crime, as well as information and links to the relevant laws of other nations, the policies of the European Council, and the United Nations' approach. You can access the site at **www.cybercrimes.net/International/IntLinks.html**.

The U.S. Department of Justice maintains a site dedicated to cyber crime at **www.usdoj.gov/criminal/cybercrime**.

REVIEWING Criminal Law and Cyber Crimes

Edward Hanousek worked for Pacific & Arctic Railway and Navigation Company (P&A) as a roadmaster of the White Pass & Yukon Railroad in Alaska. As an officer of the corporation, Hanousek was responsible "for every detail of the safe and efficient maintenance and construction of track, structures, and marine facilities of the entire railroad," including special projects. One project was a rock quarry, known as "6-mile," above the Skagway River. Next to the quarry, and just beneath the surface, ran a high-pressure oil pipeline owned by Pacific & Arctic Pipeline, Inc., P&A's sister company. When the quarry's backhoe operator punctured the pipeline, an estimated 1,000 to 5,000 gallons of oil were discharged into the river. Hanousek was charged with negligently discharging a harmful quantity of oil into a navigable water of the United States in violation of the criminal provisions of the Clean Water Act (CWA). Using the information presented in the chapter, answer the following questions.

1 Did Hanousek have the required mental state (*mens rea*) to be convicted of a crime? Why or why not?

2 Which theory discussed in the chapter would enable a court to hold Hanousek criminally liable for violating the statute regardless of whether he participated in, directed, or even knew about the specific violation?

3 Could the quarry's backhoe operator who punctured the pipeline also be charged with a crime in this situation? Explain.

4 Suppose that at trial, Hanousek argued that he could not be convicted because he was not aware of the requirements of the CWA. Would this defense be successful? Why or why not?

APPLICATION   How Can You Protect against Identity Theft?*

Identity theft is probably the fastest-growing crime in the United States. The Federal Trade Commission received 686,683 complaints of consumer fraud in 2005. Of these, 255,000 (about 37 percent) were for identity fraud. It is estimated that identity theft occurs every seventy-nine seconds and that annual losses due to this crime will have exceeded $70 billion by 2008.

Dollar loss is not the only cost. Victims of identity theft spend, on average, about six hundred hours resolving the situation after someone has fraudulently used their names to purchase goods or services, open accounts, or make unauthorized charges to their accounts. Moreover, businesses typically are unable to recoup the costs of these unauthorized purchases because they usually can hold only the thief responsible.

Sources of Information That Might Be Used

The rise in identity theft has been fueled by the vast amount of personal information stored in databases. Educational institutions, governments, and businesses all store vast quantities of information about their students, clients, and customers. As a number of recent incidents demonstrate, unless measures are taken to secure these databases, they are vulnerable to thieves.

For example, personal information was stolen from numerous universities (including Georgetown University, Ohio University, the University of Texas, and Vermont State College). Even more disturbing is the number of U.S. government databases that have been breached. For example, a laptop computer containing confidential information for about 26.5 million veterans was stolen from an employee at the U.S. Department of Veteran Affairs. The U.S. Navy reported that the records of seventy-five thousand student loan recipients, employees, and military personnel and their families were breached.

Cities, counties, Internet sources (such as Hotels.com and Neinet), insurance companies (such as Aetna), manufacturing

firms (such as Honeywell), nonprofit organizations, and even newspapers (such as the *Boston Globe*) have lost copious amounts of personal information in the last few years. In 2005, Bank of America reportedly lost tapes containing records of 1.2 million federal employees. Businesses sometimes do not publicly report incidents of theft, so the list is probably even longer. Although not all of the lost data will ultimately be used for identity theft, the potential is huge.

CHECKLIST FOR THE BUSINESS OWNER

1 Review what personal information is kept in your computer databases. Wherever possible, eliminate Social Security numbers and other personal information and code all account numbers to limit access to the account holder.

2 Review employee access to databases containing personal account information. Some employees should have no access, some limited access, some full access. Instruct your employees in how computers and personal information are to be used and not used.

3 Establish policies on what types of information may be stored on portable sources, such as laptop computers. Monitoring is important. Also maintain accurate records of where confidential data are kept and who has access to the data.

4 Consider using passwords and digital signatures to protect your computer system and data against unauthorized use.

5 Shred paper documents as much as possible—remember that identity theft can come from rummaging through your trash.

6 Be prepared for possible identity theft when your wallet, purse, credit card, checks, or mail is stolen—report the loss immediately to credit-card companies, banks, and credit bureaus. Do not keep passwords or personal identification numbers in your wallet.

7 Avoid giving any personal information over the telephone and always verify the identity of the caller.

---

* This *Application* is not meant to substitute for the services of an attorney who is licensed to practice law in your state.

KEY TERMS

actus reus 174
arson 176
beyond a reasonable doubt 172
burglary 175
computer crime 193
consent 184
crime 172
cyber crime 193
cyberterrorist 194
double jeopardy 188

duress 184
embezzlement 177
entrapment 185
exclusionary rule 189
felony 182
forgery 176
hacker 194
identity theft 194
larceny 176
mens rea 174

misdemeanor 182
money laundering 180
petty offense 182
plea bargaining 185
probable cause 186
robbery 175
search warrant 186
self-defense 184
self-incrimination 188
white-collar crime 177

CHAPTER SUMMARY — Criminal Law and Cyber Crimes

Civil Law and Criminal Law
(See pages 172–173.)

1. *Civil law*—Spells out the duties that exist between persons or between citizens and their governments, excluding the duty not to commit crimes.
2. *Criminal law*—Has to do with crimes, which are defined as wrongs against society proclaimed in statutes and, if committed, punishable by society through fines and/or imprisonment—and, in some cases, death. Because crimes are *offenses against society as a whole,* they are prosecuted by a public official, not by victims.
3. *Key differences*—An important difference between civil and criminal law is that the standard of proof is higher in criminal cases (see Exhibit 6–1 on page 172 for other differences between civil and criminal law).
4. *Civil liability for criminal acts*—A criminal act may give rise to both criminal liability and tort liability (see Exhibit 6–2 on page 173 for an example of criminal and tort liability for the same act).

Criminal Liability
(See pages 173–174.)

1. *Guilty act*—In general, some form of harmful act must be committed for a crime to exist.
2. *Intent*—An intent to commit a crime, or a wrongful mental state, is generally required for a crime to exist.

Corporate Criminal Liability
(See pages 174–175.)

1. *Liability of corporations*—Corporations normally are liable for the crimes committed by their agents and employees within the course and scope of their employment. Corporations cannot be imprisoned, but they can be fined or denied certain legal privileges.
2. *Liability of corporate officers and directors*—Corporate directors and officers are personally liable for the crimes they commit and may be held liable for the actions of employees under their supervision.

Types of Crimes
(See pages 175–182.)

1. Crimes fall into five general categories: violent crime, property crime, public order crime, white-collar crime, and organized crime.
   a. Violent crimes are those that cause others to suffer harm or death, including murder, assault and battery, sexual assault (rape), and robbery.
   b. Property crimes are the most common form of crime. The offender's goal is to obtain some economic gain or to damage property. This category includes burglary, larceny, obtaining goods by false pretenses, receiving stolen property, arson, and forgery.
   c. Public order crimes are acts, such as public drunkenness, prostitution, gambling, and illegal drug use, that a statute has established are contrary to public values and morals.
   d. White-collar crimes are illegal acts committed by a person or business using nonviolent means to obtain a personal or business advantage. Usually, such crimes are committed in the

(Continued)

CHAPTER SUMMARY   Criminal Law and Cyber Crimes—Continued

Types of Crimes—Continued	course of a legitimate occupation. Embezzlement, mail and wire fraud, bribery, bankruptcy fraud, the theft of trade secrets, and insider trading are examples of this category of crime. e. Organized crime is a form of crime conducted by groups operating illegitimately to satisfy the public's demand for illegal goods and services (such as gambling or illegal narcotics). This category of crime also includes money laundering and racketeering (RICO) violations. 2. Each type of crime may also be classified according to its degree of seriousness. Felonies are serious crimes punishable by death or by imprisonment for more than one year. Misdemeanors are less serious crimes punishable by fines or by confinement for up to one year.
Defenses to Criminal Liability (See pages 182–185.)	Defenses to criminal liability include infancy, intoxication, insanity, mistake, consent, duress, justifiable use of force, entrapment, and the statute of limitations. Also, in some cases defendants may be relieved of criminal liability, at least in part, if they are given immunity.
Constitutional Safeguards and Criminal Procedures (See pages 185–193.)	1. *Fourth Amendment*—Provides protection against unreasonable searches and seizures and requires that probable cause exist before a warrant for a search or an arrest can be issued. 2. *Fifth Amendment*—Requires due process of law, prohibits double jeopardy, and protects against self-incrimination. 3. *Sixth Amendment*—Provides guarantees of a speedy trial, a trial by jury, a public trial, the right to confront witnesses, and the right to counsel. 4. *Eighth Amendment*—Prohibits excessive bail and fines, and cruel and unusual punishment. 5. *Exclusionary rule*—A criminal procedural rule that prohibits the introduction at trial of all evidence obtained in violation of constitutional rights, as well as any evidence derived from the illegally obtained evidence. 6. *Miranda rule*—A rule set forth by the Supreme Court in *Miranda v. Arizona* holding that individuals who are arrested must be informed of certain constitutional rights, including their right to counsel. (See Exhibit 6–3 on page 190.) 7. *Arrest, indictment, and trial*—Procedures governing arrest, indictment, and trial for a crime are designed to safeguard the rights of the individual against the state. See Exhibit 6–4 on page 191 for a summary of the major procedural steps involved in prosecuting a criminal case. 8. *Sentencing guidelines*—The federal government has established sentencing laws or guidelines. The federal sentencing guidelines indicate a range of penalties for each federal crime; federal judges consider these guidelines when imposing sentences on those convicted of federal crimes.
Cyber Crime (See pages 193–196.)	Cyber crimes occur in cyberspace. Examples include cyber theft (financial crimes committed with the aid of computers, as well as identity theft), hacking, and cyberterrorism. The Computer Fraud and Abuse Act of 1984, as amended by the National Information Infrastructure Protection Act of 1996, is a significant federal statute that addresses cyber crime.

FOR REVIEW

Answers for the even-numbered questions in this **For Review** *section can be found in Appendix E at the end of this text.*

1 What two elements must exist before a person can be held liable for a crime? Can a corporation commit crimes?

2 What are five broad categories of crimes? What is white-collar crime?

3 What defenses might be raised by criminal defendants to avoid liability for criminal acts?

4 What constitutional safeguards exist to protect persons accused of crimes? What are the major procedural steps in the criminal process?

5 What is cyber crime? What laws apply to crimes committed in cyberspace?

■

QUESTIONS AND CASE PROBLEMS

 HYPOTHETICAL SCENARIOS

6.1 Criminal versus Civil Trials. In criminal trials, the defendant must be proved guilty beyond a reasonable doubt, whereas in civil trials, the defendant need only be proved guilty by a preponderance of the evidence. Discuss why a higher standard of proof is required in criminal trials.

6.2 Hypothetical Question with Sample Answer. The following situations are similar (all involve the theft of Makoto's laptop computer), yet they represent three different crimes. Identify the three crimes, noting the differences among them.

   1 While passing Makoto's house one night, Sarah sees a laptop computer left unattended on Makoto's porch. Sarah takes the computer, carries it home, and tells everyone she owns it.

   2 While passing Makoto's house one night, Sarah sees Makoto outside with a laptop computer. Holding Makoto at gunpoint, Sarah forces him to give up the computer. Then Sarah runs away with it.

   3 While passing Makoto's house one night, Sarah sees a laptop computer on a desk near a window. Sarah breaks the lock on the front door, enters, and leaves with the computer.

 For a sample answer to Question 6.2, go to Appendix F at the end of this text.

6.3 Types of Crimes. Which, if any, of the following crimes necessarily involve illegal activity on the part of more than one person?

   1 Bribery.

   2 Forgery.

   3 Embezzlement.

   4 Larceny.

   5 Receiving stolen property.

6.4 Double Jeopardy. Armington, while robbing a drugstore, shot and seriously injured Jennings, a drugstore clerk. Armington was subsequently convicted of armed robbery and assault and battery in a criminal trial. Jennings later brought a civil tort suit against Armington for damages. Armington contended that he could not be tried again for the same crime, as that would constitute double jeopardy, which is prohibited by the Fifth Amendment to the U.S. Constitution. Is Armington correct? Explain.

■

 **CASE PROBLEMS**

6.5 Fifth Amendment. The federal government was investigating a corporation and its employees. The alleged criminal wrongdoing, which included the falsification of corporate books and records, occurred between 1993 and 1996 in one division of the corporation. In 1999, the corporation pleaded guilty and agreed to cooperate in an investigation of the individuals who might have been involved in the improper corporate activities. "Doe I," "Doe II," and "Doe III" were officers of the corporation during the period when the illegal activities occurred and worked in the division where the wrongdoing took place. They were no longer working for the corporation, however, when, as part of the subsequent investigation, the government asked them to provide specific corporate documents in their possession. All three asserted the Fifth Amendment privilege against self-incrimination. The government asked a federal district court to order the three to produce the records. Corporate employees can be compelled to produce corporate records in a criminal proceeding because they hold the records as representatives of the corporation, to which the Fifth Amendment privilege against self-incrimination does not apply. Should *former* employees also be compelled to produce corporate records in their possession? Why or why not? [*In re Three Grand Jury Subpoenas Duces Tecum Dated January 29, 1999,* 191 F.3d 173 (2d Cir. 1999)]

6.6 Larceny. In February 2001, a homeowner hired Jimmy Smith, a contractor claiming to employ a crew of thirty workers, to build a garage. The homeowner paid Smith $7,950 and agreed to make additional payments as needed to complete the project, up to $15,900. Smith promised to start the next day and finish within eight weeks. Nearly a month passed with no work, while Smith lied to the homeowner that materials were on "back order." During a second month, footings were created for the foundation, and a subcontractor poured the concrete slab, but Smith did not return the homeowner's phone calls. After eight weeks, the homeowner confronted Smith, who promised to complete the job, worked on the site that day until lunch, and never returned. Three months later, the homeowner again confronted Smith, who promised to "pay [him] off" later that day but did not do so. In March 2002, the state of Georgia filed criminal charges against Smith. While his trial was pending, he promised to pay the homeowner "next week," but again failed to refund any money. The value of the labor performed before Smith abandoned the project was between $800 and $1,000, the value of the materials was $367, and the subcontractor was paid $2,270. Did Smith commit larceny? Explain. [*Smith v. State of Georgia*, 265 Ga.App.57, 592 S.E.2d 871 (2004)]

6.7 Case Problem with Sample Answer. The Sixth Amendment guarantees to a defendant who faces possible imprisonment the right to counsel at all critical stages of the criminal process, including the arraignment and the trial. In 1996, Felipe Tovar, a twenty-one-year-old college student, was arrested in Ames, Iowa, for operating a motor vehicle while under the influence of alcohol (OWI). Tovar was informed of his right to apply for court-appointed counsel and waived it. At his arraignment, he pleaded guilty. Six weeks later, he appeared for sentencing, again waived his right to counsel, and was sentenced to two days' imprisonment. In 1998, Tovar was convicted of OWI again, and in 2000, he was charged with OWI for a third time. In Iowa, a third OWI offense is a felony. Tovar asked the court not to use his first OWI conviction to enhance the third OWI charge. He argued that his 1996 waiver of counsel was not "intelligent" because the court did not make him aware of "the dangers and disadvantages of self-representation." What determines whether a person's choice in any situation is "intelligent"? What should determine whether a defendant's waiver of counsel is "intelligent" at critical stages of a criminal proceeding? [*Iowa v. Tovar*, 541 U.S. 77, 124 S.Ct. 1379, 158 L.Ed.2d 209 (2004)]

After you have answered Problem 6.7, compare your answer with the sample answer given on the Web site that accompanies this text. Go to academic.cengage.com/blaw/blt, select "Chapter 6," and click on "Case Problem with Sample Answer."

6.8 Trial. Robert Michels met Allison Formal through an online dating Web site in 2002. Michels represented himself as the retired chief executive officer of a large company that he had sold for millions of dollars. In January 2003, Michels proposed that he and Formal create a limited liability company (a special form of business organization discussed in Chapter 19)—Formal Properties Trust, LLC—to "channel their investments in real estate." Formal agreed to contribute $100,000 to the company and wrote two $50,000 checks to "Michels and Associates, LLC." Six months later, Michels told Formal that

their LLC had been formed in Delaware. Later, Formal asked Michels about her investments. He responded evasively, and she demanded that an independent accountant review the firm's records. Michels refused. Formal contacted the police. Michels was charged in a Virginia state court with obtaining money by false pretenses. The Delaware secretary of state verified, in two certified documents, that "Formal Properties Trust, L.L.C." and "Michels and Associates, L.L.C." did not exist in Delaware. Did the admission of the Delaware secretary of state's certified documents at Michels's trial violate his rights under the Sixth Amendment? Why or why not? [*Michels v. Commonwealth of Virginia*, 47 Va.App. 461, 624 S.E.2d 675 (2006)]

6.9 White-Collar Crime. Helm Instruction Co. in Maumee, Ohio, makes custom electrical control systems. Helm hired Patrick Walsh in September 1998 to work as comptroller. Walsh soon developed a close relationship with Richard Wilhelm, Helm's president, who granted Walsh's request to hire Shari Price as Walsh's assistant. Wilhelm was not aware that Walsh and Price were engaged in an extramarital affair. Over the next five years, Walsh and Price spent more than $200,000 of Helm's funds on themselves. Among other things, Walsh drew unauthorized checks on Helm's accounts to pay his personal credit cards, and issued to Price and himself unauthorized salary increases, overtime payments, and tuition reimbursement payments, altering Helm's records to hide the payments. After an investigation, Helm officials confronted Walsh. He denied the affair with Price, claimed that his unauthorized use of Helm's funds was an "interest-free loan" and argued that it was less of a burden on the company to pay his credit cards than to give him the salary increases to which he felt he was entitled. Did Walsh commit a crime? If so, what crime did he commit? Discuss. [*State v. Walsh*, __ Ohio App.3d __, __ N.E.2d __ (6 Dist. 2007)]

6.10 A Question of Ethics. *A troublesome issue concerning the constitutional privilege against self-incrimination has to do with the extent to which trickery by law enforcement officers during an interrogation may overwhelm a suspect's will to avoid self-incrimination. For example, in one case two officers questioned Charles McFarland, who was incarcerated in a state prison, about his connection to a handgun that had been used to shoot two other officers. McFarland was advised of his rights but was not asked whether he was willing to waive those rights. Instead, to induce McFarland to speak, the officers deceived him into believing that "[n]obody is going to give you charges," and he made incriminating admissions. He was indicted for possessing a handgun as a convicted felon.* [*United States v. McFarland*, 424 F.Supp.2d 427 (N.D.N.Y. 2006)]

1 Review the discussion of *Miranda v. Arizona* in this chapter. Should McFarland's statements be suppressed—that is, not be admissible at trial—because he was not asked whether he was willing to waive his rights before he made his self-incriminating statements? Does *Miranda* apply to McFarland's situation?

2 Do you think that it is fair for the police to resort to trickery and deception to bring those who may have committed crimes to justice? Why or why not? What rights or public policies must be balanced in deciding this issue?

CRITICAL THINKING AND WRITING ASSIGNMENTS

6.11 Critical Legal Thinking. Do you think that criminal procedure in this country is weighted too heavily in favor of accused persons? Can you think of a fairer way to balance the constitutional rights of accused persons against the right of society to be protected against criminal behavior? Should different criminal procedures be used when terrorism is involved? Explain.

6.12 Critical Legal Thinking. Ray steals a purse from an unattended car at a gas station. Because the purse contains money and a handgun, Ray is convicted of grand theft of property (cash) and grand theft of a firearm. On appeal, Ray claims that he is not guilty of grand theft of a firearm because he did not know that the purse contained a gun. Can Ray be convicted of the crime of grand theft of a firearm even though he did not know that the gun was in the purse?

6.13 **Video Question.** Go to this text's Web site at **academic. cengage.com/blaw/blt** and select "Chapter 6." Click on

"Video Questions" and view the video titled *Casino*. Then answer the following questions.

1 In the video, a casino manager, Ace (Robert De Niro), discusses how politicians "won their 'comp life' when they got elected." "Comps" are the free gifts that casinos give to high-stakes gamblers to keep their business. If an elected official accepts comps, is he or she committing a crime? If so, what type of crime? Explain your answers.

2 Assume that Ace committed a crime by giving politicians comps. Can the casino, Tangiers Corp., be held liable for that crime? Why or why not? How could a court punish the corporation?

3 Suppose that the Federal Bureau of Investigation wants to search the premises of Tangiers for evidence of criminal activity. If casino management refuses to consent to the search, what constitutional safeguards and criminal procedures, if any, protect Tangiers?

ONLINE ACTIVITIES

PRACTICAL INTERNET EXERCISES

Go to this text's Web site at **academic.cengage.com/blaw/blt**, select "Chapter 6," and click on "Practical Internet Exercises." There you will find the following Internet research exercises that you can perform to learn more about the topics covered in this chapter.

PRACTICAL INTERNET EXERCISE 6–1 LEGAL PERSPECTIVE—Revisiting *Miranda*

PRACTICAL INTERNET EXERCISE 6–2 MANAGEMENT PERSPECTIVE—Hackers

PRACTICAL INTERNET EXERCISE 6–3 INTERNATIONAL PERSPECTIVE—Fighting Cyber Crime Worldwide

BEFORE THE TEST

Go to this text's Web site at **academic.cengage.com/blaw/blt**, select "Chapter 6," and click on "Interactive Quizzes." You will find a number of interactive questions relating to this chapter.

CHAPTER 7
Contracts: Nature, Classification, Agreement, and Consideration

> **❝**The social order rests upon the stability and predictability of conduct, of which keeping promises is a large item.**❞**
>
> Roscoe Pound, 1870–1964
> (American jurist)

CHAPTER OUTLINE

–AN OVERVIEW OF CONTRACT LAW

–TYPES OF CONTRACTS

–AGREEMENT

–CONSIDERATION

LEARNING OBJECTIVES

AFTER READING THIS CHAPTER, YOU SHOULD BE ABLE TO ANSWER THE FOLLOWING QUESTIONS:

1 What is a contract? What are the four basic elements necessary to the formation of a valid contract?

2 What are the various types of contracts?

3 What are the requirements of an offer?

4 How can an offer be accepted?

5 What are the elements of consideration?

PROMISE
An assertion that something either will or will not happen in the future.

As the eminent jurist Roscoe Pound observed in the chapter-opening quotation, "keeping promises" is important to a stable social order. Contract law deals with, among other things, the formation and keeping of promises. A **promise** is an assertion that something either will or will not happen in the future.

Like other types of law, contract law reflects our social values, interests, and expectations at a given point in time. It shows, for example, what kinds of promises our society thinks should be legally binding. It distinguishes between promises that create only *moral* obligations (such as a promise to take a friend to lunch) and promises that are legally binding (such as a promise to pay for merchandise purchased). Contract law also demonstrates what excuses our society accepts for breaking certain types of promises. In addition, it shows what promises are considered to be contrary to public policy—against the interests of society as a whole—and therefore legally invalid. When the person making a promise is a child or is mentally incompetent, for example, a question will arise as to whether the promise should be enforced. Resolving such questions is the essence of contract law.

In this chapter, we first discuss an overview of contract law and the various types of contracts that exist. We also consider the basic requirements for a valid and enforceable contract. We then look closely at two of these requirements—agreement and consideration.

AN OVERVIEW OF CONTRACT LAW

Before we look at the numerous rules that courts use to determine whether a particular promise will be enforced, it is necessary to understand some fundamental concepts of contract law. In this section, we describe the sources and general function of contract law. We also provide the definition of a contract and present the concepts of *freedom of contract* and *freedom from contract*.

Sources of Contract Law

The common law governs all contracts except when it has been modified or replaced by statutory law, such as the Uniform Commercial Code (UCC),[1] or by administrative agency regulations. Contracts relating to services, real estate, employment, and insurance, for example, generally are governed by the common law of contracts.

Contracts for the sale and lease of goods, however, are governed by the UCC—to the extent that the UCC has modified general contract law. The relationship between general contract law and the law governing sales and leases of goods will be explored in detail in Chapter 11.

The Function of Contracts

No aspect of modern life is entirely free of contractual relationships. You acquire rights and obligations, for example, when you borrow funds, when you buy or lease a house, when you obtain insurance, when you form a business, and when you purchase goods or services. Contract law is designed to provide stability and predictability for both buyers and sellers in the marketplace.

Contract law assures the parties to private agreements that the promises they make will be enforceable. Clearly, many promises are kept because the parties involved feel a moral obligation to do so or because keeping a promise is in their mutual self-interest. The **promisor** (the person making the promise) and the **promisee** (the person to whom the promise is made) may decide to honor their agreement for other reasons. Nevertheless, the rules of contract law are often followed in business agreements to avoid potential problems.

By supplying procedures for enforcing private agreements, contract law provides an essential condition for the existence of a market economy. Without a legal framework of reasonably assured expectations within which to plan and venture, businesspersons would be able to rely only on the good faith of others. Duty and good faith are usually sufficient, but when dramatic price changes or adverse economic conditions make it costly to comply with a promise, these elements may not be enough. Contract law is necessary to ensure compliance with a promise or to entitle the innocent party to some form of relief.

PROMISOR
A person who makes a promise.
PROMISEE
A person to whom a promise is made.

The Definition of a Contract

A **contract** is an agreement that can be enforced in court. It is formed by two or more parties who agree to perform or to refrain from performing some act now or in the future. Generally, contract disputes arise when there is a promise of future performance. If the contractual promise is not fulfilled, the party who made it is subject to the sanctions of a court. That party may be required to pay monetary damages for failing to perform the contractual promise; in limited instances, the party may be required to perform the promised act.

CONTRACT
An agreement that can be enforced in court; formed by two or more competent parties who agree, for consideration, to perform or to refrain from performing some legal act now or in the future.

Requirements of a Valid Contract

The list on the next page briefly describes the four requirements that must be met for a valid contract to exist. If any of these elements is lacking, no contract will have been formed. (The first two elements—*agreement* and *consideration*—will be explained more fully later in this chapter, and the other two elements—*contractual capacity* and *legality*—will be covered in Chapter 8.)

ON THE WEB

An extensive definition of the term *contract* is offered by the 'Lectric Law Library at
www.lectlaw.com/def/c123.htm.

1. See Chapter 11 for further discussions of the significance and coverage of the Uniform Commercial Code (UCC). Articles 2 and 2A of the UCC are presented in Appendix C at the end of this book.

The manager of a Toyota dealership in Glendora, California, displays the same contract written in four different Asian languages (Chinese, Korean, Vietnamese, and Tagalog). A consumer protection law in California requires certain businesses, such as car dealers and apartment owners, that have employees who orally negotiate contracts in these languages to provide written contracts in those same languages. Why might it be important to the enforceability of a written contract that the consumer actually be able to read its provisions?
(AP Photo/Damian Dovarganes)

1 *Agreement.* An agreement to form a contract includes an *offer* and an *acceptance.* One party must offer to enter into a legal agreement, and another party must accept the terms of the offer.

2 *Consideration.* Any promises made by parties must be supported by legally sufficient and bargained-for consideration (something of value received or promised to convince a person to make a deal).

3 *Contractual capacity.* Both parties entering into the contract must have the contractual capacity to do so; the law must recognize them as possessing characteristics that qualify them as competent parties.

4 *Legality.* The contract's purpose must be to accomplish some goal that is legal and not against public policy.

Even if all of the elements of a valid contract are present, a contract may be unenforceable if the following requirements are not met. These requirements typically are raised as *defenses* to the enforceability of an otherwise valid contract.

1 *Genuineness of assent.* The consent of both parties must be genuine. For example, if a contract was formed as a result of fraud, mistake, or duress, the contract may not be enforceable (see Chapter 8).

2 *Form.* The contract must be in whatever form the law requires; for example, some contracts must be in writing to be enforceable (see Chapter 8).

Freedom of Contract and Freedom from Contract

As a general rule, the law recognizes everyone's ability to enter freely into contractual arrangements. This recognition is called *freedom of contract,* a freedom protected by the U.S. Constitution in Article I, Section 10. Because freedom of contract is a fundamental public policy of the United States, courts rarely interfere with contracts that have been voluntarily made.

Of course, as in other areas of the law, there are many exceptions to the general rule that contracts voluntarily negotiated will be enforced. For example, illegal bargains, agreements that unreasonably restrain trade, and certain unfair contracts made between one party with a great amount of bargaining power and another with little power are generally not enforced. In addition, as you will read in Chapter 8, certain contracts and clauses may not be enforceable if they are contrary to public policy, fairness, and justice. These exceptions provide *freedom from contract* for persons who may have been forced into making contracts unfavorable to themselves.

ON THE WEB

For an excellent overview of the basic principles of contract law, go to

library.findlaw.com/1999/Jan/1/ 241463.html.

TYPES OF CONTRACTS

There are numerous types of contracts. They are categorized based on legal distinctions as to their formation, performance, and enforceability. Exhibit 7–1 illustrates three classifications, or categories, of contracts based on their mode of formation.

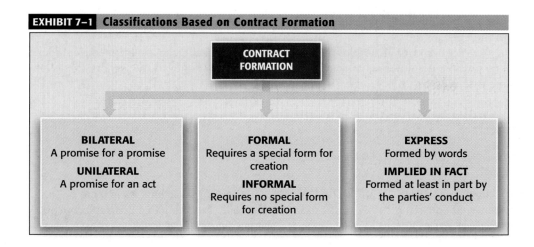

EXHIBIT 7-1 Classifications Based on Contract Formation

Contract Formation

As you can see in Exhibit 7–1, three classifications, or categories, of contracts are based on how and when a contract is formed. The best way to explain each type of contract is to compare one type with another, as we do in the following pages.

Bilateral versus Unilateral Contracts   Every contract involves at least two parties. The **offeror** is the party making the offer. The **offeree** is the party to whom the offer is made. The offeror always promises to do or not to do something and thus is also a promisor. Whether the contract is classified as *bilateral* or *unilateral* depends on what the offeree must do to accept the offer and bind the offeror to a contract.

OFFEROR
A person who makes an offer.
OFFEREE
A person to whom an offer is made.

Bilateral Contracts.   If the offeree can accept the offer simply by promising to perform, the contract is a **bilateral contract.** Hence, a bilateral contract is a "promise for a promise." An example of a bilateral contract is a contract in which one person agrees to buy another person's automobile for a specified price. No performance, such as the payment of funds or delivery of goods, need take place for a bilateral contract to be formed. The contract comes into existence at the moment the promises are exchanged. ▪**EXAMPLE 7.1** Jeff offers to buy Ann's digital camera for $200. Jeff tells Ann that he will give her the cash for the camera on the following Friday, when he gets paid. Ann accepts Jeff's offer and promises to give him the camera when he pays her on Friday. Jeff and Ann have formed a bilateral contract. ▪

BILATERAL CONTRACT
A type of contract that arises when a promise is given in exchange for a return promise.

Unilateral Contracts.   If the offer is phrased so that the offeree can accept only by completing the contract performance, the contract is a **unilateral contract.** Hence, a unilateral contract is a "promise for an act." In other words, the contract is formed not at the moment when promises are exchanged but rather when the contract is *performed.* ▪**EXAMPLE 7.2** Reese says to Celia, "If you drive my car from New York to Los Angeles, I'll give you $1,000." Only on Celia's completion of the act—bringing the car to Los Angeles—does she fully accept Reese's offer to pay $1,000. If she chooses not to accept the offer to drive the car to Los Angeles, there are no legal consequences. ▪
    Contests, lotteries, and other competitions offering prizes are also examples of offers for unilateral contracts. If a person complies with the rules of the contest—such as by submitting the right lottery number at the right place and time—a unilateral contract is

UNILATERAL CONTRACT
A contract that results when an offer can be accepted only by the offeree's performance.

formed, binding the organization offering the prize to a contract to perform as promised in the offer.

Can a school's, or an employer's, letter of tentative acceptance to a prospective student, or a possible employee, qualify as a unilateral contract? That was the issue in the following case.

CASE 7.1 **Ardito v. City of Providence**

United States District Court, District of Rhode Island, 263 F.Supp.2d 358 (2003).

FACTS In 2001, the city of Providence, Rhode Island, decided to begin hiring police officers to fill vacancies in its police department. Because only individuals who had graduated from the Providence Police Academy were eligible, the city also decided to conduct two training sessions, the "60th and 61st Police Academies." To be admitted, an applicant had to pass a series of tests and be deemed qualified by members of the department after an interview. The applicants judged most qualified were sent a letter informing them that they had been selected to attend the academy if they successfully completed a medical checkup and a psychological examination. The letter for the applicants to the 61st Academy, dated October 15, stated that it was "a conditional offer of employment." Meanwhile, a new chief of police, Dean Esserman, decided to revise the selection process, which caused some of those who had received the letter to be rejected. Derek Ardito and thirteen other newly rejected applicants filed a suit in a federal district court against the city, seeking a halt to the 61st Academy unless they were allowed to attend. They alleged in part that the city was in breach of contract.

ISSUE Was the October 15 letter a unilateral offer that the plaintiffs had accepted by passing the required medical and psychological examinations?

DECISION Yes. The court issued an injunction to prohibit the city from conducting the 61st Police Academy unless the plaintiffs were included.

REASON The court found the October 15 letter to be "a classic example of an offer to enter into a unilateral contract. The October 15 letter expressly stated that it was a 'conditional offer of employment' and the message that it conveyed was that the recipient would be admitted into the 61st Academy if he or she successfully completed the medical and psychological examinations." The court contrasted the letter with "notices sent to applicants by the City at earlier stages of the selection process. Those notices merely informed applicants that they had completed a step in the process and remained eligible to be considered for admission into the Academy. Unlike the October 15 letter, the prior notices did not purport to extend a 'conditional offer' of admission." The court concluded that "[t]he plaintiffs accepted the City's offer of admission into the Academy by satisfying the specified conditions. Each of the plaintiffs submitted to and passed lengthy and intrusive medical and psychological examinations."

WHAT IF THE FACTS WERE DIFFERENT? *Suppose that the October 15 letter had used the phrase* potential offer of employment *rather than the word* conditional. *Would the court in this case still have considered the letter to be a unilateral contract?*

ON THE WEB

For easy-to-understand definitions of legal terms and concepts, including terms and concepts relating to contract law, go to dictionary.law.com and key in a term, such as *contract* or *consideration*.

Revocation of Offers for Unilateral Contracts. A problem arises in unilateral contracts when the promisor attempts to *revoke* (cancel) the offer after the promisee has begun performance but before the act has been completed. **EXAMPLE 7.3** Suppose that Roberta offers to buy Ed's sailboat, moored in San Francisco, on delivery of the boat to Roberta's dock in Newport Beach, three hundred miles south of San Francisco. Ed rigs the boat and sets sail. Shortly before his arrival at Newport Beach, Ed receives a radio message from Roberta withdrawing her offer. Roberta's offer is to form a unilateral contract, and only Ed's delivery of the sailboat at her dock is an acceptance. ■

In contract law, offers are normally *revocable* (capable of being taken back, or canceled) until accepted. Under the traditional view of unilateral contracts, Roberta's revocation would terminate the offer. Because of the harsh effect on the offeree of the revocation of an offer to form a unilateral contract, the modern-day view is that once performance has been *substantially* undertaken, the offeror cannot revoke the offer. Thus, in our example, even though Ed has not yet accepted the offer by complete performance, Roberta is prohibited from revoking it. Ed can deliver the boat and bind Roberta to the contract.

Formal versus Informal Contracts   Another classification system divides contracts into formal contracts and informal contracts. **Formal contracts** are contracts that require a special form or method of creation (formation) to be enforceable.[2] *Contracts under seal* are a type of formal contract that involves a formalized writing with a special seal attached.[3] In the past, the seals were often made of wax and impressed on the paper document. Today, the significance of the seal in contract law has lessened, though standard-form contracts still sometimes include a place for a seal next to the signature lines. Letters of credit, which are frequently used in international sales contracts, are another type of formal contract. As will be discussed in Chapter 25, letters of credit are agreements to pay contingent on the purchaser's receipt of invoices and bills of lading (documents evidencing receipt of, and title to, goods shipped).

    Informal contracts (also called *simple contracts*) include all other contracts. No special form is required (except for certain types of contracts that must be in writing), because the contracts are usually based on their substance rather than their form. Typically, businesspersons put their contracts in writing to ensure that there is some proof of a contract's existence should problems arise.

Express versus Implied Contracts   Contracts may also be formed and categorized as express or implied by the conduct of the parties. We look here at the differences between these two types of contracts.

Express Contracts.   In an **express contract,** the terms of the agreement are fully and explicitly stated in words, oral or written. A signed lease for an apartment or a house is an express written contract. If a classmate accepts your offer to sell your textbooks from last semester for $175, an express oral contract has been made.

Implied Contracts.   A contract that is implied from the conduct of the parties is called an **implied-in-fact contract,** or an implied contract. This type of contract differs from an express contract in that the *conduct* of the parties, rather than their words, creates and defines at least some of the terms of the contract. (Note that a contract can be a mixture of an express contract and an implied-in-fact contract. In other words, a contract may contain some express terms, while others are implied.)

Requirements for an Implied-in-Fact Contract.   For an implied-in-fact contract to arise, certain requirements must be met. Normally, if the following conditions exist, a court will hold that an implied contract was formed:

FORMAL CONTRACT
A contract that by law requires a specific form, such as being executed under seal, for its validity.

INFORMAL CONTRACT
A contract that does not require a specified form or formality to be valid.

KEEP IN MIND   Not every contract is a document with "Contract" printed in block letters at the top. A contract can be expressed in a letter, a memo, or another document.

EXPRESS CONTRACT
A contract in which the terms of the agreement are stated in words, oral or written.

IMPLIED-IN-FACT CONTRACT
A contract formed in whole or in part from the conduct of the parties (as opposed to an express contract).

---

2. See *Restatement (Second) of Contracts,* Section 6, which explains that formal contracts include (1) contracts under seal, (2) recognizances, (3) negotiable instruments, and (4) letters of credit. As mentioned in Chapter 1, *Restatements of the Law* are books that summarize court decisions on a particular topic and that courts often refer to for guidance.
3. A seal may be actual (made of wax or some other durable substance), impressed on the paper, or indicated simply by the word *seal* or the letters *L.S.* at the end of the document. *L.S.* stands for *locus sigilli,* which means "the place for the seal."

What determines whether a contract for accounting, tax preparation, or any other service is an express contract or an implied-in-fact contract? (Getty Images)

1 The plaintiff furnished some service or property.

2 The plaintiff expected to be paid for that service or property, and the defendant knew or should have known that payment was expected.

3 The defendant had a chance to reject the services or property and did not.

EXAMPLE 7.4 Suppose that you need an accountant to fill out your tax return this year. You look through the Yellow Pages and find an accounting firm located in your neighborhood. You drop by the firm's office, explain your problem to an accountant, and learn what fees will be charged. The next day you return and give the receptionist all of the necessary information and documents, such as canceled checks and W-2 forms. Then you walk out the door without saying anything expressly to the accountant.

In this situation, you have entered into an implied-in-fact contract to pay the accountant the usual and reasonable fees for her accounting services. The contract is implied by your conduct and by hers. She expects to be paid for completing your tax return. By bringing in the records she will need to do the work, you have implied an intent to pay for her services. ■

Contract Performance

Contracts are also classified according to their state of performance. A contract that has been fully performed on both sides is called an **executed contract.** A contract that has not been fully performed on either side is called an **executory contract.** If one party has fully performed but the other has not, the contract is said to be executed on the one side and executory on the other, but the contract is still classified as executory.

EXAMPLE 7.5 Assume that you agree to buy ten tons of coal from Western Coal Company. Further assume that Western has delivered the coal to your steel mill, where it is now being burned. At this point, the contract is an executory contract—it is executed on the part of Western and executory on your part. After you pay Western for the coal, the contract will be executed on both sides. ■

EXECUTED CONTRACT
A contract that has been fully performed by both parties.

EXECUTORY CONTRACT
A contract that has not as yet been fully performed.

Contract Enforceability

A **valid contract** has the four elements necessary for contract formation: (1) an agreement (offer and acceptance) (2) supported by legally sufficient consideration (3) for a legal purpose and (4) made by parties who have the legal capacity to enter into the contract. As mentioned, we will discuss each of these elements in this and the following chapter. As you can see in Exhibit 7–2, valid contracts may be enforceable, voidable, or unenforceable. Additionally, a contract may be referred to as a *void contract*. We look next at the meaning of the terms *voidable, unenforceable,* and *void* in relation to contract enforceability.

Voidable Contracts   A **voidable contract** is a *valid* contract but one that can be avoided at the option of one or both of the parties. The party having the option can elect either to avoid any duty to perform or to *ratify* (make valid) the contract. If the contract is avoided, both parties are released from it. If it is ratified, both parties must fully perform their respective legal obligations.

As you will read in Chapter 8, contracts made by minors, insane persons, and intoxicated persons may be voidable. As a general rule, for example, contracts made by minors are voidable at the option of the minor. Additionally, contracts entered into under fraudulent conditions are voidable at the option of the defrauded party. Contracts entered into under legally defined duress or undue influence are voidable (see Chapter 8).

Unenforceable Contracts   An **unenforceable contract** is one that cannot be enforced because of certain legal defenses against it. It is not unenforceable because a party failed to satisfy a legal requirement of the contract; rather, it is a valid contract rendered unenforceable by some statute or law. For example, some contracts must be in writing (see Chapter 8), and if they are not, they will not be enforceable except in certain exceptional circumstances.

VALID CONTRACT
A contract that results when the elements necessary for contract formation (agreement, consideration, legal purpose, and contractual capacity) are present.

VOIDABLE CONTRACT
A contract that may be legally avoided (canceled, or annulled) at the option of one or both of the parties.

UNENFORCEABLE CONTRACT
A valid contract rendered unenforceable by some statute or law.

EXHIBIT 7–2   Enforceable, Voidable, Unenforceable, and Void Contracts

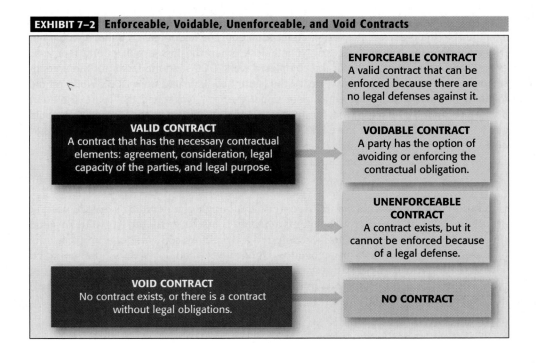

VALID CONTRACT
A contract that has the necessary contractual elements: agreement, consideration, legal capacity of the parties, and legal purpose.

ENFORCEABLE CONTRACT
A valid contract that can be enforced because there are no legal defenses against it.

VOIDABLE CONTRACT
A party has the option of avoiding or enforcing the contractual obligation.

UNENFORCEABLE CONTRACT
A contract exists, but it cannot be enforced because of a legal defense.

VOID CONTRACT
No contract exists, or there is a contract without legal obligations.

NO CONTRACT

VOID CONTRACT
A contract having no legal force or binding effect.

Void Contracts   A **void contract** is no contract at all. The terms *void* and *contract* are contradictory. None of the parties has any legal obligations if a contract is void. A contract can be void because, for example, one of the parties was previously determined by a court to be legally insane (and thus lacked the legal capacity to enter into a contract) or because the purpose of the contract was illegal.

Quasi Contracts

QUASI CONTRACT
A fictional contract imposed on the parties by a court in the interests of fairness and justice; usually imposed to avoid the unjust enrichment of one party at the expense of another.

Quasi contracts, or contracts *implied in law,* are wholly different from actual contracts. Express contracts and implied-in-fact contracts are actual or true contracts formed by the words or actions of the parties. The word *quasi* is Latin for "as if" or "analogous to." Quasi contracts are not true contracts because they do not arise from any agreement, express or implied, between the parties themselves. Rather, quasi contracts are fictional contracts that courts can impose on the parties "as if" the parties had entered into an actual contract. They are equitable rather than legal contracts. Usually, quasi contracts are imposed to avoid the *unjust enrichment* of one party at the expense of another. The doctrine of unjust enrichment is based on the theory that individuals should not be allowed to profit or enrich themselves inequitably at the expense of others.

▪**EXAMPLE 7.6**   Suppose that a vacationing physician is driving down the highway and finds Emerson lying unconscious on the side of the road. The physician renders medical aid that saves Emerson's life. Although the injured, unconscious Emerson did not solicit the medical aid and was not aware that the aid had been rendered, Emerson received a valuable benefit, and the requirements for a quasi contract were fulfilled. In such a situation, the law normally will impose a quasi contract, and Emerson will have to pay the physician for the reasonable value of the medical services provided. ▪

When does enrichment qualify as "unjust enrichment"? Sometimes a party is enriched by (benefits from) the actions of another, yet the benefits do not necessarily constitute unjust enrichment. For example, in one case the owner of a building (the lessor) leased the building to a commercial tenant (the lessee) for five years. The lessee, which assumed all responsibility for repairs, maintenance, and alterations, hired DCB Construction Company to make alterations to the premises at a cost of about $300,000. The lessor told DCB that it would not be responsible for any of the costs. Nonetheless, when the lessee quit paying rent, was evicted, and failed to pay DCB for the completed work, DCB sued the lessor for the amount still owing ($280,000). In this case, clearly the lessor had benefited from DCB's work. Yet did this benefit amount to unjust enrichment under the law? No, stated the court. The court pointed out that DCB did the work for the lessee and was notified by the lessor that it would not be liable for the costs of the work. Further, no fraud or mistake was involved. The court noted that the courts almost always reject unjust enrichment claims such as this one.[4]

▪

Limitations on Quasi-Contractual Recovery   Although quasi contracts exist to prevent unjust enrichment, the party who obtains a benefit is not liable for the fair value in some situations. Basically, a party who has conferred a benefit on someone else unnecessarily or as a result of misconduct or negligence cannot invoke the doctrine of quasi contract. The enrichment in those situations will not be considered "unjust." ▪**EXAMPLE 7.7**   You take your car to the local car wash and ask to have it run through the washer and to have the gas tank filled. While your car is being washed, you go to a nearby shopping center

---

4. *DCB Construction Co. v. Central City Development Co.,* 940 P.2d 958 (Colo.App. 1997).

for two hours. In the meantime, one of the workers at the car wash mistakenly assumes that your car is the one that he is supposed to hand wax. When you come back, you are presented with a bill for a full tank of gas, a wash job, and a hand wax. Clearly, a benefit has been conferred on you. But this benefit occurred because of a mistake by the car wash employee. You have not been *unjustly* enriched under these circumstances. People normally cannot be forced to pay for benefits "thrust" on them. ◼

When an Actual Contract Exists   The doctrine of quasi contract generally cannot be used when an actual contract covers the area in controversy. This is because a remedy already exists if a party is unjustly enriched as a result of a breach of contract: the nonbreaching party can sue the breaching party for breach of contract. In this instance, a court does not need to impose a quasi contract to achieve justice. ◼**EXAMPLE 7.8** Fung contracts with Cameron to deliver a furnace to a building owned by Bateman. Fung delivers the furnace, but Cameron never pays Fung. Bateman has been unjustly enriched in this situation, to be sure. Nevertheless, Fung cannot recover from Bateman in quasi contract because Fung had an actual contract with Cameron. Fung already has a remedy—he can sue for breach of contract to recover the price of the furnace from Cameron. No quasi contract need be imposed by the court in this situation to achieve justice. ◼

AGREEMENT

An essential element for contract formation is **agreement**—the parties must agree on the terms of the contract. Ordinarily, agreement is evidenced by two events: an *offer* and an *acceptance*. One party offers a certain bargain to another party, who then accepts that bargain.

Because words often fail to convey the precise meaning intended, the law of contracts generally adheres to the *objective theory of contracts*. Under this theory, a party's words and conduct are held to mean whatever a reasonable person in the offeree's position would think they meant. The court will give words their usual meanings even if "it were proved by twenty bishops that [the] party . . . intended something else."[5]

Requirements of the Offer

An **offer** is a promise or commitment to perform or refrain from performing some specified act in the future. As discussed earlier, the party making an offer is called the *offeror*, and the party to whom the offer is made is called the *offeree*.

Three elements are necessary for an offer to be effective:

1 There must be a serious, objective intention by the offeror.

2 The terms of the offer must be reasonably certain, or definite, so that the parties and the court can ascertain the terms of the contract.

3 The offer must be communicated to the offeree.

Once an effective offer has been made, the offeree's acceptance of that offer creates a legally binding contract (providing the other essential elements for a valid and enforceable contract are present).

In today's e-commerce world, offers are frequently made online. Essentially, the requirements for traditional offers apply to online offers as well, as you will read in Chapter 10.

AGREEMENT
A meeting of two or more minds in regard to the terms of a contract; usually broken down into two events—an offer by one party to form a contract and an acceptance of the offer by the person to whom the offer is made.

OFFER
A promise or commitment to perform or refrain from performing some specified act in the future.

5. Judge Learned Hand in *Hotchkiss v. National City Bank of New York,* 200 F. 287 (2d Cir. 1911); aff'd 231 U.S. 50, 34 S.Ct. 20, 58 L.Ed. 115 (1913). (The term *aff'd* is an abbreviation for *affirmed*; an appellate court can affirm a lower court's judgment, decree, or order, thereby declaring that it is valid and must stand as rendered.)

Intention   The first requirement for an effective offer to exist is a serious, objective intention on the part of the offeror. Intent is not determined by the *subjective* intentions, beliefs, or assumptions of the offeror. Rather, it is determined by what a reasonable person in the offeree's position would conclude the offeror's words and actions meant. Offers made in obvious anger, jest, or undue excitement do not meet the serious-and-objective-intent test. Because these offers are not effective, an offeree's acceptance does not create an agreement.

■EXAMPLE 7.9 You and three classmates ride to school each day in Julio's new automobile, which has a market value of $18,000. One cold morning, the four of you get into the car, but Julio cannot get it started. He yells in anger, "I'll sell this car to anyone for $500!" You drop $500 in his lap. A reasonable person, taking into consideration Julio's frustration and the obvious difference in value between the car's market price and the purchase price, would declare that Julio's offer was not made with serious and objective intent and that you do not have an agreement. ■

In the subsections that follow, we examine the concept of intention further as we look at the distinctions between offers and nonoffers. In the following classic case in the area of contractual agreement, the court had to decide whether an offer was intended when boasts, brags, and dares "after a few drinks" resulted in a contract to sell certain property.

CASE 7.2   Lucy v. Zehmer

LANDMARK AND CLASSIC CASES

Supreme Court of Appeals of Virginia, 196 Va. 493, 84 S.E.2d 516 (1954).

FACTS Lucy and Zehmer had known each other for fifteen to twenty years. For some time, Lucy had been wanting to buy Zehmer's farm. Zehmer had always told Lucy that he was not interested in selling. One night, Lucy stopped in to visit with the Zehmers at a restaurant they operated. Lucy said to Zehmer, "I bet you wouldn't take $50,000 for that place." Zehmer replied, "Yes, I would, too; you wouldn't give fifty." Throughout the evening, the conversation returned to the sale of the farm. At the same time, the parties were drinking whiskey. Eventually, Zehmer wrote up an agreement, on the back of a restaurant check, for the sale of the farm, and he asked his wife to sign it—which she did. When Lucy brought an action in a Virginia state court to enforce the agreement, Zehmer argued that he had been "high as a Georgia pine" at the time and that the offer had been made in jest: "two doggoned drunks bluffing to see who could talk the biggest and say the most." Lucy claimed that he had not been intoxicated and did not think Zehmer had been either, given the way Zehmer handled the transaction. The trial court ruled in favor of the Zehmers, and Lucy appealed.

ISSUE Can the agreement be avoided on the basis of intoxication?

DECISION No. The agreement to sell the farm was binding.

REASON The court held that the evidence given about the nature of the conversation, the appearance and completeness of

the agreement, and the signing all tended to show that a serious business transaction, not a casual jest, was intended. The court had to look into the objective meaning of the words and acts of the Zehmers: "An agreement or mutual assent is of course essential to a valid contract, but the law imputes to a person an intention corresponding to the reasonable meaning of his words and acts. If his words and acts, judged by a reasonable standard, manifest an intention to agree, it is immaterial what may be the real but unexpressed state of mind."

WHAT IF THE FACTS WERE DIFFERENT? *Suppose that the day after Lucy signed the real estate sales agreement, he decided that he did not want the farm after all, and Zehmer sued Lucy to perform the contract. Would this change in the facts alter the court's decision that Lucy and Zehmer had created an enforceable contract? Why or why not?*

IMPACT OF THIS CASE ON TODAY'S LAW *This is a classic case in contract law because it so clearly illustrates the objective theory of contracts with respect to determining whether an offer was intended. Today, the objective theory of contracts continues to be applied by the courts, and* Lucy v. Zehmer *is routinely cited as a significant precedent in this area.*

RELEVANT WEB SITES *To locate information on the Web concerning the* Lucy *decision, go to this text's Web site at* **academic.cengage.com/blaw/blt**, *select "Chapter 7," and click on "URLs for Landmarks."*

Expressions of Opinion. An expression of opinion is not an offer. It does not demonstrate an intention to enter into a binding agreement. **EXAMPLE 7.10** In *Hawkins v. McGee*,[6] Hawkins took his son to McGee, a physician, and asked McGee to operate on the son's hand. McGee said that the boy would be in the hospital three or four days and that the hand would *probably* heal a few days later. The son's hand did not heal for a month, but nonetheless the father did not win a suit for breach of contract. The court held that McGee did not make an offer to heal the son's hand in three or four days. He merely expressed an opinion as to when the hand would heal. ■

BE CAREFUL An opinion is not an offer and not a contract term. Goods or services can be "perfect" in one party's opinion and "poor" in another's.

Statements of Future Intent. A statement of an *intention* to do something in the future is not an offer. **EXAMPLE 7.11** If Ari says, "I *plan* to sell my stock in Novation, Inc., for $150 per share," a contract is not created if John "accepts" and tenders $150 per share for the stock. Ari has merely expressed his intention to enter into a future contract for the sale of the stock. If John accepts and tenders the $150 per share, no contract is formed, because a reasonable person would conclude that Ari was only *thinking about* selling his stock, not promising to sell it. ■

Preliminary Negotiations. A request or invitation to negotiate is not an offer; it only expresses a willingness to discuss the possibility of entering into a contract. Examples are statements such as "Will you sell Forest Acres?" and "I wouldn't sell my car for less than $8,000." A reasonable person in the offeree's position would not conclude that such a statement indicated an intention to enter into a binding obligation. Likewise, when the government and private firms need to have construction work done, they invite contractors to submit bids. The *invitation* to submit bids is not an offer, and a contractor does not bind the government or private firm by submitting a bid. (The bids that the contractors submit are offers, however, and the government or private firm can bind the contractor by accepting the bid.)

Advertisements, Catalogues, Price Lists, and Circulars. In general, advertisements, mail-order catalogues, price lists, and circular letters (meant for the general public) are treated as invitations to negotiate, not as offers to form a contract.[7] **EXAMPLE 7.12** Suppose that you put an ad in the classified section of your local newspaper offering to sell your guitar for $275. Seven people call and "accept" your "offer" before you can remove the ad from the newspaper. If the ad were truly an offer, you would be bound by seven contracts to sell your guitar. Because *initial* advertisements are treated as *invitations* to make offers rather than offers, however, you will have seven "offers" to choose from, and you can accept the best one without incurring any liability for the six you reject. ■ On some occasions, though, courts have construed advertisements to be offers because the ads contained definite terms that invited acceptance (such as an ad offering a reward for the return of a lost dog).[8]

Price lists are another form of invitation to negotiate or trade. A seller's price list is not an offer to sell at that price; it merely invites the buyer to offer to buy at that price. In fact, the seller usually puts "prices subject to change" on the price list. Only in rare circumstances will a price quotation be construed as an offer.[9]

KEEP IN MIND Advertisements are not binding, but they cannot be deceptive.

Auctions. In an auction, a seller "offers" goods for sale through an auctioneer, but this is not an offer to form a contract. Rather, it is an invitation asking bidders to submit offers. In the context of an auction, a bidder is the offeror, and the auctioneer is the offeree. The offer is accepted when the auctioneer strikes the hammer. Before the fall of the hammer, a

---

6. 84 N.H. 114, 146 A. 641 (1929).
7. *Restatement (Second) of Contracts*, Section 26, Comment b.
8. The classic example is *Lefkowitz v. Great Minneapolis Surplus Store, Inc.*, 251 Minn. 188, 86 N.W.2d 689 (1957).
9. See, for example, *Fairmount Glass Works v. Grunden-Martin Woodenware Co.*, 106 Ky. 659, 51 S.W. 196 (1899).

bidder may revoke (take back) her or his bid, or the auctioneer may reject that bid or all bids. Typically, an auctioneer will reject a bid that is below the price the seller is willing to accept.

When the auctioneer accepts a higher bid, he or she rejects all previous bids. Because rejection terminates an offer (as will be discussed later), those bids represent offers that have been terminated. Thus, if the highest bidder withdraws his or her bid before the hammer falls, none of the previous bids is reinstated. If the bid is not withdrawn or rejected, the contract is formed when the auctioneer announces, "Going once, going twice, sold!" (or something similar), and lets the hammer fall.

Traditionally, auctions have been either "with reserve" or "without reserve." In an auction with reserve, the seller (through the auctioneer) may withdraw the goods at any time before the auctioneer closes the sale by announcement or by the fall of the hammer. All auctions are assumed to be auctions with reserve unless the terms of the auction are explicitly stated to be *without reserve*. In an auction without reserve, the goods cannot be withdrawn by the seller and must be sold to the highest bidder. In auctions with reserve, the seller may reserve the right to confirm or reject the sale even after "the hammer has fallen." In this situation, the seller is obligated to notify those attending the auction that sales of goods made during the auction are not final until confirmed by the seller.[10]

How do these rules apply to an online auction of rights to a domain name? For a discussion of a case involving this issue, see this chapter's *Adapting the Law to the Online Environment* feature.

Agreements to Agree. Traditionally, agreements to agree—that is, agreements to agree to the material terms of a contract at some future date—were not considered to be binding contracts. The modern view, however, is that agreements to agree may be enforceable agreements (contracts) if it is clear that the parties intend to be bound by the agreements. In other words, under the modern view the emphasis is on the parties' intent rather than on form.

Suppose that two parties draw up a brief, handwritten memorandum of agreement, intending to set forth their decisions in a more formal document later. If the arrangements are never formalized, can the memorandum constitute a binding contract? Increasingly, the courts are holding that a preliminary agreement constitutes a binding contract if the parties have agreed on all essential terms and no disputed issues remain to be resolved.[11] In contrast, if the parties agree on certain major terms but leave other terms open for further negotiation, a preliminary agreement is binding only in the sense that the parties have committed themselves to negotiate the undecided terms in good faith in an effort to reach a final agreement.

ON THE WEB

To view the terms of a sample contract, go to the "forms" pages of the 'Lectric Law Library at www.lectlaw.com/formb.htm and select one of the types of contracts listed there to review.

Definiteness The second requirement for an effective offer involves the definiteness of its terms. An offer must have reasonably definite terms so that a court can determine if a breach has occurred and give an appropriate remedy.[12]

An offer may invite an acceptance to be worded in such specific terms that the contract is made definite. **■EXAMPLE 7.13** Suppose that Marcus Business Machines contacts your corporation and offers to sell "from one to ten MacCool copying machines for $1,600 each; state number desired in acceptance." Your corporation agrees to buy two

---

10. These rules apply under both the common law of contracts and the Uniform Commercial Code, or UCC. See UCC 2–328.

11. See, for example, *Fluorine On Call, Ltd. v. Fluorogas Limited,* No. 01-CV-186 (W.D.Tex. 2002), contract issue affirmed on appeal at 380 F.3d 849 (5th Cir. 2004).

12. *Restatement (Second) of Contracts,* Section 33. The UCC has relaxed the requirements regarding the definiteness of terms in contracts for the sale of goods. See UCC 2–204(3).

ADAPTING THE LAW TO THE ONLINE ENVIRONMENT — Can an Online Bid Constitute an Acceptance?

Under the Uniform Commercial Code, or UCC (see Chapter 11), a bid at an auction constitutes an offer. The offer (the highest bid) is accepted when the auctioneer's hammer falls. The UCC also states that auctions are "with reserve" unless the seller specifies otherwise. As noted in the text, in an auction with reserve, the seller reserves the right *not* to sell the goods to the highest bidder. Hence, even after the hammer falls, the contract for sale remains conditioned on the seller's approval. The question of how these rules should be applied to an online auction of a domain name, in which no hammer falls, came before a California court.

The Bid (or Offer?)

The case involved an online auction conducted by The.TV Corporation International (DotTV) on its Web site. DotTV posted an announcement on its Web site asking for bids for rights to the "Golf.tv" domain name and stating that the name would go to the highest bidder. Je Ho Lim submitted a bid for $1,010 and authorized DotTV to charge that amount to his credit card if his bid was the highest. Later, DotTV sent Lim an e-mail message stating that he had "won the auction" and charged the bid price of $1,010 to Lim's credit card. When DotTV subsequently refused to transfer the name, Lim sued DotTV for, among other things, breach of contract. Lim argued that his bid constituted an acceptance of DotTV's offer to sell the name. DotTV contended that Lim's bid was an offer, which it had not accepted. Furthermore, even if it had accepted Lim's offer, because the auction was "with reserve," DotTV could withdraw the domain name from the auction even after acceptance. The trial court held for DotTV, and Lim appealed.

The Court's Analysis

The appellate court first explained that the UCC's provisions concerning auctions did not apply in this case because the UCC applies only to "goods" and domain names are not goods. The court then looked at common law principles as codified in the *Restatement (Second) of Contracts*. The rules under the *Restatement* are similar to those of the UCC: a bid in an auction is an offer that is accepted when the "hammer falls," and an auction is with reserve unless otherwise specified by the seller.

The court also pointed out, however, that DotTV's charging of the bid price to Lim's credit card was inconsistent with DotTV's claim that it could withdraw the domain name from the bidding because the auction was with reserve. Furthermore, stated the court, even if it concluded that Lim's bid was an offer and not an acceptance, DotTV had accepted the offer by its e-mail to Lim stating that he had won the auction. In all, held the court, there was no evidence that a contract between DotTV and Lim had *not* been formed, and Lim had stated a valid claim against DotTV for breach of contract. The court thus reversed the lower court's decision and remanded the case for further deliberation consistent with the appellate court's opinion.[a]

FOR CRITICAL ANALYSIS *Should the UCC rules governing auctions apply to items sold on online auction sites, such as eBay? Why or why not? How can you know whether eBay's auctions are "with reserve" or "without reserve"?*

a. *Lim v. The.TV Corp. International*, 99 Cal.App.4th 684, 121 Cal.Rptr.2d 333 (2d Dist. 2002).

---

copiers. Because the quantity is specified in the acceptance, the terms are definite, and the contract is enforceable. ◾

Communication A third requirement for an effective offer is communication—the offer must be communicated to the offeree. **◾EXAMPLE 7.14** Suppose that Tolson advertises a reward for the return of her lost cat. Dirlik, not knowing of the reward, finds the cat and returns it to Tolson. Ordinarily, Dirlik cannot recover the reward because an essential element of a reward contract is that the one who claims the reward must have known it was offered. A few states would allow recovery of the reward, but not on contract principles— Dirlik would be allowed to recover on the basis that it would be unfair to deny him the reward just because he did not know about it. ◾

Termination of the Offer

The communication of an effective offer to an offeree gives the offeree the power to transform the offer into a binding, legal obligation (a contract) by an acceptance. This power of acceptance does not continue forever, though. It can be terminated by action of the parties or by operation of law.

Termination by Action of the Parties   An offer can be terminated by the action of the parties in any of three ways: by revocation, by rejection, or by counteroffer.

Revocation of the Offer.   The offeror's act of withdrawing an offer is referred to as **revocation.** Unless an offer is irrevocable, the offeror usually can revoke the offer (even if he or she has promised to keep the offer open), as long as the revocation is communicated to the offeree before the offeree accepts. Revocation may be accomplished by an express repudiation of the offer (for example, with a statement such as "I withdraw my previous offer of October 17") or by the performance of acts that are inconsistent with the existence of the offer and that are made known to the offeree.

■EXAMPLE 7.15 Geraldine offers to sell some land to Gary. A week passes, and Gary, who has not yet accepted the offer, learns from his friend Konstantine that Geraldine has in the meantime sold the property to Nunan. Gary's knowledge of Geraldine's sale of the land to Nunan, even though he learned of it through a third party, effectively revokes Geraldine's offer to sell the land to Gary. Geraldine's sale of the land to Nunan is inconsistent with the continued existence of the offer to Gary, and thus the offer to Gary is revoked. ■

The general rule followed by most states is that a revocation becomes effective when the offeree or the offeree's agent (a person who acts on behalf of another) actually receives it. Therefore, a letter of revocation mailed on April 1 and delivered at the offeree's residence or place of business on April 3 becomes effective on April 3.

An offer made to the general public can be revoked in the same manner in which the offer was originally communicated. **■EXAMPLE 7.16** Suppose that a department store offers a $10,000 reward to anyone providing information leading to the apprehension of the persons who burglarized its downtown store. The offer is published in three local papers and in four papers in neighboring communities. To revoke the offer, the store must publish the revocation in all seven papers for the same number of days it published the offer. The revocation is then accessible to the general public, and the offer is revoked even if some particular offeree does not know about the revocation. ■

Irrevocable Offers.   Although most offers are revocable, some can be made irrevocable. Increasingly, courts refuse to allow an offeror to revoke an offer when the offeree has changed position because of justifiable reliance on the offer (under the doctrine of *detrimental reliance,* or *promissory estoppel,* discussed later in this chapter). In some circumstances, "firm offers" made by merchants may also be considered irrevocable. We discuss these offers in Chapter 11.

Another form of irrevocable offer is an option contract. An **option contract** is created when an offeror promises to hold an offer open for a specified period of time in return for a payment (consideration) given by the offeree. An option contract takes away the offeror's power to revoke an offer for the period of time specified in the option. If no time is specified, then a reasonable period of time is implied. **■EXAMPLE 7.17** Suppose that you are in the business of writing movie scripts. Your agent contacts the head of development at New Line Cinema and offers to sell New Line your new movie script. New Line likes your script and agrees to pay you $25,000 for a six-month option. In this situation, you (through

A billboard offers a reward for the capture of the killer of this woman's husband. How can this offer be revoked? (AP Photo/Denis Poroy)

your agent) are the offeror, and New Line is the offeree. You cannot revoke your offer to sell New Line your script for the next six months. After six months, if no contract has been formed, New Line loses the $25,000, and you are free to sell your script to another movie studio. ▣

Option contracts are also frequently used in conjunction with the sale of real estate. **⬛EXAMPLE 7.18** You might agree with a landowner to lease a house and include in the lease contract a clause stating that you will pay $15,000 for an option to purchase the property within a specified period of time. If you decide not to purchase the home after the specified period has lapsed, you lose the $15,000, and the landlord is free to sell the property to another buyer. ▣

Rejection of the Offer by the Offeree. If the offeree rejects the offer, the offer is terminated. Any subsequent attempt by the offeree to accept will be construed as a new offer, giving the original offeror (now the offeree) the power of acceptance. A rejection is ordinarily accomplished by words or by conduct indicating an intent not to accept the offer.

As with a revocation, a rejection of an offer is effective only when it is actually received by the offeror or the offeror's agent. **⬛EXAMPLE 7.19** Suppose that Growgood Farms mails a letter to Campbell Soup Company offering to sell carrots at ten cents a pound. (Of course, today, such offers tend to be sent electronically rather than by mail, as will be discussed in Chapter 10.) Campbell Soup Company could reject the offer either by sending or faxing a letter to Growgood Farms expressly rejecting the offer or by mailing the offer back to Growgood, indicating an intent to reject it. Alternatively, Campbell could offer to buy the carrots at eight cents per pound (a counteroffer), necessarily rejecting the original offer. ▣

Merely inquiring about an offer does not constitute rejection. **⬛EXAMPLE 7.20** A friend offers to buy your DVD movie collection for $300. You respond, "Is this your best offer?" or "Will you pay me $375 for it?" A reasonable person would conclude that you did not reject the offer but merely made an inquiry for further consideration of the offer. You can still accept and bind your friend to the $300 purchase price. When the offeree merely inquires as to the firmness of the offer, there is no reason to presume that she or he intends to reject it. ▣

Counteroffer by the Offeree. A **counteroffer** is a rejection of the original offer and the simultaneous making of a new offer. **⬛EXAMPLE 7.21** Suppose that Burke offers to sell his home to Lang for $270,000. Lang responds, "Your price is too high. I'll offer to purchase

BE CAREFUL The way in which a response to an offer is phrased can determine whether the offer is accepted or rejected.

COUNTEROFFER
An offeree's response to an offer in which the offeree rejects the original offer and at the same time makes a new offer.

your house for $250,000." Lang's response is called a counteroffer because it rejects Burke's offer to sell at $270,000 and creates a new offer by Lang to purchase the home at a price of $250,000. ■

At common law, the **mirror image rule** requires that the offeree's acceptance match the offeror's offer exactly. In other words, the terms of the acceptance must "mirror" those of the offer. If the acceptance materially changes or adds to the terms of the original offer, it will be considered not an acceptance but a counteroffer—which, of course, need not be accepted. The original offeror can, however, accept the terms of the counteroffer and create a valid contract.[13]

Termination by Operation of Law   The offeree's power to transform an offer into a binding, legal obligation can be terminated by operation of law if any of four conditions occur: lapse of time, destruction of the specific subject matter, death or incompetence of the offeror or offeree, or supervening illegality of the proposed contract.

Lapse of Time.   An offer terminates automatically by law when the period of time *specified in the offer* has passed. If the offer states that it will be left open until a particular date, then the offer will terminate at midnight on that day. If the offer states that it will be left open for a number of days, such as ten days, this time period normally begins to run when the offer is actually received by the offeree, not when it is formed or sent. When the offer is delayed (through the misdelivery of mail, for example), the period begins to run from the date the offeree would have received the offer, but only if the offeree knows or should know that the offer is delayed.[14]

■EXAMPLE 7.22 Suppose that Beth offers to sell her boat to Jonah, stating that the offer will remain open until May 20. Unless Jonah accepts the offer by midnight on May 20, the offer will lapse (terminate). Now suppose that Beth writes a letter to Jonah, offering to sell him her boat if Jonah accepts the offer within twenty days of the letter's date, which is May 1. Jonah must accept within twenty days after May 1, or the offer will terminate. Suppose that instead of including the date May 1 in her letter, Beth had simply written to Jonah offering to sell him her boat if Jonah accepted within twenty days. In this instance, Jonah must accept within twenty days of receiving the letter. The same rule would apply if Beth used insufficient postage and Jonah received the letter ten days late without knowing that it had been delayed. If, however, Jonah knew that the letter was delayed, the offer would lapse twenty days after the day he ordinarily would have received the offer had Beth used sufficient postage. ■

If the offer does not specify a time for acceptance, the offer terminates at the end of a *reasonable* period of time. A reasonable period of time is determined by the subject matter of the contract, business and market conditions, and other relevant circumstances. An offer to sell farm produce, for example, will terminate sooner than an offer to sell farm equipment because farm produce is perishable and subject to greater fluctuations in market value.

Destruction of the Subject Matter.   An offer is automatically terminated if the specific subject matter of the offer is destroyed before the offer is accepted. For example, if Bekins offers to sell his prize cow to Yatsen, but the cow is struck by lightning and dies before Yatsen can accept, the offer is automatically terminated. (Note that if Yatsen accepted the offer just before lightning struck the cow, a contract would have been formed, but,

13. The mirror image rule has been greatly modified in regard to sales contracts. Section 2–207 of the UCC provides that a contract is formed if the offeree makes a definite expression of acceptance (such as signing the form in the appropriate location), even though the terms of the acceptance modify or add to the terms of the original offer (see Chapter 11).
14. *Restatement (Second) of Contracts*, Section 49.

MIRROR IMAGE RULE
A common law rule that requires that the terms of the offeree's acceptance adhere exactly to the terms of the offeror's offer for a valid contract to be formed.

ON THE WEB
For answers to some common questions about contract law, go to the Web site of the Legal Information Network, Inc., at www.contract-law.com/TheLaw.htm.

because of the cow's death, a court would likely excuse Bekins's obligation to perform the contract on the basis of impossibility of performance—see Chapter 9.)

Death or Incompetence of the Offeror or Offeree. An offeree's power of acceptance is terminated when the offeror or offeree dies or is deprived of legal capacity to enter into the proposed contract, *unless the offer is irrevocable.*[15] A revocable offer is personal to both parties and normally cannot pass to a decedent's heirs or estate or to the guardian of a mentally incompetent person. This rule applies whether or not one party had notice of the death or incompetence of the other party. **■EXAMPLE 7.23** Kapola, who is quite ill, writes to her friend Amanda, offering to sell Amanda her grand piano for only $400. That night, Kapola dies. The next day, Amanda, not knowing of Kapola's death, writes a letter to Kapola, accepting the offer and enclosing a check for $400. Is there a contract? No. There is no contract because the offer automatically terminated when Kapola died. ■

Supervening Illegality of the Proposed Contract. A statute or court decision that makes an offer illegal automatically terminates the offer. **■EXAMPLE 7.24** Suppose that Acme Finance Corporation offers to lend Jack $20,000 at 15 percent interest annually, but before Jack can accept, the state legislature enacts a statute prohibiting loans at interest rates greater than 12 percent. In this situation, the offer is automatically terminated. (If the statute is enacted after Jack accepts the offer, a valid contract is formed, but the contract may still be unenforceable—see Chapter 8.) ■

Acceptance

An **acceptance** is a voluntary act by the offeree that shows assent, or agreement, to the terms of an offer. The offeree's act may consist of words or conduct. The acceptance must be unequivocal and must be communicated to the offeror.

Who Can Accept? Generally, a third person cannot substitute for the offeree and effectively accept the offer. After all, the identity of the offeree is as much a condition of a bargaining offer as any other term contained therein. Thus, except in special circumstances, only the person to whom the offer is made or that person's agent can accept the offer and create a binding contract. For example, Lottie makes an offer to Paul. Paul is not interested, but his friend José accepts the offer. No contract is formed.

Unequivocal Acceptance To exercise the power of acceptance effectively, the offeree must accept unequivocally. This is the *mirror image rule* previously discussed. If the acceptance is subject to new conditions or if the terms of the acceptance materially change the original offer, the acceptance may be deemed a counteroffer that implicitly rejects the original offer.

Certain terms, when added to an acceptance, will not qualify the acceptance sufficiently to constitute rejection of the offer. **■EXAMPLE 7.25** Suppose that in response to a person offering to sell a painting by a well-known artist, the offeree replies, "I accept; please send a written contract." The offeree is requesting a written contract but is not making it a condition for acceptance. Therefore, the acceptance is effective without the written contract. In contrast, if the offeree replies, "I accept *if* you send a written contract," the acceptance is

ACCEPTANCE
A voluntary act by the offeree that shows assent, or agreement, to the terms of an offer; may consist of words or conduct.

DON'T FORGET When an offer is rejected, it is terminated.

---

15. *Restatement (Second) of Contracts,* Section 48. If the offer is irrevocable, it is not terminated when the offeror dies.

expressly conditioned on the request for a writing, and the statement is not an acceptance but a counteroffer. (Notice how important each word is!)[16] ■

Silence as Acceptance Ordinarily, silence cannot constitute acceptance, even if the offeror states, "By your silence and inaction, you will be deemed to have accepted this offer." This general rule applies because an offeree should not be put under a burden of liability to act affirmatively in order to reject an offer. No consideration—that is, nothing of value—has passed to the offeree to impose such a liability.

In some instances, however, the offeree does have a duty to speak; if so, his or her silence or inaction will operate as an acceptance. Silence may be an acceptance when an offeree takes the benefit of offered services even though he or she had an opportunity to reject them and knew that they were offered with the expectation of compensation. **■EXAMPLE 7.26** Suppose that John, a college student who earns extra income by washing store windows, taps on the window of a store and catches the attention of the store's manager. John points to the window and raises his cleaner, signaling that he will be washing the window. The manager does nothing to stop him. Here, the store manager's silence constitutes an acceptance, and an implied-in-fact contract is created. The store is bound to pay a reasonable value for John's work. ■

Silence can also operate as an acceptance when the offeree has had prior dealings with the offeror. If a merchant, for example, routinely receives shipments from a supplier and in the past has always notified the supplier when defective goods are rejected, then silence constitutes acceptance. Also, if a buyer solicits an offer specifying that certain terms and conditions are acceptable, and the seller makes the offer in response to the solicitation, the buyer has a duty to reject—that is, a duty to tell the seller that the offer is not acceptable. Failure to reject (silence) will operate as an acceptance.

REMEMBER A bilateral contract is a promise for a promise, and a unilateral contract is a promise for an act.

Communication of Acceptance Whether the offeror must be notified of the acceptance depends on the nature of the contract. In a bilateral contract, communication of acceptance is necessary because acceptance is in the form of a promise (not performance), and the contract is formed when the promise is made (rather than when the act is performed). Communication of acceptance is not necessary, however, if the offer dispenses with the requirement. Also, if the offer can be accepted by silence, no communication is necessary.[17]

Because a unilateral contract calls for the full performance of some act, acceptance is usually evident, and notification is unnecessary. Nevertheless, exceptions do exist, such as when the offeror requests notice of acceptance or has no way of determining whether the requested act has been performed. In addition, sometimes the law (such as Article 2 of the UCC) requires notice of acceptance, and thus notice is necessary.[18]

Mode and Timeliness of Acceptance Acceptance in bilateral contracts must be timely. The general rule is that acceptance in a bilateral contract is timely if it is made before the offer is terminated. Problems may arise, though, when the parties involved are not dealing face to face. In such situations, the offeree should use an authorized mode of communication.

---

16. As noted in footnote 13, in regard to sales contracts, the UCC provides that an acceptance may still be effective even if some terms are added. The new terms are simply treated as proposals for additions to the contract, unless both parties are merchants. If the parties are merchants, the additional terms (with some exceptions) become part of the contract [UCC 2–207(2)].
17. Under UCC 2–206(1)(b), an order or other offer to buy goods that are to be promptly shipped may be treated as either a bilateral or a unilateral offer and can be accepted by a promise to ship or by actual shipment.
18. UCC 2–206(2).

The Mailbox Rule.   Acceptance takes effect, thus completing formation of the contract, at the time the offeree sends or delivers the communication via the mode expressly or impliedly authorized by the offeror. This is the so-called **mailbox rule,** also called the *deposited acceptance rule,* which the majority of courts uphold. Under this rule, if the authorized mode of communication is the mail, then an acceptance becomes valid when it is dispatched (placed in the control of the U.S. Postal Service)—*not* when it is received by the offeror.

   The mailbox rule was formed to prevent the confusion that arises when an offeror sends a letter of revocation but, before it arrives, the offeree sends a letter of acceptance. Thus, whereas a revocation becomes effective only when it is *received* by the offeree, an acceptance becomes effective on *dispatch* (when sent, even if it is never received), provided that an *authorized* means of communication is used.

Authorized Means of Communication.   A means of communicating acceptance can be either expressly authorized—that is, expressly stipulated in the offer—or impliedly authorized by the facts and circumstances surrounding the situation or by law.[19] An acceptance sent by means not expressly or impliedly authorized normally is not effective until it is received by the offeror.

   When an offeror specifies how acceptance should be made (for example, by overnight delivery), *express authorization* is said to exist. Moreover, both the offeror and the offeree are bound in contract the moment that such a mode of acceptance is employed. **■EXAMPLE 7.27**   Shaylee & Perkins, a Massachusetts firm, offers to sell a container of antique furniture to Leaham's Antiques in Colorado. The offer states that Leaham's must accept the offer via FedEx overnight delivery. The acceptance is effective (and a binding contract is formed) the moment that Leaham's gives the overnight envelope containing the acceptance to the FedEx driver. ■

   Most offerors do not expressly specify the means of communication by which the offeree is to accept. Thus, the common law recognizes the following implied authorized means of acceptance:[20]

1 The offeror's choice of a particular mode of communication in making the offer implies that the offeree is authorized to use the same mode *or a faster* one for acceptance.

2 When two parties are at a distance, mailing is impliedly authorized.

Exceptions.   There are three basic exceptions to the rule that a contract is formed when acceptance is sent by authorized means:

1 If the acceptance is not properly dispatched (if a letter is incorrectly addressed, for example, or lacks sufficient postage), in most states it will not be effective until it is received by the offeror.

2 The offeror can stipulate in the offer that an acceptance will not be effective until it is received (usually by a specified time) by the offeror.

MAILBOX RULE
A rule providing that an acceptance of an offer becomes effective on dispatch (on being placed in an official mailbox), if mail is, expressly or impliedly, an authorized means of communication of acceptance to the offeror.

---

19. *Restatement (Second) of Contracts,* Section 30, provides that an offer invites acceptance "by any medium reasonable in the circumstances," unless the offer is specific about the means of acceptance. Under Section 65, a medium is reasonable if it is one used by the offeror or one customary in similar transactions, unless the offeree knows of circumstances that would argue against the reasonableness of a particular medium (the need for speed because of rapid price changes, for example).
20. Note that UCC 2–206(1)(a) states specifically that an acceptance of an offer for the sale of goods can be made by any medium that is *reasonable* under the circumstances.

3 Sometimes an offeree sends a rejection first, then later changes his or her mind and sends an acceptance. Obviously, this chain of events could cause confusion and even detriment to the offeror, depending on whether the rejection or the acceptance arrives first. In such situations, the law cancels the rule of acceptance on dispatch, and the first communication received by the offeror determines whether a contract is formed. If the rejection arrives first, there is no contract.[21]

PREVENTING LEGAL DISPUTES

An effective way to avoid legal disputes over contracts is to clearly communicate your intentions to the other party and express every detail in writing, even when a written contract is not legally required. If you are the offeror, be explicit in your offer about how long the offer will remain open and stipulate the authorized means of communicating the acceptance. Include a provision requiring the offeree to notify you of acceptance regardless of whether a bilateral or unilateral contract will be formed. (See the *Application* feature at the end of this chapter for additional suggestions on controlling the terms of an offer.) If you are the offeree, make sure that the language you use for any counteroffer, negotiation, or acceptance is absolutely clear and unambiguous. A simple "I accept" is best in most situations. Providing notice of the acceptance can lessen the potential for problems arising due to revocation or lost communications.

◼

CONSIDERATION
Generally, the value given in return for a promise; involves two elements—the giving of something of legally sufficient value and a bargained-for exchange. The consideration must result in a detriment to the promisee or a benefit to the promisor.

FORBEARANCE
The act of refraining from an action that one has a legal right to undertake.

If an offer expressly authorizes acceptance of the offer by first class mail or express delivery, can the offeree accept by a faster means, such as by fax or e-mail? Why or why not? (Chiaki Hayashi/Creative Commons)

Technology and Acceptances Technology, and particularly the Internet, has all but eliminated the need for the mailbox rule because online acceptances typically are communicated instantaneously to the offeror. As you will learn in Chapter 10, although online offers are not significantly different from traditional offers contained in paper documents, online acceptances have posed some unusual problems.

CONSIDERATION

In every legal system, some promises will be enforced, and other promises will not be enforced. The simple fact that a party has made a promise, then, does not mean the promise is enforceable. Under the common law, a primary basis for the enforcement of promises is consideration. **Consideration** is usually defined as the value given in return for a promise. We look here at the basic elements of consideration and then at some other contract doctrines relating to consideration.

Elements of Consideration

Often, consideration is broken down into two parts: (1) something of *legally sufficient value* must be given in exchange for the promise, and (2) there must be a *bargained-for exchange*.

Legally Sufficient Value The "something of legally sufficient value" may consist of (1) a promise to do something that one has no prior legal duty to do (to pay on receipt of certain goods, for example), (2) the performance of an action that one is otherwise not obligated to undertake (such as providing accounting services), or (3) the refraining from an action that one has a legal right to undertake (called a **forbearance**).

Consideration in bilateral contracts normally consists of a promise in return for a promise, as explained earlier. ◼**EXAMPLE 7.28** Suppose that in a contract for the sale of goods, the seller promises to ship specific goods to the buyer, and the buyer promises to pay for those goods when they are received. Each of these promises constitutes consideration for the con-

---

21. *Restatement (Second) of Contracts*, Section 40.

tract. ■ In contrast, unilateral contracts involve a promise in return for a performance. **■EXAMPLE 7.29** Anita says to her neighbor, "If you paint my garage, I will pay you $800." Anita's neighbor paints the garage. The act of painting the garage is the consideration that creates Anita's contractual obligation to pay her neighbor $800. ■

What if, in return for a promise to pay, a person refrains from pursuing harmful habits, such as the use of tobacco and alcohol? Does such a forbearance create consideration for the contract? This was the issue in *Hamer v. Sidway*, a classic case concerning consideration that we present as this chapter's *Landmark in the Law* feature on the next page.

Bargained-for Exchange   The second element of consideration is that it must provide the basis for the bargain struck between the contracting parties. The promise given by the promisor must induce the promisee to incur a legal detriment either now or in the future, and the detriment incurred must induce the promisor to make the promise. This element of bargained-for exchange distinguishes contracts from gifts. **■EXAMPLE 7.30** Roberto says to his son, "In consideration of the fact that you are not as wealthy as your brothers, I will pay you $5,000." This promise is not enforceable because Roberto's son has not given any return consideration for the $5,000 promised.[22] The son (the promisee) incurs no legal detriment; he does not have to promise anything or undertake (or refrain from undertaking) any action to receive the $5,000. Here, Roberto has simply stated his motive for giving his son a gift. The fact that the word *consideration* is used does not, by itself, mean that consideration has been given. ■

Legal Sufficiency and Adequacy of Consideration

Legal sufficiency of consideration involves the requirement that consideration be something of value in the eyes of the law. Adequacy of consideration involves "how much" consideration is given. Essentially, adequacy of consideration concerns the fairness of the bargain. On the surface, fairness would appear to be an issue when the items exchanged are of unequal value. In general, however, courts do not question the adequacy of consideration if the consideration is legally sufficient. Under the doctrine of freedom of contract, parties are usually free to bargain as they wish. If people could sue merely because they had entered into an unwise contract, the courts would be overloaded with frivolous suits.

Nevertheless, in rare situations a court will consider whether the amount or value of the consideration is adequate. This is because apparently inadequate consideration can indicate that fraud, duress, or undue influence was involved. It might also indicate that a gift was made (if a father "sells" a $100,000 house to his daughter for only $1,000, for example). When the consideration is grossly inadequate, a court may declare the contract unenforceable on the ground that it is unconscionable,[23] meaning that, generally speaking, it is so one sided under the circumstances as to be clearly unfair. (*Unconscionability* will be discussed further in Chapter 8.)

The determination of whether consideration exists does not depend on the comparative value of the things exchanged. Something need not be of direct economic or financial value to be considered legally sufficient consideration. In many situations, the exchange of promises and potential benefits is deemed sufficient as consideration.

Contracts That Lack Consideration

Sometimes, one or both of the parties to a contract may think that they have exchanged consideration when in fact they have not. Here we look at some situations in which the parties' promises or actions do not qualify as contractual consideration.

ON THE WEB

The New Hampshire attorney general's *Consumer's Sourcebook* provides information on contract law from a consumer's perspective. You can access this book online at

www.doj.nh.gov/consumer/sourcebook.

BE AWARE   A consumer's signature on a contract does not always guarantee that the contract will be enforced. Ultimately, the terms must be fair.

---

22. See *Fink v. Cox*, 18 Johns. 145, 9 Am.Dec. 191 (N.Y. 1820).
23. Pronounced un-*kon*-shun-uh-bul.

LANDMARK IN THE LAW · Hamer v. Sidway (1891)

In *Hamer v. Sidway,*[a] the issue before the court arose from a contract created in 1869 between William Story, Sr., and his nephew, William Story II. The uncle promised his nephew that if the nephew refrained from drinking alcohol, using tobacco, and playing billiards and cards for money until he reached the age of twenty-one, the uncle would pay him $5,000 (about $75,000 in today's dollars). The nephew, who indulged occasionally in all of these "vices," agreed to refrain from them and did so for the next six years. Following his twenty-first birthday in 1875, the nephew wrote to his uncle that he had performed his part of the bargain and was thus entitled to the promised $5,000. A few days later, the uncle wrote the nephew a letter stating, "[Y]ou shall have the five thousand dollars, as I promised you." The uncle said that the money was in the bank and that the nephew could "consider this money on interest."

The Issue of Consideration   The nephew left the money in the care of his uncle, who held it for the next twelve years. When the uncle died in 1887, however, the executor of the uncle's estate refused to pay the $5,000 claim brought by Louisa Hamer, a third party to whom the promise had been *assigned.* (The law allows parties to assign, or transfer, rights in contracts to third parties—see Chapter 9.) The executor, Franklin Sidway, contended that the contract was invalid because there was insufficient consideration to support it. The uncle had received nothing, and the nephew had actually benefited by fulfilling the uncle's wishes. Therefore, no contract existed.

The Court's Conclusion   Although a lower court upheld Sidway's position, the New York Court of Appeals reversed and ruled in favor of the plaintiff, Hamer. "The promisee used tobacco, occasionally drank liquor, and he had a legal right to do so," the court stated. "That right he abandoned for a period of years upon the strength of the promise of the testator [one who makes a will] that for such forbearance he would give him $5,000. We need not speculate on the effort which may have been required to give up the use of those stimulants. It is sufficient that he restricted his lawful freedom of action within certain prescribed limits upon the faith of his uncle's agreement."

APPLICATION TO TODAY'S WORLD   *Although this case was decided more than a century ago, the principles enunciated by the court remain applicable to contracts formed today, including online contracts. For a contract to be valid and binding, consideration must be given, and that consideration must be something of legally sufficient value.*

RELEVANT WEB SITES   *To locate information on the Web concerning the Hamer decision, go to this text's Web site at **academic.cengage.com/blaw/blt**, select "Chapter 7," and click on "URLs for Landmarks."*

a. 124 N.Y. 538, 27 N.E. 256 (1891).

Preexisting Duty   Under most circumstances, a promise to do what one already has a legal duty to do does not constitute legally sufficient consideration because no legal detriment is incurred.[24] The preexisting legal duty may be imposed by law or may arise out of

24. See *Foakes v. Beer*, 9 App.Cas. 605 (1884).

a previous contract. A sheriff, for example, cannot collect a reward for information leading to the capture of a criminal if the sheriff already has a legal duty to capture the criminal. Likewise, if a party is already bound by contract to perform a certain duty, that duty cannot serve as consideration for a second contract.

EXAMPLE 7.31 Suppose that Bauman-Bache, Inc., begins construction on a seven-story office building and after three months demands an extra $75,000 on its contract. If the extra $75,000 is not paid, the firm will stop working. The owner of the land, having no one else to complete construction, agrees to pay the extra $75,000. The agreement is not enforceable because it is not supported by legally sufficient consideration; Bauman-Bache had a preexisting contractual duty to complete the building. ◼

Unforeseen Difficulties. The rule regarding preexisting duty is meant to prevent extortion and the so-called holdup game. What happens, though, when an honest contractor, who has contracted with a landowner to build a house, runs into extraordinary difficulties that were totally unforeseen at the time the contract was formed? In the interests of fairness and equity, the courts sometimes allow exceptions to the preexisting duty rule. In the example just mentioned, if the landowner agrees to pay extra compensation to the contractor for overcoming the unforeseen difficulties (such as having to use dynamite and special equipment to remove an unexpected rock formation to excavate for a basement), the court may refrain from applying the preexisting duty rule and enforce the agreement. When the "unforeseen difficulties" that give rise to a contract modification are the types of risks ordinarily assumed in business, however, the courts will usually assert the preexisting duty rule.[25]

Rescission and New Contract. The law recognizes that two parties can mutually agree to rescind their contract, at least to the extent that it is executory (still to be carried out). Rescission[26] is the unmaking of a contract so as to return the parties to the positions they occupied before the contract was made. Sometimes, parties rescind a contract and make a new contract at the same time. When this occurs, it is often difficult to determine whether there was consideration for the new contract or whether the parties had a preexisting duty under the previous contract. If a court finds there was a preexisting duty, then the new contract will be invalid because there was no consideration.

Past Consideration Promises made in return for actions or events that have already taken place are unenforceable. These promises lack consideration in that the element of bargained-for exchange is missing. In short, you can bargain for something to take place now or in the future but not for something that has already taken place. Therefore, **past consideration** is no consideration. **EXAMPLE 7.32** Suppose that Elsie, a real estate agent, does her friend Judy a favor by selling Judy's house and not charging any commission. Later, Judy says to Elsie, "In return for your generous act, I will pay you $6,000." This promise is made in return for past consideration and is thus unenforceable; in effect, Judy is stating her intention to give Elsie a gift. ◼

Illusory Promises If the terms of the contract express such uncertainty of performance that the promisor has not definitely promised to do anything, the promise is said to be *illusory*— without consideration and unenforceable. **EXAMPLE 7.33** The president of Tuscan Corporation says to his employees, "All of you have worked hard, and if profits remain high, a 10 percent bonus at the end of the year will be given—if management thinks it is

ON THE WEB

To learn more about how the courts decide such issues as whether consideration was lacking for a particular contract, look at relevant case law, which can be accessed through the Web site of Cornell University's School of Law at

www.law.cornell.edu/wex/index.php/ Contracts.

RESCISSION
An act that a contract is canceled and the parties are returned to the positions they occupied before the contract was made; may be effected through the mutual consent of the parties, by the parties' conduct, or by court decree.

PAST CONSIDERATION
An act that takes place before the contract is made and that ordinarily, by itself, cannot be consideration for a later promise to pay for the act.

25. Note that under the UCC, any agreement modifying a contract within Article 2 on sales needs no consideration to be binding. See UCC 2–209(1).
26. Pronounced reh-*sih*-zhen.

warranted." This is an *illusory promise,* or no promise at all, because performance depends solely on the discretion of the president (the management). There is no bargained-for consideration. The statement declares merely that management may or may not do something in the future. ■

Option-to-cancel clauses in contracts for specified time periods sometimes present problems in regard to consideration. **■EXAMPLE 7.34** Abe contracts to hire Chris for one year at $5,000 per month, reserving the right to cancel the contract at any time. On close examination of these words, you can see that Abe has not actually agreed to hire Chris, as Abe could cancel without liability before Chris started performance. Abe has not given up the opportunity to hire someone else. This contract is therefore illusory. Now suppose that Abe contracts to hire Chris for a one-year period at $5,000 per month, reserving the right to cancel the contract at any time after Chris has begun performance by giving Chris thirty days' notice. Abe, by saying that he will give Chris thirty days' notice, is relinquishing the opportunity (legal right) to hire someone else instead of Chris for a thirty-day period. If Chris works for one month, at the end of which Abe gives him thirty days' notice, Chris has a valid and enforceable contractual claim for $10,000 in salary. ■

Settlement of Claims

Businesspersons or others can settle legal claims in several ways. It is important to understand the nature of the consideration given in these settlement agreements, or contracts. Claims are commonly settled through an *accord and satisfaction,* in which a debtor offers to pay a lesser amount than the creditor purports is owed. Two other methods that are also often used to settle claims are the *release* and the *covenant not to sue.*

ACCORD AND SATISFACTION
A common means of settling a disputed claim, whereby a debtor offers to pay a lesser amount than the creditor purports is owed. The creditor's acceptance of the offer creates an accord (agreement), and when the accord is executed, satisfaction occurs.

Accord and Satisfaction In an **accord and satisfaction,** a debtor offers to pay, and a creditor accepts, a lesser amount than the creditor originally claimed was owed. Thus, in an accord and satisfaction, the debtor attempts to terminate an existing obligation. The *accord* is the settlement agreement. In an accord, the debtor offers to give or perform something less than the parties originally agreed on, and the creditor accepts that offer in satisfaction of the claim. *Satisfaction* is the performance (usually payment), which takes place after the accord is executed. A basic rule is that there can be no satisfaction unless there is first an accord.

LIQUIDATED DEBT
A debt for which the amount has been ascertained, fixed, agreed on, settled, or exactly determined. If the amount of the debt is in dispute, the debt is considered unliquidated.

For accord and satisfaction to occur, the amount of the debt *must be in dispute.* If it is a **liquidated debt,** then accord and satisfaction cannot take place. A debt is liquidated if its amount has been ascertained, fixed, agreed on, settled, or exactly determined. An example of a liquidated debt is a loan contract in which the borrower agrees to pay a stipulated amount every month until the amount of the loan is paid. In the majority of states, acceptance of (an accord for) a lesser sum than the entire amount of a liquidated debt is not satisfaction, and the balance of the debt is still legally owed. The rationale for this rule is that the debtor has given no consideration to satisfy the obligation of paying the balance to the creditor—because the debtor has a preexisting legal obligation to pay the entire debt.

An *unliquidated debt* is the opposite of a liquidated debt. Here, reasonable persons may differ over the amount owed. It is *not* settled, fixed, agreed on, ascertained, or determined. In these circumstances, acceptance of payment of the lesser sum operates as a satisfaction, or discharge, of the debt. One argument to support this rule is that the parties give up a legal right to contest the amount in dispute, and thus consideration is given.

RELEASE
A contract in which one party forfeits the right to pursue a legal claim against the other party.

Release A **release** is a contract in which one party forfeits the right to pursue a legal claim against the other party. Releases will generally be binding if they are (1) given in good faith,

(2) stated in a signed writing (required by many states), and (3) accompanied by consideration.[27] Clearly, parties are better off if they know the extent of their injuries or damages before signing releases.

■EXAMPLE 7.35 You are involved in an automobile accident caused by Raoul's negligence. Raoul offers to give you $2,000 if you will release him from further liability resulting from the accident. You believe that this amount will cover your damages, so you agree to and sign the release. Later you discover that the repairs to your car will cost $4,200. Can you collect the balance from Raoul? The answer is normally no; you are limited to the $2,000 in the release. Why? The reason is that a valid contract existed. You and Raoul both assented to the bargain (hence, agreement existed), and sufficient consideration was present. Your consideration for the contract was the legal detriment you suffered (by releasing Raoul from liability, you forfeited your right to sue to recover damages, should they be more than $2,000). This legal detriment was induced by Raoul's promise to give you the $2,000. Raoul's promise was, in turn, induced by your promise not to pursue your legal right to sue him for damages. ■

Before agreeing to a release, a party should be certain of its terms. The following case emphasizes this point.

ON THE WEB

You can find an example of a release form and the information that should be included in a release by going to **www.legaldocs.com/htsgif.d/ xwaiverp.htm**.

---

27. Under the UCC, a written, signed waiver or renunciation by an aggrieved party discharges any further liability for a breach, even without consideration [UCC 1–107].

CASE 7.3 **BP Products North America, Inc. v. Oakridge at Winegard, Inc.**

United States District Court, Middle District of Florida, 469 F.Supp.2d 1128 (2007).

FACTS Oakridge at Winegard, Inc., and Mahammad Qureshi operated a gas station and convenience store in Orlando, Florida, subject to an exclusive fuel supply agreement with BP Products North America, Inc. Under the agreement, BP had a "right to first refusal" with respect to the sale of the premises if Oakridge received an offer. In November 2005, without notifying BP, Oakridge contracted to sell the premises to Pacific Energy, Inc., and Arooj Ahmed. Pacific wanted to sell Citgo, not BP, fuel. Qureshi told Ahmed that terminating the agreement with BP would cost $100,000—the amount that BP had provided to build the station—and agreed to reduce its price by that amount. Several months later, when BP learned of the sale and switch to Citgo fuel, it filed a suit in a federal district court against Oakridge and the others to void the deal. The parties filed claims, counterclaims, and cross-claims, and attempted unsuccessfully to mediate a resolution. Later, during a phone conference, Oakridge offered BP $263,616.95 to cover its advance of funds under the fuel supply agreement, with ownership of the premises to be retained by Pacific and all of the other claims among the parties to be released. Everyone agreed. Two weeks later, however, Oakridge refused to sign the release. BP and Pacific asked the court to order its enforcement.

ISSUE Were the settlement and release negotiated in the phone conference among the parties enforceable?

DECISION Yes. The court concluded that "there was a meeting of the minds and the parties entered into an enforceable settlement agreement" during the conference call. The court entered a judgment in favor of BP and against Oakridge and Qureshi for $263,616.95, plus interest. The court also allowed Pacific to remain in possession of the premises and dismissed the other claims.

REASON The court found that "while the exact language of the releases was not crafted during the * * * conference call, the evidence clearly establishes that the parties all agreed to release all of their claims against one another." Oakridge argued in part that the negotiations had been informal. Oakridge asserted that the agreement should not release Pacific from its alleged obligation to indemnify (compensate) the seller for $100,000 of the amount to be paid to BP. Oakridge contended that "BP and Pacific knew or had reason

CASE 7.3—Continues next page

CASE 7.3–Continued

to know that Oakridge inadvertently omitted discussion of the $100,000 reimbursement amount allegedly owed by Pacific to Oakridge for early termination of the fuel supply agreement." The court found no evidence, however, that "BP and Pacific knew or should have known that the $100,000 reimbursement amount had been inadvertently omitted."

Furthermore, the court emphasized, "the evidence clearly demonstrates that the parties all agreed to release all claims against each other arising out of the instant [present] litigation during the * * * conference call."

 FOR CRITICAL ANALYSIS–Social Consideration
Why are settlement and release agreements encouraged and readily enforced?

■

COVENANT NOT TO SUE
An agreement to substitute a contractual obligation for some other type of legal action based on a valid claim.

Covenant Not to Sue   Unlike a release, a **covenant not to sue** does not always bar further recovery. The parties simply substitute a contractual obligation for some other type of legal action based on a valid claim. Suppose (following the earlier example) that you agree with Raoul not to sue for damages in a tort action if he will pay for the damage to your car. If Raoul fails to pay, you can bring an action for breach of contract.

Promissory Estoppel

PROMISSORY ESTOPPEL
A doctrine that applies when a promisor makes a clear and definite promise on which the promisee justifiably relies. Such a promise is binding if justice will be better served by the enforcement of the promise.

ESTOPPED
Barred, impeded, or precluded.

Sometimes, individuals rely on promises, and such reliance may form a basis for contract rights and duties. Under the doctrine of **promissory estoppel** (also called *detrimental reliance*), a person who has reasonably relied on the promise of another can often obtain some measure of recovery. When the doctrine of promissory estoppel is applied, the promisor (the offeror) is **estopped** (barred or impeded) from revoking the promise. For the doctrine of promissory estoppel to be applied, the following elements are required:

1 There must be a clear and definite promise.

2 The promisee must justifiably rely on the promise.

3 The reliance normally must be of a substantial and definite character.

4 Justice will be better served by the enforcement of the promise.

■ **EXAMPLE 7.36**   Your uncle tells you, "I'll pay you $1,500 a week so that you won't have to work anymore." In reliance on your uncle's promise, you quit your job, but your uncle refuses to pay you. Under the doctrine of promissory estoppel, you may be able to enforce his promise.[28] Now your uncle makes a promise to give you $20,000 to buy a car. If you buy the car with your own funds and he does not pay you, you may once again be able to enforce the promise under this doctrine. ■

---

28. A classic example is *Ricketts v. Scothorn*, 57 Neb. 51, 77 N.W. 365 (1898).

REVIEWING Agreement and Consideration

Shane Durbin wanted to have a recording studio custom built in his home. He sent invitations to a number of local contractors to submit bids on the project. Rory Amstel submitted the lowest bid, which was $20,000 less than any of the other bids Durbin received. Durbin then called Amstel to ascertain the type and quality of the materials that were included in the bid and to find out if he could substitute a superior brand of acoustic tiles for the same bid price. Amstel said he would have to check into the price difference. The parties also discussed a possible start date for construction. Two weeks later, Durbin changed his mind and decided not to go forward with his plan to build a recording studio. Amstel filed a suit against Durbin for breach of contract. Using the information presented in the chapter, answer the following questions.

1 Did Amstel's bid meet the requirements of an offer? Explain.

2 Was there an acceptance of the offer? Why or why not?

3 Suppose that the court determines that the parties did not reach an agreement. Further suppose that Amstel, in anticipation of building Durbin's studio, had purchased materials and refused other jobs so that he would have time in his schedule for Durbin's project. Under what theory discussed in the chapter might Amstel attempt to recover these costs?

4 Now suppose that Durbin had gone forward with his plan to build the studio and immediately accepted Amstel's bid without discussing the type or quality of materials. After Amstel began construction, Durbin asked Amstel to substitute a superior brand of acoustic tiles for the tiles that Amstel had intended to use at the time that he bid on the project. Amstel installed the tiles, then asked Durbin to pay the difference in price, but Durbin refused. Can Amstel sue to obtain the price differential from Durbin in this situation? Why or why not?

APPLICATION · Controlling the Terms of the Offer*

T he courts normally attempt to "save" contracts whenever feasible, but sometimes it is impossible to do so. Two common reasons that contracts fail are that (1) the terms of the offer were too unclear or indefinite to constitute a binding contract on the offer's acceptance, and (2) the acceptance was not timely. If you are an offeror, you can control both of these factors: you can determine what the terms of the future contract will be, as well as the time and mode of acceptance.

Include Clear and Definite Terms

If a contract's terms are too unclear or indefinite, the contract will fail. Unless a court can ascertain exactly what the rights and duties of the parties are under a particular contract, the court cannot enforce those rights and duties. Therefore, as an offeror, make sure that the terms of your offer are sufficiently definite to constitute a binding contract if the offer is accepted. A statement such as "Quantity to be determined later" may allow the offeree, after acceptance, to claim that a contract was never formed because the quantity term was not specified or is ambiguous. (Note, however, that sales and lease contracts governed by the Uniform Commercial Code may be formed even though terms are missing or ambiguous.)

Another reason an offeror should make sure that the offer's terms are clear and definite is that if a contract results, any ambiguous provision may be interpreted against the party that drafted the contract.

Specify the Time and Mode of Acceptance

Problems concerning contract formation also arise when it is unclear whether an acceptance is effective or at what time it became effective. To avoid such problems, you should take some precautions when phrasing the offer. Whether your offer is made via the Internet, fax, express delivery, or mail, you can specify that the offer must be accepted (or even that you must receive the acceptance) by a certain time, and if it is not, the offer will terminate. Similarly, you can specify the mode of acceptance. In online offers, you can indicate that to accept the offer, the user must click on a certain box on the screen. If you make an offer and want the acceptance to be faxed to you, make sure that you clearly indicate that the acceptance must be faxed to you at a given fax number by a specific time, or it will not be effective.

CHECKLIST FOR THE OFFEROR

1 Make sure that the terms of the offer are sufficiently clear and definite to allow both the parties and a court to determine the specific rights and obligations of the parties. Otherwise, the contract may fail for its ambiguity.

2 Specify in the offer the date on which the offer will terminate and the authorized mode of acceptance. For example, you can indicate that an acceptance, to be effective, must be faxed to you at a specific fax number by a specific time or date. You can even specify that the acceptance will not be effective until you receive it.

---

* This Application is not meant to substitute for the services of an attorney who is licensed to practice law in your state.

KEY TERMS

acceptance 219
accord and satisfaction 226
agreement 211
bilateral contract 205
consideration 222
contract 203
counteroffer 217
covenant not to sue 228
estopped 228
executed contract 208
executory contract 208
express contract 207
forbearance 222

formal contract 207
implied-in-fact contract 207
informal contract 207
liquidated debt 226
mailbox rule 221
mirror image rule 218
offer 211
offeree 205
offeror 205
option contract 216
past consideration 225
promise 202
promisee 203

promisor 203
promissory estoppel 228
quasi contract 210
release 226
rescission 225
revocation 216
unenforceable contract 209
unilateral contract 205
valid contract 209
void contract 210
voidable contract 209

CHAPTER SUMMARY Contracts: Nature, Classification, Agreement, and Consideration

An Overview of Contract Law
(See pages 202–204.)

1. *Sources of contract law*—The common law governs all contracts except when it has been modified or replaced by statutory law, such as the Uniform Commercial Code (UCC), or by administrative agency regulations. The UCC governs contracts for the sale or lease of goods (see Chapter 11).

2. *The function of contracts*—Contract law establishes what kinds of promises will be legally binding and supplies procedures for enforcing legally binding promises, or agreements.

3. *The definition of a contract*—A contract is an agreement that can be enforced in court. It is formed by two or more competent parties who agree to perform or to refrain from performing some act in the present or in the future.

4. *Requirements of a valid contract*—Agreement, consideration, contractual capacity, and legality.

5. *Defenses to the enforcement of a contract*—Genuineness of assent and form.

Types of Contracts
(See pages 204–211.)

1. *Bilateral*—A promise for a promise.

2. *Unilateral*—A promise for an act (acceptance is the completed—or substantial—performance of the contract by the offeree).

3. *Formal*—Requires a special form for contract formation.

4. *Informal*—Requires no special form for contract formation.

5. *Express*—Formed by words (oral, written, or a combination).

6. *Implied in fact*—Formed at least in part by the conduct of the parties.

7. *Executed*—A fully performed contract.

8. *Executory*—A contract not yet fully performed.

9. *Valid*—A contract that has the necessary contractual elements of offer and acceptance, consideration, parties with legal capacity, and having been made for a legal purpose.

10. *Voidable*—A contract in which a party has the option of avoiding or enforcing the contractual obligation.

11. *Unenforceable*—A valid contract that cannot be enforced because of a legal defense.

12. *Void*—No contract exists, or there is a contract without legal obligations.

13. *Quasi contract*—A quasi contract, or a contract implied in law, is a contract that is imposed by law to prevent unjust enrichment.

CHAPTER SUMMARY	Contracts: Nature, Classification, Agreement, and Consideration–Continued
Requirements of the Offer (See pages 211–215.)	1. *Intention*—There must be a serious, objective intention by the offeror to become bound by the offer. Nonoffer situations include (a) expressions of opinion; (b) statements of future intent; (c) preliminary negotiations; (d) generally, advertisements, catalogues, price lists, and circulars; (e) solicitations for bids made by an auctioneer; and (f) traditionally, agreements to agree in the future. 2. *Definiteness*—The terms of the offer must be sufficiently definite to be ascertainable by the parties or by a court. 3. *Communication*—The offer must be communicated to the offeree.
Termination of the Offer (See pages 216–219.)	1. *By action of the parties*— a. Revocation—Unless the offer is irrevocable, it can be revoked at any time before acceptance without liability. Revocation is not effective until received by the offeree or the offeree's agent. Some offers, such as a merchant's firm offer and option contracts, are irrevocable. b. Rejection—Accomplished by words or actions that demonstrate a clear intent not to accept the offer; not effective until received by the offeror or the offeror's agent. c. Counteroffer—A rejection of the original offer and the making of a new offer. 2. *By operation of law*— a. Lapse of time—The offer terminates (1) at the end of the time period specified in the offer or (2) if no time period is stated in the offer, at the end of a reasonable time period. b. Destruction of the specific subject matter of the offer—Automatically terminates the offer. c. Death or incompetence—Terminates the offer unless the offer is irrevocable. d. Illegality—Supervening illegality terminates the offer.
Acceptance (See pages 219–222.)	1. Can be made only by the offeree or the offeree's agent. 2. Must be unequivocal. Under the common law (mirror image rule), if new terms or conditions are added to the acceptance, it will be considered a counteroffer. 3. Acceptance of a unilateral offer is effective on full performance of the requested act. Generally, no communication is necessary. 4. Acceptance of a bilateral offer can be communicated by the offeree by any authorized mode of communication and is effective on dispatch. Unless the mode of communication is expressly specified by the offeror, the following methods are impliedly authorized: a. The same mode used by the offeror or a faster mode. b. Mail, when the two parties are at a distance. c. In sales contracts, by any reasonable medium.
Elements of Consideration (See pages 222–223.)	Consideration is broken down into two parts: (1) something of *legally sufficient value* must be given in exchange for the promise, and (2) there must be a *bargained-for exchange*.
Legal Sufficiency and Adequacy of Consideration (See page 223.)	Legal sufficiency of consideration relates to the first element of consideration—something of legal value must be given in exchange for a promise. Adequacy of consideration relates to "how much" consideration is given and whether a fair bargain was reached. Courts will inquire into the adequacy of consideration (whether the consideration is legally sufficient) only when fraud, undue influence, duress, or unconscionability may be involved.

(Continued)

CHAPTER SUMMARY	Contracts: Nature, Classification, Agreement, and Consideration—Continued
Contracts That Lack Consideration (See pages 223–226.)	Consideration is lacking in the following situations: 1. *Preexisting duty*—Consideration is not legally sufficient if one is either by law or by contract under a *preexisting duty* to perform the action being offered as consideration for a new contract. 2. *Past consideration*—Actions or events that have already taken place do not constitute legally sufficient consideration. 3. *Illusory promises*—When the nature or extent of performance is too uncertain, the promise is rendered illusory (without consideration and unenforceable).
Settlement of Claims (See pages 226–228.)	1. *Accord and satisfaction*—An *accord* is an agreement in which a debtor offers to pay a lesser amount than the creditor purports to be owed. *Satisfaction* may take place when the accord is executed. 2. *Release*—An agreement in which, for consideration, a party forfeits the right to seek further recovery beyond the terms specified in the release. 3. *Covenant not to sue*—An agreement not to sue on a present, valid claim.
Promissory Estoppel (See page 228.)	The equitable doctrine of promissory estoppel applies when a promisor reasonably expects a promise to induce definite and substantial action or forbearance by the promisee, and the promisee does act in reliance on the promise. Such a promise is binding if injustice can be avoided only by enforcement of the promise. Also known as the doctrine of *detrimental reliance*.

FOR REVIEW

Answers for the even-numbered questions in this **For Review** *section can be found in Appendix E at the end of this text.*

1 What is a contract? What are the four basic elements necessary to the formation of a valid contract?

2 What are the various types of contracts?

3 What are the requirements of an offer?

4 How can an offer be accepted?

5 What are the elements of consideration?

■

QUESTIONS AND CASE PROBLEMS

HYPOTHETICAL SCENARIOS

7.1 Express versus Implied Contracts. Suppose that a local businessperson, McDougal, is a good friend of Krunch, the owner of a local candy store. Every day on his lunch hour McDougal goes into Krunch's candy store and spends about five minutes looking at the candy. After examining Krunch's candy and talking with Krunch, McDougal usually buys one or two candy bars. One afternoon, McDougal goes into Krunch's candy shop, looks at the candy, and picks up a $1 candy bar. Seeing that Krunch is very busy, he catches Krunch's eye, waves the candy bar at Krunch without saying a word, and walks out. Is there a contract? If so, classify it within the categories presented in this chapter.

7.2 Hypothetical Question with Sample Answer. Chernek, the sole owner of a small business, has a large piece of used farm equipment for sale. He offers to sell the equipment to Bollow for $10,000. Discuss the legal effects of the following events on the offer:

1 Chernek dies prior to Bollow's acceptance, and at the time she accepts, Bollow is unaware of Chernek's death.

2 The night before Bollow accepts, a fire destroys the equipment.

3 Bollow pays $100 for a thirty-day option to purchase the equipment. During this period, Chernek dies, and Bollow accepts the offer, knowing of Chernek's death.

4 Bollow pays $100 for a thirty-day option to purchase the equipment. During this period, Bollow dies, and Bollow's estate accepts Chernek's offer within the stipulated time period.

 For a sample answer to Question 7.2, go to Appendix F at the end of this text.

7.3 Contract Classification. High-Flying Advertising, Inc., contracted with Big Burger Restaurants to fly an advertisement above the Connecticut beaches. The advertisement offered $5,000 to any person who could swim from the Connecticut beaches to Long Island across the Long Island Sound in less than a day. McElfresh saw the streamer and accepted the challenge. He started his marathon swim that same day at 10 A.M. After he had been swimming for four hours and was about halfway across the sound, McElfresh saw another plane pulling a streamer that read, "Big Burger revokes." Is there a contract between McElfresh and Big Burger? If there is a contract, what type(s) of contract is (are) formed?

 CASE PROBLEMS

7.4 Implied Contract. Thomas Rinks and Joseph Shields developed Psycho Chihuahua, a caricature of a Chihuahua dog with a "do-not-back-down" attitude. They promoted and marketed the character through their company, Wrench, L.L.C. Ed Alfaro and Rudy Pollak, representatives of Taco Bell Corp., learned of Psycho Chihuahua and met with Rinks and Shields to talk about using the character as a Taco Bell "icon." Wrench sent artwork, merchandise, and marketing ideas to Alfaro, who promoted the character within Taco Bell. Alfaro asked Wrench to propose terms for Taco Bell's use of Psycho Chihuahua. Taco Bell did not accept Wrench's terms, but Alfaro continued to promote the character within the company. Meanwhile, Taco Bell hired a new advertising agency, which proposed an advertising campaign involving a Chihuahua. When Alfaro learned of this proposal, he sent the Psycho Chihuahua materials to the agency. Taco Bell made a Chihuahua the focus of its marketing but paid nothing to Wrench. Wrench filed a suit against Taco Bell in a federal district court, claiming in part that it had an implied contract with Taco Bell, which the latter breached. Do these facts satisfy the requirements for an implied contract? Why or why not? [*Wrench, L.L.C. v. Taco Bell Corp.*, 256 F.3d 446 (6th Cir. 2001), *cert.* denied, 534 U.S. 1114, 122 S.Ct. 921, 151 L.Ed.2d 885 (2002)]

7.5 Case Problem with Sample Answer. As a child, Martha Carr once visited her mother's 108-acre tract of unimproved land in Richland County, South Carolina. In 1968, Betty and Raymond Campbell leased the land. Carr, a resident of New York, was diagnosed as having schizophrenia and depression in 1986, was hospitalized five or six times, and takes prescription drugs for the illnesses. In 1996, Carr inherited the Richland property and, two years later, contacted the Campbells about selling the land. Carr asked Betty about the value of the land, and Betty said that the county tax assessor had determined that the land's *agricultural value* was $54,000.

The Campbells knew at the time that the county had assessed the total property value at $103,700 for tax purposes. On August 6, Carr signed a contract to sell the land to the Campbells for $54,000. Believing the price to be unfair, however, Carr did not deliver the deed. The Campbells filed a suit in a South Carolina state court against Carr, seeking specific performance of the contract. At trial, an expert real estate appraiser testified that the *real market value* of the property was $162,000 at the time of the contract. Under what circumstances will a court examine the adequacy of consideration? Are those circumstances present in this case? Should the court enforce the contract between Carr and the Campbells? Explain. [*Campbell v. Carr*, 361 S.C. 258, 603 S.E.2d 625 (2004)]

 After you have answered Problem 7.5, compare your answer with the sample answer given on the Web site that accompanies this text. Go to academic.cengage.com/blaw/blt, select "Chapter 7," and click on "Case Problem with Sample Answer."

7.6 Offer. In August 2000, in California, Terry Reigelsperger sought treatment for pain in his lower back from chiropractor James Siller. Reigelsperger felt better after the treatment and did not intend to return for more, although he did not mention this to Siller. Before leaving the office, Reigelsperger signed an "informed consent" form that read, in part, "I intend this consent form to cover the entire course of treatment for my present condition and for any future condition(s) for which I seek treatment." He also signed an agreement that required the parties to submit to arbitration "any dispute as to medical malpractice. . . . This agreement is intended to bind the patient and the health care provider . . . who now or in the future treat[s] the patient." Two years later, Reigelsperger sought treatment from Siller for a different condition relating to his cervical spine and shoulder. Claiming malpractice with respect to the second treatment,

Reigelsperger filed a suit in a California state court against Siller. Siller asked the court to order the submission of the dispute to arbitration. Does Reigelsperger's lack of intent to return to Siller after his first treatment affect the enforceability of the arbitration agreement and consent form? Why or why not? [*Reigelsperger v. Siller*, 40 Cal.4th 574, 53 Cal.Rptr.3d 887, 150 P.3d 764 (2007)]

7.7 Contract Enforceability. California's Subdivision Map Act (SMA) prohibits the sale of real property until a map of its subdivision is filed with, and approved by, the appropriate state agency. In November 2004, Black Hills Investments, Inc., entered into two contracts with Albertson's, Inc., to buy two parcels of property in a shopping center development. Each contract required that "all governmental approvals relating to any lot split [or] subdivision" be obtained before the sale but permitted Albertson's to waive this condition. Black Hills made a $133,000 deposit on the purchase. A few weeks later, before the sales were complete, Albertson's filed with a local state agency a map that subdivided the shopping center into four parcels, including the two that Black Hills had agreed to buy. In January 2005, Black Hills objected to concessions that Albertson's had made to a buyer of one of the other parcels, told Albertson's that it was terminating its deal, and asked for a return of its deposit. Albertson's refused. Black Hills filed a suit in a California state court against Albertson's, arguing that the contracts were void. Are these contracts valid, voidable, unenforceable, or void? Explain. [*Black Hills Investments, Inc. v. Albertson's, Inc.*, 146 Cal.App.4th 883, 53 Cal.Rptr.3d 263 (4 Dist. 2007)]

7.8 **A Question of Ethics.** *John Sasson and Emily Springer met in January 2002. John worked for the U.S. Army as an engineer. Emily was an attorney with a law firm. When, six months later, John bought a townhouse in Randolph, New Jersey, he asked Emily to live with him. She agreed, but retained the ownership of her home in Monmouth Beach. John paid the mortgage and the other expenses on the townhouse. He urged Emily to quit her job and work from "our house." In May 2003, Emily took John's advice and started her own law practice. In December, John made her the beneficiary of his $150,000 individual retirement account (IRA) and said that he would give her his 2002 BMW M3 car before the end of the next year. He proposed to her in September 2004, giving her a diamond engagement ring and promising to "take care of her" for the rest of her life. Less than a month later, John was critically injured by an accidental blow to his head during a basketball game and died. On behalf of John's estate, which was valued at $1.1 million, his brother Steven filed a complaint in a New Jersey state court to have Emily evicted from the townhouse. Given these facts, consider the following questions. [In re Estate of Sasson, 387 N.J.Super. 459, 904 A.2d 769 (App.Div. 2006)]*

1 Based on John's promise to "take care of her" for the rest of her life, Emily claimed that she was entitled to the townhouse, the BMW, and an additional portion of John's estate. Under what circumstances would such a promise constitute a valid, enforceable contract? Does John's promise meet these requirements? Why or why not?

2 Whether John's promise is legally binding, is there an ethical basis on which it should be enforced? Is there an ethical basis for *not* enforcing it? Are there any circumstances under which a promise of support should be—or should *not* be—enforced? Discuss.

CRITICAL THINKING AND WRITING ASSIGNMENTS

7.9 Critical Legal Thinking. Review the list of basic requirements for contract formation given at the beginning of this chapter. In view of those requirements, analyze the relationship entered into when a student enrolls in a college or university. Has a contract been formed? If so, is it a bilateral contract or a unilateral contract? Discuss.

7.10 Critical Legal Thinking. Under what circumstances should courts examine the adequacy of consideration?

7.11 **Video Question.** Go to this text's Web site at **academic. cengage.com/blaw/blt** and select "Chapter 7." Click on "Video Questions" and view the video titled *Bowfinger.* Then answer the following questions.

1 In the video, Renfro (Robert Downey, Jr.) says to Bowfinger (Steve Martin), "You bring me this script and Kit Ramsey and you've got yourself a 'go' picture." Assume for the purposes of this question that their agreement is a contract. Is the contract bilateral or unilateral? Is it express or implied? Is it formal or informal? Is it executed or executory? Explain your answers.

2 Recall from the video that the contract between Bowfinger and the producer was oral. Suppose that a statute requires contracts of this type to be in writing. In that situation, would the contract be void, voidable, or unenforceable? Explain.

ONLINE ACTIVITIES

 **PRACTICAL
INTERNET EXERCISES**

Go to this text's Web site at **academic.cengage.com/blaw/blt**, select "Chapter 7," and click on "Practical Internet Exercises." There you will find the following Internet research exercises that you can perform to learn more about the topics covered in this chapter.

PRACTICAL INTERNET EXERCISE 7–1   LEGAL PERSPECTIVE—Contract Terms

PRACTICAL INTERNET EXERCISE 7–2   MANAGEMENT PERSPECTIVE—Implied Employment Contracts

PRACTICAL INTERNET EXERCISE 7–3   ETHICAL PERSPECTIVE—Offers and Advertisements

BEFORE THE TEST

Go to this text's Web site at **academic.cengage.com/blaw/blt**, select "Chapter 7," and click on "Interactive Quizzes." You will find a number of interactive questions relating to this chapter.

CHAPTER 8
Contracts: Capacity, Legality, Assent, and Form

CHAPTER OUTLINE

- CONTRACTUAL CAPACITY
- LEGALITY
- GENUINENESS OF ASSENT
- THE STATUTE OF FRAUDS— REQUIREMENT OF A WRITING
- THE STATUTE OF FRAUDS— SUFFICIENCY OF THE WRITING

LEARNING OBJECTIVES

AFTER READING THIS CHAPTER, YOU SHOULD BE ABLE TO ANSWER THE FOLLOWING QUESTIONS:

1 What are some exceptions to the rule that a minor can disaffirm (avoid) any contract?

2 Does an intoxicated person have the capacity to enter into an enforceable contract?

3 In what types of situations might genuineness of assent to a contract's terms be lacking?

4 What elements must exist for fraudulent misrepresentation to occur?

5 What contracts must be in writing to be enforceable?

Courts generally want contracts to be enforceable, and much of the law is devoted to aiding the enforceability of contracts. Nonetheless, as indicated in the chapter-opening quotation, "liberty of contract" is not absolute. In other words, not all people can make legally binding contracts at all times. Contracts entered into by persons lacking the capacity to do so may be voidable. Similarly, contracts calling for the performance of an illegal act are illegal and thus void—they are not contracts at all.

In this chapter, we first examine contractual capacity and some aspects of illegal bargains. We then look at genuineness of assent. An otherwise valid contract may be unenforceable if the parties have not genuinely assented to its terms. As mentioned in Chapter 7, lack of genuine assent is a *defense* to the enforcement of a contract. A contract that is otherwise valid may also be unenforceable if it is not in the proper form. For example, if a contract is required by law to be in writing and there is no written evidence of the contract, it may not be enforceable. In the concluding section of this chapter, we examine the kinds of contracts that require a writing under what is called the *Statute of Frauds*.

CONTRACTUAL CAPACITY
The threshold mental capacity required by law for a party who enters into a contract to be bound by that contract.

CONTRACTUAL CAPACITY

Contractual capacity is the legal ability to enter into a contractual relationship. Courts generally presume the existence of contractual capacity, but in some situations, capacity is lacking or may be questionable. A person who has been determined by a court to be mentally incompetent, for example, cannot form a legally binding contract with another party. In other situations, a party may have the capacity to enter into a valid contract but may also have the right to avoid liability under it. For example, minors—or *infants*, as they are commonly referred to in the law—usually are not legally bound by contracts. In this section, we look at the effect of youth, intoxication, and mental incompetence on contractual capacity.

Minors

Today, in virtually all states, the *age of majority* (when a person is no longer a minor) for contractual purposes is eighteen years—the so-called coming of age. (The age of majority may still be twenty-one for other purposes, however, such as the purchase and consumption of alcohol.) In addition, some states provide for the termination of minority on marriage. Minority status may also be terminated by a minor's **emancipation,** which occurs when a child's parent or legal guardian relinquishes the legal right to exercise control over the child. Normally, minors who leave home to support themselves are considered emancipated. Several jurisdictions permit minors to petition a court for emancipation themselves. For business purposes, a minor may petition a court to be treated as an adult.

The general rule is that a minor can enter into any contract an adult can, provided that the contract is not one prohibited by law for minors (for example, the sale of alcoholic beverages or tobacco). A contract entered into by a minor, however, is voidable at the option of that minor, subject to certain exceptions (to be discussed shortly). To exercise the option to avoid a contract, a minor need only manifest an intention not to be bound by it. The minor "avoids" the contract by disaffirming it.

Disaffirmance   The legal avoidance, or setting aside, of a contractual obligation is referred to as **disaffirmance.** To disaffirm, a minor must express, through words or conduct, his or her intent not to be bound to the contract. The minor must disaffirm the entire contract, not merely a portion of it. For instance, a minor cannot decide to keep part of the goods purchased under a contract and return the remaining goods. When a minor disaffirms a contract, the minor can recover any property that she or he transferred to the adult as consideration for the contract, even if it is then in the possession of a third party.[1]

A contract can ordinarily be disaffirmed at any time during minority[2] or for a reasonable time after the minor comes of age. What constitutes a "reasonable" time may vary. Two months would probably be considered reasonable, but except in unusual circumstances, a court may not find it reasonable to wait a year or more after coming of age to disaffirm. If an individual fails to disaffirm an executed contract within a reasonable time after reaching the age of majority, a court will likely hold that the contract has been ratified (*ratification* will be discussed shortly).

Note that an adult who enters into a contract with a minor cannot avoid his or her contractual duties on the ground that the minor can do so. Unless the minor exercises the option to disaffirm the contract, the adult party normally is bound by it.

A Minor's Obligations on Disaffirmance   Although all states' laws permit minors to disaffirm contracts (with certain exceptions), including executed contracts, state laws differ on the extent of a minor's obligations on disaffirmance.

ON THE WEB

The Legal Information Institute at Cornell Law School provides a table with links to state statutes governing the emancipation of minors. Go to

www.law.cornell.edu/topics/ Table_Emancipation.htm.

EMANCIPATION
In regard to minors, the act of being freed from parental control; occurs when a child's parent or legal guardian relinquishes the legal right to exercise control over the child. Normally, a minor who leaves home to support himself or herself is considered emancipated.

DISAFFIRMANCE
The legal avoidance, or setting aside, of a contractual obligation.

This minor is discussing the purchase of a used car with a salesperson. When a minor disaffirms a contract, such as a contract to buy a car, most states require the minor to return whatever he or she purchased, if it is within his or her control. Why do some states require more?
(Michael Newman/PhotoEdit)

---

1. The Uniform Commercial Code, in Section 2–403(1), allows an exception if the third party is a "good faith purchaser for value."
2. In some states, however, a minor who enters into a contract for the sale of land cannot disaffirm the contract until she or he reaches the age of majority.

Majority Rule. Courts in a majority of states hold that the minor need only return the goods (or other consideration) subject to the contract, provided the goods are in the minor's possession or control. **■EXAMPLE 8.1** Jim Garrison, a seventeen-year-old, purchases a computer from Radio Shack. While transporting the computer to his home, Garrison, through no fault of his own, is involved in a car accident. As a result of the accident, the plastic casing of the computer is broken. The next day, he returns the computer to Radio Shack and disaffirms the contract. Under the majority view, this return fulfills Garrison's duty even though the computer is now damaged. Garrison is entitled to receive a refund of the purchase price (if paid in cash) or to be relieved of any further obligations under an agreement to purchase the computer on credit. ■

Minority Rule. A growing number of states, either by statute or by court decision, place an additional duty on the minor—the duty to restore the adult party to the position she or he held before the contract was made. The trend among today's courts is to hold a minor responsible for damage, ordinary wear and tear, and depreciation of goods that the minor used prior to disaffirmance.

Exceptions to the Minor's Right to Disaffirm State courts and legislatures have carved out several exceptions to the minor's right to disaffirm. Some contracts cannot be avoided simply as a matter of law, on the ground of public policy. For example, marriage contracts and contracts to enlist in the armed services fall into this category. Other contracts may not be disaffirmed for different reasons, including those discussed here.

Misrepresentation of Age. Suppose that a minor tells a seller she is twenty-one years old when she is really seventeen. Ordinarily, the minor can disaffirm the contract even though she has misrepresented her age. Moreover, in some jurisdictions the minor is not liable for the tort of fraudulent misrepresentation, the rationale being that such a tort judgment might indirectly force the minor to perform the contract.

In many jurisdictions, however, a minor who has misrepresented his or her age can be bound by a contract under certain circumstances. First, several states have enacted statutes for precisely this purpose. In these states, misrepresentation of age is enough to prohibit disaffirmance. Other statutes prohibit disaffirmance by a minor who has engaged in business as an adult. Second, some courts refuse to allow minors to disaffirm executed (fully performed) contracts unless they can return the consideration received. The combination of the minors' misrepresentations and their unjust enrichment has persuaded these courts to *estop* (prevent) the minors from asserting contractual incapacity.

Contracts for Necessaries, Insurance, and Loans. A minor who enters into a contract for necessaries may disaffirm the contract but remains liable for the reasonable value of the goods used. **Necessaries** are basic needs, such as food, clothing, shelter, and medical services, at a level of value required to maintain the minor's standard of living or financial and social status. Thus, what will be considered a necessary for one person may be a luxury for another. Additionally, what is considered a necessary depends on whether the minor is under the care or control of his or her parents, who are required by law to provide necessaries for the minor. If a minor's parents provide the minor with shelter, for example, then a contract to lease shelter (such as an apartment) normally will not be regarded as a contract for necessaries.

Generally, then, to qualify as a contract for necessaries, (1) the item contracted for must be necessary to the minor's existence, (2) the value of the necessary item may be up to a level required to maintain the minor's standard of living or financial and social status, and (3) the minor must not be under the care of a parent or guardian who is required

NECESSARIES
Necessities required for life, such as food, shelter, clothing, and medical attention; may include whatever is believed to be necessary to maintain a person's standard of living or financial and social status.

BE AWARE A minor's station in life (including financial and social status and lifestyle) is important in determining whether an item is a necessary or a luxury. For example, clothing is a necessary, but if a minor from a low-income family contracts for the purchase of a $2,000 leather coat, a court may deem the coat a luxury. In this situation, the contract would not be for "necessaries."

to supply this item. Unless these three criteria are met, the minor can normally disaffirm the contract *without* being liable for the reasonable value of the goods used.

Traditionally, insurance has not been viewed as a necessary, so minors can ordinarily disaffirm their insurance contracts and recover all premiums paid. Nevertheless, some jurisdictions prohibit disaffirming insurance contracts—for example, when minors contract for life insurance on their own lives. Financial loans are seldom considered to be necessaries, even if the minor spends the borrowed funds on necessaries. If, however, a lender makes a loan to a minor for the express purpose of enabling the minor to purchase necessaries, and the lender personally makes sure the funds are so spent, the minor normally is obligated to repay the loan.

Ratification   In contract law, **ratification** is the act of accepting and giving legal force to an obligation that previously was not enforceable. A minor who has reached the age of majority can ratify a contract expressly or impliedly. *Express* ratification occurs when the individual, on reaching the age of majority, states orally or in writing that she or he intends to be bound by the contract. *Implied* ratification takes place when the minor, on reaching the age of majority, indicates an intent to abide by the contract.

EXAMPLE 8.2 Lin enters a contract to sell her laptop to Arturo, a minor. If Arturo does not disaffirm the contract and, on reaching the age of majority, writes a letter to Lin stating that he still agrees to buy the laptop, he has expressly ratified the contract. If, instead, Arturo takes possession of the laptop as a minor and continues to use it well after reaching the age of majority, he has impliedly ratified the contract. ■

If a minor fails to disaffirm a contract within a reasonable time after reaching the age of majority, then a court must determine whether the conduct constitutes implied ratification or disaffirmance. Generally, courts presume that a contract that is *executed* (fully performed by both sides) was ratified. A contract that is still *executory* (not yet performed by both parties) is normally considered to be disaffirmed. The *Concept Summary* on this page summarizes the rules relating to contracts by minors.

RATIFICATION
The act of accepting and giving legal force to an obligation that previously was not enforceable.

Intoxicated Persons

Contractual capacity also becomes an issue when a party to a contract was intoxicated at the time the contract was made. Intoxication is a condition in which a person's normal capacity to act or think is inhibited by alcohol or some other drug. If the person was

CONCEPT SUMMARY Contracts by Minors	
General Rule	Contracts entered into by minors are voidable at the option of the minor.
Rules of Disaffirmance	A minor may disaffirm a contract at any time while still a minor and within a reasonable time after reaching the age of majority. Most states only require that the minor return the goods that were subject to the contract, regardless of any damage, wear and tear, or depreciation of those goods. Some states require that the minor pay for any damage to, or depreciation of, the goods being returned.
Exceptions to Basic Rules of Disaffirmance	1. *Fraud or misrepresentation*—In many jurisdictions, a minor who misrepresents her or his age is denied the right of disaffirmance. 2. *Necessaries*—Minors may disaffirm contracts for necessaries but remain liable for the reasonable value of the goods or services. 3. *Ratification*—After reaching the age of majority, a person can ratify a contract that he or she formed as a minor, thereby becoming fully liable on the contract.

sufficiently intoxicated to lack mental capacity, the contract may be voidable even if the intoxication was purely voluntary. For the contract to be voidable, however, the person must prove that the intoxication impaired her or his reason and judgment so severely that she or he did not comprehend the legal consequences of entering into the contract. In addition, to avoid the contract in the majority of states, the person claiming intoxication must be able to return all consideration received.

If, despite intoxication, the person understood the legal consequences of the agreement, the contract is enforceable. The fact that the terms of the contract are foolish or obviously favor the other party does not make the contract voidable (unless the other party fraudulently induced the person to become intoxicated). As a practical matter, courts rarely permit contracts to be avoided on the ground of intoxication, because it is difficult to determine whether a party was sufficiently intoxicated to avoid legal duties. Rather than inquire into the intoxicated person's mental state, many courts instead focus on objective indications of capacity to determine whether the contract is voidable owing to intoxication.[3]

Mentally Incompetent Persons

Contracts made by mentally incompetent persons can be void, voidable, or valid. If a court has previously determined that a person is mentally incompetent and has appointed a guardian to represent the person, any contract made by that mentally incompetent person is *void*—no contract exists. Only the guardian can enter into a binding contract on behalf of the mentally incompetent person.

If a court has not previously judged a person to be mentally incompetent but in fact the person was incompetent at the time, the contract may be *voidable*. A contract is voidable if the person did not know he or she was entering into the contract or lacked the mental capacity to comprehend its nature, purpose, and consequences. In such situations, the contract is voidable at the option of the mentally incompetent person but not the other party. The contract may then be disaffirmed or ratified (if the person regains mental competence). Like intoxicated persons, mentally incompetent persons must return any consideration and pay for the reasonable value of any necessaries they receive.

A contract entered into by a mentally incompetent person (whom a court has not previously declared incompetent) may also be *valid* if the person had capacity *at the time the contract was formed*. For instance, a person may be able to understand the nature and effect of entering into a certain contract yet simultaneously lack capacity to engage in other activities. In such cases, the contract ordinarily will be valid because the person is not legally mentally incompetent for contractual purposes.[4] Similarly, an otherwise mentally incompetent person may have a *lucid interval*—a temporary restoration of sufficient intelligence, judgment, and will to enter into contracts—during which she or he will be considered to have full legal capacity.

LEGALITY

To this point, we have discussed three of the requirements for a valid contract to exist—agreement, consideration, and contractual capacity. Now we examine the fourth—legality. For a contract to be valid and enforceable, it must be formed for a legal purpose. A contract

---

3. See, for example, the court's decision in *Lucy v. Zehmer*, presented as Case 7.2 in Chapter 7.
4. Modern courts no longer require a person to be completely irrational to disaffirm contracts on the basis of mental incompetence. A contract may be voidable if, by reason of a mental illness or defect, an individual was unable to act reasonably with respect to the transaction and the other party had reason to know of the condition.

to do something that is prohibited by federal or state statutory law is illegal and, as such, void from the outset and thus unenforceable. Additionally, a contract to commit a tortious act or to commit an action that is contrary to public policy is illegal and unenforceable.

Contracts Contrary to Statute

Statutes often set forth rules specifying which terms and clauses may be included in contracts and which are prohibited. We examine here several ways in which contracts may be contrary to a statute and thus illegal.

Contracts to Commit a Crime Any contract to commit a crime is a contract in violation of a statute. Thus, a contract to sell an illegal drug (the sale of which is prohibited by statute) is not enforceable. If the object or performance of the contract is rendered illegal by statute *after* the contract has been entered into, the contract is considered to be discharged by law. (See the discussion of *impossibility of performance* in Chapter 9.)

Usury Virtually every state has a statute that sets the maximum rate of interest that can be charged for different types of transactions, including ordinary loans. A lender who makes a loan at an interest rate above the lawful maximum commits **usury.** The maximum rate of interest varies from state to state, as do the consequences for lenders who make usurious loans. Some states allow the lender to recover only the principal of a loan along with interest up to the legal maximum. In effect, the lender is denied recovery of the excess interest. In other states, the lender can recover the principal amount of the loan but no interest.

USURY
Charging an illegal rate of interest.

Although usury statutes place a ceiling on allowable rates of interest, exceptions are made to facilitate business transactions. For example, many states exempt corporate loans from the usury laws. In addition, almost all states have special statutes allowing much higher interest rates on small loans to help those borrowers who need funds and could not otherwise obtain loans.

Gambling All states have statutes that regulate gambling—defined as any scheme that involves the distribution of property by chance among persons who have paid valuable consideration for the opportunity (chance) to receive the property.[5] Gambling is the creation of risk for the purpose of assuming it. Traditionally, the states have deemed gambling contracts illegal and thus void.

In several states, however, including Louisiana, Michigan, Nevada, and New Jersey, casino gambling is legal. In other states, certain forms of gambling are legal. California, for example, has not defined draw poker as a crime, although criminal statutes prohibit numerous other types of gambling games. A number of states allow gambling on horse races, and the majority of states have legalized state-operated lotteries, as well as lotteries (such as bingo) conducted for charitable purposes. Many states also allow gambling on Indian reservations.

Sometimes, it is difficult to distinguish a gambling contract from the risk sharing inherent in almost all contracts. **■EXAMPLE 8.3** In one case, five co-workers each received a free lottery ticket from a customer and agreed to split the winnings if one of the tickets turned out to be the winning one. At first glance, this may seem entirely legal. The court, however, noted that the oral contract in this case "was an exchange of promises to share winnings from the parties' individually owned lottery tickets upon the happening of the uncertain event" that one of the tickets

Payday loans are popular with individuals who do not have regular banking relationships. A client writes a check for some relatively small amount to be cashed at "pay day," usually in two weeks. About 10 million U.S. residents apply for these loans in any given year. The implicit interest rates are extremely high, sometimes more than 100 percent on an annualized basis. Why would anyone agree to pay so much for such a short-term loan?
(Seth Anderson/Creative Commons)

5. See *Wishing Well Club v. Akron*, 112 N.E.2d 41 (Ohio Com.Pl. 1951).

would win. Consequently, concluded the court, the agreement at issue was "founded on a gambling consideration" and therefore was void.[6] ▣

Online Gambling   A significant issue today is how gambling laws can be applied in the Internet context. Because state laws pertaining to gambling differ, online gambling raises a number of unique issues. For example, in those states that do not allow casino gambling or offtrack betting, what can a state government do if residents of the state place bets online? Also, where does the actual act of gambling occur? For example, suppose that a resident of New York places bets via the Internet at a gambling site located in Antigua. Is the actual act of "gambling" taking place in New York or in Antigua? According to a New York court in one case, "if the person engaged in gambling is located in New York, then New York is the location where the gambling occurred."[7] Courts of other states may take a different view, however.

Another issue that is being debated is whether entering contracts that involve gambling on sports teams that do not really exist—fantasy sports—is a form of gambling. For a discussion of this issue, see this chapter's *Adapting the Law to the Online Environment* feature.

Sabbath (Sunday) Laws   Statutes referred to as Sabbath (Sunday) laws prohibit the formation or performance of certain contracts on a Sunday. These laws, which date back to colonial times, are often called **blue laws,** as mentioned in Chapter 1. Blue laws get their name from the blue paper on which New Haven, Connecticut, printed its town ordinance in 1781 that prohibited work and required businesses to close on Sunday. According to a few state and local laws, all contracts entered into on a Sunday are illegal. Laws in other states or municipalities prohibit only the sale of certain types of merchandise, such as alcoholic beverages, on a Sunday.

In most states with such statutes, contracts that were entered into on a Sunday can be ratified during a weekday. Also, if a contract that was entered into on a Sunday has been fully performed (executed), normally it cannot be rescinded (canceled). Exceptions to Sunday laws permit contracts for necessities (such as food) and works of charity. Many states do not enforce Sunday laws, and some state courts have held these laws to be unconstitutional because they interfere with the freedom of religion.

Licensing Statutes   All states require that members of certain professions obtain licenses allowing them to practice. Physicians, lawyers, real estate brokers, architects, electricians, and stockbrokers are but a few of the people who must be licensed. Some licenses are obtained only after extensive schooling and examinations, which indicate to the public that a special skill has been acquired. Others require only that the particular person be of good moral character and pay a fee.

The Purpose of Licensing Statutes.   Generally, business licenses provide a means of regulating and taxing certain businesses and protecting the public against actions that could threaten the general welfare. For example, in nearly all states, a stockbroker must be licensed and must file a bond with the state to protect the public from fraudulent transactions in stocks. Similarly, a plumber must be licensed and bonded to protect the public against incompetent plumbers and to protect the public health. Only persons or businesses possessing the qualifications and complying with the conditions required by statute are entitled to licenses. For instance, the owner of a bar can be required to sell food as a condition of obtaining a license to serve liquor.

BLUE LAWS
State or local laws that prohibit the performance of certain types of commercial activities on a Sunday.

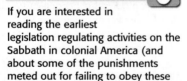

ON THE WEB

If you are interested in reading the earliest legislation regulating activities on the Sabbath in colonial America (and about some of the punishments meted out for failing to obey these regulations), go to

www.natreformassn.org/statesman/99/colfound.html.

---

6. *Dickerson v. Deno,* 770 So.2d 63 (Ala. 2000).
7. *United States v. Cohen,* 260 F.3d. 68 (2d Cir. 2001).

ADAPTING THE LAW TO THE ONLINE ENVIRONMENT — Are Online Fantasy Sports Just Another Form of Real-Life Gambling?

A ccording to the Fantasy Sports Trade Association, between 16 million and 20 million U.S. adults play some form of fantasy sports. A fantasy sport is a game in which the participants, or "owners," build a team composed of real-life players from different real-life teams. For example, an owner might include a quarterback from the New England Patriots and a running back from the San Diego Chargers. The fantasy team then competes against other fantasy sports teams with different owners. Each week during the season for the particular sport, the statistical performances of the real-life players are translated into points, and the points of all the players on an owner's fantasy team are totaled. Although fantasy baseball, basketball, golf, hockey, and other sports—even professional wrestling—are available, most participants play fantasy football.

Enter the Internet

Although the origin of fantasy sports supposedly can be traced back to 1962, when an owner of the Oakland Raiders football team and four other football fans created the Greater Oakland Professional Pigskin Prognosticators League, or GOPPPL, fantasy sports did not become big business until access to the Internet became widespread in the 1990s. Today, the number of players is increasing at a rate of 7 to 10 percent per year, and the game contributes as much as $4 billion annually to the U.S. economy. Fantasy sports sites have proliferated on the Internet, as have fantasy sports news sites, such as RotoWire.com and Fantasyfootballnews.com.

One of the appeals of online fantasy sports is that the participants can gamble on the outcome. In a fantasy football league, for example, each participant-owner adds a given amount to the pot and then "drafts" his or her fantasy team from the actual National Football League (NFL) players. Each week, as described earlier, the owner receives points based on his or her players' statistical performances. At the end of the season, the weekly points are totaled, and the owner with the most points wins the pot.

Exemption from Online Gambling Prohibitions

As online gambling has expanded, Congress has stepped in to attempt to regulate it. In October 2006, Congress passed and President George W. Bush signed into law a bill that, in essence, outlaws Internet gambling by making it illegal for credit-card companies and banking institutions to engage in transactions with Internet gambling companies.[a] Note that the act does not prohibit individuals from placing bets online, but rather focuses on restricting their ability to obtain financing for online gambling. Although the legislation seems comprehensive, it specifically exempts Internet wagers on horse racing, state lotteries, and fantasy sports. In other words, Congress explicitly determined that fantasy sports do *not* constitute a prohibited Internet gambling activity.

But Aren't Participants in Fantasy Sports Leagues Really Gambling?

In a lawsuit filed in New Jersey, Charles Humphrey claimed that media companies, including Viacom, CBS, ESPN, and *The Sporting News* had engaged in illegal gambling by hosting pay-to-play fantasy leagues. Humphrey argued that fantasy sports leagues are games of chance and not games of skill, and claimed that he was entitled to recover as gambling losses all of the entry fees paid by participants. The U.S. District Court rejected the argument, ruling that Humphrey's complaint failed to state a claim because it did not identify any individual who paid an entry fee to play in one of the fantasy sports.

Although the court dismissed the case on procedural grounds, the opinion stated that fantasy sports leagues are not bets or wagers because the entry fees are paid unconditionally. The court also found that the federal statute on Internet gambling (previously mentioned) confirms its conclusion that "fantasy sports leagues such as those operated by Defendants do not constitute gambling as a matter of law."[b]

 FOR CRITICAL ANALYSIS *What arguments can be used to support the idea that playing fantasy sports requires skill?*

a. Security and Accountability for Every Port Act, Public Law No. 109-347, Sections 5361–5367, 120 Stat. 1884 (2006). (A version of the Unlawful Internet Gambling Enforcement Act of 2006 was incorporated into this statute.) See 31 U.S.C. Section 5361 *et seq.*

b. *Humphrey v. Viacom, Inc.*, 2007 WL 1797648 (D.N.J. 2007).

Contracts with Unlicensed Practitioners. A contract with an unlicensed practitioner may still be enforceable, depending on the nature of the licensing statute. Some states expressly provide that the lack of a license in certain occupations bars the enforcement of work-related contracts. If the statute does not expressly state this, one must look to the underlying purpose of the licensing requirements for a particular occupation. If the purpose is to protect the public from unauthorized practitioners, a contract involving an unlicensed individual is illegal and unenforceable. If, however, the underlying purpose of the statute is to raise government revenues, a contract with an unlicensed practitioner is enforceable—although the unlicensed person is usually fined.

Contracts Contrary to Public Policy

Although contracts involve private parties, some are not enforceable because of the negative impact they would have on society. These contracts are said to be *contrary to public policy*. Examples include a contract to commit an immoral act, such as selling a child, and a contract that prohibits marriage. **■EXAMPLE 8.4** Everett offers a young man $10,000 if he refrains from marrying Everett's daughter. If the young man accepts, no contract is formed (the contract is void) because it is contrary to public policy. Thus, if the man marries Everett's daughter, Everett cannot sue him for breach of contract. ■ Business contracts that may be contrary to public policy include contracts in restraint of trade and unconscionable contracts or clauses.

Contracts in Restraint of Trade   Contracts in restraint of trade (anticompetitive agreements) usually adversely affect the public policy that favors competition in the economy. Typically, such contracts also violate one or more federal or state statutes.[8] An exception is recognized when the restraint is reasonable and is part of, or supplemental to, a contract for the sale of a business or an **employment contract** (a contract stating the terms and conditions of employment). Many such exceptions involve a type of restraint called a **covenant not to compete,** or a restrictive covenant.

Covenants Not to Compete and the Sale of an Ongoing Business.   Covenants (promises) not to compete are often contained as ancillary (secondary, or subordinate) clauses in contracts concerning the sale of an ongoing business. A covenant not to compete is created when a seller agrees not to open a new store in a certain geographic area surrounding the old store. Such agreements enable the seller to sell, and the purchaser to buy, the goodwill and reputation of an ongoing business. If, for example, a well-known merchant sells his or her store and opens a competing business a block away, many of the merchant's customers will likely do business at the new store. This renders less valuable the good name and reputation sold to the other merchant for a price. If a covenant not to compete is not ancillary to a sales agreement, however, it will be void because it unreasonably restrains trade and is contrary to public policy.

Covenants Not to Compete in Employment Contracts.   Agreements not to compete can also be included in employment contracts. People in middle-level and upper-level management positions commonly agree not to work for competitors or not to start a competing business for a specified period of time after terminating employment. Such agreements are generally legal so long as the specified period of time is not excessive in duration and the geographic restriction is reasonable. Basically, the restriction on competition must be reasonable—that is, not any greater than necessary to protect a legitimate business interest. Although a court might find that a time restriction of one year is reasonable, a time restriction of two, three, or five years may not be considered reasonable.

Determining what constitutes "reasonable" time and geographic restrictions in the online environment is a more difficult issue that is being addressed by the courts. The Internet environment has no physical borders, so geographic restrictions are no longer relevant. Also, a reasonable time period may be shorter in the online environment than in conventional employment contracts because the restrictions would apply worldwide.

EMPLOYMENT CONTRACT
A contract between an employer and an employee in which the terms and conditions of employment are stated.

COVENANT NOT TO COMPETE
A contractual promise of one party to refrain from conducting business similar to that of another party for a certain period of time and within a specified geographic area. Courts commonly enforce such covenants if they are reasonable in terms of time and geographic area and are part of, or supplemental to, a contract for the sale of a business or an employment contract.

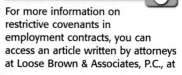

ON THE WEB
For more information on restrictive covenants in employment contracts, you can access an article written by attorneys at Loose Brown & Associates, P.C., at **www.loosebrown.com/Articles/bl2.htm**.

---

8. Federal statutes prohibiting anticompetitive agreements include the Sherman Antitrust Act, the Clayton Act, and the Federal Trade Commission Act. See Chapter 22.

Enforcement Problems. The laws governing the enforceability of covenants not to compete vary significantly from state to state. In some states, such as Texas, such a covenant will not be enforced unless the employee has received some benefit in return for signing the noncompete agreement. This is true even if the covenant is reasonable as to time and area. If the employee receives no benefit, the covenant will be deemed void. California prohibits the enforcement of covenants not to compete altogether.

Occasionally, depending on the jurisdiction, courts will *reform* covenants not to compete. If a covenant is found to be unreasonable in time or geographic area, the court may convert the terms into reasonable ones and then enforce the reformed covenant. This presents a problem, however, in that the judge has implicitly become a party to the contract. Consequently, courts usually resort to contract **reformation** only when necessary to prevent undue burdens or hardships.

REFORMATION
A court-ordered correction of a written contract so that it reflects the true intentions of the parties.

Unconscionable Contracts or Clauses   Ordinarily, a court does not look at the fairness or equity of a contract; for example, a court normally will not inquire into the adequacy of consideration. Persons are assumed to be reasonably intelligent, and the court does not come to their aid just because they have made unwise or foolish bargains. In certain circumstances, however, bargains are so oppressive that the courts relieve innocent parties of part or all of their duties. Such a bargain is called an **unconscionable contract** (or **unconscionable clause**). Both the Uniform Commercial Code (UCC) and the Uniform Consumer Credit Code (UCCC) embody the unconscionability concept—the former with regard to the sale of goods and the latter with regard to consumer loans and the waiver of rights.[9] A contract can be unconscionable on either procedural or substantive grounds, as discussed in the following subsections and illustrated graphically in Exhibit 8–1.

UNCONSCIONABLE CONTRACT (OR UNCONSCIONABLE CLAUSE)
A contract or clause that is void on the basis of public policy because one party, as a result of disproportionate bargaining power, is forced to accept terms that are unfairly burdensome and that unfairly benefit the dominating party.

9. See, for example, UCC 2–302 and 2–719, and UCCC 5–108 and 1–107.

EXHIBIT 8–1   Unconscionability

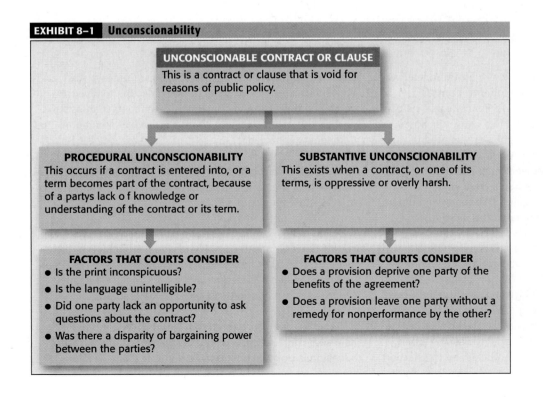

UNCONSCIONABLE CONTRACT OR CLAUSE
This is a contract or clause that is void for reasons of public policy.

PROCEDURAL UNCONSCIONABILITY
This occurs if a contract is entered into, or a term becomes part of the contract, because of a partys lack o f knowledge or understanding of the contract or its term.

SUBSTANTIVE UNCONSCIONABILITY
This exists when a contract, or one of its terms, is oppressive or overly harsh.

FACTORS THAT COURTS CONSIDER
- Is the print inconspicuous?
- Is the language unintelligible?
- Did one party lack an opportunity to ask questions about the contract?
- Was there a disparity of bargaining power between the parties?

FACTORS THAT COURTS CONSIDER
- Does a provision deprive one party of the benefits of the agreement?
- Does a provision leave one party without a remedy for nonperformance by the other?

Procedural Unconscionability. Procedural unconscionability has to do with how a term becomes part of a contract and relates to factors bearing on a party's lack of knowledge or understanding of the contract terms because of inconspicuous print, unintelligible language ("legalese"), lack of opportunity to read the contract, lack of opportunity to ask questions about the contract's meaning, and other factors. Procedural unconscionability sometimes relates to purported lack of voluntariness because of a disparity in bargaining power between the two parties. Contracts entered into because of one party's vastly superior bargaining power may be deemed unconscionable. Such contracts are often referred to as **adhesion contracts.** An adhesion contract is written exclusively by one party (the dominant party, usually the seller or creditor) and presented to the other (the adhering party, usually the buyer or borrower) on a take-it-or-leave-it basis.[10] In other words, the adhering party has no opportunity to negotiate the terms of the contract.

Standard-form contracts often contain fine-print provisions that shift a risk naturally borne by one party to the other. A variety of businesses use such contracts. Life insurance policies, residential leases, loan agreements, and employment agency contracts are often standard-form contracts. To avoid enforcement of the contract or of a particular clause, the aggrieved party must show that the parties had substantially unequal bargaining positions and that enforcement would be manifestly unfair or oppressive. If the required showing is made, the contract or particular term is deemed unconscionable and is not enforced.

In the following case, the question was whether a standard-form contract clause that mandated individual arbitration of any dispute and precluded class action[11] was unconscionable.

ADHESION CONTRACT
A "standard-form" contract, such as that between a large retailer and a consumer, in which the stronger party dictates the terms.

---

10. See, for example, *Henningsen v. Bloomfield Motors, Inc.,* 32 N.J. 358, 161 A.2d 69 (1960).
11. A *class action* is a means by which one or more individuals of a large group of persons interested in a dispute can sue as a class without every member of the group needing to appear in court.

CASE 8.1 Thibodeau v. Comcast Corp.

Superior Court of Pennsylvania, Philadelphia County, 2006 PA Super. 346, 912 A.2d 874 (2006).

FACTS Philip Thibodeau was a subscriber to Comcast Corporation's cable-television service in Pennsylvania. As part of his subscription, Thibodeau rented two converter boxes and two remote controls, which he thought were needed to receive the broadcasts. At the time, Comcast did not tell its customers that nonpremium programming could be viewed without the boxes and that the remotes were wholly unnecessary. In 2002, Comcast mailed Thibodeau and others a "customer agreement" that mandated the individual arbitration of all disputes and precluded class action. Meanwhile, also in Pennsylvania, Lorena Afroilan bought a Panasonic Corporation cell phone and contracted with the AT&T Wireless network for service. With the purchase, Afroilan was given a "Welcome Guide," which required the individual arbitration of all disputes and precluded class action. When Afroilan tried to switch providers, she discovered that her phone had a lock preventing its use on any network other than AT&T's. Thibodeau, Afroilan, and others filed class-action suits in a Pennsylvania state court against Comcast, AT&T, and Panasonic, alleging violations of state law. The trial court combined the suits and denied the defendants' requests to dismiss the complaints and compel individual arbitration. The defendants appealed.

ISSUE Should the court enforce the arbitration clauses that were part of the adhesion contracts and compel the plaintiffs to arbitrate their disputes?

DECISION No. The state appellate court affirmed the lower court's decision not to compel individual arbitration of these disputes. The court held that the preclusion of all class action in the defendants' "customer agreement" and "Welcome Guide" was "unconscionable and unenforceable."

REASON The court noted that "[n]ot every contract of adhesion contains unconscionable provisions. A contract of adhesion is only unconscionable if it unreasonably favors the

CASE 8.1–Continued

drafter." In this case, the customer contracts of both Comcast and AT&T attempted to require all customers to arbitrate all claims as individuals and to prevent them from filing class actions. According to the court, class-action suits are particularly important for consumers because they provide a means for those with limited financial resources and time to join together and assert their lawful rights. The individual members of a class often suffer only minimal damages, and no consumer would expend the time, fees, and costs of litigation for this small potential recovery. For example, defendant Thibodeau alleged that he was overcharged $9.60

per month. The court reasoned that to enforce the provisions requiring arbitration and prohibiting class actions would effectively immunize Comcast and AT&T from liability for any minor consumer claims. Because it is clearly contrary to public policy to immunize large corporations from liability, the court held that the provisions of the adhesion contracts were unconscionable and unenforceable.

 WHAT IF THE FACTS WERE DIFFERENT?
If the "customer agreement" and "Welcome Guide" had precluded only class litigation and mandated class arbitration, would the court have considered the provisions unconscionable? Why or why not?

Substantive Unconscionability. Substantive unconscionability characterizes those contracts, or portions of contracts, that are oppressive or overly harsh. Courts generally focus on provisions that deprive one party of the benefits of the agreement or leave that party without remedy for nonperformance by the other. For example, suppose that a person with little income and only a fourth-grade education agrees to purchase a refrigerator for $3,000 and signs a two-year installment contract. The same type of refrigerator usually sells for $900 on the market. Despite the general rule that the courts will not inquire into the adequacy of the consideration, some courts have held that this type of contract is unconscionable because the contract terms are so oppressive as to "shock the conscience" of the court.[12]

Exculpatory Clauses Often closely related to the concept of unconscionability are **exculpatory clauses,** which release a party from liability in the event of monetary or physical injury, *no matter who is at fault.* Indeed, courts frequently refuse to enforce such clauses because they deem them to be unconscionable. Exculpatory clauses found in rental agreements for commercial property are normally held to be contrary to public policy. Such clauses are almost universally held to be illegal and unenforceable when they are included in residential property leases. Depending on the situation, exculpatory clauses in the employment context may be deemed unconscionable.

EXCULPATORY CLAUSE
A clause that releases a contractual party from liability in the event of monetary or physical injury, no matter who is at fault.

■EXAMPLE 8.5 Suppose, for example, that Madison Manufacturing Company requires all of its employees to sign an employment contract with a clause stating that employees bear the risks incident to the position. Specifically, the contract states that the employer (Madison) is not responsible for any injury or damage that an employee may suffer as a result of accidents, carelessness, or misconduct of that employee or any other Madison worker. In this situation, because the exculpatory clause attempts to remove the employer's potential liability for any injuries to its employees, a court would usually find that the clause is contrary to public policy and unenforceable.[13] ■

Exculpatory clauses may be enforced, however, when the parties seeking their enforcement are not involved in businesses considered important to the public interest. Businesses such as health clubs, amusement parks, horse-rental concessions, golf-cart

REMEMBER Nearly everyone is liable for her or his own torts, and this responsibility cannot be contracted away.

---

12. See, for example, *Jones v. Star Credit Corp.,* 59 Misc.2d 189, 298 N.Y.S.2d 264 (1969). This case will be presented in Chapter 11 as Case 11.2.

13. For a case with similar facts, see *Little Rock & Fort Smith Railway Co. v. Eubanks,* 48 Ark. 460, 3 S.W. 808 (1887). In such a case, the exculpatory clause may also be illegal because it violates a state workers' compensation law.

concessions, and skydiving organizations frequently use exculpatory clauses to limit their liability for patrons' injuries. Because these services are not essential, the firms offering them are sometimes considered to have no relative advantage in bargaining strength, and anyone contracting for their services is considered to do so voluntarily.

ETHICAL ISSUE 8.1

Should exculpatory clauses allow the signer an opportunity to bargain? Before you may engage in a variety of activities, such as joining a gym or taking a lap around a miniature car racecourse, you may be asked to sign an agreement containing a clause releasing the owner of the operation from liability for any injury that you may suffer. Such exculpatory clauses are common. Nevertheless, courts frequently refuse to enforce them.

The Wisconsin Supreme Court, for example, has invalidated every exculpatory clause brought before it in the last twenty-five years. A recent case involved the death of a woman who drowned in a private swimming and fitness facility after signing a general waiver release statement.[14] The Wisconsin Supreme Court ruled that the exculpatory agreement was invalid because, among other things, the signer did not have "any opportunity to bargain." Indeed, waiver-of-liability agreements are almost always presented on a take-it-or-leave-it basis. Thus, if all courts were to make "an opportunity to bargain" a requirement for a valid agreement, virtually all exculpatory clauses would be deemed invalid. That would mean that under no circumstances could the creator of the waiver-of-liability agreement avoid liability—even if the signer of the agreement was 100 percent at fault and negligent. The result would be higher liability insurance rates for all businesses dealing with the public. Such higher insurance rates would be ultimately passed on to consumers in the form of higher prices for those who engage in downhill skiing, go to gyms, and do bungee jumping. Is this a fair outcome?

The Effect of Illegality

In general, an illegal contract is void: the contract is deemed never to have existed, and the courts will not aid either party. In most illegal contracts, both parties are considered to be equally at fault—*in pari delicto.* If the contract is executory (not yet fulfilled), neither party can enforce it. If it has been executed, there can be neither contractual nor quasi-contractual recovery.

That one wrongdoer in an illegal contract is unjustly enriched at the expense of the other is of no concern to the law—except under certain circumstances (to be discussed shortly). The major justification for this hands-off attitude is that it is improper to place the machinery of justice at the disposal of a plaintiff who has broken the law by entering into an illegal bargain. Another justification is the hoped-for deterrent effect of this general rule. A plaintiff who suffers a loss because of an illegal bargain will presumably be deterred from entering into similar illegal bargains in the future.

There are exceptions to the general rule that neither party to an illegal bargain can sue for breach and neither party can recover for performance rendered. We look at these exceptions here.

Justifiable Ignorance of the Facts   When one of the parties to a contract is relatively innocent (has no reason to know that the contract is illegal), that party can often recover any benefits conferred in a partially executed contract. In this situation, the courts will not enforce the contract but will allow the parties to return to their original positions.

---

14. *Atkins v. Swimwest Family Fitness Center,* 2005 WI 4, 277 Wis.2d 303, 691 N.W.2d 334 (2005).

A court may sometimes permit an innocent party who has fully performed under a contract to enforce the contract against the guilty party. **■EXAMPLE 8.6** A trucking company contracts with Gillespie to carry crated goods to a specific destination for a normal fee of $5,000. The trucker delivers the crates and later finds out that they contained illegal goods. Although the shipment, use, and sale of the goods are illegal under the law, the trucker, being an innocent party, can normally still legally collect the $5,000 from Gillespie. ■

Members of Protected Classes   When a statute protects a certain class of people, a member of that class can enforce an illegal contract even though the other party cannot. **■EXAMPLE 8.7** Statutes prohibit certain employees (such as flight attendants) from working more than a specified number of hours per month. These employees thus constitute a class protected by statute. An employee who is required to work more than the maximum can recover for those extra hours of service. ■

Other examples of statutes designed to protect a particular class of people are **blue sky laws**—state laws that regulate the offering and sale of securities for the protection of the public (see Chapter 21)—and state statutes regulating the sale of insurance. If an insurance company violates a statute when selling insurance, the purchaser can nevertheless enforce the policy and recover from the insurer.

BLUE SKY LAWS
State laws that regulate the offering and sale of securities for the protection of the public.

Withdrawal from an Illegal Agreement   If the illegal part of a bargain has not yet been performed, the party rendering performance can withdraw from the contract and recover the performance or its value. **■EXAMPLE 8.8** Suppose that Marta and Amil decide to wager (illegally) on the outcome of a boxing match. Each deposits money with a stakeholder, who agrees to pay the winner of the bet. At this point, each party has performed part of the agreement, but the illegal part of the agreement will not occur until the money is paid to the winner. Before such payment occurs, either party is entitled to withdraw from the agreement by giving notice to the stakeholder of his or her withdrawal. ■

Severable, or Divisible, Contracts   A contract that is *severable*, or divisible, consists of distinct parts that can be performed separately, with separate consideration provided for each part. With an *indivisible* contract, in contrast, the parties intended that complete performance by each party would be essential, even if the contract contains a number of seemingly separate provisions.

If a contract is divisible into legal and illegal portions, a court may enforce the legal portion but not the illegal one, so long as the illegal portion does not affect the essence of the bargain. This approach is consistent with the basic policy of enforcing the legal intentions of the contracting parties whenever possible. **■EXAMPLE 8.9** Suppose that Cole signs an employment contract that includes an overly broad and thus illegal covenant not to compete. In that situation, the court might allow the employment contract to be enforceable but reform the unreasonably broad covenant by converting its terms into reasonable ones. Alternatively, the court could declare the covenant illegal (and thus void) and enforce the remaining employment terms. ■

GENUINENESS OF ASSENT

Genuineness of assent may be lacking because of mistake, fraudulent misrepresentation, undue influence, or duress. Generally, a party who demonstrates that he or she did not genuinely assent (agree) to the terms of a contract can choose either to carry out the contract or to rescind (cancel) it and thus avoid the entire transaction.

Mistakes

We all make mistakes, so it is not surprising that mistakes are made when contracts are created. In certain circumstances, contract law allows a contract to be avoided on the basis of mistake. It is important to distinguish between *mistakes of fact* and *mistakes of value or quality*. Only a mistake of fact may allow a contract to be avoided.

■EXAMPLE 8.10 Suppose that Paco buys a violin from Beverly for $250. Although the violin is very old, neither party believes that it is extremely valuable. Later, however, an antiques dealer informs the parties that the violin is rare and worth thousands of dollars. Here, both parties were mistaken, but the mistake is a mistake of *value* rather than a mistake of *fact* that warrants contract rescission. Therefore, Beverly cannot rescind the contract. ■

Mistakes of fact occur in two forms—*unilateral* and *bilateral (mutual)*. A unilateral mistake is made by only one of the contracting parties; a mutual mistake is made by both. We look next at these two types of mistakes and illustrate them graphically in Exhibit 8–2.

Unilateral Mistakes A unilateral mistake occurs when only one party is mistaken as to a *material fact*—that is, a fact important to the subject matter of the contract. Generally, a unilateral mistake does not give the mistaken party any right to relief from the contract. In other words, the contract normally is enforceable against the mistaken party. **■EXAMPLE 8.11** Elena intends to sell her motor home for $17,500. When she learns that Chin is interested in buying a used motor home, she faxes a letter offering to sell the vehicle to him. When typing the fax, however, she mistakenly keys in the price of $15,700. Chin immediately sends Elena a fax accepting her offer. Even though Elena intended to sell her motor home for $17,500, she has made a unilateral mistake and is bound by contract to sell the vehicle to Chin for $15,700. ■

There are at least two exceptions to this rule.[15] First, if the *other* party to the contract knows or should have known that a mistake of fact was made, the contract may not be enforceable. **■EXAMPLE 8.12** In the above example, if Chin knew that Elena intended to sell her motor home for $17,500, then Elena's unilateral mistake (stating $15,700 in her offer) may render the resulting contract unenforceable. ■ The second exception arises when a unilateral mistake of fact was due to a mathematical mistake in addition, subtraction, division, or multiplication and was made inadvertently and without gross (extreme)

BE CAREFUL What a party to a contract knows or should know can determine whether the contract is enforceable.

---

15. The *Restatement (Second) of Contracts*, Section 153, liberalizes the general rule to take into account the modern trend of allowing avoidance in some circumstances even though only one party has been mistaken.

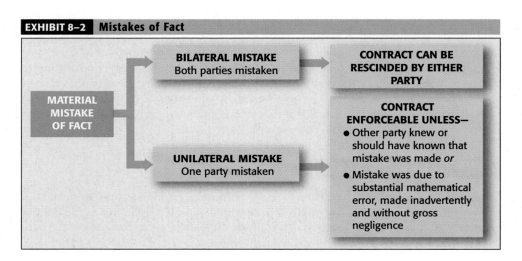

EXHIBIT 8–2 Mistakes of Fact

negligence. If a contractor's bid was significantly low because he or she made a mistake in addition when totaling the estimated costs, any contract resulting from the bid normally may be rescinded. Of course, in both situations, the mistake must still involve some *material fact*.

Bilateral (Mutual) Mistakes   When both parties are mistaken about the same material fact, the contract can be rescinded by either party.[16] Note that, as with unilateral mistakes, the mistake must be about a *material fact* (one that is important and central to the contract). **■EXAMPLE 8.13** Keeley buys a landscape painting from Umberto's art gallery. Both Umberto and Keeley believe that the painting is by the artist Vincent van Gogh. Later, Keeley discovers that the painting is a very clever fake. Because neither Umberto nor Keeley was aware of this fact when they made their deal, Keeley can rescind the contract and recover the purchase price of the painting. **■**

A word or term in a contract may be subject to more than one reasonable interpretation. In that situation, if the parties to the contract attach materially different meanings to the term, their mutual misunderstanding may allow the contract to be rescinded. **■EXAMPLE 8.14** In a classic case, *Raffles v. Wichelhaus*,[17] Wichelhaus purchased a shipment of cotton from Raffles to arrive on a ship called the *Peerless* from Bombay, India. Wichelhaus meant a ship called *Peerless* sailing from Bombay in October; Raffles meant a different ship called *Peerless* sailing from Bombay in December. When the goods arrived on the December *Peerless* and Raffles tried to deliver them, Wichelhaus refused to accept them. The British court held for Wichelhaus, concluding that no mutual assent existed because the parties had attached materially different meanings to an essential term of the contract (which ship *Peerless* was to transport the goods). **■**

In the following case, an injured worker sought to set aside a settlement agreement entered into with his employer, arguing that the agreement was based on a mutual mistake of fact—a physician's mistaken diagnosis of the worker's injury.

---

16. *Restatement (Second) of Contracts*, Section 152.
17. 159 Eng.Rep. 375 (1864).

CASE 8.2   **Roberts v. Century Contractors, Inc.**

Court of Appeals of North Carolina, 162 N.C.App. 688, 592 S.E.2d 215 (2004).
www.aoc.state.nc.us/www/public/html/opinions.htm [a]

FACTS Bobby Roberts was an employee of Century Contractors, Inc., in July 1993, when a pipe struck him in a work-related accident, causing trauma to his neck and back. Dr. James Markworth of Southeastern Orthopaedic Clinic diagnosed Roberts's injuries. After surgery and treatment, Markworth concluded that Roberts was at maximum medical improvement (MMI) and stopped treating him. Roberts agreed

with Century to accept $125,000 and payment of related medical expenses, and to waive any right to make further claims in regard to his injury. In June 1998, still experiencing pain, Roberts saw Dr. Allen Friedman, who determined that Roberts was not at MMI. Markworth then admitted that his diagnosis was a mistake. Roberts filed a claim for workers' compensation (see Chapter 18), seeking compensation and medical benefits for his injury. He alleged that his agreement with Century should be set aside due to a mutual mistake of fact. The North Carolina state administrative agency authorized to rule on workers' compensation claims awarded Roberts what he sought. Century appealed to a state intermediate appellate court.

a. Under the "Court of Appeals Opinions" heading, click on the year "2004." In your browser's "Find" box, type in the case title to access the full text of the court's opinion. The North Carolina Administrative Office of the Courts maintains this Web site.

CASE 8.2–Continues next page

CASE 8.2–Continued

ISSUE Should the agreement between Roberts and Century be set aside on the basis of a mutual mistake of fact?

DECISION Yes. The state intermediate appellate court affirmed the award of compensation and medical benefits to Roberts.

REASON The court explained that compromise settlement agreements, including settlement agreements in workers' compensation cases, are governed by general principles of contract law. The court stated that it is a well-settled principle of contract law that a valid contract exists only where there has been a meeting of the minds as to all essential terms of the agreement. "Therefore," said the court, "where a mistake is common to both parties and concerns a material past or presently existing fact, such that there is no meeting of the

minds, a contract may be avoided." The mistake "must be as to a fact which enters into and forms the basis of the contract * * * and must be such that it animates and controls the conduct of the parties." Also, "relief from a contract due to mistake of fact will be had only where *both* parties to an agreement are mistaken." The court pointed out that Markworth's MMI diagnosis was "material to the settlement of this claim" and that both parties relied on this information in entering into settlement negotiations. Later, however, "Dr. Friedman testified, and the [state agency found] as fact, that plaintiff was not at maximum medical improvement." Thus, the court concluded that there was a mutual mistake with regard to the plaintiff's medical condition at the time of the signing of the settlement agreement.

FOR CRITICAL ANALYSIS–Social Consideration
Why did the court consider Markworth's misdiagnosis a bilateral mistake rather than a unilateral mistake?

Fraudulent Misrepresentation

Although fraud is a tort, the presence of fraud also affects the genuineness of the innocent party's consent to a contract. When an innocent party consents to a contract with fraudulent terms, the contract usually can be avoided because she or he has not *voluntarily* consented to the terms.[18] Normally, the innocent party can either rescind (cancel) the contract and be restored to her or his original position or enforce the contract and seek damages for injuries resulting from the fraud.

Typically, fraud involves three elements:

1 A misrepresentation of a material fact must occur.

2 There must be an intent to deceive.

3 The innocent party must justifiably rely on the misrepresentation.

Additionally, to collect damages, a party must have been injured as a result of the misrepresentation.

Fraudulent misrepresentation can also occur in the online environment. Because curbing Internet fraud is a major challenge in today's world, we explore the topic further in Chapter 13, in the context of consumer law.

Misrepresentation Must Occur The first element of proving fraud is to show that misrepresentation of a material fact has occurred. This misrepresentation can take the form of words or actions. For example, an art gallery owner's statement, "This painting is a Picasso" is a misrepresentation of fact if the painting was done by another artist.

A statement of opinion is generally not subject to a claim of fraud. For example, claims such as "This computer will never break down" and "This car will last for years and years" are statements of opinion, not fact, and contracting parties should recognize them as such and not rely on them. A fact is objective and verifiable; an opinion is usually subject to

A woman browses through some online personal ads. Individuals who post their profiles on an Internet dating site may tend to exaggerate their attractive traits and may even make statements about themselves that they know to be false. But what happens when an Internet service provider makes fraudulent misrepresentations about its users? (Photo by Bill Stryker)

---

18. *Restatement (Second) of Contracts*, Sections 163 and 164.

debate. Therefore, a seller is allowed to "huff and puff his [or her] wares" without being liable for fraud. In certain cases, however, particularly when a naïve purchaser relies on an expert's opinion, the innocent party may be entitled to *rescission* (cancellation) or *reformation* (an equitable remedy granted by a court in which the terms of a contract are altered to reflect the true intentions of the parties).

Intent to Deceive   The second element of fraud is knowledge on the part of the misrepresenting party that facts have been misrepresented. This element, usually called *scienter*,[19] or "guilty knowledge," generally signifies that there was an intent to deceive. *Scienter* clearly exists if a party knows that a fact is not as stated. *Scienter* also exists if a party makes a statement that he or she believes not to be true or makes a statement recklessly, without regard to whether it is true or false. Finally, this element is met if a party says or implies that a statement is made on some basis, such as personal knowledge or personal investigation, when it is not.

EXAMPLE 8.15   A convicted felon, Robert Sarvis, applied for a position as an adjunct professor two weeks after his release from prison. On his résumé, he lied about his past work history by representing that he had been the president of a corporation for fourteen years and had taught business law at another college. At his interview, Sarvis stated that he was "well equipped to teach" business law and ethics and that he had "a great interest and knowledge of business law." After he was hired and began working, Sarvis's probation officer alerted the school to his criminal history. The school immediately fired Sarvis, and he brought a lawsuit against the school for breaching his employment contract. The school claimed that it was not liable for the breach because of Sarvis's fraudulent misrepresentations during the hiring process. The court agreed. Sarvis had not fully disclosed his personal history, he clearly had an intent to deceive, and the school had justifiably relied on his misrepresentations. Therefore, the school could rescind Sarvis's employment contract.[20] ■

Reliance on the Misrepresentation   The third element of fraud is *justifiable reliance* on the misrepresentation of fact. The deceived party must have a justifiable reason for relying on the misrepresentation, and the misrepresentation must be an important factor (but not necessarily the sole factor) in inducing the party to enter into the contract.

Reliance is not justified if the innocent party knows the true facts or relies on obviously extravagant statements. **EXAMPLE 8.16**   If a used-car dealer tells you, "This old Cadillac will get over sixty miles to the gallon," you normally would not be justified in relying on this statement. Suppose, however, that Merkel, a bank director, induces O'Connell, a co-director, to sign a statement that the bank has sufficient assets to meet its liabilities by telling O'Connell, "We have plenty of assets to satisfy our creditors." This statement is false. If O'Connell knows the true facts or, as a bank director, should know the true facts, he is not justified in relying on Merkel's statement. If O'Connell does not know the true facts, however, *and has no way of finding them out*, he may be justified in relying on the statement. ■

Injury to the Innocent Party   Most courts do not require a showing of injury when the action is to rescind (cancel) the contract—these courts hold that because rescission

SCIENTER
Knowledge by the misrepresenting party that material facts have been falsely represented or omitted with an intent to deceive.

REMEMBER   An opinion is neither a contract offer, nor a contract term, nor fraud.

Suppose that a city solicited bids from contractors to expand its public transportation system on this strip of land without disclosing the existence of a subsoil condition that would greatly increase the project's cost. Assuming that the city was aware of the situation, would it have had a duty to disclose the condition to bidders? What effect would the city's silence have on the resulting contract? (Michael McCauslin/Creative Commons)

---

19. Pronounced sy-*en*-ter.
20. *Sarvis v. Vermont State Colleges*, 172 Vt. 76, 772 A.2d 494 (2001).

returns the parties to the positions they held before the contract was made, a showing of injury to the innocent party is unnecessary.[21]

To recover damages caused by fraud, however, proof of an injury is universally required. The measure of damages is ordinarily equal to the property's value had it been delivered as represented, less the actual price paid for the property. In actions based on fraud, courts often award *punitive*, or *exemplary, damages*, which are granted to a plaintiff over and above the compensation for the actual loss. As pointed out in Chapter 4, punitive damages are based on the public-policy consideration of punishing the defendant or setting an example to deter similar wrongdoing by others.

PREVENTING LEGAL DISPUTES

To avoid making comments that might later be construed as a misrepresentation of material fact, business owners and managers should be careful what they say to clients and customers. Those in the business of selling products or services should assume that all customers are naïve and are relying on the seller's representations. Instruct employees to phrase their comments so that customers understand that any statements that are not factual are the employees' opinion. If someone asks a question that is beyond the employee's knowledge, it is better to say that he or she does not know than to guess and have the customer rely on a representation that turns out to be false. This can be particularly important when the questions concern topics such as compatibility or speed of electronic and digital goods, software, or related services.

Businesspersons should also be prudent about what they say when interviewing potential employees. Do not speculate on the financial health of the firm or exaggerate the company's future prospects. Exercising caution in one's statements to others in a business context is the best way to avoid potential legal actions for fraudulent misrepresentation.

Undue Influence

Undue influence arises from relationships in which one party can greatly influence another party, thus overcoming that party's free will. Minors and elderly people, for example, are often under the influence of guardians. If a guardian induces a young or elderly ward (a person placed by a court under the care of a guardian) to enter into a contract that benefits the guardian, the guardian may have exerted undue influence.

Undue influence can arise from a number of confidential or fiduciary relationships, including attorney-client, physician-patient, guardian-ward, parent-child, husband-wife, and trustee-beneficiary relationships. The essential feature of undue influence is that the party being taken advantage of does not, in reality, exercise free will in entering into a contract. A contract entered into under excessive or undue influence lacks genuine assent and is therefore voidable.[22]

Duress

ON THE WEB

To read more about contesting contracts on the grounds of fraud and duress, go to

www.lawyers.com/lawyers/A~1001073~ LDC/CONTESTING+CONTRACT.html.

Assent to the terms of a contract is not genuine if one of the parties is forced into the agreement. Forcing a party to enter into a contract because of the fear created by threats is referred to as *duress*.[23] Inducing consent to a contract through blackmail or extortion also constitutes duress. Duress is both a defense to the enforcement of a contract and a ground

---

21. For a leading case on this issue, see *Kaufman v. Jaffe*, 244 App.Div. 344, 279 N.Y.S. 392 (1935).
22. *Restatement (Second) of Contracts*, Section 177.
23. *Restatement (Second) of Contracts*, Sections 174 and 175.

for rescission of a contract. Therefore, a party who signs a contract under duress can choose to carry out the contract or to avoid the entire transaction. (The wronged party usually has this choice in cases in which assent is not real or genuine.)

Economic need is generally not sufficient to constitute duress, even when one party exacts a very high price for an item the other party needs. If the party exacting the price also creates the need, however, economic duress may be found. **■EXAMPLE 8.17** The Internal Revenue Service (IRS) assessed a large tax and penalty against Weller. Weller retained Eyman to contest the assessment. Two days before the deadline for filing a reply with the IRS, Eyman declined to represent Weller unless he agreed to pay a very high fee for Eyman's services. The agreement was held to be unenforceable.[24] Although Eyman had threatened only to withdraw his services, something that he was legally entitled to do, he was responsible for delaying his withdrawal until just before the deadline. Because Weller was forced into either signing the contract or losing his right to challenge the IRS assessment, the agreement was secured under duress. ■

THE STATUTE OF FRAUDS–REQUIREMENT OF A WRITING

Today, every state has a statute that stipulates what types of contracts must be in writing or be evidenced by a record. In this text, we refer to such a statute as the **Statute of Frauds.** The primary purpose of the statute is to ensure that, for certain types of contracts, there is reliable evidence of the contracts and their terms. These types of contracts are those historically deemed to be important or complex. Although the statutes vary slightly from state to state, the following types of contracts are normally required to be in writing or evidenced by a written memorandum:

STATUTE OF FRAUDS
A state statute under which certain types of contracts must be in writing to be enforceable.

1 Contracts involving interests in land.

2 Contracts that cannot by their terms be performed within one year from the date of formation.

3 Collateral contracts, such as promises to answer for the debt or duty of another.

4 Promises made in consideration of marriage.

5 Contracts for the sale of goods priced at $500 or more (under the Uniform Commercial Code, or UCC—see Chapter 11).

KEEP IN MIND Although only certain types of contracts must be in writing to be enforceable, it is good practice to put other contracts in writing as well to prevent disputes over contract terms.

Agreements or promises that fit into one or more of these categories are said to "fall under" or "fall within" the Statute of Frauds. (Certain exceptions are made to the Statute of Frauds, however, as you will read later in this section.)

The actual name of the Statute of Frauds is misleading because it does not apply to fraud. Rather, the statute denies enforceability to certain contracts that do not comply with its requirements. The name derives from an English act passed in 1677, which is presented as this chapter's *Landmark in the Law* feature on the following page.

Contracts Involving Interests in Land

Land is a form of *real property,* or real estate, which includes not only land but all physical objects that are permanently attached to the soil, such as buildings, plants, trees, and the soil itself. Under the Statute of Frauds, a contract involving an interest in land must be evidenced by a writing to be enforceable.[25] If Carol, for example, contracts orally to sell Seaside Shelter to Axel but later decides not to sell, Axel cannot enforce the contract. Similarly, if Axel refuses

---

24. *Thompson Crane & Trucking Co. v. Eyman,* 123 Cal.App.2d 904, 267 P.2d 1043 (1954).
25. In some states, the contract will be enforced if each party admits to the existence of the oral contract in court or admits to its existence during discovery before trial (see Chapter 3).

LANDMARK IN THE LAW The Statute of Frauds

On April 12, 1677, the English Parliament passed "An Act for the Prevention of Frauds and Perjuries." Four days later, the act was signed by King Charles II and became the law of the land. The act contained twenty-five sections and stipulated that certain types of contracts would henceforth have to be in writing or evidenced by a written memorandum if they were to be enforceable by the courts.[a]

Enforcement of Oral Promises   The English act was enacted specifically to prevent the many frauds that were being perpetrated through the perjured testimony of witnesses in cases involving breached oral agreements, for which no written evidence existed. During the early history of the common law in England, the courts generally did not enforce oral contracts, but in the fourteenth century, they began to be enforced in certain *assumpsit* actions.[b] These actions, to which the origins of modern contract law are traced, allowed a party to sue and obtain relief when a promise or contract had been breached. During the next two centuries, the king's courts commonly enforced oral promises in actions in *assumpsit*.

Problems with Oral Contracts   Because the courts enforced oral contracts on the strength of oral testimony by witnesses, it was not too difficult to evade justice by alleging that a contract had been breached and then procuring "convincing" witnesses to support the claim. The possibility of fraud in such actions was enhanced by the fact that seventeenth-century English courts did not allow oral testimony to be given by the parties to a lawsuit—or by any parties with an interest in the litigation, such as husbands or wives. Defenses against actions for breach of contract were thus limited to written evidence and the testimony given by third parties. The Statute of Frauds was enacted to minimize the possibility of fraud in oral contracts relating to certain types of transactions.

APPLICATION TO TODAY'S WORLD   *Essentially, the Statute of Frauds offers a defense against contracts that fall under the statute. Indeed, some have criticized the statute because, although it was created to protect the innocent, it can also be used as a technical defense by a party who has breached a genuine, mutually agreed-on oral contract—if the contract falls within the Statute of Frauds. For this reason, some legal scholars believe the act has caused more fraud than it has prevented. Nonetheless, U.S. courts continue to apply the Statute of Frauds to disputes involving oral contracts. The definitions of such terms as* writing *and* signature, *however, have changed to accommodate electronic documents—as you will read in Chapter 10, which covers e-contracts.*

RELEVANT WEB SITES   *To locate information on the Web concerning the Statute of Frauds, go to this text's Web site at* **academic.cengage.com/blaw/blt**, *select "Chapter 8," and click on "URLs for Landmarks."*

a. These contracts are discussed in the text of this chapter.
b. *Assumpsit* is Latin for "he or she undertook" or "he or she promised." The emergence of remedies for breached promises and duties dates to these actions. One of the earliest cases occurred in 1370, when the court allowed an individual to sue a person who, in trying to cure the plaintiff's horse, had acted so negligently that the horse died. Another such action was permitted in 1375, when a plaintiff obtained relief for having been maimed by a surgeon hired to cure him.

to close the deal, Carol cannot force Axel to pay for the land by bringing a lawsuit. The Statute of Frauds is a *defense* to the enforcement of this type of oral contract.

A contract for the sale of land ordinarily involves the entire interest in the real property, including buildings, growing crops, vegetation, minerals, timber, and anything else affixed to the land. Therefore, a *fixture* (personal property so affixed or so used as to become a part of the realty—see Chapter 24) is treated as real property.

The Statute of Frauds requires written contracts not just for the sale of land but also for the transfer of other interests in land, such as mortgages and leases. We describe these other interests in Chapter 24.

ON THE WEB

For an interesting discussion of the history and current applicability of the Statute of Frauds, both internationally and in the United States, go to

en.wikipedia.org/wiki/Statute_of_frauds.

The One-Year Rule

Contracts that cannot, *by their own terms*, be performed within one year *from the day after* the contract is formed must be in writing to be enforceable. Because disputes over such contracts are unlikely to occur until some time after the contracts are made, resolution of these disputes is difficult unless the contract terms have been put in writing. The one-year period begins to run *the day after the contract is made*.

▪**EXAMPLE 8.18** Suppose that Superior University forms a contract with Kimi San stating that San will teach three courses in history during the coming academic year (September 15 through June 15). If the contract is formed in March, it must be in writing to be enforceable—because it cannot be performed within one year. If the contract is not formed until July, however, it will not have to be in writing to be enforceable—because it can be performed within one year. ▪ Exhibit 8–3 graphically illustrates the one-year rule.

Normally, the test for determining whether an oral contract is enforceable under the one-year rule of the Statute of Frauds is whether performance is *possible* within one year from the day after the date of contract formation—not whether the agreement is *likely* to be performed within one year. When performance of a contract is objectively impossible during the one-year period, the oral contract will be unenforceable.

EXHIBIT 8–3 **The One-Year Rule**

Under the Statute of Frauds, contracts that by their terms are impossible to perform within one year from the day after the date of contract formation must be in writing to be enforceable. Put another way, if it is at all possible to perform an oral contract within one year from the day after the contract is made, the contract will fall outside the Statute of Frauds and be enforceable.

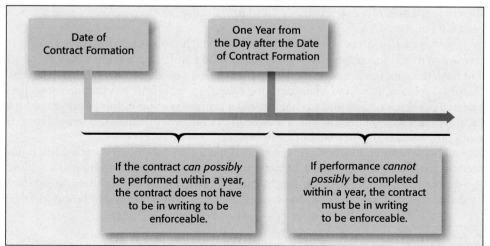

Collateral Promises

COLLATERAL PROMISE
A secondary promise that is ancillary (subsidiary) to a principal transaction or primary contractual relationship, such as a promise made by one person to pay the debts of another if the latter fails to perform. A collateral promise normally must be in writing to be enforceable.

A **collateral promise,** or secondary promise, is one that is ancillary (subsidiary) to a principal transaction or primary contractual relationship. In other words, a collateral promise is one made by a third party to assume the debts or obligations of a primary party to a contract if that party does not perform. Any collateral promise of this nature falls under the Statute of Frauds and therefore must be in writing to be enforceable. To understand this concept, it is important to distinguish between primary and secondary promises and obligations.

Primary versus Secondary Obligations   A contract in which a party assumes a primary obligation normally does not need to be in writing to be enforceable.   ▪EXAMPLE 8.19 Suppose that Kenneth orally contracts with Joanne's Floral Boutique to send his mother a dozen roses for Mother's Day. Kenneth promises to pay the boutique when he receives the bill for the flowers. Kenneth is a direct party to this contract and has incurred a *primary* obligation under the contract. Because he is a party to the contract and has a primary obligation to Joanne's Floral Boutique, this contract does not fall under the Statute of Frauds and does not have to be in writing to be enforceable. If Kenneth fails to pay the florist and the florist sues him for payment, Kenneth cannot raise the Statute of Frauds as a defense. He cannot claim that the contract is unenforceable because it was not in writing. ▪

In contrast, a contract in which a party assumes a secondary obligation does have to be in writing to be enforceable.   ▪EXAMPLE 8.20 Suppose that Kenneth's mother borrows $10,000 from the Medford Trust Company on a promissory note payable six months later. Kenneth promises the bank officer handling the loan that he will pay the $10,000 *if his mother does not pay the loan on time.* Kenneth, in this situation, becomes what is known as a *guarantor* on the loan. He is guaranteeing to the bank (the creditor) that he will pay the loan if his mother fails to do so. This kind of collateral promise, in which the guarantor states that he or she will become responsible only if the primary party does not perform, must be in writing to be enforceable. ▪ We return to the concept of guaranty and the distinction between primary and secondary obligations in Chapter 16, in the context of creditors' rights.

An Exception—The "Main Purpose" Rule   An oral promise to answer for the debt of another is covered by the Statute of Frauds *unless* the guarantor's purpose in accepting secondary liability is to secure a personal benefit. Under the "main purpose" rule, this type of contract need not be in writing.[26] The assumption is that a court can infer from the circumstances of a case whether a "leading objective" of the promisor was to secure a personal benefit.

▪EXAMPLE 8.21 Carrie Oswald contracts with Machine Manufacturing Company to have some machines custom made for her factory. To ensure that Machine Manufacturing will have the supplies it needs to make the machines, Oswald promises Allrite Materials Supply Company, Machine Manufacturing's supplier, that if Allrite continues to deliver materials to Machine Manufacturing, she will guarantee payment. This promise need not be in writing, even though the effect may be to pay the debt of another, because Oswald's main purpose is to secure a benefit for herself. ▪

Another typical application of the so-called main purpose doctrine occurs when one creditor guarantees the debtor's debt to another creditor to forestall litigation. This allows the debtor to remain in business long enough to generate profits sufficient to pay *both* creditors. In this situation, the guaranty does not need to be in writing to be enforceable.

---

26. *Restatement (Second) of Contracts,* Section 116.

BEYOND OUR BORDERS **The Statute of Frauds and International Sales Contracts**

The Convention on Contracts for the International Sale of Goods (CISG) provides rules that govern international sales contracts between citizens of countries that have ratified the convention (agreement). Article 11 of the CISG does not incorporate any Statute of Frauds provisions. Rather, it states that a "contract for sale need not be concluded in or evidenced by writing and is not subject to any other requirements as to form."

Article 11 accords with the legal customs of most nations, which no longer require contracts to meet certain formal or writing requirements to be enforceable. Ironically, even England, the nation that enacted the original Statute of Frauds in 1677, has repealed all of it except the provisions relating to collateral promises and to transfers of interests in land. Many other countries that once had such statutes have also repealed all or parts of them. Civil law countries, such as France, have never required certain types of contracts to be in writing.

 FOR CRITICAL ANALYSIS *If there was no Statute of Frauds and a dispute arose concerning an oral agreement, how would the parties substantiate their respective positions?*

Promises Made in Consideration of Marriage

A unilateral promise to make a monetary payment or to give property in consideration of marriage must be in writing. If Mr. Baumann promises to pay Joe Villard $10,000 if Villard marries Baumann's daughter, the promise must be in writing to be enforceable. The same rule applies to **prenuptial agreements**—agreements made before marriage (also called *antenuptial agreements*) that define each partner's ownership rights in the other partner's property. A prospective wife or husband may wish to limit the amount the prospective spouse can obtain if the marriage ends in divorce. Prenuptial agreements made in consideration of marriage must be in writing to be enforceable.

Contracts for the Sale of Goods

The Uniform Commercial Code (UCC) includes Statute of Frauds provisions that require written evidence of a contract. Section 2–201 contains the major provision, which generally requires a writing or memorandum for the sale of goods priced at $500 or more under the UCC (see Chapter 11). A writing that will satisfy the UCC requirement need only state the quantity term; other terms agreed on need not be stated "accurately" in the writing, as long as they adequately reflect both parties' intentions. The contract will not be enforceable, however, for any quantity greater than that set forth in the writing. In addition, the writing must be signed by the person against whom enforcement is sought. Beyond these two requirements, the writing need not designate the buyer or the seller, the terms of payment, or the price. (See this chapter's *Beyond Our Borders* feature to learn whether other countries have requirements similar to those in the Statute of Frauds.)

PRENUPTIAL AGREEMENT
An agreement made before marriage that defines each partner's ownership rights in the other partner's property. Prenuptial agreements must be in writing to be enforceable.

Exceptions to the Statute of Frauds

Exceptions to the applicability of the Statute of Frauds are made in certain situations. We describe those situations here.

Partial Performance In cases involving oral contracts for the transfer of interests in land, if the purchaser has paid part of the price, taken possession, and made valuable improvements to the property, and if the parties cannot be returned to their positions prior to the contract, a court may grant *specific performance* (performance of the contract according to its precise terms). Whether a court will enforce an oral contract for an interest in land when partial performance has taken place is usually determined by the degree of injury that would be suffered if the court chose *not* to enforce the oral contract. In some states, mere reliance on certain types of oral contracts is enough to remove them from the Statute of Frauds.

Under the UCC, an oral contract for goods priced at $500 or more is enforceable to the extent that a seller accepts payment or a buyer accepts delivery of the goods.[27] **EXAMPLE 8.22** If the president of Ajax Corporation orders by telephone thirty crates of bleach from Cloney, Inc., and repudiates the contract after ten crates have been delivered and accepted, Cloney can enforce the contract to the extent of the ten crates accepted by Ajax. ■

The existence and extent of a contract to supply computer kiosks for use in school cafeterias were in dispute in the following case.

---

27. UCC 2–201(3)(c). See Chapter 11.

CASE 8.3 **School-Link Technologies, Inc. v. Applied Resources, Inc.**

United States District Court, District of Kansas, 471 F.Supp.2d 1101 (2007).

FACTS Applied Resources, Inc. (ARI), makes computer hardware for point-of-sale systems: kiosks that consist of computers encased in chassis on which card readers or other payment devices are mounted. School-Link Technologies, Inc. (SLT), sells food-service technology to schools. In August 2003, the New York City Department of Education (NYCDOE) asked SLT to propose a cafeteria payment system that included kiosks. SLT asked ARI to participate in a pilot project, orally promising ARI that it would be the exclusive supplier of as many as 1,500 kiosks if NYCDOE awarded the contract to SLT. ARI agreed. SLT intended to cut ARI out of the deal, however, and told NYCDOE that SLT would be making its own kiosks. Meanwhile, SLT paid ARI in advance for a certain number of goods, but insisted on onerous terms for a written contract to which ARI would not agree. ARI suspended production of the prepaid items and refused to refund over $55,000 of SLT's funds. SLT filed a suit in a federal district court against ARI. ARI responded in part with a counterclaim for breach of contract, asserting that SLT failed to use ARI as an exclusive supplier as promised. ARI sought the expenses it incurred for the pilot project and the amount of

profit that it would have realized on the entire deal. SLT filed a motion for summary judgment on this claim.

ISSUE Was the oral agreement for the kiosks enforceable to the extent to which it had been performed?

DECISION Yes. The court denied SLT's motion for summary judgment on ARI's counterclaim for breach of contract "with respect to goods which SLT already received and accepted [that is,] the goods for the pilot program with the NYCDOE."

REASON The court acknowledged that, according to the Uniform Commercial Code, a contract for a sale of goods for a price of $500 or more generally must be in writing and must be signed by the party against whom enforcement is sought. The court reasoned that "[b]ecause the NYCDOE contract undisputedly involved the sale of goods in excess of $500, the parties' oral contract that ARI would be the exclusive supplier of kiosks for the project is not enforceable in the absence of an applicable exception to this general rule." Under the partial performance exception to the rule, an oral contract for a sale of goods more than $500 that would otherwise be unenforceable

CASE 8.3–Continued

for the lack of a writing is enforceable to the extent that the seller delivers the goods and the buyer accepts them. In that situation, the performance serves as a substitute for the required writing. Thus, in this case, the court concluded that the alleged oral contract between SLT and ARI, to the effect that ARI would be the exclusive supplier of kiosks for SLT's

contract with NYCDOE, was enforceable to the extent that ARI had delivered the kiosks for the pilot project and SLT had accepted them. The court added, however, that "the remaining aspect of that claim is barred by the [S]tatute of [F]rauds."

 FOR CRITICAL ANALYSIS–Social Consideration
Could ARI successfully assert a claim against SLT based on fraudulent misrepresentation? Explain.

Admissions   In some states, if a party against whom enforcement of an oral contract is sought admits in pleadings, testimony, or otherwise in court proceedings that a contract for sale was made, the contract will be enforceable.[28] A contract subject to the UCC will be enforceable, but only to the extent of the quantity admitted.[29] **EXAMPLE 8.23** Suppose that the president of Ajax Corporation in Example 8.22 admits under oath that an oral agreement was made with Cloney, Inc., for twenty crates of bleach. In this situation, even if Cloney, Inc., claims that Ajax had contracted for thirty crates, the agreement will be enforceable only to the extent admitted (for twenty rather than thirty crates of bleach). ■

Promissory Estoppel   In some states, an oral contract that would otherwise be unenforceable under the Statute of Frauds may be enforced under the doctrine of promissory estoppel, or detrimental reliance. Recall from Chapter 7 that if a promisor makes a promise on which the promisee justifiably relies to her or his detriment, a court may *estop* (prevent) the promisor from denying that a contract exists. Section 139 of the *Restatement (Second) of Contracts* provides that in these circumstances, an oral promise can be enforceable, notwithstanding the Statute of Frauds, if the reliance was foreseeable to the person making the promise and if injustice can be avoided only by enforcing the promise.

Special Exceptions under the UCC   Special exceptions to the applicability of the Statute of Frauds exist for sales contracts. Oral contracts for customized goods may be enforced in certain circumstances. Another exception has to do with oral contracts between merchants that have been confirmed in writing. We will examine these exceptions in Chapter 11. Exhibit 8–4 on the next page graphically summarizes the types of contracts that fall under the Statute of Frauds and the various exceptions that apply.

ON THE WEB

For information on the *Restatements of the Law*, including the *Restatement (Second) of Contracts*, go to the American Law Institute's Web site at

www.ali.org.

THE STATUTE OF FRAUDS–SUFFICIENCY OF THE WRITING

A written contract will satisfy the writing requirement of the Statute of Frauds. A *written memorandum* (written evidence of the oral contract) signed by the party against whom enforcement is sought will also satisfy the writing requirement.[30] The signature need not be placed at the end of the document but can be anywhere in the writing; it can even be initials rather than the full name. (See the *Application* feature at the end of this chapter for suggestions on how to prevent problems with oral contracts.)

---

28. *Restatement (Second) of Contracts*, Section 133.
29. UCC 2–201(3)(b). See Chapter 11.
30. As mentioned earlier, under the UCC's Statute of Frauds, a writing is required only for contracts for the sale of goods priced at $500 or more (see Chapter 11).

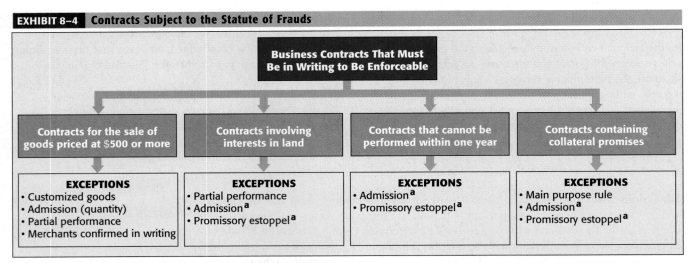

EXHIBIT 8–4   Contracts Subject to the Statute of Frauds

a. Some states follow Section 133 (on admissions) and Section 139 (on promissory estoppel) of the *Restatement (Second) of Contracts*.

A significant issue in today's business world has to do with how "signatures" can be created and verified on electronic contracts and other documents. We will examine electronic signatures in Chapter 10.

What Constitutes a Writing?

A writing can consist of any confirmation, invoice, sales slip, check, fax, or e-mail—or such items in combination. The written contract need not consist of a single document to constitute an enforceable contract. One document may incorporate another document by expressly referring to it. Several documents may form a single contract if they are physically attached, such as by staple, paper clip, or glue. Several documents may form a single contract even if they are only placed in the same envelope.

▪EXAMPLE 8.24 Sam orally agrees to sell some land next to a shopping mall to Terry. Sam gives Terry an unsigned memo that contains a legal description of the property, and Terry gives Sam an unsigned first draft of their contract. Sam sends Terry a signed letter that refers to the memo and to the first and final drafts of the contract. Terry sends Sam an unsigned copy of the final draft of the contract with a signed check stapled to it. Together, the documents can constitute a writing sufficient to satisfy the Statute of Frauds and bind both parties to the terms of the contract as evidenced by the writings. ▪

What Must Be Contained in the Writing?

A memorandum evidencing the oral contract need only contain the essential terms of the contract. Under most provisions of the Statute of Frauds, the writing must name the parties and identify the subject matter, consideration, and quantity. With respect to contracts for the sale of land, some states require that the memorandum also set forth the essential terms of the contract, such as location and price, with sufficient clarity to allow the terms to be determined from the memo itself, without reference to any outside sources.[31] Under the UCC, in regard to the sale of goods, the writing need only state the quantity and be signed by the party against whom enforcement is sought.

Because only the party against whom enforcement is sought must have signed the writing, a contract may be enforceable by one of its parties but not by the other.

---

31. *Rhodes v. Wilkins*, 83 N.M. 782, 498 P.2d 311 (1972).

EXAMPLE 8.25 Rock orally agrees to buy Betty Devlin's lake house and lot for $350,000. Devlin writes Rock a letter confirming the sale by identifying the parties and the essential terms of the sales contract—price, method of payment, and legal address—and signs the letter. Devlin has made a written memorandum of the oral land contract. Because she signed the letter, she normally can be held to the oral contract by Rock. Rock, however, because he has not signed or entered into a written contract or memorandum, can plead the Statute of Frauds as a defense, and Devlin cannot enforce the contract against him. ▣

REVIEWING Capacity and Legality

Renee Beaver started racing go-karts competitively in 2005, when she was fourteen. Many of the races required her to sign an exculpatory clause to participate, which she or her parents regularly signed. In 2008, right before her birthday, she participated in the annual Elkhart Grand Prix, a series of races in Elkhart, Indiana. During the event in which she drove, a piece of foam padding used as a course barrier was torn from its base and ended up on the track. A portion of the padding struck Beaver in the head, and another portion was thrown into oncoming traffic, causing a multikart collision during which she sustained severe injuries. Beaver filed an action against the race organizers for negligence. The organizers could not locate the exculpatory clause that Beaver was supposed to have signed. Race

organizers argued that she must have signed one to enter the race, but even if she had not signed one, her actions showed her intent to be bound by its terms. Using the information presented in the chapter, answer the following questions.

1 Did Beaver have the contractual capacity to enter a contract with an exculpatory clause? Why or why not?

2 Assuming that Beaver did, in fact, sign the exculpatory clause, did she later disaffirm or ratify the contract? Explain.

3 Now assume that Beaver had stated that she was eighteen years old at the time that she signed the exculpatory clause. How might this affect Beaver's ability to disaffirm or ratify the contract?

4 If Beaver did not actually sign the exculpatory clause, could a court conclude that she impliedly accepted its terms by participating in the race? Why or why not?

APPLICATION   How Can You Prevent Problems with Oral Contracts?*

As a general rule, most business contracts should be in writing even when they fall outside the Statute of Frauds. Businesspersons frequently make oral contracts over the telephone, however, particularly when the parties have done business with each other in the past.

Confirm the Agreement in Writing

Any time an oral contract is made, it is advisable for one of the parties to send either a written memorandum or a confir-

mation of the oral agreement by fax or e-mail to the other party. This accomplishes two purposes: (1) it demonstrates the party's clear intention to form a contract, and (2) it provides the terms of the contract as that party understood them. If the party receiving the memorandum or confirmation then disagrees with the terms as described, the issue can be addressed before performance begins.

Special Rules for Contracts between Merchants

What about the sale of goods between merchants? Under the UCC, written confirmation received by one merchant removes the Statute of Frauds requirement of a writing unless the merchant receiving the confirmation objects in writing within ten

* This *Application* is not meant to substitute for the services of an attorney who is licensed to practice law in your state.

(Continued)

days of its receipt. This law (discussed in Chapter 11) clearly points out the need for the merchant receiving the confirmation to review it carefully to ascertain that the confirmation conforms to the oral contract. If the writing does not so conform, the merchant can object in writing (the Statute of Frauds still applies), and the parties can resolve misunderstandings without legal liability. If the merchant fails to object, the written confirmation can be used as evidence to prove the terms of the oral contract. Note, however, that this ten-day rule does not apply to contracts for interests in realty or for services, to which the UCC does not apply.

CHECKLIST FOR THE BUSINESSPERSON

1 When feasible, use written contracts.
2 If you enter into an oral contract over the telephone, fax or e-mail a written confirmation outlining your understanding of the oral contract.
3 If you receive the other party's written or faxed confirmation, read it carefully to make sure that it states the terms already agreed to in the oral contract, as you understand them.
4 If you have any objections, notify the other party of these objections, in writing, within ten days.

KEY TERMS

adhesion contract 246
blue laws 242
blue sky laws 249
collateral promise 258
contractual capacity 236
covenant not to compete 244
disaffirmance 237

emancipation 237
employment contract 244
exculpatory clause 247
necessaries 238
prenuptial agreement 259
ratification 239
reformation 245

scienter 253
Statute of Frauds 255
unconscionable contract
    or clause 245
usury 241

CHAPTER SUMMARY Contracts: Capacity, Legality, Assent, and Form

CONTRACTUAL CAPACITY

Minors
(See pages 237–239.)
	A minor is a person who has not yet reached the age of majority. In most states, the age of majority is eighteen for contract purposes. Contracts with minors are voidable at the option of the minor.
	
	1. *Disaffirmance*—The legal avoidance of a contractual obligation.
	  a. Disaffirmance can take place (in most states) at any time during minority and within a reasonable time after the minor has reached the age of majority.
	  b. If a minor disaffirms part of a contract, the entire contract must be disaffirmed.
	  c. When disaffirming executed contracts, the minor has a duty to return received goods if they are still in the minor's control or (in some states) to pay their reasonable value.
	  d. A minor who has committed an act of fraud (such as misrepresentation of age) will be denied the right to disaffirm by some courts.
	  e. A minor may disaffirm a contract for necessaries but remains liable for the reasonable value of the goods.
	
	2. *Ratification*—The acceptance, or affirmation, of a legal obligation; may be express or implied.
	  a. Express ratification—Exists when the minor, through a writing or an oral agreement, explicitly assumes the obligations imposed by the contract.
	  b. Implied ratification—Exists when the conduct of the minor is inconsistent with disaffirmance or when the minor fails to disaffirm an executed contract within a reasonable time after reaching the age of majority.

CHAPTER SUMMARY	**Contracts: Capacity, Legality, Assent, and Form–Continued**
Intoxicated Persons (See pages 239–240.)	1. A contract entered into by an intoxicated person is voidable at the option of the intoxicated person if the person was sufficiently intoxicated to lack mental capacity, even if the intoxication was voluntary. 2. A contract with an intoxicated person is enforceable if, despite being intoxicated, the person understood the legal consequences of entering into the contract.
Mentally Incompetent Persons (See page 240.)	1. A contract made by a person adjudged by a court to be mentally incompetent is void. 2. A contract made by a mentally incompetent person not adjudged by a court to be mentally incompetent is voidable at the option of the mentally incompetent person.
	LEGALITY
Contracts Contrary to Statute (See pages 241–244.)	1. *Contracts to commit a crime*—Any contract to commit a crime is a contract in violation of a statute and is thus unenforceable. 2. *Usury*—Usury occurs when a lender makes a loan at an interest rate above the lawful maximum. The maximum rate of interest varies from state to state. 3. *Gambling*—Gambling contracts that contravene (go against) state statutes are deemed illegal and thus void. 4. *Sabbath (Sunday) laws*—These laws prohibit the formation or performance of certain contracts on a Sunday. Such laws vary widely from state to state, and many states do not enforce them. 5. *Licensing statutes*—Contracts entered into by persons who do not have a license, when one is required by statute, will not be enforceable *unless* the underlying purpose of the statute is to raise government revenues (and not to protect the public from unauthorized practitioners).
Contracts Contrary to Public Policy (See pages 244–248.)	1. *Contracts in restraint of trade*—Contracts to reduce or restrain free competition are illegal. Most such contracts are now prohibited by statutes. An exception is a *covenant not to compete*. It is usually enforced by the courts if the terms are ancillary to a contract (such as a contract for the sale of a business or an employment contract) and are reasonable as to time and area of restraint. Courts tend to closely scrutinize covenants not to compete. If a covenant is overbroad, a court may either reform the covenant to make the restraints more reasonable and then enforce the reformed contract or declare the covenant void and thus unenforceable. 2. *Unconscionable contracts and clauses*—When a contract or contract clause is so unfair that it is oppressive to one party, it may be deemed unconscionable; as such, it is illegal and cannot be enforced. 3. *Exculpatory clauses*—An exculpatory clause is a clause that releases a party from liability in the event of monetary or physical injury, no matter who is at fault. In certain situations, exculpatory clauses may be contrary to public policy and thus unenforceable.
The Effect of Illegality (See pages 248–249.)	In general, an illegal contract is void, and the courts will not aid either party when both parties are considered to be equally at fault (*in pari delicto*). If the contract is executory, neither party can enforce it. If the contract is executed, there can be neither contractual nor quasi-contractual recovery. Several exceptions exist to the general rule that neither party to an illegal bargain will be able to recover. In the following situations, the court may grant recovery: 1. *Justifiable ignorance of the facts*—When one party to the contract is relatively innocent. 2. *Members of protected classes*—When one party to the contract is a member of a group of persons protected by statute, such as employees. 3. *Withdrawal from an illegal agreement*—When either party seeks to recover consideration given for an illegal contract before the illegal act is performed. 4. *Severable, or divisible, contracts*—When the court can divide the contract into illegal and legal portions and the illegal portion is not essential to the bargain.

(Continued)

CHAPTER SUMMARY	Contracts: Capacity, Legality, Assent, and Form—Continued

GENUINENESS OF ASSENT

Mistakes (See pages 250–252.)	1. *Unilateral*—Generally, the mistaken party is bound by the contract *unless* (a) the other party knows or should have known of the mistake or (b) the mistake is an inadvertent mathematical error—such as an error in addition or subtraction—committed without gross negligence. 2. *Bilateral (mutual)*—When both parties are mistaken about the same material fact, such as identity, either party can avoid the contract. If the mistake concerns value or quality, either party can enforce the contract.
Fraudulent Misrepresentation (See pages 252–254.)	When fraud occurs, usually the innocent party can enforce or avoid the contract. The elements necessary to establish fraud are as follows: 1. A misrepresentation of a material fact must occur. 2. There must be an intent to deceive. 3. The innocent party must justifiably rely on the misrepresentation.
Undue Influence (See page 254.)	Undue influence arises from special relationships, such as fiduciary or confidential relationships, in which one party's free will has been overcome by the undue influence exerted by the other party. Usually, the contract is voidable.
Duress (See pages 254–255.)	Duress is the tactic of forcing a party to enter a contract under the fear of a threat—for example, the threat of violence or serious economic loss. The party forced to enter the contract can rescind the contract.

FORM—THE WRITING REQUIREMENT

| **The Statute of Frauds—Requirement of a Writing**
(See pages 255–261.) | 1. *Applicability*—The following types of contracts fall under the Statute of Frauds and must be in writing to be enforceable:

  a. Contracts involving interests in land—The statute applies to any contract for an interest in realty, such as a sale, a lease, or a mortgage.

  b. Contracts whose terms cannot be performed within one year—The statute applies only to contracts objectively impossible to perform fully within one year from the day after the contract's formation.

  c. Collateral promises—The statute applies only to express contracts made between the guarantor and the creditor that make the guarantor secondarily liable. Exception: the "main purpose" rule.

  d. Promises made in consideration of marriage—The statute applies to promises to pay money or give property in consideration of a promise to marry and to prenuptial agreements made in consideration of marriage.

  e. Contracts for the sale of goods priced at $500 or more—See the Statute of Frauds provision in Section 2–201 of the Uniform Commercial Code (UCC).

2. *Exceptions*—Partial performance, admissions, and promissory estoppel. |
| **The Statute of Frauds—Sufficiency of the Writing**
(See pages 261–263.) | To constitute an enforceable contract under the Statute of Frauds, a writing must be signed by the party against whom enforcement is sought, must name the parties, must identify the subject matter, and must state with reasonable certainty the essential terms of the contract. In a sale of land, the price and a description of the property may need to be stated with sufficient clarity to allow them to be determined without reference to outside sources. Under the UCC, a contract for a sale of goods is not enforceable beyond the quantity of goods shown in the contract. |

FOR REVIEW

Answers for the even-numbered questions in this **For Review** *section can be found in Appendix E at the end of this text.*

1 What are some exceptions to the rule that a minor can disaffirm (avoid) any contract?

2 Does an intoxicated person have the capacity to enter into an enforceable contract?

3 In what types of situations might genuineness of assent to a contract's terms be lacking?

4 What elements must exist for fraudulent misrepresentation to occur?

5 What contracts must be in writing to be enforceable?

■

QUESTIONS AND CASE PROBLEMS

 HYPOTHETICAL SCENARIOS

8.1 Contracts by Minors. Kalen is a seventeen-year-old minor who has just graduated from high school. He is attending a university two hundred miles from home and has contracted to rent an apartment near the university for one year at $500 per month. He is working at a convenience store to earn enough income to be self-supporting. After living in the apartment and paying monthly rent for four months, he becomes involved in a dispute with his landlord. Kalen, still a minor, moves out and returns the key to the landlord. The landlord wants to hold Kalen liable for the balance of the payments due under the lease. Discuss fully Kalen's liability in this situation.

8.2 Hypothetical Question with Sample Answer. A famous New York City hotel, Hotel Lux, is noted for its food as well as its luxury accommodations. Hotel Lux contracts with a famous chef, Chef Perlee, to become its head chef at $6,000 per month. The contract states that should Perlee leave the employment of Hotel Lux for any reason, he will not work as a chef for any hotel or restaurant in New York, New Jersey, or Pennsylvania for a period of one year. During the first six

months of the contract, Hotel Lux extensively advertises Perlee as its head chef, and business at the hotel is excellent. Then a dispute arises between the hotel management and Perlee, and Perlee terminates his employment. One month later, he is hired by a famous New Jersey restaurant just across the New York state line. Hotel Lux learns of Perlee's employment through a large advertisement in a New York City newspaper. It seeks to enjoin (prevent) Perlee from working in that restaurant as a chef for one year. Discuss how successful Hotel Lux will be in its action.

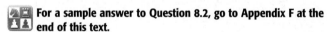 **For a sample answer to Question 8.2, go to Appendix F at the end of this text.**

8.3 Genuineness of Assent. Jerome is an elderly man who lives with his nephew, Philip. Jerome is totally dependent on Philip's support. Philip tells Jerome that unless Jerome transfers a tract of land he owns to Philip for a price 30 percent below market value, Philip will no longer support and take care of him. Jerome enters into the contract. Discuss fully whether Jerome can set aside this contract.

■

 **CASE PROBLEMS**

8.4 Oral Contracts. Robert Pinto, doing business as Pinto Associates, hired Richard MacDonald as an independent contractor in March 1992. The parties orally agreed on the terms of employment, including payment to MacDonald of a share of the company's income, but they did not put anything

in writing. In March 1995, MacDonald quit. Pinto then told MacDonald that he was entitled to $9,602.17—25 percent of the difference between the accounts receivable and the accounts payable as of MacDonald's last day. MacDonald disagreed and demanded more than $83,500—25 percent of the revenue from all invoices, less the cost of materials and outside processing, for each of the years that he worked for Pinto. Pinto refused. MacDonald filed a suit in a Connecticut state court against Pinto, alleging breach of contract. In Pinto's response and at the trial, he testified that the parties had an oral contract under which MacDonald was entitled to 25 percent of the difference between accounts receivable and payable as of the date of MacDonald's termination. Did the parties have an enforceable contract? How should the court rule, and why? [*MacDonald v. Pinto*, 62 Conn.App. 317, 771 A.2d 156 (2001)]

8.5 Case Problem with Sample Answer. In 1993, Mutual Service Casualty Insurance Co. and its affiliates (collectively, MSI) hired Thomas Brass as an insurance agent. Three years later, Brass entered into a career agent's contract with MSI. This contract contained provisions regarding Brass's activities after termination. These provisions stated that, for a period of not less than one year, Brass could not solicit any MSI customers to "lapse, cancel, or replace" any insurance contract in force with MSI in an effort to take that business to a competitor. If he did, MSI could at any time refuse to pay the commissions that it otherwise owed him. The contract also restricted Brass from working for American National Insurance Co. for three years after termination. In 1998, Brass quit MSI and immediately went to work for American National, soliciting MSI customers. MSI filed a suit in a Wisconsin state court against Brass, claiming that he had violated the noncompete terms of his MSI contract. Should the court enforce the covenant not to compete? Why or why not? [*Mutual Service Casualty Insurance Co. v. Brass*, 242 Wis.2d 733, 625 N.W.2d 648 (App. 2001)]

After you have answered Problem 8.5, compare your answer with the sample answer given on the Web site that accompanies this text. Go to **academic.cengage.com/blaw/blt**, select "Chapter 8," and click on "Case Problem with Sample Answer."

8.6 Misrepresentation of Age. Millennium Club, Inc., operates a tavern in South Bend, Indiana. In January 2003, Pamela Avila and other minors gained admission by misrepresenting that they were at least twenty-one years old. According to Millennium's representatives, the minors used false driver's licenses, "fraudulent transfer of a stamp used to gain admission by another patron or other means of false identification." To gain access, the minors also signed affidavits falsely attesting to the fact that they were twenty-one or older. When the state filed criminal charges against the Millennium Club, Millennium filed a suit in an Indiana state court against Avila and more than two hundred others, seeking damages of $3,000 each for misrepresenting their ages. The minors filed a motion to dismiss the complaint. Should the court grant the motion? What are the competing policy interests in this case? If the Millennium Club was not careful in checking the minors' identification, should it be allowed to recover? If Millennium Club reasonably relied on the minors' representations, should

the minors be allowed to avoid liability? Discuss. [*Millennium Club, Inc. v. Avila*, 809 N.E.2d 906 (Ind.App. 2004)]

8.7 Fraudulent Misrepresentation. According to the student handbook at Cleveland Chiropractic College (CCC) in Missouri, *academic misconduct* includes "selling . . . any copy of any material intended to be used as an instrument of academic evaluation in advance of its initial administration." Leonard Verni was enrolled at CCC in Dr. Aleksandr Makarov's dermatology class. Before the first examination, Verni was reported to be selling copies of the test. CCC investigated and concluded that Verni had committed academic misconduct. Verni was dismissed from CCC, which informed him of his right to an appeal. According to the handbook, at the hearing on appeal a student could have an attorney or other adviser, present witnesses' testimony and other evidence, and "question any testimony . . . against him/her." At his hearing, however, Verni did not bring his attorney, present evidence on his behalf, or question any adverse witnesses. When the dismissal was upheld, Verni filed a suit in a Missouri state court against CCC and others, claiming, in part, fraudulent misrepresentation. Verni argued that because he "relied" on the handbook's "representation" that CCC would follow its appeal procedure, he was unable to properly refute the charges against him. Can Verni succeed with this argument? Explain. [*Verni v. Cleveland Chiropractic College*, 212 S.W.3d 150 (Mo. 2007)]

8.8 Licensing Statutes. Under California law, a contract to manage a professional boxer must be in writing and the manager must be licensed by the state athletic commission. Marco Antonio Barrera is a professional boxer and two-time world champion. In May 2003, Jose Castillo, who was not licensed by the state, orally agreed to assume Barrera's management. He "understood" that he would be paid in accord with the "practice in the professional boxing industry," but in no case less than ten percent (10%) of the gross revenue" that Barrera generated as a boxer and through endorsements. Among other accomplishments, Castillo negotiated an exclusive promotion contract for Barrera with Golden Boy Promotions, Inc., which is owned and operated by Oscar De La Hoya. Castillo also helped Barrera settle three lawsuits and resolve unrelated tax problems so that Barrera could continue boxing. Castillo did not train Barrera, pick his opponents, or arrange his fights, however. When Barrera abruptly stopped communicating with Castillo, the latter filed a suit in a California state court against Barrera and others, alleging breach of contract. Under what circumstances is a contract with an unlicensed practitioner enforceable? Is the alleged contract in this case enforceable? Why or why not? [*Castillo v. Barrera*, 146 Cal.App.4th 1317, 53 Cal.Rptr.3d 494 (2 Dist. 2007)]

8.9 A Question of Ethics. *Dow AgroSciences, LLC (DAS), makes and sells agricultural seed products. In 2000, Timothy Glenn, a DAS sales manager, signed a covenant not to compete. He agreed that for two years from the date of his termination, he would not "engage in or contribute my knowl-*

edge to any work or activity involving an area of technology or business that is then competitive with a technology or business with respect to which I had access to Confidential Information during the five years immediately prior to such termination." Working with DAS business, operations, and research and development personnel, and being a member of high-level teams, Glenn had access to confidential DAS information, including agreements with DAS's business partners, marketing plans, litigation details, product secrets, new product development, future plans, and pricing strategies. In 2006, Glenn resigned to work for Pioneer Hi-Bred International, Inc., a DAS competitor. DAS filed a suit in an Indiana state court

against Glenn, asking that he be enjoined from accepting any "position that would call on him to use confidential DAS information." [*Glenn v. Dow AgroSciences, LLC*, 861 N.E.2d 1 (*Ind.App.* 2007)]

1 Generally, what interests are served by enforcing covenants not to compete? What interests are served by refusing to enforce them?

2 What argument could be made in support of reforming (and then enforcing) illegal covenants not to compete? What argument could be made against this practice?

3 How should the court rule in this case? Why?

 **CRITICAL THINKING
AND WRITING ASSIGNMENTS**

8.10 **Critical Legal Thinking.** Describe the types of individuals who might be capable of exerting undue influence on others.

8.11 **Video Question.** Go to this text's Web site at **academic.cengage.com/blaw/blt** and select "Chapter 8." Click on "Video Questions" and view the video titled *The Money Pit.* Then answer the following questions.

1 Assume that a valid contract exists between Walter (Tom Hanks) and the plumber. Recall from the video that the plumber had at least two drinks before agreeing to take on the plumbing job. If the plumber was intoxicated, is the contract voidable? Why or why not?

2 Suppose that state law requires plumbers in Walter's state to have a plumber's license and that this plumber does not have a license. Would the contract be enforceable? Why or why not?

3 In the video, the plumber suggests that Walter has been "turned down by every other plumber in the valley." Although the plumber does not even look at the house's plumbing, he agrees to do the repairs if Walter gives him a check for $5,000 right then "before he changes his mind." If Walter later seeks to void the contract because it is contrary to public policy, what should he argue?

ONLINE ACTIVITIES

 **PRACTICAL
INTERNET EXERCISES**

Go to this text's Web site at **academic.cengage.com/blaw/blt**, select "Chapter 8," and click on "Practical Internet Exercises." There you will find the following Internet research exercises that you can perform to learn more about the topics covered in this chapter.

PRACTICAL INTERNET EXERCISE 8-1   MANAGEMENT PERSPECTIVE—Minors and the Law

PRACTICAL INTERNET EXERCISE 8-2   SOCIAL PERSPECTIVE—Online Gambling

PRACTICAL INTERNET EXERCISE 8-3   LEGAL PERSPECTIVE—Promissory Estoppel and the Statute of Frauds

BEFORE THE TEST

Go to this text's Web site at **academic.cengage.com/blaw/blt**, select "Chapter 8," and click on "Interactive Quizzes." You will find a number of interactive questions relating to this chapter.

CHAPTER 9
Contracts: Third Party Rights, Discharge, Breach, and Remedies

"The laws of a state change with the changing times.**"**

Aeschylus, 525–456 B.C.E.
(Greek dramatist)

LEARNING OBJECTIVES

AFTER READING THIS CHAPTER, YOU SHOULD BE ABLE TO ANSWER THE FOLLOWING QUESTIONS:

1 What is the difference between an assignment and a delegation?

2 What factors indicate that a third party beneficiary is an intended beneficiary?

3 What is the difference between compensatory damages and consequential damages? What are nominal damages, and when do courts award nominal damages?

4 Under what circumstances will equitable remedies be available?

5 What is the rationale underlying the doctrine of election of remedies?

PRIVITY OF CONTRACT
The relationship that exists between the promisor and the promisee of a contract.

Because a contract is a private agreement between the parties who have entered into it, it is fitting that these parties alone should have rights and liabilities under the contract. This concept is referred to as **privity of contract,** and it establishes the basic principle that third parties have no rights in contracts to which they are not parties.

You may be convinced by now that for every rule of contract law, there is an exception. As times change, so must the laws, as indicated in the chapter-opening quotation. When justice cannot be served by adherence to a rule of law, exceptions to the rule must be made. In this chapter, we look at some exceptions to the rule of privity of contract. These exceptions include *assignments* and *delegations*, as well as *third party beneficiary contracts*. We also examine how contractual obligations can be *discharged*. Normally, contract discharge is accomplished by both parties performing the acts promised in the contract. We also look at the degree of performance required to discharge a contractual obligation, as well as at some other ways in which contract discharge can occur.

BREACH OF CONTRACT
The failure, without legal excuse, of a promisor to perform the obligations of a contract.

When it is no longer advantageous for a party to fulfill her or his contractual obligations, that party may breach the contract. A **breach of contract** occurs when a party fails to perform part or all of the required duties under a contract.[1] Once a party fails to perform or performs inadequately, the other party—the nonbreaching party—can choose one or more of several remedies. In the latter part of this chapter, we discuss breach of contract and remedies.

1. *Restatement (Second) of Contracts,* Section 235(2).

ASSIGNMENT AND DELEGATION

When third parties acquire rights or assume duties arising from contracts, the rights are transferred to them by *assignment*, and the duties are transferred by *delegation*.

Assignment

In a bilateral contract, the two parties have corresponding rights and duties. One party has a *right* to require the other to perform some task, and the other has a *duty* to perform it. Sometimes, though, a party will transfer her or his rights under the contract to someone else. The transfer of contract *rights* to a third person is known as an **assignment.**

Assignments are important because they are utilized in much business financing. Lending institutions, such as banks, frequently assign the rights to receive payments under their loan contracts to other firms, which pay for those rights. If you obtain a loan from your local bank to purchase a car, you may later receive in the mail a notice stating that your bank has transferred (assigned) its rights to receive payments on the loan to another firm and that, when the time comes to repay your loan, you must make the payments to that other firm.

Lenders that make *mortgage loans* (loans to allow prospective home buyers to purchase land or a home) often assign their rights to collect the mortgage payments to a third party, such as GMAC Mortgage Corporation. Following an assignment, the home buyer is notified that future payments must be made to the third party, rather than to the original lender. Billions of dollars change hands daily in the business world in the form of assignments of rights in contracts.

Effect of an Assignment In an assignment, the party assigning the rights to a third party is known as the **assignor,** and the party receiving the rights is the **assignee.** Other traditional terminology used to describe the parties in assignment relationships are the **obligee** (the person to whom a duty, or obligation, is owed) and the **obligor** (the person who is obligated to perform the duty).

When rights under a contract are assigned unconditionally, the rights of the *assignor* (the party making the assignment) are extinguished.[2] The third party (the *assignee*, or the party receiving the assignment) has a right to demand performance from the other original party to the contract (the *obligor*, the person who is obligated to perform). ▪**EXAMPLE 9.1** Brent (the obligor) owes Alex $1,000, and Alex, the obligee, assigns to Carmen the right to receive the $1,000 (thus, Alex is now the assignor). Here, a valid assignment of a debt exists. Carmen, the assignee, can enforce the contract against Brent, the obligor, if Brent fails to perform (pay the $1,000). ▪ Exhibit 9–1 on the next page illustrates assignment relationships.

The assignee obtains only those rights that the assignor originally had. Also, the assignee's rights are subject to the defenses that the obligor has against the assignor. ▪**EXAMPLE 9.2** Brent owes Alex $1,000 under a contract in which Brent agreed to buy Alex's MacBook Pro laptop. Alex assigns his right to receive the $1,000 to Carmen. Brent, in deciding to purchase the laptop, relied on Alex's fraudulent misrepresentation that the computer had two gigabytes of memory. When Brent discovers that the computer has only one gigabyte of memory, he tells Alex that he is going to return the laptop and cancel the contract. Even though Alex has assigned his "right" to receive the $1,000 to Carmen, Brent need not pay Carmen the $1,000—Brent can raise the defense of Alex's fraudulent misrepresentation to avoid payment. ▪

Rights That Cannot Be Assigned As a general rule, all rights can be assigned. Exceptions are made, however, in the following special circumstances.

ASSIGNMENT
The act of transferring to another all or part of one's rights arising under a contract.

ASSIGNOR
A party who transfers (assigns) his or her rights under a contract to another party (called the *assignee*).

ASSIGNEE
A party to whom the rights under a contract are transferred, or assigned.

OBLIGEE
One to whom an obligation is owed.

OBLIGOR
One who owes an obligation to another.

ON THE WEB

You can find a number of forms that can be used in the assignment of different types of contracts, at

www.ilrg.com/forms/#transfers.

This site is maintained by the Internet Legal Research Group.

---

2. *Restatement (Second) of Contracts*, Section 317.

EXHIBIT 9–1 | **Assignment Relationships**

In the assignment relationship illustrated here, Alex assigns his *rights* under a contract that he made with Brent to a third party, Carmen. Alex thus becomes the *assignor* and Carmen the *assignee* of the contractual rights. Brent, the *obligor* (the party owing performance under the contract), now owes performance to Carmen instead of Alex. Alex's original contract rights are extinguished after assignment.

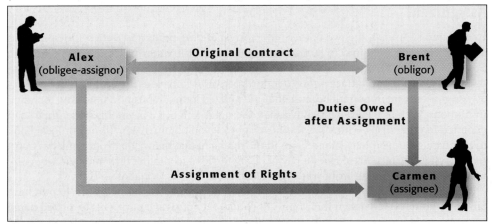

A music teacher instructs his pupil. Assuming that the boy's mother, Katherine, contracted with the teacher for his services, can Katherine assign the right to receive music lessons to another party? Why or why not? (Buccina Studios/ PhotoDisc Green)

When a Statute Expressly Prohibits Assignment. If a statute expressly prohibits assignment, the particular right in question cannot be assigned. **EXAMPLE 9.3** Marn is a new employee of CompuFuture, Inc. CompuFuture is an employer under workers' compensation statutes (see Chapter 18) in this state, so Marn is a covered employee. Marn has a relatively high-risk job. In need of a loan, she borrows from Stark, assigning to Stark all workers' compensation benefits due her should she be injured on the job. A state statute prohibits the assignment of *future* workers' compensation benefits, and thus such rights cannot be assigned. ◼

When a Contract Is Personal in Nature. When a contract is for personal services, the rights under the contract normally cannot be assigned unless all that remains is a monetary payment.[3] **EXAMPLE 9.4** Brent signs a contract to be a tutor for Alex's children. Alex then attempts to assign to Carmen his right to Brent's services. Carmen cannot enforce the contract against Brent. Brent may not like Carmen's children or for some other reason may not want to tutor them. Because personal services are unique to the person rendering them, rights to receive personal services cannot be assigned. ◼

When an Assignment Will Significantly Change the Risk or Duties of the Obligor. A right cannot be assigned if assignment will significantly increase or alter the risks or the duties of the obligor (the party owing performance under the contract).[4] **EXAMPLE 9.5** Alex has a hotel, and to insure it, he takes out a policy with Northwest Insurance Company. The policy insures against fire, theft, floods, and vandalism. Alex attempts to assign the insurance policy to Carmen, who also owns a hotel. The assignment is ineffec-

---

3. *Restatement (Second) of Contracts*, Sections 317 and 318.
4. See Section 2–210(2) of the Uniform Commercial Code (UCC).

tive because it may substantially alter the insurance company's duty of performance and the risk that the company undertakes. An insurance company evaluates the particular risk of a certain party and tailors its policy to fit that risk. If the policy is assigned to a third party, the insurance risk is materially altered. ◼

When the Contract Prohibits Assignment. If a contract stipulates that the right cannot be assigned, then *ordinarily* it cannot be assigned. **◼EXAMPLE 9.6** Brent agrees to build a house for Alex. The contract between Brent and Alex states, "This contract cannot be assigned by Alex without Brent's consent. Any assignment without such consent renders this contract void, and all rights hereunder will thereupon terminate." Alex then assigns his rights to Carmen, without first obtaining Brent's consent. Carmen cannot enforce the contract against Brent. ◼ This rule has several exceptions:

1 A contract cannot prevent an assignment of the right to receive funds. This exception exists to encourage the free flow of funds and credit in modern business settings.
2 The assignment of ownership rights in real estate often cannot be prohibited because such a prohibition is contrary to public policy in most states. Prohibitions of this kind are called restraints against **alienation** (the voluntary transfer of land ownership).
3 The assignment of negotiable instruments (see Chapter 14) cannot be prohibited.
4 In a contract for the sale of goods, the right to receive damages for breach of contract or for payment of an account owed may be assigned even though the sales contract prohibits such an assignment.[5]

ALIENATION
The process of transferring land out of one's possession (thus "alienating" the land from oneself).

Delegation

Just as a party can transfer rights to a third party through an assignment, a party can also transfer duties. Duties are not assigned, however; they are *delegated*. Normally, a **delegation of duties** does not relieve the party making the delegation (the **delegator**) of the obligation to perform in the event that the party to whom the duty has been delegated (the **delegatee**) fails to perform. No special form is required to create a valid delegation of duties. As long as the delegator expresses an intention to make the delegation, it is effective; the delegator need not even use the word *delegate*. Exhibit 9–2 on the following page graphically illustrates delegation relationships.

DELEGATION OF DUTIES
The act of transferring to another all or part of one's duties arising under a contract.
DELEGATOR
A party who transfers (delegates) her or his obligations under a contract to another party (called the *delegatee*).
DELEGATEE
A party to whom contractual obligations are transferred, or delegated.

Duties That Cannot Be Delegated As a general rule, any duty can be delegated. This rule has some exceptions, however. Delegation is prohibited in the following circumstances:

1 When performance depends on the personal skill or talents of the obligor.
2 When special trust has been placed in the obligor.
3 When performance by a third party will vary materially from that expected by the obligee (the one to whom performance is owed) under the contract.
4 When the contract expressly prohibits delegation.

The following examples will help to clarify the kinds of duties that can and cannot be delegated:

1 Brent contracts with Alex to tutor Alex in various aspects of financial underwriting and investment banking. Brent, an experienced businessperson known for his expertise in finance, delegates his duties to a third party, Carmen. This delegation is ineffective because Brent contracted to render a service that is founded on Brent's *expertise* and

---
5. UCC 2–210(2).

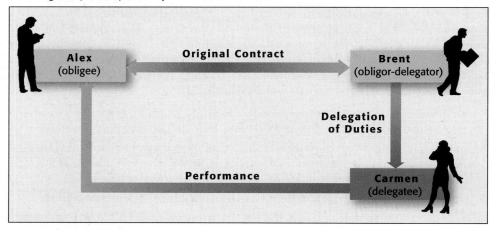

EXHIBIT 9–2 | **Delegation Relationships**

In the delegation relationship illustrated here, Brent delegates his *duties* under a contract that he made with Alex to a third party, Carmen. Brent thus becomes the *delegator* and Carmen the *delegatee* of the contractual duties. Carmen now owes performance of the contractual duties to Alex. Note that a delegation of duties normally does not relieve the delegator (Brent) of liability if the delegatee (Carmen) fails to perform the contractual duties.

Alex placed *special trust* in Brent's teaching ability. The delegation changes Alex's expectancy under the contract.

2 Brent, a famous musician, contracts with Alex to *personally* perform at a concert. Then Brent receives a better offer elsewhere and delegates his duty to perform to another musician, Miles. Regardless of Miles's exceptional musical talents, the delegation is not effective without Alex's consent because the contract was for *personal* performance.

3 Brent, an accountant, contracts to perform annual audits of Alex's business records for the next five years. The contract states that Brent must provide the services himself and cannot delegate these duties to another. Two years later, Brent is busy on other projects and delegates his obligations to perform Alex's audit to Arianna, who is a certified public accountant at the same firm. This delegation is not effective because the contract *expressly prohibited* delegation.

4 Alex is a wealthy philanthropist who just created a charitable foundation. Alex has known Brent for twenty years and knows that Brent shares his beliefs on many humanitarian issues. He contracts with Brent to be in charge of allocating funds among various charitable causes. Six months later, Brent is experiencing health problems and delegates his duties to Drew. Alex does not approve of Drew as a replacement. In this situation, Alex can claim the delegation was not effective because it *materially altered his expectations* under the contract. Alex had reasonable expectations about the types of charities to which Brent would give the foundation's funds, and substituting Drew's performance materially changes those expectations.

5 Brent contracts with Alex to pick up and deliver heavy construction machinery to Alex's property. Brent delegates this duty to Carmen, who is in the business of delivering heavy machinery. This delegation is effective. The performance required is of a routine and nonpersonal nature, and the delegation does not change Alex's expectations under the contract.

Effect of a Delegation If a delegation of duties is enforceable, the *obligee* (the one to whom performance is owed) must accept performance from the delegatee (the one to whom the duties are delegated). ▪EXAMPLE 9.7 In the fifth example in the above list, Brent delegates his duty (to pick up and deliver heavy construction machinery to Alex's property) to Carmen. In that situation, Alex (the obligee) must accept performance from Carmen (the delegatee) because the delegation was effective. The obligee can legally refuse performance from the delegatee only if the duty is one that cannot be delegated. ▪

A valid delegation of duties does not relieve the delegator of obligations under the contract.[6] In the above example, if Carmen (the delegatee) fails to perform, Brent (the delegator) is still liable to Alex (the obligee). The obligee can also hold the delegatee liable if the delegatee made a promise of performance that will directly benefit the obligee. In this situation, there is an "assumption of duty" on the part of the delegatee, and breach of this duty makes the delegatee liable to the obligee. For example, if Carmen (the delegatee) promises Brent (the delegator), in a contract, to pick up and deliver the construction equipment to Alex's property but fails to do so, Alex (the obligee) can sue Brent, Carmen, or both. Although there are many exceptions, the general rule today is that the obligee can sue both the delegatee and the delegator.

> **COMPARE** In an assignment, the assignor's original contract rights are extinguished after the assignment. In a delegation, the delegator remains liable for performance under the contract if the delegatee fails to perform.

"Assignment of All Rights" Sometimes, a contract provides for an "assignment of all rights." The traditional view was that under this type of assignment, the assignee did not assume any duties. This view was based on the theory that the assignee's agreement to accept the benefits of the contract was not sufficient to imply a promise to assume the duties of the contract.

Modern authorities, however, take the view that the probable intent in using such general words is to create both an assignment of rights and an assumption of duties.[7] Therefore, when general words are used (for example, "I assign the contract" or "all my rights under the contract"), the contract is construed as implying both an assignment of rights and an assumption of duties.

THIRD PARTY BENEFICIARIES

As mentioned earlier in this chapter, to have contractual rights, a person normally must be a party to the contract. In other words, privity of contract must exist. An exception to the doctrine of privity exists when the original parties to the contract intend, at the time of contracting, that the contract performance directly benefit a third person. In this situation, the third person becomes a **third party beneficiary** of the contract. As an **intended beneficiary** of the contract, the third party has legal rights and can sue the promisor directly for breach of the contract.

> **THIRD PARTY BENEFICIARY**
> One for whose benefit a promise is made in a contract but who is not a party to the contract.
>
> **INTENDED BENEFICIARY**
> A third party for whose benefit a contract is formed. An intended beneficiary can sue the promisor if such a contract is breached.

Types of Intended Beneficiaries

The law distinguishes between *intended* beneficiaries and *incidental* beneficiaries. Only intended beneficiaries acquire legal rights in a contract. One type of intended beneficiary is a *creditor beneficiary*. A creditor beneficiary benefits from a contract in which one party (the promisor) promises another party (the promisee) to pay a debt that the promisee owes to a third party (the creditor beneficiary). As an intended beneficiary, the creditor beneficiary can sue the promisor directly to enforce the contract.

---

6. For a classic case on this issue, see *Crane Ice Cream Co. v. Terminal Freezing & Heating Co.*, 147 Md. 588, 128 A. 280 (1925).

7. See UCC 2–210(1), (4); and *Restatement (Second) of Contracts*, Section 328.

Another type of intended beneficiary is a *donee* beneficiary. When a contract is made for the express purpose of giving a *gift* to a third party, the third party (the donee beneficiary) can sue the promisor directly to enforce the promise.[8] The most common donee beneficiary contract is a life insurance contract. **■EXAMPLE 9.8** Akins (the promisee) pays premiums to Standard Life, a life insurance company, and Standard Life (the promisor) promises to pay a certain amount on Akins's death to anyone Akins designates as a beneficiary. The designated beneficiary is a donee beneficiary under the life insurance policy and can enforce the promise made by the insurance company to pay her or him on Akins's death. ■

As the law concerning third party beneficiaries evolved, numerous cases arose in which the third party beneficiary did not fit readily into either the creditor beneficiary or the donee beneficiary category. Thus, the modern view, and the one adopted by the *Restatement (Second) of Contracts*, does not draw such clear lines and distinguishes only between intended beneficiaries (who can sue to enforce contracts made for their benefit) and incidental beneficiaries (who cannot sue, as will be discussed shortly).

When the Rights of an Intended Beneficiary Vest

An intended third party beneficiary cannot enforce a contract against the original parties until the rights of the third party have *vested*, meaning that the rights have taken effect and cannot be taken away. Until these rights have vested, the original parties to the contract—the promisor and the promisee—can modify or rescind the contract without the consent of the third party. When do the rights of third parties vest? Generally, the rights vest when one of the following occurs:

1 When the third party demonstrates manifest assent to the contract, such as sending a letter or note acknowledging awareness of and consent to a contract formed for her or his benefit.

2 When the third party materially alters his or her position in detrimental reliance on the contract, such as when a donee beneficiary contracts to have a home built in reliance on the receipt of funds promised to him or her in a donee beneficiary contract.

3 When the conditions for vesting are satisfied. For example, the rights of a beneficiary under a life insurance policy vest when the insured person dies.

If the contract expressly reserves to the contracting parties the right to cancel, rescind, or modify the contract, the rights of the third party beneficiary are subject to any changes that result. In such a situation, the vesting of the third party's rights does not terminate the power of the original contracting parties to alter their legal relationships.[9]

Incidental Beneficiaries

INCIDENTAL BENEFICIARY
A third party who incidentally benefits from a contract but whose benefit was not the reason the contract was formed. An incidental beneficiary has no rights in a contract and cannot sue to have the contract enforced.

The benefit that an **incidental beneficiary** receives from a contract between two parties is unintentional. Therefore, an incidental beneficiary cannot enforce a contract to which he or she is not a party.

■EXAMPLE 9.9 In one case, spectators at a Mike Tyson boxing match in which Tyson was disqualified for biting his opponent's ear sued Tyson and the fight's promoters for a refund of their money on the basis of breach of contract. The spectators claimed that they had standing to sue the defendants as third party beneficiaries of the contract between Tyson and the fight's promoters. The court, however, held that the spectators did not have standing to sue because they were not in contractual privity with any of the defendants. Furthermore, any

---

8. This principle was first enunciated in *Seaver v. Ransom*, 224 N.Y. 233, 120 N.E. 639 (1918).

9. Defenses raised against third party beneficiaries are given in the *Restatement (Second) of Contracts*, Section 309.

benefits they received from the contract were incidental to the contract. The court noted that the spectators got what they paid for: "the right to view whatever event transpired."[10] ■

Is a person who benefits from a contract between another party and a government entity an incidental beneficiary or an intended beneficiary? This chapter's *Adapting the Law to the Online Environment* feature on the next page discusses this issue.

Intended versus Incidental Beneficiaries

In determining whether a third party beneficiary is an intended or an incidental beneficiary, the courts generally use the *reasonable person* test. Under this test, a beneficiary will be considered an intended beneficiary if a reasonable person in the position of the beneficiary would believe that the promisor *intended* to confer on the beneficiary the right to bring suit to enforce the contract.

In determining whether a party is an intended or an incidental beneficiary, the courts also look at a number of other factors. As you can see in Exhibit 9–3, which graphically illustrates the distinction between intended and incidental beneficiaries, the presence of one or more of the following factors strongly indicates that the third party is an intended (rather than an incidental) beneficiary to the contract:

1 Performance is rendered directly to the third party.

2 The third party has the right to control the details of performance.

3 The third party is expressly designated as a beneficiary in the contract.

CONTRACT DISCHARGE

The most common way to **discharge,** or terminate, one's contractual duties is by the **performance** of those duties. The duty to perform under a contract may be *conditioned* on the occurrence or nonoccurrence of a certain event, or the duty may be *absolute*. As shown

---

DISCHARGE
The termination of an obligation. In contract law, discharge occurs when the parties have fully performed their contractual obligations or when events, conduct of the parties, or operation of law releases the parties from performance.

PERFORMANCE
In contract law, the fulfillment of one's duties arising under a contract with another; the normal way of discharging one's contractual obligations.

---

10. *Castillo v. Tyson*, 268 A.D.2d 336, 701 N.Y.S.2d 423 (Sup.Ct.App.Div. 2000).

EXHIBIT 9–3 | **Third Party Beneficiaries**

CONTRACT THAT BENEFITS A THIRD PARTY

INTENDED BENEFICIARY
An intended beneficiary is a third party—
- To whom performance is rendered directly
- Who has the right to control the details of the performance *or*
- Who is designated a beneficiary in the contract

INCIDENTAL BENEFICIARY
An incidental beneficiary is a third party—
- Who benefits from a contract but whose benefit was not the reason for the contract
- Who has no rights in the contract

CAN SUE TO ENFORCE THE CONTRACT

CANNOT SUE TO ENFORCE THE CONTRACT

ADAPTING THE LAW TO THE ONLINE ENVIRONMENT — Government Contracts and Third Party Beneficiaries

Government entities often contract with private organizations to provide certain services to the public. Are those who benefit under such contracts intended beneficiaries? This question came before the court in a case involving a person who had registered a domain name with an organization that had contracted with the federal government to provide domain name registration services.

The Domain Name Conflict

In 1994, in the early days of the Internet (as a public surfing and shopping vehicle), domain names were free for the asking. At that time, Network Solutions, Inc. (NSI), was the sole registrar of domain names. NSI had a contract with a federal government agency stating that NSI had the primary responsibility for "ensuring the quality, timeliness, and effective management" of domain name registration services.

Gary Kremen, seeing what he felt was a great opportunity, registered the name "sex.com" with NSI. Unfortunately for Kremen, Stephen Cohen also saw the potential of that domain name. Cohen, who had just gotten out of prison for impersonating a bankruptcy lawyer, knew that Kremen had already registered the name. That fact, however, in the words of the court, "was only a minor impediment for a man of Cohen's boundless resource and bounded integrity." Through forgery and deceit, Cohen succeeded in having NSI transfer the domain name to his company. When Kremen later contacted NSI, he was told that it was too late to undo the transfer. Kremen then turned to the courts for assistance.

The Legal Issues

Kremen sued Cohen, seeking as damages the substantial profits that Cohen had made by using the name. The court held in Kremen's favor and awarded him millions of dollars in damages. Kremen could not collect the judgment, however, because Cohen had disappeared—after first transferring large sums to offshore accounts. Kremen then tried to hold NSI responsible for his losses by alleging, among other things, that he was an intended third party beneficiary of NSI's contract with the government. He claimed that because NSI had not "effectively managed" its duties, as it was obligated to do under the contract, his domain name had been wrongfully transferred.

Was Kremen an intended third party beneficiary of the contract? When the case ultimately reached the U.S. Court of Appeals for the Ninth Circuit, the court held that Kremen was not an intended third party beneficiary of the contract. The court noted that a third party can enforce a contract if the contract reflects an "express or implied intention of the parties to the contract to benefit the third party." The court emphasized, however, that when a contract is with a government entity, a more stringent test applies: for a third party to be an intended beneficiary, *the contract must express a clear intent to benefit the third party.* If it does not express this clear intent, then anyone who benefits under the contract is regarded as an incidental beneficiary and, as such, cannot sue to enforce the contract.[a]

FOR CRITICAL ANALYSIS *Kremen also alleged that NSI had breached an implied-in-fact contract with him, but the court dismissed this claim. Why would the court hold that no contract existed between Kremen and NSI? Was a required element for a valid contract lacking?*

a. *Kremen v. Cohen,* 337 F.3d 1024 (9th Cir. 2003).

---

in Exhibit 9–4, in addition to performance, a contract can be discharged in numerous other ways, including discharge by agreement of the parties and discharge by operation of law.

Conditions of Performance

In most contracts, promises of performance are not expressly conditioned or qualified. Instead, they are *absolute promises.* They must be performed, or the party promising the act will be in breach of contract. **■EXAMPLE 9.10** JoAnne contracts to sell Alfonso a painting for $10,000. The parties' promises are unconditional: JoAnne's transfer of the painting to Alfonso and Alfonso's payment of $10,000 to JoAnne. The payment does not have to be made if the painting is not transferred. **■**

In some situations, however, contractual promises are conditioned. A **condition** is a possible future event, the occurrence or nonoccurrence of which will trigger the performance of a legal obligation or terminate an existing obligation under a contract. If the condition is not satisfied, the obligations of the parties are discharged. **■EXAMPLE 9.11** Suppose that

CONDITION
A qualification, provision, or clause in a contractual agreement, the occurrence or nonoccurrence of which creates, suspends, or terminates the obligations of the contracting parties.

EXHIBIT 9–4 | **Contract Discharge**

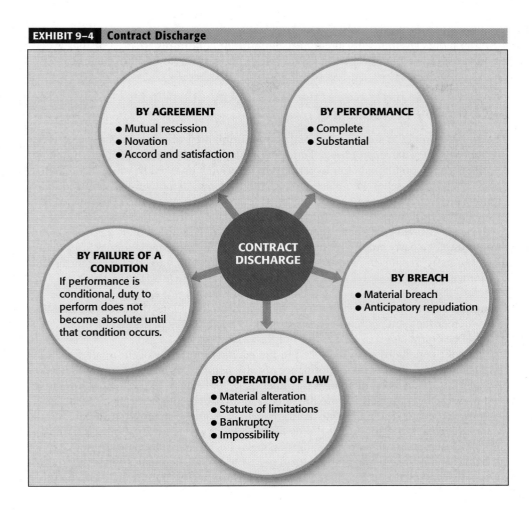

Alfonso, in the above example, offers to purchase JoAnne's painting only if an independent appraisal indicates that it is worth at least $10,000. JoAnne accepts Alfonso's offer. Their obligations (promises) are conditioned on the outcome of the appraisal. Should this condition not be satisfied (for example, if the appraiser deems the value of the painting to be only $5,000), their obligations to each other are discharged and cannot be enforced. ▣

We look here at three types of conditions that can be present in any given contract: *conditions precedent*, *conditions subsequent*, and *concurrent conditions*.

Conditions Precedent A condition that must be fulfilled before a party's promise becomes absolute is called a **condition precedent.** The condition precedes the absolute duty to perform, as in the JoAnne-Alfonso example just given. Real estate contracts frequently are conditioned on the buyer's ability to obtain financing. Insurance contracts frequently specify that certain conditions, such as passing a physical examination, must be met before the insurance company will be obligated to perform under the contract.

Conditions Subsequent When a condition operates to terminate a party's absolute promise to perform, it is called a **condition subsequent.** The condition follows, or is subsequent to, the absolute duty to perform. If the condition occurs, the party need not perform any further.

CONDITION PRECEDENT
In a contractual agreement, a condition that must be met before a party's promise becomes absolute.

CONDITION SUBSEQUENT
A condition in a contract that, if not fulfilled, operates to terminate a party's absolute promise to perform.

CONCURRENT CONDITIONS
Conditions that must occur or be performed at the same time; they are mutually dependent. No obligations arise until these conditions are simultaneously performed.

TENDER
An unconditional offer to perform an obligation by a person who is ready, willing, and able to do so.

A woman shakes hands with a salesperson after agreeing to purchase a car. Suppose that the agreement is conditioned on the dealer's installing certain optional equipment. When the woman returns to the dealership the following day, she discovers that the optional features that were agreed on have not been added to the car. Is she still obligated to buy the car? Why or why not? What type of condition is this? (Brian Teutsch/Creative Commons)

Concurrent Conditions   When each party's absolute duty to perform is conditioned on the other party's absolute duty to perform, **concurrent conditions** are present. These conditions exist only when the parties expressly or impliedly are to perform their respective duties *simultaneously.*

Discharge by Performance

The contract comes to an end when both parties fulfill their respective duties by performing the acts they have promised. Performance can also be accomplished by tender. **Tender** is an unconditional offer to perform by a person who is ready, willing, and able to do so. Therefore, a seller who places goods at the disposal of a buyer has tendered delivery and can demand payment according to the terms of the agreement. A buyer who offers to pay for goods has tendered payment and can demand delivery of the goods.

Once performance has been tendered, the party making the tender has done everything possible to carry out the terms of the contract. If the other party then refuses to perform, the party making the tender can consider the duty discharged and sue for breach of contract.

Complete Performance   When a party performs exactly as agreed, there is no question as to whether the contract has been performed. When a party's performance is perfect, it is said to be complete.

Normally, conditions expressly stated in the contract must fully occur in all aspects for complete performance (strict performance) of the contract to take place. Any deviation breaches the contract and discharges the other party's obligations to perform. For example, most construction contracts require the builder to meet certain specifications. If the specifications are conditions, complete performance is required to avoid material breach. (*Material breach* will be discussed shortly.) If the conditions are met, the other party to the contract must then fulfill her or his obligation to pay the builder. If the specifications are not conditions and if the builder, without the other party's permission, fails to meet the specifications, performance is not complete. What effect does such a failure have on the other party's obligation to pay? The answer is part of the doctrine of *substantial performance.*

Substantial Performance   A party who in good faith performs substantially all of the terms of a contract can enforce the contract against the other party under the doctrine of substantial performance. Note that good faith is required. Intentionally failing to comply with the terms is a breach of the contract.

To qualify as *substantial performance*, the performance must not vary greatly from the performance promised in the contract, and it must create substantially the same benefits as those promised in the contract. If the omission, variance, or defect in performance is unimportant and can easily be compensated for by awarding damages, a court is likely to hold that the contract has been substantially performed. Courts decide whether the performance was substantial on a case-by-case basis, examining all of the facts of the particular situation. If performance is substantial, the other party's duty to perform remains absolute (except that the party can sue for damages due to the minor deviations).

■EXAMPLE 9.12 A couple contracts with a construction company to build a house. The contract specifies that Brand X plasterboard be used for the walls. The builder cannot obtain Brand X plasterboard, and the buyers are on holiday in the mountains of Peru and virtually unreachable. The builder decides to install Brand Y instead, which he knows is identical in quality and durability to Brand X plasterboard. All other aspects of construction conform to the contract. In this situation, a court will likely hold that the builder had substantially performed his end of the bargain, and therefore the couple will be obligated to pay the builder. The court might, however, award the couple damages for the use of a different brand of plasterboard, but the couple would still have to pay the contractor the contract price, less the amount of damages. ■

Performance to the Satisfaction of Another   Contracts often state that completed work must personally satisfy one of the parties or a third person. The question is whether this satisfaction becomes a condition precedent, requiring actual personal satisfaction or approval for discharge, or whether the test of satisfaction is performance that would satisfy a *reasonable person* (substantial performance).

When the subject matter of the contract is *personal*, a contract to be performed to the satisfaction of one of the parties is conditioned, and performance must actually satisfy that party. For example, contracts for portraits, works of art, and tailoring are considered personal. Therefore, only the personal satisfaction of the party fulfills the condition—unless a court finds the party is expressing dissatisfaction only to avoid payment or otherwise is not acting in good faith.

Most other contracts need to be performed only to the satisfaction of a reasonable person unless they *expressly state otherwise*. When such contracts require performance to the satisfaction of a third party (for example, "to the satisfaction of Robert Ames, the supervising engineer"), the courts are divided. A majority of courts require the work to be satisfactory to a reasonable person, but some courts hold that the personal satisfaction of the third party designated in the contract (Robert Ames, in this example) must be met. Again, the personal judgment must be made honestly, or the condition will be excused.

Material Breach of Contract   A *breach of contract* is the nonperformance of a contractual duty. A breach is *material* when performance is not at least substantial.[11] If there is a material breach, the nonbreaching party is excused from the performance of contractual duties and can sue for damages caused by the breach. If the breach is *minor* (not material), the nonbreaching party's duty to perform may sometimes be suspended until the breach is remedied, but the duty is not entirely excused. Once the minor breach is cured, the nonbreaching party must resume performance of the contractual obligations that had been undertaken.

Any breach entitles the nonbreaching party to sue for damages, but only a material breach discharges the nonbreaching party from the contract. The policy underlying these rules is that contracts should go forward when only minor problems occur, but contracts should be terminated if major problems arise.[12]

Did a seller's failure to repair the plumbing in an apartment building within the eight-month period specified in a contract with the buyers constitute a material breach of the parties' contract? That was the issue in the following case.

---

11. *Restatement (Second) of Contracts*, Section 241.
12. See UCC 2–612, which deals with installment contracts for the sale of goods.

ON THE WEB

For a summary of how contracts may be discharged and other principles of contract law, go to

contracts.lawyers.com,

and click on the "Terminating a Contract" link.

CASE 9.1   Kim v. Park

Court of Appeals of Oregon, 192 Or.App. 365, 86 P.3d 63 (2004).
www.publications.ojd.state.or.us/appeals.htm[a]

FACTS Su Yong Kim sold an apartment building in Portland,

a. Click on "Cases decided in 2004," and scroll to the name of the case under the date 3/3/04. Then click on the case name to access the opinion. The state of Oregon's judicial branch maintains this Web site.

Oregon, to Chon Sik Park, Bok Soon Park, Johan Cen, William Itzineag, Johnny Perea, and Patricia Maldonado. At the time, the building's plumbing violated the Portland Housing Code. The contract provided the following: "Seller shall correct the plumbing code violation * * * within eight months * * *.

CASE 9.1–Continues next page

CASE 9.1–Continued

Buyer shall cooperate with seller in * * * providing access to the premises to complete repairs." Kim did not make the repairs within eight months, but twelve months after the date of the contract, Kim cut holes in the walls of the apartments to expose the plumbing. Seven weeks later, early one morning, Kim sent plumbers to the building without notice to the owners, apparently in an attempt to make repairs. The owners ordered the plumbers to leave, refused to allow Kim to send others, and stopped making payments under the contract. Kim filed a suit in an Oregon state court against the buyers, seeking the amount due. The buyers asserted that Kim's failure to repair the plumbing was a material breach that excused the performance of their obligations and counterclaimed for damages for the breach. The court concluded that Kim's breach was not material and ordered relief in his favor. The buyers appealed to a state intermediate appellate court.

ISSUE Was the seller's failure to repair the plumbing according to the parties' contract a material breach excusing the buyers' performance?

DECISION Yes. The state intermediate appellate court reversed the decision of the lower court on this issue and remanded the case for a determination of the amount of damages.

REASON The appellate court reasoned that a breach is material if it "goes to the very substance of the contract and defeats the object of the parties entering into the contract." In this case, as a result of the code violations, "the City of Portland continued to assess fines against defendants and defendants lost some tenants." The court pointed out that the requirement that the seller repair the plumbing within eight months was intended to ensure that the building's plumbing would satisfy the city code within a reasonable time after the sale. Also, the buyers had purchased the building from the seller so that they could rent out the apartments in it. According to the court, "[a]lthough the repairs to the plumbing in the building would have caused some temporary inconvenience to the tenants, the failure of plaintiff to make the repairs in accordance with the contract ultimately prevented defendants from using the building as intended by the parties' agreement. In light of that evidence, we hold that as a matter of law the plaintiff's [seller's] failure to perform as promised was a material breach of the contract." The court added that because the seller's breach was material, the buyers were not obligated to continue to perform their obligation to make the payments under the contract.

 WHY IS THIS CASE IMPORTANT? *This case emphasizes that when one party's failure to perform a contractual obligation causes another to suffer significant harm, the other party normally is entitled to a remedy. Recall from Chapter 7 that even when no contract exists, someone who justifiably relies to her or his detriment on the promise of another may be able to obtain relief under the doctrine of quasi contract or promissory estoppel.*

ANTICIPATORY REPUDIATION
An assertion or action by a party indicating that he or she will not perform an obligation that the party is contractually obligated to perform at a future time.

Anticipatory Repudiation of a Contract Before either party to a contract has a duty to perform, one of the parties may refuse to perform her or his contractual obligations. This is called **anticipatory repudiation**.[13] When anticipatory repudiation occurs, it is treated as a material breach of contract, and the nonbreaching party is permitted to bring an action for damages immediately, even though the scheduled time for performance under the contract may still be in the future.[14] Until the nonbreaching party treats this early repudiation as a breach, however, the breaching party can retract the anticipatory repudiation by proper notice and restore the parties to their original obligations.[15]

An anticipatory repudiation is treated as a present, material breach for two reasons. First, the nonbreaching party should not be required to remain ready and willing to perform when the other party has already repudiated the contract. Second, the nonbreaching party should have the opportunity to seek a similar contract elsewhere and may have the duty to do so to minimize his or her loss.

---

13. *Restatement (Second) of Contracts*, Section 253; and UCC 2–610.
14. The doctrine of anticipatory repudiation first arose in the landmark case of *Hochster v. De La Tour*, 2 Ellis and Blackburn Reports 678 (1853), when an English court recognized the delay and expense inherent in a rule requiring a nonbreaching party to wait until the time of performance before suing on an anticipatory repudiation.
15. See UCC 2–611.

Quite often, an anticipatory repudiation occurs when a sharp fluctuation in market prices creates a situation in which performance of the contract would be extremely unfavorable to one of the parties. **EXAMPLE 9.13** Martin Corporation contracts to manufacture and sell ten thousand personal computers to ComAge, a retailer of computer equipment that has five hundred outlet stores. Delivery is to be made six months from the date of the contract. The contract price is based on Martin's present costs of purchasing inventory parts from others. One month later, three suppliers of computer parts raise their prices to Martin. Because of these higher prices, Martin stands to lose $500,000 if it sells the computers to ComAge at the contract price. Martin writes to ComAge, stating that it cannot deliver the ten thousand computers at the contract price. Martin's letter is an anticipatory repudiation of the contract. ComAge has the option of treating the repudiation as a material breach and proceeding immediately to pursue remedies, even though the contract delivery date is still five months away. ■

REMEMBER The risks that prices will fluctuate and values will change are ordinary business risks for which the law does not provide relief.

Discharge by Agreement

Any contract can be discharged by agreement of the parties. The agreement can be contained in the original contract, or the parties can form a new contract for the express purpose of discharging the original contract.

Discharge by Rescission   As mentioned in previous chapters, rescission is the process in which the parties cancel the contract and are returned to the positions they occupied prior to the contract's formation. For *mutual rescission* to take place, the parties must make another agreement that also satisfies the legal requirements for a contract—there must be an *offer*, an *acceptance*, and *consideration*. Ordinarily, if the parties agree to rescind the original contract, their promises not to perform those acts promised in the original contract will be legal consideration for the second contract.

Mutual rescission can occur in this manner when the original contract is executory on both sides (that is, neither party has completed performance). Agreements to rescind most executory contracts (with the exception of real estate contracts) are enforceable even if they are made orally and even if the original agreement was in writing.[16] When one party has fully performed, however, an agreement to rescind the original contract usually is not enforceable unless additional consideration or restitution is made.[17]

Discharge by Novation   The process of **novation** substitutes a third party for one of the original parties. Essentially, the parties to the original contract and one or more new parties all get together and agree to the substitution. The requirements of a novation are as follows:

NOVATION
The substitution, by agreement, of a new contract for an old one, with the rights under the old one being terminated. Typically, novation involves the substitution of a new person who is responsible for the contract and the removal of the original party's rights and duties under the contract.

1 The existence of a previous, valid obligation.

2 Agreement by all of the parties to a new contract.

3 The extinguishing of the old obligation (discharge of the prior party).

4 A new, valid contract.

A novation may appear to be similar to an assignment or delegation. Nevertheless, there is an important distinction: a novation involves a new contract, and an assignment or delegation involves the old contract.

---

16. Agreements to rescind contracts involving transfers of realty, however, must be evidenced by a writing. Another exception has to do with the sale of goods under the UCC, when the sales contract requires written rescission.
17. Under UCC 2–209(1), however, no consideration is needed to modify a contract for a sale of goods; see also UCC 1–107. See Chapter 11 for an extended discussion of the UCC.

EXAMPLE 9.14 Suppose that you contract with Logan Enterprises to sell it your office equipment business. Logan later decides that it should not expand at this time but learns of another party, MBI Corporation, that is interested in purchasing your business. All three of you get together and agree to a novation. As long as the new contract is supported by consideration, the novation discharges the original contract between you and Logan and replaces it with the new contract between you and MBI Corporation. Logan prefers the novation because it discharges Logan's liabilities under the contract with you. If the original contract had been an installment sales contract requiring twelve monthly payments, and Logan had merely assigned the contract (assigned its rights and delegated its duties under the contract) to MBI Corporation, Logan would have remained liable to you for the payments if MBI Corporation defaulted. ◼

Discharge by Accord and Satisfaction   As Chapter 7 explained, in an *accord and satisfaction*, the parties agree to accept performance different from the performance originally promised. An *accord* is an executory contract (one that has not yet been performed) to perform some act to satisfy an existing contractual duty that is not yet discharged.[18] A *satisfaction* is the performance of the accord agreement. An *accord* and its *satisfaction* discharge the original contractual obligation.

Once the accord has been made, the original obligation is merely suspended until the accord agreement is fully performed. If it is not performed, the party to whom performance is owed can bring an action on the original obligation or for breach of the accord. **EXAMPLE 9.15** Shea obtains a judgment against Marla for $8,000. Later, both parties agree that the judgment can be satisfied by Marla's transfer of her automobile to Shea. This agreement to accept the auto in lieu of $8,000 in cash is the accord. If Marla transfers her automobile to Shea, the accord agreement is fully performed, and the $8,000 debt is discharged. If Marla refuses to transfer her car, the accord is breached. Because the original obligation is merely suspended, Shea can sue to enforce the judgment for $8,000 in cash or bring an action for breach of the accord. ◼

Discharge by Operation of Law

Under some circumstances, contractual duties may be discharged by operation of law. These circumstances include material alteration of the contract, the running of the relevant statute of limitations, bankruptcy, and impossibility of performance.

Contract Alteration   To discourage parties from altering written contracts, the law allows an innocent party to be discharged when one party has materially altered a written contract without the knowledge or consent of the other party. For example, if a party alters a material term of the contract—such as the quantity term or the price term—without the knowledge or consent of the other party, the party who was unaware of the alteration can treat the contract as discharged or terminated.

Statutes of Limitations   As mentioned earlier in this text, statutes of limitations limit the period during which a party can sue on a particular cause of action. After the applicable limitations period has passed, a suit can no longer be brought. For example, the limitations period for bringing lawsuits for breach of oral contracts is usually two to three years; for written contracts, four to five years; and for recovery of amounts awarded in judgment, ten to twenty years, depending on state law. Lawsuits for breach of a contract for the sale of goods must be brought within four years after the cause of action has accrued. By original

---

18. *Restatement (Second) of Contracts*, Section 281.

agreement, the parties can agree to reduce this four-year period to not less than a one-year period. They cannot, however, agree to extend it beyond the four-year limitations period.

Bankruptcy   A proceeding in bankruptcy attempts to allocate the debtor's assets to the creditors in a fair and equitable fashion. Once the assets have been allocated, the debtor receives a *discharge in bankruptcy* (see Chapter 16). A discharge in bankruptcy ordinarily bars the creditors from enforcing most of the debtor's contracts.

When Performance Is Impossible   After a contract has been made, performance may become impossible in an objective sense. This is known as **impossibility of performance** and may discharge the contract.[19] Performance may also become so difficult or costly due to some unforeseen event that a court will consider it commercially unfeasible, or impracticable, as discussed later in the chapter.

Objective Impossibility.   Objective impossibility ("It can't be done") must be distinguished from subjective impossibility ("I'm sorry, I simply can't do it"). An example of subjective impossibility is the inability to pay funds on time because the bank is closed.[20] In effect, the nonperforming party is saying, "It is impossible for *me* to perform," rather than "It is impossible for *anyone* to perform." Accordingly, such excuses do not discharge a contract, and the nonperforming party is normally held in breach of contract. Three basic types of situations will generally qualify as grounds for the discharge of contractual obligations based on impossibility of performance:[21]

1 *When a party whose personal performance is essential to the completion of the contract dies or becomes incapacitated prior to performance.* **■EXAMPLE 9.16** Fred, a famous dancer, contracts with Ethereal Dancing Guild to play a leading role in its new ballet. Before the ballet can be performed, Fred becomes ill and dies. His personal performance was essential to the completion of the contract. Thus, his death discharges the contract and his estate's liability for his nonperformance. ■

2 *When the specific subject matter of the contract is destroyed.* **■EXAMPLE 9.17** A-1 Farm Equipment agrees to sell Gudgel the green tractor on its lot and promises to have the tractor ready for Gudgel to pick up on Saturday. On Friday night, however, a truck veers off the nearby highway and smashes into the tractor, destroying it beyond repair. Because the contract was for this specific tractor, A-1's performance is rendered impossible owing to the accident. ■

3 *When a change in the law renders performance illegal.* An example is a contract to build an apartment building, when the zoning laws are changed to prohibit the construction of residential rental property at this location. This change renders the contract impossible to perform.

Temporary Impossibility.   An occurrence or event that makes performance temporarily impossible operates to suspend performance until the impossibility ceases. Then, ordinarily, the parties must perform the contract as originally planned. If, however, the lapse of time and the change in circumstances surrounding the contract make it substantially more burdensome for the parties to perform the promised acts, the contract is discharged.

If a fire incapacitated a commercial bakery's oven, would the bakery be excused from performing its contracts until the oven was fixed? If the bakery had a contract for a special holiday order and the oven could not be fixed until after the holiday, would that contract be discharged? Why or why not?
(Matt Biddulph/Creative Commons)

IMPOSSIBILITY OF PERFORMANCE
A doctrine under which a party to a contract is relieved of her or his duty to perform when performance becomes objectively impossible or totally impracticable (through no fault of either party).

---

19. *Restatement (Second) of Contracts,* Section 261.
20. *Ingham Lumber Co. v. Ingersoll & Co.,* 93 Ark. 447, 125 S.W. 139 (1910).
21. *Restatement (Second) of Contracts,* Sections 262–266; and UCC 2–615.

NOTE The doctrine of commercial impracticability does not provide relief from such events as ordinary price increases or easily predictable changes in the weather.

COMMERCIAL IMPRACTICABILITY
A doctrine under which a seller may be excused from performing a contract when (1) a contingency occurs, (2) the contingency's occurrence makes performance impracticable, and (3) the nonoccurrence of the contingency was a basic assumption on which the contract was made. Despite the fact that UCC Section 2–615 expressly frees only sellers under this doctrine, courts have not distinguished between buyers and sellers in applying it.

FRUSTRATION OF PURPOSE
A court-created doctrine under which a party to a contract will be relieved of her or his duty to perform when the objective purpose for performance no longer exists (due to reasons beyond that party's control).

REMEMBER The terms of a contract must be sufficiently definite for a court to determine the amount of damages to award.

EXAMPLE 9.18 The leading case on the subject, *Autry v. Republic Productions*,[22] involved an actor who was drafted into the army in 1942. Being drafted rendered the actor's contract temporarily impossible to perform, and it was suspended until the end of the war. When the actor got out of the army, the purchasing power of the dollar had so diminished that performance of the contract would have been substantially burdensome to him. Therefore, the contract was discharged. ■

Commercial Impracticability Courts may excuse parties from their performance obligations when the performance becomes much more difficult or expensive than originally contemplated at the time the contract was formed. For someone to invoke the doctrine of **commercial impracticability** successfully, however, the anticipated performance must become *extremely* difficult or costly.[23]

The added burden of performing not only must be extreme but also *must not have been known by the parties when the contract was made*. For example, in one case, a court held that a contract could be discharged because a party would have to pay ten times more than the original estimate to excavate a certain amount of gravel.[24] In another case, the court allowed a party to rescind a contract for the sale of land because of a potential problem with contaminated groundwater under the land. The court found that "the potential for substantial and unbargained-for" liability made contract performance economically impracticable. Interestingly, the court in that case also noted that the possibility of "environmental degradation with consequences extending well beyond the parties' land sale" was just as important to its decision as the economic considerations.[25] (See this chapter's *Beyond Our Borders* feature for a discussion of Germany's approach to impracticability and impossibility of performance.)

Frustration of Purpose Closely allied with the doctrine of commercial impracticability is the doctrine of **frustration of purpose**. In principle, a contract will be discharged if supervening circumstances make it impossible to attain the purpose both parties had in mind when making the contract. As with commercial impracticability, the supervening event must not have been foreseeable at the time of the contracting.

DAMAGES

As mentioned earlier, a *breach of contract* occurs when a party fails to perform part or all of the required duties under a contract. A breach of contract entitles the nonbreaching party to sue for monetary damages. As you read in Chapter 4, damages are designed to compensate a party for harm suffered as a result of another's wrongful act. In the context of contract law, damages are designed to compensate the nonbreaching party for the loss of the bargain. Often, courts say that innocent parties are to be placed in the position they would have occupied had the contract been fully performed.[26]

Types of Damages

There are basically four broad categories of damages:

1 Compensatory (to cover direct losses and costs).

2 Consequential (to cover indirect and foreseeable losses).

---

22. 30 Cal.2d 144, 180 P.2d 888 (1947).
23. *Restatement (Second) of Contracts*, Section 264.
24. *Mineral Park Land Co. v. Howard*, 172 Cal. 289, 156 P. 458 (1916).
25. *Cape-France Enterprises v. Estate of Peed*, 305 Mont. 513, 29 P.3d 1011 (2001).
26. *Restatement (Second) of Contracts*, Section 347; and Section 1–106(1) of the Uniform Commercial Code (UCC).

BEYOND OUR BORDERS | **Impossibility or Impracticability of Performance in Germany**

In the United States, when a party alleges that contract performance is impossible or impracticable because of circumstances unforeseen at the time the contract was formed, a court will either discharge the party's contractual obligations or hold the party to the contract. In other words, if a court agrees that the contract is impossible or impracticable to perform, the remedy is to rescind (cancel) the contract. Under German law, however, a court may adjust the terms of (reform) a contract in light of economic developments. If an unforeseen event affects the foundation of the agreement, the court can alter the contract's terms in view of the disruption in expectations, thus making the contract fair to the parties.

FOR CRITICAL ANALYSIS *When a contract becomes impossible or impractical to perform, which remedy would a businessperson prefer—rescission or reformation? Why?*

3 Punitive (to punish and deter wrongdoing).

4 Nominal (to recognize wrongdoing when no monetary loss is shown).

Compensatory and punitive damages were discussed in Chapter 4 in the context of tort law. Here, we look at these types of damages, as well as consequential and nominal damages, in the context of contract law.

Compensatory Damages Damages compensating the nonbreaching party for the *loss of the bargain* are known as *compensatory damages*. These damages compensate the injured party only for damages actually sustained and proved to have arisen directly from the loss of the bargain caused by the breach of contract. They simply replace what was lost because of the wrong or damage.

The standard measure of compensatory damages is the difference between the value of the breaching party's promised performance under the contract and the value of her or his actual performance. This amount is reduced by any loss that the injured party has avoided.

EXAMPLE 9.19 You contract with Marinot Industries to perform certain personal services exclusively for Marinot during August for a payment of $4,000. Marinot cancels the contract and is in breach. You are able to find another job during August but can earn only $3,000. You normally can sue Marinot for breach and recover $1,000 as compensatory damages. You may also recover from Marinot the amount that you spent to find the other job. Expenses that are directly incurred because of a breach of contract—such as those incurred to obtain performance from another source—are called **incidental damages**.

The measurement of compensatory damages varies by type of contract. Certain types of contracts deserve special mention—contracts for the sale of goods, contracts for the sale of land, and construction contracts.

Sale of Goods. In a contract for the sale of goods, the usual measure of compensatory damages is the difference between the contract price and the market price.[27]

INCIDENTAL DAMAGES
Damages awarded to compensate for expenses that are directly incurred because of a breach of contract—such as those incurred to obtain performance from another source.

27. This is the difference between the contract price and the market price at the time and place at which the goods were to be delivered or tendered. [See UCC 2–708, 2–713, and 2–715(1).]

ON THE WEB

For a summary of how contracts may be breached and other information on contract law, go to

consumer-law.lawyers.com/
Contract-Termination.html.

■EXAMPLE 9.20 MediQuick Laboratories contracts with Cal Computer Industries to purchase ten model UTS 400 network servers for $8,000 each. If Cal Computer fails to deliver the ten servers, and the current market price of the servers is $8,950, MediQuick's measure of damages is $9,500 (10 × $950), plus any incidental damages (expenses) caused by the breach. ■ If the buyer breaches and the seller has not yet produced the goods, compensatory damages normally equal the seller's lost profits on the sale, rather than the difference between the contract price and the market price.

Sale of Land. Ordinarily, because each parcel of land is unique, the remedy for a seller's breach of a contract for a sale of real estate is specific performance—that is, the buyer is awarded the parcel of property for which he or she bargained (*specific performance* is discussed more fully later in this chapter). When this remedy is unavailable (because the property has been sold, for example) or when the buyer is the party in breach, the measure of damages is typically the difference between the contract price and the market price of the land. The majority of states follow this rule.

Construction Contracts. The measure of damages in a building or construction contract varies depending on which party breaches and when the breach occurs. The owner can breach at three different stages of the construction:

1 Before performance has begun.

2 During performance.

3 After performance has been completed.

If the owner breaches *before performance has begun*, the contractor can recover only the profits that would have been made on the contract (that is, the total contract price less the cost of materials and labor). If the owner breaches *during performance*, the contractor can recover the profits plus the costs incurred in partially constructing the building. If the owner breaches *after the construction has been completed*, the contractor can recover the entire contract price plus interest.

When the contractor breaches the construction contract—either by failing to begin construction or by stopping work partway through the project—the measure of damages is the cost of completion, which includes reasonable compensation for any delay in performance. If the contractor finishes late, the measure of damages is the loss of use. (The *Application* feature at the end of this chapter offers some suggestions for a contractor who cannot perform.)

Consequential Damages Foreseeable damages that result from a party's breach of contract are referred to as **consequential damages**, or *special damages*. Consequential damages differ from compensatory damages in that they are caused by special circumstances beyond the contract itself. They flow from the consequences, or results, of a breach. When a seller fails to deliver goods, knowing that the buyer is planning to use or resell those goods immediately, consequential damages are awarded for the loss of profits from the planned resale.

To recover consequential damages, the breaching party must know (or have reason to know) that special circumstances will cause the nonbreaching party to suffer an additional loss.[28] See this chapter's *Landmark in the Law* feature on pages 290 and 291 for a discussion of *Hadley v. Baxendale*, a case decided in England in 1854.

CONSEQUENTIAL DAMAGES
Special damages that compensate for a loss that does not directly or immediately result from the breach (for example, lost profits). For the plaintiff to collect consequential damages, they must have been reasonably foreseeable at the time the breach or injury occurred.

NOTE A seller who does not wish to take on the risk of consequential damages can limit the buyer's remedies via contract.

---

28. UCC 2–715(2). See Chapter 12.

PREVENTING LEGAL DISPUTES

Business owners and managers should realize that it is sometimes impossible to prevent contract disputes. They should also understand that collecting damages through a court judgment requires litigation, which can be expensive and time consuming. Furthermore, court judgments are often difficult to enforce, particularly if the breaching party does not have sufficient assets to pay the damages awarded.[29] For these reasons, parties generally choose to settle their contract disputes before trial rather than litigate in hopes of being awarded—and being able to collect—damages (or other remedies). In sum, there is wisdom in the old saying, "a bird in the hand is worth two in the bush."

Punitive Damages   Recall from Chapter 4 that punitive damages are designed to punish a wrongdoer and to set an example to deter similar conduct in the future. Punitive damages, or *exemplary damages*, generally are not awarded in an action for breach of contract. Such damages have no legitimate place in contract law because they are, in essence, penalties, and a breach of contract is not unlawful in a criminal sense. A contract is simply a civil relationship between the parties. The law may compensate one party for the loss of the bargain—no more and no less.

In a few situations, a person's actions can cause both a breach of contract and a tort. **EXAMPLE 9.21** Two parties establish by contract a certain reasonable standard or duty of care. Failure to live up to that standard is a breach of the contract. The same act that breached the contract may also constitute negligence, or it may be an intentional tort if, for example, the breaching party committed fraud. In such a situation, it is possible for the nonbreaching party to recover punitive damages for the tort in addition to compensatory and consequential damages for the breach of contract. ■

Nominal Damages   When no actual damage or financial loss results from a breach of contract and only a technical injury is involved, the court may award **nominal damages** to the innocent party. Nominal damages awards are often small, such as one dollar, but they do establish that the defendant acted wrongfully. Most lawsuits for nominal damages are brought as a matter of principle under the theory that a breach has occurred and some damages must be imposed regardless of actual loss.

EXAMPLE 9.22 Hernandez contracts to buy potatoes at fifty cents a pound from Lentz. Lentz breaches the contract and does not deliver the potatoes. Meanwhile, the price of potatoes falls. Hernandez is able to buy them in the open market at half the price he agreed to pay Lentz. Hernandez is clearly better off because of Lentz's breach. Thus, in a suit for breach of contract, Hernandez may be awarded only nominal damages for the technical injury he sustained, as no monetary loss was involved. ■

NOMINAL DAMAGES
A small monetary award (often one dollar) granted to a plaintiff when no actual damage was suffered.

Mitigation of Damages

In most situations, when a breach of contract occurs, the injured party is held to a duty to mitigate, or reduce, the damages that he or she suffers. Under this doctrine of **mitigation of damages,** the required action depends on the nature of the situation.

MITIGATION OF DAMAGES
A rule requiring a plaintiff to do whatever is reasonable to minimize the damages caused by the defendant.

---

29. Courts dispose of cases, after trials, by entering judgments. A judgment may order the losing party to pay monetary damages to the winning party. Collecting a judgment, however, can pose problems. For example, the judgment debtor may be insolvent (unable to pay his or her bills when they come due) or have only a small net worth, or exemption laws may prevent a creditor from seizing the debtor's assets to satisfy a debt (see Chapter 16).

LANDMARK IN THE LAW *Hadley v. Baxendale* (1854)

The rule that notice of special ("consequential") circumstances must be given if consequential damages are to be recovered was first enunciated in *Hadley v. Baxendale,*[a] a landmark case decided in 1854.

Case Background   This case involved a broken crankshaft used in a flour mill run by the Hadley family in Gloucester, England. The crankshaft attached to the steam engine in the mill broke, and the shaft had to be sent to a foundry located in Greenwich so that a new shaft could be made to fit the other parts of the engine.

The Hadleys hired Baxendale, a common carrier, to transport the shaft from Gloucester to Greenwich. Baxendale received payment in advance and promised to deliver the shaft the following day. It was not delivered for several days, however. As a consequence, the mill was closed during those days because the Hadleys had no extra crankshaft on hand to use. The Hadleys sued Baxendale to recover the profits they lost during that time. Baxendale contended that the loss of profits was "too remote."

In the mid-1800s, it was common knowledge that large mills, such as that run by the Hadleys, normally had more than one crankshaft in case the main one broke and had to be repaired, as happened in this case. It is against this background that the parties argued their respective positions on whether the damages resulting from loss of profits while the crankshaft was out for repair were "too remote" to be recoverable.

The Issue before the Court and the Court's Ruling   The crucial issue before the court was whether the Hadleys had informed the carrier, Baxendale, of the special

a. 9 Exch. 341, 156 Eng.Rep. 145 (1854).

EXAMPLE 9.23 Some states require a landlord to use reasonable means to find a new tenant if a tenant abandons the premises and fails to pay rent. If an acceptable tenant becomes available, the landlord is required to lease the premises to this tenant to mitigate the damages recoverable from the former tenant. The former tenant is still liable for the difference between the amount of the rent under the original lease and the rent received from the new tenant. If the landlord has not taken the reasonable steps necessary to find a new tenant, a court will likely reduce any award by the amount of rent the landlord could have received had such reasonable means been used. ▣

In the majority of states, a person whose employment has been wrongfully terminated has a duty to mitigate damages incurred because of the employer's breach of the employment contract. In other words, wrongfully terminated employees have a duty to take similar jobs if they are available. If the employees fail to do this, the damages they receive will be equivalent to their salaries less the incomes they would have received in similar jobs obtained by reasonable means. The employer has the burden of proving that such jobs existed and that the employee could have been hired. Normally, the employee is under no duty to take a job that is not of the same type and rank.

Whether a tenant farmer acceptably attempted to mitigate his damages on his landlord's breach of their lease was at issue in the following case.

circumstances surrounding the crankshaft's repair, in particular that the mill would have to shut down while the crankshaft was being repaired. If Baxendale had been notified of this circumstance at the time the contract was formed, then the remedy for breaching the contract would have been the amount of damages that would reasonably follow from the breach—including the Hadleys' lost profits.

In the court's opinion, however, the only circumstances communicated by the Hadleys to Baxendale at the time the contract was made were that the item to be transported was a broken crankshaft of a mill and that the Hadleys were the owners and operators of that mill. The court concluded that these circumstances did not reasonably indicate that the mill would have to stop operations if the delivery of the crankshaft was delayed.

APPLICATION TO TODAY'S WORLD *Today, the rule enunciated by the court in this case still applies. When damages are awarded, compensation is given only for those injuries that the defendant could reasonably have foreseen as a probable result of the usual course of events following a breach. If the injury complained of is outside the usual and foreseeable course of events, the plaintiff must show specifically that the defendant had reason to know the facts and foresee the injury. This rule applies to contracts in the online environment as well. For example, suppose that a Web merchant loses business (and profits) due to a computer system's failure. If the failure was caused by malfunctioning software, the merchant normally may recover the lost profits from the software maker if these consequential damages were foreseeable.*

RELEVANT WEB SITES *To locate information on the Web concerning the Hadley decision, go to this text's Web site at* **academic.cengage.com/blaw/blt**, *select "Chapter 9," and click on "URLs for Landmarks."*

CASE 9.2   **Hanson v. Boeder**

Supreme Court of North Dakota, 2007 ND 20, 727 N.W.2d 280 (2007).
www.ndcourts.com/court/opinions.htm[a]

FACTS In 1998, Paul Hanson signed a five-year lease to farm 1,350 acres of Donald Boeder's land in Steele County, North Dakota, for $50 per acre beginning with the 1999 crop year. Under the lease, Hanson could use grain bins with a capacity of 93,000 bushels and two machine sheds on the property. The rent was $67,515 per year, with half due on April 1 and the balance due on November 1. In 2003, Boeder and Hanson renewed the lease for a second five-year period. During both terms, Boeder and Hanson disagreed about Hanson's farming practices, but during the second term, their disagreement escalated. In August 2005, Boeder told Hanson that their lease was over. Boeder also told Hanson not to till the land in the fall because it had been leased to a new tenant who wanted to do it himself. Hanson continued to work Boeder's land, however, while running ads in the local newspapers for other farmland to rent. Unable to find other land, Hanson filed a suit in a North Dakota state court against Boeder for breach of contract, asking the court to assess damages. The court awarded Hanson $315,194.26 to cover his lost profits, the lost use of the bins and sheds, and the value of the fall tillage. Boeder appealed to the North Dakota Supreme Court, arguing, in part, that Hanson failed to mitigate his damages.

a. Click on the "By ND citation" link. In the result, click on "2007" and then the name of the case to access the opinion. The North Dakota Supreme Court maintains this Web site.

CASE 9.2—Continues next page

CASE 9.2-Continued

ISSUE Did Hanson take appropriate steps to mitigate his damages?

DECISION Yes. The Supreme Court of North Dakota affirmed the lower court's award of damages to Hanson.

REASON The state supreme court explained that normally, "[f]or the breach of an obligation arising from contract, the measure of damages * * * is the amount which will compensate the party aggrieved for all the detriment proximately caused thereby or which in the ordinary course of things would be likely to result therefrom." The court recognized that "[a] person injured by the wrongful acts of

another has a duty to mitigate or minimize the damages and must protect himself if he can do so with reasonable exertion or at trifling expense, and can recover from the delinquent party only such damages as he could not, with reasonable effort, have avoided." In this case, Hanson had not been aware of any farmland available for lease, and he had run ads in the local newspapers seeking other farmland to rent. That Hanson was unsuccessful affected the amount of his recovery, but it did not point to a failure to mitigate his damages.

 FOR CRITICAL ANALYSIS-Social Consideration
During the trial, Boeder tried to retract his repudiation of the lease to allow Hanson to continue farming for the rest of the lease term. Should the court have considered this an acceptable substitute to mitigate Hanson's damages?

Liquidated Damages versus Penalties

LIQUIDATED DAMAGES
An amount, stipulated in a contract, that the parties to the contract believe to be a reasonable estimation of the damages that will occur in the event of a breach.

PENALTY
A contractual clause that states that a certain amount of monetary damages will be paid in the event of a future default or breach of contract. The damages are a punishment for a default and not a measure of compensation for the contract's breach. The agreement as to the penalty amount will not be enforced, and recovery will be limited to actual damages.

A **liquidated damages** provision in a contract specifies that a certain dollar amount is to be paid in the event of a future default or breach of contract. (*Liquidated* means determined, settled, or fixed.) For example, a provision requiring a construction contractor to pay $300 for every day he or she is late in completing the project is a liquidated damages provision. Liquidated damages differ from penalties. A **penalty** specifies a certain amount to be paid in the event of a default or breach of contract and is designed to penalize the breaching party. Liquidated damages provisions normally are enforceable. In contrast, if a court finds that a provision calls for a penalty, the agreement as to the amount will not be enforced, and recovery will be limited to actual damages.[30]

To determine whether a particular provision is for liquidated damages or for a penalty, the court must answer two questions:

1 At the time the contract was formed, was it apparent that damages would be difficult to estimate in the event of a breach?

2 Was the amount set as damages a reasonable estimate of those potential damages and not excessive?[31]

If the answers to both questions are yes, the provision normally will be enforced. If either answer is no, the provision normally will not be enforced. Liquidated damages provisions are frequently used in construction contracts because it is difficult to estimate the amount of damages that would be caused by a delay in completing the work.

ETHICAL ISSUE 9.1

Should a court enforce a liquidated damages clause when the amount due under that clause exceeds the actual value of the contracted goods so significantly that it seems unfair? A court had to answer this question in a case involving leased equipment. Eaton Hydraulics, Inc., entered a contract to lease nearly $9 million of computer equipment from Winthrop Resources Corporation, a computer leasing company. Four years later, Winthrop sued Eaton for breach of contract, alleging that Eaton had failed to meet numerous payment

---

30. This is also the rule under the UCC. See UCC 2–718(1).
31. *Restatement (Second) of Contracts*, Section 356(1).

obligations (often because the payments were late), failed to properly maintain the equipment, and failed to properly pack and ship the equipment back to Winthrop. The parties' contract included a liquidated damages clause that provided a formula for calculating the "Casualty Loss Value (CLV)," which would be the damages in the event of a breach.

Based on this clause, Winthrop claimed that Eaton was liable for more than $4 million in damages. Eaton argued that the CLV was an unreasonable and unenforceable penalty. Eaton presented evidence showing that when the lease ended and the computers were returned to Winthrop, each had a fair market value of about $75. The value calculated under the CLV, however, was between $500 and $700—considerably more than four times their market value. The court rejected Eaton's argument, noting that the provision was "clearly not a fair market value calculation." The court held that the liquidated damages provision was proper because of "the speculative nature of the value of the computers at termination of the lease schedules." The court reasoned that Winthrop and Eaton were both sophisticated international companies that had negotiated this contract knowing that the damages for breaching it could be several times the fair market value of the equipment. In essence, the court would not consider whether the amount due under the liquidated damages clause was fair because the parties were sophisticated businesses that had agreed on the method of calculation.[32]

The *Concept Summary* below summarizes the rules on the availability of the different types of damages.

EQUITABLE REMEDIES

In some situations, damages are an inadequate remedy for a breach of contract. In these cases, the nonbreaching party may ask the court for an equitable remedy. Equitable remedies include rescission and restitution, specific performance, and reformation.

32. *Winthrop Resources Corp. v. Eaton Hydraulics, Inc.*, 361 F.3d 465 (8th Cir. 2004).

CONCEPT SUMMARY   Damages

REMEDY	AVAILABILITY	RESULT
Compensatory Damages	A party sustains and proves an injury arising directly from the loss of the bargain.	The injured party is compensated for the loss of the bargain.
Consequential Damages	Special circumstances, of which the breaching party is aware or should be aware, cause the injured party additional loss.	The injured party is given the entire *benefit* of the bargain, such as forgone profits.
Punitive Damages	Damages are normally available only when a tort is also involved.	The wrongdoer is punished, and others are deterred from committing similar acts.
Nominal Damages	There is no financial loss.	Wrongdoing is established without actual damages being suffered. The plaintiff is awarded a nominal amount (such as $1) in damages.
Liquidated Damages	A contract provides a specific amount to be paid as damages in the event that the contract is later breached.	The nonbreaching party is paid the amount stipulated in the contract for the breach, unless the amount is construed as a penalty.

American cyclist Tyler Hamilton, leading a race, was suspended from competitive cycling for two years for transfusing himself with another person's blood. Hamilton had a contract to compete on the Phonak team, but the team terminated its contract with Hamilton after his suspension. (Jarrett Campbell/ Creative Commons)

RESTITUTION
An equitable remedy under which a person is restored to his or her original position prior to loss or injury, or placed in the position he or she would have been in had the breach not occurred.

SPECIFIC PERFORMANCE
An equitable remedy requiring exactly the performance that was specified; usually granted only when monetary damages would be an inadequate remedy and the subject matter of the contract is unique.

CONTRAST Restitution offers several advantages over traditional damages. Restitution may be available in situations when damages cannot be proved or are difficult to prove. Restitution can be used to recover specific property. Restitution sometimes results in a greater overall award.

Rescission and Restitution

As discussed earlier, *rescission* is essentially an action to undo, or cancel, a contract—to return nonbreaching parties to the positions that they occupied prior to the transaction. When fraud, mistake, duress, or failure of consideration is present, rescission is available. The failure of one party to perform under a contract entitles the other party to rescind the contract.[33] The rescinding party must give prompt notice to the breaching party.

Restitution To rescind a contract, both parties generally must make **restitution** to each other by returning goods, property, or funds previously conveyed.[34] If the physical property or goods can be returned, they must be. If the property or goods have been consumed, restitution must be made in an equivalent dollar amount.

Essentially, restitution involves the recapture of a benefit conferred on the defendant that has unjustly enriched her or him. **■EXAMPLE 9.24** Andrea pays $32,000 to Myles in return for his promise to design a house for her. The next day, Myles calls Andrea and tells her that he has taken a position with a large architectural firm in another state and cannot design the house. Andrea decides to hire another architect that afternoon. Andrea can require restitution of $32,000 because Myles has received an unjust benefit of $32,000. ■

Restitution Is Not Limited to Rescission Cases Restitution may be required when a contract is rescinded, but the right to restitution is not limited to rescission cases. Restitution may be sought in actions for breach of contract, tort actions, and other actions at law or in equity. Usually, restitution can be obtained when funds or property has been transferred by mistake or because of fraud. An award in a case may include restitution of funds or property obtained through embezzlement, conversion, theft, copyright infringement, or misconduct by a party in a confidential or other special relationship.

Specific Performance

The equitable remedy of **specific performance** calls for the performance of the act promised in the contract. This remedy is often attractive to a nonbreaching party because it provides the exact bargain promised in the contract. It also avoids some of the problems inherent in a suit for monetary damages. First, the nonbreaching party need not worry about collecting the judgment. Second, the nonbreaching party need not look around for another contract. Third, the actual performance may be more valuable than the monetary damages.

Normally, however, specific performance will not be granted unless the party's legal remedy (monetary damages) is inadequate.[35] For this reason, contracts for the sale of goods rarely qualify for specific performance. Monetary damages ordinarily are adequate in such situations because substantially identical goods can be bought or sold in the market. Only if the goods are unique will a court grant specific performance. For instance, paintings, sculptures, and rare books and coins are often unique, and monetary damages will not enable a buyer to obtain substantially identical substitutes in the market.

Sale of Land A court will grant specific performance to a buyer in an action for a breach of contract involving the sale of land. In this situation, the legal remedy of monetary damages will not compensate the buyer adequately because every parcel of land is unique;

---

33. The rescission discussed here refers to *unilateral* rescission, in which only one party wants to undo the contract. In *mutual* rescission, both parties agree to undo the contract. Mutual rescission discharges the contract; unilateral rescission is generally available as a remedy for breach of contract.
34. *Restatement (Second) of Contracts,* Section 370.
35. *Restatement (Second) of Contracts,* Section 359.

obviously, the buyer cannot obtain the same land in the same location elsewhere. Only when specific performance is unavailable (for example, when the seller has sold the property to someone else) will damages be awarded instead.

Is specific performance warranted when one of the parties has substantially—but not *fully*—performed under the contract? That was the question in the following case.

CASE 9.3 **Stainbrook v. Low**

Court of Appeals of Indiana, 842 N.E.2d 386 (2006).

FACTS In April 2004, Howard Stainbrook agreed to sell to Trent Low forty acres of land in Jennings County, Indiana, for $45,000. Thirty-two of the acres were wooded and eight were tillable. Under the agreement, Low was to pay for a survey of the property and other costs, including a tax payment due in November. Low gave Stainbrook a check for $1,000 to show his intent to fulfill the contract. They agreed to close the deal on May 11, and Low made financial arrangements to meet his obligations. On May 8, a tractor rolled over on Stainbrook, and he died. Stainbrook's son David became the executor of his father's estate. David asked Low to withdraw his offer to buy the forty acres. Low refused and filed a suit in an Indiana state court against David, seeking to enforce the contract. The court ordered specific performance. David appealed to a state intermediate appellate court, arguing, in part, that his father's contract with Low was "ambiguous and inequitable."

ISSUE Is complete performance of a contract required for the party to be entitled to the remedy of specific performance?

DECISION No. A party who has substantially performed or offered to perform his or her obligations under a contract is entitled to pursue specific performance as a remedy. The state intermediate appellate court held that specific performance was an appropriate remedy in this case and affirmed the lower court's order.

REASON The appellate court explained that a contracting party's substantial performance is sufficient to support a court's order for specific performance. Here, "Low both offered to perform and substantially performed his contractual obligations." The appellate court found that Low had offered to make the tax payment that was due, but Stainbrook's estate refused the offer. Also, Low had obtained financing before the closing date, and there was nothing to indicate that he was not prepared to meet his financial obligations and go forward with the sale. Moreover, although the survey had not yet been arranged, there was no evidence that Low would not have paid for the survey of the land as required by the contract. Because Low had substantially performed under the terms of the contract, the court held that Low was entitled to the remedy of specific performance.

WHY IS THIS CASE IMPORTANT? *The court reaffirmed the principle that "[s]pecific performance is a matter of course when it involves contracts to purchase real estate." The court also emphasized that "[a] party seeking specific performance of a real estate contract must prove that he has substantially performed his contract obligations or offered to do so." The court's reasoning underscores the importance of focusing on the elements of a principle to resolve a case fairly.*

Contracts for Personal Services Personal-service contracts require one party to work personally for another party. Courts normally refuse to grant specific performance of contracts for personal services. This is because to order a party to perform personal services against his or her will amounts to a type of involuntary servitude, which is contrary to the public policy expressed in the Thirteenth Amendment to the U.S. Constitution. Moreover, the courts do not want to monitor contracts for personal services.

EXAMPLE 9.25 If you contract with a brain surgeon to perform brain surgery on you and the surgeon refuses to perform, the court will not compel (and you certainly would not want) the surgeon to perform under these circumstances. There is no way the court can assure meaningful performance in such a situation.[36] ■

---

36. Similarly, courts often refuse to order specific performance of construction contracts because courts are not set up to operate as construction supervisors or engineers.

Reformation

Reformation is an equitable remedy used when the parties have *imperfectly* expressed their agreement in writing. Reformation allows a court to rewrite the contract to reflect the parties' true intentions. Courts order reformation most often when fraud or mutual mistake is present. **■EXAMPLE 9.26** If Keshan contracts to buy a forklift from Shelley but the written contract refers to a crane, a mutual mistake has occurred. Accordingly, a court could reform the contract so that the writing conforms to the parties' original intention as to which piece of equipment is being sold. ■

Courts frequently reform contracts in two other situations. The first occurs when two parties who have made a binding oral contract agree to put the oral contract in writing but, in doing so, make an error in stating the terms. Universally, the courts allow into evidence the correct terms of the oral contract, thereby reforming the written contract. The second situation occurs when the parties have executed a written covenant not to compete (see Chapter 8). If the covenant not to compete is for a valid and legitimate purpose (such as the sale of a business) but the area or time restraints are unreasonable, some courts will reform the restraints by making them reasonable and will enforce the entire contract as reformed. Other courts, however, will throw the entire restrictive covenant out as illegal. Exhibit 9–5 presents the remedies, including reformation, that are available to the nonbreaching party.

RECOVERY BASED ON QUASI CONTRACT

Recall from Chapter 7 that a quasi contract is not a true contract but rather a fictional contract that is imposed on the parties to prevent unjust enrichment. Hence, a quasi contract provides a basis for relief when no enforceable contract exists. The legal obligation arises because the law considers that the party accepting the benefits has made an implied promise to pay for them. Generally, when one party confers a benefit on another party, justice requires that the party receiving the benefit pay a reasonable value for it.

When Quasi Contracts Are Used

Quasi contract is a legal theory under which an obligation is imposed in the absence of an agreement. It allows the courts to act as if a contract exists when there is no actual contract or agreement between the parties. The courts can also use this theory when the parties have a contract, but it is unenforceable for some reason.

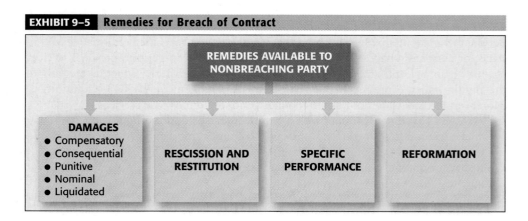

EXHIBIT 9–5 Remedies for Breach of Contract

REMEDIES AVAILABLE TO NONBREACHING PARTY

DAMAGES
- Compensatory
- Consequential
- Punitive
- Nominal
- Liquidated

RESCISSION AND RESTITUTION

SPECIFIC PERFORMANCE

REFORMATION

Quasi-contractual recovery is often granted when one party has partially performed under a contract that is unenforceable. It provides an alternative to suing for damages and allows the party to recover the reasonable value of the partial performance. **■EXAMPLE 9.27** Ericson contracts to build two oil derricks for Petro Industries. The derricks are to be built over a period of three years, but the parties do not create a written contract. Therefore, the Statute of Frauds will bar the enforcement of the contract.[37] After Ericson completes one derrick, Petro Industries informs him that it will not pay for the derrick. Ericson can sue Petro Industries under the theory of quasi contract. ■

The Requirements of Quasi Contract

To recover on a quasi contract theory, the party seeking recovery must show the following:

1 The party conferred a benefit on the other party.

2 The party conferred the benefit with the reasonable expectation of being paid.

3 The party did not act as a volunteer in conferring the benefit.

4 The party receiving the benefit would be unjustly enriched by retaining the benefit without paying for it.

■EXAMPLE 9.28 In Example 9.27, Ericson can sue in quasi contract because all of the conditions for quasi-contractual recovery have been fulfilled. Ericson built the oil derrick with the expectation of being paid. The derrick conferred an obvious benefit on Petro Industries, and Petro Industries would be unjustly enriched if it was allowed to keep the derrick without paying Ericson for the work. Therefore, Ericson should be able to recover the reasonable value of the oil derrick that was built (under the theory of *quantum meruit*[38]—"as much as he or she deserves"). The reasonable value is ordinarily equal to the fair market value. ■

ELECTION OF REMEDIES

In many cases, a nonbreaching party has several remedies available. Because the remedies may be inconsistent with one another, the common law of contracts requires the party to choose which remedy to pursue. This is called *election of remedies*. The purpose of the doctrine of election of remedies is to prevent double recovery. **■EXAMPLE 9.29** Jefferson agrees to sell his land to Adams. Then Jefferson changes his mind and repudiates the contract. Adams can sue for compensatory damages or for specific performance. If Adams receives damages as a result of the breach, she should not also be granted specific performance of the sales contract because that would mean she would unfairly end up with both the land and the damages. The doctrine of election of remedies requires Adams to choose the remedy she wants, and it eliminates any possibility of double recovery. ■

In contrast, remedies under the UCC are cumulative. They include all of the remedies available under the UCC for breach of a sales or lease contract.[39] We will examine the UCC provisions on limited remedies in Chapter 12, in the context of the remedies available on the breach of a contract for the sale or lease of goods.

DON'T FORGET The function of a quasi contract is to impose a legal obligation on a party who made no actual promise.

BE AWARE Which remedy a plaintiff elects depends on the subject of the contract, the defenses of the breaching party, any tactical advantages of choosing a particular remedy, and what the plaintiff can prove with respect to the remedy sought.

---

37. Contracts that by their terms cannot be performed within one year from the day after the date of contract formation must be in writing to be enforceable (see Chapter 8).
38. Pronounced *kwahn*-tuhm *mehr*-oo-wuht.
39. See UCC 2–703 and 2–711.

REVIEWING Third Party Rights and Discharge

Val's Foods signs a contract to buy 1,500 pounds of basil from Sun Farms, a small organic herb grower, as long as an independent organization inspects and certifies that the crop contains no pesticide or herbicide residue. Val's has a contract with several restaurant chains to supply pesto and intends to use Sun Farms' basil in the pesto to fulfill these contracts. When Sun Farms is preparing to harvest the basil, an unexpected hailstorm destroys half the crop. Sun Farms attempts to purchase additional basil from other farms, but it is late in the season and the price is twice the normal market price. Sun Farms is too small to absorb this cost and immediately notifies Val's that it will not fulfill the contract. Using the information presented in the chapter, answer the following questions.

1 Suppose that the basil does not pass the chemical-residue inspection. Which concept discussed in the chapter might allow Val's to refuse to perform the contract in this situation?

2 Under which legal theory or theories might Sun Farms claim that its obligation under the contract has been discharged by operation of law? Discuss fully.

3 Suppose that Sun Farms contacts every basil grower in the country and buys the last remaining chemical-free basil anywhere. Nevertheless, Sun Farms is able to ship only 1,475 pounds to Val's. Would this fulfill Sun Farms' obligations to Val's? Why or why not?

4 Now suppose that Sun Farms sells its operations to Happy Valley Farms. As a part of the sale, all three parties agree that Happy Valley will provide the basil as stated under the original contract. What is this type of agreement called?

APPLICATION — What Do You Do When You Cannot Perform?*

Not every contract can be performed. If you are a contractor, you may take on a job that, for one reason or another, you cannot or do not wish to perform. Simply walking away from the job and hoping for the best normally is not the most effective way to avoid litigation—which can be costly, time consuming, and emotionally draining. Instead, you should consider various options that may reduce the likelihood of litigation.

For example, suppose that you are a building contractor and you sign a contract to build a home for the Andersons according to a set of plans that they provided. Performance is to begin on June 15. On June 1, Central Enterprises offers you a position that will yield you two and a half times the amount of net income you could earn as an independent builder. To take the job, you have to start on June 15. You cannot be in two places at the same time, so to accept the new position, you must breach the contract with the Andersons.

Consider Your Options

What can you do in this situation? One option is to subcontract the work to another builder and oversee the work your-self to make sure it conforms to the contract. Another option is to negotiate with the Andersons for a release. You can offer to find another qualified builder who will build a house of the same quality at the same price. Alternatively, you can offer to pay any additional costs if another builder takes the job and is more expensive. In any event, this additional cost would be one measure of damages that a court would impose on you if the Andersons prevailed in a suit for breach of contract (in addition to any costs the Andersons suffer as a result of the breach, such as costs due to the delay in construction). Thus, by making the offer, you might be able to avoid the expense of litigation—if the Andersons accept your offer.

Settlement Offers

Often, parties are reluctant to propose compromise settlements because they fear that what they say will be used against them in court if litigation ensues. Generally, however, offers for settlement will not be admitted in court to prove that you are liable for a breach of contract (though they are at times admissible to prove a party breached the duty of good faith).

* This *Application* is not meant to substitute for the services of an attorney who is licensed to practice law in your state.

CHECKLIST FOR THE CONTRACTOR WHO CANNOT PERFORM

1 Consider a compromise.
2 Subcontract out the work and oversee it.
3 Offer to find an alternative contractor to fulfill your obligation.

4 Make a cash offer to "buy" a release from your contract. Work with an attorney in making the offer, unless only an insignificant amount is involved.

KEY TERMS

alienation 273
anticipatory repudiation 282
assignee 271
assignment 271
assignor 271
breach of contract 270
commercial impracticability 286
concurrent conditions 280
condition 278
condition precedent 279
condition subsequent 279
consequential damages 288

delegatee 273
delegation of duties 273
delegator 273
discharge 277
frustration of purpose 286
impossibility of performance 285
incidental beneficiary 276
incidental damages 287
intended beneficiary 275
liquidated damages 292
mitigation of damages 289
nominal damages 289

novation 283
obligee 271
obligor 271
penalty 292
performance 277
privity of contract 270
restitution 294
specific performance 294
tender 280
third party beneficiary 275

CHAPTER SUMMARY — Contracts: Third Party Rights, Discharge, Breach, and Remedies

THIRD PARTY RIGHTS

Assignment
(See pages 271–273.)
	1. An assignment is the transfer of rights under a contract to a third party. The person assigning the rights is the *assignor,* and the party to whom the rights are assigned is the *assignee.* The assignee has a right to demand performance from the other original party to the contract.
	2. Generally, all rights can be assigned, except in the following circumstances:
	  a. When assignment is expressly prohibited by statute (for example, workers' compensation benefits).
	  b. When a contract calls for the performance of personal services.
	  c. When the assignment will materially increase or alter the risks or duties of the *obligor* (the party that is obligated to perform).
	  d. When the contract itself stipulates that the rights cannot be assigned (with some exceptions).

Delegation
(See pages 273–275.)
	1. A delegation is the transfer of duties under a contract to a third party (the *delegatee*), who then assumes the obligation of performing the contractual duties previously held by the one making the delegation (the *delegator*).
	2. As a general rule, any duty can be delegated, except in the following circumstances:
	  a. When performance depends on the personal skill or talents of the obligor.
	  b. When special trust has been placed in the obligor.
	  c. When performance by a third party will vary materially from that expected by the obligee (the one to whom the duty is owed) under the contract.

(Continued)

CHAPTER SUMMARY	Contracts: Third Party Rights, Discharge, Breach, and Remedies–Continued
Delegation–Continued	d. When the contract expressly prohibits delegation.
	3. A valid delegation of duties does not relieve the delegator of obligations under the contract. If the delegatee fails to perform, the delegator is still liable to the obligee.
	4. An "assignment of all rights" or an "assignment of the contract" is often construed to mean that both the rights and the duties arising under the contract are transferred to a third party.
Third Party Beneficiaries (See pages 275–277.)	A third party beneficiary contract is one made for the purpose of benefiting a third party.
	1. *Intended beneficiary*–One for whose benefit a contract is created. When the promisor (the one making the contractual promise that benefits a third party) fails to perform as promised, the third party can sue the promisor directly. Examples of third party beneficiaries are creditor and donee beneficiaries.
	2. *Incidental beneficiary*–A third party who indirectly (incidentally) benefits from a contract but for whose benefit the contract was not specifically intended. Incidental beneficiaries have no rights to the benefits received and cannot sue to have the contract enforced.
	CONTRACT DISCHARGE
Discharge by Performance (See pages 280–283.)	A contract may be discharged by complete (strict) performance or by substantial performance. In some instances, performance must be to the satisfaction of another. Totally inadequate performance constitutes a material breach of the contract. An anticipatory repudiation of a contract allows the other party to sue immediately for breach of contract.
Discharge by Agreement (See pages 283–284.)	Parties may agree to discharge their contractual obligations in several ways:
	1. *By rescission*–The parties mutually agree to rescind (cancel) the contract.
	2. *By novation*–A new party is substituted for one of the primary parties to a contract.
	3. *By accord and satisfaction*–The parties agree to render and accept performance different from that on which they originally agreed.
Discharge by Operation of Law (See pages 284–286.)	Parties' obligations under contracts may be discharged by operation of law owing to one of the following:
	1. Contract alteration.
	2. Statutes of limitations.
	3. Bankruptcy.
	4. Impossibility of performance.
	COMMON REMEDIES AVAILABLE TO NONBREACHING PARTY
Damages (See pages 286–293.)	The legal remedy designed to compensate the nonbreaching party for the loss of the bargain. By awarding monetary damages, the court tries to place the parties in the positions that they would have occupied had the contract been fully performed. The nonbreaching party frequently has a duty to *mitigate* (lessen or reduce) the damages incurred as a result of the contract's breach. There are five broad categories of damages:
	1. *Compensatory damages*–Damages that compensate the nonbreaching party for injuries actually sustained and proved to have arisen directly from the loss of the bargain resulting from the breach of contract.
	a. In breached contracts for the sale of goods, the usual measure of compensatory damages is the difference between the contract price and the market price.
	b. In breached contracts for the sale of land, the measure of damages is ordinarily the same as in contracts for the sale of goods.

CHAPTER SUMMARY Contracts: Third Party Rights, Discharge, Breach, and Remedies—Continued

Damages—Continued	c. In breached construction contracts, the measure of damages depends on which party breaches and at what stage of construction the breach occurs.
	2. *Consequential damages*—Damages resulting from special circumstances beyond the contract itself; the damages flow only from the consequences of a breach. For a party to recover consequential damages, the damages must be the foreseeable result of a breach of contract, and the breaching party must have known at the time the contract was formed that special circumstances existed that would cause the nonbreaching party to incur additional loss on breach of the contract. Also called *special damages.*
	3. *Punitive damages*—Damages awarded to punish the breaching party. Usually not awarded in an action for breach of contract unless a tort is involved.
	4. *Nominal damages*—Damages small in amount (such as one dollar) that are awarded when a breach has occurred but no actual injury has been suffered. Awarded only to establish that the defendant acted wrongfully.
	5. *Liquidated damages*—Damages that may be specified in a contract as the amount to be paid to the nonbreaching party in the event the contract is breached in the future. Clauses providing for liquidated damages are enforced if the damages were difficult to estimate at the time the contract was formed and if the amount stipulated is reasonable. If the amount is construed to be a penalty, the clause will not be enforced.
Rescission and Restitution (See page 294.)	1. *Rescission*—A remedy whereby a contract is canceled and the parties are restored to the original positions that they occupied prior to the transaction. Available when fraud, a mistake, duress, or failure of consideration is present. The rescinding party must give prompt notice of the rescission to the breaching party.
	2. *Restitution*—When a contract is rescinded, both parties must make restitution to each other by returning the goods, property, or funds previously conveyed. Restitution prevents the unjust enrichment of the parties.
Specific Performance (See pages 294–295.)	An equitable remedy calling for the performance of the act promised in the contract. This remedy is available only in special situations—such as those involving contracts for the sale of unique goods or land—and when monetary damages would be an inadequate remedy. Specific performance is not available as a remedy for breached contracts for personal services.
Reformation (See page 296.)	An equitable remedy allowing a contract to be "reformed," or rewritten, to reflect the parties' true intentions. Available when an agreement is imperfectly expressed in writing.
Recovery Based on Quasi Contract (See pages 296–297.)	An equitable theory imposed by the courts to obtain justice and prevent unjust enrichment in a situation in which no enforceable contract exists. The party seeking recovery must show the following:
	1. A benefit was conferred on the other party.
	2. The party conferring the benefit did so with the expectation of being paid.
	3. The benefit was not volunteered.
	4. Retaining the benefit without paying for it would result in the unjust enrichment of the party receiving the benefit.

CONTRACT DOCTRINES RELATING TO REMEDIES

Election of Remedies (See page 297.)	A common law doctrine under which a nonbreaching party must choose one remedy from those available. This doctrine prevents double recovery. Under the UCC, remedies are cumulative for the breach of a contract for the sale of goods.

FOR REVIEW

Answers for the even-numbered questions in this **For Review** *section can be found in Appendix E at the end of this text.*

1 What is the difference between an assignment and a delegation?

2 What factors indicate that a third party beneficiary is an intended beneficiary?

3 What is the difference between compensatory damages and consequential damages? What are nominal damages, and when do courts award nominal damages?

4 Under what circumstances will equitable remedies be available?

5 What is the rationale underlying the doctrine of election of remedies?

■

QUESTIONS AND CASE PROBLEMS

HYPOTHETICAL SCENARIOS

9.1 Third Party Beneficiaries. Wilken owes Rivera $2,000. Howie promises Wilken that he will pay Rivera the $2,000 in return for Wilken's promise to give Howie's children guitar lessons. Is Rivera an intended beneficiary of the Howie-Wilken contract? Explain.

9.2 Anticipatory Repudiation. ABC Clothiers, Inc., has a contract with Taylor & Sons, a retailer, to deliver one thousand summer suits to Taylor's place of business on or before May 1. On April 1, Taylor senior receives a letter from ABC informing him that ABC will not be able to make the delivery as scheduled. Taylor is very upset, as he had planned a big ad campaign. He wants to file a suit against ABC immediately (April 2). Taylor's son, Tom, tells his father that filing a lawsuit is not proper until ABC actually fails to deliver the suits on May 1. Discuss fully who is correct, Taylor senior or Tom.

9.3 Hypothetical Question with Sample Answer. Aron, a college student, signs a one-year lease agreement that runs from September 1 to August 31. The lease agreement specifies that the lease cannot be assigned without the landlord's consent. In late May, Aron decides not to go to summer school and

assigns the balance of the lease (three months) to a close friend, Erica. The landlord objects to the assignment and denies Erica access to the apartment. Aron claims that Erica is financially sound and should be allowed the full rights and privileges of an assignee. Discuss fully whether the landlord or Aron is correct.

For a sample answer to Question 9.3, go to Appendix F at the end of this text.

9.4 Liquidated Damages. Carnack contracts to sell his house and lot to Willard for $100,000. The terms of the contract call for Willard to pay 10 percent of the purchase price as a deposit toward the purchase price, or as a down payment. The terms further stipulate that should the buyer breach the contract, Carnack will retain the deposit as liquidated damages. Willard pays the deposit, but because her expected financing of the $90,000 balance falls through, she breaches the contract. Two weeks later, Carnack sells the house and lot to Balkova for $105,000. Willard demands her $10,000 back, but Carnack refuses, claiming that Willard's breach and the contract terms entitle him to keep the deposit. Discuss who is correct.

■

CASE PROBLEMS

9.5 Substantial Performance. Adolf and Ida Krueger contracted with Pisani Construction, Inc., to erect a metal building as an addition to an existing structure. The two structures were to share a common wall, and the frames and panel heights of the new building were to match those of the existing structure. Shortly before completion of the project, however, it was

apparent that the roofline of the new building was approximately three inches higher than that of the existing structure. Pisani modified the ridge caps of the buildings to blend the rooflines. The discrepancy had other consequences, however, including misalignment of the gutters and windows of the two buildings, which resulted in an icing problem in the winter.

The Kruegers occupied the new structure but refused to make the last payment under the contract. Pisani filed a suit in a Connecticut state court to collect. Did Pisani substantially perform its obligations? Should the Kruegers be ordered to pay? Why or why not? [*Pisani Construction, Inc. v. Krueger*, 68 Conn.App. 361, 791 A.2d 634 (2002)]

9.6 Liquidated Damages versus Penalties. Every homeowner in the Putnam County, Indiana, subdivision of Stardust Hills must be a member of the Stardust Hills Owners Association, Inc., and must pay annual dues of $200 for the maintenance of common areas and other community services. Under the association's rules, dues paid more than ten days late "shall bear a delinquent fee at a rate of $2.00 per day." Phyllis Gaddis failed to pay the dues on a Stardust Hills lot that she owned. Late fees began to accrue. Nearly two months later, the association filed a suit in an Indiana state court to collect the unpaid dues and the late fees. Gaddis argued in response that the delinquent fee was an unenforceable penalty. What questions should be considered in determining the status of this fee? Should the association's rule regarding assessment of the fee be enforced? Explain. [*Gaddis v. Stardust Hills Owners Association, Inc.*, 804 N.E.2d 231 (Ind.App. 2004)]

9.7 Case Problem with Sample Answer. The National Collegiate Athletic Association (NCAA) regulates intercollegiate amateur athletics among more than 1,200 colleges and universities with which it contracts. Among other things, the NCAA maintains rules of eligibility for student participation in intercollegiate athletic events. Jeremy Bloom, a high school football and track star, was recruited to play football at the University of Colorado (CU). Before enrolling, he competed in Olympic and professional World Cup skiing events, becoming the World Cup champion in freestyle moguls. During the Olympics, Bloom appeared on MTV and was offered other paid entertainment opportunities, including a chance to host a show on Nickelodeon. Bloom was also paid to endorse certain ski equipment and contracted to model clothing for Tommy Hilfiger. On Bloom's behalf, CU asked the NCAA to waive its rules restricting student-athlete endorsement and media activities. The NCAA refused, and Bloom quit the activities to play football for CU. He filed a suit in a Colorado state court against the NCAA, however, asserting breach of contract on the ground that its rules permitted these activities if they were needed to support a professional athletic career. The NCAA responded that Bloom did not have standing to pursue this claim. What contract has allegedly been breached in this case? Is Bloom a party to this contract? If not, is he a third party beneficiary of it, and if so, is his status intended or incidental? Explain. [*Bloom v. National Collegiate Athletic Association*, 93 P.3d 621 (Colo.App. 2004)]

After you have answered Problem 9.7, compare your answer with the sample answer given on the Web site that accompanies this text. Go to **academic.cengage.com/blaw/blt**, select "Chapter 9," and click on "Case Problem with Sample Answer."

9.8 Material Breach. Kermit Johnson formed FB & I Building Products, Inc., in Watertown, South Dakota, to sell building materials. In December 1998, FB & I contracted with Superior Truss & Components in Minneota, Minnesota, "to exclusively sell Superior's open-faced wall panels, floor panels, roof trusses and other miscellaneous products." In March 2000, FB & I agreed to exclusively sell Component Manufacturing Co.'s building products in Colorado. Two months later, Superior learned of FB & I's deal with Component and terminated its contract with FB & I. That contract provided that on cancellation, "FB & I will be entitled to retain the customers that they continue to sell and service with Superior products." Superior refused to honor this provision. Between the cancellation of FB & I's contract and 2004, Superior made $2,327,528 in sales to FB & I customers without paying a commission. FB & I filed a suit in a South Dakota state court against Superior, alleging, in part, breach of contract and seeking the unpaid commissions. Superior insisted that FB & I had materially breached their contract, excusing Superior from performing. In whose favor should the court rule and why? [*FB & I Building Products, Inc. v. Superior Truss & Components, a Division of Banks Lumber, Inc.*, 727 N.W.2d 474 (S.D. 2007)]

9.9 A Question of Ethics. *King County, Washington, hired Frank Coluccio Construction Co. (FCCC) to act as general contractor for a public works project involving the construction of a small utility tunnel under the Duwamish Waterway. FCCC hired Donald B. Murphy Contractors, Inc. (DBM), as a subcontractor. DBM was responsible for constructing an access shaft at the eastern end of the tunnel. Problems arose during construction, including a "blow in" of the access shaft when it filled with water, soil, and debris. FCCC and DBM incurred substantial expenses from the repairs and delays. Under the project contract, King County was supposed to buy an insurance policy to "insure against physical loss or damage by perils included under an 'All Risk' Builder's Risk policy." Any claim under this policy was to be filed through the insured. King County, which had general property damage insurance, did not obtain an all-risk builder's risk policy. For the losses attributable to the blow-in, FCCC and DBM submitted builder's risk claims, which the county denied. FCCC filed a suit in a Washington state court against King County, alleging, among other claims, breach of contract.* [Frank Coluccio Construction Co. v. King County, 136 Wash.App. 751, 150 P.3d 1147 (Div. 1 2007)]

1 King County's property damage policy specifically excluded, at the county's request, coverage of tunnels. The county drafted its contract with FCCC to require the all-risk builder's risk policy and authorize itself to "sponsor" claims. When FCCC and DBM filed their claims, the county secretly colluded with its property damage insurer to deny payment. What do these facts indicate about the county's ethics and legal liability in this situation?

2 Could DBM, as a third party to the contract between King County and FCCC, maintain an action on the contract against King County? Discuss.

3 All-risk insurance is a promise to pay on the "fortuitous" happening of a loss or damage from any cause except those causes that are specifically excluded. Payment is not usually made on a loss that, at the time the insurance was obtained, the claimant subjectively knew would occur. If a loss results from faulty workmanship on the part of a contractor, should the obligation to pay under an all-risk policy be discharged? Explain.

CRITICAL THINKING AND WRITING ASSIGNMENTS

9.10 **Critical Legal Thinking.** The concept of substantial performance permits a party to be discharged from a contract even though the party has not fully performed her or his obligations according to the contract's terms. Is this fair? What policy interests are at issue here?

9.11 **Critical Legal Thinking.** Review the discussion of the doctrine of election of remedies in this chapter. What are some of the advantages and disadvantages of this doctrine?

9.12 **Video Question.** Go to this text's Web site at **academic.cengage.com/blaw/blt** and select "Chapter 9." Click on "Video Questions" and view the video titled *Midnight Run.* Then answer the following questions.

1 In the video, Eddie (Joe Pantoliano) and Jack (Robert De Niro) negotiate a contract for Jack to find "the Duke," a mob accountant who embezzled funds, and bring him back for trial. Assume that the contract is valid. If Jack breaches the contract by failing to bring in the Duke, what kinds of remedies, if any, can Eddie seek? Explain your answer.

2 Would the equitable remedy of specific performance be available to either Jack or Eddie in the event of a breach? Why or why not?

3 Now assume that the contract between Eddie and Jack is unenforceable. Nevertheless, Jack performs his side of the bargain by bringing in the Duke. Does Jack have any legal recourse in this situation? Explain.

ONLINE ACTIVITIES

PRACTICAL INTERNET EXERCISES

Go to this text's Web site at **academic.cengage.com/blaw/blt**, select "Chapter 9," and click on "Practical Internet Exercises." There you will find the following Internet research exercises that you can perform to learn more about the topics covered in this chapter.

PRACTICAL INTERNET EXERCISE 9-1 LEGAL PERSPECTIVE—Anticipatory Repudiation

PRACTICAL INTERNET EXERCISE 9-2 MANAGEMENT PERSPECTIVE—The Duty to Mitigate

BEFORE THE TEST

Go to this text's Web site at **academic.cengage.com/blaw/blt**, select "Chapter 9," and click on "Interactive Quizzes." You will find a number of interactive questions relating to this chapter.

CHAPTER 10
E-Contracts and E-Signatures

LEARNING OBJECTIVES

AFTER READING THIS CHAPTER, YOU SHOULD BE ABLE TO ANSWER THE FOLLOWING QUESTIONS:

1 What are some important clauses to include when making offers to form electronic contracts, or e-contracts?

2 How do shrink-wrap and click-on agreements \differ from other contracts? How have traditional laws been applied to these agreements?

3 What is an electronic signature? Are electronic signatures valid?

4 What is a partnering agreement? What purpose does it serve?

5 What is the Uniform Electronic Transactions Act (UETA)? What are some of the major provisions of this act?

> "[B]usiness models and methods for doing business have evolved to take advantage of the speed, efficiencies, and cost benefits of electronic technologies."
>
> Prefatory Note, Uniform Electronic Transactions Act

As the chapter-opening quotation indicates, electronic technology offers businesses several advantages, including speed, efficiency, and lower costs. In the 1990s, many observers argued that the development of cyberspace was revolutionary. Therefore, new legal theories, and new laws, would be needed to govern **e-contracts,** or contracts entered into electronically. To date, however, most courts have simply adapted traditional contract law principles and, when applicable, provisions of the Uniform Commercial Code to cases involving e-contract disputes.

In the first part of this chapter, we look at how traditional laws are being applied to contracts formed online. We then examine some new laws that have been created to apply in situations in which traditional laws governing contracts have sometimes been thought inadequate. For example, traditional laws governing signature and writing requirements are not easily adapted to contracts formed in the online environment. Thus, new laws have been created to address these issues.

E-CONTRACT
A contract that is formed electronically.

FORMING CONTRACTS ONLINE

Today, numerous contracts are being formed online. Although the medium through which these contracts are generated has changed, the age-old problems attending contract formation have not. Disputes concerning contracts formed online continue to center on contract terms and whether the parties voluntarily assented to those terms.

Note that online contracts may be formed not only for the sale of goods and services but also for *licensing*. The "sale" of software generally involves a license, or a right to use the software, rather than the passage of title (ownership rights) from the seller to the buyer. **■EXAMPLE 10.1** Galynn wants to obtain software that will allow her to work on spreadsheets on her BlackBerry. She goes online and purchases GridMagic. During the transaction, she has to click on several on-screen "I agree" boxes to indicate that she understands that she is purchasing only the right to use the software and will not obtain any ownership rights. After she agrees to these terms (the licensing agreement), she can download the software to her computer. ■

As you read through the following pages, keep in mind that although we typically refer to the offeror and the offeree as a *seller* and a *buyer*, in many transactions these parties would be more accurately described as a *licensor* and a *licensee*.

Online Offers

Sellers doing business via the Internet can protect themselves against contract disputes and legal liability by creating offers that clearly spell out the terms that will govern their transactions if the offers are accepted. All important terms should be conspicuous and easy to view.

Displaying the Offer The seller's Web site should include a hypertext link to a page containing the full contract so that potential buyers are made aware of the terms to which they are assenting. The contract generally must be displayed online in a readable format such as a twelve-point typeface. All provisions should be reasonably clear. **■EXAMPLE 10.2** Suppose that Netquip sells a variety of heavy equipment, such as trucks and trailers, online at its Web site. Because Netquip's pricing schedule is very complex, the schedule must be fully provided and explained on the Web site. In addition, the terms of the sale (such as any warranty and the refund policy) must be fully disclosed. ■

Provisions to Include An important rule to keep in mind is that the offeror controls the offer and thus the resulting contract. The seller should therefore anticipate the terms he or she wants to include in a contract and provide for them in the offer. In some instances, a standardized contract form may suffice. At a minimum, an online offer should include the following provisions:

1 A clause that clearly indicates what constitutes the buyer's agreement to the terms of the offer, such as a box containing the words "I accept" that the buyer can click on to indicate acceptance. (Mechanisms for accepting online offers are discussed in detail later in the chapter.)

2 A provision specifying how payment for the goods (including any applicable taxes) must be made.

3 A statement of the seller's refund and return policies.

4 Disclaimers of liability for certain uses of the goods. For example, an online seller of business forms may add a disclaimer that the seller does not accept responsibility for the buyer's reliance on the forms rather than on an attorney's advice.

5 A provision specifying the remedies available to the buyer if the goods are found to be defective or if the contract is otherwise breached. Any limitation of remedies should be clearly spelled out.

6 A statement indicating how the seller will use the information gathered about the buyer.

7 Provisions relating to dispute settlement, such as an arbitration clause or a *forum-selection clause* (discussed next).

Dispute-Settlement Provisions   Online offers frequently include provisions relating to dispute settlement. For example, the offer might include an arbitration clause specifying that any dispute arising under the contract will be arbitrated in a designated forum.

Many online contracts also contain a **forum-selection clause** (indicating the forum, or location, for the resolution of any dispute arising under the contract). As discussed in Chapter 3, significant jurisdictional issues may occur when parties are at a great distance, as they often are when they form contracts via the Internet. A forum-selection clause will help to avert future jurisdictional problems and also help to ensure that the seller will not be required to appear in court in a distant state.

> **FORUM-SELECTION CLAUSE**
> A provision in a contract designating the court, jurisdiction, or tribunal that will decide any disputes arising under the contract.

Is it fair to hold online purchasers to terms and conditions that they do not read? The purchase of a ticket for a cruise obviously constitutes a contract between the purchaser and the cruise line. Such a contract usually includes a forum-selection clause. Increasingly, people are booking their cruise ship accommodations online, but when they do, they often do not read the "fine print" of the contract that includes the forum-selection clause.

To their dismay, passengers who brought a class-action suit against Holland America after becoming ill during a cruise offered by that company learned that failing to read the details of the contract could force them to bring their suit in another state. In this case, the actual paper tickets that the passengers received had the forum-selection clause printed on them in all capital letters, but passengers who had booked their accommodations online did not receive their tickets until just before the cruise. At that point, any passengers who did not like the clause could not cancel without forfeiting their fares. Nonetheless, the court held that the forum-selection clause was enforceable because the passengers had ample time to read the terms of the contract on the cruise line's Web site. Fair or not, the dispute had to be litigated in Washington State as specified in the forum-selection clause on the cruise tickets.[1]

Online Acceptances

The *Restatement (Second) of Contracts*—a compilation of common law contract principles—states that parties may agree to a contract "by written or spoken words or by other action or by failure to act."[2] The Uniform Commercial Code (UCC), which governs sales contracts, has a similar provision. Section 2–204 of the UCC states that any contract for the sale of goods "may be made in any manner sufficient to show agreement, including conduct by both parties which recognizes the existence of such a contract."

Click-On Agreements   The courts have used these provisions to conclude that a binding contract can be created by conduct, including the act of clicking on a box indicating "I accept" or "I agree" to accept an online offer. When an online buyer indicates his or her assent to be bound by the terms of the offer by clicking on some on-screen prompt, a **click-on agreement** (sometimes referred to as a *click-on license* or *click-wrap agreement*) is formed. Exhibit 10–1 on the next page shows a portion of a click-on agreement that accompanies a package of software made and marketed by Microsoft.

Generally, the law does not require that all of the parties to a contract must actually have read all of its terms for the contract to be effective. Therefore, clicking on a button or box that states "I agree" to certain terms can be enough. The terms may be contained on a Web site through which the buyer is obtaining goods or services, or they may appear

> **CLICK-ON AGREEMENT**
> An agreement that arises when a buyer, engaging in a transaction on a computer, indicates assent to be bound by the terms of an offer by clicking on a button that says, for example, "I agree"; sometimes referred to as a *click-on license* or a *click-wrap agreement*.

---

1. *Schlessinger v. Holland America, N.V.*, 120 Cal.App.4th 552, 16 Cal.Rptr.3d 5 (2004).
2. *Restatement (Second) of Contracts*, Section 19.

EXHIBIT 10–1 A Click-On Agreement

This exhibit illustrates an online offer to form a contract. To accept the offer, the user simply scrolls down the page and clicks on the "Accept" box.

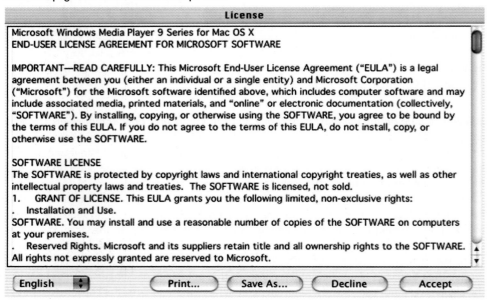

on a computer screen when software is loaded from a CD-ROM or DVD or downloaded from the Internet.

In the following case, the court considered the enforceability of a click-on (click-wrap) software licensing agreement that included a forum-selection clause.

CASE 10.1 **Mortgage Plus, Inc. v. DocMagic, Inc.**

United States District Court, District of Kansas, __ F.Supp.2d __ (2004).

FACTS In 1997, Mortgage Plus, Inc., a mortgage lender in Kansas, asked DocMagic, Inc., a California firm, for software to prepare and manage loan documents, and for document-preparation services. DocMagic sent Mortgage Plus a CD-ROM containing the software, which had to be loaded onto a computer. Before the software could be installed, a window displayed a "Software License and User Agreement" on the screen. The agreement asked, "Do you accept all terms of the preceding License Agreement? If you choose No, Setup will close." A click on a "Yes" button was needed to continue. The agreement also included a clause designating California as the venue for the resolution of any disputes. To prepare loan documents, the software asked for certain information, which it used to create a worksheet. The worksheet was e-mailed to

DocMagic, which completed the documents and returned them via e-mail. Over the next six years, people who had obtained loans from Mortgage Plus filed claims against the firm, charging it with mistakes, which cost $150,000 to resolve. Mortgage Plus filed a suit in a federal district court against DocMagic, alleging that its software failed to produce documents meeting certain legal requirements. The defendant filed a motion to transfer the suit to a federal court in California based on the clause in the click-on agreement.

ISSUE Is a forum-selection clause contained in a click-on software licensing agreement enforceable?

DECISION Yes. The court concluded that the software licensing agreement was a valid contract because a user had to agree to its terms before the software could be installed

CASE 10.1—Continued

and used. Hence, the forum-selection clause was enforceable, and the court ordered the suit to be transferred to a federal district court in California.

REASON Mortgage Plus argued that the parties had negotiated and entered into a contract before DocMagic shipped the software and that the forum-selection clause was a later, improper attempt to modify this contract. The court, however, found no evidence of this purported "original contractual agreement." Mortgage Plus also argued that it was not aware of, and thus did not accept, the licensing agreement, declaring that "a click-wrap agreement consisting of a window entitled 'Software Licensing Agreement' appearing prior to

installation of software cannot be construed as a legally binding contract." The court, however, explained that "[t]he software required users to accept the terms by clicking through a series of screens before they could access and subsequently install the software." Because Mortgage Plus had a choice as to whether to install the software and utilize the related services, "installation and use of the software with the attached license constituted an affirmative acceptance of the license terms."

WHAT IF THE FACTS WERE DIFFERENT? *Suppose that the individual who clicked on the "Yes" button and installed the software was not authorized to do this. Would the result have been different? Why or why not?*

Shrink-Wrap Agreements In many ways, click-on agreements are the Internet equivalents of *shrink-wrap agreements* (or *shrink-wrap licenses*, as they are sometimes called). A **shrink-wrap agreement** is an agreement whose terms are expressed inside a box in which the goods are packaged. (The term *shrink-wrap* refers to the plastic that covers the box.) Usually, the party who opens the box is told that she or he agrees to the terms by keeping whatever is in the box. Similarly, when the purchaser opens a software package, he or she agrees to abide by the terms of the limited license agreement.

SHRINK-WRAP AGREEMENT
An agreement whose terms are expressed in a document located inside a box in which goods (usually software) are packaged; sometimes called a *shrink-wrap license.*

■EXAMPLE 10.3 John orders a new computer from a national company, which ships the computer to him. Along with the computer, the box contains an agreement setting forth the terms of the sale, including what remedies are available. The document also states that John's retention of the computer for longer than thirty days will be construed as an acceptance of the terms. ■

In most instances, a shrink-wrap agreement is not between a retailer and a buyer, but between the manufacturer of the hardware or software and the ultimate buyer-user of the product. The terms generally concern warranties, remedies, and other issues associated with the use of the product.

Shrink-Wrap Agreements and Enforceable Contract Terms. In many cases, the courts have enforced the terms of shrink-wrap agreements in the same way as the terms of other contracts. Some courts have reasoned that by including the terms with the product, the seller proposed a contract that the buyer could accept by using the product after having an opportunity to read the terms. Thus, a buyer's failure to object to terms contained within a shrink-wrapped software package may constitute an acceptance of the terms by conduct.[3] Also, it seems practical from a business's point of view to enclose a full statement of the legal terms of a sale with the product rather than to read the statement over the phone, for example, when a buyer calls to order the product.

Shrink-Wrap Terms That May Not Be Enforced. Nevertheless, the courts have not enforced all of the terms included in shrink-wrap agreements. One important consideration is whether the parties form their contract before or after the seller communicates the terms of the shrink-wrap agreement to the buyer. If a buyer learned of the shrink-wrap terms *after* the parties entered into a contract, a court may conclude that those terms were proposals for additional terms and were not part of the contract unless the buyer expressly

---

3. For a leading case on this issue, see *ProCD, Inc. v. Zeidenberg*, 86 F.3d 1447 (7th Cir. 1996).

Avoiding Deception in Software Sales

Sometimes, businesspersons who include shrink-wrap licenses with their products may have some terms elsewhere, such as on a disk or on a download page on the Internet. Not including all of the terms in the shrink-wrap agreement, however, can lead to problems—as one software producer learned when the state of New York brought an action against its company for fraud.

The Lawsuit against Network Associates, Inc.

Network Associates, Inc. (NA), develops and sells software, including Gauntlet, a software firewall product, via the Internet. NA included a restrictive clause on its disks and on its Internet download page—but not in its license agreement that accompanied its products.

The restrictive clause provided that anyone installing the Gauntlet software accepted the terms and conditions of the license agreement in the box and urged users to read the license before installing the software. The clause also stated, among other things, that the customer "will not publish reviews of this product without prior consent from Network Associates." The problem was that the license agreement in the box stated that the agreement contained all of the rights and duties of the parties. How, then, did the restrictive clause apply to the sale?

When *Network World Fusion*, an online magazine, published a comparative review of firewall software products,

including Gauntlet, without NA's permission, NA protested. Ultimately, the state attorney general of New York brought an action against NA for fraud.

The Fraud Issue

According to the New York court hearing the case, NA's restrictive clause misled customers and was thus deceptive. First, the license agreement stated that it contained all of the terms of the agreement. Therefore, the rules and regulations listed in the restrictive clause appeared to be independent of the license contract. This could mislead purchasers of the software because they might believe that the restriction was created by some other entity, such as the federal government.

For these reasons, the court concluded that the restrictive clause was deceptive and constituted fraud. The court ordered NA to stop including the clause in its software. The court also ordered NA to reveal "the number of instances in which software was sold on disks or through the Internet containing the above-mentioned language in order for the court to determine what, if any, penalties and costs should be ordered."[a]

 FOR CRITICAL ANALYSIS *What is the difference, if any, between reading a restrictive clause in a shrink-wrap agreement and accessing it through a link as part of a click-on agreement?*

a. *People v. Network Associates, Inc.,* 195 Misc.2d 384, 758 N.Y.S.2d 466 (2003).

---

agreed to them.[4] Could any other problems arise with shrink-wrap agreements? For a discussion of a case involving an issue that arose for one firm, see this chapter's *Adapting the Law to the Online Environment* feature.

BROWSE-WRAP TERMS
Terms and conditions of use that are presented to an Internet user at the time certain products, such as software, are being downloaded but that need not be agreed to (by clicking "I agree," for example) before the user is able to install or use the product.

Browse-Wrap Terms   Like the terms of a click-on agreement, **browse-wrap terms** can occur in a transaction conducted over the Internet. Unlike a click-on agreement, however, browse-wrap terms do not require an Internet user to assent to the terms before, say, downloading or using certain software. In other words, a person can install the software without clicking "I agree" to the terms of a license. Offerors of browse-wrap terms generally assert that the terms are binding without the user's active consent.

Critics contend that browse-wrap terms are not enforceable because they do not satisfy the basic elements of contract formation. It has been suggested that to form a valid contract online, a user must at least be presented with the terms before indicating assent.[5] With respect to a browse-wrap term, this would require that a user navigate past it and agree to it before being able to obtain whatever is being granted to the user.

---

4. See, for example, *Klocek v. Gateway, Inc.,* 104 F.Supp.2d 1332 (D.Kans. 2000).
5. American Bar Association Committee on the Law of Cyberspace, "Click-Through Agreements: Strategies for Avoiding Disputes on the Validity of Assent" (document presented at the annual American Bar Association meeting in August 2001).

The following case involved the enforceability of a clause in an agreement that the court characterized as a browse-wrap license.

CASE 10.2 Specht v. Netscape Communications Corp.

United States Court of Appeals, Second Circuit, 306 F.3d 17 (2002).

FACTS Netscape Communications Corporation's "SmartDownload" software makes it easier for users to download files from the Internet without losing progress if they pause to do some other task or if their Internet connection is interrupted. Netscape offers SmartDownload free of charge on its Web site to those who indicate, by clicking on a designated box, that they wish to obtain it. John Gibson clicked on the box and downloaded the software. On the Web site's download page is a reference to a license agreement that is visible only by scrolling to the next screen. Affirmatively indicating assent to the agreement is not required to download the software. The agreement provides that any disputes arising from use of the software are to be submitted to arbitration in California. Believing that the use of SmartDownload transmits private information about its users, Gibson and others filed a suit in a federal district court in New York against Netscape, alleging violations of federal law. Netscape asked the court to order the parties to arbitration in California, according to the license agreement.

ISSUE Was the arbitration clause in the license agreement enforceable?

DECISION No. The court denied the motion to compel arbitration.

REASON The court applied Article 2 of the Uniform Commercial Code because "[a]lthough in this case the product was provided free of charge, the roles are essentially the same as when an individual uses the Internet to purchase software from a company: here, the Plaintiff requested Defendant's product by clicking on an icon marked 'Download,' and Defendant then tendered the product." The court emphasized that unless the plaintiffs agreed to the license contract, they could not be bound by the arbitration clause. After discussing the forms of license agreements that accompany sales of software (shrink-wrap, click-on, and browse-wrap licenses) and their enforceability, the court characterized Netscape's license in this case as a browse-wrap license. According to the court, Netscape's SmartDownload "allows a user to download and use the software without taking any action that plainly manifests assent to the terms of the associated license or indicates an understanding that a contract is being formed." The court pointed out that "the individual obtaining SmartDownload is not made aware that he is entering into a contract * * * . [T]he user need not view any license agreement terms or even any reference to a license agreement, and need not do anything to manifest assent." The court reasoned that the plaintiffs did not assent to the license agreement and thus were not subject to the arbitration clause.

 WHY IS THIS CASE IMPORTANT? *The ruling in this case is significant because it marks an application of traditional contract principles to a type of dispute that can arise only in the online context. In the case, the court clearly applied a long-standing principle of contract law: a person will not be bound to an agreement to which he or she did not assent.*

E-SIGNATURES

In many instances, a contract cannot be enforced unless it is signed by the party against whom enforcement is sought. In the days when many people could not write, they signed documents with an "X." Then handwritten signatures became common, followed by typed signatures, printed signatures, and, most recently, digital signatures that are transmitted electronically. Throughout the evolution of signature technology, the question of what constitutes a valid signature has arisen again and again, and with good reason—without some consensus on what constitutes a valid signature, less business and legal work could be accomplished. In this section, we look at how electronic signatures, or *e-signatures*, can be created and verified on e-contracts, as well as how the parties can enter into agreements that prevent disputes concerning e-signatures.

E-Signature Technologies

E-SIGNATURE
As defined by the Uniform Electronic Transactions Act, "an electronic sound, symbol, or process attached to or logically associated with a record and executed or adopted by a person with the intent to sign the record."

Today, numerous technologies allow electronic documents to be signed. An **e-signature** has been defined as "an electronic sound, symbol, or process attached to or logically associated with a record and executed or adopted by a person with the intent to sign the record."[6] Thus, e-signatures include encrypted digital signatures, names (intended as signatures) at the ends of e-mail messages, and "clicks" on a Web page if the click includes the identification of the person. The technologies for creating e-signatures generally fall into one of two categories, *digitized handwritten signatures* and *public-key infrastructure–based digital signatures*. A digitized signature is a graphical image of a handwritten signature that is often created using a digital pen and pad, such as an ePad, and special software. For security reasons, the strokes of a person's signature can be measured by software to authenticate the person signing (this is referred to as *signature dynamics*).

CYBERNOTARY
A legally recognized authority that can certify the validity of digital signatures.

In a public-key infrastructure (such as an *asymmetric cryptosystem*), two mathematically linked but different keys are generated—a private signing key and a public validation key. A digital signature is created when the signer uses the private key to create a unique mark on an electronic document. The appropriate software enables the recipient of the document to use the public key to verify the identity of the signer. A **cybernotary**, or legally recognized certification authority, issues the key pair, identifies the owner of the keys, and certifies the validity of the public key. The cybernotary also serves as a repository for public keys.

Other forms of e-signatures have been—or are now being—developed as well. Some e-signatures use *smart cards*, which are the size of a credit or debit card but can be used to establish a person's identity (smart cards will be discussed in Chapter 15). In addition, unique e-signatures can be created using a scanned image of a person's retina, fingerprint, or face and then matching the image to a numeric code.

State Laws Governing E-Signatures

The ePad-Ink is an electronic signature pad that can be used to insert handwritten signatures into electronic documents. What type of e-signature technology does this device utilize? What procedure is used to verify the authenticity of a signature created using this ePad?
(Photo Courtesy of Interlink Electronics)

Most states have laws governing e-signatures. The problem is that the state e-signature laws are not uniform. Some states—California is a notable example—do not allow many types of documents to be signed with e-signatures, whereas other states are more permissive. Additionally, some states recognize only digital signatures as valid, while others permit other types of e-signatures.

The National Conference of Commissioners on Uniform State Laws, in an attempt to create more uniformity among the states, promulgated the Uniform Electronic Transactions Act (UETA) in 1999. To date, the UETA has been adopted, at least in part, by forty-eight states. The UETA provides, among other things, that a signature may not be denied legal effect or enforceability solely because it is in electronic form. (Other aspects of the UETA will be discussed shortly.)

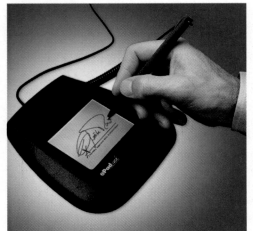

Federal Law on E-Signatures and E-Documents

In 2000, Congress enacted the Electronic Signatures in Global and National Commerce Act (E-SIGN Act)[7] to provide that no contract, record, or signature may be "denied legal effect" solely because it is in an electronic form. In other words, under this law, an electronic signature is as

---

6. This definition is from the Uniform Electronic Transactions Act, which will be discussed later in this chapter.
7. 15 U.S.C. Sections 7001 *et seq.*

valid as a signature on paper, and an electronic document can be as enforceable as a paper one.

For an electronic signature to be enforceable, the contracting parties must have agreed to use e-signatures. For an electronic document to be valid, it must be in a form that can be retained and accurately reproduced.

The E-SIGN Act does not apply to all types of documents, however. Contracts and documents that are exempt include court papers, divorce decrees, evictions, foreclosures, health-insurance terminations, prenuptial agreements, and wills. Also, the only agreements governed by the UCC that fall under this law are those covered by Articles 2 and 2A and UCC 1–107 and 1–206. Despite these limitations, the E-SIGN Act greatly expands the possibilities for contracting online.

In the following case, the court applied a variety of contract principles to determine the legal effect of an exchange of e-mails, plus a phone call.

CASE 10.3   Amber Chemical, Inc. v. Reilly Industries, Inc.

United States District Court, Eastern District of California, __ F.Supp.2d __ (2007).

FACTS Amber Chemical, Inc., a California corporation, sells chemicals to oil companies and agricultural businesses. In the fall of each year, Amber agreed to buy a minimum quantity of potassium chloride from Reilly Industries, Inc., an Indiana firm, at a price set by Reilly. Based on this price, Amber entered into contracts with its own customers. Amber then submitted periodic purchase orders to Reilly to process. In the fall of 2003, through e-mails between Reilly employee Brett Wilhelm and Amber employee Bob Brister, Reilly agreed to sell potassium chloride throughout 2004 for $122.50 per ton as long as the quantity of Amber's purchases met or exceeded the quantity of its purchases in 2003. In a phone call from Wilhelm, Brister orally confirmed that Amber would buy as much as or more than it had the previous year. In mid-March 2004, Reilly sold its potassium chloride business, and the shipments to Amber stopped. In a suit between the parties in a federal district court, Amber alleged breach of contract. Reilly filed a motion for summary judgment, claiming that the parties did not have a written contract, as the Statute of Frauds required. Amber responded by asserting the doctrine of promissory estoppel (discussed in Chapter 7).

ISSUE Did Wilhelm and Brister's e-mails and phone call establish a contract between Amber and Reilly?

DECISION Yes. The court denied Reilly's motion for summary judgment. "In sum, viewing the evidence in the light most favorable to [Amber, a] contract was formed; * * * and unconscionable injury occurred."

REASON The court acknowledged that the transaction between Amber and Reilly involved a sale of goods for a price of $500 or more and thus was subject to the writing requirement of the Statute of Frauds. The court interpreted Wilhelm's e-mail as an invitation to negotiate—to "discuss this proposal" and "work out a contract"—not an offer. Similarly, Brister's e-mailed reply to "please work the contract up" did not constitute an acceptance. And no written contract was otherwise prepared. Amber contended, however, that Reilly made a promise on which Amber relied to its detriment. The court concluded that the e-mails and phone call between Brister and Wilhelm "resulted in a two-way promise, pursuant to which Reilly promised to provide Amber a firm price for 2004, in exchange for Amber's commitment * * * to purchase at least as much potassium chloride as it had in 2003." Also, Wilhelm knew that Amber would use Reilly's price to enter into contracts to supply its own customers, and "it is undisputed that Amber suffered financial damages as a result of the alleged breach, because Amber purchased potassium chloride from other sources at unfavorable prices" to supply those customers after the shipments from Reilly stopped.

FOR CRITICAL ANALYSIS–Ethical Consideration *Reilly included with each shipment a standard invoice stating that it constituted the parties' entire agreement and that its "Standard Terms" could be modified only in a writing signed by the parties. This, Reilly asserted, made those terms "a complete expression of the parties' agreement." Could a person view Reilly's actions in this lawsuit as simply an unethical attempt to avoid its contractual obligations? Is there any possible argument leading to the opposite conclusion?*

PARTNERING AGREEMENTS

PARTNERING AGREEMENT
An agreement between a seller and a buyer who frequently do business with each other concerning the terms and conditions that will apply to all subsequently formed electronic contracts.

One way that online sellers and buyers can prevent disputes over signatures in their e-contracts, as well as disputes over the terms and conditions of those contracts, is to form partnering agreements. In a **partnering agreement,** a seller and a buyer who frequently do business with each other agree in advance on the terms and conditions that will apply to all transactions subsequently conducted electronically. The partnering agreement can also establish special access and identification codes to be used by the parties when transacting business electronically.

A partnering agreement reduces the likelihood that disputes will arise under the contract because the buyer and the seller have agreed in advance to the terms and conditions that will accompany each sale. Furthermore, if a dispute does arise, a court or arbitration forum will be able to refer to the partnering agreement when determining the parties' intent with respect to subsequent contracts. Of course, even with a partnering agreement fraud remains a possibility. If an unauthorized person uses a purchaser's designated access number and identification code, it may be some time before the problem is discovered. (Preventing unauthorized use of passwords and identification codes is one of the goals of an electronic communications policy. See the *Application* feature at the end of this chapter for suggestions on establishing such a policy.)

PREVENTING LEGAL DISPUTES

Businesspersons who are contemplating an extended contractual relationship with another party should enter into a partnering agreement—particularly if any aspect of the contract is international, involving foreign parties or deliveries. Partnering agreements are an efficient way to establish the standards between contracting parties. Such agreements can address what type of e-signature will be acceptable; who will be authorized to sign or modify the contract on behalf of the parties; and what security methods, such as passwords and identification codes, will be used. The contract should also outline the parties' understanding as to the effect of any errors, indicate which state's or nation's laws will apply, and specify how any disputes that arise will be resolved.

THE UNIFORM ELECTRONIC TRANSACTIONS ACT

As noted earlier, the Uniform Electronic Transactions Act (UETA) was set forth in 1999. It represents one of the first comprehensive efforts to create uniform laws pertaining to e-commerce.

The primary purpose of the UETA is to remove barriers to e-commerce by giving the same legal effect to electronic records and signatures as is currently given to paper documents and signatures. As mentioned earlier, the UETA broadly defines an *e-signature* as "an electronic sound, symbol, or process attached to or logically associated with a record and executed or adopted by a person with the intent to sign the record."[8] A **record** is "information that is inscribed on a tangible medium or that is stored in an electronic or other medium and is retrievable in perceivable [visual] form."[9]

RECORD
According to the Uniform Electronic Transactions Act, information that is either inscribed on a tangible medium or stored in an electronic or other medium and is retrievable.

The Scope and Applicability of the UETA

The UETA does not create new rules for electronic contracts but rather establishes that records, signatures, and contracts may not be denied enforceability solely due to their electronic form. The UETA does not apply to all writings and signatures but only to elec-

---

8. UETA 102(8).
9. UETA 102(15).

tronic records and electronic signatures *relating to a transaction*. A *transaction* is defined as an interaction between two or more people relating to business, commercial, or governmental activities.[10]

The act specifically does not apply to wills or testamentary trusts or to transactions governed by the UCC (other than those covered by Articles 2 and 2A).[11] In addition, the provisions of the UETA allow the states to exclude its application to other areas of law.

As described earlier, Congress passed the E-SIGN Act in 2000, a year after the UETA was presented to the states for adoption. Thus, a significant issue is whether and to what extent the federal E-SIGN Act preempts the UETA as adopted by the states.

The Federal E-SIGN Act and the UETA

The E-SIGN Act of 2002[12] refers explicitly to the UETA and provides that if a state has enacted the uniform version of the UETA, it is not preempted by the E-SIGN Act. In other words, if the state has enacted the UETA without modification, state law will govern. The problem is that many states have enacted nonuniform (modified) versions of the UETA, largely for the purpose of excluding other areas of state law from the UETA's terms. The E-SIGN Act specifies that those exclusions will be preempted to the extent that they are inconsistent with the E-SIGN Act's provisions.

The E-SIGN Act, however, explicitly allows the states to enact alternative requirements for the use of electronic records or electronic signatures. Generally, however, the requirements must be consistent with the provisions of the E-SIGN Act, and the state must not give greater legal status or effect to one specific type of technology. Additionally, if a state has enacted alternative requirements *after* the E-SIGN Act was adopted, the state law must specifically refer to the E-SIGN Act. The relationship between the UETA and the E-SIGN Act is illustrated in Exhibit 10–2 on the following page.

Highlights of the UETA

We look next at selected provisions of the UETA. Our discussion is, of course, based on the act's uniform provisions. Keep in mind that the states that have enacted the UETA may have adopted slightly different versions.

The Parties Must Agree to Conduct Transactions Electronically The UETA will not apply to a transaction unless each of the parties has previously agreed to conduct transactions by electronic means. The agreement need not be explicit, however, and it may be implied by the conduct of the parties and the surrounding circumstances.[13] In the comments that accompany the UETA, the drafters stated that it may be reasonable to infer that a person who gives out a business card with an e-mail address on it has consented to transact business electronically.[14] The party's agreement may also be inferred from a letter or other writing, as well as from some verbal communication.

A person who has previously agreed to an electronic transaction can also withdraw his or her consent and refuse to conduct further business electronically. Additionally, the act expressly gives parties the power to vary the UETA's provisions by contract. In other words, *parties can opt out of all or some of the terms of the UETA*. If the parties do not opt out of the terms of the UETA, however, the UETA will govern their electronic transactions.

ON THE WEB

The Web site of the National Conference of Commissioners on Uniform State Laws includes an updated list of states that have adopted the UETA. Go to

www.nccusl.org.

---

10. UETA 2(12) and 3.
11. UETA 3(b).
12. 15 U.S.C. Section 7002(2)(A)(i).
13. UETA 5(b).
14. UETA 5, Comment 4B.

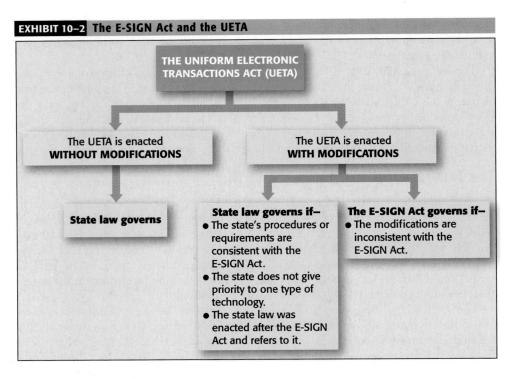

EXHIBIT 10–2 The E-SIGN Act and the UETA

THE UNIFORM ELECTRONIC TRANSACTIONS ACT (UETA)

The UETA is enacted **WITHOUT MODIFICATIONS**

The UETA is enacted **WITH MODIFICATIONS**

State law governs

State law governs if—
- The state's procedures or requirements are consistent with the E-SIGN Act.
- The state does not give priority to one type of technology.
- The state law was enacted after the E-SIGN Act and refers to it.

The E-SIGN Act governs if—
- The modifications are inconsistent with the E-SIGN Act.

ON THE WEB

At the Web site of the Consumers Union, you can read an article discussing some concerns that consumer groups have about many of the provisions in the UETA. Go to

www.consumersunion.org/finance/899nclcwc.htm.

Attribution   In the context of electronic transactions, the term *attribution* refers to the procedures that may be used to ensure that the person sending an electronic record is the same person whose e-signature accompanies the record. Under the UETA, if an electronic record or signature is the act of a particular person, the record or signature may be attributed to that person. If a person types her or his name at the bottom of an e-mail purchase order, that name would qualify as a "signature" and be attributed to the person whose name appeared. Just as in paper contracts, one may use any relevant evidence to prove that the record or signature is or is not the act of the person.[15]

Note that even if an individual's name does not appear on a record, the UETA states that the effect of the record is to be determined from the context and surrounding circumstances. In other words, a record may have legal effect even if no one has signed it. **■EXAMPLE 10.4** Darby sends a fax to Corina. The fax contains a letterhead identifying Darby as the sender, but Darby's signature does not appear on the faxed document. Depending on the circumstances, the fax may be attributed to Darby. ■

The UETA does not contain any express provisions about what constitutes fraud or whether an agent (a person who acts on behalf of another—see Chapter 17) is authorized to enter a contract. Under the UETA, other state laws control if any issues relating to agency, authority, forgery, or contract formation arise.

Notarization   If existing state law requires a document to be notarized, the UETA provides that this requirement is satisfied by the electronic signature of a notary public or other person authorized to verify signatures. **■EXAMPLE 10.5** Joel receives an offer to purchase real estate and wants to send his acceptance via e-mail. The state in which Joel resides requires his acceptance to be notarized. Under the UETA, the requirement is satisfied if a notary public is present to verify Joel's identity and affix an e-signature to his e-mail acceptance. ■

---

15. UETA 9.

The Effect of Errors The UETA encourages, but does not require, the use of security procedures (such as encryption) to verify changes to electronic documents and to correct errors. Section 10 of the UETA provides that if the parties have agreed to a security procedure and one party does not detect an error because he or she did not follow the procedure, the conforming party can legally avoid the effect of the change or error. If the parties have not agreed to use a security procedure, then other state laws (including contract law governing mistakes—see Chapter 8) will determine the effect of the error on the parties' agreement.

To avoid the effect of errors, a party must take certain steps. First, the party must promptly notify the other party of the error and of her or his intent not to be bound by the error. Second, the party must take reasonable steps to return any benefit or consideration received. Parties cannot avoid a transaction from which they have benefited. The UETA recognizes that when the consideration received is information, it may not be possible to avoid the benefit conferred. In all other situations in which a change or error occurs in an electronic record (and the parties' agreement does not specifically address errors), the UETA states that the traditional law governing mistakes will govern.

Timing Section 15 of the UETA sets forth provisions relating to the sending and receiving of electronic records. These provisions apply unless the parties agree to different terms. Under Section 15, an electronic record is considered *sent* when it is properly directed to the intended recipient in a form readable by the recipient's computer system. Once the electronic record leaves the control of the sender or comes under the control of the recipient, the UETA deems it to have been sent. An electronic record is considered *received* when it enters the recipient's processing system in a readable form—*even if no individual is aware of its receipt.*

Additionally, the UETA provides that, unless otherwise agreed, an electronic record is to be sent from or received at the party's principal place of business. If a party has no place of business, the provision then authorizes the place of sending or receipt to be the party's residence. If a party has multiple places of business, the record should be sent from or received at the location that has the closest relationship to the underlying transaction.

REVIEWING E-Contracts and E-Signatures

Ted and Betty Hyatt live in California, a state that has extensive statutory protection for consumers. The Hyatts decided to buy a computer so that they could use e-mail to stay in touch with their grandchildren, who live in another state. Over the phone, they ordered a computer from CompuEdge, Inc. When the box arrived, it was sealed with a brightly colored sticker warning that the terms enclosed within the box would govern the sale unless the customer returned the computer within thirty days. Among those terms was a clause that required any disputes to be resolved in Tennessee state courts. The Hyatts then signed up for Internet service through CyberTool, an Internet service provider. They downloaded CyberTool's software and clicked on the "quick install" box that allowed them to bypass CyberTool's "Terms of Service" page. It was possible to read this page by scrolling to the next screen, but the Hyatts did not realize this. The terms included a clause that stated all disputes were to be submitted to a Virginia state court. As soon as the Hyatts attempted to e-mail their grandchildren, they experienced problems using CyberTool's e-mail service, which continually stated that the network was busy. They also were unable to receive the photos sent by their grandchildren. Using the information presented in the chapter, answer the following questions.

(Continued)

1 Did the Hyatts accept the list of contract terms included in the computer box? Why or why not? What is the name used for this type of e-contract?

2 What type of agreement did the Hyatts form with CyberTool?

3 Suppose that the Hyatts experienced trouble with the computer's components after they had used the computer for two months. What factors will a court consider in deciding whether to enforce the forum-selection clause? Would a court be likely to enforce the clause in this contract? Why or why not?

4 Are the Hyatts bound by the contract terms specified on CyberTool's "Terms of Service" page that they did not read? Which of the required elements for contract formation might the Hyatts' claim lack? How might a court rule on this issue?

APPLICATION   Establishing an Electronic Communications Policy*

Every firm today uses computers and high-speed Internet connections. Every company also has fax machines, land-line telephones, pagers, copiers, and Internet and software assets, such as the contents stored on the company's computers and the company's domain names. Additionally, employees may use all-in-one cell phones and electronic messaging devices. Given the ubiquity of electronic communications in today's business world, no firm should be without an electronic communications policy. The policy should state that the employer owns all electronic communications resources and should also spell out what employees may and may not do when using these resources.

Limiting the Extent of Employee Usage

In the past, employees used the telephone, but today they write e-mails and use the Internet. Just as firms in the past created specific policies about personal use of the telephone, modern firms must specify how much incidental personal use of the firm's electronic communications resources is allowed. Indeed, many firms can simply keep their existing policy with respect to the telephone and add the phrase "and any other electronic communications resource" to the firm's policy document. Such a policy should explicitly cover instant messaging (IM). Many firms today specifically prohibit IM because it detracts from productivity, but other firms have found it useful and have developed IM networks for communication among team members working on large projects.

Restrictions on Internet Public Forums and on Blogs

Damaging statements made by employees in Internet public forums, such as list serves and personal blogs, can create serious problems. A comprehensive electronic communications policy should include the employer's specific restrictions on employees' statements in public forums. The employer should prohibit employees from disclosing confidential or proprietary information electronically. Additionally, an electronic communications policy should state that all employees may be audited and monitored. By doing this, the firm will warn employees that the employer will have access to all messages, files, and other information either processed through or stored on the firm's electronic communications resources.

CHECKLIST FOR CREATING AN ELECTRONIC COMMUNICATIONS POLICY

1 Indicate clearly that employees are able to use the firm's electronic communications resources, but only in accordance with the guidelines specified in the company's electronic communications policy.

2 The policy should specifically state that any personal use of the company's resources by employees must be limited and cannot affect normal business activities.

3 Every electronic communications policy should set out requirements for identification codes and passwords and indicate how employees are to protect them.

4 The policy should inform employees that the company may systematically monitor their electronic communications and their creation and use of other files.

---

* This *Application* is not meant to substitute for the services of an attorney who is licensed to practice law in your state.

KEY TERMS

browse-wrap terms 310
click-on agreement 307
cybernotary 312

e-contract 305
e-signature 312
forum-selection clause 307

partnering agreement 314
record 314
shrink-wrap agreement 309

CHAPTER SUMMARY — E-Contracts and E-Signatures

Online Offers (See pages 306–307.)	The terms of contract offers presented via the Internet should be as inclusive as the terms in an offer made in a written (paper) document. The offer should be displayed in an easily readable format and should include some mechanism, such as an "I agree" or "I accept" box, by which the customer may accept the offer. Because jurisdictional issues frequently arise with online transactions, the offer should include dispute-settlement provisions, as well as a forum-selection clause.
Online Acceptances (See pages 307–311.)	1. *Click-on agreement—* a. Definition—An agreement created when a buyer, completing a transaction on a computer, is required to indicate her or his assent to be bound by the terms of an offer by clicking on a box that says, for example, "I agree." The terms of the agreement may appear on the Web site through which the buyer is obtaining goods or services, or they may appear on a computer screen when software is downloaded. b. Enforceability—The courts have enforced click-on agreements, holding that by clicking on "I agree," the offeree has indicated acceptance by conduct. Browse-wrap terms (terms in a license that an Internet user does not have to read prior to downloading the product, such as software), however, may not be enforced on the ground that the user is not made aware that he or she is entering into a contract. 2. *Shrink-wrap agreement—* a. Definition—An agreement whose terms are expressed inside a box in which the goods are packaged. The party who opens the box is informed that, by keeping the goods that are in the box, he or she agrees to the terms of the shrink-wrap agreement. b. Enforceability—The courts have often enforced shrink-wrap agreements, even if the purchaser-user of the goods did not read the terms of the agreement. A court may deem a shrink-wrap agreement unenforceable, however, if the buyer learns of the shrink-wrap terms *after* the parties entered into the agreement.
E-Signatures (See pages 311–314.)	The Uniform Electronic Transactions Act (UETA) defines an *e-signature* as "an electronic sound, symbol, or process attached to or logically associated with a record and executed or adopted by a person with the intent to sign the record." 1. *E-signature technologies—*The two main categories of technology include digitized handwritten signatures and public-key infrastructure–based digital signatures. 2. *State laws governing e-signatures—*Although most states have laws governing e-signatures, these laws are not uniform. The UETA provides for the validity of e-signatures and may ultimately create more uniformity among the states in this respect. 3. *Federal law on e-signatures and e-documents—*The Electronic Signatures in Global and National Commerce Act (E-SIGN Act) of 2000 gave validity to e-signatures by providing that no contract, record, or signature may be "denied legal effect" solely because it is in an electronic form.

(Continued)

CHAPTER SUMMARY   E-Contracts and E-Signatures–Continued

Partnering Agreements (See page 314.)	To reduce the likelihood that disputes will arise under their e-contracts, parties who frequently do business with each other online may form a partnering agreement, setting out the terms and conditions that will apply to all their subsequent electronic transactions. The agreement may also establish access and identification codes to be used by the parties when transacting business electronically.
The Uniform Electronic Transactions Act (UETA) (See pages 314–317.)	This uniform act, which has been adopted at least in part by most states, was created by the National Conference of Commissioners on Uniform State Laws to provide rules to support the enforcement of e-contracts. Under the UETA, contracts entered into online, as well as other documents, are presumed to be valid. The UETA does not apply to certain transactions governed by the UCC or to wills or testamentary trusts.

FOR REVIEW

Answers for the even-numbered questions in this **For Review** *section can be found in Appendix E at the end of this text.*

1 What are some important clauses to include when making offers to form electronic contracts, or e-contracts?

2 How do shrink-wrap and click-on agreements differ from other contracts? How have traditional laws been applied to these agreements?

3 What is an electronic signature? Are electronic signatures valid?

4 What is a partnering agreement? What purpose does it serve?

5 What is the Uniform Electronic Transactions Act (UETA)? What are some of the major provisions of this act?

■

QUESTIONS AND CASE PROBLEMS

HYPOTHETICAL SCENARIOS

10.1 Click-On Agreements. Paul is a financial analyst for King Investments, Inc., a brokerage firm. He uses the Internet to investigate the background and activities of companies that might be good investments for King's customers. While visiting the Web site of Business Research, Inc., Paul sees on his screen a message that reads, "Welcome to businessresearch.com. By visiting our site, you have been entered as a subscriber to our e-publication, *Companies Unlimited*. This publication will be sent to you daily at a cost of $7.50 per week. An invoice will be included with *Companies Unlimited* every four weeks. You may cancel your subscription at any time." Has Paul entered into an enforceable contract to pay for *Companies Unlimited*? Why or why not?

10.2 Hypothetical Question with Sample Answer. Anne is a reporter for *Daily Business Journal*, a print publication consulted by investors and other businesspersons. She often uses the Internet to perform research for the articles that she writes for the publication. While visiting the Web site of Cyberspace Investments Corp., Anne reads a pop-up window that states, "Our business newsletter, *E-Commerce Weekly*, is available at a one-year subscription rate of $5 per issue. To subscribe, enter your e-mail address below and click 'SUBSCRIBE.' By subscribing, you agree to the terms of the subscriber's agreement. To read this agreement, click 'AGREEMENT.'" Anne enters her e-mail address, but does not click on "AGREEMENT" to read the terms. Has Anne entered into an enforceable contract to pay for *E-Commerce Weekly*? Explain.

 For a sample answer to Question 10.2, go to Appendix F at the end of this text.

10.3 Online Acceptance. Bob, a sales representative for Central Computer Co., occasionally uses the Internet to obtain information about his customers and to look for new sales leads. While visiting the Web site of Marketing World, Inc., Bob is presented with an on-screen message that offers, "To improve your ability to make deals, read our monthly online magazine, *Sales Genius*, available at a subscription rate of $15 a month. To subscribe, fill in your name, company name, and e-mail address below, and click 'YES!' By clicking 'YES!' you agree to the terms of the subscription contract. To read this contract, click 'TERMS.'" Among those terms is a clause that allows Marketing World to charge interest for subscription bills not paid within a certain time. The terms also prohibit subscribers from copying or distributing part or all of *Sales Genius* in any form. Bob subscribes without reading the terms. Marketing World later files a suit against Bob, based on his failure to pay for his subscription. Should the court hold that Bob is obligated to pay interest on the amount? Explain.

CASE PROBLEMS

10.4 Browse-Wrap Terms. Ticketmaster Corp. operates a Web site that allows customers to buy tickets to concerts, ball games, and other events. On the site's home page are instructions and an index to internal pages (one page per event). Each event page provides basic information (a short description of the event, with the date, time, place, and price) and a description of how to order tickets over the Internet, by telephone, by mail, or in person. The home page contains—if a customer scrolls to the bottom—"terms and conditions" that proscribe, among other things, linking to Ticketmaster's internal pages. A customer need not view these terms to go to an event page. Tickets.Com, Inc., operates a Web site that also publicizes special events. Tickets.Com's site includes links to the internal events pages of Ticketmaster. These links bypass Ticketmaster's home page. Ticketmaster filed a suit in a federal district court against Tickets.Com, alleging, in part, breach of contract on the ground that Tickets.Com's linking violated Ticketmaster's "terms and conditions." Tickets.Com filed a motion to dismiss. Was Tickets.Com bound by the "terms and conditions" posted on Ticketmaster's home page? Why or why not? How should the court rule on the motion? [*Ticketmaster Corp. v. Tickets.Com, Inc.,* __ F.Supp.2d __ (C.D.Cal. 2000)]

10.5 Click-On Agreements. America Online, Inc. (AOL), provided e-mail service to Walter Hughes and other members under a click-on agreement titled "Terms of Service." This agreement consisted of three parts: a "Member Agreement," "Community Guidelines," and a "Privacy Policy." The "Member Agreement" included a forum-selection clause that read, "You expressly agree that exclusive jurisdiction for any claim or dispute with AOL or relating in any way to your membership or your use of AOL resides in the courts of Virginia." When Officer Thomas McMenamon of the Methuen, Massachusetts, Police Department received threatening e-mail sent from an AOL account, he requested and obtained from AOL Hughes's name and other personal information. Hughes filed a suit in a federal district court against AOL, which filed a motion to dismiss on the basis of the forum-selection clause. Considering that the clause was a click-on provision, is it enforceable? Explain. [*Hughes v. McMenamon,* 204 F.Supp.2d 178 (D.Mass. 2002)]

10.6 Shrink-Wrap Agreements/Browse-Wrap Terms. Mary DeFontes bought a computer and a service contract from Dell Computers Corp. DeFontes was charged $950.51, of which $13.51 was identified on the invoice as "tax." This amount was paid to the state of Rhode Island. DeFontes and other Dell customers filed a suit in a Rhode Island state court against Dell, claiming that Dell was overcharging its customers by collecting a tax on service contracts and transportation costs. Dell asked the court to order DeFontes to submit the dispute to arbitration. Dell cited its "Terms and Conditions Agreement," which provides in part that by accepting delivery of Dell's products or services, a customer agrees to submit any dispute to arbitration. Customers can view this agreement through an *inconspicuous* link at the bottom of Dell's Web site, and Dell encloses a copy with an order when it is shipped. Dell argued that DeFontes accepted these terms by failing to return her purchase within thirty days, although the agreement did not state this. Is DeFontes bound to the "Terms and Conditions Agreement"? Should the court grant Dell's request? Why or why not? [*DeFontes v. Dell Computers Corp.,* __ A.2d __ (R.I. 2004)]

10.7 Case Problem with Sample Answer. Stewart Lamle invented "Farook," a board game similar to Tic Tac Toe. In May 1996, Lamle began negotiating with Mattel, Inc., to license Farook for distribution outside the United States. On June 11, 1997, the parties met and agreed on many terms, including a three-year duration, the geographic scope, a schedule for payment, and a royalty percentage. On June 26, Mike Bucher, a Mattel employee, sent Lamle an e-mail titled "Farook Deal" that repeated these terms and added that they "ha[ve] been agreed [to] . . . by . . . Mattel subject to contract. . . . Best regards Mike Bucher." Lamle faxed Mattel a more formal draft of the terms, but Mattel did not sign it. Mattel displayed Farook at its "Pre-Toy Fair" in August. After the fair, Mattel sent Lamle a fax saying that it no longer wished to license his game. Lamle filed a suit in a federal district court against Mattel, asserting, in part, breach of contract. One of the issues was whether the parties had entered into a contract. Could Bucher's name on the June 26 e-mail be considered a valid signature under the Uniform Electronic Transactions Act (UETA)? Could it be considered a valid signature outside the UETA? Why or why not? [*Lamle v. Mattel, Inc.*, 394 F.3d 1355 (Fed.Cir. 2005)]

 After you have answered Problem 10.7, compare your answer with the sample answer given on the Web site that accompanies this text. Go to **academic.cengage.com/blaw/blt**, select "Chapter 10," and click on "Case Problem with Sample Answer."

10.8 Online Acceptances. Internet Archive (IA) is devoted to preserving a record of resources on the Internet for future generations. IA uses the "Wayback Machine" to automatically browse Web sites and reproduce their contents in an archive. IA does not ask the owners' permission before copying their material but will remove it on request. Suzanne Shell, a resident of Colorado, owns www.profane-justice.org, which is dedicated to providing information to individuals accused of child abuse or neglect. The site warns, "IF YOU COPY OR DISTRIBUTE ANYTHING ON THIS SITE, YOU ARE ENTERING INTO A CONTRACT." The terms, which can be accessed only by clicking on a link, include, among other charges, a fee of $5,000 for each page copied "in advance of printing." Neither the warning nor the terms require a user to indicate assent. When Shell discovered that the Wayback Machine had copied the contents of her site—approximately eighty-seven times between May 1999 and October 2004—she asked IA to remove the copies from its archive and pay her $100,000. IA removed the copies and filed a suit in a federal district court against Shell, who responded in part with a counterclaim for breach of contract. IA filed a motion to dismiss this claim. Did IA contract with Shell? Explain. [*Internet Archive v. Shell*, __ F.Supp.2d __ (D.Colo. 2007)]

10.9 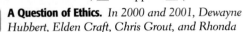 **A Question of Ethics.** *In 2000 and 2001, Dewayne Hubbert, Elden Craft, Chris Grout, and Rhonda*

Byington bought computers from Dell Corp. through its Web site. Before buying, Hubbert and the others configured their own computers. To make a purchase, each buyer completed forms on five Web pages. On each page, Dell's "Terms and Conditions of Sale" were accessible by clicking on a blue hyperlink. A statement on three of the pages read, "All sales are subject to Dell's Term[s] and Conditions of Sale," but a buyer was not required to click an assent to the terms to complete a purchase. The terms were also printed on the backs of the invoices and on separate documents contained in the shipping boxes with the computers. Among those terms was a "Binding Arbitration" clause. The computers contained Pentium 4 microprocessors, which Dell advertised as the fastest, most powerful Intel Pentium processor available. In 2002, Hubbert and the others filed a suit in an Illinois state court against Dell, alleging that this marketing was false, misleading, and deceptive. The plaintiffs claimed that the Pentium 4 microprocessor was slower and less powerful, and provided less performance, than either a Pentium III or an AMD Athlon, and at a greater cost. Dell asked the court to compel arbitration. [Hubbert v. Dell Corp., 359 Ill.App.3d 976, 835 N.E.2d 113, 296 Ill.Dec. 258 (5 Dist. 2005)]

1 Should the court enforce the arbitration clause in this case? If you were the judge, how would you rule on this issue?

2 In your opinion, do shrink-wrap, click-on, and browse-wrap terms impose too great a burden on purchasers? Why or why not?

3 An ongoing complaint about shrink-wrap, click-on, and browse-wrap terms is that sellers (often large corporations) draft them and buyers (typically individual consumers) do not read them. Should purchasers be bound in contract by terms that they have not even read? Why or why not?

 ## CRITICAL THINKING AND WRITING ASSIGNMENTS

10.10 Critical Thinking and Writing Assignment for Business. Delta Co. buys accounting software from Omega Corp. On the outside of the software box, on the inside cover of the instruction manual, and on the first screen that appears each time the program is accessed is a license that claims to cover the use of the product. The license also includes a limitation on Omega's liability arising from the use of the software. One year later, Delta discovers that the software contains a bug that has caused Delta to incur a financial loss. Delta files a lawsuit against Omega. Is the limitation-of-liability clause enforceable?

10.11 **Video Question.** Go to this text's Web site at **academic. cengage.com/blaw/blt** and select "Chapter 10." Click on "Video Questions" and view the video titled *E-Contracts: Agreeing Online*. Then answer the following questions.

1 According to the instructor in the video, what is the key factor in determining whether a particular term in an online agreement is enforceable?

2 Suppose that you click on "I accept" in order to download software from the Internet. You do not read the terms of the agreement before accepting it, even though you know that such agreements often contain forum-selection and arbitration clauses. The software later causes irreparable harm to your computer system, and you want to sue. When you go to the Web site and view the agreement, however, you discover that a choice-of-law clause in the contract specified that the law of Nigeria controls. Is this term enforceable? Is it a term that should reasonably be expected in an online contract?

3 Does it matter what the term actually says if it is a type of term that one could reasonably expect to be in the con-

tract? What arguments can be made for and against enforcing a choice-of-law clause in an online contract?

■

ONLINE ACTIVITIES

 **PRACTICAL
INTERNET EXERCISES**

Go to this text's Web site at **academic.cengage.com/blaw/blt**, select "Chapter 10," and click on "Practical Internet Exercises." There you will find the following Internet research exercises that you can perform to learn more about the topics covered in this chapter.

PRACTICAL INTERNET EXERCISE 10–1 LEGAL PERSPECTIVE—E-Contract Formation

PRACTICAL INTERNET EXERCISE 10–2 MANAGEMENT PERSPECTIVE—E-Signatures

BEFORE THE TEST

Go to this text's Web site at **academic.cengage.com/blaw/blt**, select "Chapter 10," and click on "Interactive Quizzes." You will find a number of interactive questions relating to this chapter.

■

CHAPTER 11
Sales and Leases: Formation, Title, and Risk

CHAPTER OUTLINE

—THE SCOPE OF THE UCC

—THE SCOPE OF ARTICLE 2–SALES

—THE SCOPE OF ARTICLE 2A–LEASES

—THE FORMATION OF SALES AND LEASE CONTRACTS

—TITLE, RISK, AND INSURABLE INTEREST

LEARNING OBJECTIVES

AFTER READING THIS CHAPTER, YOU SHOULD BE ABLE TO ANSWER THE FOLLOWING QUESTIONS:

1 How do Article 2 and Article 2A of the UCC differ? What types of transactions does each article cover?

2 If an offeree includes additional or different terms in an acceptance, will a contract result? If so, what happens to these terms?

3 If the parties to a contract do not expressly agree on when title to goods passes, what determines when title passes?

4 Risk of loss does not necessarily pass with title. If the parties to a contract do not expressly agree when risk passes and the goods are to be delivered without movement by the seller, when does risk pass?

5 At what point does the buyer acquire an insurable interest in goods subject to a sales contract? Can both the buyer and the seller have an insurable interest in the goods simultaneously?

A s the chapter-opening quotation states, the object of the law is to encourage commerce. This is particularly true with respect to the Uniform Commercial Code (UCC). The UCC facilitates commercial transactions by making the laws governing sales and lease contracts uniform, clearer, simpler, and more readily applicable to the numerous difficulties that can arise during such transactions. Recall from Chapter 1 that the UCC is one of many uniform (model) acts drafted by the National Conference of Commissioners on Uniform State Laws and submitted to the states for adoption. Once a state legislature has adopted a uniform act, the act becomes statutory law in that state. Thus, when we turn to sales and lease contracts, we move away from common law principles and into the area of statutory law.

We open this chapter with a discussion of the general coverage of the UCC and its significance as a legal landmark. We then look at the scope of the UCC's Article 2 (on sales) and Article 2A (on leases) as a background to the focus of this chapter, which is the formation of contracts for the sale and lease of goods.

A sale of goods transfers ownership rights in (title to) the goods from the seller to the buyer. Often, a sales contract is signed before the actual goods are available. For example, a sales contract for oranges might be signed in May, but the oranges may not be ready for picking and shipment until October. Any number of things can happen between the time the sales contract is signed and the time the goods are actually transferred into the buyer's possession. Fire, flood, or frost may destroy the orange groves, or the oranges may be lost or damaged in transit. In the latter part of this chapter, we look at the rights and liabilities of the parties between the time the contract is formed and the time the goods are actually received by the buyer (or the lessee, if the goods are being leased).

THE SCOPE OF THE UCC

The UCC attempts to provide a consistent and integrated framework of rules to deal with all phases ordinarily arising in a commercial sales or lease transaction from start to finish. For example, consider the following events, all of which may occur during a single transaction:

1 *A contract for the sale or lease of goods is formed and executed.* Article 2 and Article 2A of the UCC provide rules governing all aspects of this transaction.

2 *The transaction may involve a payment—by check, electronic fund transfer, or other means.* Article 3 (on negotiable instruments), Article 4 (on bank deposits and collections), Article 4A (on fund transfers), and Article 5 (on letters of credit) cover this part of the transaction.

3 *The transaction may involve a bill of lading or a warehouse receipt that covers goods when they are shipped or stored.* Article 7 (on documents of title) deals with this subject.

4 *The transaction may involve a demand by the seller or lender for some form of security for the remaining balance owed.* Article 9 (on secured transactions) covers this part of the transaction.

The UCC has been adopted in whole or in part by all of the states.[1] Because of its importance in the area of commercial transactions, we present the UCC as this chapter's *Landmark in the Law* feature on the following page.

THE SCOPE OF ARTICLE 2–SALES

Article 2 of the UCC governs **sales contracts,** or contracts for the sale of goods. To facilitate commercial transactions, Article 2 modifies some of the common law contract requirements that were summarized in Chapters 7 and 8. To the extent that it has not been modified by the UCC, however, the common law of contracts also applies to sales contracts. In general, the rule is that when a UCC provision addresses a certain issue, the UCC governs; when the UCC is silent, the common law governs.

For Article 2, keep two things in mind. First, Article 2 deals with the sale of *goods*; it does not deal with real property (real estate), services, or intangible property such as stocks. Thus, if a dispute involves goods, the UCC governs. If it involves real estate or services, the common law applies. The relationship between general contract law and the law governing sales of goods is illustrated in Exhibit 11–1 on page 327. Second, in some instances, the rules may vary quite a bit, depending on whether the buyer or the seller is a merchant. We look now at how the UCC defines three important terms: *sale, goods,* and *merchant status.*

What Is a Sale?

The UCC defines a **sale** as "the passing of title [evidence of ownership] from the seller to the buyer for a price" [UCC 2–106(1)]. The price may be payable in cash (or its equivalent), or in other goods or services.

ON THE WEB

To view the text of the UCC—and keep up to date on its various revisions—go to the Web site of the National Conference of Commissioners on Uniform State Laws (NCCUSL) at

www.nccusl.org.

Cornell University's Legal Information Institute also offers the full text of the UCC at

www.law.cornell.edu/uniform/ucc.html.

BE CAREFUL Although the UCC has been widely adopted without many changes, states have modified some of the details to suit their particular needs.

SALES CONTRACT
A contract for the sale of goods under which the ownership of goods is transferred from a seller to a buyer for a price.

SALE
The passing of title to property from the seller to the buyer for a price.

---

1. Louisiana has not adopted Articles 2 and 2A, however.

LANDMARK IN THE LAW **The Uniform Commercial Code**

Of all the attempts to produce a uniform body of laws relating to commercial transactions in the United States, none has been as comprehensive or successful as the Uniform Commercial Code (UCC).

The Origins of the UCC   The UCC was the brainchild of William A. Schnader, president of the National Conference of Commissioners on Uniform State Laws (NCCUSL). The drafting of the UCC began in 1945. The most significant individual involved in the project was its chief editor, Karl N. Llewellyn of the Columbia University Law School. Llewellyn's intellect, continuous efforts, and ability to compromise made the first version of the UCC—completed in 1949—a legal landmark. Over the next several years, the UCC was substantially accepted by virtually every state in the nation.

Periodic Changes and Updates   Various articles and sections of the UCC are periodically changed or supplemented to clarify certain rules or to establish new rules when changes in business customs render the existing UCC provisions inapplicable. For example, because of the increasing importance of leases of goods in the commercial context, Article 2A governing leases was added to the UCC. To clarify the rights of parties to commercial fund transfers, particularly electronic fund transfers, Article 4A was issued. Articles 3 and 4, on negotiable instruments and banking relationships, underwent significant revision in the 1990s. Because of other changes in business and in the law, the NCCUSL has recommended the repeal of Article 6 (on bulk transfers), offering a revised Article 6 to those states that prefer not to repeal it. The NCCUSL has also revised Article 9, covering secured transactions. The revised Article 9, which has been adopted by all of the states, will be discussed at length in Chapter 16.

APPLICATION TO TODAY'S WORLD   *By periodically revising the UCC's articles, the NCCUSL has been able to adapt its provisions to changing business customs and practices. UCC provisions governing sales and lease contracts have also been extended to contracts formed in the online environment.*

RELEVANT WEB SITES   *To locate information on the Web concerning the Uniform Commercial Code, go to this text's Web site at* **academic.cengage.com/blaw/blt***, select "Chapter 11," and click on "URLs for Landmarks."*

What Are Goods?

TANGIBLE PROPERTY
Property that has physical existence and can be distinguished by the senses of touch or sight. A car is tangible property; a patent right is intangible property.

INTANGIBLE PROPERTY
Property that cannot be seen or touched but exists only conceptually, such as corporate stocks and bonds, patents and copyrights, and ordinary contract rights. Article 2 of the UCC does not govern intangible property.

To be characterized as a *good*, the item of property must be *tangible*, and it must be *movable*. **Tangible property** has physical existence—it can be touched or seen. **Intangible property**—such as corporate stocks and bonds, patents and copyrights, and ordinary contract rights—has only conceptual existence and thus does not come under Article 2. A movable item can be carried from place to place. Hence, real estate is excluded from Article 2.

Two issues often give rise to disputes in determining whether the object of a contract is goods and thus whether Article 2 is applicable. One problem has to do with *goods associated with real estate*, such as crops or timber, and the other concerns contracts involving a combination of *goods and services*.

EXHIBIT 11–1 **The Law Governing Contracts**

This exhibit graphically illustrates the relationship between general contract law and statutory law (UCC Articles 2 and 2A) governing contracts for the sale and lease of goods. Sales contracts are not governed exclusively by Article 2 of the UCC but are also governed by general contract law whenever it is relevant and has not been modified by the UCC.

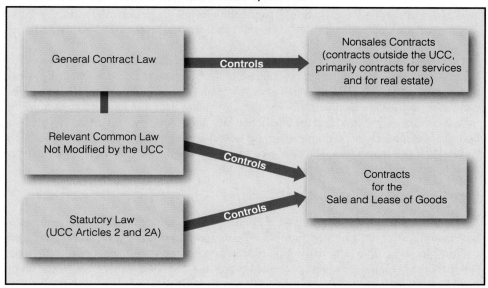

Goods Associated with Real Estate   Goods associated with real estate often fall within the scope of Article 2. Section 2–107 provides the following rules:

1 A contract for the sale of minerals or the like (including oil and gas) or a structure (such as a building) is a contract for the sale of goods if *severance,* or *separation,* is to be made by the *seller.* If the *buyer* is to sever (separate) the minerals or structure from the land, the contract is considered to be a sale of real estate governed by the principles of real property law, not the UCC.

2 A sale of growing crops (such as potatoes, carrots, wheat, and the like) or timber to be cut is considered to be a contract for the sale of goods *regardless of who severs them.*

3 Other "things attached" to realty but capable of severance without material harm to the land are considered goods *regardless of who severs them.*[2] "Things attached" that are severable without harm to realty could include such items as a portable heater, a window air conditioner in a house, and stools in a restaurant. Thus, removal of one of these things would be considered a sale of goods. The test is whether removal will cause substantial harm to the real property to which the item is attached.

Goods and Services Combined   In cases involving contracts in which goods and services are combined, courts have reached different results. For instance, is providing blood to a patient during an operation a "sale of goods" or the "performance of a medical service"? Some courts say it is a good; others say it is a service. Because the UCC does not provide the answers to such questions, the courts generally use the **predominant-factor test** to

PREDOMINANT-FACTOR TEST
A test courts use to determine whether a contract is primarily for the sale of goods or for the sale of services.

---

2. The UCC avoids the term *fixtures* here because the word has numerous definitions. A fixture is anything so firmly or permanently attached to land or to a building as to become a part of it. Once personal property becomes a fixture, it is governed by real estate law. See Chapter 24.

determine whether a contract is primarily for the sale of goods or for the sale of services.[3] This determination is important because the UCC will apply to services provided under a mixed contract that is predominantly for goods, even though the majority of courts treat services as being excluded by the UCC. In other words, if a court decides that a mixed contract is primarily a goods contract, *any* dispute, even a dispute over the services portion, will be decided under the UCC. Likewise, any dispute over a predominantly services contract will not be decided using the UCC, even if the dispute involves the goods portion of the contract.

◼EXAMPLE 11.1 An Indiana company contracts to purchase customized software from Dharma Systems. The contract states that half of the purchase price is for Dharma Systems' professional services and the other half is for the goods (the software). If the court determines that the contract is predominantly for the software, rather than the services to customize the software, the court will hold that the transaction falls under Article 2.[4] Conversely, if the court finds that the services are predominant, it will hold that the transaction is not governed by the UCC. ◼ If the transaction is not covered by the UCC, then UCC provisions, including those relating to implied warranties, will not apply.

Who Is a Merchant?

Article 2 governs the sale of goods in general. It applies to sales transactions between all buyers and sellers. In a limited number of instances, however, the UCC presumes that certain special business standards ought to be imposed on merchants because they possess a relatively high degree of commercial expertise.[5] Such standards do not apply to the casual or inexperienced seller or buyer (a "consumer"). Section 2–104 sets out three ways in which merchant status can arise:

1 A merchant is a person who *deals in goods of the kind* involved in the sales contract. Thus, a retailer, a wholesaler, or a manufacturer is a merchant of those goods sold in the business. A merchant for one type of goods is not necessarily a merchant for another type. For example, a sporting equipment retailer is a merchant when selling tennis rackets but not when selling a used computer.

2 A merchant is a person who, by occupation, holds himself or herself out as having knowledge and skill unique to the practices or goods involved in the transaction. Note that this broad definition may include banks or universities as merchants.

3 A person who *employs a merchant as a broker, agent, or other intermediary* has the status of merchant in that transaction. Hence, if a "gentleman farmer" who ordinarily does not run the farm hires a broker to purchase or sell livestock, the farmer is considered a merchant in the transaction.

In summary, a person is a **merchant** when she or he, acting in a mercantile capacity, possesses or uses an expertise specifically related to the goods being sold. Nevertheless, the distinction between merchants and nonmerchants is not always clear-cut. For example, state courts appear to be split over whether farmers should be considered merchants. In some states, farmers are considered merchants because they sell products or livestock on

MERCHANT
A person who is engaged in the purchase and sale of goods. Under the UCC, a person who deals in goods of the kind involved in the sales contract or who holds herself or himself out as having skill or knowledge peculiar to the practices or goods being purchased or sold [UCC 2–104].

---

3. UCC 2–314(1) does stipulate that serving food or drinks is a "sale of goods" for purposes of the implied warranty of merchantability, as will be discussed in Chapter 13. The UCC also specifies that selling unborn animals and rare coins qualifies as a "sale of goods."
4. See *Micro Data Base Systems, Inc. v. Dharma Systems, Inc.*, 148 F.3d 649 (7th Cir. 1998).
5. The provisions that apply only to merchants deal principally with the Statute of Frauds, firm offers, confirmatory memorandums, warranties, and contract modifications. These special rules reflect expedient business practices commonly known to merchants in the commercial setting. They will be discussed later in this chapter.

a regular basis. In other states, courts have held that the drafters of the UCC did not intend to include farmers as merchants.

THE SCOPE OF ARTICLE 2A–LEASES

In the past few decades, leases of personal property (goods) have become increasingly common. In this context, a **lease** is a transfer of the right to possess and use goods for a period of time in exchange for payment. Article 2A of the UCC was created to fill the need for uniform guidelines in this area. Article 2A covers any transaction that creates a lease of goods, as well as subleases of goods [UCC 2A–102, 2A–103(1)(k)]. Except that it applies to leases, rather than sales, of goods, Article 2A is essentially a repetition of Article 2 and varies only to reflect differences between sales and lease transactions. (Note that Article 2A is not concerned with leases of real property, such as land or buildings. The laws governing these types of transactions will be examined in Chapter 24.)

Definition of a Lease Agreement

Article 2A defines a **lease agreement** as a lessor and lessee's bargain with respect to the lease of goods, as found in their language and as implied by other circumstances, including course of dealing and usage of trade or course of performance [UCC 2A–103(1)(k)]. A **lessor** is one who transfers the right to the possession and use of goods under a lease [UCC 2A–103(1)(p)]. A **lessee** is one who acquires the right to the temporary possession and use of goods under a lease [UCC 2A–103(1)(o)]. In other words, the lessee is the party who is leasing the goods from the lessor. Article 2A applies to all types of leases of goods, including commercial leases and consumer leases. Special rules apply to certain types of leases, however, including consumer leases and finance leases.

Consumer Leases

A *consumer lease* involves three elements: (1) a lessor who regularly engages in the business of leasing or selling; (2) a lessee (except an organization) who leases the goods "primarily for a personal, family, or household purpose"; and (3) total lease payments that are less than a dollar amount set by state statute [UCC 2A–103(1)(e)]. To ensure special protection for consumers, certain provisions of Article 2A apply only to consumer leases. For example, one provision states that a consumer may recover attorneys' fees if a court finds that a term in a consumer lease contract is unconscionable [UCC 2A–108(4)(a)].

Finance Leases

A *finance lease* involves a lessor, a lessee, and a supplier. The lessor buys or leases goods from the supplier and leases or subleases them to the lessee [UCC 2A–103(1)(g)]. Typically, in a finance lease, the lessor is simply financing the transaction. **■EXAMPLE 11.2** Marlin Corporation wants to lease a crane for use in its construction business. Marlin's bank agrees to purchase the equipment from Jennco, Inc., and lease the equipment to Marlin. In this situation, the bank is the lessor-financer, Marlin is the lessee, and Jennco is the supplier. ■

Article 2A, unlike ordinary contract law, makes the lessee's obligations under a commercial finance lease irrevocable and independent from the financer's obligations [UCC 2A–407]. In other words, the lessee must perform and continue to make lease payments even if the leased equipment turns out to be defective. The lessee must look almost entirely to the supplier for warranties.

A company offering leases for automobiles. All such leases are governed by Article 2A of the UCC. What leases are not governed by the UCC? (S. Jones/Creative Commons)

LEASE
Under Article 2A of the UCC, a transfer of the right to possess and use goods for a period of time in exchange for payment.

LEASE AGREEMENT
In regard to the lease of goods, an agreement in which one person (the lessor) agrees to transfer the right to the possession and use of property to another person (the lessee) in exchange for rental payments.

LESSOR
A person who transfers the right to the possession and use of goods to another in exchange for rental payments.

LESSEE
A person who acquires the right to the possession and use of another's goods in exchange for rental payments.

THE FORMATION OF SALES AND LEASE CONTRACTS

In regard to the formation of sales and lease contracts, Article 2 and Article 2A of the UCC modify common law contract rules in several ways. Remember, though, that parties to sales contracts are free to establish whatever terms they wish. The UCC comes into play only when the parties have failed to provide in their contract for a contingency that later gives rise to a dispute. The UCC makes this clear time and again by using such phrases as "unless the parties otherwise agree" or "absent a contrary agreement by the parties."

Offer

In general contract law, the moment a definite offer is met by an unqualified acceptance, a binding contract is formed. In commercial sales transactions, the verbal exchanges, correspondence, and actions of the parties may not reveal exactly when a binding contractual obligation arises. The UCC states that an agreement sufficient to constitute a contract can exist even if the moment of its making is undetermined [UCC 2–204(2), 2A–204(2)].

> **NOTE** Under the UCC, it is the actions of the parties that determine whether they intended to form a contract.

Open Terms Remember from Chapter 7 that under the common law of contracts, an offer must be definite enough for the parties (and the courts) to ascertain its essential terms when it is accepted. In contrast, the UCC states that a sales or lease contract will not fail for indefiniteness even if one or more terms are left open as long as (1) the parties intended to make a contract and (2) there is a reasonably certain basis for the court to grant an appropriate remedy [UCC 2–204(3), 2A–204(3)].

■EXAMPLE 11.3 Mike agrees to lease from CompuQuik a highly specialized computer work station. Mike and one of CompuQuik's sales representatives sign a lease agreement that leaves some of the details blank, to be "worked out" the following week, when the leasing manager will be back from her vacation. In the meantime, CompuQuik obtains the necessary equipment from one of its suppliers and spends several days modifying the equipment to suit Mike's needs. When the leasing manager returns, she calls Mike and tells him that his work station is ready. Mike says he is no longer interested in the work station, as he has arranged to lease the same type of equipment for a lower price from another firm. CompuQuik sues Mike to recover its costs in obtaining and modifying the equipment, and one of the issues before the court is whether the parties had an enforceable contract. The court will likely hold that they did, based on their intent and conduct, despite the "blanks" in their written agreement. **■**

Relative to the common law of contracts, the UCC has radically lessened the requirement of definiteness of terms. Keep in mind, though, that the more terms left open, the less likely it is that a court will find that the parties intended to form a contract.

Open Price Term. If the parties have not agreed on a price, the court will determine a "reasonable price at the time for delivery" [UCC 2–305(1)]. If either the buyer or the seller is to determine the price, the price is to be fixed (set) in good faith [UCC 2–305(2)]. Under the UCC, *good faith* means honesty in fact and the observance of reasonable commercial standards of fair dealing in the trade [UCC 2–103(1)(b)]. The concepts of *good faith* and *commercial reasonableness* permeate the UCC. Sometimes, the price fails to be fixed through the fault of one of the parties. In that situation, the other party can treat the contract as canceled or fix a reasonable price. **■EXAMPLE 11.4** Perez and Merrick enter into a contract for the sale of unfinished doors and agree that Perez will determine the price. Perez refuses to specify the price. Merrick can either treat the contract as canceled or set a reasonable price [UCC 2–305(3)]. **■**

Are open price terms fair if the seller always seems to get the better deal? In sales law, it is acceptable for a contract to leave the price term open and to state that the seller will set the price. Such fixing of an open price term must be done in good faith, however. Consequently, when Sunoco, Inc., consistently left the price term for delivered gasoline open in twenty-two different states, a question arose as to whether the company was acting in good faith. The contracts allowed Sunoco to set the price payable in any manner it wished. Sunoco created a complicated formula that resulted in 414 pricing zones for 1,180 dealers. Sometimes, prices were set differently for adjacent price zones.

A number of gasoline dealers in New York and New Jersey sued. They argued that Sunoco was not setting prices in good faith, but rather was manipulating the price to control the dealers' business activities. Reviewing the facts, the court did not agree. It ruled that the price differentials were not attributable to "generally arbitrary, unreasonable, or capricious conduct on Sunoco's part." The court found that the fact that Sunoco charged higher prices in markets with less competition was simply the result of a capitalist system. Rather than acting with "bad motives or intention," Sunoco simply took advantage of market conditions for its own benefit.[6]

ETHICAL ISSUE 11.1

■

Open Payment Term.   When parties do not specify payment terms, payment is due at the time and place at which the buyer is to receive the goods [UCC 2–310(a)]. The buyer can tender payment using any commercially normal or acceptable means, such as a check or credit card. If the seller demands payment in cash, however, the buyer must be given a reasonable time to obtain it [UCC 2–511(2)].

■EXAMPLE 11.5 Max Alexander agreed to purchase hay from Wagner's farm. Alexander left his truck and trailer at the farm for the seller to load the hay. Nothing was said about when payment was due, and the parties were unaware of the UCC's rules. When Alexander came back to get the hay, a dispute broke out. Alexander claimed that he had been given less hay than he had ordered and argued that he did not have to pay at that time. Wagner refused to release the hay (or the vehicles on which the hay was loaded) until Alexander paid for it. Eventually, Alexander jumped into his truck and drove off without paying for the hay—for which he was later prosecuted for the crime of theft (see Chapter 6). Because the parties had failed to specify when payment was due, UCC 2–310(a) controlled and payment was due at the time Alexander picked up the hay.[7] ■

Open Delivery Term.   When no delivery terms are specified, the buyer normally takes delivery at the seller's place of business [UCC 2–308(a)]. If the seller has no place of business, the seller's residence is used. When goods are located in some other place and both parties know it, delivery is made there. If the time for shipment or delivery is not clearly specified in the sales contract, the court will infer a "reasonable" time for performance [UCC 2–309(1)].

CONTRAST The common law requires that the parties make their terms definite before they have a contract. The UCC applies general commercial standards to make the terms of a contract definite.

Duration of an Ongoing Contract.   A single contract might specify successive performances but not indicate how long the parties are required to deal with each other. In this situation, either party may terminate the ongoing contractual relationship. Principles of good faith and sound commercial practice call for reasonable notification before termination, however, to give the other party reasonable time to seek a substitute arrangement [UCC 2–309(2), (3)].

---

6. *Callahan v. Sunoco, Inc.*, ___ F.Supp.2d ___ (E.D.Pa. 2005).
7. *State v. Alexander*, 186 Or.App. 600, 64 P.3d 1148 (2003).

Options and Cooperation Regarding Performance. When the contract contemplates shipment of the goods but does not specify the shipping arrangements, the *seller* has the right to make these arrangements in good faith, using commercial reasonableness in the situation [UCC 2–311].

When a sales contract omits terms relating to the assortment of goods, the *buyer* can specify the assortment. ▣EXAMPLE 11.6 Petry Drugs, Inc., agrees to purchase one thousand toothbrushes from Marconi's Dental Supply. The toothbrushes come in a variety of colors, but the contract does not specify color. Petry, the buyer, has the right to take six hundred blue toothbrushes and four hundred green ones if it wishes. Petry, however, must exercise good faith and commercial reasonableness in making its selection [UCC 2–311]. ▣

Open Quantity Term. Normally, if the parties do not specify a quantity, a court will have no basis for determining a remedy. This is because there is almost no way to determine objectively what is a reasonable quantity of goods for someone to buy (whereas a court can objectively determine a reasonable price for particular goods by looking at the market). Nevertheless, the UCC recognizes two exceptions involving requirements and output contracts [UCC 2–306(1)].

In a **requirements contract,** the buyer agrees to purchase and the seller agrees to sell all or up to a stated amount of what the buyer *needs* or *requires.* ▣EXAMPLE 11.7 Umpqua Cannery forms a contract with Al Garcia. The cannery agrees to purchase from Garcia, and Garcia agrees to sell to the cannery, all of the green beans that the cannery needs or requires during the summer of 2008. ▣ There is implicit consideration in a requirements contract because the buyer (the cannery, in this situation) gives up the right to buy green beans from any other seller, and this forfeited right creates a legal detriment—that is, consideration. Requirements contracts are common in the business world and are normally enforceable. In contrast, if the buyer promises to purchase only if the buyer *wishes* to do so, or if the buyer reserves the right to buy the goods from someone other than the seller, the promise is illusory (without consideration) and unenforceable by either party.

In an **output contract,** the seller agrees to sell and the buyer agrees to buy all or up to a stated amount of what the seller *produces.* ▣EXAMPLE 11.8 Al Garcia forms a contract with Umpqua Cannery. Garcia agrees to sell to the cannery, and the cannery agrees to purchase from Garcia, all of the beans that Garcia produces on his farm during the summer of 2008. ▣ Again, because the seller essentially forfeits the right to sell goods to another buyer, there is implicit consideration in an output contract.

The UCC imposes a *good faith limitation* on requirements and output contracts. The quantity under such contracts is the amount of requirements or the amount of output that occurs during a *normal* production year. The actual quantity purchased or sold cannot be unreasonably disproportionate to normal or comparable prior requirements or output [UCC 2–306].

The court in the following case considered a customer's claim that its agreement to buy a supply of glass bottles from their makers was a requirements contract.

REQUIREMENTS CONTRACT
An agreement in which a buyer agrees to purchase and the seller agrees to sell all or up to a stated amount of what the buyer needs or requires.

OUTPUT CONTRACT
An agreement in which a seller agrees to sell and a buyer agrees to buy all or up to a stated amount of what the seller produces.

CASE 11.1   In re Anchor Glass Container Corp.

United States District Court, Middle District of Florida, 345 Bankr. 765 (2005).

FACTS Consumers Packaging, Inc. (CPI), owned Anchor Glass Container Corporation. Through a series of agreements beginning in 1996, CPI and Anchor supplied Encore Glass, Inc., with wine bottles of a specific type and quality. In 1999, the parties entered into an "Amended Agreement" that required the bottles to be made at CPI's plant in Lavington, British Columbia, Canada. CPI and Anchor were not obligated to

CASE 11.1–Continued

make the bottles until they accepted a purchase order from Encore. Encore could obtain volume discounts of 2 to 7 percent on its purchases through Anchor but was not obligated to buy a minimum quantity. In 2001, CPI filed for bankruptcy and sold the Lavington plant. Encore stopped sending orders to CPI and Anchor and instead bought bottles from Vitro Packaging, Inc., under a contract that provided for lower discounts than were available under the Amended Agreement. The next year, Anchor filed for bankruptcy in a federal bankruptcy court. Encore filed a claim with the court for $6,838,904.59, based on the difference between the discounts that Encore received from the two bottle makers, Anchor and Vitro Packaging. Encore argued that because the Lavington Plant was sold, it was unable to obtain the bottles from CPI and Anchor at the same discounted price. The court denied Encore's claim, ruling that the Amended Agreement was "an unenforceable indefinite quantity supply contract." Encore appealed to a federal district court, contending that the agreement was "an enforceable requirements contract."

ISSUE Was the Amended Agreement enforceable?

DECISION No. The court held that the Amended Agreement was not a requirements contract and that it was not otherwise enforceable because the parties did not contract to buy or sell "a readily ascertainable quantity." The court affirmed the lower court's judgment on Encore's claim.

REASON The court explained that under a requirements contract, a seller agrees to supply all that a buyer requires or needs in its business. In this case, "the plain language of the Amended Agreement compels the conclusion that [it is] not a requirements contract." Encore could submit purchase orders at its discretion. Encore was not required to buy any bottles from CPI and Anchor; nor was Encore required to buy all of its bottles exclusively from CPI and Anchor. Encore could take its business elsewhere at any time. The court also pointed out that "[a] contract for sale must be definite and certain as to the quantity of the goods or articles sold, or provide means, by some fixed conditions or circumstances, by which the quantities involved in the contract can be determined." The Amended Agreement "contains no definite minimum purchase amount and Encore was clearly free to purchase nothing from CPI and Anchor." Under the Amended Agreement, "Encore could choose if and when it ordered product from CPI and Anchor, as well as how much," and "CPI and Anchor were not obligated to produce a specific volume."

 FOR CRITICAL ANALYSIS–Social Consideration
If Encore could have established that the Amended Agreement was an enforceable requirements contract, what effect might the sale of the Lavington plant have had on the outcome in this case?

Merchant's Firm Offer Under regular contract principles, an offer can be revoked at any time before acceptance. The major common law exception is an *option contract* (discussed in Chapter 7), in which the offeree pays consideration for the offeror's irrevocable promise to keep the offer open for a stated period. The UCC creates a second exception for firm offers made by a merchant to sell, buy, or lease goods.

A **firm offer** arises when a merchant-offeror gives *assurances* in a *signed writing* that the offer will remain open. The merchant's firm offer is irrevocable without the necessity of consideration[8] for the stated period or, if no definite period is stated, a reasonable period (neither period to exceed three months) [UCC 2–205, 2A–205]. **■EXAMPLE 11.9** Osaka, a used-car dealer, writes a letter to Saucedo on January 1 stating, "I have a 2006 Suzuki on the lot that I'll sell you for $10,500 any time between now and January 31." This writing creates a firm offer, and Osaka will be liable for breach if he sells the Suzuki to someone other than Saucedo before January 31. **■**

It is necessary that the offer be both *written* and *signed* by the offeror.[9] When a firm offer is contained in a form contract prepared by the offeree, the offeror must also sign a separate assurance of the firm offer. This requirement ensures that the offeror is aware of

FIRM OFFER
An offer (by a merchant) that is irrevocable without the necessity of consideration for a stated period of time or, if no definite period is stated, for a reasonable time (neither period to exceed three months). A firm offer by a merchant must be in writing and must be signed by the offeror.

---

8. If the offeree pays consideration, then an option contract (not a merchant's firm offer) is formed.
9. *Signed* includes any symbol executed or adopted by a party with a present intention to authenticate a writing [UCC 1–201(39)]. A complete signature is not required. Therefore, initials, a thumbprint, a trade name, or any mark used in lieu of a written signature will suffice, regardless of its location on the document.

the offer. For instance, an offeree might respond to an initial offer by sending its own form contract containing a clause stating that the offer will remain open for three months. If the firm offer is buried amid copious language in one of the pages of the offeree's form contract, the offeror may inadvertently sign the contract without realizing that it contains a firm offer, thus defeating the purpose of the rule—which is to give effect to a merchant's deliberate intent to be bound to a firm offer.

Acceptance

The following subsections examine the UCC's provisions governing acceptance. As you will see, acceptance of an offer to buy, sell, or lease goods generally may be made in any reasonable manner and by any reasonable means.

Methods of Acceptance   The general common law rule is that an offeror can specify, or authorize, a particular means of acceptance, making that method the only one effective for contract formation. Even an unauthorized means of communication is effective, how-ever, as long as the acceptance is received by the specified deadline. **■EXAMPLE 11.10** Janel offers to sell her Humvee to Arik for $48,000. The offer states, "Answer by fax within five days." If Arik sends a letter, and Janel receives it within five days, a valid contract is formed, nonetheless. ■

Any Reasonable Means.   When the offeror does not specify a means of acceptance, the UCC provides that acceptance can be made by any means of communication that is rea-sonable under the circumstances [UCC 2–206(1), 2A–206(1)]. This broadens the com-mon law rules concerning authorized means of acceptance. (For a review of the requirements relating to mode and timeliness of acceptance, see Chapter 7.)
■EXAMPLE 11.11 Anodyne Corporation sends Bethlehem Industries a letter offering to lease $1,000 worth of postage meters. The offer states that Anodyne will keep the offer open for only ten days from the date of the letter. Before the ten days elapse, Bethlehem sends Anodyne an acceptance by fax. Is a valid contract formed? The answer is yes, because acceptance by fax is a commercially reasonable medium of acceptance under the circumstances. Acceptance is effective on Bethlehem's transmission of the fax, which occurred before the offer lapsed. ■

Promise to Ship or Prompt Shipment.   The UCC permits a seller to accept an offer to buy goods "either by a prompt *promise* to ship or by the prompt or current shipment of conforming or nonconforming goods" [UCC 2–206(1)(b)]. *Conforming* goods are goods that accord with the contract's terms; *nonconforming* goods do not. The seller's prompt shipment of *nonconforming goods* in response to the offer constitutes both an acceptance (a contract) and a *breach* of that contract.

This rule does not apply if the seller **seasonably** (within a reasonable amount of time) notifies the buyer that the nonconforming shipment is offered only as an *accommodation*, or as a favor. The notice of accommodation must clearly indicate to the buyer that the ship-ment does not constitute an acceptance and that, therefore, no contract has been formed.
■EXAMPLE 11.12 McFarrell Pharmacy orders five cases of Johnson & Johnson 3-by-5-inch gauze pads from Halderson Medical Supply, Inc. If Halderson ships five cases of Xeroform 3-by-5-inch gauze pads instead, the shipment acts as both an acceptance of McFarrell's offer and a *breach* of the resulting contract. McFarrell may sue Halderson for any appropriate damages. If, however, Halderson notifies McFarrell that the Xeroform gauze pads are being shipped *as an accommodation*—because Halderson has only Xeroform pads in stock—the shipment will constitute a counteroffer, not an acceptance. A contract will be formed only if McFarrell accepts the Xeroform gauze pads. ■

SEASONABLY
Within a specified time period or, if no period is specified, within a reasonable time.

Communication of Acceptance   Under the common law, because a unilateral offer invites acceptance by a performance, the offeree need not notify the offeror of performance unless the offeror would not otherwise know about it. In other words, beginning the requested performance is an implied acceptance. The UCC is more stringent than the common law in this regard. Under the UCC, if the offeror is not notified within a reasonable time that the offeree has accepted the contract by beginning performance, then the offeror can treat the offer as having lapsed before acceptance [UCC 2–206(2), 2A–206(2)].

Additional Terms   Under the common law, if Alderman makes an offer to Beale, and Beale in turn accepts but in the acceptance makes some slight modification to the terms of the offer, there is no contract. Recall from Chapter 7 that the so-called *mirror image rule* requires that the terms of the acceptance exactly match those of the offer. The UCC dispenses with the mirror image rule. Generally, the UCC takes the position that if the offeree's response indicates a *definite* acceptance of the offer, a contract is formed even if the acceptance includes additional or different terms from those contained in the offer [UCC 2–207(1)]. What happens to these additional terms? The answer to this question depends, in part, on whether the parties are nonmerchants or merchants.

DON'T FORGET The UCC recognizes that a proposed deal is a contract if, in commercial understanding, the deal has been closed.

Rules When One Party or Both Parties Are Nonmerchants.   If one (or both) of the parties is a *nonmerchant*, the contract is formed according to the terms of the original offer submitted by the original offeror and not according to the additional terms of the acceptance [UCC 2–207(2)]. **■EXAMPLE 11.13** Tolsen offers in writing to sell his laptop computer and printer to Valdez for $1,500. Valdez faxes a reply to Tolsen stating, "I accept your offer to purchase your laptop and printer for $1,500. I *would like* a box of laser printer paper and two extra toner cartridges to be included in the purchase price." Valdez has given Tolsen a definite expression of acceptance (creating a contract), even though the acceptance also suggests an added term for the offer. Because Tolsen is not a merchant, the additional term is merely a proposal (suggestion), and Tolsen is not legally obligated to comply with that term. ■

Rules When Both Parties Are Merchants.   In contracts *between merchants*, the additional terms automatically become part of the contract unless (1) the original offer expressly limits acceptance to the terms of the offer, (2) the new or changed terms *materially* alter the contract, or (3) the offeror objects to the new or changed terms within a reasonable period of time [UCC 2–207(2)].

What constitutes a material alteration is frequently a question that only a court can decide. Generally, if the modification involves no unreasonable element of surprise or hardship for the offeror, the court will hold that the modification did not materially alter the contract.

■EXAMPLE 11.14 Woolf has ordered meat from Tupman sixty-four times over a two-year period. Each time, Woolf placed the order over the phone, and Tupman mailed a confirmation form, and then an invoice, to Woolf. Tupman's confirmation form and invoice have always included an arbitration clause. If Woolf places another order and fails to pay for the meat, the court will likely hold that the additional term—the arbitration provision—did not materially alter the contract because Woolf should not have been surprised by the term. ■

Conditioned on Offeror's Assent.   Regardless of merchant status, the UCC provides that the offeree's expression cannot be construed as an acceptance if it contains additional or different terms that are explicitly conditioned on the offeror's assent to those terms [UCC 2–207(1)]. **■EXAMPLE 11.15** Philips offers to sell Hundert 650 pounds of turkey thighs at a specified price and with specified delivery terms. Hundert responds, "I accept your offer for 650 pounds of turkey thighs *on the condition that you give me ninety days to pay for them.*" Hundert's response will be construed not as an acceptance but as a counteroffer, which Philips may or may not accept. ▪

Additional Terms May Be Stricken. The UCC provides yet another option for dealing with conflicting terms in the parties' writings. Section 2–207(3) states that conduct by both parties that recognizes the existence of a contract is sufficient to establish a contract for the sale of goods even though the writings of the parties do not otherwise establish a contract. In this situation, "the terms of the particular contract will consist of those terms on which the writings of the parties agree, together with any supplementary terms incorporated under any other provisions of this Act." In a dispute over contract terms, this provision allows a court simply to strike from the contract those terms on which the parties do not agree.

The fact that a merchant's acceptance frequently contains additional terms or even terms that conflict with those of the offer is often referred to as the "battle of the forms." Although the drafters of UCC 2–207 tried to eliminate this battle, the problem of differing contract terms still arises in commercial settings, particularly when contracts are based on the merchants' forms, such as order forms and confirmation forms. (The *Application* feature at the end of this chapter offers suggestions on how businesspersons can avoid the "battle of the forms" and other problems with sales and lease contracts.)

Consideration

The common law rule that a contract requires consideration also applies to sales and lease contracts. Unlike the common law, however, the UCC does not require a contract modification to be supported by new consideration. An agreement modifying a contract for the sale or lease of goods "needs no consideration to be binding" [UCC 2–209(1), 2A–208(1)].

Modifications Must Be Made in Good Faith Of course, a contract modification must be sought in good faith [UCC 1–203]. **■EXAMPLE 11.16** Allied, Inc., agrees to lease a new recreational vehicle (RV) to Louise for a stated monthly payment. Subsequently, a sudden shift in the market makes it difficult for Allied to lease the new RV to Louise at the contract price without suffering a loss. Allied tells Louise of the situation, and she agrees to pay an additional sum for the lease of the RV. Later Louise reconsiders and refuses to pay more than the original price. Under the UCC, Louise's promise to modify the contract needs no consideration to be binding. Hence, she is bound by the modified contract. ▪

In this example, a shift in the market is a *good faith* reason for contract modification. What if there really was no shift in the market, however, and Allied knew that Louise needed to lease the new RV immediately but refused to deliver it unless she agreed to pay a higher price? This attempt at extortion through modification without a legitimate commercial reason would be ineffective because it would violate the duty of good faith. Allied would not be permitted to enforce the higher price.

When Modification without Consideration Requires a Writing In some situations, an agreement to modify a sales or lease contract without consideration must be in writing to be enforceable. If the contract itself prohibits any changes to the contract unless they are in a signed writing, for instance, then only those changes agreed to in a signed writing are enforceable. If a consumer (nonmerchant buyer) is dealing with a merchant and the merchant supplies the form that contains a prohibition against oral modification, the consumer must sign a separate acknowledgment of such a clause [UCC 2–209(2), 2A–208(2)].

Also, under Article 2, any modification that brings a sales contract under the Statute of Frauds must usually be in writing to be enforceable. Thus, if an oral contract for the sale of goods priced at $400 is modified so that the contract goods are now priced at $600, the modification must be in writing to be enforceable [UCC 2–209(3)]. (This is because the UCC's Statute of Frauds provision, as you will read shortly, requires a written record of sales contracts for goods priced at $500 or more.) If, however, the buyer accepts delivery of the goods after the modification, he or she is bound to the $600 price [UCC 2–201(3)(c)]. (Unlike Article 2, Article 2A does not say whether a lease as modified needs to satisfy the Statute of Frauds.)

The Statute of Frauds

The UCC contains Statute of Frauds provisions covering sales and lease contracts. Under these provisions, sales contracts for goods priced at $500 or more and lease contracts requiring payments of $1,000 or more must be in writing to be enforceable [UCC 2–201(1), 2A–201(1)].

BE AWARE It has been proposed that the UCC be revised to eliminate the Statute of Frauds.

Sufficiency of the Writing The UCC has greatly relaxed the requirements for the sufficiency of a writing to satisfy the Statute of Frauds. A writing or a memorandum will be sufficient as long as it indicates that the parties intended to form a contract and as long as it is signed by the party (or agent of the party—see Chapter 17) against whom enforcement is sought. The contract normally will not be enforceable beyond the quantity of goods shown in the writing, however. All other terms can be proved in court by oral testimony. For leases, the writing must reasonably identify and describe the goods leased and the lease term.

Special Rules for Contracts between Merchants Once again, the UCC provides a special rule for merchants. Merchants can satisfy the requirements of a writing for the Statute of Frauds if, after the parties have agreed orally, one of the merchants sends a signed written confirmation to the other merchant within a reasonable time after the oral agreement was reached. The communication must indicate the terms of the agreement, and the merchant receiving the confirmation must have reason to know of its contents. Unless the merchant who receives the confirmation gives written notice of objection to its contents within ten days after receipt, the writing is sufficient against the receiving merchant, even though she or he has not signed anything [UCC 2–201(2)].[10] What happens if a merchant sends an e-mail confirmation? For a discussion of a case involving this issue, see this chapter's *Adapting the Law to the Online Environment* feature on the next page.

EXAMPLE 11.17 Alfonso is a merchant-buyer in Cleveland. He contracts over the telephone to purchase $4,000 worth of spare aircraft parts from Goldstein, a merchant-seller in New York City. Two days later, Goldstein sends a written confirmation detailing the terms of the oral contract, and Alfonso subsequently receives it. If Alfonso does not notify Goldstein in writing of his objection to the contents of the confirmation within ten days of receipt, Alfonso cannot raise the Statute of Frauds as a defense against the enforcement of the oral contract. ▣

Exceptions In addition to the special rules for merchants, the UCC defines three exceptions to the writing requirements of the Statute of Frauds. An oral contract for the sale of goods priced at $500 or more or the lease of goods involving total payments of $1,000 or more will be enforceable despite the absence of a writing in the circumstances discussed in

An artisan creates a specially designed "bowl within a bowl" out of one piece of clay. If a restaurant orally contracted with the artisan to create twenty of the specially designed bowls for use in its business, at a price of $800, would the contract have to be in writing to be enforceable? Why or why not?
(AP Photo/Wide World Photos)

---

10. According to the comments accompanying UCC 2A–201 (Article 2A's Statute of Frauds), the "between merchants" provision was not included in Article 2A because the number of such transactions involving leases, as opposed to sales, was thought to be modest.

ADAPTING THE LAW TO THE ONLINE ENVIRONMENT

Applying the Statute of Frauds to E-Mail Confirmations

Many contracts require a writing to satisfy the Statute of Frauds. As more and more contracts are negotiated orally or through e-mail, the question arises as to whether e-mail communications can fulfill the writing requirement. This issue was at the heart of a case involving a textile merchandising company and its supplier.

Was There an Enforceable Contract?

Bazak International Corporation contracted to buy numerous pairs of jeans from Tarrant Apparel Group. The total price for the transaction was around $2 million. After a series of disputes between the companies, Tarrant sold the jeans to a third party at a higher price. Bazak sued for breach of contract. Tarrant claimed that the contract was not enforceable because there was no signed writing.

Although the parties never drew up a written contract, they did engage in a series of e-mail transmissions. In one, Bazak provided details of the purchase and attached a letter on its own company stationery. Bazak claimed that this e-mail constituted a written confirmation that satisfied the Statute of Frauds. Tarrant disagreed, arguing that because an e-mail transmission is electronic, it cannot qualify as a written confirmation of the agreement. Tarrant also contended that the e-mail was not a written memorandum between merchants because it was not signed. Finally, Tarrant argued that using e-mail transmissions between the two companies was not an appropriate means of communication in the apparel industry.

The Court Rules in Favor of E-Mail Communications

The court ruled against all three of Tarrant's arguments (and against several others as well). Even though the e-mails were "intangible messages," they still qualified as writings. After all, the court pointed out, faxes, telexes, and telegrams are all intangible forms of communication while they are being transmitted. Whether an e-mail is printed on paper or saved on a server, it remains "an objectively observable and tangible record that such a confirmation exists."

In today's online world, said the court, a signed writing does not necessarily mean a piece of paper to which a signature is physically applied. In this case, the e-mail attachment, consisting of a letter on company letterhead on which the president of the company typed in his "signature," was sufficient.

Finally, merely stating that e-mail transmissions between the two parties were an inappropriate method of communication meant very little. Tarrant would have to prove that trade usage and the course of dealing in the textile and apparel industry rarely involved e-mails. The court found that there was evidence to the contrary.[a]

FOR CRITICAL ANALYSIS *Given that the order involved $2 million worth of jeans, how might Bazak International have avoided the dispute as to whether the e-mail confirmation constituted a signed writing?*

a. *Bazak International Corp. v. Tarrant Apparel Group*, 378 F.Supp.2d 377 (S.D.N.Y. 2005).

---

the following subsections [UCC 2–201(3), 2A–201(4)]. These exceptions and other ways in which sales law differs from general contract law are summarized in the *Concept Summary*.

Specially Manufactured Goods. An oral contract is enforceable if (1) it is for goods that are specially manufactured for a particular buyer or specially manufactured or obtained for a particular lessee, (2) these goods are not suitable for resale or lease to others in the ordinary course of the seller's or lessor's business, and (3) the seller or lessor has substantially started to manufacture the goods or has made commitments for their manufacture or procurement. In this situation, once the seller or lessor has taken action, the buyer or lessee cannot repudiate the agreement claiming the Statute of Frauds as a defense.

Admissions. An oral contract for the sale or lease of goods is enforceable if the party against whom enforcement of the contract is sought admits in pleadings, testimony, or other court proceedings that a contract for sale was made. In this situation, the contract

CONCEPT SUMMARY	Major Differences between Contract Law and Sales Law	
	CONTRACT LAW	**SALES LAW**
Contract Terms	Contract must contain all material terms.	Open terms are acceptable, if parties intended to form a contract, but the contract is not enforceable beyond quantity term.
Acceptance	Mirror image rule applies. If additional terms are added in acceptance, counteroffer is created.	Additional terms will not negate acceptance unless acceptance is made expressly conditional on assent to the additional terms.
Contract Modification	Modification requires consideration.	Modification does not require consideration.
Irrevocable Offers	Option contracts (with consideration).	Merchants' firm offers (without consideration).
Statute of Frauds Requirements	All material terms must be included in the writing.	Writing is required only for the sale of goods of $500 or more, but contract is not enforceable beyond quantity specified. Merchants can satisfy the requirement by a confirmatory memorandum evidencing their agreement. *Exceptions:* 1. Contracts for specially manufactured goods are enforceable. 2. Contracts admitted to under oath by the party against whom enforcement is sought are enforceable. 3. Contracts will be enforced to the extent goods are delivered or paid for (partial performance).

will be enforceable even though it was oral, but enforceability will be limited to the quantity of goods admitted.

Partial Performance.   An oral contract for the sale or lease of goods is enforceable if payment has been made and accepted or goods have been received and accepted. This is the "partial performance" exception. The oral contract will be enforced at least to the extent that performance *actually* took place.

REMEMBER An admission can be made in documents, including internal memos and employee reports, that may be obtained during discovery prior to trial.

Unconscionability

As discussed in Chapter 8, an *unconscionable contract* is one that is so unfair and one sided that it would be unreasonable to enforce it. The UCC allows the court to evaluate a contract or any clause in a contract, and if the court deems it to have been unconscionable at the time it was made, the court can (1) refuse to enforce the contract, (2) enforce the remainder of the contract without the unconscionable clause, or (3) limit the application of any unconscionable clauses to avoid an unconscionable result [UCC 2–302, 2A–108]. The following landmark case illustrates an early application of the UCC's unconscionability provisions.

CASE 11.2 Jones v. Star Credit Corp.

LANDMARK AND CLASSIC CASES

Supreme Court of New York, Nassau County, 59 Misc.2d 189, 298 N.Y.S.2d 264 (1969).

HISTORICAL AND ECONOMIC SETTING

In the sixth century, Roman civil law allowed the courts to rescind a contract if the market value of the goods that were the subject of the contract equaled less than half the contract price. This same ratio has appeared over the last forty years in many cases in which courts have found contract clauses to be unconscionable under UCC 2–302 on the ground that the price was excessive. Most of the litigants who have used UCC 2–302 successfully have been consumers who were poor or otherwise at a disadvantage. In a Connecticut case, for example, the court held that a contract requiring a person who was poor to make payments totaling $1,248 for a television set that retailed for $499 was unconscionable.[a] The seller had not told the buyer the full purchase price. In a New York case, the court held that a contract requiring a Spanish-speaking consumer to make payments totaling nearly $1,150 for a freezer that wholesaled for less than $350 was unconscionable.[b] The contract was in English, and the salesperson did not translate or explain it.

FACTS The Joneses, the plaintiffs, agreed to purchase a freezer for $900 as the result of a salesperson's visit to their home. Tax and financing charges raised the total price to $1,234.80. At trial, the freezer was found to have a maximum retail value of approximately $300. The plaintiffs, who had made payments totaling $619.88, brought a suit in a New York state court to have the purchase contract declared unconscionable under the UCC.

ISSUE Can this contract be denied enforcement on the ground of unconscionability?

DECISION Yes. The court held that the contract was not enforceable as it stood, and the contract was reformed so that no further payments were required.

REASON The court relied on UCC 2–302(1), which states that if "the court as a matter of law finds the contract or any clause of the contract to have been unconscionable at the time it was made, the court may * * * so limit the application of any unconscionable clause as to avoid any unconscionable result." The court then examined the disparity between the $900 purchase price and the $300 retail value, as well as the fact that the credit charges alone exceeded the retail value. These excessive charges were exacted despite the seller's knowledge of the plaintiffs' limited resources. The court reformed the contract so that the plaintiffs' payments, amounting to more than $600, were regarded as payment in full.

IMPACT OF THIS CASE ON TODAY'S LAW *This early case illustrates the approach that many courts today take when deciding whether a sales contract is unconscionable—an approach that focuses on "excessive" price and unequal bargaining power.*

RELEVANT WEB SITES *To locate information on the Web concerning the Jones decision, go to this text's Web site at* **academic.cengage.com/blaw/blt***, select "Chapter 11," and then click on "URLs for Landmarks."*

a. *Murphy v. McNamara,* 36 Conn.Supp. 183, 416 A.2d 170 (1979).
b. *Frostifresh Corp. v. Reynoso,* 52 Misc.2d 26, 274 N.Y.S.2d 757 (1966); rev'd on issue of damages, 54 Misc.2d 119, 281 N.Y.S.2d 946 (1967).

TITLE, RISK, AND INSURABLE INTEREST

Before the creation of the Uniform Commercial Code (UCC), *title*—the right of ownership—was the central concept in sales law, controlling all issues of rights and remedies of the parties to a sales contract. In some situations, title is still relevant under the UCC, and the UCC has special rules for determining who has title. These rules will be discussed in the sections that follow. In most situations, however, the UCC has replaced the concept of title with three other concepts: (1) identification, (2) risk of loss, and (3) insurable interest. By breaking down the transfer of ownership into these three components, the drafters of the UCC created greater precision in the law governing sales—leaving as few points of law as possible to the decision of the courts.

In lease contracts, of course, the lessor-owner of the goods retains title. Hence, the UCC's provisions relating to passage of title do not apply to leased goods. Other concepts discussed in this chapter, though, including identification, risk of loss, and insurable interest, relate to lease contracts as well as to sales contracts.

Identification

Before any interest in specific goods can pass from the seller or lessor to the buyer or lessee, the goods must be (1) in existence and (2) identified as the specific goods designated in the contract. **Identification** takes place when specific goods are designated as the subject matter of a sales or lease contract. Title and risk of loss cannot pass from seller to buyer unless the goods are identified to the contract. (As mentioned, title to leased goods remains with the lessor—or, if the owner is a third party, with that party. The lessee does not acquire title to leased goods.) Identification is significant because it gives the buyer or lessee the right to insure (or to have an insurable interest in) the goods and the right to recover from third parties who damage the goods.

Passage of Title Once goods exist and are identified, the provisions of UCC 2–401 apply to the passage of title. In virtually all subsections of UCC 2–401, the words "unless otherwise explicitly agreed" appear, meaning that any explicit understanding between the buyer and the seller determines when title passes. Without an explicit agreement to the contrary, title passes to the buyer at the time and the place the seller performs by delivering the goods [UCC 2–401(2)]. For example, if a person buys cattle at a livestock auction, title will pass to the buyer when the cattle are physically delivered to him or her (unless, of course, the parties agree otherwise).[11]

Shipment and Destination Contracts. Unless otherwise agreed, delivery arrangements can determine when title passes from the seller to the buyer. In a **shipment contract,** the seller is required or authorized to ship goods by carrier, such as a trucking company. Under a shipment contract, the seller is required only to deliver conforming goods into the hands of a carrier, and title passes to the buyer at the time and place of shipment [UCC 2–401(2)(a)]. Generally, *all contracts are assumed to be shipment contracts if nothing to the contrary is stated in the contract.*

In a **destination contract,** the seller is required to deliver the goods to a particular destination, usually directly to the buyer, but sometimes to another party designated by the buyer. Title passes to the buyer when the goods are *tendered* at that destination [UCC 2–401(2)(b)]. As you will read in Chapter 12, *tender of delivery* occurs when the seller places or holds conforming goods at the buyer's disposal (with any necessary notice), enabling the buyer to take possession [UCC 2–503(1)].

Delivery without Movement of the Goods. When the sales contract does not call for the seller to ship or deliver the goods (when the buyer is to pick up the goods), the passage of title depends on whether the seller must deliver a **document of title,** such as a bill of lading or a warehouse receipt, to the buyer. A *bill of lading* is a receipt for goods that is signed by a carrier and serves as a contract for the transportation of the goods. A *warehouse receipt* is a receipt issued by a warehouser for goods stored in a warehouse.

When a document of title is required, title passes to the buyer *when and where the document is delivered.* Thus, if the goods are stored in a warehouse, title passes to the buyer when the appropriate documents are delivered to the buyer. The goods never

---
11. See, for example, *In re Stewart,* 274 Bankr. 503 (W.D.Ark. 2002).

IDENTIFICATION
In a sale of goods, the express designation of the goods provided for in the contract.

SHIPMENT CONTRACT
A contract for the sale of goods in which the seller is required or authorized to ship the goods by carrier. The seller assumes liability for any losses or damage to the goods until they are delivered to the carrier.

DESTINATION CONTRACT
A contract for the sale of goods in which the seller is required or authorized to ship the goods by carrier and tender delivery of the goods at a particular destination. The seller assumes liability for any losses or damage to the goods until they are tendered at the destination specified in the contract.

DOCUMENT OF TITLE
A paper exchanged in the regular course of business that evidences the right to possession of goods (for example, a bill of lading or a warehouse receipt).

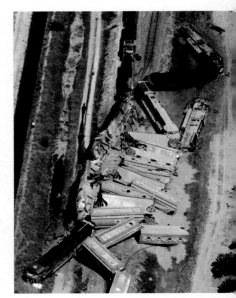

Two freight trains collide and derail. How would a court decide who held title to the goods at the time they were destroyed? (AP Photo/Eric Paul Zamora/*The Fresno Bee*)

Using International Commercial Terms, or Incoterms

With global trade growing at a rate of 5 to 10 percent per year, the number of cross-border and transcontinental shipping transactions is also increasing dramatically. The risk that goods will be lost, damaged, or destroyed in transit or at some time before the buyer takes possession also increases, however, when goods are shipped great distances, as often occurs in international sales transactions. Consequently, persons and firms engaged in global trade take steps to safeguard their interests by including in their international sales contracts terms that indicate when the risk of loss passes from the seller to the buyer.

This task is facilitated by the use of international commercial terms, or Incoterms, a set of thirteen terms commonly used in international sales contracts that have been given standardized definitions by the International Chamber of Commerce. Incoterms perform much the same function in international sales contracts as the terms in Exhibit 11–2 play in domestic contracts. Thus, Incoterms are used to indicate which party bears the risk of loss if the goods are lost or damaged, or if transportation cannot take place, as well as who pays the costs of delivery at various stages in the transportation process.

For example, a contract might state, "EXW Long Beach, California, loaded on truck, Incoterms 2000." The Incoterm EXW stands for "Ex Works," where *Ex* is from the Latin for

move. In fact, the buyer can choose to leave the goods at the same warehouse for a period of time, and the buyer's title to those goods will be unaffected.

When no documents of title are required and delivery is made without moving the goods, title passes at the time and place the sales contract is made, if the goods have already been identified. If the goods have not been identified, title does not pass until identification occurs. **■EXAMPLE 11.18** Juan sells lumber to Bodan. They agree that Bodan will pick up the lumber at the lumberyard. If the lumber has been identified (segregated, marked, or in any other way distinguished from all other lumber), title passes to Bodan when the contract is signed. If the lumber is still in large storage bins at the lumberyard, title does not pass to Bodan until the particular pieces of lumber to be sold under this contract are identified [UCC 2–401(3)]. ■

Risk of Loss

Under the UCC, risk of loss does not necessarily pass with title. When risk of loss passes from a seller or lessor to a buyer or lessee is generally determined by the contract between the parties. Sometimes, the contract states expressly when the risk of loss passes. At other times, it does not, and a court must interpret the performance and delivery terms of the contract to determine whether the risk has passed.

Delivery with Movement of the Goods—Carrier Cases   When the agreement does not state when risk of loss passes, the courts apply the following rules to cases involving movement of the goods (carrier cases).

Contract Terms.   Specific delivery terms in the contract can determine when risk of loss passes to the buyer. The terms that have traditionally been used in contracts within the United States are listed and defined in Exhibit 11–2. *Unless the parties agree otherwise,* these

"from" and *Works* refers to the seller's warehouse, factory, or other facility. When this term is used, the seller has the minimum obligations and is required only to make the goods available for pickup at his or her location. Title and risk of loss pass to the buyer at that point. Delivery by the seller is final when the goods are released to a freight forwarder (a firm that arranges shipment of goods on behalf of other firms). Thus, in this contract, the seller will load the goods on a truck at the seller's facility in Long Beach and will have no further responsibility for them. In contrast, when the Incoterm FCA, which stands for "free carrier," is used, the seller must deliver the goods, cleared for export, to the buyer's chosen carrier at the named place. The risk of loss then passes to the buyer, who pays the transportation costs and is responsible for seeing that the goods clear customs for import into another country.

The phrase "Incoterms 2000" indicates that the contract uses the latest definition, which was issued in the year 2000. Because the International Chamber of Commerce first issued Incoterms in 1936 and has published several later versions, a contract should always specify which version is meant.

 FOR CRITICAL ANALYSIS *Are there any circumstances under which the buyer or seller should* not *refer to specific Incoterms? (Hint: Are there situations in which a buyer cannot carry out the export obligations?)*

A semi-truck overturned on a New Mexico highway, spilling its cargo of fresh produce. If this was a shipment contract, and the seller was required or authorized to ship goods by carrier (but not required to deliver them to a particular final destination), when would the risk of loss pass to the buyer of the produce? (Ottmar Liebert/ Creative Commons)

terms determine which party will pay the costs of delivering the goods and who bears the risk of loss. For a discussion of the terms—called Incoterms—used in international sales contracts, see this chapter's *Beyond Our Borders* feature on the facing page.

Shipment Contracts. In a shipment contract, if the seller or lessor is required or authorized to ship goods by carrier (but is not required to deliver them to a particular final destination), risk of loss passes to the buyer or lessee when the goods are duly delivered to the carrier [UCC 2–319(1)(a), 2–509(1)(a), 2A–219(2)(a)].

EXHIBIT 11–2 **Contract Terms–Definitions**

The contract terms listed and defined in this exhibit help to determine which party will bear the costs of delivery and when risk of loss will pass from the seller to the buyer.

F.O.B. (free on board)—Indicates that the selling price of goods includes transportation costs to the specific F.O.B. place named in the contract. The seller pays the expenses and carries the risk of loss to the F.O.B. place named [UCC 2–319(1)]. If the named place is the place from which the goods are shipped (for example, the seller's city or place of business), the contract is a shipment contract. If the named place is the place to which the goods are to be shipped (for example, the buyer's city or place of business), the contract is a destination contract.

F.A.S. (free alongside)—Requires that the seller, at his or her own expense and risk, deliver the goods alongside the carrier before risk passes to the buyer [UCC 2–319(2)].

C.I.F. or **C.&F.** (cost, insurance, and freight or just cost and freight)—Requires, among other things, that the seller "put the goods in the possession of a carrier" before risk passes to the buyer [UCC 2–320(2)]. (These are basically pricing terms, and the contracts remain shipment contracts, not destination contracts.)

Delivery ex-ship (delivery from the carrying vessel)—Means that risk of loss does not pass to the buyer until the goods are properly unloaded from the ship or other carrier [UCC 2–322].

■EXAMPLE 11.19 A seller in Texas sells five hundred cases of grapefruit to a buyer in New York, F.O.B. Houston (free on board in Houston—that is, the buyer pays the transportation charges from Houston). The contract authorizes shipment by carrier; it does not require that the seller tender the grapefruit in New York. Risk passes to the buyer when conforming goods are properly placed in the possession of the carrier. If the goods are damaged in transit, the loss is the buyer's. (Actually, buyers have recourse against carriers, subject to certain limitations, and buyers usually insure the goods from the time the goods leave the seller.) ■

The following case illustrates how the application of a contract's delivery term can affect a buyer's recovery for goods damaged in transit.

CASE 11.3   **Spray-Tek, Inc. v. Robbins Motor Transportation, Inc.**

United States District Court, Western District of Wisconsin, 426 F.Supp.2d 875 (2006).

FACTS Spray-Tek, Inc., is engaged in the business of commercial dehydration of food-flavoring, pharmaceutical, and chemical products. In 2003, Spray-Tek contracted with Niro, Inc., for the design and manufacture of a customized dryer for $1,161,500. Niro agreed to ship the dryer "F.O.B. points of manufacture in the U.S.A." from its facility in Hudson, Wisconsin, to Spray-Tek's facility in Bethlehem, Pennsylvania. Niro arranged for Robbins Motor Transportation, Inc., to pick up the dryer on October 18, 2004. Robbins acknowledged in the bill of lading that it received the dryer "in apparent good order." On October 28, while in transit through Baltimore, Maryland, the dryer struck an overpass and fell off Robbins's truck. It was declared a total loss. Niro made a replacement, delivered it, and billed Spray-Tek an additional $233,100. Spray-Tek filed a suit in a federal district court against Robbins Motor under a federal statute known as the "Carmack Amendment"[a] to recover the replacement cost and other expenses. A plaintiff must show three elements to recover under the Carmack Amendment: (1) delivery of goods to a carrier in good condition, (2) their arrival in damaged condition, and (3) proof of the amount of damages. Spray-Tek filed a motion for summary judgment. Robbins argued, in part, that Spray-Tek was not entitled to recovery because it did not own the dryer during its transport.

ISSUE Does a contract that provides for the delivery of goods "F.O.B. points of manufacture in the U.S.A." mean that the goods become the buyer's property when placed in the possession of a carrier?

DECISION Yes. The court issued a summary judgment in Spray-Tek's favor on this issue. "[T]he drying chamber became plaintiff's property once it was placed on board the delivery truck at its point of manufacture in Hudson, Wisconsin." The court concluded, however, that other issues, including a possible contractual limitation on the amount of damages, involved genuine questions of material fact to be resolved at trial.

REASON The court determined that there was no dispute as to the first and second elements required for recovery under the Carmack Amendment: the dryer was delivered in good condition to Robbins, and on its "arrival," it was damaged. The question was whether, at the time the damage occurred, the title and the risk of loss had passed to Spray-Tek. The court held that the contract between Spray-Tek and Niro established Spray-Tek as the owner of the dryer when it was damaged. One clause in the contract provided that Spray-Tek would bear the risk of loss of the dryer after its delivery to the shipping point if delivery "F.O.B. shipping point" was specified. Another of the contract's terms of sale specified "F.O.B. points of manufacture in the U.S.A." Thus, "[h]ere the shipping point and the manufacturing point were identical. Accordingly, the F.O.B. points of manufacture language contained within plaintiff's contract demonstrates that plaintiff bore the risk of loss once the drying chamber departed from Niro's Hudson, Wisconsin facility." Although Robbins argued that Spray-Tek had not satisfied the third element, failing to show what "it is obligated to pay for the dryer," the court pointed out that Niro's invoice for the replacement dryer established the amount of damages.

WHAT IF THE FACTS WERE DIFFERENT? *Would the outcome of this case have been different if the contract between Spray-Tek and Niro had specified "F.O.B. Bethlehem, Pennsylvania"? Explain.*

---

a. The Carmack Amendment is part of the Interstate Commerce Act and can be found at 49 U.S.C. Section 14706. Its purpose is to remove some of the uncertainty surrounding a carrier's liability when an interstate shipment of goods is damaged.

■

Destination Contracts. In a destination contract, the risk of loss passes to the buyer or lessee when the goods are tendered to the buyer or lessee at the specified destination [UCC 2–319(1)(b), 2–509(1)(b), 2A–219(2)(b)]. In Example 11.19, if the contract had been F.O.B. New York, the risk of loss during transit to New York would have been the seller's.

Delivery without Movement of the Goods The UCC also addresses situations in which the seller or lessor is required neither to ship nor to deliver the goods. Frequently, the buyer or lessee is to pick up the goods from the seller or lessor, or the goods are held by a bailee. Under the UCC, a **bailee** is a party who, by a bill of lading, warehouse receipt, or other document of title, acknowledges possession of goods and/or contracts to deliver them. A warehousing company, for example, or a trucking company that normally issues documents of title for the goods it receives is a bailee.[12]

> **BAILEE**
> Under the UCC, a party who, by a bill of lading, warehouse receipt, or other document of title, acknowledges possession of goods and/or contracts to deliver them.

Goods Held by the Seller. If the goods are held by the seller, a document of title usually is not used. If the seller is a merchant, risk of loss to goods held by the seller passes to the buyer when the buyer *actually takes physical possession of the goods* [UCC 2–509(3)]. If the seller is not a merchant, the risk of loss to goods held by the seller passes to the buyer on *tender of delivery* [UCC 2–509(3)]. With respect to leases, the risk of loss passes to the lessee on the lessee's receipt of the goods if the lessor—or supplier, in a finance lease (see discussion earlier in this chapter)—is a merchant. Otherwise, the risk passes to the lessee on tender of delivery [UCC 2A–219(c)].

Goods Held by a Bailee. When a bailee is holding goods for a person who has contracted to sell them and the goods are to be delivered without being moved, the goods are usually represented by a negotiable or nonnegotiable document of title (a bill of lading or a warehouse receipt). Risk of loss passes to the buyer when (1) the buyer receives a negotiable document of title for the goods, (2) the bailee acknowledges the buyer's right to possess the goods, or (3) the buyer receives a nonnegotiable document of title or a writing (record) directing the bailee to deliver the goods *and* has had a *reasonable time* to present the document to the bailee and demand the goods. Obviously, if the bailee refuses to honor the document, the risk of loss remains with the seller [UCC 2–503(4)(b), 2–509(2)].

With respect to leases, if goods held by a bailee are to be delivered without being moved, the risk of loss passes to the lessee on acknowledgment by the bailee of the lessee's right to possession of the goods [UCC 2A–219(2)(b)].

> **SALE OR RETURN**
> A type of conditional sale in which title and possession pass from the seller to the buyer, but the buyer retains the option to return the goods during a specified period even though the goods conform to the contract.

Conditional Sales Buyers and sellers sometimes form sales contracts that are conditioned either on the buyer's approval of the goods or on the buyer's resale of the goods. Under such contracts, the buyer is in possession of the goods. Sometimes, however, questions arise as to whether the buyer or seller should bear the loss if, for example, the goods are damaged or stolen while in the possession of the buyer.

Sale-or-Return Contracts. A **sale or return** (sometimes called a *sale and return*) is a type of contract by which the seller sells a quantity of goods to the buyer with the understanding that the buyer can set aside the sale by returning the goods or any portion of them. The buyer is required to pay for any goods *not* returned. When the buyer receives possession of the goods under a sale-or-return contract, the title and risk of loss pass to the buyer. Title and risk of loss remain with the buyer until the buyer returns the goods to the seller within the time period specified. If the buyer fails to return the goods within this time period, the sale is finalized. The goods are returned at the buyer's risk and

A display of used watches for sale. If one of the watches was entrusted to the merchant for repair, not for sale, would a good faith purchaser of that watch have any ownership rights against a claim by the original owner? (Jeankes/Creative Commons)

---

12. Bailments will be discussed in detail in Chapter 23.

CONSIGNMENT
A transaction in which an owner of goods (the consignor) delivers the goods to another (the consignee) for the consignee to sell. The consignee pays the consignor only for the goods that are sold by the consignee.

SALE ON APPROVAL
A type of conditional sale in which the buyer may take the goods on a trial basis. The sale becomes absolute only when the buyer approves of (or is satisfied with) the goods being sold.

CURE
The right of a party who tenders nonconforming performance to correct that performance within the contract period [UCC 2–508(1)].

expense. Goods held under a sale-or-return contract are subject to the claims of the buyer's creditors while they are in the buyer's possession (even if the buyer has not paid for the goods) [UCC 2–326, 2–327].

The UCC treats a **consignment** as a sale or return. Under a consignment, the owner of goods (the *consignor*) delivers them to another (the *consignee*) for the consignee to sell. If the consignee sells the goods, the consignee must pay the consignor for them. If the consignee does not sell the goods, they may simply be returned to the consignor. While the goods are in the possession of the consignee, the consignee holds title to them, and creditors of the consignee will prevail over the consignor in any action to repossess the goods [UCC 2–326(3)].

Sale-on-Approval Contracts. When a seller offers to sell goods to a buyer and permits the buyer to take the goods on a trial basis, a **sale on approval** is usually made. The term *sale* here is a misnomer, as only an *offer* to sell has been made, along with a *bailment* created by the buyer's possession. (A bailment is a temporary delivery of personal property into the care of another—see Chapter 23.)

Therefore, title and risk of loss (from causes beyond the buyer's control) remain with the seller until the buyer accepts (approves) the offer. Acceptance can be made expressly, by any act inconsistent with the trial purpose or the seller's ownership, or by the buyer's election not to return the goods within the trial period. If the buyer does not wish to accept, the buyer may notify the seller of that fact within the trial period, and the return is made at the seller's expense and risk [UCC 2–327(1)]. Goods held on approval are not subject to the claims of the buyer's creditors until acceptance.

It is often difficult to determine whether a particular transaction involves a contract for a sale on approval, a contract for a sale or return, or a contract for sale. The UCC states that (unless otherwise agreed) "if the goods are delivered primarily for use," the transaction is a sale on approval; "if the goods are delivered primarily for resale," the transaction is a sale or return [UCC 2–326(1)].

Risk of Loss When a Sales or Lease Contract Is Breached A sales or lease contract can be breached in many ways, and the transfer of risk operates differently depending on which party breaches. Generally, the party in breach bears the risk of loss.

When the Seller or Lessor Breaches. If the goods are so nonconforming that the buyer has the right to reject them, the risk of loss does not pass to the buyer until the defects are **cured** (that is, until the goods are repaired, replaced, or discounted in price by the seller) or until the buyer accepts the goods in spite of their defects (thus waiving the right to reject). **EXAMPLE 11.20** A buyer orders ten white refrigerators from a seller, F.O.B. the seller's plant. The seller ships amber refrigerators instead. The amber refrigerators (nonconforming goods) are damaged in transit. The risk of loss falls on the seller. Had the seller shipped white refrigerators (conforming goods) instead, the risk would have fallen on the buyer [UCC 2–510(1)]. ■

If a buyer accepts a shipment of goods and later discovers a defect, acceptance can be revoked. Revocation allows the buyer to pass the risk of loss back to the seller, at least to the extent that the buyer's insurance does not cover the loss [UCC 2–510(2)].

In regard to leases, Article 2A states a similar rule. If the lessor or supplier tenders goods that are so nonconforming that the lessee has the right to reject them, the risk of loss remains with the lessor or the supplier until cure or acceptance [UCC 2A–220(1)(a)]. If the lessee, after acceptance, revokes his or her acceptance of nonconforming goods, the revocation passes the risk of loss back to the seller or supplier, to the extent that the lessee's insurance does not cover the loss [UCC 2A–220(1)(b)].

When the Buyer or Lessee Breaches. The general rule is that when a buyer or lessee breaches a contract, the risk of loss immediately shifts to the buyer or lessee. This rule has three important limitations:

1 The seller or lessor must already have identified the contract goods.

2 The buyer or lessee bears the risk for only a commercially reasonable time after the seller or lessor has learned of the breach.

3 The buyer or lessee is liable only to the extent of any deficiency in the seller's insurance coverage [UCC 2–510(3), 2A–220(2)].

Insurable Interest

Parties to sales and lease contracts often obtain insurance coverage to protect against damage, loss, or destruction of goods. Any party purchasing insurance, however, must have a sufficient interest in the insured item to obtain a valid policy. Insurance laws—not the UCC—determine sufficiency. The UCC is helpful, however, because it contains certain rules regarding insurable interests in goods.

Insurable Interest of the Buyer or Lessee A buyer or lessee has an **insurable interest** in identified goods. The moment the contract goods are identified by the seller or lessor, the buyer or lessee has a special property interest that allows the buyer or lessee to obtain necessary insurance coverage for those goods even before the risk of loss has passed [UCC 2–501(1), 2A–218(1)].

Under the rule stated in UCC 2–501(1)(c), buyers obtain an insurable interest in crops by identification, which occurs when the crops are planted or otherwise become growing crops, provided that the contract is for "the sale of crops to be harvested within twelve months or the next normal harvest season after contracting, whichever is longer." **■EXAMPLE 11.21** In March, a farmer sells a cotton crop that he hopes to harvest in October. When the crop is planted, the buyer acquires an insurable interest in it because those goods (the cotton crop) are identified to the sales contract between the seller and the buyer. ■

Insurable Interest of the Seller or Lessor A seller has an insurable interest in goods if she or he retains title to the goods. Even after title passes to the buyer, a seller who has a security interest in the goods (a right to secure payment—see Chapter 16) still has an insurable interest and can insure the goods [UCC 2–501(2)]. Hence, both a buyer and a seller can have an insurable interest in identical goods at the same time. Of course, the buyer or seller must sustain an actual loss to have the right to recover from an insurance company. In regard to leases, the lessor retains an insurable interest in leased goods until the lessee exercises an option to buy and the risk of loss has passed to the lessee [UCC 2A–218(3)].

As just explained, a seller who has a security interest in goods can still insure those goods, even though title has passed to the buyer. In today's business world, sellers frequently retain a security interest in goods because the buyer has not yet paid for the goods at the time of delivery. A business that sells and ships goods should usually maintain adequate insurance on all goods sold at least until it is assured that the buyer will pay for the goods. Losses can still occur after the goods have been delivered to the buyer. Sellers should not assume that the buyer's insurance will pay for losses the seller sustains. Insurance is essential to protect against loss.

INSURABLE INTEREST
In regard to the sale or lease of goods, a property interest in the goods that is sufficiently substantial to permit a party to insure against damage to the goods.

A freeze can destroy an orange grove. In a contract for a sale of the oranges, when does the buyer obtain an insurable interest?
(AP Photo/Gary Kazanjian)

PREVENTING
LEGAL DISPUTES

REVIEWING Sales and Leases: Formation, Title, and Risk

Guy Holcomb owns and operates Oasis Goodtime Emporium, an adult entertainment establishment. Holcomb wanted to create an adult Internet system for Oasis that would offer customers adult theme videos and "live" chat room programs using performers at the club. On May 10, Holcomb signed a work order authorizing Crossroads Consulting Group (CCG) "to deliver a working prototype of a customer chat system, demonstrating the integration of live video and chatting in a Web browser." In exchange for creating the prototype, Holcomb agreed to pay CCG $64,697. On May 20, Holcomb signed an additional work order in the amount of $12,943 for CCG to install a customized firewall system. The work orders stated that Holcomb would make monthly installment payments to CCG, and both parties expected the work would be finished by September. Due to unforeseen problems largely attributable to system configuration and software incompatibility, completion of the project required more time than anticipated. By the end of the summer, the

Web site was still not ready, and Holcomb had fallen behind in the payments to CCG. CCG was threatening to cease work and file suit for breach of contract unless the bill was paid. Rather than make further payments, Holcomb wanted to abandon the Web site project. Using the information presented in the chapter, answer the following questions.

1 Would a court be likely to decide that the transaction between Holcomb and CCG was covered by the Uniform Commercial Code (UCC)? Why or why not?

2 Would a court be likely to consider Holcomb a merchant under the UCC? Why or why not?

3 Did the parties have a valid contract under the UCC? Explain.

4 Suppose that Holcomb and CCG meet in October in an attempt to resolve their problems. At that time, the parties reach an oral agreement that CCG will continue to work without demanding full payment of the past-due amounts and Holcomb will pay CCG $5,000 per week. Assuming that the contract falls under the UCC, is the oral agreement enforceable? Why or why not?

APPLICATION   Issues for Buyers and Lessees to Note in Sales and Lease Contracts*

Businesspersons have always been involved with the sale of goods. Laws governing sales of goods date back centuries to the Middle Ages when merchants developed their own rules regarding the sale of and payment for goods (called the Law Merchant). Today, Articles 2 and 2A of the Uniform Commercial Code (UCC) establish the rules for many sales and lease contracts.

In recent years, leasing goods has become more popular, particularly when advances in technology can lead to a product becoming obsolete in a short period of time. For example, hospitals often lease rather than buy expensive technical equipment because they know that more advanced equipment will soon be available to meet the demands of diagnosis and patient care. Leasing of automobiles and trucks is becoming more popular every year.

Some Issues of Concern for Purchasers and Lessees

When entering into a contract to purchase or lease goods, a buyer or lessee needs to be familiar with the UCC's rules on several issues. (Although the remainder of this discussion applies generally to both sales and lease contracts, for simplicity it will refer only to buyers and sales.) A key issue is whether the transaction is a sale of goods or a contract for services. Determining which is the main object of the contract can be a problem when goods and services are combined. Courts and statutes have had to deal with whether providing a blood transfusion in a hospital, supplying electricity, or serving food and drink in a restaurant is a sale of a good or the performance of a service. When a contract involves both goods and services, the courts use the predominant-factor test to determine whether the UCC will apply.

Another area of concern is what terms will govern the contract. Both sellers and buyers should be aware that if their agreement leaves terms open, the UCC allows the courts to

*This *Application* is not meant to substitute for the services of an attorney who is licensed to practice law in your state.

fill in the open terms. Thus, a contract can exist even with missing terms. For example, if no delivery term is stated, the UCC stipulates that delivery takes place at the seller's place of business (or residence if the seller has no place of business).

Buyers should also be concerned with avoiding the "battle of the forms." Because sellers use their own sales forms that contain terms and conditions, and buyers use purchase orders that also include terms and conditions, disputes can arise over which terms apply to the sale. Terms in one form may conflict with those in the other, or one form may contain terms that are not in the other form. When both forms are used to create a contract and it is not clear which terms will govern, the UCC provides guidance to a court in making the determination [UCC 2–207]. If a court must make the determination, however, it is already too late because a dispute has arisen. The parties should try to avoid costly and time-consuming litigation over the terms of a contract by clarifying their intentions beforehand.

CHECKLIST FOR CONTRACT PURCHASES AND LEASES

1 If there is any doubt as to whether the contract is for a good or a service, the parties should clarify their intent in the contract. A simple statement indicating that the contract falls under the state's UCC statute is usually sufficient to indicate that a contract for goods is intended.

2 Be sure your contract includes all essential terms. Remember that a contract can be formed with open terms, such as those for price, payment, and time and place of delivery. The UCC permits the courts to supply the missing terms.

3 Try to ensure that the final contract contains terms and conditions from the form of only one party (either the seller or the buyer). The terms that will apply should be decided *before* the transaction, not afterward when a dispute can arise. (Make it a rule to always read through the other party's form prior to entering into a contract. That way you can raise any objections you might have to the form's terms or conditions before obtaining the goods.)

KEY TERMS

CHAPTER SUMMARY Sales and Leases: Formation, Title, and Risk

The Scope of the UCC (See page 325.)	The UCC attempts to provide a consistent, uniform, and integrated framework of rules to deal with all phases *ordinarily arising* in a commercial sales or lease transaction, including contract formation, passage of title and risk of loss, performance, remedies, payment for goods, warehoused goods, and secured transactions.
The Scope of Article 2—Sales (See pages 325–329.)	Article 2 governs contracts for the sale of goods (tangible, movable personal property). The common law of contracts also applies to sales contracts to the extent that the common law has not been modified by the UCC. If there is a conflict between a common law rule and the UCC, the UCC controls.
The Scope of Article 2A—Leases (See page 329.)	Article 2A governs contracts for the lease of goods. Except that it applies to leases, instead of sales, of goods, Article 2A is essentially a repetition of Article 2 and varies only to reflect differences between sales and lease transactions.

(Continued)

CHAPTER SUMMARY	Sales and Leases: Formation, Title, and Risk—Continued
Offer and Acceptance (See pages 330–336.)	1. *Offer—* a. Not all terms have to be included for a contract to be formed (only the subject matter and quantity term must be specified). b. The price does not have to be included for a contract to be formed. c. Particulars of performance can be left open. d. A written and signed offer by a *merchant,* covering a period of three months or less, is irrevocable without payment of consideration. 2. *Acceptance—* a. Acceptance may be made by any reasonable means of communication; it is effective when dispatched. b. The acceptance of a unilateral offer can be made by a promise to ship or by prompt shipment of conforming goods, or by prompt shipment of nonconforming goods if not accompanied by a notice of accommodation. c. Acceptance by performance requires notice within a reasonable time; otherwise, the offer can be treated as lapsed. d. A definite expression of acceptance creates a contract even if the terms of the acceptance vary from those of the offer, unless the varied terms in the acceptance are expressly conditioned on the offeror's assent to those terms.
Consideration (See pages 336–337.)	A modification of a contract for the sale of goods does not require consideration.
The Statute of Frauds (See pages 337–339.)	1. All contracts for the sale of goods priced at $500 or more must be in writing. A writing is sufficient as long as it indicates a contract between the parties and is signed by the party against whom enforcement is sought. A contract is not enforceable beyond the quantity shown in the writing. 2. When written confirmation of an oral contract *between merchants* is not objected to in writing by the receiver within ten days, the contract is enforceable. 3. Exceptions to the requirement of a writing exist in the following situations: a. When the oral contract is for specially manufactured goods not suitable for resale to others, and the seller has substantially started to manufacture the goods. b. When the defendant admits in pleadings, testimony, or other court proceedings that an oral contract for the sale of goods was made. In this case, the contract will be enforceable to the extent of the quantity of goods admitted. c. The oral agreement will be enforceable to the extent that payment has been received and accepted by the seller or to the extent that the goods have been received and accepted by the buyer.
Unconscionability (See page 339.)	An unconscionable contract is one that is so unfair and one sided that it would be unreasonable to enforce it. If the court deems a contract to have been unconscionable at the time it was made, the court can (1) refuse to enforce the contract, (2) refuse to enforce the unconscionable clause of the contract, or (3) limit the application of any unconscionable clauses to avoid an unconscionable result.
	TITLE, RISK, AND INSURABLE INTEREST
Shipment Contracts (See page 341.)	In the absence of an agreement, title and risk pass on the seller's or lessor's delivery of conforming goods to the carrier [UCC 2–319(1)(a), 2–401(2)(a), 2–509(1)(a), 2A–219(2)(a)].

CHAPTER SUMMARY	**Sales and Leases: Formation, Title, and Risk—Continued**
Destination Contracts (See page 341.)	In the absence of an agreement, title and risk pass on the seller's or lessor's *tender* of delivery of conforming goods to the buyer or lessee at the point of destination [UCC 2–401(2)(b), 2–319(1)(b), 2–509(1)(b), 2A–219(2)(b)].

Delivery without Movement of the Goods (See pages 341–342.)	1. In the absence of an agreement, if the goods are not represented by a document of title:
	    a. Title passes on the formation of the contract [UCC 2–401(3)(b)].
	    b. Risk passes to the buyer or lessee, if the seller or lessor (or supplier, in a finance lease) is a merchant, when the buyer or lessee receives the goods or, if the seller or lessor is a nonmerchant, when the seller or lessor *tenders* delivery of the goods [UCC 2–509(3), 2A–219(c)].
	 2. In the absence of an agreement, if the goods are represented by a document of title:
	    a. If the document is negotiable and the goods are held by a bailee, title passes on the buyer's *receipt* of the document [UCC 2–401(3)(a), 2–509(2)(a)].
	    b. If the document is nonnegotiable and the goods are held by a bailee, title and risk pass on the buyer's receipt of the document, but risk does *not* pass until the buyer, after receipt of the document, has had a reasonable time to present the document to demand the goods [UCC 2–401(3)(a), 2–509(2)(c), 2–503(4)(b)].
	 3. In the absence of an agreement, if the goods are held by a bailee and no document of title is transferred, risk passes to the buyer when the bailee acknowledges the buyer's right to the possession of the goods [UCC 2–509(2)(b)].
	 4. In respect to leases, if goods held by a bailee are to be delivered without being moved, the risk of loss passes to the lessee on acknowledgment by the bailee of the lessee's right to possession of the goods [UCC 2A–219(2)(b)].

Sale-or-Return Contracts (See pages 345–346.)	When the buyer receives possession of the goods, title and risk of loss pass to the buyer, but the buyer has the option of returning the goods to the seller. If the buyer returns the goods to the seller, title and risk of loss pass back to the seller [UCC 2–326, 2–327].
Sale-on-Approval Contracts (See page 346.)	Title and risk of loss (from causes beyond the buyer's control) remain with the seller until the buyer approves (accepts) the offer [UCC 2–327(1)].

Risk of Loss When a Sales or Lease Contract Is Breached (See page 346.)	1. If the seller or lessor breaches by tendering nonconforming goods that are rejected by the buyer or lessee, the risk of loss does not pass to the buyer or lessee until the defects are cured (unless the buyer or lessee accepts the goods in spite of their defects, thus waiving the right to reject) [UCC 2–510(1), 2A–220(1)].
	 2. If the buyer or lessee breaches the contract, the risk of loss immediately shifts to the buyer or lessee. Limitations to this rule are as follows [UCC 2–510(3), 2A–220(2)]:
	    a. The seller or lessor must already have identified the contract goods.
	    b. The buyer or lessee bears the risk for only a commercially reasonable time after the seller or lessor has learned of the breach.
	    c. The buyer or lessee is liable only to the extent of any deficiency in the seller's or lessor's insurance coverage.

Insurable Interest (See page 347.)	1. Buyers and lessees have an insurable interest in goods the moment the goods are identified to the contract by the seller or the lessor [UCC 2–501(1), 2A–218(1)]. 2. Sellers have an insurable interest in goods as long as they have (1) title to the goods or (2) a security interest in the goods [UCC 2–501(2)]. Lessors have an insurable interest in leased goods until the lessee exercises an option to buy and the risk of loss has passed to the lessee [UCC 2A–218(3)].

FOR REVIEW

Answers for the even-numbered questions in this **For Review** *section can be found in Appendix E at the end of this text.*

1 How do Article 2 and Article 2A of the UCC differ? What types of transactions does each article cover?

2 If an offeree includes additional or different terms in an acceptance, will a contract result? If so, what happens to these terms?

3 If the parties to a contract do not expressly agree on when title to goods passes, what determines when title passes?

4 Risk of loss does not necessarily pass with title. If the parties to a contract do not expressly agree when risk passes and the goods are to be delivered without movement by the seller, when does risk pass?

5 At what point does the buyer acquire an insurable interest in goods subject to a sales contract? Can both the buyer and the seller have an insurable interest in the goods simultaneously?

QUESTIONS AND CASE PROBLEMS

 HYPOTHETICAL SCENARIOS

11.1 Statute of Frauds. Fresher Foods, Inc., orally agreed to purchase from Dale Vernon, a farmer, one thousand bushels of corn for $1.25 per bushel. Fresher Foods paid $125 down and agreed to pay the remainder of the purchase price on delivery, which was scheduled for one week later. When Fresher Foods tendered the balance of $1,125 on the scheduled day of delivery and requested the corn, Vernon refused to deliver it. Fresher Foods sued Vernon for damages, claiming that Vernon had breached their oral contract. Can Fresher Foods recover? If so, to what extent?

11.2 Merchant's Firm Offer. On September 1, Jennings, a used-car dealer, wrote a letter to Wheeler, stating, "I have a 1955 Thunderbird convertible in mint condition that I will sell you for $13,500 at any time before October 9. [signed] Peter Jennings." By September 15, having heard nothing from Wheeler, Jennings sold the Thunderbird to another party. On September 29, Wheeler accepted Jennings's offer and tendered the $13,500. When Jennings told Wheeler he had sold the car to another party, Wheeler claimed Jennings had breached their contract. Is Jennings in breach? Explain.

11.3 Hypothetical Question with Sample Answer. When will risk of loss pass from the seller to the buyer under each of the following contracts, assuming the parties have not expressly agreed on when risk of loss would pass?

1 A New York seller contracts with a San Francisco buyer to ship goods to the buyer F.O.B. San Francisco.

2 A New York seller contracts with a San Francisco buyer to ship goods to the buyer in San Francisco. There is no indication as to whether the shipment will be F.O.B. New York or F.O.B. San Francisco.

3 A seller contracts with a buyer to sell goods located on the seller's premises. The buyer pays for the goods and arranges to pick them up the next week at the seller's place of business.

4 A seller contracts with a buyer to sell goods located in a warehouse.

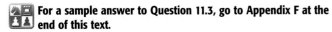 **For a sample answer to Question 11.3, go to Appendix F at the end of this text.**

 **CASE PROBLEMS**

11.4 Risk of Loss. H.S.A. II, Inc., made parts for motor vehicles. Under an agreement with Ford Motor Co., Ford provided steel to H.S.A. to make Ford parts. Ford's purchase orders for the parts contained the term "FOB Carrier Supplier's [Plant]." GMAC Business Credit, L.L.C., loaned money to H.S.A. under terms that guaranteed payment would be made, if the funds were not otherwise available, from H.S.A.'s inventory, raw materials, and finished goods. H.S.A. filed for bankruptcy on February 2, 2000, and ceased operations on June 20, when it had in its plant more than $1 million in finished goods for

Ford. Ford sent six trucks to H.S.A. to pick up the goods. GMAC halted the removal. The parties asked the bankruptcy court to determine whose interest had priority. GMAC contended in part that Ford did not have an interest in the goods because there had not yet been a sale. Ford responded that under its purchase orders, title and risk of loss transferred on completion of the parts. In whose favor should the court rule, and why? [*In re H.S.A. II, Inc.*, 271 Bankr. 534 (E.D.Mich. 2002)]

11.5 Conditional Sales. Corvette Collection of Boston, Inc. (CCB), was a used Corvette dealership located (despite its name) in Pompano Beach, Florida. In addition to selling used Corvettes, CCB serviced Corvettes and sold Corvette parts. CCB owned some of its inventory and held the rest on consignment, although there were no signs indicating the consignments. In November 2001, CCB filed a petition for bankruptcy in a federal district court. At the time, CCB possessed six Corvettes that were consigned by Chester Finley and The Corvette Experience, Inc. (TCE). Robert Furr, on CCB's behalf, asked the court to declare that CCB held the goods under a contract for a sale or return. Finley and TCE asserted that the goods were held under a contract for a sale on approval. What difference does it make? Under what circumstances would the court rule in favor of Finley and TCE? How should the court rule under the facts as stated? Why? [*In re Corvette Collection of Boston, Inc.*, 294 Bankr. 409 (S.D.Fla. 2003)]

11.6 Case Problem with Sample Answer. Propulsion Technologies, Inc., a Louisiana firm doing business as PowerTech Marine Propellers, markets small steel boat propellers that are made by a unique tooling technique. Attwood Corp., a Michigan firm, operated a foundry (a place where metal is cast) in Mexico. In 1996, Attwood offered to produce castings of the propellers. Attwood promised to maintain quality, warrant the castings against defects, and obtain insurance to cover liability. In January 1997, the parties signed a letter that expressed these and other terms—Attwood was to be paid per casting and twelve months' notice was required to terminate the deal—but the letter did not state a quantity. PowerTech provided the tooling. Attwood produced rough castings, which PowerTech refined by checking each propeller's pitch, machining its interior, grinding, balancing, polishing, and adding serial numbers and a rubber clutch. In October, Attwood told PowerTech that the foundry was closing. PowerTech filed a suit in a federal district court against Attwood, alleging, in part, breach of contract. One of the issues was whether their deal was subject to Article 2 of the Uniform Commercial Code. What type of transactions does Article 2 cover? Does the arrangement between PowerTech and Attwood qualify? Explain. [*Propulsion Technologies, Inc. v. Attwood Corp.*, 369 F.3d 896 (5th Cir. 2004)]

After you have answered Problem 11.6, compare your answer with the sample answer given on the Web site that accompanies this text. Go to academic.cengage.com/blaw/blt, select "Chapter 11," and click on "Case Problem with Sample Answer."

11.7 Title. William Bisby gave an all-terrain vehicle (ATV) to Del City Cycle in Enid, Oklahoma, to sell on his behalf. Joseph Maddox bought the ATV, but paid for it with a check written on a closed checking account. The bank refused to honor the check. Before Del City or Bisby could reclaim the ATV, however, Maddox sold it to Aaron Jordan, who sold it to Shannon Skaggs. In November 2003, the Enid Police Department seized the ATV from Skaggs. Bisby filed a suit in an Oklahoma state court against the state and Skaggs, claiming that he was the owner of the ATV and asking the court to return it to him. Skaggs objected. Is there a distinction between the ownership interests of a party who steals an item and a party who acquires the item with a check that is not honored? What was the status of Skaggs's title, if any, to the ATV? Which of the many parties involved in this case should the court rule has "good" title to the ATV? Why? [*State v. Skaggs*, 140 P.3d 576 (Okla.Civ.App. Div. 3 2006)]

11.8 Offer. In 1998, Johnson Controls, Inc. (JCI), began buying auto parts from Q. C. Onics Ventures, LP. For each part, JCI would inform Onics of its need and ask the price. Onics would analyze the specifications, contact its suppliers, and respond with a formal quotation. A quote listed a part's number and description, the price per unit, and an estimate of units available for a given year. A quote did not state payment terms, an acceptance date, the time of performance, warranties, or quantities. JCI would select a supplier and issue a purchase order for a part. The purchase order required the seller to supply all of JCI's requirements for the part but gave the buyer the right to end the deal at any time. Using this procedure, JCI issued hundreds of purchase orders. In July 2001, JCI terminated its relationship with Onics and began buying parts through another supplier. Onics filed a suit in a federal district court against Johnson, alleging breach of contract. Which documents—the price quotations or the purchase orders—constituted offers? Which were acceptances? What effect would the answers to these questions have on the result in this case? Explain. [*Q. C. Onics Ventures, LP. v. Johnson Controls, Inc.*, __ F.Supp.2d __ (N.D.Ind. 2006)]

11.9 A Question of Ethics. *Daniel Fox owned Fox & Lamberth Enterprises, Inc., a kitchen and bath remodeling business, in Dayton, Ohio. Fox leased a building from Carl and Bellulah Hussong. Craftsmen Home Improvement, Inc., also remodeled baths and kitchens. When Fox planned to close his business, Craftsmen expressed an interest in buying his showroom assets. Fox set a price of $50,000. Craftsmen's owners agreed and gave Fox a list of the desired items and "A Bill of Sale" that set the terms for payment. The parties did not discuss Fox's arrangement with the Hussongs, but Craftsmen expected to negotiate a new lease and extensively modified the premises, including removing some of the displays to its own showroom. When the Hussongs and Craftsmen could not agree on new terms, Craftsmen told Fox that the deal was off. [Fox & Lamberth Enterprises, Inc. v. Craftsmen Home Improvement, Inc., __ Ohio App.3d __, __ N.E.2d __ (2 Dist. 2006)]*

1 In Fox's suit in an Ohio state court for breach of contract, Craftsmen raised the Statute of Frauds as a defense. What are the requirements of the Statute of Frauds? Did the deal between Fox and Craftsmen meet these requirements? Did it fall under one of the exceptions? Explain.

2 Craftsmen also claimed that the "predominant factor" of its agreement with Fox was a lease for the Hussongs' building. What is the predominant-factor test? Does it apply here? In any event, is it fair to hold a party to a contract to buy a business's assets when the buyer is unable to negotiate a favorable lease of the premises on which the assets are located? Discuss.

CRITICAL THINKING
AND WRITING ASSIGNMENTS

11.10 Critical Legal Thinking. Why is the designation *merchant* or *nonmerchant* important?

11.11 **Video Question.** Go to this text's Web site at **academic. cengage.com/blaw/blt** and select "Chapter 11." Click on "Video Questions" and view the video titled *Risk of Loss.* Then answer the following questions.

1 Does Oscar have a right to refuse the shipment because

the lettuce is wilted? Why or why not? What type of contract is involved in this video?

2 Does Oscar have a right to refuse the shipment because the lettuce was not organic butter crunch lettuce? Why or why not?

3 Assume that you are in Oscar's position—that is, you are buying produce for a supermarket. What different approaches might you take to avoid having to pay for a delivery of wilted produce?

ONLINE ACTIVITIES

PRACTICAL
INTERNET EXERCISES

Go to this text's Web site at **academic.cengage.com/blaw/blt**, select "Chapter 11," and click on "Practical Internet Exercises." There you will find the following Internet research exercises that you can perform to learn more about the topics covered in this chapter.

PRACTICAL INTERNET EXERCISE 11–1 LEGAL PERSPECTIVE—Is It a Contract?

PRACTICAL INTERNET EXERCISE 11–2 MANAGEMENT PERSPECTIVE—A Checklist for Sales Contracts

PRACTICAL INTERNET EXERCISE 11–3 MANAGEMENT PERSPECTIVE—Passage of Title

BEFORE THE TEST

Go to this text's Web site at **academic.cengage.com/blaw/blt**, select "Chapter 11," and click on "Interactive Quizzes." You will find a number of interactive questions relating to this chapter.

CHAPTER 12
Sales and Leases: Performance and Breach

LEARNING OBJECTIVES

AFTER READING THIS CHAPTER, YOU SHOULD BE ABLE TO ANSWER THE FOLLOWING QUESTIONS:

1 What are the respective obligations of the parties under a contract for the sale or lease of goods?

2 What is the perfect tender rule? What are some important exceptions to this rule that apply to sales and lease contracts?

3 What options are available to the nonbreaching party when the other party to a sales or lease contract repudiates the contract prior to the time for performance?

4 What remedies are available to a seller or lessor when the buyer or lessee breaches the contract? What remedies are available to a buyer or lessee if the seller or lessor breaches the contract?

5 In contracts subject to the UCC, are parties free to limit the remedies available to the nonbreaching party on a breach of contract? If so, in what ways?

> **"It has been uniformly laid down . . . , as far back as we can remember, that good faith is the basis of all mercantile transactions."**
>
> J. Buller, 1746–1800
> (British jurist)

The performance that is required of the parties under a sales or lease contract consists of the duties and obligations each party has under the terms of the contract. Keep in mind that "duties and obligations" under the terms of the contract include those specified by the agreement, by custom, and by the Uniform Commercial Code (UCC). In this chapter, we examine the basic performance obligations of the parties under a sales or lease contract.

Sometimes, circumstances make it difficult for a person to carry out the promised performance, in which event the contract may be breached. When breach occurs, the aggrieved party looks for remedies—which we discuss in the second half of the chapter.

PERFORMANCE OBLIGATIONS

As discussed in previous chapters and stressed in the opening quotation to this chapter, the standards of good faith and commercial reasonableness are read into every contract. These standards provide a framework in which the parties can specify particulars of performance. Thus, when one party delays specifying particulars of performance for an unreasonable period of time or fails to cooperate with the other party, the innocent party is excused from any resulting delay in performance. The innocent party can proceed to perform in any reasonable manner, and the other party's failure to specify particulars or to cooperate can be treated as a breach of contract. Good faith is a question of fact for the jury.

In the performance of a sales or lease contract, the basic obligation of the seller or lessor is to *transfer and deliver conforming goods*. The basic obligation of the buyer or lessee is to *accept and pay for conforming goods* in accordance with the contract [UCC 2–301, 2A–516(1)]. Overall performance of a sales or lease contract is controlled by the agreement between the parties. When the contract is unclear and disputes arise, the courts look to the UCC.

OBLIGATIONS OF THE SELLER OR LESSOR

The major obligation of the seller or lessor under a sales or lease contract is to tender conforming goods to the buyer or lessee.

Tender of Delivery

Tender of delivery requires that the seller or lessor have and hold *conforming goods* at the disposal of the buyer or lessee and give the buyer or lessee whatever notification is reasonably necessary to enable the buyer or lessee to take delivery [UCC 2–503(1), 2A–508(1)].

Tender must occur at a *reasonable hour* and in a *reasonable manner*. In other words, a seller cannot call the buyer at 2:00 A.M. and say, "The goods are ready. I'll give you twenty minutes to get them." Unless the parties have agreed otherwise, the goods must be tendered for delivery at a reasonable hour and kept available for a reasonable period of time to enable the buyer to take possession of them [UCC 2–503(1)(a)].

All goods called for by a contract must be tendered in a single delivery unless the parties agree otherwise or the circumstances are such that either party can rightfully request delivery in lots [UCC 2–307, 2–612, 2A–510]. Hence, an order for 1,000 shirts cannot be delivered 2 shirts at a time. If, however, the seller and the buyer contemplate that the shirts will be delivered in 4 orders of 250 each, as they are produced (for summer, fall, winter, and spring stock), and the price can be apportioned accordingly, it may be commercially reasonable to deliver the shirts in this way.

Place of Delivery

The UCC provides for the place of delivery pursuant to a contract if the contract does not. Of course, the parties may agree on a particular destination, or their contract's terms or the circumstances may indicate the place of delivery.

Noncarrier Cases If the contract does not designate the place of delivery for the goods, and the buyer is expected to pick them up, the place of delivery is the *seller's place of business* or, if the seller has none, the seller's residence [UCC 2–308]. If the contract involves the sale of *identified goods*, and the parties know when they enter into the contract that these goods are located somewhere other than at the seller's place of business (such as at a warehouse), then the *location of the goods* is the place for their delivery [UCC 2–308].

■ **EXAMPLE 12.1** Rogers and Aguirre live in San Francisco. In San Francisco, Rogers contracts to sell Aguirre five used trucks, which both parties know are located in a Chicago warehouse. If nothing more is specified in the contract, the place of delivery for the trucks is Chicago. ■ The seller may tender delivery either by giving the buyer a *negotiable or nonnegotiable*

A vendor transfers boxes of produce into a store on San Francisco's Clement Street. Tender of delivery requires that the seller or lessor deliver all goods called for in the contract at a reasonable hour and keep them available for a reasonable period of time to enable the buyer to take possession of them. Under what circumstances can the goods be delivered in more than one delivery? (Mark Pritchard/Creative Commons)

document of title or by obtaining the *bailee's (warehouser's) acknowledgment* that the buyer is entitled to possession.[1]

Carrier Cases In many instances, attendant circumstances or delivery terms in the contract make it apparent that the parties intend that a carrier be used to move the goods. In carrier cases, a seller can complete performance of the obligation to deliver the goods in two ways—through a shipment contract or through a destination contract.

Shipment Contracts. Recall from Chapter 11 that a *shipment contract* requires or authorizes the seller to ship goods by a carrier. The contract does not require that the seller deliver the goods at a particular destination [UCC 2–319, 2–509]. Under a shipment contract, unless otherwise agreed, the seller must do the following:

1 Put the goods into the hands of the carrier.

2 Make a contract for their transportation that is reasonable according to the nature of the goods and their value. (For example, certain types of goods need refrigeration in transit.)

3 Obtain and promptly deliver or tender to the buyer any documents necessary to enable the buyer to obtain possession of the goods from the carrier.

4 Promptly notify the buyer that shipment has been made [UCC 2–504].

If the seller fails to notify the buyer that shipment has been made or fails to make a proper contract for transportation, the buyer can treat the contract as breached and reject the goods, but only if a *material loss* of the goods or a significant *delay* results. Of course, the parties can agree that a lesser amount of loss or that any delay will be grounds for rejection.

Destination Contracts. Under a *destination contract*, the seller agrees to see that conforming goods will be duly tendered to the buyer at a particular destination. The goods must be tendered at a reasonable hour and held at the buyer's disposal for a reasonable length of time. The seller must also give the buyer any appropriate notice that is necessary to enable the buyer to take delivery. In addition, the seller must provide the buyer with any documents of title necessary to enable the buyer to obtain delivery from the carrier [UCC 2–503].

The Perfect Tender Rule

As previously noted, the seller or lessor has an obligation to ship or tender *conforming goods*, and the buyer or lessee is required to accept and pay for the goods according to the terms of the contract. Under the common law, the seller was obligated to deliver goods in conformity with the terms of the contract in every detail. This was called the *perfect tender* doctrine. The UCC preserves the perfect tender doctrine by stating that if goods or tender of delivery fails *in any respect* to conform to the contract, the buyer or lessee has the right to accept the goods, reject the entire shipment, or accept part and reject part [UCC 2–601, 2A–509].

■EXAMPLE 12.2 A lessor contracts to lease fifty Vericlear monitors to be delivered at the lessee's place of business on or before October 1. On September 28, the lessor discovers that it has only thirty Vericlear monitors in inventory, but that it will have another forty Vericlear monitors within the next two weeks. The lessor tenders delivery of the thirty Vericlear

KEEP IN MIND If goods never arrive, the buyer or seller usually has at least some recourse against the carrier. Also, a buyer normally insures the goods from the time they leave the seller's possession.

DON'T FORGET Documents of title include bills of lading, warehouse receipts, and any other documents that, in the regular course of business, entitle a person holding these documents to obtain possession of, and title to, the goods covered.

---

1. If the seller delivers a nonnegotiable document of title or merely writes instructions to the bailee to release the goods to the buyer without the bailee's *acknowledgment* of the buyer's rights, this is also a sufficient tender, unless the buyer objects [UCC 2–503(4)]. Risk of loss, however, does not pass until the buyer has a reasonable amount of time in which to present the document or to give the bailee instructions for delivery.

monitors on October 1, with the promise that the other monitors will be delivered within two weeks. Because the lessor failed to make a perfect tender of fifty Vericlear monitors, the lessee has the right to reject the entire shipment and hold the lessor in breach. ■

Exceptions to Perfect Tender

Because of the rigidity of the perfect tender rule, several exceptions to the rule have been created, some of which are discussed here.

Agreement of the Parties   Exceptions to the perfect tender rule may be established by agreement. If the parties have agreed, for example, that defective goods or parts will not be rejected if the seller or lessor is able to repair or replace them within a reasonable period of time, the perfect tender rule does not apply.

Cure   The UCC does not specifically define the term *cure*, but it refers to the right of the seller or lessor to repair, adjust, or replace defective or nonconforming goods [UCC 2–508, 2A–513]. When any tender of delivery is rejected because of nonconforming goods and the time for performance has not yet expired, the seller or lessor can notify the buyer or lessee promptly of the intention to cure and can then do so *within the contract time for performance* [UCC 2–508(1), 2A–513(1)]. Once the time for performance has expired, the seller or lessor can still, for a reasonable time, exercise the right to cure with respect to the rejected goods if he or she had, at the time of delivery, *reasonable grounds to believe that the nonconforming tender would be acceptable to the buyer or lessee* [UCC 2–508(2), 2A–513(2)].

ON THE WEB

To view the UCC provisions discussed in this chapter, go to

www.law.cornell.edu/ucc/ucc.table.html.

Sometimes, a seller or lessor will tender nonconforming goods with some type of price allowance. The allowance serves as the "reasonable grounds" for the seller or lessor to believe that the nonconforming tender will be acceptable to the buyer or lessee. A seller or lessor might also have other reasons for assuming that a buyer or lessee will accept a nonconforming tender. **■EXAMPLE 12.3** Suppose that in the past the buyer, an office supply store, frequently accepted blue pens when the seller did not have black pens in stock. In this context, the seller has reasonable grounds to believe the store will again accept such a substitute. If the store rejects the substituted goods (blue pens) on a particular occasion, the seller nonetheless had reasonable grounds to believe that the blue pens would be acceptable. Therefore, the seller can cure within a reasonable time, even though the delivery of black pens will occur after the time limit for performance allowed under the contract. ■

The right to cure means that, to reject goods, the buyer or lessee must give notice to the seller or lessor of a particular defect. For example, if a lessee refuses a tender of goods as nonconforming but does not disclose the nature of the defect to the lessor, the lessee cannot later assert the defect as a defense if the defect is one that the lessor could have cured. Generally, buyers and lessees must act in good faith and state specific reasons for refusing to accept goods [UCC 2–605, 2A–514].

Substitution of Carriers   When an agreed-on manner of delivery (such as which carrier will be used to transport the goods) becomes impracticable or unavailable through no fault of either party, but a commercially reasonable substitute is available, the seller must use this substitute performance, which is sufficient tender to the buyer [UCC 2–614(1)]. **■EXAMPLE 12.4** A sales contract calls for the delivery of a large generator to be shipped by Roadway Trucking Corporation on or before June 1. The contract terms clearly state the importance of the delivery date. The employees of Roadway Trucking go on strike. The seller is required to make a reasonable substitute tender, perhaps by rail if that is available. Note that the seller will normally be responsible for any additional shipping costs, unless other arrangements have been made in the sales contract. ■

Installment Contracts An **installment contract** is a single contract that requires or authorizes delivery in two or more separate lots to be accepted and paid for separately. With an installment contract, a buyer or lessee can reject an installment *only if the nonconformity substantially impairs the value* of the installment and cannot be cured [UCC 2–307, 2–612(2), 2A–510(1)].

Unless the contract provides otherwise, the entire installment contract is breached only when one or more nonconforming installments *substantially* impair the value of the *whole contract.* If the buyer or lessee subsequently accepts a nonconforming installment and fails to notify the seller or lessor of cancellation, however, the contract is reinstated [UCC 2–612(3), 2A–510(2)].

A major issue to be determined is what constitutes substantial impairment of the "value of the whole contract." **■EXAMPLE 12.5** Consider an installment contract for the sale of twenty carloads of plywood. The first carload does not conform to the contract because 9 percent of the plywood deviates from the thickness specifications. The buyer cancels the contract, and immediately thereafter the second and third carloads of conforming plywood arrive at the buyer's place of business. If a lawsuit ensues, the court will have to grapple with the question of whether the 9 percent of nonconforming plywood substantially impaired the value of the whole. ■

The point to remember is that the UCC significantly alters the right of the buyer or lessee to reject the entire contract if the contract requires delivery to be made in several installments. The UCC strictly limits rejection to cases of *substantial* nonconformity.

Commercial Impracticability As mentioned in Chapter 9, occurrences unforeseen by either party when a contract was made may make performance commercially impracticable. When this occurs, the rule of perfect tender no longer holds. According to UCC 2–615(a) and 2A–405(a), a delay in delivery or nondelivery in whole or in part is not a breach when performance has been made impracticable "by the occurrence of a contingency the non-occurrence of which was a basic assumption on which the contract was made." The seller or lessor must, however, notify the buyer or lessee as soon as practicable that there will be a delay or nondelivery.

Foreseeable versus Unforeseeable Contingencies. The doctrine of commercial impracticability does not extend to problems that could have been foreseen. An increase in cost resulting from inflation, for example, does not in and of itself excuse performance, as this kind of risk is ordinarily assumed by a seller or lessor conducting business. The unforeseen contingency must be one that would have been impossible to contemplate in a given business situation. **■EXAMPLE 12.6** A major oil company that receives its supplies from the Middle East has a contract to supply a buyer with 100,000 gallons of oil. Because of an oil embargo by the Organization of Petroleum Exporting Countries (OPEC), the seller is prevented from securing oil supplies to meet the terms of the contract. Because of the same embargo, the seller cannot secure oil from any other source. This situation comes fully under the commercial impracticability exception to the perfect tender doctrine. ■

Can unanticipated increases in a seller's costs, which make performance "impracticable," constitute a valid defense to performance on the basis of commercial impracticability? The court dealt with this question in the following case.

INSTALLMENT CONTRACT
Under the UCC, a contract that requires or authorizes delivery in two or more separate lots to be accepted and paid for separately.

CASE 12.1   Maple Farms, Inc. v. City School District of Elmira

LANDMARK AND CLASSIC CASES

Supreme Court of New York, 76 Misc.2d 1080, 352 N.Y.S.2d 784 (1974).

FACTS On June 15, 1973, Maple Farms, Inc., formed an agreement with the city school district of Elmira, New York, to supply the school district with milk for the 1973–1974 school year. The agreement was in the form of a requirements contract, under which Maple Farms would sell to the school district all the milk the district required at a fixed price—which was the June market price of milk. By December 1973, the price of raw milk had increased by 23 percent over the price specified in the contract. This meant that if the terms of the contract were fulfilled, Maple Farms would lose $7,350. Because it had similar contracts with other school districts, Maple Farms stood to lose a great deal if it was held to the price stated in the contracts. When the school district would not agree to release Maple Farms from its contract, Maple Farms brought an action in a New York state court for a declaratory judgment (a determination of the parties' rights under a contract). Maple Farms contended that the substantial increase in the price of raw milk was an event not contemplated by the parties when the contract was formed and that, given the increased price, performance of the contract was commercially impracticable.

ISSUE Can Maple Farms be released from the contract on the ground of commercial impracticability?

DECISION No. The court ruled that performance in this case was not impracticable.

REASON The court reasoned that commercial impracticability arises when an event occurs that is totally unexpected and unforeseeable by the parties. The increased price of raw milk was not totally unexpected, given that in the previous year the price of milk had risen 10 percent and that the price of milk had traditionally varied. Additionally, the general inflation of prices in the United States should have been anticipated. Maple Farms had reason to know these facts and could have included a clause in its contract with the school district to protect itself from its present situation. The court also noted that the primary purpose of the contract, on the part of the school district, was to protect itself (for budgeting purposes) against price fluctuations.

WHAT IF THE FACTS WERE DIFFERENT? *Suppose that the court had ruled in the plaintiff's favor. How might that ruling have affected the plaintiff's contracts with other parties?*

IMPACT OF THIS CASE ON TODAY'S LAW *This case is a classic illustration of the UCC's commercial impracticability doctrine. Under this doctrine, parties who freely enter into contracts normally will not be excused from their contractual obligations simply because changed circumstances make performance difficult or unprofitable. Rather, to be excused from performance, a party must show that the changed circumstances were impossible to foresee at the time the contract was formed. This principle continues to be applied today.*

RELEVANT WEB SITES *To locate information on the Web concerning the* Maple Farms *decision, go to this text's Web site at* **academic.cengage.com/blaw/blt**, *select "Chapter 12," and click on "URLs for Landmarks."*

Partial Performance.   Sometimes, an unforeseen event only *partially* affects the capacity of the seller or lessor to perform, and the seller or lessor is thus able to fulfill the contract *partially* but cannot tender total performance. In this event, the seller or lessor is required to allocate in a fair and reasonable manner any remaining production and deliveries among those to whom it is contractually obligated to deliver the goods, and this allocation may take into account its regular customers [UCC 2–615(b), 2A–405(b)]. The buyer or lessee must receive notice of the allocation and has the right to accept or reject the allocation [UCC 2–615(c), 2A–405(c)].

■**EXAMPLE 12.7** A Florida orange grower, Best Citrus, Inc., contracts to sell this season's crop to a number of customers, including Martin's grocery chain. Martin's contracts to purchase two thousand crates of oranges. Best Citrus has sprayed some of its orange groves with a chemical called Karmoxin. The Department of Agriculture discovers that persons who eat products sprayed with Karmoxin may develop cancer. The department issues an order prohibiting the sale of these products. Best Citrus picks all of the oranges not sprayed with Karmoxin, but the quantity does not fully meet all the contracted-for deliveries. In this situation, Best Citrus is required to allocate its production, and it notifies Martin's that it cannot deliver the full quantity agreed on in the contract and specifies the amount it will be able to deliver under the circumstances. Martin's can either accept or reject the allocation, but Best Citrus has no further contractual liability. ◼

ETHICAL ISSUE 12.1

Should juries decide complicated issues of performance and breach under the UCC? Litigation over sales contracts is often quite complex and involves large companies and numerous transactions. Jurors usually are unfamiliar with large-scale business transactions and the UCC, yet they decide important issues such as whether a company's performance should be excused as commercially impracticable. Consider a case that arose between a honey-farming company, Adee Honey, and a wholesaler, Melford Olsen Honey, Inc. (Mel-O). In June 2002, Mel-O ordered 3.2 million pounds of honey from Adee for $1.00 a pound. The contract included a *force majeure* clause excusing performance in the event of "an act of God such as a drought or flood." Later that summer, Adee's farm began experiencing drought-like conditions, and Adee stopped shipping honey. Adee's owner informed Mel-O of the drought, and they discussed increasing the contract price to cover losses Adee would suffer. Mel-O offered to pay $1.10 per pound, but Adee wanted $1.55 per pound. In the fall of 2002, Adee started delivering honey to Mel-O at a price of $1.55 per pound, but Mel-O refused to pay.

Mel-O filed a lawsuit against Adee in federal court for breaching the contract by not fully performing. Adee claimed that its breach was excused by commercial impracticability and the *force majeure* clause. The jury determined that Adee was not excused from performing the contract due to drought and awarded Mel-O damages for the breach. Because the jury had heard evidence concerning the drought and Adee's ability to perform, the appellate court would not overturn the jury's findings of fact. Although the *force majeure* clause would have allowed Adee to stop performance (if the jury had agreed there was a drought), the court reasoned that the clause would not justify Adee's price increase to $1.55 per pound. In sum, the jury decided that Adee must pay damages, including an amount for Mel-O's lost profits, for not delivering every pound of honey required under the contract, despite the drought-like conditions. Although the appellate court noted that the amount of damages awarded by the jury resulted in Adee receiving less than $1.00 per pound for the honey, the court affirmed the decision and refused to adjust the damages.[2]

◼

Destruction of Identified Goods The UCC provides that when an unexpected event, such as a fire, totally destroys *goods identified at the time the contract is formed* through no fault of either party and *before risk passes to the buyer or lessee,* the parties are excused from performance [UCC 2–613, 2A–221]. If the goods are only partially destroyed, however, the buyer or lessee can inspect them and either treat the contract as void or accept the goods with a reduction of the contract price.

◼EXAMPLE 12.8 Atlas Sporting Equipment agrees to lease to River Bicycles sixty bicycles of a particular model that has been discontinued. No other bicycles of that model are available. River specifies that it needs the bicycles to rent to tourists. Before Atlas can deliver the bicycles, they are destroyed by a fire. In this situation, Atlas is not liable to River for failing to deliver the bicycles. The goods were destroyed through no fault of either party, before the risk

2. *Melford Olsen Honey, Inc. v. Adee*, 452 F.3d 956 (8th Cir. 2006).

A fire destroys a building holding warehoused goods in Bloomington, Illinois. Suppose that there were goods inside that had been identified to a sales contract but for which the risk of loss had not yet passed to the buyer. If the buyer sues the seller for breaching the contract by not delivering the goods, will the seller be held liable? Why or why not? ("Syslfrog"/Creative Commons)

of loss passed to the lessee. The loss was total, so the contract is avoided. Clearly, Atlas has no obligation to tender the bicycles, and River has no obligation to pay for them. ■

Assurance and Cooperation   Two other exceptions to the perfect tender doctrine apply equally to parties to sales and lease contracts: the right of assurance and the duty of cooperation.

The Right of Assurance.   The UCC provides that if one party to a contract has "reasonable grounds" to believe that the other party will not perform as contracted, he or she may *in writing* "demand adequate assurance of due performance" from the other party. Until such assurance is received, he or she may "suspend" further performance (such as payments due under the contract) without liability. What constitutes "reasonable grounds" is determined by commercial standards. If such assurances are not forthcoming within a reasonable time (not to exceed thirty days), the failure to respond may be treated as a *repudiation* of the contract [UCC 2–609, 2A–401].

■EXAMPLE 12.9 Two companies that make road-surfacing materials, Koch Materials Company and Shore Slurry Seal, Inc., enter into a contract. Koch obtains a license to use Novachip, a special material made by Shore, and Shore agrees to buy all of its asphalt from Koch for the next seven years. A few years into the contract term, Shore notifies Koch that it is planning to sell its assets to Asphalt Paving Systems, Inc. Koch demands assurances that Asphalt Paving will continue the deal, but Shore refuses to provide assurances. In this situation, Koch can treat Shore's failure to give assurances as a repudiation and file suit against Shore for breach of contract.[3] ■

A businessperson who has doubts about the other party's ability or willingness to perform a sales contract should always demand adequate assurances. The UCC comes to the aid of a party who has reasonable grounds to suspect that the other party to a contract will not perform as promised. Rather than having to "wait and see" (and possibly incur significant losses as a result), the party with such suspicions may seek adequate assurance of performance from the other party. The failure to give such assurance can be treated as an anticipatory repudiation (breach) of the contract, thus entitling the nonbreaching party to seek damages (*anticipatory repudiation* will be discussed later in this chapter). Perhaps more important, this failure allows the nonbreaching party to suspend its performance, which can save a business from sustaining substantial losses that could be recovered only through litigation. Ultimately, it may be better simply to withdraw from a deal when the other party will not provide assurances than to continue with a contract that is likely to be breached anyway and then bring a lawsuit.

■

The Duty of Cooperation.   Sometimes, the performance of one party depends on the cooperation of the other. The UCC provides that when such cooperation is not forthcoming, the other party can suspend her or his own performance without liability and hold the uncooperative party in breach or proceed to perform the contract in any reasonable manner [UCC 2–311(3)(b)].

■EXAMPLE 12.10 Aman is required by contract to deliver 1,200 model HE washing machines to various locations in California. Deliveries are to be made on or before October 1, and the locations are to be specified later by Farrell. Aman has repeatedly

3. *Koch Materials Co. v. Shore Slurry Seal, Inc.*, 205 F.Supp.2d 324 (D.N.J. 2002).

requested the delivery locations, but Farrell has not responded. On October 1, the washing machines are ready to be shipped, but Farrell still refuses to give Aman the delivery locations. Aman does not ship on October 1. Can Aman be held liable? The answer is no. Aman is excused for any resulting delay of performance because of Farrell's failure to cooperate. ◼

OBLIGATIONS OF THE BUYER OR LESSEE

The main obligation of the buyer or lessee under a sales or lease contract is to pay for the goods tendered in accordance with the contract.

Payment

Once the seller or lessor has adequately tendered delivery, the buyer or lessee is obligated to accept the goods and pay for them according to the terms of the contract. In the absence of any specific agreements, the buyer or lessee must make payment at the time and place the goods are received, even if the place of shipment is the place of delivery [UCC 2–310(a), 2A–516(1)]. Under a lease contract, a lessee must pay the lease payment that was specified in the contract [UCC 2A–516(1)].

When a sale is made on credit, the buyer is obliged to pay according to the specified credit terms (for example, 60, 90, or 120 days), not when the goods are received. The credit period usually begins on the *date of shipment* [UCC 2–310(d)].

Payment can be made by any means agreed on by the parties—cash or any other method generally acceptable in the commercial world. If the seller demands cash when the buyer offers a check, credit card, or the like, the seller must permit the buyer reasonable time to obtain legal tender [UCC 2–511].

Right of Inspection

The buyer or lessee has an absolute right to inspect the goods unless the parties have agreed otherwise. This right allows the buyer or lessee to verify, before making payment, that the goods tendered or delivered are what were contracted for or ordered. If the goods are not what were ordered, the buyer or lessee has no duty to pay. *An opportunity for inspection is therefore a condition precedent to the right of the seller or lessor to enforce payment* [UCC 2–513(1), 2A–515(1)].

Inspection can take place at any reasonable place and time and in any reasonable manner. Generally, what is reasonable is determined by custom of the trade, past practices of the parties, and the like. The buyer bears the costs of inspecting the goods (unless otherwise agreed), but if the goods are rejected because they are not conforming, the buyer can recover the costs of inspection from the seller [UCC 2–513(2)].

Acceptance

A buyer or lessee can manifest assent to the delivered goods in the following ways, each of which constitutes acceptance:

1 If, after having had a reasonable opportunity to inspect the goods, the buyer or lessee signifies to the seller or lessor that the goods either are conforming or are acceptable in spite of their nonconformity [UCC 2–606(1)(a), 2A–515(1)(a)].

2 If the buyer or lessee has had a reasonable opportunity to inspect the goods and has failed to reject them within a reasonable period of time, then acceptance is presumed [UCC 2–602(1), 2–606(1)(b), 2A–515(1)(b)].

3 In sales contracts, if the buyer performs any act inconsistent with the seller's ownership, then the buyer will be deemed to have accepted the goods. For example, any use or resale of the goods—except for the limited purpose of testing or inspecting the goods—generally constitutes an acceptance [UCC 2–606(1)(c)].

If some of the goods delivered do not conform to the contract and the seller or lessor has failed to cure, the buyer or lessee can make a *partial* acceptance [UCC 2–601(c), 2A–509(1)]. The same is true if the nonconformity was not reasonably discoverable before acceptance. (In the latter situation, the buyer or lessee may be able to revoke the acceptance, as will be discussed later in this chapter.)

A buyer or lessee cannot accept less than a single commercial unit, however. The UCC defines a *commercial unit* as a unit of goods that, by commercial usage, is viewed as a "single whole" for purposes of sale, and its division would materially impair the character of the unit, its market value, or its use [UCC 2–105(6), 2A–103(1)(c)]. A commercial unit can be a single article (such as a machine), a set of articles (such as a suite of furniture or an assortment of sizes), a quantity (such as a bale, a gross, or a carload), or any other unit treated in the trade as a single whole.

ANTICIPATORY REPUDIATION

What if, before the time for contract performance, one party clearly communicates to the other the intention not to perform? As discussed in Chapter 9, such an action is a breach of the contract by anticipatory repudiation.[4]

Suspension of Performance Obligations

When anticipatory repudiation occurs, the nonbreaching party has a choice of two responses: (1) treat the repudiation as a final breach by pursuing a remedy or (2) wait to see if the repudiating party will decide to honor the contract despite the avowed intention to renege [UCC 2–610, 2A–402]. In either situation, the nonbreaching party may suspend performance.

A Repudiation May Be Retracted

The UCC permits the breaching party (subject to some limitations) to "retract" his or her repudiation. This can be done by any method that clearly indicates the party's intent to perform. Once retraction is made, the rights of the repudiating party under the contract are reinstated. The breaching party cannot retract the repudiation, however, if since the time of the repudiation the other party has canceled or materially changed position or otherwise indicated that the repudiation is final [UCC 2–611, 2A–403].

■EXAMPLE 12.11 Cora, who owns a small inn, purchases a suite of furniture from Horton's Furniture Warehouse on April 1. The contract states, "delivery must be made on or before May 1." On April 10, Horton informs Cora that he cannot make delivery until May 10 and asks her to consent to the modified delivery date. In this situation, Cora has the option of either treating Horton's notice of late delivery as a final breach of contract and pursuing a remedy or agreeing to the later delivery date. Suppose that Cora does neither for two weeks. On April 24, Horton informs Cora that he will be able to deliver the furniture by May 1, after all. In effect, Horton has retracted his repudiation, reinstating the rights and obligations of the parties under the original contract. Note that if Cora had indicated after Horton's repudiation that she was canceling the contract, Horton would not have been able to retract his repudiation. ■

---

4. This doctrine was first enunciated in an English case decided in 1853, *Hochster v. De La Tour*, 2 Ellis and Blackburn Reports 678 (1853).

REMEDIES OF THE SELLER OR LESSOR

When the buyer or lessee is in breach, the seller or lessor has numerous remedies available under the UCC. Generally, the remedies available to the seller or lessor depend on the circumstances at the time of the breach, such as which party has possession of the goods, whether the goods are in transit, and whether the buyer or lessee has rejected or accepted the goods.

When the Goods Are in the Possession of the Seller or Lessor

Under the UCC, if the buyer or lessee breaches the contract before the goods have been delivered to her or him, the seller or lessor has the right to pursue the remedies discussed here.

> **NOTE** A buyer or lessee breaches a contract by wrongfully rejecting the goods, wrongfully revoking acceptance, refusing to pay, or repudiating the contract.

The Right to Cancel the Contract One of the options available to a seller or lessor when the buyer or lessee breaches the contract is simply to cancel (rescind) the contract [UCC 2–703(f), 2A–523(1)(a)]. The seller must notify the buyer or lessee of the cancellation, and at that point all remaining obligations of the seller or lessor are discharged. The buyer or lessee is not discharged from all remaining obligations, however; he or she is in breach, and the seller or lessor can pursue remedies available under the UCC for breach.

The Right to Withhold Delivery In general, sellers and lessors can withhold or discontinue performance of their obligations under sales or lease contracts when the buyers or lessees are in breach. If a buyer or lessee has wrongfully rejected or revoked acceptance of contract goods (rejection and revocation of acceptance will be discussed later), failed to make proper and timely payment, or repudiated a part of the contract, the seller or lessor can withhold delivery of the goods in question [UCC 2–703(a), 2A–523(1)(c)]. If the breach results from the buyer's or the lessee's insolvency (inability to pay debts as they become due), the seller or lessor can refuse to deliver the goods unless the buyer or lessee pays in cash [UCC 2–702(1), 2A–525(1)].

The Right to Resell or Dispose of the Goods When a buyer or lessee breaches or repudiates a sales contract while the seller or lessor is still in possession of the goods, the seller or lessor can resell or dispose of the goods. The seller can retain any profits made as a result of the sale and can hold the buyer or lessee liable for any loss [UCC 2–703(d), 2–706(1), 2A–523(1)(e), 2A–527(1)].

When the goods contracted for are unfinished at the time of breach, the seller or lessor can do one of two things: (1) cease manufacturing the goods and resell them for scrap or salvage value or (2) complete the manufacture and resell or dispose of them, holding the buyer or lessee liable for any deficiency. In choosing between these two alternatives, the seller or lessor must exercise reasonable commercial judgment to mitigate the loss and obtain maximum value from the unfinished goods [UCC 2–704(2), 2A–524(2)]. Any resale of the goods must be made in good faith and in a commercially reasonable manner.

In sales transactions, the seller can recover any deficiency between the resale price and the contract price, along with **incidental damages,** defined as the costs resulting from the breach [UCC 2–706(1), 2–710]. The resale can be private or public, and the goods can be sold as a unit or in parcels. The seller must give the original buyer reasonable notice of the resale, unless the goods are perishable or will rapidly decline in value [UCC 2–706(2), (3)]. A good faith purchaser in a resale takes the goods free of any of the rights of the original buyer, even if the seller fails to comply with these requirements of the UCC [UCC 2–706(5)].

INCIDENTAL DAMAGES
All costs resulting from a breach of contract, including all reasonable expenses incurred because of the breach.

In lease transactions, the lessor may lease the goods to another party and recover from the original lessee, as damages, any unpaid lease payments up to the beginning date of the lease term under the new lease. The lessor can also recover any deficiency between the lease payments due under the original lease contract and those due under the new lease contract, along with incidental damages [UCC 2A–527(2)].

The Right to Recover the Purchase Price or the Lease Payments Due   Under the UCC, an unpaid seller or lessor can bring an action to recover the purchase price or payments due under the lease contract, plus incidental damages, if the seller or lessor is unable to resell or dispose of the goods [UCC 2–709(1), 2A–529(1)].

   ■**EXAMPLE 12.12** Suppose that Southern Realty contracts with Gem Point, Inc., to purchase one thousand pens with Southern Realty's name inscribed on them. Gem Point tenders delivery of the one thousand pens, but Southern Realty wrongfully refuses to accept them. In this situation, Gem Point has, as a proper remedy, an action for the purchase price. Gem Point tendered delivery of conforming goods, and Southern Realty, by failing to accept the goods, is in breach. Gem Point obviously cannot sell to anyone else the pens inscribed with the buyer's business name, so this situation falls under UCC 2–709. ■

   If a seller or lessor is unable to resell or dispose of goods and sues for the contract price or lease payments due, the goods must be held for the buyer or lessee. The seller or lessor can resell or dispose of the goods at any time prior to collection (of the judgment) from the buyer or lessee, but must credit the net proceeds from the sale to the buyer or lessee. This is an example of the duty to mitigate damages.

The Right to Recover Damages   If a buyer or lessee repudiates a contract or wrongfully refuses to accept the goods, a seller or lessor can maintain an action to recover the damages that were sustained. Ordinarily, the amount of damages equals the difference between the contract price or lease payments and the market price or lease payments (at the time and place of tender of the goods), plus incidental damages [UCC 2–708(1), 2A–528(1)]. The time and place of tender are frequently given by such terms as F.O.B., F.A.S., and C.I.F., which determine whether there is a shipment or destination contract.[5]

When the Goods Are in Transit

If the seller or lessor has delivered the goods to a carrier or a bailee but the buyer or lessee has not as yet received them, the goods are said to be *in transit*. If, while the goods are in transit, the seller or lessor learns that the buyer or lessee is insolvent, the seller or lessor can stop the carrier or bailee from delivering the goods, regardless of the quantity of goods shipped. If the buyer or lessee is in breach but is not insolvent, the seller or lessor can stop the goods in transit only if the quantity shipped is at least a carload, a truckload, a planeload, or a larger shipment [UCC 2–705(1), 2A–526(1)].

   ■**EXAMPLE 12.13** Suppose that Arturo Ortega orders a truckload of lumber from Timber Products, Inc., to be shipped to Ortega six weeks later. Ortega, who owes Timber Products for a past shipment, promises to pay the debt immediately and to pay for the current shipment as soon as it is received. After the lumber has been shipped, Timber Products is notified by a bankruptcy court judge that Ortega has filed a petition in bankruptcy and listed Timber Products as one of his creditors (see Chapter 16). If the goods are still in transit, Timber Products can stop the carrier from delivering the lumber to Ortega. ■

Requirements for Stopping Delivery   To stop delivery, the seller or lessor must *timely notify* the carrier or other bailee that the goods are to be returned or held for the seller or

---

5. See Exhibit 11–2 on page 343 for definitions of these contract terms.

lessor. If the carrier has sufficient time to stop delivery, it must hold and deliver the goods according to the instructions of the seller or lessor, who is liable to the carrier for any additional costs incurred [UCC 2–705(3), 2A–526(3)].

The sellor or lessor has the right to stop delivery of the goods under UCC 2–705(2) and 2A–526(2) until the time when:

1 The buyer or lessee obtains possession of the goods.

2 The carrier or the bailee acknowledges the rights of the buyer or lessee in the goods (by reshipping or holding the goods for the buyer or lessee, for example).

3 A negotiable document of title covering the goods has been properly transferred to the buyer (in sales transactions only), giving the buyer ownership rights in the goods [UCC 2–705(2)].

Remedies Once the Goods Are Reclaimed   Once the seller or lessor reclaims the goods in transit, she or he can pursue the remedies allowed to sellers and lessors when the goods are in their possession. In other words, the seller or lessor who has reclaimed goods may do the following:

1 Cancel (rescind) the contract.

2 Resell the goods and recover any deficiency.

3 Sue for any deficiency between the contract price (or lease payments due) and the market price (or market lease payments), plus incidental damages.

4 Sue to recover the purchase price or lease payments due if the goods cannot be resold, plus incidental damages.

5 Sue to recover damages.

When the Goods Are in the Possession of the Buyer or Lessee

When the buyer or lessee breaches a sales or lease contract and the goods are in the buyer's or lessee's possession, the UCC gives the seller or lessor the following limited remedies.

The Right to Recover the Purchase Price or Payments Due under the Lease Contract
If the buyer or lessee has accepted the goods but refuses to pay for them, the seller or lessor can sue for the purchase price of the goods or the lease payments due, plus incidental damages [UCC 2–709(1), 2A–529(1)].

RECALL Incidental damages include all reasonable expenses incurred because of a breach of contract.

The Right to Reclaim the Goods   In a sales transaction, if a seller discovers that the buyer has received goods on credit and is insolvent, the seller can demand return of the goods. Ordinarily, the demand must be made within ten days of the buyer's receipt of the goods. The seller can demand and reclaim the goods at any time, though, if the buyer misrepresented his or her solvency in writing during the three months prior to the delivery of the goods [UCC 2–702(2)]. The seller's right to reclaim the goods, however, is subject to the rights of a good faith purchaser or other subsequent buyer in the ordinary course of business who purchases the goods from the buyer before the seller reclaims them.

Under the UCC, a seller seeking to exercise the right to reclaim goods receives preferential treatment over the buyer's other creditors—the seller need only demand the return of the goods within ten days after the buyer has received them.[6] Because of this preferential

---

6. A seller who has delivered goods to an insolvent buyer also receives preferential treatment if the buyer enters into bankruptcy proceedings (discussed in Chapter 16).

treatment, the UCC provides that reclamation *bars* the seller from pursuing any other remedy as to these goods [UCC 2–702(3)].

In regard to lease contracts, if the lessee defaults (fails to make payments that are due, for example), the lessor may reclaim the leased goods that are in the lessee's possession [UCC 2A–525(2)].

REMEDIES OF THE BUYER OR LESSEE

NOTE A seller or lessor breaches a contract by wrongfully failing to deliver the goods, delivering nonconforming goods, making an improper tender of the goods, or repudiating the contract.

When the seller or lessor breaches the contract, the buyer or lessee has numerous remedies available under the UCC in addition to recovery of as much of the price as has been paid. Like the remedies available to sellers and lessors, the remedies of buyers and lessees depend on the circumstances existing at the time of the breach. (See the *Application* feature at the end of this chapter for some suggestions on what to do when a contract is breached.)

When the Seller or Lessor Refuses to Deliver the Goods

If the seller or lessor refuses to deliver the goods or the buyer or lessee has rejected the goods, the remedies available to the buyer or lessee include those discussed here.

The Right to Cancel the Contract When a seller or lessor fails to make proper delivery or repudiates the contract, the buyer or lessee can cancel, or rescind, the contract. On notice of cancellation, the buyer or lessee is relieved of any further obligations under the contract but retains all rights to other remedies against the seller [UCC 2–711(1), 2A–508(1)(a)].

The Right to Recover the Goods If a buyer or lessee has made a partial or full payment for goods that remain in the possession of the seller or lessor, the buyer or lessee can recover the goods if the seller or lessor is insolvent or becomes insolvent within ten days after receiving the first payment and if the goods are identified to the contract. To exercise this right, the buyer or lessee must tender to the seller any unpaid balance of the purchase price [UCC 2–502, 2A–522].

The Right to Obtain Specific Performance A buyer or lessee can obtain specific performance when the goods are unique and the remedy at law is inadequate [UCC 2–716(1), 2A–521(1)]. Ordinarily, a successful suit for monetary damages is sufficient to place a buyer or lessee in the position he or she would have occupied if the seller or lessor had fully performed. When the contract is for the purchase of a particular work of art or a similarly unique item, however, monetary damages may not be sufficient. Under these circumstances, equity will require that the seller or lessor perform exactly by delivering the particular goods identified to the contract (a remedy of specific performance).

COVER
Under the UCC, a remedy that allows the buyer or lessee, on the seller's or lessor's breach, to purchase the goods, in good faith and within a reasonable time, from another seller or lessor and substitute them for the goods due under the contract. If the cost of cover exceeds the cost of the contract goods, the breaching seller or lessor will be liable to the buyer or lessee for the difference, plus incidental and consequential damages.

The Right of Cover In certain situations, buyers and lessees can protect themselves by obtaining **cover**—that is, by purchasing or leasing other goods to substitute for those due under the contract. This option is available when the seller or lessor repudiates the contract or fails to deliver the goods, or when a buyer or lessee has rightfully rejected goods or revoked acceptance.

In obtaining cover, the buyer or lessee must act in good faith and without unreasonable delay [UCC 2–712, 2A–518]. After purchasing or leasing substitute goods, the buyer or lessee can recover from the seller or lessor the difference between the cost of cover and the contract price (or lease payments), plus incidental and consequential damages, less the expenses (such as delivery costs) that were saved as a result of the breach [UCC 2–712, 2–715, 2A–518]. Consequential damages are any losses suffered by the buyer or lessee that the seller or lessor could have foreseen (had reason to know about) at the time of contract formation and any injury to the buyer's or lessee's person or property proximately resulting from the contract's breach [UCC 2–715(2), 2A–520(2)].

Buyers and lessees are not required to cover, and failure to do so will not bar them from using any other remedies available under the UCC. A buyer or lessee who fails to cover, however, may *not* be able to collect consequential damages that could have been avoided by purchasing or leasing substitute goods.

The Right to Replevy Goods   Buyers and lessees also have the right to replevy goods. Replevin[7] is an action to recover specific goods in the hands of a party who is wrongfully withholding them from the other party. Outside the UCC, the term *replevin* refers to a *prejudgment process* (a proceeding that takes place prior to a court's judgment) that permits the seizure of specific personal property in which a party claims a right or an interest. Under the UCC, the buyer or lessee can replevy goods subject to the contract if the seller or lessor has repudiated or breached the contract. To maintain an action to replevy goods, usually buyers and lessees must show that they are unable to cover for the goods after a reasonable effort [UCC 2–716(3), 2A–521(3)].

REPLEVIN
An action to recover identified goods in the hands of a party who is wrongfully withholding them from the other party. Under the UCC, this remedy is usually available only if the buyer or lessee is unable to cover.

The Right to Recover Damages   If a seller or lessor repudiates the sales contract or fails to deliver the goods, or the buyer or lessee has rightfully rejected or revoked acceptance of the goods, the buyer or lessee can sue for damages. The measure of recovery is the difference between the contract price (or lease payments) and the market price of (or lease payments that could be obtained for) the goods at the time the buyer (or lessee) *learned* of the breach. The market price or market lease payments are determined at the place where the seller or lessor was supposed to deliver the goods. The buyer or lessee can also recover incidental and consequential damages, less the expenses that were saved as a result of the breach [UCC 2–713, 2A–519].

■**EXAMPLE 12.14** Schilling orders ten thousand bushels of wheat from Valdone for $5 a bushel, with delivery due on June 14 and payment due on June 20. Valdone does not deliver on June 14. On June 14, the market price of wheat is $5.50 per bushel. Schilling chooses to do without the wheat. He sues Valdone for damages for nondelivery. Schilling can recover $0.50 × 10,000, or $5,000, plus any expenses the breach may have caused him. The measure of damages is the market price less the contract price on the day Schilling was to have received delivery. Any expenses Schilling saved by the breach would be deducted from the damages. ■

RECALL Consequential damages compensate for a loss (such as lost profits) that is not direct but was reasonably foreseeable at the time of the breach.

When the Seller or Lessor Delivers Nonconforming Goods

When the seller or lessor delivers nonconforming goods, the buyer or lessee has several remedies available under the UCC.

The Right to Reject the Goods   If either the goods or the tender of the goods by the seller or lessor fails to conform to the contract *in any respect*, the buyer or lessee can reject the goods in whole or in part [UCC 2–601, 2A–509]. If the buyer or lessee rejects the goods, she or he may then obtain cover, cancel the contract, or sue for damages for breach of contract, just as if the seller or lessor had refused to deliver the goods (see the earlier discussion of these remedies).

In the following case, the buyer of a piano that was represented to be new rejected the instrument on its delivery in an "unacceptable" condition and brought an action against the seller, seeking damages.

7. Pronounced ruh-*pleh*-vun.

CASE 12.2 Jauregui v. Bobb's Piano Sales & Service, Inc.

District Court of Appeal of Florida, Third District, 922 So.2d 303 (2006).

FACTS In November 2001, Jorge Jauregui contracted to buy a Kawai RX5 piano—"Serial No. 2392719a"—for $24,282 from Bobb's Piano Sales and Service, Inc., in Miami, Florida. The piano was represented to be in new condition and to qualify for the manufacturer's "new piano" warranty. Bobb's did not mention that the piano had been in storage for almost a year and had been moved at least six times. The piano was delivered with "unacceptable damage," according to Jauregui, who videotaped its condition. He sent a letter of complaint to the state department of consumer services, identifying at least four "necessary repairs." He then filed a suit in a Florida state court against Bobb's, claiming breach of contract. Bobb's admitted that the piano needed repair. The court concluded that Bobb's was in breach of the parties' contract and that specific performance was not possible, but ruled that Jauregui "takes nothing in damages." Jauregui appealed to a state intermediate appellate court.

ISSUE On a seller's delivery of nonconforming goods in breach of a sales contract and a buyer's rejection of the goods, is the buyer entitled to obtain damages?

DECISION Yes. The state intermediate appellate court agreed with the lower court's conclusion that the defendant had breached the parties' contract but not with the ruling that the plaintiff should not obtain damages. The appellate court awarded Jauregui the contract price with interest, the amounts of the sales tax and delivery charge, and attorneys' fees. The court also ordered Bobb's to remove the piano.

REASON The appellate court stated that the lower court's ruling was "erroneous as a matter of law." The lower court had reasoned that even in a defective condition, the piano as delivered was worth as much or more than Jauregui had paid for it, and thus no damages had been sustained. The appellate court explained, however, that "in a case such as this one, the purchaser of non-conforming goods like the offending piano retains the option to claim either the difference in value or, as plaintiff clearly did in this case, in effect, to cancel the deal and get his money back. This principle is based on the common sense idea that the purchaser is entitled to receive what he wanted to buy and pay for and that the seller is not free to supply any non-conforming item [he or] she wishes just so long as the deviant goods are worth just as much."

 FOR CRITICAL ANALYSIS–Social Consideration *If the defendant had delivered the piano in new condition and the plaintiff had refused to pay for it only out of "buyer's remorse," what might the court have ruled in this case?*

◼

Timeliness and Reason for Rejection Required. The buyer or lessee must reject the goods within a reasonable amount of time and must notify the seller or lessor *seasonably*—that is, in a timely fashion or at the proper time [UCC 2–602(1), 2A–509(2)]. If the buyer or lessee fails to reject the goods within a reasonable amount of time, acceptance will be presumed.

Note that when rejecting goods, the buyer or lessee must designate defects that would have been apparent to the seller or lessor on reasonable inspection. Failure to state the particular defects precludes the buyer or lessee from using such defects to justify rejection or to establish breach when the seller could have cured the defects if it had been notified about them in a timely fashion [UCC 2–605, 2A–514].

Duties of Merchant Buyers and Lessees When Goods Are Rejected. Suppose that a *merchant buyer* or *lessee* rightfully rejects goods and the seller or lessor has no agent or business at the place of rejection. What should the buyer or lessee do in that situation? Under the UCC, the merchant buyer or lessee has a good faith obligation to follow any reasonable instructions received from the seller or lessor with respect to the goods [UCC 2–603, 2A–511]. The buyer or lessee is entitled to be reimbursed for the care and cost entailed in following the instructions. The same requirements hold if the buyer or lessee rightfully revokes his or her acceptance of the goods at some later time [UCC 2–608(3), 2A–517(5)]. (Revocation of acceptance will be discussed shortly.)

If no instructions are forthcoming and the goods are perishable or threaten to decline in value quickly, the buyer can resell the goods in good faith, taking the appropriate reimbursement from the proceeds. In addition, the buyer is entitled to a selling commission (not to exceed 10 percent of the gross proceeds) [UCC 2–603(1), (2); 2A–511(1)]. If the goods are not perishable, the buyer or lessee may store them for the seller or lessor or reship them to the seller or lessor [UCC 2–604, 2A–512].

Buyer's Security Interest in the Goods.   Buyers who rightfully reject goods that remain in their possession or control have a *security interest* in the goods (basically, a legal claim to the goods to the extent necessary to recover expenses, costs, and the like—see Chapter 16). The security interest encompasses any payments the buyer has made for the goods, as well as any expenses incurred with regard to inspection, receipt, transportation, care, and custody of the goods [UCC 2–711(3)]. A buyer with a security interest in the goods is a "person in the position of a seller" and has the same rights as an unpaid seller. Thus, the buyer can resell, withhold delivery of, or stop delivery of the goods. A buyer who chooses to resell must account to the seller for any amounts received in excess of the security interest [UCC 2–706(6), 2–711].

An employee at a retail establishment sorts through boxes of nonconforming goods that will be returned to the manufacturers. If the merchant buyer is following the seller's instructions for rejecting the goods, who should bear the cost of having employees perform this task? (Photo Courtesy of KBToys.com and eToys.com)

Revocation of Acceptance   Acceptance of the goods precludes the buyer or lessee from exercising the right of rejection, but it does not necessarily preclude the buyer or lessee from pursuing other remedies. In certain circumstances, a buyer or lessee is permitted to *revoke* her or his acceptance of the goods. Acceptance of a lot or a commercial unit can be revoked if the nonconformity *substantially* impairs the value of the lot or unit and if one of the following factors is present:

1 If acceptance was predicated on the reasonable assumption that the nonconformity would be cured, and it has not been cured within a reasonable period of time [UCC 2–608(1)(a), 2A–517(1)(a)].

2 If the buyer or lessee did not discover the nonconformity before acceptance, either because it was difficult to discover before acceptance or because assurances made by the seller or lessor that the goods were conforming kept the buyer or lessee from inspecting the goods [UCC 2–608(1)(b), 2A–517(1)(b)].

Revocation of acceptance is not effective until the seller or lessor is notified, which must occur within a reasonable time after the buyer or lessee either discovers or *should have discovered* the grounds for revocation. Additionally, revocation must occur before the goods have undergone any substantial change (such as spoilage) not caused by their own defects [UCC 2–608(2), 2A–517(4)]. See this chapter's *Beyond Our Borders* on the next page feature for a glimpse at how the United Nations Convention on Contracts for the International Sale of Goods (CISG) views revocation of acceptance.

The Right to Recover Damages for Accepted Goods   A buyer or lessee who has accepted nonconforming goods may also keep the goods and recover damages caused by the breach. The buyer or lessee, however, must notify the seller or lessor of the breach within a reasonable time after the defect was or should have been discovered. Failure to give notice of the defects (breach) to the seller or lessor bars the buyer or lessee from pursuing any remedy [UCC 2–607(3), 2A–516(3)]. In addition, the parties to a sales or lease contract can insert a provision requiring the buyer or lessee to give notice of any defects in the goods within a set period.

When the goods delivered and accepted are not as promised, the measure of damages equals the difference between the value of the goods as accepted and their value if they had been delivered as warranted, plus incidental and consequential damages if appropriate

BEYOND OUR BORDERS — The CISG's Approach to Revocation of Acceptance

Under the UCC, a buyer or lessee who has accepted goods may be able to revoke acceptance under certain circumstances mentioned in this chapter. Provisions of the United Nations Convention on Contracts for the International Sale of Goods (CISG) similarly allow buyers to rescind their contracts after they have accepted the goods.

The CISG, however, takes a somewhat different—and more direct—approach to the problem than the UCC does. In the same circumstances that permit a buyer to revoke acceptance under the UCC, under the CISG the buyer can simply declare that the seller has *fundamentally* breached the contract and proceed to sue the seller for the breach. Article 25 of the CISG states that a "breach of contract committed by one of the parties is fundamental if it results in such detriment to the other party as substantially to deprive him [or her] of what he [or she] is entitled to expect under the contract."

FOR CRITICAL ANALYSIS *What is the essential difference between revoking acceptance and bringing a suit for breach of contract?*

[UCC 2–714(2), 2A–519(4)]. For this and other types of breaches in which the buyer or lessee has accepted the goods, the buyer or lessee is entitled to incidental and consequential damages [UCC 2–714(3), 2A–519]. The UCC also permits the buyer or lessee, with proper notice to the seller or lessor, to deduct all or any part of the damages from the price or lease payments still due and payable to the seller or lessor [UCC 2–717, 2A–516(1)].

Is two years after a sale of goods a reasonable time period in which to discover a defect in those goods and notify the seller or lessor of a breach? That was the question in the following case.

CASE 12.3 Fitl v. Strek

Supreme Court of Nebraska, 269 Neb. 51, 690 N.W.2d 605 (2005).
www.findlaw.com/11stategov/ne/neca.html[a]

FACTS Over the Labor Day weekend in 1995, James Fitl attended a sports-card show in San Francisco, California, where he met Mark Strek, doing business as Star Cards of San Francisco, an exhibitor at the show. Later, on Strek's representation that a certain 1952 Mickey Mantle Topps baseball card was in near-mint condition, Fitl bought the card from Strek for $17,750. Strek delivered it to Fitl in Omaha, Nebraska, and Fitl placed it in a safe-deposit box. In May 1997, Fitl sent the card to Professional Sports Authenticators (PSA), a sports-card grading service. PSA told Fitl that the card was ungradable because it had been discolored and doctored. Fitl

a. In the "Supreme Court Opinions" section, in the "2005" row, click on "January." In the result, click on the appropriate link next to the name of the case to access the opinion.

complained to Strek, who replied that Fitl should have initiated a return of the card within "a typical grace period for the unconditional return of a card, . . . 7 days to 1 month" of its receipt. In August, Fitl sent the card to ASA Accugrade, Inc. (ASA), another grading service, for a second opinion of the value. ASA also concluded that the card had been refinished and trimmed. Fitl filed a suit in a Nebraska state court against Strek, seeking damages. The court awarded Fitl $17,750, plus his court costs. Strek appealed to the Nebraska Supreme Court.

ISSUE Is two years after a sale of goods a reasonable time to discover a defect in those goods and notify the seller or lessor of a breach?

DECISION Yes. The state supreme court affirmed the decision of the lower court.

CASE 12.3–Continued

REASON UCC 2–607(3)(a) states, "Where a tender has been accepted * * * the buyer must within a reasonable time after he discovers or should have discovered any breach notify the seller of breach or be barred from any remedy." Under UCC 1–204(2), "[w]hat is a reasonable time for taking any action depends on the nature, purpose and circumstances of such action." The state supreme court concluded here that the buyer (Fitl) had reasonably relied on the seller's (Strek's) representation that the goods were "authentic," which they were not, and when their defects were discovered, Fitl had given a timely notice. The court reasoned that "the policies behind the notice requirement, to allow the seller to correct a defect, to prepare for negotiation and litigation, and to protect against stale claims at a time beyond which an investigation can be completed, were not unfairly prejudiced by the lack of an earlier notice to Strek. Any problem Strek may have had with the party from whom he obtained the baseball card was a separate matter from his transaction with Fitl, and an investigation into the source of the altered card would not have minimized Fitl's damages."

 WHAT IF THE FACTS WERE DIFFERENT? *Suppose that Fitl and Strek had included in their deal a written clause requiring Fitl to give notice of any defect in the card within "7 days to 1 month" of its receipt. Would the result have been different? Why or why not?*

LIMITATION OF REMEDIES

The parties to a sales or lease contract can vary their respective rights and obligations by contractual agreement. For example, a seller and buyer can expressly provide for remedies in addition to those provided in the UCC. They can also provide remedies in lieu of those provided in the UCC, or they can change the measure of damages. The seller can provide that the buyer's only remedy on breach of warranty will be repair or replacement of the item, or the seller can limit the buyer's remedy to return of the goods and refund of the purchase price. In sales and lease contracts, an agreed-on remedy is in addition to those provided in the UCC unless the parties expressly agree that the remedy is exclusive of all others [UCC 2–719(1), 2A–503(1)].

Exclusive Remedies

If the parties state that a remedy is exclusive, then it is the sole remedy. **■EXAMPLE 12.15** Standard Tool Company agrees to sell a pipe-cutting machine to United Pipe & Tubing Corporation. The contract limits United's remedy exclusively to repair or replacement of any defective parts. Thus, repair or replacement of defective parts is the buyer's exclusive remedy under this contract. ■

When circumstances cause an exclusive remedy to fail in its essential purpose, however, it is no longer exclusive, and the buyer or lessee may pursue other remedies available under the UCC [UCC 2–719(2), 2A–503(2)]. **■EXAMPLE 12.16** In the example just given, suppose that Standard Tool Company was unable to repair a defective part, and no replacement parts were available. In this situation, because the exclusive remedy failed in its essential purpose, the buyer normally is entitled to seek other remedies provided to a buyer by the UCC. ■

Limitations on Consequential Damages

As discussed in Chapter 9, *consequential damages* are special damages that compensate for indirect losses (such as lost profits) resulting from a breach of contract. For the non-breaching party to recover consequential damages, however, these damages must have been reasonably foreseeable at the time the breach occurred.

Under the UCC, parties to a contract can limit or exclude consequential damages, provided the limitation is not unconscionable. When the buyer or lessee is a consumer, any limitation of consequential damages for personal injuries resulting from consumer goods

ON THE WEB

For an example of a contract providing for an exclusive remedy, read the PrinterCare Agreement of Dell Computers at

www.dell.com/downloads/global/services/con_PrinterCare.pdf.

is *prima facie* (presumptively) unconscionable. The limitation of consequential damages is not necessarily unconscionable, however, when the loss is commercial in nature—for example, lost profits and property damage [UCC 2–719(3), 2A–503(3)].

Statute of Limitations

An action for breach of contract under the UCC must be commenced *within four years after the cause of action accrues*—that is, within four years after the breach occurs [UCC 2–725(1)]. In addition to filing suit within the four-year period, a buyer or lessee who has accepted non-conforming goods usually must notify the breaching party of the breach within a reasonable time, or the aggrieved party is barred from pursuing any remedy [UCC 2–607(3)(a), 2A–516(3)]. The parties can agree in their contract to reduce this period to not less than one year, but cannot extend it beyond four years [UCC 2–725(1), 2A–506(1)]. A cause of action accrues for breach of warranty when the seller or lessor tenders delivery. This is the rule even if the aggrieved party is unaware that the cause of action has accrued [UCC 2–725(2), 2A–506(2)].

REVIEWING **Sales and Leases: Performance and Breach**

GFI, Inc., a Hong Kong company, makes audio decoder chips, one of the essential components used in the manufacture of MP3 players. Egan Electronics contracts with GFI to buy 10,000 chips on an installment contract, with 2,500 chips to be shipped every three months, F.O.B. Hong Kong via Air Express. At the time for the first delivery, GFI delivers only 2,400 chips but explains to Egan that while the shipment is less than 5 percent short, the chips are of a higher quality than those specified in the contract and are worth 5 percent more than the contract price. Egan accepts the shipment and pays GFI the contract price. At the time for the second shipment, GFI makes a shipment identical to the first. Egan again accepts and pays for the chips. At the time for the third shipment, GFI ships 2,400 of the same chips, but this time GFI sends them via Hong Kong Air instead of Air Express.

While in transit, the chips are destroyed. When it is time for the fourth shipment, GFI again sends 2,400 chips, but this time Egan rejects the chips without explanation. Using the information presented in the chapter, answer the following questions.

1 Did GFI have a legitimate reason to expect that Egan would accept the fourth shipment? Why or why not?

2 Does the substitution of carriers in the third shipment constitute a breach of the contract by GFI? Explain.

3 Suppose that the silicon used for the chips becomes unavailable for a period of time and that GFI cannot manufacture enough chips to fulfill the contract, but does ship as many as it can to Egan. Under what doctrine might a court release GFI from further performance of the contract?

4 Under the UCC, does Egan have a right to reject the fourth shipment? Why or why not?

APPLICATION **What Can You Do When a Contract Is Breached?***

A contract for the sale of goods has been breached. Can the dispute be settled without a trip to court? The answer depends on the willingness of the parties to agree on an appropriate remedy.

Contractual Clauses on Applicable Remedies

Often, the parties to sales and lease contracts agree in advance, in their contracts, on what remedies will be applicable in the event of a breach. This may take the form of a contract provision restricting or expanding remedies available under the Uniform Commercial Code [UCC 2–719]. Such clauses help to reduce uncertainty and the necessity for costly litigation.

* This Application is not meant to substitute for the services of an attorney who is licensed to practice law in your state.

When the Contract Is Silent on Applicable Remedies

If your agreement does not cover a breach of contract and you are the nonbreaching party, the UCC gives you a variety of alternatives. What you need to do is analyze the remedies that are available if you choose to go to court, put these remedies in order of priority, and then predict how successful you might be in pursuing each remedy. Next, look at the position of the breaching party to determine the basis for negotiating a settlement.

For example, when defective goods are delivered and accepted, usually it is preferable for the buyer and seller to reach an agreement on a reduced purchase price. Practically speaking, the buyer may be unable to obtain a partial refund from the seller. UCC 2–717 allows the buyer in such circumstances to give notice of the intention to deduct the damages from any part of the purchase price not yet paid. If you are a buyer who has accepted defective goods and has not yet paid

in full, it may be appropriate for you to exercise your rights under UCC 2–717 and not pay in full when you make your final payment. Remember that most breaches of contract do not end up in court—they are settled beforehand.

CHECKLIST FOR THE NONBREACHING PARTY TO A CONTRACT

1 Ascertain if a remedy is explicitly written into your contract. Use that remedy, if possible, to avoid litigation.
2 If no specific remedy is available, look to the UCC.
3 Assess how successful you might be in pursuing a remedy if you go to court.
4 Analyze the position of the breaching party.
5 Determine whether a negotiated settlement is preferable to a lawsuit, which is best done by consulting your attorney.

KEY TERMS

CHAPTER SUMMARY Sales and Leases: Performance and Breach

REQUIREMENTS OF PERFORMANCE

Obligations of the Seller or Lessor
(See pages 356–363.)

1. The seller or lessor must tender *conforming* goods to the buyer or lessee. Tender must take place at a *reasonable hour* and in a *reasonable manner.* Under the perfect tender doctrine, the seller or lessor must tender goods that conform exactly to the terms of the contract [UCC 2–503(1), 2A–508(1)].

2. If the seller or lessor tenders nonconforming goods prior to the performance date and the buyer or lessee rejects them, the seller or lessor may *cure* (repair or replace the goods) within the contract time for performance [UCC 2–508(1), 2A–513(1)]. If the seller or lessor has reasonable grounds to believe that the buyer or lessee would accept the tendered goods, on the buyer's or lessee's rejection the seller or lessor has a reasonable time to substitute conforming goods without liability [UCC 2–508(2), 2A–513(2)].

3. If the agreed-on means of delivery becomes impracticable or unavailable, the seller must substitute an alternative means (such as a different carrier) if one is available [UCC 2–614(1)].

4. If a seller or lessor tenders nonconforming goods in any one installment under an installment contract, the buyer or lessee may reject the installment only if its value is substantially impaired and cannot be cured. The entire installment contract is breached when one or more nonconforming installments *substantially* impair the value of the *whole* contract [UCC 2–612, 2A–510].

5. When performance becomes commercially impracticable owing to circumstances that were not foreseeable when the contract was formed, the perfect tender rule no longer holds [UCC 2–615, 2A–405].

(Continued)

CHAPTER SUMMARY	Sales and Leases: Performance and Breach–Continued
Obligations of the Buyer or Lessee (See pages 363–364.)	1. On tender of delivery by the seller or lessor, the buyer or lessee must pay for the goods at the time and place the buyer or lessee *receives* the goods, even if the place of shipment is the place of delivery, unless the sale is made on credit. Payment may be made by any method generally acceptable in the commercial world unless the seller demands cash [UCC 2–310, 2–511]. In lease contracts, the lessee must make lease payments in accordance with the contract [UCC 2A–516(1)]. 2. Unless otherwise agreed, the buyer or lessee has an absolute right to inspect the goods before acceptance [UCC 2–513(1), 2A–515(1)]. 3. The buyer or lessee can manifest acceptance of delivered goods expressly in words or by conduct or by failing to reject the goods after a reasonable period of time following inspection or after having had a reasonable opportunity to inspect them [UCC 2–606(1), 2A–515(1)]. A buyer will be deemed to have accepted goods if he or she performs any act inconsistent with the seller's ownership [UCC 2–606(1)(c)].
Anticipatory Repudiation (See page 364.)	If, before the time for performance, either party clearly indicates to the other an intention not to perform, under UCC 2–610 and 2A–402 the aggrieved party may do the following: 1. Await performance by the repudiating party for a commercially reasonable time. 2. Resort to any remedy for breach. 3. In either situation, suspend performance.
	REMEDIES FOR BREACH OF CONTRACT
Remedies of the Seller or Lessor (See pages 365–368.)	1. *When the goods are in the possession of the seller or lessor*—The seller or lessor may do the following: a. Cancel the contract [UCC 2–703(f), 2A–523(1)(a)]. b. Withhold delivery [UCC 2–703(a), 2A–523(1)(c)]. c. Resell or dispose of the goods [UCC 2–703(d), 2–706(1), 2A–523(1)(e), 2A–527(1)]. d. Sue to recover the purchase price or lease payments due [UCC 2–709(1), 2A–529(1)]. e. Sue to recover damages [UCC 2–703(e), 2–708, 2A–528]. 2. *When the goods are in transit*—The seller or lessor may stop the carrier or bailee from delivering the goods [UCC 2–705, 2A–526]. 3. *When the goods are in the possession of the buyer or lessee*—The seller or lessor may do the following: a. Sue to recover the purchase price or lease payments due [UCC 2–709(1), 2A–529(1)]. b. Reclaim the goods. A seller may reclaim goods received by an insolvent buyer if the demand is made within ten days of receipt (reclaiming goods excludes all other remedies) [UCC 2–702]; a lessor may repossess goods if the lessee is in default [UCC 2A–525(2)].
Remedies of the Buyer or Lessee (See pages 368–373.)	1. *When the seller or lessor refuses to deliver the goods*—The buyer or lessee may do the following: a. Cancel the contract [UCC 2–711(1), 2A–508(1)(a)]. b. Recover the goods if the seller or lessor becomes insolvent within ten days after receiving the first payment and the goods are identified to the contract [UCC 2–502, 2A–522]. c. Obtain specific performance (when the goods are unique and when the remedy at law is inadequate) [UCC 2–716(1), 2A–521(1)]. d. Obtain cover [UCC 2–712, 2A–518].

CHAPTER SUMMARY	Sales and Leases: Performance and Breach—Continued
Remedies of the Buyer or Lessee—Continued	e. Replevy the goods (if cover is unavailable) [UCC 2–716(3), 2A–521(3)]. f. Sue to recover damages [UCC 2–713, 2A–519]. 2. *When the seller or lessor delivers or tenders delivery of nonconforming goods*—The buyer or lessee may do the following: a. Reject the goods [UCC 2–601, 2A–509]. b. Revoke acceptance if the nonconformity *substantially* impairs the value of the unit or lot and if one of the following factors is present: (1) Acceptance was predicated on the reasonable assumption that the nonconformity would be cured and it was not cured within a reasonable time [UCC 2–608(1)(a), 2A–517(1)(a)]. (2) The buyer or lessee did not discover the nonconformity before acceptance, either because it was difficult to discover before acceptance or because the seller's or lessor's assurance that the goods were conforming kept the buyer or lessee from inspecting the goods [UCC 2–608(1)(b), 2A–517(1)(b)]. c. Accept the goods and recover damages [UCC 2–607, 2–714, 2–717, 2A–519].
Limitation of Remedies (See pages 373–374.)	Remedies may be limited in sales or lease contracts by agreement of the parties. If the contract states that a remedy is exclusive, then that is the sole remedy unless the remedy fails in its essential purpose. Sellers and lessors can also limit the rights of buyers and lessees to consequential damages unless the limitation is unconscionable [UCC 2–719, 2A–503].
Statute of Limitations (See page 374.)	The UCC has a four-year statute of limitations for actions involving breach of contract. By agreement, the parties to a sales or lease contract can reduce this period to not less than one year, but they cannot extend it beyond four years [UCC 2–725(1), 2A–506(1)].

FOR REVIEW

Answers for the even-numbered questions in this For Review *section can be found in Appendix E at the end of this text.*

1 What are the respective obligations of the parties under a contract for the sale or lease of goods?

2 What is the perfect tender rule? What are some important exceptions to this rule that apply to sales and lease contracts?

3 What options are available to the nonbreaching party when the other party to a sales or lease contract repudiates the contract prior to the time for performance?

4 What remedies are available to a seller or lessor when the buyer or lessee breaches the contract? What remedies are available to a buyer or lessee if the seller or lessor breaches the contract?

5 In contracts subject to the UCC, are parties free to limit the remedies available to the nonbreaching party on a breach of contract? If so, in what ways?

■

QUESTIONS AND CASE PROBLEMS

 **HYPOTHETICAL SCENARIOS**

12.1 Remedies. Genix, Inc., has contracted to sell Larson five hundred washing machines of a certain model at list price. Genix is to ship the goods on or before December 1. Genix produces one thousand washing machines of this model but has not yet prepared Larson's shipment. On November 1, Larson repudiates the contract. Discuss the remedies available to Genix in this situation.

12.2 Hypothetical Question with Sample Answer. Cummings ordered two model X Super Fidelity speakers from Jamestown Wholesale Electronics, Inc. Jamestown shipped the speakers via United Parcel Service, C.O.D. (collect on delivery), although Cummings had not requested or agreed to a C.O.D. shipment of the goods. When the speakers were delivered, Cummings refused to accept them because he would not be able to inspect them before payment. Jamestown claimed that it had shipped conforming goods and that Cummings had breached their contract. Had Cummings breached the contract? Explain.

 For a sample answer to Question 12.2, go to Appendix F at the end of this text.

12.3 Anticipatory Repudiation. Moore contracted in writing to sell her 2002 Ford Taurus to Hammer for $8,500. Moore agreed to deliver the car on Wednesday, and Hammer promised to pay the $8,500 on the following Friday. On Tuesday, Hammer informed Moore that he would not be buying the car after all. By Friday, Hammer had changed his mind again and tendered $8,500 to Moore. Moore, although she had not sold the car to another party, refused the tender and refused to deliver. Hammer claimed that Moore had breached their contract. Moore contended that Hammer's repudiation released her from her duty to perform under the contract. Who is correct and why?

CASE PROBLEMS

12.4 Acceptance. In April 1996, Excalibur Oil Group, Inc., applied for credit and opened an account with Standard Distributors, Inc., to obtain snack foods and other items for Excalibur's convenience stores. For three months, Standard delivered the goods and Excalibur paid the invoices. In July, Standard was dissolved, and its assets were distributed to J. F. Walker Co. Walker continued to deliver the goods to Excalibur, which continued to pay the invoices until November, when the firm began to experience financial difficulties. By January 1997, Excalibur owed Walker $54,241.77. Walker then dealt with Excalibur only on a collect-on-delivery basis until Excalibur's stores closed in 1998. Walker filed a suit in a Pennsylvania state court against Excalibur and its owner to recover amounts due on unpaid invoices. To successfully plead its case, Walker had to show that there was a contract between the parties. One question was whether Excalibur had manifested acceptance of the goods delivered by Walker. How does a buyer manifest acceptance? Was there an acceptance in this case? In whose favor should the court rule, and why? [*J. F. Walker Co. v. Excalibur Oil Group, Inc.*, 792 A.2d 1269 (Pa.Super. 2002)]

12.5 Case Problem with Sample Answer. Eaton Corp. bought four air-conditioning units from Trane Co., an operating division of American Standard, Inc., in 1998. The contract stated in part, "NEITHER PARTY SHALL BE LIABLE FOR . . . CONSEQUENTIAL DAMAGES." Trane was responsible for servicing the units. During the last ten days of March 2003, Trane's employees serviced and inspected the units, changed the filters and belts, and made a material list for repairs. On April 3, a fire occurred at Eaton's facility, extensively damaging the units and the facility, although no one was hurt. Alleging that the fire started in the electric motor of one of the units, and that Trane's faulty servicing of the units caused the fire, Eaton filed a suit in a federal district court against Trane. Eaton asserted breach of contract, among other claims, seeking conse-

quential damages. Trane filed a motion for summary judgment, based on the limitation-of-remedies clause. What are consequential damages? Can these be limited in some circumstances? Is the clause valid in this case? Explain. [*Eaton Corp. v. Trane Carolina Plains*, 350 F.Supp.2d 699 (D.S.C. 2004)]

After you have answered Problem 12.5, compare your answer with the sample answer given on the Web site that accompanies this text. Go to academic.cengage.com/blaw/blt, **select "Chapter 12," and click on "Case Problem with Sample Answer."**

12.6 Right of Assurance. Advanced Polymer Sciences, Inc. (APS), based in Ohio, makes polymers and resins for use as protective coatings in industrial applications. APS also owns the technology for equipment used to make certain composite fibers. *SAVA gumarska in kemijska industria d.d.* (SAVA), based in Slovenia, makes rubber goods. In 1999, SAVA and APS contracted to form *SAVA Advanced Polymers proizvodno podjetje d.o.o.* (SAVA AP) to make and distribute APS products in Eastern Europe. Their contract provided for, among other things, the alteration of a facility to make the products using specially made equipment to be sold by APS to SAVA. Disputes arose between the parties, and in August 2000, SAVA stopped work on the new facility. APS then notified SAVA that it was stopping the manufacture of the equipment and "insist[ed] on knowing what is SAVA's intention towards this venture." In October, SAVA told APS that it was canceling their contract. In subsequent litigation, SAVA claimed that APS had repudiated the contract when it stopped making the equipment. What might APS assert in its defense? How should the court rule? Explain. [*SAVA gumarska in kemijska industria d.d. v. Advanced Polymer Sciences, Inc.*, 128 S.W.3d 304 (Tex.App.—Dallas 2004)]

12.7 Remedies of the Buyer. L.V.R.V., Inc., sells recreational vehicles (RVs) in Las Vegas, Nevada, as Wheeler's Las Vegas RV. In September 1997, Wheeler's sold a Santara RV made by

Coachmen Recreational Vehicle Co. to Arthur and Roswitha Waddell. The Waddells hoped to spend two or three years driving around the country, but almost immediately—and repeatedly—they experienced problems with the RV. Its entry door popped open. Its cooling and heating systems did not work properly. Its batteries did not maintain a charge. Most significantly, its engine overheated when ascending a moderate grade. The Waddells brought it to Wheeler's service department for repairs. Over the next year and a half, the RV spent more than seven months at Wheeler's. In March 1999, the Waddells filed a complaint in a Nevada state court against the dealer to revoke their acceptance of the RV. What are the requirements for a buyer's revocation of acceptance? Were the requirements met in this case? In whose favor should the court rule? Why? [*Waddell v. L.V.R.V., Inc.*, 122 Nev. 125, 125 P.3d 1160 (2006)]

12.8 **A Question of Ethics.** *Scotwood Industries, Inc., sells calcium chloride flake for use in ice melt products. Between July and September 2004, Scotwood delivered thirty-seven shipments of flake to Frank Miller & Sons, Inc. After each delivery, Scotwood billed Miller, which paid thirty-five of the invoices and processed 30 to 50 percent of the flake. In*

August, Miller began complaining about the quality. Scotwood assured Miller that it would remedy the situation. Finally, in October, Miller told Scotwood, "[T]his is totally unacceptable. We are willing to discuss Scotwood picking up the material." Miller claimed that the flake was substantially defective because it was chunked. Calcium chloride maintains its purity for up to five years but chunks if it is exposed to and absorbs moisture, making it unusable. In response to Scotwood's suit to collect payment on the unpaid invoices, Miller filed a counterclaim in a federal district court for breach of contract, seeking to recover based on revocation of acceptance, among other things. [*Scotwood Industries, Inc. v. Frank Miller & Sons, Inc.*, 435 F.Supp.2d 1160 (D.Kans. 2006)]

1 What is revocation of acceptance? How does a buyer effectively exercise this option? Do the facts in this case support this theory as a ground for Miller to recover damages? Why or why not?

2 Is there an ethical basis for allowing a buyer to revoke acceptance of goods and recover damages? If so, is there an ethical limit to this right? Discuss.

 ## CRITICAL THINKING AND WRITING ASSIGNMENTS

12.9 Critical Legal Thinking. Under what circumstances should courts not allow fully informed contracting parties to agree to limit remedies?

12.10 Critical Thinking and Writing Assignment for Business. Suppose that you are a collector of antique cars and you need to purchase spare parts for a 1938 engine. These parts are not made anymore and are scarce. You discover that Beem has the spare parts that you need. To get the contract

with Beem, you agree to pay 50 percent of the purchase price in advance. You send the payment on May 1, and Beem receives it on May 2. On May 3, Beem, having found another buyer willing to pay substantially more for the parts, informs you that he will not deliver as contracted. That same day, you learn that Beem is insolvent. Discuss fully any possible remedies that would enable you to take possession of these parts.

ONLINE ACTIVITIES

PRACTICAL INTERNET EXERCISES

Go to this text's Web site at **academic.cengage.com/blaw/blt**, select "Chapter 12," and click on "Practical Internet Exercises." There you will find the following Internet research exercises that you can perform to learn more about the topics covered in this chapter.

PRACTICAL INTERNET EXERCISE 12-1 MANAGEMENT PERSPECTIVE—The Right to Reject Goods

PRACTICAL INTERNET EXERCISE 12-2 LEGAL PERSPECTIVE—International Performance Requirements

BEFORE THE TEST

Go to this text's Web site at **academic.cengage.com/blaw/blt**, select "Chapter 12," and click on "Interactive Quizzes." You will find a number of interactive questions relating to this chapter.

CHAPTER 13
Warranties, Product Liability, and Consumer Law

> **"I'll warrant him heart-whole."**
>
> William Shakespeare,
> 1564–1616
> (English dramatist and poet)

LEARNING OBJECTIVES

AFTER READING THIS CHAPTER, YOU SHOULD BE ABLE TO ANSWER THE FOLLOWING QUESTIONS:

1 What factors determine whether a seller's or lessor's statement constitutes an express warranty or mere "puffing"?

2 What implied warranties arise under the UCC?

3 Can a manufacturer be held liable to any person who suffers an injury proximately caused by the manufacturer's negligently made product?

4 What defenses to liability can be raised in a product liability lawsuit?

5 What are the major federal statutes providing for consumer protection?

Warranty is an age-old concept. In sales and lease law, a warranty is an assurance by one party of the existence of a fact on which the other party can rely. Just as William Shakespeare's character in the play *As You Like It* warranted his friend "heart-whole" in the chapter-opening quotation, so sellers and lessors warrant to those who purchase or lease their goods that the goods are as represented or will be as promised.

The Uniform Commercial Code (UCC) has numerous rules governing product warranties as they occur in sales and lease contracts. Those rules are the subject matter of the first part of this chapter. A natural addition to the discussion is *product liability*: Who is liable to consumers, users, and bystanders for physical harm and property damage caused by a particular good or its use? Product liability encompasses the contract theory of warranty, as well as the tort theories of negligence and strict liability (discussed in Chapter 4).

Consumer protection law consists of all statutes, agency rules, and common law judicial rulings that serve to protect the interests of consumers. State and federal consumer laws regulate certain business activities, such as how a business may advertise, engage in mail-order and telemarketing transactions, and package and label their products. In addition, numerous local, state, and federal agencies exist to aid consumers in settling their grievances with sellers and manufacturers. In the last part of this chapter, we examine some of the sources and some of the major issues of consumer protection.

WARRANTIES

Most goods are covered by some type of warranty designed to protect consumers. Article 2 (on sales) and Article 2A (on leases) of the UCC designate several types of warranties that can arise in a sales or lease contract, including warranties of title, express warranties, and implied warranties.

Warranties of Title

Title warranty arises automatically in most sales contracts. The UCC imposes three types of warranties of title.

Good Title   In most sales, sellers warrant that they have good and valid title to the goods sold and that transfer of the title is rightful [UCC 2–312(1)(a)]. ■**EXAMPLE 13.1** Sharon steals goods from Miguel and sells them to Carrie, who does not know that the goods are stolen. If Miguel reclaims the goods from Carrie, which he has a right to do, Carrie can then sue Sharon for breach of warranty. When Sharon sold Carrie the goods, Sharon *automatically* warranted to her that the title conveyed was valid and that its transfer was rightful. Because this was not in fact the case, Sharon breached the warranty of title imposed by UCC 2–312(1)(a) and became liable to the buyer for the appropriate damages. ■

No Liens   A second warranty of title provided by the UCC protects buyers who are *unaware* of any encumbrances, or **liens** (claims, charges, or liabilities—see Chapter 16), against goods at the time the contract is made [UCC 2–312(1)(b)]. This warranty protects buyers who, for example, unknowingly purchase goods that are subject to a creditor's security interest (an interest in the goods that secures payment or performance, to be discussed in Chapter 16). If a creditor legally repossesses the goods from a buyer *who had no actual knowledge of the security interest,* the buyer can recover from the seller for breach of warranty. (A buyer who actually knows that a security interest exists has no recourse against the seller.)

> **LIEN**
> An encumbrance on a property to satisfy a debt or protect a claim for payment of a debt.

Article 2A affords similar protection for lessees. Section 2A–211(1) provides that during the term of the lease, no claim of any third party will interfere with the lessee's enjoyment of the leasehold interest.

No Infringements   A merchant-seller is also deemed to warrant that the goods delivered are free from any copyright, trademark, or patent claims of a third person [UCC 2–312(3), 2A–211(2)].[1] If this warranty is breached and the buyer is sued by the party holding copyright, trademark, or patent rights in the goods, the buyer must notify the seller of the litigation within a reasonable time to enable the seller to decide whether to defend the lawsuit. If the seller states in a writing (or record) that she or he has decided to defend and agrees to bear all expenses, then the buyer must turn over control of the litigation to the seller; otherwise, the buyer is barred from any remedy against the seller for liability established by the litigation [UCC 2–607(3)(b), 2–607(5)(b)].

In situations that involve leases rather than sales, Article 2A requires the same notice of infringement litigation [UCC 2A–516(3)(b), 2A–516(4)(b)]. There is an exception for leases to individual consumers for personal, family, or household purposes. A consumer who fails to notify the lessor within a reasonable time does not lose his or her remedy against the lessor for any liability established in the litigation [UCC 2A–516(3)(b)].

---

1. Recall from Chapter 11 that a *merchant* is defined in UCC 2–104(1) as a person who deals in goods of the kind involved in the sales contract or who, by occupation, presents himself or herself as having knowledge or skill peculiar to the goods involved in the transaction.

Disclaimer of Title Warranty   In an ordinary sales transaction, the title warranty can be disclaimed or modified only by *specific language* in the contract [UCC 2–312(2)]. For example, sellers can assert that they are transferring only such rights, title, and interest as they have in the goods. In a lease transaction, the disclaimer must be specific, be in a writing (or record), and be conspicuous [UCC 2A–214(4)].

Express Warranties

A seller or lessor can create an **express warranty** by making representations concerning the quality, condition, description, or performance potential of the goods. Under UCC 2–313 and 2A–210, express warranties arise when a seller or lessor indicates any of the following:

1 That the goods conform to any *affirmation* (declaration that something is true) or *promise* of fact that the seller or lessor makes to the buyer or lessee about the goods. Such affirmations or promises are usually made during the bargaining process. Statements such as "these drill bits will penetrate stainless steel—and without dulling" are express warranties.

2 That the goods conform to any *description* of them. For example, a label that reads "Crate contains one 150-horsepower diesel engine" or a contract that calls for the delivery of a "camel's-hair coat" creates an express warranty.

3 That the goods conform to any *sample or model* of the goods shown to the buyer or lessee.

Basis of the Bargain   To create an express warranty, a seller or lessor does not have to use formal words such as *warrant* or *guarantee* [UCC 2–313(2), 2A–210(2)]. It is only necessary that a reasonable buyer or lessee would regard the representation of fact as part of the basis of the bargain [UCC 2–313(1), 2A–210(1)]. Just what constitutes the basis of the bargain is hard to say. The UCC does not define the concept, and it is a question of fact in each case whether a representation was made at such a time and in such a way that it induced the buyer or lessee to enter into the contract. (For more information on how sellers can create—or avoid creating—warranties, see the *Application* feature at the end of this chapter.)

> **PREVENTING LEGAL DISPUTES**
>
> **Businesspersons engaged in selling or leasing goods should be careful about the words they use with customers, in writing and orally. Express warranties can be found in a seller's or lessor's advertisement, brochure, or promotional materials, in addition to being made orally or in an express warranty provision in a contract. Avoiding unintended warranties is crucial in preventing legal disputes, and all employees should be instructed on how the promises they make to buyers during a sale can create warranties.**

Statements of Opinion and Value   Only statements of fact create express warranties. If the seller or lessor makes a statement that relates to the supposed value or worth of the goods, or makes a statement of opinion or recommendation about the goods, the seller or lessor is not creating an express warranty [UCC 2–313(2), 2A–210(2)].

■EXAMPLE 13.2 A seller claims that "this is the best used car to come along in years; it has four new tires and a 250-horsepower engine just rebuilt this year." The seller has made several *affirmations of fact* that can create a warranty: the automobile has an engine; it has a 250-horsepower engine; it was rebuilt this year; there are four tires on the automobile; and the tires are new. The seller's *opinion* that the vehicle is "the best used car to come along in years," however, is known as "puffing" or "puffery" and creates no warranty. (*Puffing* is the expression of opinion by a seller or lessor that is not made as a representation of fact.) ■

A statement relating to the value of the goods, such as "this is worth a fortune" or "anywhere else you'd pay $10,000 for it," usually does not create a warranty. If the seller or lessor is an expert and gives an opinion as an expert to a layperson, though, then a warranty may be created.

It is not always easy to determine whether a statement constitutes an express warranty or puffing. The reasonableness of the buyer's or lessee's reliance appears to be the controlling criterion in many cases. For example, a salesperson's statements that a ladder "will never break" and will "last a lifetime" are so clearly improbable that no reasonable buyer should rely on them. Additionally, the context in which a statement is made might be relevant in determining the reasonableness of the buyer's or lessee's reliance. For example, a reasonable person is more likely to rely on a written statement made in an advertisement than on a statement made orally by a salesperson.

Marlboro cigarettes sit on a shelf in a retail store. Suppose that the store clerk tells a customer that these cigarettes "are the best," and the customer buys three cartons. The customer later develops lung cancer from smoking and sues the seller. In this situation, would the seller's statements be enough to create an express warranty? Why or why not?
("Ladyphoenixx"/Creative Commons)

Implied Warranties

An **implied warranty** is one that *the law derives* by implication or inference because of the circumstances of a sale, rather than by the seller's express promise. In an action based on breach of implied warranty, it is necessary to show that an implied warranty existed and that the breach of the warranty proximately caused[2] the damage sustained. We look here at some of the implied warranties that arise under the UCC.

Implied Warranty of Merchantability   Every sale or lease of goods made *by a merchant who deals in goods of the kind sold or leased* automatically gives rise to an **implied warranty of merchantability** [UCC 2–314, 2A–212]. ■**EXAMPLE 13.3** A merchant who is in the business of selling ski equipment, for instance, makes an implied warranty of merchantability every time she sells a pair of skis. A neighbor selling his skis at a garage sale does not (because he is not in the business of selling goods of this type). ■

Merchantable Goods.   Goods that are *merchantable* are "reasonably fit for the ordinary purposes for which such goods are used." They must be of at least average, fair, or medium-grade quality. The quality must be comparable to a level that will pass without objection in the trade or market for goods of the same description. To be merchantable, the goods must also be adequately packaged and labeled as provided by the agreement, and they must conform to the promises or affirmations of fact made on the container or label, if any.

It makes no difference whether the merchant knew or could have discovered that a product was defective (not merchantable). Of course, merchants are not absolute insurers against all accidents arising in connection with the goods. For example, a bar of soap is not unmerchantable merely because a user could slip and fall by stepping on it.

Merchantable Food.   The UCC recognizes the serving of food or drink to be consumed on or off the premises as a sale of goods subject to the implied warranty of merchantability [UCC 2–314(1)]. "Merchantable" food means food that is fit to eat. Courts generally determine whether food is fit to eat on the basis of consumer expectations. The courts assume that consumers should reasonably expect on occasion to find bones in fish fillets, cherry pits in cherry pie, or a nutshell in a package of shelled nuts, for example—because

IMPLIED WARRANTY
A warranty that arises by law because of the circumstances of a sale, rather than by the seller's express promise.

IMPLIED WARRANTY OF MERCHANTABILITY
A warranty that goods being sold or leased are reasonably fit for the general purpose for which they are sold or leased, are properly packaged and labeled, and are of proper quality. The warranty automatically arises in every sale or lease of goods made by a merchant who deals in goods of the kind sold or leased.

---

2. Proximate, or legal, cause exists when the connection between an act and an injury is strong enough to justify imposing liability—see Chapter 4.

such substances are natural incidents of the food. In contrast, consumers would not reasonably expect to find an inchworm in a can of peas or a piece of glass in a soft drink—because these substances are not natural to the food product.[3] In the following classic case, the court had to determine whether a fish bone was a substance that one should reasonably expect to find in fish chowder.

---

3. See, for example, *Ruvolo v. Homovich*, 149 Ohio App.3d 701, 778 N.E.2d 661 (2002).

CASE 13.1   Webster v. Blue Ship Tea Room, Inc.

LANDMARK AND CLASSIC CASES

Supreme Judicial Court of Massachusetts, 347 Mass. 421, 198 N.E.2d 309 (1964).

HISTORICAL AND CULTURAL SETTING

Chowder, a soup or stew made with fresh fish, possibly originated in the fishing villages of Brittany (a French province to the west of Paris) and was probably carried to Canada and New England by Breton fishermen. In the nineteenth century and earlier, recipes for chowder did not call for the removal of the fish bones. Chowder recipes in the first half of the twentieth century were the same as in previous centuries, sometimes specifying that the fish head, tail, and backbone were to be broken in pieces and boiled, with the "liquor thus produced . . . added to the balance of the chowder."[a] By the middle of the twentieth century, there was a considerable body of case law concerning implied warranties and foreign and natural substances in food. It was perhaps inevitable that sooner or later, a consumer injured by a fish bone in chowder would challenge the merchantability of chowder containing fish bones.

FACTS Blue Ship Tea Room, Inc., was located in Boston in an old building overlooking the ocean. Priscilla Webster, who had been born and raised in New England, went to the restaurant and ordered fish chowder. The chowder was milky in color. After three or four spoonfuls, she felt something lodged in her throat. As a result, she underwent two esophagoscopies; in the second esophagoscopy, a fish bone was found and removed. Webster filed a lawsuit against the restaurant in a Massachusetts state court for breach of the implied warranty of merchantability. The jury rendered a verdict for Webster, and the restaurant appealed to the state's highest court.

ISSUE Does serving fish chowder that contains a bone constitute a breach of an implied warranty of merchantability on the part of the restaurant?

a. Fannie Farmer, *The Boston Cooking School Cook Book* (Boston: Little, Brown, 1937), p. 166.

DECISION No. The Supreme Judicial Court of Massachusetts held that Webster could not recover against Blue Ship Tea Room because no breach of warranty had occurred.

REASON The court, citing UCC Section 2–314, stated that "a warranty that goods shall be merchantable is implied in a contract for their sale if the seller is a merchant with respect to goods of that kind. Under this section the serving for value of food or drink to be consumed either on the premises or elsewhere is a sale. * * * Goods to be merchantable must at least be * * * fit for the ordinary purposes for which such goods are used." The question here was whether a fish bone made the chowder unfit for eating. In the judge's opinion, "the joys of life in New England include the ready availability of fresh fish chowder. We should be prepared to cope with the hazards of fish bones, the occasional presence of which in chowders is, it seems to us, to be anticipated, and which, in the light of a hallowed tradition, do not impair their fitness or merchantability."

IMPACT OF THIS CASE ON TODAY'S LAW *This classic case, phrased in memorable language, was an early application of the UCC's implied warranty of merchantability to food products. The case established the rule that consumers should expect to find, on occasion, elements of food products that are natural to the product (such as fish bones in fish chowder). Courts today still apply this rule.*

RELEVANT WEB SITES *To locate information on the Web concerning the* Webster *decision, go to this text's Web site at* **academic.cengage.com/blaw/blt**, *select "Chapter 13," and click on "URLs for Landmarks."*

Implied Warranty of Fitness for a Particular Purpose   The **implied warranty of fitness for a particular purpose** arises when any seller or lessor (merchant or nonmerchant) knows the particular purpose for which a buyer or lessee will use the goods *and* knows that the buyer or lessee is relying on the skill and judgment of the seller or lessor to select suitable goods [UCC 2–315, 2A–213].

Particular versus Ordinary Purpose.   A "particular purpose" of the buyer or lessee differs from the "ordinary purpose for which goods are used" (merchantability). Goods can be merchantable but unfit for a particular purpose. ▣**EXAMPLE 13.4** Suppose that you need a gallon of paint to match the color of your living room walls—a light shade somewhere between coral and peach. You take a sample to your local hardware store and request a gallon of paint of that color. Instead, you are given a gallon of bright blue paint. Here, the salesperson has not breached any warranty of implied merchantability—the bright blue paint is of high quality and suitable for interior walls—but he or she has breached an implied warranty of fitness for a particular purpose. ▣

Knowledge and Reliance Requirements.   A seller or lessor is not required to have actual knowledge of the buyer's or lessee's particular purpose, so long as the seller or lessor "has reason to know" the purpose. For an implied warranty to be created, however, the buyer or lessee must have *relied* on the skill or judgment of the seller or lessor in selecting or furnishing suitable goods.
▣**EXAMPLE 13.5** Bloomberg leases a computer from Future Tech, a lessor of technical business equipment. Bloomberg tells the clerk that she wants a computer that will run a complicated new engineering graphics program at a realistic speed. Future Tech leases Bloomberg an Architex One computer with a CPU speed of only 2 gigahertz, even though a speed of at least 3.2 gigahertz would be required to run Bloomberg's graphics program at a "realistic speed." Bloomberg, after discovering that it takes forever to run her program, wants her money back. Here, because Future Tech has breached the implied warranty of fitness for a particular purpose, Bloomberg normally will be able to recover. The clerk knew specifically that Bloomberg wanted a computer with enough speed to run certain software. Furthermore, Bloomberg relied on the clerk to furnish a computer that would fulfill this purpose. Because Future Tech did not do so, the warranty was breached. ▣

Warranties Implied from Prior Dealings or Trade Custom   Implied warranties can also arise (or be excluded or modified) as a result of course of dealing or usage of trade [UCC 2–314(3), 2A–212(3)]. In the absence of evidence to the contrary, when both parties to a sales or lease contract have knowledge of a well-recognized trade custom, the courts will infer that both parties intended for that trade custom to apply to their contract. ▣**EXAMPLE 13.6** Suppose that it is an industrywide custom to lubricate new cars before the cars are delivered to a buyer. Latoya buys a new car from Bender Chevrolet. After the purchase, Latoya discovers that Bender failed to lubricate the car before delivering it to her. In this situation, Latoya can hold the dealer liable for damages resulting from the breach of an implied warranty. (This, of course, would also be negligence on the part of the dealer.) ▣

Overlapping Warranties

Sometimes, two or more warranties are made in a single transaction. An implied warranty of merchantability, an implied warranty of fitness for a particular purpose, or both can exist in addition to an express warranty. For example, when a sales contract for a new car states that "this car engine is warranted to be free from defects for 36,000 miles or thirty-six months, whichever occurs first," there is an express warranty against all defects and an implied warranty that the car will be fit for normal use.

IMPLIED WARRANTY OF FITNESS
FOR A PARTICULAR PURPOSE
A warranty that goods sold or leased
are fit for a particular purpose. The
warranty arises when any seller or
lessor knows the particular purpose
for which a buyer or lessee will use
the goods and knows that the buyer
or lessee is relying on the skill and
judgment of the seller or lessor to
select suitable goods.

The rule under the UCC is that express and implied warranties are construed as *cumulative* if they are consistent with one another [UCC 2–317, 2A–215]. In other words, courts interpret two or more warranties as being in agreement with each other unless this construction is unreasonable. If it is unreasonable, then a court will hold that the warranties are inconsistent and apply the following rules to interpret which warranty is most important:

1 *Express* warranties displace inconsistent *implied* warranties, except for implied warranties of fitness for a particular purpose.

2 Samples take precedence over inconsistent general descriptions.

3 Exact or technical specifications displace inconsistent samples or general descriptions.

> **BE AWARE** Express and implied warranties do not necessarily displace each other. More than one warranty can cover the same goods in the same transaction.

Warranty Disclaimers

The UCC generally permits warranties to be disclaimed or limited by specific and unambiguous language, provided that this is done in a manner that protects the buyer or lessee from surprise. Because each type of warranty is created in a special way, the manner in which a seller or lessor can disclaim warranties varies depending on the type of warranty.

Express Warranties As already stated, any affirmation of fact or promise, description of the goods, or use of samples or models by a seller or lessor creates an express warranty. Obviously, then, express warranties can be excluded if the seller or lessor carefully refrains from making any promise or affirmation of fact relating to the goods, describing the goods, or using a sample or model.

In addition, a written (or recorded) disclaimer in language that is clear and conspicuous, and called to a buyer's or lessee's attention, can negate all oral express warranties not included in the sales or lease contract [UCC 2–316(1), 2A–214(1)]. This allows the seller or lessor to avoid false allegations that oral warranties were made, and it ensures that only representations made by properly authorized individuals are included in the bargain.

Note, however, that a buyer or lessee must be made aware of any warranty disclaimers or modifications *at the time the contract is formed*. In other words, any oral or written warranties—or disclaimers—made during the bargaining process as part of a contract's formation cannot be modified at a later time by the seller or lessor.

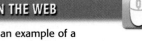

ON THE WEB

For an example of a warranty disclaimer, go to

www.bizguardian.com/terms.php.

Implied Warranties Generally speaking, implied warranties are much easier for a seller or lessor to disclaim. Under the UCC, unless circumstances indicate otherwise, all implied warranties are disclaimed by the expressions "as is," "with all faults," and other similar language that in common understanding call the buyer's or lessee's attention to the fact that there are no implied warranties [UCC 2–316(3)(a), 2A–214(3)(a)]. (Note, however, that some states have passed consumer protection statutes forbidding "as is" sales or making it illegal to disclaim warranties of merchantability on consumer goods.)

■EXAMPLE 13.7 Sue Hallett saw an advertisement offering a "lovely, eleven-year-old mare" with extensive jumping ability for sale. After visiting Mandy Morningstar's ranch and examining the horse twice, Hallett contracted to buy it for $2,950. The contract she signed described the horse as an eleven-year-old mare, but indicated that the horse was being sold "as is." Shortly after the purchase, a veterinarian determined that the horse was actually sixteen years old and in no condition for jumping. Hallett immediately notified her bank and stopped payment on the check she had written to pay for the horse. Hallett also tried to return the horse and cancel the contract with Morningstar, but Morningstar refused and filed a suit against Hallett, claiming breach of contract. The trial court found in favor of Morningstar because Hallett had examined the horse and was satisfied with its condition at the time she signed the "as is" sales contract. The appellate court reversed, however, finding that the statement in the contract describing the horse as eleven years old constituted an express warranty, which Morningstar breached. The appellate court reasoned that although the "as is" clause effectively disclaimed any implied warranties (of merchantability and fitness for a particular purpose, such as jumping), it did not disclaim the express warranty concerning the horse's age.[4] ◻

Disclaimer of the Implied Warranty of Merchantability. The UCC also permits a seller or lessor to specifically disclaim an implied warranty of merchantability [UCC 2–316(2), 2A–214(2)]. A merchantability disclaimer must specifically mention the word *merchantability.* The disclaimer need not be written, but if it is, the writing (or record) must be conspicuous [UCC 2–316(2), 2A–214(4)]. Under the UCC, a term or clause is conspicuous when it is written or displayed in such a way that a reasonable person would notice it. Conspicuous terms include words set in capital letters, in a larger font size, or in a different color so as to be set off from the surrounding text.

    ■EXAMPLE 13.8 Forbes, a merchant, sells Maves a particular lawn mower selected by Forbes with the characteristics clearly requested by Maves. At the time of the sale, Forbes orally tells Maves that he does not warrant the merchantability of the mower, as it is last year's model and has been used for demonstration purposes. If the mower proves to be defective and does not work, Maves can hold Forbes liable for breach of the warranty of fitness for a particular purpose but not for breach of the warranty of merchantability. Forbes's oral disclaimer mentioning the word *merchantability* is a proper disclaimer. ◻

WATCH OUT Courts generally view warranty disclaimers unfavorably, especially when consumers are involved.

Disclaimer of the Implied Warranty of Fitness. To specifically disclaim an implied warranty of fitness for a particular purpose, the disclaimer *must* be in a writing (or record) and must be conspicuous. The word *fitness* does not have to be mentioned; it is sufficient if, for example, the disclaimer states, "THERE ARE NO WARRANTIES THAT EXTEND BEYOND THE DESCRIPTION ON THE FACE HEREOF."

Buyer's or Lessee's Examination or Refusal to Inspect If a buyer or lessee actually examines the goods (or a sample or model) as fully as desired before entering into a contract, or if the buyer or lessee refuses to examine the goods on the seller's or lessor's demand that he or she do so, *there is no implied warranty with respect to defects that a reasonable examination would reveal or defects that are actually found* [UCC 2–316(3)(b), 2A–214(2)(b)].

    ■EXAMPLE 13.9 Suppose that Joplin buys a lamp at Gershwin's Home Store. No express warranties are made. Gershwin requests that Joplin inspect the lamp before buying it, but she refuses. Had Joplin inspected the lamp, she would have noticed that the base of the lamp was obviously cracked and the electrical cord was pulled loose. If the lamp later cracks or starts a fire in Joplin's home and she is injured, she normally will not be able to hold Gershwin's liable for breach of the warranty of merchantability. Because Joplin refused to examine the lamp when asked by Gershwin, Joplin will be deemed to have assumed the risk that it was defective. ◻

Warranty Disclaimers and Unconscionability The UCC sections dealing with warranty disclaimers do not refer specifically to unconscionability as a factor. Ultimately, however, the courts will test warranty disclaimers with reference to the UCC's unconscionability standards [UCC 2–302, 2A–108]. Such things as lack of bargaining position, "take-it-or-leave-it" choices, and a buyer's or lessee's failure to understand or know of a warranty disclaimer will become relevant to the issue of unconscionability.

---

4. *Morningstar v. Hallett,* 858 A.2d 125 (Pa.Super.Ct. 2004).

Magnuson-Moss Warranty Act

The Magnuson-Moss Warranty Act of 1975[5] was designed to prevent deception in warranties by making them easier to understand. The Federal Trade Commission (FTC) is the main agency that enforces this federal law. Additionally, the attorney general or a consumer who has been injured can bring an action to enforce the act if informal procedures for settling disputes prove to be ineffective. The act modifies UCC warranty rules to some extent when consumer transactions are involved. The UCC, however, remains the primary codification of warranty rules for commercial transactions.

Under the Magnuson-Moss Act, no seller or lessor is required to give an express written warranty for consumer goods sold. If a seller or lessor chooses to make an express written warranty, however, and the goods are priced at more than $25, the warranty must be labeled as "full" or "limited." In addition, the warrantor must make certain disclosures fully and conspicuously in a single document in "readily understood language." This disclosure must state the names and addresses of the warrantor(s), what specifically is warranted, procedures for enforcing the warranty, any limitations on warranty relief, and that the buyer has legal rights.

Full Warranty   Although a *full warranty* may not cover every aspect of the consumer product sold, what it does cover ensures some type of consumer satisfaction in the event that the product is defective. A full warranty requires free repair or replacement of any defective part; if the product cannot be repaired within a reasonable time, the consumer has the choice of a refund or a replacement without charge. Frequently, there is no time limit on a full warranty. Any limitation on consequential damages must be *conspicuously* stated. Additionally, the warrantor need not perform warranty services if the problem with the product was caused by the consumer's unreasonable use of the product.

Limited Warranty   A *limited warranty* arises when the written warranty fails to meet one of the minimum requirements of a full warranty. The fact that only a limited warranty is being given must be conspicuously stated. If the only distinction between a limited warranty and a full warranty is a time limitation, the Magnuson-Moss Warranty Act allows the warrantor to identify the warranty as a full warranty by such language as "full twelve-month warranty."

Implied Warranties   Implied warranties do not arise under the Magnuson-Moss Warranty Act; they continue to be created according to UCC provisions. Implied warranties may not be disclaimed under the Magnuson-Moss Warranty Act, however. Although a warrantor can impose a time limit on the duration of an implied warranty, it must correspond to the duration of the express warranty.[6]

PRODUCT LIABILITY

Those who make, sell, or lease goods can be held liable for physical harm or property damage caused by those goods to a consumer, user, or bystander. This is called **product liability.** Product liability claims may be based on the warranty theories just discussed, as well as on the theories of negligence, misrepresentation, and strict liability. We look here at product liability based on negligence and misrepresentation.

PRODUCT LIABILITY
The legal liability of manufacturers, sellers, and lessors of goods to consumers, users, and bystanders for injuries or damages that are caused by the goods.

Negligence

Chapter 4 defined *negligence* as the failure to exercise the degree of care that a reasonable, prudent person would have exercised under the circumstances. If a manufacturer

---

5. 15 U.S.C. Sections 2301–2312.

6. The time limit on an implied warranty occurring by virtue of the warrantor's express warranty must, of course, be reasonable, conscionable, and set forth in clear and conspicuous language on the face of the warranty.

fails to exercise "due care" to make a product safe, a person who is injured by the product may sue the manufacturer for negligence.

Due Care Must Be Exercised   The manufacturer must exercise due care in designing the product, selecting the materials, using the appropriate production process, assembling the product, and placing adequate warnings on the label informing the user of dangers of which an ordinary person might not be aware. The duty of care also extends to the inspection and testing of any purchased products that are used in the final product sold by the manufacturer.

Privity of Contract Not Required   A product liability action based on negligence does not require *privity of contract* between the injured plaintiff and the defendant manufacturer. As discussed in Chapter 9, *privity of contract* refers to the relationship that exists between the promisor and the promisee of a contract; privity is the reason that only the parties to a contract can enforce that contract. In the context of product liability law, privity is not required. This means that a person who was injured by a product need not be the one who actually purchased the product—that is, need not be in privity—to maintain a negligence suit against the manufacturer or seller of a defective product. A manufacturer is liable for its failure to exercise due care to *any* person who sustains an injury proximately caused by a negligently made (defective) product.

Relative to the long history of the common law, this exception to the privity requirement is a fairly recent development, dating to the early part of the twentieth century. A leading case in this respect is *MacPherson v. Buick Motor Co.*, which we present as this chapter's *Landmark in the Law* feature on the following page.

Misrepresentation

When a fraudulent misrepresentation has been made to a user or consumer, and that misrepresentation ultimately results in an injury, the basis of liability may be the tort of fraud. For example, the intentional mislabeling of packaged cosmetics or the intentional concealment of a product's defects would constitute fraudulent misrepresentation. The misrepresentation must be of a material fact and the seller must have had the intent to induce the buyer's reliance on the misrepresentation. Misrepresentation on a label or advertisement is enough to show an intent to induce the reliance of anyone who may use the product. In addition, the buyer must have relied on the misrepresentation.

STRICT PRODUCT LIABILITY

Under the doctrine of strict liability (discussed in Chapter 4), people may be liable for the results of their acts regardless of their intentions or their exercise of reasonable care. In addition, liability does not depend on privity of contract. The injured party does not have to be the buyer or a third party beneficiary, as required under contract warranty theory. Indeed, the provisions of the UCC do not govern this type of liability in law because it is a tort doctrine, not a principle of the law relating to sales contracts.

Strict Product Liability and Public Policy

The law imposes strict product liability as a matter of public policy. This public policy rests on the threefold assumption that (1) consumers should be protected against unsafe products; (2) manufacturers and distributors should not escape liability for faulty products simply because they are not in privity of contract with the ultimate user of those products; and (3) manufacturers, sellers, and lessors of products are generally in a better position

ON THE WEB

For an overview of product liability, go to FindLaw for Small Business at

smallbusiness.findlaw.com/business-operations/insurance/liability-product-overview.html.

LANDMARK IN THE LAW — *MacPherson v. Buick Motor Co.* (1916)

In the landmark case of *MacPherson v. Buick Motor Co.*,[a] the New York Court of Appeals—New York's highest court—dealt with the liability of a manufacturer that failed to exercise reasonable care in manufacturing a finished product.

Case Background   The case was brought by Donald MacPherson, who suffered injuries while riding in a Buick automobile that suddenly collapsed because one of the wheels was made of defective wood. The spokes crumbled into fragments, throwing MacPherson out of the vehicle and injuring him.

MacPherson had purchased the car from a Buick dealer, but he brought a lawsuit against the manufacturer, Buick Motor Company. Buick itself had not made the wheel but had bought it from another manufacturer. There was evidence, though, that the defects could have been discovered by a reasonable inspection by Buick and that no such inspection had taken place. MacPherson charged Buick with negligence for putting a human life in imminent danger.

The Issue before the Court and the Court's Ruling   The major issue before the court was whether Buick owed a duty of care to anyone except the immediate purchaser of the car—that is, the Buick dealer. In deciding the issue, Justice Benjamin Cardozo stated that "[i]f the nature of a thing is such that it is reasonably certain to place life and limb in peril when negligently made, it is then a thing of danger. . . . If to the element of danger there is added knowledge that the thing will be used by persons other than the purchaser, and used without new tests, then, irrespective of contract, the manufacturer of this thing of danger is under a duty to make it carefully."

The court concluded that "[b]eyond all question, the nature of an automobile gives warning of probable danger if its construction is defective. This automobile was designed to go 50 miles an hour. Unless its wheels were sound and strong, injury was almost certain." Although Buick had not manufactured the wheel itself, the court held that Buick had a duty to inspect the wheels and that Buick "was responsible for the finished product." Therefore, Buick was liable to MacPherson for the injuries he sustained when he was thrown from the car.

APPLICATION TO TODAY'S WORLD   *This landmark decision was a significant step in creating the legal environment of the modern world. Today, it is common for an automobile manufacturer to be held liable when its negligence causes a product user to be injured. As is often the situation, technological developments necessitated changes in the law. Had the courts continued to require privity of contract in product liability cases, today's legal landscape would be quite different indeed. Certainly, fewer cases would be pending before the courts; and just as certainly, many purchasers of products, including automobiles, would have little recourse for obtaining legal redress for injuries caused by those products.*

RELEVANT WEB SITES   *To locate information on the Web concerning the MacPherson decision, go to this text's Web site at* **academic.cengage.com/blaw/blt**, *select "Chapter 13," and click on "URLs for Landmarks."*

a. 217 N.Y. 382, 111 N.E. 1050 (1916).

than consumers to bear the costs associated with injuries caused by their products—costs that they can ultimately pass on to all consumers in the form of higher prices.

California was the first state to impose strict product liability in tort on manufacturers. In a landmark 1963 decision, *Greenman v. Yuba Power Products, Inc.*,[7] the California Supreme Court set out the reason for applying tort law rather than contract law in cases involving consumers injured by defective products. According to the court, the "purpose of such liability is to [e]nsure that the costs of injuries resulting from defective products are borne by the manufacturers . . . rather than by the injured persons who are powerless to protect themselves."

Requirements for Strict Liability

Section 402A of the *Restatement (Second) of Torts* indicates how the drafters envisioned that the doctrine of strict liability should be applied. The *Restatement* was issued in 1964, and during the next decade, Section 402A became a widely accepted statement of the liabilities of sellers of goods (including manufacturers, processors, assemblers, packagers, bottlers, wholesalers, distributors, retailers, and lessors).

The bases for an action in strict liability as set forth in Section 402A of the *Restatement (Second) of Torts*, and as the doctrine came to be commonly applied, can be summarized as a series of six requirements, which are listed here. Depending on the jurisdiction, if these requirements are met, a manufacturer's liability to an injured party can be virtually unlimited.

1 The product must be in a *defective condition* when the defendant sells it.

2 The defendant must normally be engaged in the *business of selling* (or otherwise distributing) that product.

3 The product must be *unreasonably dangerous* to the user or consumer because of its defective condition (in most states).

4 The plaintiff must incur *physical harm* to self or property by use or consumption of the product.

5 The defective condition must be the *proximate cause* of the injury or damage.

6 The *goods must not have been substantially changed* from the time the product was sold to the time the injury was sustained.

Proving a Defective Condition   Under these requirements, in any action against a manufacturer, seller, or lessor, the plaintiff does not have to show why or in what manner the product became defective. The plaintiff does, however, have to prove that the product was defective at the time it left the hands of the seller or lessor and that this defective condition makes it "unreasonably dangerous" to the user or consumer. Unless evidence can be presented that will support the conclusion that the product was defective when it was sold or leased, the plaintiff normally will not succeed. If the product was delivered in a safe condition and subsequent mishandling made it harmful to the user, the seller or lessor is not strictly liable.

Unreasonably Dangerous Products   The *Restatement* recognizes that many products cannot possibly be made entirely safe for all consumption, and thus holds sellers or lessors liable only for products that are *unreasonably* dangerous. A court may consider a product so defective as to be an **unreasonably dangerous product** in either of the following situations:

1 The product is dangerous beyond the expectation of the ordinary consumer.

2 A less dangerous alternative was economically feasible for the manufacturer, but the manufacturer failed to produce it.

---

7. 59 Cal.2d 57, 377 P.2d 897, 27 Cal.Rptr. 697 (1963).

UNREASONABLY DANGEROUS PRODUCT
In product liability law, a product that is defective to the point of threatening a consumer's health and safety. A product will be considered unreasonably dangerous if it is dangerous beyond the expectation of the ordinary consumer or if a less dangerous alternative was economically feasible for the manufacturer, but the manufacturer failed to produce it.

Sony manufactured defective lithium-ion cell batteries, some of which caught on fire. Dell and other computer companies bought these Sony batteries for use in their laptop computers. To what extent is Sony liable? To what extent are Dell and other laptop makers who purchased these batteries liable? (Photo Courtesy of theinquirer.net)

As will be discussed next, a product may be unreasonably dangerous due to a flaw in the manufacturing process, a design defect, or an inadequate warning.

Product Defects—*Restatement (Third) of Torts*

Because Section 402A of the *Restatement (Second) of Torts* did not clearly define such terms as "defective" and "unreasonably dangerous," they were interpreted differently by different courts. In 1997, to address these concerns, the American Law Institute issued the *Restatement (Third) of Torts: Products Liability*. This *Restatement* defines the three types of product defects that have traditionally been recognized in product liability law—manufacturing defects, design defects, and inadequate warnings.

Manufacturing Defects   According to Section 2(a) of the *Restatement (Third) of Torts: Products Liability*, a product "contains a manufacturing defect when the product departs from its intended design even though all possible care was exercised in the preparation and marketing of the product." Basically, a manufacturing defect is a departure from a product unit's design specifications, which results in products that are physically flawed, damaged, or incorrectly assembled. A glass bottle that is made too thin and explodes in a consumer's face is an example of a manufacturing defect. Liability is imposed on the manufacturer (and on the wholesaler and retailer) regardless of whether the manufacturer's quality control efforts were "reasonable." The idea behind holding defendants strictly liable for manufacturing defects is to encourage greater investment in product safety and stringent quality control standards.

For liability to be imposed on the basis of a manufacturing defect, the plaintiff must prove that the defect caused him or her to suffer an injury. On the question of causation in the following case, the plaintiff offered the testimony of a university professor.

CASE 13.2   **DeRienzo v. Trek Bicycle Corp.**

United States District Court, Southern District of New York, 376 F.Supp.2d 537 (2005).

FACTS   David DeRienzo of Newburgh, New York, owned a 1998 Y5 mountain bike made by Trek Bicycle Corporation. All of the Y5's parts had been replaced except the aluminum frame. DeRienzo was an aggressive rider, who enjoyed urban assault riding, dirt jumping, and mountain biking. On July 4, 2001, he jumped five to eight feet off a hillside, but as he landed, the frame broke and he crashed. Seriously injured, he filed a suit in a federal district court against Trek, claiming in part strict product liability on the basis of a manufacturing defect. He supported this claim with the testimony of Harold Paxton. Paxton is the U.S. Steel University Professor (Emeritus) of Metallurgy and Materials Science at Carnegie Mellon University and a member of related professional organizations. Paxton inspected and photographed the frame's fracture. To confirm his observations, Paxton had the frame taken apart, photographed again, analyzed chemically, and tested mechanically. Trek and its experts consented to these tests and methods. Paxton believed that the frame failed due to a defect—a crack caused by excess weld metal deposited on the inside of the tube during the manufacturing process. Trek filed

a motion for summary judgment, arguing that Paxton had never analyzed an aluminum bike frame before and did not have "the faintest idea" about the mountain biking industry. Trek also cited mistakes by Paxton's technician and misinterpretation of some of the results.

ISSUE   Was Paxton's testimony admissible, and if so, was it sufficient to defeat Trek's motion for summary judgment?

DECISION   Yes. The court ruled that Paxton could testify as an expert and, on the basis of this testimony, denied Trek's motion.

REASON   To be admissible, expert testimony must be scientifically valid and relevant to the case. Scientific validity requires that the expert's technique can be tested, that it has been subject to peer review and acceptance, that it has a known or potential rate of error, and that there are standards controlling the technique. In this case, the court held that Paxton's methods carried "sufficient indicia [indications] of scientific reliability. *   *   * Most significant in this regard is *   *   * that Defendant's own metallurgical expert and defense

CASE 13.2–Continued

counsel agreed upon the protocols by which Paxton analyzed the Bike's frame." Also, "Paxton's described procedures tend to indicate to the Court that he carried out a thorough and scientific analysis of the frame, and that these tests formed the basis for his conclusion." Paxton's testimony was offered for a proper purpose–to help the court determine what caused the Y5's frame to fail. As for Trek's objections, Paxton's "extensive education and teaching background in the field of metallurgy generally, as well as his broad and prestigious professional associations, indicate that he is qualified to undertake analysis

of an aluminum bicycle frame." Trek's other criticisms were "forensic quibbles" about which the defendant could cross-examine Paxton if "they come up at trial." The court reasoned further that Paxton's opinion that the frame failed because of a manufacturing defect gave rise to a reasonable inference that the frame's failure caused the accident.

WHY IS THIS CASE IMPORTANT? *This case illustrates that the admissibility of an expert's opinion can be essential in product liability cases to prove that a manufacturing defect exists and that the defect is what caused the plaintiff's injury.*

Design Defects   In contrast to a manufacturing defect, which is a failure of a product to meet the manufacturer's design specifications, a design defect is a flaw in the product's actual design that causes the product to create an unreasonable risk to the user. A product "is defective in design when the foreseeable risks of harm posed by the product could have been reduced or avoided by the adoption of a reasonable alternative design by the seller or other distributor, or a predecessor in the commercial chain of distribution, and the omission of the alternative design renders the product not reasonably safe."[8]

Test for Design Defects.   To successfully assert a design defect, a plaintiff has to show that a reasonable alternative design was available and that the defendant's failure to adopt the alternative design rendered the product unreasonably dangerous. In other words, a manufacturer or other defendant is liable only when the harm was reasonably preventable. **EXAMPLE 13.10** Gillespie, who cut off several of his fingers while operating a table saw, filed a lawsuit against the maker of the table saw. Gillespie alleged that the blade guards on the saw were defectively designed. At trial, however, an expert testified that the alternative design for blade guards used for table saws could not have been used for the particular cut that Gillespie was performing at the time he was injured. The court found that Gillespie's claim about defective blade guards must fail because there was no proof that the "better" design of guard would have prevented his injury.[9]

Segway, Inc., manufacturer of the Segway® Personal Transporter, voluntarily recalled all of its transporters to fix a software problem that could lead to users falling and injuring themselves. If a person was injured by such a malfunction of the software in the machine, what would the victim have to prove to establish that the device had a design defect? (Nelson Pavlosky/Creative Commons)

Factors to Be Considered.   According to the Official Comments accompanying the *Restatement (Third) of Torts*, a court can consider a broad range of factors in deciding claims of design defects. These factors include the magnitude and probability of the foreseeable risks, as well as the relative advantages and disadvantages of the product as designed and as it alternatively could have been designed.
EXAMPLE 13.11 Four-year-old Andrea suffered serious burns when she got out of bed one night to go to the bathroom and tripped on the electric cord connected to a hot-water vaporizer. Andrea's parents filed a lawsuit against the manufacturer, alleging that the vaporizer was defectively designed because the top heating unit was not secured to the jar that held the hot water. In this situation, the court said the following factors were relevant: (1) the foreseeability that the vaporizer might be accidentally tipped over, (2) the overall safety provided by an alternative design that secured the heating unit to the receptacle holding the water, (3) the consumer's knowledge or lack of knowledge that the water in the glass jar was scalding hot, (4) the added cost of the safer alternative design, and (5) the relative convenience of a vaporizer with a lift-off cap. The court also observed that

---

8. *Restatement (Third) of Torts: Products Liability*, Section 2(b).
9. *Gillespie v. Sears, Roebuck & Co.*, 386 F.3d 21 (1st Cir. 2004).

because the parents of small children are frequently told to use vaporizers to treat child-hood illnesses, it was foreseeable that the vaporizer units would be operating unattended in children's rooms. It was also foreseeable that small children might trip over the cord and be burned. As several practical and inexpensive alternative designs were available, the court found that the vaporizer that injured Andrea was defectively designed.[10] ▣

Inadequate Warnings   A product may also be deemed defective because of inadequate instructions or warnings. A product will be considered defective "when the foreseeable risks of harm posed by the product could have been reduced or avoided by the provision of reasonable instructions or warnings by the seller or other distributor, or a predecessor in the commercial chain of distribution, and the omission of the instructions or warnings renders the product not reasonably safe."[11] Generally, a seller must warn those who purchase its product of the harm that can result from the *foreseeable misuse* of the product as well.

Important factors for a court to consider under the *Restatement (Third) of Torts* include the risks of a product, the "content and comprehensibility" and "intensity of expression" of warnings and instructions, and the "characteristics of expected user groups."[12] A "reasonableness" test is applied to determine if the warnings adequately alert consumers to the product's risks. For example, children will likely respond more readily to bright, bold, simple warning labels, while educated adults might need more detailed information.

There is no duty to warn about risks that are obvious or commonly known. Warnings about such risks do not add to the safety of a product and could even detract from it by making other warnings seem less significant. The obviousness of a risk and a user's decision to proceed in the face of that risk may be a defense in a product liability suit based on a warning defect. (This defense and other defenses in product liability suits will be discussed later in this chapter.)

ETHICAL ISSUE 13.1

If a warning is provided with a product, should its manufacturer or seller be able to assume that the warning will be read and obeyed? Today, manufacturers tend to include a long list of warnings of the potential risks associated with every product. Even products that are relatively safe include warnings. Consumers are so inundated with multiple warnings for every kind of product that most people no longer pay attention to the warnings. Moreover, in some instances the warnings about a product conflict with how consumers have always used that product.

Consider a trampoline, for example. The risks of jumping on a trampoline are not new. Many children are injured on trampolines each year, but this has not decreased their popularity. The manufacturers of trampolines now warn users not to do flips or to have more than one person on a trampoline at a time—both of which have been common practices on trampolines for years. Should a manufacturer be insulated from liability because it provided warning labels in the box to be affixed on the assembled trampoline? Yes, according to the courts in several 2006 cases.[13] As long as the manufacturer provides adequate warnings, it can assume that the user will read and follow its many warnings. In other words, today's products come with many warnings so that manufacturers and sellers can avoid liability for products that might otherwise be considered defective or unreasonably dangerous. Does allowing manufacturers and sellers to avoid liability in this way make sense, given that the whole reason for imposing strict liability is the public policy of protecting consumers and making sure that manufacturers and sellers share at least some of the risks of unsafe products?

▣

---

10. This example is based on the facts of an early case on design defects, *McCormack v. Hankscraft Co.*, 278 Minn. 322, 154 N.W.2d 488 (1967).

11. *Restatement (Third) of Torts: Products Liability*, Section 2(c).

12. *Restatement (Third) of Torts: Products Liability*, Section 2, Comment h.

13. *Crosswhite v. Jumpking, Inc.*, 411 F.Supp.2d 1228 (D.Or. 2006); and *Celmer v. Jumpking, Inc.*, __ F.Supp.2d __ (D.Md. 2006).

Market-Share Liability

Generally, in all cases involving product liability, a plaintiff must prove that the defective product that caused her or his injury was the product of a specific defendant. In a few situations, however, courts have dropped this requirement when a plaintiff cannot prove which of many distributors of a harmful product supplied the particular product that caused the injuries. Under a theory of **market-share liability,** all firms that manufactured and distributed the product during the period in question are held liable for the plaintiff's injuries in proportion to the firms' respective shares of the market for that product during that period.

■EXAMPLE 13.12 In one case, a plaintiff who was a hemophiliac received injections of a blood protein known as antihemophiliac factor (AHF) concentrate. The plaintiff later tested positive for the AIDS (acquired immune deficiency syndrome) virus. Because it was not known which manufacturer was responsible for the particular AHF received by the plaintiff, the court held that all of the manufacturers of AHF could be held liable under a market-share theory of liability.[14] ■

Courts in many jurisdictions do not recognize this theory of liability, believing that it deviates too significantly from traditional legal principles.[15] In jurisdictions that do recognize market-share liability, it is usually applied in cases involving drugs or chemicals, when it is difficult or impossible to determine which company made a particular product.

> **MARKET-SHARE LIABILITY**
> A theory of sharing liability among all firms that manufactured and distributed a particular product during a certain period of time. This form of liability sharing is used only in some jurisdictions and only when the true source of the harmful product is unidentifiable.

Other Applications of Strict Liability

Virtually all courts extend the strict liability of manufacturers and other sellers to injured bystanders. **■EXAMPLE 13.13** A forklift that Trent is operating will not go into reverse, and as a result, it runs into a bystander. In this situation, the bystander can sue the manufacturer of the defective forklift under strict liability.[16] ■

The rule of strict liability is also applicable to suppliers of component parts. **■EXAMPLE 13.14** General Motors buys brake pads from a subcontractor and puts them in Chevrolets without changing their composition. If those pads are defective, both the supplier of the brake pads and General Motors will be held strictly liable for the injuries caused by the defects. ■

Statutes of Repose

As discussed in Chapter 1, *statutes of limitations* restrict the time within which an action may be brought. Many states have passed laws, called **statutes of repose,** placing outer time limits on some claims so that the defendant will not be left vulnerable to lawsuits indefinitely. These statutes may limit the time within which a plaintiff can file a product liability suit. Typically, a statute of repose begins to run at an earlier date and runs for a longer time than a statute of limitations. For example, a statute of repose may require that claims be brought within twelve years from the date of sale or manufacture of the defective product. No action can be brought if the injury occurs *after* this statutory period has lapsed. In addition, some of these legislative enactments limit the application of the doctrine of strict liability to new goods only.

> **STATUTE OF REPOSE**
> Basically, a statute of limitations that is not dependent on the happening of a cause of action. Statutes of repose generally begin to run at an earlier date and run for a longer period of time than statutes of limitations.

---

14. *Smith v. Cutter Biological, Inc.,* 72 Haw. 416, 823 P.2d 717 (1991). See also *Hymowitz v. Eli Lilly and Co.,* 73 N.Y.2d 487, 539 N.E.2d 1069, 541 N.Y.S.2d 941 (1989).

15. For the Illinois Supreme Court's position on market-share liability, see *Smith v. Eli Lilly Co.,* 137 Ill.2d 252, 560 N.E.2d 324, 148 Ill.Dec. 22 (1990).

16. See, for example, *Batts v. Tow-Motor Forklift Co.,* 978 F.2d 1386 (Miss. 1992).

DEFENSES TO PRODUCT LIABILITY

Defendants in product liability suits can raise a number of defenses. One defense, of course, is to show that there is no basis for the plaintiff's claim. For example, in a product liability case based on negligence, if a defendant can show that the plaintiff has *not* met the requirements (such as causation) for an action in negligence, generally the defendant will not be liable. In regard to strict product liability, a defendant can claim that the plaintiff failed to meet one of the requirements for an action in strict liability. If the defendant, for instance, establishes that the goods have been subsequently altered, normally the defendant will not be held liable.[17] Defendants may also assert the defenses discussed next.

Assumption of Risk

ON THE WEB

For information on the product liability litigation against tobacco companies, including defenses raised by tobacco manufacturers in trial-related documents, go to the following page of the University of California, San Francisco's Web site at

www.library.ucsf.edu/tobacco/litigation.

Assumption of risk can sometimes be used as a defense in a product liability action. For example, if a buyer fails to heed a product recall by the seller, a court might conclude that the buyer assumed the risk caused by the defect that led to the recall. To establish such a defense, the defendant must show that (1) the plaintiff knew and appreciated the risk created by the product defect and (2) the plaintiff voluntarily assumed the risk, even though it was unreasonable to do so. (See Chapter 4 for a more detailed discussion of assumption of risk.)

Product Misuse

Similar to the defense of voluntary assumption of risk is that of product misuse, which occurs when a product is used for a purpose for which it was not intended. The courts have severely limited this defense, however, and it is now recognized as a defense only when the particular use was not reasonably foreseeable. If the misuse is foreseeable, the seller must take measures to guard against it.

Comparative Negligence (Fault)

Developments in the area of comparative negligence, or fault (discussed in Chapter 4), have also affected the doctrine of strict liability—the most extreme theory of product liability. Whereas previously the plaintiff's conduct was not a defense to strict liability, today many jurisdictions, when apportioning liability and damages, consider the negligent or intentional actions of both the plaintiff and the defendant. This means that a defendant may be able to limit at least some of its liability for injuries caused by its defective product if it can show that the plaintiff's misuse of the product contributed to the injuries.

■EXAMPLE 13.15 Dan Smith, a mechanic in Alaska, was not wearing a hard hat at work when he was asked to start a diesel engine of an air compressor. Because the compressor was an older model, he had to prop open a door to start it. When he got the engine started, the door fell from its position and hit Smith's head. The injury caused him to suffer from seizures and epilepsy. Smith sued the manufacturer, claiming that the engine was defectively designed. The manufacturer argued that Smith had been negligent by failing to wear his hard hat and by propping the door open in an unsafe manner. Smith's attorney claimed that the plaintiff's ordinary negligence could not be used as a defense in product liability cases, but the Alaska Supreme Court disagreed. Alaska, like many other states, allows comparative negligence to be raised as a defense in product liability lawsuits.[18] ■

---

17. Under some state laws, the failure to properly maintain a product may constitute a subsequent alteration. See, for example, *La Plante v. American Honda Motor Co.*, 27 F.3d 731 (1st Cir. 1994).
18. *Smith v. Ingersoll-Rand Co.*, 14 P.3d 990 (Alaska 2000).

Commonly Known Dangers

The dangers associated with certain products (such as sharp knives and guns) are so commonly known that manufacturers need not warn users of those dangers. If a defendant succeeds in convincing the court that a plaintiff's injury resulted from a *commonly known danger*, the defendant normally will not be liable.

■EXAMPLE 13.16 A classic case on this issue involved a plaintiff who was injured when an elastic exercise rope that she had purchased slipped off her foot and struck her in the eye, causing a detachment of the retina. The plaintiff claimed that the manufacturer should be liable because it had failed to warn users that the exerciser might slip off a foot in such a manner. The court stated that to hold the manufacturer liable in these circumstances "would go beyond the reasonable dictates of justice in fixing the liabilities of manufacturers." After all, stated the court, "[a]lmost every physical object can be inherently dangerous or potentially dangerous in a sense. . . . A manufacturer cannot manufacture a knife that will not cut or a hammer that will not mash a thumb or a stove that will not burn a finger. The law does not require [manufacturers] to warn of such common dangers."[19] ■

A related defense is the *knowledgeable user* defense. If a particular danger (such as electrical shock) is or should be commonly known by particular users of the product (such as electricians), the manufacturer of electrical equipment need not warn these users of the danger.

CONSUMER PROTECTION LAWS

Sources of consumer protection exist at all levels of government. At the federal level, a number of laws have been passed to define the duties of sellers and the rights of consumers. Exhibit 13–1 indicates many of the areas of consumer law that are regulated by statutes. Federal administrative agencies, such as the Federal Trade Commission (FTC), also provide an important source of consumer protection. Nearly every agency and department of the federal government has an office of consumer affairs, and most states have one or more such offices, including the offices of state attorneys general, to assist consumers.

19. *Jamieson v. Woodward & Lothrop,* 247 F.2d 23, 101 D.C.App. 32 (1957).

EXHIBIT 13–1 Selected Areas of Consumer Law Regulated by Statutes

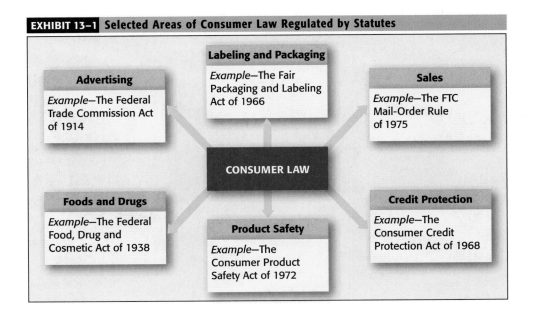

Because of the wide variation among state consumer protection laws, our primary focus here will be on federal legislation—specifically, on legislation governing deceptive advertising, telemarketing and electronic advertising, labeling and packaging, sales, health protection, product safety, and credit protection. Realize, though, that state laws often provide more sweeping and significant protections for the consumer than do federal laws.

Deceptive Advertising

DECEPTIVE ADVERTISING
Advertising that misleads consumers, either by making unjustified claims concerning a product's performance or by omitting a material fact concerning the product's composition or performance.

One of the earliest—and still one of the most important—federal consumer protection laws is the Federal Trade Commission Act of 1914 (mentioned in Chapter 22). The act created the FTC to carry out the broadly stated goal of preventing unfair and deceptive trade practices, including deceptive advertising, within the meaning of Section 5 of the act.

Generally, **deceptive advertising** occurs if a reasonable consumer would be misled by the advertising claim. Vague generalities and obvious exaggerations are permissible. These claims are known as *puffery*—that is, statements about a product that a reasonable person would not believe to be true. When a claim takes on the appearance of literal authenticity, however, it may create problems. Advertising that *appears* to be based on factual evidence but in fact is scientifically untrue will be deemed deceptive. A classic example occurred in a 1944 case in which the claim that a skin cream would restore youthful qualities to aged skin was deemed deceptive.[20]

Some advertisements contain "half-truths," meaning that the presented information is true but incomplete and, therefore, leads consumers to a false conclusion. **■EXAMPLE 13.17** The maker of Campbell's soups advertised that "most" Campbell's soups were low in fat and cholesterol and thus were helpful in fighting heart disease. What the ad did not say was that Campbell's soups were high in sodium and that high-sodium diets may increase the risk of heart disease. Hence, the FTC ruled that Campbell's claims were deceptive. ■ Advertising featuring an endorsement by a celebrity may be deemed deceptive if the celebrity does not actually use the product.

BAIT-AND-SWITCH ADVERTISING
Advertising a product at a very attractive price (the "bait") and then, once the consumer is in the store, saying that the advertised product is either not available or is of poor quality. The customer is then urged to purchase ("switched" to) a more expensive item.

Bait-and-Switch Advertising The FTC has issued rules that govern specific advertising techniques. One of the more important rules is contained in the FTC's "Guides on Bait Advertising."[21] The rule is designed to prevent **bait-and-switch advertising**—that is,

---

20. *Charles of the Ritz Distributing Corp. v. Federal Trade Commission*, 143 F.2d 676 (2d Cir. 1944).
21. 16 C.F.R. Section 288.

These stuffed teddy bears were recalled because the plastic beads inside the toys could come out and create a choking hazard for young children. According to Exhibit 13–1 on page 397, which area of consumer protection law governs such a recall? (Consumer Product Safety Commission/ Getty Images)

advertising a very low price for a particular item that will likely be unavailable to the consumer and then encouraging him or her to purchase a more expensive item. The low price is the "bait" to lure the consumer into the store. The salesperson is instructed to "switch" the consumer to a different, more expensive item. According to the FTC guidelines, bait-and-switch advertising occurs if the seller refuses to show the advertised item, fails to have reasonable quantities of it available, fails to promise to deliver the advertised item within a reasonable time, or discourages employees from selling the item.

Online Deceptive Advertising   Deceptive advertising can occur in the online environment as well. For years, the FTC has actively monitored online advertising and has identified hundreds of Web sites that have made false or deceptive advertising claims. These claims have concerned products ranging from medical treatments for various diseases to exercise equipment and weight-loss aids.

In 2000, the FTC issued guidelines to help online businesses comply with existing laws prohibiting deceptive advertising.[22] The guidelines did not set forth new rules but rather described how existing laws apply to online advertising. Generally, the rules emphasize that any ads—online or offline—must be truthful and not misleading and that any claims made in any ads must be substantiated. Additionally, ads cannot be unfair, which the FTC defines as "likely to cause substantial consumer injury that consumers could not reasonably avoid and that is not outweighed by the benefit to consumers or competition."

The guidelines also call for "clear and conspicuous" disclosure of any qualifying or limiting information. The overall impression of the ad is important in meeting this requirement. The FTC suggests that advertisers should assume that consumers will not read an entire Web page. Therefore, to satisfy the "clear and conspicuous" requirement, advertisers should place the disclosure as close as possible to the claim being qualified or include the disclosure within the claim itself. If such placement is not feasible, the next-best location is on a section of the page to which a consumer can easily scroll. Generally, hyperlinks to a disclosure are recommended only for lengthy disclosures or for disclosures that must be repeated in a variety of locations on the Web page. If the disclosure is an integral part of a claim, however, it should be placed on the same page rather than hyperlinked.

FTC Actions against Deceptive Advertising   The FTC receives complaints from many sources, including competitors of alleged violators, consumers, consumer organizations, trade associations, Better Business Bureaus, government organizations, and state and local officials. If it receives numerous and widespread complaints about a problem, the FTC will investigate. If the FTC concludes that a given advertisement is unfair or deceptive, it sends a formal complaint to the alleged offender. The company may agree to settle the complaint without further proceedings; if not, the FTC can conduct a hearing before an administrative law judge (discussed in Chapter 1) in which the company can present its defense.

If the FTC succeeds in proving that an advertisement is unfair or deceptive, it usually issues a **cease-and-desist order** requiring the company to stop the challenged advertising. It might also require **counteradvertising** in which the company advertises anew—in print, on the Internet, on radio, and on television—to inform the public about the earlier misinformation.

---
22. *Advertising and Marketing on the Internet: Rules of the Road,* September 2000. This guide is available at **www.ftc.gov/bcp/conline/pubs/buspubs/ruleroad.htm**.

ON THE WEB

A government-sponsored Web site that contains reports on consumer issues, including issues relating to online deceptive advertising and other forms of online fraud, can be accessed at

www.consumer.gov.

CEASE-AND-DESIST ORDER
An administrative or judicial order prohibiting a person or business firm from conducting activities that an agency or court has deemed illegal.

COUNTERADVERTISING
New advertising that is undertaken pursuant to a Federal Trade Commission order for the purpose of correcting earlier false claims that were made about a product.

Telemarketing and Electronic Advertising

The pervasive use of the telephone to market goods and services to homes and businesses led to the passage in 1991 of the Telephone Consumer Protection Act (TCPA).[23] The act prohibits telephone solicitation using an automatic telephone dialing system or a prerecorded voice. Most states also have laws regulating telephone solicitation. The TCPA also makes it illegal to transmit ads via fax without first obtaining the recipient's permission. (Similar issues have arisen with respect to junk e-mail, called *spam*—see Chapter 4.)

The act is enforced by the Federal Communications Commission (FCC) and also provides for a private right of action. The FCC imposes substantial fines ($11,000 each day) on companies that violate the junk fax provisions of the TCPA and has fined one company as much as $5.4 million for violations.[24] Consumers can recover any actual monetary loss resulting from a violation of the act or receive $500 in damages for each violation, whichever is greater. If a court finds that a defendant willfully or knowingly violated the act, the court has the discretion to treble (triple) the damages awarded. When many consumers file their complaints together as a class-action suit, the damages awarded can be large, as can the defendant's liability for attorneys' fees.

The Telemarketing and Consumer Fraud and Abuse Prevention Act of 1994[25] directed the FTC to establish rules governing telemarketing and to bring actions against fraudulent telemarketers. The FTC's Telemarketing Sales Rule of 1995[26] requires a telemarketer to identify the seller's name; describe the product being sold; and disclose all material facts related to the sale, including the total cost of the goods being sold, any restrictions on obtaining or using the goods, and whether a sale will be considered final and nonrefundable. The act makes it illegal for telemarketers to misrepresent information (including facts about their goods or services and earnings potential, for example). A telemarketer must also remove a consumer's name from its list of potential contacts if the consumer so requests. An amendment to the Telemarketing Sales Rule established the national Do Not Call Registry, which became effective in October 2003. Telemarketers must refrain from calling those consumers who have placed their names on the list.

Labeling and Packaging

A number of federal and state laws deal specifically with the information given on labels and packages. The rules are designed to ensure that labels provide accurate information about the product and to warn about possible dangers from its use or misuse. In general, labels must be accurate, and they must use words that are understood by the ordinary consumer. For example, a box of cereal cannot be labeled "giant" if that would exaggerate the amount of cereal contained in the box. In some instances, labels must specify the raw materials used in the product, such as the percentage of cotton, nylon, or other fibers used in a garment. In other instances, the products must carry a warning. Cigarette packages and advertising, for example, must include one of several warnings about the health hazards associated with smoking.[27]

The Fair Packaging and Labeling Act requires that food product labels identify (1) the product; (2) the net quantity of the contents and, if the number of servings is stated, the size of a serving; (3) the manufacturer; and (4) the packager or distrib-

---

REMEMBER Changes in technology often require changes in the law.

ON THE WEB

You can find current articles concerning consumer issues at the Alexander Law Firm's "Consumer Law Page." Go to consumerlawpage.com/intro.html.

Today's consumers are increasingly concerned about eating genetically modified crops and the potential presence of pesticides, hormones, and the causative agent of mad cow disease in foods. Many consumers have thus switched to buying organic foods. How might an organic label be deceptive to consumers?
(Richard Anderson)

---

23. 47 U.S.C. Sections 227 *et seq.*, as modified by the Junk Fax Protection Act of 2005.
24. See *Missouri ex rel. Nixon v. American Blast Fax, Inc.*, 323 F.3d 649 (8th Cir. 2003); *cert.* denied, 540 U.S. 1104, 124 S.Ct. 1043, 157 L.Ed.2d 888 (2004).
25. 15 U.S.C. Sections 6101–6108.
26. 16 C.F.R. Sections 310.1–310.8.
27. 15 U.S.C. Sections 1331 *et seq.*

utor.[28] The act also provides for additional requirements concerning descriptions on packages, savings claims, components of nonfood products, and standards for the partial filling of packages. Food products must bear labels detailing the food's nutrition content, including how much fat the food contains and what kind of fat it is. The Department of Health and Human Services, as well as the FTC, enforces these rules. The Nutrition Labeling and Education Act of 1990 requires standard nutrition facts (including fat content) on food labels; regulates the use of such terms as *fresh* and *low fat*; and, subject to the federal Food and Drug Administration's approval, authorizes certain health claims.

Sales

A number of statutes protect consumers by requiring the disclosure of certain terms in sales transactions and providing rules governing home or door-to-door sales, mail-order transactions, referral sales, and unsolicited merchandise. The Federal Reserve Board of Governors, for example, has issued **Regulation Z,** which governs credit provisions associated with sales contracts (discussed later in this chapter). Many states have also passed laws providing remedies to consumers in home sales. For example, a number of states have passed **"cooling-off" laws** that permit the buyers of goods sold door to door to cancel their contracts within a specified period of time, usually three to five days after the sale. An FTC regulation also requires sellers to give consumers three days to cancel any door-to-door sale, and this rule applies in addition to any state law. Furthermore, states have provided a number of consumer protection measures, such as implied warranties, through the adoption of the Uniform Commercial Code.

Telephone and Mail-Order Sales The FTC's Mail or Telephone Order Merchandise Rule of 1993, which amended the FTC's Mail-Order Rule of 1975,[29] provides specific protections for consumers who purchase goods over the phone or through the mails. The 1993 rule extended the 1975 rule to include sales in which orders are transmitted using computers, fax machines, or any similar means involving a telephone. Among other things, the rule requires mail-order merchants to ship orders within the time promised in their catalogues or advertisements, to notify consumers when orders cannot be shipped on time, and to issue a refund within a specified period of time when a consumer cancels an order.

In addition, under the Postal Reorganization Act of 1970[30] a consumer who receives *unsolicited* merchandise sent by U.S. mail can keep it, throw it away, or dispose of it in any manner that she or he sees fit. The recipient will not be obligated to the sender. **■EXAMPLE 13.18** Serena receives a copy of the "Cookbook of the Month" from a company via the U.S. mail, even though she did not order the cookbook. She gives it to her friend, Vaya, who loves to cook. The following month, Serena receives a bill for $49.99 from the company that sent the cookbook. Under the 1970 act, because the cookbook was sent to her unsolicited through the U.S. mail, Serena is not obligated to pay the bill. ■

Online Sales Protecting consumers from fraudulent and deceptive sales practices conducted via the Internet has proved to be a challenging task. Nonetheless, the FTC and other federal agencies have brought a number of enforcement actions against those who perpetrate online fraud. Additionally, the laws mentioned in previous chapters, such as the federal statute prohibiting wire fraud (see Chapter 6), apply to online transactions.

REGULATION Z
A set of rules promulgated by the Federal Reserve Board of Governors to implement the provisions of the Truth-in-Lending Act (to be discussed shortly).

"COOLING-OFF" LAWS
Laws that allow buyers a period of time, such as three days, in which to cancel door-to-door sales contracts.

ON THE WEB

To learn more about the FTC's Cooling-Off Rule, go to
www.ftc.gov/bcp/edu/pubs/consumer/products/buy01.shtm.

28. 15 U.S.C. Sections 4401–4408.
29. 16 C.F.R. Sections 435.1–435.2.
30. 39 U.S.C. Section 3009.

Some states have amended their consumer protection statutes to cover Internet transactions as well. For example, the California legislature revised its Business and Professional Code to include transactions conducted over the Internet or by "any other electronic means of communication." Previously, that code covered only telephone, mail-order catalogue, radio, and television sales. Now any entity selling over the Internet in California must explicitly create an on-screen notice indicating its refund and return policies, where its business is physically located, its legal name, and a number of other details. Various states are also setting up information sites to help consumers protect themselves.

Health and Safety Protection

The laws discussed earlier regarding the labeling and packaging of products go a long way toward promoting consumer health and safety. There is a significant distinction, however, between regulating the information dispensed about a product and regulating the actual content of the product. The classic example is tobacco products. Producers of tobacco products are required to warn consumers about the hazards associated with the use of their products, but the sale of tobacco products has not been subjected to significant restrictions or banned outright despite the obvious dangers to health. We now examine various laws that regulate the actual products made available to consumers.

BE AWARE The Food and Drug Administration is authorized to obtain, among other things, orders for the recall and seizure of certain products.

Food and Drugs   The first federal legislation regulating food and drugs was enacted in 1906 as the Pure Food and Drugs Act.[31] That law, as amended in 1938, exists now as the Federal Food, Drug and Cosmetic Act (FFDCA).[32] The act protects consumers against adulterated and misbranded foods and drugs. In its present form, the act establishes food standards, specifies safe levels of potentially hazardous food additives, and sets classifications of food and food advertising.

Most of these statutory requirements are monitored and enforced by the Food and Drug Administration (FDA). Under an extensive set of procedures established by the FDA, drugs must be shown to be effective as well as safe before they may be marketed to the public, and the use of some food additives suspected of being carcinogenic is prohibited. A 1976 amendment to the FFDCA[33] authorizes the FDA to regulate medical devices, such as pacemakers and other health devices or equipment, and to withdraw from the market any such device that is mislabeled.

ON THE WEB

The Web site of the Consumer Product Safety Commission offers a business information page that provides the text of regulations and laws, Federal Register Notices, and other information. Go to

www.cpsc.gov/businfo/businfo.html.

Consumer Product Safety   In 1972, Congress enacted the Consumer Product Safety Act,[34] which created the first comprehensive scheme of regulation over matters concerning consumer safety. The act also established the Consumer Product Safety Commission (CPSC) and gave it far-reaching authority over consumer safety.

The CPSC's Authority.   The CPSC conducts research on the safety of individual products and maintains a clearinghouse on the risks associated with various products. The Consumer Product Safety Act authorizes the CPSC to set standards for consumer products and to ban the manufacture and sale of any product that the commission deems to be potentially hazardous to consumers. The CPSC also has authority to remove from the market any products it believes to be imminently hazardous and to require manufacturers to report on any products already sold or intended for sale if the products have proved to be hazardous. Additionally, the CPSC administers other product-safety legislation,

---

31. 21 U.S.C. Sections 1–5, 7–15.
32. 21 U.S.C. Section 301.
33. 21 U.S.C. Sections 352(o), 360(j), 360(k), and 360c–360k.
34. 15 U.S.C. Section 2051.

including the Child Protection and Toy Safety Act of 1969[35] and the Federal Hazardous Substances Act of 1960.[36]

The CPSC's authority is sufficiently broad to allow it to ban any product that the commission believes poses merely an "unreasonable risk" to the consumer. Products banned by the CPSC have included various types of fireworks, cribs, and toys, as well as many products containing asbestos or vinyl chloride.

Notification Requirements. The Consumer Product Safety Act imposes notification requirements on distributors of consumer products. Distributors must immediately notify the CPSC when they receive information that a product "contains a defect which . . . creates a substantial risk to the public" or "an unreasonable risk of serious injury or death."

■**EXAMPLE 13.19** A corporation, now known as Aroma Housewares Company, had been distributing a particular model of juicer for just over a year when it began receiving letters from customers. They complained that during operation the juicer had suddenly exploded, sending pieces of glass and razor-sharp metal across the room. The company received twenty-three letters from angry consumers about the exploding juicer but waited more than six months before notifying the CPSC that the product posed a significant risk to the public. In a case filed by the federal government, the court held that when a company first receives information regarding a threat, the company is required to report the problem within twenty-four hours to the CPSC. The court also found that even if the company had to investigate the allegations, it should not have taken more than ten days to verify the information and report the problem. The court therefore held that the company had violated the law and ordered it to pay damages.[37] ■

Credit Protection

Considering the extensive use of credit by U.S. consumers, credit protection is one of the most important aspects of consumer protection legislation. A key statute regulating the credit and credit-card industries is the Truth-in-Lending Act (TILA), the name commonly given to Title 1 of the Consumer Credit Protection Act (CCPA),[38] which was passed by Congress in 1968.

Truth in Lending The TILA is basically a *disclosure law*. It is administered by the Federal Reserve Board and requires sellers and lenders to disclose credit terms or loan terms so that individuals can shop around for the best financing arrangements. TILA requirements apply only to persons who, in the ordinary course of business, lend funds, sell on credit, or arrange for the extension of credit. Thus, sales or loans made between two consumers do not come under the protection of the act. Additionally, this law protects only debtors who are *natural* persons (as opposed to the artificial "person" of a corporation); it does not extend to other legal entities.

The disclosure requirements are found in Regulation Z, which was promulgated by the Federal Reserve Board. If the contracting parties are subject to the TILA, the requirements of Regulation Z apply to any transaction involving an installment sales contract that calls for payment to be made in more than four installments. Transactions subject to Regulation Z typically include installment loans, retail and installment sales, car loans,

NOTE The Federal Reserve Board is part of the Federal Reserve System, which influences the lending and investing activities of commercial banks and the cost and availability of credit.

---

35. 15 U.S.C. Section 1262(e).

36. 15 U.S.C. Sections 1261–1273.

37. *United States v. Miram Enterprises, Inc.*, 185 F.Supp.2d 1148 (S.D.Ca. 2002).

38. 15 U.S.C. Sections 1601–1693r. The act was amended in 1980 by the Truth-in-Lending Simplification and Reform Act.

home-improvement loans, and certain real estate loans if the amount of financing is less than $25,000.

Under the provisions of the TILA, all of the terms of a credit instrument must be clearly and conspicuously disclosed. The TILA provides for contract rescission (cancellation) if a creditor fails to follow the exact procedures required by the act.[39]

Equal Credit Opportunity.   In 1974, Congress enacted, as an amendment to the TILA, the Equal Credit Opportunity Act (ECOA).[40] The ECOA prohibits the denial of credit solely on the basis of race, religion, national origin, color, gender, marital status, or age. The act also prohibits credit discrimination on the basis of whether an individual receives certain forms of income, such as public-assistance benefits.

Under the ECOA, a creditor may not require the signature of an applicant's spouse, or a cosigner, on a credit instrument if the applicant qualifies under the creditor's standards of creditworthiness for the amount requested. **■EXAMPLE 13.20** Tonja, an African American, applied for financing with a used-car dealer. The dealer reviewed Tonja's credit report and, without submitting the application to the lender, decided that she would not qualify. Instead of informing Tonja that she did not qualify, the dealer told her that she needed a cosigner on the loan to purchase the car. According to a federal appellate court in 2004, the dealership qualified as a creditor in this situation because it unilaterally denied credit. Thus, the dealer could be held liable under the ECOA.[41] ■

Credit-Card Rules.   The TILA also contains provisions regarding credit cards. One provision limits the liability of a cardholder to $50 per card for unauthorized charges made before the creditor is notified that the card has been lost. Another provision prohibits a credit-card company from billing a consumer for any unauthorized charges if the credit card was improperly issued by the company. **■EXAMPLE 13.21** Suppose that a consumer receives an unsolicited credit card in the mail and the card is later stolen and used by the thief to make purchases. In this situation, the consumer to whom the card was sent will not be liable for the unauthorized charges. ■

Other provisions of the act set out specific procedures for both the credit-card company and its cardholder to use in settling disputes related to credit-card purchases. These procedures would be used if, for example, a cardholder thinks that an error has occurred in billing or wishes to withhold payment for a faulty product purchased by credit card.

Consumer Leases.   The Consumer Leasing Act (CLA) of 1988[42] amended the TILA to provide protection for consumers who lease automobiles and other goods. The CLA applies to those who lease or arrange to lease consumer goods in the ordinary course of their business. The act applies only if the goods are priced at $25,000 or less and if the lease term exceeds four months. The CLA and its implementing regulation, Regulation M,[43] require lessors to disclose in writing all of the material terms of the lease.

Fair Credit Reporting   In 1970, to protect consumers against inaccurate credit reporting, Congress enacted the Fair Credit Reporting Act (FCRA).[44] The act provides that consumer credit reporting agencies may issue credit reports to users only for specified

---

39. Note, though, that amendments to the TILA enacted in 1995 prevent borrowers from rescinding loans because of minor clerical errors in closing documents [15 U.S.C. Sections 1605, 1631, 1635, 1640, and 1641].
40. 15 U.S.C. Section 1643.
41. *Treadway v. Gateway Chevrolet Oldsmobile, Inc.,* 362 F.3d 971 (7th Cir. 2004).
42. 15 U.S.C. Sections 1667–1667e.
43. 12 C.F.R. Part 213.
44. 15 U.S.C. Sections 1681 *et seq.*

purposes, including the extension of credit, the issuance of insurance policies, compliance with a court order, and compliance with a consumer's request for a copy of her or his own credit report. The act further provides that any time a consumer is denied credit or insurance on the basis of the consumer's credit report, or is charged more than others ordinarily would be for credit or insurance, the consumer must be notified of that fact and of the name and address of the credit reporting agency that issued the credit report.

Under the FCRA, consumers may request the source of any information being given out by a credit agency, as well as the identity of anyone who has received an agency's report. Consumers are also permitted to have access to the information contained about them in a credit reporting agency's files. If a consumer discovers that the agency's files contain inaccurate information about his or her credit standing, the agency, on the consumer's written request, must investigate the matter and delete any unverifiable or erroneous information within a reasonable period of time. The agency's investigation should include contacting the creditor whose information the consumer disputes and should involve a systematic examination of its records.

The FCRA protects consumers from inaccurate information in credit reports by requiring that lenders and other creditors report correct, relevant, and up-to-date information in a confidential and responsible manner. The FCRA allows an award of punitive damages for a "willful" violation. Did the circumstances in the following case warrant an award of punitive damages? That was the question before the court.

CASE 13.3   **Saunders v. Equifax Information Services, L.L.C.**

United States District Court, Eastern District of Virginia, Richmond Division, 469 F.Supp.2d 343 (2007).

FACTS Rex Saunders obtained an auto loan from Branch Banking & Trust Company of Virginia (BB & T). Contrary to its usual procedure, BB & T did not give Saunders a payment coupon book and rebuffed his attempts to make payments on the loan. In fact, BB & T told him that he did not have a loan from the firm. A copy of the title for the vehicle indicated no loan. Eventually, however, BB & T discovered its mistake and demanded full payment, plus interest and penalties. When payment was not immediately forthcoming, BB & T declared Saunders to be in default and repossessed and sold the car. The lender forwarded adverse credit information about Saunders, with added derogatory details, to credit reporting agencies, without noting that Saunders disputed the information. Saunders filed a suit in a federal district court against BB & T and others, alleging chiefly violations of the Fair Credit Reporting Act (FCRA). On the claims against BB & T, a jury awarded Saunders $1,000 in statutory damages and $80,000 in punitive damages. BB & T asked the court to reduce the punitive award to $4,000. BB & T argued that the credit information was "factually accurate," the mistakes in administering Saunders's loan were not "willful," and the amount of the award was arbitrary.

ISSUE Was Saunders entitled to the award of $80,000 in punitive damages?

DECISION Yes. The court held that BB & T's actions were "willful" violations of the FCRA.

REASON The court recognized the "imprecise manner" in which punitive damages are awarded. The court explained that "the most important *indicium* [indication] of the reasonableness of a punitive damages award is the degree of reprehensibility of the defendant's conduct. * * * [P]unitive damages should only be awarded if the defendant's culpability, after having paid compensatory damages, is so reprehensible [worthy of censure] as to warrant the imposition of further sanctions to achieve punishment or deterrence." Here, "BB & T caused great financial and emotional strain to a consumer by failing to properly 'book' Saunders' loan in violation of BB & T's own internal operating procedures." The jury based its decision on sufficient evidence of misconduct by BB & T, as well as the lender's economic ability, in terms of its substantial net worth of more than $3.2 billion, to pay the amount of the award. Such an assessment has "legitimate punitive and deterrent purpose[s]." Only when the amount can

CASE 13.3–Continues next page

CASE 13.3–Continued

be fairly categorized as "grossly excessive" in relation to these purposes does the award "enter the zone of arbitrariness." The amount of the award in Saunders's favor "enters no such zone of arbitrariness as it reasonably punishes BB & T for particularly egregious [appalling] conduct * * * , not for being an unsavory individual or business."

 FOR CRITICAL ANALYSIS–Social Consideration
The jury awarded Saunders only $1,000 in statutory damages, but under the circumstances, this was the maximum allowed under the FCRA. What does the fact that the jury felt compelled to award the maximum allowable amount indicate about its award of punitive damages?

ON THE WEB

The Consumer Action Web site offers useful information and links to consumer protection agencies at the city, county, and state level. Go to

www.consumeraction.gov.

Fair and Accurate Credit Transactions Act   In an effort to combat rampant identity theft (discussed in Chapter 6), Congress passed the Fair and Accurate Credit Transactions (FACT) Act of 2003.[45] The act established a national fraud alert system so that consumers who suspect that they have been or may be victimized by identity theft can place an alert in their credit files. The FACT Act also requires the major credit reporting agencies to provide consumers with a free copy of their credit reports every twelve months. Another provision requires account numbers on credit-card receipts to be shortened (truncated) so that merchants, employees, and others who have access to the receipts cannot obtain a consumer's name and full credit-card number. The act also mandates that financial institutions work with the Federal Trade Commission to identify "red flag" indicators of identity theft and to develop rules for disposing of sensitive credit information.

The FACT Act also gives consumers who have been victimized by identity theft some assistance in rebuilding their credit reputations. For example, credit reporting agencies must stop reporting allegedly fraudulent account information once the consumer establishes that identify theft has occurred. Business owners and creditors are required to provide a consumer with copies of any records that can help the consumer prove that a particular account or transaction is fraudulent (records showing that an account was created by a fraudulent signature, for example). In addition, to help prevent the spread of erroneous credit information, the act allows consumers to report the accounts affected by identity theft directly to the creditors.

Fair Debt-Collection Practices   In 1977, Congress enacted the Fair Debt Collection Practices Act (FDCPA)[46] in an attempt to curb what were perceived to be abuses by collection agencies. The act applies only to specialized debt-collection agencies that regularly attempt to collect debts on behalf of someone else, usually for a percentage of the amount owed. Creditors attempting to collect debts are not covered by the act unless, by misrepresenting themselves, they cause the debtors to believe that they are collection agencies. Attorneys who regularly try to obtain payment of consumer debts through legal proceedings, however, do meet the FDCPA's definition of "debt collector."[47]

The act explicitly prohibits a collection agency from using any of the following tactics:

1 Contacting the debtor at the debtor's place of employment if the debtor's employer objects.

2 Contacting the debtor during inconvenient or unusual times (for example, calling the debtor at three o'clock in the morning) or at any time if an attorney is representing the debtor.

3 Contacting third parties other than the debtor's parents, spouse, or financial adviser about payment of a debt unless a court authorizes such action.

---

45. Pub. L. No. 108-159, 117 Stat. 1952 (December 4, 2003).
46. 15 U.S.C. Section 1692.
47. *Heintz v. Jenkins*, 514 U.S. 291, 115 S.Ct. 1489, 131 L.Ed.2d 395 (1995).

4 Using harassment or intimidation (for example, using abusive language or threatening violence) or employing false and misleading information (for example, posing as a police officer).

5 Communicating with the debtor at any time after receiving notice that the debtor is refusing to pay the debt, except to advise the debtor of further action to be taken by the collection agency.

The enforcement of the act is primarily the responsibility of the Federal Trade Commission. The FDCPA provides that a debt collector who fails to comply with the act is liable for actual damages, plus additional damages not to exceed $1,000[48] and attorneys' fees.

---

48. According to the U.S. Court of Appeals for the Sixth Circuit, the $1,000 limit on damages applies to each lawsuit, not to each violation. See *Wright v. Finance Service of Norwalk, Inc.*, 22 F.3d 647 (6th Cir. 1994).

REVIEWING Consumer Law

Leota Sage saw a local motorcycle dealer's advertisement in a newspaper offering a MetroRider EZ electric scooter for $1,699. When she went to the dealership, however, she learned that the EZ model was sold out. The salesperson told Sage that he still had the higher-end MetroRider FX model in stock for $2,199 and would sell her one for $1,999. Sage was disappointed but decided to purchase the FX model. Sage told the sales representative that she wished to purchase the scooter on credit and was directed to the dealer's credit department. As she filled out credit forms, the clerk told Sage, an African American female, that she would need a cosigner. Sage could not understand why she would need a cosigner and asked to speak to the manager. The manager apologized, told her that the clerk was mistaken, and said that he would "speak to" the clerk. The manager completed Sage's credit application, and Sage then rode the scooter home. Seven

months later, Sage received a letter from the FTC asking questions about her transaction with the motorcycle dealer and informing her that it had received complaints from other consumers. Using the information presented in the chapter, answer the following questions.

1 Did the dealer engage in deceptive advertising? Why or why not?

2 Suppose that Sage had ordered the scooter through the dealer's Web site but the dealer had been unable to deliver it by the date promised. What would the FTC have required the merchant to do in that situation?

3 Assuming that the clerk required a cosigner based on Sage's race or gender, what act prohibits such credit discrimination?

4 What organization has the authority to ban the sale of scooters based on safety concerns?

APPLICATION How Do Sellers Create Warranties?*

Warranties are important in both commercial and consumer purchase transactions. There are three types of product warranties: express warranties, implied warranties of mer-

chantability, and implied warranties of fitness for a particular purpose. If you are a seller of products, you can make or create any one of these warranties, which are available to both consumers and commercial purchasers. First and foremost, sellers and buyers need to know whether warranties have been created.

---

* This *Application* is not meant to serve as a substitute for the services of an attorney who is licensed to practice law in your state.

(Continued)

Warranty Creation

Express warranties do not have to be labeled as such, but statements of simple opinion or value generally do not constitute express warranties. Express warranties can be made by descriptions of the goods or by showing a sample or model of the goods. Express warranties can be found in a seller's advertisement, brochure, or promotional materials or can be made orally or in an express writing. A sales representative should use care in describing the merits of a product; otherwise, the seller could be held to an express warranty. If an express warranty is not intended, the sales pitch should not promise too much.

In most sales, because the seller is a merchant, the purchased goods carry the implied warranty of merchantability. If you are a seller, you must also be aware of the importance of the implied warranty of fitness for a particular purpose. Assume that a customer comes to your sales representative, describes the work to be done in detail, and says, "I really need something that can do the job." Your sales representative replies, "This product will do the job," and the customer purchases the recommended product. An implied warranty that the product is fit for that particular purpose has been created.

Warranty Disclaimers

Many sellers, particularly in commercial sales, try to limit or disclaim warranties. The Uniform Commercial Code permits all warranties, including express warranties, to be excluded or negated. Conspicuous statements—such as "THERE ARE NO WARRANTIES WHICH EXTEND BEYOND THE DESCRIPTION ON THE FACE HEREOF" or "THERE ARE NO IMPLIED WARRANTIES OF FITNESS FOR A PARTICULAR PURPOSE OR MERCHANTABILITY WHICH ACCOMPANY THIS SALE"—can be used to disclaim the implied warranties of fitness and merchantability. Used goods are sometimes sold "as is" or "with all faults" so that implied warranties of fitness and merchantability are disclaimed. Whenever these warranties are disclaimed, a purchaser should be aware that the product may not be of even average quality.

CHECKLIST FOR THE SELLER

1 If you wish to limit warranties, do so by means of a carefully worded and prominently placed (conspicuous) written or printed provision that a reasonable person would understand and accept. Instruct your sales associates to point out the disclaimer to consumer-buyers when forming the sales contract.
2 If you are a merchant-seller, remember that in the absence of a disclaimer, almost all sales carry the implied warranty of merchantability.
3 If you do not intend to make an express warranty, do not make a promise or an affirmation of fact concerning the performance or quality of a product you are selling.

KEY TERMS

bait-and-switch advertising 398
cease-and-desist order 399
"cooling-off" laws 401
counteradvertising 399
deceptive advertising 398
express warranty 382

implied warranty 383
implied warranty of fitness
   for a particular purpose 385
implied warranty
   of merchantability 383
lien 381

market-share liability 395
product liability 388
Regulation Z 401
statute of repose 395
unreasonably dangerous
   product 391

CHAPTER SUMMARY Warranties, Product Liability, and Consumer Law

WARRANTIES

Warranties of Title (See pages 381–382.)	The UCC provides for the following warranties of title [UCC 2–312, 2A–211]: 1. *Good title*—A seller warrants that he or she has the right to pass good and rightful title to the goods. 2. *No liens*—A seller warrants that the goods sold are free of any encumbrances (claims, charges, or liabilities—usually called *liens*). A lessor warrants that the lessee will not be disturbed in her or his possession of the goods by the claims of a third party.

CHAPTER SUMMARY Warranties, Product Liability, and Consumer Law—Continued

Warranties of Title— Continued	3. *No infringements*—A merchant-seller warrants that the goods are free of infringement claims (claims that a patent, trademark, or copyright has been infringed) by third parties. Lessors make similar warranties.
Express Warranties (See pages 382–383.)	Under the UCC, an express warranty arises under the UCC when a seller or lessor indicates, as part of the basis of the bargain, any of the following: 1. An affirmation or promise of fact. 2. A description of the goods. 3. A sample shown as conforming to the contract goods [UCC 2–313, 2A–210].
Implied Warranty of Merchantability (See pages 383–384.)	When a seller or lessor is a merchant who deals in goods of the kind sold or leased, the seller or lessor warrants that the goods sold or leased are properly packaged and labeled, are of proper quality, and are reasonably fit for the ordinary purposes for which such goods are used [UCC 2–314, 2A–212].
Implied Warranty of Fitness for a Particular Purpose (See page 385.)	Arises when the buyer's or lessee's purpose or use is expressly or impliedly known by the seller or lessor, and the buyer or lessee purchases or leases the goods in reliance on the seller's or lessor's selection [UCC 2–315, 2A–213].
Other Implied Warranties (See page 385.)	Other implied warranties can arise as a result of course of dealing or usage of trade [UCC 2–314(3), 2A–212(3)].
Warranty Disclaimers (See pages 386–387.)	Express warranties can be disclaimed in a written disclaimer in language that is clear and conspicuous and called to the buyer's or lessee's attention at the time the contract is formed. A disclaimer of the implied warranty of merchantability must specifically mention the word *merchantability*. It need not be in writing, but if it is written, it must be conspicuous. A disclaimer of the implied warranty of fitness *must* be in writing and be conspicuous, though it need not mention the word *fitness*.
Magnuson-Moss Warranty Act (See page 388.)	Under the Magnuson-Moss Warranty Act, Express written warranties covering consumer goods priced at more than $25, *if made*, must be labeled as one of the following: 1. *Full warranty*—Free repair or replacement of defective parts; refund or replacement for goods if they cannot be repaired in a reasonable time. 2. *Limited warranty*—When less than a full warranty is being offered.
	PRODUCT LIABILITY
Liability Based on Negligence (See pages 388–389.)	1. The manufacturer must use due care in designing the product, selecting materials, using the appropriate production process, assembling and testing the product, and placing adequate warnings on the label or product. 2. Privity of contract is not required. A manufacturer is liable for failure to exercise due care to any person who sustains an injury proximately caused by a negligently made (defective) product.
Liability Based on Misrepresentation (See page 389.)	Fraudulent misrepresentation of a product may result in product liability based on the tort of fraud.
Requirements for Strict Liability (See pages 391–392.)	1. The defendant must sell the product in a defective condition. 2. The defendant must normally be engaged in the business of selling that product. 3. The product must be unreasonably dangerous to the user or consumer because of its defective condition (in most states).

(Continued)

CHAPTER SUMMARY	Warranties, Product Liability, and Consumer Law–Continued
Requirements for Strict Liability– Continued	4. The plaintiff must incur physical harm to self or property by use or consumption of the product. (Courts will also extend strict liability to include injured bystanders.)
	5. The defective condition must be the proximate cause of the injury or damage.
	6. The goods must not have been substantially changed from the time the product was sold to the time the injury was sustained.
Strict Liability– Product Defects (See pages 392–394.)	A product may be defective in three basic ways:
	1. In its manufacture.
	2. In its design.
	3. In the instructions or warnings that come with it.
Market-Share Liability (See page 395.)	When plaintiffs cannot prove which of many distributors of a defective product supplied the particular product that caused the plaintiffs' injuries, some courts apply market-share liability. All firms that manufactured and distributed the harmful product during the period in question are then held liable for the plaintiffs' injuries in proportion to the firms' respective shares of the market, as directed by the court.
Other Applications of Strict Liability (See page 395.)	1. Manufacturers and other sellers are liable for harms suffered by bystanders as a result of defective products.
	2. Suppliers of component parts are strictly liable for defective parts that, when incorporated into a product, cause injuries to users.
Defenses to Product Liability (See pages 396–397.)	1. *Assumption of risk*—The user or consumer knew of the risk of harm and voluntarily assumed it.
	2. *Product misuse*—The user or consumer misused the product in a way unforeseeable by the manufacturer.
	3. *Comparative negligence (fault)*—Liability may be distributed between the plaintiff and the defendant under the doctrine of comparative negligence if the plaintiff's misuse of the product contributed to the risk of injury.
	4. *Commonly known dangers*—If a defendant succeeds in convincing the court that a plaintiff's injury resulted from a commonly known danger, such as the danger associated with using a sharp knife, the defendant will not be liable.
	CONSUMER PROTECTION LAWS
Deceptive Advertising (See pages 398–399.)	1. *Definition of deceptive advertising*—Generally, an advertising claim will be deemed deceptive if it would mislead a reasonable consumer.
	2. *Bait-and-switch advertising*—Advertising a lower-priced product (the "bait") when the intention is not to sell the advertised product but to lure consumers into the store and convince them to buy a higher-priced product (the "switch") is prohibited by the FTC.
	3. *Online deceptive advertising*—The FTC has issued guidelines to help online businesses comply with existing laws prohibiting deceptive advertising. The guidelines do not set forth new rules but rather describe how existing laws apply to online advertising.
	4. *FTC actions against deceptive advertising*—
	a. Cease-and-desist orders—Requiring the advertiser to stop the challenged advertising.
	b. Counteradvertising—Requiring the advertiser to advertise to correct the earlier misinformation.
Telemarketing and Electronic Advertising (See page 400.)	The Telephone Consumer Protection Act of 1991 prohibits telephone solicitation using an automatic telephone dialing system or a prerecorded voice, as well as the transmission of advertising materials via fax without first obtaining the recipient's permission to do so.

CHAPTER SUMMARY Warranties, Product Liability, and Consumer Law–Continued

Labeling and Packaging (See pages 400–401.)	Manufacturers must comply with the labeling or packaging requirements for their specific products. In general, all labels must be accurate and not misleading.
Sales (See pages 401–402.)	1. *Telephone and mail-order sales*—Federal and state statutes and regulations govern certain practices of sellers who solicit over the telephone or through the mails and prohibit the use of the mails to defraud individuals. 2. *Online sales*—Increasingly, the Internet is being used to conduct business-to-consumer transactions. Both state and federal laws protect consumers to some extent against fraudulent and deceptive online sales practices.
Health and Safety Protection (See pages 402–403.)	1. *Food and drugs*—The Federal Food, Drug and Cosmetic Act of 1938, as amended, protects consumers against adulterated and misbranded foods and drugs. The act establishes food standards, specifies safe levels of potentially hazardous food additives, and sets classifications of food and food advertising. 2 *Consumer product safety*—The Consumer Product Safety Act of 1972 seeks to protect consumers from risk of injury from hazardous products. The Consumer Product Safety Commission has the power to remove products that are deemed imminently hazardous from the market and to ban the manufacture and sale of hazardous products.
Credit Protection (See pages 403–407.)	1. *Consumer Credit Protection Act, Title I (Truth-in-Lending Act, or TILA)*—A disclosure law that requires sellers and lenders to disclose credit terms or loan terms in certain transactions, including retail and installment sales and loans, car loans, home-improvement loans, and certain real estate loans. Additionally, the TILA provides for the following: a. Equal credit opportunity—Creditors are prohibited from discriminating on the basis of race, religion, marital status, gender, and so on. b. Credit-card protection—Credit-card users may withhold payment for a faulty product purchased by credit card, or for an error in billing, until the dispute is resolved; liability of cardholders for unauthorized charges is limited to $50, providing notice requirements are met; consumers are not liable for unauthorized charges made on unsolicited credit cards. c. Consumer leases—The Consumer Leasing Act (CLA) of 1988 protects consumers who lease automobiles and other goods priced at $25,000 or less if the lease term exceeds four months. 2. *Fair Credit Reporting Act*—Entitles consumers to request verification of the accuracy of a credit report and to have unverified or false information removed from their files. 3. *Fair Debt Collection Practices Act*—Prohibits debt collectors from using unfair debt-collection practices, such as contacting the debtor at his or her place of employment if the employer objects or at unreasonable times, contacting third parties about the debt, and harassing the debtor, for example.

FOR REVIEW

Answers for the even-numbered questions in this For Review *section can be found in Appendix E at the end of this text.*

1 What factors determine whether a seller's or lessor's statement constitutes an express warranty or mere "puffing"?

2 What implied warranties arise under the UCC?

3 Can a manufacturer be held liable to any person who suffers an injury proximately caused by the manufacturer's negligently made product?

4 What defenses to liability can be raised in a product liability lawsuit?

5 What are the major federal statutes providing for consumer protection?

■

QUESTIONS AND CASE PROBLEMS

HYPOTHETICAL SCENARIOS

13.1 Product Liability. Under what contract theory can a seller be held liable to a consumer for physical harm or property damage that is caused by the goods sold? Under what tort theories can the seller be held liable?

13.2 Product Liability. Carmen buys a television set manufactured by AKI Electronics. She is going on vacation, so she takes the set to her mother's house for her mother to use. Because the set is defective, it explodes, causing considerable damage to her mother's house. Carmen's mother sues AKI for the damages to her house. Discuss the theories under which Carmen's mother can recover from AKI.

13.3 Hypothetical Question with Sample Answer. Maria Ochoa receives two new credit cards on May 1. She had solicited one of them from Midtown Department Store, and the other arrived unsolicited from High-Flying Airlines. During the month of May, Ochoa makes numerous credit-card purchases from Midtown Department Store, but she does not use the High-Flying Airlines card. On May 31, a burglar breaks into Ochoa's home and steals both credit cards, along with other items. Ochoa notifies the Midtown Department Store of the theft on June 2, but she fails to notify High-Flying Airlines. Using the Midtown credit card, the burglar makes a $500

purchase on June 1 and a $200 purchase on June 3. The burglar then charges a vacation flight on the High-Flying Airlines card for $1,000 on June 5. Ochoa receives the bills for these charges and refuses to pay them. Discuss Ochoa's liability in these situations.

 For a sample answer to Question 13.3, go to Appendix F at the end of this text.

13.4 Implied Warranties. Sam, a farmer, needs to install a piece of equipment in his barn. The equipment, which weighs two thousand pounds, must be lifted thirty feet into a hayloft. Sam goes to Durham Hardware and tells Durham that he needs some heavy-duty rope to be used on his farm. Durham recommends a one-inch-thick nylon rope, and Sam purchases two hundred feet of it. Sam ties the rope around the piece of equipment, puts the rope through a pulley, and with the aid of a tractor lifts the equipment off the ground. Suddenly, the rope breaks. The equipment crashes to the ground and is extensively damaged. Sam files a suit against Durham for breach of the implied warranty of fitness for a particular purpose. Discuss how successful Sam will be with his suit.

■

CASE PROBLEMS

13.5 Fair Credit Reporting Act. Source One Associates, Inc., is based in Poughquag, New York. Peter Easton, Source One's president, is responsible for its daily operations. Between 1995 and 1997, Source One received requests from persons in Massachusetts seeking financial information about individuals and businesses. To obtain this information, Easton first obtained the targeted individuals' credit reports through Equifax Consumer Information Services by claiming the reports would be used only in connection with credit transactions involving the consumers. From the reports, Easton identified financial institutions at which the targeted individuals held accounts and then called the institutions to learn the account balances by impersonating either officers of the institutions or the account holders. The information was then

provided to Source One's customers for a fee. Easton did not know why the customers wanted the information. The state ("Commonwealth") of Massachusetts filed a suit in a Massachusetts state court against Source One and Easton, alleging, among other things, violations of the Fair Credit Reporting Act (FCRA). Did the defendants violate the FCRA? Explain. [*Commonwealth v. Source One Associates, Inc.*, 436 Mass. 118, 763 N.E.2d 42 (2002)]

13.6 Case Problem with Sample Answer. Mary Jane Boerner began smoking in 1945 at the age of fifteen. For a short time, she smoked Lucky Strike–brand cigarettes before switching to the Pall Mall brand, which she smoked until she quit altogether in 1981. Pall Malls had higher levels of carcinogenic tar than other cigarettes and lacked effective filters, which would have reduced the amount of tar inhaled into the lungs. In 1996, Mary Jane developed lung cancer. She and Henry Boerner, her husband, filed a suit in a federal district court against Brown & Williamson Tobacco Co., the maker of Pall Malls. The Boerners claimed, among other things, that Pall Malls contained a design defect. Mary Jane died in 1999. According to Dr. Peter Marvin, her treating physician, she died from the effects of cigarette smoke. Henry continued the suit, offering evidence that Pall Malls featured a filter that actually increased the amount of tar taken into the body. When is a product defective in design? Does this product meet the requirements? Why or why not? [*Boerner v. Brown & Williamson Tobacco Co.*, 394 F.3d 594 (8th Cir. 2005)]

After you have answered Problem 13.6, compare your answer with the sample answer given on the Web site that accompanies this text. Go to **academic.cengage.com/blaw/blt**, select "Chapter 13," and click on "Case Problem with Sample Answer."

13.7 Implied Warranties. Shalom Malul contracted with Capital Cabinets, Inc., in August 1999 for new kitchen cabinets made by Holiday Kitchens. The price was $10,900. On Capital's recommendation, Malul hired Barry Burger to install the cabinets for $1,600. Burger finished the job in March 2000, and Malul contracted for more cabinets at a price of $2,300, which Burger installed in April. Within a couple of weeks, the doors on several of the cabinets began to "melt"—the laminate (surface covering) began to pull away from the substrate (the material underneath the surface). Capital replaced several of the doors, but the problem occurred again, affecting a total of six of thirty doors. A Holiday Kitchens representative inspected the cabinets and concluded that the melting was due to excessive heat, the result of the doors being placed too close to the stove. Malul filed a suit in a New York state court against Capital, alleging, among other things, a breach of the implied warranty of merchantability. Were these goods "merchantable"? Why or why not? [*Malul v. Capital Cabinets, Inc.*, 191 Misc.2d 399, 740 N.Y.S.2d 828 (N.Y.City Civ.Ct. 2002)]

13.8 Debt Collection. 55th Management Corp. in New York City owns residential property that it leases to various tenants. In June 2000, claiming that one of the tenants, Leslie Goldman, owed more than $13,000 in back rent, 55th retained Jeffrey Cohen, an attorney, to initiate nonpayment proceedings. Cohen filed a petition in a New York state court against Goldman, seeking recovery of the unpaid rent and at least $3,000 in attorneys' fees. After receiving notice of the petition, Goldman filed a suit in a federal district court against Cohen. Goldman contended that the notice of the petition constituted an initial contact that, under the Fair Debt Collection Practices Act (FDCPA), required a validation notice. Because Cohen did not give Goldman a validation notice at the time, or within five days, of the notice of the petition, Goldman argued that Cohen was in violation of the FDCPA. Should the filing of a suit in a state court be considered "communication," requiring a debt collector to provide a validation notice under the FDCPA? Why or why not? [*Goldman v. Cohen*, 445 F.3d 152 (2d Cir. 2006)]

13.9 Express Warranties. Videotape is recorded magnetically. The magnetic particles that constitute the recorded image are bound to the tape's polyester base. The binder that holds the particles to the base breaks down over time. This breakdown, which is called sticky shed syndrome, causes the image to deteriorate. The Walt Disney Co. made many of its movies available on tape. Buena Vista Home Entertainment, Inc., sold the tapes, which it described as part of a "Gold Collection" or "Masterpiece Collection." The advertising included such statements as "Give Your Children The Memories Of A Lifetime—Collect Each Timeless Masterpiece!" and "Available For A Limited Time Only!" Charmaine Schreib and others who bought the tapes filed a suit in an Illinois state court against Disney and Buena Vista, alleging, among other things, breach of warranty. The plaintiffs claimed that the defendants' marketing promised the tapes would last for generations. In reality, the tapes were as subject to sticky shed syndrome as other tapes. Did the ads create an express warranty? In whose favor should the court rule on this issue? Explain. [*Schreib v. The Walt Disney Co.*, 219 Ill.2d 597, 852 N.E.2d 249 (2006)]

13.10 A Question of Ethics. *One of the products that McDonald's Corp. sells is the Happy Meal, which consists of a McDonald's food entrée, a small order of french fries, a small drink, and a toy. In the early 1990s, McDonald's began to aim its Happy Meal marketing at children ages one to three. In 1995, McDonald's began making nutritional information for its food products available in documents known as "McDonald's Nutrition Facts." Each document lists each food item that the restaurant serves and provides a nutritional breakdown, but the Happy Meal is not included. Marc Cohen filed a suit in an Illinois state court, alleging, among other things, that McDonald's had violated a state law prohibiting consumer fraud and deceptive business practices by failing to adhere to the National Labeling and Education Act of 1990 (NLEA). The court dismissed the suit, and Cohen appealed to a state intermediate appellate court, which affirmed the dismissal, holding that the NLEA preempted the plaintiff's claims. In view of these facts, consider the following questions. [Cohen v. McDonald's Corp., 347 Ill.App.3d 627, 808 N.E.2d 1 (1 Dist. 2004)]*

1 What does the NLEA provide? The NLEA sets out different requirements for products specifically intended for children under the age of four. Does this make sense? Is this ethical? Why or why not?

2 Because the federal government has not established certain requirements for children under the age of four, there are no regulations under the NLEA for reporting these requirements. Should a state court impose such regulations? Explain.

CRITICAL THINKING AND WRITING ASSIGNMENTS

13.11 Critical Legal Thinking. The United States has the strictest product liability laws in the world today. Why do you think many other countries, particularly developing countries, are more lax with respect to holding manufacturers liable for product defects?

13.12 Critical Thinking and Writing Assignment for Business. Many states have enacted laws that go even further than federal law to protect the interests of consumers. These laws vary tremendously from state to state. Generally, is having different laws fair to sellers who may be prohibited from engaging in a practice in one state that is legal in another? How might these different laws affect a business? Is it fair that residents of one state have more protection than residents of another? Or should all consumer protection laws be federally legislated?

13.13 **Video Question.** Go to this text's Web site at **academic. cengage.com/blaw/blt** and select "Chapter 13." Click on "Video Questions" and view the video titled *Warranties.* Then answer the following questions.

1 Discuss whether the grocery store's label of a "Party Platter for Twenty" creates an express warranty under the Uniform Commercial Code that the platter will actually serve twenty people.

2 List and describe any implied warranties discussed in the chapter that apply to this scenario.

3 How would a court determine whether Oscar had breached any express or implied warranties concerning the quantity of food on the platter?

ONLINE ACTIVITIES

PRACTICAL INTERNET EXERCISES

Go to this text's Web site at **academic.cengage.com/blaw/blt**, select "Chapter 13," and click on "Practical Internet Exercises." There you will find the following Internet research exercises that you can perform to learn more about the topics covered in this chapter.

PRACTICAL INTERNET EXERCISE 13-1 LEGAL PERSPECTIVE—Product Liability Litigation

PRACTICAL INTERNET EXERCISE 13-2 MANAGEMENT PERSPECTIVE—Warranties

PRACTICAL INTERNET EXERCISE 13-3 LEGAL PERSPECTIVE—The Food and Drug Administration

BEFORE THE TEST

Go to this text's Web site at **academic.cengage.com/blaw/blt**, select "Chapter 13," and click on "Interactive Quizzes." You will find a number of interactive questions relating to this chapter.

CHAPTER 14
Negotiable Instruments

LEARNING OBJECTIVES

AFTER READING THIS CHAPTER, YOU SHOULD BE ABLE TO ANSWER THE FOLLOWING QUESTIONS:

1 What are the four types of negotiable instruments with which Article 3 of the UCC is concerned? Which of these instruments are *orders* to pay, and which are *promises* to pay?

2 What requirements must an instrument meet to be negotiable?

3 What are the requirements for attaining HDC status?

4 What is the key to liability on a negotiable instrument? What is the difference between signature liability and warranty liability?

5 Certain defenses are valid against all holders, including HDCs. What are these defenses called? Name four defenses that fall within this category.

> **"It took many generations for people to feel comfortable accepting paper in lieu of gold or silver."**
>
> Alan Greenspan, 1926–present
> (Chair of the Board of Governors of the Federal Reserve System, 1987–2006)

Most commercial transactions would be inconceivable without negotiable instruments. A **negotiable instrument** is a signed writing (record) that contains an unconditional promise or order to pay an exact sum on demand or at a specified future time to a specific person or order, or to bearer. (The term *bearer* refers to a person in possession of an instrument that is payable to bearer or indorsed *in blank,* which will be defined later in this chapter.) Most negotiable instruments are paper documents, which is why they are sometimes referred to as *commercial paper.* The checks you write to pay for groceries, rent, your monthly car payment, insurance premiums, and other items are negotiable instruments.

A negotiable instrument can function as a substitute for cash or as an extension of credit. When a buyer writes a check to pay for goods, the check serves as a substitute for cash. When a buyer gives a seller a promissory note in which the buyer promises to pay the seller the purchase price within sixty days, the seller has essentially extended credit to the buyer for a sixty-day period. For a negotiable instrument to operate *practically* as either a substitute for cash or a credit device, or both, it is essential that the instrument be *easily transferable without danger of being uncollectible.* Each rule described in the following pages can be examined in light of this essential function of negotiable instruments.

Negotiable instruments must meet special requirements relating to form and content. These requirements, which are imposed by Article 3 of the UCC, will be discussed at

NEGOTIABLE INSTRUMENT
A signed writing (record) that contains an unconditional promise or order to pay an exact sum on demand or at an exact future time to a specific person or order, or to bearer.

length in this chapter. Article 3 also governs the process of *negotiation* (transferring an instrument from one party to another), as will be discussed. Note that UCC 3–104(b) defines *instrument* as a "negotiable instrument." For that reason, whenever the term *instrument* is used in this book, it refers to a negotiable instrument.

TYPES OF NEGOTIABLE INSTRUMENTS

For an instrument to qualify as a *negotiable instrument*, it must meet the requirements listed as numbers one through six on the facing page. (The requirements for negotiability and the UCC sections pertaining to these requirements are listed and described more fully in Exhibit 14–1 below.)

EXHIBIT 14–1 Requirements for Negotiability

REQUIREMENTS	SECTIONS	BASIC RULES
Must Be in Writing	UCC 3–103(a)(6), (9)	A writing can be on anything that is readily transferable and has a degree of permanence. [See also UCC 1–201(46).]
Must Be Signed by the Maker or Drawer	UCC 1–201(39) 3–103(a)(3), (5) 3–401(b) 3–402	1. The signature can be anyplace on the face of the instrument. 2. It can be in any form (such as a word, mark, or rubber stamp) that purports to be a signature and authenticates the writing. 3. A signature may be made in a representative capacity.
Must Be a Definite Promise or Order	UCC 3–103(a)(6), (9) 3–104(a)	1. A promise must be more than a mere acknowledgment of a debt. 2. The words "I/We promise" or "Pay" meet this criterion.
Must Be Unconditional	UCC 3–106	1. Payment cannot be expressly conditional on the occurrence of an event. 2. Payment cannot be made subject to or governed by another agreement.
Must Be an Order or Promise to Pay a Fixed Amount	UCC 3–104(a) 3–112(b)	An amount may be considered a fixed sum even if it is payable in installments, with a fixed or variable rate of interest, at a stated discount, or at an exchange rate.
Must Be Payable in Money	UCC 3–104(a)(3) 3–107	1. Any medium of exchange recognized as the currency of a government is money. 2. The maker or drawer cannot retain the option to pay the instrument in money or something else.
Must Be Payable on Demand or at a Definite Time	UCC 3–104(a)(2) 3–108(a), (b), (c)	1. Any instrument that is payable on sight, presentation, or issue, or that does not state any time for payment, is a demand instrument. 2. An instrument is still payable at a definite time, even if it is payable on or before a stated date or within a fixed period after sight or if the drawer or maker has an option to extend the time for a definite period. 3. Acceleration clauses do not affect the negotiability of the instrument.
Must Be Payable to Order or to Bearer	UCC 3–104(a)(1), (c) 3–109 3–110(a)	1. An order instrument must identify the payee with reasonable certainty. 2. An instrument that indicates it is not payable to an identified person is payable to bearer. 3. Checks are not required to be payable to order or to bearer.

1 Be in writing.

2 Be signed by the maker or the drawer.

3 Be an unconditional promise or order to pay.

4 State a fixed amount of money.

5 Be payable on demand or at a definite time.

6 Be payable to order or to bearer, unless it is a check.

The UCC specifies four types of negotiable instruments: *drafts, checks, promissory notes,* and *certificates of deposit* (CDs). These instruments, which are summarized briefly in Exhibit 14–2, are frequently divided into the two classifications that we will discuss in the following subsections: *orders to pay* (drafts and checks) and *promises to pay* (promissory notes and CDs).

Negotiable instruments may also be classified as either demand instruments or time instruments. A *demand instrument* is payable on demand; that is, it is payable immediately after it is issued and thereafter for a reasonable period of time. All checks are demand instruments because, by definition, they must be payable on demand. A *time instrument* is payable at a future date.

Drafts and Checks (Orders to Pay)

A **draft** is an unconditional written order to pay rather than a promise to pay. Drafts involve three parties. The party creating the draft (the **drawer**) orders another party (the **drawee**) to pay money, usually to a third party (the **payee**). The most common type of draft is a check, but drafts other than checks may be used in commercial transactions.

Time Drafts and Sight Drafts A *time draft* is payable at a definite future time. A *sight draft* (or demand draft) is payable on sight—that is, when it is presented to the drawee (usually a bank or financial institution) for payment. A sight draft may be payable on acceptance. **Acceptance** is the drawee's written promise to pay the draft when it comes due. The usual manner of accepting an instrument is by writing the word *accepted* across

DRAFT
Any instrument drawn on a drawee that orders the drawee to pay a certain sum of money, usually to a third party (the payee), on demand or at a definite future time.

DRAWER
The party that initiates a draft (such as a check), thereby ordering the drawee to pay.

DRAWEE
The party that is ordered to pay a draft or check. With a check, a bank or a financial institution is always the drawee.

PAYEE
A person to whom an instrument is made payable.

ACCEPTANCE
In negotiable instruments law, the drawee's signed agreement to pay a draft when it is presented.

EXHIBIT 14–2 Basic Types of Negotiable Instruments		
INSTRUMENTS	**CHARACTERISTICS**	**PARTIES**
ORDERS TO PAY		
Draft	An order by one person to another person or to bearer [UCC 3–104(e)].	Drawer—The person who signs or makes the order to pay [UCC 3–103(a)(3)].
Check	A draft drawn on a bank and payable on demand [UCC 3–104(f)].[a] (With certain types of checks, such as cashier's checks, the bank is both the drawer and the drawee—see Chapter 15 for details.)	Drawee—The person to whom the order to pay is made [UCC 3–103(a)(2)]. Payee—The person to whom payment is ordered.
PROMISES TO PAY		
Promissory note	A promise by one party to pay money to another party or to bearer [UCC 3–104(e)].	Maker—The person who promises to pay [UCC 3–103(a)(5)]. Payee—The person to whom the promise is made.
Certificate of deposit	A note issued by a bank acknowledging a deposit of funds made payable to the holder of the note [UCC 3–104(j)].	

a. Under UCC 4–105(1), banks include savings banks, savings and loan associations, credit unions, and trust companies.

the face of the instrument, followed by the date of acceptance and the signature of the drawee. A draft can be both a time and a sight draft; such a draft is payable at a stated time after sight (a draft that states it is payable ninety days after sight, for instance).

Exhibit 14–3 shows a typical time draft. For the drawee to be obligated to honor the order, the drawee must be obligated to the drawer either by agreement or through a debtor-creditor relationship. **■EXAMPLE 14.1** On January 16, Ourtown Real Estate Company orders $1,000 worth of office supplies from Eastman Supply Company, with payment due in ninety days. Also on January 16, Ourtown sends Eastman a draft drawn on its account with the First National Bank of Whiteacre as payment. In this scenario, the drawer is Ourtown, the drawee is Ourtown's bank (First National Bank of Whiteacre), and the payee is Eastman Supply Company. ■

Trade Acceptances   A **trade acceptance** is a draft that is commonly used in the sale of goods. In this type of draft, the seller is both the drawer and the payee. The buyer to whom credit is extended is the drawee. **■EXAMPLE 14.2** Jackson Street Bistro buys its restaurant supplies from Osaka Industries. When Jackson requests supplies, Osaka creates a draft ordering Jackson to pay Osaka for the supplies within ninety days. Jackson accepts the draft by signing its face and is then obligated to make the payment. If Osaka is in need of cash, it can sell the trade acceptance to a third party in the commercial money market (the market for short-term borrowing that businesses use) before the payment is due. ■ (If the draft orders the buyer's bank to pay, it is called a *banker's acceptance*.)

Checks   As mentioned, the most commonly used type of draft is a **check.** The writer of the check is the drawer, the bank on which the check is drawn is the drawee, and the person to whom the check is payable is the payee. As mentioned earlier, checks are demand instruments because they are payable on demand. (Do other countries always consider checks to be negotiable instruments? For a discussion of this issue, see this chapter's *Beyond Our Borders* feature on page 421.)

Checks will be discussed more fully in Chapter 15, but take note that with certain types of checks, such as *cashier's checks,* the bank is both the drawer and the drawee. The bank customer purchases a cashier's check from the bank—that is, pays the bank the amount of the check—and indicates to whom the check should be made payable. The bank, not the customer, is the drawer of the check, as well as the drawee. The idea behind a cashier's check is

TRADE ACCEPTANCE
A draft that is drawn by a seller of goods ordering the buyer to pay a specified sum to the seller, usually at a stated time in the future. The buyer accepts the draft by signing the face of the draft, thus creating an enforceable obligation to pay the draft when it comes due. On a trade acceptance, the seller is both the drawee and the payee.

CHECK
A draft drawn by a drawer ordering the drawee bank or financial institution to pay a certain amount of money to the holder on demand.

EXHIBIT 14–3 A Typical Time Draft

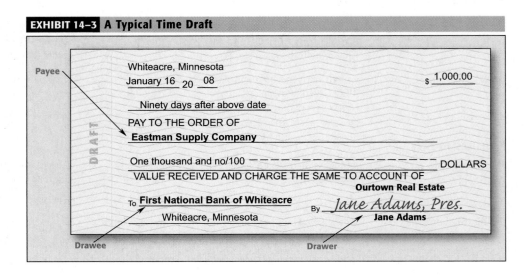

that it functions the same as cash, so there is no question about whether the check will be paid—the bank has committed itself to paying the stated amount on demand.

The following case arose from a party's petition for the discharge of a gambling debt in bankruptcy. Is a casino marker (by which a casino extends credit to a customer) the equivalent of a check? Can a "bad" check alone constitute the making of a false statement (fraud is a ground for denying a discharge in bankruptcy—see Chapter 16)? The court in this case considered these questions.

CASE 14.1 **In re Miller**

United States Bankruptcy Court, Central District of California, 310 Bankr. 185 (2004).

FACTS Obtaining credit at Mandalay Bay casino in Las Vegas, Nevada, is a four-step process. First, the customer applies for credit. Second, the casino verifies that the customer has funds in a bank account to cover the amount. Third, the casino approves the request. Fourth, the customer signs and delivers a marker to the casino, to draw money against the account and buy gambling chips. Richard Miller gambled at Mandalay Bay on at least four occasions in 1999 and 2000. Each time, he obtained credit—for $10,000, $20,000, $30,000, and $25,000, respectively—and each time, he repaid as much of the credit as he used. On his fifth trip, in August 2000, Mandalay granted him $50,000 in credit and accepted four markers—three for $10,000 and one for $20,000—based on the amount in his account with Wells Fargo Bank in Southgate, California. At the end of the month, Mandalay submitted the markers for collection, but the bank returned them unpaid. More than a year later, after paying Mandalay $19,000 of the debt, Miller filed a petition in a federal bankruptcy court, asking for a discharge of the remaining $31,000. Mandalay opposed the discharge, claiming that Miller's markers were fraudulent.

ISSUE Is a casino marker the equivalent of a check?

DECISION Yes. The court discharged the rest of Miller's debt to Mandalay. As for Mandalay's claim, the court held that the delivery of a check alone does not involve the making of a false statement, although this delivery may be part of a larger transaction in which a debtor does make false representations.

REASON To prevail on its claim of fraud, Mandalay needed to show that Miller made an untrue or false statement of fact when he issued his markers in exchange for the casino chips, as would be required if the markers were exchanged for checks. The court recognized that business transactions frequently involve statements but emphasized that these statements are found elsewhere in a transaction, not in a check. Here, Mandalay failed to offer evidence of anything that Miller said or wrote apart from his delivery of the markers. Mandalay presented only the markers, the legal equivalent of checks. In the words of the court, "[d]epositing checks that [are] not supported by sufficient funds * * * [does] not involve making a false statement * * * because a check is literally not a statement. * * * [T]he presentation of a marker, just like a check, does not involve the making of a false statement. Therefore, Miller did not make a false statement or representation by delivering the markers to Mandalay."

 WHAT IF THE FACTS WERE DIFFERENT? *Suppose that Mandalay Bay had proved that the debt represented by Miller's markers was induced by fraud. Would the result have been different? Why or why not?*

Promissory Notes and Certificates of Deposit (Promises to Pay)

A **promissory note** is a written promise made by one person (the **maker** of the promise to pay) to another (usually a payee). A promissory note, which is often referred to simply as a *note*, can be made payable at a definite time or on demand. It can name a specific payee or merely be payable to bearer (bearer instruments are discussed later in this chapter). **EXAMPLE 14.3** On April 30, Laurence and Margaret Roberts sign a writing unconditionally promising to pay "to the order of" the First National Bank of Whiteacre $3,000 (with

PROMISSORY NOTE
A written promise made by one person (the maker) to pay a fixed amount of money to another person (the payee or a subsequent holder) on demand or on a specified date.

MAKER
One who promises to pay a fixed amount of money to the holder of a promissory note or a certificate of deposit (CD).

8 percent interest) on or before June 29. This writing is a promissory note. ■ A typical promissory note is shown in Exhibit 14–4.

Types of Promissory Notes Notes are used in a variety of credit transactions and often carry the name of the transaction involved. For example, a note that is secured by personal property, such as an automobile, is called a *collateral note*, because the property pledged as security for the satisfaction of the debt is called collateral (see Chapter 16). A note secured by real estate is called a *mortgage note*. A note payable in installments, such as for payment for a suite of furniture over a twelve-month period, is called an *installment note*.

CERTIFICATE OF DEPOSIT (CD)
A note issued by a bank in which the bank acknowledges the receipt of funds from a party and promises to repay that amount, with interest, to the party on a certain date.

Certificate of Deposit A **certificate of deposit (CD)** is a type of note. A CD is issued when a party deposits funds with a bank that the bank promises to repay, with interest, on a certain date [UCC 3–104(j)]. The bank is the maker of the note, and the depositor is the payee. ■**EXAMPLE 14.4** On February 15, Sara Levin deposits $5,000 with the First National Bank of Whiteacre. The bank issues a CD, in which it promises to repay the $5,000, plus 5 percent annual interest, on August 15. ■

Certificates of deposit in small denominations (for amounts up to $100,000) are often sold by savings and loan associations, savings banks, commercial banks, and credit unions. Certificates of deposit for amounts over $100,000 are called large or jumbo CDs. Exhibit 14–5 shows a typical small CD.

Because CDs are time deposits, the purchaser-payee is typically not allowed to withdraw the funds prior to the date of maturity (except in limited circumstances, such as disability or death). If a payee wants to access the funds prior to the maturity date, he or she can sell (negotiate) the CD to a third party.

TRANSFER OF INSTRUMENTS

Once issued, a negotiable instrument can be transferred by *assignment* or by *negotiation*. Only a transfer by negotiation can result in the party obtaining the instrument receiving the rights of a holder, as discussed next.

EXHIBIT 14–4 **A Typical Promissory Note**

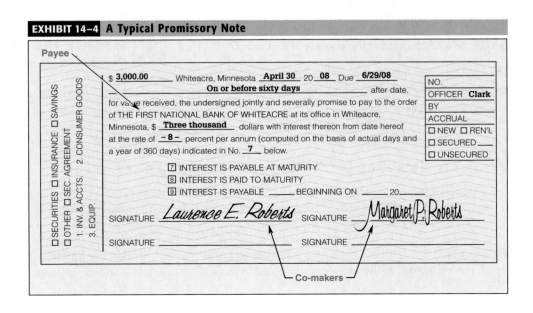

BEYOND OUR BORDERS The Negotiability of Checks in Other Nations

For many people in the United States, checks are the ultimate negotiable instrument. After all, our parents and grandparents negotiated checks. Checks have a long history of being accepted the "same as cash" at most locations in the United States. In other countries, however, checks are used less frequently and sometimes are not even negotiable.

In some European nations, such as Austria, Germany, and the Netherlands, checks are now rarely used. Direct bank transfers and electronic payments (both of which will be discussed in Chapter 15) have replaced checks in these countries. The European Union has a low-cost electronic payment system that is much faster and more efficient than the systems available in the United States. This fact—as well as the increase in identity theft and financial crimes—has contributed to the abandonment of checks elsewhere.

Even in those nations where checks are still used, they are often not actually negotiable. In France, for example, although a segment of the population still uses checks, the payee named on a check cannot indorse the check to a third party. Moreover, the payee on the check cannot walk into any bank in France and cash the check as a payee can in the United States. In France, a check can only be deposited into an account at a bank. More and more shops in France no longer accept check payments at all.

In the United Kingdom, where checks have been used even longer than in the United States, checks are rapidly becoming a thing of the past. Since 2001, businesses' electronic payments have outnumbered their payments by check. In 2006, ASDA, the second largest British supermarket chain and a subsidiary of Wal-Mart, announced that it will not accept checks as a means of payment in the future (beginning in the London area). Similarly, the largest pharmacy chain in the United Kingdom (Boots) is also phasing out checks as a payment method. British utility companies are also discouraging the use of checks by charging higher prices to customers who pay by check.

 FOR CRITICAL ANALYSIS *What are the disadvantages of not being able to indorse checks to other parties?*

EXHIBIT 14–5 A Typical Small CD

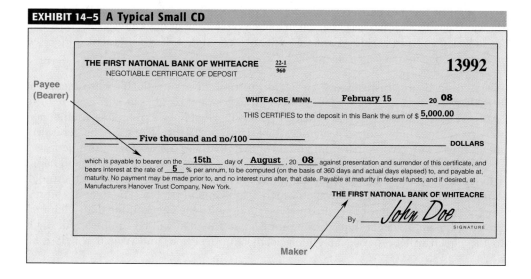

THE FIRST NATIONAL BANK OF WHITEACRE   22-1/960   13992
NEGOTIABLE CERTIFICATE OF DEPOSIT

Payee (Bearer)

WHITEACRE, MINN. _____ February 15 _____ 20 08 _____

THIS CERTIFIES to the deposit in this Bank the sum of $ 5,000.00

———— Five thousand and no/100 ————   DOLLARS

which is payable to bearer on the __15th__ day of __August__, 20 __08__ against presentation and surrender of this certificate, and bears interest at the rate of __5__ % per annum, to be computed (on the basis of 360 days and actual days elapsed) to, and payable at, maturity. No payment may be made prior to, and no interest runs after, that date. Payable at maturity in federal funds, and if desired, at Manufacturers Hanover Trust Company, New York.

THE FIRST NATIONAL BANK OF WHITEACRE

By ___*John Doe*___
                              SIGNATURE

Maker

Transfer by Assignment

Recall from Chapter 9 that an assignment is a transfer of rights under a contract. Under general contract principles, a transfer by assignment to an assignee gives the assignee only those rights that the assignor possessed. Any defenses that can be raised against an assignor can normally be raised against the assignee. This same principle applies when a negotiable instrument, such as a promissory note, is transferred by assignment. The transferee is then an *assignee* rather than a *holder*. Sometimes, a transfer fails to qualify as a negotiation because it fails to meet one or more of the requirements of a negotiable instrument, discussed on pages 416 and 417. When this occurs, the transfer becomes an assignment.

Transfer by Negotiation

NEGOTIATION
The transfer of an instrument in such form that the transferee (the person to whom the instrument is transferred) becomes a holder.

HOLDER
Any person in possession of an instrument drawn, issued, or indorsed to him or her, to his or her order, to bearer, or in blank.

Negotiation is the transfer of an instrument in such form that the transferee (the person to whom the instrument is transferred) becomes a holder [UCC 3–201(a)]. The UCC defines a **holder** as any person in the possession of an instrument drawn, issued, or indorsed to him or her, to his or her order, to bearer, or in blank. The terms *indorse* and *in blank* will be explained shortly. Under UCC principles, a transfer by negotiation creates a holder who, at the very least, receives the rights of the previous possessor [UCC 3–203(b)]. Unlike an assignment, a transfer by negotiation can make it possible for a holder to receive more rights in the instrument than the prior possessor had [UCC 3–202(b), 3–305, 3–306]. A holder who receives greater rights is known as a *holder in due course*, a concept that will be discussed shortly.

There are two methods of negotiating an instrument so that the receiver becomes a holder. The method used depends on whether the instrument is order paper or bearer paper.

ORDER INSTRUMENT
A negotiable instrument that is payable "to the order of an identified person" or "to an identified person or order."

INDORSEMENT
A signature placed on an instrument for the purpose of transferring one's ownership rights in the instrument.

Negotiating Order Instruments An **order instrument** is a negotiable instrument that is payable to the order of a specific person. In other words, it contains the name of a payee capable of indorsing it, as in "Pay to the order of Lloyd Sorenson." An order instrument is negotiated by delivery with any necessary indorsements. (An **indorsement** is a signature placed on an instrument, such as on the back of a check, for the purpose of transferring one's ownership rights in the instrument. Exhibit 14–6 shows various types of indorsements and their consequences, and the *Application* feature at the end of this chapter lists suggestions to help businesspersons avoid problems with indorsements.) **■EXAMPLE 14.5** National Express Corporation issues a payroll check "to the order of Lloyd Sorenson." Sorenson takes the check to the bank, signs his name on the back (a blank indorsement), gives it to the teller (a delivery), and receives cash. Sorenson has *negotiated* the check to the bank [UCC 3–201(b)]. ■ Note that a blank indorsement does not specify a particular indorsee and can consist of a mere signature. When an order instrument is indorsed *in blank*, it becomes a *bearer instrument*.

BEARER INSTRUMENT
Any instrument that is not payable to a specific person, including instruments payable to the "bearer" or to "cash."

Negotiating Bearer Instruments A **bearer instrument** is a negotiable instrument that is not payable to a specific person, such as an instrument payable to the "bearer" or to "cash." A bearer instrument is negotiated by delivery—that is, by transfer into another person's possession. Indorsement is not necessary [UCC 3–201(b)]. The use of bearer instruments thus involves more risk through loss or theft than the use of order instruments. **■EXAMPLE 14.6** Assume that Richard Kray writes a check "payable to cash" and hands it to Jessie Arnold (a delivery). Kray has issued the check (a bearer instrument) to Arnold. Arnold places the check in her wallet, which is subsequently stolen. The thief has possession of the check. At this point, the thief has no rights to the check. If the thief "delivers" the check to an innocent third person, however, negotiation will be complete. All rights to the check will be passed absolutely to that third person, and Arnold will lose all

EXHIBIT 14–6 Types of Indorsements and Their Consequences

WORDS CONSTITUTING THE INDORSEMENT	TYPE OF INDORSEMENT	INDORSER'S SIGNATURE LIABILITY[a]
"Mark Deitsch"	Blank	Unqualified signature liability on proper presentment and notice of dishonor.[b]
"Pay to William Hunter, Hal Cohen"	Special	Unqualified signature liability on proper presentment and notice of dishonor.
"Without recourse, Sarah Jacobs"	Qualified (blank for further negotiation)	No signature liability. Transfer warranty liability if breach occurs.[c]
"Pay to Allison Jong, without recourse, Sarah Jacobs"	Qualified (special for further negotiation)	No signature liability. Transfer warranty liability if breach occurs.
"For deposit only, Marcel Dumont"	Restrictive–for deposit (blank for further negotiation)	Signature liability only on Dumont's having amount deposited in his account. If deposit made, signature liability on proper presentment and notice of dishonor.
"Pay to Ellen Cook in trust for Roger Callahan, Roger Callahan"	Restrictive–trust (special for further negotiation)	Signature liability to original indorsee only on payment to Ellen Cook for Roger Callahan's benefit. Regardless of whether restriction is met, signature liability to subsequent indorsers on proper presentment and notice of dishonor.

a. Signature liability, discussed later in this chapter, refers to the liability of a party who signs an instrument.

b. When an instrument is dishonored—that is, when, for example, a drawer's bank refuses to cash the drawer's check on proper presentment—an indorser of the check may be liable on it if he or she is given proper notice of dishonor.

c. The transferor of an instrument makes certain warranties to the transferee and subsequent holders, and thus, even if the transferor's signature does not render him or her liable on the instrument, he or she may be liable for breach of a transfer warranty. Transfer warranties will be discussed later in this chapter.

rights to recover the proceeds of the check from that person [UCC 3–306]. Of course, Arnold could attempt to recover the funds from the thief if the thief can be found. ▣

HOLDER IN DUE COURSE (HDC)

An ordinary holder obtains only those rights that the transferor had in the instrument. In this respect, a holder has the same status as an assignee (see Chapter 9). Like an assignee, a holder normally is subject to the same defenses that could be asserted against the transferor.

In contrast, a **holder in due course (HDC)** is a holder who, by meeting certain acquisition requirements (to be discussed shortly), takes an instrument *free* of most of the defenses and claims that could be asserted against the transferor. Stated another way, an HDC can normally acquire a higher level of immunity than can an ordinary holder in regard to defenses against payment on the instrument or ownership claims to the instrument by other parties.

The basic requirements for attaining HDC status are set forth in UCC 3–302. A holder of a negotiable instrument is an HDC if she or he takes the instrument (1) for value; (2) in good faith; and (3) without notice. We now examine each of these requirements.

Taking for Value

An HDC must have given *value* for the instrument [UCC 3–302(a)(2)(i)]. A person who receives an instrument as a gift or inherits it has not met the requirement of value. In these situations, the person becomes an ordinary holder and does not possess the rights of an HDC.

The concept of value in the law of negotiable instruments is not the same as the concept of *consideration* in the law of contracts. A promise to give value in the future is clearly sufficient consideration to support a contract [UCC 1–201(44)]. A promise to give value in

HOLDER IN DUE COURSE (HDC)
A holder who acquires a negotiable instrument for value; in good faith; and without notice that the instrument is overdue, that it has been dishonored, that any person has a defense against it or a claim to it, or that the instrument contains unauthorized signatures, has been altered, or is so irregular or incomplete as to call into question its authenticity.

the future, however, normally does not constitute value sufficient to make one an HDC. A holder takes an instrument for value only to the extent that the promise has been performed [UCC 3–303(a)(1)]. Therefore, if the holder plans to pay for the instrument later or plans to perform the required services at some future date, the holder has not yet given value. In that situation, the holder is not yet an HDC.

Under UCC 3–303(a), a holder takes an instrument for value in one of five ways:

1 By performing the promise for which the instrument was issued or transferred.

2 By acquiring a security interest or other lien in the instrument, excluding a lien obtained by a judicial proceeding. (Security interests and liens will be discussed in Chapter 16.)

3 By taking the instrument in payment of, or as security for, a preexisting claim. **■EXAMPLE 14.7** Zon owes Dwyer $2,000 on a past-due account. If Zon negotiates a $2,000 note signed by Gordon to Dwyer and Dwyer accepts it to discharge the overdue account balance, Dwyer has given value for the instrument. ■

4 By giving a negotiable instrument as payment for the instrument. **■EXAMPLE 14.8** Martin has issued a $500 negotiable promissory note to Paulene. The note is due six months from the date issued. Paulene needs cash and does not want to wait for the maturity date to collect. She negotiates the note to her friend Kristen, who pays her $200 in cash and writes her a check—a negotiable instrument—for the balance of $300. Kristen has given full value for the note by paying $200 in cash and issuing Paulene the check for $300. ■

5 By giving an irrevocable commitment (such as a letter of credit—see Chapter 25) as payment for the instrument.

Taking in Good Faith

The second requirement for HDC status is that the holder must take the instrument in *good faith* [UCC 3–302(a)(2)(ii)]. This means that the holder must have acted honestly in the process of acquiring the instrument. UCC 3–103(a)(4) defines *good faith* as "honesty in fact and the observance of reasonable commercial standards of fair dealing." The good faith requirement applies only to the *holder*. It is immaterial whether the transferor acted in good faith. Thus, even a person who takes a negotiable instrument from a thief may become an HDC if the person acquires the instrument in good faith.

Because of the good faith requirement, one must ask whether the purchaser, when acquiring the instrument, honestly believed that the instrument was not defective. If a person purchases a $10,000 note for $300 from a stranger on a street corner, the issue of good faith can be raised on the grounds of both the suspicious circumstances and the grossly inadequate consideration (value).

In the following case, the court considered whether a bank observed "reasonable commercial standards of fair dealing" to fulfill the good faith requirement and become an HDC.

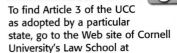

CASE 14.2   **Mid Wisconsin Bank v. Forsgard Trading, Inc.**

Wisconsin Court of Appeals, 2003 WI App. 186, 266 Wis.2d 685, 668 N.W.2d 830 (2003).
www.wisbar.org/WisCtApp/index.html[a]

FACTS Forsgard Trading, Inc., opened an account at Mid

a. Scroll down and click on "Wisconsin Court of Appeals cases 1995–present." In the result, type "2003" in the "Year" box and "100" in the "Number of cases/page" box. You will find the case at "#561." The State Bar of Wisconsin maintains this Web site.

Wisconsin Bank in July 1999. The account agreement stated, "Any items, other than cash, accepted for deposit * * * will be given provisional credit only until collection is final." Mid Wisconsin's practice is to give immediate credit on deposits, but a bank employee may place a hold on a check if, for example, there is reasonable ground for doubt about it. On May 7, 2001,

CASE 14.2–Continued

Lakeshore Truck and Equipment Sales, Inc., wrote a check payable to Forsgard in the amount of $18,500. On May 8, Forsgard deposited the check in its account at Mid Wisconsin, which gave Forsgard immediate credit. The same day, Lakeshore issued a stop-payment order (an order to its bank not to pay the check—see Chapter 15). When Mid Wisconsin received notice on May 16 that payment had been stopped, it deducted the $18,500 from Forsgard's account. Because of transfers from the account between May 8 and May 16, the deduction resulted in a negative balance. Before this incident, Forsgard had overdrawn the account twenty-four times but, on each occasion, had deposited funds to cover the overdraft. Forsgard did not do so this time. Mid Wisconsin filed a suit in a Wisconsin state court against Forsgard, Lakeshore, and others to recover the loss. The court issued a summary judgment in Mid Wisconsin's favor. Lakeshore appealed to a state intermediate appellate court.

ISSUE Did Mid Wisconsin act in good faith?

DECISION Yes. The court affirmed the lower court's judgment on this issue, holding that Mid Wisconsin was an HDC of the check.

REASON The appellate court explained that under UCC 3–305, an HDC can recover from a drawer who places a stop-payment order on a check. Under UCC 3–302, an HDC is one who takes an instrument for value and in good faith. There was no dispute that Mid Wisconsin took the check for value. UCC 3–103(a)(4) defines good faith as "honesty in fact and the observance of reasonable commercial standards of fair dealing." Lakeshore conceded that Mid Wisconsin took the check with honesty in fact. Thus, the only question was whether Mid Wisconsin's granting Forsgard immediate credit was in line with "reasonable commercial standards of fair dealing." The court found that Mid Wisconsin's acts complied with its account agreement and that "Mid Wisconsin had no reason to suspect there would be any problem if immediate credit was extended for this check." Also, "extending immediate credit is consistent with reasonable banking standards." The court pointed out, "It would hinder commercial transactions if depository banks refused to permit the withdrawal prior to the clearance of checks. * * * [B]anking practice is to the contrary. It is clear that the Uniform Commercial Code was intended * * * to protect banks [that] have given credit on deposited items prior to notice of a stop payment order."

 WHAT IF THE FACTS WERE DIFFERENT? *Suppose that Forsgard's account at Mid Wisconsin had been overdrawn when the check was deposited. How might the result in this case have been different?*

Taking without Notice

The final requirement for HDC status involves *notice* [UCC 3–302]. A person will not be afforded HDC protection if he or she acquires an instrument and is *on notice* (knows or has reason to know) that it is defective in any one of the following ways [UCC 3–302(a)]:

1 It is overdue.

2 It has been dishonored.

3 There is an uncured (uncorrected) default with respect to another instrument issued as part of the same series.

4 The instrument contains an unauthorized signature or has been altered.

5 There is a defense against the instrument or a claim to the instrument.

6 The instrument is so irregular or incomplete as to call into question its authenticity.

What Constitutes Notice? Notice of a defective instrument is given whenever the holder (1) has actual knowledge of the defect; (2) has received a notice of the defect (such as a bank's receipt of a letter listing the serial numbers of stolen bearer instruments); or (3) has reason to know that a defect exists, given all the facts and circumstances known at the time in question [UCC 1–201(25)]. The holder must also have received the notice "at a time and in a manner that gives a reasonable opportunity to act on it" [UCC 3–302(f)]. A purchaser's knowledge of certain facts, such as insolvency proceedings against the maker or drawer of the instrument, does not constitute notice that the instrument is defective [UCC 3–302(b)].

REMEMBER Demand instruments are payable immediately. Time instruments are payable at a future date.

Overdue Instruments   What constitutes notice that an instrument is overdue depends on whether it is a demand instrument (payable on demand) or a time instrument (payable at a definite time).

A purchaser has notice that a *demand instrument* is overdue if she or he either takes the instrument knowing that demand has been made or takes the instrument an unreasonable length of time after its issue. For a check, a "reasonable time" is ninety days after the date of the check. For all other demand instruments, what will be considered a reasonable time depends on the circumstances [UCC 3–304(a)].

A holder of a *time instrument* who takes the instrument at any time after its expressed due date is on notice that it is overdue [UCC 3–304(b)(2)]. Nonpayment by the due date should indicate to any purchaser that the instrument may be defective. Thus, a promissory note due on May 15 must be acquired before midnight on May 15. If it is purchased on May 16, the purchaser will be an ordinary holder, not an HDC. Sometimes, an instrument reads, "Payable in thirty days." To count thirty days, you exclude the first day and count the last day. Thus, a note dated December 1 that is payable in thirty days is due by midnight on December 31. If the payment date falls on a Sunday or holiday, the instrument is payable on the next business day.

HOLDER THROUGH AN HDC

A person who does not qualify as an HDC but who derives his or her title through an HDC can acquire the rights and privileges of an HDC. This rule, which is sometimes called the **shelter principle**, is set out in UCC 3–203(b):

> Transfer of an instrument, whether or not the transfer is a negotiation, vests in the transferee any right of the transferor to enforce the instrument, including any right as a holder in due course, but the transferee cannot acquire rights of a holder in due course by a transfer, directly or indirectly, from a holder in due course if the transferee engaged in fraud or illegality affecting the instrument.

SHELTER PRINCIPLE
The principle that the holder of a negotiable instrument who cannot qualify as a holder in due course (HDC), but who derives his or her title through an HDC, acquires the rights of an HDC.

Under this rule, anyone—no matter how far removed from an HDC—who can ultimately trace his or her title back to an HDC may acquire the rights of an HDC. By extending the benefits of HDC status, the shelter principle promotes the marketability and free transferability of negotiable instruments.

There are some limitations on the shelter principle, though. Certain persons who formerly held instruments cannot improve their positions by later reacquiring the instruments from HDCs [UCC 3–203(b)]. If a holder participated in fraud or illegality affecting the instrument, or had notice of a claim or defense against an instrument, that holder is not allowed to improve her or his status by repurchasing the instrument from a later HDC.

■EXAMPLE 14.9 Matt and Carla collaborate to defraud Lorena. Lorena is induced to give Carla a negotiable note payable to Carla's order. Carla then specially indorses the note for value to Larry, an HDC. Matt and Carla split the proceeds. Larry negotiates the note to Stuart, another HDC. Stuart then negotiates the note for value to Matt. Even though Matt obtained the note through an HDC, he does not have the rights of an HDC—and can never acquire HDC rights in this note—because he participated in the original fraud. ■

SIGNATURE LIABILITY

The key to liability on a negotiable instrument is a *signature*. The general rule is as follows: Every party, except a qualified indorser,[1] who signs a negotiable instrument is either primarily or secondarily liable for payment of that instrument when it comes due. The

---

1. A qualified indorser—one who indorses "without recourse"—undertakes no contractual obligation to pay. A qualified indorser merely assumes warranty liability, which will be discussed later in this chapter.

following subsections discuss these two types of liability, as well as the conditions that must be met before liability can arise.

Primary Liability

A person who is primarily liable on a negotiable instrument is absolutely required to pay the instrument—unless, of course, he or she has a valid defense to payment [UCC 3–305]. Only *makers* and *acceptors* of instruments are primarily liable.

The maker of a promissory note promises to pay the note. It is the maker's promise to pay that makes the note a negotiable instrument. The words "I promise to pay" embody the maker's obligation to pay the instrument according to the terms as written at the time of the signing. If the instrument was incomplete when the maker signed it, the maker is obligated to pay it according to its stated terms or according to terms that were agreed on and later filled in to complete the instrument [UCC 3–115, 3–407(a), 3–412].

An **acceptor** is a drawee who promises to pay an instrument when it is presented for payment. Once a drawee indicates acceptance by signing the draft, the drawee becomes an acceptor and is obligated to pay the draft when it is presented for payment [UCC 3–409(a)]. A drawee who refuses to accept a draft that *requires* the drawee's acceptance (such as a trade acceptance) has dishonored the instrument. Acceptance of a check is called *certification* (certified checks will be discussed in Chapter 15). Certification is not necessary on checks, and a bank is under no obligation to certify checks. On certification, however, the drawee bank occupies the position of an acceptor and is primarily liable on the check to any holder [UCC 3–409(d)].

> **ACCEPTOR**
> A drawee who is legally obligated to pay an instrument when the instrument is presented for payment.

Secondary Liability

Drawers and *indorsers* are secondarily liable. On a negotiable instrument, secondary liability is similar to the liability of a guarantor in a simple contract in the sense that it is *contingent liability*. In other words, a drawer or an indorser will be liable only if the party that is responsible for paying the instrument refuses to do so (dishonors the instrument). In regard to drafts and checks, the drawer's secondary liability does not arise until the drawee fails to pay or to accept the instrument, whichever is required [UCC 3–412, 3–415].

Dishonor of an instrument thus triggers the liability of parties who are secondarily liable on the instrument—that is, the drawer and *unqualified* indorsers. **■EXAMPLE 14.10** Nina Lee writes a check on her account at Universal Bank payable to the order of Stephen Miller. Universal Bank refuses to pay the check when Miller presents it for payment, thus dishonoring the check. In this situation, Lee will be liable to Miller on the basis of her secondary liability. ■ Drawers are secondarily liable on drafts unless they disclaim their liability by drawing the instruments "without recourse" (if the draft is a check, however, a drawer cannot disclaim liability) [UCC 3–414(e)].

Parties who are secondarily liable on a negotiable instrument promise to pay on that instrument only if the following events occur[2]:

1 The instrument is properly and timely presented.
2 The instrument is dishonored.
3 Timely notice of dishonor is given to the secondarily liable party.

Proper and Timely Presentment **Presentment** is the formal production of a negotiable instrument for acceptance or payment. The UCC requires that a holder present the

> **RECALL** A guarantor is liable on a contract to pay the debt of another only if the party who is primarily liable fails to pay.

> **PRESENTMENT**
> The act of presenting an instrument to the party liable on the instrument to collect payment. Presentment also occurs when a person presents an instrument to a drawee for a required acceptance.

---

2. These requirements are necessary for a secondarily liable party to have signature liability on a negotiable instrument, but they are not necessary for a secondarily liable party to have warranty liability (to be discussed later in the chapter).

instrument to the appropriate party, in a timely fashion, and give reasonable identification if demanded [UCC 3–414(f), 3–415(e), 3–501]. The party to whom the instrument must be presented depends on the type of instrument involved. A note or certificate of deposit must be presented to the maker for payment. A draft is presented to the drawee for acceptance, payment, or both. A check is presented to the drawee for payment [UCC 3–501(a), 3–502(b)].

Presentment can be made by any commercially reasonable means, including oral, written, or electronic communication [UCC 3–501(b)]. It is ordinarily effective when the demand for payment or acceptance is received (unless presentment takes place after an established cutoff hour, in which case it may be treated as occurring the next business day).

One of the most crucial criteria for proper presentment is timeliness [UCC 3–414(f), 3–415(e), 3–501(b)(4)]. Failure to present an instrument on time is the most common reason for improper presentment and leads to unqualified indorsers being discharged from secondary liability. Under the UCC, the holder of a domestic check must present that check for payment or collection within thirty days of its *date* to hold the drawer secondarily liable, and within thirty days after its indorsement to hold the indorser secondarily liable. Failure to meet that deadline results in a discharge of secondary liability. The time for proper presentment for different types of instruments is shown in Exhibit 14–7.

Dishonor As mentioned previously, an instrument is dishonored when the required acceptance or payment is refused or cannot be obtained within the prescribed time. An instrument is also dishonored when the required presentment is excused (as it would be, for example, if the maker had died) and the instrument is not properly accepted or paid [UCC 3–502(e), 3–504].

In certain situations, a postponement of payment or a refusal to pay an instrument will *not* dishonor the instrument. When presentment is made after an established cutoff hour (not earlier than 2:00 P.M.), for instance, a bank can postpone payment until the following business day without dishonoring the instrument. In addition, when the holder refuses to exhibit the instrument, to give reasonable identification, or to sign a receipt for the payment on the instrument, a bank's refusal to pay does not dishonor the instrument. ▪**EXAMPLE 14.11** On receiving a check from Lamar, Deere takes the check to Universal Bank and demands payment in cash. The bank requests identification, which Deere refuses to provide. In this situation, the bank would be within its rights to refuse payment to Deere, and the bank's refusal to pay would not dishonor the check. ▪

EXHIBIT 14–7	Time for Proper Presentment	
TYPE OF INSTRUMENT	**FOR ACCEPTANCE**	**FOR PAYMENT**
Time	On or before due date.	On due date.
Demand	Within a reasonable time (after date of issue or after secondary party becomes liable on the instrument).	Within a reasonable time.
Check	Not applicable.	Within thirty days of its date, to hold drawer secondarily liable. Within thirty days of indorsement, to hold indorser secondarily liable.

Proper Notice Once an instrument has been dishonored, proper notice must be given to secondary parties (drawers and indorsers) for them to be held contractually liable. Notice may be given in any reasonable manner, including an oral, written, or electronic communication, as well as notice written or stamped on the instrument itself. The bank must give any necessary notice before its midnight deadline (midnight of the next banking day after receipt). Notice by any party other than a bank must be given within thirty days following the day of dishonor or the day on which the person who is secondarily liable receives notice of dishonor [UCC 3–503].

Unauthorized Signatures

People normally are not liable to pay on negotiable instruments unless their signatures appear on the instruments. As stated previously, the general rule is that an unauthorized signature is wholly inoperative and will not bind the person whose name is forged. There are two exceptions to this general rule:

1 When the person whose name is signed ratifies (affirms) the signature, he or she will be bound [UCC 3–403(a)]. A principal can ratify an unauthorized signature made by an agent, either expressly, by affirming the validity of the signature, or impliedly, by other conduct, such as keeping any benefits received in the transaction or failing to repudiate the signature. The parties involved need not be principal and agent. **EXAMPLE 14.12** Allison Malone steals several checks from her mother, Brenda Malone; makes them out to herself; and signs "Brenda Malone." Brenda, the mother, may ratify her daughter's signature so that Allison will not be prosecuted for forgery. ■

2 When the negligence of the person whose name was forged substantially contributed to the forgery, a court may not allow the person to deny the effectiveness of an unauthorized signature [UCC 3–115, 3–406, 4–401(d)(2)]. **EXAMPLE 14.13** Rob, the owner of a business, leaves his signature stamp and a blank check on an office counter. An employee, using the stamp, fills in and cashes the check. Rob can be estopped (prevented), on the basis of negligence, from denying liability for payment of the check. Whatever loss occurs may be allocated, however, between certain parties on the basis of comparative negligence [UCC 3–406(b)]. For example, if Rob can demonstrate that the bank was negligent in paying the check, the bank may bear a portion of the loss. ■

A person who forges a check can be held personally liable for payment by an HDC [UCC 3–403(a)]. This is true even if the name of the person signing the instrument without authorization does not appear on the instrument. **EXAMPLE 14.14** If Michel Vuillard signs "Paul Richaud" without Richaud's authorization, Vuillard is personally liable just as if he had signed his own name. Vuillard's liability is limited, however, to persons who take or pay the instrument in good faith. One who knew the signature was unauthorized would not qualify as an HDC and thus could not recover from Vuillard on the instrument. (The defenses that are effective against ordinary holders versus HDCs will be discussed in detail later in this chapter.) ■

Businesspersons should be aware that although an unauthorized signature on a negotiable instrument is ineffective against the person whose name was signed, the signer remains liable. Although this rule may not be of great consequence with forgeries (because persons who commit forgery are likely to be difficult to locate and have limited financial resources), it can be very significant when dealing with unauthorized agents. A corporate agent, for instance, may have exceeded her or his authority when signing on behalf of a corporation. If you accepted an instrument from this person in good faith and paid value for it, you

PREVENTING
LEGAL DISPUTES

should be able to collect from the unauthorized agent what you cannot collect from the corporation. Because persons acting on behalf of a corporation typically have access to financial resources, pursuing this avenue may be your best chance of obtaining payment in some situations.

■

Special Rules for Unauthorized Indorsements

Generally, when an indorsement is forged or unauthorized, the burden of loss falls on the first party to take the instrument with the forged or unauthorized indorsement. This general rule is premised on the concept that the first party to take an instrument is in the best position to prevent the loss.

■EXAMPLE 14.15 Jenny Nilson steals a check drawn on Universal Bank and payable to the order of Inga Leed. Nilson indorses the check "Inga Leed" and presents the check to Universal Bank for payment. The bank, without asking Nilson for identification, pays the check, and Nilson disappears. In this situation, Leed will not be liable on the check because her indorsement was forged. The bank will bear the loss, which it might have avoided if it had requested identification from Nilson. ■

There are two important exceptions to this general rule. These exceptions arise when an indorsement is made by an imposter or by a fictitious payee. In these situations, as discussed next, the loss falls on the maker or drawer.

IMPOSTER
One who, by use of the mails, Internet, telephone, or personal appearance, induces a maker or drawer to issue an instrument in the name of an impersonated payee. Indorsements by imposters are treated as authorized indorsements under Article 3 of the UCC.

Imposter Rule An **imposter** is one who, by her or his personal appearance or use of the mails, Internet, telephone, or other communication, induces a maker or drawer to issue an instrument in the name of an impersonated payee. If the maker or drawer believes the imposter to be the named payee at the time of issue, the indorsement by the imposter is not treated as unauthorized when the instrument is transferred to an innocent party. This is because the maker or drawer *intended* the imposter to receive the instrument. In this situation, under the UCC's *imposter rule*, the imposter's indorsement will be effective—that is, not considered a forgery—insofar as the drawer or maker is concerned [UCC 3–404(a)].

■EXAMPLE 14.16 Carol impersonates Donna and induces Edward to write a check payable to the order of Donna. Carol, continuing to impersonate Donna, negotiates the check to First National Bank as payment on her loan there. As the drawer of the check, Edward is liable for its amount to First National. ■

FICTITIOUS PAYEE
A payee on a negotiable instrument whom the maker or drawer does not intend to have an interest in the instrument. Indorsements by fictitious payees are treated as authorized indorsements under Article 3 of the UCC.

Fictitious Payee Rule When a person causes an instrument to be issued to a payee who will have *no interest* in the instrument, the payee is referred to as a **fictitious payee.** A fictitious payee can be a person or firm that does not truly exist, or it may be an identifiable party that will not acquire any interest in the instrument. Under the UCC's *fictitious payee rule*, the payee's indorsement is not treated as a forgery, and an innocent holder can hold the maker or drawer liable on the instrument [UCC 3–404(b), 3–405].

Situations involving fictitious payees most often arise when (1) a dishonest employee deceives the employer into signing an instrument payable to a party with no right to receive payment on the instrument or (2) a dishonest employee or agent has the authority to issue an instrument on behalf of the employer.

How a Fictitious Payee Can Be Created—An Example. **■EXAMPLE 14.17** Blair Industries, Inc., gives its bookkeeper, Axel Ford, general authority to issue company checks drawn on First State Bank so that Ford can pay employees' wages and other corporate bills. Ford decides to cheat Blair Industries out of $10,000 by issuing a check payable to Erica Nied, an old acquaintance. Neither Blair nor Ford intends Nied to receive any of the funds, and Nied is not an employee or creditor of the company. Ford indorses the check in Nied's name, naming himself as indorsee. He then cashes the check at a local bank, which collects payment from the drawee bank, First State Bank. First State Bank charges the Blair Industries account $10,000. Blair Industries discovers the fraud and demands that the account be recredited. ▣

Who Bears the Loss? Who bears the loss? UCC 3–404(b)(2) provides the answer. **▣EXAMPLE 14.18** In the example just presented, neither the local bank that first accepted the check nor First State Bank is liable. Because Ford's indorsement in the name of a payee with no interest in the instrument is "effective," there is no "forgery." Hence, the collecting bank is protected in paying on the check, and the drawee bank is protected in charging Blair's account. Thus, the employer-drawer, Blair Industries, will bear the loss. Of course, Blair Industries has recourse against Axel Ford, if Ford has not absconded with the funds. ▣

Regardless of whether a dishonest employee actually signs the check or merely supplies his or her employer with names of fictitious creditors (or with true names of creditors having fictitious debts), the result is the same under the UCC. **▣EXAMPLE 14.19** Nathan Holtz draws up the payroll list from which employees' salary checks are written. He fraudulently adds the name Sally Vix (a fictitious person) to the payroll, and the employer signs checks to be issued to her. Again, it is the employer-drawer who bears the loss. ▣

ETHICAL ISSUE 14.1

How should the courts determine what is commercially reasonable when applying the fictitious payee rule? Remember that the UCC requires banks to observe commercially reasonable standards of fair dealing in all transactions. It is often difficult for courts to determine what is commercially reasonable when it comes to unauthorized indorsements, however, and they frequently look to the bank's own policies for guidance. Does allowing banks to set their own standards for commercial reasonableness lead to unequal application of the fictitious payee rule? Furthermore, once a bank has established a standard of reasonable behavior for itself, should the courts hold the bank to that standard?

Consider two cases with very different results. In the first, a dishonest employee, Dorothy Heck, forged indorsements on 882 employee payroll checks over a four-year period and deposited them into her bank account. Although the indorsements on the checks that Heck deposited did not exactly match the names of the payees—as was required by the bank's policy—the bank allowed Heck to deposit the checks anyway. Because the bank failed to follow its own policy, the court held that the bank had acted in bad faith and could not assert the fictitious payee rule as a defense.[3] In the second case, a dishonest insurance agent took 279 checks written to his employer, Brooks Insurance; indorsed them; and deposited them into his own bank account. The bank in this case had a policy that any checks written to a business entity should be deposited into an account with that business's name. Although the bank violated its own policy when it allowed the agent to deposit the checks into an account with a different name, the court decided that this was not enough to show bad faith. Even though the bank may have acted negligently, the court allowed the bank to assert the fictitious payee rule and avoid liability.[4] Is it fair for a court to allow a bank that violated its own policy to escape liability when the plaintiff may have known the policy and relied on the bank to follow it?

3. *Pavex, Inc. v. York Federal Savings and Loan Association,* 716 A.2d 640 (Pa.Super.Ct. 1998).
4. *Continental Casualty Co. v. Fifth/Third Bank,* 418 F.Supp.2d 964 (N.D. Ohio 2006).

WARRANTY LIABILITY

In addition to the signature liability discussed in the preceding pages, transferors make certain implied warranties regarding the instruments that they are negotiating. Liability under these warranties is not subject to the conditions of proper presentment, dishonor, or notice of dishonor. These warranties arise even when a transferor does not indorse the instrument (as in the delivery of a bearer instrument) [UCC 3–416, 3–417]. Warranty liability is particularly important when a holder cannot hold a party liable on her or his signature.

Warranties fall into two categories: those that arise on the *transfer* of a negotiable instrument and those that arise on *presentment*. Both transfer and presentment warranties attempt to shift liability back to a wrongdoer or to the person who dealt face to face with the wrongdoer and thus was in the best position to prevent the wrongdoing.

Transfer Warranties

The UCC describes five **transfer warranties** [UCC 3–416]. For transfer warranties to arise, an instrument *must be transferred for consideration.* One who transfers an instrument for consideration makes the following warranties to all subsequent transferees and holders who take the instrument in good faith (with some exceptions, as will be noted shortly):

1 The transferor is entitled to enforce the instrument.

2 All signatures are authentic and authorized.

3 The instrument has not been altered.

4 The instrument is not subject to a defense or claim of any party that can be asserted against the transferor.

5 The transferor has no knowledge of any insolvency (bankruptcy) proceedings against the maker, the acceptor, or the drawer of the instrument.[5]

The manner of transfer and the negotiation that is used determine how far and to whom a transfer warranty will run. Transfer of order paper, for consideration, by indorsement and delivery extends warranty liability to any subsequent holder who takes the instrument in good faith. The warranties of a person who transfers *without indorsement* (by the delivery of a bearer instrument), however, will extend the transferor's warranties only to the immediate transferee [UCC 3–416(a)].

Presentment Warranties

Any person who presents an instrument for payment or acceptance makes the following **presentment warranties** to any other person who in good faith pays or accepts the instrument [UCC 3–417(a), 3–417(d)]:

1 The person obtaining payment or acceptance is entitled to enforce the instrument or is authorized to obtain payment or acceptance on behalf of a person who is entitled to

TRANSFER WARRANTIES
Implied warranties, made by any person who transfers an instrument for consideration to subsequent transferees and holders who take the instrument in good faith, that (1) the transferor is entitled to enforce the instrument; (2) all signatures are authentic and authorized; (3) the instrument has not been altered; (4) the instrument is not subject to a defense or claim of any party that can be asserted against the transferor; and (5) the transferor has no knowledge of any insolvency proceedings against the maker, the acceptor, or the drawer of the instrument.

PRESENTMENT WARRANTIES
Implied warranties, made by any person who presents an instrument for payment or acceptance, that (1) the person obtaining payment or acceptance is entitled to enforce the instrument or is authorized to obtain payment or acceptance on behalf of a person who is entitled to enforce the instrument, (2) the instrument has not been altered, and (3) the person obtaining payment or acceptance has no knowledge that the signature of the drawer of the instrument is unauthorized.

---

5. A 2002 amendment to UCC 3–416(a) adds a sixth warranty: "with respect to a remotely created consumer item, that the person on whose account the item is drawn authorized the issuance of the item in the amount for which the item is drawn." UCC 3–103(16) defines a "remotely created consumer item" as an item, such as a check, drawn on a consumer account, which is not created by the payor bank and does not contain the drawer's handwritten signature. For example, a telemarketer submits an instrument to a bank for payment, claiming that the consumer on whose account the instrument purports to be drawn authorized it over the phone. Under this amendment, a bank that accepts and pays the instrument warrants to the next bank in the collection chain that the consumer authorized the item in that amount.

enforce the instrument. (This is, in effect, a warranty that there are no missing or unauthorized indorsements.)

2 The instrument has not been altered.

3 The person obtaining payment or acceptance has no knowledge that the signature of the issuer of the instrument is unauthorized.[6]

These warranties are referred to as presentment warranties because they protect the person to whom the instrument is presented. The second and third warranties do not apply to makers, acceptors, and drawers. It is assumed, for example, that a drawer or a maker will recognize his or her own signature and that a maker or an acceptor will recognize whether an instrument has been materially altered.

How should these warranties apply when two banks dispute whether a check was altered and its paper copy has been destroyed, leaving only its digital image? That was the question in the following case.

---

6. As discussed in footnote 5, the 2002 amendments to Article 3 of the UCC provide additional protection for "remotely created" consumer items [see Amended UCC 3–417(a)(4)].

CASE 14.3 **Wachovia Bank, N.A. v. Foster Bancshares, Inc.**

United States Court of Appeals, Seventh Circuit, 457 F.3d 619 (2006).

FACTS Sunjin Choi Choi deposited in her account at Foster Bank in Chicago, Illinois, a check for $133,026, on which she appeared to be the payee. The check was drawn on the account of MediaEdge, LLC, at Wachovia Bank, N.A., in Charlotte, North Carolina. Foster presented the check to Wachovia, which paid it and debited MediaEdge's account. Wachovia then made a digital copy of the check and destroyed the paper check. The payee of the check as originally issued was not Choi, however, but CMP Media, Inc. Before MediaEdge learned that CMP had not received the check, Choi withdrew the funds from her account and disappeared. MediaEdge asked Wachovia to recredit its account. Wachovia filed a suit in a federal district court against Foster Bank, seeking the amount of the check on the basis of the presentment warranty that an instrument has not been altered. The court issued a summary judgment in Wachovia's favor. Foster appealed to the U.S. Court of Appeals for the Seventh Circuit. Because the original paper check had been destroyed and it could not be determined from the digital copy whether the paper check had been altered, Foster argued that it should be assumed that the check was forged. Under that assumption, Wachovia, not Foster, would be liable for the loss. (Liability on a forged check will be discussed in detail in Chapter 15.)

ISSUE If the payee of a check presented for payment is not the payee of the check as it was originally issued, should it be assumed that the changed payee's name was forged?

DECISION No. The U.S. Court of Appeals for the Seventh Circuit affirmed the lower court's judgment. "Changing the payee's name is the classic alteration. It can with modern technology be effected by forging a check rather than by altering an original check, but since this is a novel method, the presenting bank must do more than merely assert the possibility of it."

REASON The appellate court stated that a bank in which a check is deposited may reasonably suspect the payee's name has been altered even if there is no visible evidence such as traces of a chemical wash. "The size of the check may be a warning flag that induces the bank to delay making funds deposited by the check available for withdrawal." The court also emphasized what Foster did *not* prove: that keeping a paper copy of the check would have been "a reasonable method of determining whether the drawee bank or the presenting bank should be liable for the loss"; that the forgery of checks was a more common method of bank fraud than their alteration; that banks normally contract for a different

CASE 14.3–Continues next page

CASE 14.3–Continued

allocation of liability than the UCC provides; or that Choi's *modus operandi* (usual method of operation) was to forge checks instead of to alter them. Here, the check deposited with Foster "was for a hefty $133,000, and there is no evidence that Choi had previously deposited large checks. We do not suggest that Foster was careless in deciding to make the money available for withdrawal when it did. But the uncertainties that the bank has made no effort to dispel counsel against [making the assumption] that it urges."

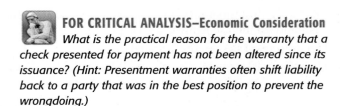

FOR CRITICAL ANALYSIS–Economic Consideration
What is the practical reason for the warranty that a check presented for payment has not been altered since its issuance? (Hint: Presentment warranties often shift liability back to a party that was in the best position to prevent the wrongdoing.)

DEFENSES TO LIABILITY

Persons who would otherwise be liable on negotiable instruments may be able to avoid liability by raising certain defenses. Two general categories of defenses—*universal defenses* and *personal defenses*—are discussed below and summarized in Exhibit 14–8 on page 436.

Universal Defenses

UNIVERSAL DEFENSES
Defenses that are valid against all holders of a negotiable instrument, including holders in due course (HDCs) and holders with the rights of HDCs.

Universal defenses (also called *real defenses*) are valid against *all* holders, including HDCs and holders who take through an HDC. Universal defenses include those described here.

Forgery Forgery of a maker's or drawer's signature cannot bind the person whose name is used unless that person ratifies (approves or validates) the signature or is barred from denying it (because the forgery was made possible by the maker's or drawer's negligence, for example) [UCC 3–403(a)]. Thus, when a person forges an instrument, the person whose name is forged normally has no liability to pay any holder or any HDC the value of the forged instrument.

Fraud in the Execution If a person is deceived into signing a negotiable instrument, believing that she or he is signing something other than a negotiable instrument (such as a receipt), *fraud in the execution*, or fraud in the inception, is committed against the signer [UCC 3–305(a)(1)]. **EXAMPLE 14.20** Gerard, a salesperson, asks Javier, a customer, to sign a paper, which Gerard says is a receipt for the delivery of goods that Javier is picking up from the store. In fact, the paper is a promissory note, but Javier is unfamiliar with the English language and does not realize this. In this situation, even if the note is negotiated to an HDC, Javier has a valid defense against payment. ■

The defense of fraud in the execution cannot be raised, however, if a reasonable inquiry would have revealed the nature and terms of the instrument.[7] Thus, the signer's age, experience, and intelligence are relevant because they frequently determine whether the signer should have known the nature of the transaction before signing.

Material Alteration An alteration is material if it changes the contract terms between any two parties *in any way*. Examples of material alterations include completing an incomplete instrument, adding words or numbers to an instrument, or making any other change to an instrument in an unauthorized manner that affects the obligation of a party

---

7. *Burchett v. Allied Concord Financial Corp.*, 74 N.M. 575, 396 P.2d 186 (1964).

to the instrument [UCC 3–407(a)]. Making any change in the amount, the date, or the rate of interest—even if the change is only one penny, one day, or 1 percent—is material.

It is not a material alteration, however, to correct the maker's address or to change the figures on a check so that they agree with the written amount. If the alteration is not material, any holder is entitled to enforce the instrument according to its terms.

Material alteration is a *complete defense* against an ordinary holder, but only a partial defense against an HDC. An ordinary holder can recover nothing on an instrument if it has been materially altered [UCC 3–407(b)]. When the holder is an HDC, by contrast, if an original term, such as the monetary amount payable, has been *altered*, the HDC can enforce the instrument against the maker or drawer according to the original terms but not for the altered amount. If the instrument was originally incomplete and was later completed in an unauthorized manner, however, alteration no longer can be claimed as a defense against an HDC, and the HDC can enforce the instrument as completed [UCC 3–407(b)]. This is because the drawer or maker of the instrument, by issuing an incomplete instrument, will normally be held responsible for the alteration, which could have been avoided by the exercise of greater care. If the alteration is readily apparent, then obviously the holder has notice of some defect or defense and therefore cannot be an HDC [UCC 3–302(a)(1)].

Discharge in Bankruptcy Discharge in bankruptcy (see Chapter 16) is an absolute defense on any instrument, regardless of the status of the holder, because the purpose of bankruptcy is to settle finally all of the insolvent party's debts [UCC 3–305(a)(1)].

Minority Minority, or infancy, is a universal defense only to the extent that state law recognizes it as a defense to a simple contract (see Chapter 8). Because state laws on minority vary, so do determinations of whether minority is a universal defense against an HDC [UCC 3–305(a)(1)(i)].

Illegality Certain types of illegality constitute universal defenses. Other types constitute personal defenses—that is, defenses that are effective against ordinary holders but not against HDCs. If a statute provides that an illegal transaction is void, then the defense is universal—that is, absolute against both an ordinary holder and an HDC. If the law merely makes the instrument voidable, then the illegality is still a personal defense against an ordinary holder but not against an HDC [UCC 3–305(a)(1)(ii)].

> **BE AWARE** Minority, illegality, mental incapacity, and duress can be universal defenses or personal defenses, depending in some circumstances on state law rather than the UCC.

Mental Incapacity If a person has been declared by a court to be mentally incompetent, then any instrument issued thereafter by that person is void. The instrument is void *ab initio* (from the beginning) and unenforceable by any holder or HDC [UCC 3–305(a)(1)(ii)]. Mental incapacity in these circumstances is thus a universal defense. If a court has not declared a person to be mentally incompetent, then mental incapacity operates as a defense against an ordinary holder but not against an HDC.

Extreme Duress When a person signs and issues a negotiable instrument under such extreme duress as an immediate threat of force or violence (for example, at gunpoint), the instrument is void and unenforceable by any holder or HDC [UCC 3–305(a)(1)(ii)]. (Ordinary duress is a defense against ordinary holders but not against HDCs.)

Personal Defenses

Personal defenses (sometimes called *limited defenses*), such as those described here, can be used to avoid payment to an ordinary holder of a negotiable instrument, but not to an HDC or a holder with the rights of an HDC.

PERSONAL DEFENSES
Defenses that can be used to avoid payment to an ordinary holder of a negotiable instrument but not a holder in due course (HDC) or a holder with the rights of an HDC.

Breach of Contract or Breach of Warranty   When there is a breach of the underlying contract for which the negotiable instrument was issued, the maker of a note can refuse to pay it, or the drawer of a check can order his or her bank to stop payment on the check. Breach of warranty can also be claimed as a defense to liability on the instrument.

■EXAMPLE 14.21   Rhoda agrees to purchase several sets of imported china from Livingston. The china is to be delivered in four weeks. Rhoda gives Livingston a promissory note for $2,000, which is the price of the china. The china arrives, but many of the pieces are broken, and several others are chipped or cracked. Rhoda refuses to pay the note on the basis of breach of contract and breach of warranty. (Recall from Chapter 13 that a seller impliedly promises that the goods are at least merchantable.) Livingston cannot enforce payment on the note because of the breach of contract and breach of warranty. If Livingston has negotiated the note to a third party, however, and the third party is an HDC, Rhoda will not be able to use breach of contract or warranty as a defense against liability on the note. ■

Lack or Failure of Consideration   The absence of consideration (value) may be a successful personal defense in some instances [UCC 3–303(b), 3–305(a)(2)]. **■EXAMPLE 14.22**   Tara gives Clem, as a gift, a note that states, "I promise to pay you $100,000." Clem accepts the note. Because there is no consideration for Tara's promise, a court will not enforce the promise. ■

Fraud in the Inducement (Ordinary Fraud)   A person who issues a negotiable instrument based on false statements by the other party will be able to avoid payment on that instrument, unless the holder is an HDC. **■EXAMPLE 14.23**   Jerry agrees to purchase Howard's used tractor for $24,500. Howard, knowing his statements to be false, tells Jerry that the tractor is in good working order, that it has been used for only one harvest, and that he owns the tractor free and clear of all claims. Jerry pays Howard $4,500

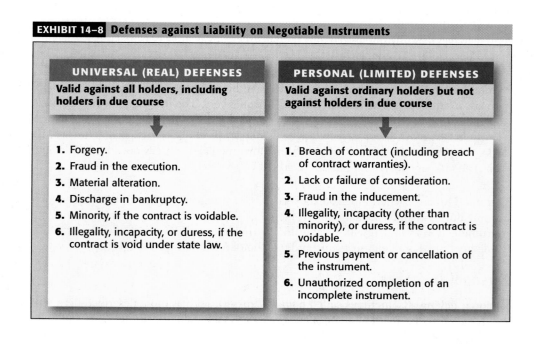

EXHIBIT 14–8 Defenses against Liability on Negotiable Instruments

UNIVERSAL (REAL) DEFENSES	PERSONAL (LIMITED) DEFENSES
Valid against all holders, including holders in due course	Valid against ordinary holders but not against holders in due course
1. Forgery.	1. Breach of contract (including breach of contract warranties).
2. Fraud in the execution.	2. Lack or failure of consideration.
3. Material alteration.	3. Fraud in the inducement.
4. Discharge in bankruptcy.	4. Illegality, incapacity (other than minority), or duress, if the contract is voidable.
5. Minority, if the contract is voidable.	5. Previous payment or cancellation of the instrument.
6. Illegality, incapacity, or duress, if the contract is void under state law.	6. Unauthorized completion of an incomplete instrument.

in cash and issues a negotiable promissory note for the balance. As it turns out, Howard still owes the original seller $10,000 on the purchase of the tractor. In addition, the tractor is three years old and has been used in three harvests. Jerry can refuse to pay the note if it is held by an ordinary holder. If Howard has negotiated the note to an HDC, however, Jerry must pay the HDC. (Of course, Jerry can then sue Howard to recover the funds paid.) ◾

Illegality   As mentioned, if a statute provides that an illegal transaction is void, a universal defense exists. If, however, the statute provides that an illegal transaction is voidable, the defense is personal.

Mental Incapacity   As mentioned, if a maker or drawer has been declared by a court to be mentally incompetent, any instrument issued by the maker or drawer is void. In that situation, mental incapacity is a universal defense [UCC 3–305(a)(1)(ii)]. If a maker or drawer issues a negotiable instrument while mentally incompetent but before a formal court hearing has declared him or her to be so, however, the instrument is voidable. In this situation, mental incapacity can serve only as a personal defense.

Other Personal Defenses   Other personal defenses that can be used to avoid payment to an ordinary holder of a negotiable instrument include the following:

1 Discharge by payment or cancellation [UCC 3–601(b), 3–602(a), 3–603, 3–604].

2 Unauthorized completion of an incomplete instrument [UCC 3–115, 3–302, 3–407, 4–401(d)(2)].

3 Nondelivery of the instrument [UCC 1–201(14), 3–105(b), 3–305(a)(2)].

4 Ordinary duress or undue influence rendering the contract voidable [UCC 3–305(a)(1)(ii)].

REVIEWING **Negotiable Instruments**

Nancy Mahar was the office manager at Golden Years Nursing Home, Inc. She was given a signature stamp to issue checks to the nursing home's employees for up to $100 as advances on their pay. The checks were drawn on Golden Years' account at First National Bank. Over a seven-year period, Mahar wrote a number of checks to employees exclusively for the purpose of embezzling funds for herself. She forged the employees' indorsements on the checks, signed her name as a second indorser, and deposited the checks in her personal account at Star Bank. The employees whose names were on the checks never actually requested

them. When the scheme was uncovered, Golden Years filed a suit against Mahar, Star Bank, and others to recover the funds. Using the information presented in the chapter, answer the following questions.

1 With regard to signature liability, which UCC provision discussed in this chapter applies to this scenario?

2 What is the rule set forth by that provision?

3 Under the UCC, which party, Golden Years or Star Bank, must bear the loss in this situation? Why?

4 Based on these facts, describe any transfer or presentment warranties that Mahar may have violated.

APPLICATION How Can You Avoid Pitfalls When Writing and Indorsing Checks?*

A s a businessperson (or as a consumer), you will certainly be writing and receiving checks. Both activities can involve pitfalls.

Checks Drawn in Blank

The danger in signing a blank check is clear. Anyone can write in an unauthorized amount and cash the check. Although you may be able to assert lack of authorization against the person who filled in the unauthorized amount, subsequent holders of the properly indorsed check may be able to enforce the check as completed. While you are haggling with the person who inserted the unauthorized figure and who may not be able to repay the amount, you will also have to honor the check for the unauthorized amount to a subsequent holder in due course.

Checks Payable to "Cash"

It is equally dangerous to write out and sign a check payable to "cash" until you are actually at the bank. Remember that checks payable to "cash" are bearer instruments. This means that if you lose or misplace the check, anybody who finds it can present it (with proper identification) to the bank for payment.

Checks Indorsed in Blank

Just as a check signed in blank or payable to "cash" may be dangerous, a negotiable instrument with a blank indorsement

also has dangers; as a bearer instrument, it may be easily transferred as cash. When you make a bank deposit, therefore, you should sign (indorse) the back of the check in blank only in the presence of a teller. If you choose to sign it ahead of time, make sure you insert the words "For deposit only" before you sign your name. As a precaution, you should consider obtaining an indorsement stamp from your bank. Then, when a check is received payable to your business, you can indorse it immediately. The stamped indorsement will indicate that the check is for deposit only to your business account specified by the number.

CHECKLIST FOR THE USE OF NEGOTIABLE INSTRUMENTS

1 A good rule of thumb is never to sign a blank check.
2 Another good rule of thumb is never to write and sign a check payable to "cash" until you are actually at the bank. If you must write the check ahead of time, consider making the check payable to the bank rather than to "cash."
3 Be wary of indorsing a check in blank unless a bank teller is simultaneously giving you a receipt for your deposit.
4 Consider obtaining an indorsement stamp from your bank so that when you receive checks you can immediately indorse them "For deposit only" to your account.

* This *Application* is not meant to substitute for the services of an attorney who is licensed to practice law in your state.

KEY TERMS

acceptance 417	holder 422	personal defenses 435
acceptor 427	holder in due course (HDC) 423	presentment 427
bearer instrument 422	imposter 430	presentment warranty 432
certificate of deposit (CD) 420	indorsement 422	promissory note 419
check 418	maker 419	shelter principle 426
draft 417	negotiable instrument 415	trade acceptance 418
drawee 417	negotiation 422	transfer warranty 432
drawer 417	order instrument 422	universal defenses 434
fictitious payee 430	payee 417	

CHAPTER SUMMARY — Negotiable Instruments

Types of Negotiable Instruments (See pages 416–420.)	To be negotiable, an instrument must meet the requirements stated below, which are explained in greater detail in Exhibit 14–1 on page 416.

1. Be in writing.
2. Be signed by the maker or drawer.
3. Be an unconditional promise or order to pay.
4. State a fixed amount of money.
5. Be payable on demand or at a definite time.
6. Be payable to order or bearer.

The UCC specifies four types of negotiable instruments: drafts, checks, promissory notes, and certificates of deposit (CDs). These instruments fall into two basic classifications:

1. *Demand instruments versus time instruments*—A demand instrument is payable on demand (when the holder presents it to the maker or drawer). A time instrument is payable at a future date.
2. *Orders to pay versus promises to pay*—Checks and drafts are *orders* to pay. Promissory notes and CDs are *promises* to pay.

Transfer of Instruments (See pages 420–423.)

1. *Transfer by assignment*—A transfer by assignment to an assignee gives the assignee only those rights that the assignor possessed. Any defenses against payment that can be raised against an assignor can normally be raised against the assignee.
2. *Transfer by negotiation*—An order instrument is negotiated by indorsement and delivery; a bearer instrument is negotiated by delivery only.

Holder in Due Course (HDC) (See pages 423–426.)

Holder in due course (HDC)—A holder who, by meeting certain acquisition requirements (summarized next), takes the instrument free of most defenses and claims to which the transferor was subject. To be an HDC, a holder must take the instrument:

1. *For value*—A holder can take an instrument for value in one of five ways [UCC 3–303]:
   a. By the complete or partial performance of the promise for which the instrument was issued or transferred.
   b. By acquiring a security interest or other lien in the instrument, excluding a lien obtained by a judicial proceeding.
   c. By taking an instrument in payment of (or as security for) a preexisting debt.
   d. By giving a negotiable instrument as payment.
   e. By giving an irrevocable commitment as payment.
2. *In good faith*—Good faith is defined as "honesty in fact and the observance of reasonable commercial standards of fair dealing" [UCC 3–103(a)(4)].
3. *Without notice*—To be an HDC, a holder must not be on notice that the instrument is defective in any of the following ways [UCC 3–302, 3–304]:
   a. The instrument is overdue.
   b. The instrument has been dishonored.
   c. There is an uncured (uncorrected) default with respect to another instrument issued as part of the same series.
   d. The instrument contains an unauthorized signature or has been altered.

(Continued)

CHAPTER SUMMARY	Negotiable Instruments—Continued
Holder in Due Course (HDC)— Continued	e. There is a defense against the instrument or a claim to the instrument. f. The instrument is so irregular or incomplete as to call into question its authenticity.
Holder through an HDC (See page 426.)	A holder who cannot qualify as an HDC has the *rights* of an HDC if he or she derives title through an HDC, unless the holder engaged in fraud or illegality affecting the instrument [UCC 3–203(b)]. This is known as the shelter principle.

Signature Liability (See pages 426–431.)	Every party (except a qualified indorser) who signs a negotiable instrument is either primarily or secondarily liable for payment of the instrument when it comes due.
	
	1. *Primary liability*—Makers and acceptors are primarily liable (an acceptor is a drawee who promises in writing to pay an instrument when it is presented for payment at a later time) [UCC 3–115, 3–407, 3–409, 3–412].
	
	2. *Secondary liability*—Drawers and indorsers are secondarily liable [UCC 3–412, 3–414, 3–415, 3–501, 3–502, 3–503]. Parties who are secondarily liable on an instrument promise to pay on that instrument if the following events occur:
	
	  a. The instrument is properly and timely presented.
	
	  b. The instrument is dishonored.
	
	  c. Timely notice of dishonor is given to the secondarily liable party.
	
	3. *Unauthorized signatures*—An unauthorized signature is wholly inoperative *unless:*
	
	  a. The person whose name is signed ratifies (affirms) it or is precluded from denying it [UCC 3–115, 3–403, 3–406, 4–401(d)(2)].
	
	  b. The instrument has been negotiated to an HDC [UCC 3–403].
	
	4. *Special rules for unauthorized indorsements*—An unauthorized indorsement will not bind the maker or drawer except in the following circumstances:
	
	  a. When an imposter induces the maker or drawer of an instrument to issue it to the imposter (imposter rule) [UCC 3–404(a)].
	
	  b. When a person signs as or on behalf of a maker or drawer, intending that the payee will have no interest in the instrument, or when an agent or employee of the maker or drawer has supplied him or her with the name of the payee, also intending the payee to have no such interest (fictitious payee rule) [UCC 3–404(b), 3–405].

Warranty Liability (See pages 432–434.)	1. *Transfer warranties*—Any person who transfers an instrument for consideration makes the following warranties to all subsequent transferees and holders who take the instrument in good faith (but when a bearer instrument is transferred by delivery only, the transferor's warranties extend only to the immediate transferee) [UCC 3–416]:
	
	  a. The transferor is entitled to enforce the instrument.
	
	  b. All signatures are authentic and authorized.
	
	  c. The instrument has not been altered.
	
	  d. The instrument is not subject to a defense or claim of any party that can be asserted against the transferor.
	
	  e. The transferor has no knowledge of any insolvency proceedings against the maker, the acceptor, or the drawer of the instrument.
	
	2. *Presentment warranties*—Any person who presents an instrument for payment or acceptance makes the following warranties to any other person who in good faith pays or accepts the instrument [UCC 3–417(a), 3–417(d)]:

CHAPTER SUMMARY Negotiable Instruments—Continued

Warranty Liability—Continued	a. The person obtaining payment or acceptance is entitled to enforce the instrument or is authorized to obtain payment or acceptance on behalf of a person who is entitled to enforce the instrument. (This is, in effect, a warranty that there are no missing or unauthorized indorsements.)
	b. The instrument has not been altered.
	c. The person obtaining payment or acceptance has no knowledge that the signature of the drawer of the instrument is unauthorized.
Defenses to Liability (See pages 434–437.)	1. *Universal (real) defenses*—The following defenses are valid against all holders, including HDCs and holders with the rights of HDCs [UCC 3–305, 3–403, 3–407]:
	a. Forgery.
	b. Fraud in the execution.
	c. Material alteration.
	d. Discharge in bankruptcy.
	e. Minority—if the contract is voidable under state law.
	f. Illegality, mental incapacity, or extreme duress—if the contract is void under state law.
	2. *Personal (limited) defenses*—The following defenses are valid against ordinary holders but not against HDCs or holders with the rights of HDCs [UCC 3–105, 3–115, 3–302, 3–305, 3–306, 3–407, 3–601, 3–602, 3–603, 3–604, 4–401]:
	a. Breach of contract or breach of warranty.
	b. Lack or failure of consideration (value).
	c. Fraud in the inducement.
	d. Illegality and mental incapacity—if the contract is voidable.
	e. Previous payment of the instrument.
	f. Unauthorized completion of the instrument.
	g. Nondelivery of the instrument.
	h. Ordinary duress or undue influence that renders the contract voidable.

FOR REVIEW

Answers for the even-numbered questions in this For Review *section can be found in Appendix E at the end of this text.*

1 What are the four types of negotiable instruments with which Article 3 of the UCC is concerned? Which of these instruments are *orders* to pay, and which are *promises* to pay?

2 What requirements must an instrument meet to be negotiable?

3 What are the requirements for attaining HDC status?

4 What is the key to liability on a negotiable instrument? What is the difference between signature liability and warranty liability?

5 Certain defenses are valid against all holders, including HDCs. What are these defenses called? Name four defenses that fall within this category.

QUESTIONS AND CASE PROBLEMS

HYPOTHETICAL SCENARIOS

14.1 Indorsements. Bertram writes a check for $200, payable to "cash." He puts the check in his pocket and drives to the bank to cash the check. As he gets out of his car in the bank's parking lot, the check slips out of his pocket and falls to the pavement. Jerrod walks by moments later, picks up the check, and later that day delivers it to Amber, to whom he owes $200. Amber indorses the check "For deposit only. [Signed] Amber Dowel" and deposits it into her checking account. In light of these circumstances, answer the following questions.

1 Is the check a bearer instrument or an order instrument?

2 Did Jerrod's delivery of the check to Amber constitute a valid negotiation? Why or why not?

3 What type of indorsement did Amber make?

4 Does Bertram have a right to recover the $200 from Amber? Explain.

14.2 Hypothetical Question with Sample Answer. Muriel Evans writes the following note on the back of an envelope: "I, Muriel Evans, promise to pay Karen Marvin or bearer $100 on demand." Is this a negotiable instrument? Discuss fully.

 **For a sample answer to Question 14.2, go to Appendix F at the end of this text.**

14.3 Signature Liability. Marion makes a promissory note payable to the order of Perry. Perry indorses the note by writing "without recourse, Perry" and transfers the note for value to Steven. Steven, in need of cash, negotiates the note to Harriet by indorsing it with the words "Pay to Harriet, [signed] Steven." On the due date, Harriet presents the note to Marion for payment, only to learn that Marion has filed for bankruptcy and will have all debts (including the note) discharged in bankruptcy. Discuss fully whether Harriet can hold Marion, Perry, or Steven liable on the note.

■

CASE PROBLEMS

14.4 Negotiability. In October 1998, Somerset Valley Bank notified Alfred Hauser, president of Hauser Co., that the bank had begun to receive what appeared to be Hauser Co. payroll checks. None of the payees were Hauser Co. employees, however, and Hauser had not written the checks or authorized anyone to sign them on his behalf. Automatic Data Processing, Inc., provided payroll services for Hauser Co. and used a facsimile signature on all its payroll checks. Hauser told the bank not to cash the checks. In early 1999, Robert Triffin, who deals in negotiable instruments, bought eighteen of the checks, totaling more than $8,800, from various check-cashing agencies. The agencies stated that they had cashed the checks expecting the bank to pay them. Each check was payable to a bearer for a fixed amount, on demand, and did not state any undertaking by the person promising payment other than the payment of money. Each check bore a facsimile drawer's signature stamp identical to Hauser Co.'s authorized stamp. Each check had been returned to an agency marked "stolen check" and stamped "do not present again." When the bank refused to cash the checks, Triffin filed a suit in a New Jersey state court against Hauser Co. Were the checks negotiable instruments? Why or why not? [*Triffin v. Somerset Valley Bank,* 343 N.J.Super. 73, 777 A.2d 993 (2001)]

14.5 Defenses. On September 13, 1979, Barbara Shearer and Barbara Couvion signed a note for $22,500, with interest at

11 percent, payable in monthly installments of $232.25 to Edgar House and Paul Cook. House and Cook assigned the note to Southside Bank in Kansas City, Missouri. In 1997, the note was assigned to Midstates Resources Corp., which assigned the note to The Cadle Co. in 2000. According to the payment history that Midstates gave to Cadle, the interest rate on the note was 12 percent. A Cadle employee noticed the discrepancy and recalculated the payments at 11 percent. When Shearer and Couvion refused to make further payments on the note, Cadle filed a suit in a Missouri state court against them to collect. Couvion and Shearer responded that they had made timely payments on the note, that Cadle and the previous holders had failed to accurately apply the payments to the reduction of principal and interest, and that the note "is either paid in full and satisfied or very close to being paid in full and satisfied." Is the makers' answer sufficient to support a verdict in their favor? If so, on what ground? If not, why not? [*The Cadle Co. v. Shearer,* 69 S.W.3d 122 (Mo.App.W.D. 2002)]

14.6 Transfer of Instruments. In July 1988, Chester Crow executed a promissory note payable "to the order of THE FIRST NATIONAL BANK OF SHREVEPORT or BEARER" in the amount of $21,578.42 at an interest rate of 3 percent per year above the "prime rate in effect at The First National Bank of Shreveport" in Shreveport, Louisiana, until paid. The note was a standard preprinted promissory note. In 1999, Credit Recoveries, Inc., filed a suit in a Louisiana state court against Crow, alleging that he owed $7,222.57 on the note, plus interest. Crow responded that the debt represented by the note had been canceled by the bank in September 1994. He further contended that in any event, to collect on the note, Credit Recoveries had to prove that it legitimately owned the note. When no evidence of ownership was forthcoming, Crow filed a motion to dismiss the suit. Is the note an order instrument or a bearer instrument? How might it have been transferred to Credit Recoveries? With this in mind, should the court dismiss the suit on the basis of Crow's contention? [*Credit Recoveries, Inc. v. Crow*, 862 So.2d 1146 (La.App. 2d Cir. 2003)]

14.7 Case Problem with Sample Answer. Harford Mutual Insurance Co. issued a check for $60,150 payable to "Andrew Michael Bogdan, Jr., Crystal Bogdan, Oceanmark Bank FSB, Goodman-Gable-Gould Company." The check was to pay a claim related to the Bogdans' commercial property. Besides the Bogdans, the payees were the mortgage holder (Oceanmark) and the insurance agent who adjusted the claim. The Bogdans and the agent indorsed the check and cashed it at Provident Bank of Maryland. Meanwhile, Oceanmark sold the mortgage to Pelican National Bank, which asked Provident to pay it the amount of the check. Provident refused. Pelican filed a suit in a Maryland state court against Provident, arguing that the check had been improperly negotiated. Was this check payable jointly or in the alternative? Whose indorsements were required to cash it? In whose favor should the court rule? Explain. [*Pelican National Bank v. Provident Bank of Maryland*, 381 Md. 327, 849 A.2d 475 (2004)]

 After you have answered Problem 14.7, compare your answer with the sample answer given on the Web site that accompanies this text. Go to academic.cengage.com/blaw/blt, select "Chapter 14," and click on "Case Problem with Sample Answer."

14.8 Requirements for HDC Status. Deola Bishop sold her home in Cameron County, Texas, to Cristobol and Juana Elisa Gonzalez in 1998. The Gonzalezes signed a note for $76,500 payable to Bishop. In January 2000, Bishop saw a newspaper ad in which American Notice Investments, Inc. (ANI), was soliciting such notes (ANI was in the business of buying notes at a discount). Bishop responded to the ad. ANI contacted First National Acceptance Co. (FNAC) to borrow the funds to make the purchase. FNAC approved the deal. ANI sent the note to FNAC, which authorized payment to Bishop on the note. ANI did not pay Bishop, however, before it ceased doing business. FNAC also did not pay Bishop, refused to return the note, and told the Gonzalezes to make their payments on the note to FNAC. Bishop and the Gonzalezes filed a suit in a Texas state court against FNAC, contending, in part, that Bishop was entitled to the note. FNAC asserted that it was a holder in due course (HDC). What is the reason for the HDC doctrine? What are the requirements for HDC status? Does FNAC qualify? Discuss. [*First National Acceptance Co. v. Bishop*, 187 S.W.3d 710 (Tex.App.—Corpus Christi 2006)]

14.9 **A Question of Ethics.** *As an assistant comptroller for Interior Crafts, Inc., in Chicago, Illinois, Todd Leparski was authorized to receive checks from Interior's customers and deposit the checks into Interior's account. Between October 2000 and February 2001, Leparski stole more than $500,000 from Interior by indorsing the checks "Interior Crafts—For Deposit Only" but depositing some of them into his own account at Marquette Bank through an automated teller machine owned by Pan American Bank. Marquette alerted Interior, which was able to recover about $250,000 from Leparski. Interior also recovered $250,000 under its policy with American Insurance Co. To collect the rest of the missing funds, Interior filed a suit in an Illinois state court against Leparski and the banks. The court ruled in favor of Interior, and Pan American appealed to a state intermediate appellate court.* [*Interior Crafts, Inc. v. Leparski*, 366 Ill.App.3d 1148, 853 N.E.2d 1244, 304 Ill.Dec. 878 (3 Dist. 2006)]

1 What type of indorsement is "Interior Crafts—For Deposit Only"? What is the obligation of a party that receives a check with this indorsement? Does the fact that Interior authorized Leparski to indorse its checks but not to deposit those checks into his own account absolve Pan American of liability? Explain.

2 From an ethical perspective, how might a business firm like Interior discourage an employee's thievery, such as Leparski's acts in this case? Discuss.

CRITICAL THINKING AND WRITING ASSIGNMENTS

14.10 Critical Legal Thinking. How does the concept of holder in due course further Article 3's general goal of encouraging the negotiability of instruments? How does it further Article 3's goal of balancing the rights of parties to negotiable instruments?

14.11 Video Question. Go to this text's Web site at academic. cengage.com/blaw/blt and select "Chapter 14." Click on "Video Questions" and view the video titled *Negotiability & Transferability: Indorsing Checks.* Then answer the following questions.

1 According to the instructor in the video, what are the two reasons why banks generally require a person to indorse a check that is made out to "cash" (a bearer instrument), even when the check is signed in the presence of the teller?

2 Suppose that your friend makes out a check payable to "cash," signs it, and hands it to you. You take the check to your bank and indorse the check with your name and the words "without recourse." What type of indorsement is this? How does this indorsement affect the bank's rights?

3 Now suppose that you go to your bank and write a check on your account payable to "cash" for $500. The teller gives you the cash *without* asking you to indorse the check. After you leave, the teller slips the check into his pocket. Later, the teller delivers it (without an indorsement) to his friend Carol in payment for a gambling debt. Carol takes your check to her bank, indorses it, and deposits the funds. Discuss whether Carol is a holder in due course.

ONLINE ACTIVITIES

PRACTICAL INTERNET EXERCISES

Go to this text's Web site at **academic.cengage.com/blaw/blt**, select "Chapter 14," and click on "Practical Internet Exercises." There you will find the following Internet research exercises that you can perform to learn more about the topics covered in this chapter.

PRACTICAL INTERNET EXERCISE 14-1 LEGAL PERSPECTIVE—Overview of Negotiable Instruments

PRACTICAL INTERNET EXERCISE 14-2 MANAGEMENT PERSPECTIVE—Holder in Due Course

PRACTICAL INTERNET EXERCISE 14-3 LEGAL PERSPECTIVE—Fictitious Payees

BEFORE THE TEST

Go to this text's Web site at **academic.cengage.com/blaw/blt**, select "Chapter 14," and click on "Interactive Quizzes." You will find a number of interactive questions relating to this chapter.

CHAPTER 15
Checks and Banking in the Digital Age

LEARNING OBJECTIVES

AFTER READING THIS CHAPTER, YOU SHOULD BE ABLE TO ANSWER THE FOLLOWING QUESTIONS:

1 On what types of checks does a bank serve as both the drawer and the drawee? What type of check does a bank agree in advance to accept when the check is presented for payment?

2 When may a bank properly dishonor a customer's check without the bank being liable to the customer? What happens if a bank wrongfully dishonors a customer's check?

3 What duties does the Uniform Commercial Code impose on a bank's customers with regard to forged and altered checks? What are the consequences of a customer's negligence in performing those duties?

4 What are the four most common types of electronic fund transfers?

5 What is e-money, and how is it stored and used? What laws apply to e-money transactions and online banking services?

> **"Money is just what we use to keep tally."**
>
> Henry Ford, 1863–1947
> (American automobile manufacturer)

Checks are the most common type of negotiable instruments regulated by the Uniform Commercial Code (UCC). It is estimated that more than 65 billion personal and commercial checks are written each year in the United States. Checks are convenient to use because they serve as a substitute for cash. Thus, as Henry Ford said in the chapter-opening quotation, checks help us to "keep tally." To be sure, most students today tend to use debit cards rather than checks for many retail transactions. Indeed, debit cards now account for more retail payments than checks. Nonetheless, commercial checks remain an integral part of the U.S. economic system.

Issues relating to checks are governed by Articles 3 and 4 of the UCC. Recall from Chapter 14 that Article 3 establishes the requirements that all negotiable instruments, including checks, must meet. Article 3 also sets forth the rights and liabilities of parties to negotiable instruments. Article 4 of the UCC governs bank deposits and collections as well as bank-customer relationships. Article 4 regulates the relationships of banks with one another as they process checks for payment, and it establishes a framework for deposit and checking agreements between a bank and its customers. A check therefore may fall within the scope of Article 3 and yet be subject to the provisions of Article 4 while in the course of collection. If a conflict between Article 3 and Article 4 arises, Article 4 controls [UCC 4–102(a)].

In this chapter, we first identify the legal characteristics of checks and the legal duties and liabilities that arise when a check is issued. Then we examine the collection process. Increasingly, credit cards, debit cards, and other devices and methods of transferring funds electronically are being used to pay for goods and services. In the latter part of this chapter, we look at the law governing electronic fund transfers.

CHECKS

A **check** is a special type of draft that is drawn on a bank, ordering the bank to pay a fixed amount of money on demand [UCC 3–104(f)]. Article 4 defines a bank as "a person engaged in the business of banking, including a savings bank, savings and loan association, credit union or trust company" [UCC 4–105(1)]. If any other institution (such as a brokerage firm) handles a check for payment or for collection, the check is *not* covered by Article 4.

Recall from Chapter 14 that a person who writes a check is called the *drawer*. The drawer is a depositor in the bank on which the check is drawn. The person to whom the check is payable is the *payee*. The bank or financial institution on which the check is drawn is the *drawee*. If Anita Cruzak writes a check from her checking account to pay her college tuition, she is the drawer, her bank is the drawee, and her college is the payee. We now look at some special types of checks.

Cashier's Checks

Checks are usually three-party instruments, but on certain types of checks, the bank can serve as both the drawer and the drawee. For example, when a bank draws a check on itself, the check is called a **cashier's check** and is a negotiable instrument on issue (see Exhibit 15–1) [UCC 3–104(g)]. Normally, a cashier's check indicates a specific payee. In effect, with a cashier's check, the bank assumes responsibility for paying the check, thus making the check more readily acceptable as a substitute for cash.

■**EXAMPLE 15.1** Kramer needs to pay a moving company $8,000 for moving his household goods to a new home in another state. The moving company requests payment in the form of a cashier's check. Kramer goes to a bank (he does not need to have an account at the bank) and purchases a cashier's check, payable to the moving company, in the amount of $8,000. Kramer has to pay the bank the $8,000 for the check, plus a small service fee. He then gives the check to the moving company. ■

Cashier's checks are sometimes used in the business community as nearly the equivalent of cash. Except in very limited circumstances, the issuing bank must honor its cashier's checks when they are presented for payment. If a bank wrongfully dishonors a cashier's check, a holder can recover from the bank all expenses incurred, interest, and consequential damages [UCC 3–411]. This same rule applies if a bank wrongfully dishonors a certified check (to be discussed shortly) or a teller's check. (A *teller's check* is a check drawn by a bank on another bank or, when drawn on a nonbank, payable at or through a bank [UCC 3–104(h)]).

Traveler's Checks

A **traveler's check** is an instrument that is payable on demand, drawn on or payable at or through a financial institution (such as a bank), and designated as a traveler's check. The

---

CHECK
A draft drawn by a drawer ordering the drawee bank or financial institution to pay a fixed amount of money to the holder on demand.

CASHIER'S CHECK
A check drawn by a bank on itself.

TRAVELER'S CHECK
A check that is payable on demand, drawn on or payable through a financial institution (bank), and designated as a traveler's check.

EXHIBIT 15–1 A Cashier's Check

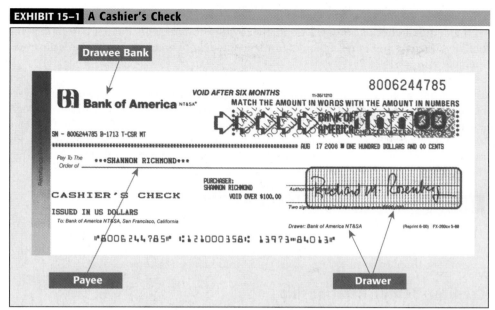

* The abbreviation *NT&SA* stands for National Trust and Savings Association. The Bank of America NT&SA is a subsidiary of BankAmerica Corporation, which is engaged in financial services, insurance, investment management, and other businesses.

institution is directly obligated to accept and pay its traveler's check according to the check's terms. Traveler's checks are designed as a safe substitute for cash when a person is on vacation or traveling and are issued for a fixed amount, such as $20, $50, or $100. The purchaser is required to sign the check at the time it is bought and again at the time it is used [UCC 3–104(i)]. Exhibit 15–2 shows an example of a traveler's check.

Certified Checks

A **certified check** is a check that has been *accepted* in writing by the bank on which it is drawn [UCC 3–409(d)]. When a drawee bank *certifies* (accepts) a check, it immediately charges the drawer's account with the amount of the check and transfers those funds to its own certified check account. In effect, the bank is agreeing in advance to accept that

CERTIFIED CHECK
A check that has been accepted in writing by the bank on which it is drawn. Essentially, the bank, by certifying (accepting) the check, promises to pay the check at the time the check is presented.

EXHIBIT 15–2 A Traveler's Check

check when it is presented for payment and to make payment from those funds reserved in the certified check account. Essentially, certification prevents the bank from denying liability. It is a promise that sufficient funds are on deposit and *have been set aside* to cover the check.

To certify a check, the bank writes or stamps the word *certified* on the face of the check and typically writes the amount that it will pay.[1] Either the drawer or the holder (payee) of a check can request certification, but the drawee bank is not required to certify a check. A bank's refusal to certify a check is not a dishonor of the check [UCC 3–409(d)]. Once a check is certified, the drawer and any prior indorsers are completely discharged from liability on the check [UCC 3–414(c), 3–415(d)]. Only the certifying bank is required to pay the instrument.

THE BANK-CUSTOMER RELATIONSHIP

The bank-customer relationship begins when the customer opens a checking account and deposits funds that the bank will use to pay for checks written by the customer. Essentially, three types of relationships come into being, as discussed next.

Creditor-Debtor Relationship

A creditor-debtor relationship is created between a customer and a bank when, for example, the customer makes cash deposits into a checking account. When a customer makes a deposit, the customer becomes a creditor, and the bank a debtor, for the amount deposited.

Agency Relationship

An agency relationship also arises between the customer and the bank when the customer writes a check on his or her account. In effect, the customer is ordering the bank to pay the amount specified on the check to the holder when the holder presents the check to the bank for payment. In this situation, the bank becomes the customer's agent and is obligated to honor the customer's request. Similarly, if the customer deposits a check into her or his account, the bank, as the customer's agent, is obligated to collect payment on the check from the bank on which the check was drawn. To transfer checkbook funds among different banks, each bank acts as the agent of collection for its customer [UCC 4–201(a)].

Contractual Relationship

Whenever a bank-customer relationship is established, certain contractual rights and duties arise. The specific rights and duties of the bank and its customer depend on the nature of the transaction. The respective rights and duties of banks and their customers are discussed in detail in the following pages.

BANK'S DUTY TO HONOR CHECKS

When a banking institution provides checking services, it agrees to honor the checks written by its customers, with the usual stipulation that the account must have sufficient funds available to pay each check [UCC 4–401(a)]. When a drawee bank *wrongfully* fails to honor a check, it is liable to its customer for damages resulting from its refusal to pay. The

---

1. If the certification does not state an amount, and the amount is later increased and the instrument negotiated to a holder in due course (HDC), the obligation of the certifying bank is the amount of the instrument when it was taken by the HDC [UCC 3–413(b)].

UCC does not attempt to specify the theory under which the customer may recover for wrongful dishonor; it merely states that the drawee (bank) is liable. Thus, the customer does not have to prove that the bank breached its contractual commitment, slandered the customer's credit, or was negligent [UCC 4–402(b)].

The customer's agreement with the bank includes a general obligation to keep sufficient funds on deposit to cover all checks written. The customer is liable to the payee or to the holder of a check in a civil suit if a check is dishonored for insufficient funds. If intent to defraud can be proved, the customer can also be subject to criminal prosecution for writing a bad check.

When the bank properly dishonors a check for insufficient funds, it has no liability to the customer. The bank may rightfully refuse payment on a customer's check in other circumstances as well. We look here at the rights and duties of both the bank and its customers in relation to specific situations.

Overdrafts

When the bank receives an item properly payable from its customer's checking account but the account contains insufficient funds to cover the amount of the check, the bank has two options. It can either (1) dishonor the item or (2) pay the item and charge the customer's account, thus creating an **overdraft,** providing that the customer has authorized the payment and the payment does not violate any bank-customer agreement [UCC 4–401(a)].[2] The bank can subtract the difference (plus a service charge) from the customer's next deposit or other customer funds because the check carries with it an enforceable implied promise to reimburse the bank.

OVERDRAFT
A check that is paid by the bank when the checking account on which the check is written contains insufficient funds to cover the check.

A bank can expressly agree with a customer to accept overdrafts through what is sometimes called an "overdraft protection agreement." If such an agreement is formed, any failure of the bank to honor a check because it would create an overdraft breaches this agreement and is treated as a wrongful dishonor [UCC 4–402(a)].

When a check "bounces," a holder can resubmit the check, hoping that at a later date sufficient funds will be available to pay it. The holder must notify any indorsers on the check of the first dishonor, however; otherwise, they will be discharged from their signature liability (see Chapter 14).

Postdated Checks

A bank may also charge a postdated check against a customer's account, unless the customer notifies the bank, in a timely manner, not to pay the check until the stated date. The notice of postdating must be given in time to allow the bank to act on the notice before committing itself to pay on the check. The UCC states that the bank should treat a notice of postdating the same as a stop-payment order—to be discussed shortly. If the bank fails to act on the customer's notice and charges the customer's account before the date on the postdated check, the bank may be liable for any damages incurred by the customer [UCC 4–401(c)].[3]

---

2. With a joint account, the bank cannot hold the nonsigning customer liable for payment of an overdraft unless that person benefited from its proceeds [UCC 4–401(b)].

3. Under the UCC, postdating does not affect the negotiability of a check. In the distant past, instead of treating postdated checks as checks payable on demand, some courts treated them as time drafts. Thus, regardless of whether the customer notified the bank of the postdating, a bank could not charge a customer's account for a postdated check without facing potential liability for the payment of later checks. Under the automated check-collection system now in use, however, a check is usually paid without respect to its date. Thus, today the bank can ignore the date on the check (treat it as a demand instrument) unless it has received notice from the customer that the check was postdated.

Stale Checks

STALE CHECK
A check, other than a certified check, that is presented for payment more than six months after its date.

Commercial banking practice regards a check that is presented for payment more than six months from its date as a **stale check**. A bank is not obligated to pay an uncertified check presented more than six months from its date [UCC 4–404]. When receiving a stale check for payment, the bank has the option of paying or not paying the check. The bank may consult the customer before paying the check. If a bank pays a stale check in good faith without consulting the customer, however, the bank has the right to charge the customer's account for the amount of the check.

Stop-Payment Orders

STOP-PAYMENT ORDER
An order by a bank customer to his or her bank not to pay or certify a certain check.

A **stop-payment order** is an order by a customer to his or her bank not to pay or certify a certain check. Only a customer or a person authorized to draw on the account can order the bank not to pay the check when it is presented for payment [UCC 4–403(a)].[4] A customer has no right to stop payment on a check that has been certified or accepted by a bank, however. The customer must issue the stop-payment order within a reasonable time and in a reasonable manner to permit the bank to act on it [UCC 4–403(a)]. Although a stop-payment order can be given orally, usually by phone, it is binding on the bank for only fourteen calendar days unless confirmed in writing.[5] A written stop-payment order (the bank typically provides a preprinted form for the customer) or an oral order confirmed in writing is effective for six months, at which time it must be renewed in writing [UCC 4–403(b)].

Bank's Liability for Wrongful Payment   If the bank pays the check in spite of a stop-payment order, the bank will be obligated to recredit the customer's account. In addition, if the bank's payment over a stop-payment order causes subsequent checks written on the drawer's account to "bounce," the bank will be liable for the resultant costs the drawer incurs. The bank is liable only for the amount of the actual damages suffered by the drawer, however [UCC 4–403(c)]. **EXAMPLE 15.2** Toshio Murano orders six bamboo palms from a local nursery at $50 each and gives the nursery a check for $300. Later that day, the nursery tells Murano that it will not deliver the palms as arranged. Murano immediately calls his bank and stops payment on the check. If the bank nonetheless honors the check, the bank will be liable to Murano for the full $300. The result would be different, however, if the nursery had delivered five palms. In that situation, Murano would owe the nursery $250 for the delivered palms, and his actual losses would be only $50. Consequently, the bank would be liable to Murano for only $50. ■

Customer's Liability for Wrongful Stop-Payment Order   A stop-payment order has its risks for a customer. The customer-drawer must have a *valid legal ground* for issuing such an order; otherwise, the holder can sue the drawer for payment. Moreover, defenses sufficient to refuse payment against a payee may not be valid grounds to prevent payment against a subsequent holder in due course [UCC 3–305, 3–306]. A person who wrongfully stops payment on a check is liable to the payee for the amount of the check and can also be liable for consequential damages incurred by the payee. See the *Application* feature at the end of this chapter for guidelines on how and when to use stop-payment orders.

---

4. For a deceased customer, any person claiming a legitimate interest in the account may issue a stop-payment order [UCC 4–405].
5. Some states do not recognize oral stop-payment orders; they must be in writing.

Death or Incompetence of a Customer

Neither the death nor the incompetence of a customer revokes a bank's authority to pay an item until the bank is informed of the situation and has had reasonable time to act on the notice. Thus, if a bank is unaware that the customer who wrote a check has been declared incompetent or has died, the bank can pay the item without incurring liability [UCC 4–405]. Even when a bank knows of the death of its customer, for ten days after the *date of death*, it can pay or certify checks drawn on or before the date of death. An exception to this rule is made if a person claiming an interest in that account, such as an heir, orders the bank to stop payment. Without this provision, banks would constantly be required to verify the continued life and competence of their drawers.

Checks Bearing Forged Drawers' Signatures

When a bank pays a check on which the drawer's signature is forged, generally the bank is liable. A bank may be able to recover at least some of the loss from the customer, however, if the customer's negligence contributed to the making of the forgery. A bank may also obtain partial recovery from the forger of the check (if he or she can be found) or from the holder who presented the check for payment (if the holder knew that the signature was forged).

The General Rule A forged signature on a check has no legal effect as the signature of a drawer [UCC 3–403(a)]. For this reason, banks require a signature card from each customer who opens a checking account. Signature cards allow the bank to verify whether the signatures on their customers' checks are genuine. The general rule is that the bank must recredit the customer's account when it pays a check with a forged signature. (Note that banks today normally verify signatures only on checks that exceed a certain threshold, such as $1,000, $2,500, or some higher amount. Even though a bank sometimes incurs liability costs when it has paid forged checks, the costs involved in verifying every check's signature would be much higher.)

Customer Negligence When the customer's negligence substantially contributes to the forgery, the bank normally will not be obligated to recredit the customer's account for the amount of the check [UCC 3–406]. The customer's liability may be reduced, however, by the amount of loss caused by negligence on the part of the bank (or other "person") paying the instrument or taking it for value if the negligence substantially contributed to the loss [UCC 3–406(b)].

■**EXAMPLE 15.3** Gemco Corporation uses special check-writing equipment to write its payroll and business checks. Gemco discovers that one of its employees used the equipment to write himself a check for $10,000 and that the bank subsequently honored it. Gemco asks the bank to recredit $10,000 to its account for improperly paying the forged check. If the bank can show that Gemco failed to take reasonable care in controlling access to the check-writing equipment, the bank will not be required to recredit Gemco's account for the amount of the forged check. If Gemco can show that negligence on the part of the bank contributed substantially to the loss, however, then Gemco's liability may be reduced proportionately. ■

In the following case, a bank that had paid a forged check claimed that the account holder's negligence had contributed to the forgery. Specifically, the bank alleged that the account holder had failed to exercise ordinary care to prevent his wife from forging a check on the account.

CASE 15.1 Nesper v. Bank of America

Court of Appeals of Ohio, Sixth District, Ottawa County, __ Ohio App.3d __, __ N.E.2d __ (2004).

FACTS Robert Nesper knew that his wife, Patricia Nesper, had engaged in financial misconduct both before and after their marriage. The misconduct included forging Robert's name on applications for credit cards and a contract to buy a vehicle. The couple continued to live together, but Robert kept a bank account in only his name at Bank of America, N.A. He kept the check pads for the account hidden in their house in a room that could be locked, although the room was not locked all of the time. In early 2002, he became aware that Patricia had forged his name to check number 275 for the account in the amount of $2,000. Robert filed a suit in an Ohio state court against the bank, seeking the return of the $2,000 to his account. Robert argued that banks have a responsibility to refuse to honor forged checks, regardless of the marital status of the forger. The court ruled in Robert's favor. The bank appealed to a state intermediate appellate court.

ISSUE Did the bank show that its account holder failed to exercise ordinary care to prevent the forgery of a check by the holder's spouse?

DECISION No. The state intermediate appellate court affirmed the judgment of the lower court. The bank was obliged to recredit its customer's account for the amount of the check.

REASON The appellate court explained that a check with a forged drawer's signature is not properly payable, and if the bank pays it, the bank is generally liable. Under UCC 3–406(a), however, "[a] person whose failure to exercise ordinary care substantially contributes to * * * the making of a forged signature on an instrument is precluded from asserting * * * the forgery against a person who, in good faith, pays the instrument." Ordinary care has been found lacking in cases in which parties who know their signatures have been forged in the past are negligent in failing to prevent further forgeries. Also, a party may ratify a forged check by affirming it—that is, by manifesting an intent to approve it while knowing the facts. Here, the bank failed to show that Robert did not exercise ordinary care with respect to Patricia's forgery of his signature on check number 275 or that he ratified the check.

WHAT IF THE FACTS WERE DIFFERENT? *If the bank had shown that Robert failed to take reasonable care in controlling access to the check pads for his account, would the outcome in this case have been different? Why or why not?*

Timely Examination of Bank Statements Required. Banks typically send or make available to their customers monthly statements detailing activity in their checking accounts. Banks are not obligated to include the canceled checks themselves with the statement sent to the customer. If the bank does not send the canceled checks (or photocopies of the canceled checks), however, it must provide the customer with information (check number, amount, and date of payment) on the statement that will allow the customer to reasonably identify the checks that the bank has paid [UCC 4–406(a), (b)]. If the bank retains the canceled checks, it must keep the checks—or legible copies of the checks—for a period of seven years [UCC 4–406(b)]. The customer may obtain a canceled check (or a copy of the check) during this period of time.

The customer has a duty to examine bank statements (and canceled checks or photocopies, if they are included with the statements) promptly and with reasonable care, and to report any alterations or forged signatures promptly [UCC 4–406(c)]. This includes forged signatures of indorsers, to be discussed later. If the customer fails to fulfill this duty and the bank suffers a loss as a result, the customer will be liable for the loss [UCC 4–406(d)]. Even if the customer can prove that she or he took reasonable care against forgeries, the UCC provides that the bank is not required to recredit the customer's account unless she or he discovers the forgeries and notifies the bank within a period of one year.

Consequences of Failing to Detect Forgeries. When the same wrongdoer has committed a series of forgeries, the UCC provides that the customer, to recover for all the forged items, must discover and report the *first* forged check to the bank within thirty calendar days of the receipt of the bank statement (and canceled checks or copies, if they are included) [UCC 4–406(d)(2)]. Failure to notify the bank within this period of time discharges the bank's liability for all forged checks that it pays prior to notification.

■EXAMPLE 15.4 Espresso Roma Corporation owns a chain of coffeehouses as well as other businesses and real properties (including dormitories at the University of California, Berkeley). Joseph Montanez, an employee and bookkeeper for Espresso Roma, used stolen computer software and blank checks to generate company checks on his home computer. The series of forged checks began in 1997 and totaled more than $330,000. When the bank statements containing the forged checks arrived in the mail, Montanez sorted through the statements and removed the checks. Espresso Roma did not discover the forgeries had occurred until May 1999. When the bank refused to recredit Espresso Roma's account, litigation followed. The court held that the bank was not liable for the forged checks because Espresso Roma failed to report the first forgeries within the UCC's time period of thirty days. Espresso Roma should have looked at the bank statements and noticed the discrepancy.[6] ■

When the Bank Is Also Negligent. In one situation, a bank customer can escape liability, at least in part, for failing to notify the bank of forged or altered checks promptly or within the required thirty-day period. If the customer can prove that the bank was also negligent—that is, that the bank failed to exercise ordinary care—then the bank will also be liable, and the loss will be allocated between the bank and the customer on the basis of comparative negligence [UCC 4–406(e)]. In other words, even though a customer may have been negligent, the bank may still have to recredit the customer's account for a portion of the loss if the bank failed to exercise ordinary care.

The UCC defines *ordinary care* as the "observance of reasonable commercial standards, prevailing in the area in which [a] person is located, with respect to the business in which that person is engaged" [UCC 3–103]. As mentioned earlier, it is customary in the banking industry to manually examine signatures only on checks over a certain amount (such as $1,000, $2,500, or some higher amount). Thus, if a bank, in accordance with prevailing banking standards, fails to examine a signature on a particular check, the bank has not necessarily breached its duty to exercise ordinary care.

Regardless of the degree of care exercised by the customer or the bank, the UCC places an absolute time limit on the liability of a bank for paying a check with a forged customer signature. A customer who fails to report a forged signature within one year from the date that the statement was made available for inspection loses the legal right to have the bank recredit his or her account [UCC 4–406(f)].

The importance of limiting access to business checking accounts and regularly reviewing bank statements cannot be overemphasized. Checks forged by employees and embezzlement of company funds are disturbingly common in today's business world. One of the best ways to avoid significant losses due to forgery or embezzlement and to prevent litigation over a bank's liability for forged items is to keep a watchful eye on business accounts. Limit the number of persons who have access to the bank accounts and bank statements of your business. Never leave company checkbooks or signature stamps in public or

KEEP IN MIND If a bank is forced to recredit a customer's account, the bank may recover from the forger or from the party that cashed the check (usually a different customer or a collecting bank).

PREVENTING LEGAL DISPUTES

---

6. *Espresso Roma Corp. v. Bank of America, N.A.,* 100 Cal.App.4th 525, 124 Cal.Rptr.2d 549 (2002).

unsecured areas. Use passwords to limit access to computerized check-writing software. Examine monthly bank statements in a timely fashion and be on the lookout for suspicious transactions. Remember that the UCC's rules pertaining to a series of forged checks are not flexible—by failing to report forgeries within thirty days of the first statement in which a forged item appears, the account holder loses the right to hold the bank liable. Businesspersons should be careful not to do anything that could be construed as negligence contributing to a forgery (or to a subsequent alteration of a check, to be discussed shortly). Businesspersons should also be diligent about reviewing bank statements and reporting discrepancies to the bank.

Checks Bearing Forged Indorsements

A bank that pays a customer's check bearing a forged indorsement must recredit the customer's account or be liable to the customer-drawer for breach of contract. ■EXAMPLE 15.5 Simon issues a $500 check "to the order of Antonio." Juan steals the check, forges Antonio's indorsement, and cashes the check. When the check reaches Simon's bank, the bank pays it and debits Simon's account. The bank must recredit the $500 to Simon's account because it failed to carry out Simon's order to pay "to the order of Antonio" [UCC 4–401(a)]. Of course, Simon's bank can in turn recover—for breach of warranty (see Chapter 14)—from the bank that cashed the check when Juan presented it [UCC 4–207(a)(2)]. ■

Eventually, the loss usually falls on the first party to take the instrument bearing the forged indorsement because, as discussed in Chapter 14, a forged indorsement does not transfer title. Thus, whoever takes an instrument with a forged indorsement cannot become a holder.

COMPARE Three years is also the limit for bringing actions for breach of warranty and to enforce other obligations, duties, and rights under Article 3.

The customer, in any event, has a duty to report forged indorsements promptly. Failure to report forged indorsements within a three-year period after the forged items have been made available to the customer relieves the bank of liability [UCC 4–111].

Altered Checks

The customer's instruction to the bank is to pay the exact amount on the face of the check to the holder. The bank has a duty to examine each check before making final payment. If it fails to detect an alteration, it is liable to its customer for the loss because it did not pay as the customer ordered. The loss is the difference between the original amount of the check and the amount actually paid [UCC 4–401(d)(1)]. ■EXAMPLE 15.6 Suppose that a check written for $11 is raised to $111. The customer's account will be charged $11 (the amount the customer ordered the bank to pay). The bank will normally be responsible for the $100. ■

Customer Negligence As in a situation involving a forged drawer's signature, a customer's negligence can shift the loss when payment is made on an altered check (unless the bank was also negligent). A common example occurs when a person carelessly writes a check and leaves large gaps around the numbers and words where additional numbers and words can be inserted (see Exhibit 15–3).

Similarly, a person who signs a check and leaves the dollar amount for someone else to fill in is barred from protesting when the bank unknowingly and in good faith pays whatever amount is shown [UCC 4–401(d)(2)]. Finally, if the bank can trace its loss on successive altered checks to the customer's failure to discover the initial alteration, then the bank can reduce its liability for reimbursing the customer's account [UCC 4–406]. The law governing the customer's duty to examine monthly statements and canceled

EXHIBIT 15–3 A Poorly Filled-Out Check

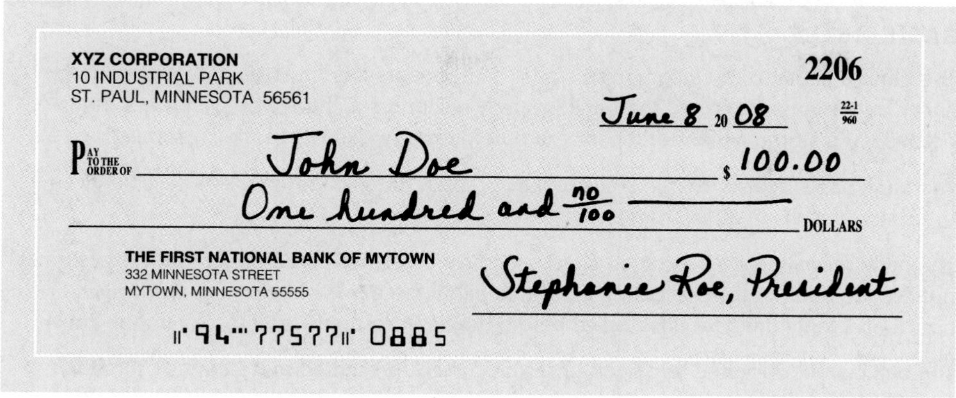

XYZ CORPORATION
10 INDUSTRIAL PARK
ST. PAUL, MINNESOTA 56561

2206

22-1/960

June 8 20 08

Pay to the order of _John Doe_ $ _100.00_

One hundred and $\frac{no}{100}$ ——————— DOLLARS

THE FIRST NATIONAL BANK OF MYTOWN
332 MINNESOTA STREET
MYTOWN, MINNESOTA 55555

Stephanie Roe, President

⑈94⑈77577⑈ 0885

checks, and to discover and report alterations to the bank, is the same as that applied to a forged drawer's signature.

In every situation involving a forged drawer's signature or an alteration, a bank must observe reasonable commercial standards of care in paying on a customer's checks [UCC 4–406(e)]. The customer's negligence can be used as a defense only if the bank has exercised ordinary care.

Other Parties from Whom the Bank May Recover   The bank is entitled to recover the amount of loss from the transferor who, by presenting the check for payment, warrants that the check has not been materially altered. This rule has two exceptions, though. If the bank is the drawer (as it is on a cashier's check and a teller's check), it cannot recover from the presenting party if the party is a holder in due course (HDC) acting in good faith [UCC 3–417(a)(2), 4–208(a)(2)]. The reason is that an instrument's drawer is in a better position than an HDC to know whether the instrument has been altered.

Similarly, an HDC who presents a certified check for payment in good faith will not be held liable under warranty principles if the check was altered before the HDC acquired it [UCC 3–417(a)(2), 4–207(a)(2)].   **■EXAMPLE 15.7**   Jordan draws a check for $500 payable to Deffen. Deffen alters the amount to $5,000. The drawee bank, First National, certifies the check for $5,000. Deffen negotiates the check to Ethan, an HDC. The drawee bank pays Ethan $5,000. On discovering the mistake, the bank cannot recover from Ethan the $4,500 paid by mistake, even though the bank was not in a superior position to detect the alteration. This is in accord with the purpose of certification, which is to obtain the definite obligation of a bank to honor a definite instrument.   ■

The *Concept Summary* on the following page summarizes the rights and liabilities of a bank and its customers in regard to checks.

BANK'S DUTY TO ACCEPT DEPOSITS

A bank has a duty to its customer to accept the customer's deposits of cash and checks. When checks are deposited, the bank must make the funds represented by those checks available within certain time frames. A bank also has a duty to collect payment on any checks payable or indorsed to its customers and deposited by them into their accounts. Cash deposits made in U.S. currency are received into customers' accounts without being subject to further collection procedures.

CONCEPT SUMMARY	Bank's Duty to Honor Checks
SITUATION	**BASIC RULES**
Wrongful Dishonor [UCC 4–402]	The bank is liable to its customer for actual damages proved if it wrongfully dishonors a check due to mistake. When the bank properly dishonors a check (for insufficient funds or because of a stop-payment order, for example), it has no liability to the customer.
Overdraft [UCC 4–401]	The bank has a right to charge a customer's account for any item properly payable, even if the charge results in an overdraft.
Postdated Check [UCC 4–401]	The bank may charge a postdated check against a customer's account, unless the customer notifies the bank of the postdating in time to allow the bank to act on the customer's notice and verify the date has passed before the bank commits itself to pay on the check.
Stale Check [UCC 4–404]	The bank is not obligated to pay an uncertified check presented more than six months after its date, but the bank may do so in good faith without liability.
Stop-Payment Order [UCC 4–403]	The customer (or a "person authorized to draw on the account") must make a stop-payment order in time for the bank to have a reasonable opportunity to act. Oral orders are binding for only fourteen days unless they are confirmed in writing. Written orders are effective for only six months unless renewed in writing. The bank is liable for wrongful payment over a timely stop-payment order to the extent that the customer suffers a loss. A customer has no right to stop payment on a check that has been certified or accepted by a bank, however. A payee can hold a person liable for actual and consequential damages if that person stopped payment on a check without a valid legal ground.
Death or Incompetence of a Customer [UCC 4–405]	So long as the bank does not know of the death or incompetence of a customer, the bank can pay an item without liability. Even with knowledge of a customer's death, a bank can honor or certify checks (in the absence of a stop-payment order) for ten days after the date of the customer's death.
Forged Signature or Alteration [UCC 4–406]	The customer has a duty to examine account statements with reasonable care on receipt and to notify the bank promptly of any forged signatures or alterations. On a series of forged signatures or alterations by the same wrongdoer, examination and report must be made within thirty calendar days of receipt of the first statement containing a forged or altered item. The customer's failure to comply with these rules releases the bank from liability unless the bank failed to exercise reasonable care; in that event, liability may be apportioned according to a comparative negligence standard. Regardless of care or lack of care, the customer is barred from holding the bank liable after one year for forged customer signatures or alterations and after three years for forged indorsements.

Availability Schedule for Deposited Checks

The Expedited Funds Availability Act of 1987[7] and Regulation CC,[8] which was issued by the Federal Reserve Board of Governors (the *Federal Reserve System* will be discussed shortly) to implement the act, require that any local check deposited must be available for withdrawal by check or as cash within one business day from the date of deposit. A check is classified as a local check if the first bank to receive the check for payment and the bank on which the check is drawn are located in the same check-processing region (check-

---

7. 12 U.S.C. Sections 4001–4010.
8. 12 C.F.R. Sections 229.1–229.42.

processing regions are designated by the Federal Reserve Board of Governors). For nonlocal checks, the funds must be available for withdrawal within not more than five business days.

Additional Requirements   In addition to the above requirements, the Expedited Funds Availability Act requires the following:

1 That funds be available on the next business day for cash deposits and wire transfers, government checks, the first $100 of a day's check deposits, cashier's checks, certified checks, and checks for which the depositary and payor banks are branches of the same institution (*depositary* and *payor banks* will be discussed shortly).

2 That the first $100 of any deposit be available for cash withdrawal on the opening of the next business day after deposit. If a local check is deposited, the next $400 is to be available for withdrawal by no later than 5:00 P.M. the next business day. If, for example, you deposit a local check for $500 on Monday, you can withdraw $100 in cash at the opening of the business day on Tuesday, and an additional $400 must be available for withdrawal by no later than 5:00 P.M. on Wednesday.

Exceptions   A different availability schedule applies to deposits made at *non-proprietary* automated teller machines (ATMs). These are ATMs that are not owned or operated by the bank receiving the deposits. Basically, a five-day hold is permitted on all deposits, including cash deposits, made at nonproprietary ATMs.

Other exceptions also exist. A depositary institution has eight days to make funds available in new accounts (those open less than thirty days). It has an extra four days on deposits that exceed $5,000 (except deposits of government and cashier's checks), on accounts with repeated overdrafts, and on checks of questionable collectibility (if the institution tells the depositor it suspects fraud or insolvency).

The Traditional Collection Process

Usually, deposited checks involve parties that do business at different banks, but sometimes checks are written between customers of the same bank. Either situation brings into play the bank collection process as it operates within the statutory framework of Article 4 of the UCC. Note that the check-collection process described in the following subsections will be modified in the future as the banking industry implements the Check Clearing in the 21st Century Act.[9] See this chapter's *Landmark in the Law* feature on pages 462 and 463 for a discussion of this act's impact on the nation's check-collection process.

Designations of Banks Involved in the Collection Process   The first bank to receive a check for payment is the **depositary bank**.[10] For example, when a person deposits an IRS tax-refund check into a personal checking account at the local bank, that bank is the depositary bank. The bank on which a check is drawn (the drawee bank) is called the **payor bank**. Any bank except the payor bank that handles a check during some phase of the collection process is a **collecting bank**. Any bank except the payor bank or the depositary bank to which an item is transferred in the course of this collection process is called an **intermediary bank**.

A woman stands at the Vcom kiosk in a 7-Eleven. These machines can provide a number of services, including ATM transactions, check cashing, money orders, wire transfers, and even bill paying in some locations. How many days after a deposit do funds normally become available for withdrawal from this type of machine?
(AP Photo/Jon Freilich)

DEPOSITARY BANK
The first bank to receive a check for payment.

PAYOR BANK
The bank on which a check is drawn (the drawee bank).

COLLECTING BANK
Any bank handling an item for collection, except the payor bank.

INTERMEDIARY BANK
Any bank to which an item is transferred in the course of collection, except the depositary or payor bank.

---

9. 12 U.S.C. Sections 5001–5018.

10. All definitions in this section are found in UCC 4–105. The terms *depositary* and *depository* have different meanings in the banking context. A depository bank refers to a *physical place* (a bank or other institution) in which deposits or funds are held or stored.

During the collection process, any bank can take on one or more of the various roles of depositary, payor, collecting, and intermediary bank. ▣**EXAMPLE 15.8** A buyer in New York writes a check on her New York bank and sends it to a seller in San Francisco. The seller deposits the check in her San Francisco bank account. The seller's bank is both a *depositary bank* and a *collecting bank*. The buyer's bank in New York is the *payor bank*. As the check travels from San Francisco to New York, any collecting bank handling the item in the collection process (other than the depositary bank and the payor bank) is also called an *intermediary bank*. Exhibit 15–4 illustrates how various banks function in the collection process in the context of this example. ▣

Check Collection between Customers of the Same Bank   An item that is payable by the depositary bank (also the payor bank) that receives it is called an "on-us item." If the bank does not dishonor the check by the opening of the second banking day following its receipt, the check is considered paid [UCC 4–215(e)(2)]. ▣**EXAMPLE 15.9** Oswald and Merkowitz both have checking accounts at State Bank. On Monday morning, Merkowitz deposits into his own checking account a $300 check drawn by Oswald. That same day, State Bank issues Merkowitz a "provisional credit" for $300. When the bank opens on Wednesday, Oswald's check is considered honored, and Merkowitz's provisional credit becomes final. ▣

Check Collection between Customers of Different Banks   Once a depositary bank receives a check, it must arrange to present it either directly or through intermediary banks to the appropriate payor bank. Each bank in the collection chain must pass the check on

EXHIBIT 15–4 **The Check-Collection Process**

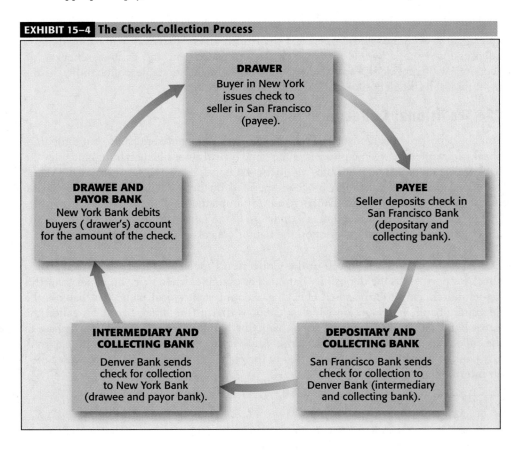

before midnight of the next banking day following its receipt [UCC 4–202(b)].[11] A "banking day" is any part of a day that the bank is open to carry on substantially all of its banking functions. Thus, if a bank has only its drive-through facilities open, a check deposited on Saturday would not trigger a bank's midnight deadline until the following Monday. When the check reaches the payor bank, that bank is liable for the face amount of the check, unless the payor bank dishonors the check or returns it by midnight on the next banking day following receipt [UCC 4–302].[12]

Because of this deadline and because banks need to maintain an even work flow in the many items they handle daily, the UCC permits what is called *deferred posting*. According to UCC 4–108, "a bank may fix an afternoon hour of 2:00 P.M. or later as a cutoff hour for the handling of money and items and the making of entries on its books." Any checks received after that hour "may be treated as being received at the opening of the next banking day." Thus, if a bank's "cutoff hour" is 3:00 P.M., a check received by a payor bank at 4:00 P.M. on Monday would be deferred for posting until Tuesday. In this situation, the payor bank's deadline would be midnight Wednesday.

Does a delay of more than one month in a bank's notice to its customer that a check deposited in his account is counterfeit reduce the customer's liability for overdrafts in his account? That was the customer's contention in the following case.

---

11. A bank may take a "reasonably longer time," such as when the bank's computer system is down due to a power failure, but the bank must show that its action is still timely [UCC 4–202(b)].

12. Most checks are cleared by a computerized process, and communication and computer facilities may fail because of electrical outages, equipment malfunction, or other conditions. If such conditions arise and a bank fails to meet its midnight deadline, the bank is "excused" from liability if the bank has exercised "such diligence as the circumstances require" [UCC 4–109(d)].

CASE 15.2   Bank One, N.A. v. Dunn

Court of Appeal of Louisiana, Second Circuit, 927 So.2d 645 (2006).

FACTS Floyd Dunn, a U.S. citizen, was hired to lobby in the United States for Zaire (now the Democratic Republic of the Congo). After three years of efforts on Zaire's behalf, Dunn submitted a bill for $500,000. Instead of paying, Zaire agreed to trade computers to Dunn, who was to sell them to Nigeria for $32,100,000. "Senator Frank," who claimed to be from Nigeria, told Dunn that he would receive the $32,100,000 after he paid alleged "back taxes" to that country. Frank offered to facilitate the payments. Dunn gave Frank the number of his account at Bank One, N.A., in Shreveport, Louisiana. As part of the deal, on August 1, 2001, a check in the amount of $315,000 drawn on the account of Argenbright Security, Inc., at First Union National Bank of Georgia was deposited into Dunn's account—which had never held more than $5,000—and sent out for collection. Because the check contained an incorrect routing number, its processing was delayed. Meanwhile, on Frank's instructions, Dunn wired $277,000 to

an account at a Virginia bank. On September 24, the $315,000 check was returned to Bank One as counterfeit. Bank One filed a suit in a Louisiana state court against Dunn, alleging that he owed $281,019.11, the amount by which his account was overdrawn. The court issued a summary judgment in Bank One's favor. Dunn appealed to a state intermediate appellate court.

ISSUE Is a bank liable to its customer for a delay in determining the counterfeit nature of a check?

DECISION No. The state intermediate appellate court affirmed the lower court's judgment. Even if Dunn had received notice of the counterfeit status of the check from Bank One before September 24, he would not have been able to collect the amount of the check from Argenbright Security.

REASON In the collection process, a bank is required to pass on a check before midnight of the next banking day

CASE 15.2–Continues next page

CASE 15.2–Continued

following the check's receipt. The appellate court acknowledged that under UCC 4–202, the bank must "exercise ordinary care in sending a notice of dishonor after learning that the item has not been paid or accepted." The court explained that "[n]otifying the customer of dishonor after the bank's midnight deadline may constitute the exercise of ordinary care if the bank took proper action within a reasonably longer time." Of course, the bank is liable for its failure to exercise ordinary care. In that situation, the measure of damages is the amount of the check "reduced by an amount that could not have been realized by the exercise of ordinary care." In other words, if a check could not have been

collected even by the use of ordinary care, the recovery for a failure to exercise ordinary care is reduced by the amount of the uncollectible check. Thus, in this case, "Dunn's liability is not diminished because of Bank One's delay in notifying Dunn that the check was counterfeit. Even if Dunn had received earlier notice from Bank One that the check was counterfeit, he still had no recourse against Argenbright Security. The $315,000 was uncollectible against Argenbright Security."

 FOR CRITICAL ANALYSIS–Ethical Consideration
Does a bank have a duty to protect its customers from their own naïveté, as exemplified in this case by Dunn's giving his bank account information to someone he did not know? Why or why not?

FEDERAL RESERVE SYSTEM
A network of twelve district banks and related branches located around the country and headed by the Federal Reserve Board of Governors. Most banks in the United States have Federal Reserve accounts.

CLEARINGHOUSE
A system or place where banks exchange checks and drafts drawn on each other and settle daily balances.

ON THE WEB

You can obtain extensive information about the Federal Reserve System by accessing "the Fed's" home page at
www.federalreserve.gov.

How the Federal Reserve System Clears Checks   The **Federal Reserve System** is a network of twelve district banks, which are located around the country and headed by the Federal Reserve Board of Governors. Most banks in the United States have Federal Reserve accounts. The Federal Reserve System greatly simplified the check-collection process by acting as a **clearinghouse**—a system or a place where banks exchange checks and drafts drawn on each other and settle daily balances.

■**EXAMPLE 15.10**   Suppose that Pamela Moy of Philadelphia writes a check to Jeanne Sutton in San Francisco. When Sutton receives the check in the mail, she deposits it in her bank. Her bank then deposits the check in the Federal Reserve Bank of San Francisco, which transfers it to the Federal Reserve Bank of Philadelphia. That Federal Reserve bank then sends the check to Moy's bank, which deducts the amount of the check from Moy's account. Exhibit 15–5 on page 464 illustrates this process. ■

Electronic Check Presentment   In the past, most checks were processed manually—the employees of each bank in the collection chain would physically handle each check that passed through the bank for collection or payment. Today, however, most checks are processed electronically. In contrast to manual check processing, which can take days, *electronic check presentment* can be done on the day of deposit. With electronic check presentment, which has been facilitated by Check 21, as described in the *Landmark in the Law* feature on pages 462 and 463, items may be encoded with information (such as the amount of the check) that is read and processed by other banks' computers. In some situations, a check may be retained at its place of deposit, and only its image or description is presented for payment under an electronic presentment agreement [UCC 4–110].[13]

A person who encodes information on an item warrants to any subsequent bank or payor that the encoded information is correct [UCC 4–209]. This is also true for a person who retains an item while transmitting its image or information describing it as presentation for payment. This person warrants that the retention and presentment of the item comply with the electronic presentment agreement.

Regulation CC provides that a returned check must be encoded with the routing number of the depositary bank, the amount of the check, and other information and adds that this "does not affect a paying bank's responsibility to return a check within the deadlines

---

13. This section of the UCC assumes that no bank will participate in an electronic presentment program without an express agreement (which is no longer true since Check 21 went into effect). See Comment 2 to UCC 4–110.

required by the U.C.C." Under UCC 4–301(d)(2), an item is returned "when it is sent or delivered to the bank's customer or transferor or pursuant to his [or her] instructions." What happens when a payor bank fails to properly encode an item and thereby causes the check to be returned to the depositary bank after the required deadline? That was the question in the following case.

CASE 15.3   **NBT Bank, N.A. v. First National Community Bank**

United States Court of Appeals, Third Circuit, 393 F.3d. 404 (2004).

FACTS Human Services Consultants, Inc. (HSC), had a checking account at First National Community Bank (FNCB) in Pennsylvania. A related firm, Human Services Consultants Management, Inc., had two checking accounts at NBT Bank, N.A., in New York, one of which was under the name PA Health. On March 8, 2001, PA Health presented a check in the amount of $706,000 for deposit in its NBT account. The check was drawn on HSC's account at FNCB. NBT credited $706,000 to PA Health's account as a provisional credit and transmitted the check to the Federal Reserve Bank of Philadelphia for presentment to FNCB, which received the check on March 12. The next morning, FNCB dishonored the check because of HSC's insufficient funds, encoded the check for return to NBT, and sent it back to the Federal Reserve bank before 11:59 P.M. Later, on the morning of March 14, FNCB phoned NBT and also sent a letter by fax, informing it of the item's dishonor. The check's encoding was in error, however, and it was wrongly routed to another bank; as a result, NBT did not receive the physical check until March 16. Ultimately, the check was revealed to be part of a fraudulent scheme that caused NBT more than $1 million in losses. NBT filed a suit in a federal district court against FNCB, asserting that FNCB's encoding error rendered FNCB's "return" of the check ineffective. The court granted FNCB's motion for summary judgment, and NBT appealed.

ISSUE If a dishonored check is not correctly encoded but is physically transferred back to the Federal Reserve bank before the midnight deadline, will the item be considered properly returned?

DECISION Yes. The U.S. Court of Appeals for the Third Circuit affirmed the lower court's judgment.

REASON The federal appellate court reasoned that the UCC's midnight deadline focuses on the physical return of a check, not encoding errors. The encoding requirement is found in Regulation CC, which explicitly states that the encoding requirements for routing numbers do not affect deadlines for a payor bank's return of the check. Regulation CC complements but does not necessarily replace the requirements of Article 4 of the UCC; the parties are bound by both. Under Regulation CC, the amount of damages for failure to exercise ordinary care in complying with the encoding provisions is "reduced by the amount of the loss that the [plaintiff] would have incurred even if the [defendant] bank had exercised ordinary care." Here, the parties agreed that NBT suffered no loss as a result of FNCB's encoding error. Thus, the court concluded that NBT could not recover the amount of the check from FNCB.

WHAT IF THE FACTS WERE DIFFERENT? *How might the result in this case have been different if NBT had committed the encoding error and FNCB had suffered the loss?*

■

ELECTRONIC FUND TRANSFERS

The application of computer technology to banking, in the form of electronic fund transfer systems, has helped to relieve banking institutions of the burden of having to move mountains of paperwork to process fund transfers. An **electronic fund transfer (EFT)** is a transfer of funds through the use of an electronic terminal, a telephone, a computer, or magnetic tape. The law governing EFTs depends on the type of transfer involved.

ELECTRONIC FUND TRANSFER (EFT)
A transfer of funds with the use of an electronic terminal, a telephone, a computer, or magnetic tape.

LANDMARK IN THE LAW — Check Clearing in the 21st Century Act (Check 21)

As described in the text, in the traditional collection process, paper checks had to be physically transported before they could be cleared. To streamline this costly and time-consuming process and improve the overall efficiency of the nation's payment system, Congress passed the Check Clearing in the 21st Century Act (Check 21), which went into effect on October 28, 2004.

Purpose of Check 21   Prior to the implementation of Check 21, banks had to present the original paper check for payment in the absence of an agreement for presentment in some other form. Although the Uniform Commercial Code authorizes banks to use other means of presentment, such as electronic presentment, a broad-based system of electronic presentment failed to develop because it required agreements among individual banks.[a] Check 21 has changed this situation by creating a new negotiable instrument called a *substitute check.* While the act does not require that any bank change its current check-collection practices, the creation of substitute checks will certainly facilitate the use of electronic check processing over time.

What Is a Substitute Check?   A substitute check is a paper reproduction of the front and back of an original check that contains all of the same information required on checks for automated processing. Banks create a substitute check from a digital image of an original check. Every substitute check must include the following statement somewhere on it: "This is a legal copy of your check. You can use it in the same way you would use the original check."

In essence, those financial institutions that exchange digital images of checks do not have to send the original paper checks. They can simply transmit the information electronically and replace the original checks with the paper reproductions—the substitute checks. Banks that do not exchange checks electronically are required to accept substitute checks in the same way that they accept original checks.

The Gradual Elimination of Paper Checks   Because financial institutions must accept substitute checks as if they were original checks, the original checks will no longer be needed and will probably be destroyed after their digital images are created. By eliminating the original check after a substitute check is created, the financial system can prevent the check from being paid twice. Also, eliminating original checks and retaining only digital images will reduce the expense of storage and retrieval. Nevertheless, at least for quite a while, not all checks will be converted to substitute checks. That means that if a bank returns canceled checks to deposit holders at the end

a. UCC 3-501(b)(2) and 4-110.

Consumer fund transfers are governed by the Electronic Fund Transfer Act (EFTA) of 1978.[14] Commercial fund transfers are governed by Article 4A of the UCC.

The benefits of electronic banking are obvious. Automatic payments, direct deposits, and other fund transfers are now made electronically; no physical transfers of cash, checks, or other negotiable instruments are involved.

---

14. 15 U.S.C. Sections 1693–1693r. The EFTA amended Title IX of the Consumer Credit Protection Act.

of each month, some of those returned checks may be substitute checks, and some may be original canceled paper checks.

Since the passage of Check 21, financial institution customers cannot demand an original canceled check. Check 21 is a federal law and applies to all financial institutions, other businesses, and individuals in the United States. In other words, no customers can opt out of Check 21 and demand that their original canceled checks be returned with their monthly statements. Also, businesses and individuals must accept a substitute check as proof of payment because it is the legal equivalent of the original check.

The New System Means Reduced "Float" Time   Sometimes, individuals and businesses write checks even though they have insufficient funds in their accounts to cover those checks. Such check writers are relying on "float," or the time between when a check is written and when the amount is actually deducted from the account. When all checks had to be physically transported, the float time could be several days, but as Check 21 is implemented, the time required to process checks will be substantially reduced—and so will float time. Thus, account holders who plan to cover their checks after writing them may experience unexpected overdrafts.

Though consumers and businesses will no longer be able to rely on float time, they may benefit in another way from Check 21. The Expedited Funds Availability Act requires that the Federal Reserve Board revise the availability schedule for funds from deposited checks to correspond to reductions in check-processing time.[b] Therefore, as the speed of check processing increases under Check 21, the Federal Reserve Board will reduce the maximum time that a bank can hold funds from deposited checks before making them available to the depositor. Thus, account holders will have faster access to their deposited funds.

APPLICATION TO TODAY'S WORLD   *As more financial institutions make agreements to transfer digital images of checks, the check-processing system will become more efficient and therefore less costly, affecting banking fees everywhere. Businesspersons (and consumers as well) increasingly will be less able to rely on banking float when they are low on current funds. To avoid disputes and potential litigation, businesspersons should make sure that the funds are available to cover checks at the time they are written.*

RELEVANT WEB SITES   *To locate information on the Web concerning the Check 21 Act, go to this text's Web site at* academic.cengage.com/blaw/blt, *select "Chapter 15," and click on "URLs for Landmarks."*

b. 12 U.S.C. Sections 4001–4010.

Not surprisingly, though, electronic banking also poses difficulties on occasion. It is difficult to issue stop-payment orders with electronic banking. Also, fewer records are available to prove or disprove that a transaction took place. The possibilities for tampering with a person's private banking information have increased. As mentioned earlier, customers can no longer rely on having time between the writing of a check and the deduction of the funds from an account (float time). Electronic funds and digital cash can also be used

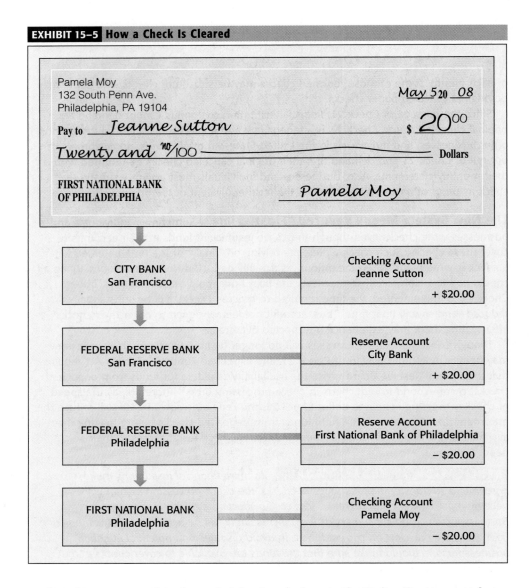

EXHIBIT 15–5 How a Check Is Cleared

to launder money, as this chapter's *Adapting the Law to the Online Environment* feature on pages 466 and 467 explains.

Types of EFT Systems

Most banks today offer EFT services to their customers. The following are the four most common types of EFT systems used by bank customers:

1 *Automated teller machines (ATMs)*—The machines are connected online to the bank's computers. A customer inserts a plastic card (called an *ATM* or *debit card*) issued by the bank and keys in a *personal identification number* (PIN) to access her or his accounts and conduct banking transactions.

2 *Point-of-sale systems*—Online terminals allow consumers to transfer funds to merchants to pay for purchases using a debit card.

3 *Direct deposits and withdrawals*—Customers can authorize the bank to allow another party—such as the government or an employer—to make direct deposits into their accounts. Similarly, customers can request the bank to make automatic payments to a third party at regular, recurrent intervals from the customer's funds (insurance premiums or loan payments, for example).

4 *Internet payment systems* — Many financial institutions permit their customers to access the institution's computer system via the Internet and direct a transfer of funds between accounts or pay a particular bill, such as a utility bill, for example.

Consumer Fund Transfers

The Electronic Fund Transfer Act (EFTA) provides a basic framework for the rights, liabilities, and responsibilities of users of EFT systems. Additionally, the act gave the Federal Reserve Board authority to issue rules and regulations to help implement the act's provisions. The Federal Reserve Board's implemental regulation is called **Regulation E**.

The EFTA governs financial institutions that offer electronic fund transfers involving consumer accounts. The types of accounts covered include checking accounts, savings accounts, and any other asset accounts established for personal, family, or household purposes. Note that telephone transfers are covered by the EFTA only if they are made in accordance with a prearranged plan under which periodic or recurring transfers are contemplated.[15] What rights did the EFTA establish for consumers engaged in EFT transactions? In the subsections that follow, we look more closely at the act's provisions concerning three important issues: disclosure requirements, unauthorized transfers, and error resolution.

REGULATION E
A set of rules issued by the Federal Reserve System's Board of Governors to protect users of elecronic fund transfer systems.

Disclosure Requirements The EFTA is essentially a disclosure law benefiting consumers. The act requires financial institutions to inform consumers of their rights and responsibilities, including those listed here, with respect to EFT systems.

1 If a customer's debit card is lost or stolen and used without his or her permission, the customer may be required to pay no more than $50. The customer, however, must notify the bank of the loss or theft within two days of learning about it. Otherwise, the liability increases to $500. The customer may be liable for more than $500 if he or she does not report the unauthorized use within sixty days after it appears on the customer's statement. (If a customer voluntarily gives her or his debit card to another, who then uses it improperly, the protections just mentioned do not apply.)

2 The customer must discover any error on the monthly statement within sixty days and must notify the bank. The bank then has ten days to investigate and must report its conclusions to the customer in writing. If the bank takes longer than ten days, it must return the disputed amount to the customer's account until it finds the error. If there is no error, the customer has to return the disputed funds to the bank.

3 The bank must furnish receipts for transactions made through computer terminals, but it is not obligated to do so for telephone transfers.

4 The bank must provide a monthly statement for every month in which there is an electronic transfer of funds. Otherwise, the bank must provide statements every quarter. The statement must show the amount and date of the transfer, the names of the retailers or other third parties involved, the location or identification of the terminal, and the fees. Additionally, the statement must give an address and a phone number for inquiries and error notices.

5 Any preauthorized payment for utility bills and insurance premiums can be stopped three days before the scheduled transfer if the customer notifies the financial institution orally or in writing. (The institution may require the customer to provide written confirmation within fourteen days of an oral notification.)

---

15. *Kashanchi v. Texas Commerce Medical Bank, N.A.*, 703 F.2d 936 (5th Cir. 1983).

ADAPTING THE LAW TO THE ONLINE ENVIRONMENT — Digital Funds Provide New Opportunities for Money Laundering

Recall from Chapter 6 that criminals often engage in money laundering to make their illegitimate funds appear legitimate. The profits obtained from illegal activities, such as drug trafficking, are processed through various financial transactions in an effort to conceal their illegal source. Money laundering has been going on for many years, but in the past criminals had to physically transport the cash. The advantages of digital cash—in particular, the ability to exchange it anonymously—have provided an avenue for more effective money laundering (sometimes referred to as *cyberlaundering*). Today, terrorist groups and criminal enterprises use two types of electronic cash to transfer funds and evade detection by law enforcement: prepaid ATM cards and ATM cards offered by online gaming companies that convert virtual cash to real cash.

Reporting Requirements for Cash Transfers

Under federal law, financial institutions must report any financial transactions or fund transfers involving more than $10,000 in cash.[a] Given the vast amounts of cash produced by criminal enterprises—$65 billion per year from sales of illicit drugs in

the United States, for example[b]—this requirement makes it difficult for them to avoid detection by the government. Nevertheless, on a global scale, about $600 billion in drug-trafficking profits are laundered every year—an amount equal to between 2 and 5 percent of the world's gross domestic product.[c] Previously, to avoid running afoul of the reporting requirements, drug traffickers had to move their cash a little at a time in numerous transactions or smuggle bundles of cash across borders. The requirements also limited the amount that could be laundered through more traditional means, such as wiring funds through Western Union. Terrorist groups also had difficulty transferring cash across borders to fund their terrorist activities. Today, however, both criminals and terrorist groups are turning to prepaid ATM cards and virtual cash.

Advantages of Prepaid ATM Cards

From a would-be money launderer's perspective, a prepaid ATM card offers several advantages over an ATM or debit card issued by a bank. A bank-issued card is linked to the customer's bank account, so using the card creates a paper trail that can easily be traced if the customer is suspected of criminal or terrorist activity. Furthermore, as mentioned, banks must report to the government any transactions, including

a. The Bank Secrecy Act of 1970, 18 U.S.C. Sections 1956–1957, as amended by the Money Laundering Control Act of 1986, 31 C.F.R. Section 103.22(a)(1).

b. This estimate is from the White House Office of National Drug Control Policy, as cited in Adrienne Lewis, "Drug, Terror Rings Find New Ways to Launder Money," *USA Today*, January 12, 2006.

c. This statistic was taken from the Web site of the U.S. Department of Justice at **www.usdoj.gov/dea/programs/money.htm**.

BE CAREFUL The EFTA does not provide for the reversal of an electronic transfer of funds once it has occurred.

Unauthorized Electronic Fund Transfers   Unauthorized electronic fund transfers are one of the hazards of electronic banking. A paper check leaves visible evidence of a transaction, and a customer can easily detect a forgery or an alteration on a check with ordinary vigilance. Evidence of an electronic transfer, however, is often only an entry in a computer printout of the various debits and credits made to a particular account during a specified time period.

Because of the vulnerability of EFT systems to fraudulent activities, the EFTA clearly defined what constitutes an unauthorized transfer. Under the act, a transfer is unauthorized if (1) it is initiated by a person other than the consumer who has no actual authority to initiate the transfer; (2) the consumer receives no benefit from it; and (3) the consumer did not furnish the person "with the card, code, or other means of access" to her or his account. Unauthorized access to an EFT system constitutes a federal felony, and those convicted may be fined up to $10,000 and sentenced to as long as ten years in prison.

Violations and Damages   Banks must strictly comply with the terms of the EFTA. If they fail to adhere to the letter of the law of the EFTA, they will be held liable for violation. For a bank's violation of the EFTA, a consumer may recover both actual damages (including attorneys' fees and costs) and punitive damages of not less than $100 and not more than

those using ATM cards, that involve more than $10,000 in cash (and banks often have their own limits on the size of transactions using ATM cards).

In contrast, a prepaid ATM card is not linked to a bank account but is essentially a *stored-value card*. The purchaser simply pays a specific amount to the card provider, and that amount is loaded onto the card (as will be discussed further later in the chapter). The user can then access those funds anywhere in the world without having to provide identification or have a bank account. Students and travelers often find prepaid ATM cards a convenient and safer substitute for cash, as do the approximately 75 million people in the United States who do not have bank accounts.

More important for money laundering purposes is that prepaid ATM cards can be purchased anonymously at retail and check-cashing stores across the nation—locations that are not subject to the government's reporting requirements. Thus, criminals and terrorist groups can pay for the cards with large amounts of cash and then use the cards to move funds across borders—a much easier process than smuggling cash past customs agents.

Money Laundering through Virtual Gaming Currency

The dramatic increase in virtual gaming has also opened the door to cyberlaundering. As mentioned in the *Adapting the Law to the Online Environment* feature in Chapter 8 on fantasy sports, online gaming has become extremely popular worldwide. For years, gamers who participate in these virtual worlds (using digital personas, or "Avatars") have been selling their digital monies, goods, or properties for real-world compensation. A number of Avatars have managed to create wealth for the persons controlling them by selling (or taxing) assets in the virtual world.

Initially, players were able to convert their virtual dollars or credits to real-world cash only by selling them on online auction sites. (Gamers could always do the reverse and use real cash or credit cards to add monies to their online accounts.) Soon, Web sites developed at which gamers could exchange virtual currency. Then, in 2006, the makers of Entropia Universe—a multiplayer game involving a virtual universe that transacted more than $165 million of business in 2005—began offering real-world ATM cards.

With these new ATM cards, a gamer can instantly convert his or her Avatar's virtual world assets into physical currency and withdraw "real" cash from any Versatel brand ATM in the world. In essence, a person can generate and hold significant financial assets anonymously in the virtual world without paying taxes on them or having to report the proceeds to the government. In addition, these assets can be purchased, transferred, and accessed from any place in the world and are completely unregulated and unreported. Once the funds are withdrawn from a virtual account, they are "clean" and cannot be traced to an identifiable source. What more could a criminal or terrorist want? The anonymous virtual world holds great appeal for those who want to hide their assets from governmental view and transfer funds internationally without risking detection.

FOR CRITICAL ANALYSIS *Should only banks and regulated financial institutions be allowed to issue ATM cards? Why or why not? How else might the government regulate digital funds to reduce the potential for cyberlaundering?*

$1,000. (Unlike actual damages, *punitive damages* are assessed to punish a defendant or to deter similar wrongdoers.) Failure to investigate an error in good faith makes the bank liable for treble damages (three times the amount of damages). Even when a customer has sustained no actual damage, the bank may be liable for legal costs and punitive damages if it fails to follow the proper procedures outlined by the EFTA in regard to error resolution.

Commercial Transfers

Funds are also transferred electronically "by wire" between commercial parties. In fact, the dollar volume of payments by wire transfer is more than $1 trillion a day—an amount that far exceeds the dollar volume of payments made by other means. The two major wire payment systems are the Federal Reserve's wire transfer network (Fedwire) and the Clearing House Interbank Payment System (CHIPS).

Commercial wire transfers are governed by Article 4A of the UCC, which has been adopted by most states. The following example illustrates the type of fund transfer covered by Article 4A. **EXAMPLE 15.11** Jellux, Inc., owes $5 million to Perot Corporation. Instead of sending Perot a check or some other instrument that would enable Perot to obtain payment, Jellux tells its bank, East Bank, to credit $5 million to Perot's account in West Bank.

NOTE If any part of an electronic fund transfer is covered by the EFTA, the entire transfer is excluded from UCC Article 4A.

East Bank debits Jellux's East Bank account and wires $5 million to Perot's West Bank account. In more complex transactions, additional banks would be involved. ■

In these and similar circumstances, ordinarily a financial institution's instruction is transmitted electronically. Any means may be used, however, including first-class mail. To reflect this fact, Article 4A uses the term *funds transfer* rather than wire transfer to describe the overall payment transaction.

E-MONEY AND ONLINE BANKING

New forms of electronic payments (e-payments) have the potential to replace *physical* cash—coins and paper currency—with *virtual* cash in the form of electronic impulses. This is the unique promise of **digital cash**, which consists of funds stored on microchips and on other computer devices. Online banking has also become a reality in today's world. In a few minutes, anybody with the proper software can access his or her account, transfer funds, write "checks," pay bills, monitor investments, and often even buy and sell stocks.

Various forms of electronic money, or **e-money**, are emerging. The simplest kind of e-money system uses **stored-value cards.** These are plastic cards embossed with magnetic strips containing magnetically encoded data. In some applications, a stored-value card can be used only to purchase specific goods and services offered by the card issuer. For example, university libraries typically have copy machines that students operate by inserting a stored-value card. Each time a student makes copies, the machine deducts the per-copy fee from the card. As mentioned earlier, though, stored-value cards in the form of prepaid ATM cards can be used anyplace that accepts ATM cards.

Another form of e-money is the smart card. **Smart cards** are plastic cards containing computer microchips that can hold more information than a magnetic strip. A smart card carries and processes security programming. This capability gives smart cards a technical advantage over stored-value cards. The microprocessors on smart cards can also authenticate the validity of transactions. Retailers can program electronic cash registers to confirm the authenticity of a smart card by examining a unique digital signature stored on its microchip. (Digital signatures were discussed in Chapter 10.)

Online Banking Services

Most online bank customers use three kinds of services. One of the most popular is bill consolidation and payment. Another is transferring funds among accounts. These online services are now offered via the Internet as well as by phone. The third is applying for loans, which many banks permit customers to do over the Internet. Customers typically have to appear in person to finalize the terms of a loan.

Two important banking activities generally are not yet available online: depositing and withdrawing funds. With smart cards, people could transfer funds on the Internet, thereby effectively transforming their personal computers into ATMs. Many observers believe that online banking is the way to introduce people to e-money and smart cards.

Since the late 1990s, several banks have operated exclusively on the Internet. These "virtual banks" have no physical branch offices. Because few people are equipped to send funds to virtual banks via smart-card technology, the virtual banks have accepted deposits through physical delivery systems, such as the U.S. Postal Service, FedEx, UPS, or DHL.

Regulatory Compliance

Banks have an interest in seeing the widespread use of online banking because of its significant potential for reducing costs and thus increasing profits. As in other areas of cyberspace, however, determining how laws apply to online banking activities can be difficult.

DIGITAL CASH
Funds contained on computer software, in the form of secure programs stored on microchips and on other computer devices.

E-MONEY
Prepaid funds recorded on a computer or a card (such as a smart card or a stored-value card).

STORED-VALUE CARD
A card bearing a magnetic strip that holds magnetically encoded data, providing access to stored funds.

SMART CARD
A card containing a microprocessor that permits storage of funds via security programming, can communicate with other computers, and does not require online authorization for fund transfers.

ON THE WEB

For tips on how to bank over the Internet safely, read the information provided by the Federal Deposit Insurance Corporation (FDIC) at

www.fdic.gov/bank/individual/online/safe.html.

The Home Mortgage Disclosure Act[16] and the Community Reinvestment Act (CRA) of 1977,[17] for example, require a bank to define its market area and also to provide information to regulators about its deposits and loans. Under the CRA, banks establish market areas in communities situated next to their branch offices. The banks map these areas, using boundaries defined by counties or standard metropolitan areas, and annually review the maps. The purpose of these requirements is to prevent discrimination in lending practices.

But how does a successful "cyberbank" delineate its community? If, for instance, Bank of Internet becomes a tremendous success, does it really have a physical community? Will regulators simply allow a written description of a cybercommunity for Internet customers? Such regulatory issues are new, challenging, and certain to become more complicated as Internet banking widens its scope internationally.

A consumer uses a smart card to pay for lunch at a restaurant. Can the financial institution that issued the card disclose the consumer's personal information to a third party without the consumer's consent? Why or why not? (Courtesy of ViVOtech)

Privacy Protection

At the present time, it is not clear which, if any, laws apply to the security of e-money payment information and e-money issuers' financial records. This is partly because it is not clear whether e-money issuers fit within the traditional definition of a financial institution.

E-Money Payment Information The Federal Reserve has decided not to impose Regulation E, which governs certain electronic fund transfers, on e-money transactions. Federal laws prohibiting unauthorized access to electronic communications might apply, however. For example, the Electronic Communications Privacy Act of 1986[18] prohibits any person from knowingly divulging to any other person the contents of an electronic communication while that communication is in transmission or in electronic storage.

E-Money Issuers' Financial Records Under the Right to Financial Privacy Act of 1978,[19] before a financial institution may give financial information about you to a federal agency, you must explicitly consent. If you do not, a federal agency wishing to access your financial records must obtain a warrant. A digital cash issuer may be subject to this act if that issuer is deemed to be (1) a bank by virtue of its holding customer funds or (2) any entity that issues a physical card similar to a credit or debit card.

Consumer Financial Data In 1999, Congress passed the Financial Services Modernization Act,[20] also known as the Gramm-Leach-Bliley Act, in an attempt to delineate how financial institutions can treat customer data. In general, the act and its rules[21] place restrictions and obligations on financial institutions to protect consumer data and privacy. Every financial institution must provide its customers with information on its privacy policies and practices. No financial institution can disclose nonpublic personal information about a consumer to an unaffiliated third party unless the act's disclosure and opt-out requirements are met.

---

16. 12 U.S.C. Sections 2801–2810.
17. 12 U.S.C. Sections 2901–2908.
18. 18 U.S.C. Sections 2510–2521.
19. 12 U.S.C. Sections 3401 *et seq.*
20. 12 U.S.C. Sections 24a, 248b, 1820a, 1828b, 1831v–1831y, 1848a, 2908, 4809; 15 U.S.C. Sections 80b–10a, 6701, 6711–6717, 6731–6735, 6751–6766, 6781, 6801–6809, 6821–6827, 6901–6910; and others.
21. 12 C.F.R. Part 40.

REVIEWING Checks and Banking in the Digital Age

RPM Pizza, Inc., issued a check for $96,000 to Systems Marketing for an advertising campaign. A few days later, RPM decided not to go through with the deal and placed a written stop-payment order on the check. RPM and Systems had no further contact for many months. Three weeks after the stop-payment order expired, however, Toby Rierson, an employee at Systems, cashed the check. Bank One Cambridge, RPM's bank, paid the check with funds from RPM's account. Because the check was more than six months old, it was stale, and thus, according to standard banking procedures as well as Bank One's own policies, the signature on the check should have been specially verified, but it was not. RPM filed a suit in a federal district court against Bank One to recover the amount of the check. Using the information presented in the chapter, answer the following questions.

1 How long is a written stop-payment order effective? What could RPM have done to further prevent this check from being cashed?

2 What would happen if it turned out that RPM did not have a legitimate reason for stopping payment on the check?

3 What are a bank's obligations with respect to stale checks?

4 Would a court be likely to hold the bank liable for the amount of the check because it failed to verify the signature on the check? Why or why not?

APPLICATION How to Use Stop-Payment Orders*

For a variety of reasons, a drawer should not misuse stop-payment orders. We look at some of those reasons here.

Monetary Costs and Risks

One reason is monetary: banks usually charge between $20 and $30 for a stop-payment order, so stopping payment is not cost-effective for a check written for a small amount. Another reason is the risk attached to the issuing of a stop-payment order for any drawer-customer. The bank is entitled to take a reasonable amount of time to put your stop-payment order into effect before it has liability for improper payment. Hence, the payee or another holder may be able to cash the check despite your stop-payment order if he or she acts quickly. Indeed, you could be writing out a stop-payment order in the bank lobby while the payee or holder cashes the check in the drive-in facility outside. In addition, even if a bank pays over your proper stop-payment order, the bank will be liable to the drawer-customer only for the amount of loss the drawer suffers from the improper payment.

When You Can Stop Payment

Remember that, to avoid liability, a drawer must have a legal reason for issuing a stop-payment order. You cannot stop payment on a check simply because you have had a change of heart about the wisdom of your purchase. Generally, you can safely stop payment if you clearly did not get what you paid for or were fraudulently induced to make a purchase. You can also stop payment if a "cooling-off" law governs the transaction—that is, if you legally have a few days in which to change your mind about a purchase. Any wrongful stop-payment order subjects the *drawer* to liability to the payee or a holder, and this liability may include special damages that resulted from the order. When all is considered, it may be unwise to stop payment hastily on a check because of a minor dispute with the payee.

CHECKLIST FOR STOP-PAYMENT ORDERS

1 Compare the stop-payment fee with the disputed sum to make sure it is worthwhile to issue a stop-payment order.
2 Make sure that your bank will honor your stop-payment order before the payee cashes the check.
3 Make sure that you have a legal reason for issuing the stop-payment order.

* This *Application* is not meant to substitute for the services of an attorney who is licensed to practice law in your state.

KEY TERMS

cashier's check 446
certified check 447
check 446
clearinghouse 460
collecting bank 457
depositary bank 457
digital cash 468

electronic fund transfer (EFT) 461
e-money 468
Federal Reserve System 460
intermediary bank 457
overdraft 449
payor bank 457
Regulation E 465

smart card 468
stale check 450
stop-payment order 450
stored-value card 468
traveler's check 446

CHAPTER SUMMARY — Checks and Banking in the Digital Age

Checks (See pages 446–448.)	1. *Cashier's check*—A check drawn by a bank on itself (the bank is both the drawer and the drawee) and purchased by a customer. In effect, the bank assumes responsibility for paying the check, thus making the check nearly the equivalent of cash.
	2. *Traveler's check*—An instrument on which a financial institution is both the drawer and the drawee. The purchaser must provide his or her signature as a countersignature for a traveler's check to become a negotiable instrument.
	3. *Certified check*—A check for which the drawee bank certifies in writing that it has set aside funds from the drawer's account to ensure payment of the check on presentation. On certification, the drawer and all prior indorsers are completely discharged from liability on the check.
The Bank-Customer Relationship (See page 448.)	1. *Creditor-debtor relationship*—The bank and its customer have a creditor-debtor relationship (the bank is the debtor because it holds the customer's funds on deposit).
	2. *Agency relationship*—Because a bank must act in accordance with the customer's orders in regard to the customer's deposited money, an agency relationship also arises—the bank is the agent for the customer, who is the principal.
	3. *Contractual relationship*—The bank's relationship with its customer is also contractual; both the bank and the customer assume certain contractual duties when a customer opens a bank account.
Bank's Duty to Honor Checks (See pages 448–455.)	Generally, a bank has a duty to honor its customers' checks, provided that the customers have sufficient funds on deposit to cover the checks [UCC 4–401(a)]. The bank is liable to its customers for actual damages proved to be due to wrongful dishonor. The bank's duty to honor its customers' checks is not absolute. See the *Concept Summary* on page 456 for a detailed list of the rights and liabilities of the bank and the customer in various situations, such as overdrafts and forged signatures.
Bank's Duty to Accept Deposits (See pages 455–461.)	A bank has a duty to accept deposits made by its customers into their accounts. Funds represented by checks deposited must be made available to customers according to a schedule mandated by the Expedited Funds Availability Act of 1987 and Regulation CC. A bank also has a duty to collect payment on any checks deposited by its customers. When checks deposited by customers are drawn on other banks, as they often are, the check-collection process comes into play (summarized next).
	1. *Definitions of banks*—UCC 4–105 provides the following definitions of banks involved in the collection process:
	a. Depositary bank—The first bank to accept a check for payment.
	b. Payor bank—The bank on which a check is drawn.

(Continued)

CHAPTER SUMMARY	Checks and Banking in the Digital Age—Continued
Bank's Duty to Accept Deposits— Continued	c. Collecting bank—Any bank except the payor bank that handles a check during the collection process. d. Intermediary bank—Any bank except the payor bank or the depositary bank to which an item is transferred in the course of the collection process. 2. *Check collection between customers of the same bank*—A check payable by the depositary bank that receives it is an "on-us item"; if the bank does not dishonor the check by the opening of the second banking day following its receipt, the check is considered paid [UCC 4–215(e)(2)]. 3. *Check collection between customers of different banks*—Each bank in the collection process must pass the check on to the next appropriate bank before midnight of the next banking day following its receipt [UCC 4–108, 4–202(b), 4–302]. 4. *How the Federal Reserve System clears checks*—The Federal Reserve System facilitates the check-clearing process by serving as a clearinghouse for checks. 5. *Electronic check presentment*—When checks are presented electronically, items may be encoded with information (such as the amount of the check) that is read and processed by other banks' computers. In some situations, a check may be retained at its place of deposit, and only its image or information describing it is presented for payment under a Federal Reserve agreement, clearinghouse rule, or other agreement [UCC 4–110].
Electronic Fund Transfers (See pages 461–468.)	1. *Types of EFT systems*— a. Automated teller machines (ATMs). b. Point-of-sale systems. c. Direct deposits and withdrawals. d. Internet payment systems. 2. *Consumer fund transfers*—Consumer fund transfers are governed by the Electronic Fund Transfer Act (EFTA) of 1978. The EFTA is basically a disclosure law that sets forth the rights and duties of the bank and the customer with respect to EFT systems. Banks must comply strictly with EFTA requirements. 3. *Commercial transfers*—Article 4A of the UCC, which has been adopted by almost all of the states, governs fund transfers not subject to the EFTA or other federal or state statutes.
E-Money and Online Banking (See pages 468–469.)	1. *New forms of e-payments*—These include stored-value cards and smart cards. 2. *Current online banking services*— a. Bill consolidation and payment. b. Transferring funds among accounts. c. Applying for loans. 3. *Regulatory compliance*—Banks must define their market areas, in communities situated next to their branch offices, under the Home Mortgage Disclosure Act and the Community Reinvestment Act. It is not clear how an online bank would define its market area or its community. 4. *Privacy protection*—It is not entirely clear which, if any, laws apply to e-money and online banking. The Financial Services Modernization Act (the Gramm-Leach-Bliley Act) outlines how financial institutions can treat consumer data and privacy in general. The Right to Financial Privacy Act may also apply.

FOR REVIEW

Answers for the even-numbered questions in this For Review *section can be found in Appendix E at the end of this text.*

1 On what types of checks does a bank serve as both the drawer and the drawee? What type of check does a bank agree in advance to accept when the check is presented for payment?

2 When may a bank properly dishonor a customer's check without the bank being liable to the customer? What happens if a bank wrongfully dishonors a customer's check?

3 What duties does the Uniform Commercial Code impose on a bank's customers with regard to forged and altered checks? What are the consequences of a customer's negligence in performing those duties?

4 What are the four most common types of electronic fund transfers?

5 What is e-money, and how is it stored and used? What laws apply to e-money transactions and online banking services?

QUESTIONS AND CASE PROBLEMS

 **HYPOTHETICAL SCENARIOS**

15.1 Error Resolution. Sheridan has a checking account at Gulf Bank. She frequently uses her access card to obtain money from the automated teller machines. She always withdraws $50 when she makes a withdrawal, but she never withdraws more than $50 in any one day. When she received the April statement on her account, she noticed that on April 13 two withdrawals for $50 each had been made from the account. Believing this to be a mistake, she went to her bank on May 10 to inform the bank of the error. A bank officer told her that the bank would investigate and inform her of the result. On May 26, the bank officer called her and said that bank personnel were having trouble locating the error but would continue to try to find it. On June 20, the bank sent her a full written report advising her that no error had been made. Sheridan, unhappy with the bank's explanation, filed suit against the bank, alleging that it had violated the Electronic Fund Transfer Act. What was the outcome of the suit? Would it matter if the bank could show that on the day in question it had deducted $50 from Sheridan's account to cover a check that Sheridan had written to a local department store and that had cleared the bank on that day?

15.2 Hypothetical Question with Sample Answer. First Internet Bank operates exclusively on the Web with no physical

branch offices. Although some of First Internet's business is transacted with smart-card technology, most of its business with its customers is conducted through the mail. First Internet offers free checking, no-fee money market accounts, mortgage refinancing, and other services. With what regulation covering banks might First Internet find it difficult to comply, and what is the difficulty?

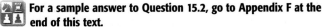 **For a sample answer to Question 15.2, go to Appendix F at the end of this text.**

15.3 Forged Checks. Roy Supply, Inc., and R. M. R. Drywall, Inc., had checking accounts at Wells Fargo Bank. Both accounts required all checks to carry two signatures—that of Edward Roy and that of Twila June Moore, both of whom were executive officers of both companies. Between January 1989 and March 1991, the bank honored hundreds of checks on which Roy's signature was forged by Moore. On January 31, 1992, Roy and the two corporations notified the bank of the forgeries and then filed a suit in a California state court against the bank, alleging negligence. Who is liable for the amounts of the forged checks? Why?

CASE PROBLEMS

15.4 Debit Cards. On April 20, 1999, while visiting her daughter and son-in-law Michael Dowdell, Carol Farrow asked Dowdell to fix her car. She gave him her car keys, attached

to which was a small wallet containing her debit card. Dowdell repaired her car and returned the keys. Two days later, Farrow noticed that her debit card was missing and contacted Auburn Bank, which had issued the card. Farrow reviewed her automated teller machine (ATM) transaction record and noticed that a large amount of cash had been withdrawn from her checking account on April 22 and April 23. When Farrow reviewed the photos taken by the ATM cameras at the time of the withdrawals, she recognized Dowdell as the person using her debit card. Dowdell was convicted in an Alabama state court of the crime of fraudulent use of a debit card. What procedures are involved in a debit-card transaction? What problems with debit-card transactions are apparent from the facts of this case? How might these problems be prevented? [*Dowdell v. State*, 790 So.2d 359 (Ala.Crim.App. 2000)]

15.5 **Check Collection.** Robert Santoro was the manager of City Check Cashing, Inc., a check-cashing service in New Jersey, and Peggyann Slansky was the clerk. On July 14, Misir Koci presented Santoro with a $290,000 check signed by Melvin Green and drawn on Manufacturers Hanover Trust Co. (a bank). The check was stamped with a Manufacturers certification stamp. The date on the check had clearly been changed from August 8 to July 7. Slansky called the bank to verify the check and was told that the serial number "did not sound like one belonging to the bank." Slansky faxed a copy of the check to the bank with a query about the date, but she received no reply. Slansky also called Green, who stated that the date on the check was altered before it was certified. Check Cashing cashed and deposited the check within two hours. The drawee bank found the check to be invalid and timely returned it unpaid. Check Cashing filed a suit in a New Jersey state court against Manufacturers and others, asserting that the bank should have responded to the fax before the midnight deadline in Section 4–302 of the Uniform Commercial Code. Did the bank violate the midnight deadline rule? Explain. [*City Check Cashing, Inc. v. Manufacturers Hanover Trust Co.*, 166 N.J. 49, 764 A.2d 411 (2001)]

15.6 **Forged Indorsement.** Visiting Nurses Association of Telfair County, Inc. (VNA), maintained a checking account at Security State Bank in Valdosta, Georgia. Wanda Williamson, a VNA clerk, was responsible for making VNA bank deposits, but she was not a signatory on the association's account. Over a four-year period, Williamson embezzled more than $250,000 from VNA by forging its indorsement on checks, cashing them at the bank, and keeping a portion of the proceeds. Williamson was arrested, convicted, sentenced to a prison term, and ordered to pay restitution. VNA filed a suit in a Georgia state court against the bank, alleging, among other things, negligence. The bank filed a motion for summary judgment on the ground that VNA was precluded by Section 4–406(f) of the Uniform Commercial Code from recovering on checks with forged indorsements. Should the court grant the motion? Explain. [*Security State Bank v. Visiting Nurses Association of Telfair County, Inc.*, 568 S.E.2d 491 (Ga.App. 2002)]

15.7 **Case Problem with Sample Answer.** In December 1999, Jenny Triplett applied for a bookkeeping position with

Spacemakers of America, Inc., in Atlanta, Georgia. Spacemakers hired Triplett and delegated to her all responsibility for maintaining the company checkbook and reconciling it with the monthly statements from SunTrust Bank. Triplett also handled invoices from vendors. Spacemakers' president, Dennis Rose, reviewed the invoices and signed the checks to pay them, but no other employee checked Triplett's work. By the end of her first full month of employment, Triplett had forged six checks totaling more than $22,000, all payable to Triple M Entertainment, which was not a Spacemakers vendor. By October 2000, Triplett had forged fifty-nine more checks, totaling more than $475,000. A SunTrust employee became suspicious of an item that required sight inspection under the bank's fraud detection standards, which exceeded those of other banks in the area. Triplett was arrested. Spacemakers filed a suit in a Georgia state court against SunTrust. The bank filed a motion for summary judgment. On what basis could the bank avoid liability? In whose favor should the court rule, and why? [*Spacemakers of America, Inc. v. SunTrust Bank*, 271 Ga.App. 335, 609 S.E.2d 683 (2005)]

After you have answered Problem 15.7, compare your answer with the sample answer given on the Web site that accompanies this text. Go to academic.cengage.com/blaw/blt, select "Chapter 15," and click on "Case Problem with Sample Answer."

15.8 **Forged Signatures.** Cynthia Stafford worked as an administrative professional at Gerber & Gerber, P.C. (professional corporation), a law firm, for more than two years. During that time, she stole ten checks payable to Gerber & Gerber (G&G), which she indorsed in blank by forging one of the attorney's signatures. She then indorsed the forged checks in her name and deposited them in her account at Regions Bank. Over the same period, G&G deposited in its accounts at Regions Bank thousands of checks amounting to $300 million to $400 million. Each G&G check was indorsed with a rubber stamp for deposit into the G&G account. The thefts were made possible in part because G&G kept unindorsed checks in an open file accessible to all employees and Stafford was sometimes the person assigned to stamp the checks. When the thefts were discovered, G&G filed a suit in a Georgia state court against Regions Bank to recover the stolen funds, alleging, among other things, negligence. Regions Bank filed a motion for summary judgment. What principles apply to attribute liability between these parties? How should the court rule on the bank's motion? Explain. [*Gerber & Gerber, P.C. v. Regions Bank*, 596 S.E.2d 174 (Ga.App. 2004)]

15.9 **Forged Indorsements.** In 1994, Brian and Penny Grieme bought a house in Mandan, North Dakota. They borrowed for the purchase through a loan program financed by the North Dakota Housing Finance Agency (NDHFA). The Griemes obtained insurance for the house from Center Mutual Insurance Co. When a hailstorm damaged the house in 2001, Center Mutual determined that the loss was $4,378 and issued a check for that amount, drawn on

Bremer Bank, N.A. The check's payees included Brian Grieme and the NDHFA. Grieme presented the check for payment to Wells Fargo Bank of Tempe, Arizona. The back of the check bore his signature and in hand-printed block letters the words "ND Housing Finance." The check was processed for collection and paid, and the canceled check was returned to Center Mutual. By the time the insurer learned that NDHFA's indorsement had been forged, the Griemes had canceled their policy, defaulted on their loan, and filed for bankruptcy. The NDHFA filed a suit in a North Dakota state court against Center Mutual for the amount of the check. Who is most likely to suffer the loss in this case? Why? [*State ex rel. North Dakota Housing Finance Agency v. Center Mutual Insurance Co.*, 720 N.W.2d 425 (N.Dak. 2006)]

15.10 **A Question of Ethics.** *From the 1960s, James Johnson served as Bradley Union's personal caretaker and assistant, and was authorized by Union to handle his banking transactions. Louise Johnson, James's wife, wrote checks on Union's checking account to pay his bills, normally signing the checks "Brad Union." Branch Banking & Trust Co. (BB&T) managed Union's account. In December 2000, on the basis of Union's deteriorating mental and physical condi-* tion, *a North Carolina state court declared him incompetent. Douglas Maxwell was appointed as Union's guardian. Maxwell "froze" Union's checking account and asked BB&T for copies of the canceled checks, which were provided by July 2001. Maxwell believed that Union's signature on the checks had been forged. In August 2002, Maxwell contacted BB&T, which refused to recredit Union's account. Maxwell filed a suit on Union's behalf in a North Carolina state court against BB&T.* [*Union v. Branch Banking & Trust Co.*, 176 N.C.App. 711, 627 S.E.2d 276 (2006)]

1 Before Maxwell's appointment, BB&T sent monthly statements and canceled checks to Union, and Johnson reviewed them, but no unauthorized signatures were ever reported. On whom can liability be imposed in the case of a forged drawer's signature on a check? What are the limits set by Section 4–406(f) of the Uniform Commercial Code? Should Johnson's position, Union's incompetence, or Maxwell's appointment affect the application of these principles? Explain.

2 Why was this suit brought against BB&T? Is BB&T liable? If not, who is? Why? Regardless of any violations of the law, did anyone act unethically in this case? If so, who and why?

CRITICAL THINKING AND WRITING ASSIGNMENTS

15.11 Critical Legal Thinking. Under the 1990 revision of Article 4, a bank is not required to include the customer's canceled checks when it sends monthly statements to the customer. Banks may simply itemize the checks (by number, date, and amount) or, in addition to this itemization, also provide photocopies of the checks. What implications do the revised rules have for bank customers in terms of liability for unauthorized signatures and indorsements?

ONLINE ACTIVITIES

 ## PRACTICAL INTERNET EXERCISES

Go to this text's Web site at **academic.cengage.com/blaw/blt**, select "Chapter 15," and click on "Practical Internet Exercises." There you will find the following Internet research exercises that you can perform to learn more about the topics covered in this chapter.

PRACTICAL INTERNET EXERCISE 15–1 MANAGEMENT PERSPECTIVE—Check Fraud

PRACTICAL INTERNET EXERCISE 15–2 LEGAL PERSPECTIVE—Smart Cards

BEFORE THE TEST

Go to this text's Web site at **academic.cengage.com/blaw/blt**, select "Chapter 15," and click on "Interactive Quizzes." You will find a number of interactive questions relating to this chapter.

CHAPTER 16
Creditors' Rights and Bankruptcy

CHAPTER OUTLINE

- SECURED TRANSACTIONS
- ADDITIONAL LAWS ASSISTING CREDITORS
- ADDITIONAL LAWS ASSISTING DEBTORS
- BANKRUPTCY PROCEEDINGS

LEARNING OBJECTIVES

AFTER READING THIS CHAPTER, YOU SHOULD BE ABLE TO ANSWER THE FOLLOWING QUESTIONS:

1 What is a security interest? What three requirements must be met to create an enforceable security interest?

2 What is a prejudgment attachment? What is a writ of execution? How does a creditor use these remedies?

3 What is garnishment? When might a creditor undertake a garnishment proceeding?

4 In a bankruptcy proceeding, what constitutes the debtor's estate in property? What property is exempt from the estate under federal bankruptcy law?

5 In a Chapter 11 reorganization, what is the role of the debtor in possession?

SECURED TRANSACTION
Any transaction in which the payment of a debt is guaranteed, or secured, by personal property owned by the debtor or in which the debtor has a legal interest.

ON THE WEB
To find Article 9 of the UCC as adopted by a particular state, go to the Web site of Cornell University's Law School at
www.law.cornell.edu/ucc/ucc.table.html.

Whenever the payment of a debt is guaranteed, or *secured*, by personal property owned by the debtor or in which the debtor has a legal interest, the transaction becomes known as a **secured transaction.** The concept of the secured transaction is as basic to modern business practice as the concept of credit. Logically, sellers and lenders do not want to risk nonpayment, so they usually will not sell goods or lend funds unless the payment is somehow guaranteed. Indeed, business as we know it could not exist without laws permitting and governing secured transactions.

Article 9 of the Uniform Commercial Code (UCC) governs secured transactions as applied to personal property, *fixtures* (certain property that is attached to land—see Chapter 24), accounts, instruments, commercial assignments of $1,000 or more, *chattel paper* (any writing evidencing a debt secured by personal property), agricultural liens, and what are called general intangibles (such as patents and copyrights). Article 9 does not cover other creditor devices, such as liens and real estate mortgages.

In this chapter, after first examining the law governing secured transactions, we discuss other laws that assist creditors and debtors in resolving their disputes. In the last part of this chapter, we focus on bankruptcy as a last resort in resolving debtor-creditor disputes.

SECURED TRANSACTIONS

The importance of being a secured creditor cannot be overemphasized. Secured creditors generally are not hampered by state laws favorable to debtors, and if their security interest meets certain requirements, they have a favored position should the debtor enter into bankruptcy.

The Terminology of Secured Transactions

The UCC's terminology is now uniformly adopted in all documents used in situations involving secured transactions. A brief summary of the UCC's definitions of terms relating to secured transactions follows.

1 A **secured party** is any creditor who has a *security interest* in the *debtor's collateral*. This creditor can be a seller, a lender, a cosigner, or even a buyer of accounts or chattel paper [UCC 9–102(a)(72)].

2 A **debtor** is the "person" who *owes payment* or other performance of a secured obligation [UCC 9–102(a)(28)].

3 A **security interest** is the *interest* in the collateral (such as personal property or fixtures) that *secures payment or performance of an obligation* [UCC 1–201(37)].

4 A **security agreement** is an *agreement* that *creates* or provides for a *security interest* [UCC 9–102(a)(73)].

5 **Collateral** is the *subject* of the *security interest* [UCC 9–102(a)(12)].

6 A **financing statement**—referred to as the UCC-1 form—is the *instrument normally filed* to give *public notice* to *third parties* of the *secured party's security interest* [UCC 9–102(a)(39)].

These basic definitions form the concept under which a debtor-creditor relationship becomes a secured transaction relationship (see Exhibit 16–1).

Creating a Security Interest

A creditor has two main concerns if the debtor **defaults** (fails to pay the debt as promised): (1) Can the debt be satisfied through the possession and (usually) sale of the collateral? (2) Will the creditor have priority over any other creditors or buyers who may have rights in the same collateral? These two concerns are met through the creation and perfection of a security interest. We begin by examining how a security interest is created.

SECURED PARTY
A lender, seller, or any other person in whose favor there is a security interest, including a person to whom accounts or chattel paper have been sold.

DEBTOR
Under Article 9 of the UCC, any party who owes payment or performance of a secured obligation, whether or not the party actually owns or has rights in the collateral.

SECURITY INTEREST
Any interest in personal property or fixtures that secures payment or performance of an obligation.

SECURITY AGREEMENT
An agreement that creates or provides for a security interest between the debtor and a secured party.

COLLATERAL
Under Article 9 of the UCC, the property subject to a security interest, including accounts and chattel paper that have been sold.

FINANCING STATEMENT
A document prepared by a secured creditor, and filed with the appropriate state or local official, to give notice to the public that the creditor has a security interest in collateral belonging to the debtor named in the statement. The financing statement must contain the names and addresses of both the debtor and the secured party and must describe the collateral by type or item.

DEFAULT
Failure to observe a promise or discharge an obligation; commonly used to refer to failure to pay a debt when it is due.

EXHIBIT 16–1 Secured Transactions—Concept and Terminology

In a security agreement, a debtor and a creditor agree that the creditor will have a security interest in collateral in which the debtor has rights. In essence, the collateral secures the loan and ensures the creditor of payment should the debtor default.

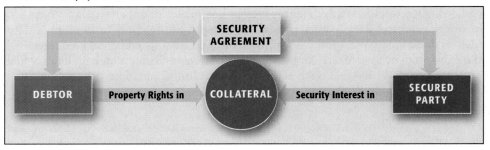

To become a secured party, the creditor must obtain a security interest in the collateral of the debtor. Three requirements must be met for a creditor to have an enforceable security interest:

1 Either (a) the collateral must be in the possession of the secured party in accordance with an agreement, or (b) there must be a written or authenticated security agreement that describes the collateral subject to the security interest and is signed or authenticated by the debtor.

2 The secured party must give something of value to the debtor.

3 The debtor must have "rights" in the collateral.

Once these requirements have been met, the creditor's rights are said to attach to the collateral. **Attachment** gives the creditor an enforceable security interest in the collateral [UCC 9–203].[1]

Written or Authenticated Security Agreement   When the collateral is *not* in the possession of the secured party, the security agreement must be either written or authenticated, and it must describe the collateral. Note here that *authentication* means to sign, execute, or adopt any symbol on an electronic record that verifies the person signing has the intent to adopt or accept the record [UCC 9–102(a)(7)(69)]. If the security agreement is in writing or authenticated, *only the debtor's signature or authentication* is required to create the security interest. The reason authentication is acceptable is to provide for electronic filing (the filing process will be discussed later).

A security agreement must contain a description of the collateral that reasonably identifies it. Generally, such phrases as "all the debtor's personal property" or "all the debtor's assets" would *not* constitute a sufficient description [UCC 9–108(c)].

Secured Party Must Give Value   The secured party must give to the debtor something of value. Some examples would be a binding commitment to extend credit or consideration to support a simple contract [UCC 1–201(44)]. Normally, the value given by a secured party is in the form of a direct loan or a commitment to sell goods on credit.

Debtor Must Have Rights in the Collateral   The debtor must have rights in the collateral; that is, the debtor must have some ownership interest in or right to obtain possession of that collateral. The debtor's rights can represent either a current or a future legal interest in the collateral. For example, a retail seller-debtor can give a secured party a security interest not only in existing inventory owned by the retailer but also in *future* inventory to be acquired by the retailer.

Perfecting a Security Interest

Perfection is the legal process by which secured parties protect themselves against the claims of third parties who may wish to have their debts satisfied out of the same collateral. Whether a secured party's security interest is perfected or unperfected may have serious consequences for the secured party if, for example, the debtor defaults on the debt or files for bankruptcy. What if the debtor has borrowed from two different creditors, using the same property as collateral for both loans? If the debtor defaults on both loans, which of the two creditors has first rights to the collateral? In this situation, the creditor with a perfected security interest will prevail.

ATTACHMENT
In a secured transaction, the process by which a secured creditor's interest "attaches" to the property of another (collateral) and the creditor's security interest becomes enforceable.

PERFECTION
The legal process by which secured parties protect themselves against the claims of third parties who may wish to have their debts satisfied out of the same collateral; usually accomplished by filing a financing statement with the appropriate government official.

---

1. Note that in the context of judicial liens, discussed later in this chapter, the term *attachment* has a different meaning. In that context, it refers to a court-ordered seizure and taking into custody of property prior to the securing of a court judgment for a past-due debt.

Usually, perfection is accomplished by filing a financing statement, but in some circumstances, a security interest becomes perfected without the filing of a financing statement. Where or how a security interest is perfected sometimes depends on the type of collateral. Collateral is generally divided into two classifications: *tangible collateral* (collateral that can be seen, felt, and touched) and *intangible collateral* (collateral that consists of or generates rights). (See the *Application* feature at the end of this chapter for additional information on perfecting a security interest.)

If a tractor used for harvesting became collateral for a secured loan, how would the collateral be classified? (Camera_Art/Creative Commons)

Perfection by Filing   The most common means of perfection is by filing a *financing statement*—a document that gives public notice to third parties of the secured party's security interest—with the office of the appropriate government official. The security agreement itself can also be filed to perfect the security interest. The financing statement must provide the names of the debtor and the secured party and must indicate the collateral covered by the financing statement. Once completed, filings are indexed in the name of the debtor so that they can be located by subsequent searchers.

In most states, a financing statement must be filed in the appropriate state office, such as the office of the secretary of state, in the state where the debtor is located. Filing in the county where the collateral is located is required only when the collateral consists of timber to be cut, fixtures, or collateral to be extracted—such as oil, coal, gas, or minerals [UCC 9–301(3), (4), and 9–502(b)].

The Debtor's Name.   The UCC requires that a financing statement be filed under the name of the debtor [UCC 9–502(a)(1)]. Slight variations in names normally will not be considered misleading if a search of the filing office's records, using a standard computer search engine routinely used by that office, would disclose the filings [UCC 9–506(c)].[2] If the debtor is identified by the correct name at the time of the filing of a financing statement, the secured party's interest retains its priority even if the debtor later changes his or her name. Because most states use electronic filing systems, UCC 9–503 sets out some detailed rules for determining when the debtor's name as it appears on a financing statement is sufficient.

For corporations, which are organizations that have registered with the state, the debtor's name on the financing statement must be "the name of the debtor indicated on the public record of the debtor's jurisdiction of organization" [UCC 9–503(a)(1)]. If the debtor is a trust or a trustee with respect to property held in trust, the filed financing statement must disclose this information and must provide the trust's name as specified in its official documents [UCC 9–503(a)(3)]. For all others, the filed financing statement must disclose "the individual or organizational name of the debtor" [UCC 9–503(a)(4)(A)]. As used here, the word *organization* includes unincorporated associations, such as clubs and some churches, as well as joint ventures and general partnerships. If an organizational debtor does not have a group name, the names of the individuals in the group must be listed.

Providing only the debtor's trade name (or a fictitious name) in a financing statement is *not* sufficient for perfection [UCC 9–503(c)]. **■EXAMPLE 16.1** A loan is being made

---

2. If the name listed in the financing statement is so inaccurate that a search using the standard search engine will not disclose the debtor's name, then it is deemed seriously misleading under UCC 9–506. This may also occur when a debtor changes names after the financing statement is filed. See also UCC 9–507, which governs the effectiveness of financing statements found to be seriously misleading.

to a sole proprietorship owned by Peter Jones. The trade, or fictitious, name is Pete's Plumbing. A financing statement filed in the trade name Pete's Plumbing would not be sufficient because it does not identify Peter Jones as the debtor. The financing statement must be filed under the name of the actual debtor—in this instance, Peter Jones. ▣ The reason for this rule is to ensure that the debtor's name on a financing statement is one that prospective lenders can locate and recognize in future searches.

Description of the Collateral. The UCC requires that both the security agreement and the financing statement contain a description of the collateral in which the secured party has a security interest. The security agreement must describe the collateral because no security interest in goods can exist unless the parties agree on which goods are subject to the security interest. The financing statement must also describe the collateral because the purpose of filing the statement is to give public notice of the fact that certain goods of the debtor are subject to a security interest. Other parties who might later wish to lend funds to the debtor or buy the collateral can thus learn of the security interest by checking with the state or local office in which a financing statement for that type of collateral would be filed. For land-related security interests, a legal description of the realty is also required [UCC 9–502(b)].

Consequences of an Improper Filing. Any improper filing renders the security interest unperfected and reduces the secured party's claim in bankruptcy to that of an unsecured creditor. For instance, if the debtor's name on the financing statement is seriously misleading or if the collateral is not sufficiently described in the financing statement, the filing may not be effective. The following case provides an illustration.

CASE 16.1   Corona Fruits & Veggies, Inc. v. Frozsun Foods, Inc.

Court of Appeal of California, Second District, Division 6, 143 Cal.App.4th 319, 48 Cal.Rptr.3d 868 (2006).

FACTS In July 2001, Corona Fruits & Veggies, Inc., and Corona Marketing Company sublet farmland in Santa Barbara County, California, to Armando Munoz Juarez, a strawberry farmer. The Corona companies also loaned funds to Juarez for payroll and production expenses. The sublease and other documents involved in the transaction set out Juarez's full name, but Juarez generally went by the name "Munoz" and signed the sublease "Armando Munoz." The Coronas filed UCC-1 financing statements that identified the debtor as "Armando Munoz." In December, Juarez contracted to sell strawberries to Frozsun Foods, Inc., which advanced funds secured by a financing statement that identified the debtor as "Armando Juarez." By the next July, Juarez owed the Coronas $230,482.52 and Frozsun $19,648.52. When Juarez did not repay the Coronas, they took possession of the farmland, harvested and sold the strawberries, and kept the proceeds. The Coronas and Frozsun filed a suit in a California state court against Juarez to collect the rest of his debt. The court ruled that Frozsun's interest took priority because only its financing

statement was recorded properly. The Coronas appealed to a state intermediate appellate court.

ISSUE Does a creditor fail to perfect a security interest if a financing statement lists a debtor's name incorrectly?

DECISION Yes. The state intermediate appellate court affirmed the lower court's ruling. "Shakespeare asked, 'What's in a name?' We supply an answer * * * : Everything when the last name is true and nothing when the last name is false."

REASON The appellate court recognized that "minor errors in a UCC financing statement do not affect the effectiveness of the financing statement." It is only when "errors render the document seriously misleading to other creditors" that the effectiveness of a statement is undercut. "When a creditor files a UCC-1 financing statement, the debtor's true last name is crucial because the financing statements are indexed by last names. A subsequent creditor who loans [funds] to a debtor with the same name is put on notice that its lien is secondary."

CASE 16.1–Continued

In this case, Juarez's identification cards and tax returns stated his true, full name, and the Coronas identified him by this name in their contracts, business records, and checks, and even in their pleadings filed with the court. The Coronas could have used this name in their financing statements, too, to protect the priority of their security interests, but they did not.

Frozsun searched the UCC records under the name "Juarez" and did not find the Coronas' statements. For these reasons, Frozsun's interest was superior.

 FOR CRITICAL ANALYSIS–Technological Consideration *Under what circumstances might a financing statement be considered effective even if it does not identify the debtor correctly?*

Perfection without Filing   In two types of situations, security interests can be perfected without filing a financing statement. The first occurs when the collateral is transferred into the possession of the secured party. The second occurs when the security interest is one of a limited number (thirteen) under the UCC that can be perfected on attachment (without a filing and without having to possess the goods) [UCC 9–309]. The phrase *perfected on attachment* means that these security interests are automatically perfected at the time of their creation. Two of the more common security interests that are perfected on attachment are a *purchase-money security interest* in consumer goods (defined and explained below) and an assignment of a beneficial interest in a decedent's estate [UCC 9–309(1), (13)].

Perfection by Possession.   Under the common law, one of the most widespread means of obtaining financing was to **pledge** certain collateral as security for the debt and transfer the collateral into the creditor's possession. When the debt was paid, the collateral was returned to the debtor. Although the debtor usually entered into a written security agreement, an oral security agreement was also enforceable as long as the secured party possessed the collateral. Article 9 of the UCC retained the common law pledge and the principle that the security agreement need not be in writing to be enforceable if the collateral is transferred to the secured party [UCC 9–310, 9–312(b), 9–313].

PLEDGE
A common law security device (retained in Article 9 of the UCC) in which personal property is transferred into the possession of the creditor as security for the payment of a debt and retained by the creditor until the debt is paid.

Perfection by Attachment—The Purchase-Money Security Interest in Consumer Goods.
A **purchase-money security interest (PMSI)** is created when a person buys consumer goods (items bought primarily for personal, family, or household purposes) and the seller or lender agrees to extend credit for part or all of the purchase price of the goods. The entity that extends the credit and obtains the PMSI can be either the seller (a store, for example) or a financial institution that lends the buyer the funds with which to purchase the goods [UCC 9–102(a)(2)].

A PMSI in consumer goods is perfected automatically at the time of a credit sale—that is, at the time the PMSI is created. The seller in this situation need do nothing more to perfect her or his interest. **■EXAMPLE 16.2** Jamie wants to purchase a new high-definition television from ABC Television, Inc. The purchase price is $2,500. Not being able to pay the entire amount in cash, Jamie signs a purchase agreement to pay $1,000 down and $100 per month until the balance plus interest is fully paid. ABC is to retain a security interest in the purchased goods until full payment has been made. Because the security interest was created as part of the purchase agreement, it is a PMSI in consumer goods. ABC does not need to do anything else to perfect its security interest. ■

PURCHASE-MONEY SECURITY INTEREST (PMSI)
A security interest that arises when a seller or lender extends credit for part or all of the purchase price of goods purchased by a buyer.

Exceptions to the Rule of Automatic Perfection.   There are exceptions to this rule of automatic perfection. First, certain types of security interests that are subject to other federal or state laws may require additional steps to be perfected [UCC 9–311]. For example,

If a couple purchases a plasma TV on an installment plan, what kind of security interest is created?
(AP Photo/Mark Lennihan)

CONTINUATION STATEMENT
A statement that, if filed within six months prior to the expiration date of the original financing statement, continues the perfection of the original security interest for another five years. The perfection of a security interest can be continued in the same manner indefinitely.

PROCEEDS
Under Article 9 of the UCC, whatever is received when collateral is sold or otherwise disposed of, such as by exchange.

most states have certificate-of-title statutes that establish perfection requirements for specific goods, such as automobiles, trailers, boats, mobile homes, and farm tractors. If a consumer in these jurisdictions purchases a boat, for example, the secured party will need to file a certificate of title with the appropriate state official to perfect the PMSI. A second exception involves PMSIs in nonconsumer goods, such as livestock or a business's inventory, which are not automatically perfected (these types of PMSIs are discussed later in this chapter in the context of priorities).

Effective Time Duration of Perfection   A financing statement is effective for five years from the date of filing [UCC 9–515]. If a **continuation statement** is filed within six months *prior to* the expiration date, the effectiveness of the original statement is continued for another five years, starting with the expiration date of the first five-year period [UCC 9–515(d), (e)]. The effectiveness of the statement can be continued in the same manner indefinitely. Any attempt to file a continuation statement outside the six-month window will render the continuation ineffective, and the perfection will lapse at the end of the five-year period.

If a financing statement lapses, the security interest that had been perfected by the filing now becomes unperfected. A purchaser for value can acquire the collateral as if the security interest had never been perfected as against a purchaser for value [UCC 9–515(c)].

The Scope of a Security Interest

In addition to covering collateral already in the debtor's possession, a security agreement can cover various other types of property, including the proceeds of the sale of collateral, after-acquired property, and future advances.

Proceeds   **Proceeds** are whatever cash or property is received when collateral is sold or disposed of in some other way [UCC 9–102(a)(64)]. A security interest in the collateral gives the secured party a security interest in the proceeds acquired from the sale of that collateral. **■EXAMPLE 16.3** A bank has a perfected security interest in the inventory of a retail seller of heavy farm machinery. The retailer sells a tractor out of this inventory to a farmer, who is by definition a *buyer in the ordinary course of business* (this term will be discussed later in the chapter). The farmer agrees, in a security agreement, to make monthly payments to the retailer for a period of twenty-four months. If the retailer goes into default on the loan from the bank, the bank is entitled to the remaining payments the farmer owes to the retailer as proceeds. ■

A security interest in proceeds perfects automatically on the *perfection* of the secured party's security interest in the original collateral and remains perfected for twenty days after the debtor receives the proceeds. One way to extend the twenty-day automatic perfection period is to provide for such extended coverage in the original security agreement [UCC 9–315(c), (d)]. This is typically done when the collateral is the type that is likely to be sold, such as a retailer's inventory—for example, of computers or DVD recorders. The UCC also permits a security interest in identifiable cash proceeds to remain perfected after twenty days [UCC 9–315(d)(2)].

AFTER-ACQUIRED PROPERTY
Property that is acquired by the debtor after the execution of a security agreement.

After-Acquired Property   **After-acquired property** is property that the debtor acquired after the execution of the security agreement. The security agreement may provide for a security interest in after-acquired property [UCC 9–204(1)]. This is particularly useful for inventory financing arrangements because a secured party whose security interest is in existing inventory knows that the debtor will sell that inventory, thereby reducing the collateral subject to the security interest. Generally, the debtor will purchase new inventory to replace the inventory sold. The secured party wants this newly acquired inventory to be subject to the original security interest. Thus, the after-acquired property clause continues the secured party's claim to any inventory acquired thereafter. (This is not to say that the original security interest will take priority over the rights of all other creditors with regard to this after-acquired inventory, as will be discussed later.)

Future Advances   Often, a debtor will arrange with a bank to have a *continuing line of credit* under which the debtor can borrow funds intermittently. Advances against lines of credit can be subject to a properly perfected security interest in certain collateral. The security agreement may provide that any future advances made against that line of credit are also subject to the security interest in the same collateral [UCC 9–204(c)].

A security agreement that provides for a security interest in proceeds, in after-acquired property, or in collateral subject to future advances by the secured party (or in all three) is often characterized as a **floating lien**. This type of security interest continues in the collateral or proceeds even if the collateral is sold, exchanged, or disposed of in some other way.

Priorities

The importance of perfection to a secured party cannot be overemphasized, particularly when another party is claiming an interest in the same collateral covered by the perfected secured party's security interest. The general rule is that a perfected secured party's interest has priority over the interests of the following parties [UCC 9–317, 9–322]:

1 An unsecured creditor.

2 An unperfected secured party.

3 A subsequent lien creditor, such as a judgment creditor who acquires a lien on the collateral by execution and levy—a process discussed later in this chapter.

4 A trustee in bankruptcy (to be discussed later in this chapter)—at least, the perfected secured party has priority to the proceeds from the sale of the collateral by the trustee.

5 Buyers who *do not* purchase the collateral in the ordinary course of a seller's business.

Buyers of the Collateral   When someone purchases collateral in which a creditor has a perfected security interest, the question arises as to whether the buyer or the secured party has priority to the goods. The UCC recognizes five types of buyers whose interest in purchased goods could conflict with those of a perfected secured party on the debtor's default. These five types are as follows (see Exhibit 16–2 on the next page for details):

1 Buyers in the ordinary course of business.

2 Buyers of consumer goods purchased outside the ordinary course of business.

3 Buyers of chattel paper [UCC 9–330].

4 Buyers of instruments, documents, or securities [UCC 9–330(d), 9–331(a)].

5 Buyers of farm products.[3]

Under the UCC, a person who buys "in the ordinary course of business" takes the goods free from any security interest created by the seller *even if the security interest is perfected and the buyer knows of its existence* [UCC 9–320(a)]. The rationale for this rule is obvious:

This woman owns a store that sells antique clocks and other used objects. As a creditor, why would you want a floating lien in a debtor's inventory? (BohPhoto/ Creative Commons)

FLOATING LIEN
A security interest in proceeds, after-acquired property, or collateral subject to future advances by the secured party (or all three); a security interest in collateral that is retained even when the collateral changes in character, classification, or location.

---

3. Under the Food Security Act of 1985, buyers in the ordinary course of business include buyers of farm products from a farmer. Under this act, these buyers are protected from prior perfected security interests unless the secured parties perfected centrally by a special form called an *effective financing statement* (EFS) or the buyers received proper notice of the secured party's security interest.

EXHIBIT 16–2	Priority of Claims to a Debtor's Collateral
PARTIES	**PRIORITY**
Perfected Secured Party versus **Unsecured Parties and Creditors**	A perfected secured party's interest has priority over the interests of most other parties, including unsecured creditors, unperfected secured parties, subsequent lien creditors, trustees in bankruptcy, and buyers who do not purchase the collateral in the ordinary course of business.
Perfected Secured Party versus **Perfected Secured Party**	Between two perfected secured parties in the same collateral, the general rule is that the first in time of perfection is the first in right to the collateral [UCC 9–322(a)(1)].
Perfected Secured Party versus **Perfected PMSI**	A PMSI, even if second in time of perfection, has priority providing that the following conditions are met: 1. *Other collateral*—A PMSI has priority, providing it is perfected within twenty days after the debtor takes possession [UCC 9–324(a)]. 2. *Inventory*—A PMSI has priority if it is perfected and proper written or authenticated notice is given to the other security-interest holder *on* or *before* the time the debtor takes possession [UCC 9–324(b)]. 3. *Software*—Applies to a PMSI in software only if used in goods subject to a PMSI. If the goods are inventory, priority is determined the same as for inventory; if they are not, priority is determined as for goods other than inventory [UCC 9–103(c), 9–324(f)].
Perfected Secured Party versus **Purchaser of Debtor's Collateral**	1. *Buyer of goods in the ordinary course of the seller's business*—Buyer prevails over a secured party's security interest, even if perfected and even if the buyer knows of the security interest [UCC 9–320(a)]. 2. *Buyer of consumer goods purchased outside the ordinary course of business*—Buyer prevails over a secured party's interest, even if perfected by attachment, providing the buyer purchased as follows: a. For value. b. Without actual knowledge of the security interest. c. For use as a consumer good. d. Prior to the secured party's perfection by *filing* [UCC 9–320(b)]. 3. *Buyer of chattel paper*—Buyer prevails if the buyer: a. Gave new value in making the purchase. b. Took possession in the ordinary course of the buyer's business. c. Took without knowledge of the security interest [UCC 9–330]. 4. *Buyer of instruments, documents, or securities*—Buyer who is a holder in due course, a holder to whom negotiable documents have been duly negotiated, or a bona fide purchaser of securities has priority over a previously perfected security interest [UCC 9–330(d), 9–331(a)]. 5. *Buyer of farm products*—Buyer from a farmer takes free and clear of perfected security interests unless, where permitted, a secured party files centrally an effective financing statement (EFS) or the buyer receives proper notice of the security interest before the sale.
Unperfected Secured Party versus **Unsecured Creditor**	An unperfected secured party prevails over unsecured creditors and creditors who have obtained judgments against the debtor but who have not begun the legal process to collect on those judgments [UCC 9–201(a)].

if buyers could not obtain the goods free and clear of any security interest the merchant had created—for example, in inventory—the free flow of goods in the marketplace would be hindered. A *buyer in the ordinary course of business* is a person who in good faith, and without knowledge that the sale violates the rights of another in the goods, buys goods in the ordinary course from a person in the business of selling goods of that kind [UCC 1–201(9)]. Note that the buyer can know about the existence of a perfected security interest, so long as he or she does not know that buying the goods violates the rights of any third party.

■EXAMPLE 16.4 On August 1, West Bank has a perfected security interest in all of ABC Television's existing inventory and any inventory thereafter acquired. On September 1, Carla, a student at Central University, purchases one of the television sets in ABC's inventory. On December 1, ABC goes into default. Can West Bank repossess the TV set sold to Carla? The answer is no, because Carla is a buyer in the ordinary course of business (ABC is in the business of selling goods of that kind) and takes free and clear of West Bank's perfected security interest. This is true even if Carla knew that West Bank had a security interest in ABC's inventory when she purchased the TV. ■

Creditors or Secured Parties Sometimes, several secured parties may have perfected security interests in the same collateral. Conversely, on occasion no creditor may have a perfected security interest in the goods. Other problems may arise when two or more secured parties have perfected security interests in goods that have been so combined that they have lost their separate identities. In these situations, the following UCC rules generally apply:

> **KEEP IN MIND** Secured creditors—perfected or not—have priority over unsecured creditors.

1 *Conflicting perfected security interests.* When two or more secured parties have perfected security interests in the same collateral, generally the first to perfect (file or take possession of the collateral) has priority, unless the state's statute provides otherwise [UCC 9–322(a)(1)].

2 *Conflicting unperfected security interests.* When two conflicting security interests are unperfected, the first to attach has priority [UCC 9–322(a)(3)].

3 *Conflicting perfected security interests in commingled or processed goods.* When goods to which two or more perfected security interests attach are so manufactured or commingled that they lose their identities into a product or mass, the perfected parties' security interests attach to the new product or mass "according to the ratio that the cost of goods to which each interest originally attached bears to the cost of the total product or mass" [UCC 9–336].

Default

Article 9 defines the rights, duties, and remedies of the secured party and of the debtor on the debtor's default. Should the secured party fail to comply with her or his duties, the debtor is afforded particular rights and remedies. Although any breach of the terms of the security agreement can constitute default, default occurs most commonly when the debtor fails to meet the scheduled payments that the parties have agreed on or when the debtor becomes bankrupt.

Basic Remedies The rights and remedies under UCC 9–601(a), (b) are *cumulative* [UCC 9–601(c)]. Therefore, if a creditor is unsuccessful in enforcing rights by one method, he or she can pursue another method. Generally, a secured party's remedies can be divided into the two basic categories discussed next.

Repossession of the Collateral—The Self-Help Remedy. On the debtor's default, a secured party can take peaceful possession of the collateral without the use of judicial process [UCC 9–609(b)]. This provision is often referred to as the "self-help" provision of Article 9. The UCC does not define *peaceful possession,* however. The general rule is that the collateral has been taken peacefully if the secured party can take possession

RECALL A trespass to land occurs when a person, without permission, enters onto another's land and is established as a trespasser.

EXECUTION
An action to carry into effect the directions in a court decree or judgment.

LEVY
The obtaining of funds by legal process through the seizure and sale of nonsecured property, usually done after a writ of execution has been issued.

without committing (1) trespass onto land, (2) assault and/or battery, or (3) breaking and entering. On taking possession, the secured party may either retain the collateral for satisfaction of the debt [UCC 9–620] or resell the goods and apply the proceeds toward the debt [UCC 9–610].

Judicial Remedies. Alternatively, a secured party can relinquish the security interest and use any judicial remedy available, such as obtaining a judgment on the underlying debt, followed by execution and levy. (**Execution** is the implementation of a court's decree or judgment. **Levy** is the obtaining of funds by legal process through the seizure and sale of nonsecured property, usually done after a writ of execution has been issued.) Execution and levy are rarely undertaken unless the collateral is no longer in existence or has declined so much in value that it is worth substantially less than the amount of the debt and the debtor has other assets available that may be legally seized to satisfy the debt [UCC 9–601(a)].

Disposition of Collateral Once default has occurred and the secured party has obtained possession of the collateral, the secured party may either retain the collateral in full satisfaction of the debt or sell, lease, or otherwise dispose of the collateral in any commercially reasonable manner and apply the proceeds toward satisfaction of the debt [UCC 9–602(7), 9–603, 9–610(a), 9–620]. Any sale is always subject to procedures established by state law.

Proceeds from the Disposition. Proceeds from the disposition of collateral after default on the underlying debt are distributed in the following order:

1 Expenses incurred by the secured party in repossessing, storing, and reselling the collateral.

2 Balance of the debt owed to the secured party.

3 Junior lienholders who have made written or authenticated demands.

4 Unless the collateral consists of accounts, payment intangibles, promissory notes, or chattel paper, any surplus goes to the debtor [UCC 9–608(a); 9–615(a), (e)].

Whenever the secured party receives noncash proceeds from the disposition of collateral after default, the secured party must make a value determination and apply this value in a commercially reasonable manner [UCC 9–608(a)(3), 9–615(c)].

Deficiency Judgment. Often, after proper disposition of the collateral, the secured party has not collected all that the debtor still owes. Unless otherwise agreed, the debtor is liable for any deficiency, and the creditor can obtain a **deficiency judgment** from a court to collect the deficiency. Note, however, that if the underlying transaction was, for example, a sale of accounts or of chattel paper, the debtor is entitled to any surplus or is liable for any deficiency only if the security agreement so provides [UCC 9–615(d), (e)].

DEFICIENCY JUDGMENT
A judgment against a debtor for the amount of a debt remaining unpaid after the collateral has been repossessed and sold.

Redemption Rights. At any time before the secured party disposes of the collateral or enters into a contract for its disposition, or before the debtor's obligation has been discharged through the secured party's retention of the collateral, the debtor or any other secured party can exercise the right of *redemption* of the collateral. The debtor or other secured party can do this by tendering performance of all obligations secured by the collateral and by paying the expenses reasonably incurred by the secured party in retaking and maintaining the collateral [UCC 9–623].

ADDITIONAL LAWS ASSISTING CREDITORS

Both the common law and statutory laws other than Article 9 of the UCC create various rights and remedies for creditors. Here we discuss some of these rights and remedies.

Liens

As explained in Chapter 13, a *lien* is an encumbrance on (claim against) property to satisfy a debt or protect a claim for the payment of a debt. Creditors' liens may arise under the common law or under statutory law. Statutory liens include *mechanic's liens*. Liens created at common law include *artisan's liens*. *Judicial liens* include those that represent a creditor's efforts to collect on a debt before or after a judgment is entered by a court.

Generally, a lien creditor has priority over an unperfected secured party but not over a perfected secured party. In other words, if a person becomes a lien creditor *before* another party perfects a security interest in the same property, the lienholder has priority. If a lien is obtained *after* another's security interest in the property is perfected, the lienholder does not have priority. This is true for all liens except mechanic's and artisan's liens, which normally have priority over perfected security interests—unless a statute provides otherwise.

Mechanic's Lien   When a person contracts for labor, services, or materials to be furnished for the purpose of making improvements on real property (land and objects attached to the land, such as buildings and trees—see Chapter 24) but does not immediately pay for the improvements, the creditor can file a **mechanic's lien** on the property. This creates a special type of debtor-creditor relationship in which the real estate itself becomes security for the debt. Note that state law governs the procedures that must be followed to create a mechanic's lien.

Artisan's Lien   An **artisan's lien** is a security device created at common law through which a creditor can recover payment from a debtor for labor and materials furnished for the repair or improvement of personal property. In contrast to a mechanic's lien, an artisan's lien is *possessory*. The lienholder ordinarily must have retained possession of the property and have expressly or impliedly agreed to provide the services on a cash, not a credit, basis. The lien remains in existence as long as the lienholder maintains possession, and the lien is terminated once possession is voluntarily surrendered—unless the surrender is only temporary.

EXAMPLE 16.5 Tenetia leaves her diamond ring at the jeweler's to be repaired and to have her initials engraved on the band. In the absence of an agreement, the jeweler can keep the ring until Tenetia pays for the services. Should Tenetia fail to pay, the jeweler has a lien on Tenetia's ring for the amount of the bill and normally can sell the ring in satisfaction of the lien. ■

Modern statutes permit the holder of an artisan's lien to foreclose and sell the property subject to the lien to satisfy payment of the debt. As with a mechanic's lien, the holder of an artisan's lien is required to give notice to the owner of the property prior to foreclosure and sale. The sale proceeds are used to pay the debt and the costs of the legal proceedings, and the surplus, if any, is paid to the former owner.

Judicial Liens   When a debt is past due, a creditor can bring a legal action against the debtor to collect the debt. If the creditor is successful in the action, the court awards the creditor a judgment against the debtor (usually for the amount of the debt plus any interest and legal costs incurred in obtaining the judgment). Frequently, however, the creditor is unable to collect the awarded amount.

Painters finish the trim on a house. If the homeowner does not pay for the work, what can the painters do to collect what they are owed?
(Joshin Yamada/Creative Commons)

MECHANIC'S LIEN
A statutory lien on the real property of another, created to ensure payment for work performed and materials furnished in the repair or improvement of real property, such as a building.

ARTISAN'S LIEN
A possessory lien given to a person who has made improvements and added value to another person's personal property as security for payment for services performed.

To ensure that a judgment in the creditor's favor will be collectible, the creditor is permitted to request that certain nonexempt property of the debtor be seized to satisfy the debt. (As will be discussed later in this chapter, under state or federal statutes, certain property is exempt from attachment by creditors.) If the court orders the debtor's property to be seized prior to a judgment in the creditor's favor, the court's order is referred to as a *writ of attachment*. If the court orders the debtor's property to be seized following a judgment in the creditor's favor, the court's order is referred to as a *writ of execution*.

Writ of Attachment. Recall from earlier in this chapter that *attachment*, in the context of secured transactions, refers to the process through which a security interest in a debtor's collateral becomes enforceable. In the context of judicial liens, this word has another meaning: *attachment* is a court-ordered seizure and taking into custody of property prior to the securing of a judgment for a past-due debt. Attachment rights are created by state statutes. Normally, attachment is a *prejudgment* remedy occurring either at the time a lawsuit is filed or immediately afterwards. To attach before judgment, a creditor must comply with the specific state's statutory restrictions and requirements. The due process clause of the Fourteenth Amendment to the U.S. Constitution also applies and requires that the debtor be given notice and an opportunity to be heard (see Chapter 1).

The creditor must have an enforceable right to payment of the debt under law and must follow certain procedures. Otherwise, the creditor can be liable for damages for wrongful attachment. She or he must file with the court an *affidavit* (a written or printed statement, made under oath or sworn to) stating that the debtor is in default and indicating the statutory grounds under which attachment is sought. The creditor must also post a bond to cover at least the court costs, the value of the loss of use of the good suffered by the debtor, and the value of the property attached. When the court is satisfied that all the requirements have been met, it issues a **writ of attachment**, which directs the sheriff or other public officer to seize nonexempt property. If the creditor prevails at trial, the seized property can be sold to satisfy the judgment.

Writ of Execution. If the creditor wins and the debtor will not or cannot pay the judgment, the creditor is entitled to go back to the court and request a **writ of execution**. This writ is a court order directing the sheriff to seize (levy) and sell any of the debtor's nonexempt real or personal property that is within the court's geographic jurisdiction (usually the county in which the courthouse is located). The proceeds of the sale are used to pay off the judgment, accrued interest, and the costs of the sale. Any excess is paid to the debtor. The debtor can pay the judgment and redeem the nonexempt property any time before the sale takes place. (Because of exemption laws and bankruptcy laws, however, many judgments are virtually uncollectible.)

Garnishment

An order for **garnishment** permits a creditor to collect a debt by seizing property of the debtor that is being held by a third party. In a garnishment proceeding, the third party—the person or entity that the court is ordering to garnish an individual's property—is called the *garnishee*. Frequently, a garnishee is the debtor's employer. A creditor may seek a garnishment judgment against the debtor's employer so that part of the debtor's usual paycheck will be paid to the creditor. In some situations, however, the garnishee is a third party that holds funds belonging to the debtor (such as a bank) or has possession of, or exercises control over, other types of property belonging to the debtor. Almost all types of property can be garnished, including tax refunds, pensions, and trust funds—so long as the property is not exempt from garnishment and is in the possession of a third party.

WRIT OF ATTACHMENT
A court's order, issued prior to a trial to collect a debt, directing the sheriff or other public officer to seize nonexempt property of the debtor. If the creditor prevails at trial, the seized property can be sold to satisfy the judgment.

WRIT OF EXECUTION
A court's order, issued after a judgment has been entered against a debtor, directing the sheriff to seize (levy) and sell any of the debtor's nonexempt real or personal property. The proceeds of the sale are used to pay off the judgment, accrued interest, and costs of the sale; any surplus is paid to the debtor.

GARNISHMENT
A legal process used by a creditor to collect a debt by seizing property of the debtor (such as wages) that is being held by a third party (such as the debtor's employer).

The legal proceeding for a garnishment action is governed by state law, and garnishment operates differently from state to state. As a result of a garnishment proceeding, as noted, the court orders a third party (such as the debtor's employer) to turn over property owned by the debtor (such as wages) to pay the debt. Garnishment can be a prejudgment remedy, requiring a hearing before a court, but is most often a postjudgment remedy. According to the laws in some states, the creditor needs to obtain only one order of garnishment, which will then apply continuously to the debtor's wages until the entire debt is paid. In other states, the judgment creditor must go back to court for a separate order of garnishment for each pay period.

Both federal and state laws limit the amount that can be taken from a debtor's weekly take-home pay through garnishment proceedings.[4] Federal law provides a framework to protect debtors from suffering unduly when paying judgment debts.[5] State laws also provide dollar exemptions, and these amounts are often larger than those provided by federal law. Under federal law, an employer cannot dismiss an employee because his or her wages are being garnished.

Mortgage Foreclosure

A **mortgage** is a written instrument giving a creditor an interest in (lien on) the debtor's real property as security for the payment of a debt. Financial institutions grant mortgage loans for the purchase of property—usually a dwelling and the land on which it sits (*real property* will be discussed in Chapter 24). Given the relatively large sums that many individuals borrow to purchase a home, defaults are not uncommon.

Mortgage holders have the right to foreclose on mortgaged property in the event of a debtor's default. The usual method of foreclosure is by judicial sale of the property, although the statutory methods of foreclosure vary from state to state. If the proceeds of the foreclosure sale are sufficient to cover both the costs of the foreclosure and the mortgaged debt, the debtor receives any surplus. If the sale proceeds are insufficient to cover the foreclosure costs and the mortgaged debt, however, the **mortgagee** (the creditor-lender) can seek to recover the difference from the **mortgagor** (the debtor) by obtaining a deficiency judgment representing the difference between the mortgaged debt and the amount actually received from the proceeds of the foreclosure sale.

The mortgagee obtains a deficiency judgment in a separate legal action pursued subsequent to the foreclosure action. The deficiency judgment entitles the mortgagee to recover the amount of the deficiency from other property owned by the debtor.

Suretyship and Guaranty

When a third person promises to pay a debt owed by another in the event the debtor does not pay, either a *suretyship* or a *guaranty* relationship is created. Suretyship and guaranty provide creditors with the right to seek payment from the third party if the primary debtor defaults on her or his obligations. Exhibit 16–3 on the following page illustrates the relationship between a suretyship or guaranty party and the creditor.

Surety   A contract of strict **suretyship** is a promise made by a third person to be responsible for the debtor's obligation. It is an express contract between the **surety** (the third

MORTGAGE
A written instrument giving a creditor an interest in (lien on) the debtor's real property as security for payment of a debt.

MORTGAGEE
Under a mortgage agreement, the creditor who takes a security interest in the debtor's property.

MORTGAGOR
Under a mortgage agreement, the debtor who gives the creditor a security interest in the debtor's property in return for a mortgage loan.

SURETYSHIP
An express contract in which a third party to a debtor-creditor relationship (the surety) promises to be primarily responsible for the debtor's obligation.

SURETY
A person, such as a cosigner on a note, who agrees to be primarily responsible for the debt of another.

---

4. Some states (for example, Texas) do not permit garnishment of wages by private parties except under a child-support order.

5. For example, the federal Consumer Credit Protection Act of 1968, 15 U.S.C. Sections 1601–1693r, provides that a debtor can retain either 75 percent of the disposable earnings per week or a sum equivalent to thirty hours of work paid at federal minimum-wage rates, whichever is greater.

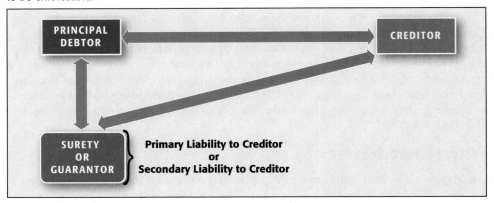

EXHIBIT 16–3 Suretyship and Guaranty Parties

In a suretyship or guaranty arrangement, a third party promises to be responsible for a debtor's obligations. A third party who agrees to be responsible for the debt even if the primary debtor does not default is known as a surety; a third party who agrees to be *secondarily* responsible for the debt—that is, responsible only if the primary debtor defaults—is known as a guarantor. As noted in Chapter 8, normally a promise of guaranty (a collateral, or secondary, promise) must be in writing to be enforceable.

party) and the creditor. The surety in the strictest sense is primarily liable for the debt of the principal. The creditor need not exhaust all legal remedies against the principal debtor before holding the surety responsible for payment. The creditor can demand payment from the surety from the moment the debt is due.

Guaranty   With a suretyship arrangement, the surety is *primarily* liable for the debtor's obligation. With a guaranty arrangement, the **guarantor**—the third person making the guaranty—is *secondarily* liable. The guarantor can be required to pay the obligation *only after the principal debtor defaults*, and default usually takes place only after the creditor has made an attempt to collect from the debtor.

The Statute of Frauds requires that a guaranty contract between the guarantor and the creditor must be in writing to be enforceable unless the *main purpose* exception (discussed in Chapter 8) applies.[6] A suretyship agreement, by contrast, need not be in writing to be enforceable. In other words, surety agreements can be oral, whereas guaranty contracts must be written.

GUARANTOR
A person who agrees to satisfy the debt of another (the debtor) only after the principal debtor defaults. Thus, a guarantor's liability is secondary.

PREVENTING LEGAL DISPUTES

Businesspersons should be careful when signing guaranty contracts and should explicitly indicate if they are signing on behalf of a company rather than personally. If a corporate officer or director, for example, signs her or his name on a guaranty for a third party without indicating that she or he is signing as a representative of the corporation, that individual might be held personally liable as the guarantor. Although a guaranty contract may be preferable to a suretyship contract in many situations because it creates secondary rather than primary liability, nevertheless substantial risk is involved. Moreover, depending on the wording used in a guaranty

---

6. Briefly, the main purpose exception provides that if the main purpose of the guaranty agreement is to benefit the guarantor, then the contract need not be in writing to be enforceable.

contract, the extent of the guarantor's liability may be unlimited or may continue over a series of transactions. Be absolutely clear about the potential liability before agreeing to serve as a guarantor, and contact an attorney for guidance.

Defenses of the Surety and the Guarantor   The defenses of the surety and the guarantor are basically the same. Therefore, the following discussion applies to both, although it refers only to the surety.

Actions Releasing the Surety.   Certain actions will release the surety from the obligation. For example, making any material modification in the terms of the original contract between the principal debtor and the creditor—including a binding extension of time for payment—without first obtaining the consent of the surety will discharge a gratuitous surety completely. (A *gratuitous surety* is one who receives no consideration in return for acting as a surety, such as a father who agrees to assume responsibility for his daughter's obligation.) A surety who is compensated (such as a venture capitalist who will profit from a loan made to the principal debtor) will be discharged to the extent that the surety suffers a loss. Naturally, if the principal obligation is paid by the debtor or by another person on behalf of the debtor, the surety is discharged from the obligation. Similarly, if valid tender of payment is made, and the creditor rejects it with knowledge of the surety's existence, the surety is released from any obligation on the debt.

In addition, if a creditor surrenders the collateral to the debtor or impairs the collateral while knowing of the surety and without the surety's consent, the surety is released to the extent of any loss suffered as a result of the creditor's actions. The primary reason for this requirement is to protect a surety who agreed to become obligated only because the debtor's collateral was in the possession of the creditor.

Defenses of the Principal Debtor.   Generally, the surety can use any defenses available to a principal debtor to avoid liability on the obligation to the creditor. The ability of the surety to assert any defenses the debtor may have against the creditor is the most important concept in suretyship. Therefore, it means that most of the defenses available to the debtor are also those of the surety. A few exceptions do exist, however. The surety cannot assert the principal debtor's incapacity or bankruptcy as a defense, nor can the surety assert the statute of limitations as a defense.

Obviously, a surety may also have his or her own defenses—for example, his or her own incapacity or bankruptcy. If the creditor fraudulently induced the surety to guarantee the debt of the debtor, the surety can assert fraud as a defense. In most states, the creditor has a legal duty to inform the surety, prior to the formation of the suretyship contract, of material facts known by the creditor that would substantially increase the surety's risk. Failure to so inform may constitute fraud and makes the suretyship obligation voidable.

Rights of the Surety and the Guarantor   Generally, when the surety or guarantor pays the debt owed to the creditor, the surety or guarantor is entitled to certain rights. The rights of the surety and guarantor are basically the same.

ADDITIONAL LAWS ASSISTING DEBTORS

The law protects debtors as well as creditors. Certain property of the debtor, for example, is exempt from creditors' actions. Probably the most familiar exemption is the **homestead exemption.** Each state permits the debtor to retain the family home, either in its entirety

HOMESTEAD EXEMPTION
A law permitting a debtor to retain the family home, either in its entirety or up to a specified dollar amount, free from the claims of unsecured creditors or trustees in bankruptcy.

Livestock, such as the cattle shown here, is usually considered exempt property under laws that assist debtors. Why do you think that lawmakers have made cattle exempt? (PhotoDisc)

or up to a specified dollar amount, free from the claims of unsecured creditors or trustees in bankruptcy (a *bankruptcy trustee* is appointed by the court to hold and protect the debtor's property, as will be discussed later in this chapter). The purpose of the homestead exemption is to ensure that the debtor will retain some form of shelter.

■**EXAMPLE 16.6** Suppose that Van Cleave owes Acosta $40,000. The debt is the subject of a lawsuit, and the court awards Acosta a judgment of $40,000 against Van Cleave. Van Cleave's home is valued at $50,000, and the state exemption on homesteads is $25,000. There are no outstanding mortgages or other liens. To satisfy the judgment debt, Van Cleave's family home is sold at public auction for $45,000. The proceeds of the sale are distributed as follows:

1 Van Cleave is given $25,000 as his homestead exemption.

2 Acosta is paid $20,000 toward the judgment debt, leaving a $20,000 deficiency judgment that can be satisfied from any other nonexempt property (personal or real) that Van Cleave may have, if allowed by state law. ■

Various types of personal property may also be exempt from satisfaction of judgment debts. Personal property that is most often exempt includes the following:

1 Household furniture up to a specified dollar amount.

2 Clothing and certain personal possessions, such as family pictures or a Bible or other religious text.

3 A vehicle (or vehicles) for transportation (at least up to a specified dollar amount).

4 Certain classified animals, usually livestock but including pets.

5 Equipment that the debtor uses in a business or trade, such as tools or professional instruments, up to a specified dollar amount.

BANKRUPTCY PROCEEDINGS

Bankruptcy law in the United States has two goals—to protect a debtor by giving him or her a fresh start, free from creditors' claims, and to ensure equitable treatment to creditors who are competing for a debtor's assets. Bankruptcy law is federal law, but state laws on secured transactions, liens, judgments, and exemptions also play a role in federal bankruptcy proceedings. Bankruptcy proceedings are held in federal bankruptcy courts, which are under the authority of U.S. district courts, and rulings by bankruptcy courts can be appealed to the district courts.

Bankruptcy law prior to 2005 was based on the Bankruptcy Reform Act of 1978, as amended (called the Bankruptcy Code). In 2005, Congress enacted a new Bankruptcy Reform Act.[7] As you will read in the following sections, the 2005 act significantly overhauled certain provisions of the Bankruptcy Code for the first time in twenty-five years. Because of its significance for creditors and debtors alike, we present the Bankruptcy Reform Act as this chapter's *Landmark in the Law* feature.

The Bankruptcy Code is contained in Title 11 of the *United States Code* (U.S.C.) and has eight "chapters." Chapters 1, 3, and 5 of the Code include general definitional provisions and provisions governing case administration and procedures, creditors, the debtor, and the estate. These three chapters of the Code normally apply to all types of bankruptcies. There are five other chapters that set forth the different types of relief that debtors may

---

7. The full title of the act is the Bankruptcy Abuse Prevention and Consumer Protection Act of 2005, Pub. L. No. 109-8, 119 Stat. 23 (April 20, 2005).

The Bankruptcy Reform Act of 2005

When Congress enacted the Bankruptcy Reform Act of 1978, many claimed that the new act made it too easy for debtors to file for bankruptcy protection. The Bankruptcy Reform Act of 2005 was passed, in part, in response to businesses' concerns about the rise in personal bankruptcy filings. Certainly, the facts cannot be denied: from 1978 to 2005, personal bankruptcy filings increased ninefold, reaching a peak of 1,613,097 in the year ending June 30, 2003. By the early 2000s, various business groups—including credit-card companies, banks, and firms providing loans for automobile purchases—were claiming that the bankruptcy process was being abused and that reform was necessary. As Mallory Duncan of the National Retail Federation put it, bankruptcy had gone from being a "stigma" to being a "financial planning tool" for many debtors.[a]

More Repayment Plans, Fewer Liquidation Bankruptcies   One of the major goals of the Bankruptcy Reform Act of 2005 is to require consumers to pay as many of their debts as they possibly can instead of having those debts fully discharged in bank-ruptcy. Prior to the new law, the vast majority of bankruptcies were filed under Chapter 7 of the Bankruptcy Code, which permits debtors, with some exceptions, to have *all* of their debts discharged in bankruptcy. Only about 20 percent of personal bankruptcies were filed under Chapter 13 of the Bankruptcy Code. As you will read later in this chapter, this part of the Bankruptcy Code requires the debtor to establish a repayment plan and pay off as many of his or her debts as possible over a maximum period of five years. Under the 2005 legislation, more debtors have to file for bankruptcy under Chapter 13.

Other Significant Provisions of the Act   Another important provision of the Bankruptcy Reform Act of 2005 involves the homestead exemption. Prior to the passage of the act, some states allowed debtors petitioning for bankruptcy to exempt all of the equity (the market value minus the outstanding mortgage owed) in their homes during bankruptcy proceedings. The 2005 act leaves these exemptions in place but puts some limits on their use. The 2005 act also includes a number of other changes. For example, one provision gives child-support obligations priority over other debts and allows enforcement agencies to continue efforts to collect child-support payments.

APPLICATION TO TODAY'S WORLD   *The Bankruptcy Reform Act of 2005 subjects a large class of individuals in the United States to increased financial risk. Supporters of the law hope that it will curb abuse by deterring financially troubled debtors from viewing bankruptcy as a mere "planning tool" instead of as a last resort. Certainly, fewer debtors are allowed to have their debts discharged in Chapter 7 liquidation proceedings. At the same time, the 2005 act makes it more difficult for debtors to obtain a "fresh start" financially—one of the major goals of bankruptcy law in the United States. Under the 2005 act, more debtors are forced to file under Chapter 13. Additionally, the act has made the bankruptcy process more time consuming and costly because it requires more extensive documentation and certification.*

RELEVANT WEB SITES   *To locate information on the Web concerning the 2005 bankruptcy reform legislation, go to this text's Web site at* **academic.cengage.com/blaw/blt**, *select "Chapter 16," and click on "URLs for Landmarks."*

a. As cited in Nedra Pickler, "Bush Signs Big Rewrite of Bankruptcy Law," *Los Angeles Times,* April 20, 2005.

RECALL Congress regulates the jurisdiction of the federal courts, within the limits set by the U.S. Constitution. Congress can expand or reduce the number of federal courts at any time.

LIQUIDATION
The sale of all of the nonexempt assets of a debtor and the distribution of the proceeds to the debtor's creditors. Chapter 7 of the Bankruptcy Code provides for liquidation bankruptcy proceedings.

CONSUMER-DEBTOR
An individual whose debts are primarily consumer debts (debts for purchases made primarily for personal, family, or household use).

DISCHARGE
In bankruptcy proceedings, the extinction of the debtor's dischargeable debts, thereby relieving the debtor of the obligation to pay the debts.

PETITION IN BANKRUPTCY
The document that is filed with a bankruptcy court to initiate bankruptcy proceedings. The official forms required for a petition in bankruptcy must be completed accurately, sworn to under oath, and signed by the debtor.

U.S. TRUSTEE
A government official who performs certain administrative tasks that a bankruptcy judge would otherwise have to perform.

seek. Chapter 7 provides for **liquidation** proceedings (the selling of all nonexempt assets and the distribution of the proceeds to the debtor's creditors). Chapter 9 governs the adjustment of the debts of municipalities. Chapter 11 governs reorganizations. Chapter 12 (for family farmers) and Chapter 13 (for individuals) provide for adjustment of the debts of parties with regular income.[8] A debtor (except for a municipality) need not be insolvent[9] to file for bankruptcy relief under the Bankruptcy Code. Anyone obligated to a creditor can declare bankruptcy.

To fully inform a consumer-debtor of the various types of relief available, the Code requires that the clerk of the court provide certain information to all consumer-debtors prior to the commencement of a bankruptcy filing. A **consumer-debtor** is a debtor whose debts result primarily from the purchase of goods for personal, family, or household use. First, the clerk must give consumer-debtors written notice of the general purpose, benefits, and costs of each chapter of bankruptcy under which they may proceed. Second, the clerk must provide consumer-debtors with informational materials on the types of services available from credit counseling agencies.

In the following pages, we deal first with liquidation proceedings under Chapter 7 of the Code. We then examine the procedures required for Chapter 11 reorganizations and for Chapter 12 and Chapter 13 plans.

Chapter 7–Liquidation

Liquidation is the most familiar type of bankruptcy proceeding and is often referred to as an *ordinary,* or *straight, bankruptcy.* Put simply, a debtor in a liquidation bankruptcy turns all assets over to a trustee. The trustee sells the nonexempt assets and distributes the proceeds to creditors. With certain exceptions, the remaining debts are then **discharged** (extinguished), and the debtor is relieved of the obligation to pay the debts.

Any "person"—defined as including individuals, partnerships, and corporations[10]— may be a debtor under Chapter 7. Railroads, insurance companies, banks, savings and loan associations, investment companies licensed by the Small Business Administration, and credit unions *cannot* be Chapter 7 debtors, however. Other chapters of the Code or other federal or state statutes apply to them. A husband and wife may file jointly for bankruptcy under a single petition.

A straight bankruptcy may be commenced by the filing of either a voluntary or an involuntary **petition in bankruptcy**—the document that is filed with a bankruptcy court to initiate bankruptcy proceedings. If a debtor files the petition, then it is a *voluntary bankruptcy.* If one or more creditors file a petition to force the debtor into bankruptcy, then it is called an *involuntary bankruptcy.*

Voluntary Bankruptcy   To bring a voluntary petition in bankruptcy, the debtor files official forms designated for that purpose in the bankruptcy court. The Bankruptcy Reform Act of 2005 specifies that *before* debtors can file a petition, they must receive credit counseling from an approved nonprofit agency within the 180-day period preceding the date of filing. The act provides detailed criteria for the **U.S. trustee** (a government official who

---

8. There are no Chapters 2, 4, 6, 8, or 10 in Title 11. Such "gaps" are not uncommon in the *United States Code.* They occur because, when a statute is enacted, chapter numbers (or other subdivisional unit numbers) are sometimes reserved for future use. (A gap may also appear if a law has been repealed.)

9. The inability to pay debts as they become due is known as *equitable* insolvency. A *balance-sheet* insolvency, which exists when a debtor's liabilities exceed assets, is not the test. Thus, it is possible for debtors to petition voluntarily for bankruptcy even though their assets far exceed their liabilities. This situation may occur when a debtor's cash-flow problems become severe.

10. The definition of *corporation* includes unincorporated companies and associations. It also covers labor unions.

performs appointment and other administrative tasks that a bankruptcy judge would otherwise have to perform) to approve nonprofit budget and counseling agencies and requires a list of approved agencies to be made publicly available. A debtor filing a Chapter 7 petition must include a certificate proving that he or she attended an individual or group briefing from an approved counseling agency within the last 180 days (roughly six months).

The Code requires a consumer-debtor who has opted for liquidation bankruptcy proceedings to confirm the accuracy of the petition's contents. The debtor must also state in the petition, at the time of filing, that he or she understands the relief available under other chapters of the Code and has chosen to proceed under Chapter 7. If an attorney is representing the consumer-debtor, the attorney must file an affidavit stating that she or he has informed the debtor of the relief available under each chapter of bankruptcy. In addition, the 2005 act requires the attorney to reasonably attempt to verify the accuracy of the consumer-debtor's petition and schedules (described below). Failure to do so is considered perjury.

Chapter 7 Schedules.   The voluntary petition contains the following schedules:

1 A list of both secured and unsecured creditors, their addresses, and the amount of debt owed to each.

2 A statement of the financial affairs of the debtor.

3 A list of all property owned by the debtor, including property claimed by the debtor to be exempt.

4 A listing of current income and expenses.

5 A certificate of credit counseling (as discussed previously).

6 Copies of evidence of payments received from employers within sixty days prior to the filing of the petition.

7 A statement of the amount of monthly income, itemized to show how the amount is calculated.

8 A copy of the debtor's federal income tax return for the most recent year ending immediately before the filing of the petition.

As previously noted, the official forms must be completed accurately, sworn to under oath, and signed by the debtor. To conceal assets or knowingly supply false information on these schedules is a crime under the bankruptcy laws. At the request of the court, the U.S. trustee, or any party of interest, the debtor must file tax returns at the end of each tax year while the case is pending and provide copies to the court. This requirement also applies to Chapter 11 and 13 bankruptcies (discussed later in this chapter).

With the exception of tax returns, failure to file the required schedules within forty-five days after the filing of the petition (unless an extension up to forty-five days is granted) will result in an automatic dismissal of the petition. The debtor has up to seven days before the date of the first creditors' meeting to provide a copy of the most current tax returns to the trustee.

When Substantial Abuse Will Be Presumed.   The Bankruptcy Reform Act of 2005 established a new system of "means testing"—based on the debtor's income—to determine whether a debtor's petition is presumed to be a "substantial abuse" of Chapter 7. If the debtor's family income is greater than the median family income in the state in which the petition is filed, the trustee or any party in interest (such as a creditor) can bring a motion to dismiss the Chapter 7 petition. State median incomes vary from state to state and are calculated and reported by the U.S. Bureau of the Census.

The debtor's current monthly income is calculated using the last six months' average income, less certain "allowed expenses" reflecting the basic needs of the debtor. The monthly amount is then multiplied by twelve. If the resulting income exceeds the state median income by $6,000 or more,[11] abuse is presumed, and the trustee or any creditor can file a motion to dismiss the petition. A debtor can rebut (refute) the presumption of abuse "by demonstrating special circumstances that justify additional expenses or adjustments of current monthly income for which there is no reasonable alternative." (An example might be anticipated medical costs not covered by health insurance.) These additional expenses or adjustments must be itemized and their accuracy attested to under oath by the debtor.

When Substantial Abuse Will Not Be Presumed. If the debtor's income is below the state median (or if the debtor has successfully rebutted the means-test presumption), abuse will not be presumed. In these situations, the court may still find substantial abuse, but the creditors will not have standing (see Chapter 1) to file a motion to dismiss. Basically, this leaves intact the prior law on substantial abuse, allowing the court to consider such factors as the debtor's bad faith or circumstances indicating substantial abuse.

Can a debtor seeking relief under Chapter 7 exclude voluntary contributions to a retirement plan as a reasonably necessary expense in calculating her income? The Code does not disallow the contributions, but whether their exclusion constitutes substantial abuse requires a review of the debtor's circumstances, as in the following case.

---

11. This amount ($6,000) is the equivalent of $100 per month for five years, indicating that the debtor could pay at least $100 per month under a Chapter 13 five-year repayment plan.

CASE 16.2 Hebbring v. U.S. Trustee

United States Court of Appeals, Ninth Circuit, 463 F.3d 902 (2006).

FACTS In 2003, Lisa Hebbring owned a single-family home in Reno, Nevada, valued at $160,000, on which she owed $154,103. She also owned a 2001 Volkswagen Beetle valued at $14,000, on which she owed $18,839, and other personal property valued at $1,775. She earned $49,000 per year as a customer service representative for SBC Nevada. In June, Hebbring filed a Chapter 7 petition in a federal bankruptcy court, seeking relief from $11,124 in credit-card debt. Her petition listed monthly net income of $2,813 and expenditures of $2,897, for a deficit of $84. In calculating her income, Hebbring excluded a $232 monthly pretax deduction for a contribution to a retirement plan maintained by her employer and an $81 monthly after-tax deduction for a contribution to her own retirement savings. At the time, Hebbring was thirty-three years old. The U.S. trustee assigned to oversee her case filed a motion to dismiss her petition for substantial abuse,

arguing in part that the retirement savings contributions should be disallowed. According to the trustee, these and other adjustments would leave Hebbring $615 per month in disposable income, which would be enough to repay 100 percent of her credit-card debt over three years. The court dismissed her petition. She appealed to a federal district court, which affirmed the dismissal. Hebbring appealed to the U.S. Court of Appeals for the Ninth Circuit.

ISSUE Based on Hebbring's age and financial circumstances, would granting her petition in bankruptcy constitute substantial abuse?

DECISION Yes. The U.S. Court of Appeals for the Ninth Circuit affirmed the lower court's decision, "finding that Hebbring's retirement contributions are not reasonably necessary based on her age and financial circumstances, and that she is therefore capable of paying her unsecured debts."

CASE 16.2–Continued

REASON The appellate court emphasized the facts of Hebbring's situation. She was thirty-three years old, earning $49,000 per year, making mortgage payments on a house, and contributing about 8 percent of her income toward her retirement savings. "In light of these circumstances, the bankruptcy court's conclusion that Hebbring's retirement contributions are not a reasonably necessary expense is not clearly erroneous." Furthermore, based on the information that Hebbring provided on the schedules she submitted with her bankruptcy petition, even excluding her voluntary retirement plan contributions, she "has $172 per month in disposable income, sufficient to repay 56% of her unsecured [credit-card] debt over three years or 93% over five years * * * . The bankruptcy court thus did not err in finding that Hebbring is able to [pay at least] a substantial portion of the unsecured claims."

 FOR CRITICAL ANALYSIS–Ethical Consideration
Is it fair for the court to treat retirement payments differently depending on a person's age?

Additional Grounds for Dismissal.   As noted, a debtor's voluntary petition for Chapter 7 relief may be dismissed for substantial abuse or for failing to provide the necessary documents (such as schedules and tax returns) within the specified time. In addition, a motion to dismiss a Chapter 7 filing might be granted in two other situations under the Bankruptcy Reform Act of 2005. First, if the debtor has been convicted of a violent crime or a drug-trafficking offense, the victim can file a motion to dismiss the voluntary petition.[12] Second, if the debtor fails to pay postpetition domestic-support obligations (which include child and spousal support), the court may dismiss the debtor's Chapter 7 petition.

ETHICAL ISSUE 16.1

Is it fair to increase the costs for debtors seeking bankruptcy relief? The 2005 Bankruptcy Reform Act has increased the costs of filing for bankruptcy. Not only has the filing fee for Chapter 7 bankruptcies increased from $155 to $200, but attorneys' fees will likely increase also—and attorneys' fees, rather than filing fees, typically constitute the major expense for bankruptcy filings. Attorneys will likely raise the fees they charge to handle bankruptcy cases in the wake of the 2005 act because they will be assuming greater risk. Under the new law, the debtor's attorney must certify the accuracy of all factual allegations in the bankruptcy petition and schedules under the penalty of perjury. In other words, attorneys may be subject to sanctions (fines) if there are any factual inaccuracies.

Because the attorney will be held accountable for factual inaccuracies, she or he will most likely want to independently investigate the truth of the facts stated in the petition and schedules. This may entail hiring private investigators, appraisers, and auditors for assistance in researching and accounting for all of the debtor's income and assets. Ultimately, the debtor will end up paying these costs. Is this fair considering that a main goal of bankruptcy is to give debtors a fresh start?

Order for Relief.   If the voluntary petition for bankruptcy is found to be proper, the filing of the petition will itself constitute an order for relief. (An **order for relief** is the court's grant of assistance to a debtor.) Once a consumer-debtor's voluntary petition has been filed, the clerk of the court (or other appointee) must give the trustee and creditors

ORDER FOR RELIEF
A court's grant of assistance to a debtor. In bankruptcy proceedings, the order relieves the debtor of the immediate obligation to pay the debts listed in the bankruptcy petition.

---

12. Note that the court may not dismiss a case on this ground if the debtor's bankruptcy is necessary to satisfy a claim for a domestic-support obligation.

notice of the order for relief by mail not more than twenty days after the entry of the order.

Involuntary Bankruptcy An involuntary bankruptcy occurs when the debtor's creditors force the debtor into bankruptcy proceedings. An involuntary case cannot be commenced against a farmer[13] or a charitable institution. For an involuntary action to be filed against other debtors, the following requirements must be met: If the debtor has twelve or more creditors, three or more of those creditors having unsecured claims totaling at least $13,475 must join in the petition. If a debtor has fewer than twelve creditors, one or more creditors having a claim of $13,475 or more may file.

If the debtor challenges the involuntary petition, a hearing will be held, and the bankruptcy court will determine if the involuntary petition is appropriate. An involuntary petition should not be used as an everyday debt-collection device, however, and the Code provides penalties for the filing of frivolous (unjustified) petitions against debtors. If the court allows the bankruptcy to proceed, the debtor will be required to supply the same information in the bankruptcy schedules as in a voluntary bankruptcy.

Automatic Stay The moment a petition, either voluntary or involuntary, is filed, an **automatic stay,** or suspension, of virtually all actions by creditors against the debtor or the debtor's property normally goes into effect. In other words, once a petition has been filed, creditors cannot contact the debtor by phone or mail or start any legal proceedings to recover debts or to repossess property. A secured creditor or other party in interest, however, may petition the bankruptcy court for relief from the automatic stay. If a creditor knowingly violates the automatic stay (a willful violation), any injured party, including the debtor, is entitled to recover actual damages, costs, and attorneys' fees and may be entitled to recover punitive damages as well.

Exceptions to the Automatic Stay. The 2005 Bankruptcy Reform Act provides several exceptions to the automatic stay. A new exception is created for domestic-support obligations, which include any debt owed to or recoverable by a spouse, former spouse, child of the debtor, a child's parent or guardian, or a governmental unit. In addition, proceedings against the debtor related to divorce, child custody or visitation, domestic violence, and support enforcement are not stayed.

Limitations on the Automatic Stay. Under the new Code, if a creditor or other party in interest requests relief from the stay, the stay will automatically terminate sixty days after the request, unless the court grants an extension[14] or the parties agree otherwise. Also, the automatic stay on secured debts normally will terminate thirty days after the petition is filed if the debtor had filed a bankruptcy petition that was dismissed within the prior year. Any party in interest can request the court to extend the stay by showing that the filing is in good faith.

If two or more bankruptcy petitions are dismissed during the prior year, the Code presumes bad faith, and the automatic stay does not go into effect until the court determines that the filing was made in good faith. In addition, if the petition is subsequently dismissed because the debtor failed to file the required documents within thirty days of filing, for example, the stay is terminated. Finally, the automatic stay on secured property termi-

AUTOMATIC STAY
In bankruptcy proceedings, the suspension of virtually all litigation and other action by creditors against the debtor or the debtor's property. The stay is effective the moment the debtor files a petition in bankruptcy.

---

13. The definition of *farmer* includes persons who receive more than 50 percent of their gross income from farming operations, such as tilling the soil; dairy farming; ranching; or the production or raising of crops, poultry, or livestock. Corporations and partnerships, as well as individuals, can be farmers.
14. The court might grant an extension, for example, on a motion by the trustee that the property is of value to the estate.

nates forty-five days after the creditors' meeting (to be discussed shortly) unless the debtor redeems or reaffirms certain debts. In other words, the debtor cannot keep the secured property (such as a financed automobile), even if she or he continues to make payments on it, without reinstating the rights of the secured party to collect on the debt.

Property of the Estate   On the commencement of a liquidation proceeding under Chapter 7, an **estate in property** is created. The estate consists of all the debtor's interests in property currently held, wherever located, together with community property (property jointly owned by a husband and wife in certain states—see Chapter 23), property transferred in a transaction voidable by the trustee, proceeds and profits from the property of the estate, and certain after-acquired property. Interests in certain property—such as gifts, inheritances, property settlements (from divorce), and life insurance death proceeds—to which the debtor becomes entitled *within 180 days after filing* may also become part of the estate. Under the 2005 act, withholdings for employee benefit plan contributions are excluded from the estate. Generally, though, the filing of a bankruptcy petition fixes a dividing line: property acquired prior to the filing of the petition becomes property of the estate, and property acquired after the filing of the petition, except as just noted, remains the debtor's.

Creditors' Meeting and Claims   Within a reasonable time after the order of relief has been granted (not less than ten days or more than thirty days), the trustee must call a meeting of the creditors listed in the schedules filed by the debtor. The bankruptcy judge does not attend this meeting, but the debtor must attend and submit to an examination under oath. At the meeting, the trustee ensures that the debtor is aware of the potential consequences of bankruptcy and of his or her ability to file under a different chapter of the Bankruptcy Code. To be entitled to receive a portion of the debtor's estate, each creditor normally files a *proof of claim* with the bankruptcy court clerk within ninety days of the creditors' meeting.[15] The proof of claim lists the creditor's name and address, as well as the amount that the creditor asserts is owed to the creditor by the debtor. A proof of claim is necessary if there is any dispute concerning the claim but not if the debtor's schedules list the creditor's claim as liquidated (exactly determined).

Exemptions   The trustee takes control over the debtor's property, but an individual debtor is entitled to exempt certain property from the bankruptcy. The Bankruptcy Code exempts the following property:[16]

1 Up to $20,200 in equity in the debtor's residence and burial plot (the homestead exemption).

2 Interest in a motor vehicle up to $3,225.

3 Interest, up to $525 for a particular item, in household goods and furnishings, wearing apparel, appliances, books, animals, crops, and musical instruments (the aggregate total of all items is limited, however, to $10,775).

4 Interest in jewelry up to $1,350.

5 Interest in any other property up to $1,075, plus any unused part of the $20,200 homestead exemption up to $10,125.

6 Interest in any tools of the debtor's trade up to $2,025.

7 Any unmatured life insurance contracts owned by the debtor.

ESTATE IN PROPERTY
In bankruptcy proceedings, all of the debtor's interests in property currently held, wherever located, together with certain jointly owned property, property transferred in transactions voidable by the trustee, proceeds and profits from the property of the estate, and certain property interests to which the debtor becomes entitled within 180 days after filing for bankruptcy.

---

15. This ninety-day rule applies in Chapter 12 and Chapter 13 bankruptcies as well.

16. The dollar amounts stated in the Bankruptcy Code are adjusted automatically every three years on April 1 based on changes in the Consumer Price Index. The adjusted amounts are rounded to the nearest $25. The amounts stated in this chapter are in accordance with those computed on April 1, 2007.

Because of Florida's unlimited homestead exemption law, the state has been a haven for wealthy individuals looking to shield equity from creditors. This house in Boca Raton, Florida, shown while still under construction, belonged to Scott Sullivan, former chief financial officer of WorldCom. WorldCom, now known as MCI, filed the largest bankruptcy in U.S. history about the same time this picture was taken in 2002. In 2005, Sullivan settled the WorldCom Securities Class Action Litigation by, among other things, surrendering the proceeds from the sale of the Florida house. The ten-bedroom, twelve-bath mansion with a boathouse, dock, and wine cellar went for $9.7 million, although the asking price was once $22.5 million. Under the 2005 Code, would Sullivan have thought he could take advantage of Florida's unlimited homestead exemption? Why or why not? (Joe Raedle/Getty Images)

8 Certain interests in accrued dividends and interest under life insurance contracts owned by the debtor, not to exceed $10,775.

9 Professionally prescribed health aids.

10 The right to receive Social Security and certain welfare benefits, alimony and support, certain retirement funds and pensions, and education savings accounts held for specific periods of time.

11 The right to receive certain personal-injury and other awards up to $20,200.

Individual states have the power to pass legislation precluding debtors from using the federal exemptions within the state; a majority of the states have done this, as mentioned earlier in this chapter. In those states, debtors may use only state, not federal, exemptions. In the rest of the states, an individual debtor (or a husband and wife filing jointly) may choose either the exemptions provided under state law or the federal exemptions.

The Homestead Exemption The 2005 Bankruptcy Reform Act significantly changed the law for those debtors seeking to use state homestead exemption statutes (which were discussed previously). In six states, including Florida and Texas, homestead exemptions allow debtors petitioning for bankruptcy to shield unlimited amounts of equity in their homes from creditors. Under the prior Bankruptcy Code, the debtor had to have been domiciled in the state for at least six months to apply any of the state exemptions. The 2005 act increased the domicile period to two years. In other words, now the debtor must have lived in the state for two years prior to filing the petition to be able to use the state homestead exemption.

In addition, if the homestead was acquired within three and one-half years preceding the date of filing, the maximum equity exempted is $136,875, even if the state law would permit a higher amount. Also, if the debtor owes a debt arising from a violation of securities law or if the debtor committed certain criminal or tortious acts in the previous five years that indicate the filing was substantial abuse, the debtor may not exempt any amount of equity.

The Trustee Promptly after the order for relief has been entered, an interim, or provisional, trustee is appointed by the U.S. trustee. The interim, or provisional, trustee presides over the debtor's property until the first meeting of creditors. At this first meeting, either a permanent trustee is elected, or the interim trustee becomes the permanent trustee.

The basic duty of the trustee is to collect the debtor's available estate and reduce it to cash for distribution, preserving the interests of both the debtor and the unsecured creditors. This requires that the trustee be accountable for administering the debtor's estate. To enable the trustee to accomplish this duty, the Code gives the trustee certain powers, stated in both general and specific terms. These powers must be exercised within two years of the order for relief.

New Duties under the 2005 Act. Under the new law, the U.S. trustee or bankruptcy administrator is required to promptly review all materials filed by the debtor. Not later than ten days after the first meeting of the creditors, the trustee must file a statement as to whether the case is presumed to be an abuse under the means test. The trustee must then provide a copy of this statement concerning abuse to all creditors within five days. Not later than forty days after the first creditors' meeting, the trustee must either file a motion to dismiss the petition (or convert it to a Chapter 13 case) or file a statement setting forth the reasons why the motion would not be appropriate.

Under the 2005 act, the trustee also has new duties designed to protect domestic-support creditors (those to whom a domestic-support obligation is due). The trustee is required to provide written notice of the bankruptcy to the claim holder (a former spouse who is owed child support, for example). The notice must also include certain information, such as the debtor's address, the name and address of the debtor's last known employer, and the address and phone number of the state child-support enforcement agency. (Note that these requirements are not limited to Chapter 7 bankruptcies, and the trustee may have additional duties in other types of bankruptcy to collect assets for distribution to the domestic-support creditor.)

Trustee's Powers. The trustee occupies a position *equivalent* in rights to that of certain other parties. For example, the trustee has the same rights as a creditor who could have obtained a judicial lien or levy execution on the debtor's property. This means that a trustee has priority over an unperfected secured party to the debtor's property. This right of a trustee, equivalent to that of a lien creditor, is known as the *strong-arm power.*

The trustee has the power to require persons holding the debtor's property at the time the petition is filed to deliver the property to the trustee. Usually, a trustee does not take actual physical possession of a debtor's property but instead takes constructive possession by exercising control over the property. **■EXAMPLE 16.7** Suppose that a trustee needs to obtain possession of a debtor's trucks. The trustee could notify the debtor and take the keys to the trucks—without actually moving the trucks—to effectively take possession of them. ■

The trustee also has specific powers of *avoidance*—that is, the trustee can set aside a sale or other transfer of the debtor's property, taking it back as a part of the debtor's estate. These powers include any voidable rights available to the debtor, preferences, certain statutory liens, and fraudulent transfers by the debtor. Each of these powers is discussed in more detail below. Note that under the 2005 act, the trustee no longer has the power to avoid any transfer that was a bona fide payment of a domestic-support debt.

The debtor shares most of the trustee's avoidance powers. Thus, if the trustee does not take action to enforce one of the rights mentioned above, the debtor in a liquidation bankruptcy can still enforce that right.[17]

A trustee steps into the shoes of the debtor. Thus, any reason that a debtor can use to obtain the return of his or her property can be used by the trustee as well. These grounds for recovery include fraud, duress, incapacity, and mutual mistake.

Distribution of Property The Code provides specific rules for the distribution of the debtor's property to secured and unsecured creditors (to be discussed shortly.) If any amount remains after the priority classes of creditors have been satisfied, it is turned over to the debtor. Exhibit 16–4 on the next page illustrates graphically the collection and distribution of property in most voluntary bankruptcies.

In a bankruptcy case in which the debtor has no assets,[18] creditors are notified of the debtor's petition for bankruptcy but are instructed not to file a claim. In such a case, the unsecured creditors will receive no payment, and most, if not all, of these debts will be discharged.

Distribution to Secured Creditors. The rights of perfected secured creditors were discussed earlier in this chapter. The Code provides that a consumer-debtor, either within thirty days of filing a liquidation petition or before the date of the first meeting of the creditors (whichever is first), must file with the clerk a statement of intention with respect to the secured collateral. The statement must indicate whether the debtor will redeem the collateral (make a single payment equal to the current value of the property), reaffirm the debt (continue making payments on the debt), or surrender the property to the secured

---

17. Under a Chapter 11 bankruptcy (to be discussed later in this chapter), for which no trustee other than the debtor generally exists, the debtor has the same avoidance powers as a trustee under Chapter 7. Under Chapters 12 and 13 (also to be discussed later in this chapter), a trustee must be appointed.
18. This type of bankruptcy is called a "no-asset" case.

EXHIBIT 16-4 Collection and Distribution of Property in Most Voluntary Bankruptcies

This exhibit illustrates the property that might be collected in a debtor's voluntary bankruptcy and how it might be distributed to creditors. Involuntary bankruptcies and some voluntary bankruptcies could include additional types of property and other creditors.

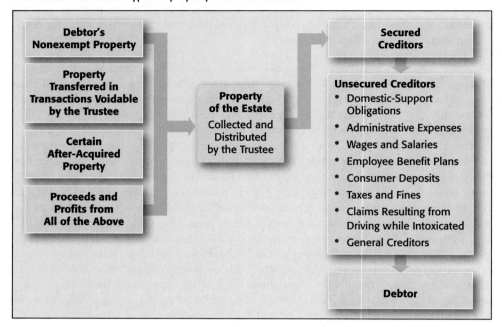

party.[19] The trustee is obligated to enforce the debtor's statement within forty-five days after the meeting of the creditors. As noted previously, failure of the debtor to redeem or reaffirm within forty-five days terminates the automatic stay.

If the collateral is surrendered to the perfected secured party, the secured creditor can enforce the security interest either by accepting the property in full satisfaction of the debt or by foreclosing on the collateral and using the proceeds to pay off the debt. Thus, the perfected secured party has priority over unsecured parties as to the proceeds from the disposition of the collateral.

Distribution to Unsecured Creditors. Bankruptcy law establishes an order of priority for classes of debts owed to *unsecured* creditors, and they are paid in the order of their priority. Each class must be fully paid before the next class is entitled to any of the remaining proceeds. If there are insufficient proceeds to pay fully all the creditors in a class, the proceeds are distributed *proportionately* to the creditors in that class, and classes lower in priority receive nothing. If there is any balance remaining after all the creditors are paid, it is returned to the debtor.

The new bankruptcy law elevated domestic-support (mainly child-support) obligations to the highest priority of unsecured claims—so these are the first debts to be paid. After that, administrative expenses related to the bankruptcy (such as court costs, trustee fees, and attorneys' fees) are paid; next come any expenses that a debtor in an involuntary bankruptcy incurs in the ordinary course of business. Unpaid wages, salaries, and commissions earned within ninety days prior to the petition are paid next, followed by certain claims for contributions to employee benefit plans, claims by farmers and fishermen, consumer deposits,

---

19. Also, if applicable, the debtor must specify whether the collateral will be claimed as exempt property.

and certain taxes. Claims of general creditors rank last in the order of priority, which is why these unsecured creditors often receive little, if anything, in a Chapter 7 bankruptcy.

Discharge From the debtor's point of view, the purpose of a liquidation proceeding is to obtain a fresh start through the discharge of debts.[20] As mentioned earlier, once the debtor's assets have been distributed to creditors as permitted by the Code, the debtor's remaining debts are then discharged, meaning that the debtor is not obligated to pay them. Certain debts, however, are not dischargeable in bankruptcy. Also, certain debtors may not qualify to have all debts discharged in bankruptcy. These situations are discussed below.

BE AWARE Often, a discharge in bankruptcy—even under Chapter 7— does not free a debtor of *all* of her or his debts.

Exceptions to Discharge. Discharge of a debt may be denied because of the nature of the claim or the conduct of the debtor. A court will not discharge claims that are based on a debtor's willful or malicious conduct or fraud, or claims related to property or funds that the debtor obtained by false pretenses, embezzlement, or larceny. Any monetary judgment against the debtor for driving while intoxicated cannot be discharged in bankruptcy. When a debtor fails to list a creditor on the bankruptcy schedules (and thus the creditor is not notified of the bankruptcy), that creditor's claims are not dischargeable.

Claims that are not dischargeable in a liquidation bankruptcy include amounts due to the government for taxes, fines, or penalties.[21] Additionally, amounts borrowed by the debtor to pay these taxes will not be discharged. Domestic-support obligations and property settlements arising from a divorce or separation cannot be discharged. Certain student loans or educational debts are not dischargeable (unless payment of the loans imposes an undue hardship on the debtor and the debtor's dependents), nor are amounts due on a retirement account loan. Consumer debts for purchasing luxury items worth more than $550 and cash advances totaling more than $825 are generally not dischargeable.

Objections to Discharge. In addition to the exceptions to discharge previously listed, a bankruptcy court may also deny the discharge of the *debtor* (as opposed to the debt). Grounds for the denial of discharge of the debtor include the following:

1 The debtor's concealment or destruction of property with the intent to hinder, delay, or defraud a creditor.

2 The debtor's fraudulent concealment or destruction of financial records.

3 The granting of a discharge to the debtor within eight years prior to the filing of the petition.

4 The debtor's failure to complete the required consumer education course (unless such a course is unavailable).

5 Proceedings in which the debtor could be found guilty of a felony.

The purpose of denying a discharge on these or other grounds is to prevent a debtor from avoiding, through bankruptcy, the consequences of his or her wrongful conduct. When a discharge is denied under these circumstances, the debtor's assets are still distributed to the creditors, but the debtor remains liable for the unpaid portions of all claims.

---

20. Discharges are granted under Chapter 7 only to *individuals*, not to corporations or partnerships. The latter may use Chapter 11, or they may terminate their existence under state law.

21. Taxes accruing within three years prior to bankruptcy are nondischargeable, including federal and state income taxes, employment taxes, taxes on gross receipts, property taxes, excise taxes, customs duties, and any other taxes for which the government claims the debtor is liable in some capacity. See 11 U.S.C. Sections 507(a)(8), 523(a)(1).

Chapter 11–Reorganization

The type of bankruptcy proceeding used most commonly by corporate debtors is the Chapter 11 *reorganization*. In a reorganization, the creditors and the debtor formulate a plan under which the debtor pays a portion of its debts and the rest of the debts are discharged. The debtor is allowed to continue in business. Although this type of bankruptcy is generally a corporate reorganization, any debtors (including individuals but excluding stockbrokers and commodities brokers) who are eligible for Chapter 7 relief are eligible for relief under Chapter 11. In 1994, Congress established a "fast-track" Chapter 11 procedure for small-business debtors whose liabilities do not exceed $2.19 million and who do not own or manage real estate. This allows bankruptcy proceedings without the appointment of committees and can save time and costs.

The same principles that govern the filing of a liquidation (Chapter 7) petition apply to reorganization (Chapter 11) proceedings. The case may be brought either voluntarily or involuntarily. The same guidelines govern the entry of the order for relief. The automatic-stay provision applies in reorganizations as well. The 2005 Bankruptcy Reform Act's exceptions to the automatic stay also apply to Chapter 11 proceedings, as do the new provisions regarding substantial abuse and additional grounds for dismissal (or conversion) of bankruptcy petitions. Also, the 2005 act contains specific rules and limitations for *individual* debtors who file a Chapter 11 petition. For example, an individual debtor's postpetition acquisitions and earnings become the property of the bankruptcy estate.

Under Section 305(a) of the Bankruptcy Code, a court, after notice and a hearing, may dismiss or suspend all proceedings in a case at any time if dismissal or suspension would better serve the interests of the creditors. Section 1112 also allows a court, after notice and a hearing, to dismiss a case under reorganization "for cause." Cause includes the absence of a reasonable likelihood of rehabilitation, the inability to effect a plan, and an unreasonable delay by the debtor that is prejudicial to (may harm the interests of) creditors.[22]

In some instances, creditors may prefer private, negotiated adjustments of creditor-debtor relations, also known as **workouts,** to bankruptcy proceedings. Often, these out-of-court workouts are much more flexible and thus more conducive to a speedy settlement. Speed is critical because delay is one of the most costly elements in any bankruptcy proceeding. Another advantage of workouts is that they avoid the various administrative costs of bankruptcy proceedings.

On entry of the order for relief, the debtor in Chapter 11 generally continues to operate the business as a **debtor in possession (DIP).** The court, however, may appoint a trustee (often referred to as a *receiver*) to operate the debtor's business if gross mismanagement of the business is shown or if appointing a trustee is in the best interests of the estate.

The DIP's role is similar to that of a trustee in a liquidation. The DIP is entitled to avoid preferential payments made to creditors and fraudulent transfers of assets. The DIP has the power to decide whether to cancel or assume prepetition executory contracts (those that are not yet performed) or unexpired leases.

The Reorganization Plan   A reorganization plan to rehabilitate the debtor is a plan to conserve and administer the debtor's assets in the hope of an eventual return to successful operation and solvency.

Filing the Plan.   Only the debtor may file a plan within the first 120 days after the date of the order for relief. Under the 2005 act, the 120-day period may be extended, but not beyond 18 months from the date of the order for relief. If the debtor does not meet the

WORKOUT
An out-of-court agreement between a debtor and creditors in which the parties work out a payment plan or schedule under which the debtor's debts can be discharged.

DEBTOR IN POSSESSION (DIP)
In Chapter 11 bankruptcy proceedings, a debtor who is allowed to continue in possession of the estate in property (the business) and to continue business operations.

---

22. See 11 U.S.C. Section 1112(b). Debtors are not prohibited from filing successive petitions, however. A debtor whose petition is dismissed, for example, can file a new Chapter 11 petition (which may be granted unless it is filed in bad faith).

120-day deadline or get an extension, and if the debtor fails to obtain the required creditor consent (discussed below) within 180 days, any party may propose a plan up to 20 months from the date of the order for relief. (In other words, the 180-day period cannot be extended beyond 20 months past the date of the order for relief.) For a small-business debtor, the time for the debtor's filing is 180 days.

The plan must be fair and equitable and must do the following:

1 Designate classes of claims and interests.

2 Specify the treatment to be afforded the classes. (The plan must provide the same treatment for all claims in a particular class.)

3 Provide an adequate means for execution. (The 2005 Bankruptcy Reform Act requires individual debtors to utilize postpetition assets as necessary to execute the plan.)

4 Provide for payment of tax claims over a five-year period.

Acceptance and Confirmation of the Plan.   Once the plan has been developed, it is submitted to each class of creditors for acceptance. Each class must accept the plan unless the class is not adversely affected by it. A class has accepted the plan when a majority of the creditors, representing two-thirds of the amount of the total claim, vote to approve it. Confirmation is conditioned on the debtor's certifying that all postpetition domestic-support obligations have been paid in full. For small-business debtors, if the plan meets the listed requirements, the court must confirm the plan within forty-five days (unless this period is extended). Even when all classes of creditors accept the plan, the court may refuse to confirm it if it is not "in the best interests of the creditors."[23] The plan can also be modified upon the request of the debtor, trustee, U.S. trustee, or holder of the unsecured claim.

Even if only one class of creditors has accepted the plan, the court may still confirm the plan under the Code's so-called **cram-down provision.** In other words, the court may confirm the plan over the objections of a class of creditors. Before the court can exercise this right of cram-down confirmation, it must be demonstrated that the plan is fair and equitable, and does not discriminate unfairly against any creditors.

Discharge.   The plan is binding on confirmation. The Bankruptcy Reform Act of 2005, however, provides that confirmation of a plan does not discharge an individual debtor. Individual debtors must complete the plan prior to discharge, unless the court orders otherwise. For all other debtors, the court may order discharge at any time after the plan is confirmed. This discharge does not apply to any claims that would be denied discharge under liquidation.

Chapter 13–Individuals' Repayment Plan

Chapter 13 of the Bankruptcy Code provides for the "Adjustment of Debts of an Individual with Regular Income." Individuals (not partnerships or corporations) with regular income who owe fixed unsecured debts of less than $336,900 or fixed secured debts of less than $1,010,650 may take advantage of bankruptcy repayment plans. Among those eligible are salaried employees; sole proprietors; and individuals who live on welfare, Social Security, fixed pensions, or investment income. Many small-business debtors have a choice of filing under either Chapter 11 or Chapter 13. Repayment plans offer several advantages, however. One advantage is that they are less expensive and less complicated than reorganization proceedings or, for that matter, even liquidation proceedings.

CRAM-DOWN PROVISION
A provision of the Bankruptcy Code that allows a court to confirm a debtor's Chapter 11 reorganization plan even though only one class of creditors has accepted it. To exercise the court's right under this provision, the court must demonstrate that the plan does not discriminate unfairly against any creditors and is fair and equitable.

---

23. The plan need not provide for full repayment to unsecured creditors. Instead, creditors receive a percentage of each dollar owed to them by the debtor.

Filing the Petition A Chapter 13 repayment plan case can be initiated only by the filing of a voluntary petition by the debtor or by the conversion of a Chapter 7 petition (because of a finding of substantial abuse under the means test, for example). Certain liquidation and reorganization cases may be converted to Chapter 13 with the consent of the debtor.[24] A trustee, who will make payments under the plan, must be appointed. On the filing of a repayment plan petition, the automatic stay previously discussed takes effect. Although the stay applies to all or part of the debtor's consumer debt, it does not apply to any business debt incurred by the debtor. The automatic stay also does not apply to domestic-support obligations.

The Bankruptcy Code imposes the requirement of good faith on a debtor at both the time of the filing of the petition and the time of the filing of the plan. The Code does not define good faith—it is determined in each case through a consideration of "the totality of the circumstances." Bad faith can be cause for the dismissal of a Chapter 13 petition, as the following case illustrates.

---

24. A Chapter 13 repayment plan may be converted to a Chapter 7 liquidation either at the request of the debtor or, under certain circumstances, "for cause" by a creditor. A Chapter 13 case may be converted to a Chapter 11 case after a hearing.

CASE 16.3 **In re Buis**

United States Bankruptcy Court, Northern District of Florida, Pensacola Division, 337 Bankr. 243 (2006).

FACTS In 2000, Roger and Pauline Buis bought an air show business, including a helicopter, a trailer, and props, from Robert and Annette Hosking. The price was $275,000, which the Buises agreed to pay in installments. The Buises formed Otto Airshows and decorated the helicopter as "Otto the Clown." They performed in air shows and took passengers on flights for a fee. In 2003, the Buises began accusing a competitor, Army Aviation Heritage Foundation and Museum, Inc. (AAHF), of safety lapses. AAHF filed a suit in a federal district court against the Buises and their company, alleging defamation. The court issued a summary judgment in AAHF's favor. While a determination of the amount of the damages was pending, the Buises stopped doing business as Otto Airshows. They formed a new firm, Prop and Rotor Aviation, Inc., to which they leased the Otto equipment. Within a month, they filed a bankruptcy petition under Chapter 13. The plan and the schedules did not mention AAHF, the Prop and Rotor lease, a settlement that the Buises received in an unrelated suit, and other items. AAHF filed a motion to dismiss the case, asserting, among other things, that the Buises filed their petition in bad faith.

ISSUE Was the dismissal of the Buises' petition warranted on the ground of bad faith?

DECISION Yes. The court dismissed the Buises' petition. The debtors had not included all of their assets and liabilities on their initial petition, and had timed its filing to avoid

payment on the judgment to AAHF. They had also attempted to transfer interests in some of their assets in preference to certain creditors.

REASON In particular, "[t]he debtors failed to list AAHF as a creditor, which is especially hard for the court to comprehend when the debtor admitted that it was AAHF's judgment that pushed them into bankruptcy." The Buises also failed to "report any income from leases in their statement of financial affairs or list any agreement with Prop and Rotor anywhere in their schedules." They did not disclose the $55,000 that they obtained in their unrelated suit, as well as "a Kubota lawn tractor worth $10,000 and their generator, worth $400." The debtors filed their petition "after they were found liable in the District Court Action and after an unsuccessful mediation with AAHF, but before a final judgment could be entered." The court saw this as an attempt to "keep the debtors eligible to file for relief under Chapter 13, because the debts owed to AAHF would be dischargeable." The court interpreted the Buises' transfers of assets to creditors as "suspect," because the debtors granted the interests and "waited 90 days so they would 'stick,' then filed their petition." Besides, "the debtor admitted that he began planning to avoid AAHF's judgment through a Chapter 13 bankruptcy shortly after the adverse ruling."

WHAT IF THE FACTS WERE DIFFERENT?
If AAHF had lost its defamation suit against the Buises, would the result in this case have been the same? Why or why not?

The Repayment Plan A plan of rehabilitation by repayment must provide for the following:

1 The turning over to the trustee of such future earnings or income of the debtor as is necessary for execution of the plan.

2 Full payment through deferred cash payments of all claims entitled to priority.[25]

3 Identical treatment of all claims within a particular class. (The Code permits the debtor to list co-debtors, such as guarantors or sureties, as a separate class.)

Filing the Plan. Only the debtor may file for a repayment plan. This plan may provide either for payment of all obligations in full or for payment of a lesser amount. Prior to the 2005 act, the time for repayment was usually three years unless the court approved an extension for up to five years. Under the new Code, the length of the payment plan (three or five years) is determined by the debtor's family income. If the debtor's family income is greater than the state median family income under the means test (previously discussed), the proposed plan must be for five years. The term may not exceed five years, however.

The Code requires the debtor to make "timely" payments from her or his disposable income, and the trustee must ensure that the debtor commences these payments. The debtor must begin making payments under the proposed plan within thirty days after the plan has been *filed*. Failure of the debtor to make timely payments or to commence payments within the thirty-day period will allow the court to convert the case to a liquidation bankruptcy or to dismiss the petition.

Confirmation of the Plan. After the plan is filed, the court holds a confirmation hearing, at which interested parties (such as creditors) may object to the plan. Under the 2005 act, the hearing must be held at least twenty days, but no more than forty-five days, after the meeting of the creditors. Confirmation of the plan is dependent on the debtor's certification that postpetition domestic-support obligations have been paid in full and that all prepetition tax returns have been filed. The court will confirm a plan with respect to each claim of a secured creditor under any of the following circumstances:

1 If the secured creditors have accepted the plan.

2 If the plan provides that secured creditors retain their liens until there is payment in full or until the debtor receives a discharge.

3 If the debtor surrenders the property securing the claims to the creditors.

Discharge After the completion of all payments, the court grants a discharge of all debts provided for by the repayment plan. Except for allowed claims not provided for by the plan, certain long-term debts provided for by the plan, certain tax claims, payments on retirement accounts, and claims for domestic-support obligations, all other debts are dischargeable. Under prior law, a discharge of debts under a Chapter 13 repayment plan was sometimes referred to as a "superdischarge" because it allowed the discharge of fraudulently incurred debt and claims resulting from malicious or willful injury.

The 2005 Bankruptcy Reform Act, however, deleted most of the "superdischarge" provisions, especially for debts based on fraud. Today, debts for trust fund taxes, taxes for which returns were never filed or filed late (within two years of filing), domestic-support payments, student loans, and debts related to injury or property damage caused while driving under the influence of alcohol or drugs are nondischargeable. The new law also excludes fraudulent tax obligations, criminal fines and restitution, fraud by a person

BE CAREFUL Courts, trustees, and creditors carefully monitor Chapter 13 debtors. If payments are not made, a court can require the debtor to explain why and may allow a creditor to take back her or his property.

25. As with a Chapter 11 reorganization plan, full repayment of all claims is not always required.

acting in a fiduciary capacity, and restitution for willfully and maliciously causing personal injury or death.

Chapter 12–Family Farmers and Fishermen

In 1986, to help relieve economic pressure on small farmers, Congress created Chapter 12 of the Bankruptcy Code. In 2005, Congress extended this protection to family fishermen,[26] modified its provisions somewhat, and made it a permanent chapter in the Bankruptcy Code (previously, the statutes authorizing Chapter 12 had to be periodically renewed by Congress).

For purposes of Chapter 12, a *family farmer* is one whose gross income is at least 50 percent farm dependent and whose debts are at least 80 percent farm related.[27] The total debt must not exceed $3,544,525. A partnership or a closely held corporation (see Chapter 20) that is at least 50 percent owned by the farm family can also qualify as a family farmer.

A *family fisherman* is defined by the 2005 act as one whose gross income is at least 50 percent dependent on commercial fishing operations and whose debts are at least 80 percent related to commercial fishing. The total debt for a family fisherman must not exceed $1,642,500. As with family farmers, a partnership or closely held corporation can also qualify.

The procedure for filing a family-farmer or family-fisherman bankruptcy plan is very similar to the procedure for filing a repayment plan under Chapter 13. Court confirmation of the plan is the same as for a repayment plan. In summary, the plan must provide for payment of secured debts at the value of the collateral. If the secured debt exceeds the value of the collateral, the remaining debt is unsecured. For unsecured debtors, the plan must be confirmed if either the value of the property to be distributed under the plan equals the amount of the claim or the plan provides that all of the debtor's disposable income to be received in a three-year period (or longer, by court approval) will be applied to making payments. Completion of payments under the plan discharges all debts provided for by the plan.

---

26. Although the Code uses the terms *fishermen* and *fisherman,* Chapter 12 provisions apply equally to men and women.

27. Note that the Bankruptcy Code defines a *family farmer* and a *farmer* differently. To be a farmer, a person or business must receive 50 percent of gross income from a farming operation that the person or business owns or operates—see footnote 13.

REVIEWING **Creditors' Rights and Bankruptcy**

Three months ago, Janet Hart's husband of twenty years died of cancer. Although he had medical insurance, he left Janet with outstanding medical bills of more than $50,000. Janet has worked at the local library for the past ten years, earning $1,500 per month. Since her husband's death, Janet also has received $1,500 in Social Security benefits and $1,100 in life insurance proceeds every month, giving her a monthly income of $4,300. After she pays the mortgage payment of $1,500 and the amounts due on other debts each month, Janet barely has enough left over to buy groceries for her family (she has two teenage daughters at home). She decides to file for Chapter 7 bankruptcy, hoping for a fresh start. Using the information provided in the chapter, answer the following questions.

1 Under the Bankruptcy Code after the 2005 act, what must Janet do prior to filing a petition for relief under Chapter 7?

2 How much time does Janet have after filing the bankruptcy petition to submit the required schedules? What happens if Janet does not meet the deadline?

3 Assume that Janet files a petition under Chapter 7. Further assume that the median family income in the state in

which Janet lives is $49,300. What steps would a court take to determine whether Janet's petition is presumed to be "substantial abuse" under the means test?

4 Suppose that the court determines that no presumption of substantial abuse applies in Janet's case. Nevertheless, the court finds that Janet does have the ability to pay at least a portion of the medical bills out of her disposable income. What would the court likely order in that situation?

APPLICATION — How Do You Perfect a Security Interest?*

The importance of perfecting your security interest as a creditor cannot be overemphasized, particularly when the debt is large and you wish to protect the priority of your security interest over others who have an interest in the debtor's collateral. Failure to perfect or to perfect properly may result in your becoming the equivalent of an unsecured creditor.

Perfection by Filing

As discussed in this chapter, perfection is most commonly accomplished by filing a financing statement in the appropriate location. (Less commonly, perfection can be achieved by possession or attachment.) Generally, the moment the filing takes place, your priority is established over the other creditors—as well as over some purchasers of the collateral and a subsequent trustee in bankruptcy.

When you create a security agreement, describe the collateral in terms that are specific enough to put third parties on notice of your security interest in that collateral. Although the UCC permits broad general descriptions (such as "all assets") in the financing statement (as opposed to the security agreement), if your description is insufficient or misleading, your security interest will not be perfected.

Priority between Two Perfected Secured Parties

Sometimes, two secured parties have a security interest in the same debtor's collateral. On the debtor's default, the question arises as to which perfected secured party prevails. The answer is important for businesspersons because the loser most often ends up with the same status as an unsecured creditor.

The general rule is that the first creditor to perfect will have priority. An exception to the first-in-time rule applies, however, if the first perfection does not involve a purchase-money security interest (PMSI) and the second is a PMSI. This exception can be extremely important if the collateral is inventory or other goods, such as equipment, and the security agreement for the first-in-time non-PMSI contains an after-acquired property clause. This clause and the "timely" perfection of the PMSI (with proper notice for inventory) will come into conflict. In this situation, the perfected PMSI holder has priority to the debtor's newly acquired inventory or equipment.

CHECKLIST FOR PERFECTING YOUR SECURITY INTEREST

1 File a financing statement promptly.
2 Describe the collateral sufficiently—sometimes, it is better to err by giving too much detail than by giving too little.
3 If you are a holder of a PMSI, be sure that it is properly perfected (give proper notice if it involves inventory) so that you have priority over a previously perfected non-PMSI in the same collateral.

* This *Application* is not meant to substitute for the services of an attorney who is licensed to practice law in your state.

KEY TERMS

after-acquired property 482
artisan's lien 487
attachment 478
automatic stay 498

collateral 477
consumer-debtor 494
continuation statement 482
cram-down provision 505

debtor 477
debtor in possession (DIP) 504
default 477
deficiency judgment 486

CHAPTER SUMMARY Creditors' Rights and Bankruptcy

SECURED TRANSACTIONS

Creating a Security Interest (See pages 477–478.)	1. Unless the creditor has possession of the collateral, there must be a written or authenticated security agreement that is signed or authenticated by the debtor and describes the collateral subject to the security interest.
	2. The secured party must give value to the debtor.
	3. The debtor must have rights in the collateral—some ownership interest in or right to obtain possession of the specified collateral.
Perfecting a Security Interest (See pages 478–482.)	1. *Perfection by filing*—The most common method of perfection is by filing a financing statement containing the names of the secured party and the debtor and indicating the collateral covered by the financing statement.
	a. Communication of the financing statement to the appropriate filing office, together with the correct filing fee, constitutes a filing.
	b. The financing statement must be filed under the name of the debtor; fictitious (trade) names normally are not accepted.
	c. The classification of collateral determines whether filing is necessary and, if it is, where to file.
	2. *Perfection without filing*—
	a. By transfer of collateral—The debtor can transfer possession of the collateral to the secured party. A *pledge* is an example of this type of transfer.
	b. By attachment, such as the attachment of a purchase-money security interest (PMSI) in consumer goods—If the secured party has a PMSI in consumer goods (goods bought or used by the debtor for personal, family, or household purposes), the secured party's security interest is perfected automatically. In all, thirteen types of security interests can be perfected by attachment.
The Scope of a Security Interest (See pages 482–483.)	A security agreement can cover the following types of property:
	1. *Collateral in the present possession or control of the debtor.*
	2. *Proceeds from a sale, exchange, or disposition of secured collateral.*
	3. *After-acquired property*—A security agreement may provide that property acquired after the execution of the security agreement will also be secured by the agreement. This provision often accompanies security agreements covering a debtor's inventory.
	4. *Future advances*—A security agreement may provide that any future advances made against a line of credit will be subject to the initial security interest in the same collateral.
Priorities (See pages 483–485.)	See Exhibit 16–2 on page 484.

CHAPTER SUMMARY	Creditors' Rights and Bankruptcy—Continued

Default
(See pages 485–486.)
	On the debtor's default, the secured party may do either of the following:
	
	1. Take possession (peacefully or by court order) of the collateral covered by the security agreement and then pursue one of two alternatives:
	
	   a. Retain the collateral (unless the secured party has a PMSI in consumer goods and the debtor has paid 60 percent or more of the selling price or loan).
	
	   b. Dispose of the collateral in accordance with the requirements of UCC 9–602(7), 9–603, 9–610(a), and 9–613.
	
	2. Relinquish the security interest and use any judicial remedy available, such as proceeding to judgment on the underlying debt, followed by execution and levy on the nonexempt assets of the debtor.

ADDITIONAL LAWS ASSISTING CREDITORS

Liens
(See pages 487–488.)
	1. *Mechanic's lien*—A nonpossessory, filed lien on an owner's real estate for labor, services, or materials furnished to or made on the realty.
	
	2. *Artisan's lien*—A possessory lien on an owner's personal property for labor performed or value added.
	
	3. *Judicial liens*—
	
	   a. Writ of attachment—A court's order for seizure of property, issued prior to the court's final determination of the creditor's rights to the property. Attachment is available only on the creditor's posting of a bond and strict compliance with the applicable state statutes.
	
	   b. Writ of execution—A court order directing the sheriff to seize (levy) and sell a debtor's nonexempt real or personal property to satisfy a court's judgment in the creditor's favor.

Garnishment (See pages 488–489.)	A collection remedy that allows the creditor to attach a debtor's funds (such as wages owed or bank accounts) and property that are held by a third person.
Mortgage Foreclosure (See page 489.)	On the debtor's default, the entire mortgage debt is due and payable, allowing the creditor to foreclose on the realty by selling it to satisfy the debt.
Suretyship and Guaranty (See pages 489–491.)	Under contract, a third person agrees to be primarily or secondarily liable for the debt owed by the principal debtor. A creditor can turn to this third person for satisfaction of the debt.

ADDITIONAL LAWS ASSISTING DEBTORS

Exemptions
(See pages 491–492.)
	Numerous laws assist debtors. Additionally, state laws exempt certain types of real and personal property.
	
	1. *Exempted real property*—Each state permits the debtor to retain the family home, either in its entirety or up to a specified dollar amount, free from the claims of unsecured creditors or trustees in bankruptcy (homestead exemption).
	
	2. *Exempted personal property*—Personal property that is most often exempt from satisfaction of judgment debts includes the following:
	
	   a. Household furniture up to a specified dollar amount.
	
	   b. Clothing and certain personal possessions.
	
	   c. Transportation vehicles up to a specified dollar amount.
	
	   d. Certain classified animals, such as livestock and pets.
	
	   e. Equipment used in a business or trade up to a specified dollar amount.

(Continued)

CHAPTER SUMMARY	Creditors' Rights and Bankruptcy—Continued		
BANKRUPTCY—A COMPARISON OF CHAPTERS 7, 11, 12, AND 13			
Issue	**Chapter 7**	**Chapter 11**	**Chapters 12 and 13**
Purpose	Liquidation.	Reorganization.	Adjustment.
Who Can Petition	Debtor (voluntary) or creditors (involuntary).	Debtor (voluntary) or creditors (involuntary).	Debtor (voluntary) only.
Who Can Be a Debtor	Any "person" (including partnerships and corporations) except railroads, insurance companies, banks, savings and loan institutions, investment companies licensed by the U.S. Small Business Administration, and credit unions. Farmers and charitable institutions cannot be involuntarily petitioned.	Any debtor eligible for Chapter 7 relief; railroads are also eligible.	*Chapter 12*—Any family farmer (one whose gross income is at least 50 percent farm dependent and whose debts are at least 80 percent farm related) or family fisherman (one whose gross income is at least 50 percent dependent on commercial fishing) or any partnership or closely held corporation at least 50 percent owned by a family farmer or fisherman, when total debt does not exceed $3,544,525 for a family farmer and $1,642,500 for a family fisherman. *Chapter 13*—Any individual (not partnerships or corporations) with regular income who owes fixed unsecured debts of less than $336,900 or fixed secured debts of less than $1,010,650.
Procedure Leading to Discharge	Nonexempt property is sold with proceeds to be distributed (in order) to priority groups. Dischargeable debts are terminated.	Plan is submitted; if it is approved and followed, debts are discharged.	Plan is submitted and must be approved if the value of the property to be distributed equals the amount of the claims or if the debtor turns over disposable income for a three-year or five-year period; if the plan is followed, debts are discharged.
Advantages	On liquidation and distribution, most debts are discharged, and the debtor has an opportunity for a fresh start.	Debtor continues in business. Creditors can either accept the plan, or it can be "crammed down" on them. The plan allows for the reorganization and liquidation of debts over the plan period.	Debtor continues in business or possession of assets. If the plan is approved, most debts are discharged after a three-year period.

FOR REVIEW

Answers for the even-numbered questions in this **For Review** *section can be found in Appendix E at the end of this text.*

1 What is a security interest? What three requirements must be met to create an enforceable security interest?

2 What is a prejudgment attachment? What is a writ of execution? How does a creditor use these remedies?

3 What is garnishment? When might a creditor undertake a garnishment proceeding?

4 In a bankruptcy proceeding, what constitutes the debtor's estate in property? What property is exempt from the estate under federal bankruptcy law?

5 In a Chapter 11 reorganization, what is the role of the debtor in possession?

QUESTIONS AND CASE PROBLEMS

 HYPOTHETICAL SCENARIOS

16.1 Priority Disputes. Redford is a seller of electric generators. He purchases a large quantity of generators from a manufacturer, Mallon Corp., by making a down payment and signing an agreement to pay the balance over a period of time. The agreement gives Mallon Corp. a security interest in the generators and the proceeds. Mallon Corp. properly files a financing statement on its security interest. Redford receives the generators and immediately sells one of them to Garfield on an installment contract with payment to be made in twelve equal installments. At the time of the sale, Garfield knows of Mallon's security interest. Two months later, Redford goes into default on his payments to Mallon.

Discuss Mallon's rights against purchaser Garfield in this situation.

16.2 Hypothetical Question with Sample Answer. Marsh has a prize horse named Arabian Knight. Marsh is in need of working capital. She borrows $5,000 from Mendez, who takes possession of Arabian Knight as security for the loan. No written agreement is signed. Discuss whether, in the absence of a written agreement, Mendez has a security interest in Arabian Knight. If Mendez does have a security interest, is it a perfected security interest? Explain.

 For a sample answer to Question 16.2, go to Appendix F at the end of this text.

 **CASE PROBLEMS**

16.3 Automatic Stay. On January 22, 2001, Marlene Moffett bought a used 1998 Honda Accord from Hendrick Honda in Woodbridge, Virginia. Moffett agreed to pay $20,024.25, with interest, in sixty monthly installments, and Hendrick retained a security interest in the car. (As discussed in this chapter, Hendrick thus had the right to repossess the car in the event of default, subject to Moffett's right of redemption.) Hendrick assigned its rights under the sales agreement to Tidewater Finance Co., which perfected its security interest. The car was Moffett's only means of traveling the forty miles from her home to her workplace. In March and April 2002, Moffett missed two monthly payments. On April 25, Tidewater repossessed the car. On the same day, Moffett filed a Chapter 13 plan in a federal bankruptcy court. Moffett asked that the car be returned to her, in part, under

the Bankruptcy Code's automatic-stay provision. Tidewater asked the court to terminate the automatic stay so that it could sell the car. How can the interests of both the debtor and the creditor be fully protected in this case? What should the court rule? Explain. [*In re Moffett*, 356 F.3d 518 (4th Cir. 2004)]

16.4 Case Problem with Sample Answer. James Stout, a professor of economics and business at Cornell College in Mount Vernon, Iowa, filed a petition in bankruptcy under Chapter 7, seeking to discharge about $95,000 in credit-card debts. At the time, Stout had been divorced for ten years and had custody of his children: Z. S., who attended college, and G. S., who was twelve years old. Stout's ex-wife did not contribute child support. According to Stout, G. S. was an "elite" ice-skater

514 BUSINESS LAW TODAY: THE ESSENTIALS

who practiced twenty hours a week and had placed between first and third at more than forty competitive events. He had decided to home school G. S., whose achievements were average for her grade level despite her frequent absences from public school. His petition showed monthly income of $4,227 and expenses of $4,806. The expenses included annual home school costs of $8,400 and annual skating expenses of $6,000. They did not include Z. S.'s college costs, such as airfare for his upcoming studies in Europe, and other items. The trustee allowed monthly expenses of $3,227—with nothing for skating—and asked the court to dismiss the petition. Can the court grant this request? Should it? If so, what might it encourage Stout to do? Explain. [*In re Stout*, 336 Bankr. 138 (N.D. Iowa 2006)]

After you have answered Problem 16.4, compare your answer with the sample answer given on the Web site that accompanies this text. Go to academic.cengage.com/blaw/blt, select "Chapter 16," and click on "Case Problem with Sample Answer."

16.5 Security Interest. In St. Louis, Missouri, in August 2000, Richard Miller orally agreed to loan Jeff Miller $35,000 in exchange for a security interest in a 1999 Kodiak dump truck. The Millers did not put anything in writing concerning the loan, its repayment terms, or Richard's security interest or rights in the truck. Jeff used the amount of the loan to buy the truck, which he kept in his possession. In June 2004, Jeff filed a petition to obtain a discharge of his debts in bankruptcy. Richard claimed that he had a security interest in the truck and thus was entitled to any proceeds from its sale. What are a creditor's main concerns on a debtor's default? How does a creditor satisfy these concerns? What are the requirements for a creditor to have an enforceable security interest? Are these requirements met in this case? Considering these points, what is the court likely to rule with respect to Richard's claim? [*In re Miller*, 320 Bankr. 911 (E.D.Mo. 2005)]

16.6 Creating a Security Interest. In 2002, Michael Sabol, doing business in the recording industry as Sound Farm Productions, applied to Morton Community Bank in Bloomington, Illinois, for a $58,000 loan to expand his business. Besides the loan application, Sabol signed a promissory note that referred to the bank's rights in "any collateral." Sabol also signed a letter that stated, "the undersigned does hereby authorize Morton Community Bank to execute, file and record all financing statements, amendments, termination statements and all other statements authorized by Article 9 of the Illinois Uniform Commercial Code, as to any security interest." Sabol did not sign any other documents, including the financing statement, which contained a description of the collateral. Less than three years later, without having repaid the loan, Sabol filed a petition in a federal bankruptcy court to declare bankruptcy. The bank claimed a security interest in Sabol's sound equipment. What are the elements of an enforceable security interest?

What are the requirements of each of those elements? Does the bank have a valid security interest in this case? Explain. [*In re Sabol*, 337 Bankr. 195 (C.D.Ill. 2006)]

16.7 Exceptions to Discharge. Between 1988 and 1992, Lorna Nys took out thirteen student loans, totaling about $30,000, to finance an associate of arts degree in drafting from the College of the Redwoods and a bachelor of arts degree from Humboldt State University (HSU) in California. In 1996, Nys began working at HSU as a drafting technician. As a "Drafter II," the highest-paying drafting position at HSU, Nys's gross income in 2002 was $40,244. She was fifty-one years old, her net monthly income was $2,299.33, and she had $2,295.05 in monthly expenses, including saving $140 for her retirement, which she planned for age sixty-five. When Educational Credit Management Corp. (ECMC) began to collect payments on Nys's student loans, she filed a Chapter 7 petition in a federal bankruptcy court, seeking a discharge of the loans. ECMC argued that Nys did not show any "additional circumstances" that would impede her ability to repay. What is the standard for the discharge of student loans under Chapter 7? Does Nys meet that standard? Why or why not? [*In re Nys*, 446 F.3d 938 (9th Cir. 2006)]

16.8 A Question of Ethics. *In October 1994, Charles Edwards formed ETS Payphones, Inc., to sell and lease payphones as investment opportunities—an investor would buy a phone from ETS, which would lease it back. ETS promised returns of 14 to 15 percent but consistently lost money. To meet its obligations to existing investors, ETS had to continually attract new investors. Eventually, ETS defrauded thousands of investors of more than $300 million. Edwards transferred the funds from ETS to himself. In 2000, ETS filed a petition in a federal bankruptcy court to declare bankruptcy. Darryl Laddin was appointed trustee. On the debtor's behalf, Laddin filed a suit against Reliance Trust Co. and others, alleging, among other things, that the defendants helped defraud investors by "ignoring the facts" and "funneling" the investors' funds to ETS, causing it to "incur millions of dollars in additional debt." Laddin sought treble (triple) damages.* [Official Committee of Unsecured Creditors of PSA, Inc. v. Edwards, 437 F.3d 1145 (11th Cir. 2006)]

1 The defendants argued, in part, that the doctrine of *in pari delicto*, which provides that a wrongdoer may not profit from his or her wrongful acts, barred Laddin's claim. Who should be considered ethically responsible for the investors' losses? Explain.

2 Laddin contended that his actions, as trustee on behalf of the debtor, should not be subject to the doctrine of *in pari delicto* because that doctrine depends on the "personal malfeasance of the individual seeking to recover." The defendants filed a motion to dismiss Laddin's complaint. Do you think that the court should rule in favor of Laddin or the defendants? Why?

**CRITICAL THINKING
AND WRITING ASSIGNMENTS**

16.9 **Critical Legal Thinking.** Review the three requirements for an enforceable security interest. Why is each of these requirements necessary?

16.10 **Video Question.** Go to this text's Web site at **academic. cengage.com/blaw/blt** and select "Chapter 16." Click on "Video Questions" and view the video titled *The River*. Then answer the following questions.

1 In the video, a crowd (including Mel Gibson) is gathered at a farm auction in which a neighbor's (Jim Antonio's) farming goods are being sold. The people in the crowd, who are upset because they believe that the bank is selling out the farmer, begin chanting "no sale, no sale." In an effort to calm the situation, the farmer tells the crowd that "they've already foreclosed" on his farm. What does he mean?

2 Assume that the auction is a result of Chapter 7 bankruptcy proceedings. Was the farmer's petition for bankruptcy voluntary or involuntary? Explain.

3 Suppose that the farmer purchased the homestead three years prior to filing a petition in bankruptcy and that the current market value of the farm is $215,000. What is the maximum amount of equity that the farmer could claim as exempt under the 2005 Bankruptcy Reform Act?

4 Compare the results of a Chapter 12 bankruptcy as opposed to a Chapter 7 bankruptcy for the farmer in the video.

ONLINE ACTIVITIES

**PRACTICAL
INTERNET EXERCISES**

Go to this text's Web site at **academic.cengage.com/blaw/blt**, select "Chapter 16," and click on "Practical Internet Exercises." There you will find the following Internet research exercises that you can perform to learn more about the topics covered in this chapter.

PRACTICAL INTERNET EXERCISE 16–1 LEGAL PERSPECTIVE—Repossession

PRACTICAL INTERNET EXERCISE 16–2 MANAGEMENT PERSPECTIVE—Bankruptcy Alternatives

BEFORE THE TEST

Go to this text's Web site at **academic.cengage.com/blaw/blt**, select "Chapter 16," and click on "Interactive Quizzes." You will find a number of interactive questions relating to this chapter.

CHAPTER 17
Agency

"[It] is a universal principle in the law of agency, that the powers of the agent are to be exercised for the benefit of the principal only, and not of the agent or of third parties."

Joseph Story, 1779–1845
(Associate justice of the
United States Supreme Court,
1811–1844)

AGENCY
A relationship between two parties
in which one party (the agent)
agrees to represent or act for the
other (the principal).

LEARNING OBJECTIVES

AFTER READING THIS CHAPTER, YOU SHOULD BE ABLE
TO ANSWER THE FOLLOWING QUESTIONS:

1 What is the difference between an employee and an independent contractor?

2 How do agency relationships arise?

3 What duties do agents and principals owe to each other?

4 When is a principal liable for the agent's actions with respect to third parties? When is the agent liable?

5 What are some of the ways in which an agency relationship can be terminated?

One of the most common, important, and pervasive legal relationships is that of **agency.** As discussed in Chapter 14, in an agency relationship between two parties, one of the parties, called the *agent*, agrees to represent or act for the other, called the *principal*. The principal has the right to control the agent's conduct in matters entrusted to the agent, and the agent must exercise his or her powers "for the benefit of the principal only," as Justice Joseph Story indicated in the chapter-opening quotation. By using agents, a principal can conduct multiple business operations simultaneously in various locations. Thus, for example, contracts that bind the principal can be made at different places with different persons at the same time.

Agency relationships permeate the business world. Indeed, agency law is essential to the existence and operation of a corporate entity, because only through its agents can a corporation function and enter into contracts. A familiar example of an agent is a corporate officer who serves in a representative capacity for the owners of the corporation. In this capacity, the officer has the authority to bind the principal (the corporation) to a contract.

AGENCY RELATIONSHIPS

Section 1(1) of the *Restatement (Second) of Agency*[1] defines agency as "the fiduciary relation which results from the manifestation of consent by one person to another that the other shall act in his [or her] behalf and subject to his [or her] control, and consent by the other so to act." In other words, in a principal-agent relationship, the parties have

---

1. The *Restatement (Second) of Agency* is an authoritative summary of the law of agency and is often referred to by judges and other legal professionals.

agreed that the agent will act *on behalf and instead of* the principal in negotiating and transacting business with third parties.

The term **fiduciary** is at the heart of agency law. The term can be used both as a noun and as an adjective. When used as a noun, it refers to a person having a duty created by her or his undertaking to act primarily for another's benefit in matters connected with the undertaking. When used as an adjective, as in "fiduciary relationship," it means that the relationship involves trust and confidence.

Agency relationships commonly exist between employers and employees. Agency relationships may sometimes also exist between employers and independent contractors who are hired to perform special tasks or services.

FIDUCIARY
As a noun, a person having a duty created by his or her undertaking to act primarily for another's benefit in matters connected with the undertaking. As an adjective, a relationship founded on trust and confidence.

Employer-Employee Relationships

Normally, all employees who deal with third parties are deemed to be agents. A salesperson in a department store, for instance, is an agent of the store's owner (the principal) and acts on the owner's behalf. Any sale of goods made by the salesperson to a customer is binding on the principal. Similarly, most representations of fact made by the salesperson with respect to the goods sold are binding on the principal.

Because employees who deal with third parties are normally deemed to be agents of their employers, agency law and employment law overlap considerably. Agency relationships, though, as will become apparent, can exist outside an employer-employee relationship and thus have a broader reach than employment laws do. Additionally, bear in mind that agency law is based on the common law. In the employment realm, many common law doctrines have been displaced by statutory law and government regulations relating to employment relationships.

Employment laws (state and federal) apply only to the employer-employee relationship. Statutes governing Social Security, withholding taxes, workers' compensation, unemployment compensation, workplace safety, employment discrimination, and the like (see Chapter 18) are applicable only if employer-employee status exists. *These laws do not apply to an independent contractor.*

ON THE WEB

For information on the *Restatements of the Law,* including planned revisions, go to the American Law Institute's Web site at **www.ali.org.**

Employer–Independent Contractor Relationships

Independent contractors are not employees because, by definition, those who hire them have no control over the details of their physical performance. Section 2 of the *Restatement (Second) of Agency* defines an **independent contractor** as follows:

> [An independent contractor is] a person who contracts with another to do something for him [or her] but who is not controlled by the other nor subject to the other's right to control with respect to his [or her] physical conduct in the performance of the undertaking. *He [or she] may or may not be an agent.* [Emphasis added.]

Building contractors and subcontractors are independent contractors; a property owner does not control the acts of either of these professionals. Truck drivers who own their equipment and hire themselves out on a per-job basis are independent contractors, but truck drivers who drive company trucks on a regular basis are usually employees.

The relationship between a person or firm and an independent contractor may or may not involve an agency relationship. To illustrate: An owner of real estate who hires a real estate broker to negotiate a sale of his or her property not only has contracted with an independent contractor (the real estate broker) but also has established an agency relationship for the specific purpose of assisting in the sale of the property. Another example is an insurance agent, who is both

INDEPENDENT CONTRACTOR
One who works for, and receives payment from, an employer but whose working conditions and methods are not controlled by the employer. An independent contractor is not an employee but may be an agent.

An independent contractor communicates from a building site. What are some significant differences between employees and independent contractors? (Greg Younger/ Creative Commons)

an independent contractor and an agent of the insurance company for which she or he sells policies. (Note that an insurance *broker,* in contrast, normally is an agent of the person obtaining insurance and not of the insurance company.)

Determining Employee Status

The courts are frequently asked to determine whether a particular worker is an employee or an independent contractor. How a court decides this issue can have a significant effect on the rights and liabilities of the parties. For example, employers are required to pay certain taxes, such as Social Security and unemployment taxes, for employees but not for independent contractors.

Criteria Used by the Courts In determining whether a worker has the status of an employee or an independent contractor, the courts often consider the following questions:

1 How much control can the employer exercise over the details of the work? (If an employer can exercise considerable control over the details of the work, this would indicate employee status. This is perhaps the most important factor weighed by the courts in determining employee status.)

2 Is the worker engaged in an occupation or business distinct from that of the employer? (If so, this points to independent-contractor status, not employee status.)

3 Is the work usually done under the employer's direction or by a specialist without supervision? (If the work is usually done under the employer's direction, this would indicate employee status.)

4 Does the employer supply the tools at the place of work? (If so, this would indicate employee status.)

5 For how long is the person employed? (If the person is employed for a long period of time, this would indicate employee status.)

6 What is the method of payment—by time period or at the completion of the job? (Payment by time period, such as once every two weeks or once a month, would indicate employee status.)

7 What degree of skill is required of the worker? (If little skill is required, this may indicate employee status.)

Sometimes, workers may benefit from having employee status—for tax purposes and to be protected under certain employment laws, for example. As mentioned earlier, federal statutes governing employment discrimination apply only when an employer-employee relationship exists. The question in the following case was whether, for the purpose of applying one of these statutes, a television show's co-host was an employee or an independent contractor.

CASE 17.1 **Alberty-Vélez v. Corporación de Puerto Rico**

United States Court of Appeals, First Circuit, 361 F.3d 1 (2004).
www.ca1.uscourts.gov[a]

FACTS In July 1993, Victoria Lis Alberty-Vélez (Alberty) began to co-host a new television show, *Desde Mi Pueblo,* on WIPR,

a. In the right-hand column, click on "Opinions." When that page opens, under "General Search," in the "Opinion Number begins with" box, type "02-2187" and click on "Submit Search." In the result, click on the appropriate link to access the opinion. The U.S. Court of Appeals for the First Circuit maintains this Web site.

a television station in Puerto Rico. The show profiled Puerto Rican cities and towns. Instead of signing a single contract, Alberty signed a new contract for each episode. Each contract obligated her to work a certain number of days. She was not obliged to do other work for WIPR, and WIPR was not obliged to contract with her for other work. During the filming, Alberty was responsible for providing her clothing, shoes, accessories,

CASE 17.1–Continued

hairstylist, and other services and materials. She was paid a lump sum, ranging from $400 to $550, for each episode. WIPR did not withhold income or Social Security taxes and did not provide health insurance, life insurance, a retirement plan, paid sick leave, maternity leave, or vacation time. Alberty became pregnant, and after November 1994, WIPR stopped contracting with her. She filed a suit in a federal district court against WIPR's owner, Corporación de Puerto Rico para la Difusión Pública, alleging, among other things, discrimination on the basis of her pregnancy in violation of a federal statute. The court issued a judgment in the defendant's favor. Alberty appealed to the U.S. Court of Appeals for the First Circuit.

ISSUE Was Alberty an independent contractor and therefore outside the application of the federal statute restricting employment discrimination on the basis of pregnancy?

DECISION Yes. The U.S. Court of Appeals for the First Circuit affirmed the lower court's judgment in WIPR's favor.

REASON The appellate court explained that in determining whether a party is an independent contractor, a court considers the employer's right to control the manner and means by which the party does the job for which he or she is

hired. Important factors include the required skills, the source of the tools for the job, the location of the work, the duration of the relationship between the parties, whether the employer has the right to assign other projects to the hired party, the parties' discretion over when and how long the work is done, the method of payment, whether the work is part of the employer's regular business, whether the employer is in business, the provision of employee benefits, and the tax treatment of the hired party. In this case, the court found that "[t]he parties structured their relationship through the use of set length contracts that permitted Alberty the freedom to pursue other opportunities and assured WIPR that it would not have to pay Alberty for the weeks that it was not filming. Further, the lack of benefits, the method of payment, and the parties' own description of their relationship in tax documents all indicate independent-contractor status."

 WHAT IF THE FACTS WERE DIFFERENT? *Suppose that Alberty had been a full-time, hourly worker and that such status was common among television hosts, but WIPR had manipulated the benefits and tax withholdings to favor independent-contractor status. Would the result have been different? Why or why not?*

Criteria Used by the IRS Businesspersons should be aware that the Internal Revenue Service (IRS) has established its own criteria for determining whether a worker is an independent contractor or an employee. Although the IRS once considered twenty factors in determining a worker's status, guidelines that took effect in 1997 encourage IRS examiners to focus on just one of those factors—the degree of control the business exercises over the worker.

The IRS tends to closely scrutinize a firm's classification of its workers because, as mentioned, employers can avoid certain tax liabilities by hiring independent contractors instead of employees. Even when a firm classifies a worker as an independent contractor, if the IRS decides that the worker is actually an employee, the employer will be responsible for paying any applicable Social Security, withholding, and unemployment taxes.

EXAMPLE 17.1 Microsoft Corporation had required a number of workers to become associated with employment agencies so that they could work for Microsoft as temporary workers. The workers sued, alleging that they were actually employees of Microsoft (rather than independent contractors) and thus entitled to participate in the company's stock option plan. The IRS determined that the workers were employees because Microsoft had exercised significant control over their work performance. A court affirmed this decision on appeal. Ultimately, Microsoft was required to pay back payroll taxes for hundreds of workers who had contractually agreed to work for Microsoft as independent contractors.[2]

---

2. *Vizcaino v. U.S. District Court for the Western District of Washington,* 173 F.3d 713 (9th Cir. 1999).

Businesspersons should be aware that the mere designation of a person as an independent contractor does not mean the employer can necessarily avoid tax liability. The courts and the IRS look behind the label to ascertain the true relationship between the worker and the business entity. Control is the most significant factor. Because of the potentially significant tax liability if the IRS determines that independent contractors are actually employees, businesspersons should seek the advice of an attorney when classifying workers as independent contractors. The *Application* feature at the end of the chapter offers more suggestions for using independent contractors.

Employee Status and "Works for Hire"   Under the Copyright Act of 1976, any copyrighted work created by an employee within the scope of her or his employment at the request of the employer is a "work for hire," and the employer owns the copyright to the work. When an employer hires an independent contractor—a freelance artist, writer, or computer programmer, for example—the independent contractor owns the copyright *unless* the parties agree in writing that the work is a "work for hire" and the work falls into one of nine specific categories, including audiovisual and other works.

■**EXAMPLE 17.2** Graham marketed CD-ROM discs containing compilations of software programs that are available free to the public. Graham hired James to create a file-retrieval program that allowed users to access the software on the CDs. James built into the final version of the program a notice stating that he was the author of the program and owned the copyright. Graham removed the notice. When James sold the program to another CD-ROM publisher, Graham filed a suit claiming that James's file-retrieval program was a "work for hire" and that Graham owned the copyright to the program. The court, however, decided that James—a skilled computer programmer who controlled the manner and method of his work—was an independent contractor and not an employee for hire. Thus, James owned the copyright to the file-retrieval program.[3] ■

HOW AGENCY RELATIONSHIPS ARE FORMED

Agency relationships normally are consensual; that is, they come about by voluntary consent and agreement between the parties. Generally, the agreement need not be in writing,[4] and consideration is not required.

A person must have contractual capacity to be a principal.[5] Those who cannot legally enter into contracts directly should not be allowed to do so indirectly through an agent. Any person can be an agent, though, regardless of whether he or she has the capacity to enter a contract. Because an agent derives the authority to enter into contracts from the principal and because a contract made by an agent is legally viewed as a contract of the principal, it is immaterial whether the agent personally has the legal capacity to make that contract. Thus, even a minor or a person who is legally incompetent can be appointed as an agent (but generally cannot be a principal).

---

3. *Graham v. James,* 144 F.3d 229 (2d Cir. 1998).
4. There are two main exceptions to the statement that agency agreements need not be in writing: (1) Whenever agency authority empowers the agent to enter into a contract that the Statute of Frauds requires to be in writing, the agent's authority from the principal must likewise be in writing (this is called the *equal dignity rule,* to be discussed later in this chapter). (2) A power of attorney, which confers authority to an agent, must be in writing.
5. Note that some states allow a minor to be a principal. When a minor is permitted to be a principal, however, any resulting contracts will be voidable by the minor principal but not by the adult third party.

An agency relationship can be created for any legal purpose. An agency relationship that is created for an illegal purpose or that is contrary to public policy is unenforceable. **EXAMPLE 17.3** Sharp (as principal) contracts with Blesh (as agent) to sell illegal narcotics. This agency relationship is unenforceable because selling illegal narcotics is a felony and is contrary to public policy. ■ It is also illegal for physicians and other licensed professionals to employ unlicensed agents to perform professional actions.

Generally, an agency relationship can arise in four ways: by agreement of the parties, by ratification, by estoppel, and by operation of law. Here we look at each of these possibilities.

Agency by Agreement

Most agency relationships are based on an express or implied agreement that the agent will act for the principal and that the principal agrees to have the agent so act. An agency agreement can take the form of an express written contract. **EXAMPLE 17.4** Renato enters into a written agreement with Troy, a real estate agent, to sell Renato's house. An agency relationship exists between Renato and Troy for the sale of the house and is detailed in a document that both parties sign. ■

Many express agency relationships are created by oral agreements rather than written contracts. **EXAMPLE 17.5** Reese asks Cary, a gardener, to contract with others for the care of his lawn on a regular basis. Cary agrees. In this situation, an agency relationship exists between Reese and Cary for the lawn care. ■

An agency agreement can also be implied by conduct. **EXAMPLE 17.6** A hotel expressly allows only Boris Koontz to park cars, but Boris has no employment contract there. The hotel's manager tells Boris when to work, as well as where and how to park the cars. The hotel's conduct amounts to a manifestation of its willingness to have Boris park its customers' cars, and Boris can infer from the hotel's conduct that he has authority to act as a parking valet. It can be inferred that Boris is an agent-employee for the hotel, his purpose being to provide valet parking services for hotel guests. ■

Agency by Ratification

On occasion, a person who is in fact not an agent (or who is an agent acting outside the scope of her or his authority) may make a contract on behalf of another (a principal). If the principal approves or affirms that contract by word or by action, an agency relationship is created by **ratification.** Ratification involves a question of intent, and intent can be expressed by either words or conduct. The basic requirements for ratification are discussed later in this chapter.

Agency by Estoppel

When a principal causes a third person to believe that another person is his or her agent, and the third person deals with the supposed agent, the principal is "estopped to deny" the agency relationship. In such a situation, the principal's actions create the *appearance* of an agency that does not in fact exist. The third person must prove that she or he *reasonably* believed that an agency relationship existed, though.[6] Facts and circumstances must show that an ordinary, prudent person familiar with business practice and custom would have been justified in concluding that the agent had authority.

EXAMPLE 17.7 Andrew accompanies Grant, a seed sales representative, to call on a customer, Steve, the proprietor of the General Seed Store. Andrew has done independent

ON THE WEB

An excellent source for information on agency, including court cases involving agency concepts, is the Legal Information Institute (LII) at Cornell University. You can access the LII's Web page on this topic at

www.law.cornell.edu/wex/index.php/Agency.

RATIFICATION
The act of accepting and giving legal force to an obligation that previously was not enforceable.

A restaurant offers valet parking services. Can it be inferred that the parking attendant shown here is an agent of the restaurant? Why or why not? (Valerie Everett/Creative Commons)

---

6. These concepts also apply when a person who is in fact an agent undertakes an action that is beyond the scope of her or his authority, as will be discussed later in this chapter.

sales work but has never signed an employment agreement with Grant. Grant boasts to Steve that he wishes he had three more assistants "just like Andrew." By making this representation, Grant creates the impression that Andrew is his agent and has authority to solicit orders. Steve has reason to believe from Grant's statements that Andrew is an agent for Grant. Steve then places seed orders with Andrew. If Grant does not correct the impression that Andrew is an agent, Grant will be bound to fill the orders just as if Andrew were really his agent. Grant's representation to Steve created the impression that Andrew was Grant's agent and had authority to solicit orders. ▣

Note that the acts or declarations of a purported *agent* in and of themselves do not create an agency by estoppel. Rather, it is the deeds or statements *of the principal* that create an agency by estoppel. ▣**EXAMPLE 17.8** If Andrew walks into Steve's store and claims to be Grant's agent, when in fact he is not, and Grant has no knowledge of Andrew's representations, Grant will not be bound to any deal struck by Andrew and Steve. Andrew's acts and declarations alone do not create an agency by estoppel. ▣

Under what other circumstances might a third party reasonably believe that an agent has the authority to act for a principal when the agent actually does not have this authority? The following case provides an illustration.

CASE 17.2   **Motorsport Marketing, Inc. v. Wiedmaier, Inc.**

Missouri Court of Appeals, Western District, 195 S.W.3d 492 (2006).
www.courts.mo.gov[a]

FACTS Wiedmaier, Inc., owns and operates Wiedmaier Truck Stop in St. Joseph, Missouri. The owners are Marsha Wiedmaier and her husband, Jerry. Their son Michael does not own an interest in the firm, but in 2002 and 2003, he worked for it as a fuel truck operator. Motorsport Marketing, Inc., sells racing collectibles and memorabilia to retail outlets. In April 2003, Michael faxed a credit application to Motorsport's sales manager, Lesa James. Michael's mother, Marsha, signed the form as "Secretary-Owner" of Wiedmaier; after she signed, Michael added himself to the list of owners. Motorsport approved a credit line. Michael formed Extreme Diecast, LLC, which he told Motorsport was part of Wiedmaier, and began ordering Motorsport merchandise. By early 2004, however, Michael had stopped making payments on the account, quit his job, and moved to Columbus, Ohio. Patrick Rainey, the president of Motorsport, contacted Marsha. She refused to pay. Motorsport filed a suit in a Missouri state court against Wiedmaier and others to collect the unpaid amount. The court entered a judgment in favor of Motorsport, assessing liability against the defendants for the outstanding balance of

$93,388.58, plus $13,406.38 in interest and $25,165.93 in attorneys' fees. The defendants appealed to a state intermediate appellate court.

ISSUE Did Motorsport reasonably believe that Michael acted as Wiedmaier's agent in ordering merchandise?

DECISION Yes. The state intermediate appellate court affirmed the judgment of the lower court, echoing the conclusion that "Michael acted as an apparent agent of Wiedmaier, Inc., in its dealings with Motorsport."

REASON The appellate court emphasized that "[t]he credit application constituted a direct communication from Wiedmaier, Inc. (through Marsha) to Motorsport causing Motorsport to reasonably believe that Michael had authority to act for Wiedmaier, Inc." Marsha signed the application, on which Michael was listed as an owner. The defendants argued that Michael paid Motorsport with checks drawn on Extreme Diecast's account, which should have led Motorsport to investigate further. In response, the court pointed out that, as Motorsport was aware, "it is a common practice for a truck stop to have a separate division with a separate name to handle its diecast and other related merchandise, and that Michael represented that this is exactly what Extreme Diecast was." In good faith reliance on the credit application and Michael's representations, Motorsport extended credit to Wiedmaier and filled Michael's orders. "If the transaction[s]

---

a. In the "Quick Links" box, click on "Opinion & Minutes." When that page opens, click on the "Missouri Court of Appeals, Western District opinions" link. At the bottom of the next page, click on the "Search Opinions" link. In that page's "Search for" box, type "Wiedmaier" and click on "Search." In the result, click on the name of the case to access the opinion. The Missouri state courts maintain this Web site.

CASE 17.2–Continued

executed by Michael [do] not bind Wiedmaier, Inc., Motorsport will suffer the loss of the balance due on the account."

 WHAT IF THE FACTS WERE DIFFERENT?
Suppose that Motorsport's sales manager had telephoned Marsha Wiedmaier rather than just faxing the credit

application. Further suppose that Marsha had vouched for Michael's creditworthiness but informed Motorsport that she and her husband owned Wiedmaier and that Michael worked for them. How might the outcome of this case have been different in that situation?

Agency by Operation of Law

The courts may find an agency relationship in the absence of a formal agreement in other situations as well. This can occur in family relationships. For instance, suppose that one spouse purchases certain basic necessaries and charges them to the other spouse's charge account. The courts will often rule that the latter is liable to pay for the necessaries, either because of a social policy of promoting the general welfare of the spouse or because of a legal duty to supply necessaries to family members.

Agency by operation of law may also occur in emergency situations, when the agent's failure to act outside the scope of his or her authority would cause the principal substantial loss. If the agent is unable to contact the principal, the courts will often grant this emergency power. For instance, a railroad engineer may contract on behalf of her or his employer for medical care for an injured motorist hit by the train.

DUTIES OF AGENTS AND PRINCIPALS

Once the principal-agent relationship has been created, both parties have duties that govern their conduct. As discussed previously, an agency relationship is *fiduciary*—one of trust. In a fiduciary relationship, each party owes the other the duty to act with the utmost good faith. We now examine the various duties of agents and principals.

In general, for every duty of the principal, the agent has a corresponding right, and vice versa. When one party to the agency relationship violates his or her duty to the other party, the remedies available to the nonbreaching party arise out of contract and tort law. These remedies include monetary damages, termination of the agency relationship, an injunction, and required accountings.

Agent's Duties to the Principal

Generally, the agent owes the principal five duties—performance, notification, loyalty, obedience, and accounting.

Performance   An implied condition in every agency contract is the agent's agreement to use reasonable diligence and skill in performing the work. When an agent fails entirely to perform her or his duties, liability for breach of contract normally will result. The degree of skill or care required of an agent is usually that expected of a reasonable person under similar circumstances. Generally, this is interpreted to mean ordinary care. If an agent has represented himself or herself as possessing special skills, however, the agent is expected to exercise the degree of skill or skills claimed. Failure to do so constitutes a breach of the agent's duty.

A real estate agent meets with clients in her office. Suppose that the agent knows a buyer who is willing to pay more than the asking price for a property. What duty would the agent breach if she bought the property from the seller and sold it at a profit to that buyer? (Yoon Hernandez/Creative Commons)

Not all agency relationships are based on contract. In some situations, an agent acts gratuitously—that is, not for monetary compensation. A gratuitous agent cannot be liable for breach of contract, as there is no contract; he or she is subject only to tort liability. Once a gratuitous agent has begun to act in an agency capacity, he or she has the duty to continue to perform in that capacity in an acceptable manner and is subject to the same standards of care and duty to perform as other agents.

Notification An agent is required to notify the principal of all matters that come to her or his attention concerning the subject matter of the agency. This is the *duty of notification,* or the duty to inform. **■EXAMPLE 17.9** Lang, an artist, is about to negotiate a contract to sell a series of paintings to Barber's Art Gallery for $25,000. Lang's agent learns that Barber is insolvent and will be unable to pay for the paintings. Lang's agent has a duty to inform Lang of this fact because it is relevant to the subject matter of the agency—the sale of Lang's paintings. ■ Generally, the law assumes that the principal knows of any information acquired by the agent that is relevant to the agency—regardless of whether the agent actually passes on this information to the principal. It is a basic tenet of agency law that notice to the agent is notice to the principal.

Loyalty Loyalty is one of the most fundamental duties in a fiduciary relationship. Basically, the agent has the duty to act *solely for the benefit of his or her principal* and not in the interest of the agent or a third party. For example, an agent cannot represent two principals in the same transaction unless both know of the dual capacity and consent to it. The duty of loyalty also means that any information or knowledge acquired through the agency relationship is considered confidential. It would be a breach of loyalty to disclose such information either during the agency relationship or after its termination. Typical examples of confidential information are trade secrets and customer lists compiled by the principal.

BE AWARE An agent's disclosure of confidential information could constitute the business tort of misappropriation of trade secrets.

In short, the agent's loyalty must be undivided. The agent's actions must be strictly for the benefit of the principal and must not result in any secret profit for the agent. The following case involved a real estate agent who discovered, while working for a principal, that a property owner would only sell the desired property as a package deal with another parcel. One of the questions the court had to decide was whether the agent breached the duty of loyalty by buying the property to resell it to the principal.

CASE 17.3   **Cousins v. Realty Ventures, Inc.**

Court of Appeal of Louisiana, Fifth Circuit, 844 So.2d 860 (2003).

FACTS Don Cousins, an insurance agent, sought commercial real estate in Metairie, Louisiana, for Eagle Ventures, Inc., to buy as an investment. Cousins engaged the services of Leo Hodgins, a real estate agent and the owner of Realty Ventures, Inc. (RVI). In June 1991, on Eagle's behalf, Hodgins submitted an offer of $90,000 to Westinghouse Credit Corporation to buy an 8,000-square-foot office building at 3330 Lake Villa Drive. Westinghouse responded that it could not sell the property immediately due to an agreement with its property management company. Through Hodgins, Eagle resubmitted the offer in October. Hodgins learned that Westinghouse would sell the building only with its neighboring property, a 33,000-square-foot office building at 4141 Veterans Boulevard, for $425,000. Hodgins estimated the two properties' worth to be about $1 million. Without telling Eagle about the package, Hodgins, his brother Paul, and RVI formed 4141 Vets Limited Partnership to buy the two buildings on May 7, 1992, for $420,000. Hodgins then offered to sell 3330 Lake Villa to Eagle for $175,000. Cousins and others filed a suit in a Louisiana state court against RVI and others, alleging breach of fiduciary duties. A jury returned a verdict in

CASE 17.3–Continued

favor of the plaintiffs and awarded damages in the amount of $1.75 million. The defendants appealed to a state intermediate appellate court.

ISSUE Did Hodgins breach the agent's duty of loyalty?

DECISION Yes. The state intermediate appellate court affirmed the judgment of the lower court. "Leo Hodgins' failure to communicate the package sale to plaintiffs the moment he learned of it constituted a breach of his fiduciary duties to them."

REASON The appellate court specified that "Hodgins' duty was to give plaintiffs the information that Westinghouse rejected their offer for a single property sale and allow them to decide whether they wished to purchase both properties." The court explained that an agent's "precise duties" are defined by "the nature of the task the * * * agent

undertakes to perform and the agreements he makes with the involved parties." Here, Cousins engaged Hodgins to find commercial investment property for Eagle to buy, and Hodgins called the principal's attention to Westinghouse's office building at 3330 Lake Villa Drive. Despite Eagle's offer to buy the property, submitted through Hodgins, and Westinghouse's response, Hodgins arranged a sale of the property to his firm, 4141 Vets Limited Partnership. The court pointed out that a real estate agent has "a duty to communicate to his principal all offers received and may be liable in damages for failure to do so. Moreover, a realtor has a duty to relay accurate information about property, a duty which extends to both vendor and purchaser, and may be held liable if such duty is breached."

 FOR CRITICAL ANALYSIS–Social Consideration *What steps do the facts in the* Cousins *case indicate that an investor might want to consider when dealing through an agent?*

Obedience When acting on behalf of a principal, an agent has a duty to follow all lawful and clearly stated instructions of the principal. Any deviation from such instructions is a violation of this duty. During emergency situations, however, when the principal cannot be consulted, the agent may deviate from the instructions without violating this duty. Whenever instructions are not clearly stated, the agent can fulfill the duty of obedience by acting in good faith and in a manner reasonable under the circumstances.

Accounting Unless an agent and a principal agree otherwise, the agent has the duty to keep and make available to the principal an account of all property and funds received and paid out on behalf of the principal. This includes gifts from third parties in connection with the agency. For example, a gift from a customer to a salesperson for prompt deliveries made by the salesperson's firm, in the absence of a company policy to the contrary, belongs to the firm. The agent has a duty to maintain separate accounts for the principal's funds and for the agent's personal funds, and the agent must not intermingle these accounts.

Principal's Duties to the Agent

The principal also owes certain duties to the agent. These duties relate to compensation, reimbursement and indemnification, cooperation, and safe working conditions.

Compensation In general, when a principal requests certain services from an agent, the agent reasonably expects payment. The principal therefore has a duty to pay the agent for services rendered. For example, when an accountant or an attorney is asked to act as an agent, an agreement to compensate the agent for such service is implied. The principal also has a duty to pay that compensation in a timely manner. Except in a gratuitous agency relationship, in which an agent does not act for payment in return, the principal must pay the agreed-on value for an agent's services. If no amount has been expressly agreed on, the principal owes the agent the customary compensation for such services.

Reimbursement and Indemnification   Whenever an agent disburses funds to fulfill the request of the principal or to pay for necessary expenses in the course of a reasonable performance of his or her agency duties, the principal has the duty to reimburse the agent for these payments. Agents cannot recover for expenses incurred through their own misconduct or negligence, though.

Subject to the terms of the agency agreement, the principal has the duty to compensate, or *indemnify*, an agent for liabilities incurred because of authorized and lawful acts and transactions. For instance, if the principal fails to perform a contract formed by the agent with a third party and the third party then sues the agent, the principal is obligated to compensate the agent for any costs incurred in defending against the lawsuit.

Additionally, the principal must indemnify (pay) the agent for the value of benefits that the agent confers on the principal. The amount of indemnification is usually specified in the agency contract. If it is not, the courts will look to the nature of the business and the type of loss to determine the amount. Note that this rule applies to acts by gratuitous agents as well. If the finder of a dog that becomes sick takes the dog to a veterinarian and pays the required fees for the veterinarian's services, the agent is entitled to be reimbursed by the owner of the dog for those fees.

Cooperation   A principal has a duty to cooperate with the agent and to assist the agent in performing her or his duties. The principal must do nothing to prevent such performance.

When a principal grants an agent an exclusive territory, for example, the principal creates an *exclusive agency* and cannot compete with the agent or appoint or allow another agent to so compete. If the principal does so, she or he will be exposed to liability for the agent's lost sales or profits. **■EXAMPLE 17.10**   Akers (the principal) creates an exclusive agency by granting Johnson (the agent) an exclusive territory within which Johnson may sell Akers's products. In this situation, Akers cannot compete with Johnson within that territory—or appoint or allow another agent to so compete—because this would violate the exclusive agency. If Akers does so, he can be held liable for Johnson's lost sales or profits. ■

Safe Working Conditions   Under the common law, a principal is required to provide safe working premises, equipment, and conditions for all agents and employees. The principal has a duty to inspect the working conditions and to warn agents and employees about any unsafe areas. When the agent is an employee, the employer's liability is frequently covered by state workers' compensation insurance, and federal and state statutes often require the employer to meet certain safety standards (to be discussed in Chapter 18).

AGENT'S AUTHORITY

An agent's authority to act can be either *actual* (express or implied) or *apparent*. If an agent contracts outside the scope of his or her authority, the principal may still become liable by ratifying the contract.

Actual Authority

As indicated, an agent's actual authority can be express or implied. We look here at both of these forms of actual authority.

EQUAL DIGNITY RULE
In most states, a rule stating that express authority given to an agent must be in writing if the contract to be made on behalf of the principal is required to be in writing.

Express Authority   *Express authority* is authority declared in clear, direct, and definite terms. Express authority can be given orally or in writing. In most states, the **equal dignity rule** requires that if the contract being executed is or must be in writing, then the agent's authority must also be in writing. Failure to comply with the equal dignity rule can make a contract voidable *at the option of the principal*. The law regards the contract at that point as a mere offer. If the principal decides to accept the offer, acceptance must be ratified, or affirmed, in writing.

■EXAMPLE 17.11 Klee (the principal) orally asks Parkinson (the agent) to sell a ranch that Klee owns. Parkinson finds a buyer and signs a sales contract (a contract for an interest in realty must be in writing) on behalf of Klee to sell the ranch. The buyer cannot enforce the contract unless Klee subsequently ratifies Parkinson's agency status *in writing*. Once Parkinson's agency status is ratified, either party can enforce rights under the contract. ■

Exceptions to the Equal Dignity Rule. Modern business practice allows an exception to the equal dignity rule. An executive officer of a corporation normally is not required to obtain written authority from the corporation to conduct *ordinary* business transactions. The equal dignity rule does not apply when an agent acts in the presence of a principal or when the agent's act of signing is merely perfunctory. Thus, if Dickens (the principal) negotiates a contract but is called out of town the day it is to be signed and orally authorizes Santini to sign the contract, the oral authorization is sufficient.

Power of Attorney. Giving an agent a **power of attorney** confers express authority.[7] The power of attorney normally is a written document and is usually notarized. (A document is notarized when a **notary public**—a public official authorized to attest to the authenticity of signatures—signs and dates the document and imprints it with his or her seal of authority.) Most states have statutory provisions for creating a power of attorney. A power of attorney can be special (permitting the agent to do specified acts only), or it can be general (permitting the agent to transact all business for the principal). Because a general power of attorney grants extensive authority to an agent to act on behalf of the principal in many ways (see Exhibit 17–1 on the next page), it should be used with great caution. Ordinarily, a power of attorney terminates on the incapacity or death of the person giving the power.[8]

Implied Authority An agent has the *implied authority* to do what is reasonably necessary to carry out express authority and accomplish the objectives of the agency. Authority can also be implied by custom or inferred from the position the agent occupies.

■EXAMPLE 17.12 Mueller is employed by Al's Supermarket to manage one of its stores. Al's has not expressly stated that Mueller has authority to contract with third persons. In this situation, though, authority to manage a business implies authority to do what is reasonably required (as is customary or can be inferred from a manager's position) to operate the business. This includes forming contracts to hire employees, to buy merchandise and equipment, and to advertise the products sold in the store. ■

Does an agent's breach of loyalty terminate the agent's authority? Suppose that an employee-agent who is authorized to access company trade secrets contained in computer files takes those secrets to a competitor for whom the employee is about to begin working. Clearly, in this situation the agent has violated the ethical—and legal—duty of loyalty to the principal. Does this breach of loyalty mean that the employee's act of accessing the trade secrets was unauthorized? The question has significant implications because if the act was unauthorized, the employee will be subject to state and federal laws prohibiting unauthorized access to computer information and data. If the act was authorized, the employee will not be

> **POWER OF ATTORNEY**
> A written document, which is usually notarized, authorizing another to act as one's agent; can be special (permitting the agent to do specified acts only) or general (permitting the agent to transact all business for the principal).
>
> **NOTARY PUBLIC**
> A public official authorized to attest to the authenticity of signatures.

ETHICAL ISSUE 17.1

---

7. An agent who holds the power of attorney is called an *attorney-in-fact* for the principal. The holder does not have to be an attorney-at-law (and often is not).

8. A *durable* power of attorney, however, continues to be effective despite the principal's incapacity. An elderly person, for example, might grant a durable power of attorney to provide for the handling of property and investments or specific health-care needs should she or he become incompetent.

EXHIBIT 17–1 A Sample General Power of Attorney

GENERAL POWER OF ATTORNEY

Know All Men by These Present:

That I, _____ , hereinafter referred to as PRINCIPAL, in the County of _____
State of _____ , do(es) appoint _____ as my true and lawful attorney.

In principal's name, and for principal's use and benefit, said attorney is authorized hereby;

(1) To demand, sue for, collect, and receive all money, debts, accounts, legacies, bequests, interest, dividends, annuities, and demands as are now or shall hereafter become due, payable, or belonging to principal, and take all lawful means, for the recovery thereof and to compromise the same and give discharges for the same;

(2) To buy and sell land, make contracts of every kind relative to land, any interest therein or the possession thereof, and to take possession and exercise control over the use thereof;

(3) To buy, sell, mortgage, hypothecate, assign, transfer, and in any manner deal with goods, wares and merchandise, choses in action, certificates or shares of capital stock, and other property in possession or in action, and to make, do, and transact all and every kind of business of whatever nature;

(4) To execute, acknowledge, and deliver contracts of sale, escrow instructions, deeds, leases including leases for minerals and hydrocarbon substances and assignments of leases, covenants, agreements and assignments of agreements, mortgages and assignments of mortgages, conveyances in trust, to secure indebtedness or other obligations, and assign the beneficial interest thereunder, subordinations of liens or encumbrances, bills of lading, receipts, evidences of debt, releases, bonds, notes, bills, requests to reconvey deeds of trust, partial or full judgments, satisfactions of mortgages, and other debts, and other written instruments of whatever kind and nature, all upon such terms and conditions as said attorney shall approve.

GIVING AND GRANTING to said attorney full power and authority to do all and every act and thing whatsoever requisite and necessary to be done relative to any of the foregoing as fully to all intents and purposes as principal might or could do if personally present.

All that said attorney shall lawfully do or cause to be done under the authority of this power of attorney is expressly approved.

Dated: _____   /s/ _____

State of _____   } SS.
County of _____

On _____ , before me, the undersigned, a Notary Public in and for said State, personally appeared _____

known to me to be the person _____ whose name _____ subscribed
to the within instrument and acknowledged that _____ executed the same.

Witness my hand and official seal.

(Seal) _____
Notary Public in and for said State.

subject to such laws. Although one court has held that the moment the employee accessed trade secrets for the purpose of divulging them to a competitor, the employee's authority as an agent terminated,[9] most courts have held that an agent's authority continues.

In one case, for example, three employees of Lockheed Martin Corporation copied confidential information and trade secrets from Lockheed's computer network onto compact discs and BlackBerries (personal digital assistants). Lockheed had authorized the employee-agents to access these files but was understandably upset when the three resigned and went to work for a competitor, taking the trade secrets with them. Lockheed sued the former agents under the Computer Fraud and Abuse Act (discussed in Chapter 6), arguing that they accessed the data without authorization. The federal district court, however, held that the individuals did

---

9. *Shurgard Storage Centers, Inc. v. Safeguard Self Storage, Inc.*, 119 F.Supp.2d 1121 (W.D.Wash. 2000).

have authorization to access the computer network and did not lose this authorization when they breached the duty of loyalty. Therefore, the court dismissed the case.[10] This ruling is important for businesspersons because it means that an employee-agent who steals confidential data or trade secrets may not be liable for unauthorized access.

Apparent Authority

Actual authority (express or implied) arises from what the principal manifests *to the agent.* An agent has **apparent authority** when the principal, by either words or actions, causes a *third party* reasonably to believe that an agent has authority to act, even though the agent has no express or implied authority. If the third party changes her or his position in reliance on the principal's representations, the principal may be *estopped* (prevented) from denying that the agent had authority.

EXAMPLE 17.13 A traveling salesperson, Ling (the agent), is authorized to take customers' orders. Ling does not deliver the ordered goods and is not authorized to collect payments for the goods. A customer, Byron, pays Ling for a solicited order. Ling then takes the payment to the principal's accounting department, and an accountant accepts the payment and sends Byron a receipt. This procedure is thereafter followed for other orders solicited from and paid for by Byron. Later, Ling solicits an order, and Byron pays her as before. This time, however, Ling absconds with the payment. Can Byron claim that the payment to the agent was authorized and was thus, in effect, a payment to the principal?

The answer is normally yes, because the principal's *repeated* acts of accepting Byron's payment led him reasonably to expect that Ling had authority to receive payments for goods solicited. Although Ling did not have express or implied authority, the principal's conduct gave Ling *apparent* authority to collect. In this situation, the principal would be estopped from denying that Ling had authority to collect payments.

APPARENT AUTHORITY
Authority that is only apparent, not real. In agency law, a person may be deemed to have had the power to act as an agent for another party if the other party's manifestations to a third party led the third party to believe that an agency existed when, in fact, it did not.

Ratification

As already mentioned, ratification occurs when the principal affirms an agent's *unauthorized* act. When ratification occurs, the principal is bound to the agent's act, and the act is treated as if it had been authorized by the principal *from the outset.* Ratification can be either express or implied.

If the principal does not ratify the contract, the principal is not bound, and the third party's agreement with the agent is viewed as merely an unaccepted offer. Because the third party's agreement is an unaccepted offer, the third party can revoke the offer at any time, without liability, before the principal ratifies the contract.

The requirements for ratification can be summarized as follows:

1 The agent must have acted on behalf of an identified principal who subsequently ratifies the action.

2 The principal must know of all material facts involved in the transaction. If a principal ratifies a contract without knowing all of the facts, the principal can rescind (cancel) the contract.

3 The principal must affirm the agent's act in its entirety.

4 The principal must have the legal capacity to authorize the transaction at the time the agent engages in the act and at the time the principal ratifies. The third party must also have the legal capacity to engage in the transaction.

BE AWARE An agent who exceeds his or her authority and enters into a contract that the principal does not ratify may be liable to the third party on the ground of misrepresentation.

---

10. *Lockheed Martin Corp. v. Speed*, ___ F.Supp.2d ___ (M.D.Fla. 2006).

5 The principal's affirmation must occur before the third party withdraws from the transaction.

6 The principal must observe the same formalities when approving the act done by the agent as would have been required to authorize it initially.

The *Concept Summary* below outlines the rules concerning an agent's authority to bind the principal and a third party.

LIABILITY IN AGENCY RELATIONSHIPS

Frequently, a question arises as to which party, the principal or the agent, should be held liable for contracts formed by the agent or for torts or crimes committed by the agent. We look here at these aspects of agency law.

Liability for Contracts

Liability for contracts formed by an agent depends on how the principal is classified and on whether the actions of the agent were authorized or unauthorized. Principals are classified as disclosed, partially disclosed, or undisclosed.[11]

A **disclosed principal** is a principal whose identity is known by the third party at the time the contract is made by the agent. A **partially disclosed principal** is a principal whose identity is not known by the third party, but the third party knows that the agent is or may be acting for a principal at the time the contract is made. **EXAMPLE 17.14** Sarah has contracted with a real estate agent to sell certain property. She wishes to keep her identity a secret, but the agent makes it perfectly clear to potential buyers of the property that the agent is acting in an agency capacity. In this situation, Sarah is a partially disclosed principal. ■ An **undisclosed principal** is a principal whose identity is totally

DISCLOSED PRINCIPAL
A principal whose identity is known to a third party at the time the agent makes a contract with the third party.

PARTIALLY DISCLOSED PRINCIPAL
A principal whose identity is unknown by a third party, but the third party knows that the agent is or may be acting for a principal at the time the agent and the third party form a contract.

UNDISCLOSED PRINCIPAL
A principal whose identity is unknown by a third person, and the third person has no knowledge that the agent is acting for a principal at the time the agent and the third person form a contract.

---

11. *Restatement (Second) of Agency*, Section 4.

CONCEPT SUMMARY Authority of Agent to Bind Principal and Third Party

AUTHORITY OF AGENT	DEFINITION	EFFECT ON PRINCIPAL AND THIRD PARTY
Express Authority	Authority expressly given by the principal to the agent.	Principal and third party are bound in contract.
Implied Authority	Authority implied (1) because such authority is necessary if the agent is to carry out expressly authorized duties and responsibilities, (2) by custom, or (3) from the position in which the principal has placed the agent.	Principal and third party are bound in contract.
Apparent Authority	Authority created when the conduct of the principal leads a third party to believe that the principal's agent has authority.	Principal and third party are bound in contract.
Unauthorized Acts	Acts committed by an agent that are outside the scope of his or her express, implied, or apparent authority.	Principal and third party are not bound in contract—*unless* the principal ratifies prior to the third party's withdrawal.

unknown by the third party, and the third party has no knowledge that the agent is acting in an agency capacity at the time the contract is made.

Authorized Acts   If an agent acts within the scope of her or his authority, normally the principal is obligated to perform the contract regardless of whether the principal was disclosed, partially disclosed, or undisclosed. Whether the agent may also be held liable under the contract, however, depends on the disclosed, partially disclosed, or undisclosed status of the principal.

Disclosed or Partially Disclosed Principal.   A disclosed or partially disclosed principal is liable to a third party for a contract made by an agent who is acting within the scope of her or his authority. If the principal is disclosed, an agent has no contractual liability for the nonperformance of the principal or the third party. If the principal is partially disclosed, in most states the agent is also treated as a party to the contract, and the third party can hold the agent liable for contractual nonperformance.[12]

   EXAMPLE 17.15   Walgreens leased commercial property to operate a drugstore at a mall owned by Kedzie Plaza Associates. A property management company, Taxman Corporation, signed the lease on behalf of the principal, Kedzie. The lease required the landlord to keep the sidewalks free of snow and ice, so Taxman, on behalf of Kedzie, contracted with another company to remove ice and snow from the sidewalks surrounding the Walgreens store. When a Walgreens employee slipped on ice outside the store and was injured, she sued Taxman for negligence. Because the principal's identity (Kedzie) was fully disclosed in the snow-removal contract, however, the Illinois court ruled that the agent, Taxman, could not be held liable. Taxman did not assume a contractual obligation to remove the snow but merely retained a contractor to do so on behalf of the owner.[13] ▪

Undisclosed Principal.   When neither the fact of agency nor the identity of the principal is disclosed, the undisclosed principal is bound to perform just as if the principal had been fully disclosed at the time the contract was made. The agent is also liable as a party to the contract.

   When a principal's identity is undisclosed and the agent is forced to pay the third party, the agent is entitled to be indemnified (compensated) by the principal. The principal had a duty to perform, even though his or her identity was undisclosed, and failure to do so will make the principal ultimately liable. Once the undisclosed principal's identity is revealed, the third party generally can elect to hold either the principal or the agent liable on the contract. Conversely, the undisclosed principal can require the third party to fulfill the contract, *unless* (1) the undisclosed principal was expressly excluded as a party in the contract; (2) the contract is a negotiable instrument signed by the agent with no indication of signing in a representative capacity; or (3) the performance of the agent is personal to the contract, allowing the third party to refuse the principal's performance.

Unauthorized Acts   If an agent has no authority but nevertheless contracts with a third party, the principal cannot be held liable on the contract. It does not matter whether the principal was disclosed, partially disclosed, or undisclosed. The *agent* is liable, however.

   EXAMPLE 17.16   Scranton signs a contract for the purchase of a truck, purportedly acting as an agent under authority granted by Johnson. In fact, Johnson has not given Scranton any such authority. Johnson refuses to pay for the truck, claiming that Scranton had

---

12. *Restatement (Second) of Agency*, Section 321.
13. *McBride v. Taxman Corp.*, 327 Ill.App.3d 992, 765 N.E.2d 51 (2002).

no authority to purchase it. The seller of the truck is entitled to hold Scranton liable for payment. ■

If the principal is disclosed or partially disclosed, the agent is liable to the third party as long as the third party relied on the agency status. The agent's liability here is based on the breach of an *implied warranty of authority* (an agent impliedly warrants that he or she has the authority to enter a contract on behalf of the principal), not on breach of the contract itself.[14] If the third party knows at the time the contract is made that the agent does not have authority—or if the agent expresses to the third party *uncertainty* as to the extent of her or his authority—then the agent is not personally liable.

Liability for E-Agents Although in the past standard agency principles applied only to *human* agents, today these same principles are being applied to electronic agents. An electronic agent, or **e-agent,** is a semiautonomous computer program that is capable of executing specific tasks. E-agents used in e-commerce include software that can search through many databases and retrieve only information that is relevant for the user.

The Uniform Electronic Transactions Act (UETA), which was discussed in detail in Chapter 10 and has been adopted by the majority of the states, contains several provisions relating to the principal's liability for the actions of e-agents. Section 15 of the UETA states that e-agents may enter into binding agreements on behalf of their principals. Presumably, then—at least in those states that have adopted the act—the principal will be bound by the terms in a contract entered into by an e-agent. Thus, if you place an order over the Internet, the company (principal) whose system took the order via an e-agent cannot claim that it did not receive your order.

The UETA also stipulates that if an e-agent does not provide an opportunity to prevent errors at the time of the transaction, the other party to the transaction can avoid the transaction. For instance, if an e-agent fails to provide an on-screen confirmation of a purchase or sale, the other party can avoid the effect of any errors.

E-AGENT
A computer program that by electronic or other automated means can independently initiate an action or respond to electronic messages or data without review by an individual.

Liability for Torts and Crimes

Obviously, any person, including an agent, is liable for her or his own torts and crimes. Whether a principal can also be held liable for an agent's torts and crimes depends on several factors, which we examine here. In some situations, a principal may be held liable not only for the torts of an agent but also for the torts committed by an independent contractor.

A serious ski accident occurs under the supervised instruction of a ski resort employee. Are there any circumstances under which the principal (the resort) will not be liable? (Rob Lee/Creative Commons)

Principal's Tortious Conduct A principal conducting an activity through an agent may be liable for harm resulting from the principal's own negligence or recklessness. Thus, a principal may be liable for giving improper instructions, authorizing the use of improper materials or tools, or establishing improper rules that resulted in the agent's committing a tort. **■EXAMPLE 17.17** Jack knows that Suki cannot drive but nevertheless tells her to use the company truck to deliver some equipment to a customer. In this situation, Jack (the principal) will be liable for his own negligence to anyone injured by Suki's negligent driving. ■

Principal's Authorization of Agent's Tortious Conduct A principal who authorizes an agent to commit a tort may be liable to persons or property injured thereby, because the act is considered to be the

---

14. The agent is not liable on the contract because the agent was never intended personally to be a party to the contract.

principal's. **EXAMPLE 17.18** Selkow directs his agent, Warren, to cut the corn on specific acreage, which neither of them has the right to do. The harvest is therefore a trespass (a tort), and Selkow is liable to the owner of the corn. ■

Note also that an agent acting at the principal's direction can be liable as a *tortfeasor* (one who commits a wrong, or tort), along with the principal, for committing the tortious act even if the agent was unaware of the wrongfulness of the act. Assume in the above example that Warren, the agent, did not know that Selkow had no right to harvest the corn. Warren can be held liable to the owner of the field for damages, along with Selkow, the principal.

Liability for Agent's Misrepresentation   A principal is exposed to tort liability whenever a third person sustains a loss due to the agent's misrepresentation. The principal's liability depends on whether the agent was actually or apparently authorized to make representations and whether such representations were made within the scope of the agency. The principal is always directly responsible for an agent's misrepresentation made within the scope of the agent's authority. **EXAMPLE 17.19** Bassett is a demonstrator for Moore's products. Moore sends Bassett to a home show to demonstrate the products and to answer questions from consumers. Moore has given Bassett authority to make statements about the products. If Bassett makes only true representations, all is fine; but if he makes false claims, Moore will be liable for any injuries or damages sustained by third parties in reliance on Bassett's false representations. ■

Liability for Agent's Negligence   As mentioned, an agent is liable for his or her own torts. A principal may also be liable for harm an agent caused to a third party under the doctrine of *respondeat superior*,[15] a Latin term meaning "let the master respond." This doctrine, which is discussed in this chapter's *Landmark in the Law* feature on the following page, is similar to the theory of strict liability discussed in Chapter 4. The doctrine imposes **vicarious liability,** or indirect liability, on the employer—that is, liability without regard to the personal fault of the employer for torts committed by an employee in the course or scope of employment.

Determining the Scope of Employment.   The key to determining whether a principal may be liable for the torts of an agent under the doctrine of *respondeat superior* is whether the torts are committed within the scope of the agency or employment. The *Restatement (Second) of Agency,* Section 229, indicates the factors that today's courts will consider in determining whether a particular act occurred within the course and scope of employment. These factors are as follows:

1 Whether the employee's act was authorized by the employer.
2 The time, place, and purpose of the act.
3 Whether the act was one commonly performed by employees on behalf of their employers.
4 The extent to which the employer's interest was advanced by the act.
5 The extent to which the private interests of the employee were involved.
6 Whether the employer furnished the means or instrumentality (for example, a truck or a machine) by which the injury was inflicted.
7 Whether the employer had reason to know that the employee would do the act in question and whether the employee had ever done it before.
8 Whether the act involved the commission of a serious crime.

RESPONDEAT SUPERIOR
Latin for "let the master respond." A doctrine under which a principal or an employer is held liable for the wrongful acts committed by agents or employees while acting within the course and scope of their agency or employment.

VICARIOUS LIABILITY
Legal responsibility placed on one person for the acts of another; indirect liability imposed on a supervisory party (such as an employer) for the actions of a subordinate (such as an employee) because of the relationship between the two parties.

---

15. Pronounced ree-*spahn*-dee-uht soo-*peer*-ee-your.

LANDMARK IN THE LAW — The Doctrine of *Respondeat Superior*

The idea that a master (employer) must respond to third persons for losses negligently caused by the master's servant (employee) first appeared in Lord Holt's opinion in *Jones v. Hart* (1698).[a] By the early nineteenth century, this maxim had been adopted by most courts and was referred to as the doctrine of *respondeat superior.*

Theories of Liability   The vicarious (indirect) liability of the master for the acts of the servant has been supported primarily by two theories. The first theory rests on the issue of *control,* or *fault:* the master has control over the acts of the servant and is thus responsible for injuries arising out of such service. The second theory is economic in nature: because the master takes the benefits or profits of the servant's service, he or she should also suffer the losses; moreover, the master is better able than the servant to absorb such losses.

The *control* theory is clearly recognized in the *Restatement (Second) of Agency,* which defines a master as "a principal who employs an agent to perform service in his [or her] affairs and who controls, or has the right to control, the physical conduct of the other in the performance of the service." Accordingly, a servant is defined as "an agent employed by a master to perform service in his [or her] affairs whose physical conduct in his [or her] performance of the service is controlled, or is subject to control, by the master."

Limitations on the Employer's Liability   There are limitations on the master's liability for the acts of the servant, however. An employer (master) is responsible only for the wrongful conduct of an employee (servant) that occurs in "the scope of employment." The criteria used by the courts in determining whether an employee is acting within the scope of employment are set forth in the *Restatement (Second) of Agency* and discussed in the text. Generally, the act must be of a kind the servant was employed to do; must have occurred within "authorized time and space limits"; and must have been "activated, at least in part, by a purpose to serve the master."

APPLICATION TO TODAY'S WORLD   *The courts have accepted the doctrine of* respondeat superior *for nearly two centuries. This theory of vicarious liability is laden with practical implications in all situations in which a principal-agent (master-servant, employer-employee) relationship exists. Today, the small-town grocer with one clerk and the multinational corporation with thousands of employees are equally subject to the doctrinal demand of "let the master respond." (For a further discussion of employers' liability for wrongs committed by their employees, including wrongs committed in the online employment environment, see Chapter 18.)*

RELEVANT WEB SITES   *To locate information on the Web concerning the doctrine of* respondeat superior, *go to this text's Web site at* **academic.cengage.com/blaw/blt***, select "Chapter 17," and click on "URLs for Landmarks."*

a. K.B. 642, 90 Eng. Reprint 1255 (1698).

The Distinction between a "Detour" and a "Frolic." A useful insight into the "scope of employment" concept may be gained from the judge's classic distinction between a "detour" and a "frolic" in the case of *Joel v. Morison* (1834).[16] In this case, the English court held that if a servant merely took a detour from his master's business, the master will be responsible. If, however, the servant was on a "frolic of his own" and not in any way "on his master's business," the master will not be liable.

■EXAMPLE 17.20 Mandel, a traveling salesperson, while driving his employer's vehicle to call on a customer, decides to stop at the post office—which is one block off his route—to mail a personal letter. As Mandel approaches the post office, he negligently runs into a parked vehicle owned by Chan. In this situation, because Mandel's detour from the employer's business is not substantial, he is still acting within the scope of employment, and the employer is liable. The result would be different, though, if Mandel had decided to pick up a few friends for cocktails in another city and in the process had negligently run into Chan's vehicle. In that circumstance, the departure from the employer's business would be substantial, and the employer normally would not be liable to Chan for damages. Mandel would be considered to have been on a "frolic" of his own. ■

Employee Travel Time. An employee going to and from work or to and from meals is usually considered outside the scope of employment. If travel is part of a person's position, however, such as a traveling salesperson or a regional representative of a company, then travel time is normally considered within the scope of employment. Thus, the duration of the business trip, including the return trip home, is within the scope of employment unless there is a significant departure from the employer's business.

NOTE An agent-employee going to or from work or meals usually is not considered to be within the scope of employment. An agent-employee whose job requires travel, however, is considered to be within the scope of employment for the entire trip, including the return.

Notice of Dangerous Conditions. The employer is charged with knowledge of any dangerous conditions discovered by an employee and pertinent to the employment situation.
■EXAMPLE 17.21 Chad, a maintenance employee in Martin's apartment building, notices a lead pipe protruding from the ground in the building's courtyard. The employee neglects either to fix the pipe or to inform the employer of the danger. John falls on the pipe and is injured. The employer is charged with knowledge of the dangerous condition regardless of whether or not Chad actually informed the employer. That knowledge is imputed to the employer by virtue of the employment relationship. ■

Liability for Agent's Intentional Torts Most intentional torts that employees commit have no relation to their employment; thus, their employers will not be held liable. Nevertheless, under the doctrine of *respondeat superior*, the employer can be liable for intentional torts of the employee that are committed within the course and scope of employment, just as the employer is liable for negligence. For instance, an employer is liable when an employee (such as a "bouncer" at a nightclub or a security guard at a department store) commits the tort of assault and battery or false imprisonment while acting within the scope of employment.

In addition, an employer who knows or should know that an employee has a propensity for committing tortious acts is liable for the employee's acts even if they would not ordinarily be considered within the scope of employment. For example, if the employer hires a bouncer knowing that he has a history of arrests for assault and battery, the employer may be liable if the employee viciously attacks a patron in the parking lot after hours.

An employer may also be liable for permitting an employee to engage in reckless actions that can injure others. ■EXAMPLE 17.22 An employer observes an employee smoking while

---

16. 6 Car. & P. 501, 172 Eng. Reprint 1338 (1834).

filling containerized trucks with highly flammable liquids. Failure to stop the employee will cause the employer to be liable for any injuries that result if a truck explodes. ■ (See this chapter's *Beyond Our Borders* feature for a discussion of another approach to an employer's liability for an employee's acts.)

Liability for Independent Contractor's Torts   Generally, an employer is not liable for physical harm caused to a third person by the negligent act of an independent contractor in the performance of the contract. This is because the employer does not have *the right to control* the details of an independent contractor's performance. Exceptions to this rule are made in certain situations, though, such as when unusually hazardous activities are involved. Typical examples of such activities include blasting operations, the transportation of highly volatile chemicals, or the use of poisonous gases. In these situations, an employer cannot be shielded from liability merely by using an independent contractor. Strict liability is imposed on the employer-principal as a matter of law. Also, in some states, strict liability may be imposed by statute.

Liability for Agent's Crimes   An agent is liable for his or her own crimes. A principal or employer is not liable for an agent's crime even if the crime was committed within the scope of authority or employment—unless the principal participated by conspiracy or other action. In some jurisdictions, under specific statutes, a principal may be liable for an agent's violation, in the course and scope of employment, of regulations, such as those governing sanitation, prices, weights, and the sale of liquor.

HOW AGENCY RELATIONSHIPS ARE TERMINATED

Agency law is similar to contract law in that both an agency and a contract can be terminated by an act of the parties or by operation of law. Once the relationship between the principal and the agent has ended, the agent no longer has the right (*actual* authority) to bind the principal. For an agent's *apparent* authority to be terminated, though, third persons may also need to be notified that the agency has been terminated.

Termination by Act of the Parties

An agency may be terminated by act of the parties in several ways, including those discussed here.

Lapse of Time   An agency agreement may specify the time period during which the agency relationship will exist. If so, the agency ends when that time period expires. For instance, if the parties agree that the agency will begin on January 1, 2008, and end on December 31, 2009, the agency is automatically terminated on December 31, 2009. If no definite time is stated, then the agency continues for a reasonable time and can be terminated at will by either party. What constitutes a "reasonable time" depends, of course, on the circumstances and the nature of the agency relationship.

Purpose Achieved   An agent can be employed to accomplish a particular objective, such as the purchase of stock for a cattle rancher. In that situation, the agency automatically ends after the cattle have been purchased. If more than one agent is employed to accomplish the same purpose, such as the sale of real estate, the first agent to complete the sale automatically terminates the agency relationship for all the others.

Occurrence of a Specific Event   An agency can be created to terminate on the happening of a certain event. If Posner appoints Rubik to handle her business affairs while she is away, the agency automatically terminates when Posner returns.

Mutual Agreement   Recall from the chapters on contract law that parties can cancel (rescind) a contract by mutually agreeing to terminate the contractual relationship. The same holds true in agency law regardless of whether the agency contract is in writing or whether it is for a specific duration.

Termination by One Party   As a general rule, either party can terminate the agency relationship (the act of termination is called *revocation* if done by the principal and *renunciation* if done by the agent). Although both parties have the *power* to terminate the agency, they may not possess the *right*. Wrongful termination can subject the canceling party to a suit for breach of contract. ■**EXAMPLE 17.23** Rawlins has a one-year employment contract with Munro to act as an agent in return for $65,000. Munro has the *power* to discharge Rawlins before the contract period expires. If Munro discharges Rawlins, however, Munro can be sued for breaching the contract and will be liable to Rawlins for damages because he had no *right* to terminate the agency. ■

A special rule applies in an *agency coupled with an interest*. This type of agency is not an agency in the usual sense because it is created for the agent's benefit instead of the principal's benefit. ■**EXAMPLE 17.24** Julie borrows $5,000 from Rob, giving Rob some of her jewelry and signing a letter giving Rob the power to sell the jewelry as her agent if she fails to repay the loan. After receiving the $5,000 from Rob, Julie attempts to revoke Rob's authority to sell the jewelry as her agent. Julie would not succeed in this attempt because a principal cannot revoke an agency created for the agent's benefit. ■

Notice of Termination   When an agency has been terminated by act of the parties, it is the principal's duty to inform any third parties who know of the existence of the agency that it has been terminated (although notice of the termination may be given by others). Although an agent's actual authority ends when the agency is terminated, an agent's *apparent authority* continues until the third party receives notice (from any source) that such authority has been terminated. If the principal knows that a third party has dealt with the agent, the principal is expected to notify that person *directly*. For third parties who have heard about the agency but have not yet dealt with the agent, *constructive notice* is sufficient.[17]

No particular form is required for notice of agency termination to be effective. The principal can personally notify the agent, or the agent can learn of the termination through some other means. **[■EXAMPLE 17.25]** Manning bids on a shipment of steel, and Stone is hired as an agent to arrange transportation of the shipment. When Stone learns that Manning has lost the bid, Stone's authority to make the transportation arrangement terminates. **[■]** If the agent's authority is written, however, it normally must be revoked in writing.

Termination by Operation of Law

Termination of an agency by operation of law occurs in the circumstances discussed here. Note that when an agency terminates by operation of law, there is no duty to notify third persons.

Death or Insanity The general rule is that the death or mental incompetence of either the principal or the agent automatically and immediately terminates the ordinary agency relationship. Knowledge of the death is not required. **[■EXAMPLE 17.26]** Geer sends Pyron to China to purchase a rare painting. Before Pyron makes the purchase, Geer dies. Pyron's agent status is terminated at the moment of Geer's death, even though Pyron does not know that Geer has died. **[■]** Some states, however, have enacted statutes changing this common law rule to make knowledge of the principal's death a requirement for agency termination.

An agent's transactions that occur after the death of the principal are not binding on the principal's estate.[18] **[■EXAMPLE 17.27]** Carson is hired by Perry to collect a debt from Thomas (a third party). Perry dies, but Carson, not knowing of Perry's death, still collects the funds from Thomas. Thomas's payment to Carson is no longer legally sufficient to discharge the debt to Perry because Carson's authority to collect ended on Perry's death. If Carson absconds with the funds, Thomas is still liable for the debt to Perry's estate. **[■]**

Impossibility When the specific subject matter of an agency is destroyed or lost, the agency terminates. **[■EXAMPLE 17.28]** Bullard employs Gonzalez to sell Bullard's house. Prior to any sale, the house is destroyed by fire. In this situation, Gonzalez's agency and authority to sell Bullard's house terminate. **[■]** Similarly, when it is impossible for the agent to perform the agency lawfully because of a change in the law, the agency terminates.

Changed Circumstances When an event occurs that has such an unusual effect on the subject matter of the agency that the agent can reasonably infer that the principal will not want the agency to continue, the agency terminates. **[■EXAMPLE 17.29]** Roberts hires Mullen to sell a tract of land for $20,000. Subsequently, Mullen learns that there is oil under the land and that the land is worth $1 million. The agency and Mullen's authority to sell the land for $20,000 are terminated. **[■]**

Bankruptcy If either the principal or the agent petitions for bankruptcy, the agency is *usually* terminated. In certain circumstances, as when the agent's financial status is irrel-

---

17. *Constructive notice* is information or knowledge of a fact imputed by law to a person if he or she could have discovered the fact by proper diligence. Constructive notice is often accomplished by newspaper publication.

18. Recall from Chapter 15 that special rules apply when the agent is a bank. Banks can continue to exercise specific types of authority even after a customer has died or become mentally incompetent unless they have knowledge of the death or incompetence [Section 4–405 of the Uniform Commercial Code]. Even with knowledge of the customer's death, the bank has authority to honor checks for ten days following the customer's death in the absence of a stop-payment order.

evant to the purpose of the agency, the agency relationship may continue. Insolvency (defined as the inability to pay debts when they become due or when liabilities exceed assets), as distinguished from bankruptcy, does not necessarily terminate the relationship.

War When the principal's country and the agent's country are at war with each other, the agency is terminated. In this situation, the agency is automatically suspended or terminated because there is no way to enforce the legal rights and obligations of the parties.

REVIEWING Agency

Lynne Meyer, on her way to a business meeting and in a hurry, stopped by a Buy-Mart store for a new pair of nylons to wear to the meeting. There was a long line at one of the checkout counters, but a cashier, Valerie Watts, opened another counter and began loading the cash drawer. Meyer told Watts that she was in a hurry and asked Watts to work faster. Watts, however, only slowed her pace. At this point, Meyer hit Watts. It is not clear from the record whether Meyer hit Watts intentionally or, in an attempt to retrieve the nylons, hit her inadvertently. In response, Watts grabbed Meyer by the hair and hit her repeatedly in the back of the head, while Meyer screamed for help. Management personnel separated the two women and questioned them about the incident. Watts was immediately fired for violating the store's no-fighting policy. Meyer subsequently sued Buy-Mart, alleging that the store was liable for the tort (assault and battery) committed by its employee. Using the information presented in the chapter, answer the following questions.

1 Under what doctrine discussed in this chapter might Buy-Mart be held liable for the tort committed by Watts?

2 What is the key factor in determining whether Buy-Mart is liable under this doctrine?

3 How is Buy-Mart's potential liability affected depending on whether Watts's behavior constituted an intentional tort or a tort of negligence?

4 Suppose that when Watts applied for the job at Buy-Mart, she disclosed in her application that she had previously been convicted of felony assault and battery. Nevertheless, Buy-Mart hired Watts as a cashier. How might this fact affect Buy-Mart's liability for Watts's actions?

APPLICATION How Can an Employer Use Independent Contractors?*

As an employer, you may at some time consider hiring an independent contractor. Hiring workers as independent contractors instead of as employees may help you reduce both your potential tort liability and your tax liability.

Minimizing Potential Tort Liability

One reason for using an independent contractor is that employers are usually not liable for torts that an independent contractor commits against third parties. Nevertheless, there are exceptions. If an employer exercises significant control over the activities of the independent contractor, for example, the contractor may be considered an employee, and the employer can then be liable for the contractor's torts.

To minimize even the possibility of being liable for the negligence of an independent contractor, you should check the contractor's qualifications before hiring him or her. The degree to which you should investigate depends, of course, on the nature of the work. For example, hiring an independent contractor to maintain the landscaping around your building should require less investigation than employing an independent contractor to install the electrical systems that you sell. Also, a more thorough investigation is necessary when the

* This *Application* is not meant to substitute for the services of an attorney who is licensed to practice law in your state.

(Continued)

contractor's activities present a potential danger to the public (as in delivering explosives).

Generally, it is a good idea to have the independent contractor assume, in a written contract, liability for harms caused to third parties by the contractor's negligence. You should also require the independent contractor to purchase liability insurance to cover the costs of potential lawsuits for harms caused to third persons by the independent contractor's hazardous activities or negligence.

Reducing Tax Liability and Other Costs

Another reason for hiring independent contractors is that you do not need to pay or withhold Social Security, income, or unemployment taxes on their behalf. The independent contractor is responsible for paying these taxes. Additionally, the independent contractor is not eligible for any retirement or medical plans or other fringe benefits that you provide for yourself and your employees, and this is a cost saving to you.

A word of caution, though: simply designating a person as an independent contractor does not make her or him one. The Internal Revenue Service (IRS) will reclassify individuals as employees if it determines that they are "in fact" employees, regardless of how you have designated them. Thus, the IRS will not treat an office assistant as an independent contractor simply because you designate him or her as such. If the IRS determines that you exercise significant control over the assistant, the IRS may decide that the assistant is, in fact, an employee.

If you improperly designate an employee as an independent contractor, the penalty may be high. Usually, you will be liable for back Social Security and unemployment taxes, plus interest and penalties. When in doubt, seek professional assistance in such matters.

CHECKLIST FOR THE EMPLOYER

1 Check the qualifications of any independent contractor you plan to use to reduce the possibility that you might be legally liable for the contractor's negligence.
2 It is best to require in any contract with an independent contractor that the contractor assume liability for harm to a third person caused by the contractor's negligence.
3 In your contracts with independent contractors, require that they carry liability insurance. Examine the policy to make sure that it is current, particularly when the contractor will be undertaking actions that are more than normally hazardous to the public.
4 Do not do anything that would lead a third person to believe that an independent contractor is your employee, and do not allow independent contractors to represent themselves as your employees.
5 Regularly inspect the work of the independent contractor to make sure that it is being performed in accordance with contract specifications. Such supervision on your part will not change the worker's status as an independent contractor.

KEY TERMS

agency 516
apparent authority 529
disclosed principal 530
e-agent 532
equal dignity rule 526

fiduciary 517
independent contractor 517
notary public 527
partially disclosed principal 530
power of attorney 527

ratification 521
respondeat superior 533
undisclosed principal 530
vicarious liability 533

CHAPTER SUMMARY Agency

Agency Relationships (See pages 516–520.)	In a *principal-agent* relationship, an agent acts on behalf of and instead of the principal in dealing with third parties. An employee who deals with third parties is normally an agent. An independent contractor is not an employee, and the employer has no control over the details of physical performance. An independent contractor may or may not be an agent.
How Agency Relationships Are Formed (See pages 520–523.)	Agency relationships may be formed by agreement, by ratification, by estoppel, and by operation of law.

CHAPTER SUMMARY Agency–Continued

Duties of Agents and Principals (See pages 523–526.)	1. *Duties of the agent*—
	
	    a. Performance—The agent must use reasonable diligence and skill in performing her or his duties or use the special skills that the agent has represented to the principal that the agent possesses.
	
	    b. Notification—The agent is required to notify the principal of all matters that come to his or her attention concerning the subject matter of the agency.
	
	    c. Loyalty—The agent has a duty to act solely for the benefit of the principal and not in the interest of the agent or a third party.
	
	    d. Obedience—The agent must follow all lawful and clearly stated instructions of the principal.
	
	    e. Accounting—The agent has a duty to make available to the principal records of all property and funds received and paid out on behalf of the principal.
	
	 2. *Duties of the principal*—
	
	    a. Compensation—Except in a gratuitous agency relationship, the principal must pay the agreed-on value (or reasonable value) for an agent's services.
	
	    b. Reimbursement and indemnification—The principal must reimburse the agent for all funds disbursed at the request of the principal and for all funds the agent disburses for necessary expenses in the course of reasonable performance of his or her agency duties.
	
	    c. Cooperation—A principal must cooperate with and assist an agent in performing her or his duties.
	
	    d. Safe working conditions—A principal must provide safe working conditions for the agent-employee.

Agent's Authority (See pages 526–530.)	1. *Express authority*—Can be oral or in writing. Authorization must be in writing if the agent is to execute a contract that must be in writing. 2. *Implied authority*—Authority customarily associated with the position of the agent or authority that is deemed necessary for the agent to carry out expressly authorized tasks. 3. *Apparent authority*—Exists when the principal, by word or action, causes a third party reasonably to believe that an agent has authority to act, even though the agent has no express or implied authority. 4. *Ratification*—The affirmation by the principal of an agent's unauthorized action or promise. For the ratification to be effective, the principal must be aware of all material facts.

Liability in Agency Relationships (See pages 530–536.)	1. *Liability for contracts*—If the principal's identity is disclosed or partially disclosed at the time the agent forms a contract with a third party, the principal is liable to the third party under the contract if the agent acted within the scope of his or her authority. If the principal's identity is undisclosed at the time of contract formation, the agent is personally liable to the third party, but if the agent acted within the scope of his or her authority, the principal is also bound by the contract.
	
	 2. *Liability for agent's negligence*—Under the doctrine of *respondeat superior,* the principal is liable for any harm caused to another through the agent's torts if the agent was acting within the scope of her or his employment at the time the harmful act occurred.
	
	 3. *Liability for agent's intentional torts*—Usually, employers are not liable for the intentional torts that their agents commit, *unless:*
	
	    a. The acts are committed within the scope of employment, and thus the doctrine of *respondeat superior* applies.
	
	    b. The employer allowed an employee to engage in reckless acts that caused injury to another.

(Continued)

CHAPTER SUMMARY Agency—Continued

Liability in Agency Relationships— Continued

c. The agent's misrepresentation causes a third party to sustain damage, and the agent had either actual or apparent authority to act.

4. *Liability for independent contractor's torts*—A principal is not liable for harm caused by an independent contractor's negligence, unless hazardous activities are involved (in this situation, the principal is strictly liable for any resulting harm) or other exceptions apply.

5. *Liability for agent's crimes*—An agent is responsible for his or her own crimes, even if the crimes were committed while the agent was acting within the scope of authority or employment. A principal will be liable for an agent's crime only if the principal participated by conspiracy or other action or (in some jurisdictions) if the agent violated certain government regulations in the course of employment.

How Agency Relationships Are Terminated (See pages 536–539.)

1. *By act of the parties*—

a. Lapse of time (if the parties specified a definite time for the duration of the agency when the agency was established).

b. Purpose achieved.

c. Occurrence of a specific event.

d. Mutual rescission (requires mutual consent of principal and agent).

e. Termination by act of either the principal (revocation) or the agent (renunciation). (A principal cannot revoke an agency coupled with an interest.)

f. Notice to third parties is required when an agency is terminated by act of the parties. Direct notice is required for those who have previously dealt with the agency; constructive notice will suffice for all other third parties.

2. *By operation of law*—

a. Death or mental incompetence of either the principal or the agent.

b. Impossibility (when the purpose of the agency cannot be achieved because of an event beyond the parties' control).

c. Changed circumstances (in which it would be inequitable to require that the agency be continued).

d. Bankruptcy of the principal or the agent, or war between the principal's and agent's countries.

e. Notice to third parties is not required when an agency is terminated by operation of law.

FOR REVIEW

Answers for the even-numbered questions in this For Review *section can be found in Appendix E at the end of this text.*

1 What is the difference between an employee and an independent contractor?

2 How do agency relationships arise?

3 What duties do agents and principals owe to each other?

4 When is a principal liable for the agent's actions with respect to third parties? When is the agent liable?

5 What are some of the ways in which an agency relationship can be terminated?

QUESTIONS AND CASE PROBLEMS

 **HYPOTHETICAL SCENARIOS**

17.1 Ratification by Principal. Springer was a political candidate running for Congress. He was operating on a tight budget and instructed his campaign staff not to purchase any campaign materials without his explicit authorization. In spite of these instructions, one of his campaign workers ordered Dubychek Printing Co. to print some promotional materials for Springer's campaign. When the printed materials arrived, Springer did not return them but instead used them during his campaign. When Springer failed to pay for the materials, Dubychek sued for recovery of the price. Springer contended that he was not liable on the sales contract because he had not authorized his agent to purchase the printing services. Dubychek argued that the campaign worker was Springer's agent and that the worker had authority to make the printing contract. Additionally, Dubychek claimed that even if the purchase was unauthorized, Springer's use of the materials constituted ratification of his agent's unauthorized purchase. Is Dubychek correct? Explain.

17.2 Hypothetical Question with Sample Answer. Paul Gett is a well-known, wealthy financial expert living in the city of Torris. Adam Wade, Gett's friend, tells Timothy Brown that he is Gett's agent for the purchase of rare coins. Wade even shows Brown a local newspaper clipping mentioning Gett's interest in coin collecting. Brown, knowing of Wade's friendship with Gett, contracts with Wade to sell a rare coin valued at $25,000 to Gett. Wade takes the coin and disappears with it. On the payment due date, Brown seeks to collect from Gett, claiming that Wade's agency made Gett liable. Gett does not deny that Wade was a friend, but he claims that Wade was never his agent. Discuss fully whether an agency was in existence at the time the contract for the rare coin was made.

 **For a sample answer to Question 17.2, go to Appendix F at the end of this text.**

17.3 Employee versus Independent Contractor. Stephen Hemmerling was a driver for the Happy Cab Co. Hemmerling paid certain fixed expenses and abided by a variety of rules relating to the use of the cab, the hours that could be worked, and the solicitation of fares, among other things. Rates were set by the state. Happy Cab did not withhold taxes from Hemmerling's pay. While driving the cab, Hemmerling was injured in an accident and filed a claim against Happy Cab in a Nebraska state court for workers' compensation benefits. Such benefits are not available to independent contractors. On what basis might the court hold that Hemmerling is an employee? Explain.

 **CASE PROBLEMS**

17.4 Agency Formation. Ford Motor Credit Co. is a subsidiary of Ford Motor Co. with its own offices, officers, and directors. Ford Credit buys contracts and leases of automobiles entered into by dealers and consumers. Ford Credit also provides inventory financing for dealers' purchases of Ford and non-Ford vehicles and makes loans to Ford and non-Ford dealers. Dealers and consumers are not required to finance their purchases or leases of Ford vehicles through Ford Credit. Ford Motor is not a party to the agreements between Ford Credit and its customers and does not directly receive any payments under those agreements. Also, Ford Credit is not subject to any agreement with Ford Motor "restricting or conditioning" its ability to finance the dealers' inventories or the consumers' purchases or leases of vehicles. A number of plaintiffs filed a product liability suit in a Missouri state court against Ford Motor. Ford Motor claimed that the court did not have venue. The plaintiffs asserted that Ford Credit, which had an office in the jurisdiction, acted as Ford's "agent for the transaction of its usual and customary business" there. Is Ford Credit an agent of Ford Motor? Discuss. [*State ex rel. Ford Motor Co. v. Bacon*, 63 S.W.3d 641 (Mo. 2002)]

17.5 Liability for Independent Contractor's Torts. Greif Brothers Corp., a steel drum manufacturer, owned and operated a manufacturing plant in Youngstown, Ohio. In 1987, Lowell Wilson, the plant superintendent, hired Youngstown Security Patrol, Inc. (YSP), a security company, to guard Greif property and "deter thieves and vandals." Some YSP security guards, as Wilson knew, carried firearms. Eric Bator, a YSP security guard, was not certified as an armed guard but nevertheless took his gun, in a briefcase, to work. While working at the Greif plant on August 12, 1991, Bator fired his gun at Derrell Pusey, in the belief that Pusey was an intruder. The bullet struck and killed Pusey. Pusey's mother filed a suit in an Ohio state court against Greif and others, alleging, in part, that her son's death was the result of YSP's negligence, for which Greif was responsible. Greif filed a motion for a directed verdict. What is the plaintiff's best argument that Greif is responsible for YSP's actions? What is Greif's best defense? Explain. [*Pusey v. Bator*, 94 Ohio St.3d 275, 762 N.E.2d 968 (2002)]

17.6 Case Problem with Sample Answer. Sam and Theresa Daigle decided to build a home in Cameron Parish, Louisiana. To obtain financing, they contacted Trinity United Mortgage Co. In a meeting with Joe Diez on Trinity's behalf, on July 18, 2001, the Daigles signed a temporary loan agreement with Union Planters Bank. Diez assured them that they did not need to make payments on this loan until their house was built and that permanent financing had been secured. Because the Daigles did not make payments on the Union loan, Trinity declined to make the permanent loan. Meanwhile, Diez left Trinity's employ. On November 1, the Daigles moved into their new house. They tried to contact Diez at Trinity but were told that he was unavailable and would get back to them. Three weeks later, Diez came to the Daigles' home and had them sign documents that they believed were to secure a permanent loan but that were actually an application with Diez's new employer. Union filed a suit in a Louisiana state court against the Daigles for failing to pay on its loan. The Daigles paid Union, obtained permanent financing through another source, and filed a suit against Trinity to recover the cost. Who should have told the Daigles that Diez was no longer Trinity's agent? Could Trinity be liable to the Daigles on this basis? Explain. [*Daigle v. Trinity United Mortgage, L.L.C.*, 890 So.2d 583 (La.App. 3 Cir. 2004)]

After you have answered Problem 17.6, compare your answer with the sample answer given on the Web site that accompanies this text. Go to academic.cengage.com/blaw/blt, select "Chapter 17," and click on "Case Problem with Sample Answer."

17.7 Principal's Duties to Agent. Josef Boehm was an officer and the majority shareholder of Alaska Industrial Hardware, Inc. (AIH), in Anchorage, Alaska. In August 2001, Lincolnshire Management, Inc., in New York, created AIH Acquisition Corp. to buy AIH. The three firms signed a "commitment letter" to negotiate "a definitive stock purchase agreement" (SPA). In September, Harold Snow and Ronald Braley began to work, on Boehm's behalf, with Vincent Coyle, an agent for AIH Acquisition, to produce an SPA. They exchanged many drafts and dozens of e-mails. Finally, in February 2002, Braley told Coyle that Boehm would sign the SPA "early next week." That did not occur, however, and at the end of March, after more negotiations and drafts, Boehm demanded a higher price. AIH Acquisition agreed, and following more work by the agents, another SPA was drafted. In April, the parties met in Anchorage. Boehm still refused to sign. AIH Acquisition and others filed a suit in a federal district court against AIH. Did Boehm violate any of the duties that principals owe to their agents? If so, which duty, and how was it violated? Explain. [*AIH Acquisition Corp. v. Alaska Industrial Hardware, Inc.*, __ F.Supp.2d __ (S.D.N.Y. 2004)]

17.8 Agent's Duties to Principal. In July 2001, John Warren viewed a condominium in Woodland Hills, California, as a potential buyer. Hildegard Merrill was the agent for the seller. Because Warren's credit rating was poor, Merrill told him he needed a co-borrower to obtain a mortgage at a reasonable rate. Merrill said that her daughter Charmaine would "go on title" until the loan and sale were complete if Warren would pay her $10,000. Merrill also offered to defer her commission on the sale as a loan to Warren so that he could make a 20 percent down payment on the property. He agreed to both plans. Merrill applied for and secured the mortgage in Charmaine's name alone by misrepresenting her daughter's address, business, and income. To close the sale, Merrill had Warren remove his name from the title to the property. In October, Warren moved into the condominium, repaid Merrill the amount of her deferred commission, and began paying the mortgage. Within a few months, Merrill had Warren evicted. Warren filed a suit in a California state court against Merrill and Charmaine. Who among these parties was in an agency relationship? What is the basic duty that an agent owes a principal? Was the duty breached here? Explain. [*Warren v. Merrill*, 143 Cal.App.4th 96, 49 Cal.Rptr.3d 122 (2 Dist. 2006)]

17.9 A Question of Ethics. *Emergency One, Inc. (EO), makes fire and rescue vehicles. Western Fire Truck, Inc., contracted with EO to be its exclusive dealer in Colorado and Wyoming through December 2003. James Costello, a Western salesperson, was authorized to order EO vehicles for his customers. Without informing Western, Costello e-mailed EO about Western's difficulties in obtaining cash to fund its operations. He asked about the viability of Western's contract and his possible employment with EO. On EO's request, and in disregard of Western's instructions, Costello sent some payments for EO vehicles directly to EO. In addition, Costello, with EO's help, sent a competing bid to a potential Western customer. EO's representative e-mailed Costello, "You have my permission to kick [Western's] ass." In April 2002, EO terminated its contract with Western, which, after reviewing Costello's e-mail, fired Costello. Western filed a suit in a Colorado state court against Costello and EO, alleging, among other things, that Costello breached his duty as an agent and that EO aided and abetted the breach. [Western Fire Truck, Inc. v. Emergency One, Inc., 134 P.3d 570 (Colo.App. 2006)]*

1 Was there an agency relationship between Western and Costello? Western required monthly reports from its sales staff, but Costello did not report regularly. Does this indicate that Costello was *not* Western's agent? In determining whether an agency relationship exists, is the *right* to control or the *fact* of control more important? Explain.

2 Did Costello owe Western a duty? If so, what was the duty? Did Costello breach it? How?

3 A Colorado state statute allows a court to award punitive damages in "circumstances of fraud, malice, or willful and wanton conduct." Did any of these circumstances exist in this case? Should punitive damages be assessed against either defendant? Why or why not?

CRITICAL THINKING
AND WRITING ASSIGNMENTS

17.10 Critical Legal Thinking. What policy is served by the law that employers do not have copyright ownership in works created by independent contractors (unless there is a written "work for hire" agreement)?

17.11 **Video Question.** Go to this text's Web site at **academic.cengage.com/blaw/blt** and select "Chapter 17." Click on "Video Questions" and view the video titled *Fast Times at Ridgemont High.* Then answer the following questions.

1 Recall from the video that Brad (Judge Reinhold) is told to deliver an order of Captain Hook Fish and Chips to IBM. Is Brad an employee or an independent contractor? Why?

2 Assume that Brad is an employee and agent of Captain Hook Fish and Chips. What duties does he owe Captain Hook? What duties does Captain Hook Fish and Chips, as principal, owe to Brad?

3 In the video, Brad throws part of his uniform and several bags of the food that he is supposed to deliver out of his car window while driving. If Brad is an agent-employee and his actions cause injury to a person or property, can Captain Hook Fish and Chips be held liable? Why or why not? What should Captain Hook argue to avoid liability for Brad's actions?

ONLINE ACTIVITIES

 # PRACTICAL
INTERNET EXERCISES

Go to this text's Web site at **academic.cengage.com/blaw/blt**, select "Chapter 17," and click on "Practical Internet Exercises." There you will find the following Internet research exercises that you can perform to learn more about the topics covered in this chapter.

PRACTICAL INTERNET EXERCISE 17-1   LEGAL PERSPECTIVE—Employees or Independent Contractors?

PRACTICAL INTERNET EXERCISE 17-2   MANAGEMENT PERSPECTIVE—Liability in Agency Relationships

BEFORE THE TEST

Go to this text's Web site at **academic.cengage.com/blaw/blt**, select "Chapter 17," and click on "Interactive Quizzes." You will find a number of interactive questions relating to this chapter.

CHAPTER 18
Employment Law

LEARNING OBJECTIVES

AFTER READING THIS CHAPTER, YOU SHOULD BE ABLE TO ANSWER THE FOLLOWING QUESTIONS:

1 What is the employment-at-will doctrine? When and why are exceptions to this doctrine made?

2 What federal statute governs working hours and wages?

3 Under the Family and Medical Leave Act of 1993, under what circumstances may an employee take family or medical leave?

4 What federal acts prohibit discrimination in the workplace?

5 What are three defenses to claims of employment discrimination?

Until the early 1900s, most employer-employee relationships were governed by the common law. Today, the workplace is regulated extensively by statutes and administrative agency regulations. Recall from Chapter 1 that common law doctrines apply only to areas *not* covered by statutory law. Common law doctrines have thus been displaced to a large extent by statutory law.

In the 1930s, during the Great Depression, both state and federal governments began to regulate employment relationships. Out of the 1960s civil rights movement to end racial and other forms of discrimination grew a body of law protecting employees against discrimination in the workplace. This protective legislation further eroded the common law that had been governing employer-employee relationships. In the decades since, judicial decisions, administrative agency actions, and legislation have restricted the ability of employers to discriminate against workers on the basis of race, color, religion, national origin, gender, age, or disability. As a result, today employers must comply with a myriad of laws and regulations to ensure that employee rights are protected. In this chapter, we look at the most significant laws regulating employment relationships.

EMPLOYMENT AT WILL

Traditionally, employment relationships have generally been governed by the common law doctrine of **employment at will.** Other common law rules governing employment relationships—including rules under contract, tort, and agency law—have already been discussed at length in previous chapters of this text.

Given that many employees (those who deal with third parties) are normally deemed agents of an employer, agency concepts are especially relevant in the employment context. The distinction under agency law between employee status and independent-contractor status is also relevant to employment relationships. Generally, the laws discussed in this chapter apply only to the employer-employee relationship; they do not apply to independent contractors.

Under the employment-at-will doctrine, either party may terminate the employment relationship at any time and for any reason, unless doing so would violate the provisions of an employment contract. The majority of U.S. workers continue to have the legal status of "employees at will." In other words, this common law doctrine is still in widespread use, and only one state (Montana) does not apply the doctrine. Nonetheless, as mentioned in the chapter introduction, federal and state statutes governing employment relationships prevent the doctrine from being applied in a number of circumstances. Today, an employer is not permitted to fire an employee if doing so would violate a federal or state employment statute, such as one prohibiting employment termination for discriminatory reasons.

EMPLOYMENT AT WILL
A common law doctrine under which either party may terminate an employment relationship at any time for any reason, unless a contract specifies otherwise.

Exceptions to the Employment-at-Will Doctrine

Under the employment-at-will doctrine, as mentioned, an employer may hire and fire employees at will (regardless of the employees' performance) without liability, unless doing so violates the terms of an employment contract or statutory law. Because of the harsh effects of the employment-at-will doctrine for employees, the courts have carved out various exceptions to the doctrine. These exceptions are based on contract theory, tort theory, and public policy.

Exceptions Based on Contract Theory   Some courts have held that an *implied* employment contract exists between an employer and an employee. If an employee is fired outside the terms of the implied contract, he or she may succeed in an action for breach of contract even though no written employment contract exists. **EXAMPLE 18.1** Suppose that an employer's manual or personnel bulletin states that, as a matter of policy, workers will be dismissed only for good cause. If an employee is aware of this policy and continues to work for the employer, a court may find that there is an implied contract based on the terms stated in the manual or bulletin.[1] Generally, the key consideration in determining whether an employment manual creates an implied contractual obligation is the employee's reasonable expectations.

REMEMBER An implied contract may exist if a party furnishes a service expecting to be paid, and the other party, who knows (or should know) of this expectation, has a chance to reject the service and does not.

An employer's oral promises to employees regarding discharge policy may also be considered part of an implied contract. If the employer fires a worker in a manner contrary to what was promised, a court may hold that the employer has violated the implied contract and is liable for damages. Most state courts will judge a claim of breach of an implied employment contract by traditional contract standards. In some cases, courts have held that an implied employment contract exists even though employees agreed in writing to be employees at will.[2]

---

1. See, for example, *Pepe v. Rival Co.,* 85 F.Supp.2d 349 (D.N.J. 1999).
2. See, for example, *Kuest v. Regent Assisted Living, Inc.,* 111 Wash.App. 36, 43 P.3d 23 (2002).

Courts in a few states have gone further and held that all employment contracts contain an implied covenant of good faith. This means that both sides promise to abide by the contract in good faith. If an employer fires an employee for an arbitrary or unjustified reason, the employee can claim that the covenant of good faith was breached and the contract violated.

Exceptions Based on Tort Theory In a few situations, the discharge of an employee may give rise to an action for wrongful discharge under tort theories. Abusive discharge procedures may result in a suit for intentional infliction of emotional distress or defamation. In addition, some courts have permitted workers to sue their employers under the tort theory of fraud. ■EXAMPLE 18.2 Suppose that an employer induces a prospective employee to leave a lucrative job and move to another state by offering "a long-term job with a thriving business." In fact, the employer is not only having significant financial problems but is also planning a merger that will result in the elimination of the position offered to the prospective employee. If the employee takes the job in reliance on the employer's representations and is fired shortly thereafter, the employee may be able to bring an action against the employer for fraud.[3] ■

Exceptions Based on Public Policy The most widespread common law exception to the employment-at-will doctrine is made on the basis of public policy. Courts may apply this exception when an employer fires a worker for reasons that violate a fundamental public policy of the jurisdiction.

Sometimes, an employer will direct employees to perform an illegal act and fire them if they refuse to do so. At other times, an employer will fire or discipline employees who "blow the whistle" on the employer's wrongdoing. **Whistleblowing** occurs when an employee tells government authorities, upper-level managers, or the press that her or his employer is engaged in some unsafe or illegal activity. Whistleblowers on occasion have been protected from wrongful discharge for reasons of public policy.

■EXAMPLE 18.3 Diane Lins, the regional manager for a corporation that owned child-care centers, was involved in a work-related auto accident with five of her subordinates. After the accident, the employees filed workers' compensation claims. (As will be discussed later in this chapter, *workers' compensation laws* enable employees to be compensated for injuries incurred on the job, regardless of fault.) Lins's superiors became concerned that the employees would file lawsuits against the company and told Lins to fire them, but she refused and was subsequently terminated. In this situation, a court held that Lins's discharge was wrongful. Because it is illegal to fire an employee for filing a workers' compensation claim, the court held that public policy prevented the employer from discharging Lins in retaliation for refusing to carry out an unlawful order.[4] ■

Today, whistleblowers have some protection under statutory law. Most states have enacted so-called whistleblower statutes that protect a whistleblower from subsequent retaliation by the employer. On the federal level, the Whistleblower Protection Act of 1989[5] protects federal employees who blow the whistle on their employers from retaliatory actions. Whistleblower statutes sometimes also offer an incentive to disclose information by providing the whistleblower with a monetary reward. For instance, a whistleblower who has disclosed information relating to a fraud perpetrated against the U.S. government will receive between 15 and 25 percent of the proceeds if the government brings a suit against the wrongdoer.[6]

WHISTLEBLOWING
An employee's disclosure to government authorities, upper-level managers, or the press that the employer is engaged in unsafe or illegal activities.

---

3. See, for example, *Lazar v. Superior Court of Los Angeles County*, 12 Cal.4th 631, 909 P.2d 981, 49 Cal.Rptr.2d 377 (1996); and *McConkey v. AON Corp.*, 354 N.J.Super. 25, 804 A.2d 572 (A.D. 2002).
4. *Lins v. Children's Discovery Centers of America, Inc.*, 95 Wash.App. 486, 976 P.2d 168 (1999).
5. 5 U.S.C. Section 1201.
6. The False Claims Reform Act of 1986, which amended the False Claims Act of 1863, 31 U.S.C. Sections 3729–3733.

Wrongful Discharge

Whenever an employer discharges an employee in violation of an employment contract or a statute protecting employees, the employee may bring an action for **wrongful discharge.** Even if an employer's actions do not violate any provisions in an employment contract or a statute, the employer may still be subject to liability under a common law doctrine, such as a tort theory or agency.

WRONGFUL DISCHARGE
An employer's termination of an employee's employment in violation of the law.

WAGE AND HOUR LAWS

In the 1930s, Congress enacted several laws regulating the wages and working hours of employees. In 1931, Congress passed the Davis-Bacon Act,[7] which requires contractors and subcontractors working on government construction projects to pay "prevailing wages" to their employees. In 1936, the Walsh-Healey Act[8] was passed. This act requires that a minimum wage, as well as overtime pay at 1.5 times regular pay rates, be paid to employees of manufacturers or suppliers entering into contracts with agencies of the federal government.

In 1938, Congress passed the Fair Labor Standards Act[9] (FLSA). This act extended wage and hour requirements to cover all employers engaged in interstate commerce or in the production of goods for interstate commerce, plus selected types of other businesses. We examine here the FLSA's provisions in regard to child labor, maximum hours, and minimum wages.

MINIMUM WAGE
The lowest wage, either by government regulation or union contract, that an employer may pay an hourly worker.

Child Labor

The FLSA prohibits oppressive child labor. Children under fourteen years of age are allowed to do certain types of work, such as deliver newspapers, work for their parents, and work in the entertainment and (with some exceptions) agricultural areas. Children who are fourteen or fifteen years of age are allowed to work, but not in hazardous occupations. There are also numerous restrictions on how many hours per day and per week they can work.

■EXAMPLE 18.4 Children under the age of sixteen cannot work during school hours, for more than three hours on a school day (or eight hours on a nonschool day), for more than eighteen hours during a school week (or forty hours during a nonschool week), or before 7 A.M. or after 7 P.M. (9 P.M. during the summer). ■ Many states require persons under sixteen years of age to obtain work permits.

Working times and hours are not restricted for persons between the ages of sixteen and eighteen, but they cannot be employed in hazardous jobs or in jobs detrimental to their health and well-being. None of these restrictions apply to persons over the age of eighteen.

Wages and Hours

The FLSA provides that a **minimum wage** of a specified amount must be paid to employees in covered industries. In 2007, President George W. Bush signed the Fair Minimum Wage Act, which amends the FLSA and gradually raises the federal minimum wage from $5.15 per hour to $7.25 per hour over a two-year period.[10] Under the FLSA, the term *wages* includes the reasonable cost of the

This photo, taken in 1938, the same year the FLSA was passed by Congress, shows children working in a cranberry bog in Burlington County, New Jersey. Would this type of work involving children harvesting and carrying crates of fruit be considered oppressive?
(Arthur Rothstein/Library of Congress)

---

7. 40 U.S.C. Sections 276a–276a-5.
8. 41 U.S.C. Sections 35–45.
9. 29 U.S.C. Sections 201–260.
10. Note that many state and local governments also have minimum-wage laws; these laws can provide for higher minimum-wage rates than that required by the federal government.

employer in furnishing employees with board, lodging, and other facilities if they are customarily furnished by that employer.

Under the FLSA, employees who work more than forty hours per week normally must be paid 1.5 times their regular pay for all hours over forty. Note that the FLSA overtime provisions apply only after an employee has worked more than forty hours per *week*. Thus, employees who work for ten hours a day, four days per week, are not entitled to overtime pay because they do not work more than forty hours per week.

Overtime Exemptions

Certain employees are exempt from the overtime provisions of the FLSA. These exemptions include employees whose jobs are categorized as executive, administrative, or professional, as well as outside salespersons and computer employees. In the past, to fall into one of these exemptions, an employee had to earn more than a specified salary threshold and devote a certain percentage of work time to the performance of specific types of duties. Because the salary limits were low and the duties tests were complex and confusing, some employers in the last few decades have been able to avoid paying overtime wages to their employees. This prompted the U.S. Department of Labor to substantially revise the regulations pertaining to overtime for the first time in more than fifty years.

New rules implemented in August 2004 expanded the number of workers eligible for overtime by nearly tripling the salary threshold.[11] Under these provisions, workers earning less than $23,660 a year are guaranteed overtime pay for working more than forty hours per week (the previous ceiling was $8,060). Employers can continue to pay overtime to ineligible employees if they want to do so, but cannot waive or reduce the overtime requirements of the FLSA.

The exemptions to the overtime-pay requirement do not apply to manual laborers or other workers who perform work involving repetitive operations with their hands (such as nonmanagement production-line employees, for example). The exemptions also do not apply to police, firefighters, licensed nurses, and other public safety workers. White-collar workers who earn more than $100,000 per year, computer programmers, dental hygienists, and insurance adjusters are typically exempt—though they must also meet certain other criteria. Under the new provisions, an employer cannot deny overtime wages to an employee based only on the employee's job title.

Under the overtime-pay regulations, an employee qualifies for the executive exemption if, among other requirements, his or her "primary duty" is management. This requirement was the focus of the dispute in the following case.

---

11. 29 C.F.R. Section 541.

ON THE WEB

For more details about the regulations concerning overtime that became effective on August 23, 2004, go to the Web site of the U.S. Department of Labor at

www.dol.gov.

CASE 18.1 **Mims v. Starbucks Corp.**

United States District Court, Southern District of Texas, __ F.Supp.2d __ (2007).

FACTS In Starbucks Corporation's stores, baristas (coffee-making specialists) wait on customers, make drinks for customers, serve customers, operate the cash register, clean the store, and maintain its equipment. In each store, a manager supervises and motivates six to thirty employees, including baristas, shift supervisors, and assistant managers. The manager oversees customer service and processes employee records, payrolls, and inventory counts. He or she also develops strategies to increase revenues, control costs, and comply with corporate policies. Kevin Keevican was hired as a barista in March 2000. Keevican was promoted to shift

CASE 18.1–Continued

supervisor, assistant manager, and, in November 2001, manager. During his tenure, Keevican doubled pastry sales at one store, nearly tripled revenues at another, and won sales awards at both. As a manager, Keevican worked seventy hours a week for $650 to $800, a 10 to 20 percent bonus, and fringe benefits such as paid sick leave, not available to baristas. Keevican resigned in 2004. He and other former managers, including Kathleen Mims, filed a suit in a federal district court against Starbucks, seeking unpaid overtime and other amounts. The plaintiffs admitted that they performed many managerial tasks, but argued that they spent 70 to 80 percent of their time on barista chores. Starbucks filed a motion for summary judgment.

ISSUE During their employment, was management the plaintiffs' "primary duty"?

DECISION Yes. The court issued a summary judgment in Starbucks's favor and dismissed the claims of the plaintiffs, who were exempt from the FLSA's overtime provisions as executive employees.

REASON The court held that an employee's "primary duty" is "what the employee does that is of principal value to the employer, not the collateral tasks that she may also perform,

even if they consume more than half her time." The determining factors are "(1) the relative importance of managerial duties compared to other duties; (2) the frequency with which the employee makes discretionary decisions; (3) the employee's relative freedom from supervision; and (4) the relationship between the employee's salary and the wages paid to employees who perform relevant non-exempt work." In this case, the barista chores "quite obviously were of minor importance to Defendant when compared to the significant management responsibilities * * * that directly influenced the ultimate commercial and financial success or failure of the store." Also, each plaintiff was "the single highest-ranking employee in his [or her] particular store and was responsible on site for that store's day-to-day overall operations." He or she was "vested with enough discretionary power and freedom from supervision to qualify for the executive exemption." Finally, the "marked disparity in pay and benefits between Plaintiffs and the non-exempt employees is a hallmark of exempt status."

 WHAT IF THE FACTS WERE DIFFERENT? *Suppose that Keevican's job title had been "glorified barista" instead of "manager." Would the result have been different? Explain.*

WORKER HEALTH AND SAFETY

Under the common law, employees injured on the job had to rely on tort law or contract law theories in suits they brought against their employers. Additionally, workers had some recourse under the common law governing agency relationships (discussed in Chapter 17), which imposes a duty on a principal-employer to provide a safe workplace for an agent-employee. Today, numerous state and federal statutes protect employees and their families from the risk of accidental injury, death, or disease resulting from their employment. This section discusses the primary federal statute governing health and safety in the workplace, along with state workers' compensation laws.

The Occupational Safety and Health Act

At the federal level, the primary legislation protecting employees' health and safety is the Occupational Safety and Health Act of 1970.[12] Congress passed this act in an attempt to ensure safe and healthful working conditions for practically every employee in the country. The act requires employers to meet specific standards in addition to their general duty to keep workplaces safe.

Enforcement Agencies Three federal agencies develop and enforce the standards set by the Occupational Safety and Health Act. The Occupational Safety and Health

---

12. 29 U.S.C. Sections 553, 651–678.

BE AWARE To check for compliance with safety standards without being cited for violations, an employer can often obtain advice from an insurer, a trade association, or a state agency.

WORKERS' COMPENSATION LAWS State statutes establishing an administrative procedure for compensating workers' injuries that arise out of—or in the course of—their employment, regardless of fault.

Administration (OSHA) is part of the U.S. Department of Labor and has the authority to promulgate standards, make inspections, and enforce the act. OSHA has developed safety standards governing many workplace details, such as the structural stability of ladders and the requirements for railings. OSHA also establishes standards that protect employees against exposure to substances that may be harmful to their health.

The National Institute for Occupational Safety and Health is part of the U.S. Department of Health and Human Services. Its main duty is to conduct research on safety and health problems and to recommend standards for OSHA to adopt. Finally, the Occupational Safety and Health Review Commission is an independent agency set up to handle appeals from actions taken by OSHA administrators.

Procedures and Violations OSHA compliance officers may enter and inspect facilities of any establishment covered by the Occupational Safety and Health Act.[13] Employees may also file complaints of violations. Under the act, an employer cannot discharge an employee who files a complaint or who, in good faith, refuses to work in a high-risk area if bodily harm or death might reasonably result.

Employers with eleven or more employees are required to keep occupational injury and illness records for each employee. Each record must be made available for inspection when requested by an OSHA inspector. Whenever a work-related injury or disease occurs, employers must make reports directly to OSHA. Whenever an employee is killed in a work-related accident or when five or more employees are hospitalized as a result of one accident, the employer must notify the Department of Labor within forty-eight hours. If the company fails to do so, it will be fined. Following the accident, a complete inspection of the premises is mandatory.

Criminal penalties for willful violation of the Occupational Safety and Health Act are limited. Employers may also be prosecuted under state laws, however. In other words, the act does not preempt state and local criminal laws.[14]

State Workers' Compensation Laws

State **workers' compensation laws** establish an administrative procedure for compensating workers injured on the job. Instead of suing, an injured worker files a claim with the administrative agency or board that administers local workers' compensation claims.

Employees Covered by Workers' Compensation Most workers' compensation statutes are similar. No state covers all employees. Typically, domestic workers, agricultural workers, temporary employees, and employees of common carriers (companies that provide transportation services to the public) are excluded, but minors are covered. Usually, the statutes allow employers to purchase insurance from a private insurer or a state fund to pay workers' compensation benefits in the event of a claim. Most states also allow employers to be self-insured—that is, employers that show an ability to pay claims do not need to buy insurance.

Requirements for Receiving Workers' Compensation In general, the right to recover benefits is predicated wholly on the existence of an employment relationship and the fact that the injury was *accidental* and *occurred on the job or in the course of employment*,

---

13. In the past, warrantless inspections were conducted. In 1978, however, the United States Supreme Court held that warrantless inspections violated the warrant clause of the Fourth Amendment to the U.S. Constitution. See *Marshall v. Barlow's, Inc.*, 436 U.S. 307, 98 S.Ct. 1816, 56 L.Ed.2d 305 (1978).
14. *Pedraza v. Shell Oil Co.*, 942 F.2d 48 (1st Cir. 1991); *cert.* denied, *Shell Oil Co. v. Pedraza*, 502 U.S. 1082, 112 S.Ct. 993, 117 L.Ed.2d 154 (1992).

regardless of fault. Intentionally inflicted self-injury, for example, would not be considered accidental and hence would not be covered. If an injury occurs while an employee is commuting to or from work, it usually will not be considered to have occurred on the job or in the course of employment and hence will not be covered.

An employee must notify her or his employer promptly (usually within thirty days) of an injury. Generally, an employee must also file a workers' compensation claim with the appropriate state agency or board within a certain period (sixty days to two years) from the time the injury is first noticed, rather than from the time of the accident.

Workers' Compensation versus Litigation   An employee's acceptance of workers' compensation benefits bars the employee from suing for injuries caused by the employer's negligence. By barring lawsuits for negligence, workers' compensation laws also prevent employers from raising common law defenses to negligence, such as contributory negligence, assumption of risk, or injury caused by a "fellow servant" (another employee). A worker may sue an employer who *intentionally* injures the worker, however.

INCOME SECURITY

Federal and state governments participate in insurance programs designed to protect employees and their families by covering the financial impact of retirement, disability, death, hospitalization, and unemployment. The key federal law on this subject is the Social Security Act of 1935.[15]

Social Security

The Social Security Act provides for old-age (retirement), survivors, and disability insurance. The act is therefore often referred to as OASDI. Both employers and employees must "contribute" under the Federal Insurance Contributions Act (FICA)[16] to help pay for benefits that will partially make up for the employees' loss of income on retirement.

The basis for the employee's and the employer's contributions is the employee's annual wage base—the maximum amount of the employee's wages that are subject to the tax. The employer withholds the employee's FICA contribution from the employee's wages and then matches this contribution. (In 2007, employers were required to withhold 6.2 percent of each employee's wages, up to a maximum wage base of $97,500, and to match this contribution.)

Retired workers are then eligible to receive monthly payments from the Social Security Administration, which administers the Social Security Act. Social Security benefits are fixed by statute but increase automatically with increases in the cost of living.

NOTE   Social Security covers almost all jobs in the United States. Nine out of ten workers "contribute" to this protection for themselves and their families.

Medicare

Medicare, a federal government health-insurance program, is administered by the Social Security Administration for people sixty-five years of age and older and for some under the age of sixty-five who are disabled. It has two parts, one pertaining to hospital costs and the other to nonhospital medical costs, such as visits to physicians' offices. People who have Medicare hospital insurance can also obtain additional federal medical insurance if they pay small monthly premiums, which increase as the cost of medical care increases.

As with Social Security contributions, both the employer and the employee "contribute" to Medicare, but unlike Social Security, there is no cap on the amount of wages subject to the Medicare tax. In 2007, both the employer and the employee were

---

15. 42 U.S.C. Sections 301–1397e.
16. 26 U.S.C. Sections 3101–3125.

required to pay 1.45 percent of *all* wages and salaries to finance Medicare. Thus, for Social Security and Medicare together, in 2007 the employer and employee each paid 7.65 percent of the first $97,500 of income (6.2 percent for Social Security + 1.45 percent for Medicare) for a combined total of 15.3 percent. In addition, all wages and salaries above $97,500 were taxed at a combined (employer and employee) rate of 2.9 percent for Medicare. Self-employed persons pay both the employer and the employee portions of the Social Security and Medicare taxes (15.3 percent of income up to $97,500 and 2.9 percent of income above that amount in 2007).

Private Pension Plans

Significant legislation has been enacted to regulate employee retirement plans set up by employers to supplement Social Security benefits. The major federal act covering these retirement plans is the Employee Retirement Income Security Act (ERISA) of 1974.[17] This act empowers the Labor Management Services Administration of the U.S. Department of Labor to enforce its provisions governing employers who have private pension funds for their employees. ERISA does not require an employer to establish a pension plan. When a plan exists, however, ERISA establishes standards for its management.

A key provision of ERISA concerns vesting. **Vesting** gives an employee a legal right to receive pension benefits at some future date when he or she stops working. Before ERISA was enacted, some employees who had worked for companies for as long as thirty years received no pension benefits when their employment terminated, because those benefits had not vested. ERISA establishes complex vesting rules. Generally, however, all employee contributions to pension plans vest immediately, and employee rights to employer contributions to a plan vest after five years of employment.

In an attempt to prevent mismanagement of pension funds, ERISA has established rules on how they must be invested. Pension managers must be cautious in choosing investments and must diversify the plan's investments to minimize the risk of large losses. ERISA also contains detailed record-keeping and reporting requirements.

VESTING
The creation of an absolute or unconditional right or power.

Unemployment Insurance

To ease the financial impact of unemployment, the United States has a system of unemployment insurance. The Federal Unemployment Tax Act (FUTA) of 1935[18] created a state-administered system that provides unemployment compensation to eligible individuals. Under this system, employers pay into a fund, and the proceeds are paid out to qualified unemployed workers. The FUTA and state laws require employers that fall under the provisions of the act to pay unemployment taxes at regular intervals.

To be eligible for unemployment compensation, a worker must be willing and able to work and be actively seeking employment. Workers who have been fired for misconduct or who have voluntarily left their jobs are not eligible for benefits. To leave a job voluntarily is to leave it without good cause.

WATCH OUT If an employer does not pay unemployment taxes, a state government can place a lien (claim) on the property to secure the debt. Liens were discussed in Chapter 16.

COBRA

Federal legislation also addresses the issue of health insurance for workers whose jobs have been terminated—and who are thus no longer eligible for group health-insurance plans. The Consolidated Omnibus Budget Reconciliation Act (COBRA) of 1985[19] prohibits an employer from eliminating a worker's medical, optical, or dental insurance on

---

17. 29 U.S.C. Sections 1001 *et seq.*
18. 26 U.S.C. Sections 3301–3310.
19. 29 U.S.C. Sections 1161–1169.

the voluntary or involuntary termination of the worker's employment. The act applies to most workers who have either lost their jobs or had their hours decreased so that they are no longer eligible for coverage under the employer's health plan. Only workers fired for gross misconduct are excluded from protection.

Application of COBRA   The worker has sixty days (beginning with the date that the group coverage would stop) to decide whether to continue with the employer's group insurance plan. If the worker chooses to discontinue the coverage, the employer has no further obligation. If the worker chooses to continue coverage, though, the employer is obligated to keep the policy active for up to eighteen months. If the worker is disabled, the employer must extend coverage up to twenty-nine months. The coverage provided must be the same as that enjoyed by the worker prior to the termination or reduction of work. If family members were originally included, for example, COBRA prohibits their exclusion. The worker does not receive the insurance coverage for free, however. To receive continued benefits, she or he may be required to pay all of the premiums, as well as a 2 percent administrative charge.

Employers' Obligations under COBRA   Employers, with some exceptions, must comply with COBRA if they employ twenty or more workers and provide a benefit plan to those workers. An employer must inform an employee of COBRA's provisions when that worker faces termination or a reduction of hours that would affect his or her eligibility for coverage under the plan.

The employer is relieved of the responsibility to provide benefit coverage if the employer completely eliminates its group benefit plan. An employer is also relieved of responsibility if the worker fails to pay the premium or becomes eligible for Medicare, is covered under a spouse's health plan, or is insured under a different plan (with a new employer, for example). An employer that does not comply with COBRA risks substantial penalties, such as a tax of up to 10 percent of the annual cost of the group plan or $500,000, whichever is less.

Employer-Sponsored Group Health Plans

The Health Insurance Portability and Accountability Act (HIPAA),[20] which was discussed in Chapter 1 in the context of privacy protections, contains provisions that affect employer-sponsored group health plans. HIPAA does not require employers to provide health insurance, but it does establish requirements for those that do provide such coverage. For example, under HIPAA, an employer's ability to exclude persons from coverage for "preexisting conditions" is strictly limited to the previous six months. The act defines *preexisting conditions* as those for which medical advice, diagnosis, care, or treatment was recommended or received within the previous six months (excluding pregnancy).

In addition, employers that are plan sponsors have significant responsibilities regarding the manner in which they collect, use, and disclose the health information of employees and their families. Essentially, the act requires employers to comply with a number of administrative, technical, and procedural safeguards (such as training employees, designating privacy officials, and distributing privacy notices) to ensure that employees' health information is not disclosed to unauthorized parties. Failure to comply with HIPAA regulations can result in civil penalties of up to $100 per person per violation (with a cap of $25,000 per year). The employer is also subject to criminal prosecution for certain types of HIPAA violations and can face up to $250,000 in criminal fines and imprisonment for up to ten years if convicted.

---

20. 29 U.S.C.A. Sections 1181 *et seq.*

FAMILY AND MEDICAL LEAVE

In 1993, Congress passed the Family and Medical Leave Act (FMLA)[21] to allow employees to take time off from work for family or medical reasons. A majority of the states also have legislation allowing for a leave from employment for family or medical reasons, and many employers maintain private family-leave plans for their workers.

Coverage and Applicability of the FMLA

The FMLA requires employers that have fifty or more employees to provide employees with up to twelve weeks of unpaid family or medical leave during any twelve-month period. The FMLA expressly covers private and public (government) employees.[22] Generally, an employee may take family leave to care for a newborn baby, an adopted child, or a foster child and take medical leave when the employee or the employee's spouse, child, or parent has a "serious health condition" requiring care.[23] The employer must continue the worker's health-care coverage and guarantee employment in the same position or a comparable position when the employee returns to work. An important exception to the FMLA, however, allows the employer to avoid reinstating a *key employee*—defined as an employee whose pay falls within the top 10 percent of the firm's workforce. Also, the act does not apply to part-time or newly hired employees (those who have worked for less than one year).

Employees suffering from certain chronic health conditions, such as asthma, diabetes, and pregnancy, may take FMLA leave for their own incapacities that require absences of less than three days. **■EXAMPLE 18.5** Estel, an employee who has asthma, suffers from periodic episodes of illness. According to regulations issued by the U.S. Department of Labor, employees with such conditions are covered by the FMLA. Thus, Estel may take a medical leave. ■

Violations of the FMLA

An employer that violates the FMLA may be held liable for damages to compensate an employee for unpaid wages (or salary), lost benefits, denied compensation, and actual monetary losses (such as the cost of providing for care of the family member) up to an amount equivalent to the employee's wages for twelve weeks. Supervisors may also be subject to personal liability, as employers, for violations of the act.[24] A court may require the employer to reinstate the employee in her or his job or to grant a promotion that had been denied. A successful plaintiff is entitled to court costs; attorneys' fees; and, in cases involving bad faith on the part of the employer, two times the amount of damages awarded by a judge or jury.

Employers generally are required to notify employees when an absence will be counted against leave authorized under the act. If an employer fails to provide such notice, and the employee consequently suffers an injury because he or she did not receive notice, the employer may be sanctioned.[25] **■EXAMPLE 18.6** An employee, Isha Hartung, is

A boy leans against his pregnant mother's belly. The mother hopes to take time off from her full-time corporate job when the baby is born. What is required for the Family and Medical Leave Act (FMLA) to apply to her employer? If the employer is covered by the FMLA, how much family leave does the act authorize?
(PhotoDisc Red)

---

21. 29 U.S.C. Sections 2601, 2611–2619, 2651–2654.

22. The United States Supreme Court affirmed that government employers could be sued for violating the FMLA in *Nevada Department of Human Resources v. Hibbs*, 538 U.S. 721, 123 S.Ct. 1972, 152 L.Ed.2d 953 (2003).

23. The foster care must be state sanctioned before such an arrangement falls within the coverage of the FMLA.

24. See, for example, *Rupnow v. TRC, Inc.*, 999 F.Supp. 1047 (N.D. Ohio 1998).

25. *Ragsdale v. Wolverine World Wide, Inc.*, 535 U.S. 81, 122 S.Ct. 1155, 152 L.Ed.2d 167 (2002).

absent from work for thirty weeks while undergoing treatment for cancer. Her employer did not inform Isha that this time off would count as FMLA leave. At the end of twelve weeks, the employer sent Isha a notice stating that she must return to work the following Monday, but she had not completed her chemotherapy and did not go back to work. In this situation, because the employer did not notify Isha that her absence would be considered FMLA leave, a court might allow her to take additional protected time off. ■

Is the FMLA fair to unmarried or childless employees? Some employees who do not have a spouse or children complain that they are being treated unfairly in the workplace because employees with families are entitled to more legally protected leave under the FMLA. In certain areas, such as nursing, law enforcement, and the airline industry, someone must always be on duty, and usually those employees who are single and have no children are assigned to work during holidays. The FMLA adds to their predicament because it allows employees to take extended leave when they have a baby or when their spouse, child, or parent is ill. Both women and men frequently take up to three months' leave when their children are born. Do men and women who do not have a spouse or children deserve a legally protected period of extended leave at any point? According to some estimates, unmarried people without children make up 40 percent of the workforce, yet they have no legal right to take an extended period of leave from work—unless, of course, they develop a serious health condition or need to care for a sick parent.

■

EMPLOYEE PRIVACY RIGHTS

In the last twenty-five years, concerns about the privacy rights of employees have arisen in response to the sometimes invasive tactics used by employers to monitor and screen workers. Perhaps the greatest privacy concern in today's employment arena has to do with electronic performance monitoring. Clearly, employers need to protect themselves from liability for their employees' online activities. They also have a legitimate interest in monitoring the productivity of their workers. At the same time, employees expect to have a certain zone of privacy in the workplace. Indeed, many lawsuits have involved allegations that employers' intrusive monitoring practices violate employees' privacy rights.

Electronic Monitoring in the Workplace

According to a survey by the American Management Association, more than two-thirds of employers engage in some form of surveillance of their employees.[26] Types of monitoring include reviewing employees' e-mail and computer files, video recording of employee job performance, and recording and reviewing telephone conversations and voice mail.

Various specially designed software products have made it easier for an employer to track employees' Internet use. Software now allows an employer to track almost every move made by an employee using the Internet, including the specific Web sites visited and the time spent surfing the Web. Filtering software, which was discussed in Chapter 1, can also be used to prevent employees from accessing certain Web sites, such as sites containing pornographic or sexually explicit images. Other filtering software may be used to screen incoming e-mail for viruses and to block junk e-mail (spam).

Although the use of filtering software by public employers (government agencies) has led to charges that blocking access to Web sites violates employees' rights to free speech,

---

26. For a discussion of this survey and its results, see Allison R. Michael and Scott M. Lidman, "Monitoring of Employees Still Growing," *The National Law Journal,* January 29, 2001, p. B9.

Employers are increasingly using sophisticated surveillance systems to monitor their employees' conduct in the workplace. What legitimate interests might employers have for using surveillance cameras?
("Redjar"/Creative Commons)

this issue does not arise in private businesses. This is because the First Amendment's protection of free speech applies only to *government* restraints on speech, and normally not to restraints imposed in the private sector.

Laws Protecting Employee Privacy Rights   A number of laws protect privacy rights. We look here at laws that apply in the employment context.

Protection under Constitutional and Tort Law.   Recall from Chapter 1 that the U.S. Constitution does not contain a provision that explicitly guarantees a right to privacy. A personal right to privacy, however, has been inferred from other constitutional guarantees provided by the First, Third, Fourth, Fifth, and Ninth Amendments to the Constitution. Tort law (see Chapter 4), state constitutions, and a number of state and federal statutes also provide for privacy rights.

The Electronic Communications Privacy Act.   The major statute with which employers must comply is the Electronic Communications Privacy Act (ECPA) of 1986.[27] This act amended existing federal wiretapping law to cover electronic forms of communications, such as communications via cellular telephones or e-mail. The ECPA prohibits the intentional interception of any wire or electronic communication and the intentional disclosure or use of the information obtained by the interception. Excluded from coverage, however, are any electronic communications through devices that are "furnished to the subscriber or user by a provider of wire or electronic communication service" and that are being used by the subscriber or user, or by the provider of the service, "in the ordinary course of its business."

This "business-extension exception" to the ECPA permits employers to monitor employees' electronic communications made in the ordinary course of business. It does not, however, permit employers to monitor employees' personal communications. Under another exception to the ECPA, however, an employer may avoid liability under the act if the employees consent to having their electronic communications intercepted by the employer. Thus, an employer may be able to avoid liability under the ECPA by simply requiring employees to sign forms indicating that they consent to such monitoring.

Clearly, the law allows employers to engage in electronic monitoring in the workplace. In fact, cases in which courts have held that an employer's monitoring of electronic communications in the workplace violated employees' privacy rights are relatively rare. Courts have even found that employers have a right to monitor the e-mail of an independent contractor (such as an insurance agent) when the employer provided the e-mail service and was authorized to access stored messages.[28]

Factors Considered by the Courts in Employee Privacy Cases   When determining whether an employer should be held liable for violating an employee's privacy rights, the courts generally weigh the employer's interests against the employee's reasonable expectation of privacy. Generally, if employees are informed that their communications are being monitored, they cannot reasonably expect those communications to be private. If employees are not informed that certain communications are being monitored, however, the employer may be held liable for invading their privacy.

■**EXAMPLE 18.7**   In one case, an employer secretly recorded conversations among his four employees by placing a tape recorder in their common office. The conversations

---

27. 18 U.S.C. Sections 2510–2521.
28. See *Fraser v. Nationwide Mutual Insurance Co.*, 352 F.3d 107 (3d Cir. 2004).

were of a highly personal nature and included harsh criticisms of the employer. The employer immediately fired two of the employees, informing them that their termination was due to their comments on the tape. In the ensuing suit, one of the issues was whether the employees, in these circumstances, had a reasonable expectation of privacy. The court held that they did and granted summary judgment in their favor. The employees clearly would not have criticized their boss if they had not assumed that their conversations were private. Furthermore, the office was small, and the employees were careful that no third parties ever overheard their comments.[29] ▣

Privacy Expectations and E-Mail Systems   In cases brought by employees alleging that their privacy has been invaded by e-mail monitoring, the courts have tended to hold for the employers. This is true even when the employees were not informed that their e-mail would be monitored.

▣**EXAMPLE 18.8**   In a leading case on this issue, the Pillsbury Company promised its employees that it would not read their e-mail or terminate or discipline them based on the content of their e-mail. Despite this promise, Pillsbury intercepted employee Michael Smyth's e-mail, decided that it was unprofessional and inappropriate, and fired him. In Pennsylvania, where the discharge occurred, it is against public policy for an employer to fire an employee based on a violation of the employee's right to privacy. In Smyth's suit against the company, he claimed that his termination was a violation of this policy. The court, however, found no "reasonable expectation of privacy in e-mail communications voluntarily made by an employee to his supervisor over the company e-mail system."[30] ▣

Other Types of Monitoring

In addition to monitoring their employees' online activities, employers also engage in other types of employee screening and monitoring practices. These practices, which have included lie-detector tests, drug tests, AIDS tests, and employment screening, have often been subject to challenge as violations of employee privacy rights.

Lie-Detector Tests   At one time, many employers required employees or job applicants to take polygraph examinations (lie-detector tests) in connection with their employment. To protect the privacy interests of employees and job applicants, in 1988 Congress passed the Employee Polygraph Protection Act.[31] The act prohibits employers from (1) requiring or causing employees or job applicants to take lie-detector tests or suggesting or requesting that they do so; (2) using, accepting, referring to, or asking about the results of lie-detector tests taken by employees or applicants; and (3) taking or threatening negative employment-related action against employees or applicants based on results of lie-detector tests or on their refusal to take the tests.

Employers excepted from these prohibitions include federal, state, and local government employers; certain security service firms; and companies manufacturing and distributing controlled substances. Other employers may use polygraph tests when investigating losses attributable to theft, including embezzlement and the theft of trade secrets.

Drug Testing   In the interests of public safety, many employers, including the government, require their employees to submit to drug testing. State laws relating to the privacy rights and drug testing of private-sector employees vary from state to state. Many states

---

29. *Dorris v. Absher*, 179 F.3d 420 (6th Cir. 1999).
30. *Smyth v. Pillsbury Co.*, 914 F.Supp. 97 (E.D.Pa. 1996).
31. 29 U.S.C. Sections 2001 *et seq.*

have statutes that allow drug testing by private employers but place restrictions on when the testing is appropriatee and how it is performed. A collective bargaining agreement may also provide protection against drug testing. In some instances, employees have brought an action against the employer for the tort of invasion of privacy (discussed in Chapter 4).

Government employers, of course, are constrained in drug testing by the Fourth Amendment to the U.S. Constitution, which prohibits unreasonable searches and seizures (see Chapter 4). When there was a reasonable basis for suspecting government employees of using drugs, however, drug tests have been held constitutional. Additionally, when drug use in a particular government job could threaten public safety, testing has been upheld.

The permissibility of a private employer's drug tests hinges on the determination of whether the testing was reasonable. Is a private employer's zero-tolerance substance abuse policy that denies a "second chance" to employees who test positive for drugs reasonable? That was the question in the following case.

CASE 18.2   **CITGO Asphalt Refining Co. v. Paper, Allied-Industrial, Chemical, and Energy Workers Int'l. Union Local No. 2-991**

United States Court of Appeals, Third Circuit, 385 F.3d 809 (2004).

FACTS CITGO Petroleum Corporation operates more than sixty oil-refining facilities, including CITGO Asphalt Refining Company (CARCO) in Paulsboro, New Jersey. Paper, Allied-Industrial, Chemical, and Energy Workers International Union (PACE) represents some of CITGO's workers. Under an agreement between CITGO and PACE, the company has the right to "make and enforce rules for the maintenance of discipline and safety." In December 1998, CITGO implemented a new substance abuse policy, which included a zero-tolerance provision. Local 2-991 of PACE challenged the policy at CARCO. During arbitration on the dispute, PACE representatives testified that policies at smaller facilities owned by other companies— Motiva and Sun Oil—did not include zero-tolerance provisions. John DeLeon, a CITGO manager, testified that Tosco, Marathon, and Exxon, three major companies in the industry, had zero-tolerance policies. He also testified that CITGO's safety record is the best in the industry. The arbitrator ruled that CITGO should modify its policy to allow a rehabilitation opportunity, or "second chance." CARCO filed a suit in a federal district court against PACE, challenging the arbitrator's ruling. The court issued an order to enforce the award. CARCO appealed to the U.S. Court of Appeals for the Third Circuit.

ISSUE Is a private employer's substance abuse policy that denies a "second chance" to employees who test positive for drugs reasonable?

DECISION Yes. The U.S. Court of Appeals for the Third Circuit reversed the lower court's order and remanded the case for an order vacating the arbitrator's award.

REASON The appellate court was aware that other, smaller companies do not have zero-tolerance policies but stated that this fact is not enough to support a finding that CITGO's zero-tolerance policy is unreasonable. With respect to the practices of other companies—whose safety records are inferior to CITGO's—"one could just as readily conclude that it was unreasonable for [those companies] not to have" zero-tolerance policies, which "the three largest companies in the industry" have imposed. The arbitrator also referred to a certain federal statute and its implementing regulations that allow a second chance, but "that does not mean that a decision to the contrary is unreasonable. This is especially true when we consider the hazardous nature of CITGO's facilities [and] the need for prompt and unimpaired action in the event of an emergency." In fact, added the court, "the statute and the regulations at issue leave it to the parties to define appropriate discipline." CITGO's facility, "a hazardous work environment susceptible to explosions," the safety-sensitive positions of CITGO's workers, and the firm's right under its agreement with PACE outweigh the facts on which the arbitrator relied.

WHAT IF THE FACTS WERE DIFFERENT? *Suppose that CITGO's safety record was the worst in the oil-refining industry rather than the best. Would the result have been different? Why or why not?*

AIDS Testing A number of employers test their workers for acquired immune deficiency syndrome (AIDS). Some state laws restrict AIDS testing, and federal statutes offer some protection to employees or job applicants who have AIDS or have tested positive for HIV, the virus that causes AIDS. The federal Americans with Disabilities Act (ADA) of 1990[32] (discussed later in this chapter), for example, prohibits discrimination against persons with disabilities, and the term *disability* has been broadly defined to include diseases such as AIDS. The ADA also requires employers to reasonably accommodate the needs of persons with disabilities. As a rule, although the ADA generally does not prohibit AIDS testing, it does prevent an employer from discharging employees based on the results of those tests or disclosing the test results to unauthorized parties.

Genetic Testing A serious privacy issue arose when some employers began conducting genetic testing of employees or prospective employees in an effort to identify individuals who might develop significant health problems in the future. To date, however, only a few cases involving this issue have come before the courts. In one case, the Lawrence Berkeley Laboratory screened prospective employees for the gene that causes sickle-cell anemia, although the applicants were not informed of this. In a lawsuit subsequently brought by the prospective employees, a federal appellate court held that they had a cause of action for violation of their privacy rights.[33] The case was later settled for $2.2 million.

In another case, the Equal Employment Opportunity Commission (EEOC), the federal agency in charge of administering laws prohibiting employment discrimination, brought an action against a railroad company that had genetically tested its employees. The EEOC contended that the genetic testing violated the Americans with Disabilities Act. In 2002, this case was settled out of court, also for $2.2 million.[34]

Screening Procedures Preemployment screening procedures are another area of concern to potential employees. What kinds of questions are permissible on an employment application or a preemployment test? What kinds of questions go too far in invading the applicant's privacy? Is it an invasion of privacy, for example, to ask questions about the prospective employee's sexual orientation or religious convictions? Although an employer may believe that such information is relevant to the job for which the individual has applied, the applicant may feel differently about the matter. Generally, questions on an employment application must have a reasonable nexus, or connection, with the job for which the person is applying.

KEEP IN MIND An employer may act on the basis of any professionally developed test, provided the test relates to the employment and does not violate the law.

EMPLOYMENT DISCRIMINATION

Out of the 1960s civil rights movement to end racial and other forms of discrimination grew a body of law protecting employees against discrimination in the workplace. This protective legislation further eroded the employment-at-will doctrine, which was discussed earlier in this chapter. In the past several decades, judicial decisions, administrative agency actions, and legislation have restricted the ability of employers, as well as unions, to discriminate against workers on the basis of race, color, religion, national origin, gender, age, or disability. A class of persons defined by one or more of these criteria is known as a **protected class**.

Several federal statutes prohibit **employment discrimination** against members of protected classes. The most important statute is Title VII of the Civil Rights Act of 1964.[35]

PROTECTED CLASS
A group of persons protected by specific laws because of the group's defining characteristics. Under laws prohibiting employment discrimination, these characteristics include race, color, religion, national origin, gender, age, and disability.

EMPLOYMENT DISCRIMINATION
Treating employees or job applicants unequally on the basis of race, color, national origin, religion, gender, age, or disability; prohibited by federal statutes.

---

32. 42 U.S.C. Sections 12102–12118.

33. *Norman-Bloodsaw v. Lawrence Berkeley Laboratory*, 135 F.3d 1260 (9th Cir. 1998).

34. For a discussion of this settlement, see David Hechler, "Railroad to Pay $2.2 Million over Genetic Testing," *The National Law Journal*, May 13, 2002, p. A22.

35. 42 U.S.C. Sections 2000e–2000e-17.

Title VII prohibits discrimination on the basis of race, color, religion, national origin, or gender at any stage of employment. The Age Discrimination in Employment Act of 1967[36] and the Americans with Disabilities Act of 1990[37] prohibit discrimination on the basis of age and disability, respectively.

This section focuses on the kinds of discrimination prohibited by these federal statutes. Note, though, that discrimination against employees on the basis of any of these criteria may also violate state human rights statutes or other state laws or public policies prohibiting discrimination.

Title VII of the Civil Rights Act of 1964

Title VII of the Civil Rights Act of 1964 and its amendments prohibit job discrimination against employees, applicants, and union members on the basis of race, color, national origin, religion, or gender at any stage of employment. Title VII applies to employers with fifteen or more employees, labor unions with fifteen or more members, labor unions that operate hiring halls (to which members go regularly to be rationed jobs as they become available), employment agencies, and state and local governing units or agencies. A special section of the act prohibits discrimination in most federal government employment.

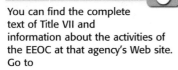

ON THE WEB

You can find the complete text of Title VII and information about the activities of the EEOC at that agency's Web site. Go to

www.eeoc.gov.

The Equal Employment Opportunity Commission   Compliance with Title VII is monitored by the Equal Employment Opportunity Commission (EEOC). A victim of alleged discrimination, before bringing a suit against the employer, must first file a claim with the EEOC. The EEOC may investigate the dispute and attempt to obtain the parties' voluntary consent to an out-of-court settlement. If a voluntary agreement cannot be reached, the EEOC may then file a suit against the employer on the employee's behalf. If the EEOC decides not to investigate the claim, the victim may bring her or his own lawsuit against the employer.

The EEOC does not investigate every claim of employment discrimination, regardless of the merits of the claim. Generally, it investigates only "priority cases," such as cases involving retaliatory discharge (firing an employee in retaliation for submitting a claim to the EEOC) and cases involving types of discrimination that are of particular concern to the EEOC.

Intentional and Unintentional Discrimination   Title VII prohibits both intentional and unintentional discrimination.

Intentional Discrimination.   Intentional discrimination by an employer against an employee is known as **disparate-treatment discrimination.** Because intent may sometimes be difficult to prove, courts have established certain procedures for resolving disparate-treatment cases. Suppose that a woman applies for employment with a construction firm and is rejected. If she sues on the basis of disparate-treatment discrimination in hiring, she must show that (1) she is a member of a protected class, (2) she applied and was qualified for the job in question, (3) she was rejected by the employer, and (4) the employer continued to seek applicants for the position or filled the position with a person not in a protected class.

If the woman can meet these relatively easy requirements, she has made out a *prima facie* case of illegal discrimination. Making out a *prima facie* case of discrimination means that the plaintiff has met her initial burden of proof and will win in the absence of a legally acceptable employer defense (defenses to claims of employment discrimination

DISPARATE-TREATMENT DISCRIMINATION
A form of employment discrimination that results when an employer intentionally discriminates against employees who are members of protected classes.

***PRIMA FACIE* CASE**
A case in which the plaintiff has produced sufficient evidence of his or her claim that the case can go to a jury; a case in which the evidence compels a decision for the plaintiff if the defendant produces no affirmative defense or evidence to disprove the plaintiff's assertion.

---

36. 29 U.S.C. Sections 621–634.
37. 42 U.S.C. Sections 12102–12118.

will be discussed later in this chapter). The burden then shifts to the employer-defendant, who must articulate a legal reason for not hiring the plaintiff. To prevail, the plaintiff must then show that the employer's reason is a *pretext* (not the true reason) and that discriminatory intent actually motivated the employer's decision.

Unintentional Discrimination.   Employers often use interviews and testing procedures to choose from among a large number of applicants for job openings. Minimum educational requirements are also common. These practices and procedures may have an unintended discriminatory impact on a protected class. **Disparate-impact discrimination** occurs when a protected group of people is adversely affected by an employer's practices, procedures, or tests, even though they do not appear to be discriminatory. In a disparate-impact discrimination case, the complaining party must first show statistically that the employer's practices, procedures, or tests are discriminatory in effect. Once the plaintiff has made out a *prima facie* case, the burden of proof shifts to the employer to show that the practices or procedures in question were justified. There are two ways of proving that disparate-impact discrimination exists, as discussed next.

> **DISPARATE-IMPACT DISCRIMINATION**
> A form of employment discrimination that results from certain employer practices or procedures that, although not discriminatory on their face, have a discriminatory effect.

A plaintiff can prove a disparate impact by comparing the employer's workforce to the pool of qualified individuals available in the local labor market. The plaintiff must show that as a result of educational or other job requirements or hiring procedures, the percentage of nonwhites, women, or members of other protected classes in the employer's workforce does not reflect the percentage of that group in the pool of qualified applicants. If a person challenging an employment practice can show a connection between the practice and the disparity, he or she has made out a *prima facie* case and need not provide evidence of discriminatory intent.

Disparate-impact discrimination can also occur when an educational or other job requirement or hiring procedure excludes members of a protected class from an employer's workforce at a substantially higher rate than nonmembers, regardless of the racial balance in the employer's workforce. This "rates analysis" compares the selection rate for whites with that for nonwhites (or other members of a protected class). The plaintiff does not have to prove that the workforce does not reflect the percentage of qualified nonwhite persons available in the local labor market.

The EEOC has devised a test, called the "four-fifths rule," to determine whether an employment examination is discriminatory on its face. Under this rule, a selection rate for protected classes that is less than four-fifths, or 80 percent, of the rate for the group with the highest rate will generally be regarded as evidence of disparate impact. **EXAMPLE 18.9** One hundred white applicants take an employment test, and fifty pass the test and are hired. One hundred minority applicants take the test, and twenty pass the test and are hired. Because twenty is less than four-fifths (80 percent) of fifty, the test would be considered discriminatory under the EEOC guidelines. ◼

Discrimination Based on Race, Color, and National Origin   If a company's standards or policies for selecting or promoting employees have the effect of discriminating against employees or job applicants on the basis of race, color, or national origin, they are illegal. Employers can avoid liability for the discriminatory effect of certain policies (except those that discriminate on the basis of race) by showing a substantial, demonstrable relationship to realistic qualifications for the job in question. Discrimination against these protected classes in regard to employment conditions and benefits is also illegal.

EXAMPLE 18.10 Cynthia McCullough, an African American woman with a college degree, had worked at a deli in a grocery store for more than a year, but the owner of the store promoted a white woman to the position of "deli manager." The white woman had worked in the deli for only three months, had only a sixth-grade education, and could not calculate prices or read recipes. Although the owner gave various reasons for promoting the white woman instead of McCullough, a federal appellate court held that these reasons were likely just excuses and that the real reason was discriminatory intent.[38] ◼

Note that discrimination based on race can also take the form of "reverse discrimination," or discrimination against "majority" individuals, such as white males. **◼EXAMPLE 18.11** In one Pennsylvania case, an African American woman fired four white men from their management positions at a school district. The men filed a lawsuit for racial discrimination, alleging that the woman was trying to eliminate white males from the department. The woman claimed that the terminations were part of a reorganization plan to cut costs in the department. The jury sided with the men and awarded them nearly $3 million in damages. The verdict was upheld on appeal (though the damages award was reduced slightly).[39] ◼

Discrimination Based on Religion   Title VII of the Civil Rights Act of 1964 also prohibits government employers, private employers, and unions from discriminating against persons because of their religion. An employer must "reasonably accommodate" the religious practices of its employees, unless to do so would cause undue hardship to the employer's business. For example, if an employee's religion prohibits him or her from working on a certain day of the week or at a certain type of job, the employer must make a reasonable attempt to accommodate these religious requirements. Employers must reasonably accommodate an employee's religious belief even if the belief is not based on the tenets or dogma of a particular church, sect, or denomination. The only requirement is that the belief be sincerely held by the employee.

Discrimination Based on Gender   Under Title VII, as well as other federal acts (including the Equal Pay Act of 1963, which we also discuss here), employers are forbidden from discriminating against employees on the basis of gender. Employers are prohibited from classifying jobs as male or female and from advertising in help-wanted columns that are designated male or female unless the employer can prove that the gender of the applicant is essential to the job. Furthermore, employers cannot have separate male and female seniority lists. Generally, to succeed in a suit for gender discrimination, a plaintiff must demonstrate that gender was a determining factor in the employer's decision to hire, fire, or promote her or him. Typically, this involves looking at all of the surrounding circumstances.

The Equal Pay Act of 1963, which amended the Fair Labor Standards Act of 1938, prohibits employers from gender-based wage discrimination. For the act's equal pay requirements to apply, the male and female employees must work at the same establishment doing similar work (a barber and a beautician, for example). To determine whether the Equal Pay Act has been violated, a court will look to the primary duties of the two jobs. It is the job content rather than the job description that controls in all cases. If a court finds that the wage differential is due to any factor other than gender, such as a seniority or merit system, then it does not violate the Equal Pay Act.

The Pregnancy Discrimination Act of 1978,[40] which amended Title VII, expanded the definition of gender discrimination to include discrimination based on pregnancy. Women affected by pregnancy, childbirth, or related medical conditions must be treated—for all employment-related purposes, including the receipt of benefits under

---

38. *McCullough v. Real Foods, Inc.,* 140 F.3d 1123 (8th Cir. 1998). The federal district court had granted summary judgment for the employer in this case. The U.S. Court of Appeals for the Eighth Circuit reversed the district court's decision and remanded the case for trial.
39. *Johnston v. School District of Philadelphia,* ___ F.Supp.2d ___ (E.D.Pa. 2006).
40. 42 U.S.C. Section 2000e(k).

employee benefit programs—the same as other persons not so affected but similar in ability to work.

Constructive Discharge   The majority of Title VII complaints involve unlawful discrimination in decisions to hire or fire employees. In some situations, however, employees who leave their jobs voluntarily can claim that they were "constructively discharged" by the employer. **Constructive discharge** occurs when the employer causes the employee's working conditions to be so intolerable that a reasonable person in the employee's position would feel compelled to quit.

Proving Constructive Discharge.   The plaintiff must present objective proof of intolerable working conditions, which the employer knew or had reason to know about yet failed to correct within a reasonable time period. Courts generally also require the employee to show causation—that the employer's unlawful discrimination caused the working conditions to be intolerable. Put a different way, the employee's resignation must be a foreseeable result of the employer's discriminatory action.

■EXAMPLE 18.12 Khalil's employer humiliates him by informing him in front of his co-workers that he is being demoted to an inferior position. Khalil, who was born in Iraq, is then subjected to continued insults, harassment, and derogatory remarks about his national origin by his co-workers. The employer is aware of this discriminatory treatment but does nothing to remedy the situation, despite repeated complaints from Khalil. After several months, Khalil quits his job and files a Title VII claim. In this situation, Khalil would likely have sufficient evidence to maintain an action for constructive discharge in violation of Title VII. ■ Although courts weigh the facts on a case-by-case basis, employee demotion is one of the most frequently cited reasons for a finding of constructive discharge, particularly when the employee was subjected to humiliation.

Applies to All Title VII Discrimination.   Note that constructive discharge is a theory that plaintiffs can use to establish any type of discrimination claims under Title VII, including race, color, national origin, religion, gender, pregnancy, and sexual harassment. Constructive discharge has also been successfully used in situations that involve discrimination based on age or disability (both of which will be discussed later in this chapter). Constructive discharge is most commonly asserted in cases involving sexual harassment, however.

When constructive discharge is claimed, the employee can pursue damages for loss of income, including back pay. These damages ordinarily would not be available to an employee who left a job voluntarily.

Sexual Harassment   Title VII also protects employees against **sexual harassment** in the workplace. Sexual harassment can take two forms: *quid pro quo* harassment and hostile-environment harassment. *Quid pro quo* is a Latin phrase that is often translated to mean "something in exchange for something else." *Quid pro quo* harassment occurs when sexual favors are demanded in return for job opportunities, promotions, salary increases, and the like. According to the United States Supreme Court, hostile-environment harassment occurs when "the workplace is permeated with discriminatory intimidation, ridicule, and insult, that is sufficiently severe or pervasive to alter the conditions of the victim's employment and create an abusive working environment."[41]

Generally, the courts apply this Supreme Court guideline on a case-by-case basis. Some courts have held that just one incident of sexually offensive conduct—such as a sexist remark by a co-worker or a photo on an employer's desk of his bikini-clad wife—can

---

41. *Harris v. Forklift Systems,* 510 U.S. 17, 114 S.Ct. 367, 126 L.Ed.2d 295 (1993).

create a hostile environment. Other courts, however, require more than one instance of sexually offensive conduct to find that an abusive working environment exists.

PREVENTING LEGAL DISPUTES

It is essential for business owners and managers to be familiar with the laws pertaining to sexual harassment and gender discrimination, and to understand what constitutes a hostile environment. Remember that harassment in the workplace can take many forms and be based on many characteristics (gender, race, national origin, religion, age, and disability) but that sexual harassment must be on the basis of an employee's gender. Establish written policies and review them annually. Any complaint should be taken seriously and investigated. Some employment specialists even suggest that employers assume that hostile-environment harassment has occurred if an employee claims that it has. Prompt remedial action is key, but it must not include any immediate adverse action against the complainant (such as termination). Most importantly, immediately seek the advice of counsel when a complaint arises.

ON THE WEB

The New York State Governor's Office of Employee Relations maintains an interactive site on sexual harassment and how to prevent sexual harassment in the workplace. Go to

www.goer.state.ny.us/Train/onlinelearning/SH/intro.html.

Harassment by Supervisors. For an employer to be held liable for a supervisor's sexual harassment, the supervisor must have taken a tangible employment action against the employee. A *tangible employment action* is a significant change in employment status, such as firing or failing to promote an employee, reassigning the employee to a position with significantly different responsibilities, or effecting a significant change in employment benefits. Only a supervisor, or another person acting with the authority of the employer, can cause this sort of injury.

In 1998, in two separate cases, the United States Supreme Court issued some significant guidelines relating to the liability of employers for their supervisors' harassment of employees in the workplace.[42] On the one hand, employees benefit by the ruling that employers may be held liable for their supervisors' harassment even though the employers were unaware of the actions and even though the employees suffered no adverse job consequences. On the other hand, the Court made it clear in both decisions that employers have an affirmative defense against liability for their supervisors' harassment of employees if the employers can show the following:

1 That they have taken "reasonable care to prevent and correct promptly any sexually harassing behavior" (by establishing effective harassment policies and complaint procedures, for example).

2 That the employees suing for harassment failed to follow these policies and procedures.

In 2004, the Supreme Court further clarified the tangible employment action requirement as applied to constructive discharge claims. The case involved a police department employee who was sexually harassed by her supervisor and claimed that she was constructively discharged. The Court noted that a constructive discharge may or may not involve official employer action (such as a demotion). When there is no official employer action, the employer should be given a chance to establish an affirmative defense against liability, unless the plaintiff quit in reasonable response to a tangible employment action.[43]

In 2006, the United States Supreme Court settled another issue on which the federal courts had been reaching different conclusions—the level of proof required in retaliation

42. See *Faragher v. City of Boca Raton,* 524 U.S. 775, 118 S.Ct. 2275, 141 L.Ed.2d 662 (1998); and *Burlington Industries v. Ellerth,* 524 U.S. 742, 118 S.Ct. 2257, 141 L.Ed.2d 633 (1998).
43. *Pennsylvania State Police v. Suders,* 542 U.S. 129, 124 S.Ct. 2342, 159 L.Ed.2d 204 (2004).

claims. In a *retaliation claim,* an individual asserts that she or he has suffered a harm as a result of making a charge, testifying, or participating in a Title VII investigation or proceeding. The Court unanimously held that plaintiffs in retaliation claims do not have to prove that the challenged action adversely affected their workplace or employment. Instead, to prove retaliation, they must show only that the challenged action was one that would likely have dissuaded a reasonable worker from making or supporting a charge of discrimination. Retaliation claims will continue to be analyzed on a case-by-case basis under this ruling.[44]

Harassment by Co-Workers and Nonemployees. Often, employees alleging harassment complain that the actions of co-workers, not supervisors, are responsible for creating a hostile working environment. In such cases, the employee may still have a cause of action against the employer. Normally, though, the employer will be held liable only if the employer knew, or should have known, about the harassment and failed to take immediate remedial action.

Employers may also be liable for harassment by *nonemployees* in certain circumstances. **EXAMPLE 18.13** If a restaurant owner or manager knows that a certain customer repeatedly harasses a waitress and permits the harassment to continue, the restaurant owner may be liable under Title VII even though the customer is not an employee of the restaurant. The issue turns on the control that the employer exerts over a nonemployee. In one case, an owner of a Pizza Hut franchise was held liable for the harassment of a waitress by two male customers because no steps were taken to prevent the harassment.[45] ■

Same-Gender Harassment The courts have also had to address the issue of whether men who are harassed by other men, or women who are harassed by other women, are protected by laws that prohibit gender-based discrimination in the workplace. For example, what if the male president of a firm demands sexual favors from a male employee? Does this action qualify as sexual harassment? For some time, the courts were widely split on this issue. In 1998, in *Oncale v. Sundowner Offshore Services, Inc.,*[46] the United States Supreme Court resolved the issue by holding that Title VII protection extends to situations in which individuals are harassed by members of the same gender.

Nevertheless, it can be difficult to prove that the harassment in same-gender harassment cases is "based on sex." **EXAMPLE 18.14** Suppose that a gay man is harassed by another man at the workplace. The harasser is not a homosexual and does not treat all men with hostility—just this one man. Does the victim in this situation have a cause of action under Title VII? A court may find that the harasser's conduct does not qualify as sexual harassment under Title VII because it was based on the employee's sexual orientation, not on his "sex."[47] ■ Although Title VII does not prohibit discrimination or harassment based on a person's sexual orientation, a growing number of companies are voluntarily establishing nondiscrimination policies that include sexual orientation. (Workers in the United States often have more protection against sexual harassment in the workplace than workers in other countries, as this chapter's *Beyond Our Borders* feature on the next page explains.)

Online Harassment Employees' online activities can create a hostile working environment in many ways. Racial jokes, ethnic slurs, or other comments contained in e-mail

---

44. *Burlington Northern and Santa Fe Railroad Co. v. White,* ___ U.S. ___, 126 S.Ct. 2405, 165 L.Ed.2d 345 (2006).
45. *Lockard v. Pizza Hut, Inc.,* 162 F.3d 1062 (10th Cir. 1998).
46. 523 U.S. 75, 118 S.Ct. 998, 140 L.Ed.2d 207 (1998).
47. See, for example, *McCown v. St. John's Health System,* 349 F.3d 540 (8th Cir. 2003); and *Rene v. MGM Grand Hotel, Inc.,* 305 F.3d 1061 (9th Cir. 2002).

BEYOND OUR BORDERS Sexual Harassment in Other Nations

The problem of sexual harassment in the workplace is not confined to the United States. Indeed, it is a worldwide problem for female workers. In Argentina, Brazil, Egypt, Turkey, and many other countries, there is no legal protection against any form of employment discrimination. Even in those countries that do have laws prohibiting discriminatory employment practices, including gender-based discrimination, those laws often do not specifically include sexual harassment as a discriminatory practice. Several countries have attempted to remedy this omission by passing new laws or amending others to specifically prohibit sexual harassment in the workplace. Japan, for example, has amended its Equal Employment Opportunity Law to include a provision making sexual harassment illegal. Thailand has also passed its first sexual-harassment law. In 2002, the European Union, which some years ago outlawed gender-based discrimination, adopted a directive that specifically identifies sexual harassment as a form of discrimination. Nevertheless, women's groups throughout Europe contend that corporations in European countries tend to view sexual harassment with "quiet tolerance." They contrast this attitude with that of most U.S. corporations, which have implemented specific procedures to deal with harassment claims.

FOR CRITICAL ANALYSIS *Why do you think U.S. corporations are more aggressive than European companies in taking steps to prevent sexual harassment in the workplace?*

■

may become the basis for a claim of hostile-environment harassment or other forms of discrimination. A worker who sees sexually explicit images on a co-worker's computer screen may find the images offensive and claim that they create a hostile working environment.

Nevertheless, employers may be able to avoid liability for online harassment if they take prompt remedial action. **■EXAMPLE 18.15** In *Daniels v. WorldCom, Inc.*,[48] Angela Daniels, an employee of Robert Half International under contract to WorldCom, Inc., received racially harassing e-mailed jokes from another employee. After receiving the jokes, Daniels complained to WorldCom managers. Shortly afterward, the company issued a warning to the offending employee about the proper use of the e-mail system and held two meetings to discuss company policy on the use of the system. In Daniels's suit against WorldCom for racial discrimination, a federal district court concluded that the employer was not liable for its employee's racially harassing e-mails because the employer took prompt remedial action. ■ This chapter's *Adapting the Law to the Online Environment* feature on pages 570 and 571 discusses some new issues related to employees' computer use.

Remedies under Title VII   Employer liability under Title VII may be extensive. If the plaintiff successfully proves that unlawful discrimination occurred, he or she may be awarded reinstatement, back pay, retroactive promotions, and damages. Compensatory damages are available only in cases of intentional discrimination. Punitive damages may be recovered against a private employer only if the employer acted with malice or reckless indifference to an individual's rights. The statute limits the total amount of compen-

48. ___ F.Supp. ___ (N.D.Tex. 1998). See also *Musgrove v. Mobil Oil Corp.*, ___ F.Supp.2d ___ (N.D.Tex. 2003).

satory and punitive damages that the plaintiff can recover from specific employers—ranging from $50,000 against employers with one hundred or fewer employees to $300,000 against employers with more than five hundred employees.

Discrimination Based on Age

Age discrimination is potentially the most widespread form of discrimination, because anyone—regardless of race, color, national origin, or gender—could be a victim at some point in life. The Age Discrimination in Employment Act (ADEA) of 1967, as amended, prohibits employment discrimination on the basis of age against individuals forty years of age or older. The act also prohibits mandatory retirement for nonmanagerial workers. For the act to apply, an employer must have twenty or more employees, and the employer's business activities must affect interstate commerce. The EEOC administers the ADEA, but the act also permits private causes of action against employers for age discrimination.

Procedures under the ADEA   The burden-shifting procedure under the ADEA is similar to that under Title VII. If a plaintiff can establish that she or he (1) was a member of the protected age group, (2) was qualified for the position from which she or he was discharged, and (3) was discharged under circumstances that give rise to an inference of discrimination, the plaintiff has established a *prima facie* case of unlawful age discrimination. The burden then shifts to the employer, who must articulate a legitimate reason for the discrimination. If the plaintiff can prove that the employer's reason is only a pretext (excuse) and that the plaintiff's age was a determining factor in the employer's decision, the employer will be held liable under the ADEA.

If an employer offers several nondiscriminatory reasons, based on a variety of events, for an act of alleged discrimination, does the employee need to rebut every reason by proving that the events did not occur? That was the question in the following case.

> **REMEMBER** The Fourteenth Amendment prohibits any state from denying any person "the equal protection of the laws." This prohibition applies to the *federal* government through the due process clause of the Fifth Amendment.

CASE 18.3   **Cash Distributing Co. v. Neely**

Mississippi Supreme Court, 947 So.2d 286 (2007).
www.mssc.state.ms.us[a]

FACTS Cash Distributing Company is a distributorship for Anheuser-Busch Corporation products, including Budweiser and Michelob beers, with offices in Starkville, Columbus, and Tupelo, Mississippi. In 1973, James Neely began to work for Cash. At the time, the company often relaxed or ignored Anheuser-Busch rules. By the late 1990s, Neely had become the manager of the Columbus office. In 1997, Anheuser-Busch began to require Cash to comply with certain standards. Danny Cash, Cash's chief executive officer (CEO), announced that he intended to strictly enforce the new rules. Part of the

a. In the center of the page, click on the "Search this Site" link. On the next page, click on "Plain English." When that page opens, in the "Enter the ISYS Plain English query:" box, type "2004-CT-01124-SCT" and click "Search." In the result, click on the item that includes that number to access the opinion. The Mississippi Supreme Court maintains this Web site.

newly required documentation was a tracking form to detect out-of-date beer. Danny also required Neely to, among other things, submit daily call sheets to disclose where he had been and what he had done and to submit regular written employee evaluations. Neely generally refused to provide the new documents. In March 2000, Danny terminated Neely's employment, replacing him with Tony Carley, who was then thirty-eight years old. Neely filed a suit in a Mississippi state court against Cash, alleging a violation of the ADEA, among other things. Neely was awarded $120,000 in back pay. Both parties appealed to a state intermediate appellate court, which reversed the lower court's failure to grant additional remedies to Neely. Cash appealed to the Mississippi Supreme Court.

ISSUE Can an employee prevail in an ADEA suit without rebutting every nondiscriminatory reason that the employer offers for an act of discrimination?

CASE 18.3—Continues next page

ADAPTING THE LAW TO THE ONLINE ENVIRONMENT — New Issues in Online Privacy and Employment Discrimination

A s computers come to be used for more and more aspects of both personal and professional life, the line between personal use and work-related use is becoming blurred. As this chapter has explained, employers are legally required to prevent discrimination in the workplace, including a hostile environment created by workers' online activities. That employers have a right—or even an obligation—to monitor their employees' computer use to this end is generally established. Indeed, courts have generally held that employees have no expectation of privacy in their workplace computers when a private employer supplies the equipment. The limits of this privacy exception are still being tested, however, as a number of issues related to computers, privacy, and employment discrimination remain unresolved. A new issue that is just emerging is whether employers can obtain information about job applicants by conducting online searches when asking for the same information on a job application or in an interview might be illegal.

Searches of Workplace Computers

An employee who uses his or her workplace computer to view sexually explicit photographs may create a hostile environment if the photographs can be seen by other employees. Furthermore, if the photographs involve children, the employee's activities may be illegal. Courts have generally held that employers can search a workplace computer for evidence of employee misconduct[a] and that they can also consent to a search by government officials. If the computer is in a locked office, however, does the employee have a greater expectation of privacy? In *United States v. Ziegler*[b] in 2007, the court had to answer this question.

The Internet service provider for Frontline Processing Corporation informed the Federal Bureau of Investigation (FBI) that one of Frontline's computers had been used to access child-pornography Web sites in violation of federal criminal law. The FBI investigated and determined that Jeffrey Ziegler, Frontline's director of operations, had used the computer in his office to search for and view online photos of "very young girls in various states of undress." Frontline agreed to cooperate with the FBI, and at some point corporate employees entered Ziegler's locked office and made a backup copy of the hard drive on his computer without his consent.

Ziegler appealed his subsequent conviction for possessing child pornography on the ground that the search of his computer violated his Fourth Amendment rights against unreasonable search and seizure. The U.S. Court of Appeals for the Ninth Circuit first held that Ziegler had no reasonable expectation of privacy, but on rehearing, the court changed its ruling and held that Ziegler did have a reasonable expectation of privacy in the contents of the computer in his locked office. Because the employer (Frontline) owned the

a. See, for example, *Twymon v. Wells Fargo & Co.*, 462 F.3d 925 (8th Cir. 2006); and *Griffis v. Pinal County*, 213 Ariz. 300, 141 P.3d 780 (2006).
b. 474 F.3d 1184 (9th Cir. 2007).

CASE 18.3–Continued

DECISION Yes. The Mississippi Supreme Court affirmed the lower court's judgment. Neely did not have to prove that the events that Cash claimed led to his dismissal did not actually happen.

REASON Neely did not deny the occurrence of most of the events that Cash claimed were the nondiscriminatory reasons for Neely's discharge. Instead, Neely offered proof that these events were not the real reasons for his termination. For example, Cash claimed that it discharged Neely for "insubordination and his failure to discover and report out-of-date product on a particular occasion." Neely responded that "his operation in Columbus received perfect scores following several evaluations" by Anheuser-Busch. Neely also showed that "out-of-date product was fairly common and that the extremely meticulous audit of his territory," preceding his

discharge, "was unprecedented, * * * a 'witch hunt.'" Neely also claimed that Danny Cash made derogatory comments about his age. For example, in a document titled "Jim Neely Time Line," Danny referred to "too much older supervisors that were riding their time out." The state supreme court concluded, "The jury in this case obviously credited Neely's account of his dismissal and the evidence supporting it over explanations supplied by Cash. This Court has no basis to disturb that decision on appeal. The jury was free to find that even if, as Cash claimed, Neely had been insubordinate, that justification was pretextual based on evidence of unequal treatment [and] age-related statements made by Cash's CEO."

WHAT IF THE FACTS WERE DIFFERENT?
If Neely had admitted that he had committed all of the "wrongful" acts attributed to him by Cash, would the outcome of this case have been different? Why or why not?

computer, however, the court held that Frontline's consent validated the search. According to the court, a "computer is the type of workplace property that remains within control of the employer 'even if the employee has placed personal items in it.'"

Unresolved Issues

Certainly, the trend is clearly toward limiting employees' expectations of privacy in employer-owned computers in the workplace, but several questions still remain open. What expectations of privacy does an employee have in a laptop computer that is provided by the company but is used by the employee at home or on the road? Similarly, if the employee works at home on an employer-owned computer, to what degree can the employer justify monitoring the employee's online activities? Although computers in remote locations could be used to send harassing e-mail, other employees are unlikely to view offensive material on such computers, so that justification for monitoring Internet use seems less valid.

Other issues have to do with whether employers must tell employees that their computer use will be monitored and the degree to which employers should monitor employees' online activities that are mostly personal. To date, only two states (Connecticut and Delaware) have passed laws specifically requiring private employers to inform employees that their workplace Internet activities will be monitored. Personal blogs raise an even more complex issue: Does an employer have the right to monitor its employees' personal blogs? If an employee's personal blog contains racially or sexually offensive comments about co-workers, what should the employer do? Thus far, in most of the cases involving employees dismissed for computer misuse, the employer had a written

Internet policy and presented evidence that the employee knew about and disregarded the policy. According to recent surveys, however, most organizations do not have policies on employees' blogs.

Even more problematic is another issue that is just emerging. Today, many college students and recent graduates belong to social networking sites such as Facebook.com and MySpace.com where they can post photographs, comments, blogs, or even videos about themselves. Some of this material is suggestive, to say the least. A number of employers have begun to use search engines to search for information on job applicants. A search may turn up not just photos that the applicant intended to be viewed only by close friends but also information about the applicant's marital status, sexual orientation, or political or religious views that the employer could not ask for on a job application or discuss in a job interview. Nevertheless, this information is now readily available to employers. Some colleges and employment counselors are beginning to advise job seekers to make sure that they remove any information they do not want a prospective employer to see, but the issue of whether employers have a right to search for this information is likely to persist.

FOR CRITICAL ANALYSIS *Suppose that an employee writes a message to like-minded persons concerning religious beliefs or political views. Can the employee be fired in that situation? Who decides what is acceptable Internet activity when there is no written policy?*

Replacing Older Workers with Younger Workers Numerous age discrimination cases have been brought against employers who, to cut costs, replaced older, higher-salaried employees with younger, lower-salaried workers. Whether a firing is discriminatory or simply part of a rational business decision to prune the company's ranks is not always clear. Companies often defend a decision to discharge a worker by asserting that the worker could no longer perform his or her duties or that the worker's skills were no longer needed. The employee must prove that the discharge was motivated, at least in part, by age bias. Proof that qualified older employees are generally discharged before younger employees or that co-workers continually made unflattering age-related comments about the discharged worker may be enough.

The plaintiff need not prove that he or she was replaced by a person outside the protected class—that is, by a person under the age of forty years.[49] Rather, the issue in all ADEA cases is whether age discrimination has, in fact, occurred, regardless of the age of the replacement worker.

State Employees Not Covered by the ADEA Generally, the states are immune from lawsuits brought by private individuals in federal court—unless a state consents to the suit.

49. *O'Connor v. Consolidated Coin Caterers Corp.*, 517 U.S. 308, 116 S.Ct. 1307, 134 L.Ed.2d 433 (1996).

This immunity stems from the United States Supreme Court's interpretation of the Eleventh Amendment (the text of this amendment is included in Appendix B). **EXAMPLE 18.16** In two Florida cases, professors and librarians contended that their employers—two Florida state universities—denied them salary increases and other benefits because they were getting old and their successors could be hired at lower cost. The universities claimed that as agencies of a sovereign state, they could not be sued in federal court without the state's consent. The cases ultimately reached the United States Supreme Court, which held that the Eleventh Amendment bars private parties from suing state employers for violations of the ADEA.[50] ■

State immunity under the Eleventh Amendment is not absolute, however, as the Supreme Court explained in 2004. In some situations, such as when fundamental rights are at stake, Congress has the power to abrogate (abolish) state immunity to private suits through legislation that unequivocally shows Congress's intent to subject states to private suits.[51] As a general rule, though, the Court has found that state employers are immune from private suits brought by employees under the ADEA (for age discrimination, as noted above), the Americans with Disabilities Act[52] (for disability discrimination), and the Fair Labor Standards Act.[53] In contrast, states are not immune from the requirements of the Family and Medical Leave Act.[54]

Discrimination Based on Disability

The Americans with Disabilities Act (ADA) of 1990 is designed to eliminate discriminatory employment practices that prevent otherwise qualified workers with disabilities from fully participating in the national labor force. Prior to 1990, the major federal law providing protection to those with disabilities was the Rehabilitation Act of 1973. That act covered only federal government employees and those employed under federally funded programs. The ADA extends federal protection against disability-based discrimination to all workplaces with fifteen or more workers (with the exception of state government employers, who are generally immune under the Eleventh Amendment, as was just discussed). Basically, the ADA requires that employers "reasonably accommodate" the needs of persons with disabilities unless to do so would cause the employer to suffer an "undue hardship."

Procedures under the ADA To prevail on a claim under the ADA, a plaintiff must show that he or she (1) has a disability, (2) is otherwise qualified for the employment in question, and (3) was excluded from the employment solely because of the disability. As in Title VII cases, a claim alleging a violation of the ADA may be commenced only after the plaintiff has pursued the claim through the EEOC. Plaintiffs may sue for many of the same remedies available under Title VII. The EEOC may decide to investigate and perhaps even sue the employer on behalf of the employee. If the EEOC decides not to sue, then the employee is entitled to sue.

Significantly, the United States Supreme Court held in 2002 that the EEOC could bring a suit against an employer for disability-based discrimination even though the employee had agreed to submit any job-related disputes to arbitration (see Chapter 3). The Court reasoned that because the EEOC was not a party to the arbitration agreement, the agreement was not binding on the EEOC.[55]

---

50. *Kimel v. Florida Board of Regents*, 528 U.S. 62, 120 S.Ct. 631, 145 L.Ed.2d 522 (2000).
51. *Tennessee v. Lane*, 541 U.S. 509, 124 S.Ct. 1978, 158 L.Ed.2d 820 (2004).
52. *Board of Trustees of the University of Alabama v. Garrett*, 531 U.S. 356, 121 S.Ct. 955, 148 L.Ed.2d 866 (2001).
53. *Alden v. Maine*, 527 U.S. 706, 119 S.Ct. 2240, 144 L.Ed.2d 636 (1999).
54. *Nevada Department of Human Resources v. Hibbs*, 538 U.S. 721, 123 S.Ct. 1972, 155 L.Ed.2d 953 (2003).
55. *EEOC v. Waffle House, Inc.*, 534 U.S. 279, 122 S.Ct. 754, 151 L.Ed.2d 75 (2002).

Plaintiffs in lawsuits brought under the ADA may seek many of the same remedies available under Title VII. These include reinstatement, back pay, a limited amount of compensatory and punitive damages (for intentional discrimination), and certain other forms of relief. Repeat violators may be ordered to pay fines of up to $100,000.

What Is a Disability?   The ADA is broadly drafted to cover persons with a wide range of disabilities. Specifically, the ADA defines *disability* as "(1) a physical or mental impairment that substantially limits one or more of the major life activities of such individuals; (2) a record of such impairment; or (3) being regarded as having such an impairment."

Health conditions that have been considered disabilities under the federal law include blindness, alcoholism, heart disease, cancer, muscular dystrophy, cerebral palsy, paraplegia, diabetes, acquired immune deficiency syndrome (AIDS), testing positive for the human immunodeficiency virus (HIV), and morbid obesity (defined as existing when an individual's weight is two times that of a normal person).[56] The ADA excludes from coverage certain conditions, such as kleptomania (the obsessive desire to steal).

Although the ADA's definition of disability is broad, starting in 1999, the United States Supreme Court has issued a series of decisions narrowing the definition of what constitutes a disability under the act.

Co-workers discuss business matters. What is a disability under the Americans with Disabilities Act? (Johnny Stockshooter/Image State)

Correctable Conditions.   In 1999, in *Sutton v. United Airlines, Inc.*,[57] the Supreme Court reviewed a case raising the issue of whether severe myopia, or nearsightedness, which can be corrected with lenses, qualifies as a disability under the ADA. The Supreme Court ruled that it does not. The determination of whether a person is substantially limited in a major life activity is based on how the person functions when taking medication or using corrective devices, not on how the person functions without these measures.

In a similar case in 2002, a federal appellate court held that a pharmacist suffering from diabetes, which could be corrected by insulin, did not have a cause of action against his employer under the ADA.[58] In other cases decided in the early 2000s, the courts have held that plaintiffs with bipolar disorder, epilepsy, and other such conditions do *not* fall under the ADA's protections if the conditions can be corrected.

Repetitive-Stress Injuries.   For some time, the courts were divided on the issue of whether carpal tunnel syndrome (or other repetitive-stress injury) constitutes a disability under the ADA. Carpal tunnel syndrome is a condition of pain and weakness in the hand caused by repetitive compression of a nerve in the wrist. In 2002, in a case involving this issue, the Supreme Court unanimously held that it does not. The Court stated that although the employee could not perform the manual tasks associated with her job, the condition did not constitute a disability under the ADA because it did not "substantially limit" the major life activity of performing manual tasks.[59]

Reasonable Accommodation   The ADA does not require that employers accommodate the needs of job applicants or employees with disabilities who are not otherwise qualified

ON THE WEB

An abundance of helpful information on disability-based discrimination, including the text of the ADA, can be found online at

www.jan.wvu.edu/portals/dbtac.htm.

---

56. *Cook v. Rhode Island Department of Mental Health,* 10 F.3d 17 (1st Cir. 1993).
57. 527 U.S. 471, 119 S.Ct. 2139, 144 L.Ed.2d 450 (1999).
58. *Orr v. Walmart Stores, Inc.,* 297 F.3d 720 (8th Cir. 2002).
59. *Toyota Motor Manufacturing, Kentucky, Inc. v. Williams,* 534 U.S. 184, 122 S.Ct. 681, 151 L.Ed.2d 615 (2002).

for the work. If a job applicant or an employee with a disability, with reasonable accommodation, can perform essential job functions, however, the employer must make the accommodation. Required modifications may include installing ramps for a wheelchair, establishing more flexible working hours, creating or modifying job assignments, and creating or improving training materials and procedures.

Generally, employers should give primary consideration to employees' preferences in deciding what accommodations should be made. What happens if a job applicant or employee does not indicate to the employer how her or his disability can be accommodated so that the employee can perform essential job functions? In this situation, the employer may avoid liability for failing to hire or retain the individual on the ground that the applicant or employee has failed to meet the "otherwise qualified" requirement.[60]

ON THE WEB

The Equal Employment Opportunity Commission posts a manual that provides guidance on reasonable accommodation and undue hardship under the ADA. Go to

www.eeoc.gov/policy/docs/accommodation.html.

Undue Hardship. Employers who do not accommodate the needs of persons with disabilities must demonstrate that the accommodations will cause "undue hardship." Generally, the law offers no uniform standards for identifying what is an undue hardship other than the imposition of a "significant difficulty or expense" on the employer. In other words, the focus is on the resources and circumstances of the particular employer in relation to the cost or difficulty of providing a specific accommodation.

Usually, the courts decide whether an accommodation constitutes an undue hardship on a case-by-case basis. **■EXAMPLE 18.17** Bryan Lockhart, who uses a wheelchair, works for a cell phone company that provides parking to its employees. Lockhart informs the company supervisors that the parking spaces are so narrow that he is unable to extend the ramp on his van that allows him to get in and out of the vehicle. Lockhart therefore requests that the company reasonably accommodate his needs by paying a monthly fee for him to use a larger parking space in an adjacent lot. In this situation, a court would likely find that it would not be an undue hardship for the employer to pay for additional parking for Lockhart. ■

Job Applications and Preemployment Physical Exams. Employers must modify their job-application process so that those with disabilities can compete for jobs with those who do not have disabilities. **■EXAMPLE 18.18** A job announcement that includes only a phone number would discriminate against potential job applicants with hearing impairments. Thus, the job announcement must also provide an address. ■

Employers are restricted in the kinds of questions they may ask on job-application forms and during preemployment interviews (see the *Application* feature at the end of this chapter for guidelines on this topic). Furthermore, they cannot require persons with disabilities to submit to preemployment physicals unless such exams are required of all other applicants. Employers can condition an offer of employment on the applicant's successfully passing a medical examination, but can disqualify the applicant only if the medical problems they discover would render the applicant unable to perform the job.

DON'T FORGET Preemployment screening procedures must be applied equally in regard to all job applicants.

Dangerous Workers. Employers are not required to hire or retain workers who, because of their disabilities, pose a direct threat to the health or safety of their co-workers or the public.[61] This danger must be substantial and immediate; it cannot be speculative. In the wake of the AIDS epidemic, many employers have been concerned about hiring or con-

---

60. See, for example, *Beck v. University of Wisconsin Board of Regents*, 75 F.3d 1130 (7th Cir. 1996); and *White v. York International Corp.*, 45 F.3d 357 (10th Cir. 1995).

61. The United States Supreme Court has also upheld regulations that permit an employer to refuse to hire a worker when the job would pose a threat to that person's own health. *Chevron USA, Inc. v. Echazabal*, 536 U.S. 73, 122 S.Ct. 2045, 153 L.Ed.2d 82 (2002).

tinuing to employ a worker who has AIDS under the assumption that the worker might pose a direct threat to the health or safety of others in the workplace. Courts have generally held, however, that AIDS is not so contagious as to disqualify employees in most jobs. Therefore, employers must reasonably accommodate job applicants or employees who have AIDS or who test positive for HIV, the virus that causes AIDS.

Substance Abusers. Drug addiction is a disability under the ADA because drug addiction is a substantially limiting impairment. Those who are using illegal drugs at the present time are not protected by the act, however. The ADA protects only persons with *former* drug addictions—those who have completed a supervised drug-rehabilitation program or are in a supervised rehabilitation program. Individuals who have used drugs casually in the past are not protected under the act. They are not considered addicts and therefore do not have a disability (addiction).

People suffering from alcoholism are protected by the ADA. Employers cannot legally discriminate against employees simply because they are suffering from alcoholism and must treat them in the same way they treat other employees. In other words, an employee with alcoholism who comes to work late because she or he was drinking the night before cannot be disciplined any differently than someone else who is late for another reason. Of course, employers have the right to prohibit the use of alcohol in the workplace and can require that employees not be under the influence of alcohol while working. Employers can also fire or refuse to hire a person with alcoholism if he or she poses a substantial risk of harm either to himself or herself or to others and the risk cannot be reduced by reasonable accommodation.

Health-Insurance Plans. Workers with disabilities must be given equal access to any health insurance provided to other employees. Employers can exclude from coverage pre-existing health conditions and certain types of diagnostic or surgical procedures, though. An employer can also put a limit, or cap, on health-care payments under its particular group health policy—as long as such caps are "applied equally to all insured employees" and do not "discriminate on the basis of disability." Whenever a group health-care plan makes a disability-based distinction in its benefits, the plan violates the ADA. The employer must then be able to justify the distinction by proving one of the following:

1 That limiting coverage of certain ailments is required to keep the plan financially sound.

2 That coverage of certain ailments would cause such a significant increase in premium payments or their equivalent that the plan would be unappealing to a significant number of workers.

3 That the disparate treatment is justified by the risks and costs associated with a particular disability.

Hostile-Environment Claims under the ADA As discussed earlier in this chapter, under Title VII of the Civil Rights Act of 1964, an employee may base certain types of employment-discrimination causes of action on a hostile-environment theory. Using this theory, a worker may successfully sue her or his employer, even if the worker was not fired or otherwise discriminated against.

Although the ADA does not expressly provide for hostile-environment claims, a number of courts have allowed such actions. Only a few plaintiffs have been successful, however.[62]

---

62. See, for example, *Shaver v. Independent Stave Co.*, 350 F.3d 716 (8th Cir. 2003); *Johnson v. North Carolina Department of Health and Human Services*, 454 F.Supp.2d 467 (M.D.N.C. 2006); and *Lucenti v. Potter*, 432 F.Supp.2d 347 (S.D.N.Y. 2006).

For a claim to succeed, the conduct complained of must be sufficiently severe or pervasive to permeate the workplace and alter the conditions of employment such that a reasonable person would find the environment hostile or abusive. **■EXAMPLE 18.19** Lester Wenigar was a fifty-seven-year-old man with a low IQ and limited mental capacity who worked at a farm doing manual labor and serving as a night watchman. His employer frequently shouted at him and called him names, did not allow him to take breaks, and provided him with substandard living quarters (a storeroom over a garage without any heat or windows). In this situation, because the employer's conduct was severe and offensive, a court would likely find that the working conditions constituted a hostile environment under the ADA.[63] ■

DEFENSES TO EMPLOYMENT DISCRIMINATION

The first line of defense for an employer charged with employment discrimination is, of course, to assert that the plaintiff has failed to meet his or her initial burden of proving that discrimination occurred. As noted, plaintiffs bringing cases under the ADA sometimes find it difficult to meet this initial burden because they must prove that their alleged disabilities are disabilities covered by the ADA. Furthermore, plaintiffs in ADA cases must prove that they were otherwise qualified for the job and that their disabilities were the sole reason they were not hired or were fired.

Once a plaintiff succeeds in proving that discrimination occurred, the burden shifts to the employer to justify the discriminatory practice. Often, employers attempt to justify the discrimination by claiming that it was the result of a business necessity, a bona fide occupational qualification, or a seniority system. In some cases, as noted earlier, an effective antiharassment policy and prompt remedial action when harassment occurs may shield employers from liability for sexual harassment under Title VII.

Business Necessity

BUSINESS NECESSITY
A defense to allegations of employment discrimination in which the employer demonstrates that an employment practice that discriminates against members of a protected class is related to job performance.

An employer may defend against a claim of disparate-impact (unintentional) discrimination by asserting that a practice that has a discriminatory effect is a **business necessity**. **■EXAMPLE 18.20** If requiring a high school diploma is shown to have a discriminatory effect, an employer might argue that a high school education is necessary for workers to perform the job at a required level of competence. If the employer can demonstrate to the court's satisfaction that a definite connection exists between a high school education and job performance, the employer will normally succeed in this business necessity defense. ■

Bona Fide Occupational Qualification

BONA FIDE OCCUPATIONAL QUALIFICATION (BFOQ)
Identifiable characteristics reasonably necessary to the normal operation of a particular business. These characteristics can include gender, national origin, and religion, but not race.

Another defense applies when discrimination against a protected class is essential to a job—that is, when a particular trait is a **bona fide occupational qualification (BFOQ)**. Race, however, can never be a BFOQ. Generally, courts have restricted the BFOQ defense to instances in which the employee's gender is essential to the job.[64] **■EXAMPLE 18.21** A women's clothing store might legitimately hire only female sales attendants if part of an attendant's job involves assisting clients in the store's dressing rooms. Similarly, the Federal Aviation Administration can legitimately impose age limits for airline pilots—but an airline cannot impose weight limits only on female flight attendants. ■

---

63. *Wenigar v. Johnson*, 712 N.W.2d 190 (Minn.App. 2006). This case involved a hostile-environment claim under the Minnesota disability statute rather than the ADA, but the court relied on another court's decision under the ADA.
64. A classic example is *United Auto Workers v. Johnson Controls, Inc.*, 499 U.S. 187, 111 S.Ct. 1196, 113 L.Ed.2d 158 (1991), in which the Supreme Court held that a policy adopted to protect unborn children of female employees from the harmful effects of lead exposure was an unacceptable BFOQ.

Seniority Systems

An employer with a history of discrimination might have no members of protected classes in upper-level positions. Even if the employer now seeks to be unbiased, it may face a lawsuit in which the plaintiff asks a court to order that minorities be promoted ahead of schedule to compensate for past discrimination. If no present intent to discriminate is shown, however, and if promotions or other job benefits are distributed according to a fair **seniority system** (in which workers with more years of service are promoted first or laid off last), the employer has a good defense against the suit.

According to the United States Supreme Court in 2002, this defense may also apply to alleged discrimination under the ADA. If an employee with a disability requests an accommodation (such as an assignment to a particular position) that conflicts with an employer's seniority system, the accommodation will generally not be considered "reasonable" under the act.[65]

SENIORITY SYSTEM
In regard to employment relationships, a system in which those who have worked longest for the employer are first in line for promotions, salary increases, and other benefits. They are also the last to be laid off if the workforce must be reduced.

After-Acquired Evidence of Employee Misconduct

In some situations, employers have attempted to avoid liability for employment discrimination on the basis of "after-acquired evidence"—that is, evidence that the employer discovers after a lawsuit is filed—of an employee's misconduct. **■EXAMPLE 18.22** Suppose that an employer fires a worker, who then sues the employer for employment discrimination. During pretrial investigation, the employer learns that the employee made material misrepresentations on his or her employment application—misrepresentations that, had the employer known about them, would have served as a ground to fire the individual. ■

According to the United States Supreme Court, after-acquired evidence of wrongdoing cannot be used to shield an employer entirely from liability for employment discrimination. It may, however, be used to limit the amount of damages for which the employer is liable.[66]

---

65. *U.S. Airways, Inc. v. Barnett*, 535 U.S. 391, 122 S.Ct. 1516, 152 L.Ed.2d 589 (2002).
66. *McKennon v. Nashville Banner Publishing Co.*, 513 U.S. 352, 115 S.Ct. 879, 130 L.Ed.2d 852 (1995).

REVIEWING **Employment Law**

Rick Saldona began working as a traveling salesperson for Aimer Winery in 1977. Sales constituted 90 percent of Saldona's work time. Saldona worked an average of fifty hours per week but received no overtime pay. In June 2007, Saldona's new supervisor, Caesar Braxton, claimed that Saldona had been inflating his reported sales calls and required Saldona to submit to a polygraph test. Saldona reported Braxton to the U.S. Department of Labor, which prohibited Aimer from requiring Saldona to take a polygraph test for this purpose. In August 2007, Saldona's wife, Venita, fell from a ladder and sustained a head injury while employed as a full-time agricultural harvester. Saldona delivered to Aimer's human resources department a letter from his wife's physician indicating that she would need daily care for several months, and Saldona took leave until December 2007. Aimer had sixty-three employees at that time. When Saldona returned to Aimer, he was informed that his position had been eliminated because his sales territory had been combined with an adjacent territory. Using the information presented in the chapter, answer the following questions.

1 Would Saldona have been legally entitled to receive overtime pay at a higher rate? Why or why not?

2 What is the maximum length of time Saldona would have been allowed to take leave to care for his injured spouse?

3 Under what circumstances would Aimer have been allowed to require an employee to take a polygraph test?

4 Would Aimer likely be able to avoid reinstating Saldona under the *key employee* exception? Why or why not?

Many employers have been held liable under the Americans with Disabilities Act (ADA) of 1990 simply because they asked the wrong questions when interviewing job applicants with disabilities. If you are an employer, you can do several things to avoid violating the ADA.

Become Familiar with the EEOC Guidelines

As a preliminary step, you should become familiar with the guidelines on job interviews issued by the Equal Employment Opportunity Commission (EEOC). These guidelines indicate the kinds of questions that employers may—and may not—ask job applicants with disabilities. Often, the line between permissible and impermissible questions is a fine one. Consider these examples:

- *Ability to perform the job.* As an employer, you may ask a job applicant, "Can you do the job?" You may also ask whether the applicant can perform specific tasks related to the job. You may not ask the candidate, "How would you do the job?"—*unless* the disability is obvious, the applicant brings up the subject during the interview, or you ask the question of all applicants.

- *Absenteeism.* You may ask, "Can you meet our attendance requirements?" or "How many days were you absent last year?" You may not ask, "How many days were you sick last year?"

- *Drug use.* Generally, employers may ask about current or past use of illegal drugs but not about drug addiction. Therefore, as an employer, you may ask, "Have you ever used illegal drugs?" or "Have you done so in the last six months?" You may not ask, "How often did you use illegal drugs?" or "Have you been treated for drug abuse?"

- *Alcohol use.* Generally, employers may ask about a candidate's drinking habits but not about alcoholism. Therefore, you may ask, "Do you drink alcohol?" or "Have you been arrested for driving while intoxicated?" but you may not ask, "How often do you drink?"

- *History of job-related injuries.* Employers may not ask a job candidate with a disability any questions about the applicant's previous job-related injuries or about workers' compensation claims submitted in the past.

Once you have made a job offer, though, you may ask the applicant questions concerning his or her disability, including questions about previous workers' compensation claims or about the extent of a drinking problem. You may also ask for medical documents verifying the nature of the applicant's disability. Generally, however, you should ask such questions only if you ask them of all applicants or if they are follow-up questions concerning information about the applicant's disability that she or he already disclosed during a job interview.

Obtain Legal Assistance and Instruct Staff Members

To avoid liability under the ADA, the wisest thing you can do is consult with an attorney. You should inform the attorney of the kinds of questions you typically ask job applicants during interviews or following employment offers. Then, you should work with the attorney in modifying these questions so that they are consistent with the EEOC's guidelines on permissible and impermissible questions. Finally, you should make sure that anyone on your staff who interviews job applicants receives thorough instructions on what questions may and may not be asked of candidates with disabilities. You might also remind your staff that under the ADA, the words and phraseology the interviewer uses may result in a violation of the ADA regardless of the interviewer's intentions.

CHECKLIST FOR THE EMPLOYER

1 Familiarize yourself with the EEOC's guidelines indicating what questions are and are not permissible when interviewing job applicants with disabilities.
2 Work with an attorney to create a list of particular types of questions that are and are not permissible under the EEOC's guidelines with respect to job candidates with disabilities.
3 Make sure that all persons in your firm who interview job applicants are thoroughly instructed as to the types of questions that they may and may not ask when interviewing job applicants with disabilities.

* This *Application* is not meant to substitute for the services of an attorney who is licensed to practice law in your state.

KEY TERMS

bona fide occupational
   qualification (BFOQ) 576
business necessity 576
constructive discharge 565
disparate-impact
   discrimination 563
disparate-treatment
   discrimination 562

employment at will 547
employment discrimination 561
minimum wage 549
prima facie case 562
protected class 561
seniority system 577
sexual harassment 565
vesting 554

whistleblowing 548
workers' compensation laws 552
wrongful discharge 549

CHAPTER SUMMARY Employment Law

Employment at Will
(See pages 547–549.)

1. *Employment-at-will doctrine*—Under this common law doctrine, either party may terminate the employment relationship at any time and for any reason ("at will"). This doctrine is still in widespread use throughout the United States, although federal and state statutes prevent it from being applied in certain circumstances.

2. *Exceptions to the employment-at-will doctrine*—To protect employees from some of the harsh results of the employment-at-will doctrine, courts have made exceptions to the doctrine on the basis of contract theory, tort theory, and public policy.

3. *Whistleblower statutes*—Most states have passed whistleblower statutes specifically to protect employees who "blow the whistle" on their employers from subsequent retaliation by those employers. The federal Whistleblower Protection Act of 1989 protects federal employees who report their employers' wrongdoing. The federal False Claims Reform Act of 1986 provides monetary rewards for whistleblowers who disclose information relating to fraud perpetrated against the U.S. government. Whistleblowers have occasionally received protection under the common law for reasons of public policy.

4. *Wrongful discharge*—Whenever an employer discharges an employee in violation of an employment contract or statutory law protecting employees, the employee may bring a suit for wrongful discharge.

Wage and Hour Laws
(See pages 549–551.)

1. *Davis-Bacon Act (1931)*—Requires contractors and subcontractors working on federal government construction projects to pay their employees "prevailing wages."

2. *Walsh-Healey Act (1936)*—Requires firms that contract with federal agencies to pay their employees a minimum wage and overtime pay.

3. *Fair Labor Standards Act (1938)*—Extended wage and hour requirements to cover all employers whose activities affect interstate commerce plus certain other businesses. The act has specific requirements in regard to child labor, maximum hours, and minimum wages.

Worker Health and Safety
(See pages 551–553.)

1. *Occupational Safety and Health Act (1970)*—Requires employers to meet specific safety and health standards that are established and enforced by the Occupational Safety and Health Administration (OSHA).

2. *State workers' compensation laws*—Establish an administrative procedure for compensating workers who are injured in accidents that occur on the job, regardless of fault.

Income Security
(See pages 553–555.)

1. *Social Security and Medicare*—The Social Security Act of 1935 provides for old-age (retirement), survivors, and disability insurance. Both employers and employees must make contributions under the Federal Insurance Contributions Act (FICA) to help pay for benefits that will partially make up for the employees' loss of income on retirement. The Social Security Administration also administers Medicare, a health-insurance program for older or disabled persons.

(Continued)

CHAPTER SUMMARY Employment Law—Continued

Income Security—Continued	2. *Private pension plans*—The federal Employee Retirement Income Security Act (ERISA) of 1974 establishes standards for the management of employer-provided pension plans.
	3. *Unemployment insurance*—The Federal Unemployment Tax Act of 1935 created a system that provides unemployment compensation to eligible individuals. Covered employers are taxed to help defray the costs of unemployment compensation.
	4. *COBRA*—The Consolidated Omnibus Budget Reconciliation Act (COBRA) of 1985 requires employers to give employees, on termination of employment, the option of continuing their medical, optical, or dental insurance coverage for a certain period.
	5. *HIPAA*—The Health Insurance Portability and Accountability Act (HIPAA) does not require employers to provide health insurance, but it does establish certain requirements for employer-sponsored health insurance. Employers must comply with a number of administrative, technical, and procedural safeguards to ensure the privacy of employees' health information.
Family and Medical Leave (See pages 556–557.)	The Family and Medical Leave Act (FMLA) of 1993 requires employers with fifty or more employees to provide their employees (except for key employees) with up to twelve weeks of unpaid family or medical leave during any twelve-month period for the following reasons:
	1. *Family leave*—May be taken to care for a newborn baby, an adopted child, or a foster child.
	2. *Medical leave*—May be taken when the employee or the employee's spouse, child, or parent has a serious health condition requiring care.
Employee Privacy Rights (See pages 557–561.)	A right to privacy has been inferred from guarantees provided by the First, Third, Fourth, Fifth, and Ninth Amendments to the U.S. Constitution. State laws may also provide for privacy rights. Employer practices that are often challenged by employees as invasive of their privacy rights include electronic performance monitoring, lie-detector tests, drug testing, AIDS testing, and screening procedures.
Title VII of the Civil Rights Act of 1964 (See pages 562–569.)	Title VII prohibits employment discrimination based on race, color, national origin, religion, or gender.
	1. *Procedures*—Employees must file a claim with the Equal Employment Opportunity Commission (EEOC). The EEOC may sue the employer on the employee's behalf; if not, the employee may sue the employer directly.
	2. *Types of discrimination*—Title VII prohibits both intentional (disparate-treatment) and unintentional (disparate-impact) discrimination. Disparate-impact discrimination occurs when an employer's practice, such as hiring only persons with a certain level of education, has the effect of discriminating against a class of persons protected by Title VII. Title VII also extends to discriminatory practices, such as various forms of harassment, in the online environment.
	3. *Remedies for discrimination under Title VII*—If a plaintiff proves that unlawful discrimination occurred, he or she may be awarded reinstatement, back pay, and retroactive promotions. Damages (both compensatory and punitive) may be awarded for intentional discrimination.
Discrimination Based on Age (See pages 569–572.)	The Age Discrimination in Employment Act (ADEA) of 1967 prohibits employment discrimination on the basis of age against individuals forty years of age or older. Procedures for bringing a case under the ADEA are similar to those for bringing a case under Title VII.
Discrimination Based on Disability (See pages 572–576.)	The Americans with Disabilities Act (ADA) of 1990 prohibits employment discrimination against persons with disabilities who are otherwise qualified to perform the essential functions of the jobs for which they apply.
	1. *Procedures and remedies*—To prevail on a claim under the ADA, the plaintiff must show that she or he has a disability, is otherwise qualified for the employment in question, and was excluded from the employment solely because of the disability. Procedures under the ADA are similar to those required in Title VII cases; remedies are also similar to those under Title VII.

CHAPTER SUMMARY Employment Law—Continued

Discrimination Based on Disability— Continued	2. *Definition of disability*—The ADA defines the term *disability* as a physical or mental impairment that substantially limits one or more major life activities, a record of such impairment, or being regarded as having such an impairment. 3. *Reasonable accommodation*—Employers are required to reasonably accommodate the needs of persons with disabilities. Reasonable accommodations may include altering job-application procedures, modifying the physical work environment, and permitting more flexible work schedules. Employers are not required to accommodate the needs of all workers with disabilities. For example, employers need not accommodate workers who pose a definite threat to health and safety in the workplace or those who are not otherwise qualified for their jobs.
Defenses to Employment Discrimination (See pages 576–577.)	If a plaintiff proves that employment discrimination occurred, employers may avoid liability by successfully asserting certain defenses. Employers may assert that the discrimination was required for reasons of business necessity, to meet a bona fide occupational qualification, or to maintain a legitimate seniority system. Evidence of prior employee misconduct acquired after the employee has been fired is not a defense to discrimination.

FOR REVIEW

Answers for the even-numbered questions in this **For Review** *section can be found in Appendix E at the end of this text.*

1 What is the employment-at-will doctrine? When and why are exceptions to this doctrine made?

2 What federal statute governs working hours and wages?

3 Under the Family and Medical Leave Act of 1993, under what circumstances may an employee take family or medical leave?

4 What federal acts prohibit discrimination in the workplace?

5 What are three defenses to claims of employment discrimination?

◾

QUESTIONS AND CASE PROBLEMS

 HYPOTHETICAL SCENARIOS

18.1 Title VII Violations. Discuss fully whether any of the following actions would constitute a violation of Title VII of the 1964 Civil Rights Act, as amended.

  1 Tennington, Inc., is a consulting firm and has ten employees. These employees travel on consulting jobs in seven states. Tennington has an employment record of hiring only white males.

  2 Novo Films, Inc., is making a film about Africa and needs to employ approximately one hundred extras for this picture. To hire these extras, Novo advertises in all major newspapers in Southern California. The ad states that only African Americans need apply.

18.2 Hypothetical Question with Sample Answer. Denton and Carlo were employed at an appliance plant. Their job

required them to do occasional maintenance work while standing on a wire mesh twenty feet above the plant floor. Other employees had fallen through the mesh; one was killed by the fall. When Denton and Carlo were asked by their supervisor to do work that would likely require them to walk on the mesh, they refused due to their fear of bodily harm or death. Because of their refusal to do the requested work, the two employees were fired from their jobs. Was their discharge wrongful? If so, under what federal employment law? To what federal agency or department should they turn for assistance?

 For a sample answer to Question 18.2, go to Appendix F at the end of this text.

◾

CASE PROBLEMS

18.3 Employee Privacy. Patience Oyoyo worked as a claims analyst in the claims management department of Baylor Healthcare Network, Inc. When questions arose about Oyoyo's performance on several occasions, department manager Debbie Outlaw met with Oyoyo to discuss, among other things, Oyoyo's personal use of a business phone. Outlaw reminded Oyoyo that company policy prohibited excessive personal calls and that these would result in the termination of her employment. Outlaw began to monitor Oyoyo's phone usage, noting lengthy outgoing calls on several occasions, including some long-distance calls. Eventually, Outlaw terminated Oyoyo's employment, and Oyoyo filed a suit in a federal district court against Baylor. Oyoyo asserted, in part, that by monitoring her phone calls, the employer had invaded her privacy. Baylor asked the court to dismiss this claim. In whose favor should the court rule, and why? [*Oyoyo v. Baylor Health Network, Inc.*, __ F.Supp.2d __ (N.D.Tex. 2000)]

18.4 Discrimination Based on Age. The United Auto Workers (UAW) is the union that represents the employees of General Dynamics Land Systems, Inc. In 1997, a collective bargaining agreement between UAW and General Dynamics eliminated the company's obligation to provide health insurance to employees who retired after the date of the agreement, except for current workers at least fifty years old. Dennis Cline and 194 other employees, who were over forty years old but under fifty, objected to this term. They complained to the Equal Employment Opportunity Commission, claiming that the agreement violated the Age Discrimination in Employment Act (ADEA) of 1967. The ADEA forbids discriminatory preference for the "young" over the "old." Does the ADEA also prohibit favoring the old over the young? How should the court rule? Explain. [*General Dynamics Land Systems, Inc. v. Cline*, 540 U.S. 581, 124 S.Ct. 1236, 157 L.Ed.2d 1094 (2004)]

18.5 Workers' Compensation. The Touch of Class Lounge is in a suburban shopping plaza, or strip mall, in Omaha, Nebraska. Patricia Bauer, the Lounge's owner, does not own the parking lot, which is provided for the common use of all of the businesses in the plaza. Stephanie Zoucha was a bartender at the Lounge. Her duties ended when she locked the door after closing. On June 4, 2001, at 1:15 A.M., Zoucha closed the bar and locked the door. An hour later, she walked to her car in the parking lot, where she was struck with "[l]ike a tire iron on the back of my head." Zoucha sustained a skull fracture and other injuries, including significant cognitive impairment (speech and thought formation). Her purse, containing her tip money, was stolen. She identified her attacker as William Nunez, who had been in the Lounge earlier that night. Zoucha filed a petition in a Nebraska state court to obtain workers' compensa-

tion. What are the requirements for receiving workers' compensation? Should Zoucha's request be granted or denied? Why? [*Zoucha v. Touch of Class Lounge*, 269 Neb. 89, 690 N.W.2d 610 (2005)]

18.6 Case Problem with Sample Answer. Jennifer Willis worked for Coca Cola Enterprises, Inc. (CCE), in Louisiana as a senior account manager. On a Monday in May 2003, Willis called her supervisor to tell him that she was sick and would not be able to work that day. She also said that she was pregnant, but she did not say she was sick *because* of the pregnancy. On Tuesday, she called to ask where to report to work and was told that she could not return without a doctor's release. She said that she had a doctor's appointment on "Wednesday," which her supervisor understood to be the next day. Willis meant the *following* Wednesday. More than a week later, during which time Willis did not contact CCE, she was told that she had violated CCE's "No Call/No Show" policy. Under this policy "an employee absent from work for three consecutive days without notifying the supervisor during that period will be considered to have voluntarily resigned." She was fired. Willis filed a suit in a federal district court against CCE under the Family and Medical Leave Act (FMLA). To be eligible for FMLA leave, an employee must inform an employer of the reason for the leave. Did Willis meet this requirement? Did CCE's response to Willis's absence violate the FMLA? Explain. [*Willis v. Coca Cola Enterprises, Inc.*, 445 F.3d 413 (5th Cir. 2006)]

After you have answered Problem 18.6, compare your answer with the sample answer given on the Web site that accompanies this text. Go to academic.cengage.com/blaw/blt, select "Chapter 18," and click on "Case Problem with Sample Answer."

18.7 Unemployment Insurance. Mary Garas, a chemist, sought work in Missouri through Kelly Services, Inc. Kelly is a staffing agency that places individuals in jobs of varying duration with other companies. Through Kelly, Garas worked at Merial Co. from April 2005 to February 2006. After the assignment ended, Garas asked Kelly for more work. Meanwhile, she filed a claim for unemployment benefits with the Missouri Division of Employment Security (DES). In March, Kelly recruiter Rebecca Cockrum told Garas about a temporary assignment with Celsis Laboratory. Garas said that she would prefer a "more stable position," but later asked Cockrum to submit her résumé to Celsis. Before the employer responded, Kelly told the DES that Garas had refused suitable work. Under a Missouri state statute, a claim for unemployment benefits must be denied if "the claimant failed without good cause . . . to accept suitable work when offered the claimant . . . by an employer by whom the individual was formerly employed." The DES denied Garas's claim for benefits. She filed an appeal with a state court. Was the DES's denial right or wrong? Why? [*Garas v. Kelly Services, Inc.*, 211 S.W.3d 149 (Mo.App. E.D. 2007)]

18.8 Discrimination Based on Disability. Cerebral palsy limits Steven Bradley's use of his legs. He uses forearm crutches for short-distance walks and a wheelchair for longer distances. Standing for more than ten or fifteen minutes is difficult. With support, however, Bradley can climb stairs and get on and off a stool. His condition also restricts the use of his fourth finger to, for example, type, but it does not limit his ability to write—he completed two years of college. His grip strength is normal, and he can lift heavy objects. In 2001, Bradley applied for a "greeter" or "cashier" position at a Wal-Mart Stores, Inc., Supercenter in Richmond, Missouri. The job descriptions stated, "No experience or qualification is required." Bradley indicated that he was available for full- or part-time work from 4:00 P.M. to 10:00 P.M. any evening. His employment history showed that he currently worked as a proofreader and that he had previously worked as an administrator. His application was rejected, according to Janet Daugherty, the personnel manager, based on his "work history" and the "direct threat" that he posed to the safety of himself and others. Bradley claimed, however, that the store refused to hire him due to his disability. What steps must Bradley follow to pursue his claim? What does he need to show to prevail? Is he likely to meet these requirements? Discuss. [*EEOC v. Wal-Mart Stores, Inc.*, 477 F.3d 561 (8th Cir. 2007)]

18.9 **A Question of Ethics.** *Beverly Tull had worked for Atchison Leather Products, Inc., in Kansas for ten years when, in 1999, she began to complain of hand, wrist, and shoulder pain. Atchison recommended that she contact a certain physician, who in April 2000 diagnosed the condition* as carpal tunnel syndrome "severe enough" for surgery. In August, Tull filed a claim with the state workers' compensation board. Because Atchison changed workers' compensation insurance companies every year, a dispute arose as to which company should pay Tull's claim. Fearing liability, no insurer would authorize treatment, and Tull was forced to delay surgery until December. The board granted her temporary total disability benefits for the subsequent six weeks that she missed work. On April 23, 2002, Berger Co. bought Atchison. The new employer adjusted Tull's work to be less demanding and stressful, but she continued to suffer pain. In July, a physician diagnosed her condition as permanent. The board granted her permanent partial disability benefits. By May 2005, the bickering over the financial responsibility for Tull's claim involved five insurers—four of which had each covered Atchison for a single year and one of which covered Berger. [*Tull v. Atchison Leather Products, Inc.*, 37 Kan.App.2d 87, 150 P.3d 316 (2007)]

1 When an injured employee files a claim for workers' compensation, there is a proceeding to assess the injury and determine the amount of compensation. Should a dispute between insurers over the payment of the claim be resolved in the same proceeding? Why or why not?

2 The board designated April 23, 2002, as the date of Tull's injury. What is the reason for determining the date of a worker's injury? Should the board in this case have selected this date or a different date? Why?

3 How should the board assess liability for the payment of Tull's medical expenses and disability benefits? Would it be appropriate to impose joint and several liability on the insurers, or should the individual liability of each of them be determined? Explain.

CRITICAL THINKING AND WRITING ASSIGNMENTS

18.10 Critical Legal Thinking. Employees have a right to privacy, but employers also have a right to create and maintain an efficient and safe workplace. Do you think that existing laws strike an appropriate balance between employers' rights and employees' rights?

18.11 **Video Question.** Go to this text's Web site at **academic. cengage.com/blaw/blt** and select "Chapter 18." Click on "Video Questions" and view the video titled *Parenthood*. Then answer the following questions.

1 In the video, Gil (Steve Martin) threatens to leave his job when he discovers that his boss is promoting another person to partner instead of him. His boss (Dennis Dugan) laughs and tells him that the threat is not realistic because if Gil leaves, he will be competing for positions with workers who are younger than he is and willing to accept lower salaries. If Gil takes his employer's advice and stays in his current position, can he sue his boss for age discrimination based on the boss's statements? Why or why not?

2 Suppose that Gil leaves his current position and applies for a job at another firm. The prospective employer refuses to hire him based on his age. What would Gil have to prove to establish a *prima facie* case of age discrimination? Explain your answer.

3 What defenses might Gil's current employer raise if Gil sues for age discrimination?

ONLINE ACTIVITIES

 **PRACTICAL INTERNET EXERCISES**

Go to this text's Web site at **academic.cengage.com/blaw/blt**, select "Chapter 18," and click on "Practical Internet Exercises." There you will find the following Internet research exercises that you can perform to learn more about the topics covered in this chapter.

PRACTICAL INTERNET EXERCISE 18-1 LEGAL PERSPECTIVE—Workers' Compensation

PRACTICAL INTERNET EXERCISE 18-2 MANAGEMENT PERSPECTIVE—Workplace Monitoring and Surveillance

PRACTICAL INTERNET EXERCISE 18-3 LEGAL PERSPECTIVE—Americans with Disabilities

BEFORE THE TEST

Go to this text's Web site at **academic.cengage.com/blaw/blt**, select "Chapter 18," and click on "Interactive Quizzes." You will find a number of interactive questions relating to this chapter.

CHAPTER 19
The Entrepreneur's Options

CHAPTER OUTLINE

—MAJOR BUSINESS FORMS

—SPECIAL BUSINESS FORMS

—PRIVATE FRANCHISES

LEARNING OBJECTIVES

AFTER READING THIS CHAPTER, YOU SHOULD BE ABLE TO ANSWER THE FOLLOWING QUESTIONS:

1 What are some of the major forms of business organization used by entrepreneurs in the United States?

2 What advantages and disadvantages are associated with each major business form?

3 Why have limited liability companies and limited liability partnerships come into widespread use in recent years?

4 What is a joint venture? What are some other special business organizational forms, and why are they used?

5 What is a franchise, and how does a franchising relationship arise?

> "[E]veryone thirsteth after gaine."
>
> Sir Edward Coke, 1552–1634
> (English jurist and politician)

Many Americans would agree with Sir Edward Coke's comment in the chapter-opening quotation that most people, at least, "thirsteth after gaine." Certainly, an entrepreneur's primary motive for undertaking a business enterprise is to make profits. An **entrepreneur** is by definition one who initiates and assumes the financial risks of a new enterprise and undertakes to provide or control its management.

One of the questions faced by anyone who wishes to start up a business is what form of business organization should be chosen for the business endeavor. In this chapter, we first examine and compare the basic features of the several major business forms in use today. We then look at some special business forms that may be used to organize a business venture. A discussion of private franchises concludes the chapter.

ENTREPRENEUR
One who initiates and assumes the financial risk of a new business enterprise and undertakes to provide or control its management.

MAJOR BUSINESS FORMS

Traditionally, entrepreneurs have used three major forms to organize their business enterprises—the sole proprietorship; the partnership, including the limited partnership; and the corporation. In the last several years, two other business forms have come into widespread use—the limited liability company and the limited liability partnership. We examine each of these forms in this section.

Sole Proprietorships

SOLE PROPRIETORSHIP
The simplest form of business organization, in which the owner is the business. The owner reports business income on his or her personal income tax return and is legally responsible for all debts and obligations incurred by the business.

The simplest form of business organization is a **sole proprietorship.** In this form, the owner is the business; thus, anyone who does business without creating a separate business organization has a sole proprietorship. More than two-thirds of all U.S. businesses are sole proprietorships. They are usually small enterprises—about 99 percent of the sole proprietorships in the United States have revenues of less than $1 million per year. Sole proprietors can own and manage any type of business, ranging from an informal, home-office undertaking to a large restaurant or construction firm. Today, a number of online businesses that sell goods and services on a nationwide basis are organized as sole proprietorships.

Advantages of the Sole Proprietorship   A major advantage of the sole proprietorship is that the proprietor owns the entire business and has a right to receive all of the profits (because he or she assumes all of the risk). In addition, it is often easier and less costly to start a sole proprietorship than to start any other kind of business, as few legal formalities are involved.[1] One does not need to file any documents with the government to start a sole proprietorship (though a state business license may be required to operate certain businesses).

This type of business organization also entails more flexibility than does a partnership or a corporation. The sole proprietor is free to make any decision she or he wishes concerning the business—including whom to hire, when to take a vacation, and what kind of business to pursue, for example. In addition, the proprietor can sell or transfer all or part of the business to another party at any time and does not need approval from anyone else (as would be required from partners in a partnership or normally from shareholders in a corporation).

A sole proprietor pays only personal income taxes (including Social Security, or self-employment, tax) on the business's profits, which are reported as personal income on the proprietor's personal income tax return. Sole proprietors are also allowed to establish certain tax-exempt retirement accounts.

This woman creates floral arrangements. She owns the business by herself. What are the advantages of doing business as a sole proprietorship? (Salim Fadhley/ Creative Commons)

Disadvantages of the Sole Proprietorship   The major disadvantage of the sole proprietorship is that the proprietor alone bears the burden of any losses or liabilities incurred by the business enterprise. In other words, the sole proprietor has unlimited liability, or legal responsibility, for all obligations incurred in doing business. Any lawsuit against the business or its employees can lead to unlimited personal liability for the owner of a sole proprietorship. Creditors can go after the owner's personal assets to satisfy any business debts. This unlimited liability is a major factor to be considered in choosing a business form. The sole proprietorship also has the disadvantage of lacking continuity on the death of the proprietor. When the owner dies, so does the business—it is automatically dissolved. Another disadvantage is that the proprietor's opportunity to raise capital is limited to personal funds and the funds of those who are willing to make loans.

The personal liability of the owner of a sole proprietorship was at issue in the following case. The case involved the federal Cable Communications Act, which prohibits a commercial establishment from broadcasting television programs to its patrons without authorization. The court had to decide whether the owner of a sole proprietorship that installed a satellite television system was personally liable for violating this act by identifying a restaurant as a "residence" for billing purposes.

---

1. Although starting up a sole proprietorship involves relatively few legal formalities compared to other business organizational forms, even small sole proprietorships may need to comply with certain zoning requirements, obtain appropriate licenses, and the like.

CASE 19.1 Garden City Boxing Club, Inc. v. Dominguez

United States District Court, Northern District of Illinois, Eastern Division, __ F.Supp.2d __ (2006).

FACTS Garden City Boxing Club, Inc. (GCB), which is based in San Jose, California, owned the exclusive right to broadcast via closed-circuit television several prizefights, including the match between Oscar De La Hoya and Fernando Vargas on September 14, 2002. GCB sold the right to receive the broadcasts to bars and other commercial venues. The fee was $20 multiplied by an establishment's maximum fire code occupancy. Antenas Enterprises in Chicago, Illinois, sells and installs satellite television systems under a contract with DISH Network. After installing a system, Antenas sends the buyer's address and other identifying information to DISH. In January 2002, Luis Garcia, an Antenas employee, identified a new customer as José Melendez at 220 Hawthorn Commons in Vernon Hills. The address was a restaurant—Mundelein Burrito—but Garcia designated the account as residential. Mundelein's patrons watched the De La Hoya–Vargas match on September 14, as well as three other fights on other dates, for which the restaurant paid only the residential rate to DISH and nothing to GCB. GCB filed a suit in a federal district court against Luis Dominguez, the sole proprietor of Antenas, to collect the fee.

ISSUE Is Dominguez personally liable for the amount of Mundelein's fee?

DECISION Yes. The court issued a summary judgment in GCB's favor, holding that the plaintiff was entitled to the amount of the fee, plus damages and attorneys' fees.

REASON The court found that Mundelein was clearly a commercial establishment. "The structure of the building, an exterior identification sign, and its location in a strip mall made this obvious." Under the Cable Communications Act, "[a]n authorized intermediary of a communication violates the Act when it divulges communication through an electronic channel to one other than the addressee." Antenas's improper designation of Mundelein as residential allowed the unauthorized broadcast of four prizefights to the restaurant. Antenas is a sole proprietorship. A sole proprietorship has no legal identity apart from that of the individual who owns it. Furthermore, a sole proprietor is personally responsible for the acts that his or her employees commit within the scope of their employment. Dominguez owns Antenas, and Garcia is Dominguez's employee. "Accordingly, Dominguez is personally liable for the damages caused by the violation of * * * the [Cable Communications] Act."

WHAT IF THE FACTS WERE DIFFERENT? *If Mundelein had identified itself as a residence when ordering the satellite system, how might the result in this case have been different?*

Partnerships

A **partnership** arises from an agreement, express or implied, between two or more persons to carry on a business for profit. Partners are co-owners of a business and have joint control over its operation and the right to share in its profits. No particular form of partnership agreement is necessary for the creation of a general partnership, but for practical reasons, the agreement should be in writing. Basically, in a partnership agreement, called **articles of partnership,** the partners may agree to almost any terms when establishing the partnership so long as they are not illegal or contrary to public policy.

The Law Governing Partnerships The Uniform Partnership Act (UPA) governs the operation of partnerships *in the absence of express agreement* and has done much to reduce controversies in the law relating to partnerships. The UPA defines a *partnership* as "an association of two or more persons to carry on as co-owners a business for profit" [UPA 101(6)]. The *intent* to associate is a key element of a partnership, and one cannot join a partnership unless all other partners consent [UPA 401(i)].

PARTNERSHIP
An agreement by two or more persons to carry on, as co-owners, a business for profit.

ARTICLES OF PARTNERSHIP
A written agreement that sets forth each partner's rights and obligations with respect to the partnership.

Conflicts commonly arise over whether a business enterprise is legally a partnership, especially in the absence of a formal, written partnership agreement. In resolving disputes over whether partnership status exists, courts will usually look for the following three essential elements of partnership implicit in the UPA's definition of the term:

1 A sharing of profits and losses.
2 A joint ownership of the business.
3 An equal right in the management of the business.

Under the UPA, all partners have equal rights in managing the partnership [UPA 401(f)]. Each partner in an ordinary partnership has one vote in management matters *regardless of the proportional size of his or her interest in the firm.* Each partner is entitled to the proportion of business profits and losses designated in the partnership agreement. If the agreement does not apportion profits or losses, the UPA provides that *profits shall be shared equally and losses shall be shared in the same ratio as profits* [UPA 401(b)]. Each partner, however, can be held fully liable for all debts of the partnership.

Advantages and Disadvantages of Partnerships   As with a sole proprietorship, one of the advantages of a partnership is that it can be organized fairly easily and inexpensively. Additionally, the partnership form of business offers important tax advantages. The partnership itself files only an informational tax return with the Internal Revenue Service. In other words, the firm itself pays no taxes. Rather, a partner's profit from the partnership (whether distributed or not) is "passed through" and taxed as individual income to the individual partner.

A partnership may also allow for greater capital contributions to the business than is possible in a sole proprietorship. Two or more persons can invest in the business, and lenders may be more willing to make loans to a partnership than they would be to a sole proprietorship.

The main disadvantage of the partnership form of business is that the partners are subject to personal liability for partnership obligations. If the partnership cannot pay its debts, the personal assets of the partners are subject to creditors' claims. Moreover, the acts of one partner in the ordinary course of business subject the other partners to personal liability [UPA 305].

Limited Partnerships

A special form of partnership is the **limited partnership**, which consists of at least one general partner and one or more limited partners. A limited partnership is a creature of statute, because it does not come into existence until a *certificate of limited partnership* is filed with the appropriate state office. A **general partner** assumes responsibility for the management of the partnership and liability for all partnership debts. A **limited partner** has no right to participate in the general management or operation of the partnership and assumes no liability for partnership debts beyond the amount of capital that he or she has contributed. Thus, one of the major benefits of becoming a limited partner is this limitation on liability, both with respect to lawsuits brought against the partnership and the amount of funds placed at risk.

LIMITED PARTNERSHIP
A partnership consisting of one or more general partners (who manage the business and are liable to the full extent of their personal assets for debts of the partnership) and one or more limited partners (who contribute only assets and are liable only up to the amount contributed by them).

GENERAL PARTNER
In a limited partnership, a partner who assumes responsibility for the management of the partnership and liability for all partnership debts.

LIMITED PARTNER
In a limited partnership, a partner who contributes capital to the partnership but has no right to participate in the management and operation of the business. The limited partner assumes no liability for partnership debts beyond the capital contributed.

Should a limited partner be able to sue a third party whose negligence caused the partnership to fail?   Limited partners in a limited partnership have a number of rights, yet these rights are limited. For example, if a third party with whom a limited partnership has contracted causes the limited partnership to fail, a limited partner may not sue that third party. Generally, the limited partnership itself must bring the suit—the limited partners have no standing to sue for losses that result in the failure of the enterprise. For example, in one case a limited partner invested $16 million in BCH Energy, L.P., in reliance on BCH's representations that it would build and manage plants that convert waste products into energy. BCH hired Metric Constructors to construct an energy-generating project. Serious problems caused the project to lose all funds invested. The limited partner sued Metric Constructors, contending that Metric was negligent in its construction. The court, however, held that the limited partner did not have standing to sue the contractor (Metric). The court held that any complaint brought against the contractor had to be brought by the partnership, not by its limited partner or partners.[2] While this ruling may seem unfair to the limited partner, it is consistent with the principle that limited partners should not have a say in the management of limited partnerships.

Corporations

A third and widely used type of business organizational form is the **corporation.** The corporation, like the limited partnership, is a creature of statute. The corporation's existence as a legal entity, which can be perpetual, depends generally on state law.

Corporations are owned by *shareholders*—those who have purchased ownership shares in the business. A *board of directors*, elected by the shareholders, manages the business. The board of directors normally employs *officers* to oversee day-to-day operations.

One of the key advantages of the corporate form of business is that the liability of its owners (shareholders) is limited to their investments. The shareholders usually are not personally liable for the obligations of the corporation. A disadvantage of the corporate form is that profits are taxed twice (double taxation). First, the corporation as an entity pays income taxes on corporate profits, and second, the shareholders pay income taxes on those profits that are distributed to them. (The corporate business form will be discussed in detail in Chapter 20.)

Limited Liability Companies

Traditionally, the two most common forms of business organization selected by two or more persons entering into business together were the partnership and the corporation. For many entrepreneurs and investors, the ideal business form would combine the tax advantages of the partnership form of business with the limited liability of the corporate enterprise. A relatively new form of business organization, the **limited liability company (LLC),** is a hybrid form of business enterprise that meets these needs by offering the limited liability of the corporation and the tax advantages of a partnership. Increasingly, LLCs are becoming an organizational form of choice among businesspersons, a trend encouraged by state statutes permitting their use. The origins and evolution of the LLC are discussed in this chapter's *Landmark in the Law* feature on the next page.

Like corporations, LLCs must be formed and operated in compliance with state statutes. Statutes governing LLCs vary, of course, from state to state. In an attempt to create more uniformity among the states in this respect, in 1995 the National Conference of Commissioners on Uniform State Laws issued the Uniform Limited Liability Company Act (ULLCA). To date, less than one-fifth of the states have adopted the ULLCA, and thus the law governing LLCs remains far from uniform.

Operating an LLC   Some provisions are common to most state statutes, however. For example, in an LLC the owners (who are called *members*) themselves can normally decide how to operate the various aspects of the business by forming an **operating agreement.**

CORPORATION
A legal entity formed in compliance with statutory requirements. The entity is distinct from its shareholder-owners.

LIMITED LIABILITY COMPANY (LLC)
A hybrid form of business enterprise that offers the limited liability of the corporation but the tax advantages of a partnership.

OPERATING AGREEMENT
In a limited liability company, an agreement in which the members set forth the details of how the business will be managed and operated. State statutes typically give the members wide latitude in deciding for themselves the rules that will govern their organization.

---

2. *Energy Investors Fund, L.P. v. Metric Constructors, Inc.,* 351 N.C. 331, 525 S.E.2d 441 (2000).

LANDMARK IN THE LAW · Limited Liability Company (LLC) Statutes

In 1977, Wyoming became the first state to pass legislation authorizing the creation of a limited liability company (LLC). Although LLCs emerged in the United States only in 1977, they have been used for more than a century in other areas, including several European and South American nations.

Taxation of LLCs   In the United States, after Wyoming's adoption of an LLC statute, it still was not known how the Internal Revenue Service (IRS) would treat the LLC for tax purposes. In 1988, however, the IRS ruled that Wyoming LLCs would be taxed as partnerships instead of as corporations, providing that certain requirements were met. Prior to this ruling, only one other state—Florida, in 1982—had authorized LLCs. The 1988 IRS ruling encouraged other states to enact LLC statutes, and in less than a decade, all states had done so.

IRS rules that went into effect on January 1, 1997, also encouraged more widespread use of LLCs in the business world. Under these rules, any unincorporated business is automatically taxed as a partnership unless it indicates otherwise on the tax form. The exceptions involve publicly traded companies, companies formed under a state incorporation statute, and certain foreign-owned companies. If a business prefers to be taxed as a corporation, it can check a box on the IRS form to indicate this choice.

Foreign Entities May Be LLC Members   Part of the impetus behind the creation of LLCs in this country is that foreign investors are allowed to become LLC members. Generally, in an era increasingly characterized by global business efforts and investments, the LLC offers U.S. firms and potential investors from other countries greater flexibility and opportunities than are available through partnerships or corporations.

APPLICATION TO TODAY'S WORLD   *Once it became clear that LLCs could be taxed as partnerships, the LLC form of business organization was widely adopted. Members could avoid the personal liability associated with the partnership form of business as well as the double taxation of the corporate form of business. Today, LLCs, which were virtually unheard of twenty years ago, are a widely used form of business organization.*

RELEVANT WEB SITES   *To locate information on the Web concerning limited liability company statutes, go to this text's Web site at* academic.cengage.com/blaw/blt, *select "Chapter 19," and click on "URLs for Landmarks."*

Operating agreements typically contain provisions relating to management, how profits will be divided, the transfer of membership interests, whether the LLC will be dissolved on the death or departure of a member, and other important issues.

As with any business arrangement, disputes may arise over any number of issues. If there is no agreement covering the topic under dispute, such as how profits will be divided, the state LLC statute will govern the outcome. For example, most LLC statutes provide that if the members have not specified how profits will be divided, they will be divided equally among the members. Generally, when an issue is not covered by an operating agreement or by an LLC statute, the principles of partnership law are applied.

Advantages of the LLC   A key advantage of the LLC is that the liability of members is limited to the amount of their investments. Another advantage is the flexibility of the LLC in regard to both taxation and management.

An LLC that has *two or more members* can choose to be taxed either as a partnership or as a corporation. As mentioned earlier, a corporate entity must pay income taxes on its profits, and the shareholders pay personal income taxes on profits distributed as dividends. An LLC that wants to distribute profits to the members may prefer to be taxed as a partnership to avoid the double-taxation characteristic of the corporate entity. Unless an LLC indicates that it wishes to be taxed as a corporation, the IRS automatically taxes it as a partnership. This means that the LLC as an entity pays no taxes; rather, as in a partnership, profits are "passed through" the LLC to the members who then personally pay taxes on the profits. If an LLC's members want to reinvest the profits in the business, however, rather than distribute the profits to members, they may prefer that the LLC be taxed as a corporation. Corporate income tax rates may be lower than personal tax rates. Part of the attractiveness of the LLC is this flexibility with respect to taxation.

For federal income tax purposes, one-member LLCs are automatically taxed as sole proprietorships unless they indicate that they wish to be taxed as corporations. With respect to state taxes, most states follow the IRS rules. Still another advantage of the LLC for businesspersons is the flexibility it offers in terms of business operations and management. Finally, because foreign investors can participate in an LLC, the LLC form of business is attractive as a way to encourage investment.

Disadvantages of the LLC   The disadvantages of the LLC are relatively few. Although initially there was uncertainty over how LLCs would be taxed, that disadvantage no longer exists. One remaining disadvantage is that state LLC statutes are not yet uniform. Until all of the states have adopted the ULLCA, an LLC in one state will have to check the rules in the other states in which the firm does business to ensure that it retains its limited liability. Generally, though, most—if not all—states apply to a foreign LLC (an LLC formed in another state) the law of the state where the LLC was formed.

Still another disadvantage is the lack of case law dealing with LLCs. How the courts interpret statutes provides important guidelines for businesses. Given the relative newness of the LLC as a business form in the United States, there is not, as yet, a substantial body of case law to provide this kind of guidance.

Stan Ovshinsky, founder of Ovonic Hydrogen Systems, LLC, a developer of alternative energy technologies. What are some of the advantages of doing business as an LLC instead of a corporation? Are there any disadvantages? (Photo Courtesy of ECD Ovonics)

REMEMBER   A uniform law is a "model" law. It does not become the law of any state until the state legislature adopts it, either in part or in its entirety.

Limited Liability Partnerships

The **limited liability partnership (LLP)** is similar to the LLC but is designed more for professionals who normally do business as partners in a partnership. The major advantage of the LLP is that it allows a partnership to continue as a *pass-through entity* for tax purposes but limits the personal liability of the partners. For this reason, the LLP has become a widely preferred business organizational form for those who have traditionally conducted their business as a general partnership.

In 1991, Texas became the first state to enact an LLP statute. Other states quickly followed suit, and by 1997, virtually all of the states had enacted LLP statutes. LLPs must also be formed and operated in compliance with state statutes. In most states, it is relatively easy to convert a traditional partnership into an LLP because the firm's basic organizational structure remains the same. Additionally, all of the statutory and common law rules governing partnerships still apply (apart from those modified by the LLP statute). Normally, an LLP statute is simply an amendment to a state's already existing partnership law.

The LLP allows professionals to avoid personal liability for the malpractice of other partners. Remember that a major disadvantage of the partnership is the unlimited personal

LIMITED LIABILITY PARTNERSHIP (LLP)
A business organizational form that is similar to the LLC but that is designed more for professionals who normally do business as partners in a partnership. The LLP is a pass-through entity for tax purposes, like the general partnership, but it limits the personal liability of the partners.

ON THE WEB

For an example of a state law (that of Iowa) governing limited liability partnerships, go to

www.sos.state.ia.us/business/limliabpart.html.

liability of its partners. **▪EXAMPLE 19.1** A group of five attorneys is operating as a partnership. One of the attorneys, Dan Kolcher, is sued for malpractice and loses. If the firm was organized as a general partnership and the firm did not have sufficient malpractice insurance to pay the judgment, the personal assets of other attorneys could be used to satisfy the obligation. Because the firm is organized as a limited liability partnership, however, no other partner at the law firm can be held *personally* liable for Kolcher's malpractice, unless she or he acted as Kolcher's supervisor. In the absence of a supervisor, only Kolcher's personal assets could be used to satisfy the judgment (to the extent that the judgment exceeds the liability insurance coverage.) ▪

Although LLP statutes vary from state to state, generally each state statute limits the liability of partners in some way. For example, Delaware law protects each innocent partner from the "debts and obligations of the partnership arising from negligence, wrongful acts, or misconduct." In North Carolina, Texas, and Washington, D.C., the statutes protect innocent partners from obligations arising from "errors, omissions, negligence, incompetence, or malfeasance." Although the language of these statutes may seem to apply specifically to attorneys, virtually any group of professionals can use the LLP.

Major Business Forms Compared

When deciding which form of business organization would be most appropriate, businesspersons normally consider several factors, including ease of creation, the liability of the owners, tax considerations, and the need for capital. Each major form of business organization offers distinct advantages and disadvantages with respect to these and other factors. Exhibit 19–1 on pages 594 and 595 summarizes the essential advantages and disadvantages of each of the forms of business organization discussed in this chapter.

SPECIAL BUSINESS FORMS

Besides the business forms discussed previously, there are several other forms that can be used to organize a business. For the most part, these other business forms are hybrid organizations—that is, they have characteristics similar to those of partnerships or corporations or combine features of both. These forms include joint ventures, syndicates, joint stock companies, business trusts, and cooperatives.

Joint Ventures

JOINT VENTURE
A joint undertaking of a specific commercial enterprise by an association of persons. A joint venture is normally not a legal entity and is treated like a partnership for federal income tax purposes.

CONTRAST A partnership involves a continuing relationship of the partners. A joint venture is essentially a one-time association.

A **joint venture** is an enterprise in which two or more persons or business entities combine their efforts or their property for a single transaction or project, or a related series of transactions or projects. **▪EXAMPLE 19.2** When several contractors combine their resources to build and sell houses in a single development, their relationship is a joint venture. The joint venture is treated much like a partnership, but it differs in that it is created in contemplation of a limited activity or a single transaction. ▪ Joint ventures are taxed like partnerships, and, unless otherwise agreed, joint venturers share profits and losses equally.

Members of a joint venture usually have limited powers to bind their co-venturers. A joint venture is normally not a legal entity and therefore cannot be sued as such, but its members can be sued individually. Joint ventures range in size from very small activities to huge, multimillion-dollar joint actions engaged in by some of the world's largest corporations.

Syndicates

SYNDICATE
An investment group of persons or firms brought together for the purpose of financing a project that they would not or could not undertake independently.

A group of individuals getting together to finance a particular project, such as the building of a shopping center or the purchase of a professional basketball franchise, is called a **syndicate** or an *investment group*. The form of such groups varies considerably. A syndicate may exist as a corporation or as a general or limited partnership. In some cases, the members merely purchase and own property jointly but have no legally recognized business arrangement.

Joint Stock Companies

A **joint stock company** is a true hybrid of a partnership and a corporation. It has many characteristics of a corporation in that (1) its ownership is represented by transferable shares of stock, (2) it is usually managed by directors and officers of the company or association, and (3) it can have a perpetual existence. Most of its other features, however, are more characteristic of a partnership, and it is usually treated like a partnership. As with a partnership, it is formed by agreement (not statute), property is usually held in the names of the members, shareholders have personal liability, and generally the company is not treated as a legal entity for purposes of a lawsuit.

JOINT STOCK COMPANY
A hybrid form of business organization that combines characteristics of a corporation and a partnership. Usually, the joint stock company is regarded as a partnership for tax and other legally related purposes.

Business Trusts

A **business trust** is created by a written trust agreement that sets forth the interests of the beneficiaries and the obligations and powers of the trustees. With a business trust, legal ownership and management of the property of the business stay with one or more of the trustees, and the profits are distributed to the beneficiaries.

The business trust was started in Massachusetts in an attempt to obtain the limited liability advantage of corporate status while avoiding certain restrictions on a corporation's ownership and development of real property. The business trust resembles a corporation in many respects. Beneficiaries of the trust, for example, are not personally responsible for the debts or obligations of the business trust. In fact, in a number of states, business trusts must pay corporate taxes.

BUSINESS TRUST
A form of business organization in which investors (trust beneficiaries) transfer cash or property to trustees in exchange for trust certificates that represent their investment shares. The certificate holders share in the trust's profits but have limited liability.

Cooperatives

A **cooperative** is an association that is organized to provide an economic service to its members (or shareholders); it may or may not be incorporated. Most cooperatives are organized under state statutes for cooperatives, general business corporations, or LLCs. Generally, an incorporated cooperative will distribute dividends, or profits, to its owners on the basis of their transactions with the cooperative rather than on the basis of the amount of capital they contributed. Members of incorporated cooperatives have limited liability, as do shareholders of corporations or members of LLCs. Cooperatives that are unincorporated are often treated like partnerships. The members have joint liability for the cooperative's acts.

This form of business is generally adopted by groups of individuals who wish to pool their resources to gain some advantage in the marketplace. Consumer purchasing co-ops are formed to obtain lower prices through quantity discounts. Seller marketing co-ops are formed to control the market and thereby obtain higher sales prices from consumers. Co-ops range in size from small, local, consumer cooperatives to national businesses such as Ace Hardware and Land O' Lakes, the well-known producer of dairy products.

COOPERATIVE
An association, which may or may not be incorporated, that is organized to provide an economic service to its members.

PRIVATE FRANCHISES

Instead of setting up a business form through which to market their own products or services, many entrepreneurs opt to purchase a franchise. A **franchise** is defined as any arrangement in which the owner of a trademark, a trade name, or a copyright licenses others to use the trademark, trade name, or copyright in the selling of goods or services. A

FRANCHISE
Any arrangement in which the owner of a trademark, trade name, or copyright licenses another to use that trademark, trade name, or copyright in the selling of goods or services.

EXHIBIT 19–1 Major Forms of Business Compared

CHARACTERISTIC	SOLE PROPRIETORSHIP	PARTNERSHIP	CORPORATION
Method of creation	Created at will by owner.	Created by agreement of the parties.	Authorized by the state under the state's corporation law.
Legal position	Not a separate entity; owner is the business.	Is a separate legal entity in most states.	Always a legal entity separate and distinct from its owners—a legal fiction for the purposes of owning property and being a party to litigation.
Liability	Unlimited liability.	Unlimited liability.	Limited liability of shareholders—shareholders are not liable for the debts of the corporation.
Duration	Determined by owner; automatically dissolved on owner's death.	Terminated by agreement of the partners, but can continue to do business even when a partner dissociates from the partnership.	Can have perpetual existence.
Transferability of interest	Interest can be transferred, but individual's proprietorship then ends.	Although partnership interest can be assigned, assignee does not have full rights of a partner.	Shares of stock can be transferred.
Management	Completely at owner's discretion.	Each general partner has a direct and equal voice in management unless expressly agreed otherwise in the partnership agreement.	Shareholders elect directors, who set policy and appoint officers.
Taxation	Owner pays personal taxes on business income.	Each partner pays pro rata share of income taxes on net profits, whether or not they are distributed.	Double taxation—corporation pays income tax on net profits, with no deduction for dividends, and shareholders pay income tax on disbursed dividends they receive.
Organizational fees, annual license fees, and annual reports	None or minimal.	None or minimal.	All required.
Transaction of business in other states	Generally no limitation.	Generally no limitation.[a]	Normally must qualify to do business and obtain certificate of authority.

a. A few states have enacted statutes requiring that foreign partnerships qualify to do business there.

EXHIBIT 19-1 Major Forms of Business Compared—Continued

CHARACTERISTIC	LIMITED PARTNERSHIP	LIMITED LIABILITY COMPANY	LIMITED LIABILITY PARTNERSHIP
Method of creation	Created by agreement to carry on a business for a profit. At least one party must be a general partner and the other(s) limited partner(s). Certificate of limited partnership is filed. Charter must be issued by the state.	Created by an agreement of the member-owners of the company. Articles of organization are filed. Charter must be issued by the state.	Created by agreement of the partners. A statement of qualification for the limited liability partnership is filed.
Legal position	Treated as a legal entity.	Treated as a legal entity.	Generally, treated same as a general partnership.
Liability	Unlimited liability of all general partners; limited partners are liable only to the extent of capital contributions.	Member-owners' liability is limited to the amount of capital contributions or investments.	Varies, but under the Uniform Partnership Act, liability of a partner for acts committed by other partners is limited.
Duration	By agreement in certificate, or by termination of the last general partner (retirement, death, and the like) or last limited partner.	Unless a single-member LLC, can have perpetual existence (same as a corporation).	Remains in existence until cancellation or revocation.
Transferability of interest	Interest can be assigned (same as general partnership), but if assignee becomes a member with consent of other partners, certificate must be amended.	Member interests are freely transferable.	Interest can be assigned same as in a general partnership.
Management	General partners have equal voice or by agreement. Limited partners may not retain limited liability if they actively participate in management.	Member-owners can fully participate in management, or management is selected by member-owners who manage on behalf of the members.	Same as a general partnership.
Taxation	Generally taxed as a partnership.	LLC is not taxed, and members are taxed personally on profits "passed through" the LLC.	Same as a general partnership.
Organizational fees, annual license fees, and annual reports	Organizational fee required; usually not others.	Organizational fee required; others vary with states.	Fees are set by each state for filing statements of qualification, foreign qualification, and annual reports.
Transaction of business in other states	Generally no limitations.	Generally no limitation, but may vary depending on state.	Must file a statement of foreign qualification before doing business in another state.

FRANCHISEE
One receiving a license to use another's (the franchisor's) trademark, trade name, or copyright in the sale of goods and services.

FRANCHISOR
One licensing another (the franchisee) to use the owner's trademark, trade name, or copyright in the selling of goods or services.

KEEP IN MIND Because a franchise involves the licensing of a trademark, a trade name, or a copyright, the law governing intellectual property may apply in some cases.

franchisee (a purchaser of a franchise) is generally legally independent of the **franchisor** (the seller of the franchise). At the same time, the franchisee is economically dependent on the franchisor's integrated business system. In other words, a franchisee can operate as an independent businessperson but still obtain the advantages of a regional or national organization.

Today, it is estimated that franchising companies and their franchisees account for a significant portion of all retail sales in this country. Well-known franchises include McDonald's, 7-Eleven, and Burger King. Franchising has also become a popular way for businesses to expand their operations internationally, as discussed in this chapter's *Beyond Our Borders* feature.

Types of Franchises

Because the franchising industry is so extensive and so many different types of businesses sell franchises, it is difficult to summarize the many types of franchises that now exist. Generally, though, the majority of franchises fall into one of three classifications: distributorships, chain-style business operations, or manufacturing or processing-plant arrangements. We briefly describe these types of franchises here.

Distributorship   A *distributorship* arises when a manufacturing concern (franchisor) licenses a dealer (franchisee) to sell its product. Often, a distributorship covers an exclusive territory. An example of this type of franchise is an automobile dealership or beer distributorship. **■EXAMPLE 19.3** Anheuser-Busch distributes its brands of beer through a network of authorized wholesale distributors, each with an assigned territory. Marik signs a distributorship contract for the area from Gainesville to Ocala, Florida. If the contract states that Marik is the exclusive distributor in that area, then no other franchisee may distribute Anheuser-Busch beer in that region. ■

Chain-Style Business Operation   In a *chain-style business operation*, a franchise operates under a franchisor's trade name and is identified as a member of a select group of dealers that engage in the franchisor's business. The franchisee is generally required to follow standardized or prescribed methods of operation. Often, the franchisor requires that the franchisee maintain certain standards of operation. In addition, sometimes the franchisee is obligated to obtain materials and supplies exclusively from the franchisor. Examples of this type of franchise are McDonald's and most other fast-food chains. Chain-style franchises are also common in service-related businesses, including real estate brokerage firms, such as Century 21, and tax-preparing services, such as H&R Block, Inc.

Manufacturing or Processing-Plant Arrangement   In a *manufacturing or processing-plant arrangement*, the franchisor transmits to the franchisee the essential ingredients or formula to make a particular product. The franchisee then markets the product either at wholesale or at retail in accordance with the franchisor's standards. Examples of this type of franchise are Coca-Cola and other soft-drink bottling companies.

The Franchise Contract

The franchise relationship is defined by a contract between the franchisor and the franchisee. The franchise contract specifies the terms and conditions of the franchise and spells out the rights and duties of the franchisor and the franchisee. If either party fails to perform the contractual duties, that party may be subject to a lawsuit for breach of contract. Generally, statutes and case law governing franchising tend to emphasize the importance of good faith and fair dealing in franchise relationships.

ON THE WEB

A good source for information on the purchase and sale of franchises is Franchising.org, which is online at **www.franchising.org**.

BEYOND OUR BORDERS Franchising in Foreign Nations

In the last twenty years, many U.S. companies (particularly fast-food chains and coffeehouses) have successfully expanded through franchising in nations around the globe. Franchises offer businesses a way to expand internationally without violating the legal restrictions that many nations impose on foreign ownership of businesses. Although Canada has been the most popular location for franchises in the past, during the last few years, franchisors have expanded their target locations to Asia, South America, Central America, and Mexico.

Businesspersons must exercise caution when entering international franchise relationships—perhaps even more so than when entering other types of international contracts. Differences in language, culture, laws, and business practices can seriously complicate the franchising relationship. If a U.S. franchisor has quality control standards that do not mesh with local business practices, for example, how can the franchisor maintain the quality of its product and protect its good reputation? If the law in China, for example, does not provide for the same level of intellectual property protection, how can a U.S. franchisor protect its trademark rights or prevent its "secret recipe or formula" from being copied?

Because of the complexities of international franchising, successful franchisors recommend that a company seeking to franchise overseas conduct thorough research to determine whether its particular type of business will be well received in that location. It is important to know the political and cultural climate of the target country, as well as the economic trends. Marketing surveys to assess the potential success of the franchise location are crucial in international markets. Also, because complying with U.S. disclosure laws may not satisfy the legal requirements of other nations, most successful franchisors retain counsel knowledgeable in the laws of the target location. Competent counsel can draft dispute-settlement provisions (such as an arbitration clause) for international franchising contracts and advise the parties about the tax implications of operating a foreign franchise (such as import taxes and customs duties).

 FOR CRITICAL ANALYSIS *Should a U.S.-based franchisor be allowed to impose different contract terms and quality control standards on franchisees in foreign nations than it does on domestic franchisees? Why or why not?*

Because each type of franchise relationship has its own characteristics, it is difficult to describe the broad range of details a franchising contract may include. In the remaining pages of this chapter, we look at some of the major issues that typically are addressed in a franchise contract. The *Application* feature at the end of this chapter further describes some steps a franchisee can take to avoid problems common in franchise agreements.

Payment for the Franchise The franchisee ordinarily pays an initial fee or lump-sum price for the franchise license (the privilege of being granted a franchise). This fee is separate from the various products that the franchisee purchases from or through the franchisor. In some industries, the franchisor relies heavily on the initial sale of the franchise for realizing a profit. In other industries, the continued dealing between the parties brings profit to both. In most situations, the franchisor will receive a stated percentage of the annual sales

Franchises can extend to foreign countries, even for very American brands such as Disney. In 2006, the RJ Corporation of India signed a franchise agreement with Disney Consumer Products. What do you think some of the elements of that agreement were? (AP Photo/ Saurabh Das)

or annual volume of business done by the franchisee. The franchise agreement may also require the franchisee to pay a percentage of advertising costs and certain administrative expenses.

Business Premises The franchise agreement may specify whether the premises for the business must be leased or purchased outright. In some cases, a building must be constructed or remodeled to meet the terms of the agreement. The agreement usually will specify whether the franchisor supplies equipment and furnishings for the premises or whether this is the responsibility of the franchisee.

Location of the Franchise Typically, the franchisor will determine the territory to be served. Some franchise contracts give the franchisee exclusive rights, or "territorial rights," to a certain geographic area. Other franchise contracts, though they define the territory allotted to a particular franchise, either specifically state that the franchise is nonexclusive or are silent on the issue of territorial rights.

Many franchise cases involve disputes over territorial rights, and the implied covenant of good faith and fair dealing often comes into play in this area of franchising. For example, suppose that the franchise contract either does not give a franchisee exclusive territorial rights or is silent on the issue. If the franchisor allows a competing franchise to be established nearby, the franchisee may suffer a significant loss in profits. In this situation, a court may hold that the franchisor's actions breached an implied covenant of good faith and fair dealing.

Business Organization of the Franchisee The business organization of the franchisee is of great concern to the franchisor. Depending on the terms of the franchise agreement, the franchisor may specify particular requirements for the form and capital structure of the business. The franchise agreement may also require that the franchisee adhere to certain standards of operation in such aspects of the business as sales quotas, quality, and record keeping. Furthermore, a franchisor may wish to retain stringent control over the training of personnel involved in the operation and over administrative aspects of the business.

Quality Control by the Franchisor Although the day-to-day operation of the franchise business is normally left to the franchisee, the franchise agreement may provide for the amount of supervision and control agreed on by the parties. When the franchisee prepares a product, such as food, or provides a service, such as a motel, the contract often provides that the franchisor will establish certain standards for the facility. Typically, the contract will state that the franchisor is permitted to make periodic inspections to ensure that the standards are being maintained so as to protect the franchise's name and reputation.

RECALL Under the doctrine of *respondeat superior* (see Chapter 17), an employer may be liable for the torts of employees if they occur within the scope of employment, without regard to the personal fault of the employer.

As a general rule, the validity of a provision permitting the franchisor to establish and enforce certain quality standards is unquestioned. Because the franchisor has a legitimate interest in maintaining the quality of the product or service to protect its name and reputation, it can exercise greater control in this area than would otherwise be tolerated. Increasingly, however, franchisors are finding that if they exercise too much control over the operations of their franchisees, they may incur vicarious (indirect) liability under agency theory for the acts of their franchisees' employees. The actual exercise of control, or at least the right to control, is the key consideration. If the franchisee controls the day-to-day operations of the business to a significant degree, the franchisor may be able to avoid liability, as the following case illustrates.

CASE 19.2 Kerl v. Dennis Rasmussen, Inc.

Wisconsin Supreme Court, 273 Wis.2d 106, 682 N.W.2d 328 (2004).

FACTS Arby's, Inc., is a national franchisor of fast-food restaurants. Dennis Rasmussen, Inc. (DRI), is an Arby's franchisee. Under the terms of their franchise contract, DRI agreed to follow Arby's specifications for several aspects of operating the business. DRI hired Cathy Propp as manager for its Arby's restaurant in 1994. In early 1999, Propp hired Harvey Pierce, a local county jail inmate with work-release privileges after a conviction for sexual assault. On June 11, Pierce left his shift at the restaurant without permission, walked half a mile to a discount store parking lot, and shot his former girlfriend Robin Kerl, her fiancé David Jones, and himself. Pierce and Jones died. Kerl survived but is permanently disabled. Kerl and others filed a suit in a Wisconsin state court against DRI and Arby's, claiming, among other things, that Arby's was vicariously liable (see Chapter 17) for DRI's allegedly negligent hiring and supervision of Pierce. Arby's filed a motion for summary judgment, which the court granted. A state intermediate appellate court affirmed this judgment. The plaintiffs appealed to the Wisconsin Supreme Court.

ISSUE Was Arby's vicariously liable for DRI's actions?

DECISION No. The Wisconsin Supreme Court affirmed the lower court's decision, holding that Arby's was not vicariously liable for DRI's actions. Arby's had neither a right of control nor actual control over DRI's allegedly negligent actions.

REASON The state supreme court pointed out that "[v]icarious liability under the doctrine of *respondeat superior* depends upon the existence of a master/servant agency relationship," but "the license agreement between Arby's and DRI contains a provision that disclaims any agency relationship." Further, the "plethora of general controls on the operation of DRI's restaurant" in the parties' franchise contract "are consistent with the quality and operational standards commonly contained in franchise agreements to achieve product and marketing uniformity and to protect the franchisor's trademark. They are insufficient to establish a master/servant relationship. More particularly, they do not establish that Arby's controlled or had the right to control DRI's hiring and supervision of employees." And "a franchisor may be subject to vicarious liability for the tortious conduct of its franchisee only if the franchisor had control or a right of control over the daily operation of the specific aspect of the franchisee's business that is alleged to have caused the harm."

WHY IS THIS CASE IMPORTANT TO BUSINESSPERSONS? *This case addresses an important issue for franchisors—vicarious (indirect) liability for franchisees' actions. Many franchisors understandably want to exercise enough control over the franchisee to protect the identity and reputation of the franchise. Yet the more control a franchisor exercises, the more likely it is that a court will hold the franchisor liable for any injuries sustained at the franchise or as a result of the franchisee's conduct.*

Pricing Arrangements Franchises provide the franchisor with an outlet for the firm's goods and services. Depending on the nature of the business, the franchisor may require the franchisee to purchase certain supplies from the franchisor at an established price.[3] A franchisor cannot, however, set the prices at which the franchisee will resell the goods because such price setting may be a violation of state or federal antitrust laws, or both. A franchisor can suggest retail prices but cannot mandate them.

Termination of the Franchise The duration of the franchise is a matter to be determined between the parties. Sometimes, a franchise will start out for a short period, such as a year,

---

3. Although a franchisor can require franchisees to purchase supplies from it, requiring a franchisee to purchase exclusively from the franchisor may violate federal antitrust laws (see Chapter 22). For two landmark cases in this area, see *United States v. Arnold, Schwinn & Co.*, 388 U.S. 365, 87 S.Ct. 1856, 18 L.Ed.2d 1249 (1967); and *Fortner Enterprises, Inc. v. U.S. Steel Corp.*, 394 U.S. 495, 89 S.Ct. 1252, 22 L.Ed.2d 495 (1969).

so that the franchisor can determine whether it wants to stay in business with the franchisee. Other times, the duration of the franchise contract correlates with the term of the lease for the business premises and both are renewable at the end of that period. Usually, the franchise agreement will specify that termination must be "for cause," such as death or disability of the franchisee, insolvency of the franchisee, breach of the franchise agreement, or failure to meet specified sales quotas. Most franchise contracts provide that notice of termination must be given. If no set time for termination is specified, then a reasonable time, with notice, will be implied. A franchisee must be given reasonable time to wind up the business—that is, to do the accounting and return the copyright or trademark or any other property of the franchisor.

Wrongful Termination. Because a franchisor's termination of a franchise often has adverse consequences for the franchisee, much franchise litigation involves claims of wrongful termination. Generally, the termination provisions of contracts are more favorable to the franchisor. This means that the franchisee, who normally invests a substantial amount of time and funds to make the franchise operation successful, may receive little or nothing for the business on termination. The franchisor owns the trademark and hence the business.

It is in this area that statutory and case law become important. Federal and state laws protect franchisees from the arbitrary or unfair termination of their franchises by the franchisors. Generally, both statutory and case law emphasize the importance of good faith and fair dealing in terminating a franchise relationship.

PREVENTING LEGAL DISPUTES

To avoid potential disputes regarding franchise termination, a prospective franchisee should always do preliminary research on a franchisor before agreeing to enter into a franchise contract. Find out whether the franchisor has terminated franchises in the past, how many times, and for what reasons. Contact five to ten franchisees of the same franchisor and ask questions about their relationships and any problems. Learning whether the franchisor has been honest, reliable, and reasonable with its franchisees in the past can be invaluable in preventing disputes over termination and bad faith actions of a franchisor.

◼

The Importance of Good Faith and Fair Dealing. In determining whether a franchisor has acted in good faith when terminating a franchise agreement, the courts generally try to balance the rights of both parties. If a court perceives that a franchisor has arbitrarily or unfairly terminated a franchise, the franchisee will be provided with a remedy for wrongful termination. If a franchisor's decision to terminate a franchise was made in the normal course of the franchisor's business operations, however, and reasonable notice of termination was given to the franchisee, generally a court will not consider the termination wrongful.

At issue in the following case was whether General Motors Corporation acted wrongfully in terminating its franchise with a motor vehicle dealer in Connecticut.

CASE 19.3 | **Chic Miller's Chevrolet, Inc. v. General Motors Corp.**

United States District Court, District of Connecticut, 352 F.Supp.2d 251 (2005).

FACTS Chapin Miller began work as a mail clerk with General Motors Acceptance Corporation (GMAC). By 1967, Miller had succeeded sufficiently within the organization to

CASE 19.3–Continued

acquire Chic Miller's Chevrolet, a General Motors Corporation (GM) dealership, in Bristol, Connecticut. As part of its operations, Chic Miller's entered into lending agreements, commonly known as floor plan financing, to enable it to buy new vehicles from GM. At first, the dealership had floor plan financing through GMAC. In 2001, however, Miller believed that GMAC was charging interest "at an inappropriately high rate" and negotiated a lower rate from Chase Manhattan Bank. In November 2002, Chase declined to provide further financing. Unable to obtain a loan from any other lender, Chic Miller's contacted GMAC, which also refused to make a deal. Under the parties' "Dealer Sales and Service Agreement," GM could terminate a dealership for "Failure of Dealer to maintain the line of credit." GM sent several notices of termination, but Chic Miller's remained open until March 2003, when it closed for seven days. GM sent a final termination notice. Chic Miller's filed a suit in a federal district court against GM, alleging, among other things, a failure to act in good faith in terminating the franchise. GM filed a motion for summary judgment.

ISSUE Did GM act wrongfully in terminating its franchise with Chic Miller's?

DECISION No. The court granted GM's motion for summary judgment. GM acted in good faith, with good cause

under the applicable state statute, in terminating Chic Miller's franchise.

REASON The court stated that to terminate a franchise under the Connecticut Franchise Act, "a franchisor must: provide notice that complies with statutory requirements; have 'good cause' for the termination; and act 'in good faith.'" The court explained that there is "good cause" under the statute "if there is a failure by the dealer to comply with a provision of the franchise which is both reasonable and of material significance to the franchise relationship." In this case, the dealer failed to maintain floor plan financing, a material requirement under the franchise agreement. "[W]ithout floor plan financing, a dealership is unable to purchase motor vehicle inventory, which, in turn, severely limits a dealership's ability to earn income from vehicle sales." The dealership "will eventually lose its ability to generate revenues and become financially insolvent, and will not be able to conduct customary sales and service operations." Here, the dealer also failed to conduct sales and service operations for seven consecutive business days, another material requirement under the parties' contract.

 WHAT IF THE FACTS WERE DIFFERENT? *Suppose that in March 2003, Chic Miller's had placed one newspaper ad promoting its services and had sold one car. Would the result have been different? Why or why not?*

REVIEWING **The Entrepreneur's Options**

Carlos Del Rey decided to open a fast-food Mexican restaurant and signed a franchise contract with a national chain called La Grande Enchilada. Under the franchise agreement, Del Rey purchased the building and La Grande Enchilada supplied the equipment. The contract required the franchisee to strictly follow the franchisor's operating manual and stated that failure to do so would be grounds for terminating the franchise contract. The manual set forth detailed operating procedures and safety standards, and provided that a La Grande Enchilada representative would inspect the restaurant monthly to ensure compliance. Nine months after Del Rey began operating his La Grande Enchilada, a spark from the grill ignited an oily towel in the kitchen. No one was injured, but by the time firefighters were able to put out the fire, the kitchen had sustained extensive damage. The cook told the fire department that the towel was "about two feet from the grill" when it caught fire, which was

in compliance with the franchisor's manual that required towels to be at least one foot from the grills. Nevertheless, the next day La Grande Enchilada notified Del Rey that his franchise would terminate in thirty days for failure to follow the prescribed safety procedures. Using the information presented in the chapter, answer the following questions.

1 What type of franchise was Del Rey's La Grande Enchilada restaurant?

2 If Del Rey operates the restaurant as a sole proprietorship, who bears the loss for the damaged kitchen? Explain.

3 Assume that Del Rey files a lawsuit against La Grande Enchilada, claiming that his franchise was wrongfully terminated. What is the main factor a court would consider in determining whether the franchise was wrongfully terminated?

4 Would a court be likely to rule that La Grande Enchilada had good cause to terminate Del Rey's franchise in this situation? Why or why not?

A franchise arrangement appeals to many prospective businesspersons for several reasons. Entrepreneurs who purchase franchises can operate independently and without the risks associated with products that have never before been marketed. Additionally, the franchisee can usually rely on the assistance and guidance of a management network that is regional or national in scope and has been in place for some time. Franchisees do face potential problems, however. Generally, to avoid possibly significant economic and legal difficulties, it is imperative that you obtain all relevant details about the business and that you have an attorney evaluate the franchise contract for possible pitfalls.

The Franchise Fee

Virtually all franchise contracts require a franchise fee payable up front or in installments. This fee often ranges between $10,000 and $50,000. For nationally known franchises, such as McDonald's, the fee may be $500,000 or more. To calculate the true cost of the franchise, however, you must also include the fees that are paid once the franchise opens for business. For example, as a franchisee, you would probably pay 2 to 8 percent of your gross sales as royalties to the franchisor (for the use of the franchisor's trademark, for example). Another 1 to 2 percent of gross sales might go to the franchisor to cover advertising costs. Although your business would benefit from the advertising, the cost of that advertising might exceed the benefits you would realize.

Electronic Encroachment and Termination Provisions

Even when the franchise contract gives the franchisee exclusive territorial rights, a problem that many franchisees do not anticipate is the adverse effects on their businesses of so-called electronic encroachment. For example, suppose that a franchise contract gives the franchisee exclusive rights to operate a franchise in a certain territory. Nothing in the contract, though, indicates what will happen if the franchisor sells its products to customers located within the franchisee's territory via telemarketing, mail-order catalogues, or online services. As

a prospective franchisee, you should make sure that your franchise contract covers such contingencies and protects you against any losses you might incur if you face these types of competition in your area.

A major economic consequence, usually of a negative nature, will occur if the franchisor can or does terminate your franchise agreement. Before you sign a franchise contract, make sure that the contract provisions regarding termination are reasonable, clearly specified, and provide you with adequate notice and sufficient time to wind up business.

CHECKLIST FOR THE FRANCHISEE

1 Find out all you can about the franchisor: How long has the franchisor been in business? How profitable is the business? Is there a healthy market for the product?

2 Obtain the most recent financial statement from the franchisor and a complete description of the business.

3 Obtain a clear and complete statement of all fees that you will be required to pay.

4 Determine whether the franchisor will help you find a suitable location, train management and employees, assist with promotion and advertising, and supply capital or credit.

5 Visit other franchisees in the same business. Ask them about their profitability and their experiences with the product, the market, and the franchisor.

6 Evaluate your training and experience in the business on which you are about to embark. Are they sufficient to ensure success as a franchisee?

7 Carefully examine the franchise contract provisions relating to termination of the franchise agreement. Are they specific enough to allow you to sue for breach of contract in the event the franchisor wrongfully terminates the contract? Find out how many franchises have been terminated in the past several years.

8 Will you have an exclusive geographic territory and, if so, for how many years? Does the franchisor have a right to engage in telemarketing, electronic marketing, and Internet or mail-order sales to customers within this territory?

9 Finally, the most important way to protect yourself is to have an attorney familiar with franchise law examine the contract before you sign it.

---

* This *Application* is not meant to substitute for the services of an attorney who is licensed to practice law in your state.

KEY TERMS

articles of partnership   587
business trust   593
cooperative   593
corporation   589
entrepreneur   585
franchise   593
franchisee   596
franchisor   596

general partner   588
joint stock company   593
joint venture   592
limited liability
   company (LLC)   589
limited liability
   partnership (LLP)   591
limited partner   588

limited partnership   588
operating agreement   589
partnership   587
sole proprietorship   586
syndicate   592

CHAPTER SUMMARY   The Entrepreneur's Options

Major Business Forms
(See pages 585–592.)

1. *Sole proprietorships*—The simplest form of business; used by anyone who does business without creating an organization. The owner is the business. The owner pays personal income taxes on all profits and is personally liable for all business debts.

2. *Partnerships*—Created by agreement of the parties; not treated as an entity except for limited purposes. Partners have unlimited liability for partnership debts, and each partner normally has an equal voice in management. Income is "passed through" the partnership to the individual partners, who pay personal taxes on the income.

3. *Limited partnerships*—Must be formed in compliance with statutory requirements. A limited partnership consists of one or more general partners, who have unlimited liability for partnership losses, and one or more limited partners, who are liable only to the extent of their contributions. Only general partners can participate in management.

4. *Corporations*—A corporation is formed in compliance with statutory requirements, is a legal entity separate and distinct from its owners, and can have perpetual existence. The shareholder-owners elect directors, who set policy and hire officers to run the day-to-day business of the corporation. Shareholders normally are not personally liable for the debts of the corporation. The corporation pays income tax on net profits; shareholders pay income tax on disbursed dividends.

5. *Limited liability companies (LLCs)*—The LLC is a hybrid form of business organization that offers the limited liability feature of corporations but the tax benefits of partnerships. LLC members participate in management. Members of LLCs may be corporations or partnerships, are not restricted in number, and may be residents of other countries.

6. *Limited liability partnerships (LLPs)*—Typically, an LLP is formed by professionals who work together as partners in a partnership. Under most state LLP statutes, it is relatively easy to convert a traditional partnership into an LLP. LLP statutes vary, but generally they allow professionals to avoid personal liability for the malpractice of other partners.

Special Business Forms
(See pages 592–593.)

1. *Joint venture*—An organization created by two or more persons in contemplation of a limited activity or a single transaction; otherwise, similar to a partnership.

2. *Syndicate*—An investment group that undertakes to finance a particular project; may exist as a corporation or as a general or limited partnership.

3. *Joint stock company*—A business form similar to a corporation in some respects (transferable shares of stock, management by directors and officers, perpetual existence) but otherwise resembling a partnership.

4. *Business trust*—Created by a written trust agreement that sets forth the interests of the beneficiaries and obligations and powers of the trustee(s). Similar to a corporation in many respects. Beneficiaries are not personally liable for the debts or obligations of the business trust.

(Continued)

CHAPTER SUMMARY	The Entrepreneur's Options—Continued
Special Business Forms—Continued	5. *Cooperative*—An association organized to provide an economic service to its members. May be incorporated or unincorporated.
Private Franchises (See pages 593–601.)	1. *Types of franchises*—
	a. Distributorship (for example, automobile dealerships).
	b. Chain-style operation (for example, fast-food chains).
	c. Manufacturing/processing-plant arrangement (for example, soft-drink bottling companies, such as Coca-Cola).
	2. *The franchise contract*—
	a. Ordinarily requires the franchisee (purchaser) to pay a price for the franchise license.
	b. Specifies the territory to be served by the franchisee's firm.
	c. May require the franchisee to purchase certain supplies from the franchisor at an established price.
	d. May require the franchisee to abide by certain standards of quality relating to the product or service offered but cannot set retail resale prices.
	e. Usually provides for the date and/or conditions of termination of the franchise arrangement. Both federal and state statutes attempt to protect certain franchisees from franchisors who unfairly or arbitrarily terminate franchises.

FOR REVIEW

Answers for the even-numbered questions in this For Review *section can be found in Appendix E at the end of this text.*

1 What are some of the major forms of business organization used by entrepreneurs in the United States?

2 What advantages and disadvantages are associated with each major business form?

3 Why have limited liability companies and limited liability partnerships come into widespread use in recent years?

4 What is a joint venture? What are some other special business organizational forms, and why are they used?

5 What is a franchise, and how does a franchising relationship arise?

QUESTIONS AND CASE PROBLEMS

HYPOTHETICAL SCENARIOS

19.1 Forms of Business Organization. In each of the following situations, determine whether Georgio's Fashions is a sole proprietorship, a partnership, a limited partnership, or a corporation.

  1 Georgio's defaults on a payment to supplier Dee Creations. Dee sues Georgio's and each of the owners of Georgio's personally for payment of the debt.

  2 Georgio's raises $200,000 through the sale of shares of its stock.

  3 At tax time, Georgio's files a tax return with the IRS and pays taxes on the firm's net profits.

  4 Georgio's is owned by three persons, two of whom are not allowed to participate in the firm's management.

19.2 Choice of Business Form. Jorge, Marta, and Jocelyn are college graduates, and Jorge has come up with an idea for a new product that he believes could make the three of them very rich. His idea is to manufacture soft-drink dispensers for home use and market them to consumers throughout the

Midwest. Jorge's personal experience qualifies him to be both first-line supervisor and general manager of the new firm. Marta is a born salesperson. Jocelyn has little interest in sales or management but would like to invest a large sum of money that she has inherited from her aunt. What factors should Jorge, Marta, and Jocelyn consider in deciding which form of business organization to adopt?

19.3 Hypothetical Question with Sample Answer. Omega Computers, Inc., is a franchisor that grants exclusive physical territories to its franchisees with retail locations, including Pete's Digital Products. Omega sells more than two

hundred of the franchises before establishing an interactive Web site. On the site, a customer can order Omega's products directly from the franchisor. When Pete's sets up a Web site through which a customer can also order Omega's products, Omega and Pete's file suits against each other, alleging that each is in violation of the franchise relationship. To decide this issue, what factors should the court consider? How might these parties have avoided this conflict? Discuss.

 For a sample answer to Question 19.3, go to Appendix F at the end of this text.

■

 **CASE PROBLEMS**

19.4 Franchise Termination. In 1985, Bruce Byrne, with his sons Scott and Gordon, opened Lone Star R.V. Sales, Inc., a motor home dealership in Houston, Texas. In 1994, Lone Star became a franchised dealer for Winnebago Industries, Inc., a manufacturer of recreational vehicles. The parties renewed the franchise in 1995, but during the next year, their relationship began to deteriorate. Lone Star did not maintain a current inventory, its sales did not meet goals agreed to between the parties, and Lone Star disparaged Winnebago products to consumers and otherwise failed to actively promote them. Several times, the Byrnes subjected Winnebago employees to verbal abuse. During one phone conversation, Bruce threatened to throw a certain Winnebago sales manager off Lone Star's lot if he appeared at the dealership. Bruce was physically incapable of carrying out the threat, however. In 1998, Winnebago terminated the franchise, claiming, among many other things, that it was concerned for the safety of its employees. Lone Star filed a protest with the Texas Motor Vehicle Board. Did Winnebago have good cause to terminate Lone Star's franchise? Discuss. [*Lone Star R.V. Sales, Inc. v. Motor Vehicle Board of the Texas Department of Transportation*, 49 S.W.3d 492 (Tex.App.—Austin, 2001)]

19.5 Case Problem with Sample Answer. At least six months before the 1996 Summer Olympic Games in Atlanta, Georgia, Stafford Fontenot, Steve Turner, Mike Montelaro, Joe Sokol, and Doug Brinsmade agreed to sell Cajun food at the games and began making preparations. Calling themselves "Prairie Cajun Seafood Catering of Louisiana," on May 19 the group applied for a license with the Fulton County, Georgia, Department of Public Health–Environmental Health Services. Later, Ted Norris sold a mobile kitchen for an $8,000 check drawn on the "Prairie Cajun Seafood Catering of Louisiana" account and two promissory notes, one for $12,000 and the other for $20,000. The notes, which were

dated June 12, listed only Fontenot "d/b/a Prairie Cajun Seafood" as the maker (*d/b/a* is an abbreviation for "doing business as"). On July 31, Fontenot and his friends signed a partnership agreement, which listed specific percentages of profits and losses. They drove the mobile kitchen to Atlanta, but business was "disastrous." When the notes were not paid, Norris filed a suit in a Louisiana state court against Fontenot, seeking payment. What are the elements of a partnership? Was there a partnership among Fontenot and the others? Who is liable on the notes? Explain. [*Norris v. Fontenot*, 867 So.2d 179 (La.App. 3 Cir. 2004)]

 After you have answered Problem 19.5, compare your answer with the sample answer given on the Web site that accompanies this text. Go to academic.cengage.com/blaw/blt, **select "Chapter 19," and click on "Case Problem with Sample Answer."**

19.6 Sole Proprietorship. James Ferguson operates "Jim's 11-E Auto Sales" in Jonesborough, Tennessee, as a sole proprietorship. In 1999, Consumers Insurance Co. issued a policy to "Jim Ferguson, Jim's 11E Auto Sales" covering "Owned 'Autos' Only." *Auto* was defined to include "a land motor vehicle," which was not further explained in the policy. Coverage extended to damages caused by the owner or driver of an underinsured motor vehicle. In 2000, Ferguson bought and titled in his own name a 1976 Harley-Davidson motorcycle, intending to repair and sell the cycle through his dealership. In October 2001, while driving the motorcycle, Ferguson was struck by an auto driven by John Jenkins. Ferguson filed a suit in a Tennessee state court against Jenkins—who was underinsured with respect to Ferguson's medical bills—and Consumers. The insurer argued, among other things, that because the motorcycle was bought and titled in Ferguson's own name, and he was driving it at the time of the accident, it was his personal vehicle and thus was not covered under the dealership's policy. What is the relationship between a sole proprietor and a sole proprietorship?

How might this status affect the court's decision in this case? [*Ferguson v. Jenkins*, 204 S.W.3d 779 (Tenn.App. 2006)]

19.7 Indications of Partnership. In August 2003, Tammy Duncan began working as a waitress at Bynum's Diner, which was owned by her mother, Hazel Bynum, and her stepfather, Eddie Bynum, in Valdosta, Georgia. Less than a month later, the three signed an agreement under which Eddie was to relinquish his management responsibilities, allowing Tammy to be co-manager. At the end of this six-month period, Eddie would revisit this agreement and could then extend it for another six-month period. The diner's bank account was to remain in Eddie's name. There was no provision with regard to the diner's profit, if any, and the parties did not change the business's tax information. Tammy began doing the bookkeeping, as well as waiting tables and performing other duties. On October 30, she slipped off a ladder and injured her knees. At the end of the six-month term, Tammy quit working at the diner. The Georgia State Board of Workers' Compensation determined that she had been the diner's employee and awarded her benefits under the diner's workers' compensation policy with Cypress Insurance Co. Cypress filed a suit in a Georgia state court against Tammy, arguing that she was not an employee, but a co-owner. What are the essential elements of a partnership? Was Tammy a partner in the business of the diner? Explain. [*Cypress Insurance Co. v. Duncan*, 281 Ga.App. 469, 636 S.E.2d 159 (2006)]

19.8 **A Question of Ethics.** *Blushing Brides, L.L.C., a publisher of wedding planning magazines in Columbus,* *Ohio, opened an account with Gray Printing Co. in July 2000. On behalf of Blushing Brides, Louis Zacks, the firm's member-manager, signed a credit agreement that identified the firm as the "purchaser" and required payment within thirty days. Despite the agreement, Blushing Brides typically took up to six months to pay the full amount for its orders. Gray printed and shipped 10,000 copies of a fall/winter 2001 issue for Blushing Brides but had not been paid when the firm ordered 15,000 copies of a spring/summer 2002 issue. Gray refused to print the new order without an assurance of payment. Zacks signed a promissory note for $14,778, plus interest at 6 percent per year, payable to Gray on June 22. Gray printed the new order but by October had been paid only $7,500. Gray filed a suit in an Ohio state court against Blushing Brides and Zacks to collect the balance.* [Gray Printing Co. v. Blushing Brides, L.L.C., __ Ohio App.3d __, __ N.E.2d __ (10 Dist. 2006)]

1 Under what circumstances is a member of an LLC liable for the firm's debts? In this case, is Zacks personally liable under the credit agreement for the unpaid amount on Blushing Brides' account? Did Zacks's promissory note affect the parties' liability on the account? Explain.

2 Should a member of an LLC assume an ethical responsibility to meet the obligations of the firm? Discuss.

CRITICAL THINKING AND WRITING ASSIGNMENTS

19.9 Critical Legal Thinking. Suppose that a franchisor requires the franchisee to purchase a particular type of van that will be used to deliver the franchised carpet-cleaning services to the public. If the van is involved in an accident that causes injury to a person, should the franchisor be held liable for the injuries? What are the arguments for and against holding the franchisor liable under the circumstances? Would it be better if the law established a clear rule regarding the degree of control a franchisor must exert before being subjected to liability for the franchisee's actions? Why or why not?

19.10 Critical Thinking and Writing Assignment for Business. Sandra Lerner met Patricia Holmes at Holmes's horse training facility, and they became friends. One evening, while applying nail polish to Lerner, Holmes layered a raspberry color over black to produce a new color, which Lerner liked. Later, the two created other colors with names like "Bruise," "Smog,"

and "Oil Slick," and titled their concept "Urban Decay." Lerner and Holmes started a firm to produce and market the polishes but never discussed the sharing of profits and losses. They agreed to build the business and then sell it. Together, they did market research, experimented with colors, worked on a logo and advertising, obtained capital from an investment firm, and hired employees. Then Lerner began working to edge Holmes out of the firm.

1 Lerner claimed that there was no partnership agreement because there was no agreement to divide profits. Was Lerner right? Why or why not?

2 Suppose that Lerner, but not Holmes, had contributed a significant amount of personal funds into developing and marketing the new nail polish. Would this entitle Lerner to receive more of the profits? Explain.

ONLINE ACTIVITIES

 **PRACTICAL
INTERNET EXERCISES**

Go to this text's Web site at **academic.cengage.com/blaw/blt**, select "Chapter 19," and click on "Practical Internet Exercises." There you will find the following Internet research exercises that you can perform to learn more about the topics covered in this chapter.

PRACTICAL INTERNET EXERCISE 19-1   LEGAL PERSPECTIVE—Starting a Business

PRACTICAL INTERNET EXERCISE 19-2   MANAGEMENT PERSPECTIVE—Franchises

PRACTICAL INTERNET EXERCISE 19-3   MANAGEMENT PERSPECTIVE—Limited Partnerships and Limited Liability Partnerships

BEFORE THE TEST

Go to this text's Web site at **academic.cengage.com/blaw/blt**, select "Chapter 19," and click on "Interactive Quizzes." You will find a number of interactive questions relating to this chapter.

CHAPTER 20
Corporations

CHAPTER OUTLINE

- THE NATURE AND CLASSIFICATION OF CORPORATIONS
- CORPORATE FORMATION
- CORPORATE FINANCING
- CORPORATE MANAGEMENT– DIRECTORS AND OFFICERS
- CORPORATE OWNERSHIP– SHAREHOLDERS
- MERGER AND CONSOLIDATION
- PURCHASE OF ASSETS OR STOCK
- TERMINATION

LEARNING OBJECTIVES

AFTER READING THIS CHAPTER, YOU SHOULD BE ABLE TO ANSWER THE FOLLOWING QUESTIONS:

1 What are the express and implied powers of corporations? On what sources are these powers based?

2 What are the duties of corporate directors and officers?

3 What must directors do to avoid liability for honest mistakes of judgment and poor business decisions?

4 What role do corporate shareholders play in the corporate enterprise? What are some important rights of shareholders?

5 What is the difference between a corporate merger and a corporate consolidation?

I n the previous chapter, we described several forms of business organization. In this chapter, we look at corporations. The corporation is a creature of statute. As John Marshall indicated in the chapter-opening quotation, a corporation is an artificial being, existing only in law and neither tangible nor visible. Its existence generally depends on state law, although some corporations, especially public organizations, can be created under state or federal law.

Each state has its own body of corporate law, and these laws are not entirely uniform. The Model Business Corporation Act (MBCA) is a codification of modern corporation law that has been influential in the drafting and revision of state corporation statutes. Today, the majority of state statutes are guided by the revised version of the MBCA, which is often referred to as the Revised Model Business Corporation Act (RMBCA).[1]

THE NATURE AND CLASSIFICATION OF CORPORATIONS

A corporation is a legal entity created and recognized by state law. It can consist of one or more *natural persons* (as opposed to the artificial *legal person* of the corporation) identified under a common name. A corporation can be owned by a single person, or it can

---

1. Excerpts from the Revised Model Business Corporation Act (RMBCA) are presented on the Web site that accompanies this text.

have hundreds, thousands, or even millions of owners (shareholders). The corporation substitutes itself for its shareholders in conducting corporate business and in incurring liability, yet its authority to act and the liability for its actions are separate and apart from the individuals who own it.

In a corporation, the responsibility for the overall management of the firm is entrusted to a *board of directors*, whose members are elected by the shareholders. The board of directors hires *corporate officers* and other employees to run the daily business operations of the corporation. When an individual purchases a share of stock in a corporation, that person becomes a shareholder and thus an owner of the corporation. Unlike the members of a partnership, the body of shareholders can change constantly without affecting the continued existence of the corporation. A shareholder can sue the corporation, and the corporation can sue a shareholder. Also, under certain circumstances, a shareholder can sue on behalf of a corporation. The rights and duties of corporate personnel will be examined in detail later in this chapter.

CONTRAST The death of a sole proprietor or a partner can result in the dissolution of a business. The death of a corporate shareholder, however, rarely, if ever, causes the dissolution of a corporation.

The shareholder form of business organization emerged in Europe at the end of the seventeenth century. These organizations, called *joint stock companies*, frequently collapsed because their organizers absconded with the funds or proved to be incompetent. Because of this history of fraud and collapse, organizations resembling corporations were regarded with suspicion in the United States during its early years. Although several business corporations were formed after the Revolutionary War, the corporation did not come into common use for private business until the nineteenth century.

The Constitutional Rights of Corporations

A corporation is recognized as a "person" under state and federal law, and it enjoys many of the same rights and privileges that U.S. citizens enjoy. The Bill of Rights guarantees persons certain protections, and corporations are considered persons in most instances. Accordingly, a corporation as an entity has the same right of access to the courts as a natural person and can sue or be sued. It also has a right to due process before denial of life, liberty, or property, as well as freedom from unreasonable searches and seizures (see Chapter 6 for a discussion of searches and seizures in the business context) and from double jeopardy.

Under the First Amendment, corporations are entitled to freedom of speech. As we pointed out in Chapter 1, however, commercial speech (such as advertising) and political speech (such as contributions to political causes or candidates) receive significantly less protection than noncommercial speech.

Generally, a corporation is not entitled to claim the Fifth Amendment privilege against self-incrimination. Agents or officers of the corporation therefore cannot refuse to produce corporate records on the ground that it might incriminate them.[2] Additionally, the privileges and immunities clause of the U.S. Constitution (Article IV, Section 2) does not protect corporations, nor does it protect an unincorporated association.[3] This clause requires each state to treat citizens of other states equally with respect to certain rights, such as access to the courts and travel rights. This constitutional clause does not apply to corporations because corporations are legal persons only, not natural citizens.

ON THE WEB

Corporate statutes for all but a few states are now online at

www.law.cornell.edu/topics/state_statutes.html#corporations.

The Limited Liability of Shareholders

One of the key advantages of the corporate form is the limited liability of its owners (shareholders). Corporate shareholders normally are not personally liable for the obligations of

---

2. *Braswell v. United States*, 487 U.S. 99, 108 S.Ct. 2284, 101 L.Ed. 98 (1988). A court might allow an officer or employee to assert the Fifth Amendment privilege against self-incrimination in only a few circumstances. See, for example, *In re Three Grand Jury Subpoenas Duces Tecum Dated January 29, 1999*, 191 F.3d 173 (2d Cir. 1999).
3. *W. C. M. Window Co. v. Bernardi*, 730 F.2d 486 (7th Cir. 1984).

the corporation beyond the extent of their investments. In certain limited situations, however, the "corporate veil" can be pierced and liability for the corporation's obligations extended to shareholders. Additionally, to enable the firm to obtain credit, shareholders in small companies sometimes voluntarily assume personal liability, as guarantors, for corporate obligations.

Corporate Taxation

Corporate profits are taxed by various levels of government. Corporations can do one of two things with corporate profits—retain them or pass them on to shareholders in the form of **dividends.** The corporation normally receives no tax deduction for dividends distributed to shareholders. Dividends are again taxable (except when they represent distributions of capital) as income to the shareholder receiving them. This double-taxation feature of the corporation is one of its major disadvantages—although a 2003 law mitigated this double-taxation feature to some extent by providing a reduced federal tax rate on qualifying dividends.[4]

Profits that are not distributed are retained by the corporation. These **retained earnings,** if invested properly, will yield higher corporate profits in the future and thus cause the price of the company's stock to rise. Individual shareholders can then reap the benefits of these retained earnings in the capital gains they receive when they sell their shares. The consequences of a corporation's failure to pay taxes can be severe. The state can suspend corporate status until the taxes are paid, or it can dissolve a corporation for failing to pay taxes.[5]

DIVIDEND
A distribution to corporate shareholders of corporate profits or income, disbursed in proportion to the number of shares held.

RETAINED EARNINGS
The portion of a corporation's profits that has not been paid out as dividends to shareholders.

ETHICAL ISSUE 20.1

HOLDING COMPANY
A company whose business activity is holding shares in another company.

Is it ethical for a corporation to establish an offshore holding company to reduce U.S. taxes? In recent years, some U.S. corporations have been using holding companies to reduce—or at least defer—their U.S. income taxes. At its simplest, a **holding company** (sometimes referred to as a *parent company*) is a company whose business activity consists of holding shares in another company. Typically, the holding company is established in a low-tax or no-tax offshore jurisdiction. Among the best known are the Cayman Islands, Dubai, Hong Kong, Luxembourg, Monaco, and Panama.

Sometimes, a major U.S. corporation sets up an investment holding company in a low-tax offshore environment. The corporation then transfers its cash, bonds, stocks, and other investments to the holding company. In general, any profits received by the holding company on these investments are taxed at the rate of the offshore jurisdiction in which the company is registered, not the rates applicable to the parent company or its shareholders in their country of residence. Thus, deposits of cash, for example, may earn interest that is taxed at only a minimal rate. Once the profits are brought "onshore," though, they are taxed at the federal corporate income tax rate, and any payments received by the shareholders are also taxable at the full U.S. rates.

Occasionally, a member of Congress or the media learns that a large U.S. corporation has used an offshore holding company to reduce its U.S. tax liability. The company's actions are then decried as both unethical and unpatriotic. Others are not so sure. They point out that those who run corporations have a duty to minimize (legally, of course) taxes owed by the corporation and by its shareholders.

---

4. The Jobs Growth Tax Relief Reconciliation Act of 2003, Pub. L. No. 108-27, May 28, 2003, codified at 26 U.S.C.A. Section 6429 and 42 U.S.C.A. Section 801.

5. See, for example, *Bullington v. Palangio*, 345 Ark. 320, 45 S.W.3d 834 (2001).

Torts and Criminal Acts

A corporation is liable for the torts committed by its agents or officers within the course and scope of their employment. This principle applies to a corporation exactly as it applies to the ordinary agency relationships discussed in Chapter 17. It follows the doctrine of *respondeat superior.*

As discussed in Chapter 6, under modern criminal law a corporation may be held liable for the criminal acts of its agents and employees, provided the punishment is one that can be applied to the corporation. Although corporations cannot be imprisoned, they can be fined. (Of course, corporate directors and officers can be imprisoned, and in recent years, many have faced criminal penalties for their own actions or for the actions of employees under their supervision.)

Recall from Chapter 6 that the U.S. Sentencing Commission created standardized sentencing guidelines for federal crimes. These guidelines went into effect in 1987. The commission subsequently created specific sentencing guidelines for crimes committed by corporate employees (white-collar crimes).[6] The net effect of the guidelines has been a significant increase in criminal penalties for crimes committed by corporate personnel. Penalties depend on such factors as the seriousness of the offense, the amount involved, and the extent to which top company executives are implicated. Corporate lawbreakers can face fines amounting to hundreds of millions of dollars, though the guidelines allow judges to impose less severe penalties in certain circumstances.

The question in the following case was whether a corporation could be convicted for its employee's criminal negligence.

---

6. Note that the Sarbanes-Oxley Act of 2002, discussed in Chapter 2 and Chapter 21, stiffened the penalties for certain types of corporate crime and ordered the U.S. Sentencing Commission to revise the sentencing guidelines accordingly.

CASE 20.1 **Commonwealth v. Angelo Todesca Corp.**

Supreme Judicial Court of Massachusetts, 446 Mass. 128, 842 N.E.2d 930 (2006).
www.findlaw.com/11stategov/ma/maca.html[a]

FACTS Brian Gauthier worked as a truck driver for Angelo Todesca Corporation, a trucking and paving company. During 2000, Gauthier drove a ten-wheel tri-axle dump truck, which was designated as AT-56. Angelo's safety manual required its trucks to be equipped with back-up alarms, which were to sound automatically whenever the vehicles were in reverse gear. In November, Gauthier discovered that AT-56's alarm was missing. Angelo ordered a new alarm. Meanwhile, Gauthier continued to drive AT-56. On December 1, Angelo assigned Gauthier to haul asphalt to a work site in Centerville, Massachusetts. At the site, as Gauthier backed up AT-56 to dump its load, he struck a police officer who was directing traffic through the site and facing away from the truck. The officer died of his injuries. The commonwealth of Massachusetts charged Gauthier and Angelo in a Massachusetts state court with, among other wrongful acts, vehicular homicide. Angelo was convicted and fined $2,500. On Angelo's appeal, a state intermediate appellate court reversed Angelo's conviction. The state appealed to the Massachusetts Supreme Judicial Court, the state's highest court.

ISSUE Can a corporation be convicted for its employee's criminal negligence?

DECISION Yes. The Massachusetts Supreme Judicial Court affirmed Angelo's conviction.

REASON The court identified three elements required to prove a corporation guilty of a criminal offense: (1) an individual commits a criminal offense; (2) at the time of commission, the individual is engaged in corporate business;

a. In the "Supreme Court Opinions" section, in the "2006" row, click on "March." When that page opens, scroll to the name of the case and click on its docket number to access the opinion.

CASE 20.1—Continues next page

CASE 20.1–Continued

and (3) the corporation vested the individual with the authority to engage in that business on its behalf. The focus in this case was on the first element, with the defendant arguing that a "corporation" could not be guilty of vehicular homicide because it cannot "operate" a vehicle. The court recognized that a corporation is not a "living person" but pointed out that it can act through its agents, which may include its employees. The court reasoned that if an employee commits a crime "while engaged in corporate business that the employee has been authorized to conduct," a corporation can be held liable for the crime. The defendant also contended that operating a truck without a back-up alarm is not a crime. The court conceded this point but explained that "the criminal conduct was Gauthier's negligent operation of the defendant's truck, resulting in the victim's death."

 WHY IS THIS CASE IMPORTANT TO BUSINESSPERSONS? *Other states' courts that have considered the question at issue in this case have concluded that a corporation may be criminally liable for vehicular homicide under those states' statutes. This was the first case in which Massachusetts state courts ruled on the question under a Massachusetts statute.*

Corporate Powers

When a corporation is created, the express and implied powers necessary to achieve its purpose also come into existence. The express powers of a corporation are found in its **articles of incorporation** (a document filed with the state that contains information about the corporation, including its organization and functions), in the law of the state of incorporation, and in the state and federal constitutions. Corporate **bylaws,** which are internal rules of management adopted by the corporation at its first organizational meeting, also establish the express powers of the corporation. Because state corporation statutes frequently provide default rules that apply if the company's bylaws are silent on an issue, it is important that the bylaws set forth the specific operating rules of the corporation. In addition, after the bylaws are adopted, the corporation's board of directors will pass resolutions that also grant or restrict corporate powers.

The following order of priority is used when conflicts arise among documents involving corporations:

1 The U.S. Constitution.

2 State constitutions.

3 State statutes.

4 The articles of incorporation.

5 Bylaws.

6 Resolutions of the board of directors.

Certain implied powers attach when a corporation is created. Barring express constitutional, statutory, or other prohibitions, the corporation has the implied power to perform all acts reasonably appropriate and necessary to accomplish its corporate purposes. For this reason, a corporation has the implied power to borrow funds within certain limits, to lend funds, and to extend credit to those with whom it has a legal or contractual relationship.

To borrow funds, the corporation acts through its board of directors to authorize the loan. Most often, the president or chief executive officer of the corporation will execute the necessary papers on behalf of the corporation. In so doing, corporate officers have the implied power to bind the corporation in matters directly connected with the *ordinary* business affairs of the enterprise.

ARTICLES OF INCORPORATION
The document filed with the appropriate governmental agency, usually the secretary of state, when a business is incorporated. State statutes usually prescribe what kind of information must be contained in the articles of incorporation.

BYLAWS
A set of governing rules adopted by a corporation or other association.

Classification of Corporations

The classification of a corporation normally depends on its location, purpose, and ownership characteristics. A **close corporation** is one whose shares are held by members of a family or by relatively few persons. Close corporations are also referred to as *closely held, family,* or *privately held* corporations. Usually, the members of the small group constituting a close corporation are personally known to each other. Because the number of shareholders is so small, there is no trading market for the shares. An **S corporation** is a close business corporation that has met certain requirements as set by the Internal Revenue Code and thus qualifies for special income tax treatment (all other corporations are C corporations). Essentially, an S corporation is taxed the same as a partnership, but its owners enjoy the privilege of limited liability. A *professional corporation* is a corporation formed by professional persons, such as accountants, attorneys, dentists, and physicians, to gain tax benefits.

A corporation is referred to as a **domestic corporation** by its home state (the state in which it incorporates). A corporation formed in one state but doing business in another is referred to in the second state as a **foreign corporation.** A corporation formed in another country (say, Mexico) but doing business in the United States is referred to in the United States as an **alien corporation.**

A corporation does not have an automatic right to do business in a state other than its state of incorporation. In some instances, it must obtain a *certificate of authority* in any state in which it plans to do business. Once the certificate has been issued, the powers conferred on a corporation by its home state generally can be exercised in the other state.

CLOSE CORPORATION
A corporation whose shareholders are limited to a small group of persons, often including only family members.

S CORPORATION
A close business corporation that has met certain requirements set out in the Internal Revenue Code and thus qualifies for special income tax treatment. Essentially, an S corporation is taxed the same as a partnership, but its owners enjoy the privilege of limited liability.

DOMESTIC CORPORATION
In a given state, a corporation that does business in, and is organized under the law of, that state.

FOREIGN CORPORATION
In a given state, a corporation that does business in the state without being incorporated therein.

ALIEN CORPORATION
A designation in the United States for a corporation formed in another country but doing business in the United States.

CORPORATE FORMATION

Up to this point, we have discussed some of the general characteristics of corporations. We now examine the process by which corporations come into existence. Incorporating a business is much simpler today than it was twenty years ago, and many states allow businesses to incorporate online.

Note that one of the most common reasons for creating a corporation is the need for additional capital to finance expansion. Many of the Fortune 500 companies were originally sole proprietorships or partnerships before converting to a corporate entity. A sole proprietor in need of funds can seek partners who will bring capital with them. Although a partnership may be able to secure more funds from potential lenders than a sole proprietor could, the amount is still limited. When a firm wants significant growth, simply increasing the number of partners can result in so many partners that the firm can no longer operate effectively. Therefore, incorporation may be the best choice for an expanding business organization because a corporation can obtain more capital by issuing shares of *stock* (to be discussed shortly).

Promotional Activities

In the past, preliminary steps were taken to organize and promote the business before incorporating. Contracts were made with investors and others on behalf of the future corporation. Today, however, due to the relative ease of forming a corporation in most states, persons incorporating their business rarely, if ever, engage in preliminary promotional activities. Nevertheless, it is important for businesspersons to understand that they are personally liable for all preincorporation contracts made with investors, accountants, or others on behalf of the future corporation. This personal liability continues until the corporation assumes the preincorporation contracts by *novation* (discussed in Chapter 9).

Incorporation Procedures

Exact procedures for incorporation differ among states, but the basic steps are as follows: (1) select a state of incorporation, (2) secure the corporate name by confirming its availability, and (3) prepare and file the articles of incorporation with the secretary of state accompanied by payment of the specified fees.

Selecting the State of Incorporation   The first step in the incorporation process is to select a state in which to incorporate. Because state incorporation laws differ, individuals may look for the states that offer the most advantageous tax or incorporation provisions. (See the *Application* feature at the end of this chapter for details on how you can find out each state's requirements and incorporate your business online.) Another consideration is the fee that a particular state charges to incorporate, as well as the annual fees and the fees for specific transactions (such as stock transfers).

Delaware has historically had the least restrictive laws and provisions that favor corporate management. Consequently, many corporations, including a number of the largest, have incorporated there. Close corporations, particularly those of a professional nature, generally incorporate in the state where their principal shareholders live and work. For reasons of convenience and cost, businesses often choose to incorporate in the state in which the corporation's business will primarily be conducted.

ON THE WEB

For answers to "frequently asked questions" on the topic of incorporation, go to

www.bizfilings.com/products/ccorp.asp.

Securing the Corporate Name   The choice of a corporate name is subject to state approval to ensure against duplication or deception. State statutes usually require that the secretary of state run a check on the proposed name in the state of incorporation. Some states require that the persons incorporating a firm, at their own expense, run a check on the proposed name, which can often be accomplished via Internet-based services. Once cleared, a name can be reserved for a short time, for a fee, pending the completion of the articles of incorporation. All corporate statutes require the corporation name to include the word *Corporation*, *Incorporated*, *Company*, or *Limited*, or abbreviations of these terms.

Businesspersons should be cautious when choosing a corporate name. Recognize that even if a particular state does not require the incorporator to run a name check, doing so is always advisable and can help prevent future disputes. Many states provide online search capabilities, but these searches are usually limited and will only compare the proposed name to the names of active corporations within that state. Trade name disputes, however, are not limited to corporations. Thus, using a business name that is deceptively similar to the name of a partnership or limited liability company can also lead to a dispute. Disputes are even more likely to arise among firms that do business over the Internet. Always check on the availability of a particular domain name before selecting a corporate name. This is an area in which it pays to be overly cautious and incur some additional cost to hire an attorney or specialized firm to conduct a name search. If you learn that another business is using a similar name, you can contact that business and ask for its consent to your proposed name.

Preparing and Filing the Articles of Incorporation   The primary document needed to incorporate a business is the *articles of incorporation*. The articles include basic information about the corporation and serve as a primary source of authority for its future organization and business functions. The person or persons who execute (sign) the articles are called *incorporators*. After the articles of incorporation have been prepared, signed, and authenticated by the incorporators, they are sent to the appropriate state official, usually the secretary of state, along with the required filing fee. Once the secretary of state approves and returns the articles, the corporation officially exists.

CORPORATE FINANCING

Part of the process of corporate formation involves corporate financing. Corporations are financed by the issuance and sale of corporate securities. **Securities** (*stocks* and *bonds*) evidence the right to participate in earnings and the distribution of corporate property or the obligation to pay funds.

Stocks, or *equity securities*, represent the purchase of ownership in the business firm. **Bonds** (debentures), or *debt securities*, represent the borrowing of funds by firms (and governments). Of course, not all debt is in the form of debt securities. For example, some debt is in the form of accounts payable and notes payable, which typically are short-term debts. Bonds are simply a way for the corporation to split up its long-term debt so that it can market it more easily.

Bonds

Bonds are issued by business firms and by governments at all levels as evidence of the funds they are borrowing from investors. Bonds normally have a designated *maturity date*—the date when the principal, or face, amount of the bond is returned to the investor. They are sometimes referred to as *fixed-income securities* because their owners (that is, the creditors) receive fixed-dollar interest payments, usually semiannually, during the period of time prior to maturity. Because debt financing represents a legal obligation on the part of the corporation, various features and terms of a particular bond issue are specified in a lending agreement called a **bond indenture.** The bond indenture specifies the maturity date of the bond and the pattern of interest payments until maturity.

Stocks

Corporations can also obtain financing by issuing stocks. Exhibit 20–1 on the next page summarizes the types of stocks issued by corporations. The true ownership of a corporation is represented by **common stock.** Common stock provides a proportionate interest in the corporation with regard to (1) control, (2) earnings, and (3) net assets. A shareholder's interest generally is in proportion to the number of shares he or she owns out of the total number of shares issued. A holder of common stock generally has the right to vote on any proposed changes in the firm's ownership structure, such as a *merger* that can change the proportion of ownership. In terms of receiving payment for their investments, holders of common stock are last in line. They are entitled to the earnings that are left after preferred stockholders, bondholders, suppliers, employees, and other groups have been paid. Once those groups are paid, however, the owners of common stock may be entitled to *all* the remaining earnings as dividends. (The board of directors normally is not under any duty to declare the remaining earnings as dividends, however.)

Preferred stock is stock with *preferences*. Usually, this means that holders of preferred stock have priority over holders of common stock as to dividends and as to payment on dissolution of the corporation. Holders of preferred stock may or may not have the right to vote.

Preferred stock is not included among the liabilities of a business because it is equity. Like other equity securities, preferred shares have no fixed maturity date on which the firm must pay them off. Although firms occasionally buy back preferred stock, they are not legally obligated to do so. Holders of preferred stock are investors who have assumed

SECURITIES
Generally, stock certificates, bonds, notes, debentures, warrants, or other documents given as evidence of an ownership interest in a corporation or as a promise of repayment by a corporation.

STOCK
An equity (ownership) interest in a corporation, measured in units of shares.

BOND
A certificate that evidences a corporate (or government) debt. It is a security that involves no ownership interest in the issuing entity.

BOND INDENTURE
A contract between the issuer of a bond and the bondholder.

COMMON STOCK
Shares of ownership in a corporation that give the owner of the stock a proportionate interest in the corporation with regard to control, earnings, and net assets. Shares of common stock are lowest in priority with respect to payment of dividends and distribution of the corporation's assets on dissolution.

PREFERRED STOCK
Classes of stock that have priority over common stock as to both payment of dividends and distribution of assets on the corporation's dissolution.

EXHIBIT 20–1	Types of Stocks
Common stock	Voting shares that represent ownership interest in a corporation. Common stock has the lowest priority with respect to payment of dividends and distribution of assets on the corporation's dissolution.
Preferred stock	Shares of stock that have priority over common-stock shares as to payment of dividends and distribution of assets on dissolution. Dividend payments are usually a fixed percentage of the face value of the share.
Cumulative preferred stock	Required dividends not paid in a given year must be paid in a subsequent year before any common-stock dividends are paid.
Participating preferred stock	Stock entitling the owner to receive the preferred-stock dividend and additional dividends if the corporation has paid dividends on common stock.
Convertible preferred stock	Stock entitling the owners to convert their shares into a specified number of common shares either in the issuing corporation or, sometimes, in another corporation.
Redeemable, or callable, preferred stock	Preferred shares issued with the express condition that the issuing corporation has the right to repurchase the shares as specified.

a rather cautious position in their relationship to the corporation. They have a stronger position than common shareholders with respect to dividends and claims on assets, but they will not share in the full prosperity of the firm if it grows successfully over time. This is because the value of preferred shares will not rise as rapidly as that of common shares during a period of financial success. Preferred stockholders do receive fixed dividends periodically, however, and they may benefit to some extent from changes in the market price of the shares.

CORPORATE MANAGEMENT—DIRECTORS AND OFFICERS

A corporation typically is governed by a board of directors. A director occupies a position of responsibility unlike that of other corporate personnel. Directors are sometimes inappropriately characterized as *agents* because they act on behalf of the corporation. No *individual* director, however, can act as an agent to bind the corporation; and as a group, directors collectively control the corporation in a way that no agent is able to control a principal. Directors are also often incorrectly characterized as *trustees* because they occupy positions of trust and control over the corporation. Unlike trustees, however, they do not own or hold title to property for the use and benefit of others.

Election of Directors

Subject to statutory limitations, the number of directors is set forth in the corporation's articles or bylaws. Historically, the minimum number of directors has been three, but today many states permit fewer. Indeed, the Revised Model Business Corporation Act (RMBCA), in Section 8.01, permits corporations with fewer than fifty shareholders to eliminate the board of directors.

Normally, the incorporators appoint the initial board of directors at the time the corporation is created, or the corporation itself names the directors in the articles. The first

ON THE WEB

One of the best sources on the Web for information on corporations, including their directors, is the EDGAR database of the Securities and Exchange Commission at

www.sec.gov/edgar.shtml.

board serves until the first annual shareholders' meeting. Subsequent directors are elected by a majority vote of the shareholders.

The term of office for a director is usually one year—from annual meeting to annual meeting. Longer and staggered terms are permissible under most state statutes. A common practice is to elect one-third of the board members each year for a three-year term. In this way, there is greater management continuity.

Removal of Directors   A director can be removed *for cause*—that is, for failing to perform a required duty—either as specified in the articles or bylaws or by shareholder action. Even the board of directors itself may be given power to remove a director for cause, subject to shareholder review. In most states, a director cannot be removed without cause unless the corporation has previously authorized such an action.

> **BE AWARE** The articles of incorporation may provide that a director can be removed only for cause.

Whether shareholders should be able to remove a director without cause is part of an ongoing debate about the balance of power between a corporation and its shareholders. It was also the pivotal question at the heart of the battle for corporate control in the following case.

CASE 20.2   Relational Investors, LLC v. Sovereign Bancorp, Inc.

United States District Court, Southern District of New York, 417 F.Supp.2d 438 (2006).

FACTS In June 2004, Relational Investors, LLC, a Delaware corporation, began acquiring a significant number of shares of stock in Sovereign Bancorp, Inc., a Pennsylvania firm. By 2005, Relational held about 8 percent of Sovereign's stock and had become its largest shareholder. Relational expressed dissatisfaction with Sovereign's management and, in May, announced that it would seek representation on Sovereign's board at the next annual shareholders' meeting in April 2006. (Sovereign elects one-third of its six board members at each annual meeting.) Sovereign then announced that it would sell 19.8 percent of its stock for $2.4 billion to Santander Central Hispano, S.A., a bank incorporated under the laws of Spain. Relational responded that it intended to seek the removal of Sovereign's *entire* board at the next shareholders' meeting. Sovereign filed a suit in a federal district court against Relational, seeking a declaration that its directors could be removed only for cause. Relational filed a motion for judgment on the pleadings.

ISSUE Could Sovereign's shareholders remove its directors without cause?

DECISION Yes. The court granted Relational's motion for judgment on the pleadings, declaring that Sovereign's shareholders had the right to remove its directors without cause. "[T]he tension is * * * resolved in favor of shareholder autonomy."

REASON The court pointed out that "[a]t the time of Sovereign's incorporation in 1987, Pennsylvania law expressly provided for the removal of directors without cause." The court acknowledged that "as concerns about hostile corporate takeovers grew, several states began enacting legislation to limit the ability of shareholders to remove directors," and in 1989, Pennsylvania likewise "limit[ed] the ability of shareholders to remove directors without cause to situations where the company's charter and bylaws permitted such actions." In this case, Sovereign's articles of incorporation "clearly and unambiguously" allowed for directors to be removed without cause. "Article Eighth [of Sovereign's articles of incorporation] provides, simply and clearly, that a majority vote of qualified shareholders may remove directors from office." Sovereign argued that because Article Eighth was adopted before Pennsylvania amended its law to restrict the removal of directors, the article "could not have been intended as an 'opt out' to the revised statute which thereafter provided for a presumption of removal only for cause." The court refused to accept this argument: "The plain language of Article Eighth, and an analysis of the law in effect at the time of its enactment in 1987, makes clear that the original Articles of Incorporation provided for removal without cause. The enactment of [the revised statute] did not alter this original intent."

FOR CRITICAL ANALYSIS–Social Consideration
If you could dictate a corporation's rule with respect to the removal of its directors, what would you prescribe? Why?

Vacancies on the Board of Directors   Vacancies can occur on the board of directors if a director dies or resigns or if a new position is created through amendment of the articles or bylaws. In these situations, either the shareholders or the board itself can fill the position, depending on state law or on the provisions of the bylaws. Note, however, that even when the bylaws appear to authorize an election, a court can invalidate the election if the directors were attempting to diminish the shareholders' influence in it.

Board of Directors' Meetings

The board of directors conducts business by holding formal meetings with recorded minutes. The dates of regular meetings are usually established in the articles or bylaws or by board resolution, and no further notice is customarily required. Special meetings can be called, with notice sent to all directors.

Quorum requirements vary among jurisdictions. (A **quorum** is the minimum number of members of a body of officials or other group that must be present in order for business to be validly transacted.) Many states leave the decision as to quorum requirements to the corporate articles or bylaws. In the absence of specific state statutes, most states provide that a quorum is a majority of the number of directors authorized in the articles or bylaws. Voting is done in person (unlike voting at shareholders' meetings, which can be done by proxy, as discussed later in this chapter).[7] The rule is one vote per director. Ordinary matters generally require a simple majority vote; certain extraordinary issues may require a greater-than-majority vote.

Directors' Rights and Compensation

A director of a corporation has a number of rights, including the rights of participation, inspection, compensation, and indemnification. The right to participation means that directors are entitled to participate in all board of directors' meetings and have a right to be notified of these meetings. The dates of regular board meetings usually are established by the bylaws or by board resolution, and no notice of these meetings is required. If special meetings are called, however, notice is required unless waived by the director. A director must have access to all of the corporate books and records to make decisions and to exercise the necessary supervision over corporate officers and employees. This right of inspection is virtually absolute and cannot be restricted.

In the past, directors rarely were paid. Today, in contrast, corporate directors are often paid at least nominal sums and may receive more substantial compensation in large corporations because of the time, work, effort, and especially risk involved. Most states permit the corporate articles or bylaws to authorize compensation for directors; sometimes, the directors are allowed to set their own compensation. In many corporations, directors are also chief corporate officers (president or chief executive officer, for example) and receive compensation in their managerial positions.

Directors' Management Responsibilities

Directors have responsibility for all policymaking decisions necessary to the management of corporate affairs. Just as shareholders cannot act individually to bind the corporation, the directors must act as a body in carrying out routine corporate business. The general areas of responsibility of the board of directors include the following:

1 Declaration and payment of corporate dividends to shareholders.

---

7. Except in Louisiana, which allows a director to vote by proxy under certain circumstances.

2 Authorization for major corporate policy decisions—for example, the initiation of proceedings for the sale or lease of corporate assets outside the regular course of business, the determination of new product lines, and the overseeing of major contract negotiations and major management-labor negotiations.

3 Appointment, supervision, and removal of corporate officers and other managerial employees and the determination of their compensation.

4 Financial decisions, such as the decision to issue authorized shares and bonds.

In most states, the board of directors can delegate some of its functions to an executive committee or to corporate officers. In doing so, the board is not relieved of its overall responsibility for directing the affairs of the corporation, but corporate officers and managerial personnel are empowered to make decisions relating to ordinary, daily corporate affairs within well-defined guidelines.

Corporate Officers and Executives

Corporate officers and other executive employees are hired by the board of directors or, in rare instances, by the shareholders. In addition to carrying out the duties articulated in the bylaws, corporate and managerial officers act as agents of the corporation, and the ordinary rules of agency (discussed in Chapter 17) normally apply to their employment. The qualifications required of officers and executive employees are determined at the discretion of the corporation and are included in the articles or bylaws. In most states, a person can hold more than one office and can be both an officer and a director of the corporation.

Corporate officers and other high-level managers are employees of the company, so their rights are defined by employment contracts. The board of directors, though, normally can remove corporate officers at any time with or without cause and regardless of the terms of the employment contracts—although in so doing, the corporation may be liable for breach of contract. The duties of corporate officers are the same as those of directors because both groups are involved in decision making and are in similar positions of control. Hence, officers are viewed as having the same fiduciary duties of care and loyalty in their conduct of corporate affairs as directors have, a subject to which we now turn.

Duties and Liabilities of Directors and Officers

Directors and officers are deemed *fiduciaries* of the corporation because their relationship with the corporation and its shareholders is one of trust and confidence. These fiduciary duties include the duty of care and the duty of loyalty.

Duty of Care   Directors and officers must exercise due care in performing their duties. The standard of *due care* has been variously described in judicial decisions and codified in many corporation codes. Generally, a director or officer is expected to act in good faith, to exercise the care that an ordinarily prudent person would exercise in similar circumstances, and to act in what he or she considers to be the best interests of the corporation [RMBCA 8.30]. Directors and officers who have not exercised the required duty of care can be held liable for the harms suffered by the corporation as a result of their negligence. (Directors and officers also have a duty not to destroy evidence in the event of a lawsuit involving the corporation.)

Duty to Make Informed and Reasonable Decisions.   Directors and officers are expected to be informed on corporate matters and to make reasonable decisions. To be

Corporate executives discuss the business of their firm. Can the same person be both a director and an officer of a corporation? (John Terence Turner/Getty Images)

CONTRAST   Shareholders own a corporation and directors make policy decisions, but officers who run the daily business of the corporation often have significant decision-making power.

informed, the director or officer must do what is necessary to become informed: attend presentations, ask for information from those who have it, read reports, and review other written materials such as contracts. In other words, directors and officers must carefully study a situation and its alternatives before making a decision. Depending on the nature of the business, directors and officers are often expected to act in accordance with their own knowledge and training. Nevertheless, most states (and Section 8.30 of the RMBCA) allow a director to make decisions in reliance on information furnished by competent officers or employees, professionals such as attorneys and accountants, or even an executive committee of the board without being accused of acting in bad faith or failing to exercise due care if such information turns out to be faulty.

Duty to Exercise Reasonable Supervision. Directors are also expected to exercise a reasonable amount of supervision when they delegate work to corporate officers and employees. **■EXAMPLE 20.1** Dale, a corporate bank director, fails to attend any board of directors' meetings for five years. In addition, Dale never inspects any of the corporate books or records and generally fails to supervise the efforts of the bank president and the loan committee. Meanwhile, Brennan, the bank president, who is a corporate officer, makes various improper loans and permits large overdrafts. In this situation, Dale (the corporate director) can be held liable to the corporation for losses resulting from the unsupervised actions of the bank president and the loan committee. ■

Duty of Loyalty   *Loyalty* can be defined as faithfulness to one's obligations and duties. In the corporate context, the duty of loyalty requires directors and officers to subordinate their personal interests to the welfare of the corporation. Among other things, this means that directors may not use corporate funds or confidential corporate information for personal advantage. They must also refrain from self-dealing. For instance, a director should not oppose a *tender offer* (a takeover bid—to be discussed later in this chapter) that is in the corporation's best interest simply because its acceptance may cost the director her or his position. Cases dealing with fiduciary duty may involve one or more of the following:

1 Competing with the corporation.

2 Usurping (taking advantage of) a corporate opportunity.

3 Having an interest that conflicts with the interest of the corporation.

4 Engaging in insider trading (using information that is not public to make a profit trading securities, as will be discussed in Chapter 21).

5 Authorizing a corporate transaction that is detrimental to minority shareholders.

Conflicts of Interest   The duty of loyalty also requires officers and directors to *fully disclose* to the board of directors any potential conflict of interest that might arise in any corporate transaction. The various state statutes contain different standards, but a contract generally will *not* be voidable if all of the following are true: if the contract was fair and reasonable to the corporation at the time it was made, if there was a full disclosure of the interest of the officers or directors involved in the transaction, and if the contract was approved by a majority of the disinterested directors or shareholders.

■EXAMPLE 20.2 Southwood Corporation needs office space. Lambert Alden, one of its five directors, owns the building adjoining the corporation's main office building. He negotiates a lease with Southwood for the space, making a full disclosure to Southwood and the other four board directors. The lease arrangement is fair and reasonable, and it is unanimously approved by the corporation's board of directors. In this situation, Alden has not breached his duty of loyalty to the corporation, and thus the contract is valid. If it were otherwise, directors would be prevented from ever transacting business with the corporations they serve. ■

The Business Judgment Rule Directors and officers are expected to exercise due care and to use their best judgment in guiding corporate management, but they are not insurers of business success. Honest mistakes of judgment and poor business decisions on their part do not make them liable to the corporation for resulting damages. Under the **business judgment rule,** a corporate director or officer may be able to avoid liability to the corporation or to its shareholders for poor business judgments. The business judgment rule generally immunizes directors and officers from liability for the consequences of a decision that is within managerial authority, as long as the decision complies with management's fiduciary duties, and as long as acting on the decision is within the powers of the corporation. Consequently, if there is a reasonable basis for a business decision, it is unlikely that the court will interfere with that decision, even if the corporation suffers as a result.

To benefit from the rule, directors and officers must act in good faith, in what they consider to be the best interests of the corporation, and with the care that an ordinarily prudent person in a similar position would exercise in similar circumstances. This requires an informed decision, with a rational basis, and with no conflict between the decision maker's personal interest and the interest of the corporation.

BUSINESS JUDGMENT RULE
A rule that immunizes corporate management from liability for actions that result in corporate losses or damages if the actions are undertaken in good faith and are within both the power of the corporation and the authority of management to make.

CORPORATE OWNERSHIP–SHAREHOLDERS

The acquisition of a share of stock makes a person an owner and shareholder in a corporation. Shareholders thus own the corporation. Although they have no legal title to corporate property, such as buildings and equipment, they do have an equitable (ownership) interest in the firm.

As a general rule, shareholders have no responsibility for the daily management of the corporation, although they are ultimately responsible for choosing the board of directors, which does have such control. Ordinarily, corporate officers and directors owe no duty to individual shareholders unless some contract or special relationship exists between them in addition to the corporate relationship. Their duty is to act in the best interests of the corporation and its shareholder-owners as a whole. In turn, as you will read later in this chapter, controlling shareholders owe a fiduciary duty to minority shareholders. Normally, there is no legal relationship between shareholders and creditors of the corporation. Shareholders can, in fact, be creditors of the corporation and thus have the same rights of recovery against the corporation as any other creditor.

In this section, we look at the powers and voting rights of shareholders, which are generally established in the articles of incorporation and under the state's general incorporation law.

BE AWARE Shareholders normally are not agents of the corporation.

Shareholders' Powers

Shareholders must approve fundamental changes affecting the corporation before the changes can be implemented. Hence, shareholders are empowered to amend the articles of incorporation (charter) and bylaws, approve a merger or the dissolution of the corporation, and approve the sale of all or substantially all of the corporation's assets. Some of these powers are subject to prior board approval.

Directors are elected to (and removed from) the board of directors by a vote of the shareholders. The first board of directors is either named in the articles of incorporation or chosen by the incorporators to serve until the first shareholders' meeting. From that time on, the selection and retention of directors are exclusively shareholder functions.

Directors usually serve their full terms; if they are unsatisfactory, they are simply not reelected. Shareholders have the inherent power, however, to remove a director from office *for cause* (breach of duty or misconduct) by a majority vote.[8] Some state statutes (and some corporate articles) even permit removal of directors without cause by the vote of a majority of the holders of outstanding shares entitled to vote.

Shareholders' Meetings

Shareholders' meetings must occur at least annually, and additional, special meetings can be called to deal with urgent matters. Because it is usually not practical for owners of only a few shares of stock of publicly traded corporations to attend shareholders' meetings, such shareholders normally give third parties written authorization to vote their shares at the meeting. This authorization is called a **proxy** (from the Latin *procurare*, "to manage, take care of"). Proxies are often solicited by management, but any person can solicit proxies to concentrate voting power.

When shareholders want to change a company policy, they can put their idea up for a shareholder vote. They can do this by submitting a shareholder proposal to the board of directors and asking the board to include the proposal in the proxy materials that are sent to all shareholders before meetings.

The Securities and Exchange Commission (SEC), which regulates the purchase and sale of securities (see Chapter 21), has special provisions relating to proxies and shareholder proposals. SEC Rule 14a-8 provides that all shareholders who own stock worth at least $1,000 are eligible to submit proposals for inclusion in corporate proxy materials. The corporation is required to include information on whatever proposals will be considered at the shareholders' meeting along with proxy materials. Only those proposals that relate to significant policy considerations rather than ordinary business operations must be included. For a discussion of how the SEC is adapting its rules regarding proxy solicitation to take advantage of today's communications technology, see this chapter's *Adapting the Law to the Online Environment* feature.

Shareholder Voting

Shareholders exercise ownership control through the power of their votes. Corporate business matters are presented in the form of *resolutions*, which shareholders vote to approve or disapprove. Each shareholder is entitled to one vote per share, although the voting techniques that will be discussed shortly all enhance the power of the shareholder's vote. The articles of incorporation can exclude or limit voting rights, particularly for certain classes of shares, such as *preferred shares*.

Quorum Requirements   For shareholders to conduct business at a meeting, a quorum must be present. Generally, a quorum exists when shareholders holding more than 50 percent of the outstanding shares are present. In some states, obtaining the unanimous written consent of shareholders is a permissible alternative to holding a shareholders' meeting [RMBCA 7.25].

Once a quorum is present, voting can proceed. A majority vote of the shares represented at the meeting is usually required to pass resolutions. ◾**EXAMPLE 20.3** Novo Pictures, Inc., has 10,000 outstanding shares of voting stock. Its articles of incorporation set the quorum at 50 percent of outstanding shares and provide that a majority vote of the shares present is necessary to pass resolutions concerning ordinary matters. Therefore, for

---

PROXY
In corporate law, a written agreement between a stockholder and another party in which the stockholder authorizes the other party to vote the stockholder's shares in a certain manner.

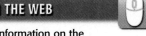

ON THE WEB

For information on the SEC's rulings, including rulings on proxy materials, go to

www.sec.gov/rules/final.shtml.

BE CAREFUL   Once a quorum is present, a vote can be taken even if some shareholders leave without casting their votes.

---

8. A director can often demand court review of removal for cause.

ADAPTING THE LAW TO THE ONLINE ENVIRONMENT

The SEC Adopts New E-Proxy Rules

In the past, anyone wishing to solicit proxies from shareholders had to mail each shareholder numerous paper documents relating to the proxy. Required materials often include notice of the meeting, proxy statements and consent solicitation statements, proxy cards, information statements, annual reports, additional soliciting materials, and any amendments made to these materials. Providing all of these documents in paper form can be very costly.

In January 2007, the Securities and Exchange Commission (SEC) adopted voluntary e-proxy rules that went into effect on July 1, 2007.[a] Essentially, the new rules allow companies to furnish proxy materials to shareholders by posting them on a Web site and providing shareholders with notice of the availability of the proxy materials online. This is a significant development that will reduce the printing and mailing costs associated with furnishing proxy materials to shareholders. Because the rules are voluntary, a company may still provide paper proxy documents if it so chooses.

The Notice and Access Model

Under the SEC's new rules, a company may now furnish proxy materials to shareholders using the notice and access model, which includes the following steps:

- The company posts the proxy materials on a publicly accessible Web site.
- The company then sends a (paper) notice to each shareholder at least forty calendar days prior to the date of the shareholders' meeting for which the proxy is being solicited.
- No other materials (such as a proxy card) can be sent along with the initial notice (unless the proxy is being combined with a meeting notice required by state law).
- The notice must be written in plain English and include a prominent statement of the following: the date, time, and location of the shareholders' meeting; the specific Web site at which the shareholders can access the proxy materials; an explanation of how they can obtain paper copies of the

proxy materials at no cost (by calling a toll-free phone number, for instance); and a clear and impartial description of each matter to be considered at the shareholders' meeting.
- After sending the initial notice, the company must wait at least ten days before sending a (paper) proxy card to the shareholders. This ten-day waiting period is designed to provide shareholders with sufficient time to access the proxy materials online or request paper copies.
- If a shareholder requests paper proxy materials, the company must send them to the shareholder within three business days.
- After receiving the initial paper notice, a shareholder can permanently elect to receive all future proxy materials on paper or by e-mail.

Shareholders and other parties conducting their own proxy solicitations can also use the notice and access model with slight modifications. The notice must still be sent forty days before the meeting date and include substantially the same information, but the notice need not be provided to all shareholders. In contrast to company solicitations, other parties can selectively choose the shareholders from whom they wish to solicit proxies without sending information to all other shareholders.

Should E-Proxy Rules Be Mandatory?

The SEC has also proposed making the new e-proxy rules mandatory for all proxy solicitations in the future. The mandatory notice and access model would operate substantially the same as just outlined, except that the initial notice could be accompanied by a paper or e-mail copy of the proxy statement, annual report, and proxy card. The main difference between the mandatory and voluntary models is that under the voluntary rule, the company (or other party seeking proxies) can choose whether to use electronic or paper means, whereas under a mandatory rule, the SEC would require the use of electronic means. Under either rule, the shareholder can always choose to receive paper documents rather than accessing the materials online.

FOR CRITICAL ANALYSIS *Why might a company or other party choose to solicit proxies the old-fashioned way, by providing paper documents instead of Internet access, despite the added costs?*

a. 17 C.F.R. Parts 240, 249, and 274.

this firm, a quorum of shareholders representing 5,000 outstanding shares must be present at a shareholders' meeting to conduct business. If exactly 5,000 shares are represented at the meeting, a vote of at least 2,501 of those shares is needed to pass a resolution. If 6,000 shares are represented, a vote of 3,001 will be required, and so on. ◼

At times, more than a simple majority vote will be required either by a state statute or by the corporate articles. Extraordinary corporate matters, such as a *merger, consolidation,* or *dissolution* of the corporation (as will be discussed later in this chapter), require a higher percentage of all corporate shares entitled to vote and not just a majority of those present at that particular meeting.

Cumulative Voting   Most states permit or even require shareholders to elect directors by *cumulative voting,* a voting method designed to allow minority shareholders to be represented on the board of directors.[9] With cumulative voting, the number of board members to be elected is multiplied by the number of voting shares a shareholder owns. The result equals the number of votes the shareholder has, and this total can be cast for one or more nominees for director. All nominees stand for election at the same time. When cumulative voting is not required either by statute or under the articles, the entire board can be elected by a simple majority of shares at a shareholders' meeting.

Cumulative voting can best be understood by an example. **■EXAMPLE 20.4** A corporation has 10,000 shares issued and outstanding. One group of shareholders (the minority shareholders) holds only 3,000 shares, and the other group of shareholders (the majority shareholders) holds the other 7,000 shares. Three members of the board are to be elected. The majority shareholders' nominees are Acevedo, Barkley, and Craycik. The minority shareholders' nominee is Drake. Can Drake be elected by the minority shareholders?

If cumulative voting is allowed, the answer is yes. Together, the minority shareholders have 9,000 votes (the number of directors to be elected times the number of shares held by the minority shareholders equals 3 times 3,000, which equals 9,000 votes). All of these votes can be cast to elect Drake. The majority shareholders have 21,000 votes (3 times 7,000 equals 21,000 votes), but these votes have to be distributed among their three nominees. The principle of cumulative voting is that no matter how the majority shareholders cast their 21,000 votes, they will not be able to elect all three directors if the minority shareholders cast all of their 9,000 votes for Drake, as illustrated in Exhibit 20–2. ■

Rights of Shareholders

Shareholders possess numerous rights. A significant right—the right to vote their shares— has already been discussed. We now look at some additional rights of shareholders.

STOCK CERTIFICATE
A certificate issued by a corporation evidencing the ownership of a specified number of shares in the corporation.

Stock Certificates   A **stock certificate** is a certificate issued by a corporation that evidences ownership of a specified number of shares in the corporation. In jurisdictions that

9. See, for example, California Corporate Code Section 708. Under RMBCA 7.28, however, no cumulative voting rights exist unless the articles of incorporation so provide.

EXHIBIT 20–2   Results of Cumulative Voting

This exhibit illustrates how cumulative voting gives minority shareholders a greater chance of electing a director of their choice. By casting all of their 9,000 votes for one candidate (Drake), the minority shareholders will succeed in electing Drake to the board of directors.

BALLOT	MAJORITY SHAREHOLDERS' VOTES			MINORITY SHAREHOLDERS' VOTES	DIRECTORS ELECTED
	Acevedo	**Barkley**	**Craycik**	**Drake**	
1	10,000	10,000	1,000	9,000	Acevedo/Barkley/Drake
2	9,001	9,000	2,999	9,000	Acevedo/Barkley/Drake
3	6,000	7,000	8,000	9,000	Barkley/Craycik/Drake

require the issuance of stock certificates, shareholders have the right to demand that the corporation issue certificates. In most states and under RMBCA 6.26, boards of directors may provide that shares of stock will be uncertificated—that is, no actual, physical stock certificates will be issued. When shares are uncertificated, the corporation may be required to send each shareholder a letter or some other form of notice that contains the same information that would normally appear on the face of stock certificates.

Stock is intangible personal property, and the ownership right exists independently of the certificate itself. If a stock certificate is lost or destroyed, ownership is not destroyed with it. A new certificate can be issued to replace one that has been lost or destroyed.[10] Notice of shareholders' meetings, dividends, and operational and financial reports are all distributed according to the recorded ownership listed in the corporation's books, not on the basis of possession of the certificate.

Stock certificates are displayed. To be a shareholder, is it necessary to have physical possession of a certificate? Why or why not? (PhotoDisc)

Preemptive Rights   A **preemptive right** entitles a shareholder to purchase newly issued shares of a corporation's stock, equal in percentage to shares already held, before the stock is offered to other outside buyers. This allows each shareholder to maintain her or his proportionate control, voting power, or financial interest in the corporation. Most statutes either (1) grant preemptive rights but allow them to be negated in the corporation's articles or (2) deny preemptive rights except to the extent that they are granted in the articles. The result is that the articles of incorporation determine the existence and scope of preemptive rights. Generally, preemptive rights apply only to additional, newly issued stock sold for cash, and the preemptive rights must be exercised within a specified time period, which is usually thirty days.

PREEMPTIVE RIGHT
A right held by shareholders that entitles them to purchase newly issued shares of a corporation's stock, equal in percentage to shares already held, before the stock is offered to any outside buyers. Preemptive rights enable shareholders to maintain their proportionate ownership and voice in the corporation.

Dividends   As mentioned earlier in this chapter, a *dividend* is a distribution of corporate profits or income *ordered by the directors* and paid to the shareholders in proportion to their respective shares in the corporation. Dividends can be paid in cash, property, stock of the corporation that is paying the dividends, or stock of other corporations.[11]

State laws vary, but each state determines the general circumstances and legal requirements under which dividends are paid. State laws also control the sources of revenue to be used; only certain funds are legally available for paying dividends. Depending on state law, dividends may be paid from the following sources:

1 *Retained earnings.* All states allow dividends to be paid from the undistributed net profits earned by the corporation, including capital gains from the sale of fixed assets. As mentioned earlier in this chapter, the undistributed net profits are called *retained earnings.*

2 *Net profits.* A few states allow dividends to be issued from current net profits without regard to deficits in prior years.

3 *Surplus.* A number of states allow dividends to be paid out of any kind of surplus.

---

10. The Uniform Commercial Code (UCC) provides that for a lost or destroyed certificate to be reissued, a shareholder normally must furnish an *indemnity bond.* An indemnity bond is a written promise to reimburse the holder for any actual or claimed loss caused by the issuer's or some other person's conduct. The bond protects the corporation against potential loss should the original certificate reappear at some future time in the hands of a bona fide purchaser [UCC 8–302, 8–405(2)].

11. Technically, dividends paid in stock are not dividends. They maintain each shareholder's proportionate interest in the corporation. On one occasion, a distillery declared and paid a "dividend" in bonded whiskey.

Illegal Dividends. A dividend paid while the corporation is insolvent is automatically an illegal dividend, and shareholders may be required to return the payment to the corporation or its creditors. Whenever dividends are illegal or improper, the board of directors can be held personally liable for the amount of the payment. When directors can show that a shareholder knew that a dividend was illegal when it was received, however, the directors are entitled to reimbursement from the shareholder.

Directors' Failure to Declare a Dividend. When directors fail to declare a dividend, shareholders can ask a court to compel the directors to meet and to declare a dividend. To succeed, the shareholders must show that the directors have acted so unreasonably in withholding the dividend that their conduct is an abuse of their discretion.

Often, large cash reserves are accumulated for a bona fide purpose, such as expansion, research, or other legitimate corporate goals. The mere fact that sufficient corporate earnings or surplus is available to pay a dividend is not enough to compel directors to distribute funds that, in the board's opinion, should not be paid. The courts are reluctant to interfere with corporate operations and will not compel directors to declare dividends unless abuse of discretion is clearly shown.

Inspection Rights Shareholders in a corporation enjoy both common law and statutory inspection rights. The shareholder's right of inspection is limited, however, to the inspection and copying of corporate books and records for a *proper purpose*, provided the request is made in advance. The shareholder can inspect in person, or an attorney, accountant, or other type of assistant can do so as the shareholder's agent. The RMBCA requires the corporation to maintain an alphabetical voting list of shareholders with addresses and number of shares owned; this list must be kept open at the annual meeting for inspection by any shareholder of record [RMBCA 7.20].

Transfer of Shares Stock certificates generally are negotiable and freely transferable by indorsement and delivery. Transfer of stock in closely held corporations, however, usually is restricted by the bylaws, by a restriction stamped on the stock certificate, or by a shareholder agreement.

Sometimes, corporations or their shareholders restrict transferability by reserving the option to purchase any shares offered for resale by a shareholder. This **right of first refusal** remains with the corporation or the shareholders for only a specified time or a reasonable period. Variations on the purchase option are possible. For example, a shareholder might be required to offer the shares to other shareholders first or to the corporation first.

When shares are transferred, a new entry is made in the corporate stock book to indicate the new owner. Until the corporation is notified and the entry is complete, all rights—including voting rights, the right to notice of shareholders' meetings, and the right to dividend distributions—remain with the current record owner.

RIGHT OF FIRST REFUSAL
The right to purchase personal or real property—such as corporate shares or real estate—before the property is offered for sale to others.

Rights on Dissolution When a corporation is dissolved and its outstanding debts and the claims of its creditors have been satisfied, the remaining assets are distributed to the shareholders in proportion to the percentage of shares owned by each shareholder. Certain classes of preferred stock can be given priority. If no class of stock has been given preferences in the distribution of assets on liquidation, then all of the stockholders share the remaining assets.

In some circumstances, shareholders may petition a court to have the corporation dissolved. If, for example, the minority shareholders know that the board of directors is mishandling corporate assets, those shareholders can petition a court to appoint a *receiver* who will wind up corporate affairs and liquidate the business assets of the corporation.

The RMBCA permits any shareholder to initiate such an action in any of the following circumstances [RMBCA 14.30]:

1 The directors are deadlocked in the management of corporate affairs. The shareholders are unable to break that deadlock, and irreparable injury to the corporation is being suffered or threatened.

2 The acts of the directors or those in control of the corporation are illegal, oppressive, or fraudulent.

3 Corporate assets are being misapplied or wasted.

4 The shareholders are deadlocked in voting power and have failed, for a specified period (usually two annual meetings), to elect successors to directors whose terms have expired or would have expired with the election of successors.

The Shareholder's Derivative Suit   When those in control of a corporation—the corporate directors—fail to sue in the corporate name to redress a wrong suffered by the corporation, shareholders are permitted to do so "derivatively" in what is known as a **shareholder's derivative suit.** Before a derivative suit can be brought, some wrong must have been done to the corporation, and the shareholders must have presented their complaint to the board of directors. Only if the directors fail to solve the problem or to take appropriate action can the derivative suit go forward.

SHAREHOLDER'S DERIVATIVE SUIT
A suit brought by a shareholder to enforce a corporate cause of action against a third person.

The right of shareholders to bring a derivative action is especially important when the wrong suffered by the corporation results from the actions of corporate directors or officers. This is because the directors and officers would probably want to prevent any action against themselves.

The shareholder's derivative suit is unusual in that those suing are not pursuing rights or benefits for themselves personally but are acting as guardians of the corporate entity. Therefore, any damages recovered by the suit normally go into the corporation's treasury, not to the shareholders. (Derivative actions are less common in other countries than in the United States, as this chapter's *Beyond Our Borders* feature on page 628 explains.)

Duties of Majority Shareholders

In some instances, a majority shareholder is regarded as having a fiduciary duty to the corporation and to the minority shareholders. This occurs when a single shareholder (or a few shareholders acting in concert) owns a sufficient number of shares to exercise *de facto* (actual) control over the corporation. In these situations, majority shareholders owe a fiduciary duty to the minority shareholders.

A breach of fiduciary duty can also occur when the majority shareholders of a closely held corporation use their control to exclude the minority from certain benefits of participating in the firm. **EXAMPLE 20.5** Three brothers, Alfred, Carl, and Eugene, each owned a one-third interest in a corporation and had worked for the corporation for most of their adult lives. When a dispute arose concerning discrepancies in the corporation's accounting records, Carl and Eugene fired Alfred and told the company's employees that Alfred had had a nervous breakdown, which was not true. Alfred sued Carl and Eugene, alleging that they had breached their fiduciary duties. The brothers argued that because there was no reduction in the value of the corporation or the value of Alfred's shares in the company, they had not breached their fiduciary duties. The court, however, held that the brothers' conduct was unfairly prejudicial toward Alfred and supported a finding of a breach of fiduciary duty.[12] ■

---

12. See, for example, *Swanson v. Upper Midwest Industries, Inc.,* ___ N.W.2d ___ (Minn.App. 2002).

Today, most of the claims brought against directors and officers in the United States are those alleged in shareholders' derivative suits. Other nations, however, put more restrictions on the use of such suits. German law, for example, does not provide for derivative litigation, and a corporation's duty to its employees is just as significant as its duty to the shareholder-owners of the company. The United Kingdom has no statute authorizing derivative actions, which are permitted only to challenge directors' actions that the shareholders could not legally ratify. Japan authorizes derivative actions but also permits a company to sue the plaintiff-shareholder for damages if the action is unsuccessful.

FOR CRITICAL ANALYSIS *Do corporations benefit from shareholders' derivative suits? If so, how?*

■

MERGER AND CONSOLIDATION

A corporation typically extends its operations by combining with another corporation through a merger, a consolidation, a purchase of assets, or a purchase of a controlling interest in the other corporation. The terms *merger* and *consolidation* are often used interchangeably, but they refer to two legally distinct proceedings. The rights and liabilities of the corporation, its shareholders, and its creditors are the same for both, however.

Merger

A **merger** involves the legal combination of two or more corporations in such a way that only one of the corporations continues to exist. **■EXAMPLE 20.6** Corporation A and Corporation B decide to merge. They agree that A will absorb B. Therefore, on merging, B ceases to exist as a separate entity, and A continues as the *surviving corporation.* ■ Exhibit 20–3 graphically illustrates this process.

After the merger, A is recognized as a single corporation, possessing all the rights, privileges, and powers of itself and B. It automatically acquires all of B's property and assets without the necessity of a formal transfer. Additionally, A becomes liable for all of B's debts and obligations. Finally, A's articles of incorporation are deemed amended to include any changes that are stated in the *articles of merger* (a document setting forth the terms and conditions of the merger that is filed with the secretary of state).

In a merger, the surviving corporation inherits the disappearing corporation's preexisting legal rights and obligations. For example, if the disappearing corporation had a right of action against a third party, the surviving corporation can bring suit after the merger to recover the disappearing corporation's damages. The common law similarly recognizes that, following a merger, a right to bring an action to enforce a property right will *vest* with the successor (surviving) corporation, and no right of action will remain with the disappearing corporation.

Consolidation

In a **consolidation,** two or more corporations combine in such a way that each corporation ceases to exist and a new one emerges. **■EXAMPLE 20.7** Corporation A and Corporation B

MERGER
A contractual and statutory process in which one corporation (the surviving corporation) acquires all of the assets and liabilities of another corporation (the merged corporation). The shareholders of the merged corporation either are paid for their shares or receive shares in the surviving corporation.

CONSOLIDATION
A contractual and statutory process in which two or more corporations join to become a completely new corporation. The original corporations cease to exist, and the new corporation acquires all their assets and liabilities.

EXHIBIT 20–3 **Merger**

In this illustration, Corporation A and Corporation B decide to merge. They agree that A will absorb B, so after the merger, B no longer exists as a separate entity, and A continues as the surviving corporation.

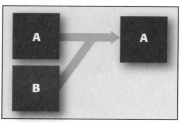

consolidate to form an entirely new organization, Corporation C. In the process, A and B both terminate, and C comes into existence as an entirely new entity. Exhibit 20–4 graphically illustrates this process.

The results of a consolidation are essentially the same as the results of a merger. C is recognized as a new corporation and a single entity; A and B cease to exist. C inherits all of the rights, privileges, and powers previously held by A and B. Title to any property and assets owned by A and B passes to C without a formal transfer. C assumes liability for all of the debts and obligations owed by A and B. The *articles of consolidation*, which state the terms of the consolidation, take the place of A's and B's original corporate articles and are thereafter regarded as C's corporate articles. ■

PURCHASE OF ASSETS OR STOCK

When a corporation acquires all or substantially all of the assets of another corporation by direct purchase, the purchasing, or *acquiring*, corporation simply extends its ownership and control over more physical assets. Because no change in the legal entity occurs, the acquiring corporation is not required to obtain shareholder approval for the purchase.[13] The U.S. Department of Justice and the Federal Trade Commission, however, have issued guidelines that significantly constrain and often prohibit mergers that could result from a purchase of assets, including takeover bids. (These guidelines are part of the federal antitrust laws that will be discussed in Chapter 22.)

Note that the corporation that is *selling* all of its assets is substantially changing its business position and perhaps its ability to carry out its corporate purposes. For that reason, the corporation whose assets are being sold must obtain the approval of both the board of directors and the shareholders. In most states and under RMBCA 13.02, a dissenting shareholder of the selling corporation can demand **appraisal rights.**

Potential Liability in Purchases of Assets

Generally, a corporation that purchases the assets of another corporation is not responsible for the liabilities of the selling corporation. Exceptions to this rule are made in certain circumstances, however. In any of the following situations, the acquiring corporation will be held to have assumed *both* the assets and the liabilities of the selling corporation:

1 When the purchasing corporation impliedly or expressly assumes the seller's liabilities.

2 When the sale amounts to what is in fact a merger or consolidation.

3 When the purchaser continues the seller's business and retains the same personnel (same shareholders, directors, and officers).

4 When the sale is fraudulently executed to escape liability.

Purchase of Stock and Tender Offers

An alternative to the purchase of another corporation's assets is the purchase of a substantial number of the voting shares of its stock. This enables the acquiring corporation to control the **target corporation** (the corporation being acquired). The process of acquiring control over a corporation in this way is commonly referred to as a corporate **takeover.**

EXHIBIT 20–4 **Consolidation**

In this illustration, Corporation A and Corporation B consolidate to form an entirely new organization, Corporation C. In the process, A and B terminate, and C comes into existence as an entirely new entity.

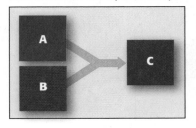

APPRAISAL RIGHT
The right of a dissenting shareholder, who objects to an extraordinary transaction of the corporation (such as a merger or a consolidation), to have his or her shares appraised and to be paid the fair value of those shares by the corporation.

TARGET CORPORATION
The corporation to be acquired in a corporate takeover; a corporation whose shareholders receive a tender offer.

TAKEOVER
The acquisition of control over a corporation through the purchase of a substantial number of the voting shares of the corporation.

13. If the acquiring corporation plans to pay for the assets with its own corporate stock and not enough authorized unissued shares are available, the shareholders must vote to approve the issuance of additional shares by amendment of the corporate articles. Additionally, acquiring corporations whose stock is traded on a national stock exchange can be required to obtain their own shareholders' approval if they plan to issue a significant number of shares, such as a number equal to 20 percent or more of the outstanding shares.

TENDER OFFER
An offer to purchase made by one company directly to the shareholders of another (target) company; sometimes referred to as a *takeover bid*.

The acquiring corporation deals directly with the target company's shareholders in seeking to purchase the shares they hold. It does this by making a **tender offer** to all of the shareholders of the target corporation. The tender offer can be conditioned on receiving a specified number of shares by a certain date. The price offered is generally higher than the market price of the target corporation's stock prior to the announcement of the tender offer as a means of inducing shareholders to accept the offer. For instance, in the 2006 merger of AT&T and BellSouth, BellSouth shareholders reportedly received approximately $37.09 per share—a 16 percent premium over the market price of the stock. Federal securities laws strictly control the terms, duration, and circumstances under which most tender offers are made.

A firm may respond to a tender offer in numerous ways. Sometimes, a target firm's board of directors will see a tender offer as favorable and will recommend to the shareholders that they accept it. To resist a takeover, a target company can make a *self-tender*, which is an offer to acquire stock from its own shareholders and thereby retain corporate control. Alternatively, a target corporation might resort to one of several other defensive tactics to resist a takeover. In one commonly used tactic, known as a "poison pill," a target company gives its shareholders rights to purchase additional shares at low prices when there is a takeover attempt. The use of poison pills is an attempt to prevent takeovers by making a takeover prohibitively expensive.

TERMINATION

The termination of a corporation's existence has two phases—dissolution and winding up. **Dissolution** is the legal death of the artificial "person" of the corporation. *Winding up* is the process by which corporate assets are liquidated, or converted into cash and distributed among creditors and shareholders.[14]

DISSOLUTION
The formal disbanding of a partnership or a corporation. Dissolution of a corporation can take place by (1) an act of the state legislature, (2) agreement of the shareholders and the board of directors, (3) the expiration of a time period stated in the certificate of incorporation, or (4) court order.

Voluntary Dissolution

Dissolution can be brought about voluntarily by the directors and the shareholders. State incorporation statutes establish the required procedures to voluntarily dissolve a corporation. Basically, there are two possible methods: by the shareholders' unanimous vote to initiate dissolution proceedings[15] or by a proposal of the board of directors that is submitted to the shareholders at a shareholders' meeting. When a corporation is dissolved voluntarily, the corporation must file *articles of dissolution* with the state and notify its creditors of the dissolution. The corporation must also establish a date (at least 120 days following the date of dissolution) by which all claims against the corporation must be received [RMBCA 14.06].

Involuntary Dissolution

Because corporations are creatures of statute, the state can also dissolve a corporation in certain circumstances. The secretary of state or the state attorney general can bring an action to dissolve a corporation that has failed to pay its annual taxes or to submit required annual reports, for example. A state court can also dissolve a corporation that has committed fraud or misrepresentation to the state during incorporation.

---

14. Some prefer to call this phase *liquidation*, but we use the term *winding up* to mean all acts needed to bring the legal and financial affairs of the business to an end, including liquidating the assets and distributing them among creditors and shareholders. See RMBCA 14.05.

15. See, for example, Delaware Code Section 275(c). Not every state allows shareholders to initiate corporate dissolution, however.

Sometimes, a shareholder or a group of shareholders petitions a court for corporate dissolution. A court may dissolve a corporation if the controlling shareholders or directors have engaged in fraudulent, illegal, or oppressive conduct.[16]

Shareholders may also petition a court for dissolution when the board of directors is deadlocked. Courts hesitate to order involuntary dissolution in such situations unless there is specific statutory authorization to do so. In the following case, the issue was whether the circumstances satisfied the statutory requirements for a court to dissolve a trucking corporation.

CASE 20.3   Sartori v. S & S Trucking, Inc.

Supreme Court of Montana, 2006 MT 164, 332 Mont. 503, 139 P.3d 806 (2006).

FACTS Tony Stacy approached his friend, Justin Sartori, about buying a trucking business and operating it together. Sartori agreed, and because he had a good credit standing and Stacy did not, Sartori borrowed $78,493.68 from First Interstate Bank in Eureka, Montana, to buy the business. In September 2003, they formed S & S Trucking, Inc., and agreed to be its only directors, officers, and shareholders, with each owning an equal number of shares. Within weeks, however, they realized that they were incompatible. For example, Sartori often did not appear when and where Stacy expected, and they differed over the payment of earnings from S & S's income. In October, Sartori incorporated Brimstone Enterprise to undermine S & S. He had S & S's mail forwarded to Brimstone, transferred S & S's licenses to Brimstone, and attempted to attract S & S's customers to Brimstone. In mid-November, he quit working for S & S and filed a suit in a Montana state court against S & S and Stacy, demanding that the firm be dissolved. The court set a deadline for the dissolution. The defendants appealed to the Montana Supreme Court.

ISSUE Can a court order the dissolution of a corporation without finding that the firm has suffered or is threatened with an injury?

DECISION Yes. The Montana Supreme Court affirmed the decision of the lower court, holding that the order for the dissolution of S & S was correct.

REASON The state supreme court pointed out that under Montana Code Section 35-1-938(2)(a), a court can dissolve a corporation in a proceeding by a shareholder if "the directors are deadlocked in the management of the corporate affairs, the shareholders are unable to break the deadlock, and irreparable injury to the corporation is threatened or being suffered or the business and affairs of the corporation can no longer be conducted to the advantage of the shareholders generally because of the deadlock." The court conceded that S & S had not suffered an "irreparable injury," but reasoned that the deadlock between Sartori and Stacy had led Sartori to sabotage the corporation. "As a result, the business and affairs of S & S could no longer be conducted to the advantage of the shareholders."

FOR CRITICAL ANALYSIS–Social Consideration
At the time of the defendants' appeal, S & S had twelve employees and, according to Stacy, its business was thriving. Should the court have taken these factors into consideration when deciding whether to order the dissolution of the firm? Why or why not?

Winding Up

When dissolution takes place by voluntary action, the members of the board of directors act as trustees of the corporate assets. As trustees, they are responsible for winding up the affairs of the corporation for the benefit of corporate creditors and shareholders. This makes the board members personally liable for any breach of their fiduciary trustee duties.

When the dissolution is involuntary—or if board members do not wish to act as trustees of the assets—the court will appoint a **receiver** to wind up the corporate affairs

RECEIVER
In a corporate dissolution, a court-appointed person who winds up corporate affairs and liquidates corporate assets.

---

16. See, for example, *Colt v. Mt. Princeton Trout Club, Inc.*, 78 P.3d 1115 (Colo.App. 2003).

and liquidate corporate assets. Courts may also appoint a receiver when shareholders or creditors can show that the board of directors should not be permitted to act as trustees of the corporate assets.

REVIEWING Corporations

David Brock is on the board of directors of Firm Body Fitness, Inc., which owns a string of fitness clubs in New Mexico. Brock owns 15 percent of the Firm Body stock, and he is also employed as a tanning technician at one of the fitness clubs. After the January financial report showed that Firm Body's tanning division was operating at a substantial net loss, the board of directors, led by Marty Levinson, discussed terminating the tanning operations. Brock successfully convinced a majority of the board that the tanning division was necessary to market the club's overall fitness package. By April, the tanning division's financial losses had risen. The board hired a business analyst who conducted surveys and determined that the tanning operations did not significantly increase membership. A shareholder, Diego Peñada, discovered that Brock owned stock in Sunglow, Inc., the company from which Firm Body purchased

its tanning equipment. Peñada notified Levinson, who privately reprimanded Brock. Shortly afterwards, Brock and Mandy Vail, who owned 37 percent of Firm Body stock and also held shares of Sunglow, voted to replace Levinson on the board of directors. Using the information presented in the chapter, answer the following questions.

1 What duties did Brock, as a director, owe to Firm Body?

2 Does the fact that Brock owned shares in Sunglow establish a conflict of interest? Why or why not?

3 Suppose that Firm Body brought an action against Brock claiming that he had breached the duty of loyalty by not disclosing his interest in Sunglow to the other directors. What theory might Brock use in his defense?

4 Now suppose that Firm Body did not bring an action against Brock. What type of lawsuit might Peñada be able to bring based on these facts?

APPLICATION How Can Online Services Facilitate the Incorporation Process?*

Today, just about anybody can form a corporation for any lawful purpose in any state. The requirements differ from state to state. You do not even have to form your corporation in the state where you live or the state where you are doing business. In fact, many individuals form their corporations in the state of Delaware because it has the fewest legal restrictions on corporate formation and operation. Today, Delaware is also the state most often chosen for incorporation via the Internet, often through online companies that offer incorporation services.

Finding Information on Incorporation Requirements

Nearly every state has a Web site at which you can find the individual state's requirements for incorporation. (To locate

your state's Web site, go to **www.statelocalgov.net**.) Most state sites post guidelines or instructions on forming corporations (and other business entities), fee schedules, and frequently asked questions (FAQs). Many also provide downloadable corporate forms.

In addition, hundreds of companies now provide incorporation services online, and you can obtain a great deal of information at their Web sites. For example, at the Web site of The Company Corporation (TCC) of Delaware (**www. corporate.com**), you can read about the advantages and costs of incorporating in your state or any other state, as well as the pros and cons of the different types of corporate entities. Similar information is available via an online seminar at the Web site of Harvard Business Services, Inc. (**www.delawareinc.com**). In addition, this site provides free downloadable forms and will act as the corporation's registered agent for a fixed annual fee of $50.

Another useful site is that of the Corporation Service Company (CSC) (**www.incspot.com/public**), which has more than a hundred years' experience in forming corporations. In addition to the standard services, CSC will scan and upload documents related to any corporate transaction or litigation into an online database. This service provides centralized access to important documents for authorized users anywhere in the world and allows multiple parties to track ongoing negotiations.

Incorporating Online

If you wish to incorporate via an online incorporation service, all you need to do is fill out a form online. For example, if you fill out the incorporation forms at the TCC Web site, TCC will then file the forms with the appropriate state office and obtain the state's authorization of the corporation for you. You can also arrange for the online incorporation service to perform other services such as acting as registered agent for your corporation, obtaining a tax identification number, and registering a domain name for your business.

CHECKLIST OF FACTORS TO CONSIDER WHEN INCORPORATING ONLINE OR OFFLINE

1 Determine how important the state of incorporation is to your business.
2 Decide which state's incorporation requirements and restrictions best suit the needs of your business.
3 Find out not only the initial cost of incorporation but also any continuing costs, such as annual fees and possible fees for attorneys and accountants.
4 Learn what formalities are necessary and the amount of record keeping that will be required.
5 Is "do-it-yourself" online incorporation appropriate? (Depending on the nature and potential growth of your business, you may decide to contact an attorney who can take you through the necessary steps in incorporating your business.)

KEY TERMS

alien corporation 613
appraisal right 629
articles of incorporation 612
bond 615
bond indenture 615
business judgment rule 621
bylaws 612
close corporation 613
common stock 615
consolidation 628
dissolution 630

dividend 610
domestic corporation 613
foreign corporation 613
holding company 610
merger 628
preemptive right 625
preferred stock 615
proxy 622
quorum 618
receiver 631
retained earnings 610

right of first refusal 626
S corporation 613
securities 615
shareholder's derivative suit 627
stock 615
stock certificate 624
takeover 629
target corporation 629
tender offer 630

CHAPTER SUMMARY Corporations

The Nature and Classification of Corporations
(See pages 608–613.)

A corporation is a legal entity distinct from its owners. Formal statutory requirements, which vary somewhat from state to state, must be followed in forming a corporation. The corporation can have perpetual existence or be chartered for a specific period of time.

1. *Corporate parties*—The shareholders own the corporation. They elect a board of directors to govern the corporation. The board of directors hires corporate officers and other employees to run the daily business of the firm.

2. *Corporate taxation*—The corporation pays income tax on net profits; shareholders pay income tax on the disbursed dividends that they receive from the corporation (double-taxation feature).

3. *Torts and criminal acts*—The corporation is liable for the torts committed by its agents or officers within the course and scope of their employment (under the doctrine of *respondeat superior*). In some circumstances, a corporation can be held liable (and be fined) for the criminal acts of its agents and employees. In certain situations, corporate officers may be held personally liable for corporate crimes.

(Continued)

CHAPTER SUMMARY	Corporations–Continued
The Nature and Classification of Corporations— Continued	4. *Corporate powers*— a. Express powers—The express powers of a corporation are granted by the following laws and documents (listed according to their priority): federal constitution, state constitutions, state statutes, articles of incorporation, bylaws, and resolutions of the board of directors. b. Implied powers—Barring express constitutional, statutory, or other prohibitions, the corporation has the implied power to do all acts reasonably appropriate and necessary to accomplish its corporate purposes. 5. *Classification of corporations*— a. Close corporations—Corporations owned by a family or a relatively small number of individuals; transfer of shares is usually restricted, and the corporation cannot make a public offering of its securities. b. S corporations—Small domestic corporations (must have one hundred or fewer shareholders as members) that under Subchapter S of the Internal Revenue Code are given special tax treatment. These corporations allow shareholders to enjoy the limited legal liability of the corporate form but avoid its double-taxation feature (taxes are paid by shareholders as personal income, and the S corporation is not taxed separately). c. Professional corporations—Corporations formed by professionals (for example, doctors and lawyers) to obtain the benefits of incorporation (such as tax benefits and limited liability). In most situations, the professional corporation is treated like other corporations, but sometimes the courts will disregard the corporate form and treat the shareholders as partners. d. Domestic, foreign, and alien corporations—A corporation is referred to as a *domestic corporation* within its home state (the state in which it incorporates). A corporation is referred to as a *foreign corporation* by any state that is not its home state. A corporation is referred to as an *alien corporation* if it originates in another country but does business in the United States.
Corporate Formation (See pages 613–615.)	1. *Promotional activities*—Preliminary promotional activities are rarely if ever engaged in today. A person who enters into contracts with investors and others on behalf of a future corporation is personally liable on all preincorporation contracts. Liability remains until the corporation is formed and assumes the contract by *novation*. 2. *Incorporation procedures*—Exact procedures for incorporation differ among states, but the basic steps are as follows: (1) select a state of incorporation, (2) secure the corporate name by confirming its availability, (3) prepare the articles of incorporation, and (4) file the articles of incorporation with the secretary of state accompanied by payment of the specified fees.
Corporate Financing (See pages 615–616.)	1. *Bonds*—Corporate bonds are securities representing corporate debt—funds borrowed by a corporation. 2. *Stocks*—Stocks are equity securities issued by a corporation that represent the purchase of ownership in the business firm. Exhibit 20–1 on page 616 describes the various types of stock and preferred stock.
Corporate Management— Directors and Officers (See pages 616–621.)	1. *Election of directors*—The first board of directors is usually appointed by the incorporators; thereafter, directors are elected by the shareholders. Directors usually serve a one-year term, although the term can be longer and staggered terms are permitted under most state statutes. 2. *Board of directors' meetings*—The board of directors conducts business by holding formal meetings with recorded minutes. The date of regular meetings is usually established in the corporate articles or bylaws; special meetings can be called, with notice sent to all directors. Quorum requirements vary from state to state; usually, a quorum is a majority of the corporate directors. Voting must usually be done in person, and in ordinary matters only a majority vote is required.

CHAPTER SUMMARY Corporations–Continued

Corporate Management– Directors and Officers–Continued

3. *Directors' rights and compensation*—A director has several rights, including the rights of participation, inspection, compensation, and indemnification. Compensation is usually specified in the corporate articles or bylaws.

4. *Directors' management responsibilities*—Directors are responsible for declaring and paying corporate dividends to shareholders; authorizing major corporate decisions; appointing, supervising, and removing corporate officers and other managerial employees; making financial decisions necessary to the management of corporate affairs; and issuing authorized shares and bonds. Directors may delegate some of their responsibilities to executive committees and corporate officers and executives.

5. *Corporate officers and executives*—Corporate officers and other executive employees are normally hired by the board of directors. In most states, a person can hold more than one office and can be both an officer and a director of a corporation. The rights of corporate officers and executives are defined by employment contracts. The duties of corporate officers are the same as those of directors.

6. *Duties and liabilities of directors and officers*—

   a. Duty of care—Directors are obligated to act in good faith, to use prudent business judgment in the conduct of corporate affairs, and to act in the corporation's best interests. If a director fails to exercise this duty of care, he or she can be answerable to the corporation and to the shareholders for breaching the duty.

   b. Duty of loyalty—Directors have a fiduciary duty to subordinate their own interests to those of the corporation in matters relating to the corporation.

   c. Conflicts of interest—To fulfill their duty of loyalty, directors and officers must make a full disclosure of any potential conflicts of interest between their personal interests and those of the corporation.

   d. Business judgment rule—This rule immunizes a director from liability for a corporate decision as long as the decision was within the powers of the corporation and the authority of the director to make, and was an informed, reasonable, and loyal decision.

Corporate Ownership– Shareholders (See pages 621–628.)

1. *Shareholders' powers*—Shareholders' powers include the approval of all fundamental changes affecting the corporation and the election of the board of directors.

2. *Shareholders' meetings*—Shareholders' meetings must occur at least annually; special meetings can be called when necessary. Notice of the date, time, and place of the meeting (and its purpose, if it is specially called) must be sent to shareholders. Shareholders may vote by proxy (authorizing someone else to vote their shares) and may submit proposals to be included in the company's proxy materials sent to shareholders before meetings.

3. *Shareholder voting*—Shareholder voting requirements and procedures are as follows:

   a. A minimum number of shareholders (a quorum—generally, more than 50 percent of shares held) must be present at a meeting for business to be conducted; resolutions are passed (usually) by simple majority vote.

   b. Cumulative voting may or may not be required or permitted. Cumulative voting gives minority shareholders a better chance to be represented on the board of directors.

4. *Rights of shareholders*—Shareholders have numerous rights, which may include the following:

   a. Voting rights.

   b. The right to a stock certificate and preemptive rights (depending on the articles of incorporation).

   c. The right to obtain a dividend (at the discretion of the directors).

(Continued)

CHAPTER SUMMARY	Corporations–Continued
Corporate Ownership— Shareholders— Continued	d. The right to inspect the corporate records.
	e. The right to transfer shares (this right may be restricted in close corporations).
	f. The right to a share of corporate assets when the corporation is dissolved.
	g. The right to sue on behalf of the corporation (bring a shareholder's derivative suit) when the directors fail to do so.
Merger and Consolidation (See pages 628–629.)	1. *Merger*—The legal combination of two or more corporations, with the result that the surviving corporation acquires all the assets and obligations of the other corporation, which then ceases to exist.
	2. *Consolidation*—The legal combination of two or more corporations, with the result that each corporation ceases to exist and a new one emerges. The new corporation assumes all the assets and obligations of the former corporations.
Purchase of Assets or Stock (See pages 629–630.)	A purchase of assets occurs when one corporation acquires all or substantially all of the assets of another corporation. A purchase of stock occurs when one corporation acquires a substantial number of the voting shares of the stock of another (target) corporation.
	1. *Acquiring corporation*—The acquiring (purchasing) corporation is not required to obtain shareholder approval; the corporation is merely increasing its assets, and no fundamental business change occurs.
	2. *Acquired corporation*—The acquired (purchased) corporation is required to obtain the approval of both its directors and its shareholders for the sale of its assets, because this creates a substantially change the corporation's business position.
	3. *Tender offer*—A public offer to all shareholders of the target corporation to purchase its stock at a price that is generally higher than the market price of the target stock prior to the announcement of the tender offer. Federal and state securities laws strictly control the terms, duration, and circumstances under which most tender offers are made.
	4. *Target responses*—Ways in which target corporations respond to takeover bids. These include self-tenders, poison pills, and numerous other strategies.
Termination (See pages 630–632.)	The termination of a corporation involves the following two phases:
	1. *Dissolution*—The legal death of the artificial "person" of the corporation. Dissolution can be brought about voluntarily by the directors and shareholders or involuntarily by the state or through a court order.
	2. *Winding up (liquidation)*—The process by which corporate assets are converted into cash and distributed to creditors and shareholders according to specified rules of preference. May be supervised by members of the board of directors (when dissolution is voluntary) or by a receiver appointed by the court to wind up corporate affairs.

FOR REVIEW

Answers for the even-numbered questions in this **For Review** *section can be found in Appendix E at the end of this text.*

1 What are the express and implied powers of corporations? On what sources are these powers based?

2 What are the duties of corporate directors and officers?

3 What must directors do to avoid liability for honest mistakes of judgment and poor business decisions?

4 What role do corporate shareholders play in the corporate enterprise? What are some important rights of shareholders?

5 What is the difference between a corporate merger and a corporate consolidation?

QUESTIONS AND CASE PROBLEMS

HYPOTHETICAL SCENARIOS

20.1 Voting Techniques. Algonquin Corp. has issued and has outstanding 100,000 shares of common stock. Four stockholders own 60,000 of these shares, and for the past six years they have nominated a slate of people for membership on the board, all of whom have been elected. Sergio and twenty other shareholders, owning 20,000 shares, are dissatisfied with corporate management and want a representative on the board who shares their views. Explain under what circumstances Sergio and the minority shareholders can elect their representative to the board.

20.2 Hypothetical Question with Sample Answer. Jolson is the chair of the board of directors of Artel, Inc., and Douglas is the chair of the board of directors of Fox Express, Inc. Artel is a manufacturing corporation, and Fox Express is a transportation corporation. Jolson and Douglas meet to consider the possibility of combining their corporations and activities into a single corporate entity. They consider two alternative courses of action: Artel could acquire all of the stock and assets of Fox Express, or the corporations could combine to form a new corporation, called A&F Enterprises, Inc. Both Jolson and Douglas are concerned about the necessity of a formal transfer of property, liability for existing debts, and the need to amend the articles of incorporation. Discuss what the two proposed combinations are called and the legal effect each has on the transfer of property, the liabilities of the combined corporations, and the need to amend the articles of incorporation.

 For a sample answer to Question 20.2, go to Appendix F at the end of this text.

CASE PROBLEMS

20.3 Inspection Rights. Craig Johnson founded Distributed Solutions, Inc. (DSI), in 1991 to make software and provide consulting services, including payroll services, for small companies. Johnson was the sole officer and director and the majority shareholder. Jeffrey Hagen was a minority shareholder. In 1993, Johnson sold DSI's payroll services to himself and a few others and set up Distributed Payroll Solutions, Inc. (DPSI). In 1996, DSI had revenues of $739,034 and assets of $541,168. DSI's revenues in 1997 were $934,532. Within a year, however, all of DSI's assets were sold, and Johnson told Hagen that he was dissolving the firm because, among other things, it conducted no business and had no prospects for future business. Hagen asked for corporate records to determine the value of DSI's stock, DSI's financial condition, and "whether unauthorized and oppressive acts had occurred in connection with the operation of the corporation which impacted the value of" the stock. When there was no response, Hagen filed a suit in an Illinois state court against DSI and Johnson, seeking an order to compel the inspection. The defendants filed a motion to dismiss, arguing that Hagen had failed to plead a proper purpose. Should the court grant Hagen's request? Discuss. [*Hagen v. Distributed Solutions, Inc.*, 328 Ill.App.3d 132, 764 N.E.2d 1141, 262 Ill.Dec. 24 (1 Dist. 2002)]

20.4 Torts and Criminal Acts. Greg Allen is an employee, a shareholder, a director, and the president of Greg Allen Construction Co. In 1996, Daniel and Sondra Estelle hired Allen's firm to renovate a home they owned in Ladoga, Indiana. To finance the cost, they obtained a line of credit from Banc One, Indiana, which required periodic inspections to disburse funds. Allen was on the job every day and supervised all of the work. He designed all of the structural changes, including a floor system for the bedroom over the living room, the floor system of the living room, and the stairway to the second floor. He did all of the electrical, plumbing, and carpentry work and installed all of the windows. He did most of the drywall taping and finishing and most of the painting. The Estelles found much of this work to be unacceptable, and the bank's inspector agreed that it was of poor quality. When Allen failed to act on the Estelles' complaints, they filed a suit in an Indiana state court against Allen Construction and Allen personally, alleging, in part, that his individual work on the project was negligent. Can both Allen and his corporation be held liable for this tort? Explain. [*Greg Allen Construction Co. v. Estelle*, 798 N.E.2d 171 (Ind. 2003)]

20.5 Duty of Loyalty. Digital Commerce, Ltd., designed software to enable its clients to sell their products or services over the Internet. Kevin Sullivan served as a Digital vice president until 2000, when he became president. Sullivan was dissatisfied that his compensation did not include stock in Digital, but he was unable to negotiate a deal that included equity (referring to shares of ownership in the company). In May, Sullivan solicited ASR Corp.'s business for Digital while he investigated employment opportunities with ASR for himself. When ASR would not include an "equity component" in a job offer, Sullivan refused to negotiate further on Digital's behalf. A few months later, Sullivan began to form his own firm to compete with Digital, conducting organizational and marketing activities on Digital's time, including soliciting ASR's business. In August, Sullivan resigned after first having all e-mail pertaining to the new firm deleted from Digital's computers. ASR signed a contract with Sullivan's new firm and paid it $400,000 for work through October 2001. Digital filed a suit in a federal district court against Sullivan, claiming that he had usurped a corporate opportunity. Did Sullivan breach his fiduciary duty to Digital? Explain. [*In re Sullivan*, 305 Bankr. 809 (W.D.Mich. 2004)]

20.6 Case Problem with Sample Answer. Thomas Persson and Jon Nokes founded Smart Inventions, Inc., in 1991 to market household consumer products. The success of their first product, the Smart Mop, continued with later products, which were sold through infomercials and other means. Persson and Nokes were the firm's officers and equal shareholders, with Persson responsible for product development and Nokes operating the day-to-day activities. By 1998, they had become dissatisfied with each other's efforts. Nokes represented the firm as financially "dying," "in a grim state, . . . worse than ever," and offered to buy all of Persson's shares for $1.6 million. Persson accepted. On the day that they signed the agreement to transfer the shares, Smart Inventions began marketing a new product—the Tap Light, which was an instant success, generating millions of dollars in revenues. In negotiating with Persson, Nokes had intentionally kept the Tap Light a secret. Persson filed a suit in a California state court against Smart Inventions and others, asserting fraud and other claims. Under what principle might Smart Inventions be liable for Nokes's fraud? Is Smart Inventions liable in this case? Explain. [*Persson v. Smart Inventions, Inc.*, 125 Cal.App.4th 1141, 23 Cal.Rptr.3d 335 (2 Dist. 2005)]

After you have answered Problem 20.6, compare your answer with the sample answer given on the Web site that accompanies this text. Go to academic.cengage.com/blaw/blt, select "Chapter 20," and click on "Case Problem with Sample Answer."

20.7 Purchase of Assets. In January 1999, General Star Indemnity Co. agreed to insure Indianapolis Racing League (IRL) racecars against damage during on-track accidents. In connection with the insurance, General Star deposited $400,000 with G Force, LLC (GFCO), a Colorado firm, to enable it to buy and provide, without delay, parts for damaged cars. GFCO agreed to return any unspent funds. Near the end of the season, Elan Motorsports Technologies (EMT) acquired GFCO. In 2000, EMT incorporated G Force, LLC, in Georgia (GFGA), and GFCO ceased to exist. GFGA renewed the arrangement with General Star and engaged in the same operations as GFCO, but EMT employees conducted GFGA's business at EMT's offices. In 2002, EMT assumed ownership of GFGA's assets and continued the business. EMT also assumed GFGA's liabilities,

except for the obligation to return General Star's unspent funds. General Star filed a suit in a Georgia state court against EMT, seeking to recover its deposit. What is the rule concerning the liability of a corporation that buys the assets of another? Are there exceptions? Which principles apply in this case? Explain. [*General Star Indemnity Co. v. Elan Motorsports Technologies, Inc.*, 356 F.Supp.2d 1333 (N.D.Ga. 2004)]

20.8 Dissolution. Clara Mahaffey operated Mahaffey's Auto Salvage, Inc., in Dayton, Ohio, as a sole proprietorship. In 1993, Kenneth Stumpff and Mahaffey's son, Richard Harris, joined the firm. Stumpff ran the wrecker and bought the vehicles for salvage. Harris handled the day-to-day operations and the bookkeeping. They became the company's equal 50 percent shareholders on Mahaffey's death in 2002. Harris, who inherited the land on which the firm was located, increased the rent to $1,500 per month. Within two years of Mahaffey's death, and without consulting Stumpff, Harris raised the rent to $2,500. Stumpff's wife died, and he took a leave of absence, during which the company paid him $2,500 a month and provided health insurance. After two years, Harris stopped the payments, discontinued the health benefits, and fired Stumpff, threatening to call the police if he came on the premises. Stumpff withdrew $16,000 from the firm's account, leaving a balance of $113. Harris offered to buy Stumpff's interest in the business, but Stumpff refused and filed a suit in an Ohio state court against Harris. A state statute permits the dissolution of a corporation if the owners are deadlocked in its management. Should the court order the dissolution of Mahaffey's? Why or why not? [*Stumpff v. Harris*, __ N.E.2d __, __ Ohio App.3d __ (2 Dist. 2006)]

20.9 A Question of Ethics. *New Orleans Paddlewheels, Inc. (NOP), is a Louisiana corporation formed in 1982 when James Smith, Sr., and Warren Reuther were its only shareholders, with each holding 50 percent of the stock. NOP is part of a sprawling enterprise of tourism and hospitality companies in New Orleans. The positions on the board of each company were split equally between the Smith and Reuther families. At Smith's request, his son James Smith, Jr. (JES), became involved in the businesses. In 1999, NOP's board elected JES the president, in charge of day-to-day operations, and Reuther the chief executive officer (CEO), in charge of marketing and development. Over the next few years, animosity developed between Reuther and JES. In October 2001, JES terminated Reuther as CEO and denied him access to the offices and books of NOP and the other companies, literally changing the locks on the doors. At the next meetings of the boards of NOP and the overall enterprise, deadlock ensued, with the directors voting along family lines on every issue. Complaining that the meetings were a "waste of time," JES began to run the entire enterprise by taking advantage of an unequal balance of power on the companies' executive committees. In NOP's subsequent bankruptcy proceeding, Reuther filed a motion for the appointment of a* *trustee to formulate a plan for the firm's reorganization, alleging, among other things, misconduct by NOP's management. [In re New Orleans Paddlewheels, Inc., 350 Bankr. 667 (E.D.La. 2006)]*

1 Was Reuther legally entitled to have access to the books and records of NOP and the other companies? JES maintained, among other things, that NOP's books were "a mess." Was JES's denial of that access unethical? Explain.

2 How would you describe JES's attempt to gain control of NOP and the other companies? Were his actions duplicitous and self-serving in the pursuit of personal gain or legitimate and reasonable in the pursuit of a business goal? Discuss.

 ## CRITICAL THINKING AND WRITING ASSIGNMENTS

20.10 Critical Legal Thinking. What are some of the ways in which the limited liability of corporate shareholders serves the public interest? Are there any ways in which this limited liability is harmful to the public interest? Explain.

20.11 Critical Legal Thinking. In general, courts are reluctant to grant shareholders' petitions for corporate dissolution except in extreme circumstances, such as when corporate directors or shareholders are deadlocked and the corporation suffers as a result. Rather, a court will attempt to "save" the corporate entity whenever possible. Why is this?

ONLINE ACTIVITIES

 ## PRACTICAL INTERNET EXERCISES

Go to this text's Web site at **academic.cengage.com/blaw/blt**, select "Chapter 20," and click on "Practical Internet Exercises." There you will find the following Internet research exercises that you can perform to learn more about the topics covered in this chapter.

PRACTICAL INTERNET EXERCISE 20-1 LEGAL PERSPECTIVE—Mergers

PRACTICAL INTERNET EXERCISE 20-2 MANAGEMENT PERSPECTIVE—Online Incorporation

PRACTICAL INTERNET EXERCISE 20-3 LEGAL PERSPECTIVE—Liability of Directors and Officers

BEFORE THE TEST

Go to this text's Web site at **academic.cengage.com/blaw/blt**, select "Chapter 20," and click on "Interactive Quizzes." You will find a number of interactive questions relating to this chapter.

CHAPTER 21
Investor Protection, Insider Trading, and Corporate Governance

LEARNING OBJECTIVES

AFTER READING THIS CHAPTER, YOU SHOULD BE ABLE TO ANSWER THE FOLLOWING QUESTIONS:

1 What is meant by the term *securities*?

2 What are the two major statutes regulating the securities industry? When was the Securities and Exchange Commission created, and what are its major purposes and functions?

3 What is insider trading? Why is it prohibited?

4 What are some of the features of state securities laws?

5 What certification requirements does the Sarbanes-Oxley Act impose on corporate executives?

After the stock market crash of 1929, many members of Congress argued in favor of regulating securities markets. Basically, legislation for such regulation was enacted to provide investors with more information to help them make buying and selling decisions about *securities*—generally defined as any documents or records evidencing corporate ownership *(stock)* or debts *(bonds)*—and to prohibit deceptive, unfair, and manipulative practices. (See Chapter 20 for a brief discussion of stocks and bonds.) Today, the sale and transfer of securities are heavily regulated by federal and state statutes and by government agencies.

This chapter discusses the nature of federal securities regulation and its effect on the business world. We first examine the major traditional laws governing securities offerings and trading. We then discuss corporate governance and the Sarbanes-Oxley Act of 2002,[1] which affects certain types of securities transactions. Finally, we look at how securities laws are being adapted to the online environment. Before we begin, though, the important role played by the Securities and Exchange Commission (SEC) in the regulation of federal securities laws requires some attention. We examine the origin and functions of the SEC in this chapter's *Landmark in the Law* feature on pages 642 and 643.

SECURITIES ACT OF 1933

The Securities Act of 1933[2] governs initial sales of stock by businesses. The act was designed to prohibit various forms of fraud and to stabilize the securities industry by requiring that all essential information concerning the issuance of securities be made available

---

1. 15 U.S.C. Sections 7201 *et seq.*
2. 15 U.S.C. Sections 77–77aa.

to the investing public. Basically, the purpose of this act is to require disclosure. The 1933 act provides that all securities transactions must be registered with the SEC or be exempt from registration requirements.

What Is a Security?

Section 2(1) of the Securities Act states that securities include the following:

> [A]ny note, stock, treasury stock, bond, debenture, evidence of indebtedness, certificate of interest or participation in any profit-sharing agreement, collateral-trust certificate, preorganization certificate or subscription, transferable share, investment contract, voting-trust certificate, certificate of deposit for a security, fractional undivided interest in oil, gas, or other mineral rights, or, in general, any interest or instrument commonly known as a "security," or any certificate of interest or participation in, temporary or interim certificate for, receipt for, guarantee of, or warrant or right to subscribe to or purchase, any of the foregoing.[3]

During the stock market crash of 1929, hordes of investors crowded Wall Street to find out the latest news. How did this crash affect the future stock market?
(National Archives)

The courts have had to interpret what the act's statement of what constitutes a security[4] means by "investment contracts." An investment contract is any transaction in which a person (1) invests (2) in a common enterprise (3) reasonably expecting profits (4) derived *primarily* or *substantially* from others' managerial or entrepreneurial efforts.[5]

For our purposes, it is probably convenient to think of securities in their most common forms—stocks and bonds issued by corporations. Bear in mind, though, that securities can take many forms and have been held to include whiskey, cosmetics, worms, beavers, boats, vacuum cleaners, muskrats, and cemetery lots, as well as investment contracts in condominiums, franchises, limited partnerships, oil or gas or other mineral rights, and farm animals accompanied by care agreements.

■EXAMPLE 21.1 Alpha Telcom sold, installed, and maintained pay-phone systems. As part of its pay-phone program, Alpha guaranteed buyers a 14 percent return on the amount of their purchase. Alpha was operating at a net loss, however, and continually borrowed funds to pay investors the fixed rate of return it had promised. Eventually, the company filed for bankruptcy, and the SEC brought an action alleging that Alpha had violated the Securities Act of 1933. In this situation, a federal court concluded that the pay-phone program was a security because it involved an investment contract.[6] ■

Businesspersons should be aware that securities are not limited to stocks and bonds but can encompass a wide variety of interests. The analysis hinges on the nature of the transaction rather than the instrument or substance involved. Because Congress enacted securities laws to regulate *investments,* in whatever form and by whatever name they are called, virtually any type of security that might be sold as an investment can be subject to securities laws. When in doubt about whether an investment transaction involves securities, businesspersons should always seek the advice of an attorney.

PREVENTING
LEGAL DISPUTES

■

---

3. 15 U.S.C. Section 77b(1). Amendments in 1982 added stock options.

4. See 15 U.S.C. Section 77b(a)(1).

5. *SEC v. W. J. Howey Co.,* 328 U.S. 293, 66 S.Ct. 1100, 90 L.Ed. 1244 (1946).

6. *SEC v. Alpha Telcom, Inc.,* 187 F.Supp.2d 1250 (2002). See also *SEC v. Edwards,* 540 U.S. 389, 124 S.Ct. 892, 157 L.Ed.2d 813 (2004), in which the United States Supreme Court held that an investment scheme offering contractual entitlement to a fixed rate of return can be an investment contract and therefore can be considered a security under federal law.

LANDMARK IN THE LAW **The Securities and Exchange Commission**

In 1931, the U.S. Senate passed a resolution calling for an extensive investigation of securities trading. The investigation led, ultimately, to the passage by Congress of the Securities Act of 1933, which is also known as the *truth-in-securities* bill. In the following year, Congress passed the Securities Exchange Act. This 1934 act created the Securities and Exchange Commission (SEC).

Major Responsibilities of the SEC The SEC was created as an independent regulatory agency with the function of administering the 1933 and 1934 acts. Its major responsibilities in this respect are as follows:

1 Requiring disclosure of facts concerning offerings of securities listed on national securities exchanges and of certain securities traded over the counter (OTC).
2 Regulating the trade in securities on national and regional securities exchanges and in the OTC markets.
3 Investigating securities fraud.
4 Regulating the activities of securities brokers, dealers, and investment advisers and requiring their registration.
5 Supervising the activities of mutual funds.
6 Recommending administrative sanctions, injunctive remedies, and criminal prosecution against those who violate securities laws. (The SEC can bring enforcement actions for civil violations of federal securities laws. The Fraud Section of the Criminal Division of the U.S. Department of Justice prosecutes criminal violations.)

The SEC's Expanding Regulatory Powers Since its creation, the SEC's regulatory functions have gradually been increased by legislation granting it authority in different areas. For example, to further curb securities fraud, the Securities Enforcement Remedies and Penny Stock Reform Act of 1990[a] amended existing securities laws to allow SEC administrative law judges to hear cases involving many more types of alleged

a. 15 U.S.C. Section 77g.

ON THE WEB

The Securities and Exchange Commission provides a list of downloadable forms pertinent to securities filings, including registration statements, as well as information on other matters discussed in this chapter. Go to

www.sec.gov/about/forms/secforms.htm.

PROSPECTUS
A written document, required by securities laws, that describes the security being sold, the financial operations of the issuing corporation, and the investment or risk attaching to the security. It is designed to provide sufficient information to enable investors to evaluate the risk involved in purchasing the security.

Registration Statement

Section 5 of the Securities Act of 1933 broadly provides that unless a security qualifies for an exemption, that security must be *registered* before it is offered to the public. Issuing corporations must file a *registration statement* with the SEC and must provide all investors with a *prospectus*. A **prospectus** is a written disclosure document that describes the security being sold, the financial operations of the issuing corporation, and the investment or risk attaching to the security. The 1933 act requires a prospectus to be delivered to investors, and issuers use this document as a selling tool. In principle, the registration statement and the prospectus supply sufficient information to enable unsophisticated investors to evaluate the financial risk involved.

Contents of the Registration Statement The registration statement must be written in plain English and fully describe the following:

securities law violations; the SEC's enforcement options were also greatly expanded. In addition, the act provides that courts can prevent persons who have engaged in securities fraud from serving as officers and directors of publicly held corporations. The Securities Acts Amendments of 1990 authorized the SEC to seek sanctions against those who violate foreign securities laws.[b]

The National Securities Markets Improvement Act of 1996 expanded the power of the SEC to exempt persons, securities, and transactions from the requirements of the securities laws.[c] (This part of the act is also known as the Capital Markets Efficiency Act.) The act also limited the authority of the states to regulate certain securities transactions and particular investment advisory firms.[d] The Sarbanes-Oxley Act of 2002,[e] which you will read about later in this chapter, further expanded the authority of the SEC by directing the agency to issue new rules relating to corporate disclosure requirements and by creating an oversight board to regulate public accounting firms.

APPLICATION TO TODAY'S WORLD *Congress and the SEC have been attempting to streamline the regulatory process generally. The goal is to make it more efficient and more relevant to today's securities trading practices, including those occurring in the online environment. Another goal is to establish more oversight over securities transactions and accounting practices. Additionally, as the number and types of online securities frauds increase, the SEC is trying to keep pace by expanding its online fraud division.*

RELEVANT WEB SITES *To locate information on the Web concerning the SEC, go to this text's Web site at* **academic.cengage.com/blaw/blt**, *select "Chapter 21," and click on "URLs for Landmarks."*

b. 15 U.S.C. Section 78a.
c. 15 U.S.C. Sections 77z-3, 78mm.
d. 15 U.S.C. Section 80b-3a.
e. 15 U.S.C. Sections 7201 *et seq.*

Shown here is the New York Stock Exchange. It is only one of the many markets in which securities are publicly traded. Indeed, in today's global context, New York is no longer the "king" of financial markets. In any event, security trading in the United States is heavily regulated. Does this regulation mean that investors face less risk? (Luis Villa del Campo/ Creative Commons)

DON'T FORGET The purpose of the Securities Act of 1933 is disclosure—the SEC does not consider whether a security is worth the investment price.

1 The securities being offered for sale, including their relationship to the registrant's other capital securities.

2 The corporation's properties and business (including a financial statement certified by an independent public accounting firm).

3 The management of the corporation, including managerial compensation, stock options, pensions, and other benefits. Any interests of directors or officers in any material transactions with the corporation must be disclosed.

4 How the corporation intends to use the proceeds of the sale.

5 Any pending lawsuits or special risk factors.

Registration Process The registration statement does not become effective until after it has been reviewed and approved by the SEC. The 1933 act restricts the types of activities that an issuer can engage in at each stage in the registration process. If an issuer violates the restrictions discussed here, investors can rescind their contracts to purchase the securities. During the *prefiling* period (before filing the registration statement), the issuer cannot either sell or offer to sell the securities. No advertising of an upcoming securities offering is allowed during the prefiling period.

Waiting Period.   Once the registration statement has been filed, a waiting period of at least twenty days begins during which the SEC reviews the registration statement for completeness. Typically, the staff members at the SEC who review the registration statement ask the registrant to make numerous changes and additions, which can extend the length of the waiting period.[7] During the waiting period, the issuing corporation may make *oral* offers to sell the securities to interested investors and may distribute a *preliminary prospectus*, called a **red herring prospectus**.[8] A red herring prospectus contains most of the information that will be included in the final prospectus but often does not include a price. Only general advertising is permitted, such as a **tombstone ad,** so named because historically the format resembled a tombstone. Such ads simply tell the investor where and how to obtain a prospectus. Normally, any other type of advertising—as well as written offers or actual sales—is prohibited until the registration becomes effective.

RED HERRING PROSPECTUS
A preliminary prospectus that can be distributed to potential investors after the registration statement (for a securities offering) has been filed with the Securities and Exchange Commission. The name derives from the red legend printed across the prospectus stating that the registration has been filed but has not become effective.

TOMBSTONE AD
An advertisement, historically in a format resembling a tombstone, of a securities offering. The ad tells potential investors where and how they may obtain a prospectus.

Posteffective Period.   Once the SEC has reviewed and approved the registration statement and the twenty-day period has elapsed, the registration is effective. The issuer can now offer and sell the securities without restrictions. If the company issued a preliminary prospectus to investors, it must provide those investors with a final prospectus either prior to or at the time they purchase the securities. The issuer can require investors to download the final prospectus from a Web site.

     ■**EXAMPLE 21.2** Delphia, Inc., wants to make a public offering of its common stock. The firm files a registration statement and a prospectus with the SEC on May 1. On the same day, the company can make its first *offers* to sell the stock, but an actual sale can take place only *after* the SEC declares the registration to be effective. On May 10, Delphia places tombstone ads in certain trade publications to announce the offering and to tell investors how to get a prospectus. The firm issues a preliminary prospectus on May 15. On May 20, the registration statement becomes effective, and the company makes the final prospectus available to potential buyers. On this date, Delphia can sell the first shares in the issue. ■

Exempt Securities

A number of specific securities are exempt from the registration requirements of the Securities Act of 1933. These securities—which can also generally be resold without being registered—include the following:[9]

1 Government-issued securities.

2 Bank and financial institution securities, which are regulated by banking authorities.

3 Short-term notes and drafts (negotiable instruments that have a maturity date that does not exceed nine months).

---

7. It is common for the SEC to require a registrant to provide additional information more than once. After the registration statement has gone through several rounds of changes, the SEC gives its approval. In these circumstances, because the process may have taken months to complete, registrants frequently request an acceleration of the twenty-day waiting period. If the SEC grants the request, registration can become effective without the issuer having to wait the full twenty days.

8. The name *red herring* comes from the red legend printed across the prospectus stating that the registration has been filed but has not become effective.

9. 15 U.S.C. Section 77c.

4 Securities of nonprofit, educational, and charitable organizations.

5 Securities issued by common carriers (railroads and trucking companies).

6 Any insurance, endowment, or annuity contract issued by a state-regulated insurance company.

7 Securities issued in a corporate reorganization in which one security is exchanged for another or in a bankruptcy proceeding.

8 Securities issued in stock dividends and stock splits.

Exhibit 21–1 summarizes the securities and transactions (discussed next) that are exempt from the registration requirements under the Securities Act of 1933 and SEC regulations.

Exempt Transactions

In addition to the exempt securities listed in the previous subsection, certain *transactions* are exempt from registration requirements. These transaction exemptions are very broad

EXHIBIT 21–1 Exemptions under the 1933 Securities Act

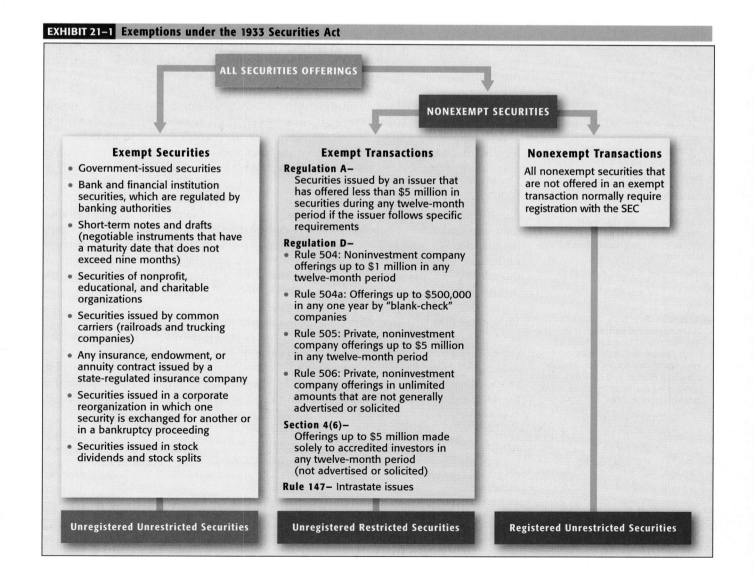

and can enable an issuer to avoid the high cost and complicated procedures associated with registration. Because the coverage of the exemptions overlaps somewhat, an offering may qualify for more than one. Therefore, many sales occur without registration.

BE AWARE The issuer of an exempt security does not have to disclose the same information that other issuers do.

Regulation A Offerings Securities issued by an issuer that has offered less than $5 million in securities during any twelve-month period are exempt from registration.[10] Under Regulation A,[11] the issuer must file with the SEC a notice of the issue and an offering circular, which must also be provided to investors before the sale. This is a much simpler and less expensive process than the procedures associated with full registration. Companies are allowed to "test the waters" for potential interest before preparing the offering circular. To *test the waters* means to determine potential interest without actually selling any securities or requiring any commitment on the part of those who express interest. Small-business issuers (companies with annual revenues of less than $25 million) can also use an integrated registration and reporting system that uses simpler forms than the full registration system.

Small Offerings—Regulation D The SEC's Regulation D contains four separate exemptions from registration requirements for limited offers (offers that either involve a small dollar amount or are made in a limited manner). Regulation D provides that any of these offerings made during any twelve-month period are exempt from the registration requirements.

INVESTMENT COMPANY
A company that acts on behalf of many smaller shareholders/owners by buying a large portfolio of securities and professionally managing that portfolio.

MUTUAL FUND
A specific type of investment company that continually buys or sells to investors shares of ownership in a portfolio.

Rule 504. Noninvestment company offerings up to $1 million in any twelve-month period are exempt.[12] Noninvestment companies are firms that are not engaged primarily in the business of investing or trading in securities. (In contrast, an **investment company** is a firm that buys a large portfolio of securities and professionally manages it on behalf of many smaller shareholders/owners. **A mutual fund** is a type of investment company.)

Rule 504a. Offerings up to $500,000 in any one year by so-called blank-check companies—companies with no specific business plans except to locate and acquire currently unknown businesses or opportunities—are exempt if no general solicitation or advertising is used; the SEC is notified of the sales; and precaution is taken against nonexempt, unregistered resales.[13] The limits on advertising and unregistered resales do not apply if the offering is made solely in states that provide for registration and disclosure and the securities are sold in compliance with those provisions.[14]

ACCREDITED INVESTORS
In the context of securities offerings, "sophisticated" investors, such as banks, insurance companies, investment companies, the issuer's executive officers and directors, and persons whose income or net worth exceeds certain limits.

Rule 505. Private, noninvestment company offerings up to $5 million in any twelve-month period are exempt, regardless of the number of **accredited investors** (banks, insurance companies, investment companies, the issuer's executive officers and directors, and persons whose income or net worth exceeds certain limits), so long as there are no more than thirty-five unaccredited investors; no general solicitation or advertising is used; the SEC is notified of the sales; and precaution is taken against nonexempt, unregistered resales. If the sale involves

---

10. 15 U.S.C. Section 77c(b).
11. 17 C.F.R. Sections 230.251–230.263.
12. 17 C.F.R. Section 230.504. Rule 504 is the exemption used by most small businesses, but that could change under new SEC Rule 1001. This rule permits, under certain circumstances, "testing the waters" for offerings of up to $5 million *per transaction*. These offerings can be made only to "qualified purchasers" (knowledgeable, sophisticated investors), though.
13. Precautions to be taken against nonexempt, unregistered resales include asking the investor whether he or she is buying the securities for others; before the sale, disclosing to each purchaser in writing that the securities are unregistered and thus cannot be resold, except in an exempt transaction, without first being registered; and indicating on the certificates that the securities are unregistered and restricted.
14. 17 C.F.R. Section 230.504a.

any unaccredited investors, *all* investors must be given material information about the offering company, its business, and the securities before the sale. Unlike Rule 506 (discussed next), Rule 505 does not require that the issuer believe each unaccredited investor "has such knowledge and experience in financial and business matters that he [or she] is capable of evaluating the merits and the risks of the prospective investment."[15]

Rule 506.   Private, noninvestment company offerings in unlimited amounts that are not generally solicited or advertised are exempt if the SEC is notified of the sales; precaution is taken against nonexempt, unregistered resales; and the issuer believes that each unaccredited investor has sufficient knowledge or experience in financial matters to be capable of evaluating the investment's merits and risks. There may be no more than thirty-five unaccredited investors, but there are no limits on the number of accredited investors. If there are *any* unaccredited investors, the issuer must provide *all* purchasers with material information about itself, its business, and the securities before the sale.[16]

This exemption is perhaps most important to those firms that want to raise funds through the sale of securities without registering them. It is often referred to as the *private placement* exemption because it exempts "transactions not involving any public offering."[17] This provision applies to private offerings to a limited number of persons who are sufficiently sophisticated and able to assume the risk of the investment (and who thus have no need for federal registration protection). It also applies to private offerings to similarly situated institutional investors.

Small Offerings—Section 4(6)   Under Section 4(6) of the Securities Act of 1933, an offer made *solely* to accredited investors is exempt if its amount is not more than $5 million. Any number of accredited investors may participate, but no unaccredited investors may do so. No general solicitation or advertising may be used; the SEC must be notified of all sales; and precautions must be taken against nonexempt, unregistered resales. Precautions are necessary because these are *restricted* securities and may be resold only by registration or in an exempt transaction.[18] (The securities purchased and sold by most people who deal in stock are called, in contrast, *unrestricted* securities.)

Intrastate Offerings—Rule 147   Also exempt are intrastate transactions involving purely local offerings.[19] This exemption applies to most offerings that are restricted to residents of the state in which the issuing company is organized and doing business. For nine months after the last sale, virtually no resales may be made to nonresidents, and precautions must be taken against this possibility. These offerings remain subject to applicable laws in the state of issue.

Resales   Most securities can be resold without registration (although some resales may be subject to restrictions, as discussed above in connection with specific exemptions). The Securities Act of 1933 provides exemptions for resales by most persons other than issuers or underwriters. The average investor who sells shares of stock does not have to file a registration statement with the SEC. Resales of restricted securities acquired under Rule 504a, Rule 505, Rule 506, or Section 4(6), however, trigger the registration requirements unless the party selling them complies with Rule 144 or Rule 144A. These rules are sometimes referred to as "safe harbors."

KEEP IN MIND An investor can be "sophisticated" by virtue of his or her education and experience or by investing through a knowledgeable, experienced representative.

15. 17 C.F.R. Section 230.505.
16. 17 C.F.R. Section 230.506.
17. 15 U.S.C. Section 77d(2).
18. 15 U.S.C. Section 77d(6).
19. 15 U.S.C. Section 77c(a)(11); 17 C.F.R. Section 230.147.

Rule 144. Rule 144 exempts restricted securities from registration on resale if there is adequate current public information about the issuer, the person selling the securities has owned them for at least one year, they are sold in certain limited amounts in unsolicited brokers' transactions, and the SEC is given notice of the resale.[20] "Adequate current public information" refers to the reports that certain companies are required to file under the Securities Exchange Act of 1934. A person who has owned the securities for at least one year is subject to none of these requirements, unless the person is an affiliate. An *affiliate* is one who controls, is controlled by, or is in common control with the issuer.

CONTRAST Securities do not have to be held for one year to be exempt from registration on a resale under Rule 144A, as they do under Rule 144.

Rule 144A. Securities that at the time of issue are not of the same class as securities listed on a national securities exchange or quoted in a U.S. automated interdealer quotation system may be resold under Rule 144A.[21] They may be sold only to a qualified institutional buyer (an institution, such as an insurance company or a bank that owns and invests at least $100 million in securities). The seller must take reasonable steps to ensure that the buyer knows that the seller is relying on the exemption under Rule 144A. A sample restricted stock certificate is shown in Exhibit 21–2.

Violations of the 1933 Act

As mentioned, the SEC has the power to investigate and bring civil enforcement actions against companies that violate federal securities laws. It is a violation of the Securities Act of 1933 to intentionally defraud investors by misrepresenting or omitting facts in a registration statement or prospectus. Liability is also imposed on those who are negligent for not discovering the fraud. Selling securities before the effective date of the registration statement or under an exemption for which the securities do not qualify results in liability.

Criminal violations are prosecuted by the U.S. Department of Justice. Violators may be fined up to $10,000, imprisoned for up to five years, or both. The SEC is authorized

---

20. 17 C.F.R. Section 230.144.
21. 17 C.F.R. Section 230.144A.

EXHIBIT 21–2 **A Sample Restricted Stock Certificate**

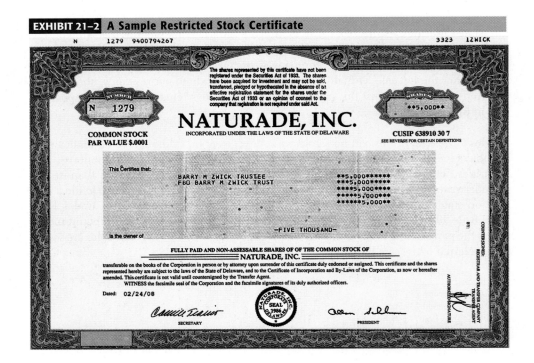

to seek civil sanctions against those who willfully violate the 1933 act. It can request an injunction to prevent further sales of the securities involved or ask the court to grant other relief, such as an order to a violator to refund profits. Those parties who purchase securities and suffer harm as a result of false or omitted statements may also bring suits in a federal court to recover their losses and other damages.

SECURITIES EXCHANGE ACT OF 1934

The Securities Exchange Act of 1934 provides for the regulation and registration of securities exchanges, brokers, dealers, and national securities associations, such as the National Association of Securities Dealers (NASD). Unlike the 1933 act, which is a one-time disclosure law, the 1934 act provides for continuous periodic disclosures by publicly held corporations to enable the SEC to regulate subsequent trading. The Securities Exchange Act of 1934 applies to companies that have assets in excess of $10 million and five hundred or more shareholders. These corporations are referred to as Section 12 companies because they are required to register their securities under Section 12 of the 1934 act. Section 12 companies are required to file reports with the SEC annually and quarterly, and sometimes even monthly if specified events occur (such as a merger).

The act also authorizes the SEC to engage in market surveillance to deter undesirable market practices such as fraud, market manipulation (attempts at illegally influencing stock prices), and misrepresentation. In addition, the act provides for the SEC's regulation of proxy solicitations for voting (discussed in Chapter 20).

Section 10(b), SEC Rule 10b-5, and Insider Trading

Section 10(b) is one of the most important sections of the Securities Exchange Act of 1934. This section proscribes the use of any manipulative or deceptive device in violation of SEC rules and regulations. Among the rules that the SEC has promulgated pursuant to the 1934 act is **SEC Rule 10b-5,** which prohibits the commission of fraud in connection with the purchase or sale of any security.

One of the major goals of Section 10(b) and SEC Rule 10b-5 is to prevent so-called **insider trading,** which occurs when persons buy or sell securities on the basis of information that is not available to the public. Corporate directors, officers, and others such as majority shareholders, for instance, often have advance inside information that can affect the future market value of the corporate stock. Obviously, their positions give them a trading advantage over the general public and other shareholders. The 1934 Securities Exchange Act defines inside information and extends liability to those who take advantage of such information in their personal transactions when they know that the information is unavailable to those with whom they are dealing. Section 10(b) of the 1934 act and SEC Rule 10b-5 cover not only corporate officers, directors, and majority shareholders but also any persons having access to or receiving information of a nonpublic nature on which trading is based.

Disclosure under SEC Rule 10b-5   Any material omission or misrepresentation of material facts in connection with the purchase or sale of a security may violate not only the Securities Act of 1933 but also the antifraud provisions of Section 10(b) of the 1934 act and SEC Rule 10b-5. The key to liability (which can be civil or criminal) under Section 10(b) and SEC Rule 10b-5 is whether the insider's information is *material.*

Examples of Material Facts Calling for Disclosure.   The following are some examples of material facts calling for disclosure under the rule:

SEC RULE 10b-5
A rule of the Securities and Exchange Commission that makes it unlawful, in connection with the purchase or sale of any security, to make any untrue statement of a material fact or to omit a material fact if such omission causes the statement to be misleading.

INSIDER TRADING
The purchase or sale of securities on the basis of information that has not been made available to the public.

Evidence in an insider-trading case against the former chief executive officer of Qwest Communications gets delivered to a Denver courthouse. Why is insider trading deemed illegal? (AP Photo/ Ed Andrieski)

1 Fraudulent trading in the company stock by a broker-dealer.

2 A dividend change (whether up or down).

3 A contract for the sale of corporate assets.

4 A new discovery, a new process, or a new product.

5 A significant change in the firm's financial condition.

6 Potential litigation against the company.

Note that any one of these facts, by itself, is not *automatically* considered a material fact. Rather, it will be regarded as a material fact if it is significant enough that it would likely affect an investor's decision as to whether to purchase or sell the company's securities.

The following is one of the landmark cases interpreting SEC Rule 10b-5. The SEC sued Texas Gulf Sulphur Company for issuing a misleading press release. The release underestimated the magnitude and value of a mineral discovery. The SEC also sued several of Texas Gulf Sulphur's directors, officers, and employees under SEC Rule 10b-5 for purchasing large amounts of the corporate stock prior to the announcement of the corporation's rich ore discovery.

CASE 21.1   SEC v. Texas Gulf Sulphur Co.

LANDMARK AND CLASSIC CASES

United States Court of Appeals, Second Circuit, 401 F.2d 833 (1968).

HISTORICAL AND ENVIRONMENTAL SETTING

No court has ever held that every buyer or seller is entitled to all of the information relating to all of the circumstances in every stock transaction. By the mid-1950s, however, significant understatement of the value of the assets of a company had been held to be materially misleading.[a] In 1957, the Texas Gulf Sulphur Company (TGS) began exploring for minerals in eastern Canada. In March 1959, aerial geophysical surveys were conducted over more than fifteen thousand square miles of the area. The operations revealed numerous and extraordinary variations in the conductivity of the rock, which indicated a remarkable concentration of commercially exploitable minerals. One site of such variations was near Timmins, Ontario. On October 29 and 30, 1963, a ground survey of the site near Timmins indicated a need to drill for further evaluation.

FACTS On November 12, 1963, the Texas Gulf Sulphur Company drilled a hole that appeared to yield a core with an exceedingly high mineral content, although further drilling would be necessary to establish whether there was enough

a. *Speed v. Transamerica Corp.*, 99 F.Supp. 808 (D.Del. 1951).

ore to be mined commercially. TGS kept secret the results of the core sample. After learning of the ore discovery, officers and employees of the company made substantial purchases of TGS's stock or accepted stock options. On April 11, 1964, an unauthorized report of the mineral find appeared in the newspapers. On the following day, April 12, TGS issued a press release that played down the discovery and stated that it was too early to tell whether the ore find would be a significant one. Later on, TGS announced a strike of at least 25 million tons of ore. The news led to a substantial increase in the price of TGS stock. The Securities and Exchange Commission (SEC) brought a suit in a federal district court against the officers and employees of TGS for violating the insider-trading prohibition of SEC Rule 10b-5. The officers and employees argued that the prohibition did not apply. They reasoned that the information on which they had traded was not material, as the find had not been commercially proved. The trial court held that most of the defendants had not violated SEC Rule 10b-5, and the SEC appealed.

ISSUE Did the officers and employees of TGS violate SEC Rule 10b-5 by buying the stock, even though they did not know the full extent and profit potential of the ore discovery at the time of their purchases?

CASE 21.1–Continued

DECISION Yes. The U.S. Court of Appeals for the Second Circuit reversed the lower court's decision and remanded the case for further proceedings, holding that the employees and officers had violated SEC Rule 10b-5's prohibition against insider trading.

REASON For SEC Rule 10b-5 purposes, the test of materiality is whether the information would affect the judgment of reasonable investors. Reasonable investors include speculative as well as conservative investors. "[A] major factor in determining whether the * * * discovery [of the ore] was a material fact is the importance attached to the drilling results by those who knew about it. * * * [T]he timing by those who knew of it of their stock purchases and their purchases of short-term calls [rights to buy shares at a specified price within a specified time period]—purchases in some cases by individuals who had never before purchased calls or even TGS stock—virtually compels the inference that

the insiders were influenced by the drilling results. * * * We hold, therefore, that all transactions in TGS stock or calls by individuals apprised of the drilling results * * * were made in violation of Rule 10b-5."

IMPACT OF THIS CASE ON TODAY'S LAW *This landmark case affirmed the principle that the test of whether information is "material," for SEC Rule 10b-5 purposes, is whether it would affect the judgment of reasonable investors. The corporate insiders' purchases of stock and stock options (rights to purchase stock) indicated that they were influenced by the drilling results and that the information about the drilling results was material. The courts continue to cite this case when applying SEC Rule 10b-5 to other cases of alleged insider trading.*

RELEVANT WEB SITES *To locate information on the Web concerning the SEC v. Texas Gulf Suphur Co. decision, go to this text's Web site at* **academic.cengage.com/blaw/blt**, *select "Chapter 21," and click on "URLs for Landmarks."*

The Private Securities Litigation Reform Act of 1995. One of the unintended effects of SEC Rule 10b-5 was to deter the disclosure of some material information, such as financial forecasts. To understand why, consider an example. **■EXAMPLE 21.3** A company announces that its projected earnings in a certain time period will be X amount. It turns out that the forecast is wrong. The earnings are in fact much lower, and the price of the company's stock is affected—negatively. The shareholders then bring a class-action suit against the company, alleging that the directors violated SEC Rule 10b-5 by disclosing misleading financial information. ■

In an attempt to rectify this problem and promote disclosure, Congress passed the Private Securities Litigation Reform Act of 1995. Among other things, the act provides a "safe harbor" for publicly held companies that make forward-looking statements, such as financial forecasts. Those who make such statements are protected against liability for securities fraud as long as the statements are accompanied by "meaningful cautionary statements identifying important factors that could cause actual results to differ materially from those in the forward-looking statement."[22]

After the 1995 act was passed, a number of securities class-action suits were filed in state courts to skirt the requirements of the 1995 federal act. In response to this problem, Congress passed the Securities Litigation Uniform Standards Act of 1998 (SLUSA).[23] The act placed stringent limits on the ability of plaintiffs to bring class-action suits in state courts against firms whose securities are traded on national stock exchanges.

Outsiders and SEC Rule 10b-5 The traditional insider-trading case involves true insiders—corporate officers, directors, and majority shareholders who have access to (and trade on) inside information. Increasingly, liability under Section 10(b) of the 1934 act and SEC Rule 10b-5 is being extended to include certain "outsiders"—those persons who

---

22. 15 U.S.C. Sections 77z-2, 78u-5.
23. Pub. L. No. 105-353. This act amended many sections of Title 15 of the *United States Code.*

trade on inside information acquired indirectly. Two theories have been developed under which outsiders may be held liable for insider trading: the *tipper/tippee theory* and the *misappropriation theory.*

Tipper/Tippee Theory. Anyone who acquires inside information as a result of a corporate insider's breach of his or her fiduciary duty can be liable under SEC Rule 10b-5. This liability extends to **tippees** (those who receive "tips" from insiders) and even remote tippees (tippees of tippees).

The key to liability under this theory is that the inside information must be obtained as a result of someone's breach of a fiduciary duty to the corporation whose shares are involved in the trading. The tippee is liable under this theory only if (1) there is a breach of a duty not to disclose inside information, (2) the disclosure is in exchange for personal benefit, and (3) the tippee knows (or should know) of this breach and benefits from it.[24]

Misappropriation Theory. Liability for insider trading may also be established under the misappropriation theory. This theory holds that an individual who wrongfully obtains (misappropriates) inside information and trades on it for her or his personal gain should be held liable because, in essence, she or he stole information rightfully belonging to another.

The misappropriation theory has been controversial because it significantly extends the reach of SEC Rule 10b-5 to outsiders who ordinarily would not be deemed fiduciaries of the corporations in whose stock they trade. The United States Supreme Court, however, has held that liability under SEC Rule 10b-5 can be based on the misappropriation theory.[25]

It is not always wrong to disclose material, nonpublic information about a company to a person who would not otherwise be privy to it. A corporate officer might discuss business events with his or her spouse, for example, with the understanding that the spouse will not repeat the conversation to anyone. What if the spouse says that she will disclose the information? In the following case, the defendants argued that there should be no liability under the misappropriation theory in this situation.

24. See, for example, *Chiarella v. United States,* 445 U.S. 222, 100 S.Ct. 1108, 63 L.Ed.2d 348 (1980); and *Dirks v. SEC,* 463 U.S. 646, 103 S.Ct. 3255, 77 L.Ed.2d 911 (1983).
25. *United States v. O'Hagan,* 521 U.S. 642, 117 S.Ct. 2199, 138 L.Ed.2d 724 (1997).

TIPPEE
A person who receives inside information.

CASE 21.2 **SEC v. Rocklage**

United States Court of Appeals, First Circuit, 470 F.3d 1 (2006).
www.ca1.uscourts.gov[a]

FACTS Patricia Rocklage was the wife of Scott Rocklage, the chairman and chief executive officer of Cubist Pharmaceuticals, Inc. Scott had sometimes disclosed material, nonpublic information about Cubist to Patricia, and she had always kept the information confidential. On December 31, 2001, Scott

a. Click on "Opinions." On the next page, in the "General Search" section, in the "Short title contains" box, type "Rocklage" and then click on "Submit Search." In the result, in the "Click for Opinion" column, click on the first number to access the opinion. The U.S. Court of Appeals for the First Circuit maintains this Web site.

told Patricia that one of Cubist's key drugs had failed its clinical trial and reminded her not to discuss this information with anyone. Patricia was aware that her brother, William Beaver, owned Cubist stock, and she told Scott that she wanted to tell her brother about the failed trial. Scott tried to discourage her. Patricia had an "understanding" with William, however, and told him that she had heard significant negative news about Cubist. He sold his 5,583 shares of its stock and tipped his friend David Jones, who sold his 7,500 shares. On January 16, 2002, Cubist publicly announced the trial results, and the price of its stock dropped. William and David had

CASE 21.2–Continued

avoided losses of $99,527 and $133,222, respectively, by selling when they did. The Securities and Exchange Commission (SEC) filed a suit in a federal district court against Patricia, William, and David, alleging insider trading in violation of Section 10(b) of the Securities Exchange Act of 1934 and SEC Rule 10b-5. The court denied the defendants' motion to dismiss. They appealed to the U.S. Court of Appeals for the First Circuit.

ISSUE Could Patricia, William, and David avoid liability for insider trading under the misappropriation theory on the ground that Patricia had told Scott she would tell William what Scott had told her?

DECISION No. The U.S. Court of Appeals for the First Circuit affirmed the lower court's decision and remanded the case for further proceedings.

REASON The U.S. Court of Appeals for the First Circuit recognized that the misappropriation theory bases liability on the deception of the source of the information. In this case, "Mrs. Rocklage engaged in deceptive devices, in connection

with a securities transaction, when she tricked her husband into revealing confidential information to her so that she could, and did, assist her brother with the sale of his Cubist stock. * * * [B]efore her husband's initial disclosure about the clinical trial, Mrs. Rocklage did absolutely nothing to correct his mistaken understanding that she would keep the trial results confidential." And she did this, "knowing full well that in obtaining that information she would enable her brother to execute a securities transaction. She then actively facilitated a securities transaction by tipping her brother, and securities were in fact sold based on her information." The court conceded that Patricia's disclosure to Scott might have eliminated any deception involved in her tip to William, but it did not "negate the original deception. * * * [B]ecause of the way in which Mrs. Rocklage first acquired this information, her overall scheme was still deceptive: it had as part of it at least one deceptive device."

 FOR CRITICAL ANALYSIS–Social Consideration
Are there any circumstances in which the disclosure to the source that his or her information will be revealed to others might serve to avoid liability? Explain.

Insider Reporting and Trading–Section 16(b)

Officers, directors, and certain large stockholders[26] of Section 12 corporations (corporations that are required to register their securities under Section 12 of the 1934 act) must file reports with the SEC concerning their ownership and trading of the corporations' securities.[27] To discourage such insiders from using nonpublic information about their companies for their personal benefit in the stock market, Section 16(b) of the 1934 act provides for the recapture by the corporation of all profits realized by an insider on any purchase and sale or sale and purchase of the corporation's stock within any six-month period.[28] It is irrelevant whether the insider actually uses inside information; *all such* **short-swing profits** *must be returned to the corporation.*

Section 16(b) applies not only to stock but also to warrants, options, and securities convertible into stock. The courts have fashioned complex rules for determining profits. Note that the SEC exempts a number of transactions under Rule 16b-3.[29] For all of these reasons, corporate insiders are wise to seek specialized counsel before trading in the corporation's stock. Exhibit 21–3 on the next page compares the effects of SEC Rule 10b-5 and Section 16(b).

Proxy Statements

Section 14(a) of the Securities Exchange Act of 1934 regulates the solicitation of proxies from shareholders of Section 12 companies. The SEC regulates the content of proxy

ON THE WEB

For information on investor protection, including answers to frequently asked questions on the topic of securities fraud, go to

www.securitieslaw.com.

SHORT-SWING PROFITS
Profits earned within six months of a trade. Section 12 of the 1934 Securities Exchange Act requires company insiders to return any profits made from the purchase and sale of company stock if both transactions occur within a six-month period.

---

26. Those stockholders owning 10 percent of the class of equity securities registered under Section 12 of the 1934 act.
27. 15 U.S.C. Section 78*l*.
28. A person who expects the price of a particular stock to decline can realize profits by "selling short"—selling at a high price and repurchasing later at a lower price to cover the "short sale."
29. 17 C.F.R. Section 240.16b-3.

EXHIBIT 21–3 Comparison of Coverage, Application, and Liability under SEC Rule 10b-5 and Section 16(b)

AREA OF COMPARISON	SEC RULE 10b–5	SECTION 16(b)
What is the subject matter of the transaction?	Any security (does not have to be registered).	Any security (does not have to be registered).
What transactions are covered?	Purchase or sale.	Short-swing purchase and sale or short-swing sale and purchase.
Who is subject to liability?	Virtually anyone with inside information under a duty to disclose—including officers, directors, controlling shareholders, and tippees.	Officers, directors, and certain 10 percent shareholders.
Is omission or misrepresentation necessary for liability?	Yes.	No.
Are there any exempt transactions?	No.	Yes, there are a number of exemptions.
Who may bring an action?	A person transacting with an insider, the SEC, or a purchaser or seller damaged by a wrongful act.	A corporation or a shareholder by derivative action.

A proxy statement. Who regulates the content of proxy statements and how? (Courtesy of Prudential Financial)

statements. As discussed in Chapter 20, a proxy statement is sent to shareholders when corporate officials are requesting authority to vote on behalf of the shareholders in a particular election on specified issues. Whoever solicits a proxy must fully and accurately disclose in the proxy statement all of the facts that are pertinent to the matter on which the shareholders are to vote. SEC Rule 14a-9 is similar to the antifraud provisions of SEC Rule 10b-5. Remedies for violations are extensive; they range from injunctions that prevent a vote from being taken to monetary damages.

Violations of the 1934 Act

As mentioned earlier, violations of Section 10(b) of the Securities Exchange Act of 1934 and SEC Rule 10b-5, including insider trading, may be subject to criminal or civil liability. For either criminal or civil sanctions to be imposed, however, *scienter* must exist—that is, the violator must have had an intent to defraud or knowledge of her or his misconduct (see Chapter 8). *Scienter* can be proved by showing that the defendant made false statements or wrongfully failed to disclose material facts.

Violations of Section 16(b) include the sale by insiders of stock acquired less than six months before the sale (or less than six months after the sale if selling short). These violations are subject to civil sanctions. Liability under Section 16(b) is strict liability. Thus, liability is imposed regardless of whether *scienter* or negligence existed.

Criminal Penalties For violations of Section 10(b) and Rule 10b-5, an individual may be fined up to $5 million, imprisoned for up to twenty years, or both.[30] A partnership or a corporation may be fined up to $25 million. Under Section 807 of the Sarbanes-Oxley Act of 2002, for a *willful* violation of the 1934 act the violator may, in addition to being subject to a fine, be imprisoned for up to twenty-five years.

---

30. These numbers reflect the increased penalties imposed by the Sarbanes-Oxley Act of 2002.

In a criminal prosecution under the securities laws, a jury is not allowed to speculate on whether a defendant acted willfully—there can be no reasonable doubt that the defendant knew he or she was acting wrongfully. The issue in the following case was whether, in light of this principle, there was enough evidence to present to a jury the question of whether Martha Stewart, founder of a well-known media and homemaking empire, intended to deceive investors.

CASE 21.3 **United States v. Stewart**

United States District Court, Southern District of New York, 305 F.Supp.2d 368 (2004).

FACTS Samuel Waksal, the chief executive officer of ImClone Systems, Inc., a biotechnology company, was a client of stockbroker Peter Bacanovic. Bacanovic's other clients included Martha Stewart, then the chief executive officer of Martha Stewart Living Omnimedia (MSLO). On December 27, 2001, Waksal began selling his ImClone stock. Bacanovic allegedly had Stewart informed of Waksal's sales, and she also sold her ImClone shares. The next day, ImClone announced that the Food and Drug Administration had rejected the company's application for approval of the greatly anticipated medication called Erbitux. The government began to investigate Stewart's ImClone trades, the media began to report on the investigation, and the value of MSLO stock began to drop. In June 2002, at a "Mid-Year Media Review" conference attended by investment professionals and investors, Stewart said that she had previously agreed with Bacanovic to sell her ImClone stock if the price fell to $60 per share. "I have nothing to add on this matter today. And I'm here to talk about our terrific company." Her statements were followed by a forty-minute presentation on MSLO. Subsequently, Stewart was charged with, among other things, fraud in connection with the purchase and sale of MSLO securities in violation of the Securities Exchange Act of 1934. She filed a motion asking for an acquittal on this charge.

ISSUE Could a reasonable juror find beyond a reasonable doubt that Stewart lied to influence the market for the securities of her company?

DECISION No. The court concluded that in Stewart's case, "to find the essential element of criminal intent beyond a reasonable doubt, a rational juror would have to speculate."[a]

REASON The government argued that Stewart was aware that the negative publicity about her ImClone trade was having an impact on the market value of MSLO securities and that she deliberately directed her statement to investors. The government pointed out that Stewart was aware that she was speaking to analysts and investors at the conference and began by saying that she was embarking on a topic about which her audience was "probably interested." According to the government, Stewart's awareness of her audience (investors and analysts) and the timing of her statement as the price of MSLO stock was falling were sufficient to permit a jury to infer that she intended to deceive investors when she made the statement. The court reasoned, however, that "any inference to be drawn from the makeup of the audience must also take into account the fact that Stewart was only one of several representatives of MSLO, and that MSLO was only one of several corporations making presentations at the conference. * * * There is no evidence that the negative publicity about ImClone influenced Stewart's decision to attend and take advantage of a platform from which to reach investors directly. To the contrary, her statement—a very brief portion of a much longer presentation—indicates otherwise."

FOR CRITICAL ANALYSIS–Social Consideration
Why might a court require more evidence of scienter, or intent, in the context of criminal securities fraud prosecution than it would in the context of civil securities fraud action?

---

a. Stewart was later convicted on other charges related to her ImClone trades and was sentenced to five months in prison and five months under house arrest. Although she appealed the decision in an attempt to clear her name, the U.S. Court of Appeals for the Second Circuit upheld her conviction in 2006.

Civil Sanctions The SEC can also bring suit in a federal district court against anyone violating or aiding in a violation of the 1934 act or SEC rules by purchasing or selling a security while in the possession of material nonpublic information.[31] The violation must occur on or through the facilities of a national securities exchange or from or through a broker or dealer. The court may assess as a penalty as much as triple the profits gained or the loss avoided by the guilty party. Profit or loss is defined as "the difference between the purchase or sale price of the security and the value of that security as measured by the trading price of the security at a reasonable period of time after public dissemination of the nonpublic information."[32]

The Insider Trading and Securities Fraud Enforcement Act of 1988 enlarged the class of persons who may be subject to civil liability for insider-trading violations. This act also gave the SEC authority to award **bounty payments** (rewards given by government officials for acts beneficial to the state) to persons providing information leading to the prosecution of insider-trading violations.[33]

Private parties may also sue violators of Section 10(b) and Rule 10b-5. A private party may obtain rescission (cancellation) of a contract to buy securities or damages to the extent of the violator's illegal profits. Those found liable have a right to seek contribution from those who share responsibility for the violations, including accountants, attorneys, and corporations.[34] For violations of Section 16(b), a corporation can bring an action to recover the short-swing profits.

STATE SECURITIES LAWS

Today, all states have their own corporate securities laws, or "blue sky laws," that regulate the offer and sale of securities within individual state borders. (As mentioned in Chapter 8, the phrase *blue sky laws* dates to a 1917 decision by the United States Supreme Court in which the Court declared that the purpose of such laws was to prevent "speculative schemes which have no more basis than so many feet of 'blue sky.'")[35] Article 8 of the Uniform Commercial Code, which has been adopted by all of the states, also imposes various requirements relating to the purchase and sale of securities.

Requirements under State Securities Laws

Despite some differences in philosophy, all state blue sky laws have certain features. Typically, state laws have disclosure requirements and antifraud provisions, many of which are patterned after Section 10(b) of the Securities Exchange Act of 1934 and SEC Rule 10b-5. State laws also provide for the registration or qualification of securities offered or issued for sale within the state and impose disclosure requirements. Unless an exemption from registration is applicable, issuers must register or qualify their stock with the appropriate state official, often called a *corporations commissioner*. Additionally, most state securities laws regulate securities brokers and dealers.

BOUNTY PAYMENT
A reward (payment) given to a person or persons who perform a certain service, such as informing legal authorities of illegal actions.

BE AWARE Federal securities laws do not take priority over state securities laws.

---

31. The Insider Trading Sanctions Act of 1984, 15 U.S.C. Section 78u(d)(2)(A).
32. 15 U.S.C. Section 78u(d)(2)(C).
33. 15 U.S.C. Section 78u-1.
34. The United States Supreme Court has ruled that a private party cannot bring an action against those who "aid and abet" under Section 10(b) and SEC Rule 10b-5. *Central Bank of Denver, N.A. v. First Interstate Bank of Denver, N.A.*, 511 U.S. 164, 114 S.Ct. 1439, 128 L.Ed.2d 119 (1994). Only the SEC can bring actions against so-called aiders and abettors. Nevertheless, some courts have held accountants and attorneys liable as primary violators under Section 10(b), and a conflict exists in the federal circuit courts as to precisely what conduct subjects accountants and attorneys to liability.
35. *Hall v. Geiger-Jones Co.*, 242 U.S. 539, 37 S.Ct. 217, 61 L.Ed. 480 (1917).

Concurrent Regulation

State securities laws apply mainly to intrastate transactions. Since the adoption of the 1933 and 1934 federal securities acts, the state and federal governments have regulated securities concurrently. Issuers must comply with both federal and state securities laws, and exemptions from federal law are not exemptions from state laws.

The dual federal and state system has not always worked well, particularly during the early 1990s, when the securities markets underwent considerable expansion. In response, Congress passed the National Securities Markets Improvement Act of 1996, which eliminated some of the duplicate regulations and gave the SEC exclusive power to regulate most national securities activities. The National Conference of Commissioners on Uniform State Laws then substantially revised the Uniform Securities Act and recommended it to the states for adoption in 2002. Unlike the previous version of this law, the new act is designed to coordinate state and federal securities regulation and enforcement efforts. Eleven states have already adopted the Uniform Securities Act, and several other states are considering adoption.[36]

CORPORATE GOVERNANCE

Corporate governance can be narrowly defined as the relationship between a corporation and its shareholders. The Organization for Economic Cooperation and Development (OECD) provides a broader definition:

> Corporate governance is the system by which business corporations are directed and controlled. The corporate governance structure specifies the distribution of rights and responsibilities among different participants in the corporation, such as the board of directors, managers, shareholders, and other stakeholders, and spells out the rules and procedures for making decisions on corporate affairs.[37]

Although this definition has no legal value, it does set the tone for the ways in which modern corporations should be governed. In other words, effective corporate governance requires more than compliance with laws and regulations. The definition and focus of corporate governance principles vary around the world. For a discussion of corporate governance in other nations, see this chapter's *Beyond Our Borders* feature on the following page.

CORPORATE GOVERNANCE
A set of policies or procedures affecting the way a corporation is directed or controlled.

The Need for Good Corporate Governance

The need for effective corporate governance arises in large corporations because corporate ownership (by shareholders) is separated from corporate control (by officers and managers). In the real world, officers and managers are tempted to advance their own interests, even when such interests conflict with those of the shareholders. The collapse of Enron Corporation and other well-publicized scandals in the corporate world in the early 2000s provide a clear illustration of the reasons for concern about managerial opportunism.

Attempts at Aligning the Interests of Officers with Those of Shareholders

Some corporations have sought to align the financial interests of their offficers with those of the company's shareholders by providing the officers with **stock options,** which enable

STOCK OPTIONS
An agreement that grants the owner the option to buy a given number of shares of stock, usually within a set time period.

---

36. At the time this book went to press, the Uniform Securities Act had been adopted in Hawaii, Idaho, Iowa, Kansas, Maine, Minnesota, Missouri, Oklahoma, South Carolina, South Dakota, and Vermont, as well as in the U.S. Virgin Islands. Adoption legislation was pending in Indiana and Washington State. You can find current information on state adoptions at www.nccusl.org.

37. *Governance in the 21st Century: Future Studies* (OECD, 2001).

BEYOND OUR BORDERS Corporate Governance in Other Nations

Corporate governance has become an issue of concern not only for U.S. corporations, but also for corporate entities around the world. With the globalization of business, a corporation's bad acts (or lack of control systems) can have far-reaching consequences. Different models of corporate governance exist, often depending on the degree of capitalism in the particular nation. In the United States, corporate governance tends to give priority to shareholders' interests. This approach encourages significant innovation and cost and quality competition. In contrast, the coordinated model of governance that prevails in continental Europe and Japan considers the interests of so-called stakeholders—employees, managers, suppliers, customers, and the community—to be a priority. The coordinated model still encourages innovation and cost and quality competition, but not to the same extent as the U.S. model.

FOR CRITICAL ANALYSIS *Why does the presence of a capitalist system affect a nation's perspective on corporate governance?*

them to purchase shares of the corporation's stock at a set price. When the market price rises above that level, the officers can sell their shares for a profit. Because a stock's market price generally increases as the corporation prospers, the options give the officers a financial stake in the corporation's well-being and supposedly encourage them to work hard for the benefit of the shareholders.

Options have turned out to be an imperfect device for providing effective governance, however. Executives in some companies have been tempted to "cook" the company's books in order to keep share prices higher so that they could sell their stock for a profit. Executives in other corporations have experienced no losses when share prices dropped; instead, their options were "repriced" so that they did not suffer from the share price decline and could still profit from future increases above the lowered share price. Thus, although stock options theoretically can motivate officers to protect shareholder interests, stock option plans have often become a way for officers to take advantage of shareholders.

With stock options generally failing to work as planned and numerous headline-making scandals occurring within major corporations, there has been an outcry for more "outside" directors (those with no formal employment affiliation with the company). The theory is that independent directors will more closely monitor the actions of corporate officers. Hence, today we see more boards with outside directors. Note, though, that outside directors may not be truly independent of corporate officers; they may be friends or business associates of the leading officers. A study of board appointments found that the best way to increase one's probability of appointment was to "suck up" to the chief executive officer.[38]

Corporate Governance and Corporate Law

Good corporate governance standards are designed to address problems (such as those briefly discussed above) and to motivate officers to make decisions to promote the financial interests of the company's shareholders. Generally, corporate governance entails corporate decision-making structures that monitor employees (particularly officers) to ensure

---

38. Jennifer Reingold, "Suck Up and Move Fast," *Fast Company*, January 2005, p. 34.

that they are acting for the benefit of the shareholders. Thus, corporate governance involves, at a minimum:

1 The audited reporting of financial progress at the corporation, so that managers can be evaluated.

2 Legal protections for shareholders, so that violators of the law, who attempt to take advantage of shareholders, can be punished for misbehavior and victims may recover damages for any associated losses.

The Practical Significance of Good Corporate Governance   Effective corporate governance may have considerable practical significance. A study by researchers at Harvard University and the Wharton School of Business found that firms providing greater shareholder rights had higher profits, higher sales growth, higher firm value, and other economic advantages.[39] Better corporate governance in the form of greater accountability to investors may therefore offer the opportunity to increase corporations' valuations.

Governance and Corporation Law   Corporate governance is the essential purpose of corporation law in the United States. These statutes set up the legal framework for corporate governance. Under the corporate law of Delaware, where most major companies incorporate, all corporations must have in place certain structures of corporate governance. The key structure of corporate law is, of course, the board of directors. Directors make the most important decisions about the future of the corporation and monitor the actions of corporate officers. Directors are elected by shareholders to look out for their best interests.

The Board of Directors   Some argue that shareholder democracy is key to improving corporate governance. If shareholders could vote on major corporate decisions, shareholders could presumably have more control over the corporation. Essential to shareholder democracy is the concept of electing the board of directors, usually at the corporation's annual meeting. Under corporate law, a corporation must have a board of directors elected by the shareholders. Virtually anyone can become a director, though some organizations, such as the New York Stock Exchange, require certain standards of service for directors of their listed corporations.

Directors have the responsibility of ensuring that officers are operating wisely and in the exclusive interest of shareholders. Directors receive reports from the officers and give them managerial directions. The board in theory controls the compensation of officers (presumably tied to performance). The reality, though, is that corporate directors devote a relatively small amount of time to monitoring officers.

Ideally, shareholders would monitor the directors' supervision of officers. As one leading board monitor commented, "Boards of directors are like subatomic particles—they behave differently when they are observed." Consequently, monitoring of directors, and holding them responsible for corporate failings, can induce the directors to do a better job of monitoring officers and ensuring that the company is being managed in the interest of shareholders. Although the directors can be sued for failing to do their jobs effectively, directors are rarely held personally liable.

Importance of the Audit Committee   One crucial board committee is known as the *audit committee*. The audit committee oversees the corporation's accounting and financial reporting processes, including both internal and outside auditors. Unless the committee

---

39. Paul A. Gompers, Joy L. Ishii, and Andrew Metrick, "Corporate Governance and Equity Prices," *Quarterly Journal of Economics*, Vol. 118 (2003), p. 107.

members have sufficient expertise and are willing to spend the time to carefully examine the corporation's bookkeeping methods, however, the audit committee may be ineffective.

The audit committee also oversees the corporation's "internal controls." These are the measures taken to ensure that reported results are accurate; they are carried out largely by the company's internal auditing staff. As an example, these controls help to determine whether a corporation's debts are collectible. If the debts are not collectible, it is up to the audit committee to make sure that the corporation's financial officers do not simply pretend that payment will eventually be made.

The Compensation Committee   Another important committee of the board of directors is the *compensation committee*. This committee monitors and determines the compensation to be paid to the company's officers. As part of this process, it is responsible for assessing the officers' performance and for designing a compensation system that will better align the officers' interests with those of shareholders. (The *Application* feature at the end of this chapter discusses other corporate governance issues that a business owner may encounter.)

The Sarbanes-Oxley Act of 2002

As discussed in Chapter 2, in 2002 following a series of corporate scandals, Congress passed the Sarbanes-Oxley Act. The act separately addresses certain issues relating to corporate governance. Generally, the act attempts to increase corporate accountability by imposing strict disclosure requirements and harsh penalties for violations of securities laws. Among other things, the act requires chief corporate executives to take responsibility for the accuracy of financial statements and reports that are filed with the SEC. Chief executive officers and chief financial officers must personally certify that the statements and reports are accurate and complete.

Additionally, the new rules require that certain financial and stock-transaction reports must be filed with the SEC earlier than was required under the previous rules. The act also mandates SEC oversight over a new entity, called the Public Company Accounting Oversight Board, which regulates and oversees public accounting firms. Other provisions of the act created new private civil actions and expanded the SEC's remedies in administrative and civil actions.

Because of the importance of this act for corporate leaders and for those dealing with securities transactions, we present excerpts and explanatory comments in Appendix D. We also highlight some of its key provisions relating to corporate accountability in Exhibit 21–4.

More Internal Controls and Accountability   The Sarbanes-Oxley Act includes some traditional securities law provisions but also introduces direct *federal* corporate governance requirements for public companies (companies whose shares are traded in the public securities markets). The law addresses many of the corporate governance procedures just discussed and creates new requirements in an attempt to make the system work more effectively. The requirements deal with independent monitoring of company officers by both the board of directors and auditors.

Sections 302 and 404 of Sarbanes-Oxley require high-level managers (the most senior officers) to establish and maintain an effective system of internal controls. Moreover, senior management must reassess the system's effectiveness on an annual basis. Some companies already had strong and effective internal control systems in place before the passage of the act, but others had to take expensive steps to bring their internal controls up to the new federal standard. These include "disclosure controls and procedures" to ensure that company financial reports are accurate and timely. Assessment must involve

EXHIBIT 21–4 **Some Key Provisions of the Sarbanes-Oxley Act of 2002 Relating to Corporate Accountability**

Certification Requirements—Under Section 906 of the Sarbanes-Oxley Act, the chief executive officers (CEOs) and chief financial officers (CFOs) of most major companies listed on public stock exchanges must now certify financial statements that are filed with the SEC. For virtually all filed financial reports, CEOs and CFOs have to certify that such reports "fully comply" with SEC requirements and that all of the information reported "fairly represents in all material respects, the financial conditions and results of operations of the issuer."

Under Section 302 of the act, for each quarterly and annual filing with the SEC, CEOs and CFOs of reporting companies are required to certify that a signing officer reviewed the report and that it contains no untrue statements of material fact. Also, the signing officer or officers must certify that they have established an internal control system to identify all material information, and that any deficiencies in the system were disclosed to the auditors.

Loans to Directors and Officers—Section 402 prohibits any reporting company, as well as any private company that is filing an initial public offering, from making personal loans to directors and executive officers (with a few limited exceptions, such as for certain consumer and housing loans).

Protection for Whistleblowers—Section 806 protects "whistleblowers"—those employees who report ("blow the whistle" on) securities violations by their employers—from being fired or in any way discriminated against by their employers.

Blackout Periods—Section 306 prohibits certain types of securities transactions during "blackout periods"—periods during which the issuer's ability to purchase, sell, or otherwise transfer funds in individual account plans (such as pension funds) is suspended.

Enhanced Penalties for—

- *Violations of Section 906 Certification Requirements*—A CEO or CFO who certifies a financial report or statement filed with the SEC knowing that the report or statement does not fulfill all of the requirements of Section 906 will be subject to criminal penalties of up to $1 million in fines, ten years in prison, or both. *Willful* violators of the certification requirements may be subject to $5 million in fines, twenty years in prison, or both.

- *Violations of the Securities Exchange Act of 1934*—Penalties for securities fraud under the 1934 act were also increased (as discussed earlier in this chapter). Individual violators may be fined up to $5 million, imprisoned for up to twenty years, or both. *Willful* violators may be imprisoned for up to twenty-five years in addition to being fined.

- *Destruction or Alteration of Documents*—Anyone who alters, destroys, or conceals documents or otherwise obstructs any official proceeding will be subject to fines, imprisonment for up to twenty years, or both.

- *Other Forms of White-Collar Crime*—The act stiffened the penalties for certain criminal violations, such as federal mail and wire fraud, and ordered the U.S. Sentencing Commission to revise the sentencing guidelines for white-collar crimes (see Chapter 6).

Statute of Limitations for Securities Fraud—Section 804 provides that a private right of action for securities fraud may be brought no later than two years after the discovery of the violation or five years after the violation, whichever is earlier.

the documenting of financial results and accounting policies before reporting the results. By the beginning of 2008, hundreds of companies had reported that they had identified and corrected shortcomings in their internal control systems.

Certification and Monitoring Requirements   Section 906 requires that chief executive officers (CEOs) and chief financial officers (CFOs) certify that the information in the corporate financial statements "fairly represents in all material respects, the financial conditions and results of operations of the issuer." These corporate officers are subject to both civil and criminal penalties for violation of this section. This requirement makes officers directly accountable for the accuracy of their financial reporting and avoids any "ignorance defense" if shortcomings are later discovered.

Sarbanes-Oxley also includes requirements to improve directors' monitoring of officers' activities. All members of the corporate audit committee for public companies must be outside directors. The New York Stock Exchange (NYSE) has a similar rule that also extends to the board's compensation committee. The audit committee must have a written charter that sets out its duties and provides for performance appraisal. At least one "financial expert" must serve on the audit committee, which must hold executive meetings without company officers being present. The audit committee must establish procedures for "whistleblowers" to report violations. In addition to reviewing the internal controls, the committee also monitors the actions of the outside auditor.

ETHICAL ISSUE 21.1

*Is scienter **required for corporate executives to be liable for securities fraud based on financial statements that contain accounting misstatements or omissions?*** Section 906 of the Sarbanes-Oxley Act makes signing officers (CEOs and CFOs) directly accountable for the accuracy of their financial reports. One concern since the passage of the act is whether signing officers can be liable for fraud if the reports contain any errors or inaccurate information. Is mere negligence sufficient for liability, or must the officer have intended to deceive (*scienter*)? State courts have been split on the degree of intent required to impose liability. In 2006, however, a federal appellate court ruled that to be liable for securities fraud, an executive must either have had an intent to deceive or have been severely reckless in certifying a financial report.

The case involved a Georgia company, NDC Health Corporation; six of its executives; and the New York–based accounting firm Ernst & Young. An investor, Robert Garfield, filed a class-action suit claiming that the company's executives had certified financial reports that understated corporate expenses due to errors in amortization and capitalization. The trial court concluded that the specific accounting errors alleged were vague and difficult to evaluate and held that although the signing executives might have been negligent, they could not be liable for securities fraud. The federal appellate court agreed and affirmed the lower court's dismissal of the complaint. The appellate court held that to interpret Sarbanes-Oxley as imposing liability on corporate executives regardless of whether they had any intent to deceive would conflict with the plain language of the Private Securities Litigation Reform Act (discussed earlier in this chapter).[40]

ONLINE SECURITIES OFFERINGS AND DISCLOSURES

The Spring Street Brewing Company, headquartered in New York, made history when it became the first company to attempt to sell securities via the Internet. Through its online initial public offering (IPO), which ended in early 1996, Spring Street raised about $1.6 million—without having to pay any commissions to brokers or underwriters. The offering was made pursuant to Regulation A, which, as mentioned earlier in this chapter, allows small-business issuers to use a simplified registration procedure.

Such online IPOs (sometimes referred to as DPOs, which stands for *direct public offerings*) are particularly attractive to small companies and start-up ventures that may find it difficult to raise capital from institutional investors or through underwriters. By making the offering online under Regulation A, the company can avoid both commissions and the costly and time-consuming filings required for a traditional IPO under federal and state law.

Regulations Governing Online Securities Offerings

One of the early questions posed by online offerings was whether the delivery of securities *information* via the Internet met the requirements of the 1933 Securities Act, which traditionally were applied to the delivery of paper documents. In an interpretive release issued

---

40. *Garfield v. NDC Health Corp.*, 466 F.3d 1255 (11th Cir. 2006).

in 1995, the SEC stated that "[t]he use of electronic media should be at least an equal alternative to the use of paper-based media" and that anything that can be delivered in paper form under the current securities laws might also be delivered in electronic form.[41]

Basically, there has been no change in the substantive law of disclosure; only the delivery vehicle has changed. When the Internet is used for delivery of a prospectus, the same rules apply as for the delivery of a paper prospectus. Timely and adequate notice is required, however. The only unique consideration is how to provide timely and adequate notice of the delivery of information. Posting a prospectus on a Web site does not constitute adequate notice, but sending separate e-mails or even postcards stating the URL where the prospectus can be viewed will satisfy the SEC's notice requirements.

An issue that has come up in the last few years is whether Web site postings and blogs can satisfy the requirement that companies provide "widespread dissemination" of material information about a stock to investors. See this chapter's *Adapting the Law to the Online Environment* feature on the next page for a discussion of this topic.

Potential Liability Created by Online Offering Materials

Every printed prospectus indicates that only the information given in the prospectus can be used in making an investment decision about the securities offered. The same wording, of course, appears on Web-based offerings. What happens if an electronic prospectus contains information that conflicts with the information provided in a printed prospectus?

As anyone who is familiar with the Internet knows, the graphics, images, and audio files created by one computer are not always readable by another computer when they are exchanged online. The SEC has issued Rule 304 to deal with this situation.[42] The first part of the rule states that if graphic, image, or audio material in a prospectus cannot be reproduced in an electronic form on the SEC's EDGAR system, the electronic prospectus must include a fair and accurate narrative description of the omitted data. The second part of Rule 304 provides that the graphic, image, and audio material contained in the version of a document delivered to investors is *deemed to be part of the electronic document* filed with the SEC. As a result, a corporation can have two versions of a prospectus—a print version that contains graphics and an electronic version that describes the information shown in the graphics.

Hyperlinks to Other Web Pages   Those who create such Web-based offerings may be tempted to insert hyperlinks to other Web pages. They may include links to other sites that have analyzed the future prospects of the company, the products and services sold by the company, or the offering itself. To avoid potential liability, however, online offerors (the entities making the offerings) need to exercise caution when including such hyperlinks.

Regulation D Offerings   Potential problems may also occur with some Regulation D offerings, if the offeror places the offering circular on its Web site for general consumption by anybody on the Internet. Because Regulation D offerings are private placements, general solicitation is restricted. If anyone can have access to the offering circular on the Web, the Regulation D exemption may be disqualified.

ON THE WEB

The SEC's Electronic Data Gathering, Analysis, and Retrieval (EDGAR) system contains information about the SEC's operations, the statutes it implements, its proposed and final rules, and its enforcement actions, as well as corporate financial information. Go to

www.sec.gov/edgar.shtml.

---

41. "Use of Electronic Media for Delivery Purposes," Securities Act Release No. 33-7233 (October 6, 1995). The rules governing the use of electronic transmissions for delivery purposes were subsequently confirmed in Securities Act Release No. 33-7289 (May 9, 1996) and expanded in Securities Act Release No. 33-7856 (April 28, 2000).
42. 17 C.F.R. Section 232.304.

ADAPTING THE LAW TO THE ONLINE ENVIRONMENT

Should the SEC Recognize Internet Postings and Blogs as a Means of Disseminating Financial Information?

I n 2000, the SEC issued Regulation Fair Disclosure,[a] or Regulation FD, in an attempt to ensure that some investors do not have more information than the general public. Under Regulation FD, when a company gives "material nonpublic information" about its prospects to certain individuals or entities, such as stock analysts or Wall Street professionals, it must also disclose that information to the public. To comply with the regulation, corporate executives typically first meet in person or by phone conference with analysts and then hold a press conference to disseminate the information to the public.

Now at least one corporate executive would like to use the company's Web site to disseminate the required information. On September 25, 2006, Jonathan Schwartz, the CEO of Sun Microsystems, Inc., sent a letter to the chair of the SEC. Pointing out "the utility of the Internet to inform investors," Schwartz said that he wanted to avoid "consuming trees with press releases." According to Schwartz, Sun Microsystems' Web site (**www.sun.com**), which includes a blog written by Schwartz himself (**www.blogs.sun.com/jonathan**) as well as blogs from almost four thousand employees, receives nearly a million hits per day. His letter stated emphatically, "we believe that the proliferation of the Internet supports a new policy that online communications fully satisfy Regulation FD's broad distribution requirement."[b] As of mid-2007, however, the SEC has not taken a position on whether the "widespread dissemination" required by the regulation can be satisfied by posting the information on the company's Web site or blog.

FOR CRITICAL ANALYSIS *What are the pros and cons of the SEC allowing Web site postings to satisfy the fair disclosure rule? Should blogs be treated differently than Web sites? Why or why not?*

a. 17 C.F.R. Section 243.101(e)(2).

b. Schwartz's letter is posted with a short article titled "One Small Step for the Blogosphere" at **www.blogs.sun.com/jonathan/entry/one_small_step_for_the**.

Online Securities Offerings by Foreign Companies

Another question raised by Internet transactions has to do with securities offerings by foreign companies. Traditionally, foreign companies have not been able to offer new shares to the U.S. public without first registering them with the SEC. Today, however, anybody in the world can offer shares of stock worldwide via the Web.

The SEC asks that foreign issuers on the Internet implement measures to warn U.S. investors. For instance, a foreign company offering shares of stock on the Internet must add a disclaimer on its Web site stating that it has not gone through the registration procedure in the United States. If the SEC believes that a Web site's offering of foreign securities is targeting U.S. residents, it will pursue that company in an attempt to require it to register in the United States.[43]

ONLINE SECURITIES FRAUD

A major problem facing the SEC today is how to enforce the antifraud provisions of the securities laws in the online environment. In 1999, in the first cases involving illegal online securities offerings, the SEC filed suit against three individuals for illegally offering securities on an Internet auction site.[44] In essence, all three indicated that their companies would go public soon and attempted to sell unregistered securities via the Web

43. International Series Release No. 1125 (March 23, 1998).
44. *In re Davis*, SEC Administrative File No. 3-10080 (October 20, 1999); *In re Haas*, SEC Administrative File No. 3-10081 (October 20, 1999); *In re Sitaras*, SEC Administrative File No. 3-10082 (October 20, 1999).

auction site. All of these actions were in violation of Sections 5, 17(a)(1), and 17(a)(3) of the 1933 Securities Act. Since then, the SEC has brought a variety of Internet-related fraud cases, including cases involving investment scams and the manipulation of stock prices in Internet chat rooms.

Investment Scams

An ongoing problem is how to curb online investment scams. One fraudulent investment scheme involved twenty thousand investors, who lost, in all, more than $3 million. Some cases have involved false claims about the earnings potential of home business programs, such as the claim that one could "earn $4,000 or more each month." Others have concerned claims of "guaranteed credit repair."

Using Chat Rooms to Manipulate Stock Prices

"Pumping and dumping" occurs when a person who has purchased a particular stock heavily promotes ("pumps up") that stock—thereby creating a great demand for it and driving up its price—and then sells ("dumps") it. The practice of pumping up a stock and then dumping it is quite old. In the online world, however, the process can occur much more quickly and efficiently.

EXAMPLE 21.4 The most famous case in this area involved Jonathan Lebed, a fifteen-year-old stock trader and Internet user from New Jersey. Lebed was the first minor ever charged with securities fraud by the SEC, but it is unlikely that he will be the last. The SEC charged that Lebed bought thinly traded stocks. After purchasing a stock, he would flood stock-related chat rooms, particularly at Yahoo's finance boards, with messages touting the stock's virtues. He used numerous false names so that no one would know that a single person was posting the messages. He would say that the stock was the most "undervalued stock in history" and that its price would jump by 1,000 percent "very soon." When other investors would then buy the stock, the price would go up quickly, and Lebed would sell out. The SEC forced the teenager to repay almost $300,000 in gains plus interest but allowed him to keep about $500,000 of the profits he made by trading small-company stocks that he also touted on the Internet. ■

The SEC has been bringing an increasing number of cases against those who manipulate stock prices in this way. Many of these online investment scams are perpetrated through mass e-mails (spam), online newsletters, and chat rooms.

Hacking into Online Stock Accounts The last few years have seen the emergence of a new form of "pumping and dumping" stock involving hackers who break into existing online stock accounts and make unauthorized transfers. Millions of people now buy and sell investments online through online brokerage companies such as E*Trade and Ameritrade. Sophisticated hackers have learned to use online investing to their advantage.

By installing keystroke-monitoring software on computer terminals in public places, such as hotels, libraries, and airports, hackers can gain access to online account information. All they have to do is wait for a person to access an online trading account and then monitor the next several dozen keystrokes to determine the customer's account number and password. Once they have the log-in information, they can access the customer's account and liquidate her or his existing stock holdings. The hackers then use the customer's funds to purchase thinly traded, microcap securities, also known as penny stocks. The goal is to boost the price of a stock that the hacker has already purchased at a lower price. Then, when the stock price goes up, the hacker sells all the stock and wires the funds to either an offshore account or a dummy corporation, making it difficult for the SEC to trace the transactions and prosecute the offender.

■EXAMPLE 21.5 Aleksey Kamardin, a twenty-one-year-old Florida student, purchased 55,000 shares of stock in Fuego Entertainment using an E*Trade account in his own name. Kamardin then hacked into other customers' accounts at E*Trade, Ameritrade, Schwab, and other brokerage companies, and used their funds to purchase a total of 458,000 shares of Fuego stock. When the stock price rose from $.88 per share to $1.28 per share, Kamardin sold all of his shares of Fuego, making a profit of $9,164.28 in about three hours. Kamardin did this with other thinly traded stocks as well, allegedly making $82,960 in about five weeks, and prompting the SEC to file charges against him in January 2007.[45] ■

So far, the brokerage companies have been covering their customers' losses from this new wave of frauds, but the potential for loss is substantial. E*Trade and Ameritrade have also increased security measures and are changing their software to prevent further intrusions into customers' online stock accounts.

---

45. You can read the SEC's complaint against Kamardin by going to the SEC's Web site at **www.sec.gov**, clicking on the link to litigation releases, and selecting "LR-19981." The case had not been resolved by the time this book went to press.

REVIEWING Investor Protection, Insider Trading, and Corporate Governance

Dale Emerson served as the chief financial officer for Reliant Electric Company, a distributor of electricity serving portions of Montana and North Dakota. Reliant was in the final stages of planning a takeover of Dakota Gasworks, Inc., a natural gas distributor that operated solely within North Dakota. Emerson went on a weekend fishing trip with his uncle, Ernest Wallace. Emerson mentioned to Wallace that he had been putting in a lot of extra hours at the office planning a takeover of Dakota Gasworks. On returning from the fishing trip, Wallace met with a broker from Chambers Investments and purchased $20,000 of Reliant stock. Three weeks later, Reliant made a tender offer to Dakota Gasworks stockholders and purchased 57 percent of Dakota Gasworks stock. Over the next two weeks, the price of Reliant stock rose 72 percent before leveling out. Wallace then sold his Reliant stock for a gross profit of $14,400. Using the information presented in the chapter, answer the following questions.

1 Would registration with the SEC be required for Dakota Gasworks securities? Why or why not?

2 Did Emerson violate Section 10(b) of the Securities Exchange Act of 1934 and SEC Rule 10b-5? Why or why not?

3 What theory or theories might a court use to hold Wallace liable for insider trading?

4 Under the Sarbanes-Oxley Act of 2002, who would be required to certify the accuracy of financial statements filed with the SEC?

APPLICATION   What Venture Capital Financing and Corporate Governance Issues Might a Business Owner Encounter?*

As pointed out in Chapter 20, corporations obtain financing in a variety of ways, including selling corporate securities in the form of stocks and bonds. Nevertheless, a rea-

son that many new businesses fail is that they are undercapitalized. Thus, obtaining proper financing for your new or existing business is extremely important.

Start-Up Businesses

Start-up businesses, particularly in the high-tech industry, are good examples of the need for proper financing. Many new

---

* This *Application* is not meant to substitute for the services of an attorney who is licensed to practice law in your state.

businesses rely for funding on the owners' personal assets, loans from the owners' relatives or friends, and, sometimes, loans from outsiders. If a new business has a viable product or service, it may seek financing from venture capitalists—that is, businesses and individuals who lend funds to a start-up business. Generally, to obtain this "loan," the start-up business gives up a share of its ownership to the venture capitalist.

When venture capitalists provide financing, their primary goals are to enable the business to enhance its product or service; have the business properly incorporated; and, by the proper filing of a registration statement, take the corporation public through an IPO. Most often, it is the issuance and sale of these shares that affords the owners, including the venture capitalists, with operating costs and modest to substantial profits.

The Dangers of Venture Capitalist Financing

There are dangers to this type of financing. First, the start-up must find a venture capitalist willing to invest in the business. Whether this will happen depends largely on how viable the product or service is or will be. Many start-ups die simply because venture capitalists declined to invest, and the owners' personal funds were exhausted. Second, as mentioned, the start-up business will most likely be giving up a percentage of its ownership. Despite the old saying "do not give the farm away," the developers of the product or service may have to give up part of their control over the business or a significant portion of the financial rewards it produces. Third, when the business goes public, investors may not purchase the shares in sufficient amount or at a price that will provide the hoped-for profits.

Corporate Governance Issues

Once the venture capital financing is secured and the corporation has been formed, the owners may become members of the board of directors or officers. Corporate governance is important today regardless of the corporation's size. Increasingly, the SEC and shareholders are closely scrutinizing whether the stock options granted to corporate officers as a form of compensation are excessive or unfair in other ways.

Several corporations have recently come under investigation for "backdating" stock options—that is, for dating the options earlier than they were actually issued in order to lower the set price (the price that the option recipient must pay for stock purchased with the options). For example, suppose that options are issued on December 31 when the market price of the company's stock is $50. In this situation, the set price would be $50. If, however, the options issued on December 31 were backdated to February 1, when the market price was $30 per share, the options recipient would have to pay only $30 per share and would have an immediate profit of $20 per share. Backdating is illegal, however.

If you become an officer or board member, you will have access to information concerning your corporation that is not available to the public. Never use this information to gain an advantage on the stock market or give this information to others who can get a trading advantage. *Insider trading* is illegal, and liability extends to those to whom you give the information.

CHECKLIST FOR VENTURE CAPITAL FINANCING AND CORPORATE GOVERNANCE ISSUES

1 Be sure you have a viable product or service before seeking venture capital financing.
2 If the venture capitalist wants a percentage of the ownership of your business, be sure you "do not give the farm away" (lose control or substantially reduce the value of your interest in the business).
3 Take care when granting stock options as a form of compensation and never backdate the set price for stock options.
4 If you are a corporate officer or director, do not trade on the stock market based on nonpublic information or give inside information to others.

KEY TERMS

CHAPTER SUMMARY	Investor Protection, Insider Trading, and Corporate Governance
Securities Act of 1933 (See pages 640–649.)	Prohibits fraud and stabilizes the securities industry by requiring disclosure of all essential information relating to the issuance of securities to the investing public. 1. *Registration requirements*—Securities, unless exempt, must be registered with the SEC before being offered to the public. The *registration statement* must include detailed financial information about the issuing corporation; the intended use of the proceeds of the securities being issued; and certain disclosures, such as interests of directors or officers and pending lawsuits. 2. *Prospectus*—The issuer must provide investors with a *prospectus* that describes the security being sold, the issuing corporation, and the risk attaching to the security. 3. *Exemptions*—The SEC has exempted certain offerings from the requirements of the Securities Act of 1933. Exemptions may be determined on the basis of the size of the issue, whether the offering is private or public, and whether advertising is involved. Exemptions are summarized in Exhibit 21–1 on page 645.

Securities Exchange Act of 1934
(See pages 649–656.)
	Provides for the regulation and registration of securities exchanges, brokers, dealers, and national securities associations (such as the NASD). Maintains a continuous disclosure system for all corporations with securities on the securities exchanges and for those companies that have assets in excess of $10 million and five hundred or more shareholders (Section 12 companies).
	
	1. *SEC Rule 10b-5 [under Section 10(b) of the 1934 act]*—
	
	   a. Applies in virtually all cases concerning the trading of securities—a firm's securities do not have to be registered under the 1933 act for the 1934 act to apply.
	
	   b. Applies only when the requisites of federal jurisdiction (such as use of the mails, stock exchange facilities, or any facility of interstate commerce) are present.
	
	   c. Applies to insider trading by corporate officers, directors, majority shareholders, and any persons receiving inside information (information not available to the investing public) who base their trading on this information.
	
	   d. Liability for violations can be civil or criminal.
	
	   e. May be violated by failing to disclose "material facts" that must be disclosed under this rule.
	
	   f. Liability may be based on the tipper/tippee or the misappropriation theory.
	
	2. *Insider trading [under Section 16(b) of the 1934 act]*—To prevent corporate officers and directors from taking advantage of inside information, the 1934 act requires officers, directors, and shareholders owning 10 percent or more of the issued stock of a corporation to turn over to the corporation all short-term profits (called *short-swing profits*) realized from the purchase and sale or sale and purchase of corporate stock within any six-month period.
	
	3. *Proxies [under Section 14(a) of the 1934 act]*—The SEC regulates the content of proxy statements sent to shareholders by corporate managers of Section 12 companies who are requesting authority to vote on behalf of the shareholders in a particular election on specified issues. Section 14(a) is essentially a disclosure law, with provisions similar to the antifraud provisions of SEC Rule 10b-5.

State Securities Laws (See pages 656–657.)	All states have corporate securities laws (*blue sky laws*) that regulate the offer and sale of securities within state borders; these laws are designed to prevent "speculative schemes which have no more basis than so many feet of 'blue sky.'" States regulate securities concurrently with the federal government. The Uniform Securities Act of 2002, which has been adopted by eleven states and is being considered by several others, is designed to promote coordination and reduce duplication between state and federal securities regulation.

CHAPTER SUMMARY	**Investor Protection, Insider Trading, and Corporate Governance–Continued**
Corporate Governance (See pages 657–662.)	1. *Definition*—Corporate governance is the system by which business corporations are governed, including policies and procedures for making decisions on corporate affairs. 2. *The need for corporate governance*—Corporate governance is necessary in large corporations because corporate ownership (by the shareholders) is separated from corporate control (by officers and managers). This separation of corporate ownership and control can often result in conflicting interests. Corporate governance standards address such issues. 3. *Sarbanes-Oxley Act of 2002*—This act attempts to increase corporate accountability by imposing strict disclosure requirements and harsh penalties for violations of securities laws.
Online Securities Offerings and Disclosures (See pages 662–664.)	In 1995, the SEC announced that anything that can be delivered in paper form under current securities laws may also be delivered in electronic form. Generally, when the Internet is used for the delivery of a prospectus, the same rules apply as for the delivery of a paper prospectus. When securities offerings are made online, the offerors should be careful that any hyperlinked materials do not mislead investors. Caution should also be used when making Regulation D offerings (private placements), because general solicitation is restricted with these offerings.
Online Securities Fraud (See pages 664–666.)	A major problem facing the SEC today is how to enforce the antifraud provisions of the securities laws in the online environment. Internet-related forms of securities fraud include investment scams and the manipulation of stock prices in online chat rooms.

FOR REVIEW

Answers for the even-numbered questions in this **For Review** *section can be found in Appendix E at the end of this text.*

1 What is meant by the term *securities*?

2 What are the two major statutes regulating the securities industry? When was the Securities and Exchange Commission created, and what are its major purposes and functions?

3 What is insider trading? Why is it prohibited?

4 What are some of the features of state securities laws?

5 What certification requirements does the Sarbanes-Oxley Act impose on corporate executives?

■

QUESTIONS AND CASE PROBLEMS

 **HYPOTHETICAL SCENARIOS**

21.1 Registration Requirements. Langley Brothers, Inc., a corporation incorporated and doing business in Kansas, decides to sell common stock worth $1 million to the public. The stock will be sold only within the state of Kansas. Joseph Langley, the chairman of the board, says the offering need not be registered with the Securities and Exchange Commission. His brother, Harry, disagrees. Who is right? Explain.

21.2 Hypothetical Question with Sample Answer. Huron Corp. has 300,000 common shares outstanding. The owners of these outstanding shares live in several different states. Huron has decided to split the 300,000 shares two for one. Will Huron Corp. have to file a registration statement and prospectus on the 300,000 new shares to be issued as a result of the split? Explain.

 For a sample answer to Question 21.2, go to Appendix F at the end of this text.

■

CASE PROBLEMS

21.3 Definition of a Security. The W. J. Howey Co. owned large tracts of citrus acreage in Lake County, Florida. For several years, it planted about five hundred acres annually, keeping half of the groves itself and offering the other half to the public to help finance additional development. Howey-in-the-Hills Service, Inc., was a service company engaged in cultivating and developing these groves, including harvesting and marketing the crops. Each prospective customer was offered both a land sales contract and a service contract, after being told that it was not feasible to invest in a grove unless service arrangements were made. Of the acreage sold by Howey, 85 percent was sold with a service contract with Howey-in-the-Hills Service. Howey did not register with the Securities and Exchange Commission (SEC) or meet the other administrative requirements that issuers of securities must fulfill. The SEC sued to enjoin Howey from continuing to offer the land sales and service contracts. Howey responded that no SEC violation existed because no securities had been issued. Evaluate the definition of a security given in this chapter, and then determine whether Howey or the SEC should prevail in court. [*SEC v. W. J. Howey Co.*, 328 U.S. 293, 66 S.Ct. 1100, 90 L.Ed. 1244 (1946)]

21.4 Violations of the 1934 Act. 2TheMart.com, Inc., was conceived in January 1999 to launch an auction Web site to compete with eBay, Inc. On January 19, 2TheMart announced that its Web site was in its "final development" stages and was expected to be active by the end of July as a "preeminent" auction site. The company also said that it had "retained the services of leading Web site design and architecture consultants to design and construct" the site. Based on the announcement, investors rushed to buy 2TheMart's stock, causing a rapid increase in the price. On February 3, 2TheMart entered into an agreement with IBM to take preliminary steps to plan the site. Three weeks later, 2TheMart announced that the site was "currently in final development." On June 1, 2TheMart signed a contract with IBM to design, build, and test the site, with a target delivery date of October 8. When 2TheMart's site did not debut as announced, Mary Harrington and others who had bought the stock filed a suit in a federal district court against the firm's officers, alleging violations of the Securities Exchange Act of 1934. The defendants responded, in part, that any alleged misrepresentations were not material and asked the court to dismiss the suit. How should the court rule, and why? [*In re 2TheMart.com, Inc. Securities Litigation*, 114 F.Supp.2d 955 (C.D.Ca. 2000)]

21.5 Insider Reporting and Trading. Ronald Bleakney, an officer at Natural Microsystems Corp. (NMC), a Section 12 corporation, directed NMC sales in North America, South America, and Europe. In November 1998, Bleakney sold more than 7,500 shares of NMC stock. The following March, Bleakney resigned from the firm, and the next

month, he bought more than 20,000 shares of its stock. NMC provided some guidance to employees concerning the rules of insider trading, but with regard to Bleakney's transactions, the corporation said nothing about potential liability. Richard Morales, an NMC shareholder, filed a suit against NMC and Bleakney to compel recovery, under Section 16(b) of the Securities Exchange Act of 1934, of Bleakney's profits from the sale and purchase of his shares. (When Morales died, his executor Deborah Donoghue became the plaintiff.) Bleakney argued that he should not be liable because he relied on NMC's advice. Should the court order Bleakney to disgorge his profits? Explain. [*Donoghue v. Natural Microsystems Corp.*, 198 F.Supp.2d 487 (S.D.N.Y. 2002)]

21.6 Case Problem with Sample Answer. Scott Ginsburg was chief executive officer (CEO) of Evergreen Media Corp., which owned and operated radio stations. In 1996, Evergreen became interested in acquiring EZ Communications, Inc., which also owned radio stations. To initiate negotiations, Ginsburg met with EZ's CEO, Alan Box, on Friday, July 12. Two days later, Scott phoned his brother Mark, who, on Monday, bought 3,800 shares of EZ stock. Mark discussed the deal with their father, Jordan, who bought 20,000 EZ shares on Thursday. On July 25, the day before the EZ bid was due, Scott phoned his parents' home, and Mark bought another 3,200 EZ shares. The same routine was followed over the next few days, with Scott periodically phoning Mark or Jordan, both of whom continued to buy EZ shares. Evergreen's bid was refused, but on August 5, EZ announced its merger with another company. The price of EZ stock rose 30 percent, increasing the value of Mark and Jordan's shares by $664,024 and $412,875, respectively. The Securities and Exchange Commission (SEC) filed a civil suit in a federal district court against Scott. What was the most likely allegation? What is required to impose sanctions for this offense? Should the court hold Scott liable? Why or why not? [*SEC v. Ginsburg*, 362 F.3d 1292 (11th Cir. 2004)]

After you have answered Problem 21.6, compare your answer with the sample answer given on the Web site that accompanies this text. Go to academic.cengage.com/blaw/blt, select "Chapter 21," and click on "Case Problem with Sample Answer."

21.7 Securities Laws. In 1997, WTS Transnational, Inc., required financing to develop a prototype of an unpatented fingerprint-verification system. At the time, WTS had no revenue, $655,000 in liabilities, and only $10,000 in assets. Thomas Cavanagh and Frank Nicolois, who operated an investment banking company called U.S. Milestone (USM), arranged the financing using Curbstone Acquisition Corp. Curbstone had no assets but had registered approximately 3.5 million shares of stock with the Securities and Exchange Commission (SEC). Under the terms of the deal, Curbstone acquired

WTS, and the resulting entity was named Electro-Optical Systems Corp. (EOSC). New EOSC shares were issued to all of the WTS shareholders. Only Cavanagh and others affiliated with USM could sell EOSC stock to the public, however. Over the next few months, these individuals issued false press releases, made small deceptive purchases of EOSC shares at high prices, distributed hundreds of thousands of shares to friends and relatives, and sold their own shares at inflated prices through third party companies they owned. When the SEC began to investigate, the share price fell to its actual value, and innocent investors lost over $15 million. Were any securities laws violated in this case? If so, what might be an appropriate remedy? [*SEC v. Cavanagh*, 445 F.3d 105 (2d Cir. 2006)]

21.8 Securities Trading. Between 1994 and 1998, Richard Svoboda, a credit officer for NationsBank N.A., in Dallas, Texas, evaluated and approved his employer's extensions of credit to clients. These responsibilities gave Svoboda access to nonpublic information about the clients' earnings, performance, acquisitions, and business plans in confidential memos, e-mail, credit applications, and other sources. Svoboda devised a scheme with Michael Robles, an independent accountant, to use this information to trade securities. Pursuant to their scheme, Robles traded in the securities of more than twenty different companies and profited by more than $1 million. Svoboda also executed trades for his own profit of more than $200,000, despite their agreement that Robles would do all of the trading. Aware that their scheme violated NationsBank's policy, they attempted to conduct their trades to avoid suspicion. When NationsBank questioned Svoboda about his actions, he lied, refused to cooperate, and was fired. Did Svoboda or Robles commit any crimes? Are they subject to civil liability? If so, who could file a suit and on what ground? What are the possible sanctions? What might be a defense? How should a court rule? Discuss. [*SEC v. Svoboda*, 409 F.Supp.2d 331 (S.D.N.Y. 2006)]

21.9 **A Question of Ethics.** *Melvin Lyttle told John Montana and Paul Knight about a "Trading Program" that pur-*

portedly would buy and sell securities in deals that were fully insured, as well as monitored and controlled by the Federal Reserve Bank. Without checking the details or even verifying whether the Program existed, Montana and Knight, with Lyttle's help, began to sell interests in the Program to investors. For a minimum investment of $1 million, the investors were promised extraordinary rates of return—from 10 percent to as much as 100 percent per week—without risk. They were told, among other things, that the Program would "utilize banks that can ensure full bank integrity of The Transaction whose undertaking[s] are in complete harmony with international banking rules and protocol and who [sic] guarantee maximum security of a Funder's Capital Placement Amount." Nothing was required but the investors' funds and their silence—the Program was to be kept secret. Over a four-month period in 1999, Montana raised approximately $23 million from twenty-two investors. The promised gains did not accrue, however. Instead, Montana, Lyttle, and Knight depleted investors' funds in high-risk trades or spent the funds on themselves. [*SEC v. Montana*, 464 F.Supp.2d 772 (S.D.Ind. 2006)]

1 The Securities and Exchange Commission (SEC) filed a suit in a federal district court against Montana and the others, seeking an injunction, civil penalties, and disgorgement with interest. The SEC alleged, among other things, violations of Section 10(b) of the Securities Exchange Act of 1934 and SEC Rule 10b-5. What is required to establish a violation of these laws? Describe how and why the facts in this case meet, or fail to meet, these requirements.

2 It is often remarked, "There's a sucker born every minute!" Does that phrase describe the Program's investors? Ultimately, about half of the investors recouped the amount they invested. Should the others be considered at least partly responsible for their own losses? Why or why not?

CRITICAL THINKING AND WRITING ASSIGNMENTS

21.10 Critical Legal Thinking. Do you think that the tipper/tippee and misappropriation theories extend liability under SEC Rule 10b-5 too far? Why or why not?

21.11 Critical Thinking and Writing Assignment for Business. Insider trading, as you learned, is illegal. Not everyone agrees that it should be, though. A small group of legal scholars believe that insider trading should be completely legal. They argue that insider trading, if more widespread, would cause stock prices to almost instantly adjust to new information. They further argue that "insiders," if able to make profits from

insider trading, would therefore accept lower salaries and benefits.

1 Why is insider trading illegal in the first place? Who is supposed to be protected and why?

2 What is wrong with the argument advanced by the legal scholars who want insider trading made legal? Or, are they right? Explain your answer.

21.12 **Video Question.** Go to this text's Web site at **academic. cengage.com/blaw/blt** and select "Chapter 21."

Click on "Video Questions" and view the video titled *Mergers and Acquisitions*. Then answer the following questions.

1 Analyze whether the purchase of Onyx Advertising is a material fact that the Quigley Company had a duty to disclose under SEC Rule 10b-5.

2 Does it matter whether Quigley personally knew about or authorized the company spokesperson's statements? Why or why not?

3 Which case discussed in the chapter presented issues that are very similar to those raised in the video? Under the holding of that case, would Onyx Advertising be able to maintain a suit against the Quigley Company for violation of SEC Rule 10b-5?

4 Who else might be able to bring a suit against the Quigley Company for insider trading under SEC Rule 10b-5?

ONLINE ACTIVITIES

PRACTICAL INTERNET EXERCISES

Go to this text's Web site at **academic.cengage.com/blaw/blt**, select "Chapter 21," and click on "Practical Internet Exercises." There you will find the following Internet research exercises that you can perform to learn more about the topics covered in this chapter.

PRACTICAL INTERNET EXERCISE 21-1   LEGAL PERSPECTIVE—Electronic Delivery

PRACTICAL INTERNET EXERCISE 21-2   MANAGEMENT PERSPECTIVE—The SEC's Role

BEFORE THE TEST

Go to this text's Web site at **academic.cengage.com/blaw/blt**, select "Chapter 21," and click on "Interactive Quizzes." You will find a number of interactive questions relating to this chapter.

CHAPTER 22
Promoting Competition in a Global Context

LEARNING OBJECTIVES

AFTER READING THIS CHAPTER, YOU SHOULD BE ABLE TO ANSWER THE FOLLOWING QUESTIONS:

1 What is a monopoly? What is market power? How do these concepts relate to each other?

2 What type of activity is prohibited by Section 1 of the Sherman Act? What type of activity is prohibited by Section 2 of the Sherman Act?

3 What are the four major provisions of the Clayton Act, and what types of activities do these provisions prohibit?

4 What agencies of the federal government enforce the federal antitrust laws?

5 What are four activities that are exempt from the antitrust laws?

> **"Free competition is worth more to society than it costs."**
>
> Oliver Wendell Holmes, Jr.,
> 1841–1935
> (Associate justice of the
> United States Supreme Court,
> 1902–1932)

T oday's antitrust laws are the direct descendants of common law actions intended to limit *restraints on trade* (agreements between firms that have the effect of reducing competition in the marketplace). Such actions date to the fifteenth century in England. In the United States, concern over monopolistic practices arose following the Civil War with the growth of large corporate enterprises and their attempts to reduce competition. To thwart competition, they legally tied themselves together in business trusts. A *business trust* is a form of business organization in which trustees hold title to property for the benefit of others. The most powerful of these trusts, the Standard Oil trust, is examined in this chapter's *Landmark in the Law* feature on pages 676 and 677.

Many states tried to curb such monopolistic behavior by enacting statutes outlawing the use of trusts. That is why all the laws regulating economic competition today are referred to as **antitrust laws.** At the national level, Congress passed the Sherman Antitrust Act in 1890. In 1914, Congress passed the Clayton Act and the Federal Trade Commission Act to further curb anticompetitive or unfair business practices. Congress later amended the 1914 acts to broaden and strengthen their coverage.

This chapter examines these major antitrust statutes, focusing particularly on the Sherman Act and the Clayton Act, as amended, and the types of activities they prohibit. Remember in reading this chapter that the basis of antitrust legislation is the desire to foster competition. Antitrust legislation was initially created—and continues to be enforced—because of our belief that competition leads to lower prices, generates more

ANTITRUST LAW
Laws protecting commerce from unlawful restraints.

product information, and results in a more equitable distribution of wealth between consumers and producers. As Oliver Wendell Holmes, Jr., indicated in the chapter-opening quotation, free competition is worth more to our society than the cost we pay for it. The cost includes government regulation of business behavior.

THE SHERMAN ANTITRUST ACT

In 1890, Congress passed "An Act to Protect Trade and Commerce against Unlawful Restraints and Monopolies"—commonly known as the Sherman Antitrust Act or, more simply, as the Sherman Act. The Sherman Act was and remains one of the government's most powerful weapons in the effort to maintain a competitive economy, as noted in this chapter's *Landmark in the Law* feature on pages 676 and 677.

Major Provisions of the Sherman Act

Sections 1 and 2 contain the main provisions of the Sherman Act:

1 Every contract, combination in the form of trust or otherwise, or conspiracy, in restraint of trade or commerce among the several States, or with foreign nations, is hereby declared to be illegal [and is a felony punishable by a fine and/or imprisonment].

2 Every person who shall monopolize, or attempt to monopolize, or combine or conspire with any other person or persons, to monopolize any part of the trade or commerce among the several States, or with foreign nations, shall be deemed guilty of a felony [and is similarly punishable].

Differences between Section 1 and Section 2

These two sections of the Sherman Act are quite different. Violation of Section 1 requires two or more persons, as a person cannot contract or combine or conspire alone. Thus, the essence of the illegal activity is *the act of joining together*. Section 2, though, can apply either to one person or to two or more persons because it refers to "[e]very person." Thus, unilateral conduct can result in a violation of Section 2.

The cases brought to court under Section 1 of the Sherman Act differ from those brought under Section 2. Section 1 cases are often concerned with finding an agreement (written or oral) that leads to a restraint of trade. Section 2 cases deal with the structure of a monopoly that already exists in the marketplace. The term **monopoly** generally is used to describe a market in which there is a single seller or a very limited number of sellers. Whereas Section 1 focuses on agreements that are restrictive—that is, agreements that have a wrongful purpose—Section 2 looks at the so-called misuse of **monopoly power** in the marketplace.

MONOPOLY
A term generally used to describe a market in which there is a single seller or a very limited number of sellers.

MONOPOLY POWER
The ability of a monopoly to dictate what takes place in a given market.

MARKET POWER
The power of a firm to control the market price of its product. A monopoly has the greatest degree of market power.

Monopoly power exists when a firm has an extremely great amount of **market power**—the power to affect the market price of its product. Both Section 1 and Section 2 seek to curtail market practices that result in undesired monopoly pricing and output behavior. For a case to be brought under Section 2, however, the "threshold" or "necessary" amount of monopoly power must already exist. We will return to a discussion of these two sections of the Sherman Act after we look at the act's jurisdictional requirements.

Jurisdictional Requirements

The Sherman Act applies only to restraints that have a substantial impact on interstate commerce. The Sherman Act also extends to U.S. nationals abroad who are engaged in activities that have an effect on U.S. foreign commerce. (The extraterritorial application of U.S. antitrust laws will be discussed in the last section of this chapter as well as in Chapter 25.) State laws regulate local restraints on competition.

Courts have generally held that any activity that substantially affects interstate commerce falls within the scope of the Sherman Act. As discussed in Chapter 1, courts have construed the meaning of *interstate commerce* broadly, bringing even local activities within the regulatory power of the national government.

SECTION 1 OF THE SHERMAN ACT

The underlying assumption of Section 1 of the Sherman Act is that society's welfare is harmed if rival firms are permitted to join in an agreement that consolidates their market power or otherwise restrains competition. The types of trade restraints that Section 1 of the Sherman Act prohibits generally fall into two broad categories: *horizontal restraints* and *vertical restraints*, both of which will be discussed shortly. First, though, we look at the rules that the courts may apply when assessing the anticompetitive impact of alleged restraints on trade.

Per Se Violations versus the Rule of Reason

Some restraints are so blatantly and substantially anticompetitive that they are deemed *per se violations*—illegal *per se* (on their face, or inherently)—under Section 1. Other agreements, however, even though they result in enhanced market power, do not *unreasonably* restrain trade. Using what is called the **rule of reason,** the courts analyze anticompetitive agreements that allegedly violate Section 1 of the Sherman Act to determine whether they may, in fact, constitute reasonable restraints on trade.

The need for a rule-of-reason analysis of some agreements in restraint of trade is obvious—if the rule of reason had not been developed, virtually any business agreement could conceivably be held to violate the Sherman Act. Justice Louis Brandeis effectively phrased this sentiment in *Chicago Board of Trade v. United States*, a case decided in 1918:

> Every agreement concerning trade, every regulation of trade, restrains. To bind, to restrain, is of their very essence. The true test of legality is whether the restraint imposed is such as merely regulates and perhaps thereby promotes competition or whether it is such as may suppress or even destroy competition.[1]

When analyzing an alleged Section 1 violation under the rule of reason, a court will consider several factors. These factors include the purpose of the agreement, the parties' power to implement the agreement to achieve that purpose, and the effect or potential effect of the agreement on competition. Another factor that a court might consider is whether the parties could have relied on less restrictive means to achieve their purpose.

---

1. 246 U.S. 231, 38 S.Ct. 242, 62 L.Ed. 683 (1918).

ON THE WEB

You can find a discussion of the *per se* rule and the rule of reason, as well as an extensive summary of antitrust laws, at **www.findlaw.com/01topics/01antitrust/index.html.**

PER SE VIOLATION
A type of anticompetitive agreement that is considered to be so injurious to the public that there is no need to determine whether it actually injures market competition. Rather, it is in itself (*per se*) a violation of the Sherman Act.

RULE OF REASON
A test by which a court balances the positive effects (such as economic efficiency) of an agreement against its potentially anticompetitive effects. In antitrust litigation, many practices are analyzed under the rule of reason.

One of Standard Oil's refineries in Richmond, California, around 1900. (Library of Congress)

LANDMARK IN THE LAW: The Sherman Antitrust Act of 1890

The author of the Sherman Antitrust Act of 1890, Senator John Sherman, was the brother of the famed Civil War general William Tecumseh Sherman and a recognized financial authority. Sherman had been concerned for years with the diminishing competition within U.S. industry and the emergence of monopolies, such as the Standard Oil trust.

The Standard Oil Trust   By 1890, the Standard Oil trust had become the foremost petroleum refining and marketing combination in the United States. Streamlined, integrated, and centrally and efficiently controlled, Standard Oil maintained a monopoly over the industry that could not be disputed. The trust controlled 90 percent of the U.S. market for refined petroleum products, and small manufacturers were incapable of competing with such an industrial leviathan.

The increasing consolidation occurring in U.S. industry, and particularly the Standard Oil trust, came to the attention of the public in March 1881. Henry Demarest Lloyd, a young journalist from Chicago, published an article in the *Atlantic Monthly* entitled "The Story of a Great Monopoly." The article discussed the success of the Standard Oil Company and clearly demonstrated that the petroleum industry in the United States was dominated by one firm—Standard Oil. Lloyd's article, which was so popular that the issue was reprinted six times, marked the beginning of the U.S. public's growing awareness of, and concern over, the rise of monopolies.

The Passage of the Sherman Antitrust Act   The common law regarding trade regulation was not always consistent. Certainly, it was not very familiar to the members of

Horizontal Restraints

HORIZONTAL RESTRAINT
Any agreement that in some way restrains competition between rival firms competing in the same market.

The term **horizontal restraint** is encountered frequently in antitrust law. A horizontal restraint is any agreement that in some way restrains competition between rival firms competing in the same market. In the following subsections, we look at several types of horizontal restraints.

PRICE-FIXING AGREEMENT
An agreement between competitors to fix the prices of products or services at a certain level.

Price Fixing   Any **price-fixing agreement**—an agreement among competitors to fix prices—constitutes a *per se* violation of Section 1. Perhaps the definitive case regarding price-fixing agreements is still the 1940 case of *United States v. Socony-Vacuum Oil Co.*[2] In that case, a group of independent oil producers in Texas and Louisiana were caught between falling demand due to the Great Depression of the 1930s and increasing supply from newly discovered oil fields in the region. In response to these conditions, a group of major refining companies agreed to buy "distress" gasoline (excess supplies) from the independents so as to dispose of it in an "orderly manner." Although there was no explicit agreement as to price, it was clear that the purpose of the agreement was to limit the supply of gasoline on the market and thereby raise prices.

There may have been good business reasons for the agreement. Nonetheless, the United States Supreme Court recognized the dangerous effects that such an agreement could have on open and free competition. The Court held that the reasonableness of a price-fixing agreement is never a defense; any agreement that restricts output or artificially

---

2. 310 U.S. 150, 60 S.Ct. 811, 84 L.Ed. 1129 (1940).

PROMOTING COMPETITION
IN A GLOBAL CONTEXT

Congress. The public concern over large business integrations and trusts was familiar, however. In 1888, 1889, and again in 1890, Senator Sherman introduced in Congress bills designed to destroy the large combinations of capital that, he felt, were creating a lack of balance within the nation's economy. Sherman told Congress that the Sherman Act "does not announce a new principle of law, but applies old and well-recognized principles of the common law."[a] In 1890, the Fifty-First Congress enacted the bill into law.

In this chapter, we look closely at the major provisions of this act. Generally, the act prohibits business combinations and conspiracies that restrain trade and commerce, as well as certain monopolistic practices.

APPLICATION TO TODAY'S WORLD   *The Sherman Antitrust Act remains very relevant to today's world. The widely publicized monopolization case brought in 2001 by the U.S. Department of Justice and a number of state attorneys general against Microsoft Corporation is just one example of the relevance of the Sherman Act to modern business developments and practices.[b]*

RELEVANT WEB SITES   *To locate information on the Web concerning the Sherman Antitrust Act, go to this text's Web site at* academic.cengage.com/blaw/blt, *select "Chapter 22," and click on "URLs for Landmarks."*

a. 21 *Congressional Record* 2456 (1890).
b. *United States v. Microsoft Corp.,* 253 F.3d 34 (D.D.C. 2001). This case will also be discussed in Example 22.5.

---

fixes price is a *per se* violation of Section 1. The rationale of the *per se* rule was best stated in what is now the most famous portion of the Court's opinion—footnote 59. In that footnote, Justice William O. Douglas compared a freely functioning price system to a body's central nervous system, condemning price-fixing agreements as threats to "the central nervous system of the economy."

■EXAMPLE 22.1 The manufacturer of the prescription drug Cardizem CD, which can help prevent heart attacks, was about to lose its patent on the drug. Another company developed a generic version in anticipation of the patent expiring. After the two firms became involved in litigation over the patent, the first company agreed to pay the second company $40 million per year not to market the generic version until their dispute was resolved. This agreement was held to be a *per se* violation of the Sherman Act because it restrained competition between rival firms and delayed the entry of generic versions of Cardizem into the market.[3] ■

Group Boycotts   A **group boycott** is an agreement by two or more sellers to refuse to deal with (boycott) a particular person or firm. Such group boycotts have been held to constitute *per se* violations of Section 1 of the Sherman Act. Section 1 has been violated if it can be demonstrated that the boycott or joint refusal to deal was undertaken with the intention of eliminating competition or preventing entry into a given market. Some boycotts, such

GROUP BOYCOTT
The refusal by a group of competitors to deal with a particular person or firm; prohibited by the Sherman Act.

3. *In re Cardizem CD Antitrust Litigation,* 332 F.3d 896 (6th Cir. 2003).

as group boycotts against a supplier for political reasons, may be protected under the First Amendment right to freedom of expression, however.

Horizontal Market Division   It is a *per se* violation of Section 1 of the Sherman Act for competitors to divide up territories or customers. ▣**EXAMPLE 22.2** Manufacturers A, B, and C compete against each other in the states of Kansas, Nebraska, and Iowa. By agreement, A sells products only in Kansas, B sells only in Nebraska, and C sells only in Iowa. This concerted action not only reduces marketing costs but also allows all three (assuming there is no other competition) to raise the price of the goods sold in their respective states. The same violation would take place if A, B, and C simply agreed that A would sell only to institutional purchasers (such as school districts, universities, state agencies and departments, and cities) in all three states, B only to wholesalers, and C only to retailers. ▣

Trade Associations   Businesses in the same general industry or profession frequently organize trade associations to pursue common interests. The joint activities of the trade association may include exchanges of information, representation of the members' business interests before governmental bodies, advertising campaigns, and the setting of regulatory standards to govern the industry or profession.

Generally, the rule of reason is applied to many of these horizontal actions. If a court finds that a trade association practice or agreement that restrains trade is sufficiently beneficial both to the association and to the public, it may deem the restraint reasonable.

Other trade association agreements may have such substantially anticompetitive effects that the court will consider them to be in violation of Section 1 of the Sherman Act. ▣**EXAMPLE 22.3** A professional engineering society's code of ethics prohibited members from discussing prices with a potential customer until after the customer had chosen an engineer. When this ban on competitive bidding was challenged as a violation of Section 1, the United States Supreme Court held that it was "nothing less than a frontal assault on the basic policy of the Sherman Act."[4] ▣ For a discussion of how federal regulators are looking into alleged anticompetitive practices involving the Web-based multiple listing services of trade associations in the real estate industry, see this chapter's *Adapting the Law to the Online Environment* feature on pages 680 and 681. (For other potential problems with online advertising of real property, see the *Adapting the Law to the Online Environment* feature in Chapter 24 on page 737.)

Vertical Restraints

A **vertical restraint** of trade results from an agreement between firms at different levels in the manufacturing and distribution process. In contrast to horizontal relationships, which occur at the same level of operation, vertical relationships encompass the entire chain of production. The chain of production normally includes the purchase of inventory, basic manufacturing, distribution to wholesalers, and eventual sale of a product at the retail level. For some products, these distinct phases may be carried out by different firms. In other instances, a single firm carries out two or more of the separate functional phases. Such enterprises are considered to be **vertically integrated firms.**

Even though firms operating at different functional levels are not in direct competition with one another, they are in competition with other firms. Thus, agreements between firms standing in a vertical relationship may affect competition. Some vertical restraints are *per se* violations of Section 1; others are judged under the rule of reason.

Territorial or Customer Restrictions   In arranging for the distribution of its products, a manufacturing firm often wishes to insulate dealers from direct competition with other

ON THE WEB

The Federal Trade Commission (FTC) offers an abundance of information on antitrust law, including "A Plain English Guide to Antitrust Laws," at its Web site. Go to

www.ftc.gov/bc/compguide/index.

VERTICAL RESTRAINT
  Any restraint on trade created by agreements between firms at different levels in the manufacturing and distribution process.

VERTICALLY INTEGRATED FIRM
  A firm that carries out two or more functional phases (manufacture, distribution, and retailing, for example) of the chain of production.

---

4. *National Society of Professional Engineers v. United States,* 435 U.S. 679, 98 S.Ct. 1355, 55 L.Ed.2d 637 (1978).

dealers selling the product. To this end, it may institute territorial restrictions or attempt to prohibit wholesalers or retailers from reselling the product to certain classes of buyers, such as competing retailers.

A firm may have legitimate reasons for imposing such territorial or customer restrictions. **■EXAMPLE 22.4** A computer manufacturer may wish to prevent a dealer from cutting costs and undercutting rivals by selling computers without promotion or customer service, while relying on nearby dealers to provide these services. In this situation, the cost-cutting dealer reaps the benefits (sales of the product) paid for by other dealers who undertake promotion and arrange for customer service. By not providing customer service, the cost-cutting dealer may also harm the manufacturer's reputation. ■

Territorial and customer restrictions are judged under the rule of reason. In *United States v. Arnold, Schwinn & Co.*,[5] a case decided in 1967, a bicycle manufacturer, Schwinn, was assigning specific territories to its wholesale distributors and authorizing certain retail dealers only if they agreed to advertise Schwinn bikes and give them the same prominence as other brands. The United States Supreme Court held that these vertical territorial and customer restrictions were *per se* violations of Section 1 of the Sherman Act. Ten years later, however, in *Continental T.V., Inc. v. GTE Sylvania, Inc.*,[6] a case involving similar restrictions imposed on retailers by a television manufacturer, the Supreme Court overturned the *Schwinn* decision. In the *Continental* decision, the Court held that such vertical restrictions should be judged under the rule of reason, and this rule is still applied in most vertical restraint cases.[7] The *Continental* decision marked a definite shift from rigid characterization of these kinds of vertical restraints to a more flexible, economic analysis of the restraints under the rule of reason.

Resale Price Maintenance Agreements An agreement between a manufacturer and a distributor or retailer in which the manufacturer specifies what the retail prices of its products must be is referred to as a **resale price maintenance agreement.** This type of agreement may violate Section 1 of the Sherman Act. Though once considered a *per se* violation, such vertical price fixing is now judged under the rule of reason because the practice may increase competition and benefit consumers.[8]

RESALE PRICE MAINTENANCE AGREEMENT
An agreement between a manufacturer and a retailer in which the manufacturer specifies what the retail prices of its products must be.

Refusals to Deal As discussed previously, joint refusals to deal (group boycotts) are subject to close scrutiny under Section 1 of the Sherman Act. A single manufacturer acting unilaterally, though, is generally free to deal, or not to deal, with whomever it wishes. In vertical arrangements, even though a manufacturer cannot set retail prices for its products, it can refuse to deal with retailers or dealers that cut prices to levels substantially below the manufacturer's suggested retail prices. In *United States v. Colgate & Co.*,[9] for example, the United States Supreme Court held that a manufacturer's advance announcement that it would not sell to price cutters was not a violation of the Sherman Act.

Nevertheless, in some instances, a unilateral refusal to deal will violate antitrust laws. These instances involve offenses proscribed under Section 2 of the Sherman Act and occur only if (1) the firm refusing to deal has—or is likely to acquire—monopoly power and (2) the refusal is likely to have an anticompetitive effect on a particular market.

---

5. 388 U.S. 365, 87 S.Ct. 1856, 18 L.Ed.2d 1249 (1967).

6. 433 U.S. 36, 97 S.Ct. 2549, 53 L.Ed.2d 568 (1977).

7. Note that there is some disagreement in the case law on when a vertical restraint should be considered unreasonable. See, for example, *State of New York by Abrams v. Anheuser-Busch*, 811 F.Supp. 848 (E.D.N.Y. 1993), which calls into doubt one of the holdings of the *Continental* case.

8. *State Oil Co. v. Khan*, 522 U.S. 3, 118 S.Ct. 275, 139 L.Ed.2d 199 (1997).

9. 250 U.S. 300, 39 S.Ct. 465, 63 L.Ed. 992 (1919).

Can Realtor® Associations Limit Listings on Their Web Sites?

L ike almost every other product, homes are now being sold via the Internet on hundreds of thousands of Web sites. The most extensive listings of homes for sale, though, are found on the multiple listing services (MLS) sites that are available for every locality in the United States. An MLS site is developed through a cooperative agreement by real estate brokers in a particular market area to pool information about the properties they have for sale. Today, the majority of residential real estate sales involve the use of MLS. Although MLS sites offer convenience by combining listings from many brokers, the sites have also raised antitrust concerns by restricting how certain brokers may use the sites. The Federal Trade Commission (FTC) and the U.S. Department of Justice have brought antitrust actions against both local real estate associations and the National Association of Realtors®, a national trade association for real estate brokers and agents, for attempting to restrict the use of MLS databases.

Boards of Realtors® Have Attempted to Limit Listings on Their Web Sites

In a given market area, the MLS listings are put together by the members of a local real estate association, typically called a Board of Realtors®, for the members' exclusive use. In many areas, Boards of Realtors® have attempted to restrict the homes that can be listed on the official MLS Web site. In particular, the boards have tried to prevent discount brokers from listing the homes they have for sale.

The FTC's Bureau of Competition filed a complaint for violation of antitrust laws against the Board of Realtors® in Austin, Texas, which had a rule prohibiting discount brokers from listing on its MLS site. After several months of negotiations, the FTC prevented the Austin board from adopting and enforcing "any rule that treats different types of real estate listing agreements differently." The FTC is now pursuing similar negotiations in other cities including Cleveland, Columbus, Detroit, and Indianapolis.

The NAR Tries to Restrict Virtual Brokers

The National Association of Realtors (NAR) represents more than 1 million individual member brokers and their affiliated agents and sales associates. Its policies govern the conduct of its members throughout the United States. In the 1990s, many members of the NAR began to create password-protected Web sites through which prospective home buyers could search the MLS database. The password would be given only to potential buyers who had registered as customers of the broker. The brokers who worked through these virtual office Web sites, or VOWs, came to be known as VOW-operating brokers. Because they had no need of a physical office, their operating

SECTION 2 OF THE SHERMAN ACT

Section 1 of the Sherman Act proscribes certain concerted, or joint, activities that restrain trade. In contrast, Section 2 condemns "every person who shall monopolize, or attempt to monopolize." Thus, two distinct types of behavior are subject to sanction under Section 2: *monopolization* and *attempts to monopolize.* One tactic that may be involved in either offense is **predatory pricing.** Predatory pricing involves an attempt by one firm to drive its competitors from the market by selling its product at prices substantially *below* the normal costs of production. Once the competitors are eliminated, the firm will attempt to recapture its losses and go on to earn higher profits by driving prices up far above their competitive levels.

PREDATORY PRICING
The pricing of a product below cost with the intent to drive competitors out of the market.

Monopolization

MONOPOLIZATION
The possession of monopoly power in the relevant market and the willful acquisition or maintenance of that power, as distinguished from growth or development as a consequence of a superior product, business acumen, or historic accident.

In *United States v. Grinnell Corp.,*[10] the United States Supreme Court defined the offense of **monopolization** as involving the following two elements: "(1) the possession of monopoly power in the relevant market and (2) the willful acquisition or maintenance of [that] power as distinguished from growth or development as a consequence of a superior

---

10. 384 U.S. 563, 86 S.Ct. 1698, 16 L.Ed.2d 778 (1966).

expenses were lower than those of traditional brokers. Soon both Cendant and RE/MAX, the largest and second-largest U.S. real estate franchisors, respectively, expressed concern that VOW-operating brokers would put downward pressure on brokers' commissions.

In response, the NAR developed a new policy for Web listings. The policy included an opt-out provision "that forbade any broker participating in a multiple listing service from conveying a listing to his or her customers via the Internet without the permission of the listing broker." In other words, a traditional broker could prevent her or his listings in the MLS database from being displayed on the Web site of a VOW-operating broker.

The U.S. Department of Justice Enters the Fray

The Antitrust Division of the U.S. Department of Justice, however, contended that the opt-out policy was anticompetitive and harmful to consumers. When the Justice Department indicated that it would bring an antitrust action against the NAR, the association modified its policy and eliminated the selective opt-out provision aimed specifically at VOW-operating brokers. Nevertheless, the revised policy still allowed brokers to prevent their listings from being displayed on any competitor's Web site. Thus, under the new policy, traditional brokers could still prevent VOW-operating brokers from providing the same MLS information via the Internet that traditional brokers could provide in person. The policy also permitted MLS sites to lower the quality of the data feed they provide brokers, thereby restraining brokers from using Internet-based features to enhance the services they offer customers.

In response, the Justice Department filed a suit in federal district court against the NAR, asserting that the association's policies had violated Section 1 of the Sherman Act by preventing real estate brokers from offering better services as well as lower costs to online consumers. The department contends that the NAR's policies constitute a "contract, combination, and conspiracy between NAR and its members which unreasonably restrains competition in brokerage service markets throughout the United States to the detriment of American consumers." In 2006, finding that the Justice Department had shown sufficient evidence of anticompetitive effects to allow the suit to go forward, the court denied the NAR's motion to dismiss the case.[a]

FOR CRITICAL ANALYSIS *Why couldn't discount brokers simply create their own Web sites to list the houses they have for sale?*

a. *United States v. National Association of Realtors,* 2006 WL 3434263 (N.D.Ill. 2006).

product, business acumen, or historic accident." A violation of Section 2 requires that both these elements—monopoly power and an intent to monopolize—be established.

Monopoly Power   The Sherman Act does not define *monopoly.* In economic parlance, monopoly refers to control of a single market by a single entity. It is well established in antitrust law, however, that a firm may be deemed a monopolist even though it is not the sole seller in a market. Additionally, size alone does not determine whether a firm is a monopoly. For example, a "mom and pop" grocery located in an isolated desert town is a monopolist if it is the only grocery serving that particular market. Size in relation to the market is what matters because monopoly involves the power to affect prices.

Market Power.   *Monopoly power,* as mentioned earlier in this chapter, exists when a firm has an extremely large amount of market power. If a firm has sufficient market power to control prices and exclude competition, that firm has monopoly power. As difficult as it is to define market power precisely, it is even more difficult to measure it. In determining the extent of a firm's market power, courts often use the so-called **market-share test**,[11] which measures the firm's percentage share of the "relevant market." A firm may be considered

MARKET-SHARE TEST
The primary measure of monopoly power. A firm's market share is the percentage of a market that the firm controls.

---

11. Other measures of market power have been devised, but the market-share test is the most widely used.

to have monopoly power if its share of the relevant market is 70 percent or more. This is merely a rule of thumb, though; it is not a binding principle of law. In some instances, a smaller share may be held to constitute monopoly power.[12]

Relevant Market. The relevant market consists of two elements: (1) a relevant product market and (2) a relevant geographic market. What should the relevant product market include? No doubt, it must include all products that, although produced by different firms, have identical attributes, such as sugar. Products that are not identical, however, may sometimes be substituted for one another. Coffee may be substituted for tea, for example. In defining the relevant product market, the key issue is the degree of interchangeability between products. If one product is a sufficient substitute for another, the two products are considered to be part of the same product market.

The second component of the relevant market is the geographic extent of the market. For products that are sold nationwide, the geographic boundaries of the market encompass the entire United States. If a producer and its competitors sell in only a limited area (one in which customers have no access to other sources of the product), the geographic market is limited to that area. A national firm may thus compete in several distinct areas and have monopoly power in one area but not in another.

The geographic size of a relevant market was at issue in the following case.

---

12. This standard was first articulated by Judge Learned Hand in *United States v. Aluminum Co. of America*, 148 F.2d 416 (2d Cir. 1945). A 90 percent share was held to be clear evidence of monopoly power. Anything less than 64 percent, said Judge Hand, made monopoly power doubtful, and anything less than 30 percent was clearly not monopoly power.

CASE 22.1   Heerwagen v. Clear Channel Communications

United States Court of Appeals, Second Circuit, 435 F.3d 219 (2006).

FACTS Clear Channel Communications, Inc., owns nearly 1,200 U.S. radio stations and has interests in 240 radio stations overseas. It also promotes or produces more than 26,000 live entertainment events per year; owns more than 135 live entertainment venues; and controls 900 music-related Web sites, 19 television stations, and more than 700,000 outdoor-advertising displays. In 2001, Clear Channel accounted for 70 percent of U.S. concert ticket revenue. Its combined ownership of media and concert halls enabled it to book and sell nationwide tours for performers without involving other parties. Malinda Heerwagen lived in Chicago, Illinois. Over a five-year period beginning in 1997, she attended ten rock concerts in Chicago, including performances by U2, the Grateful Dead, the Rolling Stones, and Paul McCartney. In 2002, on behalf of "[a]ll persons * * * who purchased tickets to any live rock concert in the United States" from Clear Channel, Heerwagen filed a suit in a federal district court. She claimed that Clear Channel had used anticompetitive practices to acquire and maintain monopoly power in a national ticket market for live rock concerts in violation of Section 2 of the Sherman Act, thereby forcing audiences to pay inflated prices for tickets. The court denied Heerwagen's petition. She appealed to the U.S. Court of Appeals for the Second Circuit.

ISSUE Is the relevant market for tickets to live rock concerts national?

DECISION No. The U.S. Court of Appeals for the Second Circuit affirmed the lower court's ruling, which was based on the conclusion that "the market at issue here is local."

REASON During the relevant five-year period, Heerwagen did not go to a live rock concert outside Chicago, nor did she check out the ticket prices of performances elsewhere. The U.S. Court of Appeals for the Second Circuit reasoned that, as Heerwagen's own experience demonstrated, "there is little cross-elasticity of demand for live rock concert tickets between geographic areas. A purchaser of a concert ticket is hardly likely to look outside of her own area, even if the price for

CASE 22.1–Continued

tickets has increased inside her region and decreased for the same tour in other places. Tours are promoted nationally, but a higher price in Boston will not lead Boston purchasers to buy tickets for the same concert held in New York." Evidence of this fact, which was presented to the lower court, "accords with common sense in the calculus for the availability of substitutes. The cost to attend a concert in a remote geographic region would be substantially greater than whatever increment a concert promoter might add to the cost

of a concert ticket. Hence, from the standpoint of the individual concertgoer the two concert tickets are not substitutes for one another."

FOR CRITICAL ANALYSIS–Economic Consideration
Around the United States, prices vary for tickets to live rock concerts by the same performing artists. What might this indicate about any one promoter's power to control prices and exclude competition nationally?

The Intent Requirement Monopoly power, in and of itself, does not constitute the offense of monopolization under Section 2 of the Sherman Act. The offense also requires an *intent* to monopolize. A dominant market share may be the result of business acumen or the development of a superior product. It may simply be the result of historic accident. In these situations, the acquisition of monopoly power is not an antitrust violation. Indeed, it would be contrary to society's interest to condemn every firm that acquired a position of power because it was well managed and efficient and marketed a product desired by consumers.

If a firm possesses market power as a result of carrying out some purposeful act to acquire or maintain that power through anticompetitive means, then it is in violation of Section 2. In most monopolization cases, intent may be inferred from evidence that the firm had monopoly power and engaged in anticompetitive behavior.

■EXAMPLE 22.5 Navigator, the first popular graphical Internet browser, used Java technology that was able to run on a variety of platforms. When Navigator was introduced, Microsoft perceived a threat to its dominance of the operating-system market. Microsoft developed a competing browser, Internet Explorer, and then began to require computer makers that wanted to install Windows to also install Explorer and exclude Navigator. In addition, Microsoft included codes in Windows that would cripple the operating system if Explorer was deleted, and it also paid Internet service providers to distribute Explorer and exclude Navigator. Because of this pattern of exclusionary conduct, a court found that Microsoft was guilty of monopolization in violation of Section 2 of the Sherman Act. The court reasoned that Microsoft's pattern of conduct could be rational only if the firm knew that it possessed monopoly power.[13] ■

KEEP IN MIND Section 2 of the Sherman Act essentially condemns the act of monopolizing, not the possession of monopoly power.

PREVENTING LEGAL DISPUTES

Because exclusionary conduct can have legitimate efficiency-enhancing effects, it can be difficult to determine when conduct will be viewed as anticompetitive and a violation of Section 2 of the Sherman Act. Thus, a business that possesses monopoly power must be careful that its actions cannot be inferred to be evidence of intent to monopolize. Even if your business does not have a dominant market share, you would be wise to take precautions. Make sure that you can articulate clear, legitimate reasons for the particular conduct or contract and that you do not provide any direct evidence (damaging e-mails, for example) of an intent to exclude competitors. A court will be less likely to infer the intent to monopolize if the specific conduct was aimed at increasing output and

---

13. *United States v. Microsoft Corp.*, 253 F.3d 34 (D.D.C. 2001). Microsoft has faced numerous antitrust claims and has settled a number of lawsuits in which it was accused of antitrust violations and anticompetitive tactics.

lowering per-unit costs, improving product quality, or protecting a patented technology or innovation. Exclusionary conduct and agreements that have no redeeming qualities are much more likely to be deemed illegal.

Attempts to Monopolize

ATTEMPTED MONOPOLIZATION
Any actions by a firm to eliminate competition and gain monopoly power.

Section 2 also prohibits **attempted monopolization** of a market. Any action challenged as an attempt to monopolize must have been specifically intended to exclude competitors and garner monopoly power. In addition, the attempt must have had a "dangerous" probability of success—only *serious* threats of monopolization are condemned as violations. The probability cannot be dangerous unless the alleged offender possesses some degree of market power.

ETHICAL ISSUE 22.1

Are we destined for more monopolies in the future? Knowledge and information form the building blocks of the so-called new economy. Some observers believe that the nature of this new economy means that we will see an increasing number of monopolies similar to Microsoft. Consider that the justification for all antitrust law is that monopoly leads to restricted output and hence higher prices for consumers. That is how a monopolist maximizes profits relative to a competitive firm. In the knowledge-based sector, however, firms face *economies of scale* (defined as decreases in long-run average costs resulting from increases in output), so they will do the exact opposite of a traditional monopolist—they will increase output and reduce prices. That is exactly what Microsoft has done over the years—the prices of its operating system and applications have fallen, particularly when corrected for inflation.

This characteristic of knowledge-based monopolies may mean that antitrust authorities will have to have greater tolerance for these monopolies to allow them to benefit from full economies of scale. After all, consumers are the ultimate beneficiaries of such economies of scale. In the early 1900s, economist Joseph Schumpeter argued in favor of allowing monopolies. According to his theory of "creative destruction," monopolies stimulate innovation and economic growth because firms that capture monopoly profits have a greater incentive to innovate. Those that do not survive—the firms that are "destroyed"—leave room for the more efficient firms that will survive.

THE CLAYTON ACT

In 1914, Congress attempted to strengthen federal antitrust laws by enacting the Clayton Act. The Clayton Act was aimed at specific anticompetitive or monopolistic practices that the Sherman Act did not cover. The substantive provisions of the act deal with four distinct forms of business behavior, which are declared illegal but not criminal. With regard to each of the four provisions, the act's prohibitions are qualified by the general condition that the behavior is illegal only if it substantially tends to lessen competition or create monopoly power. The major offenses under the Clayton Act are set out in Sections 2, 3, 7, and 8 of the act.

Section 2—Price Discrimination

PRICE DISCRIMINATION
Setting prices in such a way that two competing buyers pay two different prices for an identical product or service.

Section 2 of the Clayton Act prohibits **price discrimination,** which occurs when a seller charges different prices to competitive buyers for identical goods or services. Because businesses frequently circumvented Section 2 of the act, Congress strengthened this section by amending it with the passage of the Robinson-Patman Act in 1936.

As amended, Section 2 prohibits price discrimination that cannot be justified by differences in production costs or transportation costs, or cost differences due to other reasons. To violate Section 2, the seller must be engaged in interstate commerce, and the effect of the price discrimination must be to substantially lessen competition or create a competitive injury. In other words, a seller is prohibited from reducing a price to one buyer below the price charged to that buyer's competitor. Even offering goods to different customers at the same price but with different delivery arrangements may violate Section 2 in some circumstances.[14]

An exception is made if the seller can justify the price reduction by demonstrating that the lower price was charged temporarily and in good faith to meet another seller's equally low price to the buyer. To be predatory, a seller's pricing policies must also include a reasonable prospect that the seller will recoup its losses.[15]

Section 3—Exclusionary Practices

Under Section 3 of the Clayton Act, sellers or lessors cannot sell or lease goods "on the condition, agreement or understanding that the . . . purchaser or lessee thereof shall not use or deal in the goods . . . of a competitor or competitors of the seller." In effect, this section prohibits two types of vertical agreements involving exclusionary practices—exclusive-dealing contracts and tying arrangements.

Exclusive-Dealing Contracts A contract under which a seller forbids a buyer to purchase products from the seller's competitors is called an **exclusive-dealing contract.** A seller is prohibited from making an exclusive-dealing contract under Section 3 if the effect of the contract is "to substantially lessen competition or tend to create a monopoly."

■EXAMPLE 22.6 In *Standard Oil Co. of California v. United States*,[16] a leading case decided by the United States Supreme Court in 1949, the then-largest gasoline seller in the nation made exclusive-dealing contracts with independent stations in seven western states. The contracts involved 16 percent of all retail outlets, with sales amounting to approximately 7 percent of all retail sales in that market. The Court noted that the market was substantially concentrated because the seven largest gasoline suppliers all used exclusive-dealing contracts with their independent retailers and together controlled 65 percent of the market. Looking at market conditions after the arrangements were instituted, the Court found that market shares were extremely stable and that entry into the market was apparently restricted. Thus, the Court held that Section 3 of the Clayton Act had been violated because competition was "foreclosed in a substantial share" of the relevant market. ■

Note that since the Supreme Court's 1949 decision in the *Standard Oil* case, a number of subsequent decisions have called the holding in this case into doubt.[17] Today, it is clear that to violate antitrust law, an exclusive-dealing agreement (or tying arrangement, discussed next) must qualitatively and substantially harm competition. To prevail, a plaintiff must present affirmative evidence that the performance of the agreement will foreclose competition and harm consumers.

Suppose that the owner of this gas station agrees to buy gas only from Shell Oil Company. Does this agreement necessarily violate the Clayton Act? Why or why not?
("Iotae/Aaron"/Creative Commons)

EXCLUSIVE-DEALING CONTRACT
An agreement under which a seller forbids a buyer to purchase products from the seller's competitors.

14. *Bell v. Fur Breeders Agricultural Cooperative*, 3 F.Supp.2d 1241 (D. Utah 1998).

15. See, for example, *Brooke Group, Ltd. v. Brown & Williamson Tobacco Corp.*, 509 U.S. 209, 113 S.Ct. 2578, 125 L.Ed.2d 168 (1993), in which the United States Supreme Court held that a seller's price-cutting policies could not be predatory "[g]iven the market's realities"—the size of the seller's market share and the expanding output by other sellers, as well as additional factors.

16. 337 U.S. 293, 69 S.Ct. 1051, 93 L.Ed. 1371 (1949).

17. See, for example, *Illinois Tool Works, Inc. v. Independent Ink, Inc.*, 547 U.S. 28, 126 S.Ct. 1281, 164 L.Ed.2d 26 (2006), also presented as Case 22.2; *Stop & Shop Supermarket Co. v. Blue Cross & Blue Shield of Rhode Island*, 373 F.3d 57 (1st Cir. 2004); *Yeager's Fuel, Inc. v. Pennsylvania Power & Light Co.*, 953 F.Supp. 617 (E.D.Pa. 1997); and *Tampa Electric Co. v. Nashville Coal Co.*, 365 U.S. 320, 81 S.Ct. 632, 5 L.Ed.2d 580 (1961).

TYING ARRANGEMENT
An agreement between a buyer and a seller in which the buyer of a specific product or service becomes obligated to purchase additional products or services from the seller.

Tying Arrangements   When a seller conditions the sale of a product (the tying product) on the buyer's agreement to purchase another product (the tied product) produced or distributed by the same seller, a **tying arrangement,** or *tie-in sales agreement,* results. The legality of a tie-in agreement depends on many factors, particularly the purpose of the agreement and its likely effect on competition in the relevant markets (the market for the tying product and the market for the tied product).

■**EXAMPLE 22.7**   In 1936, the United States Supreme Court held that International Business Machines and Remington Rand had violated Section 3 of the Clayton Act by requiring the purchase of their own machine cards (the tied product) as a condition for leasing their tabulation machines (the tying product). Because only these two firms sold completely automated tabulation machines, the Court concluded that each possessed market power sufficient to "substantially lessen competition" through the tying arrangements.[18] ■

Section 3 of the Clayton Act has been held to apply only to commodities, not to services. Tying arrangements, however, can also be considered agreements that restrain trade in violation of Section 1 of the Sherman Act. Thus, cases involving tying arrangements of services have been brought under Section 1 of the Sherman Act. Although earlier cases condemned tying arrangements as illegal *per se,* courts now evaluate tying agreements under the rule of reason.

When an arrangement ties patented and unpatented products, can the relevant market and the patent holder's power in that market be presumed without proof? That was the question in the following case.

18. *International Business Machines Corp. v. United States,* 298 U.S. 131, 56 S.Ct. 701, 80 L.Ed. 1085 (1936).

CASE 22.2   Illinois Tool Works, Inc. v. Independent Ink, Inc.

Supreme Court of the United States, 547 U.S. 28, 126 S.Ct. 1281, 164 L.Ed.2d 26 (2006).
www.findlaw.com/casecode/supreme.html[a]

FACTS Illinois Tool Works, Inc., in Glenview, Illinois, owns Trident, Inc. The firms make printing systems that include three components: a patented inkjet printhead, a patented ink container that attaches to the printhead, and specially designed, but unpatented, ink. They sell the systems to original equipment manufacturers (OEMs) that incorporate the systems into printers that are sold to other companies to use in printing bar codes on packaging materials. As part of each deal, the OEMs agree to buy ink exclusively from Illinois and Trident and not to refill the patented containers with ink of any other kind. Independent Ink, Inc., in Gardena, California, sells ink with the same chemical composition as Illinois and Trident's product at lower prices. Independent filed a suit in a federal district court against Illinois and Trident, alleging, among other things, that they were engaged in illegal tying in violation of the Sherman Act. Independent filed a motion for summary judgment, arguing that because the defendants owned patents in their

products, market power could be presumed. The court issued a summary judgment in the defendants' favor, holding that market power could not be presumed. The U.S. Court of Appeals for the Federal Circuit reversed this judgment. Illinois and Trident appealed to the United States Supreme Court.

ISSUE Does a party claiming a violation of antitrust law in a deal tying patented and unpatented products have to offer proof of the relevant market and the patent holder's power in that market?

DECISION Yes. The United States Supreme Court vacated the judgment of the appellate court and remanded the case to the trial court to give Independent "a fair opportunity" to offer evidence of the relevant market and the defendants' power within it. The Supreme Court ruled that a plaintiff that alleges an illegal tying arrangement involving a patented product must prove that the defendant has market power in the tying product.

REASON The Court pointed out that the presumption that a company automatically possesses market power in a

a. In the "Browsing" section, click on "2006 Decisions." When that page opens, scroll to the name of the case and click on it to read the opinion.

CASE 22.2–Continued

patented product arose outside the area of antitrust law as part of the patent misuse doctrine. The assumption was that "by tying the purchase of unpatented goods to the sale of [a] patented good, the patentee was restraining competition or securing a limited monopoly of an unpatented material." The patent misuse doctrine "presumed the requisite economic power over the tying product such that the patentee could extend its economic control to unpatented products." Over the years, however, Congress "chipp[ed] away at the assumption in the patent misuse context" and finally amended the patent laws to eliminate the presumption in that context. "[G]iven the fact that the patent misuse doctrine provided the basis for the market power presumption, it would be anomalous to preserve the presumption in antitrust after Congress has

eliminated its foundation." Instead, tying arrangements involving patented products should be evaluated according to such factors as those that apply in a rule-of-reason analysis.

 WHY IS THIS CASE IMPORTANT TO BUSINESSPERSONS? *This case effectively reversed more than forty years of case law. Prior to this decision, the mere fact that a patent existed gave rise to a presumption that the patent holder had market power for purposes of a tying claim. In this case, the Court rejected the presumption of market power and required the plaintiff to provide affirmative evidence of market power over the tied product in all future tying claims. Further, by recognizing that tying arrangements can have legitimate business justifications, the Court signaled a shift in its view of tying claims.*

■

Section 7–Mergers

Under Section 7 of the Clayton Act, a person or business organization cannot hold stock and/or assets in another entity "where the effect . . . may be to substantially lessen competition." Section 7 is the statutory authority for preventing mergers or acquisitions that could result in monopoly power or a substantial lessening of competition in the marketplace. Section 7 applies to horizontal mergers and vertical mergers, both of which we discuss in the following subsections.

A crucial consideration in most merger cases is the **market concentration** of a product or business. Determining market concentration involves allocating percentage market shares among the various companies in the relevant market. When a small number of companies control a large share of the market, the market is concentrated. For example, if the four largest grocery stores in Chicago accounted for 80 percent of all retail food sales, the market clearly would be concentrated in those four firms. Competition, however, is not necessarily diminished solely as a result of market concentration, and other factors will be considered in determining whether a merger will violate Section 7. One factor of particular importance in evaluating the effects of a merger is whether the merger will make it more difficult for potential competitors to enter the relevant market.

MARKET CONCENTRATION
The degree to which a small number of firms control a large percentage share of a relevant market; determined by calculating the percentages held by the largest firms in that market.

Horizontal Mergers Mergers between firms that compete with each other in the same market are called **horizontal mergers.** If a horizontal merger creates an entity with anything other than a small percentage market share, the merger will be presumed illegal. This is because the United States Supreme Court has held that Congress, in amending Section 7 of the Clayton Act in 1950, intended to prevent mergers that increase market concentration.[19] When analyzing the legality of a horizontal merger, the courts also consider three other factors: overall concentration of the relevant product market, the relevant market's history of tending toward concentration, and whether the apparent design of the merger is to establish market power or to restrict competition.

The Federal Trade Commission and the U.S. Department of Justice have established guidelines indicating which mergers will be challenged. Under the guidelines, the first

HORIZONTAL MERGER
A merger between two firms that are competing in the same marketplace.

---

19. *Brown Shoe v. United States,* 370 U.S. 294, 82 S.Ct. 1502, 8 L.Ed.2d 510 (1962).

factor to be considered is the degree of concentration in the relevant market. Other factors to be considered include the ease of entry into the relevant market, economic efficiency, the financial condition of the merging firms, and the nature and price of the product or products involved. If a firm is a leading one—having at least a 35 percent share and twice the share of the next leading firm—any merger with a firm having as little as a 1 percent share will be closely scrutinized.

Vertical Mergers   A **vertical merger** occurs when a company at one stage of production acquires a company at a higher or lower stage of production. An example of a vertical merger is a company merging with one of its suppliers or retailers. In the past, courts focused almost exclusively on "foreclosure" in assessing vertical mergers. Foreclosure occurs because competitors of the merging firms lose opportunities to sell or buy products from the merging firms.

> ■**EXAMPLE 22.8** In *United States v. E. I. du Pont de Nemours & Co.*,[20] du Pont was challenged for acquiring a considerable amount of General Motors (GM) stock. In holding that the transaction was illegal, the United States Supreme Court noted that the stock acquisition would enable du Pont to prevent other sellers of fabrics and finishes from selling to GM, which then accounted for 50 percent of all auto fabric and finishes purchases. ■

Today, whether a vertical merger will be deemed illegal generally depends on several factors, such as whether the merger would produce a firm controlling an undue percentage share of the relevant market. The courts also analyze whether the merger would result in a significant increase in the concentration of firms in that market, the barriers to entry into the market, and the apparent intent of the merging parties.[21] Mergers that do not prevent competitors of either merging firm from competing in a segment of the market will not be condemned as "foreclosing" competition and are legal.

Section 8—Interlocking Directorates

Section 8 of the Clayton Act deals with *interlocking directorates*—that is, the practice of having individuals serve as directors on the boards of two or more competing companies simultaneously. Specifically, no person may be a director in two or more competing corporations at the same time if either of the corporations has capital, surplus, or undivided profits aggregating more than $24,001,000 or competitive sales of $2,400,100 or more. The Federal Trade Commission (FTC) adjusts the threshold amounts each year. (The amounts given here are those announced by the FTC in 2007.)

ENFORCEMENT OF ANTITRUST LAWS

The federal agencies that enforce the federal antitrust laws are the U.S. Department of Justice (DOJ) and the Federal Trade Commission (FTC). The FTC was established by the Federal Trade Commission Act of 1914. Section 5 of that act condemns all forms of anticompetitive behavior that are not covered under other federal antitrust laws.

Only the DOJ can prosecute violations of the Sherman Act, which can be either criminal or civil offenses. Either the DOJ or the FTC can enforce the Clayton Act, but violations of that statute are not crimes and can be pursued only through civil proceedings. The DOJ or the FTC may ask the courts to impose various remedies, including **divestiture** (making a company give up one or more of its operating functions) and dissolution. A

VERTICAL MERGER
The acquisition by a company at one level in a marketing chain of a company at a higher or lower level in the chain (such as a company merging with one of its suppliers or retailers).

CONTRAST   Section 5 of the Federal Trade Commission Act is broader than the other antitrust laws. It covers virtually all anticompetitive behavior, including conduct that does not violate either the Sherman Act or the Clayton Act.

DIVESTITURE
The act of selling one or more of a company's divisions or parts, such as a subsidiary or plant; often mandated by the courts in merger or monopolization cases.

---

20. 353 U.S. 586, 77 S.Ct. 872, 1 L.Ed.2d 1057 (1957).
21. *United States v. Dairy Farmers of America, Inc.*, 426 F.3d 850 (6th Cir. 2005); *United States v. Philadelphia National Bank*, 374 U.S. 321, 83 S.Ct. 1715, 10 L.Ed.2d 915 (1963).

meatpacking firm, for example, might be forced to divest itself of control or ownership of butcher shops. (To find out how you can avoid antitrust problems, see the *Application* feature at the end of this chapter.)

The FTC has the sole authority to enforce violations of Section 5 of the Federal Trade Commission Act. FTC actions are effected through administrative orders, but if a firm violates an FTC order, the FTC can seek court sanctions for the violation.

Private Actions

A private party who has been injured as a result of a violation of the Sherman Act or the Clayton Act can sue for damages and attorneys' fees. In some instances, private parties may also seek injunctive relief to prevent antitrust violations. The courts have determined that the ability to sue depends on the directness of the injury suffered by the would-be plaintiff. Thus, a person wishing to sue under the Sherman Act must prove (1) that the antitrust violation either caused or was a substantial factor in causing the injury that was suffered and (2) that the unlawful actions of the accused party affected business activities of the plaintiff that were protected by the antitrust laws.

Treble Damages

In recent years, more than 90 percent of all antitrust actions have been brought by private plaintiffs. One reason for this is that successful plaintiffs may recover **treble damages**—three times the damages that they have suffered as a result of the violation. Such recoveries by private plaintiffs for antitrust violations have been rationalized as encouraging people to act as "private attorneys general" who will vigorously pursue antitrust violators on their own initiative. In a situation involving a price-fixing agreement, normally each competitor is jointly and severally liable for the total amount of any damages, including treble damages if they are imposed.

EXEMPTIONS FROM ANTITRUST LAWS

There are many legislative and constitutional limitations on antitrust enforcement. Most statutory and judicially created exemptions to the antitrust laws apply to the following areas or activities:

1 *Labor.* Section 6 of the Clayton Act generally permits labor unions to organize and bargain without violating antitrust laws. Section 20 of the Clayton Act specifies that strikes and other labor activities are not violations of any law of the United States. A union can lose its exemption, however, if it combines with a nonlabor group rather than acting simply in its own self-interest.

2 *Agricultural associations and fisheries.* Section 6 of the Clayton Act (along with the Capper-Volstead Act of 1922) exempts agricultural cooperatives from the antitrust laws. The Fisheries Cooperative Marketing Act of 1976 exempts from antitrust legislation individuals in the fishing industry who collectively catch, produce, and prepare for market their products. Both exemptions allow members of such co-ops to combine and set prices for a particular product, but do not allow them to engage in exclusionary practices or restraints of trade directed at competitors.

3 *Insurance.* The McCarran-Ferguson Act of 1945 exempts the insurance business from the antitrust laws whenever state regulation exists. This exemption does not cover boycotts, coercion, or intimidation on the part of insurance companies.

ON THE WEB

You can find links to the home pages for federal government agencies, including the Department of Justice and the Federal Trade Commission, at

www.usa.gov.

TREBLE DAMAGES
Damages that, by statute, are three times the amount that the fact finder determines is owed.

Congress named an act after baseball player Curt Flood. Why?
(Courtesy of the National Baseball Hall of Fame)

NOTE State actions include the regulation of public utilities, whose rates may be set by the states in which they do business.

4 *Foreign trade.* Under the provisions of the Webb-Pomerene Act, of 1918, U.S. exporters may engage in cooperative activity to compete with similar foreign associations. This type of cooperative activity may not, however, restrain trade within the United States or injure other U.S. exporters. The Export Trading Company Act of 1982 broadened the Webb-Pomerene Act by permitting the Department of Justice to certify properly qualified export trading companies. Any activity within the scope described by the certificate is exempt from public prosecution under the antitrust laws.

5 *Professional baseball.* In 1922, the United States Supreme Court held that professional baseball was not within the reach of federal antitrust laws because it did not involve "interstate commerce."[22] Some of the effects of this decision, however, were modified by the Curt Flood Act of 1998. Essentially, the act allows players the option of suing team owners for anticompetitive practices if, for example, the owners collude to "blacklist" players, hold down players' salaries, or force players to play for specific teams.[23]

6 *Oil marketing.* The Interstate Oil Compact of 1935 allows states to determine quotas on oil that will be marketed in interstate commerce.

7 *Cooperative research and production.* Cooperative research among small-business firms is exempt under the Small Business Act of 1958, as amended. Research or production of a product, process, or service by joint ventures consisting of competitors is exempt under special federal legislation, including the National Cooperative Research Act of 1984 and the National Cooperative Production Amendments of 1993.

8 *Joint efforts by businesspersons to obtain legislative or executive action.* This is often referred to as the *Noerr-Pennington* doctrine.[24] For example, DVD producers may jointly lobby Congress to change the copyright laws without being held liable for attempting to restrain trade. Though selfish rather than purely public-minded conduct is permitted, there is an exception: an action will not be protected if it is clear that the action is "objectively baseless in the sense that no reasonable [person] could reasonably expect success on the merits" and it is an attempt to make anticompetitive use of government processes.[25]

9 *Other exemptions.* Other activities exempt from antitrust laws include activities approved by the president in furtherance of the defense of our nation (under the Defense Production Act of 1950, as amended); state actions, when the state policy is clearly articulated and the policy is actively supervised by the state;[26] and activities of regulated industries (such as the communication and banking industries) when federal commissions, boards, or agencies (such as the Federal Communications Commission and the Federal Maritime Commission) have primary regulatory authority.

The issue in the following case was whether a National Football League eligibility rule fell within the labor exemption from the antitrust laws.

22. *Federal Baseball Club of Baltimore, Inc. v. National League of Professional Baseball Clubs,* 259 U.S. 200, 42 S.Ct. 465, 66 L.Ed. 898 (1922).

23. Note that in 2003, a federal appellate court held that because baseball was exempt from federal antitrust laws, it was also exempt from the reach of state antitrust laws due to the supremacy clause. *Major League Baseball v. Crist,* 331 F.3d 1177 (11th Cir. 2003).

24. See *Eastern Railroad Presidents Conference v. Noerr Motor Freight, Inc.,* 365 U.S. 127, 81 S.Ct. 523, 5 L.Ed.2d 464 (1961); and *United Mine Workers of America v. Pennington,* 381 U.S. 657, 85 S.Ct. 1585, 14 L.Ed.2d 626 (1965).

25. *Professional Real Estate Investors, Inc. v. Columbia Pictures Industries, Inc.,* 508 U.S. 49, 113 S.Ct. 1920, 123 L.Ed.2d 611 (1993).

26. See *Parker v. Brown,* 317 U.S. 341, 63 S.Ct. 307, 87 L.Ed. 315 (1943).

CASE 22.3   **Clarett v. National Football League**

United States Court of Appeals, Second Circuit, 369 F.3d 124 (2004).

FACTS Maurice Clarett was a star football player attending Ohio State University (OSU). In his freshman year, Clarett led his team to an undefeated season and a double-overtime victory over the University of Miami in the Fiesta Bowl that resulted in OSU's first national championship in thirty-four years. Clarett's goal was to play in the National Football League (NFL) in the fall of 2004. The NFL, an unincorporated association of thirty-two member clubs, consistently outperforms all other professional sports leagues, in both revenues and television ratings, representing an unparalleled opportunity for an aspiring football player in terms of salary and level of competition. The only thing preventing Clarett from achieving his goal was an NFL rule that limited eligibility to players three seasons removed from their high school graduation. Clarett filed a suit in a federal district court against the NFL, claiming that the rule was an illegal restraint of trade. Clarett argued that by adopting the rule, the NFL teams had agreed to exclude a broad class of players from the NFL labor market. The court issued a summary judgment in Clarett's favor. The NFL appealed to the U.S. Court of Appeals for the Second Circuit.

ISSUE Does the NFL rule that limits eligibility to players three seasons removed from their high school graduation constitute an illegal restraint of trade?

DECISION No. The U.S. Court of Appeals for the Second Circuit reversed the judgment of the lower court and remanded the case for the entry of a judgment in favor of the NFL. The appellate court vacated the order designating Clarett eligible to participate in the year's NFL draft.

REASON The U.S. Court of Appeals for the Second Circuit reasoned that, as a mandatory bargaining subject between employer and employees, the eligibility rule was exempt from the application of the antitrust laws. The court explained, "[T]o accommodate the collective bargaining process, certain concerted activity among and between labor and employers [is] held to be beyond the reach of the antitrust laws." The court acknowledged that the NFL has maintained draft eligibility rules in one form or another throughout most of its history, but noted that the beginning of a collective bargaining relationship between the NFL and its players' union more than thirty years ago "irrevocably altered the governing legal regime." Today, players cannot negotiate directly with the NFL teams over the terms and conditions of their employment. Instead, the NFL and the players' union engage in collective bargaining. The court stated that the eligibility rules constitute a mandatory bargaining subject "because they have tangible effects on the wages and working conditions of current NFL players."

 FOR CRITICAL ANALYSIS–Social Consideration
Why are the NFL's member clubs permitted to agree that a player will not be hired until three full football seasons after the player's high school graduation?

U.S. ANTITRUST LAWS IN THE GLOBAL CONTEXT

U.S. antitrust laws have a broad application. Not only may persons in foreign nations be subject to their provisions, but the laws may also be applied to protect foreign consumers and competitors from violations committed by U.S. business firms. Consequently, *foreign persons*, a term that by definition includes foreign governments, may sue under U.S. antitrust laws in U.S. courts. (For a discussion of how antitrust lawsuits in the United Kingdom are beginning to resemble those in the United States, see this chapter's *Beyond Our Borders* feature on the next page.)

The Extraterritorial Application of U.S. Antitrust Laws

Section 1 of the Sherman Act provides for the extraterritorial effect of the U.S. antitrust laws. The United States is a major proponent of free competition in the global economy, and thus any conspiracy that has a *substantial effect* on U.S. commerce is within the reach of the Sherman Act. The violation may even occur outside the United States, and foreign governments as well as persons can be sued for violation of U.S. antitrust laws. Before U.S. courts will exercise jurisdiction and apply antitrust laws, it must be shown that the alleged

BEYOND OUR BORDERS — U.S.-Style Antitrust Lawsuits Become More Popular in the United Kingdom

In recent years, several multinational corporations that had participated in an international cartel to fix the prices of vitamins paid out more than $4 billion to those harmed by the price-fixing scheme. Although companies based in several countries suffered damages, the only plaintiffs that received a share of the settlement were those with operations in the United States. Such anomalies may change in the future, though, at least for businesses and individuals in the United Kingdom, where antitrust regulators are encouraging private parties to bring suits for antitrust violations.

As explained earlier in this chapter, U.S. law encourages private antitrust actions by allowing successful plaintiffs to recover treble damages and attorneys' fees. In contrast, British law has discouraged such suits by generally requiring the losing party to pay the winning party's legal expenses and by limiting attorneys' fees. Caps on attorneys' fees are common throughout Europe, and in Britain, the most the attorney for the winning party can do is to ask the judge to approve the doubling of the attorney's hourly rate. Consequently, attorneys are often reluctant to undertake private antitrust suits.

Today, however, both of these disincentives are being removed. In an effort to promote more private antitrust litigation, the British antitrust agency is encouraging judges to waive "loser-pays" rules more often. Furthermore, to counter the problem of limits on attorneys' fees, a new lawsuit-financing industry is emerging in London. Private investors, insurers, and hedge funds have begun financing lawsuits in exchange for a share of any awards.

These changes are being watched closely by other European countries. The United Kingdom is a member of the twenty-seven-nation European Union (EU), and what happens there with respect to lawsuits against international cartels may start a trend. Indeed, the EU's antitrust commissioner, Neelie Kroes, has publicly supported such a movement. Because cartels today typically are international, plaintiffs believe that successful price-fixing claims should result in *global* settlements that include all businesses and individuals who can prove they were injured by the scheme, regardless of where they are located. Already, British victims of price-fixing cartels are allowed to sue for lost profits throughout Europe.

 FOR CRITICAL ANALYSIS *What effect does private funding of lawsuits in exchange for a percentage of the award have on attorneys' incentive to undertake lawsuits against international cartels?*

violation had a substantial effect on U.S. commerce. U.S. jurisdiction is automatically invoked, however, when a *per se* violation occurs.

If a domestic firm, for example, joins a foreign cartel to control the production, price, or distribution of goods, and this cartel has a *substantial effect* on U.S. commerce, a *per se* violation may exist. Hence, both the domestic firm and the foreign cartel could be sued for violation of the U.S. antitrust laws. Likewise, if a foreign firm doing business in the United States enters into a price-fixing or other anticompetitive agreement to control a portion of U.S. markets, a *per se* violation may exist.

The Application of Foreign Antitrust Laws

Large U.S. companies increasingly need to worry about the application of foreign antitrust laws as well. The European Union (EU), for example, has antitrust laws that are stricter in many respects than those of the United States. The EU blocked a bid by General Electric Company to acquire Honeywell International, Inc., in 2001. The EU entered into its own antitrust settlement with Microsoft Corporation, with remedies (including a potential fine of $665 million) that went beyond those imposed in the United States. The EU has also threatened additional fines for Microsoft's alleged failure to comply with requirements that it offer Windows without its proprietary Media Player video and music applications.

Many other nations also have laws that promote competition and prohibit trade restraints. For example, Japanese antitrust laws forbid unfair trade practices, monopolization, and restrictions that unreasonably restrain trade. Several nations in Southeast Asia, including Indonesia, Malaysia, and Vietnam, have enacted statutes protecting competition. Argentina, Brazil, Chile, Peru, and several other Latin American countries have adopted modern antitrust laws as well. Most of the antitrust laws apply extraterritorially, as U.S. antitrust laws do. This means that a U.S. company may be subject to another nation's antitrust laws if the company's conduct has a substantial effect on that nation's commerce.

REVIEWING Promoting Competition in a Global Context

The Internet Corporation for Assigned Names and Numbers (ICANN) is a nonprofit entity that organizes Internet domain names. It is governed by a board of directors elected by various groups with commercial interests in the Internet. One of ICANN's functions is to authorize an entity to serve as a registrar for certain "top level domains" (TLDs). ICANN entered into an agreement with VeriSign to provide registry services for the ".com" TLD in accordance with ICANN's specifications. VeriSign complained that ICANN was restricting the services that it could make available as a registrar and was blocking new services, imposing unnecessary conditions on those services, and setting prices at which the services were offered. VeriSign claimed that ICANN's control of the registry services for domain names violated Section 1 of the Sherman Act. Using the information presented in the chapter, answer the following questions.

1 Should ICANN's actions be judged under the rule of reason or deemed a *per se* violation of Section 1 of the Sherman Act?

2 Should ICANN's action be viewed as a horizontal or a vertical restraint of trade?

3 Does it matter that ICANN's leadership is chosen by those with a commercial interest in the Internet?

4 If the dispute is judged under the rule of reason, what might be ICANN's defense for having a standardized set of registry services that must be used?

APPLICATION How Can You Avoid Antitrust Problems?*

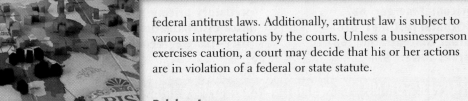

Business managers need to be aware of how antitrust legislation may affect their activities. In addition to the federal antitrust laws covered in this chapter, the states also have antitrust and unfair competition laws. Moreover, state authorities have the power to bring civil lawsuits to enforce federal antitrust laws. Additionally, antitrust law is subject to various interpretations by the courts. Unless a businessperson exercises caution, a court may decide that his or her actions are in violation of a federal or state statute.

Pricing Issues

Almost all businesses have competitors and want to outsell those competitors. The pricing of a business's goods or

* This *Application* is not meant to substitute for the services of an attorney who is licensed to practice law in your state.

(Continued)

BUSINESS LAW TODAY: THE ESSENTIALS

services is extremely important not only for its volume of sales, but also for its bottom-line profit. When setting or changing a price, businesses frequently hire a cost accountant to perform an analysis. This is only a start because a firm must also consider the price of a competitor's similar or identical products. Most businesses do not want a "price war" with rapidly declining prices. Thus, it is not uncommon for a business to charge basically the same price as its competitors. A problem arises when there is an agreement (express or implied) to fix the price. This is a *per se* violation of Section 1 of the Sherman Act and can result in criminal or civil actions (including treble damages).

Knowing the price a competitor charges—and meeting that price—is not a violation in and of itself. Frequently, its legality depends on how the information was obtained. Violations occur when there is a communication (regardless of purpose) between a business owner (or employee) and a direct competitor. If concerned that a communication may cause antitrust pricing problems, businesspersons should consult with an attorney who can explain what is legal when dealing with competitors.

Another problem in pricing can occur when a business wants to have some control over the price that its retailers charge when selling its product to customers. Historically, resale price maintenance agreements were automatically deemed illegal as vertical restraints of trade. Today, the courts use the rule of reason to test for illegality. There are a variety of legitimate reasons for price maintenance agreements, including product image and resale value. For example, a

BMW automobile has both a price and a value image, and to sell it at a Hyundai price could seriously damage BMW's image.

Implications of Foreign Law

Antitrust issues are not limited to domestic businesses doing business in the United States. Because of today's global economy, many companies conduct business in other nations and with foreign businesses. Antitrust laws in other countries differ from U.S. law and can apply to a U.S. firm that has dealings with businesses located in a foreign nation even though the firm does not have a physical presence there. Always be aware of the antitrust laws of any country in which you are doing business. Generally, any businessperson who is considering doing business overseas should seek counsel from a competent attorney concerning potential antitrust violations.

CHECKLIST FOR AVOIDING ANTITRUST PROBLEMS

1 Exercise caution when communicating and dealing with competitors.
2 Seek the advice of an attorney specializing in antitrust law to ensure that your business practices and agreements do not violate antitrust laws.
3 If you conduct business ventures in other nations, obtain the advice of an attorney who is familiar with the antitrust laws of those nations.

KEY TERMS

antitrust law 673
attempted monopolization 684
divestiture 688
exclusive-dealing contract 685
group boycott 677
horizontal merger 687
horizontal restraint 676
market concentration 687
market power 674

market-share test 681
monopolization 680
monopoly 674
monopoly power 674
per se violation 675
predatory pricing 680
price discrimination 684
price-fixing agreement 676

resale price maintenance
    agreement 679
rule of reason 675
treble damages 689
tying arrangement 686
vertical merger 688
vertical restraint 678
vertically integrated firm 678

CHAPTER SUMMARY Promoting Competition in a Global Context

The Sherman Antitrust Act (1890)
(See pages 674–684.)

1. *Major provisions*—

  a. Section 1—Prohibits contracts, combinations, and conspiracies in restraint of trade.

    (1) Horizontal restraints subject to Section 1 include price-fixing agreements, group boycotts (joint refusals to deal), horizontal market divisions, and trade association agreements.

CHAPTER SUMMARY	Promoting Competition in a Global Context–Continued
The Sherman Antitrust Act (1890)—Continued	(2) Vertical restraints subject to Section 1 include territorial or customer restrictions, resale price maintenance agreements, and refusals to deal. b. Section 2—Prohibits monopolies and attempts to monopolize. 2. *Jurisdictional requirements*—The Sherman Act applies only to activities that have a significant impact on interstate commerce. 3. *Interpretive rules*— a. *Per se* rule—Applied to restraints on trade that are so inherently anticompetitive that they cannot be justified and are deemed illegal as a matter of law. b. Rule of reason—Applied when an anticompetitive agreement may be justified by legitimate benefits. Under the rule of reason, the lawfulness of a trade restraint will be determined by the purpose and effects of the restraint.
The Clayton Act (1914) (See pages 684–688.)	The major provisions are as follows: 1. *Section 2*—As amended in 1936 by the Robinson-Patman Act, prohibits price discrimination that substantially lessens competition and prohibits a seller engaged in interstate commerce from selling to two or more buyers goods of similar grade and quality at different prices when the result is a substantial lessening of competition or the creation of a competitive injury. 2. *Section 3*—Prohibits exclusionary practices, such as exclusive-dealing contracts and tying arrangements, when the effect may be to substantially lessen competition. 3. *Section 7*—Prohibits mergers when the effect may be to substantially lessen competition or to tend to create a monopoly. a. Horizontal merger—The acquisition by merger or consolidation of a competing firm engaged in the same relevant market. Will be presumed unlawful if the entity created by the merger will have anything other than a small percentage market share. b. Vertical merger—The acquisition by a seller of one of its buyers or vice versa. Will be unlawful if the merger prevents competitors of either merging firm from competing in a segment of the market that otherwise would be open to them, resulting in a substantial lessening of competition. 4. *Section 8*—Prohibits interlocking directorates.
Enforcement of Antitrust Laws (See pages 688–689.)	Federal agencies that enforce antitrust laws are the Department of Justice and the Federal Trade Commission, which was established by the Federal Trade Commission Act of 1914. Private parties who have been injured as a result of violations of the Sherman Act or Clayton Act may also bring civil suits. In recent years, many private parties have filed such suits largely because, if successful, they may be awarded treble damages and attorneys' fees.
Exemptions from Antitrust Laws (See pages 689–691.)	1. Labor unions. 2. Agricultural associations and fisheries. 3. Insurance when state regulation exists. 4. Export trading companies. 5. Professional baseball. 6. Oil marketing. 7. Cooperative research and production. 8. Joint efforts by businesspersons to obtain legislative or executive action. 9. Other activities, including certain national defense activities, state actions, and activities of certain regulated industries.

(Continued)

CHAPTER SUMMARY	**Promoting Competition in a Global Context–Continued**
U.S. Antitrust Laws in the Global Context (See pages 691–693.)	1. *U.S. laws application*—U.S. antitrust laws are broad and can be applied in foreign nations to protect foreign consumers and competitors. Foreign governments and persons can also bring actions under U.S. antitrust laws. Section 1 of the Sherman Act applies to any conspiracy that has a substantial effect on U.S. commerce.
	2. *Foreign laws application*—Many other nations also have laws that promote competition and prohibit trade restraints and some are more restrictive than U.S. laws. These foreign antitrust laws are increasingly being applied to U.S. firms.

FOR REVIEW

Answers for the even-numbered questions in this **For Review** *section can be found in Appendix E at the end of this text.*

1 What is a monopoly? What is market power? How do these concepts relate to each other?

2 What type of activity is prohibited by Section 1 of the Sherman Act? What type of activity is prohibited by Section 2 of the Sherman Act?

3 What are the four major provisions of the Clayton Act, and what types of activities do these provisions prohibit?

4 What agencies of the federal government enforce the federal antitrust laws?

5 What are four activities that are exempt from the antitrust laws?

QUESTIONS AND CASE PROBLEMS

 **HYPOTHETICAL SCENARIOS**

22.1 Sherman Act. An agreement that is blatantly and substantially anticompetitive is deemed a *per se* violation of Section 1 of the Sherman Act. Under what rule is an agreement analyzed if it appears to be anticompetitive but is not a *per se* violation? In making this analysis, what factors will a court consider?

22.2 Hypothetical Question with Sample Answer. Allitron, Inc., and Donovan, Ltd., are interstate competitors selling similar appliances, principally in the states of Illinois, Indiana, Kentucky, and Ohio. Allitron and Donovan agree that Allitron will no longer sell in Indiana and Ohio and that Donovan will no longer sell in Illinois and Kentucky. Have Allitron and Donovan violated any antitrust laws? If so, which law? Explain.

 For a sample answer to Question 22.2, go to Appendix F at the end of this text.

22.3 Exclusionary Practices. Instant Foto Corp. is a manufacturer of photography film. At the present time, Instant Foto has approximately 50 percent of the market. Instant Foto advertises that the purchase price for its film includes photo processing by Instant Foto Corp. Instant Foto claims that its film processing is specially designed to improve the quality of photos taken with Instant Foto film. Is Instant Foto's combination of film and film processing an antitrust violation? Explain.

 **CASE PROBLEMS**

22.4 Tying Arrangement. Public Interest Corp. (PIC) owned and operated the television station WTMV-TV in Lakeland, Florida. MCA Television, Ltd., owns and licenses syndicated television programs. The parties entered into a licensing contract with respect to several television shows. MCA conditioned the license on PIC's agreeing to take another show, *Harry and the Hendersons*. PIC agreed to this arrangement, although it would not have chosen to license *Harry* if it had not had to do so to secure the licenses for the other shows. More than two years into the contract, a dispute arose over

PIC's payments, and negotiations failed to resolve the dispute. In a letter, MCA suspended PIC's broadcast rights for all of its shows and stated that "[a]ny telecasts of MCA programming by WTMV-TV . . . will be deemed unauthorized and shall constitute an infringement of MCA's copyrights." PIC nonetheless continued broadcasting MCA's programs, with the exception of *Harry*. MCA filed a suit in a federal district court against PIC, alleging breach of contract and copyright infringement. PIC filed a counterclaim, contending, in part, that MCA's deal was an illegal tying arrangement. Is PIC correct? Explain. [*MCA Television, Ltd. v. Public Interest Corp.*, 171 F.3d 1265 (11th Cir. 1999)]

22.5 Case Problem with Sample Answer. Moist snuff is a smokeless tobacco product sold in small round cans from racks, which include point-of-sale (POS) ads. POS ads are critical because tobacco advertising is restricted and the number of people who use smokeless tobacco products is relatively small. In the moist snuff market in the United States, there are only four competitors, including U.S. Tobacco Co. and its affiliates (USTC) and Conwood Co. In 1990, USTC, which held 87 percent of the market, began to convince major retailers, including Wal-Mart Stores, Inc., to use USTC's "exclusive racks" to display its products and those of all other snuff makers. USTC agents would then destroy competitors' racks. USTC also began to provide retailers with false sales data to convince them to maintain its poor-selling items and drop competitors' less expensive products. Conwood's Wal-Mart market share fell from 12 percent to 6.5 percent. In stores in which USTC did not have rack exclusivity, however, Conwood's market share increased to 25 percent. Conwood filed a suit in a federal district court against USTC, alleging, in part, that USTC used its monopoly power to exclude competitors from the moist snuff market. Should the court rule in Conwood's favor? What is USTC's best defense? Discuss. [*Conwood Co., L.P. v. U.S. Tobacco Co.*, 290 F.3d 768 (6th Cir. 2002)]

After you have answered Problem 22.5, compare your answer with the sample answer given on the Web site that accompanies this text. Go to **academic.cengage.com/blaw/blt**, select "Chapter 22," and click on "Case Problem with Sample Answer."

22.6 Restraint of Trade. Visa U.S.A., Inc., MasterCard International, Inc., American Express (Amex), and Discover are the four major credit- and charge-card networks in the United States. Visa and MasterCard are joint ventures, owned by the thousands of banks that are their members. The banks issue the cards, clear transactions, and collect fees from the merchants that accept the cards. In contrast, Amex and Discover themselves issue cards to customers, process transactions, and collect fees. Since 1995, Amex has asked banks to issue its cards. No bank has been willing to do so, however, because it would have to stop issuing Visa and MasterCard cards under those networks' rules barring member banks from issuing cards on rival networks. The U.S. Department of Justice filed a suit in a federal district court against Visa and MasterCard, alleging, among other things, that the rules were illegal restraints of trade under the Sherman Act. Do the rules harm competition? If so, how? What relief might the court order to stop any anticompetitiveness? [*United States v. Visa U.S.A., Inc.*, 344 F.3d 229 (2d Cir. 2003)]

22.7 Sherman Act. Dentsply International, Inc., is one of a dozen manufacturers of artificial teeth for dentures and other restorative devices. Dentsply sells its teeth to twenty-three dealers in dental products. The dealers supply the teeth to dental laboratories, which fabricate dentures for sale to dentists. There are hundreds of other dealers who compete with one another on the basis of price and service. Some manufacturers sell directly to the laboratories. There are also thousands of laboratories that compete with one another on the basis of price and service. Because of advances in dental medicine, however, artificial tooth manufacturing has low growth potential, and Dentsply dominates the industry. Dentsply's market share is greater than 75 percent and is about fifteen times larger than that of its closest competitor. Dentsply prohibits its dealers from marketing competitor's teeth unless they were selling the teeth before 1993. The federal government filed a suit in a federal district court against Dentsply, alleging, in part, a violation of Section 2 of the Sherman Act. What must the government show to succeed in its suit? Are those elements present in this case? What should the court rule? Explain. [*United States v. Dentsply International, Inc.*, 399 F.3d 181 (3d Cir. 2005)]

22.8 Price Fixing. Texaco Inc. and Shell Oil Co. are competitors in the national and international oil and gasoline markets. They refine crude oil into gasoline and sell it to service station owners and others. Between 1998 and 2002, Texaco and Shell engaged in a joint venture, Equilon Enterprises, to consolidate their operations in the western United States and a separate venture, Motiva Enterprises, for the same purpose in the eastern United States. This ended their competition in the domestic refining and marketing of gasoline. As part of the ventures, Texaco and Shell agreed to pool their resources and share the risks and profits of their joint activities. The Federal Trade Commission and several states approved the formation of these entities without restricting the pricing of their gasoline, which the ventures began to sell at a single price under the original Texaco and Shell brand names. Fouad Dagher and other station owners filed a suit in a federal district court against Texaco and Shell, alleging that the defendants were engaged in illegal price fixing. Do the circumstances in this case fit the definition of a price-fixing agreement? Explain. [*Texaco Inc. v. Dagher*, 547 U.S. 1, 126 S.Ct. 1276, 164 L.Ed.2d 1 (2006)]

22.9 Restraint of Trade. In 1999, residents of the city of Madison, Wisconsin, became concerned that overconsumption of liquor seemed to be increasing near the campus of the University of Wisconsin–Madison (UW), leading to more frequent use of detoxification facilities and calls for police services in the campus area. Under pressure from UW, which shared these concerns, the city initiated a new policy, imposing conditions on area taverns to discourage price-reduction "specials" believed to encourage high-volume and dangerous drinking. In 2002, the city began to draft an ordinance to ban all drink specials. Tavern owners responded by announcing that they had "voluntarily" agreed to discontinue drink specials on Friday and Saturday nights after 8 P.M. The city put its ordinance on hold. UW student Nic Eichenseer and others filed a suit in a Wisconsin state court against the Madison-Dane County Tavern League, Inc. (an association of local tavern owners), and others, alleging violations of antitrust law. On what might the plaintiffs base a claim for relief? Are the defendants in this case exempt from the antitrust laws? What should the court rule? Why? [*Eichenseer v. Madison-Dane County Tavern League, Inc.*, 2006 WI App. 226, 725 N.W.2d 274 (2006)]

22.10 **A Question of Ethics.** *In the 1990s, DuCoa, L.P., made choline chloride, a B-complex vitamin essential for the growth and development of animals. The U.S. market for choline chloride was divided into thirds among DuCoa, Bioproducts, Inc., and Chinook Group Ltd. To stabilize the market and keep the price of the vitamin higher than it would otherwise be, the companies agreed to fix the price and allocate market share by deciding which of them would offer the lowest price to each customer. At times, however, the compa-*

nies disregarded the agreement. During an increase in competitive activity in August 1997, Daniel Rose became president of DuCoa. The next month, a subordinate advised him of the conspiracy. By February 1998, Rose had begun to implement a strategy to persuade DuCoa's competitors to rejoin the conspiracy. By April, the three companies had reallocated their market shares and increased their prices. In June, the U.S. Department of Justice began to investigate allegations of price fixing in the vitamin market. Ultimately, a federal district court convicted Rose of conspiracy to violate Section 1 of the Sherman Act. [*United States v. Rose*, 449 F.3d 627 (5th Cir. 2006)]

1 The court "enhanced" Rose's sentence to thirty months' imprisonment, one year of supervised release, and a $20,000 fine based, among other things, on his role as "a manager or supervisor" in the conspiracy. Rose appealed this enhancement to the U.S. Court of Appeals for the Fifth Circuit. Was it fair to increase Rose's sentence on this ground? Why or why not?

2 Was Rose's participation in the conspiracy unethical? If so, how might Rose have behaved ethically instead? If not, could any of the participants' conduct be considered unethical? Explain.

 ## CRITICAL THINKING AND WRITING ASSIGNMENTS

22.11 Critical Legal Thinking. Critics of antitrust law claim that in the long run, competitive market forces will eliminate private monopolies unless they are fostered by government regulation. Can you think of any examples of monopolies that continue to be fostered by government in the United States?

22.12 Critical Thinking and Writing Assignment for Business. In what ways might antitrust laws place too great a burden on commerce in the global marketplace?

ONLINE ACTIVITIES

PRACTICAL INTERNET EXERCISES

Go to this text's Web site at **academic.cengage.com/blaw/blt**, select "Chapter 22," and click on "Practical Internet Exercises." There you will find the following Internet research exercises that you can perform to learn more about the topics covered in this chapter.

PRACTICAL INTERNET EXERCISE 22-1 LEGAL PERSPECTIVE—The Standard Oil Trust

PRACTICAL INTERNET EXERCISE 22-2 MANAGEMENT PERSPECTIVE—Avoiding Antitrust Problems

BEFORE THE TEST

Go to this text's Web site at **academic.cengage.com/blaw/blt**, select "Chapter 22," and click on "Interactive Quizzes." You will find a number of interactive questions relating to this chapter.

CHAPTER 23
Personal Property, Bailments, and Insurance

LEARNING OBJECTIVES

AFTER READING THIS CHAPTER, YOU SHOULD BE ABLE TO ANSWER THE FOLLOWING QUESTIONS:

1 What is real property? What is personal property?

2 What are the three elements necessary for an effective gift? How else can property be acquired?

3 What are the three elements of a bailment?

4 What are the basic rights and duties of a bailee? What are the rights and duties of a bailor?

5 What clauses are typically included in insurance contracts?

> "The great ... end ... of men united into commonwealths, and putting themselves under government, is the preservation of their property."
>
> John Locke, 1632–1704
> (English political philosopher)

Property consists of the legally protected rights and interests a person has in anything with an ascertainable value that is subject to ownership. Property would have little value (and the word would have little meaning) if the law did not define the right to use it, to sell or dispose of it, and to prevent trespass on it. Indeed, John Locke, as indicated in the chapter-opening quotation, considered the preservation of property to be the primary reason for the establishment of government.

Property is divided into real property and personal property. **Real property** (sometimes called *realty* or *real estate*) means the land and everything permanently attached to it. Everything else is **personal property,** or *personalty.* Attorneys sometimes refer to personal property as **chattel,** a term used under the common law to denote all forms of personal property. Personal property can be tangible or intangible. *Tangible* personal property, such as a television set or a car, has physical substance. *Intangible* personal property represents some set of rights and interests but has no real physical existence. Stocks and bonds, patents, and copyrights are examples of intangible personal property.

In the first part of this chapter, we look at the ways in which title to property is held; the methods of acquiring ownership of personal property; and issues relating to mislaid, lost, and abandoned personal property. In the second part of the chapter, we examine bailment relationships. A *bailment* is created when personal property is temporarily delivered into the care of another without a transfer of title, such as when you take an item of clothing to the dry cleaner. This is the distinguishing characteristic of a bailment compared with a sale or a gift—there is no passage of title and no intent to transfer title. In the last

PROPERTY
Legally protected rights and interests in anything with an ascertainable value that is subject to ownership.

REAL PROPERTY
Land and everything attached to it, such as trees and buildings.

PERSONAL PROPERTY
Property that is movable; any property that is not real property.

CHATTEL
All forms of personal property.

part of this chapter, we consider insurance, which is a foremost concern of property owners and others. By insuring our property, and our lives, we protect ourselves against damage and loss.

PROPERTY OWNERSHIP

Property ownership[1] can be viewed as a bundle of rights, including the right to possess property and to dispose of it—by sale, gift, lease, or other means.

Fee Simple

FEE SIMPLE
An absolute form of property ownership entitling the property owner to use, possess, or dispose of the property as he or she chooses during his or her lifetime. On death, the interest in the property descends to the owner's heirs.

A person who holds the entire bundle of rights to property is said to be the owner in **fee simple.** The owner in fee simple is entitled to use, possess, or dispose of the property as he or she chooses during his or her lifetime, and on this owner's death, the interests in the property descend to his or her heirs. We will return to this form of property ownership in Chapter 24, in the context of ownership rights in real property.

Concurrent Ownership

CONCURRENT OWNERSHIP
Joint ownership.

Persons who share ownership rights simultaneously in a particular piece of property are said to be *concurrent* owners. There are two principal types of **concurrent ownership:** *tenancy in common* and *joint tenancy.* Other types of concurrent ownership include *tenancy by the entirety* and *community property.*

TENANCY IN COMMON
Co-ownership of property in which each party owns an undivided interest that passes to her or his heirs at death.

Tenancy in Common   The term **tenancy in common** refers to a form of co-ownership in which each of two or more persons owns an *undivided* interest in the property. The interest is undivided because each tenant has rights in the *whole* property. ■**EXAMPLE 23.1** Rosa and Chad own a rare stamp collection together as tenants in common. This does not mean that Rosa owns some particular stamps and Chad others. Rather, it means that Rosa and Chad each have rights in the *entire* collection. (If Rosa owned some of the stamps and Chad owned others, then the interest would be *divided*.) ■

On the death of a tenant in common, that tenant's interest in the property passes to her or his heirs. ■**EXAMPLE 23.2** Should Rosa die before Chad, a one-half interest in the stamp collection will become the property of Rosa's heirs. If Rosa sells her interest to Fred before she dies, Fred and Chad will be co-owners as tenants in common. If Fred dies, his interest in the personal property will pass to his heirs, and they in turn will own the property with Chad as tenants in common. ■

JOINT TENANCY
The joint ownership of property by two or more co-owners in which each co-owner owns an undivided portion of the property. On the death of one of the joint tenants, his or her interest automatically passes to the surviving joint tenant(s).

Joint Tenancy   In a **joint tenancy,** each of two or more persons owns an undivided interest in the property, and a deceased joint tenant's interest passes to the surviving joint tenant or tenants. The rights of a surviving joint tenant to inherit a deceased joint tenant's ownership interest—which are referred to as *survivorship rights*—distinguish the joint tenancy from the tenancy in common. A joint tenancy can be terminated before a joint tenant's death by gift or by sale; in this situation, the person who receives the property as a gift or who purchases the property becomes a tenant in common, not a joint tenant.

■**EXAMPLE 23.3** If, in the preceding example, Rosa and Chad held their stamp collection in a joint tenancy and if Rosa died before Chad, the entire collection would become the property of Chad; Rosa's heirs would receive absolutely no interest in the collection. If Rosa, while living, sold her interest to Fred, however, the sale would terminate the joint tenancy, and Fred and Chad would become owners as tenants in common. ■

---

1. The principles discussed in this section apply equally to real property ownership (to be discussed in Chapter 24).

Generally, it is presumed that a co-tenancy is a tenancy in common unless there is a clear intention to establish a joint tenancy. Thus, language such as "to Jerrold and Eva as joint tenants with right of survivorship, and not as tenants in common" would be necessary to create a joint tenancy.

Tenancy by the Entirety   A **tenancy by the entirety** is a less common form of ownership that can be created by a conveyance (transfer) of real property to a husband and wife. It differs from a joint tenancy only by the fact that neither spouse can make a separate lifetime transfer of his or her interest without the consent of the other spouse. In some states where statutes give the wife the right to convey her property, this form of concurrent ownership has been effectively abolished. A divorce, either spouse's death, or mutual agreement will terminate a tenancy by the entirety.

Community Property   A married couple is allowed to own property as **community property** in only a limited number of states.[2] If property is held as community property, each spouse technically owns an undivided one-half interest in property acquired during the marriage. Generally, community property does not include property acquired prior to the marriage or property acquired by gift or inheritance as separate property during the marriage. After a divorce, community property is divided equally in some states and according to the discretion of the court in other states.

The *Concept Summary* below illustrates the primary types of property ownership.

TENANCY BY THE ENTIRETY
The joint ownership of property by a husband and wife. Neither party can transfer her or his interest in the property without the consent of the other.

COMMUNITY PROPERTY
A form of concurrent ownership of property in which each spouse technically owns an undivided one-half interest in property acquired during the marriage. This form of joint ownership occurs in only ten states and Puerto Rico.

ACQUIRING OWNERSHIP OF PERSONAL PROPERTY

The most common way of acquiring personal property is by purchasing it. We have already discussed the purchase and sale of personal property (goods) in Chapters 11 through 13. Here, we look at additional ways in which ownership of personal property can be acquired, including acquisition by possession, production, gift, accession, and confusion.

---

2. These states include Alaska, Arizona, California, Idaho, Louisiana, Nevada, New Mexico, Texas, Washington, and Wisconsin. Puerto Rico allows property to be owned as community property as well.

CONCEPT SUMMARY | **Common Types of Property Ownership**

CONCEPT	DESCRIPTION
Fee Simple	Owners of property in fee simple have the fullest ownership rights in property. They have the right to use, possess, or dispose of the property as they choose during their lifetimes and to pass on the property to their heirs at death.
Tenancy in Common	Co-ownership in which two or more persons own an undivided interest in property; on one tenant's death, that tenant's property interest passes to his or her heirs.
Joint Tenancy	Co-ownership in which two or more persons own an undivided interest in property; on the death of a joint tenant, that tenant's property interest transfers to the remaining tenant(s), *not* to the heirs of the deceased.
Tenancy by the Entirety	A form of co-ownership between a husband and wife that is similar to a joint tenancy, except that a spouse cannot separately transfer her or his interest during her or his lifetime.
Community Property	A form of co-ownership between a husband and wife in which each spouse technically owns an undivided one-half interest in property acquired during the marriage. This type of ownership exists in only some states.

Possession

One example of acquiring ownership by possession is the capture of wild animals. Wild animals belong to no one in their natural state, and the first person to take possession of a wild animal normally owns it. The killing of a wild animal amounts to assuming ownership of it. Merely being in hot pursuit does not give title, however. This basic rule has two exceptions. First, any wild animals captured by a trespasser are the property of the landowner, not the trespasser. Second, if wild animals are captured or killed in violation of wild-game statutes, the state, and not the capturer, obtains title to the animals.

Those who find lost or abandoned property can also acquire ownership rights through mere possession of the property, as will be discussed later in the chapter. (Ownership rights in real property can also be acquired through possession, such as adverse possession—see Chapter 24.)

Production

Production—the fruits of labor—is another means of acquiring ownership of personal property. For instance, writers, inventors, and manufacturers all produce personal property and thereby acquire title to it. (In some situations, though, as when a researcher is hired to invent a new product or technique, the researcher-producer may not own what is produced.)

Gifts

GIFT
Any voluntary transfer of property made without consideration, past or present.

A **gift** is another fairly common means of acquiring and transferring ownership of real and personal property. A gift is essentially a voluntary transfer of property ownership for which no consideration is given. As discussed in Chapter 7, the presence of consideration is what distinguishes a contract from a gift.

To be an effective gift, three requirements must be met: (1) donative intent on the part of the *donor* (the one giving the gift); (2) delivery; and (3) acceptance by the *donee* (the one receiving the gift). We examine each of these requirements here, as well as the requirements of a gift made in contemplation of imminent death. Until these three requirements are met, no effective gift has been made. ■**EXAMPLE 23.4** Suppose that your aunt tells you that she *intends* to give you a new Mercedes-Benz for your next birthday. This is simply a promise to make a gift. It is not considered a gift until the Mercedes-Benz is delivered and accepted. ■

ON THE WEB

Who owns a gift received by a married person—the spouse who received the gift or the husband and wife jointly? To learn the answer to this question, go to Scott Law Firm's Web page at

www.scottlawfirm.com/property.htm.

Donative Intent   When a gift is challenged in court, the court will determine whether donative intent exists by looking at the language of the donor and the surrounding circumstances. ■**EXAMPLE 23.5** A court may look at the relationship between the parties and the size of the gift in relation to the donor's other assets. A gift to a mortal enemy is viewed with suspicion. Similarly, when a gift represents a large portion of a person's assets, the court will scrutinize the transaction closely to determine the mental capacity of the donor and ascertain whether any element of fraud or duress is present. ■

CONSTRUCTIVE DELIVERY
An act equivalent to the actual, physical delivery of property that cannot be physically delivered because of difficulty or impossibility. For example, the transfer of a key to a safe constructively delivers the contents of the safe.

Delivery   The gift must be delivered to the donee. Delivery is obvious in most cases, but some objects cannot be relinquished physically. Then the question of delivery depends on the surrounding circumstances.

Constructive Delivery.   When the object itself cannot be physically delivered, a symbolic, or constructive, delivery will be sufficient. **Constructive delivery** does not confer actual possession of the object in question, only the right to take actual possession. Thus, *constructive delivery* is a general term used to describe an action that the law holds to be the equivalent of real delivery. **EXAMPLE 23.6** Suppose that you want to make a gift of various rare coins that you have stored in a safe-deposit box at your bank. You certainly cannot deliver the box itself to the donee, and you do not want to take the coins out of the bank. In this situation, you can simply deliver the key to the box to the donee and authorize the donee's access to the box and its contents. This action constitutes a constructive delivery of the contents of the box. ■

The delivery of intangible property—such as stocks, bonds, insurance policies, and contracts, for example—must always be accomplished by symbolic, or constructive, delivery. This is because the documents represent rights and are not, in themselves, the true property.

Delivery by Agents. Delivery may be accomplished by means of a third person who is the agent of either the donor or the donee. If the third person is the agent of the donor, the delivery is effective when the agent delivers the gift to the donee. If the third person is the agent of the donee, the gift is effectively delivered when the donor delivers the property to the donee's agent. Naturally, no delivery is necessary if the gift is already in the hands of the donee. All that is necessary to complete the gift in such a situation is that the donor had the required intent and the donee accepted the gift.

Relinquishing Dominion and Control. An effective delivery also requires giving up complete control and **dominion** (ownership rights) over the subject matter of the gift. The outcome of disputes often turns on whether control has actually been relinquished. The Internal Revenue Service scrutinizes transactions between relatives when one claims to have given income-producing property to the other. A relative who does not relinquish complete control over a piece of property will have to pay taxes on the income from that property, as opposed to the family member who received the "gift."

In the following classic case, the court focused on the requirement that a donor must relinquish complete control and dominion over property given to the donee before a gift can be effectively delivered.

DOMINION
Ownership rights in property, including the right to possess and control the property.

CASE 23.1 **In re Estate of Piper**

LANDMARK AND CLASSIC CASES

Missouri Court of Appeals, 676 S.W.2d 897 (1984).

FACTS Gladys Piper died intestate (without a will) in 1982. At her death, she owned miscellaneous personal property worth $5,000 and had in her purse $200 in cash and two diamond rings, known as the Andy Piper rings. The contents of her purse were taken by her niece Wanda Brown, allegedly to preserve them for the estate. Clara Kaufmann, a friend of Piper's, filed a claim against the estate for $4,800. From October 1974 until Piper's death, Kaufmann had taken Piper to the doctor, beauty shop, and grocery store; had written her checks to pay her bills; and had helped her care for her home. Kaufmann maintained that Piper had promised to pay her for these services and had given her the diamond rings as a gift. A Missouri state trial court denied her request for payment; the court found that her services had been

voluntary. Kaufmann then filed a petition for delivery of personal property—the rings—which was granted by the trial court. Brown, other heirs, and the administrator of Piper's estate appealed.

ISSUE Had Gladys Piper made an effective gift of the rings to Clara Kaufmann?

DECISION No. The state appellate court reversed the judgment of the trial court on the ground that Piper had never delivered the rings to Kaufmann.

REASON Kaufmann claimed that the rings belonged to her by reason of a "consummated gift long prior to the death of Gladys Piper." Two witnesses testified for Kaufmann at the trial that Piper had told them the rings belonged to Kaufmann but

CASE 23.1–Continues next page

CASE 23.1–Continued

that she was going to wear them until she died. The appellate court found "no evidence of any actual delivery." The court held that the essentials of a gift are (1) a present intention to make a gift on the part of the donor, (2) a delivery of the property by the donor to the donee, and (3) an acceptance by the donee. The evidence in the case showed only an intent to make a gift. Because there was no delivery—either actual or constructive—a valid gift was not made. For Piper to have made a gift, her intention would have to have been executed by the complete and unconditional delivery of the property or the delivery of a proper written instrument evidencing the gift. As this did not occur, the court found that there had been no gift.

 WHAT IF THE FACTS WERE DIFFERENT? *Suppose that Gladys Piper had told Clara Kaufmann that she was giving the rings to Clara but wished to keep them*

in her possession for a few more days. Would this have affected the court's decision in this case? Why or why not?

IMPACT OF THIS CASE ON TODAY'S LAW *This case clearly illustrates the delivery requirement when making a gift. Assuming that Piper did, indeed, intend for Kaufmann to have the rings, it was unfortunate that Kaufmann had no right to receive them after Piper's death. Yet the alternative could lead to perhaps even more unfairness. The policy behind the delivery requirement is to protect alleged donors and their heirs from fraudulent claims based solely on oral testimony. If not for this policy, an alleged donee could easily claim that a gift was made when, in fact, it was not.*

RELEVANT WEB SITES *To locate information on the Web concerning the Piper decision, go to this text's Web site at academic.cengage.com/blaw/blt, select "Chapter 23," and click on "URLs for Landmarks."*

Acceptance The final requirement of a valid gift is acceptance by the donee. This rarely presents any problem, as most donees readily accept their gifts. The courts generally assume acceptance unless the circumstances indicate otherwise.

GIFT *INTER VIVOS*
A gift made during one's lifetime and not in contemplation of imminent death, in contrast to a gift *causa mortis.*

GIFT *CAUSA MORTIS*
A gift made in contemplation of death. If the donor does not die of that ailment, the gift is revoked.

Gifts *Inter Vivos* and Gifts *Causa Mortis* A gift made during one's lifetime is termed a **gift *inter vivos*. Gifts *causa mortis*** (so-called *deathbed gifts*), in contrast, are made in contemplation of imminent death. A gift *causa mortis* does not become absolute until the donor dies from the contemplated illness, and it is automatically revoked if the donor recovers from the illness. Moreover, the donee must survive to take the gift. To be effective, a gift *causa mortis* must also meet the three requirements discussed earlier—donative intent, delivery, and acceptance by the donee.

■**EXAMPLE 23.7** Yang is to be operated on for a cancerous tumor. Before the operation, he delivers an envelope to a close business associate. The envelope contains a letter saying, "I realize my days are numbered, and I want to give you this check for $1 million in the event of my death from this operation." The business associate cashes the check. The surgeon performs the operation and removes the tumor. Yang recovers fully. Several months later, Yang dies from a heart attack that is totally unrelated to the operation. If Yang's personal representative (the party charged with administering Yang's estate) tries to recover the $1 million, normally she will succeed. The gift *causa mortis* is automatically revoked if the donor recovers. The *specific event* that was contemplated in making the gift was death from a particular operation. Because Yang's death was not the result of this event, the gift is revoked, and the $1 million passes to Yang's estate. ■

Accession

ACCESSION
Occurs when an individual adds value to personal property by the use of either labor or materials. In some situations, a person may acquire ownership rights in another's property through accession.

Accession means "something added." Accession occurs when someone adds value to an item of personal property by the use of either labor or materials. Generally, there is no dispute about who owns the property after the accession occurs, especially when the accession is accomplished with the owner's consent. ■**EXAMPLE 23.8** A Corvette-customizing specialist comes to Hoshi's house. Hoshi has all the materials necessary to customize the car. The customizing specialist uses them to add a unique bumper to Hoshi's Corvette.

Hoshi simply pays the customizer for the value of the labor, obviously retaining title to the property. ■

When a Party Wrongfully Causes the Accession   When accession occurs without the permission of the owner, the courts tend to favor the owner over the improver—the one who improves the property—provided that the accession was wrongful and undertaken in bad faith. This is true even if the accession increased the value of the property substantially. In addition, many courts will deny the improver (wrongdoer) any compensation for the value added. **■EXAMPLE 23.9** Patti steals a car and puts expensive new tires on it. Obviously, a car thief will not be compensated for the value of the new tires if the rightful owner recovers the car. ■

Increased Property Value Due to a Good Faith Accession   If the accession is performed in good faith, however, even without the owner's consent, ownership of the improved item most often depends on whether the accession has increased the value of the property or changed its identity. The greater the increase in value, the more likely that ownership will pass to the improver. If ownership does pass, the improver must compensate the original owner for the value of the property prior to the accession. If the increase in value is not sufficient for ownership to pass to the improver, most courts will require the owner to compensate the improver for the value added.

Confusion

Confusion is the commingling (mixing together) of goods so that one person's personal property cannot be distinguished from another's. Confusion frequently occurs when the goods are *fungible*. *Fungible goods* are goods consisting of identical particles, such as grain or oil. For instance, if two farmers put their number 2–grade winter wheat into the same storage bin, confusion will occur and the farmers become tenants in common.

When goods are confused due to a wrongful and willful act and the wrongdoer is unable to prove what percentage of the confused goods belongs to him or her, then the innocent party ordinarily acquires title to the whole. If confusion occurs as a result of agreement, an honest mistake, or the act of some third party, the owners share ownership as tenants in common and will share any loss in proportion to their ownership interests in the property.

■EXAMPLE 23.10 Five farmers in a small Iowa community enter a cooperative arrangement. Each fall, the farmers harvest the same amount of number 2–grade yellow corn and store it in silos that are held by the cooperative. Each farmer thus owns one-fifth of the total corn in the silos. If one farmer harvests and stores more corn than the others in the cooperative silos and wants to claim a greater ownership interest, that farmer must keep careful records. Otherwise, the courts will presume that each farmer has an equal interest in the corn. ■

MISLAID, LOST, AND ABANDONED PROPERTY

As already mentioned, one of the methods of acquiring ownership of property is to possess it. Simply finding something and holding on to it, however, does not necessarily give the finder any legal rights in the property. Different rules apply, depending on whether the property was mislaid, lost, or abandoned.

Mislaid Property

Property that has voluntarily been placed somewhere by the owner and then inadvertently forgotten is **mislaid property.** **■EXAMPLE 23.11** Suppose that you go to a movie theater.

CONFUSION
The mixing together of goods belonging to two or more owners so that the separately owned goods cannot be identified.

MISLAID PROPERTY
Property with which the owner has voluntarily parted and then cannot find or recover.

While paying for popcorn at the concession stand, you set your iPod on the counter and then leave it there. The iPod is mislaid property, and the theater owner is entrusted with the duty of reasonable care for it. ■ When mislaid property is found, the finder does not obtain title to the goods. Instead, the owner of the place where the property was mislaid becomes the caretaker of the property because it is highly likely that the true owner will return.[3]

Lost Property

LOST PROPERTY
Property with which the owner has involuntarily parted and then cannot find or recover.

Property that is involuntarily left and forgotten is **lost property.** A finder of the property can claim title to the property against the whole world *except the true owner.*[4] If the true owner demands that the lost property be returned, the finder must return it. If a third party attempts to take possession of lost property from a finder, the third party cannot assert a better title than the finder. The law that finders of lost property may obtain good title to the property has a long history, as discussed in this chapter's *Landmark in the Law* feature on pages 708 and 709.

■EXAMPLE 23.12 Khalia works in a large library at night. As she crosses the courtyard on her way home, she finds a piece of gold jewelry set with stones that look like precious stones to her. She takes it to a jeweler to have it appraised. While pretending to weigh the jewelry, the jeweler's employee removes several of the stones. If Khalia brings an action to recover the stones from the jeweler, she normally will win because she found lost property and holds valid title against everyone *except the true owner.* Because the property was lost, rather than mislaid, the finder is the caretaker of the jewelry, and the finder acquires title good against the whole world (except the true owner). ■

Conversion of Lost Property   When a finder knows who the true owner of the property is and fails to return it to that person, the finder is guilty of the tort of *conversion* (the wrongful taking of another's property—see Chapter 4). Many states require the finder to make a reasonably diligent search to locate the true owner of lost property.

ESTRAY STATUTE
A statute defining finders' rights in property when the true owners are unknown.

Estray Statutes   Many states have **estray statutes,** which encourage and facilitate the return of property to its true owner and then reward the finder for honesty if the property remains unclaimed. These laws provide an incentive for finders to report their discoveries by making it possible for them, after the passage of a specified period of time, to acquire legal title to the property they have found. Such statutes usually require the county clerk to advertise the property in an attempt to help the owner recover what has been lost. Generally, the item must be lost property, not merely mislaid property, for estray statutes to apply.

Abandoned Property

ABANDONED PROPERTY
Property with which the owner has voluntarily parted, with no intention of recovering it.

Property that has been discarded by the true owner, with no intention of reclaiming title to it, is **abandoned property.** Someone who finds abandoned property acquires title to it, and such title is good against the whole world, *including the original owner.* The owner of lost property who eventually gives up any further attempt to find it is frequently held to have abandoned the property. If a person finds abandoned property while trespassing on the property of another, title vests in the owner of the land, not in the finder.

ON THE WEB

Some states and government agencies now post online a list of unclaimed property. For an example of the various types of property that may go unclaimed, go to the following Web page, which is part of the state of Delaware's Web site:

revenue.delaware.gov/information/ Escheat.shtml.

---

3. The finder of mislaid property is an involuntary bailee (to be discussed later in this chapter).
4. See *Armory v. Delamirie*, discussed in this chapter's *Landmark in the Law* feature on pages 708 and 709.

■**EXAMPLE 23.13** Aleka is driving with the windows down in her car. Somewhere along her route, a valuable scarf blows out the window. She retraces her route and searches for the scarf but cannot find it. She finally gives up her search and proceeds to her destination five hundred miles away. Six months later, Frye, a hitchhiker, finds the scarf. Frye has acquired title, which is good even against Aleka. By completely giving up her search, Aleka abandoned the scarf just as effectively as if she had intentionally discarded it. ■

BAILMENTS

A **bailment** is formed by the delivery of personal property, without transfer of title, by one person, called a **bailor,** to another, called a **bailee,** usually under an agreement for a particular purpose—for example, to loan, lease, store, repair, or transport the property. On completion of the purpose, the bailee is obligated to return the bailed property in the same or better condition to the bailor or a third person or to dispose of it as directed.

Bailments are usually created by agreement, but not necessarily by contract, because in many bailments not all of the elements of a contract (such as mutual assent and consideration) are present. ■**EXAMPLE 23.14** If you lend your bicycle to a friend, a bailment is created, but not by contract, because there is no consideration. Many commercial bailments, such as the delivery of clothing to the cleaners for dry cleaning, are based on contract, though. ■

Businesspersons need to be aware that the law of bailments applies to many routine personal and business transactions. Indeed, a vast number of bailments are created daily in the business community. When dealing with bailments, whether you realize it or not, you are subject to the obligations and duties that arise from the bailment relationship. Consequently, every person should understand the elements necessary for the creation of a bailment. Knowing how bailment relationships are created, and what rights, duties, and liabilities flow from ordinary bailments, is critical in avoiding legal disputes. Also important is understanding that bailees can limit the dollar amount of their liability by contract.

Elements of a Bailment

Not all transactions involving the delivery of property from one person to another create a bailment. For such a transfer to become a bailment, the following three elements must be present:

1 Personal property.

2 Delivery of possession (without title).

3 Agreement that the property will be returned to the bailor or otherwise disposed of according to its owner's directions.

Personal Property Requirement Only personal property is bailable; there can be no bailment of persons. Although a bailment of your luggage is created when it is transported by an airline, as a passenger you are not the subject of a bailment. Additionally, you cannot bail realty; thus, leasing your house to a tenant does not create a bailment. Although bailments commonly involve *tangible* items—such as jewelry, cattle, or vehicles—*intangible* personal property, such as promissory notes or shares of corporate stock, may also be bailed.

A man found the Super Bowl ring of a Chicago Bears football player in a couch that the player had once owned. Is the ring mislaid, lost, or abandoned property? Did the finder acquire valid title to the ring? Why or why not? What, if anything, might the finder be required to do?
(AP Photo/Kevin Howell)

PREVENTING LEGAL DISPUTES

BAILMENT
A situation in which the personal property of one person (a bailor) is entrusted to another (a bailee), who is obligated to return the bailed property to the bailor or dispose of it as directed.

BAILOR
One who entrusts goods to a bailee.

BAILEE
One to whom goods are entrusted by a bailor.

ON THE WEB

For a discussion of the origins of the term *bailment* and how bailment relationships have been defined, go to

www.lectlaw.com/def/b005.htm.

LANDMARK IN THE LAW — The Law of Finders

The well-known children's adage "Finders keepers, losers weepers," is actually written into law—provided that the loser (the rightful owner) cannot be found. A finder of lost personal property may acquire good title to the property *against everyone except the true owner*. A number of landmark cases have made this principle clear. An early English case, *Armory v. Delamirie*,[a] is considered a landmark in Anglo-American jurisprudence concerning finders' rights in property.

Finders' Rights   The plaintiff in the case was Armory, a chimney sweep who found a jewel in its setting during the course of his work. He took the jewel to a goldsmith to have it appraised. The goldsmith refused to return the jewel to Armory, claiming that Armory was not the rightful owner of the property. Because the true owner of the jewel had not come forward to claim it, the court held that the finder, as prior possessor of the item, had rights to the jewel superior to those of all others except the rightful owner. The court stated, "The finder of a jewel, though he does not by such finding acquire an absolute property or ownership, yet . . . has such a property as will enable him to keep it against all but the rightful owner."

Who Has Rights to Wrongfully Obtained Goods?   A curious situation arises when goods wrongfully obtained by one person are in turn wrongfully obtained by another, and the two parties contest each other's rights to possession. In such a situation, does the *Armory* rule still apply—that is, does the first (illegal) possessor have more rights in the property than the second (illegal) possessor? In a case that came before the Minnesota Supreme Court in 1892, *Anderson v. Gouldberg*,[b] the court said yes.

a. 93 Eng.Rep. 664 (K.B. [King's Bench] 1722).
b. 51 Minn. 294, 53 N.W. 636 (1892).

Delivery of Possession   *Delivery of possession* means the transfer of possession of the property to the bailee. For delivery to occur, the bailee must be given exclusive possession and control over the property, and the bailee must *knowingly* accept the personal property.[5] In other words, the bailee must *intend* to exercise control over it.

If either delivery of possession or knowing acceptance is lacking, there is no bailment relationship. **■EXAMPLE 23.15** Kim takes a friend out to dinner at an expensive restaurant. When they enter the restaurant, Kim's friend checks her coat. In the pocket of the coat is a $20,000 diamond necklace. The bailee, by accepting the coat, does not knowingly also accept the necklace. Thus, a bailment of the coat exists—because the restaurant has exclusive possession and control over the coat and knowingly accepted it—but not a bailment of the necklace. ■

Physical versus Constructive Delivery.   Either *physical* or *constructive* delivery will result in the bailee's exclusive possession of and control over the property. As discussed earlier in the context of gifts, constructive delivery is a substitute, or symbolic, delivery.

---

5. We are dealing here with *voluntary bailments*. This does not apply to *involuntary bailments*.

In the *Anderson* case, the plaintiffs trespassed on another's land, wrongfully cut timber, and hauled the logs to a mill. The defendants later stole the logs from the mill site, allegedly in the name of the owner of the property on which the timber had been cut. The evidence at trial indicated that both parties had illegally acquired the property. The court instructed the jury that even if the plaintiffs were trespassers when they cut the logs, they were entitled to recover them from later possessors—except the true owner or an agent of the true owner. The jury found for the plaintiffs, a decision affirmed later by the Minnesota Supreme Court.

Thus, even persons who wrongfully obtain property can bring an action to repossess the property from another who takes it from them. More than a century after the *Anderson* decision, another court noted that it is a "well-settled common law rule that a thief in possession of stolen goods has an ownership interest superior to the world at large, save one with a better claim to the property."[c]

APPLICATION TO TODAY'S WORLD *Although the* Armory *case was decided nearly three hundred years ago, the principle enunciated by the court in that case remains applicable today. Finders of lost property continue to acquire good title to the property against all but the true owner.*

RELEVANT WEB SITES *To locate information on the Web concerning the* Armory *decision, go to this text's Web site at* **academic.cengage.com/blaw/blt***, select "Chapter 23," and click on "URLs for Landmarks."*

---

c. *People v. Wilson,* 93 N.Y.2d 222, 689 N.Y.S.2d 419 (1999). See also *Payne v. TK Auto Wholesalers,* 98 Conn.App. 533, 911 A.2d 747 (2006). Note, however, that today when the police catch a thief with stolen goods, the police can confiscate the property.

◼

BE AWARE A finder who appropriates the personal property of another, knowing who the true owner is, can be guilty of *conversion*—see Chapter 4.

What is delivered to the bailee is not the actual property bailed (such as a car) but something so related to the property (such as the car keys) that the requirement of delivery is satisfied.

Involuntary Bailments. In certain situations, a bailment is found despite the apparent lack of the requisite elements of control and knowledge. One example of such a situation occurs when the bailee acquires the property accidentally or by mistake—as in finding someone else's lost or mislaid property. A bailment is created even though the bailor did not voluntarily deliver the property to the bailee. Such bailments are called *constructive* or *involuntary* bailments.

◼**EXAMPLE 23.16** Several corporate managers are asked to attend an urgent meeting at the law firm of Jacobs & Matheson. One of the corporate officers, Kyle Gustafson, inadvertently leaves his briefcase at the firm at the conclusion of the meeting. In this situation, a court could find that an involuntary bailment was created even though Gustafson did not voluntarily deliver the briefcase and the law firm did not intentionally accept it. If an involuntary bailment existed, the firm would be responsible for taking care of the briefcase and returning it to Gustafson. ◼

Bailment Agreement A bailment agreement, or contract, can be express or implied. Although a written agreement is not required for bailments of less than one year (that is, the Statute of Frauds does not apply—see Chapter 8), it is a good idea to have one, especially when valuable property is involved.

The bailment agreement expressly or impliedly provides for the return of the bailed property to the bailor or to a third person, or for disposal of the property by the bailee. The agreement presupposes that the bailee will return the identical goods originally given by the bailor. In certain types of bailments, though, such as bailments of fungible goods, the property returned need only be equivalent property.

EXAMPLE 23.17 If Holman stores his grain (fungible goods) in Joe's Warehouse, a bailment is created. At the end of the storage period, however, the warehouse is not obligated to return to Holman exactly the same grain that he stored. As long as the warehouse returns grain of the same *type, grade,* and *quantity,* the warehouse—the bailee—has performed its obligation. ■

Ordinary Bailments

Bailments are either *ordinary* or *special (extraordinary).* There are three types of ordinary bailments. They are distinguished according to *which party receives a benefit from the bailment.* This factor will dictate the rights and liabilities of the parties, and the courts may use it to determine the standard of care required of the bailee in possession of the personal property. The three types of ordinary bailments are as follows:

1 *Bailment for the sole benefit of the bailor.* This is a gratuitous bailment (a bailment without consideration) for the convenience and benefit of the bailor. **EXAMPLE 23.18** Allen asks his friend, Sumi, to store his car in her garage while he is away. If Sumi agrees to do so, then it is a gratuitous bailment because the bailment of the car is for the sole benefit of the bailor (Allen). ■

2 *Bailment for the sole benefit of the bailee.* This type of bailment typically occurs when one person lends an item to another person (the bailee) solely for the bailee's convenience and benefit. **EXAMPLE 23.19** Allen asks to borrow Sumi's boat so that he can go sailing over the weekend. The bailment of the boat is for Allen's (the bailee's) sole benefit. ■

3 *Bailment for the mutual benefit of the bailee and the bailor.* This is the most common kind of bailment and involves some form of compensation for storing items or holding property while it is being serviced. It is a contractual bailment and may be referred to as a *bailment for hire* or a *commercial bailment.* **EXAMPLE 23.20** Allen leaves his car at a service station for an oil change. Because the service station will be paid to change Allen's oil, this is a mutual-benefit bailment. ■ Many lease arrangements in which the lease involves goods (leases were discussed in Chapters 11 through 13) also fall into this category of bailment once the lessee takes possession.

Rights of the Bailee Certain rights are implicit in the bailment agreement. Generally, the bailee has the right to take possession, to utilize the property for accomplishing the purpose of the bailment, to receive some form of compensation, and to limit her or his liability for the bailed goods. These rights of the bailee are present (with some limitations) in varying degrees in all bailment transactions.

Right of Possession. A hallmark of the bailment agreement is that the bailee acquires the *right to control and possess the property temporarily.* The bailee's right of possession permits the bailee to recover damages from any third person for damage or loss of the property. If the property is stolen, the bailee has a legal right to regain possession of it or to obtain damages from any third person who has wrongfully interfered with the bailee's possessory rights. The bailee's right to regain possession of the property or to obtain damages is important because, as you will read shortly, a bailee is liable to the bailor for any loss or damage to bailed property resulting from the bailee's negligence.

Right to Use Bailed Property. Depending on the type of bailment and the terms of the bailment agreement, a bailee may also have a right to use the bailed property. When no provision is made, the extent of use depends on how necessary it is for the goods to be at the bailee's disposal for the ordinary purpose of the bailment to be carried out. ■**EXAMPLE 23.21** If you borrow a friend's car to drive to the airport, you, as the bailee, would obviously be expected to use the car. In a bailment involving the long-term storage of a car, however, the bailee is not expected to use the car because the ordinary purpose of a storage bailment does not include use of the property. ▣

Right of Compensation. Except in a gratuitous bailment, a bailee has a right to be compensated as provided for in the bailment agreement, to be reimbursed for costs and services rendered in the keeping of the bailed property, or both. Even in a gratuitous bailment, a bailee has a right to be reimbursed or compensated for costs incurred in the keeping of the bailed property. ■**EXAMPLE 23.22** Margo loses her pet dog, and Justine finds it. Justine takes Margo's dog to her home and feeds it. Even though she takes good care of the dog, it becomes ill, and she takes it to a veterinarian. Justine pays the bill for the veterinarian's services and the medicine. Justine normally will be entitled to be reimbursed by Margo for all reasonable costs incurred in the keeping of Margo's dog. ▣

To enforce the right of compensation, the bailee has a right to place a *possessory lien* (which entitles a creditor to retain possession of the debtor's goods until a debt is paid) on the specific bailed property until he or she has been fully compensated. This type of lien, sometimes referred to as an *artisan's lien* or a *bailee's lien*, was discussed in Chapter 16.

Right to Limit Liability. In ordinary bailments, bailees have the right to limit their liability as long as the limitations are called to the attention of the bailor and are not against public policy. It is essential that the bailor be informed of the limitation in some way. Even when the bailor knows of the limitation, certain types of disclaimers of liability have been considered to be against public policy and therefore illegal. The courts carefully scrutinize *exculpatory clauses*, or clauses that limit a person's liability for her or his own wrongful acts, and in bailments they are often held to be illegal. This is particularly true in bailments for the mutual benefit of the bailor and the bailee. ■**EXAMPLE 23.23** A receipt from a parking garage expressly disclaims liability for any damage to parked cars, regardless of the cause. Because the bailee has attempted to exclude liability for the bailee's own negligence, including the parking attendant's negligence, the clause will likely be deemed unenforceable because it is against public policy. ▣

Duties of the Bailee The bailee has two basic responsibilities: (1) to take appropriate care of the property and (2) to surrender the property to the bailor or dispose of it in accordance with the bailor's instructions at the end of the bailment.

The Duty of Care. The bailee must exercise reasonable care in preserving the bailed property. What constitutes reasonable care in a bailment situation normally depends on the nature and specific circumstances of the bailment. Traditionally, the courts have determined the appropriate standard of care on the basis of the type of bailment involved. In a bailment for the sole benefit of the bailor, for example, the bailee need exercise only a slight degree of care. In a bailment for the sole benefit of the bailee, however, the bailee must exercise great care. In a mutual-benefit bailment, courts normally impose a reasonable standard of care—that is, the bailee must exercise the degree of care that a reasonable and prudent person would exercise in the same circumstances. Exhibit 23–1 illustrates these concepts. A bailee's failure to exercise appropriate care in handling the bailor's property results in tort liability.

Duty to Return Bailed Property. At the end of the bailment, the bailee normally must hand over the original property to either the bailor or someone the bailor designates or must otherwise dispose of it as directed. This is usually a *contractual* duty arising from the bailment agreement (contract). Failure to give up possession at the time the bailment ends is a breach of contract and could result in the tort of conversion or an action based on bailee negligence. If the bailed property has been lost or is returned damaged, a court will presume that the bailee was negligent. The bailee's obligation is excused, however, if the goods or chattels were destroyed, lost, or stolen through no fault of the bailee (or claimed by a third party with a superior claim).

Because the bailee has a duty to return the bailed goods to the bailor, a bailee may be liable if the goods being held or delivered are given to the wrong person. Hence, a bailee must be satisfied that a person (other than the bailor) to whom the goods are being delivered is the actual owner or has authority from the owner to take possession of the goods. Should the bailee deliver in error, then the bailee may be liable for conversion or misdelivery.

Duties of the Bailor It goes without saying that the duties of a bailor are essentially the same as the rights of a bailee. Obviously, a bailor has a duty to compensate the bailee either as agreed or as reimbursement for costs incurred by the bailee in keeping the bailed property. A bailor also has an all-encompassing duty to provide the bailee with goods or chattels that are free from known defects that could cause injury to the bailee.

Bailor's Duty to Reveal Defects. The bailor's duty to reveal defects to the bailee translates into two rules:

1 In a *mutual-benefit bailment*, the bailor must notify the bailee of all known defects and any hidden defects that the bailor knows of or could have discovered with reasonable diligence and proper inspection.

2 In a *bailment for the sole benefit of the bailee*, the bailor must notify the bailee of any known defects.

The bailor's duty to reveal defects is based on a negligence theory of tort law. A bailor who fails to give the appropriate notice is liable to the bailee and to any other person who might reasonably be expected to come into contact with the defective article.

■**EXAMPLE 23.24** Rentco (the bailor) rents a tractor to Hal Iverson. Unknown to Rentco (but *discoverable* by reasonable inspection), the brake mechanism on the tractor is defective at the time the bailment is made. Iverson uses the defective tractor without knowledge of the brake problem and is injured along with two other field workers when the tractor rolls out of control. Because this is a mutual-benefit bailment, Rentco has a *duty* to notify Iverson of the discoverable brake defect. Rentco's failure to fulfill this duty is the *proximate cause* (discussed in Chapter 4) of injuries to farm workers who might be

EXHIBIT 23–1 Degree of Care Required of a Bailee		
Bailment for the Sole Benefit of the Bailor	Mutual-Benefit Bailment	Bailment for the Sole Benefit of the Bailee
DEGREE OF CARE →		
SLIGHT	REASONABLE	GREAT

expected to use, or have contact with, the tractor. Therefore, Rentco is liable under a negligence theory for the injuries sustained by Iverson and the two others. ■

Warranty Liability for Defective Goods. A bailor can also incur *warranty liability* based on contract law (see Chapter 13) for injuries resulting from the bailment of defective articles. Property leased by a bailor must be *fit for the intended purpose of the bailment.* Warranties of fitness arise by law in sales contracts and leases, and judges have extended these warranties to situations in which the bailees are compensated for the bailment (such as when one leaves a car with a parking attendant). Article 2A of the Uniform Commercial Code (UCC) extends the implied warranties of merchantability and fitness for a particular purpose to bailments whenever the bailments include rights to use the bailed goods.[6]

Special Types of Bailments

Up to this point, our discussion of bailments has been concerned with ordinary bailments—bailments in which bailees are expected to exercise ordinary care in the handling of bailed property. Some bailment transactions warrant special consideration. These include bailments in which the bailee's duty of care is *extraordinary*—that is, the bailee's liability for loss or damage to the property is absolute—as is generally true in bailments involving common carriers and innkeepers. Warehouse companies have the same duty of care as ordinary bailees, but, like carriers, they are subject to extensive regulation under federal and state laws, including Article 7 of the UCC.

Common Carriers *Common carriers* are publicly licensed to provide transportation services to the general public. They are distinguished from private carriers, which operate transportation facilities for a select clientele. A private carrier is not required to provide service to every person or company making a request. A common carrier, however, must arrange carriage for all who apply, within certain limitations.[7]

The delivery of goods to a common carrier creates a bailment relationship between the shipper (bailor) and the common carrier (bailee). Unlike ordinary bailees, the common carrier is held to a standard of care based on *strict liability*, rather than reasonable care, in protecting the bailed personal property. This means that the common carrier is absolutely liable, regardless of due care, for all loss or damage to goods except damage caused by one of the following common law exceptions: (1) an act of God, (2) an act of a public enemy, (3) an order of a public authority, (4) an act of the shipper, or (5) the inherent nature of the goods.

Common carriers cannot contract away their liability for damaged goods. Subject to government regulations, however, they are permitted to limit their dollar liability to an amount stated on the shipment contract or rate filing.[8] This point is illustrated in the following case.

---

6. UCC 2A–212, 2A–213.

7. A common carrier is not required to take any and all property anywhere in all instances. Public regulatory agencies govern common carriers, and carriers can be restricted to geographic areas. They can also be limited to carrying certain kinds of goods or to providing only special types of transportation equipment.

8. Federal laws require common carriers to offer shippers the opportunity to obtain higher dollar limits for loss by paying a higher fee for the transport.

CASE 23.2 **Treiber & Straub, Inc. v. United Parcel Service, Inc.**

United States Court of Appeals, Seventh Circuit, 474 F.3d 379 (2007).

FACTS Michael Straub is the president of Treiber & Straub, Inc., a fine-jewelry store in Wisconsin. To return a diamond ring to Norman Silverman Company, a wholesaler in California,

CASE 23.2–Continues next page

CASE 23.2—Continued

Straub chose United Parcel Service, Inc. (UPS), and, through www.ups.com, arranged to ship the ring via "Next Day Air." To ship a package using the Web site, a customer has to click on two on-screen boxes to agree to "My UPS Terms and Conditions." Among these terms, UPS and its insurer, UPS Capital Insurance Agency, Inc., limit their liability and the amount of insurance coverage on packages to $50,000. UPS refuses to ship items of "unusual value"—those worth more than $50,000—and the carrier and its insurer disclaim liability *entirely* for such items. The ring was worth $105,000. Undeterred, Straub opted for the maximum coverage and indicated on the air bill that the value was "$50,000 or less." UPS lost the ring. Treiber & Straub reimbursed the wholesaler for the full loss and filed a suit in a federal district court against UPS and its insurer to recover $50,000 under the insurance policy. The court issued a summary judgment in the defendants' favor based on the disclaimer. The plaintiff appealed to the U.S. Court of Appeals for the Seventh Circuit, arguing, among other things, that the disclaimer was "literally buried among all the other extensive terms and conditions on the vast UPS Web site."

ISSUE Was the carrier's disclaimer enforceable?

DECISION Yes. The U.S. Court of Appeals for the Seventh Circuit affirmed the judgment of the lower court. The appellate court held that the carrier's disclaimer was prominent enough.

REASON The court examined the relevant pages on the UPS Web site. On those pages, UPS initially limits its liability to $100 but offers customers an opportunity to buy insurance for coverage up to $50,000. If a customer wants to ship a package with a value of more than $50,000, UPS refuses to accept it or to insure it. UPS does not explain all of the details about these limits on a single page, but the court ruled that this "does not call for a different result in light of everything else that was available to the shipper." The limitation and the disclaimer are repeated several times on the Web site. This ensures "clear and reasonable notice" of the terms, to which a customer has to click twice in agreement to arrange a shipment. Further, the court reasoned that if UPS accepted packages with values greater than $50,000 but insured them for no more than that amount, "it would distort the mix of claims it is insuring, skewing it toward the high-value end, necessitating a significant change in premiums. The risk of theft would also increase for packages with higher declared values." The court also pointed out that in this case, "by indicating on the air bill the insured value (of $50,000 or less) rather than the actual value" of the ring, "Treiber [& Straub] effectively breached the shipping contract."

WHAT IF THE FACTS WERE DIFFERENT? *If Straub had claimed that he had not read the terms, would the result in this case have been different? Why or why not?*

ON THE WEB

You will find a hypertext version of Article 7 of the Uniform Commercial Code, which pertains to warehouse receipts, bills of lading, and other documents of title, at Cornell Law School's Legal Information Institute. Go to www.law.cornell.edu/ucc/7/overview.html.

Warehouse Companies *Warehousing* is the business of providing storage of property for compensation.[9] Like ordinary bailees, warehouse companies are liable for loss or damage to property resulting from *negligence*. A warehouse company, however, is a professional bailee and is therefore expected to exercise a high degree of care to protect and preserve the goods. A warehouse company can limit the dollar amount of its liability, but the bailor must be given the option of paying an increased storage rate for an increase in the liability limit.

Unlike ordinary bailees, a warehouse company can issue *documents of title*—in particular, *warehouse receipts*—and is subject to extensive government regulation, including Article 7 of the UCC.[10] A warehouse receipt describes the bailed property and the terms of the bailment contract. It can be negotiable or nonnegotiable, depending on how it is written. It is negotiable if its terms provide that the warehouse company will deliver the goods "to the bearer" of the receipt or "to the order of" a person named on the receipt.[11] The warehouse receipt represents the goods (that is, it indicates title) and hence has value and utility in financing commercial transactions.

EXAMPLE 23.25 Ossip delivers 6,500 cases of canned corn to Chaney, the owner of a warehouse. Chaney issues a negotiable warehouse receipt payable "to bearer" and gives it

---

9. UCC 7–102(h) defines the person engaged in the storing of goods for hire as a "warehouseman."
10. A *document of title* is defined in UCC 1–201(15) as any "document which in the regular course of business or financing is treated as adequately evidencing that the person in possession of it is entitled to receive, hold, and dispose of the document and the goods it covers." A *warehouse receipt* is a document of title issued by a person engaged in the business of storing goods for hire.
11. UCC 7–104.

to Ossip. Ossip sells and delivers the warehouse receipt to Better Foods, Inc. Better Foods is now the owner of the corn and has the right to obtain the cases by simply presenting the warehouse receipt to Chaney. ◼

Innkeepers At common law, innkeepers and hotel owners were strictly liable for the loss of any cash or property that guests brought into their rooms. Today, only those who provide lodging to the public for compensation as a *regular* business are covered under this rule of strict liability. Moreover, the rule applies only to those who are guests, as opposed to lodgers, who are persons that permanently reside at the hotel or inn.

In many states, innkeepers can avoid strict liability for loss of guests' cash and valuables by (1) providing a safe in which to keep them and (2) notifying guests that a safe is available. In addition, statutes often limit the liability of innkeepers with regard to articles that are not kept in the safe and may limit the availability of damages in the absence of innkeeper negligence. Most statutes require that the innkeeper post these limitations or otherwise notify the guest. Such postings, or notices, are frequently found on the doors of the rooms in motels and hotels.

◼**EXAMPLE 23.26** Joyce stays for a night at the Harbor Hotel. When she returns from eating breakfast in the hotel restaurant, she discovers that her suitcase has been stolen and sees that the lock on the door between her room and the room next door is broken. Joyce claims that the hotel is liable for her loss. Because the hotel was not negligent, however, normally it is not liable under state law. ◼

INSURANCE

Many precautions may be taken to protect against the hazards of life. For instance, an individual may wear a seat belt to protect against injuries from automobile accidents or install smoke detectors to guard against injury from fire. Of course, no one can predict whether an accident or a fire will ever occur, but individuals and businesses must establish plans to protect their personal and financial interests should some event threaten to undermine their security.

Insurance is a contract by which the insurance company (the insurer) promises to pay a sum of money or give something of value to another (either the insured or the beneficiary) in the event that the insured is injured, dies, or sustains damage to her or his property as a result of particular, stated contingencies. Basically, insurance is an arrangement for *transferring and allocating risk*. In many instances, **risk** can be described as a prediction concerning potential loss based on known and unknown factors. Insurance, however, involves much more than a game of chance.

Risk management normally involves the transfer of certain risks from the individual to the insurance company by a contractual agreement. The insurance contract and its provisions will be examined shortly. First, however, we look at the different types of insurance that can be obtained, insurance terminology, and the concept of insurable interest.

Classifications of Insurance

Insurance is classified according to the nature of the risk involved. For instance, fire insurance, casualty insurance, life insurance, and title insurance apply to different types of risk. Furthermore, policies of these types protect different persons and interests. This is reasonable because the types of losses that are expected and that are foreseeable or unforeseeable vary with the nature of the activity. Exhibit 23–2 on pages 716 and 717 presents a list of insurance classifications. (For a discussion of insurance policies designed to cover the special kinds of risks faced by online businesses, see the *Application* feature at the end of this chapter.)

INSURANCE
A contract in which, for a stipulated consideration, one party agrees to compensate the other for loss on a specific subject by a specified peril.

RISK
A prediction concerning potential loss based on known and unknown factors.

RISK MANAGEMENT
Planning that is undertaken to protect one's interest should some event threaten to undermine its security. In the context of insurance, risk management involves transferring certain risks from the insured to the insurance company.

EXHIBIT 23–2	**Insurance Classifications**
TYPE OF INSURANCE	**COVERAGE**
Accident	Covers expenses, losses, and suffering incurred by the insured because of accidents causing physical injury and any consequent disability; sometimes includes a specified payment to heirs of the insured if death results from an accident.
All-risk	Covers all losses that the insured may incur except those that are specifically excluded. Typical exclusions are war, pollution, earthquakes, and floods.
Automobile	May cover damage to automobiles resulting from specified hazards or occurrences (such as fire, vandalism, theft, or collision); normally provides protection against liability for personal injuries and property damage resulting from the operation of the vehicle.
Casualty	Protects against losses incurred by the insured as a result of being held liable for personal injuries or property damage sustained by others.
Credit	Pays to a creditor the balance of a debt on the disability, death, insolvency, or bankruptcy of the debtor; often offered by lending institutions.
Decreasing-term life	Provides life insurance; requires uniform payments over the life (term) of the policy, but with a decreasing face value (amount of coverage).
Employer's liability	Insures employers against liability for injuries or losses sustained by employees during the course of their employment; covers claims not covered under workers' compensation insurance.
Fidelity or guaranty	Provides indemnity against losses in trade or losses caused by the dishonesty of employees, the insolvency of debtors, or breaches of contract.
Fire	Covers losses incurred by the insured as a result of fire.
Floater	Covers movable property, as long as the property is within the territorial boundaries specified in the contract.
Group	Provides individual life, medical, or disability insurance coverage but is obtainable through a group of persons, usually employees. The policy premium is paid either entirely by the employer or partially by the employer and partially by the employee.

Insurance Terminology

POLICY
In insurance law, a contract between the insurer and the insured in which, for a stipulated consideration, the insurer agrees to compensate the insured for loss on a specific subject by a specified peril.

PREMIUM
In insurance law, the price paid by the insured for insurance protection for a specified period of time.

UNDERWRITER
In insurance law, the insurer, or the one assuming a risk in return for the payment of a premium.

An insurance contract is called a **policy**; the consideration paid to the insurer is called a **premium**; and the insurance company is sometimes called an **underwriter**. The parties to an insurance policy are the *insurer* (the insurance company) and the *insured* (the person covered by its provisions or the holder of the policy).

Insurance contracts are usually obtained through an *agent*, who ordinarily works for the insurance company, or through a *broker*, who is ordinarily an *independent contractor*. When a broker deals with an applicant for insurance, the broker is, in effect, the applicant's agent and not an agent of the insurance company. In contrast, an insurance agent is an agent of the insurance company, not of the applicant. As a general rule, the insurance company is bound by the acts of its insurance agents when they act within the agency relationship (discussed in Chapter 17). In most situations, state law determines the status of all parties writing or obtaining insurance.

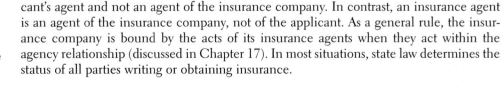

Does an insurance agent have a duty to advise insurance applicants about coverage? When a person applies for insurance coverage through an insurance company's agent, is the agent obligated to advise that person as to what coverage he or she should obtain? If the agent does not advise a client about certain types of coverage, has the agent breached a duty to the applicant? For example, suppose that someone applies for auto insurance, and the insurance agent does not advise him that he should sign up for uninsured motorist coverage. Later, the insured

EXHIBIT 23–2	Insurance Classifications—Continued
TYPE OF INSURANCE	**COVERAGE**
Health	Covers expenses incurred by the insured as a result of physical injury or illness and other expenses relating to health and life maintenance.
Homeowners'	Protects homeowners against some or all risks of loss to their residences and the residences' contents or liability arising from the use of the property.
Key-person	Protects a business in the event of the death or disability of a key employee.
Liability	Protects against liability imposed on the insured as a result of injuries to the person or property of another.
Life	Covers the death of the policyholder. On the death of the insured, the insurer pays the amount specified in the policy to the insured's beneficiary.
Major medical	Protects the insured against major hospital, medical, or surgical expenses.
Malpractice	Protects professionals (physicians, lawyers, and others) against malpractice claims brought against them by their patients or clients; a form of liability insurance.
Marine	Covers movable property (including ships, freight, and cargo) against certain perils or navigation risks during a specific voyage or time period.
Mortgage	Covers a mortgage loan. The insurer pays the balance of the mortgage to the creditor on the death or disability of the debtor.
No-fault auto	Covers personal injuries and (sometimes) property damage resulting from automobile accidents. The insured submits his or her claims to his or her own insurance company, regardless of who was at fault. A person may sue the party at fault or that party's insurer only when an accident results in serious medical injury and consequent high medical costs. Governed by state "no-fault" statutes.
Term life	Provides life insurance for a specified period of time (term) with no cash surrender value; usually renewable.
Title	Protects against any defects in title to real property and any losses incurred as a result of existing claims against or liens on the property at the time of purchase.

is involved in an accident with an uninsured motorist, and the insurance company refuses to compensate him for his injuries and losses. The insured claims that the insurance agent was negligent in not advising him to sign up for uninsured motorist coverage. Was the agent negligent? No. As mentioned earlier, an insurance agent is an agent of the insurer, not the insured. As such, the agent owes fiduciary duties to the insurer (the insurance company), but not to the insured. The agent's only duties to the insured are contractual in nature.

Although some may think that this rule is unfair to insurance applicants, who may know less about the need for certain types of insurance coverage than the agent does, a contrary rule might create even more unfairness. An insurance agent could be held liable for failure to advise a client of every possible insurance option, and the insured would be relieved of any burden to take care of her or his own financial needs and expectations. Also, as one court noted, if the state legislature does not require such coverage, why should the courts require insurance companies to offer or explain available optional coverage?[12]

Insurable Interest

A person can insure anything in which she or he has an **insurable interest**. Without this insurable interest, there is no enforceable contract, and a transaction to purchase insurance coverage would have to be treated as a wager. In regard to real and personal

INSURABLE INTEREST
An interest either in a person's life or well-being or in property that is sufficiently substantial that insuring against injury to (or the death of) the person or against damage to the property does not amount to a mere wagering (betting) contract.

---

12. *Jones v. Kennedy*, 108 S.W.3d 203 (Mo.App. 2003).

property, an insurable interest exists when the insured derives a pecuniary benefit (a benefit consisting of or relating to money) from the preservation and continued existence of the property. Put another way, one has an insurable interest in property when one would sustain a financial loss from its destruction. In regard to life insurance, a person must have a reasonable expectation of benefit from the continued life of another in order to have an insurable interest in that person's life. The benefit may be pecuniary (as with so-called *key-person insurance*, which insures the lives of important employees, usually in small companies), or it may be founded on the relationship between the parties (by blood or affinity).

For property insurance, the insurable interest must exist at the time the loss occurs but need not exist when the policy is purchased. In contrast, for life insurance, the insurable interest must exist at the time the policy is obtained. The existence of an insurable interest is a primary concern in determining liability under an insurance policy. Whether a party had an insurable interest in property was at issue in the following case.

CASE 23.3   **Zurich American Insurance Co. v. ABM Industries, Inc.**

United States Court of Appeals, Second Circuit, 397 F.3d 158 (2005).

FACTS ABM Industries, Inc., is an engineering, lighting, and janitorial service contractor that, in 2001, occupied office and storage space in the World Trade Center (WTC) in New York City. This space included a call center to which WTC tenants reported problems. ABM operated the heating, ventilating, and air-conditioning (HVAC) systems for the WTC, essentially running the physical plant, and serviced the common areas. At the time, ABM employed more than 800 persons at the WTC. Zurich American Insurance Company insured ABM against losses resulting from "business interruption * * * caused by direct physical loss or damage * * * to property owned, controlled, used, leased or intended for use by the Insured." After the terrorist attacks on September 11, 2001, ABM filed a claim with Zurich to recover for the loss of all income derived from ABM's WTC operations. Zurich asked a federal district court for a declaratory judgment on the extent of its liability. The court issued a summary judgment in Zurich's favor, limiting the amount of ABM's recovery to the income it lost from "the destruction of the [WTC] space that ABM itself occupied or caused by the destruction of ABM's own supplies and equipment." ABM appealed to the U.S. Court of Appeals for the Second Circuit.

ISSUE Did ABM have an insurable interest in property at the time of its loss?

DECISION Yes. The U.S. Court of Appeals for the Second Circuit reversed the ruling of the lower court and issued a summary judgment in ABM's favor.

REASON The appellate court stated, "The only prerequisite to coverage mandated by New York law is that an entity have an insurable interest in the property it insures." The court pointed out that under the applicable New York state statute, this term includes "any lawful and substantial economic interest in the safety or preservation of property from loss, destruction or pecuniary damage." The court emphasized that in this case, the insurance "policy's scope expressly includes real or personal property that the insured 'used,' 'controlled,' or 'intended for use.'" Because ABM's income depends on "the common areas and leased premises in the WTC complex, * * * ABM meets New York's requirement of having an insurable interest in that property."

WHAT IF THE FACTS WERE DIFFERENT? *Suppose that before September 11, ABM had transferred its operations at the WTC to another firm. Additionally, assume that it had sold its supplies and equipment to that firm but, as of September 11, ABM had not notified Zurich to cancel its insurance. Would the result have been different? Why or why not?*

The Insurance Contract

An insurance contract is governed by the general principles of contract law, although the insurance industry is heavily regulated by each state. Several aspects of the insurance contract will be treated here, including the application for insurance, the date when the contract takes effect, and some of the important provisions typically found in insurance contracts. In addition, we will also discuss the cancellation of an insurance policy and defenses that insurance companies can raise against payment on a policy.

These steel columns will support the Freedom Towers that will replace the World Trade Center towers that were destroyed in the terrorist attacks on September 11, 2001. Congress passed legislation guaranteeing federal government financial assistance for insurance companies should there be terrorist attacks in the future. (AP Photo/Mark Lennihan)

Application   The filled-in application form for insurance is usually attached to the policy and made a part of the insurance contract. Thus, an insurance applicant is bound by any false statements that appear in the application (subject to certain exceptions). Because the insurance company evaluates the risk factors based on the information included in the insurance application, misstatements or misrepresentations can void a policy, especially if the insurance company can show that it would not have extended insurance if it had known the true facts.

Effective Date   The effective date of an insurance contract—that is, the date on which the insurance coverage begins—is important. In some instances, the insurance applicant is not protected until a formal written policy is issued. In other situations, the applicant is protected between the time the application is received and the time the insurance company either accepts or rejects it. Four facts should be kept in mind:

1 A broker is merely the agent of an applicant. Therefore, until the broker obtains a policy, the applicant normally is not insured.

2 A person who seeks insurance from an insurance company's agent will usually be protected from the moment the application is made, provided that some form of premium has been paid. Between the time the application is received and either rejected or accepted, the applicant is covered (possibly subject to passing a physical examination). Usually, the agent will write a memorandum, or **binder,** indicating that a policy is pending and stating its essential terms.

3 If the parties agree that the policy will be issued and delivered at a later time, the contract is not effective until the policy is issued and delivered or sent to the applicant, depending on the agreement. Thus, any loss sustained between the time of application and the delivery of the policy is not covered.

4 The parties may agree that a life insurance policy will be binding at the time the insured pays the first premium, or the policy may be expressly contingent on the applicant's passing a physical examination. If the applicant pays the premium and passes the examination, the policy coverage is continuously in effect. If the applicant pays the premium but dies before having the physical examination, then in order to collect, the applicant's estate must show that the applicant *would have passed* the examination had he or she not died.

NOTE The federal government has the power to regulate the insurance industry under the commerce clause of the U.S. Constitution. Instead of exercising this power itself, Congress allows the states to regulate insurance.

BINDER
A written, temporary insurance policy.

Coinsurance Clauses   Often, when taking out fire insurance policies, property owners insure their property for less than full value because most fires do not result in a total loss. To encourage owners to insure their property for an amount as close to full value as possible, fire insurance policies commonly include a coinsurance clause. Typically, a *coinsurance clause* provides that if the owner insures the property up to a specified percentage—usually

80 percent—of its value, she or he will recover any loss up to the face amount of the policy. If the insurance is for less than the fixed percentage, the owner is responsible for a proportionate share of the loss.

Coinsurance applies only in instances of partial loss. ▪**EXAMPLE 23.27** If the owner of property valued at $100,000 takes out a policy in the amount of $40,000 and suffers a loss of $30,000, the recovery will be $15,000. The formula for calculating the recovery amount is as follows:

$$\frac{\text{amount of insurance (\$40,000)}}{\text{coinsurance percentage (80\%)} \times \text{property value (\$100,000)}} = \frac{\text{recovery percentage}}{(50\%)}$$

recovery percentage (50%) × amount of loss ($30,000) = recovery amount ($15,000)

If the owner had taken out a policy in the amount of $80,000, then, according to the same formula, the full loss would have been recovered up to the face value of the policy. ▪

Other Provisions and Clauses   Some other important provisions and clauses contained in insurance contracts are listed and defined in Exhibit 23–3. The courts are aware that most people do not have the special training necessary to understand the intricate terminology used in insurance policies. Thus, the words used in an insurance contract have their ordinary meanings. They are interpreted by the courts in light of the nature of the coverage involved—see, for example, this chapter's *Adapting the Law to the Online Environment* feature on page 722.

When there is an ambiguity in the policy, the provision generally is interpreted against the insurance company. Also, when it is unclear whether an insurance contract actually exists because the written policy has not been delivered, the uncertainty normally is resolved against the insurance company. The court presumes that the policy is in effect unless the company can show otherwise. Similarly, an insurer must make sure that the insured is adequately notified of any change in coverage under an existing policy.

Cancellation   The insured can cancel a policy at any time, and the insurer can cancel under certain circumstances. When an insurance company can cancel its insurance contract, the policy or a state statute usually requires that the insurer give advance written notice

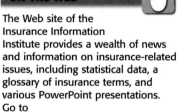

ON THE WEB

The Web site of the Insurance Information Institute provides a wealth of news and information on insurance-related issues, including statistical data, a glossary of insurance terms, and various PowerPoint presentations. Go to

www.iii.org.

EXHIBIT 23–3   **Insurance Contract Provisions and Clauses**

Antilapse clause	An antilapse clause provides that the policy will not automatically lapse if no payment is made on the date due. Ordinarily, under such a provision, the insured has a *grace period* of thirty or thirty-one days within which to pay an overdue premium before the policy is canceled.
Appraisal clause	Insurance policies frequently provide that if the parties cannot agree on the amount of a loss covered under the policy or the value of the property lost, an appraisal, or estimate, by an impartial and qualified third party can be demanded.
Arbitration clause	Many insurance policies include clauses that call for arbitration of disputes that may arise between the insurer and the insured concerning the settlement of claims.
Incontestability clause	An incontestability clause provides that after a policy has been in force for a specified length of time—usually two or three years—the insurer cannot contest statements made in the application.
Multiple insurance	Many insurance policies include a clause providing that if the insured has multiple insurance policies that cover the same property and the amount of coverage exceeds the loss, the loss will be shared proportionally by the insurance companies.

of the cancellation to the insured. The same requirement applies when only part of a policy is canceled. Any premium paid in advance may be refundable on the policy's cancellation. The insured may also be entitled to a life insurance policy's cash surrender value.

The insurer may cancel an insurance policy for various reasons, depending on the type of insurance. For example, automobile insurance can be canceled for nonpayment of premiums or suspension of the insured's driver's license. Property insurance can be canceled for nonpayment of premiums or for other reasons, including the insured's fraud or misrepresentation, conviction for a crime that increases the hazard insured against, or gross negligence that increases the risk assumed by the insurer. Life and health policies can be canceled because of false statements made by the insured in the application, but the cancellation must take place before the effective date of an incontestability clause. An insurer cannot cancel— or refuse to renew—a policy for discriminatory reasons or other reasons that violate public policy, or because the insured has appeared as a witness in a case against the company.

Good Faith Obligations   Both parties to an insurance contract are responsible for the obligations they assume under the contract (contract law was discussed in Chapters 7 through 10). In addition, both the insured and the insurer have an implied duty to act in good faith.

Good faith requires the party who is applying for insurance to reveal everything necessary for the insurer to evaluate the risk. In other words, the applicant must disclose all material facts, including all facts that an insurer would consider in determining whether to charge a higher premium or to refuse to issue a policy altogether. Many insurance companies today require that an applicant give the company permission to access other information, such as private medical records and credit ratings, for the purpose of evaluating the risk.

Once the insurer has accepted the risk, and some event occurs that gives rise to a claim, the insurer has a duty to investigate to determine the facts. When a policy provides insurance against third party claims, the insurer is obligated to make reasonable efforts to settle such a claim. If a settlement cannot be reached, then regardless of the claim's merit, the insurer must defend any suit against the insured. Usually, a policy provides that in this situation the insured must cooperate, and sometimes the insured is required to attend hearings and trials.

Bad Faith Actions   Although the law of insurance generally follows contract law, most states now recognize a "bad faith" tort action against insurers. Thus, if an insurer in bad faith denies coverage of a claim, the insured may recover in tort in an amount exceeding the policy's coverage limits and may even recover millions of dollars in punitive damages. Some courts have held insurers liable for bad faith refusals to settle claims for reasonable amounts within the policy limits.[13]

Defenses against Payment   An insurance company can raise any of the defenses that would be valid in an ordinary action on a contract, as well as some defenses that do not apply in ordinary contract actions. If the insurance company can show that the policy was procured by fraud or misrepresentation, it may have a valid defense for not paying on a claim. (The insurance company may also have the right to disaffirm or rescind an insurance contract.) An absolute defense exists if the insurer can show that the insured lacked an insurable interest—thus rendering the policy void from the beginning. Improper actions, such as those that are against public policy or that are otherwise illegal, can also give the insurance company a defense against the payment of a claim or allow it to rescind the contract.

---

13. See, for example, *Columbia National Insurance Co. v. Freeman*, 347 Ark. 423, 64 S.W.3d 720 (2002).

ADAPTING THE LAW TO THE ONLINE ENVIRONMENT — Recovering for the Loss of Computer Data

Over the past decade, hackers have spread numerous viruses that can cause computer systems to fail and stored data to be lost. When a business's computer system comes under attack, often the damage is extensive. Nevertheless, traditional business insurance policies usually do not specifically cover the risks associated with the loss of computer information. Typically, business insurance covers only "physical loss," and a number of courts have held that computer information is not physical.[a] Only in rare circumstances have courts held that general business insurance policies cover the loss of computerized information.

A Computer Virus Caused Significant Damage

In one case, the operating system of an employment agency, Lambrecht & Associates, Inc., was attacked by a computer virus. All of Lambrecht's employees were networked into a large central server that was equipped with certain pre-packaged software programs, such as Microsoft Office and Norton AntiVirus.™ One day when the employees came to work, they discovered the computers were having difficulty booting up and were performing strange operations. Ultimately, the entire system froze up, and all of the information that had previously been stored on the system was deleted. As a result, Lambrecht's employees were unable to use their computers to communicate with prospective employers and employees, and the business lost income. In addition, Lambrecht had to replace its server, buy a new operating system and new software, and manually reenter a large amount of data. When Lambrecht filed a claim with its insurer, State Farm Lloyd's, State Farm denied coverage. Lambrecht filed a suit, but the trial court agreed with the insurer that the loss was not covered. Lambrecht appealed.

The Exact Language of the Insurance Policy

Lambrecht had a business insurance policy that provided coverage for "accidental direct physical loss to business personal property." In addition, Lambrecht had purchased $100,000 of additional coverage for replacement of valuable "papers or records, including those which exist on electronic or magnetic media," provided that the loss is not "caused by an error in programming." State Farm contended that the damage to Lambrecht's computer system was neither "accidental" nor "physical," as the insurance policy required for coverage.

The Meaning of "Accidental" and "Physical" Loss

According to State Farm, the damage was not accidental because the hacker's act of infecting Lambrecht's computer system with a virus was voluntary and intentional. The state appellate court, however, held that the question of whether an occurrence was "accidental" should be determined by looking at the incident from the perspective of the insured. Here, there was no evidence to indicate "that Lambrecht was involved in any voluntary or intentional conduct or took any action which caused the damage Lambrecht suffered." Thus, the court held that the damage was unexpected and accidental.

The court also rejected State Farm's argument that the data loss was not "physical" because data are not tangible (capable of being touched). Although the court recognized that other judges have focused on this distinction, in this case, the plain terms of the policy expressly covered electronic records and storage media. Hence, the court held that the language of the policy dictated a finding that the data losses Lambrecht suffered were "physical" as a matter of law.[b]

 FOR CRITICAL ANALYSIS *If the policy in this case had not expressly mentioned loss of electronic records, would the court have found that the loss was "physical"? Why or why not?*

a. See, for example, *America Online, Inc. v. St. Paul Mercury Insurance Co.,* 207 F.Supp.2d 459 (E.D.Va. 2002).

b. *Lambrecht & Associates, Inc. v. State Farm Lloyd's,* 119 S.W.3d 16 (Tex.App. 2003).

An insurance company can be prevented from asserting some defenses that are normally available, however. **EXAMPLE 23.28** Farmers' Co-op Insurance Company tells an insured, Berta Rydell, that information requested on a form is optional, but she provides it anyway. The company cannot use the information to avoid its contractual obligation under the insurance contract. Similarly, an insurance company normally cannot escape payment on the death of an insured on the ground that the person's age was stated incorrectly on the application. ◼

REVIEWING Personal Property and Bailments

Vanessa Denai owned forty acres of land in rural Louisiana with a 1,600-square-foot house on it and a metal barn near the house. Denai later met Lance Finney, who had been seeking a small plot of rural property to rent. After several meetings, Denai invited Finney to live in a corner of her property in exchange for Finney's assistance in cutting wood and tending her property. Denai agreed to store Finney's sailboat in her barn. With Denai's consent, Finney constructed a concrete and oak foundation on Denai's property and purchased a 190-square-foot dome from Dome Baja for $3,395. The dome was shipped by Doty Express, a transportation company licensed to serve the public. When it arrived, Finney installed the dome frame and fabric exterior so that the dome was detachable from the foundation. A year after Finney installed the dome, Denai wrote Finney a note stating, "I've decided to give you four acres of land surrounding your dome as drawn on this map." This gift violated no local land-use restrictions. Using the information presented in the chapter, answer the following questions.

1 Is the dome real property or personal property? Explain.

2 Is Denai's gift of land to Finney a testamentary gift, a gift *causa mortis,* or a gift *inter vivos?*

3 What type of bailment relationship was created when Denai agreed to store Finney's boat? What degree of care was Denai required to exercise in storing the boat?

4 What standard of care applied to the shipment of the dome by Doty Express?

APPLICATION How Can You Manage Risk in Cyberspace?*

As mentioned elsewhere, companies doing business online face many risks that are not covered by traditional types of insurance (see Exhibit 23–2 on pages 716 and 717). Not surprisingly, a growing number of companies are now offering policies designed to cover Web-related risks.

Insurance Coverage for Web-Related Risks

Insurance to cover Web-related incidents is frequently referred to as *network intrusion insurance.* Such insurance protects companies from losses stemming from hacking and computer viruses; programming errors; network and Web site disruptions; theft of electronic data and assets, including intellectual property; Web-related defamation, copyright infringement, and false advertising; and violations of users' privacy rights.

InsureTrust.com, an insurer affiliated with three leading insurance companies—American International Group, Lloyd's of London, and Reliance National—is a leading provider of cyberinsurance coverage. Other insurers, such as Hartford Insurance and the Chubb Group of Insurance Companies, have also added insurance for Web-related perils to their offerings. Clearly, the market for these types of insurance coverage is rapidly evolving, and new policies will continue to appear.

Customized Policies

Unlike traditional insurance policies, which are generally drafted by insurance companies and presented to insurance applicants on a take-it-or-leave-it basis, cyberinsurance policies are usually customized to provide protection against specific risks faced by a particular type of business. For example, an Internet service provider will face different risks than an online merchant, and a banking institution will face different risks than a law firm. The specific business-related risks are taken into consideration when determining the policy premium.

Qualifying Criteria

Many companies that offer network intrusion insurance require applicants to meet high security standards. In other

---

* This *Application* is not meant to substitute for the services of an attorney who is licensed to practice law in your state.

(Continued)

words, to qualify for a policy under an insurance company's risk management processes, a business must have Web-related security measures in place. Several companies assess the applicant's security system before underwriting a policy. For example, an insurer might assess the applicant's security measures and refuse to provide coverage unless the business scores higher than 60 percent. If the business does not score that high, it can contract with the company to improve its Web-related security.

CHECKLIST FOR THE BUSINESSPERSON

1 Determine the types of risks that your Web business is exposed to and try to obtain an insurance policy that protects you against those specific risks.

2 As when procuring any type of insurance coverage, read the policy carefully, including any exclusions contained in the fine print, before committing to it.
3 Do not be "penny wise and pound foolish" when it comes to insurance protection. Though insurance coverage may seem expensive, it may be much less costly than the loss of intellectual property or the cost of defending against a lawsuit. Opting for a higher deductible can reduce the amount you pay in premiums.
4 Find out what the company's underwriting standards are and determine whether your Web security measures meet its standards.

KEY TERMS

abandoned property 706
accession 704
bailee 707
bailment 707
bailor 707
binder 719
chattel 699
community property 701
concurrent ownership 700
confusion 705
constructive delivery 702

dominion 703
estray statute 706
fee simple 700
gift 702
gift *causa mortis* 704
gift *inter vivos* 704
insurable interest 717
insurance 715
joint tenancy 700
lost property 706
mislaid property 705

personal property 699
policy 716
premium 716
property 699
real property 699
risk 715
risk management 715
tenancy by the entirety 701
tenancy in common 700
underwriter 716

CHAPTER SUMMARY — Personal Property, Bailments, and Insurance

PERSONAL PROPERTY

Definition of Personal Property (See page 699.)	Personal property (personalty) includes all property not classified as real property (realty). Personal property can be tangible (such as a TV set or a car) or intangible (such as stocks or bonds). Personal property may be referred to legally as *chattel*—a term used under the common law to denote all forms of personal property.
Property Ownership (See pages 700–701.)	Having the fullest ownership rights in property is called *fee simple* ownership. There are various ways of co-owning property, including *tenancy in common, joint tenancy, tenancy by the entirety,* and *community property.*
Acquiring Ownership of Personal Property (See pages 701–705.)	The most common means of acquiring ownership in personal property is by purchasing it (see Chapters 11 through 13). Another way in which personal property is often acquired is by will or inheritance. The following are additional methods of acquiring personal property: 1. *Possession*—Ownership may be acquired by possession if no other person has ownership title (for example, capturing wild animals or finding abandoned property).

CHAPTER SUMMARY	Personal Property, Bailments, and Insurance–Continued
Acquiring Ownership of Personal Property– Continued	2. *Production*–Any product or item produced by an individual (with minor exceptions) becomes the property of that individual. 3. *Gift*–An effective gift exists when the following conditions exist: a. There is evidence of *intent* to make a gift of the property in question. b. The gift is *delivered* (physically or constructively) to the donee or the donee's agent. c. The gift is *accepted* by the donee or the donee's agent. 4. *Accession*–When someone adds value to an item of personal property by labor or materials, the added value generally becomes the property of the owner of the original property (includes accessions made in bad faith or wrongfully). Good faith accessions that substantially increase the property's value or change the identity of the property may cause title to pass to the improver. 5. *Confusion*–In the case of fungible goods, if a person wrongfully and willfully commingles goods with those of another in order to render them indistinguishable, the innocent party acquires title to the whole. Otherwise, the owners become tenants in common of the commingled goods.
Mislaid, Lost, and Abandoned Property (See pages 705–707.)	1. *Mislaid property*–Property that is placed somewhere voluntarily by the owner and then inadvertently forgotten. A finder of mislaid property will not acquire title to the goods, and the owner of the place where the property was mislaid becomes a caretaker of the mislaid property. 2. *Lost property*–Property that is involuntarily left and forgotten. A finder of lost property can claim title to the property against the whole world *except the true owner.* 3. *Abandoned property*–Property that has been discarded by the true owner, who has no intention of claiming title to the property in the future. A finder of abandoned property can claim title to it against the whole world, *including the original owner.*
	BAILMENTS
Elements of a Bailment (See pages 707–710.)	1. *Personal property*–Bailments involve only personal property. 2. *Delivery of possession*–For an effective bailment to exist, the bailee (the one receiving the property) must be given exclusive possession and control over the property, and in a voluntary bailment, the bailee must knowingly accept the personal property. 3. *The bailment agreement*–Expressly or impliedly provides for the return of the bailed property to the bailor or a third party, or for the disposal of the bailed property by the bailee.
Ordinary Bailments (See pages 710–713.)	1. *Types of bailments*– a. Bailment for the sole benefit of the bailor–A gratuitous bailment undertaken for the sole benefit of the bailor (for example, as a favor to the bailor). b. Bailment for the sole benefit of the bailee–A gratuitous loan of an article to a person (the bailee) solely for the bailee's benefit. c. Mutual-benefit (contractual) bailment–The most common kind of bailment; involves compensation between the bailee and bailor for the service provided. 2. *Rights of a bailee (duties of a bailor)*– a. The right of possession–Allows actions against third persons who damage or convert the bailed property and allows actions against the bailor for wrongful breach of the bailment. b. The right to use bailed property–A bailee may also have the right to use the bailed property, depending on the type of bailment and the terms of the agreement.

(Continued)

CHAPTER SUMMARY	Personal Property, Bailments, and Insurance—Continued
Ordinary Bailments— Continued	c. The right to be compensated and reimbursed for expenses—In the event of nonpayment, the bailee has the right to place a possessory (bailee's) lien on the bailed property.
	d. The right to limit liability—An ordinary bailee can limit his or her liability for loss or damage, provided proper notice is given and the limitation is not against public policy. In special bailments, limitations on liability for negligence or on types of losses usually are not allowed, but limitations on the monetary amount of liability are permitted.
	3. *Duties of a bailee (rights of a bailor)*—
	a. A bailee must exercise appropriate care over property entrusted to her or him. What constitutes appropriate care normally depends on the nature and circumstances of the bailment.
	b. Bailed goods in a bailee's possession must be either returned to the bailor or disposed of according to the bailor's directions. A bailee's failure to return the bailed property creates a presumption of negligence and constitutes a breach of contract or the tort of conversion of goods.
Special Types of Bailments (See pages 713–715.)	1. *Common carriers*—Carriers that are publicly licensed to provide transportation services to the general public. A common carrier is held to a standard of care based on *strict liability* unless the bailed property is lost or destroyed due to (a) an act of God, (b) an act of a public enemy, (c) an order of a public authority, (d) an act of the shipper, or (e) the inherent nature of the goods.
	2. *Warehouse companies*—Professional bailees that differ from ordinary bailees in that they (a) can issue documents of title (warehouse receipts) and (b) are subject to state and federal statutes, including Article 7 of the UCC (as are common carriers). They must exercise a high degree of care over the bailed property and are liable for loss of or damage to property if they fail to do so.
	3. *Innkeepers (hotel operators)*—Those who provide lodging to the public for compensation as a *regular* business. The common law strict liability standard to which innkeepers were once held is limited today by state statutes, which vary from state to state.
	INSURANCE
Classifications (See page 715.)	See Exhibit 23–2 on pages 716 and 717.
Insurance Terminology (See page 716.)	1. *Policy*—The insurance contract.
	2. *Premium*—The consideration paid to the insurer for a policy.
	3. *Underwriter*—The insurance company.
	4. *Parties*—Include the insurer (the insurance company), the insured (the person covered by insurance), and an agent (a representative of the insurance company) or a broker (ordinarily an independent contractor).
Insurable Interest (See pages 717–718.)	An insurable interest exists whenever an individual or entity benefits from the preservation of the health or life of the insured or the property to be insured. For life insurance, an insurable interest must exist at the time the policy is issued. For property insurance, an insurable interest must exist at the time of the loss.
The Insurance Contract (See pages 719–723.)	1. *Laws governing*—The general principles of contract law are applied; the insurance industry is also heavily regulated by the states.
	2. *Application*—An insurance applicant is bound by any false statements that appear in the application (subject to certain exceptions), which is part of the insurance contract. Misstatements or misrepresentations may be ground for voiding the policy.

CHAPTER SUMMARY	Personal Property, Bailments, and Insurance—Continued
The Insurance Contract—Continued	3. *Effective date*—Coverage on an insurance policy can begin when a *binder* (a written memorandum indicating that a formal policy is pending and stating its essential terms) is written; when the policy is issued; at the time of contract formation; or depending on the terms of the contract, when certain conditions are met. 4. *Provisions and clauses*—See Exhibit 23–3 on page 720. Words will be given their ordinary meanings, and any ambiguity in the policy will be interpreted against the insurance company. When the written policy has not been delivered and it is unclear whether an insurance contract actually exists, the uncertainty will be resolved against the insurance company. The court will presume that the policy is in effect unless the company can show otherwise. 5. *Defenses against payment to the insured*—Defenses include misrepresentation or fraud by the applicant.

FOR REVIEW

Answers for the even-numbered questions in this **For Review** *section can be found in Appendix E at the end of this text.*

1 What is real property? What is personal property?

2 What are the three elements necessary for an effective gift? How else can property be acquired?

3 What are the three elements of a bailment?

4 What are the basic rights and duties of a bailee? What are the rights and duties of a bailor?

5 What clauses are typically included in insurance contracts?

■

QUESTIONS AND CASE PROBLEMS

HYPOTHETICAL SCENARIOS

23.1 Duties of the Bailee. Discuss the standard of care traditionally required of the bailee for the bailed property in each of the following situations, and determine whether the bailee breached that duty.

  1 Ricardo borrows Steve's lawn mower because his own lawn mower needs repair. Ricardo mows his front yard. To mow the backyard, he needs to move some hoses and lawn furniture. He leaves the mower in front of his house while doing so. When he returns to the front yard, he discovers that the mower has been stolen.

  2 Alicia owns a valuable speedboat. She is going on vacation and asks her neighbor, Maureen, to store the boat in one stall of Maureen's double garage. Maureen consents, and the boat is moved into the garage. Maureen needs some grocery items for dinner and drives to the store. She leaves the garage door open while she is gone, as is her custom, and the speedboat is stolen during that time.

23.2 Gifts. Jaspal has a severe heart attack and is taken to the hospital. He is aware that he is not expected to live. Because he is a bachelor with no close relatives nearby, Jaspal gives his car keys to his close friend, Friedrich, telling Friedrich that he is expected to die and that the car is Friedrich's. Jaspal survives the heart attack, but two months later he dies from pneumonia. Sam, Jaspal's uncle and the executor of his estate, wants Friedrich to return the car. Friedrich refuses, claiming that the car was given to him by Jaspal as a gift. Discuss whether Friedrich will be required to return the car to Jaspal's estate.

23.3 Hypothetical Question with Sample Answer. Curtis is an executive on a business trip to the West Coast. He has driven his car on this trip and checks into the Hotel Ritz. The hotel has a guarded underground parking lot. Curtis gives his car keys to the parking lot attendant but fails to notify the attendant that his wife's $10,000 fur coat is in a box in the trunk. The next day, on checking out, he discovers that his car has been stolen. Curtis wants to hold the hotel liable for both the car and the coat. Discuss the probable success of his claim.

For a sample answer to Question 23.3, go to Appendix F at the end of this text.

23.4 Found Property. Bill Heise is a janitor for the First Mercantile Department Store. While walking to work, Bill discovers an expensive watch lying on the curb. Bill gives the watch to his son, Otto. Two weeks later, Martin Avery, the true owner of the watch, discovers that Bill found the watch and demands it back from Otto. Discuss who is entitled to the watch and why.

23.5 Timing of Insurance Coverage. On October 10, Joleen Vora applied for a $50,000 life insurance policy with Magnum Life Insurance Co.; she named her husband, Jay, as the beneficiary. Joleen paid the insurance company the first year's policy premium on making the application. Two days later, before she had a chance to take the physical examination required by the insurance company and before the policy was issued, Joleen was killed in an automobile accident. Jay submitted a claim to the insurance company for the $50,000. Can Jay collect? Explain.

CASE PROBLEMS

23.6 Found Property. A. D. Lock owned Lock Hospitality, Inc., which in turn owned the Best Western Motel in Conway, Arkansas. Joe Terry and David Stocks were preparing the motel for renovation. As they were removing the ceiling tiles in room 118, with Lock present in the room, they noticed a dusty cardboard box near the heating and air-supply vent where it had apparently been concealed. Terry climbed a ladder to reach the box, opened it, and handed it to Stocks. The box was filled with more than $38,000 in old currency. Lock took possession of the box and its contents. Terry and Stocks filed a suit in an Arkansas state court against Lock and his corporation to obtain the cash. Should the cash be characterized as lost, mislaid, or abandoned property? To whom should the court award it? Explain. [*Terry v. Lock*, 343 Ark. 452, 37 S.W.3d 202 (2001)]

23.7 Case Problem with Sample Answer. Vincent Slavin was a partner at Cantor Fitzgerald Securities in the World Trade Center (WTC) in New York City. In 1998, Slavin and Anna Baez became engaged and began living together. They placed both of their names on three accounts at Chase Manhattan Bank according to the bank's terms, which provided that "accounts with multiple owners are joint, payable to either owner or the survivor." Slavin arranged for the direct deposit of his salary and commissions into one of the accounts. On September 11, 2001, Slavin died when two planes piloted by terrorists crashed into the WTC towers, causing their collapse. At the time, the balance in the three accounts was $656,944.36. On September 14, Cantor Fitzgerald deposited an additional $58,264.73 into the direct-deposit account. Baez soon withdrew the entire amount from all of the accounts. Mary Jelnek, Slavin's mother, filed a suit in a New York state court against Baez to determine the ownership of the funds that had been in the accounts. In what form of ownership were the accounts held? Who is entitled to which of the funds and why? [*In re Jelnek*, 3 Misc.3d 725, 777 N.Y.S.2d 871 (2004)]

After you have answered Problem 23.7, compare your answer with the sample answer given on the Web site that accompanies this text. Go to academic.cengage.com/blaw/blt, select "Chapter 23," and click on "Case Problem with Sample Answer."

23.8 Cancellation of Insurance Policy. James Mitchell bought a building in Los Angeles, California, in February 2000 and applied to United National Insurance Co. for a fire insurance policy. The application stated, among other things, that the building measured 3,420 square feet, it was to be used as a video production studio, the business would generate $300,000 in revenue, and the building had no uncorrected fire code violations. In fact, the building measured less than 2,000 square feet; it was used to film only one music video over a two-day period; the business generated only $6,500 in revenue; and the city had cited the building for combustible debris, excessive weeds, broken windows, missing doors, damaged walls, and other problems. In November, Mitchell met Carl Robinson, who represented himself as a business consultant. Mitchell gave Robinson the keys to the property to show it to a prospective buyer. On November 22, Robinson set fire to the building and was killed in the blaze. Mitchell filed a claim for the loss. United denied the claim and rescinded the policy. Mitchell filed a suit in a California state court against United. Can an insurer cancel a policy? If so, on what ground might United have justifiably canceled Mitchell's policy? What might Mitchell argue to oppose a cancellation? What should the court rule? Explain. [*Mitchell v. United National Insurance Co.*, 127 Cal.App.4th 457, 25 Cal.Rptr.3d 627 (2 Dist. 2005)]

23.9 Concurrent Ownership. In July 2003, Chester Dellinger and his son Michael opened a joint bank account with Advancial Federal Credit Union in Dallas, Texas. Both of them signed the "Account Application," which designated Chester as a "member" and Michael as a "joint owner."

Both of them received a copy of the "Account Agreement, Disclosures and Privacy Policy," which provided that "a multiple party account includes rights of survivorship." Chester died in February 2005. His will designated Michael as the executor of the estate, most of which was to be divided equally between Michael and his brother, Joseph, Chester's other son. Michael determined the value of the estate to be about $117,000. He did not include the Advancial account balance, which was about $234,000. Joseph filed a suit in a Texas state court against Michael, contending that the funds in the Advancial account should be included in the estate. Michael filed a motion for summary judgment. Who owned the Advancial account when Chester was alive? Who owned it after he died? What should the court rule? Explain. [*In re Estate of Dellinger*, 224 S.W.3d 434 (Tex.App.—Dallas 2007)]

23.10 **A Question of Ethics.** *Marcella Lashmett was engaged in the business of farming in Illinois. Her daughter Christine Montgomery was also a farmer. Christine often borrowed Marcella's farm equipment. More than once, Christine used the equipment as a trade-in on the purchase of new equipment titled in Christine's name alone. After each transaction, Christine paid Marcella an agreed-to sum of money, and Marcella filed a gift tax return. Marcella died on December 19, 1999. Her heirs included Christine and Marcella's other daughter, Cheryl Thomas. Marcella's will gave whatever farm equipment remained on her death to Christine. If Christine chose to sell or trade any of the items, however, the proceeds were to be split equally with Cheryl. The will designated Christine to handle the disposition of the estate, but she did nothing. Eventually, Cheryl filed a petition with an Illinois state court, which appointed her to administer the will. Cheryl then filed a suit against her sister to discover what assets their mother had owned. [In re Estate of Lashmett, 369 Ill.App.3d 1013, ___ N.E.2d ___ (4 Dist. 2007)]*

1 Cheryl learned that three months before Marcella's death, Christine had used Marcella's tractor as a trade-in on the purchase of a new tractor. The trade-in credit had been $55,296.28. Marcella had been paid nothing, and no gift tax return had been filed. Christine claimed, among other things, that the old tractor had been a gift. What is a "gift"? What are the elements of a gift? What do the facts suggest on this claim? Discuss.

2 Christine also claimed that she had tried to pay Marcella $20,000 on the trade-in of the tractor but that her mother had refused to accept it. Christine showed a check made out to Marcella for that amount and marked "void." Would you rule in Christine's favor on this claim? Why or why not?

 **CRITICAL THINKING
AND WRITING ASSIGNMENTS**

23.11 Critical Legal Thinking. Suppose that a certificate of deposit (CD) owned by two joint tenants (with the right of survivorship) is given by one of the joint tenants as security for a loan (without the other joint tenant's knowledge). Further suppose that the joint tenant dies after defaulting on the loan. Who has superior rights in the CD, the creditor or the other surviving joint tenant?

23.12 **Video Question.** Go to this text's Web site at **academic. cengage.com/blaw/blt** and select "Chapter 23." Click on "Video Questions" and view the video titled *Double Indemnity*. Then answer the following questions.

1 Recall from the video that Mrs. Dietrichson (Barbara Stanwyck) is attempting to take out an "accident insurance" policy (similar to life insurance) on her husband without his knowledge. Does Mrs. Dietrichson have an insurable interest in the life of her husband? Why or why not?

2 Why would Walter (Fred MacMurray), the insurance agent, refuse to sell Mrs. Dietrichson an insurance policy covering her husband's life without her husband's knowledge?

3 Suppose that Mrs. Dietrichson contacts a different insurance agent and does not tell the agent that she wants to obtain insurance on her husband without his knowledge. Instead, she asks the agent to leave an insurance application for her husband to sign. Without her husband's knowledge, Mrs. Dietrichson then fills out the application for insurance, which includes a two-year incontestability clause, and forges Mr. Dietrichson's signature. Mr. Dietrichson dies three years after the policy is issued. Will the insurance company be obligated to pay on the policy? Why or why not?

ONLINE ACTIVITIES

PRACTICAL INTERNET EXERCISES

Go to this text's Web site at **academic.cengage.com/blaw/blt**, select "Chapter 23," and click on "Practical Internet Exercises." There you will find the following Internet research exercises that you can perform to learn more about the topics covered in this chapter.

PRACTICAL INTERNET EXERCISE 23-1   LEGAL PERSPECTIVE—Lost Property

PRACTICAL INTERNET EXERCISE 23-2   MANAGEMENT PERSPECTIVE—Bailments

PRACTICAL INTERNET EXERCISE 23-3   MANAGEMENT PERSPECTIVE—Risk Management in Cyberspace

BEFORE THE TEST

Go to this text's Web site at **academic.cengage.com/blaw/blt**, select "Chapter 23," and click on "Interactive Quizzes." You will find a number of interactive questions relating to this chapter.

CHAPTER 24
Real Property and Environmental Law

LEARNING OBJECTIVES

AFTER READING THIS CHAPTER, YOU SHOULD BE ABLE
TO ANSWER THE FOLLOWING QUESTIONS:

1 What are the requirements for acquiring property
by adverse possession?

2 What limitations may be imposed on the rights
of property owners?

3 What are the respective duties of the landlord
and tenant concerning the use and maintenance
of leased property?

4 What is contained in an environmental impact
statement, and who must file one?

5 What is Superfund, and who is potentially liable
under Superfund?

> **"**The right of
> property is the
> most sacred of
> all the rights of
> citizenship.**"**
>
> Jean-Jacques Rousseau, 1712–1778
> (French writer and philosopher)

rom earliest times, property has provided a means for survival. Primitive peoples lived
off the fruits of the land, eating the vegetation and wildlife. Later, as the wildlife was
domesticated and the vegetation cultivated, property provided pasturage and farmland. In
the twelfth and thirteenth centuries in Europe, the power of feudal lords was determined by
the amount of land they held—the more land, the more powerful they were. After the age
of feudalism passed, property continued to be an indicator of family wealth and social position. In the Western world, an individual's right to his or her property has become, in the
words of Jean-Jacques Rousseau, one of the "most sacred of all the rights of citizenship."

In this chapter, we first examine the nature of real property. We then look at the various ways in which real property can be owned and at how ownership rights in real property are transferred from one person to another. We conclude the chapter with a
discussion of the major statutes that help to protect our environment.

THE NATURE OF REAL PROPERTY

Real property consists of land and the buildings, plants, and trees that are on it. Real property also includes subsurface and airspace rights, as well as personal property that has
become permanently attached to real property. Whereas personal property is movable,
real property—also called *real estate* or *realty*—is immovable.

Land

Land includes the soil on the surface of the earth and the natural or artificial structures that are attached to it. It further includes all the waters contained on or under the surface and much, but not necessarily all, of the airspace above it. The exterior boundaries of land extend down to the center of the earth and up to the farthest reaches of the atmosphere (subject to certain qualifications).

Airspace and Subsurface Rights

The owner of real property has rights to the airspace above the land, as well as to the soil and minerals underneath it. Limitations on either airspace rights or subsurface rights normally have to be indicated on the document that transfers title at the time of purchase. When no such limitations, or *encumbrances*, are noted, a purchaser can normally expect to have an unlimited right to possession of the property.

Airspace Rights Early cases involving airspace rights dealt with such matters as whether a telephone wire could be run across a person's property when the wire did not touch any of the property[1] and whether a bullet shot over a person's land constituted trespass.[2] Today, disputes concerning airspace rights may involve the right of commercial and private planes to fly over property and the right of individuals and governments to seed clouds and produce rain artificially. Flights over private land normally do not violate property rights unless the flights are so low and so frequent that they directly interfere with the owner's enjoyment and use of the land.[3] Leaning walls or buildings and projecting eave spouts or roofs may also violate the airspace rights of an adjoining property owner.

Subsurface Rights In many states, land ownership may be separated, in that the surface of a piece of land and the subsurface may have different owners. Subsurface rights can be extremely valuable, as these rights include the ownership of minerals, oil, and natural gas. Subsurface rights would be of little value, however, if the owner could not use the surface to exercise those rights. Hence, a subsurface owner will have a right (called a *profit,* to be discussed later in this chapter) to go onto the surface of the land to, for example, discover and mine minerals.

When the ownership is separated into surface and subsurface rights, each owner can pass title to what she or he owns without the consent of the other owner. Of course, conflicts can arise between a surface owner's use and the subsurface owner's need to extract minerals, oil, or natural gas. One party's interest may become subservient (secondary) to the other party's interest either by statute or case law. At common law and generally today, if the owners of the subsurface rights excavate (dig), they are absolutely liable if their excavation causes the surface to collapse. Depending on the circumstances, the excavators may also be liable for any damage to structures on the land. Many states have statutes that extend excavators' liability to include damage to structures on the property. Typically, these statutes provide precise requirements for excavations of various depths.

Plant Life and Vegetation

Plant life, both natural and cultivated, is also considered to be real property. In many instances, the natural vegetation, such as trees, adds greatly to the value of the realty.

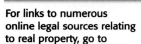
---

1. *Butler v. Frontier Telephone Co.,* 186 N.Y. 486, 79 N.E. 716 (1906).
2. *Herrin v. Sutherland,* 74 Mont. 587, 241 P. 328 (1925). Shooting over a person's land constitutes trespass.
3. *United States v. Causby,* 328 U.S. 256, 66 S.Ct. 1062, 90 L.Ed. 1206 (1946).

When a parcel of land is sold and the land has growing crops on it, the sale includes the crops, unless otherwise specified in the sales contract. When crops are sold by themselves, however, they are considered to be personal property or goods. Consequently, the sale of crops is a sale of goods and thus is governed by the Uniform Commercial Code (UCC) rather than by real property law.[4]

Fixtures

Certain personal property can become so closely associated with the real property to which it is attached that the law views it as real property. Such property is known as a **fixture**—a thing *affixed* to realty, meaning that it is attached to the real property by roots; embedded in it; permanently situated on it; or permanently attached by means of cement, plaster, bolts, nails, or screws. The fixture can be physically attached to real property, be attached to another fixture, or even be without any actual physical attachment to the land (such as a statue). As long as the owner intends the property to be a fixture, normally it will be a fixture.

FIXTURE
A thing that was once personal property but has become attached to real property in such a way that it takes on the characteristics of real property and becomes part of that real property.

Fixtures are included in the sale of land if the sales contract does not provide otherwise. The sale of a house includes the land and the house and the garage on the land, as well as the cabinets, plumbing, and windows. Because these are permanently affixed to the property, they are considered to be a part of it. Certain items, such as drapes and window-unit air conditioners, are difficult to classify. Thus, a contract for the sale of a house or commercial realty should indicate which items of this sort are included in the sale.

■EXAMPLE 24.1 A farm had an eight-tower center-pivot irrigation system, bolted to a cement slab and connected to an underground well. The bank held a mortgage note on the farm secured by "all buildings, improvements, and fixtures." The farm's owners had also used the property as security for other loans, but the contracts for those loans did not specifically mention fixtures or the irrigation system. Later, when the farmers were unable to repay their debts and filed for bankruptcy, a dispute arose between the bank and another creditor over the irrigation system. Ultimately, a court held that the irrigation system was a fixture because it was firmly attached to the land and integral to the operation of the farm. Therefore, the bank's security interest had priority over that of the other creditor.[5] ■

One way to avoid certain disputes over real property is to make sure that any contract specifically lists which fixtures the parties intend to be included in a sale or transfer or subjected to a security interest. Without such a list, the parties may have very different ideas as to what is being transferred with the real property (or included as collateral for a loan). In the end, it is much simpler and less expensive to itemize fixtures in a contract than to engage in litigation.

PREVENTING
LEGAL DISPUTES

OWNERSHIP INTERESTS IN REAL PROPERTY

Ownership of property is an abstract concept that cannot exist independently of the legal system. No one can actually possess or *hold* a piece of land, the airspace above it, the earth below it, and all the water contained on it. The legal system therefore recognizes certain rights and duties that constitute ownership interests in real property.

---

4. See UCC 2–107(2).
5. *In re Sand & Sage Farm & Ranch, Inc.,* 266 Bankr. 507 (D.Kans. 2001).

Recall from Chapter 23 that property ownership is often viewed as a bundle of rights. One who possesses the entire bundle of rights is said to hold the property in *fee simple*, which is the most complete form of ownership. When only some of the rights in the bundle are transferred to another person, the effect is to limit the ownership rights of both the transferor of the rights and the recipient.

Ownership in Fee Simple

FEE SIMPLE ABSOLUTE
An ownership interest in land in which the owner has the greatest possible aggregation of rights, privileges, and power. Ownership in fee simple absolute is limited absolutely to a person and her or his heirs.

In a **fee simple absolute,** the owner has the greatest aggregation of rights, privileges, and power possible. The owner can give the property away or dispose of the property by *deed* (the instrument used to transfer property, as will be discussed later in this chapter) or by will. When there is no will, the fee simple passes to the owner's legal heirs on her or his death. A fee simple is potentially infinite in duration and is assigned forever to a person and her or his heirs without limitation or condition. The owner has the rights of *exclusive* possession and use of the property.

The rights that accompany a fee simple include the right to use the land for whatever purpose the owner sees fit. Of course, other laws, including applicable zoning, noise, and environmental laws, may limit the owner's ability to use the property in certain ways.

In the following case, the court had to decide whether the noise—rock and roll music, conversation, and clacking pool balls—coming from a local bar (called a "saloon" during the days of cowboys in the United States) unreasonably interfered with a neighboring property owner's rights.

CASE 24.1 **Biglane v. Under the Hill Corp.**

Mississippi Supreme Court, 949 So.2d 9 (2007).
www.mssc.state.ms.us[a]

FACTS In 1967, Nancy and James Biglane bought and refurbished a building at 27 Silver Street in Natchez, Mississippi, and opened the lower portion as a gift shop. In 1973, Andre Farish and Paul O'Malley bought the building next door, at 25 Silver Street, and opened the Natchez Under the Hill Saloon (the Saloon). Later, the Biglanes converted the upper floors of their building into an apartment and moved into it. Even though the Biglanes installed insulated walls and windows, located their bedroom on the side of the building away from the Saloon, and placed the air-conditioning unit on the side nearest the Saloon, the noise from the Saloon kept them awake at night. During the summer, the Saloon, which had no air-conditioning, opened its windows and doors, and live music echoed up and down the street. After the Biglanes complained about the noise, the Saloon installed thicker windows, replaced the loudest band, and asked the other bands to keep their output below a certain level of decibels.

Still dissatisfied, the Biglanes filed a suit in a Mississippi state court against the Saloon. The court enjoined the defendant from opening doors or windows when music was playing and ordered it to prevent its patrons from loitering in the street. Both parties appealed to the Mississippi Supreme Court.

ISSUE Did the Saloon's noise unreasonably interfere with the Biglanes' property rights?

DECISION Yes. The Mississippi Supreme Court affirmed the lower court's injunction: "One landowner may not use his land so as to unreasonably annoy, inconvenience, or harm others."

REASON The state supreme court pointed out that an owner may be subject to liability when the owner's conduct is "an invasion of another's interest in the private use and enjoyment of land and that invasion is * * * intentional and unreasonable." Reasonable use of property does not include "obnoxious noises, which in turn result in a material injury to owners of property in the vicinity, causing them to suffer substantial annoyance, inconvenience, and discomfort." An owner does not have to be driven from his or her property. The interference can be sufficient if "the enjoyment of life and property is rendered materially uncomfortable and annoying."

a. In the center of the page, click on the "Search this Site" link. On the next page, click on "Plain English." When that page opens, in the "Enter the ISYS Plain English query:" box, type "2005-CA-01751-SCT" and click on "Search." In the result, click on the first item in the list that includes that number to access the opinion. The Mississippi Supreme Court maintains this Web site.

CASE 24.1–Continued

Each case is to be decided on its own facts, including the location of the property and the surrounding circumstances. Here, the court balanced the interests of the Biglanes and the Saloon "in a quest for an equitable remedy that allowed the couple to enjoy their private apartment * * * while protecting a popular business and tourist attraction from over-regulation."

FOR CRITICAL ANALYSIS–Ethical Consideration
At one point in their dispute, the Biglanes blocked off two parking lots that served the Saloon. Was this an unreasonable interference with the Saloon's rights? Explain.

Life Estates

A **life estate** is an estate that lasts for the life of some specified individual. A **conveyance**, or transfer of real property, "to A for his life" creates a life estate. In a life estate, the life tenant's ownership rights cease to exist on the life tenant's death.[6] The life tenant has the right to use the land, provided that he or she commits no waste (injury to the land). In other words, the life tenant cannot use the land in a manner that would adversely affect its value. The life tenant is entitled to any rents generated by the land and can harvest crops from the land. If mines and oil wells are already on the land, the life tenant can extract minerals and oil and is entitled to the royalties, but he or she cannot exploit the land by creating new wells or mines.

The life tenant can create liens, *easements* (discussed below), and leases, but none can extend beyond the life of the tenant. In addition, with few exceptions, the owner of a life estate has an exclusive right to possession during her or his life.

Along with these rights, the life tenant also has some duties—to keep the property in repair and to pay property taxes. In short, the owner of the life estate has the same rights as a fee simple owner except that the life tenant must maintain the value of the property during her or his tenancy.

Nonpossessory Interests

In contrast to the types of property interests just described, some interests in land do not include any rights to possess the property. These interests, known as **nonpossessory interests**, include easements, profits, and licenses.

An **easement** is the right of a person to make limited use of another person's real property without taking anything from the property. An easement, for instance, can be the right to walk or drive across another's property. In contrast, a **profit**[7] is the right to go onto land owned by another and take away some part of the land itself or some product of the land. **EXAMPLE 24.2** Akmed owns Sandy View. Akmed gives Carmen the right to go there to remove all the sand and gravel that she needs for her cement business. Carmen has a profit. ■

In the context of real property, a **license** is the revocable right of a person to come onto another person's land. It is a personal privilege that arises from the consent of the owner of the land and can be revoked by the owner. A ticket to attend a movie at a theater is an

LIFE ESTATE
An interest in land that exists only for the duration of the life of some person, usually the holder of the estate.

CONVEYANCE
The transfer of title to land from one person to another by deed; a document (such as a deed) by which an interest in land is transferred from one person to another.

NONPOSSESSORY INTEREST
In the context of real property, an interest in land that does not include any right to possess the property.

EASEMENT
A nonpossessory right to use another's property in a manner established by either express or implied agreement.

PROFIT
In real property law, the right to enter onto and remove things from the property of another (for example, the right to enter onto a person's land and remove sand and gravel).

LICENSE
A revocable right or privilege of a person to come onto another person's land.

---

6. Because a life tenant's rights in the property cease at death, life estates are frequently used to avoid probate proceedings. The person who owns the property deeds it to the person who would eventually inherit the property and reserves a life estate for herself or himself. That way, the property owner can live there until death, and the property then passes to the intended heir without the need for legal proceedings.

7. The term *profit*, as used here, does not refer to the "profits" made by a business firm. Rather, it means a gain or an advantage.

example of a license. **■EXAMPLE 24.3** The owner of a Broadway theater issues Alena a ticket to see a play. If Alena is refused entry into the theater because she is improperly dressed, she has no right to force her way into the theater. The ticket is only a revocable license, not a conveyance of an interest in property. ■

TRANSFER OF OWNERSHIP

Ownership of real property can pass from one person to another in several ways. Commonly, ownership interests in land are transferred by sale, and the terms of the transfer are specified in a real estate sales contract. Often, real estate brokers or agents who are licensed by the state assist the buyers and sellers during the sales transaction. (For a discussion of some issues involving online advertising by real estate professionals, see this chapter's *Adapting the Law to the Online Environment* feature. We discussed the antitrust implications of real property listings on the Internet in Chapter 22's *Adapting the Law to the Online Environment* feature on pages 680 and 681.) Real property ownership can also be transferred by gift, by will or inheritance, by possession, or by *eminent domain*. When ownership rights in real property are transferred, the type of interest being transferred and the conditions of the transfer normally are set forth in a *deed* executed by the person who is conveying the property.

Deeds

DEED
A document by which title to property (usually real property) is passed.

Possession and title to land are passed from person to person by means of a **deed**—the instrument of conveyance of real property. A deed is a writing signed by an owner of real property that transfers title to another. Deeds must meet certain requirements, but unlike a contract, a deed does not have to be supported by legally sufficient consideration. Gifts of real property are common, and they require deeds even though there is no consideration for the gift. To be valid, a deed must include the following:

1 The names of the *grantor* (the giver or seller) and the *grantee* (the donee or buyer).

2 Words evidencing an intent to convey the property (for example, "I hereby bargain, sell, grant, or give").

3 A legally sufficient description of the land.

4 The grantor's (and usually her or his spouse's) signature.

5 Delivery of the deed.

WARRANTY DEED
A deed in which the grantor assures (warrants to) the grantee that the grantor has title to the property conveyed in the deed, that there are no encumbrances on the property other than what the grantor has represented, and that the grantee will enjoy quiet possession of the property; a deed that provides the greatest amount of protection for the grantee.

Warranty Deeds   Different types of deeds provide different degrees of protection against defects of title. A **warranty deed** makes the greatest number of warranties and thus provides the greatest protection against defects of title. In most states, special language is required to create a general warranty deed.

Warranty deeds commonly include a number of *covenants*, or promises, that the grantor makes to the grantee. These covenants include a covenant that the grantor has the title to, and the power to convey, the property; a covenant of quiet enjoyment (a warranty that the buyer will not be disturbed in her or his possession of the land); and a covenant that transfer of the property is made without knowledge of adverse claims of third parties. Generally, the warranty deed makes the grantor liable for all defects of title by the grantor and previous titleholders.

■EXAMPLE 24.4 Julio sells a two-acre lot and office building by warranty deed. Subsequently, a third person shows up who has better title than Julio had and forces the buyer off the property. Here, the covenant of quiet enjoyment has been breached, and the buyer can sue Julio to recover the purchase price of the land plus any other damages incurred as a result. ■

ADAPTING THE LAW TO THE ONLINE ENVIRONMENT **Potential Problems When Real Estate Is Advertised Online**

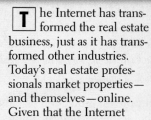

T he Internet has transformed the real estate business, just as it has transformed other industries. Today's real estate professionals market properties—and themselves—online. Given that the Internet knows no physical borders, what happens when an online advertisement reaches people outside the state in which the real estate professional is licensed? Is this illegal? Can the agent be sued for fraud if the ad contains misrepresentations?

State Licensing Statutes and Advertising

Every state requires anyone who sells or offers to sell real property in that state to obtain a license. To be licensed, a person normally must pass a state examination and pay a fee and then must take a minimum number of continuing education courses periodically (every year or two) to maintain the license. Usually, a person must also be licensed to list real property for sale or to negotiate the purchase, sale, lease, or exchange of real property or a business opportunity involving real property.[a] Often, a state agency, such as a real estate commission, is in charge of granting licenses and enforcing the laws and regulations governing real estate professionals.

State laws can differ on the exact activities that require a real estate license, though. Consider, for example, the problems faced by Stroman Realty, Inc., a licensed Realtor® in Texas. (The term *Realtor* is "a registered collective membership mark that identifies a real estate professional who is a member of the National Association of Realtors.") Stroman's business focuses on reselling time shares (which allow the owner to use the property for a specified interval of time per year) on the secondary market. The company used a computerized service to match potential buyers with properties and maintained a Web site where buyers could view available time shares. Stroman advertised its time-share resale services both in print and via the Internet and frequently engaged in transactions involving parties in multiple states.

After a complaint from an Illinois resident, the Illinois agency in charge of enforcing licensing requirements sent Stroman a cease-and-desist letter. The agency stated that Stroman had engaged in a number of activities in Illinois that required a real estate license, and ordered the company to stop these activities. Stroman filed a lawsuit asking a federal district court to stay (suspend) the administrative action, arguing that Illinois licensing law was unconstitutional and violated the dormant commerce clause (see Chapter 1). The federal court, however, refused to exercise jurisdiction on the constitutionality issue and dismissed Stroman's complaint. The court noted that the regulation of the real estate profession is clearly an important state interest and that Illinois was merely enforcing its Licensing Act when it took action against Stroman.[b]

Actions for Misrepresentations (Fraud)

Suppose that a real estate agent, either inadvertently or intentionally, makes a misstatement online about some important aspect of real property that is for sale. Someone, relying on the statements, responds to the ad and eventually contracts to buy the property, only to discover later that the ad misrepresented it. What remedies does the buyer have? In this situation, the buyer can complain to the state authority that granted the agent's license, and the state may even revoke the license for such conduct. If the buyer wants to obtain damages or cancel the contract, however, he or she will have to sue the agent for fraud (see Chapters 4 and 8). At this point, jurisdictional problems may arise.

If the real estate agent and the buyer are located in different states and the Internet ad was the agent's only contact with the buyer's state, the buyer may have to travel to the agent's state to file the suit. Courts have reached different conclusions on the type of Internet advertising that permits a court to have jurisdiction over an out-of-state advertiser. In addition, courts may sometimes refuse to exercise jurisdiction over an out-of-state defendant even if they could do so (as the court did in the case just discussed involving Stroman Realty). Thus, people who are deceived when buying real property from an online ad and wish to sue the perpetrator of the fraud may be in a precarious position depending on the state where they live.

FOR CRITICAL ANALYSIS *Do you think that the federal government should regulate the advertising of real property on the Internet to protect consumers from potential fraud? If so, what kind of regulations would be appropriate, and how might they be enforced?*

---

a. See, for example, California Business and Professions Code Section 10131 and 26 Vermont Statutes Annotated Sections 2211–2212.

b. *Stroman Realty, Inc. v. Grillo*, 438 F.Supp.2d 929 (N.D.Ill. 2006).

Special Warranty Deeds   In contrast to a warranty deed, a **special warranty deed,** which is also referred to as a *limited warranty deed*, warrants only that the grantor or seller held good title during his or her ownership of the property. In other words, the grantor is not warranting that there were no defects of title when the property was held by previous owners.

If the special warranty deed discloses all liens or other encumbrances, the seller will not be liable to the buyer if a third person subsequently interferes with the buyer's ownership. If the third person's claim arises out of, or is related to, some act of the seller, however, the seller will be liable to the buyer for damages.

Quitclaim Deeds   A **quitclaim deed** offers the least amount of protection against defects in the title. Basically, a quitclaim deed conveys to the grantee whatever interest the grantor had; so, if the grantor had no interest, then the grantee receives no interest. Naturally, if the grantor had a defective title or no title at all, a conveyance by warranty deed or special warranty deed would not cure the defects. Such deeds, however, will give the buyer a cause of action to sue the seller.

A quitclaim deed can and often does serve as a release of the grantor's interest in a particular parcel of property. **■EXAMPLE 24.5** After ten years of marriage, Sandi and Jim are getting a divorce. During the marriage, Sandi purchased a parcel of waterfront property next to her grandparents' home in Louisiana. Jim helped make some improvements to the property, but he is not sure what ownership interests, if any, he has in the property because Sandi used her own funds (acquired before the marriage) to purchase the lot. Jim agrees to quitclaim the property to Sandi as part of the divorce settlement, releasing any interest he might have in that piece of property. ■

Recording Statutes   Every jurisdiction has **recording statutes,** which allow deeds to be recorded for a fee. The grantee normally pays this fee because he or she is the one who will be protected by recording the deed.

Recording a deed gives notice to the public that a certain person is now the owner of a particular parcel of real estate. Thus, prospective buyers can check the public records to see whether there have been earlier transactions creating interests or rights in specific parcels of real property. Putting everyone on notice as to the identity of the true owner is intended to prevent the previous owners from fraudulently conveying the land to other purchasers. Deeds are recorded in the county where the property is located. Many state statutes require that the grantor sign the deed in the presence of two witnesses before it can be recorded.

Will or Inheritance

Property that is transferred on an owner's death is passed either by will or by state inheritance laws. If the owner of land dies with a will, the land passes in accordance with the terms of the will. If the owner dies without a will, state inheritance statutes prescribe how and to whom the property will pass.

Adverse Possession

Adverse possession is a means of obtaining title to land without delivery of a deed. Essentially, when one person possesses the property of another for a certain statutory period of time (three to thirty years, with ten years being most common), that person, called the *adverse possessor*, acquires title to the land and cannot be removed from it by the original owner. The adverse possessor may ultimately obtain a perfect title just as if there had been a conveyance by deed.

For property to be held adversely, four elements must be satisfied:

1 Possession must be actual and exclusive—that is, the possessor must take sole physical occupancy of the property.

2 The possession must be open, visible, and notorious, not secret or clandestine. The possessor must occupy the land for all the world to see.

3 Possession must be continuous and peaceable for the required period of time. This requirement means that the possessor must not be interrupted in the occupancy by the true owner or by the courts.

4 Possession must be hostile and adverse. In other words, the possessor must claim the property as against the whole world. He or she cannot be living on the property with the permission of the owner.

There are a number of public-policy reasons for the adverse possession doctrine. These include society's interest in resolving boundary disputes, in quieting (determining) title when title to property is in question, and in ensuring that real property remains in the stream of commerce. More fundamentally, policies behind the doctrine include rewarding possessors for putting land to productive use and punishing owners who sit on their rights too long and do not take action when they see adverse possession.

Eminent Domain

Even ownership in real property in fee simple absolute is limited by a superior ownership. Just as in medieval England the king was the ultimate landowner, so in the United States the government has an ultimate ownership right in all land. This right, known as **eminent domain,** is sometimes referred to as the *condemnation power* of government to take land for public use. It gives the government the right to acquire possession of real property in the manner directed by the U.S. Constitution and the laws of the state whenever the public interest requires it. Property may be taken only for public use, not for private benefit.

EXAMPLE 24.6 When a new public highway is to be built, the government must decide where to build it and how much land to condemn. After the government determines that a particular parcel of land is necessary for public use, it will first offer to buy the property. If the owner refuses the offer, the government brings a judicial (**condemnation**) proceeding to obtain title to the land. Then, in another proceeding, the court determines the *fair value* of the land, which is usually approximately equal to its market value. ■

When the government takes land owned by a private party for public use, it is referred to as a **taking,** and the government must compensate the private party. Under the so-called *takings clause* of the Fifth Amendment to the U.S. Constitution, the government may not take private property for public use without "just compensation." State constitutions contain similar provisions.

Can the power of eminent domain be used to further economic development? That was the question in the following case.

Should the government be permitted to take undeveloped coastal property from private citizens for public use without compensation? Why or why not?
(Greg Chimitris/Creative Commons)

EMINENT DOMAIN
The power of a government to take land from private citizens for public use on the payment of just compensation.

CONDEMNATION
The process of taking private property for public use through the government's power of eminent domain.

TAKING
The taking of private property by the government for public use. The government may not take private property for public use without "just compensation."

CASE 24.2 **Kelo v. City of New London, Connecticut**

Supreme Court of the United States, 545 U.S. 469, 125 S.Ct. 2655, 162 L.Ed.2d 439 (2005).
www.findlaw.com/casecode/supreme.html[a]

FACTS After decades of economic decline, the city of New London was designated as a "distressed municipality" by a Connecticut state agency in 1990, but conditions continued to deteriorate. In 1996, the federal government closed the

a. In the "Browsing" section, click on "2005 Decisions." In the result, click on the name of the case to access the opinion.

Naval Undersea Warfare Center, which had been located in the Fort Trumbull area of the city and had employed more than 1,500 people. Within two years, the city's unemployment rate was nearly double that of the state. In 1998, Pfizer, Inc., announced that it would build a $300 million research facility on a site next to Fort Trumbull. Hoping that this would draw new business to the city, the city council approved a plan to

CASE 24.2–Continues next page

CASE 24.2–Continued

redevelop the area that once housed the federal facility. The city bought most of the land for the project, but negotiations with some of the property owners fell through, and the city began condemnation proceedings. Susette Kelo and other affected owners filed a suit in a Connecticut state court against the city and others. The plaintiffs claimed, among other things, that the taking of their property would violate the "public use" restriction in the U.S. Constitution's Fifth Amendment. The court issued a ruling partly in favor of both sides. On appeal, the Connecticut Supreme Court held that all of the city's proposed takings were valid. The owners appealed to the United States Supreme Court.

ISSUE Can a city use its power of eminent domain to take private property for the purpose of economic development?

DECISION Yes. The United States Supreme Court affirmed the lower court's judgment. The Court held that economic development can constitute a "public use" within the meaning of the Fifth Amendment's takings clause to justify a local government's exercise of its power of eminent domain.

REASON The Court concluded that the city's plan "unquestionably serves a public purpose," even though it

would also benefit private parties. The Court explained, "Viewed as a whole, our jurisprudence has recognized that the needs of society have varied between different parts of the Nation, just as they have evolved over time in response to changed circumstances. Our earliest cases in particular embodied a strong theme of federalism, emphasizing the great respect that we owe to state legislatures and state courts in discerning local public needs. For more than a century, our public use jurisprudence has wisely eschewed rigid formulas and intrusive scrutiny in favor of affording legislatures broad latitude in determining what public needs justify the use of the takings power." Thus, the city's "determination that the area was sufficiently distressed to justify a program of economic rejuvenation is entitled to our deference. The City has carefully formulated an economic development plan that it believes will provide appreciable benefits to the community. * * * Because that plan unquestionably serves a public purpose, the takings challenged here satisfy the public use requirement of the Fifth Amendment."

 FOR CRITICAL ANALYSIS–Economic Consideration
Considering the impact of the ruling in this case, what are some arguments against the decision?

ETHICAL ISSUE 24.1

Should eminent domain be used to promote private developments? Issues of fairness often arise when the government takes private property for public use. One issue is whether it is fair for a government to take property by eminent domain and then convey it to private developers. For example, suppose that a city government decides that it is in the public interest to have a larger parking lot for a local, privately owned sports stadium or to have a manufacturing plant locate in the city to create more jobs. The government may condemn certain tracts of existing housing or business property and then convey the land to the privately owned stadium or to the owner of the manufacturing plant. Such acts bring in private developers and businesses that provide jobs and increase tax revenues, thus revitalizing communities. But is the land really being taken for "public use," as required by the Fifth Amendment to the U.S. Constitution?

The increasingly widespread use of eminent domain for such purposes has generated substantial controversy. Although the United States Supreme Court approved this type of taking in the *Kelo* case (see Case 24.2), the Court also recognized that individual states have the right to pass laws that prohibit takings for economic development. Thirty-five states have done exactly that, limiting the government's ability to take private property and give it to private developers. At least eight states have amended their state constitutions, and a number of other states have passed ballot measures. Thus, the debate over whether it is fair for the government to take its citizens' property for economic redevelopment continues.

LEASEHOLD ESTATES

A **leasehold estate** is created when a real property owner or lessor (landlord) agrees to convey the right to possess and use the property to a lessee (tenant) for a certain period of time. In every leasehold estate, the tenant has a *qualified* right to exclusive possession (qualified by the right of the landlord to enter on the premises to ensure that waste is not being committed). The *temporary* nature of possession, under a lease, is what distinguishes a tenant from a purchaser, who acquires title to the property. The tenant can use the land—for example, by harvesting crops—but cannot injure it by such activities as cutting down timber for sale or extracting oil.

The respective rights and duties of the landlord and tenant that arise under a lease agreement will be discussed shortly. Here, we look at the types of leasehold estates, or tenancies, that can be created when real property is leased.

LEASEHOLD ESTATE
An estate in realty held by a tenant under a lease. In every leasehold estate, the tenant has a qualified right to possess and/or use the land.

Fixed-Term Tenancy or Tenancy for Years

A **fixed-term tenancy,** also called a *tenancy for years,* is created by an express contract by which property is leased for a specified period of time, such as a day, a month, a year, or a period of years. Signing a one-year lease to occupy an apartment, for instance, creates a fixed-term tenancy. Note that the term need not be specified by date and can be conditioned on the occurrence of an event, such as leasing a cabin for the summer or an apartment during Mardi Gras. At the end of the period specified in the lease, the lease ends (without notice), and possession of the apartment returns to the lessor. If the tenant dies during the period of the lease, the lease interest passes to the tenant's heirs as personal property. Often, leases include renewal or extension provisions.

FIXED-TERM TENANCY
A type of tenancy under which property is leased for a specified period of time, such as a month, a year, or a period of years; also called a *tenancy for years.*

Periodic Tenancy

A **periodic tenancy** is created by a lease that does not specify how long it is to last but does specify that rent is to be paid at certain intervals. This type of tenancy is automatically renewed for another rental period unless properly terminated. **■EXAMPLE 24.7** Kayla enters a lease with Capital Properties. The lease states, "Rent is due on the tenth day of every month." This provision creates a periodic tenancy from month to month. ■ This type of tenancy can also extend from week to week or from year to year.

Under the common law, to terminate a periodic tenancy, the landlord or tenant must give at least one period's notice to the other party. If the tenancy extends from month to month, for example, one month's notice must be given prior to the last month's rent payment. State statutes may require a different period for notice of termination in a periodic tenancy, however.

PERIODIC TENANCY
A lease interest in land for an indefinite period involving payment of rent at fixed intervals, such as week to week, month to month, or year to year.

Tenancy at Will

When a leasehold interest is created in which either party can terminate the tenancy without notice, it is called a **tenancy at will.** This type of tenancy can arise if a landlord rents certain property to a tenant "for as long as both agree" or allows a person to live on the premises without paying rent. Tenancy at will is rare in today's world because most state statutes require a landlord to provide some period of notice to terminate a tenancy (as previously noted). States may also require a landowner to have sufficient cause (reason) to end a residential tenancy. Certain events, such as the death of either party or the voluntary commission of waste by the tenant, automatically terminate a tenancy at will.

TENANCY AT WILL
A type of tenancy that either party can terminate without notice; usually arises when a tenant who has been under a tenancy for years retains possession, with the landlord's consent, after the tenancy for years has terminated.

Tenancy at Sufferance

TENANCY AT SUFFERANCE
A type of tenancy under which a tenant who, after rightfully being in possession of leased premises, continues (wrongfully) to occupy the property after the lease has terminated. The tenant has no rights to possess the property and occupies it only because the person entitled to evict the tenant has not done so.

The mere possession of land without right is called a **tenancy at sufferance.** A tenancy at sufferance is not a true tenancy because it is created when a tenant *wrongfully* retains possession of property. Whenever a tenancy for years or a periodic tenancy ends and the tenant continues to retain possession of the premises without the owner's permission, a tenancy at sufferance is created.

LANDLORD-TENANT RELATIONSHIPS

ON THE WEB

You can find online links to most uniform laws, including the Uniform Residential Landlord and Tenant Act (URLTA), at www.lawsource.com.

In the past several decades, landlord-tenant relationships have become much more complex, as has the law governing them. Generally, the law has come to apply contract doctrines, such as those relating to implied warranties and unconscionability, to the landlord-tenant relationship. Increasingly, landlord-tenant relationships have become subject to specific state and local statutes and ordinances as well. In 1972, in an effort to create more uniformity in the law governing landlord-tenant relationships, the National Conference of Commissioners on Uniform State Laws issued the Uniform Residential Landlord and Tenant Act (URLTA). More than one-third of the states have adopted variations of the URLTA. We look now at how a landlord-tenant relationship is created and at the respective rights and duties of landlords and tenants.

Creating the Landlord-Tenant Relationship

A landlord-tenant relationship is established by a lease contract. As mentioned, a lease contract arises when a property owner (landlord) agrees to give another party (the tenant) the exclusive right to possess the property—usually for a price and for a specified term.

NOTE Sound business practice dictates that a lease for commercial property should be written carefully and should clearly define the parties' rights and obligations.

Form of the Lease A lease contract may be oral or written. Under the common law, an oral lease is valid. As with most oral contracts, however, a party who seeks to enforce an oral lease may have difficulty proving its existence. In most states, statutes mandate that leases be in writing for some tenancies (such as those exceeding one year). Therefore, to ensure the validity of a lease agreement, it should be in writing and do the following:

1 Express an intent to establish the relationship.

2 Provide for the transfer of the property's possession to the tenant at the beginning of the term.

3 Provide for the landlord's *reversionary* (future) interest, which entitles the property owner to retake possession at the end of the term.

4 Describe the property—for example, give its street address.

5 Indicate the length of the term, the amount of the rent, and how and when it is to be paid.

Illegality State or local law often dictates permissible lease terms. For example, a statute or ordinance might prohibit the leasing of a structure that is in a certain physical condition or is not in compliance with local building codes. Similarly, a statute may prohibit the leasing of property for a particular purpose. For instance, a state law might prohibit gambling houses. Thus, if a landlord and tenant intend that the leased premises be used only to house an illegal betting operation, their lease is unenforceable.

A property owner cannot legally discriminate against prospective tenants on the basis of race, color, national origin, religion, gender, or disability. In addition, a tenant cannot legally promise to do something counter to laws prohibiting discrimination. A commercial tenant, for example, cannot legally promise to do business only with members of a particular race. The public policy underlying these prohibitions is to treat all people equally.

Rights and Duties

The rights and duties of landlords and tenants generally pertain to four broad areas of concern—the possession, use, maintenance, and, of course, rent of leased property.

Possession   A landlord is obligated to give a tenant possession of the property that the tenant has agreed to lease. Many states follow the "English" rule, which requires the landlord to provide actual *physical possession* to the tenant (making sure that the previous tenant has vacated). Other states follow the "American" rule, which requires the landlord to transfer only the *legal right to possession* (thus, the new tenant is responsible for removing a previous tenant). After obtaining possession, the tenant retains the property exclusively until the lease expires, unless the lease states otherwise.

The covenant of quiet enjoyment mentioned previously also applies to leased premises. Under this covenant, the landlord promises that during the lease term, neither the landlord nor anyone having a superior title to the property will disturb the tenant's use and enjoyment of the property. This covenant forms the essence of the landlord-tenant relationship, and if it is breached, the tenant can terminate the lease and sue for damages.

If the landlord deprives the tenant of possession of the leased property or interferes with the tenant's use or enjoyment of it, an **eviction** occurs. An eviction occurs, for instance, when the landlord changes the lock and refuses to give the tenant a new key. A **constructive eviction** occurs when the landlord wrongfully performs or fails to perform any of the duties the lease requires, thereby making the tenant's further use and enjoyment of the property exceedingly difficult or impossible. Examples of constructive eviction include a landlord's failure to provide heat in the winter, light, or other essential utilities.

Use and Maintenance of the Premises   If the parties do not limit by agreement the uses to which the property may be put, the tenant may make any use of it, as long as the use is legal and reasonably relates to the purpose for which the property is adapted or ordinarily used and does not injure the landlord's interest.

The tenant is responsible for any damage to the premises that he or she causes, intentionally or negligently, and may be held liable for the cost of returning the property to the physical condition it was in at the lease's inception. Also, the tenant is not entitled to create a *nuisance* by substantially interfering with others' quiet enjoyment of their property rights. Unless the parties have agreed otherwise, the tenant is not responsible for ordinary wear and tear and the property's consequent depreciation in value.

In some jurisdictions, landlords of residential property are required by statute to maintain the premises in good repair. Landlords must also comply with any applicable state statutes and city ordinances regarding maintenance and repair of buildings.

Implied Warranty of Habitability   The **implied warranty of habitability** requires a landlord who leases residential property to ensure that the premises are habitable—that is, in a condition that is safe and suitable for people to live there. Also, the landlord must make repairs to maintain the premises in that condition for the lease's duration. Some state legislatures have enacted this warranty into law. In other jurisdictions, courts have based the warranty on the existence of a landlord's statutory duty to keep leased premises in good repair, or they have simply applied it as a matter of public policy.

Generally, this warranty applies to major, or *substantial*, physical defects that the landlord knows or should know about and has had a reasonable time to repair—for example, a large hole in the roof. An unattractive or annoying feature, such as a crack in the wall, may

ON THE WEB

Many Web sites now provide information on laws and other topics relating to landlord-tenant relationships. One of them is TenantNet™ at

www.tenant.net.

EVICTION
A landlord's act of depriving a tenant of possession of the leased premises.

CONSTRUCTIVE EVICTION
A form of eviction that occurs when a landlord fails to perform adequately any of the duties (such as providing heat in the winter) required by the lease, thereby making the tenant's further use and enjoyment of the property exceedingly difficult or impossible.

IMPLIED WARRANTY OF HABITABILITY
An implied promise by a landlord that rented residential premises are fit for human habitation—that is, in a condition that is safe and suitable for people to live there.

be unpleasant, but unless the crack is a structural defect or affects the residence's heating capabilities, it is probably not sufficiently substantial to make the place uninhabitable.

Rent   *Rent* is the tenant's payment to the landlord for the tenant's occupancy or use of the landlord's real property. Usually, the tenant must pay the rent even if she or he refuses to occupy the property or moves out, as long as the refusal or the move is unjustified and the lease is in force. Under the common law, if the leased premises were destroyed by fire or flood, the tenant still had to pay rent. Today, however, most state's statutes provide that if an apartment building burns down, tenants are not required to continue to pay rent.

In some situations, such as when a landlord breaches the implied warranty of habitability, a tenant may be allowed to withhold rent as a remedy. When rent withholding is authorized under a statute, the tenant must usually put the amount withheld into an *escrow account*. This account is held in the name of the depositor (the tenant) and an *escrow agent* (usually the court or a government agency), and the funds are returnable to the depositor if the third person (the landlord) fails to make the premises habitable. Generally, the tenant may withhold an amount equal to the amount by which the defect rendering the premises unlivable reduces the property's rental value. How much that is may be determined in different ways, and a tenant who withholds more than is legally permissible is liable to the landlord for the excessive amount withheld.

Transferring Rights to Leased Property

Either the landlord or the tenant may wish to transfer her or his rights to the leased property during the term of the lease.

Transferring the Landlord's Interest   Just as any other real property owner can sell, give away, or otherwise transfer his or her property, so can a landlord—who is, of course, the leased property's owner. If complete title to the leased property is transferred, the tenant becomes the tenant of the new owner. The new owner may collect subsequent rent but must abide by the terms of the existing lease agreement.

Transferring the Tenant's Interest   The tenant's transfer of his or her entire interest in the leased property to a third person is an *assignment of the lease*. The tenant's transfer of all or part of the premises for a period shorter than the lease term is a *sublease*.

Assignment.   A lease assignment is an agreement to transfer all rights, title, and interest in the lease to the assignee. It is a complete transfer. Many leases require that the assignment have the landlord's written consent. An assignment that lacks consent can be avoided (nullified) by the landlord. State statutes may specify that the landlord may not unreasonably withhold such consent, though. Also, a landlord who knowingly accepts rent from the assignee may be held to have waived the consent requirement.

When an assignment is valid, the assignee acquires all of the tenant's rights under the lease. An assignment, however, does not release the assigning tenant from the obligation to pay rent should the assignee default. Also, if the assignee exercises an option under the original lease to extend the term, the assigning tenant remains liable for the rent during the extension, unless the landlord agrees otherwise.

Subleases.   The tenant's transfer of all or part of the premises for a period shorter than the lease term is a **sublease**. The same restrictions that apply to an assignment of the tenant's interest in leased property apply to a sublease. If the landlord's consent is required, a sublease without such permission is ineffective. Also, a sublease does not release the tenant from her or his obligations under the lease any more than an assignment does.

NOTE   Options that may be available to a tenant on a landlord's breach of the implied warranty of habitability include repairing the defect and deducting the cost from the rent, canceling the lease, and suing for damages.

SUBLEASE
A lease executed by the lessee of real estate to a third person, conveying the same interest that the lessee enjoys but for a shorter term than that held by the lessee.

■EXAMPLE 24.8 Derek, a student, leases an apartment for a two-year period. Although Derek had planned on attending summer school, he is offered a job in Europe for the summer months, and he accepts. Because he does not wish to pay three months' rent for an unoccupied apartment, Derek subleases the apartment to Adva, who becomes a sublessee. (Derek may have to obtain his landlord's consent for this sublease if the lease requires it.) Adva is bound by the same terms of the lease as Derek. As in a lease assignment, the landlord can hold Derek liable if Adva violates the lease terms. **■**

ENVIRONMENTAL LAW

We now turn to a discussion of the various ways in which businesses are regulated by the government in the interest of protecting the environment. To a great extent, environmental law consists of statutes passed by federal, state, or local governments and regulations issued by administrative agencies. (See the *Application* feature at the end of this chapter for information on how to avoid facing penalties for violating environmental laws.)

State and Local Regulation

Many states regulate the degree to which the environment may be polluted. Thus, for example, even when state zoning laws permit a business's proposed development, the proposal may have to be altered to lessen the development's impact on the environment. State laws may restrict a business's discharge of chemicals into the air or water or regulate its disposal of toxic wastes. States may also regulate the disposal or recycling of other wastes, including glass, metal, and plastic containers and paper. Additionally, states may restrict the emissions from motor vehicles.

City, county, and other local governments control some aspects of the environment. For instance, local zoning laws control some land use. These laws may be designed to inhibit or regulate the growth of cities and suburbs or to protect the natural environment. In the interest of safeguarding the environment, such laws may prohibit certain land uses. An issue subject to ongoing debate is whether landowners should be compensated when restrictions are placed on the use of their property.

Other aspects of the environment may be subject to local regulation for other reasons. Methods of waste and garbage removal and disposal, for example, can have a substantial impact on a community. The appearance of buildings and other structures, including advertising signs and billboards, may affect traffic safety, property values, or local aesthetics. Noise generated by a business or its customers may be annoying, disruptive, or damaging to neighbors. The location and condition of parks, streets, and other publicly used land subject to local control affect the environment and can also affect business.

Federal Regulation

Congress has enacted a number of statutes to control the impact of human activities on the environment. Some of these laws have been passed to improve the quality of air and water. Some of them specifically regulate toxic chemicals, including pesticides, herbicides, and hazardous wastes.

Environmental Regulatory Agencies   Much of the body of federal law governing business activities consists of the regulations issued and enforced by administrative agencies. The primary agency regulating environmental law is, of course, the Environmental Protection Agency (EPA), which was created in 1970 to coordinate federal environmental responsibilities. Other federal agencies with authority to regulate specific environmental matters include the Department of the Interior, the Department of Defense, the Department of Labor, the Food and Drug Administration, and the Nuclear Regulatory Commission. These regulatory agencies—and all other agencies of the federal government—must take environmental factors into consideration when making significant decisions.

Most federal environmental laws provide that private parties can sue to enforce environmental regulations if government agencies fail to do so—or if agencies go too far in their enforcement actions. Typically, a threshold hurdle in such suits is meeting the requirements for standing to sue.

State and local regulatory agencies also play a significant role in implementing federal environmental legislation. Typically, the federal government relies on state and local governments to enforce federal environmental statutes and regulations such as those regulating air quality.

Environmental Impact Statements   The National Environmental Policy Act (NEPA) of 1969[8] requires that an **environmental impact statement (EIS)** be prepared for every major federal action that significantly affects the quality of the environment. An EIS must analyze (1) the impact on the environment that the action will have, (2) any adverse effects on the environment and alternative actions that might be taken, and (3) irreversible effects the action might generate.

An action qualifies as "major" if it involves a substantial commitment of resources (monetary or otherwise). An action is "federal" if a federal agency has the power to control it. Construction by a private developer of a ski resort on federal land, for example, may require an EIS.[9] Building or operating a nuclear plant, which requires a federal permit,[10] would require an EIS, as would constructing a dam as part of a federal project.[11] If an agency decides that an EIS is unnecessary, it must issue a statement supporting this conclusion. EISs have become instruments for private individuals, consumer interest groups, businesses, and others to challenge federal agency actions on the basis that the actions improperly threaten the environment.

Air Pollution

Federal involvement with air pollution goes back to the 1950s, when Congress authorized funds for air-pollution research. In 1963, the federal government passed the Clean Air Act,[12] which focused on multistate air pollution and provided assistance to the states. Various amendments, particularly in 1970, 1977, and 1990, have strengthened the government's authority to regulate the quality of air. These laws provide the basis for issuing regulations to control pollution coming primarily from mobile sources (such as automobiles) and stationary sources (such as electric utilities and industrial plants).

Mobile Sources of Pollution   Regulations governing air pollution from automobiles and other mobile sources specify pollution standards and establish time schedules for meeting the standards. For example, under the 1990 amendments to the Clean Air Act, automobile manufacturers were required to cut new automobiles' exhaust emissions of nitrogen oxide by 60 percent and of other pollutants by 35 percent by 1998. Regulations that became effective beginning with 2004 model cars called for nitrogen oxide tailpipe emissions to be cut by nearly 10 percent by 2007. For the first time, sport utility vehicles (SUVs) and light trucks were required to meet the same standards as automobiles. The amendments also required service stations to sell gasoline with a higher oxygen content in certain cities, and to sell even cleaner-burning gasoline in the most polluted urban areas.

ENVIRONMENTAL IMPACT STATEMENT (EIS)
A statement required by the National Environmental Policy Act for any major federal action that will significantly affect the quality of the environment. The statement must analyze the action's impact on the environment and explore alternative actions that might be taken.

---

8. 42 U.S.C. Sections 4321–4370d.
9. *Robertson v. Methow Valley Citizens' Council*, 490 U.S. 332, 109 S.Ct. 1835, 104 L.Ed.2d 351 (1989).
10. *Calvert Cliffs' Coordinating Committee v. Atomic Energy Commission*, 449 F.2d 1109 (D.C.Cir. 1971).
11. *Marsh v. Oregon Natural Resources Council*, 490 U.S. 360, 109 S.Ct. 1851, 104 L.Ed.2d 377 (1989).
12. 42 U.S.C. Sections 7401 et seq.

Updating Pollution-Control Standards The EPA attempts to update pollution-control standards when new scientific information becomes available. For example, studies conducted in the 1990s showed that very small particles (2.5 microns, or about one-thirtieth the width of a human hair) of soot might affect our health as significantly as larger particles. Based on this evidence, in 1997 the EPA issued new particulate standards for motor vehicle exhaust systems and other sources of pollution. The EPA also instituted a more rigorous standard for ozone (the basic ingredient of smog), which is formed when sunlight combines with pollutants from cars and other sources.

The EPA's particulate standards and ozone standard were challenged in court by a number of business groups that claimed that the EPA had exceeded its authority under the Clean Air Act by issuing the stricter rules. Additionally, the groups claimed that the EPA had to take economic costs into account when developing new regulations. In 2000, however, the United States Supreme Court upheld the EPA's authority under the Clean Air Act to issue the standards. The Court also held that the EPA did not have to take economic costs into account when creating new rules.[13]

In 2006, the EPA again reevaluated its particulate standards and found that more than two hundred counties were not meeting the standards set in 1997. The EPA issued new regulations for daily (twenty-four-hour) exposure to particles of soot but did not change the annual particulate standards.[14]

ON THE WEB

For information on EPA standards, guidelines, and regulations, go to the EPA's Web site at

www.epa.gov.

Stationary Sources of Pollution The Clean Air Act authorizes the EPA to establish air-quality standards for stationary sources (such as manufacturing plants) but recognizes that the primary responsibility for preventing and controlling air pollution rests with state and local governments. The EPA sets primary and secondary levels of ambient standards—that is, the maximum levels of certain pollutants—and the states formulate plans to achieve those standards. Different standards apply depending on whether the sources of pollution are located in clean areas or polluted areas and whether they are already existing sources or major new sources.

The standards are aimed at controlling hazardous air pollutants—that is, those likely to cause death or serious irreversible or incapacitating illness such as cancer or neurological and reproductive damage. In all, 189 substances, including asbestos, benzene, beryllium, cadmium, and vinyl chloride, have been classified as hazardous. They are emitted from stationary sources by a variety of business activities, including smelting (melting ore to produce metal), dry cleaning, house painting, and commercial baking. Instead of establishing specific emissions standards for each hazardous air pollutant, the 1990 amendments to the Clean Air Act require major sources of pollutants to use pollution-control equipment that represents the *maximum achievable control technology*, or MACT, to reduce emissions. The EPA issues guidelines as to what equipment meets these standards. The EPA has also issued rules to regulate hazardous air pollutants emitted by landfills.[15]

Under the 1990 amendments to the Clean Air Act, 110 of the oldest coal-burning power plants in the United States had to cut their emissions by 40 percent by the year 2001 to reduce acid rain. Utilities were granted "credits" to emit certain amounts of sulfur dioxide, and those that emit less than the allowed amounts can sell their credits to other polluters. The amendments also required an end to the production of chlorofluorocarbons, carbon tetrachloride, and methyl chloroform, which are used in air-conditioning, refrigeration, and insulation and have been linked to depletion of the ozone layer. In 2002, a federal district court held that these amendments to the

An area in an office building undergoing the removal of asbestos, a hazardous air pollutant. (Aaron Suggs/Creative Commons)

13. *Whitman v. American Trucking Associations*, 531 U.S. 457, 121 S.Ct. 903, 149 L.Ed.2d 1 (2000).
14. 40 C.F.R. Part 50.
15. 40 C.F.R. Sections 60.750–759.

Clean Air Act effectively preempted a New York state pollution-control law that set more stringent requirements than the federal statute.[16]

Violations of the Clean Air Act For violations of emission limits under the Clean Air Act, the EPA can assess civil penalties of up to $25,000 per day. Additional fines of up to $5,000 per day can be assessed for other violations, such as failing to maintain the required records. To penalize those who find it more cost-effective to violate the act than to comply with it, the EPA is authorized to obtain a penalty equal to the violator's economic benefits from noncompliance. Persons who provide information about violators may be paid up to $10,000. Private individuals can also sue violators.

Those who knowingly violate the act may be subject to criminal penalties, including fines of up to $1 million and imprisonment for up to two years (for false statements or failures to report violations). Corporate officers are among those who may be subject to these penalties.

Water Pollution

Water pollution stems mostly from industrial, municipal, and agricultural sources. Pollutants entering streams, lakes, and oceans include organic wastes, heated water, sediments from soil runoff, nutrients (including fertilizers and human and animal wastes), and toxic chemicals and other hazardous substances. We look here at laws and regulations governing water pollution.

Federal regulations governing the pollution of water can be traced back to the Rivers and Harbors Appropriations Act of 1899.[17] These regulations prohibited ships and manufacturers from discharging or depositing refuse in navigable waterways without a permit. In 1948, Congress passed the Federal Water Pollution Control Act (FWPCA),[18] but its regulatory system and enforcement powers proved to be inadequate.

The Clean Water Act In 1972, amendments to the FWPCA—known as the Clean Water Act—established the following goals: (1) make waters safe for swimming, (2) protect fish and wildlife, and (3) eliminate the discharge of pollutants into the water. The amendments set specific time schedules, which were extended by amendment in 1977 and by the Water Quality Act of 1987.[19] Under these schedules, the EPA limits the discharge of various types of pollutants based on the technology available for controlling them. The 1972 act also requires municipal and industrial polluters to apply for permits before discharging wastes into navigable waters.

Under the act, violators are subject to a variety of civil and criminal penalties. Depending on the violation, civil penalties range from $10,000 per day to $25,000 per day, but not more than $25,000 per violation. Criminal penalties, which apply only if a violation was intentional, range from a fine of $2,500 per day and imprisonment for up to one year to a fine of $1 million and fifteen years' imprisonment. Injunctive relief and damages can also be imposed. The polluting party can be required to clean up the pollution or pay for the cost of doing so.

Before a company can obtain a federal license to "discharge" into navigable waters, the affected state must certify that water-protection laws will not be violated. Can a river routed through a hydropower dam "discharge" into itself for purposes of the Clean Water Act, thus requiring the dam's owner to obtain state approval? That was the question in the following case.

16. *Clean Air Markets Group v. Pataki*, 194 F.Supp.2d 147 (N.D.N.Y. 2002).
17. 33 U.S.C. Sections 401–418.
18. 33 U.S.C. Sections 1251–1387.
19. This act amended 33 U.S.C. Section 1251.

CASE 24.3 · S. D. Warren Co. v. Maine Board of Environmental Protection

Supreme Court of the United States, __ U.S. __, 126 S.Ct. 1843, 164 L.Ed.2d 625 (2006).
www.findlaw.com/casecode/supreme.html[a]

FACTS S. D. Warren Company operates hydropower dams to generate electricity for a paper mill on the Presumpscot River, which runs for twenty-five miles through southern Maine. Each dam creates a pond, from which water funnels into a canal, through turbines, and back to the riverbed. Operating the dams requires a license from the Federal Energy Regulatory Commission (FERC). Under the Clean Water Act, a license for an activity that causes a "discharge" into navigable waters requires the state in which the activity occurs to certify that the discharge will not violate water-quality standards. To renew the licenses for the dams in 1999, Warren applied for certification from the Maine Department of Environmental Protection. The agency told Warren to maintain a minimum stream flow in the river and to allow passage for migratory fish and eels. Warren appealed to the state board of environmental protection, which upheld the requirements. FERC licensed the dams subject to these conditions. Warren filed a suit in a Maine state court against the state agency, arguing that the dams do not result in discharges. The court ruled in the agency's favor. Warren appealed to the Supreme Judicial Court of Maine, the state's highest court, which affirmed the lower court's ruling. Warren appealed to the United States Supreme Court.

ISSUE Does water flowing through a hydropower dam operated under a federal license constitute a "discharge" into navigable waters requiring state approval?

a. In the "Browsing" section, click on "2006 Decisions." When that page opens, scroll to the name of the case, and click on it to read the opinion.

DECISION Yes. The United States Supreme Court affirmed the decision of the Maine Supreme Judicial Court.

REASON The Court pointed out that in cases involving water, the term *discharge* has consistently been applied to mean a "flowing or issuing out." The federal Environmental Protection Agency (EPA), FERC, and the Court "have each regularly read 'discharge' as having its plain meaning and thus covering releases from hydroelectric dams." The goal of the Clean Water Act is to achieve "water quality which provides for the protection and propagation of fish, shellfish, and wildlife and provides for recreation in and on the water." In line with this goal, the act defines *pollution* to mean "the man-made or man-induced alteration of the chemical, physical, biological, and radiological integrity of water." Controlling the release of water through turbines changes the flow of the river, causing it to absorb less oxygen, which "aquatic organisms" need to breathe. Due to Warren's dams, parts of the river's bed are dry and "unavailable as habitat for indigenous populations of fish and other aquatic organisms." Opportunities for fishing and other recreational uses are curtailed. These conditions "fall within a State's legitimate legislative business." State certification under the Clean Water Act is "essential in the scheme to preserve state authority to address the broad range of pollution."

 WHAT IF THE FACTS WERE DIFFERENT? *Would the result in this case have been different if the quality of the water flowing through the turbines of Warren's dams improved before returning to the river? Why or why not?*

Wetlands The Clean Water Act prohibits the filling or dredging of **wetlands** unless a permit is obtained from the Army Corps of Engineers. The EPA defines *wetlands* as "those areas that are inundated or saturated by surface or ground water at a frequency and duration sufficient to support, and that under normal circumstances do support, a prevalence of vegetation typically adapted for life in saturated soil conditions." In recent years, the EPA's broad interpretation of what constitutes a wetland subject to the regulatory authority of the federal government has generated substantial controversy.

■**EXAMPLE 24.9** One of the most controversial regulations was the "migratory-bird rule" issued by the Army Corps of Engineers. Under this rule, any bodies of water that could affect interstate commerce, including seasonal ponds or waters "used or suitable for use by migratory birds" that fly over state borders, were "navigable waters" subject to federal regulation as wetlands under the Clean Water Act. The rule was challenged in a case brought by a group of communities that wanted to build a landfill in a tract of land northwest of Chicago. The Army Corps of Engineers refused to grant a permit for the landfill on the ground that

WETLANDS
Water-saturated areas of land that are designated by a government agency (such as the Army Corps of Engineers or the Environmental Protection Agency) as protected areas that support wildlife and therefore cannot be filled in or dredged by private contractors or parties without a permit.

the shallow ponds formed a habitat for migratory birds. Ultimately, the United States Supreme Court held that the Army Corps of Engineers had exceeded its authority under the Clean Water Act. The Court stated that it was not prepared to hold that isolated and seasonal ponds, puddles, and "prairie potholes" become "navigable waters of the United States" simply because they serve as a habitat for migratory birds.[20] ☐

The United States Supreme Court revisited the issue of wetlands in 2006, again scaling back the reach of the Clean Water Act. Two disputes had arisen as to whether certain properties in Michigan could be developed by the owners or were protected as wetlands, and the Court consolidated them on appeal. One involved property deemed to be wetlands because it was near an unnamed ditch that flowed into the Sutherland-Oemig Drain, which ultimately connected to Lake St. Clair. The other involved acres of marshy land, some of which was adjacent to a creek that flowed into a river, which flowed into yet another river, eventually reaching Saginaw Bay. Although the lower courts had concluded that both properties were wetlands under the Clean Water Act, the Supreme Court reversed these decisions. The Court held that the act covers "only those wetlands with a continuous surface connection to bodies that are waters of the United States in their own right." The Court further held that navigable waters under the act include only relatively permanent, standing or flowing bodies of water—not intermittent or temporary flows of water.[21]

Drinking Water   Another statute governing water pollution is the Safe Drinking Water Act of 1974.[22] This act requires the EPA to set maximum levels for pollutants in public water systems. Public water system operators must come as close as possible to meeting the EPA's standards by using the best available technology that is economically and technologically feasible. The EPA is particularly concerned about contamination from underground sources. Pesticides and wastes leaked from landfills or disposed of in underground injection wells are among the more than two hundred pollutants known to exist in groundwater used for drinking in at least thirty-four states. Many of these substances are associated with cancer and may cause damage to the central nervous system, liver, and kidneys.

The act was amended in 1996 to give the EPA more flexibility in setting regulatory standards. These amendments also imposed new requirements on suppliers of drinking water. Each supplier must send to every household it supplies with water an annual statement describing the source of its water, the level of any contaminants contained in the water, and any possible health concerns associated with the contaminants.

Ocean Dumping   The Marine Protection, Research, and Sanctuaries Act of 1972[23] (popularly known as the Ocean Dumping Act), as amended in 1983, regulates the transportation and dumping of material into ocean waters. It prohibits entirely the ocean dumping of radiological, chemical, and biological warfare agents and high-level radioactive waste. The act also establishes a permit program for transporting and dumping other materials, and designates certain areas as marine sanctuaries. Each violation of any provision in the Ocean Dumping Act may result in a civil penalty of up to $50,000. A knowing violation is a criminal offense that may result in a $50,000 fine, imprisonment for not more than a year, or both. The court may also grant an injunction to prevent an imminent or continuing violation of the Ocean Dumping Act.

---

20. *Solid Waste Agency of Northern Cook County v. U.S. Army Corps of Engineers*, 531 U.S. 159, 121 S.Ct. 675, 148 L.Ed.2d 576 (2001).
21. *Rapanos v. United States*, __U.S. __, 126 S.Ct. 2208, 165 L.Ed.2d 159 (2006).
22. 42 U.S.C. Sections 300f to 300j-25.
23. 16 U.S.C. Sections 1401–1445.

Oil Pollution   In response to the worst oil spill in North American history—more than 10 million gallons of oil leaked into Alaska's Prince William Sound from the *Exxon Valdez* supertanker in 1989—Congress passed the Oil Pollution Act of 1990.[24] Under this act, any onshore or offshore oil facility, oil shipper, vessel owner, or vessel operator that discharges oil into navigable waters or onto an adjoining shore can be liable for clean-up costs, as well as damages.

Under the act, damage to natural resources, private property, and the local economy, including the increased cost of providing public services, is compensable. The penalties range from $2 million to $350 million, depending on the size of the vessel and on whether the oil spill came from a vessel or an offshore facility. The party held responsible for the clean-up costs can bring a civil suit for contribution from other potentially liable parties. The act also decreed that by the year 2011, oil tankers using U.S. ports must be double hulled to limit the severity of accidental spills.

Clean-up efforts in Alaska's Prince William Sound following the Exxon Valdez *oil spill. How did this disaster change the law regarding oil spills? Who can be held responsible for clean-up costs? (*Exxon Valdez* Oil Spill Trustee Council/National Oceanic & Atmospheric Adminstration)*

Toxic Chemicals

Originally, most environmental clean-up efforts were directed toward reducing smog and making water safe for fishing and swimming. Today, the control of toxic chemicals used in agriculture and in industry has become increasingly important.

Pesticides and Herbicides   The Federal Insecticide, Fungicide, and Rodenticide Act (FIFRA) of 1947 regulates pesticides and herbicides.[25] Under FIFRA, pesticides and herbicides must be (1) registered before they can be sold, (2) certified and used only for approved applications, and (3) used in limited quantities when applied to food crops. The EPA can cancel or suspend registration of substances that are identified as harmful and may also inspect factories where the chemicals are made. Under 1996 amendments to FIFRA, there must be no more than a one-in-a-million risk to people of developing cancer from any kind of exposure to the substance, including eating food that contains pesticide residues.[26]

It is a violation of FIFRA to sell a pesticide or herbicide that is either unregistered or has had its registration canceled or suspended. It is also a violation to sell a pesticide or herbicide with a false or misleading label or to destroy or deface any labeling required under the act. Penalties for commercial dealers include imprisonment for up to one year and a fine of no more than $25,000. Farmers and other private users of pesticides or herbicides who violate the act are subject to a $1,000 fine and incarceration for up to thirty days.

Toxic Substances   The first comprehensive law covering toxic substances was the Toxic Substances Control Act of 1976.[27] The act was passed to regulate chemicals and chemical compounds that are known to be toxic—such as asbestos and polychlorinated biphenyls, popularly known as PCBs—and to institute investigation of any possible harmful effects from new chemical compounds. The regulations authorize the EPA to require that manufacturers, processors, and other organizations planning to use chemicals first determine their effects on human health and the environment. The EPA can regulate

24. 33 U.S.C. Sections 2701–2761.
25. 7 U.S.C. Sections 135–136y.
26. 21 U.S.C. Section 346a.
27. 15 U.S.C. Sections 2601–2692.

A hazardous waste–disposal team cleans up toxic chemicals that spilled from a semi-trailer onto a public highway. (Courtesy of Minnesota Pollution Control Agency)

substances that potentially pose an imminent hazard or an unreasonable risk of injury to health or the environment. The EPA may require special labeling, limit the use of a substance, set production quotas, or prohibit the use of a substance altogether.

Hazardous Waste Disposal

Some industrial, agricultural, and household wastes pose more serious threats than others. If not properly disposed of, these toxic chemicals may present a substantial danger to human health and the environment. If released into the environment, they may contaminate public drinking water resources.

Resource Conservation and Recovery Act In 1976, Congress passed the Resource Conservation and Recovery Act (RCRA)[28] in reaction to the growing concern over the effects of hazardous waste materials on the environment. The RCRA required the EPA to determine which forms of solid waste should be considered hazardous and to establish regulations to monitor and control hazardous waste disposal. The act also requires all producers of hazardous waste materials to label and package properly any hazardous waste to be transported. The RCRA was amended in 1984 and 1986 to decrease the use of land containment in the disposal of hazardous waste and to require smaller generators of hazardous waste to comply with the act.

Under the RCRA, a company may be assessed a civil penalty of up to $25,000 for each violation.[29] Penalties are based on the seriousness of the violation, the probability of harm, and the extent to which the violation deviates from RCRA requirements. Criminal penalties include fines of up to $50,000 for each day of violation, imprisonment for up to two years (in most instances), or both.[30] Criminal fines and the period of imprisonment can be doubled for certain repeat offenders.

Superfund In 1980, Congress passed the Comprehensive Environmental Response, Compensation, and Liability Act (CERCLA),[31] commonly known as Superfund, to regulate the clean-up of leaking hazardous waste–disposal sites. A special federal fund was created for that purpose. Because of its impact on the business community, the act is presented as this chapter's *Landmark in the Law* feature.

Potentially Responsible Parties under Superfund. Superfund provides that when a release or a threatened release of hazardous chemicals from a site occurs, the EPA can clean up the site and recover the cost of the clean-up from the following persons: (1) the person who generated the wastes disposed of at the site, (2) the person who transported the wastes to the site, (3) the person who owned or operated the site at the time of the disposal, or (4) the current owner or operator. A person falling within one of these categories is referred to as a **potentially responsible party (PRP)**.

POTENTIALLY RESPONSIBLE PARTY (PRP)
A party liable for the costs of cleaning up a hazardous waste–disposal site under the Comprehensive Environmental Response, Compensation, and Liability Act (CERCLA). Any person who generated the hazardous waste, transported it, owned or operated the waste site at the time of disposal, or owns or operates the site at the present time may be responsible for some or all of the clean-up costs.

---

28. 42 U.S.C. Sections 6901 *et seq.*
29. 42 U.S.C. Section 6928(a).
30. 42 U.S.C. Section 6928(d).
31. 42 U.S.C. Sections 9601–9675.

LANDMARK IN THE LAW   Superfund

The origins of the Comprehensive Environmental Response, Compensation, and Liability Act (CERCLA) of 1980, commonly referred to as Superfund, can be traced to drafts that the Environmental Protection Agency (EPA) started to circulate in 1978.

Dump Sites Characterized as "Ticking Time Bombs"   EPA officials emphasized the necessity of new legislation by pointing to what they characterized as "ticking time bombs"—dump sites around the country that were ready to explode and injure the public with toxic fumes. The popular press was also running prominent stories about hazardous waste–dump sites at the time. The New York Love Canal disaster first made headlines in 1978 when residents in the area complained about health problems, contaminated sludge oozing into their basements, and chemical "volcanoes" erupting in their yards. These problems were the result of approximately 21,000 tons of chemicals that Hooker Chemical had dumped into the canal from 1942 to 1953. By the middle of May 1980, the Love Canal situation was making the national news virtually every day, and it remained in the headlines for a month.

CERCLA–Its Purpose and Primary Elements   The basic purpose of CERCLA, which was amended in 1986, is to regulate the clean-up of leaking hazardous waste–disposal sites. The act has four primary elements:

1   It established an information-gathering and analysis system that enables the government to identify chemical dump sites and determine the appropriate action.
2   It authorized the EPA to respond to hazardous substance emergencies and to arrange for the clean-up of a leaking site directly if the persons responsible for the problem fail to clean up the site.
3   It created a Hazardous Substance Response Trust Fund (Superfund) to pay for the clean-up of hazardous sites using funds obtained through taxes on certain businesses.
4   It allowed the government to recover the cost of clean-up from the persons who were (even remotely) responsible for hazardous substance releases.

APPLICATION TO TODAY'S WORLD   *The provisions of CERCLA profoundly affect today's businesses. Virtually any business decision relating to the purchase and sale of property, for example, requires an analysis of previous activities on the property to determine whether they resulted in contamination. Additionally, to avoid violating CERCLA, owners and managers of manufacturing plants must be extremely careful in arranging for the removal and disposal of any hazardous waste materials. Unless Congress significantly changes CERCLA and the way that it is implemented, businesses will continue to face potentially extensive liability for violations under this act.*

RELEVANT WEB SITES   *To locate information on the Web concerning Superfund, go to this text's Web site at* **academic.cengage.com/blaw/blt**, *select "Chapter 24," and click on "URLs for Landmarks."*

Joint and Several Liability under Superfund. Liability under Superfund is usually joint and several—that is, a person who generated *only a fraction of the hazardous waste* disposed of at the site may nevertheless be liable for *all* of the clean-up costs. CERCLA authorizes a party who has incurred clean-up costs to bring a "contribution action" against any other person who is liable or potentially liable for a percentage of the costs.

REVIEWING Real Property

Vern Shoepke purchased a two-story home from Walter and Eliza Bruster in the town of Roche, Maine. The warranty deed did not specify what covenants would be included in the conveyance. The property was adjacent to a public park that included a popular Frisbee golf course. (Frisbee golf is a sport similar to golf but using Frisbees.) Wayakichi Creek ran along the north end of the park and along Shoepke's property. The deed allowed Roche citizens the right to walk across a five-foot-wide section of the lot beside Wayakichi Creek as part of a two-mile public trail system. Teenagers regularly threw Frisbee golf discs from the walking path behind Shoepke's property over his yard to the adjacent park. Shoepke habitually shouted and cursed at the teenagers, demanding that they not throw objects over his yard. Two months after

moving into his Roche home, Shoepke leased the second floor to Lauren Slater for nine months. (The lease agreement did not specify that Shoepke's consent would be required to sublease the second floor.) After three months of tenancy, Slater sublet the second floor to a local artist, Javier Indalecio. Over the remaining six months, Indalecio's use of oil paints damaged the carpeting in Shoepke's home. Using the information presented in the chapter, answer the following questions.

1 What is the term for the right of Roche citizens to walk across Shoepke's land on the trail?

2 In the warranty deed that was used in the property transfer from the Brusters to Shoepke, what covenants would be inferred by most courts?

3 Can Shoepke hold Slater financially responsible for the damage to the carpeting caused by Indalecio?

APPLICATION How Can You Keep Abreast of Environmental Laws?*

Businesspersons today increasingly face the threat of severe civil or criminal penalties if they violate environmental laws and regulations. Thus, it is crucial to be aware of what those laws and regulations are, how to monitor changes in them, and when to consult with an attorney during the normal course of business. Consider some areas of concern that affect businesses.

Factors to Consider When Purchasing Business Property

When purchasing business property, keep in mind the environmental problems that may arise. Realize that it is up to

you as a purchaser of the property to raise environmental issues—sellers, title insurance companies, and real estate brokers will rarely pursue such matters. (A bank financing the property may worry about the potential environmental hazards of the property, however.)

As a purchaser of business property, you should find out whether there are any restrictions regarding the use of the land, such as whether it can be cleared of trees for construction purposes. The most important environmental concern, though, is whether the property has been contaminated by hazardous wastes created by the previous owners.

Investigate Land-Use History

Purchasers of property can be held liable under Superfund for the clean-up of hazardous wastes dumped by previous property

---

* This *Application* is not meant to substitute for the services of an attorney who is licensed to practice law in your state.

owners. Although current property owners who pay clean-up costs can sue the previous owners for contribution, such litigation is expensive and the outcome uncertain. Clearly, a more prudent course is to investigate the history of the use of the land prior to purchasing the property. You might even want to hire a private environmental site inspector to determine, at a minimum, whether the land has any obvious signs of former contamination.

Investigate and Correct Environmental Violations

Today's companies have an incentive to discover their own environmental wrongdoings. As mentioned in Chapter 6, the federal sentencing guidelines encourage companies to promptly detect, disclose, and correct wrongdoing, including environmental crimes. Companies that do so are subject to lighter penalties for violations of environmental laws. Thus, a company would be well advised to conduct environmental compliance audits regularly.

Small businesses (those with up to one hundred employees) will find it particularly advantageous to investigate and correct environmental violations. Under current EPA guide-lines, the EPA will waive all fines if a small company corrects environmental violations within 180 days after being notified of the violations (or 360 days if pollution-prevention techniques are involved). The policy does not apply to criminal violations of environmental laws or to actions that pose a significant threat to public health, safety, or the environment.

CHECKLIST FOR THE BUSINESSPERSON

1 If you are going to purchase real estate, use land, or engage in activities that might cause environmental damage, check with your attorney immediately and investigate the land-use history.
2 If you want to avoid liability for violating environmental regulations or statutes, conduct environmental compliance audits on a regular basis.
3 If you are ever charged with violating an environmental regulation or law, immediately cease the activity you are being charged with and contact your attorney.
4 In general, environmental law is sufficiently complex that you should never attempt to deal with it without the help of an attorney.

KEY TERMS

adverse possession 738
condemnation 739
constructive eviction 743
conveyance 735
deed 736
easement 735
eminent domain 739
environmental impact
   statement (EIS) 746
eviction 743
fee simple absolute 734

fixed-term tenancy 741
fixture 733
implied warranty
   of habitability 743
leasehold estate 741
license 735
life estate 735
nonpossessory interest 735
periodic tenancy 741
potentially responsible
   party (PRP) 752

profit 735
quitclaim deed 738
recording statutes 738
special warranty deed 738
sublease 744
taking 739
tenancy at sufferance 742
tenancy at will 741
warranty deed 736
wetlands 749

CHAPTER SUMMARY Real Property and Environmental Law

REAL PROPERTY

The Nature of Real Property (See pages 731–733.)	Real property (also called real estate or realty) is immovable. It includes land, subsurface and airspace rights, plant life and vegetation, and fixtures.
Ownership Interests in Real Property (See pages 733–736.)	1. *Fee simple absolute*—The most complete form of ownership. 2. *Life estate*—An estate that lasts for the life of a specified individual during which time the individual is entitled to possess, use, and benefit from the estate; ownership rights in a life estate are subject to the rights of the future-interest holder. 3. *Nonpossessory interest*—An interest that involves the right to use real property but not to possess it. Easements, profits, and licenses are nonpossessory interests.

(Continued)

CHAPTER SUMMARY	Real Property and Environmental Law—Continued
Transfer of Ownership (See pages 736–740.)	1. *By deed*—When real property is sold or transferred as a gift, title to the property is conveyed by means of a deed. A deed must meet specific legal requirements. A *warranty deed* warrants the most extensive protection against defects of title. A *quitclaim deed* conveys to the grantee only whatever interest the grantor had in the property. A deed may be recorded in the manner prescribed by *recording statutes* in the appropriate jurisdiction to give third parties notice of the owner's interest.
	2. *By will or inheritance*—If the owner dies after having made a valid will, the land passes as specified in the will. If the owner dies without having made a will, the heirs inherit according to state inheritance statutes.
	3. *By adverse possession*—When a person possesses the property of another for a statutory period of time (three to thirty years, with ten years being the most common), that person acquires title to the property, provided the possession is actual and exclusive, open and visible, continuous and peaceable, and hostile and adverse (without the permission of the owner).
	4. *By eminent domain*—The government can take land for public use, with just compensation, when the public interest requires the taking.
Leasehold Estates (See pages 741–742.)	A leasehold estate is an interest in real property that is held for only a limited period of time, as specified in the lease agreement. Types of tenancies relating to leased property include the following:
	1. *Fixed-term tenancy*—Tenancy for a period of time stated by express contract.
	2. *Periodic tenancy*—Tenancy for a period determined by the frequency of rent payments; automatically renewed unless proper notice is given.
	3. *Tenancy at will*—Tenancy for as long as both parties agree; no notice of termination is required.
	4. *Tenancy at sufferance*—Possession of land without legal right.
Landlord-Tenant Relationships (See pages 742–745.)	1. *Lease agreement*—The landlord-tenant relationship is created by a lease agreement. State or local laws may dictate whether the lease must be in writing and what lease terms are permissible.
	2. *Rights and duties*—The rights and duties that arise under a lease agreement generally pertain to the following areas:
	a. Possession—The tenant has an exclusive right to possess the leased premises, which must be available to the tenant at the agreed-on time. Under the covenant of quiet enjoyment, the landlord promises that during the lease term neither the landlord nor anyone having superior title to the property will disturb the tenant's use and enjoyment of the property.
	b. Use and maintenance of the premises—Unless the parties agree otherwise, the tenant may make any legal use of the property. The tenant is responsible for any damage that he or she causes. The landlord must comply with laws that set specific standards for the maintenance of real property. The implied warranty of habitability requires that a landlord furnish and maintain residential premises in a habitable condition (that is, in a condition safe and suitable for human life).
	c. Rent—The tenant must pay the rent as long as the lease is in force, unless the tenant justifiably refuses to occupy the property or withholds the rent because of the landlord's failure to maintain the premises properly.
	3. *Transferring rights to leased property*—
	a. If the landlord transfers complete title to the leased property, the tenant becomes the tenant of the new owner. The new owner may then collect the rent but must abide by the existing lease.

CHAPTER SUMMARY   Real Property and Environmental Law—Continued

Landlord-Tenant Relationships— Continued	b. Generally, in the absence of an agreement to the contrary, tenants may assign their rights (but not their duties) under a lease contract to a third person. Tenants may also sublease leased property to a third person, but the original tenant is not relieved of any obligations to the landlord under the lease. In either situation, the landlord's consent may be required, but statutes may prohibit the landlord from unreasonably withholding such consent.

ENVIRONMENTAL LAW

State and Local Regulation (See page 745.)	Activities affecting the environment are controlled at the local and state levels through regulations relating to land use, the disposal and recycling of garbage and waste, and pollution-causing activities in general.
Federal Regulation (See pages 745–754.)	1. *Environmental regulatory agencies*—The most well known of the agencies regulating environmental law is the federal Environmental Protection Agency (EPA), which was created in 1970 to coordinate federal environmental programs. The EPA administers most federal environmental policies and statutes.
	2. *Assessing environmental impact*—The National Environmental Policy Act of 1969 imposes environmental responsibilities on all federal agencies and requires the preparation of an environmental impact statement (EIS) for every major federal action. An EIS must analyze the action's impact on the environment, its adverse effects and possible alternatives, and its irreversible effects on environmental quality.
	3. *Important areas regulated by the federal government*—Important areas regulated by the federal government include the following:
	a. Air pollution—Regulated under the authority of the Clean Air Act of 1963 and its amendments, particularly those of 1970, 1977, and 1990.
	b. Water pollution—Regulated under the authority of the Rivers and Harbors Appropriations Act of 1899, as amended, and the Federal Water Pollution Control Act of 1948, as amended by the Clean Water Act of 1972.
	c. Toxic chemicals and hazardous waste—Pesticides and herbicides, toxic substances, and hazardous waste are regulated under the authority of the Federal Insecticide, Fungicide, and Rodenticide Act of 1947, the Toxic Substances Control Act of 1976, and the Resource Conservation and Recovery Act of 1976, respectively. The Comprehensive Environmental Response, Compensation, and Liability Act (CERCLA) of 1980, as amended, regulates the clean-up of hazardous waste–disposal sites.

FOR REVIEW

Answers for the even-numbered questions in this **For Review** *section can be found in Appendix E at the end of this text.*

1 What are the requirements for acquiring property by adverse possession?

2 What limitations may be imposed on the rights of property owners?

3 What are the respective duties of the landlord and tenant concerning the use and maintenance of leased property?

4 What is contained in an environmental impact statement, and who must file one?

5 What is Superfund, and who is potentially liable under Superfund?

■

QUESTIONS AND CASE PROBLEMS

HYPOTHETICAL SCENARIOS

24.1 Clean Air Act. Current scientific knowledge indicates that there is no safe level of exposure to a cancer-causing agent. In theory, even one molecule of such a substance has the potential for causing cancer. Section 112 of the Clean Air Act requires that all cancer-causing substances be regulated to ensure a margin of safety. Some environmental groups have argued that all emissions of such substances must be eliminated if a margin of safety is to be reached. Such a total elimination would likely shut down many major U.S. industries. Should the Environmental Protection Agency totally eliminate all emissions of cancer-causing chemicals? Discuss.

24.2 Hypothetical Question with Sample Answer. Wiley and Gemma are neighbors. Wiley's lot is extremely large, and his present and future use of it will not involve the entire area. Gemma wants to build a single-car garage and driveway along the present lot boundary. Because the placement of her existing structures makes it impossible for her to comply with an ordinance requiring buildings to be set back fifteen feet from an adjoining property line, Gemma cannot build the garage. Gemma contracts to purchase ten feet of Wiley's property along their boundary line for $3,000. Wiley is willing to sell but will give Gemma only a quitclaim deed, whereas Gemma wants a warranty deed. Discuss the differences between these deeds as they would affect the rights of the parties if the title to this ten feet of land later proves to be defective.

 For a sample answer to Question 24.2, go to Appendix F at the end of this text.

24.3 Landlord's Responsibilities. Sarah has rented a house from Frank. The house is only two years old, but the roof leaks every time it rains. The water that has accumulated in the attic has caused plaster to fall off ceilings in the upstairs bedrooms, and one ceiling has started to sag. Sarah has complained to Frank and asked him to have the roof repaired. Frank says that he has caulked the roof, but the roof still leaks. Frank claims that because Sarah has sole control of the leased premises, she has the duty to repair the roof. Sarah insists that the repair of the roof is Frank's responsibility. Discuss fully who is responsible for repairing the roof and, if the responsibility belongs to Frank, what remedies are available to Sarah.

CASE PROBLEMS

24.4 Environmental Impact Statement. Greers Ferry Lake is in Arkansas, and its shoreline is under the management of the U.S. Army Corps of Engineers, which is part of the U.S. Department of Defense (DOD). The Corps's 2000 Shoreline Management Plan (SMP) rezoned numerous areas along the lake, authorized the Corps to issue permits for the construction of new boat docks in the rezoned areas, increased by 300 percent the area around habitable structures that could be cleared of vegetation, and instituted a Wildlife Enhancement Permit to allow limited modifications of the shoreline. In relation to the SMP's adoption, the Corps issued a Finding of No Significant Impact, which declared that no environmental impact statement (EIS) was necessary. The Corps issued thirty-two boat dock construction permits under the SMP before Save Greers Ferry Lake, Inc., filed a suit in a federal district court against the DOD, asking the court to, among other things, stop the Corps from acting under the SMP and order it to prepare an EIS. What are the requirements for an EIS? Is an EIS needed in this case? Explain. [*Save Greers Ferry Lake, Inc. v. Department of Defense*, 255 F.3d 498 (8th Cir. 2001)]

24.5 Commercial Lease Terms. Metropolitan Life Insurance Co. leased space in its Trail Plaza Shopping Center in Florida to Winn-Dixie Stores, Inc., to operate a supermarket. Under the lease, the landlord agreed not to permit "any [other] property located within the shopping center to be used for or occupied by any business dealing in or which shall keep in stock or sell for off-premises consumption any staple or fancy groceries" in more than "500 square feet of sales area." In 1999, Metropolitan leased 22,000 square feet of space in Trail Plaza to 99 Cent Stuff–Trail Plaza, LLC, under a lease that prohibited it from selling "groceries" in more than 500 square feet of "sales area." Shortly after 99 Cent Stuff opened, it began selling food and other products, including soap, matches, and paper napkins. Alleging that these sales violated the parties' leases, Winn-Dixie filed a suit in a Florida state court against 99 Cent Stuff and others. The defendants argued, among other things, that the groceries provision covered only food and that the 500-square-foot restriction included only shelf space, not store aisles. How should these lease terms be interpreted? Should the court grant an injunction in Winn-Dixie's favor? Explain. [*Winn-*

Dixie Stores, Inc. v. 99 Cent Stuff–Trail Plaza, LLC, 811 So.2d 719 (Fla.App. 3 Dist. 2002)]

24.6 Easements. The Wallens family owned a cabin on Lummi Island in the state of Washington. A driveway ran from the cabin across their property to South Nugent Road. In 1952, Floyd Massey bought the adjacent lot and built a cabin. To gain access to his property, he used a bulldozer to extend the driveway, without the Wallenses' permission but also without their objection. In 1975, the Wallenses sold their property to Wright Fish Co. Massey continued to use and maintain the driveway without permission or objection. In 1984, Massey sold his property to Robert Drake. Drake and his employees continued to use and maintain the driveway without permission or objection, although Drake knew it was located largely on Wright's property. In 1997, Wright sold its lot to Robert Smersh. The next year, Smersh told Drake to stop using the driveway. Drake filed a suit in a Washington state court against Smersh, claiming an easement by prescription (which is created by meeting the same requirements as adverse possession). Does Drake's use of the driveway meet all of the requirements? What should the court rule? Explain. [*Drake v. Smersh*, 122 Wash.App. 147, 89 P.3d 726 (Div. 1 2004)]

24.7 Case Problem with Sample Answer. The Hope Partnership for Education, a religious organization, proposed to build a private independent middle school in a blighted neighborhood in Philadelphia, Pennsylvania. In 2002, the Hope Partnership asked the Redevelopment Authority of the City of Philadelphia to acquire specific land for the project and sell it to the Hope Partnership for a nominal price. The land included a house at 1839 North Eighth Street owned by Mary Smith, whose daughter Veronica lived there with her family. The Authority offered Smith $12,000 for the house and initiated a taking of the property. Smith filed a suit in a Pennsylvania state court against the Authority, admitting that the house was a "substandard structure in a blighted area," but arguing that the taking was unconstitutional because its beneficiary was private. The Authority asserted that only the public purpose of the taking should be considered, not the status of the property's developer. On what basis can a government entity use the power of eminent domain to take property? What are the limits to this power? How should the court rule? Why? [*In re Redevelopment Authority of City of Philadelphia*, 588 Pa. 789, 906 A.2d 1197 (2006)]

After you have answered Problem 24.7, compare your answer with the sample answer given on the Web site that accompanies this text. Go to **academic.cengage.com/blaw/blt**, select "Chapter 24," and click on "Case Problem with Sample Answer."

24.8 Clean Water Act. The Anacostia River, which flows through Washington, D.C., is one of the ten most polluted rivers in the country. For bodies of water such as the Anacostia, the Clean Water Act requires states (which, under the act, include the District of Columbia) to set a "total maximum daily load" (TMDL) for pollutants. A TMDL is to be set "at a level necessary to implement the applicable water-quality standards with seasonal variations." The Anacostia contains biochemical pollutants that consume oxygen, putting the river's aquatic life at risk for suffocation. In addition, the river is murky, stunting the growth of plants that rely on sunlight and impairing recreational use. The Environmental Protection Agency (EPA) approved one TMDL limiting the *annual* discharge of oxygen-depleting pollutants and a second limiting the *seasonal* discharge of pollutants contributing to turbidity. Neither TMDL limited daily discharges. Friends of the Earth, Inc. (FoE), asked a federal district court to review the TMDLs. What is FoE's best argument in this dispute? What is the EPA's likely response? What should the court rule and why? [*Friends of the Earth, Inc. v. Environmental Protection Agency*, 446 F.3d 140 (D.C.Cir. 2006)]

24.9 Ownership in Fee Simple. Thomas and Teresa Cline built a house on a 76-acre parcel of real estate next to Roy Berg's home and property in Augusta County, Virginia. The homes were about 1,800 feet apart but in view of each other. After several disagreements between the parties, Berg equipped an 11-foot tripod with motion sensors and floodlights that intermittently illuminated the Clines' home. Berg also installed surveillance cameras that tracked some of the movement on the Clines' property. The cameras transmitted on an open frequency, which could be received by any television within range. The Clines asked Berg to turn off, or at least redirect, the lights. When he refused, they erected a fence for 200 feet along the parties' common property line. The 32-foot-high fence consisted of 20 utility poles spaced 10 feet apart with plastic wrap stretched between the poles. This effectively blocked the lights and cameras. Berg filed a suit against the Clines in a Virginia state court, complaining that the fence interfered unreasonably with his use and enjoyment of his property. He asked the court to order the Clines to take the fence down. What are the limits on an owner's use of property? How should the court rule in this case? Why? [*Cline v. Berg*, 639 S.E.2d 231 (Va. 2007)]

24.10 A Question of Ethics. *In 1999, Stephen and Linda Kailin bought the Monona Center, a mall in Madison, Wisconsin, from Perry Armstrong for $760,000. The contract provided, "Seller represents to Buyer that as of the date of acceptance Seller had no notice or knowledge of conditions affecting the Property or transaction" other than certain items disclosed at the time of the offer. Armstrong told the Kailins of the Center's eight tenants, their lease expiration dates, and the monthly and annual rent due under each lease. One of the lessees, Ring's All-American Karate, occupied about a third of the Center's space under a five-year lease. Because of Ring's financial difficulties, Armstrong had agreed to reduce its rent for nine months in 1997. By the time of the sale to the Kailins, Ring owed $13,910 in unpaid rent, but Armstrong did not tell the Kailins, who did not ask. Ring continued to fail to pay rent and finally vacated the Center. The Kailins filed a suit in a Wisconsin state court against Armstrong and others, alleging, among other things,* *misrepresentation.* [Kailin v. Armstrong, 2002 WI App. 70, 252 Wis.2d 676, 643 N.W.2d 132 (2002)]

1 Did Armstrong have a duty to disclose Ring's delinquency and default to the Kailins? Explain.

2 What obligation, if any, did Ring have to the Kailins or Armstrong after failing to pay the rent and eventually defaulting on the lease? Why?

CRITICAL THINKING AND WRITING ASSIGNMENTS

24.11 Critical Thinking and Writing Assignment for Business. Garza Construction Co. erects a silo (a grain storage facility) on Reeve's ranch. Garza also lends Reeve funds to pay for the silo under an agreement providing that the silo is not to become part of the land until Reeve completes the loan payments. Before the silo is paid for, Metropolitan State Bank, the mortgage holder on Reeve's land, forecloses on the property. Metropolitan contends that the silo is a fixture to the realty and that the bank is therefore entitled to the proceeds from its sale. Garza argues that the silo is personal property and that the proceeds should therefore go to Garza. Is the silo a fixture? Why or why not?

24.12 Critical Legal Thinking. It has been estimated that for every dollar spent cleaning up hazardous waste sites, administrative agencies spend seven dollars in overhead. Can you think of any way to trim the administrative costs associated with the clean-up of contaminated sites?

ONLINE ACTIVITIES

PRACTICAL INTERNET EXERCISES

Go to this text's Web site at **academic.cengage.com/blaw/blt**, select "Chapter 24," and click on "Practical Internet Exercises." There you will find the following Internet research exercises that you can perform to learn more about the topics covered in this chapter.

PRACTICAL INTERNET EXERCISE 24-1   LEGAL PERSPECTIVE—Eminent Domain

PRACTICAL INTERNET EXERCISE 24-2   MANAGEMENT PERSPECTIVE—Complying with Environmental Regulations

PRACTICAL INTERNET EXERCISE 24-3   SOCIAL PERSPECTIVE—The Rights of Tenants

BEFORE THE TEST

Go to this text's Web site at **academic.cengage.com/blaw/blt**, select "Chapter 24," and click on "Interactive Quizzes." You will find a number of interactive questions relating to this chapter.

CHAPTER 25
International Law in a Global Economy

LEARNING OBJECTIVES

AFTER READING THIS CHAPTER, YOU SHOULD BE ABLE TO ANSWER THE FOLLOWING QUESTIONS:

1 What is the principle of comity, and why do courts deciding disputes involving a foreign law or judicial decree apply this principle?

2 What is the act of state doctrine? In what circumstances is this doctrine applied?

3 Under the Foreign Sovereign Immunities Act of 1976, on what bases might a foreign state be considered subject to the jurisdiction of U.S. courts?

4 In what circumstances will U.S. antitrust laws be applied extraterritorially?

5 Do U.S. laws prohibiting employment discrimination apply in all circumstances to U.S. employees working for U.S. employers abroad?

> **"**Our interests are those of the open door—a door of friendship and mutual advantage. This is the only door we care to enter.**"**
>
> Woodrow Wilson, 1856–1924
> (Twenty-eighth president of the United States, 1913–1921)

nternational business transactions are not unique to the modern world. Indeed, as suggested by President Woodrow Wilson's statement in the chapter-opening quotation, people have always found that they can benefit from exchanging goods with others. What is new in our day is the dramatic growth in world trade and the emergence of a global business community. Because the exchange of goods, services, and ideas on a global level is now routine, students of business law and the legal environment should be familiar with the laws pertaining to international business transactions. In this chapter, we first examine the legal context of international business transactions. We then look at some selected areas relating to business activities in a global context, including international sales contracts, civil dispute resolution, letters of credit, and investment protection. We conclude the chapter with a discussion of the application of certain U.S. laws in a transnational setting.

INTERNATIONAL PRINCIPLES AND DOCTRINES

Recall from our discussion in Chapter 1 that **international law** can be defined as a body of law—formed as a result of international customs, treaties, and organizations—that governs relations among or between nations. International law may be public, creating standards for the nations themselves or it may be private, establishing international standards for private transactions that cross national borders. **National law,** in contrast, is the law of a particular nation, such as Brazil, Germany, Japan, or the United States. Here, we look

INTERNATIONAL LAW
The law that governs relations among nations. International customs and treaties are important sources of international law.

NATIONAL LAW
Laws that pertain to a particular nation (as opposed to international law).

at some legal principles and doctrines of international law that have evolved over time and that the courts of various nations have employed—to a greater or lesser extent—to resolve or reduce conflicts that involve a foreign element. The three important legal principles and doctrines discussed in the following subsections are based primarily on courtesy and respect and are applied in the interests of maintaining harmonious relations among nations.

The Principle of Comity

COMITY
The principle by which one nation defers to and gives effect to the laws and judicial decrees of another nation. This recognition is based primarily on respect.

Under what is known as the principle of **comity,** one nation will defer to and give effect to the laws and judicial decrees of another country, as long as those laws and judicial decrees are consistent with the law and public policy of the accommodating nation.

■EXAMPLE 25.1 A Swedish seller and a U.S. buyer have formed a contract, which the buyer breaches. The seller sues the buyer in a Swedish court, which awards damages. The buyer's assets, however, are in the United States and cannot be reached unless the judgment is enforced by a U.S. court of law. In this situation, if a U.S. court determines that the procedures and laws applied in the Swedish court were consistent with U.S. national law and policy, that court will likely defer to (and enforce) the foreign court's judgment. ■

One way to understand the principle of comity (and the *act of state doctrine*, which will be discussed shortly) is to consider the relationships among the states in our federal form of government. Each state honors (gives "full faith and credit" to) the contracts, property deeds, wills, and other legal obligations formed in other states, as well as judicial decisions with respect to such obligations. On a worldwide basis, nations similarly attempt to honor judgments rendered in other countries when it is feasible to do so. Of course, in the United States the states are constitutionally required to honor other states' actions, whereas internationally, nations are not *required* to honor the actions of other nations.

The Act of State Doctrine

ACT OF STATE DOCTRINE
A doctrine providing that the judicial branch of one country will not examine the validity of public acts committed by a recognized foreign government within its own territory.

EXPROPRIATION
The seizure by a government of a privately owned business or personal property for a proper public purpose and with just compensation.

CONFISCATION
A government's taking of a privately owned business or personal property without a proper public purpose or an award of just compensation.

The **act of state doctrine** is a judicially created doctrine that provides that the judicial branch of one country will not examine the validity of public acts committed by a recognized foreign government within its own territory.

When a Foreign Government Takes Private Property The **act of state doctrine** can have important consequences for individuals and firms doing business with, and investing in, other countries. For example, this doctrine is frequently employed in situations involving expropriation or confiscation. **Expropriation** occurs when a government seizes a privately owned business or privately owned goods for a proper public purpose and awards just compensation. When a government seizes private property for an illegal purpose or without just compensation, the taking is referred to as a **confiscation.** The line between these two forms of taking is sometimes blurred because of differing interpretations of what is illegal and what constitutes just compensation.

■EXAMPLE 25.2 Flaherty, Inc., a U.S. company, owns a mine in Brazil. The government of Brazil seizes the mine for public use and claims that the profits that Flaherty realized from the mine in preceding years constitute just compensation. Flaherty disagrees, but the act of state doctrine may prevent the company's recovery in a U.S. court. ■ Note that in a case alleging that a foreign government has wrongfully taken the plaintiff's property, the defendant government has the burden of proving that the taking was an expropriation, not a confiscation.

On May 1, 2007, Venezuela's president, Hugo Chavez, told an enthusiastic crowd that he had completed the nationalization of all of that country's formerly private oil companies. What long-term effects might such an action have on foreign investments in Venezuela? (AP Photo/ Fernando Llano)

May Immunize a Foreign Government's Actions   When applicable, both the act of state doctrine and the doctrine of *sovereign immunity* (to be discussed next) tend to immunize (protect) foreign governments from the jurisdiction of U.S. courts. This means that firms or individuals who own property overseas often have diminished legal protection against government actions in the countries in which they operate.

The Doctrine of Sovereign Immunity

When certain conditions are satisfied, the doctrine of **sovereign immunity** immunizes foreign nations from the jurisdiction of U.S. courts. In 1976, Congress codified this rule in the Foreign Sovereign Immunities Act (FSIA).[1] The FSIA exclusively governs the circumstances in which an action may be brought in the United States against a foreign nation, including attempts to attach a foreign nation's property.

Section 1605 of the FSIA sets forth the major exceptions to the jurisdictional immunity of a foreign state or country. A foreign state is not immune from the jurisdiction of U.S. courts when the state has "waived its immunity either explicitly or by implication" or when the action is taken "in connection with a commercial activity carried on in the United States by the foreign state" or having "a direct effect in the United States."[2] The FSIA also contains an exception for torts committed in the United States and for some violations of international law. Generally, because the law is jurisdictional in nature, a plaintiff has the burden of showing that a defendant is not entitled to sovereign immunity.

The question frequently arises as to whether an entity falls within the category of a foreign state. The question of what is a commercial activity has also been the subject of dispute. Under Section 1603 of the FSIA, a *foreign state* includes both a political subdivision of a foreign state and an instrumentality (department or agency of any branch of a government) of a foreign state. Section 1603 broadly defines a *commercial activity* as a commercial activity that is carried out by a foreign state within the United States, but it does not describe the particulars of what constitutes a commercial activity. Thus, the courts are left to decide whether a particular activity is governmental or commercial in nature. In the following case, the United States Supreme Court considered whether the principles of the FSIA should apply to a dispute dating back to World War II, before the FSIA was enacted.

SOVEREIGN IMMUNITY
A doctrine that immunizes foreign nations from the jurisdiction of U.S. courts when certain conditions are satisfied.

ON THE WEB

FindLaw's Web site includes an extensive array of links to international doctrines, treaties, and other nations' laws. Go to

library.findlaw.com

and select "International Law."

---

1. 28 U.S.C. Section 1602–1611.
2. See, for example, *Keller v. Central Bank of Nigeria*, 277 F.3d 811 (6th Cir. 2002), in which the court held that failure to pay promised funds to a Cleveland account was an action having a direct effect in the United States.

CASE 25.1   **Republic of Austria v. Altmann**

Supreme Court of the United States, 541 U.S. 677, 124 S.Ct. 2240, 159 L.Ed.2d 1 (2004).
www.findlaw.com/casecode/supreme.html[a]

FACTS   Maria Altmann escaped from Austria and moved to California after Nazi Germany annexed Austria in 1938. Altmann was an heir of Ferdinand Bloch-Bauer, who had owned valuable artworks, including paintings by Gustav Klimt, which the Nazis seized. The Austrian Gallery, an "instrumentality" of the Republic of Austria, eventually displayed the Klimt paintings along with other art that the Nazis had seized or Austria had expropriated after World War II. Altmann filed a suit in a U.S. federal district court against Austria and the gallery to recover the Klimt paintings. The defendants filed a motion to dismiss the complaint on the basis of sovereign immunity under the Foreign Sovereign Immunities Act (FSIA), even though the FSIA was not enacted until 1976. The court ruled in Altmann's favor. The defendants appealed to the U.S. Court of Appeals for the Ninth Circuit, which affirmed the lower court's ruling. The defendants appealed to the United States Supreme Court.

ISSUE   Does the FSIA apply to acts that were committed before 1976?

a. In the "Browsing" section, click on "2004 Decisions." When that page opens, scroll to the name of the case and click on it to read the opinion.

CASE 25.1–Continues next page

CASE 25.1—Continued

DECISION   Yes. The United States Supreme Court affirmed the lower court's decision "because the Act * * * clearly applies to conduct, like petitioners' alleged wrongdoing, that occurred prior to 1976." The complaint was not dismissed, and the case was remanded for trial.

REASON   The Supreme Court first recognized that there was no doubt that the FSIA's procedural provisions applied to all "pending" cases. The Court reasoned further that the FSIA, according to these and other provisions, applied to "all postenactment claims of sovereign immunity," which were to be "henceforth" decided by the courts. The Court stated that the language in these provisions "suggests Congress intended courts to resolve *all* such claims in conformity with the principles set forth in the Act, regardless of when the underlying conduct occurred." Citing the FSIA's "comprehensive framework"

for resolving claims of sovereign immunity, the Court concluded that "[m]any of the [FSIA's] provisions unquestionably apply to cases arising out of conduct that occurred before 1976." The Court explained that "[a]pplying the FSIA to all pending cases regardless of when the underlying conduct occurred is most consistent with two of the Act's principal purposes: clarifying the rules that judges should apply in resolving sovereign immunity claims and eliminating political participation in the resolution of such claims." These purposes would be "frustrated if, in postenactment cases concerning preenactment conduct, courts were to continue to follow the * * * standards that the FSIA replaced."

 WHAT IF THE FACTS WERE DIFFERENT?   *If the Court had held that the FSIA did not apply to Altmann's claim, could Altmann still have established that the U.S. courts had jurisdiction over Austria? Why or why not?*

DOING BUSINESS INTERNATIONALLY

EXPORT
The sale of goods and services by domestic firms to buyers located in other countries.

A U.S. domestic firm can engage in international business transactions in a number of ways. The simplest way is to seek out foreign markets for domestically produced products or services. In other words, U.S. firms can **export** their goods and services to markets abroad. Alternatively, a U.S. firm can establish foreign production facilities so as to be closer to the foreign market or markets in which its products are sold. The advantages may include lower labor costs, fewer government regulations, and lower taxes and trade barriers. A domestic firm can also obtain revenues by licensing its technology to an existing foreign company or by selling franchises to overseas entities.

Exporting

Exporting can take two forms: direct exporting and indirect exporting. In *direct exporting*, a U.S. company signs a sales contract with a foreign purchaser that provides for the conditions of shipment and payment for the goods. (How payments are made in international transactions is discussed later in this chapter.) If sufficient business develops in a foreign country, a U.S. corporation may set up a specialized marketing organization in that foreign market by appointing a foreign agent or a foreign distributor. This is called *indirect exporting*.

When a U.S. firm desires to limit its involvement in an international market, it will typically establish an *agency relationship* with a foreign firm (*agency* was discussed in Chapter 17). The foreign firm then acts as the U.S. firm's agent and can enter contracts in the foreign location on behalf of the principal (the U.S. company).

DISTRIBUTION AGREEMENT
A contract between a seller and a distributor of the seller's products setting out the terms and conditions of the distributorship.

EXCLUSIVE DISTRIBUTORSHIP
A distributorship in which the seller and the distributor of the seller's products agree that the distributor will distribute only the seller's products.

When a substantial market exists in a foreign country, a U.S. firm may wish to appoint a distributor located in that country. The U.S. firm and the distributor enter into a **distribution agreement,** which is a contract between the seller and the distributor setting out the terms and conditions of the distributorship. These terms and conditions—for example, price, currency of payment, availability of supplies, and method of payment—primarily involve contract law. Disputes concerning distribution agreements may involve jurisdictional or other issues (discussed in detail later in this chapter). In addition, in some instances an **exclusive distributorship**—in which the distributor agrees to distribute only the seller's goods—has raised antitrust problems.

Manufacturing Abroad

An alternative to direct or indirect exporting is the establishment of foreign manufacturing facilities. Typically, U.S. firms establish manufacturing plants abroad if they believe that doing so will reduce their costs—particularly for labor, shipping, and raw materials—and enable them to compete more effectively in foreign markets. Foreign firms have done the same in the United States. Sony, Nissan, and other Japanese manufacturers have established U.S. plants to avoid import duties that the U.S. Congress may impose on Japanese products entering this country.

A U.S. firm can manufacture goods in other countries in several ways. They include licensing, franchising, and investing in a wholly owned subsidiary or a joint venture.

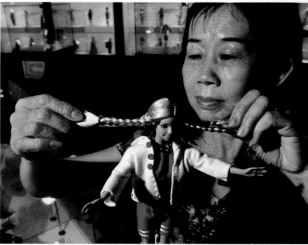

A woman holds a Barbie doll that was manufactured in Taiwan. Why would a U.S. corporation, such as Mattel, Inc., outsource its manufacturing jobs to a foreign firm? (AP Photo/Wally Santana)

Licensing A U.S. firm can obtain business from abroad by licensing a foreign manufacturing company to use its copyrighted, patented, or trademarked intellectual property or trade secrets. Like any other licensing agreement (see Chapters 5 and 10), a licensing agreement with a foreign-based firm calls for a payment of royalties on some basis—such as so many cents per unit produced or a certain percentage of profits from units sold in a particular geographic territory.

In some circumstances, even in the absence of a patent, a firm may be able to license the "know-how" associated with a particular manufacturing process—for example, a plant design or a secret formula. The foreign firm that agrees to sign the licensing agreement further agrees to keep the know-how confidential and to pay royalties. **■EXAMPLE 25.3** The Coca-Cola Bottling Company licenses firms worldwide to use (and keep confidential) its secret formula for the syrup used in its soft drink. In return, the foreign firms licensed to make the syrup pay Coca-Cola a percentage of the income earned from the sale of the soft drink. ■

The licensing of intellectual property rights benefits all parties to the transaction. The firm that receives the license can take advantage of an established reputation for quality. The firm that grants the license receives income from the foreign sales of its products and also establishes a global reputation. Additionally, once a firm's trademark is known worldwide, the firm may experience increased demand for other products it manufactures or sells—obviously an important consideration.

ON THE WEB

For information on the legal requirements of doing business abroad, a good source is the Internet Law Library's collection of laws of other nations. Go to

www.lawguru.com/ilawlib.

Franchising Franchising is a well-known form of licensing. Recall from Chapter 19 that in a franchise arrangement the owner of a trademark, trade name, or copyright (the franchisor) licenses another (the franchisee) to use the trademark, trade name, or copyright under certain conditions or limitations in the selling of goods or services. In return, the franchisee pays a fee, which is usually based on a percentage of gross or net sales. Examples of international franchises include Holiday Inn and Hertz.

Investing in a Wholly Owned Subsidiary or a Joint Venture Another way to expand into a foreign market is to establish a wholly owned subsidiary firm in a foreign country. When a wholly owned subsidiary is established, the parent company, which remains in the United States, retains complete ownership of all the facilities in the foreign country, as well as complete authority and control over all phases of the operation. A U.S. firm can also expand into international markets through a joint venture. In a joint venture, the U.S. company owns only part of the operation; the rest is owned either by local owners in the foreign country or by another foreign entity. All of the firms involved in a joint venture share responsibilities, as well as profits and liabilities.

COMMERCIAL CONTRACTS IN AN INTERNATIONAL SETTING

Like all commercial contracts, an international contract should be in writing. For an example of an actual international sales contract, see Exhibit 25–1.

Contract Clauses

Language and legal differences among nations can create special problems for parties to international contracts when disputes arise. It is possible to avoid these problems by including in a contract special provisions designating the official language of the contract, the legal forum (court or place) in which disputes under the contract will be settled, and the substantive law that will be applied in settling any disputes. Parties to international contracts should also indicate in their contracts what acts or events will excuse the parties from performance under the contract and whether disputes under the contract will be arbitrated or litigated.

Choice of Language   A deal struck between a U.S. company and a company in another country normally involves two languages. Typically, many phrases in one language are not readily translatable into another. Consequently, the complex contractual terms involved may not be understood by one party in the other party's language. To make sure that no disputes arise out of this language problem, an international sales contract should have a **choice-of-language clause** designating the official language by which the contract will be interpreted in the event of disagreement.

CHOICE-OF-LANGUAGE CLAUSE
A clause in a contract designating the official language by which the contract will be interpreted in the event of a future disagreement over the contract's terms.

PREVENTING LEGAL DISPUTES

When entering into international contracts, businesspersons should always determine whether the foreign nation has any applicable language requirements. Some nations have mandatory language requirements. In France, for instance, certain legal documents, such as the prospectuses used in securities offerings, must be written in French. In addition, contracts with any state or local authority in France, instruction manuals, and warranties for goods and services offered for sale in France must also be written in French. To avoid disputes, know the law of the jurisdiction before you enter into any agreements in that nation. Remember that certain legal terms or phrases in documents may not easily translate from one language to another. Finding out that a nation has language requirements may influence your decision whether to enter into a contract in that location and will definitely affect your decision whether to include a choice-of-law clause (to be discussed shortly).

FORUM-SELECTION CLAUSE
A provision in a contract designating the court, jurisdiction, or tribunal that will decide any disputes arising under the contract.

Choice of Forum   When parties from several countries are involved, litigation may be pursued in courts in different nations. There are no universally accepted rules as to which court has jurisdiction over particular subject matter or parties to a dispute. Consequently, parties to an international transaction should always include in the contract a **forum-selection clause** indicating what court, jurisdiction, or tribunal will decide any disputes arising under the contract. It is especially important to indicate the specific court that will have jurisdiction. The forum does not necessarily have to be within the geographic boundaries of the home nation of either party.

EXAMPLE 25.4   Garware Polyester, Ltd., based in Mumbai, India, develops and makes plastics and high-tech polyester film. Intermax Trading Corporation, based in New York, acted as Garware's North American sales agent and sold its products on a commission basis. Garware and Intermax had executed a series of agency agreements under which the

EXHIBIT 25–1 Sample International Sales Contract

Sample Sales Contract for Purchase of Green Coffee

Starbucks Coffee Company was founded in 1971, when it opened its first store in Seattle's Pike Place Market. Today, Starbucks is the leading roaster and retailer of specialty coffee in the world. The company has nearly 6,000 stores in thirty-seven countries. Starbucks's chairman and chief global strategist, Howard Schultz, who has been instrumental in the company's expansion, hopes to have 10,000 stores in fifty countries by the end of 2007.

Schultz joined the company in 1982, when Starbucks was still only a small, but highly respected roaster and retailer of whole-bean and ground coffee. A business trip to Italy opened Schultz's eyes to the rich tradition and popularity of the espresso bar. Espresso drinks became the foundation of his vision for the company, and when Schultz purchased Starbucks in 1987, Starbucks started brewing. In a few years, the company had expanded to numerous locations in the United States and was available in restaurants, hotels, and airports, as well as by mail-order catalogue. In 1992, Starbucks began to sell shares of the company's stock to the public. The price of Starbucks stock initially was $17 per share. The same share of stock today would be worth about $400—a gain of 2,200 percent.

"In the early days, there were only a few members of the financial community who believed in our viability and staying power," says Schultz. No one dreamed that Starbucks would grow from a company that was worth approximately $270 million in 1992 into a company that is worth nearly $10 billion today. With the forward-thinking Schultz at the helm, however, Starbucks blossomed into one of the world's most admired brands. Since opening its first international location in 1996, Starbucks has expanded to 1,200 international locations throughout North America and Europe, as well as in the Middle East and Pacific Rim. Starbucks coffee is now available in supermarkets and online.

In addition to its uncompromising commitment to buying, roasting, and serving only the finest coffees in the world, Starbucks also produces and sells bottled Frappuccino®, a line of premium ice creams, Tazo® Tea, and a line of compact discs.

The company has also given back to the communities in which it operates—sponsoring cultural events, such as jazz and film festivals, and donating money to charities, especially those that benefit children. Starbucks provides funding for education and literacy programs, college scholarship programs, and international relief organizations. Starbucks is also strongly committed to promoting environmentally sound methods of growing coffee and gives to organizations supporting coffee farmers.

(Photo Courtesy of Jill Doran for Starbucks Coffee)

(Continued)

EXHIBIT 25–1	Sample International Sales Contract–Continued

① OVERLAND COFFEE IMPORT CONTRACT
OF THE
GREEN COFFEE ASSOCIATION
OF
NEW YORK CITY, INC.*

Contract Seller's No.: **504617**
Buyer's No.: **P9264**
Date: **9/11/08**

SOLD BY: **XYZ Co.**
TO: **Starbucks**

② QUANTITY: **Five Hundred** (**500**) Tons of (Bags) **Mexican** coffee
③ weighing about **152.117 lbs.** per bag.

PACKAGING: **④** Coffee must be packed in clean sound bags of uniform size made of sisal, henequen, jute, burlap, or similar woven material, without inner lining or outer covering of any material properly sewn by hand and/or machine.
Bulk shipments are allowed if agreed by mutual consent of Buyer and Seller.

DESCRIPTION: **⑤** **High grown Mexican Altura**

PRICE: **⑥** At **Ten/$10.00 dollars** U. S. Currency, per **lb.** net, (U.S. Funds)
Upon delivery in Bonded Public Warehouse at **Laredo, TX**
(City and State)

PAYMENT: **⑦** **Cash against warehouse receipts**

⑧ Bill and tender to DATE when all import requirements and governmental regulations have been satisfied, and coffee delivered or discharged (as per contract terms). Seller is obliged to give the Buyer two (2) calendar days free time in Bonded Public Warehouse following but not including date of tender.

ARRIVAL: **⑨** During **December** via **truck**
(Period) (Method of Transportation)
from **Mexico** for arrival at **Laredo, TX USA**
(Country of Exportation) (Country of Importation)
Partial shipments permitted.

ADVICE OF ARRIVAL: **⑩** Advice of arrival with warehouse name and location, together with the quantity, description, marks and place of entry, must be transmitted directly, or through Seller's Agent/Broker, to the Buyer or his Agent/Broker. Advice will be given as soon as known but not later than the fifth business day following arrival at the named warehouse. Such advice may be given verbally with written confirmation to be sent the same day.

WEIGHTS: **⑪** (1) DELIVERED WEIGHTS: Coffee covered by this contract is to be weighed at location named in tender. Actual tare to be allowed.
(2) SHIPPING WEIGHTS: Coffee covered by this contract is sold on shipping weights. Any loss in weight exceeding **1/2** percent at location named in tender is for account of Seller at contract price.
(3) Coffee is to be weighed within fifteen (15) calendar days after tender. Weighing expenses, if any, for account of **seller** (Seller or Buyer)

MARKINGS: Bags to be branded in English with the name of Country of Origin and otherwise to comply with laws and regulations of the Country of Importation, in effect at the time of entry, governing marking of import merchandise. Any expense incurred by failure to comply with these regulations to be borne by Exporter/Seller.

RULINGS: **⑫** The "Rulings on Coffee Contracts" of the Green Coffee Association of New York City, Inc., in effect on the date this contract is made, is incorporated for all purposes as a part of this agreement, and together herewith, constitute the entire contract. No variation or addition hereto shall be valid unless signed by the parties to the contract.
Seller guarantees that the terms printed on the reverse hereof, which by reference are made a part hereof, are identical with the terms as printed in By-Laws and Rules of the Green Coffee Association of New York City, Inc., heretofore adopted.
Exceptions to this guarantee are:

ACCEPTED: **XYZ Co.**
BY_____ Seller
_____ Agent

Starbucks
BY_____ Buyer
_____ Agent

COMMISSION TO BE PAID BY: **seller**

ABC Brokerage
⑬ Broker(s)

When this contract is executed by a person acting for another, such person hereby represents that he is fully authorized to commit his principal.

* Reprinted with permission of the Green Coffee Association of New York City, Inc.

EXHIBIT 25–1 | **Sample International Sales Contract–Continued**

① This is a contract for a sale of coffee to be *imported*. If the parties' principal places of business are located in different countries, the contract may be subject to the United Nations Convention on Contracts for the International Sale of Goods (CISG). If the parties' principal places of business are located in the United States, the contract may be subject to the Uniform Commercial Code (UCC).

② Quantity is one of the most important terms to include in a contract. Without it, a court may not be able to enforce the contract. See Chapter 11.

③ Weight per unit (bag) can be exactly stated or approximately stated. If it is not so stated, usage of trade in international contracts determines standards of weight.

④ Packaging requirements can be conditions for acceptance and payment. Bulk shipments are not permitted without the consent of the buyer. See Chapter 7 for an explanation of contract conditions.

⑤ A description of the coffee and the "Markings" constitute express warranties. Warranties in contracts for domestic sales of goods were discussed in Chapter 13. International contracts rely more heavily on descriptions and models or samples.

⑥ Under the UCC, parties can enter into a valid contract even though the price is not set. See Chapter 11. Under the CISG, a contract must provide for an exact determination of the price.

⑦ The terms of payment can take one of two forms: credit or cash. Credit terms can be complicated. A cash term can be simple, and payment can be made by any means acceptable in the ordinary course of business (for example, a personal check or a letter of credit). If the seller insists on actual cash, the buyer must be given a reasonable time to get it. See Chapter 12.

⑧ *Tender* means the seller places goods that conform to the contract at the buyer's disposition. What constitutes a valid tender was explained in Chapter 12. This contract requires that the coffee meet all import regulations and that it be ready for pickup by the buyer at a "Bonded Public Warehouse." (A *bonded warehouse* is a place in which goods can be stored without paying taxes until the goods are removed.) For a discussion of the responsibilities of the parties when goods are in a warehouse, see Chapter 23.

⑨ The delivery date is significant because, if it is not met, the buyer can hold the seller in breach of the contract. Under this contract, the seller can be given a "period" within which to deliver the goods, instead of being required to deliver on a specific day, which could present problems. The seller is also given some time to rectify goods that do not pass inspection (see the "Guarantee" clause on page 770). For a discussion of the remedies of the buyer and seller, see Chapter 12.

⑩ As part of a proper tender, the seller (or its agent) must inform the buyer (or its agent) when the goods have arrived at their destination. The responsibilities of agents were set out in Chapter 17.

⑪ In some contracts, delivered and shipped weights can be important. During shipping, some loss can be attributed to the type of goods (spoilage of fresh produce, for example) or to the transportation itself. A seller and buyer can agree on the extent to which either of them will bear such losses.

⑫ Documents are often incorporated in a contract by reference, because including them word for word can make a contract difficult to read. If the document is later revised, the whole contract might have to be reworked. Documents that are typically incorporated by reference include detailed payment and delivery terms, special provisions, and sets of rules, codes, and standards.

⑬ In international sales transactions, and for domestic deals involving certain products, brokers are used to form the contracts. When so used, the brokers are entitled to a commission. See Chapter 17.

(Continued)

EXHIBIT 25–1	Sample International Sales Contract–Continued

TERMS AND CONDITIONS

ARBITRATION: All controversies relating to, in connection with, or arising out of this contract, its modification, making or the authority or obligations of the signatories hereto, and whether involving the principals, agents, brokers, or others who actually sub-scribe hereto, shall be settled by arbitration in accordance with the "Rules of Arbitration" of the Green Coffee Association of New York City, Inc., as they exist at the time of the arbitration (including provisions as to payment of fees and ex-penses). Arbitration is the sole remedy hereunder, and it shall be held in accordance with the law of New York State, and judgment of any award may be entered in the courts of that State, or in any other court of competent jurisdiction. All notices or judicial service in reference to arbitration or enforcement shall be deemed given if transmitted as required by the aforesaid rules. **⑭**

GUARANTEE: (a) If all or any of the coffee is refused admission into the country of importation by reason of any violation of govern-mental laws or acts, which violation existed at the time the coffee arrived at Bonded-Public Warehouse, seller is required, as to the amount not admitted and as soon as possible, to deliver replacement coffee in conformity to all terms and condi-tions of this contract, excepting only the Arrival terms, but not later than thirty (30) days after the date of the violation notice. Any payment made and expenses incurred for any coffee denied entry shall be refunded within ten (10) calendar days of denial of entry, and payment shall be made for the replacement delivery in accordance with the terms of this con-tract. Consequently, if Buyer removes the coffee from the Bonded Public Warehouse, Seller's responsibility as to such portion hereunder ceases. **⑮**
(b) Contracts containing the overstamp "No Pass-No Sale" on the face of the contract shall be interpreted to mean: If any or all of the coffee is not admitted into the country of Importation in its original condition by reason of failure to meet requirements of the government's laws or Acts, the contract shall be deemed null and void as to that portion of the coffee which is not admitted in its original condition. Any payment made and expenses incurred for any coffee denied entry shall be refunded within ten (10) calendar days of denial of entry.

CONTINGENCY: This contract is not contingent upon any other contract.

CLAIMS: Coffee shall be considered accepted as to quality unless within _fifteen_ (15) calendar days after delivery at Bonded Public Warehouse or within _fifteen_ (15) calendar days after all Government clearances have been received, whichever is later, either: **⑯**
(a) Claims are settled by the parties hereto, or,
(b) Arbitration proceedings have been filed by one of the parties in accordance with the provisions hereof.
(c) If neither (a) nor (b) has been done in the stated period or if any portion of the coffee has been removed from the Bonded Public Warehouse before representative sealed samples have been drawn by the Green Coffee Association of New York City, Inc., in accordance with its rules, Seller's responsibility for quality claims ceases for that portion so removed.
(d) Any question of quality submitted to arbitration shall be a matter of allowance only, unless otherwise provided in the contract.

DELIVERY: (a) No more than three (3) chops may be tendered for each lot of 250 bags. **⑰**
(b) Each (chop) of coffee tendered is to be uniform in grade and appearance. All expense necessary to make coffee uniform shall be for account of seller.
(c) Notice of arrival and/or sampling order constitutes a tender, and must be given not later than the fifth business day fol-lowing arrival at Bonded Public Warehouse stated on the contract.

INSURANCE: Seller is responsible for any loss or damage, or both, until Delivery and Discharge of coffee at the Bonded Public Warehouse in the Country of Importation. **⑱**
All Insurance Risks, costs and responsibility are for Seller's Account until Delivery and Discharge of coffee at the Bonded Public Warehouse in the Country of Importation.
Buyer's insurance responsibility begins from the day of importation or from the day of tender, whichever is later. **⑲**

FREIGHT: Seller to provide and pay for all transportation and related expenses to the Bonded Public Warehouse in the Country of Importation.

EXPORT DUTIES/TAXES: Exporter is to pay all Export taxes, duties or other fees or charges, if any, levied because of exportation. **⑳**

IMPORT DUTIES/TAXES: Any Duty or Tax whatsoever, imposed by the government or any authority of the Country of Importation, shall be borne by the Importer/Buyer.

INSOLVENCY OR FINANCIAL FAILURE OF BUYER OR SELLER: If, at any time before the contract is fully executed, either party hereto shall meet with creditors because of inability gener-ally to make payment of obligations when due, or shall suspend such payments, fail to meet his general trade obligations in the regular course of business, shall file a petition in bankruptcy or, for an arrangement, shall become insolvent, or commit an act of bankruptcy, then the other party may at his option, expressed in writing, declare the aforesaid to consti-tute a breach and default of this contract, and may, in addition to other remedies, decline to deliver further or make pay-ment or may sell or purchase for the defaulter's account, and may collect damage for any injury or loss, or shall account for the profit, if any, occasioned by such sale or purchase. **㉑**
This clause is subject to the provisions of (11 USC 365 (e) 1) if invoked.

BREACH OR DEFAULT OF CONTRACT: In the event either party hereto fails to perform, or breaches or repudiates this agreement, the other party shall subject to the specific provisions of this contract be entitled to the remedies and relief provided for by the Uniform Commercial Code of the State of New York. The computation and ascertainment of damages, or the determination of any other dispute as to relief, shall be made by the arbitrators in accordance with the Arbitration Clause herein. **㉒**
Consequential damages shall not, however, be allowed.

EXHIBIT 25–1 **Sample International Sales Contract–Continued**

⑭ Arbitration involves settling a dispute by submitting it to a disinterested party (other than a court), that renders a decision. The procedures and costs can be provided for in an arbitration clause or incorporated through other documents. To enforce an award rendered in an arbitration, the winning party can "enter" (submit) the award in a court "of competent jurisdiction." For a general discussion of arbitration and other forms of alternative dispute resolution (other than courts), see Chapter 3.

⑮ When goods are imported internationally, they must meet certain import requirements before being released to the buyer. Because of this, buyers frequently want a guaranty clause that covers the goods not admitted into the country and that either requires the seller to replace the goods within a stated time or allows the contract for those goods not admitted to be void. See Chapter 12.

⑯ In the "Claims" clause, the parties agree that the buyer has a certain time within which to reject the goods. The right to reject is a right by law and does not need to be stated in a contract. If the buyer does not exercise the right within the time specified in the contract, the goods will be considered accepted. See Chapter 12.

⑰ Many international contracts include definitions of terms so that parties understand what they mean. Some terms are used in a particular industry in a specific way. Here, the word "chop" refers to a unit of like-grade coffee bean. The buyer has a right to inspect ("sample") the coffee. If the coffee does not conform to the contract, the seller must correct the nonconformity. See Chapter 12.

⑱ The "Delivery," "Insurance," and "Freight" clauses, with the "Arrival" clause on page one, indicate that this is a destination contract. The seller has the obligation to deliver the goods to the destination, not simply deliver them into the hands of a carrier. Under this contract, the destination is a "Bonded Public Warehouse" in a specific location. The seller bears the risk of loss until the goods are delivered at their destination. Typically, the seller will have bought insurance to cover the risk. See Chapter 11 for a discussion of delivery terms and the risk of loss and Chapter 23 for a general discussion of insurance.

⑲ Delivery terms are commonly placed in all sales contracts. Such terms determine who pays freight and other costs and, in the absence of an agreement specifying otherwise, who bears the risk of loss. International contracts may use delivery terms as provided under the UCC (see Chapter 11), or can use INCOTERMS, which are published by the International Chamber of Commerce. INCOTERMS differ slightly from UCC terms in legal effect. For example, the INCOTERM "DDP" ("delivered duty paid") requires the seller to arrange shipment, obtain and pay for import or export permits, and get the goods through customs to a named destination.

⑳ Exported and imported goods are subject to duties, taxes, and other charges imposed by the governments of the countries involved. International contracts spell out who is responsible for these charges.

㉑ This clause protects a party if the other party should become financially unable to fulfill the obligations under the contract. Thus, if the seller cannot afford to deliver or the buyer cannot afford to pay, for the stated reasons, the other party can consider the contract breached. This right is subject to "11 USC 365(e)(1)," which refers to a specific provision of the U.S. Bankruptcy Code dealing with executory contracts. Bankruptcy provisions were covered in Chapter 16.

㉒ In the "Breach or Default of Contract" clause, the parties agree that the remedies under this contract are the remedies (except for consequential damages) provided by the UCC, as in effect in the state of New York. The amount and "ascertainment" of damages, as well as other disputes about relief, are to be determined by arbitration. UCC remedies were discussed in Chapter 12. Arbitration was discussed in Chapter 3.

㉓ Three clauses frequently included in international contracts are omitted here. There is no "choice of language" clause designating the official language to be used in interpreting the contract terms. There is no "choice of forum" clause designating the place in which disputes will be litigated, except for arbitration (law of New York State). Finally, there is no *"force majeure"* clause relieving the sellers or buyers from nonperformance due to events beyond their control.

Workers at a manufacturing plant owned by Ford Motor Company in Chongqing, China. The factory produces 150,000 cars per year. What contract clauses would affect where and how these foreign workers are able to resolve disputes with their U.S. employer? (AP Photo/ Joachim Ladefoged)

CHOICE-OF-LAW CLAUSE
A clause in a contract designating the law (such as the law of a particular state or nation) that will govern the contract.

FORCE MAJEURE CLAUSE
A provision in a contract stipulating that certain unforeseen events—such as war, political upheavals, or acts of God—will excuse a party from liability for nonperformance of contractual obligations.

courts of Bombay (Mumbai), India, would have exclusive jurisdiction over any disputes relating to their agreement. When Intermax fell behind in its payments to Garware, Garware filed a lawsuit in a U.S. court to collect the balance due, claiming that the forum-selection clause did not apply to sales of warehoused goods. The court, however, sided with Intermax. Because the forum-selection clause was valid and enforceable, Garware had to bring its complaints against Intermax in a court in India.[3] ◼

Choice of Law A contractual provision designating the applicable law—such as the law of Germany or the United Kingdom or California—is called a **choice-of-law clause.** Every international contract typically includes a choice-of-law clause. At common law (and in European civil law systems), parties are allowed to choose the law that will govern their contractual relationship, provided that the law chosen is the law of a jurisdiction that has a substantial relationship to the parties and to the international business transaction.

Under Section 1–105 of the Uniform Commercial Code, parties may choose the law that will govern the contract as long as the choice is "reasonable." Article 6 of the United Nations Convention on Contracts for the International Sale of Goods, however, imposes no limitation on the parties' choice of what law will govern the contract. The 1986 Hague Convention on the Law Applicable to Contracts for the International Sale of Goods— often referred to as the Choice-of-Law Convention—allows unlimited autonomy in the choice of law. The Hague Convention indicates that whenever a contract does not specify a choice of law, the governing law is that of the country in which the *seller's* place of business is located.

Force Majeure Clause Every contract, particularly those involving international transactions, should have a ***force majeure* clause.** *Force majeure* is a French term meaning "impossible or irresistible force"—sometimes loosely identified as "an act of God." In international business contracts, *force majeure* clauses commonly stipulate that in addition to acts of God, a number of other eventualities (such as government orders or embargoes, for example) may excuse a party from liability for nonperformance.

Civil Dispute Resolution

International contracts frequently include arbitration clauses. By means of such clauses, the parties agree in advance to be bound by the decision of a specified third party in the event of a dispute, as discussed in Chapter 3. The third party may be a neutral entity (such as the International Chamber of Commerce), a panel of individuals representing both parties' interests, or some other group or organization. (For an example of an arbitration clause in an international contract, refer to page 770 in Exhibit 25–1.) The United Nations Convention on the Recognition and Enforcement of Foreign Arbitral Awards (often referred to as the New York Convention) assists in the enforcement of arbitration clauses, as do provisions in specific treaties among nations. The New York Convention has been implemented in nearly one hundred countries, including the United States.

If a sales contract does not include an arbitration clause, litigation may occur. If the contract contains forum-selection and choice-of-law clauses, the lawsuit will be heard by a court in the specified forum and decided according to that forum's law. If no forum and choice of law have been specified, however, legal proceedings will be more complex and

---

3. *Garware Polyester, Ltd. v. Intermax Trading Corp.,* ___ F.Supp.2d ___ (S.D.N.Y. 2001).

attended by much more uncertainty. For instance, litigation may take place in two or more countries, with each country applying its own choice-of-law rules to determine the substantive law that will be applied to the particular transactions. Even if a plaintiff wins a favorable judgment in a lawsuit litigated in the plaintiff's country, there is no way to predict whether courts in the defendant's country will enforce the judgment. (For a further discussion of this issue, see this chapter's *Beyond Our Borders* feature on the next page.)

PAYMENT METHODS FOR INTERNATIONAL TRANSACTIONS

Currency differences between nations and the geographic distance between parties to international sales contracts add a degree of complexity to international sales that does not exist in the domestic market. Because international contracts involve greater financial risks, special care should be taken in drafting these contracts to specify both the currency in which payment is to be made and the method of payment.

Monetary Systems

Although our national currency, the U.S. dollar, is one of the primary forms of international currency, any U.S. firm undertaking business transactions abroad must be prepared to deal with one or more other currencies. After all, just as a U.S. firm wants to be paid in U.S. dollars for goods and services sold abroad, so, too, does a Japanese firm want to be paid in Japanese yen for goods and services sold outside Japan. Both firms therefore must rely on the convertibility of currencies.

Foreign Exchange Markets Currencies are convertible when they can be freely exchanged one for the other at some specified market rate in a **foreign exchange market.** Foreign exchange markets make up a worldwide system for the buying and selling of foreign currencies. At any point in time, the foreign exchange rate is set by the forces of supply and demand in unrestricted foreign exchange markets. The foreign exchange rate is simply the price of a unit of one country's currency in terms of another country's currency. For example, if today's exchange rate is one hundred Japanese yen for one dollar, that means that anybody with one hundred yen can obtain one dollar, and vice versa.

FOREIGN EXCHANGE MARKET
A worldwide system in which foreign currencies are bought and sold.

Correspondent Banking Frequently, a U.S. company can rely on its domestic bank to take care of all international transfers of funds. Commercial banks often transfer funds internationally through their **correspondent banks** in other countries.

CORRESPONDENT BANK
A bank in which another bank has an account (and vice versa) for the purpose of facilitating fund transfers.

■**EXAMPLE 25.5** A customer of Citibank wishes to pay a bill in euros to a company in Paris. Citibank can draw a bank check payable in euros on its account in Crédit Agricole, a Paris correspondent bank, and then send the check to the French company to which its customer owes the funds. Alternatively, Citibank's customer can request a wire transfer of the funds to the French company. Citibank instructs Crédit Agricole by wire to pay the necessary amount in euros. ■

The Clearing House Interbank Payment System (CHIPS) handles about 90 percent of both national and international interbank transfers of U.S. funds. In addition, the Society for Worldwide International Financial Telecommunications (SWIFT) is a communication system that provides banks with messages concerning international transactions.

Letters of Credit

Because buyers and sellers engaged in international business transactions are frequently separated by thousands of miles, special precautions are often taken to ensure performance under the contract. Sellers want to avoid delivering goods for which they might not be paid. Buyers desire the assurance that sellers will not be paid until there is evidence that

BEYOND OUR BORDERS Arbitration versus Litigation

One of the reasons many businesspersons find it advantageous to include arbitration clauses in their international contracts is that arbitration awards are usually easier to enforce than court judgments. As mentioned, the New York Convention provides for the enforcement of arbitration awards in those countries that have signed the convention. In contrast, the enforcement of court judgments normally depends on the principle of comity and bilateral agreements providing for such enforcement.

How the principle of comity is applied varies from one nation to another, though, and many countries have not signed bilateral agreements agreeing to enforce judgments rendered in U.S. courts. Furthermore, a U.S. court may not enforce a foreign court's judgment if it conflicts with U.S. laws or policies, especially if the case involves important constitutional rights such as freedom of the press or freedom of religion. For example, a U.S. federal appellate court refused to enforce the judgment of a British court in a libel (defamation) case. The court pointed out that the judgment was contrary to the public policy of the United States, which generally favors a much broader and more protective freedom of the press than has ever been provided by English law.[a]

Similarly, a U.S. federal district court refused to enforce a French default judgment against Viewfinder, Inc., a U.S. firm that operated a Web site. The firm's Web site posted photographs from fashion shows and information about the fashion industry. Several French clothing designers filed an action in a French court alleging that the Web site showed photos of their clothing designs. Because Viewfinder defaulted and did not appear in the French court to contest the allegations, the French court awarded the designers the equivalent of more than $175,000. When the designers came to the United States to enforce the judgment, Viewfinder asserted a number of arguments as to why the U.S. court should not enforce the French judgment. Ultimately, Viewfinder convinced the U.S. court that its conduct on the Web site was protected expression under the First Amendment.[b]

 FOR CRITICAL ANALYSIS   *What might be some other advantages of arbitrating disputes involving international transactions? Are there any disadvantages?*

a. *Matusevitch v. Telnikoff,* 159 F.3d 636 (D.C.Cir. 1998). Note that a U.S. court may be less likely to have public-policy concerns when enforcing a foreign judgment based on a contract. See, for example, *Society of Lloyd's v. Siemon-Netto,* 457 F.3d 94 (C.A.D.C. 2006).
b. *Sarl Louis Feraud International v. Viewfinder, Inc.,* 406 F.Supp.2d 274 (S.D.N.Y. 2005).

◼

LETTER OF CREDIT
A written instrument, usually issued by a bank on behalf of a customer or other person, in which the issuer promises to honor drafts or other demands for payment by third persons in accordance with the terms of the instrument.

the goods have been shipped. Thus, **letters of credit** are frequently used to facilitate international business transactions.

In a simple letter-of-credit transaction, the *issuer* (a bank) agrees to issue a letter of credit and to ascertain whether the *beneficiary* (seller) performs certain acts. In return, the *account party* (buyer) promises to reimburse the issuer for the amount paid to the beneficiary. The transaction may also involve an *advising bank* that transmits information and a *paying bank* that expedites payment under the letter of credit. See Exhibit 25–2 for an illustration of a letter-of-credit transaction.

EXHIBIT 25-2 A Letter-of-Credit Transaction

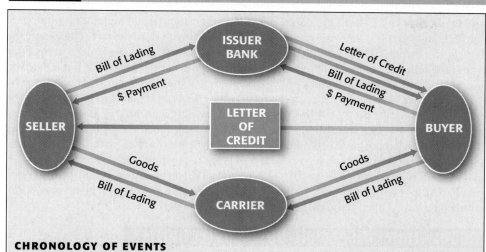

CHRONOLOGY OF EVENTS

1. Buyer contracts with issuer bank to issue a letter of credit; this sets forth the banks obligation to pay on the letter of credit and buyer's obligation to pay the bank.

2. Letter of credit is sent to seller informing seller that on compliance with the terms of the letter of credit (such as presentment of necessary documents—in this example, a bill of lading), the bank will issue payment for the goods.

3. Seller delivers goods to carrier and receives a bill of lading.

4. Seller delivers the bill of lading to issuer bank and, if the document is proper, receives payment.

5. Issuer bank delivers the bill of lading to buyer.

6. Buyer delivers the bill of lading to carrier.

7. Carrier delivers the goods to buyer.

8. Buyer settles with issuer bank.

Under a letter of credit, the issuer is bound to pay the beneficiary (seller) when the beneficiary has complied with the terms and conditions of the letter of credit. The beneficiary looks to the issuer, not to the account party (buyer), when it presents the documents required by the letter of credit. Typically, the letter of credit will require that the beneficiary deliver a *bill of lading* to the issuing bank to prove that shipment has been made. A letter of credit assures the beneficiary (seller) of payment and at the same time assures the account party (buyer) that payment will not be made until the beneficiary has complied with the terms and conditions of the letter of credit.

The Value of a Letter of Credit   The basic principle behind letters of credit is that payment is made against the documents presented by the beneficiary and not against the facts that the documents purport to reflect. Thus, in a letter-of-credit transaction, the issuer does not police the underlying contract; a letter of credit is independent of the underlying contract between the buyer and the seller. Eliminating the need for banks (issuers) to inquire into whether actual contractual conditions have been satisfied greatly reduces the costs of letters of credit. Moreover, the use of a letter of credit protects both buyers and sellers.

DON'T FORGET A letter of credit is independent of the underlying contract between the buyer and the seller.

Compliance with a Letter of Credit   A letter-of-credit transaction generally involves at least three separate and distinct contracts: the contract between the account party (buyer) and the beneficiary (seller); the contract between the issuer (bank) and the account party (buyer); and, finally, the letter of credit itself, which involves the issuer (bank) and the beneficiary (seller). These contracts are separate and distinct, and the issuer's obligations under the letter of credit do not concern the underlying contract between the buyer and the seller. Rather, it is the issuer's duty to ascertain whether the documents presented by the beneficiary (seller) comply with the terms of the letter of credit.

If the documents presented by the beneficiary comply with the terms of the letter of credit, the issuer (bank) must honor the letter of credit. If the issuing bank refuses to pay the beneficiary (seller) even though the beneficiary has complied with all the requirements, the beneficiary can bring an action to enforce payment. Sometimes, however, it can be difficult to determine exactly what a letter of credit requires. Traditionally, courts required strict compliance with the terms of a letter of credit, but in recent years, some courts have moved to a standard of *reasonable* compliance.

REGULATION OF SPECIFIC BUSINESS ACTIVITIES

Doing business abroad can affect the economies, foreign policies, domestic policies, and other national interests of the countries involved. For this reason, nations impose laws to restrict or facilitate international business. Controls may also be imposed by international agreements. We discuss here how different types of international activities are regulated.

Investing

Firms that invest in foreign nations face the risk that the foreign government may take possession of the investment property. Expropriation, as already mentioned, occurs when property is taken and the owner is paid just compensation for what is taken. Expropriation does not violate generally observed principles of international law. Such principles are normally violated, however, when a government confiscates property without compensation (or without adequate compensation). Few remedies are available for confiscation of property by a foreign government. Claims are often resolved by lump-sum settlements after negotiations between the United States and the taking nation.

To counter the deterrent effect that the possibility of confiscation may have on potential investors, many countries guarantee that foreign investors will be compensated if their property is taken. A guaranty can take the form of national constitutional or statutory laws or provisions in international treaties. As further protection for foreign investments, some countries provide insurance for their citizens' investments abroad.

Export Controls

The U.S. Constitution provides in Article I, Section 9, that "No Tax or Duty shall be laid on Articles exported from any State." Thus, Congress cannot impose any export taxes. Congress can, however, use a variety of other devices to control exports. Congress may set export quotas on various items, such as grain being sold abroad. Under the Export Administration Act of 1979,[4] the flow of technologically advanced products and technical data can be restricted. In recent years, the U.S. Department of Commerce has made a controversial attempt to restrict the export of encryption software.

While restricting certain exports, the United States (and other nations) also uses devices such as export incentives and subsidies to stimulate other exports and thereby aid

NOTE   Most countries restrict exports for the same reasons: to protect national security, to further foreign policy objectives, and to prevent the spread of nuclear weapons.

---

4. 50 U.S.C. Sections 2401–2420.

domestic businesses. The Revenue Act of 1971,[5] for instance, gave tax benefits to firms marketing their products overseas through certain foreign sales corporations by exempting income produced by the exports. Under the Export Trading Company Act of 1982,[6] U.S. banks are encouraged to invest in export trading companies, which are formed when exporting firms join together to export a line of goods. The Export-Import Bank of the United States provides financial assistance, consisting primarily of credit guaranties given to commercial banks that in turn lend funds to U.S. exporting companies.

Import Controls

All nations have restrictions on imports, and the United States is no exception. Restrictions include strict prohibitions, quotas, and tariffs. Under the Trading with the Enemy Act of 1917,[7] for instance, no goods may be imported from nations that have been designated enemies of the United States. Other laws prohibit the importation of illegal drugs, books that urge insurrection against the United States, and agricultural products that pose dangers to domestic crops or animals.

Importing goods that infringe U.S. patents is also prohibited. The International Trade Commission (ITC) investigates allegations that imported goods infringe U.S. patents and imposes penalties if necessary. In the following case, a party fined more than $13.5 million for importing certain disposable cameras appealed to the U.S. Court of Appeals for the Federal Circuit.

---

5. 26 U.S.C. Sections 991–994.
6. 15 U.S.C. Sections 4001, 4003.
7. 12 U.S.C. Section 95a.

CASE 25.2 | **Fuji Photo Film Co. v. International Trade Commission**

United States Court of Appeals, Federal Circuit, 474 F.3d 1281 (2007).

FACTS Fuji Photo Film Company owns fifteen U.S. patents for "lens-fitted film packages" (LFFPs), popularly known as disposable cameras. An LFFP consists of a plastic shell preloaded with film. To develop the film, a consumer gives the LFFP to a film processor and receives back the negatives and prints, but not the shell. Fuji makes and sells LFFPs. Jazz Photo Corporation collected used LFFP shells in the United States, shipped them abroad to have new film inserted, and then imported them back into the United States for sale. The International Trade Commission (ITC) determined that Jazz's resale of shells originally sold outside the United States infringed Fuji's patents. In 1999, the ITC issued a cease-and-desist order to stop the imports. While the order was being disputed at the ITC and in the courts, between August 2001 and December 2003 Jazz imported and sold 27 million refurbished LFFPs. Fuji complained to the ITC, which fined Jazz more than $13.5 million. Jack Benun, Jazz's chief operating officer, appealed to the U.S. Court of Appeals for the Federal Circuit.

ISSUE Did Jazz violate the cease-and-desist order?

DECISION Yes. The U.S. Court of Appeals for the Federal Circuit affirmed this part of the ITC's decision. The court held, among other things, that "substantial evidence supports the finding that the majority of the cameras were first sold abroad."

REASON The court explained that to determine Jazz's violations of Fuji's patents, the ITC had used identifying numbers printed on Fuji's LFFPs and Fuji's production and shipping databases to pinpoint where Jazz's refurbished LFFPs were first sold. Against this evidence, Benun asserted that Jazz utilized its own "informed compliance program" to track the LFFP shells from their collection to their sale. Benun argued that this tracking system ensured that only shells collected from the United States were refurbished for sale here. The court reasoned, however, that this tracking program would ensure "at most" only that Jazz refurbished LFFPs collected from the United States, not that Jazz refurbished LFFPs first sold here.

CASE 25.2–Continues next page

CASE 25.2–Continued

Besides, Jazz's tracking program was "too incomplete and disorganized to be credible." Because "there was no suggestion that the incomplete and disorganized nature of the program was due to Fuji's actions, this ground alone was sufficient to justify a conclusion that Benun" did not prove the refurbished LFFPs had been sold first in the United States.

 FOR CRITICAL ANALYSIS–Ethical Consideration
Suppose that, after this decision, Jazz fully compensated Fuji for the infringing sales of the LFFPs. Would Jazz have acquired the right to refurbish those LFFPs in the future? Explain.

QUOTA
A set limit on the amount of goods that can be imported.

TARIFF
A tax on imported goods.

DUMPING
The selling of goods in a foreign country at a price below the price charged for the same goods in the domestic market.

NORMAL TRADE RELATIONS (NTR) STATUS
A status granted in an international treaty by a provision stating that the citizens of the contracting nations may enjoy the privileges accorded by either party to citizens of its NTR nations. Generally, this status is designed to establish equality of international treatment.

Quotas and Tariffs Limits on the amounts of goods that can be imported are known as **quotas.** At one time, the United States had legal quotas on the number of automobiles that could be imported from Japan. Today, Japan "voluntarily" restricts the number of automobiles exported to the United States. **Tariffs** are taxes on imports. A tariff is usually a percentage of the value of the import, but it can be a flat rate per unit (for example, per barrel of oil). Tariffs raise the prices of goods, causing some consumers to purchase more domestically manufactured goods and less imported goods.

Dumping The United States has specific laws directed at what it sees as unfair international trade practices. **Dumping,** for example, is the sale of imported goods at "less than fair value." "Fair value" is usually determined by the price of those goods in the exporting country. Foreign firms that engage in dumping in the United States hope to undersell U.S. businesses to obtain a larger share of the U.S. market. To prevent this, an extra tariff—known as an *antidumping duty*—may be assessed on the imports.

Minimizing Trade Barriers Restrictions on imports are also known as *trade barriers.* The elimination of trade barriers is sometimes seen as essential to the world's economic well-being. Most of the world's leading trading nations are members of the World Trade Organization (WTO), which was established in 1995. To minimize trade barriers among nations, each member country of the WTO is required to grant **normal trade relations (NTR) status** (formerly known as *most-favored-nation status*) to other member countries. This means each member is obligated to treat other members at least as well as it treats the country that receives its most favorable treatment with regard to imports or exports.

Various regional trade agreements and associations also help to minimize trade barriers between nations. The European Union (EU), for example, is working to minimize or remove barriers to trade among its member countries. The EU is a single integrated trading unit made up of twenty-seven European nations. Another important regional trade agreement is the North American Free Trade Agreement (NAFTA). NAFTA, which became effective on January 1, 1994, created a regional trading unit consisting of Canada, Mexico, and the United States. The primary goal of NAFTA is to eliminate tariffs among these three countries on substantially all goods over a period of fifteen to twenty years.

A more recent trade agreement is the Central America–Dominican Republic–United States Free Trade Agreement (CAFTA-DR), which was signed into law by President George W. Bush in 2005. This agreement was formed by Costa Rica, the Dominican Republic, El Salvador, Guatemala, Honduras, Nicaragua, and the United States. The purpose of the agreement was to reduce trade tariffs and improve market access among all of the signatory nations, including the United States. As of 2008, legislatures from all seven countries had approved CAFTA-DR, despite significant opposition in certain nations, including Costa Rica, where nationwide strikes erupted in response to legislation adopting the treaty.

Bribing Foreign Officials

Giving cash or in-kind benefits to foreign government officials to obtain business contracts and other favors is often considered normal practice. To reduce such bribery by representatives of U.S. corporations, Congress enacted the Foreign Corrupt Practices Act in 1977.[8] This act and its implications for American businesspersons engaged in international business transactions were discussed in Chapter 2.

U.S. LAWS IN A GLOBAL CONTEXT

The internationalization of business raises questions about the extraterritorial application of a nation's laws—that is, the effect of the country's laws outside its boundaries. To what extent do U.S. domestic laws apply to other nations' businesses? To what extent do U.S. domestic laws apply to U.S. firms doing business abroad? Here, we discuss the extraterritorial application of certain U.S. laws, including the Sarbanes-Oxley Act, antitrust laws, and laws prohibiting employment discrimination.

The Sarbanes-Oxley Act

The Sarbanes-Oxley Act of 2002, which was discussed in Chapters 2 and 21, is designed to improve the quality and clarity of financial reporting and auditing of public companies. The act prescribes the issuance of codes of ethics, increases the criminal penalties for securities fraud, and utilizes other means to hold public companies to higher reporting standards.

Three provisions of the act protect whistleblowers. One section requires public companies to adopt procedures that encourage employees to expose "questionable" accounting. Another section imposes criminal sanctions for retaliation against anyone who reports the commission of any federal offense to law enforcement officers.

A third section—18 U.S.C. Section 1514A—creates an administrative complaint procedure and a federal civil cause of action for employees who report violations of the federal laws relating to fraud against the shareholders of public companies. The extraterritorial application of this section was at issue in the following case.

---

8. 15 U.S.C. Sections 78m–78ff.

CASE 25.3   Carnero v. Boston Scientific Corp.

United States Court of Appeals, First Circuit, 433 F.3d 1 (2006).
www.ca1.uscourts.gov[a]

FACTS Boston Scientific Corporation (BSC) is a Delaware corporation with headquarters in Natick, Massachusetts. BSC, which makes medical equipment, operates in many countries throughout the world. Its subsidiaries include Boston Scientific Argentina, S.A. (BSA), in Argentina and Boston Scientific Do

a. In the right-hand column, click on "Opinions." When that page opens, in the "Short Title contains" box, type in "Carnero" and click on "Submit Search." In the result, in the "Click for Opinion" column, click on one of the numbers to access the opinion.

Brasil, Ltda. (BSB), in Brazil. In 1997, Ruben Carnero, a citizen of Argentina, began working for BSA in Buenos Aires. Four years later, Carnero accepted a simultaneous assignment with BSB. Soon afterward, he reported to BSC that its Latin American subsidiaries were improperly inflating sales figures and engaging in other accounting misconduct. His employment with BSA and BSB was terminated. Carnero filed a complaint with the U.S. Department of Labor (DOL) against BSC under the Sarbanes-Oxley Act, seeking reinstatement. The DOL rejected the claim. Carnero filed a suit in a federal district

CASE 25.3–Continues next page

CASE 25.3–Continued

court against BSC on the same basis. When the court dismissed the complaint, Carnero appealed to the U.S. Court of Appeals for the First Circuit.

ISSUE Does 18 U.S.C. Section 1514A apply to acts that occur outside the United States?

DECISION No. The U.S. Court of Appeals for the First Circuit affirmed the lower court's dismissal of Carnero's complaint under 18 U.S.C. Section 1514A. This section of the Sarbanes-Oxley Act "does not reflect the necessary clear expression of congressional intent to extend its reach beyond our nation's borders."

REASON The appellate court pointed out that "when a statute is silent as to its territorial reach, and no contrary congressional intent clearly appears, there is generally a presumption against its extraterritorial application." This presumption recognizes that Congress is chiefly focused on domestic situations and prevents "unintended clashes" with other nations' laws. In this case, the Sarbanes-Oxley Act is silent as to the application of 18 U.S.C. Section 1514A abroad. The enforcement of this section is the responsibility of the DOL, whose jurisdiction and resources are entirely domestic. The section's venue provisions (which establish the appropriate location to file a civil lawsuit) apply only to plaintiffs and violations within U.S. borders, "with no corresponding basis being provided for venue as to foreign complainants claiming violations in foreign countries." The legislative history of the statute also reveals that Congress did not consider "the possibility or the problems of overseas application" of this section. In contrast, other sections of the statute were expressly tailored for "extraterritorial enforcement."

 FOR CRITICAL ANALYSIS–Economic Consideration *How might the court's decision in this case frustrate the basic purpose of the Sarbanes-Oxley Act, which is to protect investors in U.S. securities markets and the integrity of those markets?*

U.S. Antitrust Laws

U.S. antitrust laws (discussed in Chapter 22) have a wide application. They may *subject* persons in foreign nations to their provisions, as well as *protect* foreign consumers and competitors from violations committed by U.S. citizens. Section 1 of the Sherman Act provides for the extraterritorial effect of the U.S. antitrust laws. The United States is a major proponent of free competition in the global economy. Thus, any conspiracy that has a *substantial effect* on U.S. commerce is within the reach of the Sherman Act. The law applies even if the violation occurs outside the United States, and foreign governments as well as persons can be sued for violations.

Before U.S. courts will exercise jurisdiction and apply antitrust laws, however, it must be shown that the alleged violation had a substantial effect on U.S. commerce. **EXAMPLE 25.6** A number of companies that manufacture and sell paper on the global market meet in Japan on several occasions and reach a price-fixing agreement (an agreement to set prices). Although several of the companies are based in foreign nations, they sell paper in the United States through their wholly owned subsidiaries. Thus, the agreement to sell paper at above-normal prices throughout North America has a *substantial restraining effect* on U.S. commerce. In this situation, a U.S. court has jurisdiction over the defendant companies even though the price-fixing activities took place entirely outside the United States. ■

Antidiscrimination Laws

As explained in Chapter 18, federal laws in the United States prohibit discrimination on the basis of race, color, national origin, religion, gender, age, and disability. These laws, as they affect employment relationships, generally apply extraterritorially. Since 1984, for example, the Age Discrimination in Employment Act of 1967 has covered U.S. employees working abroad for U.S. employers. The Americans with Disabilities Act of 1990, which requires employers to accommodate the needs of workers with disabilities, also applies to U.S. nationals working abroad for U.S. firms.

For some time, it was uncertain whether the major U.S. law regulating discriminatory practices in the workplace, Title VII of the Civil Rights Act of 1964, applied extraterritorially. The Civil Rights Act of 1991 addressed this issue. The act provides that Title VII applies extraterritorially to all U.S. employees working for U.S. employers abroad. Generally, U.S. employers must abide by U.S. discrimination laws unless to do so would violate the laws of the country where their workplaces are located. This "foreign laws exception" allows employers to avoid being subjected to conflicting laws.

REVIEWING International Law in a Global Economy

Robco, Inc., was a Florida arms dealer. The armed forces of Honduras contracted to purchase weapons from Robco over a six-year period. After the government was replaced and a democracy installed, the Honduran government sought to reduce the size of its military, and its relationship with Robco deteriorated. Honduras refused to honor the contract by purchasing the inventory of arms, which Robco could sell only at a much lower price. Robco filed a suit in a federal district court in the United States to recover damages for this breach of contract by the government of Honduras. Using the information provided in the chapter, answer the following questions.

1 Should the Foreign Sovereign Immunities Act (FSIA) preclude this lawsuit? Why or why not?

2 Does the act of state doctrine bar Robco from seeking to enforce the contract? Explain.

3 Suppose that prior to this lawsuit, the new government of Honduras had enacted a law making it illegal to purchase weapons from foreign arms dealers. What doctrine might lead a U.S. court to dismiss Robco's case in that situation?

4 Now suppose that the U.S. court hears the case and awards damages to Robco, but the government of Honduras has no assets in the United States that can be used to satisfy the judgment. Under which doctrine might Robco be able to collect the damages by asking another nation's court to enforce the U.S. judgment?

APPLICATION — Issues and Risks in International Transactions*

The global economy has changed the way we do business and made us all realize the importance of having at least a passing understanding of international law.

Increasingly, U.S. businesses are establishing production facilities in other countries. They do this because of fewer government regulations and taxes and, of course, lower labor costs. U.S. businesses also contract to buy directly from foreign manufacturers. Often, U.S. firms have their branded products manufactured outside the United States (outsourcing). Any U.S. business that engages in outsourcing, however, faces a risk of uneven quality, even if it is outsourcing services, such as call centers. Thus, every U.S. firm must have in place a mechanism to protect the goodwill generated by its brand even when the product (or service) is made entirely at a foreign facility.

Other Risks Involved

A U.S. firm that does business internationally may also face other risks. Products manufactured or purchased abroad may

* This *Application* is not meant to substitute for the services of an attorney who is licensed to practice law in your state.

(Continued)

be subject to import quotas and to tariffs (taxes on the imported goods). These quotas and tariffs may change during the course of a manufacturing cycle or a selling season.

Contract interpretation is always a potential problem. Thus, it is important to make sure that both parties understand all contract terms. You are well advised to include a choice-of-language clause in every contract. Nevertheless, even when two countries have a common language, such as England and the United States, a word or phrase may still have different meanings. For example, a *lamp* in England is a *flashlight* in the United States.

A choice-of-law clause and a forum-selection clause should be included in every contract involving international transactions. These clauses should be very specific, stating where any arbitration or litigation will take place. Legal systems around the world vary significantly, even in regard to simple sales transactions.

International Treaties and Agreements

International treaties and agreements continue to have as their goal the promotion of trade. Consequently, anyone con-

templating doing business globally should become familiar with these laws. Numerous international organizations also seek to facilitate international business. Some of them can provide assistance in settling disputes.

CHECKLIST FOR DOING BUSINESS INTERNATIONALLY

1 Be aware that the law governing your transactions in another country may be different from U.S. domestic law.
2 Always include choice-of-language and forum-selection clauses in your contracts, and try to ensure that these clauses are as favorable as possible to you.
3 Consider adding an arbitration clause to your contract to avoid the expenses of a trial if a dispute arises.
4 Become familiar with treaties and international agreements that might affect your international business dealings.

KEY TERMS

act of state doctrine 762
choice-of-language clause 766
choice-of-law clause 772
comity 762
confiscation 762
correspondent bank 773
distribution agreement 764
dumping 778

exclusive distributorship 764
export 764
expropriation 762
force majeure clause 772
foreign exchange market 773
forum-selection clause 766
international law 761
letter of credit 774

national law 761
normal trade relations
(NTR) status 778
quota 778
sovereign immunity 763
tariff 778

CHAPTER SUMMARY International Law in a Global Economy

International Principles and Doctrines (See pages 761–764.)	1. *The principle of comity*—Under this principle, nations give effect to the laws and judicial decrees of other nations for reasons of courtesy and international harmony.
	2. *The act of state doctrine*—A doctrine under which U.S. courts avoid passing judgment on the validity of public acts committed by a recognized foreign government within its own territory.
	3. *The doctrine of sovereign immunity*—When certain conditions are satisfied, foreign nations are immune from U.S. jurisdiction under the Foreign Sovereign Immunities Act of 1976. Exceptions are made (a) when a foreign state has "waived its immunity either explicitly or by implication" or (b) when the action is taken "in connection with a commercial activity carried on in the United States by the foreign state."
Doing Business Internationally (See pages 764–765.)	Ways in which U.S. domestic firms engage in international business transactions include (a) exporting, which may involve foreign agents or distributors, and (b) manufacturing abroad through licensing arrangements, franchising operations, wholly owned subsidiaries, or joint ventures.

CHAPTER SUMMARY International Law in a Global Economy–Continued

Commercial Contracts in an International Setting (See pages 766–773.)	International business contracts often include choice-of-language, forum-selection, and choice-of-law clauses to reduce the uncertainties associated with interpreting the language of the agreement and dealing with legal differences. Most domestic and international contracts include *force majeure* clauses. They commonly stipulate that certain events, such as floods, fire, accidents, labor strikes, and government orders, may excuse a party from liability for nonperformance of the contract. Arbitration clauses are also frequently found in international contracts.
Payment Methods for International Transactions (See pages 773–776.)	1. *Currency conversion*—Because nations have different monetary systems, payment on international contracts requires currency conversion at a rate specified in a foreign exchange market. 2. *Correspondent banking*—Correspondent banks facilitate the transfer of funds from a buyer in one country to a seller in another. 3. *Letters of credit*—Letters of credit facilitate international transactions by ensuring payment to sellers and assuring buyers that payment will not be made until the sellers have complied with the terms of the letters of credit. Typically, compliance occurs when a bill of lading is delivered to the issuing bank.
Regulation of Specific Business Activities (See pages 776–779.)	In the interests of their economies, foreign policies, domestic policies, or other national priorities, nations impose laws that restrict or facilitate international business. Such laws regulate foreign investments, exporting, and importing. The World Trade Organization attempts to minimize trade barriers among nations, as do regional trade agreements and associations, including the European Union, the North American Free Trade Agreement, and the Central America–Dominican Republic–United States Free Trade Agreement.
U.S. Laws in a Global Context (See pages 779–781.)	1. *Antitrust laws*—U.S. antitrust laws may be applied beyond the borders of the United States. Any conspiracy that has a substantial effect on commerce within the United States may be subject to the Sherman Act, even if the violation occurs outside the United States. 2. *Antidiscrimination laws*—The major U.S. laws prohibiting employment discrimination, including Title VII of the Civil Rights Act of 1964, the Age Discrimination in Employment Act of 1967, and the Americans with Disabilities Act of 1990, cover U.S. employees working abroad for U.S. firms—*unless* to apply the U.S. laws would violate the laws of the host country.

FOR REVIEW

Answers for the even-numbered questions in this For Review *section can be found in Appendix E at the end of this text.*

1 What is the principle of comity, and why do courts deciding disputes involving a foreign law or judicial decree apply this principle?

2 What is the act of state doctrine? In what circumstances is this doctrine applied?

3 Under the Foreign Sovereign Immunities Act of 1976, on what bases might a foreign state be considered subject to the jurisdiction of U.S. courts?

4 In what circumstances will U.S. antitrust laws be applied extraterritorially?

5 Do U.S. laws prohibiting employment discrimination apply in all circumstances to U.S. employees working for U.S. employers abroad?

QUESTIONS AND CASE PROBLEMS

HYPOTHETICAL SCENARIOS

25.1 Letters of Credit. The Swiss Credit Bank issued a letter of credit in favor of Antex Industries to cover the sale of 92,000 electronic integrated circuits manufactured by Electronic Arrays. The letter of credit specified that the chips would be transported to Tokyo by ship. Antex shipped the circuits by air. Payment on the letter of credit was dishonored because the shipment by air did not fulfill the precise terms of the letter of credit. Should a court compel payment? Explain.

25.2 Hypothetical Question with Sample Answer. As China and other formerly Communist nations move toward free enterprise, they must develop a new set of business laws. If you could start from scratch, what kind of business law system would you adopt, a civil law system or a common law system? What kind of business regulations would you impose?

For a sample answer to Question 25.2, go to Appendix F at the end of this text.

CASE PROBLEMS

25.3 Dumping. In response to a petition filed on behalf of the U.S. pineapple industry, the U.S. Commerce Department initiated an investigation of canned pineapple imported from Thailand. The investigation concerned Thai producers of the canned fruit, including the Thai Pineapple Public Co. The Thai producers also turned out products, such as pineapple juice and juice concentrate, outside the scope of the investigation. These products use separate parts of the same fresh pineapple, so they share raw material costs. To determine fair value and antidumping duties, the Commerce Department had to calculate the Thai producers' cost of production and, in so doing, had to allocate a portion of the shared fruit costs to the canned fruit. These allocations were based on the producers' own financial records, which were consistent with Thai generally accepted accounting principles. The result was a determination that more than 90 percent of the canned fruit sales were below the cost of production. The producers filed a suit in the U.S. Court of International Trade against the federal government, challenging this allocation. The producers argued that their records did not reflect actual production costs, which instead should be based on the weight of fresh fruit used to make the products. Did the Commerce Department act reasonably in determining the cost of production? Why or why not? [*Thai Pineapple Public Co. v. United States*, 187 F.3d 1362 (Fed.Cir. 1999)]

25.4 Sovereign Immunity. Tonoga, Ltd., doing business as Taconic Plastics, Ltd., is a manufacturer incorporated in Ireland with its principal place of business in New York. In 1997, Taconic entered into a contract with a German construction company to supply special material for a tent project designed to shelter religious pilgrims visiting holy sites in Saudi Arabia. Most of the material was made in, and shipped from, New York. The company did not pay Taconic and eventually filed for bankruptcy. Another German firm, Werner Voss Architects and Engineers, acting as an agent for the government of Saudi Arabia, guaranteed the payments due Taconic to induce it to complete the project. When it did not receive the final payment, Taconic filed a suit in a U.S. district court against the government of Saudi Arabia, claiming a breach of the guaranty and seeking to collect, in part, about $3 million. The defendant filed a motion to dismiss based, among other things, on the doctrine of sovereign immunity. Under what circumstances does this doctrine apply? What are its exceptions? Should this suit be dismissed under the "commercial activity" exception? Explain. [*Tonoga, Ltd. v. Ministry of Public Works and Housing of Kingdom of Saudi Arabia*, 135 F.Supp.2d 350 (N.D.N.Y. 2001)]

25.5 Case Problem with Sample Answer. DaimlerChrysler Corp. makes and markets motor vehicles. DaimlerChrysler assembled the 1993 and 1994 model years of its trucks at plants in Mexico. Assembly involved sheet metal components sent from the United States. DaimlerChrysler subjected some of the parts to a complicated treatment process, which included applying coats of paint to prevent corrosion, impart color, and protect the finish. Under U.S. law, goods that are assembled abroad using U.S.-made parts can be imported tariff free. A U.S. *statute* provides that painting is "incidental" to assembly and does not affect the status of the goods. A U.S. *regulation*, however, states that "painting primarily intended to enhance the appearance of an article or to impart distinctive features or characteristics" is not incidental. The U.S. Customs Service levied a tariff on the trucks. DaimlerChrysler filed a suit in the U.S. Court of International Trade, challenging the levy. Should the court rule in DaimlerChrysler's favor? Why or why not?

[*DaimlerChrysler Corp. v. United States*, 361 F.3d 1378 (Fed.Cir. 2004)]

After you have answered Problem 25.5, compare your answer with the sample answer given on the Web site that accompanies this text. Go to academic.cengage.com/blaw/blt, select "Chapter 25," and click on "Case Problem with Sample Answer."

25.6 Comity. E&L Consulting, Ltd., is a U.S. corporation that sells lumber products in New Jersey, New York, and Pennsylvania. Doman Industries, Ltd., is a Canadian corporation that also sells lumber products, including green hem-fir, a durable product used for homebuilding. Doman supplies more than 95 percent of the green hem-fir for sale in the northeastern United States. In 1990, Doman contracted to sell green hem-fir through E&L, which received monthly payments plus commissions. In 1998, Sherwood Lumber Corp., a New York firm and an E&L competitor, approached E&L about a merger. The negotiations were unsuccessful. According to E&L, Sherwood and Doman then conspired to monopolize the green hem-fir market in the United States. When Doman terminated its contract with E&L, the latter filed a suit in a federal district court against Doman, alleging violations of U.S. antitrust law. Doman filed for bankruptcy in a Canadian court and asked the U.S. court to dismiss E&L's suit under the principle of comity, among other things. What is the "principle of comity"? On what basis would it apply in this case? What would be the likely result? Discuss. [*E&L Consulting, Ltd. v. Doman Industries, Ltd.*, 360 F.Supp.2d 465 (E.D.N.Y. 2005)]

25.7 Dumping. A newspaper printing press system is more than one hundred feet long, stands four or five stories tall, and weighs 2 million pounds. Only about ten of the systems are sold each year in the United States. Because of the size and cost, a newspaper may update its system, rather than replace it, by buying "additions." By the 1990s, Goss International Corp. was the only domestic maker of the equipment in the United States and represented the entire U.S. market. Tokyo Kikai Seisakusho (TKSC), a Japanese corporation, makes the systems in Japan. In the 1990s, TKSC began to compete in the U.S. market, forcing Goss to cut its prices below cost. TKSC's tactics included offering its customers "secret" rebates on prices that were ultimately substantially less than the products' actual market value in Japan. According to TKSC office memos, the goal was to "win completely this survival game" against Goss, the "enemy." Goss filed a suit in a federal district court against TKSC and others, alleging illegal dumping. At what point does a foreign firm's attempt to compete with a domestic manufacturer in the United States become illegal dumping? Was that point reached in this case? Discuss. [*Goss International Corp. v. Man Roland Druckmaschinen Aktiengesellschaft*, 434 F.3d 1081 (8th Cir. 2006)]

25.8 International Principles. Jan Voda, M.D., a resident of Oklahoma City, Oklahoma, owns three U.S. patents related to guiding catheters for use in interventional cardiology, as well as corresponding foreign patents issued by the European Patent Office, Canada, France, Germany, and Great Britain. Voda filed a suit in a federal district court against Cordis Corp., a U.S. firm, alleging infringement of the U.S. patents under U.S. patent law and of the corresponding foreign patents under the patent law of the various foreign countries. Cordis admitted, "[T]he XB catheters have been sold domestically and internationally since 1994. The XB catheters were manufactured in Miami Lakes, Florida, from 1993 to 2001 and have been manufactured in Juarez, Mexico, since 2001." Cordis argued, however, that Voda could not assert infringement claims under foreign patent law because the court did not have jurisdiction over such claims. Which of the important international legal principles discussed in this chapter would be most likely to apply in this case? How should the court apply it? Explain. [*Voda v. Cordis Corp.*, 476 F.3d 887 (Fed.Cir. 2007)]

25.9 A Question of Ethics. On December 21, 1988, Pan Am Flight 103 exploded 31,000 feet in the air over Lockerbie, Scotland, killing all 259 passengers and crew on board and 11 people on the ground. Among those killed was Roger Hurst, a U.S. citizen. An investigation determined that a portable radio–cassette player packed in a brown Samsonite suitcase smuggled onto the plane was the source of the explosion. The explosive device was constructed with a digital timer specially made for, and bought by, Libya. Abdel Basset Ali Al-Megrahi, a Libyan government official and an employee of the Libyan Arab Airline (LAA), was convicted by the Scottish High Court of Justiciary on criminal charges that he planned and executed the bombing in association with members of the Jamahiriya Security Organization (JSO) (an agency of the Libyan government that performs security and intelligence functions) or the Libyan military. Members of the victims' families filed a suit in a U.S. federal district court against the JSO, the LAA, Al-Megrahi, and others. The plaintiffs claimed violations of U.S. federal law, including the Anti-Terrorism Act, and state law, including the intentional infliction of emotional distress. [Hurst v. Socialist People's Libyan Arab Jamahiriya, 474 F.Supp.2d 19 (D.D.C. 2007)]

1 Under what doctrine, codified in which federal statute, might the defendants claim to be immune from the jurisdiction of a U.S. court? Should this law include an exception for "state-sponsored terrorism"? Why or why not?

2 The defendants agreed to pay $2.7 billion, or $10 million per victim, to settle all claims for "compensatory death damages." The families of eleven victims, including Hurst, were excluded from the settlement because they were "not wrongful death beneficiaries under applicable state law." These plaintiffs continued the suit. The defendants filed a motion to dismiss. Should the motion be granted on the ground that the settlement bars the plaintiffs' claims? Explain.

CRITICAL THINKING
AND WRITING ASSIGNMENTS

25.10 Critical Legal Thinking. Business cartels and monopolies that are legal in some countries may engage in practices that violate U.S. antitrust laws. In view of this fact, what are some of the implications of applying U.S. antitrust laws extraterritorially?

25.11 **Video Question.** Go to this text's Web site at **academic. cengage.com/blaw/blt** and select "Chapter 25." Click on "Video Questions" and view the video titled *International: Letter of Credit*. Then answer the following questions.

1 Do banks always require the same documents to be presented in letter-of-credit transactions? If not, who dictates what documents will be required in the letter of credit?

2 At what point does the seller receive payment in a letter-of-credit transaction?

3 What assurances does a letter of credit provide to the buyer and the seller involved in the transaction?

ONLINE ACTIVITIES

PRACTICAL
INTERNET EXERCISES

Go to this text's Web site at **academic.cengage.com/blaw/blt**, select "Chapter 25," and click on "Practical Internet Exercises." There you will find the following Internet research exercises that you can perform to learn more about the topics covered in this chapter.

PRACTICAL INTERNET EXERCISE 25-1 LEGAL PERSPECTIVE—The World Trade Organization

PRACTICAL INTERNET EXERCISE 25-2 MANAGEMENT PERSPECTIVE—Overseas Business Opportunities

BEFORE THE TEST

Go to this text's Web site at **academic.cengage.com/blaw/blt**, select "Chapter 25," and click on "Interactive Quizzes." You will find a number of interactive questions relating to this chapter.

APPENDIX A
How to Brief Cases and Analyze Case Problems

HOW TO BRIEF CASES

To fully understand the law with respect to business, you need to be able to read and understand court decisions. To make this task easier, you can use a method of case analysis that is called *briefing*. There is a fairly standard procedure that you can follow when you "brief" any court case. You must first read the case opinion carefully. When you feel you understand the case, you can prepare a brief of it.

Although the format of a case brief may vary, typically it will present the essentials of the case under headings such as those listed below. This is basically the format followed by the authors when briefing the cases that have been included in this text.

1 Citation. Give the full citation for the case, including the name of the case, the date it was decided, and the court that decided it.
2 Facts. Briefly indicate (a) the reasons for the lawsuit; (b) the identity and arguments of the plaintiff(s) and defendant(s), respectively; and (c) the lower court's decision—if appropriate.
3 Issue. Concisely phrase, in the form of a question, the essential issue before the court. (If more than one issue is involved, you may have two—or even more—questions here.)
4 Decision. Indicate here—with a "yes" or "no," if possible—the court's answer to the question (or questions) in the *Issue* section above.
5 Reason. Summarize as briefly as possible the reasons given by the court for its decision (or decisions) and the case or statutory law relied on by the court in arriving at its decision.

For a case-specific example of what should be included under each of the above headings when briefing a case, see the review of the sample court case presented in the appendix to Chapter 1 of this text.

HOW TO ANALYZE CASE PROBLEMS

In addition to learning how to brief cases, students of business law and the legal environment also find it helpful to know how to analyze case problems. Part of the study of business law and the legal environment usually involves analyzing case problems, such as those included in this text at the end of each chapter.

For each case problem in this book, we provide the relevant background and facts of the lawsuit and the issue before the court. When you are assigned one of these problems, your job will be to determine how the court should decide the issue, and why. In other words, you will need to engage in legal analysis and reasoning. Here we offer some suggestions on how to make this task less daunting. We begin by presenting a sample problem:

> While Janet Lawson, a famous pianist, was shopping in Quality Market, she slipped and fell on a wet floor in one of the aisles. The floor had recently been mopped by one of the store's employees, but there were no signs warning customers that the floor in that area was wet. As a result of the fall, Lawson injured her right arm and was unable to perform piano concerts for the next six months. Had she been able to perform the scheduled concerts, she would have earned approximately $60,000 over that period of time. Lawson sued Quality Market for this amount, plus another $10,000 in medical expenses. She claimed that the store's failure to warn customers of the wet floor constituted negligence and therefore the market was liable for her injuries. Will the court agree with Lawson? Discuss.

Understand the Facts

This may sound obvious, but before you can analyze or apply the relevant law to a specific set of facts, you must clearly understand those facts. In other words, you should read through the case problem carefully and more than once, if necessary, to make sure you understand the identity of the plaintiff(s) and defendant(s) in the case and the progression of events that led to the lawsuit.

In the sample case just given, the identity of the parties is fairly obvious. Janet Lawson is the one bringing the suit; therefore, she is the plaintiff. Quality Market, against whom she is bringing the suit, is the defendant. Some of the case problems you may work on have multiple plaintiffs or defendants. Often, it is helpful to use abbreviations for the parties. To indicate a reference to a plaintiff, for example, the *pi* symbol—π—is often used, and a defendant is denoted by a *delta*—Δ—a triangle.

The events leading to the lawsuit are also fairly straightforward. Lawson slipped and fell on a wet floor, and she contends that Quality Market should be liable for her injuries because it was negligent in not posting a sign warning customers of the wet floor.

When you are working on case problems, realize that the facts should be accepted as they are given. For example, in our sample problem, it should be accepted that the floor was wet and that there was no sign. In other words, avoid making conjectures, such as "Maybe the floor wasn't too wet" or "Maybe an employee was getting a sign to put up," or "Maybe someone stole the sign." Questioning the facts as they are presented only adds confusion to your analysis.

Legal Analysis and Reasoning

Once you understand the facts given in the case problem, you can begin to analyze the case. The **IRAC method** is a helpful tool to use in the legal analysis and reasoning process. IRAC is an acronym for *Issue, Rule, Application, Conclusion.* Applying this method to our sample problem would involve the following steps:

1 First, you need to decide what legal **issue** is involved in the case. In our sample case, the basic issue is whether Quality Market's failure to warn customers of the wet floor constituted negligence. As discussed in Chapter 4, negligence is a *tort*—a civil wrong. In a tort lawsuit, the plaintiff seeks to be compensated for another's wrongful act. A defendant will be deemed negligent if he or she breached a duty of care owed to the plaintiff and the breach of that duty caused the plaintiff to suffer harm.

2 Once you have identified the issue, the next step is to determine what **rule of law** applies to the issue. To make this determination, you will want to review carefully the text of the chapter in which the problem appears to find the relevant rule of law. Our sample case involves the tort of negligence, covered in Chapter 4. The applicable rule of law is the tort law principle that business owners owe a duty to exercise reasonable care to protect their customers ("business invitees"). Reasonable care, in this context, includes either removing—or warning customers of—*foreseeable* risks about which the owner *knew* or *should have known.* Business owners need not warn customers of "open and obvious" risks, however. If a business owner breaches this duty of care (fails to exercise the appropriate degree of care toward customers), and the breach of duty causes a customer to be injured, the business owner will be liable to the customer for the customer's injuries.

3 The next—and usually the most difficult—step in analyzing case problems is the **application** of the relevant rule of law to the specific facts of the case you are studying. In our sample problem, applying the tort law principle just discussed presents few difficulties. An employee of the store had mopped the floor in the aisle where Lawson slipped and fell, but no sign was present indicating that the floor was wet. That a customer might fall on a wet floor is clearly a foreseeable risk. Therefore, the failure to warn customers about the wet floor was a breach of the duty of care owed by the business owner to the store's customers.

4 Once you have completed Step 3 in the IRAC method, you should be ready to draw your **conclusion.** In our sample case, Quality Market is liable to Lawson for her injuries, because the market's breach of its duty of care caused Lawson's injuries.

The fact patterns in the case problems presented in this text are not always as simple as those presented in our sample problem. Often, for example, there may be more than one plaintiff or defendant. There also may be more than one issue involved in a case and more than one applicable rule of law. Furthermore, in some case problems the facts may indicate that the general rule of law should not apply. For example, suppose a store employee advised Lawson not to walk on the floor in the aisle because it was wet, but Lawson decided to walk on it anyway. This fact could alter the outcome of the case because the store could then raise the defense of assumption of risk (see Chapter 4). Nonetheless, a careful review of the chapter should always provide you with the knowledge you need to analyze the problem thoroughly and arrive at accurate conclusions.

APPENDIX B
The Constitution of the United States

PREAMBLE

We the People of the United States, in Order to form a more perfect Union, establish Justice, insure domestic Tranquility, provide for the common defence, promote the general Welfare, and secure the Blessings of Liberty to ourselves and our Posterity, do ordain and establish this Constitution for the United States of America.

ARTICLE I

Section 1. All legislative Powers herein granted shall be vested in a Congress of the United States, which shall consist of a Senate and House of Representatives.

Section 2. The House of Representatives shall be composed of Members chosen every second Year by the People of the several States, and the Electors in each State shall have the Qualifications requisite for Electors of the most numerous Branch of the State Legislature.

No Person shall be a Representative who shall not have attained to the Age of twenty five Years, and been seven Years a Citizen of the United States, and who shall not, when elected, be an Inhabitant of that State in which he shall be chosen.

Representatives and direct Taxes shall be apportioned among the several States which may be included within this Union, according to their respective Numbers, which shall be determined by adding to the whole Number of free Persons, including those bound to Service for a Term of Years, and excluding Indians not taxed, three fifths of all other Persons. The actual Enumeration shall be made within three Years after the first Meeting of the Congress of the United States, and within every subsequent Term of ten Years, in such Manner as they shall by Law direct. The Number of Representatives shall not exceed one for every thirty Thousand, but each State shall have at Least one Representative; and until such enumeration shall be made, the State of New Hampshire shall be entitled to chuse three, Massachusetts eight, Rhode Island and Providence Plantations one, Connecticut five, New York six, New Jersey four, Pennsylvania eight, Delaware one, Maryland six, Virginia ten, North Carolina five, South Carolina five, and Georgia three.

When vacancies happen in the Representation from any State, the Executive Authority thereof shall issue Writs of Election to fill such Vacancies.

The House of Representatives shall chuse their Speaker and other Officers; and shall have the sole Power of Impeachment.

Section 3. The Senate of the United States shall be composed of two Senators from each State, chosen by the Legislature thereof, for six Years; and each Senator shall have one Vote.

Immediately after they shall be assembled in Consequence of the first Election, they shall be divided as equally as may be into three Classes. The Seats of the Senators of the first Class shall be vacated at the Expiration of the second Year, of the second Class at the Expiration of the fourth Year, and of the third Class at the Expiration of the sixth Year, so that one third may be chosen every second Year; and if Vacancies happen by Resignation, or otherwise, during the Recess of the Legislature of any State, the Executive thereof may make temporary Appointments until the next Meeting of the Legislature, which shall then fill such Vacancies.

No Person shall be a Senator who shall not have attained to the Age of thirty Years, and been nine Years a Citizen of the United States, and who shall not, when elected, be an Inhabitant of that State for which he shall be chosen.

The Vice President of the United States shall be President of the Senate, but shall have no Vote, unless they be equally divided.

The Senate shall chuse their other Officers, and also a President pro tempore, in the Absence of the Vice President, or when he shall exercise the Office of President of the United States.

The Senate shall have the sole Power to try all Impeachments. When sitting for that Purpose, they shall be on Oath or Affirmation. When the President of the United States is tried, the Chief Justice shall preside: And no Person shall be convicted without the Concurrence of two thirds of the Members present.

Judgment in Cases of Impeachment shall not extend further than to removal from Office, and disqualification to hold and enjoy any Office of honor, Trust, or Profit under the United States: but the Party convicted shall nevertheless be liable and subject to Indictment, Trial, Judgment, and Punishment, according to Law.

Section 4. The Times, Places and Manner of holding Elections for Senators and Representatives, shall be prescribed in each State by the Legislature thereof; but the Congress may at any time by Law make or alter such Regulations, except as to the Places of chusing Senators.

The Congress shall assemble at least once in every Year, and such Meeting shall be on the first Monday in December, unless they shall by Law appoint a different Day.

Section 5. Each House shall be the Judge of the Elections, Returns, and Qualifications of its own Members, and a Majority of each shall constitute a Quorum to do Business; but a smaller Number may adjourn from day to day, and may be authorized to compel the Attendance of absent Members, in such Manner, and under such Penalties as each House may provide.

Each House may determine the Rules of its Proceedings, punish its Members for disorderly Behavior, and, with the Concurrence of two thirds, expel a Member.

Each House shall keep a Journal of its Proceedings, and from time to time publish the same, excepting such Parts as may in their Judgment require Secrecy; and the Yeas and Nays of the Members of either House on any question shall, at the Desire of one fifth of those Present, be entered on the Journal.

Neither House, during the Session of Congress, shall, without the Consent of the other, adjourn for more than three days, nor to any other Place than that in which the two Houses shall be sitting.

Section 6. The Senators and Representatives shall receive a Compensation for their Services, to be ascertained by Law, and paid out of the Treasury of the United States. They shall in all Cases, except Treason, Felony and Breach of the Peace, be privileged from Arrest during their Attendance at the Session of their respective Houses, and in going to and returning from the same; and for any Speech or Debate in either House, they shall not be questioned in any other Place.

No Senator or Representative shall, during the Time for which he was elected, be appointed to any civil Office under the Authority of the United States, which shall have been created, or the Emoluments whereof shall have been increased during such time; and no Person holding any Office under the United States, shall be a Member of either House during his Continuance in Office.

Section 7. All Bills for raising Revenue shall originate in the House of Representatives; but the Senate may propose or concur with Amendments as on other Bills.

Every Bill which shall have passed the House of Representatives and the Senate, shall, before it become a Law, be presented to the President of the United States; If he approve he shall sign it, but if not he shall return it, with his Objections to the House in which it shall have originated, who shall enter the Objections at large on their Journal, and proceed to reconsider it. If after such Reconsideration two thirds of that House shall agree to pass the Bill, it shall be sent together with the Objections, to the other House, by which it shall likewise be reconsidered, and if approved by two thirds of that House, it shall become a Law. But in all such Cases the Votes of both Houses shall be determined by Yeas and Nays, and the Names of the Persons voting for and against the Bill shall be entered on the Journal of each House respectively. If any Bill shall not be returned by the President within ten Days (Sundays excepted) after it shall have been presented to him, the Same shall be a Law, in like Manner as if he had signed it, unless the Congress by their Adjournment prevent its Return in which Case it shall not be a Law.

Every Order, Resolution, or Vote, to which the Concurrence of the Senate and House of Representatives may be necessary (except on a question of Adjournment) shall be presented to the President of the United States; and before the Same shall take Effect, shall be approved by him, or being disapproved by him, shall be repassed by two thirds of the Senate and House of Representatives, according to the Rules and Limitations prescribed in the Case of a Bill.

Section 8. The Congress shall have Power To lay and collect Taxes, Duties, Imposts and Excises, to pay the Debts and provide for the common Defence and general Welfare of the United States; but all Duties, Imposts and Excises shall be uniform throughout the United States;

To borrow Money on the credit of the United States;

To regulate Commerce with foreign Nations, and among the several States, and with the Indian Tribes;

To establish an uniform Rule of Naturalization, and uniform Laws on the subject of Bankruptcies throughout the United States;

To coin Money, regulate the Value thereof, and of foreign Coin, and fix the Standard of Weights and Measures;

To provide for the Punishment of counterfeiting the Securities and current Coin of the United States;

To establish Post Offices and post Roads;

To promote the Progress of Science and useful Arts, by securing for limited Times to Authors and Inventors the exclusive Right to their respective Writings and Discoveries;

To constitute Tribunals inferior to the supreme Court;

To define and punish Piracies and Felonies committed on the high Seas, and Offenses against the Law of Nations;

To declare War, grant Letters of Marque and Reprisal, and make Rules concerning Captures on Land and Water;

To raise and support Armies, but no Appropriation of Money to that Use shall be for a longer Term than two Years;

To provide and maintain a Navy;

To make Rules for the Government and Regulation of the land and naval Forces;

To provide for calling forth the Militia to execute the Laws of the Union, suppress Insurrections and repel Invasions;

To provide for organizing, arming, and disciplining, the Militia, and for governing such Part of them as may be employed in the Service of the United States, reserving to the States respectively, the Appointment of the Officers, and the Authority of training the Militia according to the discipline prescribed by Congress;

To exercise exclusive Legislation in all Cases whatsoever, over such District (not exceeding ten Miles square) as may, by Cession of particular States, and the Acceptance of Congress, become the Seat of the Government of the United States, and to exercise like Authority over all Places purchased by the Consent of the Legislature of the State in which the Same shall be, for the Erection of Forts, Magazines, Arsenals, dock-Yards, and other needful Buildings;—And

To make all Laws which shall be necessary and proper for carrying into Execution the foregoing Powers, and all other Powers vested by this Constitution in the Government of the United States, or in any Department or Officer thereof.

Section 9. The Migration or Importation of such Persons as any of the States now existing shall think proper to admit, shall not be prohibited by the Congress prior to the Year one thousand eight hundred and eight, but a Tax or duty may be imposed on such Importation, not exceeding ten dollars for each Person.

The privilege of the Writ of Habeas Corpus shall not be suspended, unless when in Cases of Rebellion or Invasion the public Safety may require it.

No Bill of Attainder or ex post facto Law shall be passed.

No Capitation, or other direct, Tax shall be laid, unless in Proportion to the Census or Enumeration herein before directed to be taken.

No Tax or Duty shall be laid on Articles exported from any State.

No Preference shall be given by any Regulation of Commerce or Revenue to the Ports of one State over those of another: nor shall Vessels bound to, or from, one State be obliged to enter, clear, or pay Duties in another.

No Money shall be drawn from the Treasury, but in Consequence of Appropriations made by Law; and a regular Statement and Account of the Receipts and Expenditures of all public Money shall be published from time to time.

No Title of Nobility shall be granted by the United States: And no Person holding any Office of Profit or Trust under them, shall, without the Consent of the Congress, accept of any present, Emolument, Office, or Title, of any kind whatever, from any King, Prince, or foreign State.

Section 10. No State shall enter into any Treaty, Alliance, or Confederation; grant Letters of Marque and Reprisal; coin Money; emit Bills of Credit; make any Thing but gold and silver Coin a Tender in Payment of Debts; pass any Bill of Attainder, ex post facto Law, or Law impairing the Obligation of Contracts, or grant any Title of Nobility.

No State shall, without the Consent of the Congress, lay any Imposts or Duties on Imports or Exports, except what may be absolutely necessary for executing its inspection Laws: and the net Produce of all Duties and Imposts, laid by any State on Imports or Exports, shall be for the Use of the Treasury of the United States; and all such Laws shall be subject to the Revision and Controul of the Congress.

No State shall, without the Consent of Congress, lay any Duty of Tonnage, keep Troops, or Ships of War in time of Peace, enter into any Agreement or Compact with another State, or with a foreign Power, or engage in War, unless actually invaded, or in such imminent Danger as will not admit of delay.

ARTICLE II

Section 1. The executive Power shall be vested in a President of the United States of America. He shall hold his Office during the Term of four Years, and, together with the Vice President, chosen for the same Term, be elected, as follows:

Each State shall appoint, in such Manner as the Legislature thereof may direct, a Number of Electors, equal to the whole Number of Senators and Representatives to which the State may be entitled in the Congress; but no Senator or Representative, or Person holding an Office of Trust or Profit under the United States, shall be appointed an Elector.

The Electors shall meet in their respective States, and vote by Ballot for two Persons, of whom one at least shall not be an Inhabitant of the same State with themselves. And they shall make a List of all the Persons voted for, and of the Number of Votes for each; which List they shall sign and certify, and transmit sealed to the Seat of the Government of the United States, directed to the President of the Senate. The President of the Senate shall, in the Presence of the Senate and House of Representatives, open all the Certificates, and the Votes shall then be counted. The Person having the greatest Number of Votes shall be the President, if such Number be a Majority of the whole Number of Electors appointed; and if there be more than one who have such Majority, and have an equal Number of Votes, then the House of Representatives shall immediately chuse by Ballot one of them for President; and if no Person have a Majority, then from the five highest on the List the said House shall in like Manner chuse the President. But in chusing the President, the Votes shall be taken by States, the Representation from each State having one Vote; A quorum for this Purpose shall consist of a Member or Members from two thirds of the States, and a Majority of all the States shall be necessary to a Choice. In every Case, after the Choice of the President, the Person having the greater Number of Votes of the Electors shall be the Vice President. But if there should remain two or more who have equal Votes, the Senate shall chuse from them by Ballot the Vice President.

The Congress may determine the Time of chusing the Electors, and the Day on which they shall give their Votes; which Day shall be the same throughout the United States.

No person except a natural born Citizen, or a Citizen of the United States, at the time of the Adoption of this Constitution, shall be eligible to the Office of President; neither shall any Person be eligible to that Office who shall not have attained to the Age of thirty five Years, and been fourteen Years a Resident within the United States.

In Case of the Removal of the President from Office, or of his Death, Resignation or Inability to discharge the Powers and Duties of the said Office, the same shall devolve on the Vice President, and the Congress may by Law provide for the Case of Removal, Death, Resignation or Inability, both of the President and Vice President, declaring what Officer shall then act as President, and such Officer shall act accordingly, until the Disability be removed, or a President shall be elected.

The President shall, at stated Times, receive for his Services, a Compensation, which shall neither be increased nor diminished during the Period for which he shall have been elected, and he shall not receive within that Period any other Emolument from the United States, or any of them.

Before he enter on the Execution of his Office, he shall take the following Oath or Affirmation: "I do solemnly swear (or affirm) that I will faithfully execute the Office of President of the United States, and will to the best of my Ability, preserve, protect and defend the Constitution of the United States."

Section 2. The President shall be Commander in Chief of the Army and Navy of the United States, and of the Militia of the several States, when called into the actual Service of the United States; he may require the Opinion, in writing, of the principal Officer in each of the executive Departments, upon any Subject relating to the Duties of their respective Offices, and he shall have Power to grant Reprieves and Pardons for Offenses against the United States, except in Cases of Impeachment.

He shall have Power, by and with the Advice and Consent of the Senate to make Treaties, provided two thirds of the Senators present concur; and he shall nominate, and by and with the Advice and Consent of the Senate, shall appoint Ambassadors, other public Ministers and Consuls, Judges of the supreme Court, and all other Officers of the United States, whose Appointments are not herein otherwise provided for, and which shall be established by Law; but the Congress may by Law vest the Appointment of such inferior Officers, as they think proper, in the President alone, in the Courts of Law, or in the Heads of Departments.

The President shall have Power to fill up all Vacancies that may happen during the Recess of the Senate, by granting Commissions which shall expire at the End of their next Session.

Section 3. He shall from time to time give to the Congress Information of the State of the Union, and recommend to their Consideration such Measures as he shall judge necessary and expedient; he may, on extraordinary Occasions, convene both Houses, or either of them, and in Case of Disagreement between them, with Respect to the Time of Adjournment, he may adjourn them to such Time as he shall think proper; he shall receive Ambassadors and other public Ministers; he shall take Care that the Laws be faithfully executed, and shall Commission all the Officers of the United States.

Section 4. The President, Vice President and all civil Officers of the United States, shall be removed from Office on Impeachment for, and Conviction of, Treason, Bribery, or other high Crimes and Misdemeanors.

ARTICLE III

Section 1. The judicial Power of the United States, shall be vested in one supreme Court, and in such inferior Courts as the Congress may from time to time ordain and establish. The Judges, both of the supreme and inferior Courts, shall hold their Offices during good Behaviour, and shall, at stated Times, receive for their Services a Compensation, which shall not be diminished during their Continuance in Office.

Section 2. The judicial Power shall extend to all Cases, in Law and Equity, arising under this Constitution, the Laws of the United States, and Treaties made, or which shall be made, under their Authority;—to all Cases affecting Ambassadors, other public Ministers and Consuls;—to all Cases of admiralty and maritime Jurisdiction;—to Controversies to which the United States shall be a Party;—to Controversies between two or more States;—between a State and Citizens of another State;—between Citizens of different States;—between Citizens of the same State claiming Lands under Grants of different States, and between a State, or the Citizens thereof, and foreign States, Citizens or Subjects.

In all Cases affecting Ambassadors, other public Ministers and Consuls, and those in which a State shall be a Party, the supreme Court shall have original Jurisdiction. In all the other Cases before mentioned, the supreme Court shall have appellate Jurisdiction, both as to Law and Fact, with such Exceptions, and under such Regulations as the Congress shall make.

The Trial of all Crimes, except in Cases of Impeachment, shall be by Jury; and such Trial shall be held in the State where the said Crimes shall have been committed; but when not committed within any State, the Trial shall be at such Place or Places as the Congress may by Law have directed.

Section 3. Treason against the United States, shall consist only in levying War against them, or, in adhering to their Enemies, giving them Aid and Comfort. No Person shall be convicted of Treason unless on the Testimony of two Witnesses to the same overt Act, or on Confession in open Court.

The Congress shall have Power to declare the Punishment of Treason, but no Attainder of Treason shall work Corruption of Blood, or Forfeiture except during the Life of the Person attainted.

ARTICLE IV

Section 1. Full Faith and Credit shall be given in each State to the public Acts, Records, and judicial Proceedings of every other State. And the Congress may by general Laws prescribe the Manner in which such Acts, Records and Proceedings shall be proved, and the Effect thereof.

Section 2. The Citizens of each State shall be entitled to all Privileges and Immunities of Citizens in the several States.

A Person charged in any State with Treason, Felony, or other Crime, who shall flee from Justice, and be found in another State, shall on Demand of the executive Authority of the State from which he fled, be delivered up, to be removed to the State having Jurisdiction of the Crime.

No Person held to Service or Labour in one State, under the Laws thereof, escaping into another, shall, in Consequence of any Law or Regulation therein, be discharged from such Service or Labour, but shall be delivered up on Claim of the Party to whom such Service or Labour may be due.

Section 3. New States may be admitted by the Congress into this Union; but no new State shall be formed or erected within the Jurisdiction of any other State; nor any State be formed by the Junction of two or more States, or Parts of States, without the Consent of the Legislatures of the States concerned as well as of the Congress.

The Congress shall have Power to dispose of and make all needful Rules and Regulations respecting the Territory or other Property belonging to the United States; and nothing in this Constitution shall be so construed as to Prejudice any Claims of the United States, or of any particular State.

Section 4. The United States shall guarantee to every State in this Union a Republican Form of Government, and shall protect each of them against Invasion; and on Application of the Legislature, or of the Executive (when the Legislature cannot be convened) against domestic Violence.

ARTICLE V

The Congress, whenever two thirds of both Houses shall deem it necessary, shall propose Amendments to this Constitution, or, on the Application of the Legislatures of two thirds of the several States, shall call a Convention for proposing Amendments, which, in either Case, shall be valid to all Intents and Purposes, as part of this Constitution, when ratified by the Legislatures of three fourths of the several States, or by Conventions in three fourths thereof, as the one or the other Mode of Ratification may be proposed by the Congress; Provided that no Amendment which may be made prior to the Year One thousand eight hundred and eight shall in any Manner affect the first and fourth Clauses in the Ninth Section of the first Article; and that no State, without its Consent, shall be deprived of its equal Suffrage in the Senate.

ARTICLE VI

All Debts contracted and Engagements entered into, before the Adoption of this Constitution shall be as valid against the United States under this Constitution, as under the Confederation.

This Constitution, and the Laws of the United States which shall be made in Pursuance thereof; and all Treaties made, or which shall be made, under the Authority of the United States, shall be the supreme Law of the Land; and the Judges in every State shall be bound thereby, any Thing in the Constitution or Laws of any State to the Contrary notwithstanding.

The Senators and Representatives before mentioned, and the Members of the several State Legislatures, and all executive and judicial Officers, both of the United States and of the several States, shall be bound by Oath or Affirmation, to support this Constitution; but no religious Test shall ever be required as a Qualification to any Office or public Trust under the United States.

ARTICLE VII

The Ratification of the Conventions of nine States shall be sufficient for the Establishment of this Constitution between the States so ratifying the Same.

AMENDMENT I [1791]

Congress shall make no law respecting an establishment of religion, or prohibiting the free exercise thereof; or abridging the freedom of speech, or of the press; or the right of the people peaceably to assembly, and to petition the Government for a redress of grievances.

AMENDMENT II [1791]

A well regulated Militia, being necessary to the security of a free State, the right of the people to keep and bear Arms, shall not be infringed.

AMENDMENT III [1791]

No Soldier shall, in time of peace be quartered in any house, without the consent of the Owner, nor in time of war, but in a manner to be prescribed by law.

AMENDMENT IV [1791]

The right of the people to be secure in their persons, houses, papers, and effects, against unreasonable searches and seizures, shall not be violated, and no Warrants shall issue, but upon probable cause, supported by Oath or affirmation, and particularly describing the place to be searched, and the persons or things to be seized.

AMENDMENT V [1791]

No person shall be held to answer for a capital, or otherwise infamous crime, unless on a presentment or indictment of a Grand Jury, except in cases arising in the land or naval forces, or in the Militia, when in actual service in time of War or public danger; nor shall any person be subject for the same offence to be twice put in jeopardy of life or limb; nor shall be compelled in any criminal case to be a witness against himself, nor be deprived of life, liberty, or property, without due process of law; nor shall private property be taken for public use, without just compensation.

AMENDMENT VI [1791]

In all criminal prosecutions, the accused shall enjoy the right to a speedy and public trial, by an impartial jury of the State and district wherein the crime shall have been committed, which district shall have been previously ascertained by law, and to be informed of the nature and cause of the accusation; to be confronted with the witnesses against him; to have compulsory process for obtaining witnesses in his favor, and to have the Assistance of Counsel for his defence.

AMENDMENT VII [1791]

In Suits at common law, where the value in controversy shall exceed twenty dollars, the right of trial by jury shall be preserved, and no fact tried by jury, shall be otherwise re-examined in any Court of the United States, than according to the rules of the common law.

AMENDMENT VIII [1791]

Excessive bail shall not be required, nor excessive fines imposed, nor cruel and unusual punishments inflicted.

AMENDMENT IX [1791]

The enumeration in the Constitution, of certain rights, shall not be construed to deny or disparage others retained by the people.

AMENDMENT X [1791]

The powers not delegated to the United States by the Constitution, nor prohibited by it to the States, are reserved to the States respectively, or to the people.

AMENDMENT XI [1798]

The Judicial power of the United States shall not be construed to extend to any suit in law or equity, commenced or prosecuted against one of the United States by Citizens of another State, or by Citizens or Subjects of any Foreign State.

AMENDMENT XII [1804]

The Electors shall meet in their respective states, and vote by ballot for President and Vice-President, one of whom, at least, shall not be an inhabitant of the same state with themselves; they shall name in their ballots the person voted for as President, and in distinct ballots the person voted for as Vice-President, and they shall make distinct lists of all persons voted for as President, and of all persons voted for as Vice-President, and of the number of votes for each, which lists they shall sign and certify, and transmit sealed to the seat of the government of the United States, directed to the President of the Senate;—The President of the Senate shall, in the presence of the Senate and House of Representatives, open all the certificates and the votes shall then be counted;—The person having the greatest number of votes for President, shall be the President, if such number be a majority of the whole number of Electors appointed; and if no person have such majority, then from the persons having the highest numbers not exceeding three on the list of those voted for as President, the House of Representatives shall choose immediately, by ballot, the President. But in choosing the President, the votes shall be taken by states, the representation from each state having one vote; a quorum for this purpose shall consist of a member or members from two-thirds of the states, and a majority of all states shall be necessary to a choice. And if the House of Representatives shall not choose a President whenever the right of choice shall devolve upon them, before the fourth day of March next following, then the Vice-President shall act as President, as in the case of the death or other constitutional disability of the President.—The person having the greatest number of votes as Vice-President, shall be the Vice-President, if such number be a majority of the whole number of Electors appointed, and if no person have a majority, then from the two highest numbers on the list, the Senate shall choose the Vice-President; a quorum for the purpose shall consist of two-thirds of the whole number of Senators, and a majority of the whole number shall be necessary to a choice. But no person constitutionally ineligible to the office of President shall be eligible to that of Vice-President of the United States.

AMENDMENT XIII [1865]

Section 1. Neither slavery nor involuntary servitude, except as a punishment for crime whereof the party shall have been duly convicted, shall exist within the United States, or any place subject to their jurisdiction.

Section 2. Congress shall have power to enforce this article by appropriate legislation.

Amendment XIV [1868]

Section 1. All persons born or naturalized in the United States, and subject to the jurisdiction thereof, are citizens of the United States and of the State wherein they reside. No State shall make or enforce any law which shall abridge the privileges or immunities of citizens of the United States; nor shall any State deprive any person of life, liberty, or property, without due process of law; nor deny to any person within its jurisdiction the equal protection of the laws.

Section 2. Representatives shall be apportioned among the several States according to their respective numbers, counting the whole number of persons in each State, excluding Indians not taxed. But when the right to vote at any election for the choice of electors for President and Vice President of the United States, Representatives in Congress, the Executive and Judicial officers of a State, or the members of the Legislature thereof, is denied to any of the male inhabitants of such State, being twenty-one years of age, and citizens of the United States, or in any way abridged, except for participation in rebellion, or other crime, the basis of representation therein shall be reduced in the proportion which the number of such male citizens shall bear to the whole number of male citizens twenty-one years of age in such State.

Section 3. No person shall be a Senator or Representative in Congress, or elector of President and Vice President, or hold any office, civil or military, under the United States, or under any State, who having previously taken an oath, as a member of Congress, or as an officer of the United States, or as a member of any State legislature, or as an executive or judicial officer of any State, to support the Constitution of the United States, shall have engaged in insurrection or rebellion against the same, or given aid or comfort to the enemies thereof. But Congress may by a vote of two-thirds of each House, remove such disability.

Section 4. The validity of the public debt of the United States, authorized by law, including debts incurred for payment of pensions and bounties for services in suppressing insurrection or rebellion, shall not be questioned. But neither the United States nor any State shall assume or pay any debt or obligation incurred in aid of insurrection or rebellion against the United States, or any claim for the loss or emancipation of any slave; but all such debts, obligations and claims shall be held illegal and void.

Section 5. The Congress shall have power to enforce, by appropriate legislation, the provisions of this article.

Amendment XV [1870]

Section 1. The right of citizens of the United States to vote shall not be denied or abridged by the United States or by any State on account of race, color, or previous condition of servitude.

Section 2. The Congress shall have power to enforce this article by appropriate legislation.

Amendment XVI [1913]

The Congress shall have power to lay and collect taxes on incomes, from whatever source derived, without apportionment among the several States, and without regard to any census or enumeration.

Amendment XVII [1913]

Section 1. The Senate of the United States shall be composed of two Senators from each State, elected by the people thereof, for six years; and each Senator shall have one vote. The electors in each State shall have the qualifications requisite for electors of the most numerous branch of the State legislatures.

Section 2. When vacancies happen in the representation of any State in the Senate, the executive authority of such State shall issue writs of election to fill such vacancies: *Provided,* That the legislature of any State may empower the executive thereof to make temporary appointments until the people fill the vacancies by election as the legislature may direct.

Section 3. This amendment shall not be so construed as to affect the election or term of any Senator chosen before it becomes valid as part of the Constitution.

Amendment XVIII [1919]

Section 1. After one year from the ratification of this article the manufacture, sale, or transportation of intoxicating liquors within, the importation thereof into, or the exportation thereof from the United States and all territory subject to the jurisdiction thereof for beverage purposes is hereby prohibited.

Section 2. The Congress and the several States shall have concurrent power to enforce this article by appropriate legislation.

Section 3. This article shall be inoperative unless it shall have been ratified as an amendment to the Constitution by the legislatures of the several States, as provided in the Constitution, within seven years from the date of the submission hereof to the States by the Congress.

Amendment XIX [1920]

Section 1. The right of citizens of the United States to vote shall not be denied or abridged by the United States or by any State on account of sex.

Section 2. Congress shall have power to enforce this article by appropriate legislation.

Amendment XX [1933]

Section 1. The terms of the President and Vice President shall end at noon on the 20th day of January, and the terms of Senators and Representatives at noon on the 3d day of January, of the years in which such terms would have ended if this article had not been ratified; and the terms of their successors shall then begin.

Section 2. The Congress shall assemble at least once in every year, and such meeting shall begin at noon on the 3d day of January, unless they shall by law appoint a different day.

Section 3. If, at the time fixed for the beginning of the term of the President, the President elect shall have died, the Vice President elect shall become President. If the President shall not have been chosen before the time fixed for the beginning of his term, or if the President elect shall have failed to qualify, then the Vice President elect shall act as President until a President shall have qualified; and the Congress may by law provide for the case wherein neither a President elect nor a Vice President elect shall have qualified, declaring who shall then act as President, or the manner in which one who is to act shall be selected, and such person shall act accordingly until a President or Vice President shall have qualified.

Section 4. The Congress may by law provide for the case of the death of any of the persons from whom the House of Representatives may choose a President whenever the right of choice shall have devolved upon them, and for the case of the death of any of the persons from whom the Senate may choose a

Vice President whenever the right of choice shall have devolved upon them.

Section 5.   Sections 1 and 2 shall take effect on the 15th day of October following the ratification of this article.

Section 6.   This article shall be inoperative unless it shall have been ratified as an amendment to the Constitution by the legislatures of three-fourths of the several States within seven years from the date of its submission.

AMENDMENT XXI [1933]

Section 1.   The eighteenth article of amendment to the Constitution of the United States is hereby repealed.

Section 2.   The transportation or importation into any State, Territory, or possession of the United States for delivery or use therein of intoxicating liquors, in violation of the laws thereof, is hereby prohibited.

Section 3.   This article shall be inoperative unless it shall have been ratified as an amendment to the Constitution by conventions in the several States, as provided in the Constitution, within seven years from the date of the submission hereof to the States by the Congress.

AMENDMENT XXII [1951]

Section 1.   No person shall be elected to the office of the President more than twice, and no person who has held the office of President, or acted as President, for more than two years of a term to which some other person was elected President shall be elected to the office of President more than once. But this Article shall not apply to any person holding the office of President when this Article was proposed by the Congress, and shall not prevent any person who may be holding the office of President, or acting as President, during the term within which this Article becomes operative from holding the office of President or acting as President during the remainder of such term.

Section 2.   This article shall be inoperative unless it shall have been ratified as an amendment to the Constitution by the legislatures of three-fourths of the several States within seven years from the date of its submission to the States by the Congress.

AMENDMENT XXIII [1961]

Section 1.   The District constituting the seat of Government of the United States shall appoint in such manner as the Congress may direct:

A number of electors of President and Vice President equal to the whole number of Senators and Representatives in Congress to which the District would be entitled if it were a State, but in no event more than the least populous state; they shall be in addition to those appointed by the states, but they shall be considered, for the purposes of the election of President and Vice President, to be electors appointed by a state; and they shall meet in the District and perform such duties as provided by the twelfth article of amendment.

Section 2.   The Congress shall have power to enforce this article by appropriate legislation.

AMENDMENT XXIV [1964]

Section 1.   The right of citizens of the United States to vote in any primary or other election for President or Vice President, for electors for President or Vice President, or for Senator or Representative in Congress, shall not be denied or abridged by the United States, or any State by reason of failure to pay any poll tax or other tax.

Section 2.   The Congress shall have power to enforce this article by appropriate legislation.

AMENDMENT XXV [1967]

Section 1.   In case of the removal of the President from office or of his death or resignation, the Vice President shall become President.

Section 2.   Whenever there is a vacancy in the office of the Vice President, the President shall nominate a Vice President who shall take office upon confirmation by a majority vote of both Houses of Congress.

Section 3.   Whenever the President transmits to the President pro tempore of the Senate and the Speaker of the House of Representatives his written declaration that he is unable to discharge the powers and duties of his office, and until he transmits to them a written declaration to the contrary, such powers and duties shall be discharged by the Vice President as Acting President.

Section 4.   Whenever the Vice President and a majority of either the principal officers of the executive departments or of such other body as Congress may by law provide, transmit to the President pro tempore of the Senate and the Speaker of the House of Representatives their written declaration that the President is unable to discharge the powers and duties of his office, the Vice President shall immediately assume the powers and duties of the office as Acting President.

Thereafter, when the President transmits to the President pro tempore of the Senate and the Speaker of the House of Representatives his written declaration that no inability exists, he shall resume the powers and duties of his office unless the Vice President and a majority of either the principal officers of the executive department or of such other body as Congress may by law provide, transmit within four days to the President pro tempore of the Senate and the Speaker of the House of Representatives their written declaration that the President is unable to discharge the powers and duties of his office. Thereupon Congress shall decide the issue, assembling within forty-eight hours for that purpose if not in session. If the Congress, within twenty-one days after receipt of the latter written declaration, or, if Congress is not in session, within twenty-one days after Congress is required to assemble, determines by two-thirds vote of both Houses that the President is unable to discharge the powers and duties of his office, the Vice President shall continue to discharge the same as Acting President; otherwise, the President shall resume the powers and duties of his office.

AMENDMENT XXVI [1971]

Section 1.   The right of citizens of the United States, who are eighteen years of age or older, to vote shall not be denied or abridged by the United States or by any State on account of age.

Section 2.   The Congress shall have power to enforce this article by appropriate legislation.

AMENDMENT XXVII [1992]

No law, varying the compensation for the services of the Senators and Representatives, shall take effect, until an election of Representatives shall have intervened.

APPENDIX C
Articles 2 and 2A of the Uniform Commercial Code

Article 2
SALES

Part 1 Short Title, General Construction and Subject Matter

§ 2–101. Short Title.

This Article shall be known and may be cited as Uniform Commercial Code—Sales.

§ 2–102. Scope; Certain Security and Other Transactions Excluded From This Article.

Unless the context otherwise requires, this Article applies to transactions in goods; it does not apply to any transaction which although in the form of an unconditional contract to sell or present sale is intended to operate only as a security transaction nor does this Article impair or repeal any statute regulating sales to consumers, farmers or other specified classes of buyers.

§ 2–103. Definitions and Index of Definitions.

(1) In this Article unless the context otherwise requires

    (a) "Buyer" means a person who buys or contracts to buy goods.

    (b) "Good faith" in the case of a merchant means honesty in fact and the observance of reasonable commercial standards of fair dealing in the trade.

    (c) "Receipt" of goods means taking physical possession of them.

    (d) "Seller" means a person who sells or contracts to sell goods.

(2) Other definitions applying to this Article or to specified Parts thereof, and the sections in which they appear are:

"Acceptance". Section 2–606.
"Banker's credit". Section 2–325.
"Between merchants". Section 2–104.
"Cancellation". Section 2–106(4).
"Commercial unit". Section 2–105.
"Confirmed credit". Section 2–325.
"Conforming to contract". Section 2–106.
"Contract for sale". Section 2–106.
"Cover". Section 2–712.
"Entrusting". Section 2–403.
"Financing agency". Section 2–104.
"Future goods". Section 2–105.
"Goods". Section 2–105.

"Identification". Section 2–501.
"Installment contract". Section 2–612.
"Letter of Credit". Section 2–325.
"Lot". Section 2–105.
"Merchant". Section 2–104.
"Overseas". Section 2–323.
"Person in position of seller". Section 2–707.
"Present sale". Section 2–106.
"Sale". Section 2–106.
"Sale on approval". Section 2–326.
"Sale or return". Section 2–326.
"Termination". Section 2–106.

(3) The following definitions in other Articles apply to this Article:
"Check". Section 3–104.
"Consignee". Section 7–102.
"Consignor". Section 7–102.
"Consumer goods". Section 9–109.
"Dishonor". Section 3–507.
"Draft". Section 3–104.

(4) In addition Article 1 contains general definitions and principles of construction and interpretation applicable throughout this Article.

As amended in 1994 and 1999.

§ 2–104. Definitions: "Merchant"; "Between Merchants"; "Financing Agency".

(1) "Merchant" means a person who deals in goods of the kind or otherwise by his occupation holds himself out as having knowledge or skill peculiar to the practices or goods involved in the transaction or to whom such knowledge or skill may be attributed by his employment of an agent or broker or other intermediary who by his occupation holds himself out as having such knowledge or skill.

(2) "Financing agency" means a bank, finance company or other person who in the ordinary course of business makes advances against goods or documents of title or who by arrangement with either the seller or the buyer intervenes in ordinary course to make or collect payment due or claimed under the contract for sale, as by purchasing or paying the seller's draft or making advances against it or by merely taking it for collection whether or not documents of title accompany the draft. "Financing agency" includes also a bank or other person who similarly intervenes between persons who are in the position of seller and buyer in respect to the goods (Section 2–707).

(3) "Between merchants" means in any transaction with respect to which both parties are chargeable with the knowledge or skill of merchants.

§ 2–105. Definitions: Transferability; "Goods"; "Future" Goods; "Lot"; "Commercial Unit".

(1) "Goods" means all things (including specially manufactured goods) which are movable at the time of identification to the contract for sale other than the money in which the price is to be paid, investment securities (Article 8) and things in action. "Goods" also includes the unborn young of animals and growing crops and other identified things attached to realty as described in the section on goods to be severed from realty (Section 2–107).

(2) Goods must be both existing and identified before any interest in them can pass. Goods which are not both existing and identified are "future" goods. A purported present sale of future goods or of any interest therein operates as a contract to sell.

(3) There may be a sale of a part interest in existing identified goods.

(4) An undivided share in an identified bulk of fungible goods is sufficiently identified to be sold although the quantity of the bulk is not determined. Any agreed proportion of such a bulk or any quantity thereof agreed upon by number, weight or other measure may to the extent of the seller's interest in the bulk be sold to the buyer who then becomes an owner in common.

(5) "Lot" means a parcel or a single article which is the subject matter of a separate sale or delivery, whether or not it is sufficient to perform the contract.

(6) "Commercial unit" means such a unit of goods as by commercial usage is a single whole for purposes of sale and division of which materially impairs its character or value on the market or in use. A commercial unit may be a single article (as a machine) or a set of articles (as a suite of furniture or an assortment of sizes) or a quantity (as a bale, gross, or carload) or any other unit treated in use or in the relevant market as a single whole.

§ 2–106. Definitions: "Contract"; "Agreement"; "Contract for Sale"; "Sale"; "Present Sale"; "Conforming" to Contract; "Termination"; "Cancellation".

(1) In this Article unless the context otherwise requires "contract" and "agreement" are limited to those relating to the present or future sale of goods. "Contract for sale" includes both a present sale of goods and a contract to sell goods at a future time. A "sale" consists in the passing of title from the seller to the buyer for a price (Section 2–401). A "present sale" means a sale which is accomplished by the making of the contract.

(2) Goods or conduct including any part of a performance are "conforming" or conform to the contract when they are in accordance with the obligations under the contract.

(3) "Termination" occurs when either party pursuant to a power created by agreement or law puts an end to the contract otherwise than for its breach. On "termination" all obligations which are still executory on both sides are discharged but any right based on prior breach or performance survives.

(4) "Cancellation" occurs when either party puts an end to the contract for breach by the other and its effect is the same as that of "termination" except that the cancelling party also retains any remedy for breach of the whole contract or any unperformed balance.

§ 2–107. Goods to Be Severed From Realty: Recording.

(1) A contract for the sale of minerals or the like (including oil and gas) or a structure or its materials to be removed from realty is a contract for the sale of goods within this Article if they are to be severed by the seller but until severance a purported present sale thereof which is not effective as a transfer of an interest in land is effective only as a contract to sell.

(2) A contract for the sale apart from the land of growing crops or other things attached to realty and capable of severance without material harm thereto but not described in subsection (1) or of timber to be cut is a contract for the sale of goods within this Article whether the subject matter is to be severed by the buyer or by the seller even though it forms part of the realty at the time of contracting, and the parties can by identification effect a present sale before severance.

(3) The provisions of this section are subject to any third party rights provided by the law relating to realty records, and the contract for sale may be executed and recorded as a document transferring an interest in land and shall then constitute notice to third parties of the buyer's rights under the contract for sale.

As amended in 1972.

Part 2 Form, Formation and Readjustment of Contract

§ 2–201. Formal Requirements; Statute of Frauds.

(1) Except as otherwise provided in this section a contract for the sale of goods for the price of $500 or more is not enforceable by way of action or defense unless there is some writing sufficient to indicate that a contract for sale has been made between the parties and signed by the party against whom enforcement is sought or by his authorized agent or broker. A writing is not insufficient because it omits or incorrectly states a term agreed upon but the contract is not enforceable under this paragraph beyond the quantity of goods shown in such writing.

(2) Between merchants if within a reasonable time a writing in confirmation of the contract and sufficient against the sender is received and the party receiving it has reason to know its contents, its satisfies the requirements of subsection (1) against such party unless written notice of objection to its contents is given within ten days after it is received.

(3) A contract which does not satisfy the requirements of subsection (1) but which is valid in other respects is enforceable

    (a) if the goods are to be specially manufactured for the buyer and are not suitable for sale to others in the ordinary course of the seller's business and the seller, before notice of repudiation is received and under circumstances which reasonably indicate that the goods are for the buyer, has made either a substantial beginning of their manufacture or commitments for their procurement; or

    (b) if the party against whom enforcement is sought admits in his pleading, testimony or otherwise in court that a contract for sale was made, but the contract is not enforceable under this provision beyond the quantity of goods admitted; or

    (c) with respect to goods for which payment has been made and accepted or which have been received and accepted (Sec. 2–606).

§ 2–202. Final Written Expression: Parol or Extrinsic Evidence.

Terms with respect to which the confirmatory memoranda of the parties agree or which are otherwise set forth in a writing intended by the parties as a final expression of their agreement with respect to such terms as are included therein may not be contradicted by evidence of any prior agreement or of a contemporaneous oral agreement but may be explained or supplemented

(a) by course of dealing or usage of trade (Section 1–205) or by course of performance (Section 2–208); and

(b) by evidence of consistent additional terms unless the court finds the writing to have been intended also as a complete and exclusive statement of the terms of the agreement.

§ 2–203. **Seals Inoperative.**

The affixing of a seal to a writing evidencing a contract for sale or an offer to buy or sell goods does not constitute the writing a sealed instrument and the law with respect to sealed instruments does not apply to such a contract or offer.

§ 2–204. **Formation in General.**

(1) A contract for sale of goods may be made in any manner sufficient to show agreement, including conduct by both parties which recognizes the existence of such a contract.

(2) An agreement sufficient to constitute a contract for sale may be found even though the moment of its making is undetermined.

(3) Even though one or more terms are left open a contract for sale does not fail for indefiniteness if the parties have intended to make a contract and there is a reasonably certain basis for giving an appropriate remedy.

§ 2–205. **Firm Offers.**

An offer by a merchant to buy or sell goods in a signed writing which by its terms gives assurance that it will be held open is not revocable, for lack of consideration, during the time stated or if no time is stated for a reasonable time, but in no event may such period of irrevocability exceed three months; but any such term of assurance on a form supplied by the offeree must be separately signed by the offeror.

§ 2–206. **Offer and Acceptance in Formation of Contract.**

(1) Unless other unambiguously indicated by the language or circumstances

(a) an offer to make a contract shall be construed as inviting acceptance in any manner and by any medium reasonable in the circumstances;

(b) an order or other offer to buy goods for prompt or current shipment shall be construed as inviting acceptance either by a prompt promise to ship or by the prompt or current shipment of conforming or nonconforming goods, but such a shipment of non-conforming goods does not constitute an acceptance if the seller seasonably notifies the buyer that the shipment is offered only as an accommodation to the buyer.

(2) Where the beginning of a requested performance is a reasonable mode of acceptance an offeror who is not notified of acceptance within a reasonable time may treat the offer as having lapsed before acceptance.

§ 2–207. **Additional Terms in Acceptance or Confirmation.**

(1) A definite and seasonable expression of acceptance or a written confirmation which is sent within a reasonable time operates as an acceptance even though it states terms additional to or different from those offered or agreed upon, unless acceptance is expressly made conditional on assent to the additional or different terms.

(2) The additional terms are to be construed as proposals for addition to the contract. Between merchants such terms become part of the contract unless:

(a) the offer expressly limits acceptance to the terms of the offer;

(b) they materially alter it; or

(c) notification of objection to them has already been given or is given within a reasonable time after notice of them is received.

(3) Conduct by both parties which recognizes the existence of a contract is sufficient to establish a contract for sale although the writings of the parties do not otherwise establish a contract. In such case the terms of the particular contract consist of those terms on which the writings of the parties agree, together with any supplementary terms incorporated under any other provisions of this Act.

§ 2–208. **Course of Performance or Practical Construction.**

(1) Where the contract for sale involves repeated occasions for performance by either party with knowledge of the nature of the performance and opportunity for objection to it by the other, any course of performance accepted or acquiesced in without objection shall be relevant to determine the meaning of the agreement.

(2) The express terms of the agreement and any such course of performance, as well as any course of dealing and usage of trade, shall be construed whenever reasonable as consistent with each other; but when such construction is unreasonable, express terms shall control course of performance and course of performance shall control both course of dealing and usage of trade (Section 1–205).

(3) Subject to the provisions of the next section on modification and waiver, such course of performance shall be relevant to show a waiver or modification of any term inconsistent with such course of performance.

§ 2–209. **Modification, Rescission and Waiver.**

(1) An agreement modifying a contract within this Article needs no consideration to be binding.

(2) A signed agreement which excludes modification or rescission except by a signed writing cannot be otherwise modified or rescinded, but except as between merchants such a requirement on a form supplied by the merchant must be separately signed by the other party.

(3) The requirements of the statute of frauds section of this Article (Section 2–201) must be satisfied if the contract as modified is within its provisions.

(4) Although an attempt at modification or rescission does not satisfy the requirements of subsection (2) or (3) it can operate as a waiver.

(5) A party who has made a waiver affecting an executory portion of the contract may retract the waiver by reasonable notification received by the other party that strict performance will be required of any term waived, unless the retraction would be unjust in view of a material change of position in reliance on the waiver.

§ 2–210. **Delegation of Performance; Assignment of Rights.**

(1) A party may perform his duty through a delegate unless otherwise agreed or unless the other party has a substantial interest in having his original promisor perform or control the acts required by the

contract. No delegation of performance relieves the party delegating of any duty to perform or any liability for breach.

(2) Except as otherwise provided in Section 9–406, unless otherwise agreed, all rights of either seller or buyer can be assigned except where the assignment would materially change the duty of the other party, or increase materially the burden or risk imposed on him by his contract, or impair materially his chance of obtaining return performance. A right to damages for breach of the whole contract or a right arising out of the assignor's due performance of his entire obligation can be assigned despite agreement otherwise.

(3) The creation, attachment, perfection, or enforcement of a security interest in the seller's interest under a contract is not a transfer that materially changes the duty of or increases materially the burden or risk imposed on the buyer or impairs materially the buyer's chance of obtaining return performance within the purview of subsection (2) unless, and then only to the extent that, enforcement actually results in a delegation of material performance of the seller. Even in that event, the creation, attachment, perfection, and enforcement of the security interest remain effective, but (i) the seller is liable to the buyer for damages caused by the delegation to the extent that the damages could not reasonably by prevented by the buyer, and (ii) a court having jurisdiction may grant other appropriate relief, including cancellation of the contract for sale or an injunction against enforcement of the security interest or consummation of the enforcement.

(4) Unless the circumstances indicate the contrary a prohibition of assignment of "the contract" is to be construed as barring only the delegation to the assignee of the assignor's performance.

(5) An assignment of "the contract" or of "all my rights under the contract" or an assignment in similar general terms is an assignment of rights and unless the language or the circumstances (as in an assignment for security) indicate the contrary, it is a delegation of performance of the duties of the assignor and its acceptance by the assignee constitutes a promise by him to perform those duties. This promise is enforceable by either the assignor or the other party to the original contract.

(6) The other party may treat any assignment which delegates performance as creating reasonable grounds for insecurity and may without prejudice to his rights against the assignor demand assurances from the assignee (Section 2–609).

As amended in 1999.

Part 3 General Obligation and Construction of Contract

§ 2–301. General Obligations of Parties.

The obligation of the seller is to transfer and deliver and that of the buyer is to accept and pay in accordance with the contract.

§ 2–302. Unconscionable Contract or Clause.

(1) If the court as a matter of law finds the contract or any clause of the contract to have been unconscionable at the time it was made the court may refuse to enforce the contract, or it may enforce the remainder of the contract without the unconscionable clause, or it may so limit the application of any unconscionable clause as to avoid any unconscionable result.

(2) When it is claimed or appears to the court that the contract or any clause thereof may be unconscionable the parties shall be afforded a reasonable opportunity to present evidence as to its com-

mercial setting, purpose and effect to aid the court in making the determination.

§ 2–303. Allocations or Division of Risks.

Where this Article allocates a risk or a burden as between the parties "unless otherwise agreed", the agreement may not only shift the allocation but may also divide the risk or burden.

§ 2–304. Price Payable in Money, Goods, Realty, or Otherwise.

(1) The price can be made payable in money or otherwise. If it is payable in whole or in part in goods each party is a seller of the goods which he is to transfer.

(2) Even though all or part of the price is payable in an interest in realty the transfer of the goods and the seller's obligations with reference to them are subject to this Article, but not the transfer of the interest in realty or the transferor's obligations in connection therewith.

§ 2–305. Open Price Term.

(1) The parties if they so intend can conclude a contract for sale even though the price is not settled. In such a case the price is a reasonable price at the time for delivery if

(a) nothing is said as to price; or

(b) the price is left to be agreed by the parties and they fail to agree; or

(c) the price is to be fixed in terms of some agreed market or other standard as set or recorded by a third person or agency and it is not so set or recorded.

(2) A price to be fixed by the seller or by the buyer means a price for him to fix in good faith.

(3) When a price left to be fixed otherwise than by agreement of the parties fails to be fixed through fault of one party the other may at his option treat the contract as cancelled or himself fix a reasonable price.

(4) Where, however, the parties intend not to be bound unless the price be fixed or agreed and it is not fixed or agreed there is no contract. In such a case the buyer must return any goods already received or if unable so to do must pay their reasonable value at the time of delivery and the seller must return any portion of the price paid on account.

§ 2–306. Output, Requirements and Exclusive Dealings.

(1) A term which measures the quantity by the output of the seller or the requirements of the buyer means such actual output or requirements as may occur in good faith, except that no quantity unreasonably disproportionate to any stated estimate or in the absence of a stated estimate to any normal or otherwise comparable prior output or requirements may be tendered or demanded.

(2) A lawful agreement by either the seller or the buyer for exclusive dealing in the kind of goods concerned imposes unless otherwise agreed an obligation by the seller to use best efforts to supply the goods and by the buyer to use best efforts to promote their sale.

§ 2–307. Delivery in Single Lot or Several Lots.

Unless otherwise agreed all goods called for by a contract for sale must be tendered in a single delivery and payment is due only on such tender but where the circumstances give either party the right to make or demand delivery in lots the price if it can be apportioned may be demanded for each lot.

§ 2–308. Absence of Specified Place for Delivery.

Unless otherwise agreed

(a) the place for delivery of goods is the seller's place of business or if he has none his residence; but

(b) in a contract for sale of identified goods which to the knowledge of the parties at the time of contracting are in some other place, that place is the place for their delivery; and

(c) documents of title may be delivered through customary banking channels.

§ 2–309. Absence of Specific Time Provisions; Notice of Termination.

(1) The time for shipment or delivery or any other action under a contract if not provided in this Article or agreed upon shall be a reasonable time.

(2) Where the contract provides for successive performances but is indefinite in duration it is valid for a reasonable time but unless otherwise agreed may be terminated at any time by either party.

(3) Termination of a contract by one party except on the happening of an agreed event requires that reasonable notification be received by the other party and an agreement dispensing with notification is invalid if its operation would be unconscionable.

§ 2–310. Open Time for Payment or Running of Credit; Authority to Ship Under Reservation.

Unless otherwise agreed

(a) payment is due at the time and place at which the buyer is to receive the goods even though the place of shipment is the place of delivery; and

(b) if the seller is authorized to send the goods he may ship them under reservation, and may tender the documents of title, but the buyer may inspect the goods after their arrival before payment is due unless such inspection is inconsistent with the terms of the contract (Section 2–513); and

(c) if delivery is authorized and made by way of documents of title otherwise than by subsection (b) then payment is due at the time and place at which the buyer is to receive the documents regardless of where the goods are to be received; and

(d) where the seller is required or authorized to ship the goods on credit the credit period runs from the time of shipment but post-dating the invoice or delaying its dispatch will correspondingly delay the starting of the credit period.

§ 2–311. Options and Cooperation Respecting Performance.

(1) An agreement for sale which is otherwise sufficiently definite (subsection (3) of Section 2–204) to be a contract is not made invalid by the fact that it leaves particulars of performance to be specified by one of the parties. Any such specification must be made in good faith and within limits set by commercial reasonableness.

(2) Unless otherwise agreed specifications relating to assortment of the goods are at the buyer's option and except as otherwise provided in subsections (1)(c) and (3) of Section 2–319 specifications or arrangements relating to shipment are at the seller's option.

(3) Where such specification would materially affect the other party's performance but is not seasonally made or where one party's cooperation is necessary to the agreed performance of the other but is not seasonally forthcoming, the other party in addition to all other remedies

(a) is excused for any resulting delay in his own performance; and

(b) may also either proceed to perform in any reasonable manner or after the time for a material part of his own performance treat the failure to specify or to cooperate as a breach by failure to deliver or accept the goods.

§ 2–312. Warranty of Title and Against Infringement; Buyer's Obligation Against Infringement.

(1) Subject to subsection (2) there is in a contract for sale a warranty by the seller that

(a) the title conveyed shall be good, and its transfer rightful; and

(b) the goods shall be delivered free from any security interest or other lien or encumbrance of which the buyer at the time of contracting has no knowledge.

(2) A warranty under subsection (1) will be excluded or modified only by specific language or by circumstances which give the buyer reason to know that the person selling does not claim title in himself or that he is purporting to sell only such right or title as he or a third person may have.

(3) Unless otherwise agreed a seller who is a merchant regularly dealing in goods of the kind warrants that the goods shall be delivered free of the rightful claim of any third person by way of infringement or the like but a buyer who furnishes specifications to the seller must hold the seller harmless against any such claim which arises out of compliance with the specifications.

§ 2–313. Express Warranties by Affirmation, Promise, Description, Sample.

(1) Express warranties by the seller are created as follows:

(a) Any affirmation of fact or promise made by the seller to the buyer which relates to the goods and becomes part of the basis of the bargain creates an express warranty that the goods shall conform to the affirmation or promise.

(b) Any description of the goods which is made part of the basis of the bargain creates an express warranty that the goods shall conform to the description.

(c) Any sample or model which is made part of the basis of the bargain creates an express warranty that the whole of the goods shall conform to the sample or model.

(2) It is not necessary to the creation of an express warranty that the seller use formal words such as "warrant" or "guarantee" or that he have a specific intention to make a warranty, but an affirmation merely of the value of the goods or a statement purporting to be merely the seller's opinion or commendation of the goods does not create a warranty.

§ 2–314. Implied Warranty: Merchantability; Usage of Trade.

(1) Unless excluded or modified (Section 2–316), a warranty that the goods shall be merchantable is implied in a contract for their sale if the seller is a merchant with respect to goods of that kind.

Under this section the serving for value of food or drink to be consumed either on the premises or elsewhere is a sale.

(2) Goods to be merchantable must be at least such as

(a) pass without objection in the trade under the contract description; and

(b) in the case of fungible goods, are of fair average quality within the description; and

(c) are fit for the ordinary purposes for which such goods are used; and

(d) run, within the variations permitted by the agreement, of even kind, quality and quantity within each unit and among all units involved; and

(e) are adequately contained, packaged, and labeled as the agreement may require; and

(f) conform to the promises or affirmations of fact made on the container or label if any.

(3) Unless excluded or modified (Section 2–316) other implied warranties may arise from course of dealing or usage of trade.

§ 2–315. Implied Warranty: Fitness for Particular Purpose.

Where the seller at the time of contracting has reason to know any particular purpose for which the goods are required and that the buyer is relying on the seller's skill or judgment to select or furnish suitable goods, there is unless excluded or modified under the next section an implied warranty that the goods shall be fit for such purpose.

§ 2–316. Exclusion or Modification of Warranties.

(1) Words or conduct relevant to the creation of an express warranty and words or conduct tending to negate or limit warranty shall be construed wherever reasonable as consistent with each other; but subject to the provisions of this Article on parol or extrinsic evidence (Section 2–202) negation or limitation is inoperative to the extent that such construction is unreasonable.

(2) Subject to subsection (3), to exclude or modify the implied warranty of merchantability or any part of it the language must mention merchantability and in case of a writing must be conspicuous, and to exclude or modify any implied warranty of fitness the exclusion must be by a writing and conspicuous. Language to exclude all implied warranties of fitness is sufficient if it states, for example, that "There are no warranties which extend beyond the description on the face hereof."

(3) Notwithstanding subsection (2)

(a) unless the circumstances indicate otherwise, all implied warranties are excluded by expressions like "as is", "with all faults" or other language which in common understanding calls the buyer's attention to the exclusion of warranties and makes plain that there is no implied warranty; and

(b) when the buyer before entering into the contract has examined the goods or the sample or model as fully as he desired or has refused to examine the goods there is no implied warranty with regard to defects which an examination ought in the circumstances to have revealed to him; and

(c) an implied warranty can also be excluded or modified by course of dealing or course of performance or usage of trade.

(4) Remedies for breach of warranty can be limited in accordance with the provisions of this Article on liquidation or limitation of damages and on contractual modification of remedy (Sections 2–718 and 2–719).

§ 2–317. Cumulation and Conflict of Warranties Express or Implied.

Warranties whether express or implied shall be construed as consistent with each other and as cumulative, but if such construction is unreasonable the intention of the parties shall determine which warranty is dominant. In ascertaining that intention the following rules apply:

(a) Exact or technical specifications displace an inconsistent sample or model or general language of description.

(b) A sample from an existing bulk displaces inconsistent general language of description.

(c) Express warranties displace inconsistent implied warranties other than an implied warranty of fitness for a particular purpose.

§ 2–318. Third Party Beneficiaries of Warranties Express or Implied.

Note: If this Act is introduced in the Congress of the United States this section should be omitted. (States to select one alternative.)

Alternative A

A seller's warranty whether express or implied extends to any natural person who is in the family or household of his buyer or who is a guest in his home if it is reasonable to expect that such person may use, consume or be affected by the goods and who is injured in person by breach of the warranty. A seller may not exclude or limit the operation of this section.

Alternative B

A seller's warranty whether express or implied extends to any natural person who may reasonably be expected to use, consume or be affected by the goods and who is injured in person by breach of the warranty. A seller may not exclude or limit the operation of this section.

Alternative C

A seller's warranty whether express or implied extends to any person who may reasonably be expected to use, consume or be affected by the goods and who is injured by breach of the warranty. A seller may not exclude or limit the operation of this section with respect to injury to the person of an individual to whom the warranty extends.

As amended 1966.

§ 2–319. F.O.B. and F.A.S. Terms.

(1) Unless otherwise agreed the term F.O.B. (which means "free on board") at a named place, even though used only in connection with the stated price, is a delivery term under which

(a) when the term is F.O.B. the place of shipment, the seller must at that place ship the goods in the manner provided in this Article (Section 2–504) and bear the expense and risk of putting them into the possession of the carrier; or

(b) when the term is F.O.B. the place of destination, the seller must at his own expense and risk transport the goods to that place and there tender delivery of them in the manner provided in this Article (Section 2–503);

(c) when under either (a) or (b) the term is also F.O.B. vessel, car or other vehicle, the seller must in addition at his own expense and risk load the goods on board. If the term is F.O.B. vessel the buyer must name the vessel and in an appropriate case the seller must comply with the provisions of this Article on the form of bill of lading (Section 2–323).

(2) Unless otherwise agreed the term F.A.S. vessel (which means "free alongside") at a named port, even though used only in connection with the stated price, is a delivery term under which the seller must

(a) at his own expense and risk deliver the goods alongside the vessel in the manner usual in that port or on a dock designated and provided by the buyer; and

(b) obtain and tender a receipt for the goods in exchange for which the carrier is under a duty to issue a bill of lading.

(3) Unless otherwise agreed in any case falling within subsection (1)(a) or (c) or subsection (2) the buyer must seasonably give any needed instructions for making delivery, including when the term is F.A.S. or F.O.B. the loading berth of the vessel and in an appropriate case its name and sailing date. The seller may treat the failure of needed instructions as a failure of cooperation under this Article (Section 2–311). He may also at his option move the goods in any reasonable manner preparatory to delivery or shipment.

(4) Under the term F.O.B. vessel or F.A.S. unless otherwise agreed the buyer must make payment against tender of the required documents and the seller may not tender nor the buyer demand delivery of the goods in substitution for the documents.

§ 2–320. C.I.F. and C. & F. Terms.

(1) The term C.I.F. means that the price includes in a lump sum the cost of the goods and the insurance and freight to the named destination. The term C. & F. or C.F. means that the price so includes cost and freight to the named destination.

(2) Unless otherwise agreed and even though used only in connection with the stated price and destination, the term C.I.F. destination or its equivalent requires the seller at his own expense and risk to

(a) put the goods into the possession of a carrier at the port for shipment and obtain a negotiable bill or bills of lading covering the entire transportation to the named destination; and

(b) load the goods and obtain a receipt from the carrier (which may be contained in the bill of lading) showing that the freight has been paid or provided for; and

(c) obtain a policy or certificate of insurance, including any war risk insurance, of a kind and on terms then current at the port of shipment in the usual amount, in the currency of the contract, shown to cover the same goods covered by the bill of lading and providing for payment of loss to the order of the buyer or for the account of whom it may concern; but the seller may add to the price the amount of the premium for any such war risk insurance; and

(d) prepare an invoice of the goods and procure any other documents required to effect shipment or to comply with the contract; and

(e) forward and tender with commercial promptness all the documents in due form and with any indorsement necessary to perfect the buyer's rights.

(3) Unless otherwise agreed the term C. & F. or its equivalent has the same effect and imposes upon the seller the same obligations and risks as a C.I.F. term except the obligation as to insurance.

(4) Under the term C.I.F. or C. & F. unless otherwise agreed the buyer must make payment against tender of the required documents and the seller may not tender nor the buyer demand delivery of the goods in substitution for the documents.

§ 2–321. C.I.F. or C. & F.: "Net Landed Weights"; "Payment on Arrival"; Warranty of Condition on Arrival.

Under a contract containing a term C.I.F. or C. & F.

(1) Where the price is based on or is to be adjusted according to "net landed weights", "delivered weights", "out turn" quantity or quality or the like, unless otherwise agreed the seller must reasonably estimate the price. The payment due on tender of the documents called for by the contract is the amount so estimated, but after final adjustment of the price a settlement must be made with commercial promptness.

(2) An agreement described in subsection (1) or any warranty of quality or condition of the goods on arrival places upon the seller the risk of ordinary deterioration, shrinkage and the like in transportation but has no effect on the place or time of identification to the contract for sale or delivery or on the passing of the risk of loss.

(3) Unless otherwise agreed where the contract provides for payment on or after arrival of the goods the seller must before payment allow such preliminary inspection as is feasible; but if the goods are lost delivery of the documents and payment are due when the goods should have arrived.

§ 2–322. Delivery "Ex-Ship".

(1) Unless otherwise agreed a term for delivery of goods "ex-ship" (which means from the carrying vessel) or in equivalent language is not restricted to a particular ship and requires delivery from a ship which has reached a place at the named port of destination where goods of the kind are usually discharged.

(2) Under such a term unless otherwise agreed

(a) the seller must discharge all liens arising out of the carriage and furnish the buyer with a direction which puts the carrier under a duty to deliver the goods; and

(b) the risk of loss does not pass to the buyer until the goods leave the ship's tackle or are otherwise properly unloaded.

§ 2–323. Form of Bill of Lading Required in Overseas Shipment; "Overseas".

(1) Where the contract contemplates overseas shipment and contains a term C.I.F. or C. & F. or F.O.B. vessel, the seller unless otherwise agreed must obtain a negotiable bill of lading stating that the goods have been loaded on board or, in the case of a term C.I.F. or C. & F., received for shipment.

(2) Where in a case within subsection (1) a bill of lading has been issued in a set of parts, unless otherwise agreed if the documents are not to be sent from abroad the buyer may demand tender of the full

set; otherwise only one part of the bill of lading need be tendered. Even if the agreement expressly requires a full set

(a) due tender of a single part is acceptable within the provisions of this Article on cure of improper delivery (subsection (1) of Section 2–508); and

(b) even though the full set is demanded, if the documents are sent from abroad the person tendering an incomplete set may nevertheless require payment upon furnishing an indemnity which the buyer in good faith deems adequate.

(3) A shipment by water or by air or a contract contemplating such shipment is "overseas" insofar as by usage of trade or agreement it is subject to the commercial, financing or shipping practices characteristic of international deep water commerce.

§ 2–324. "No Arrival, No Sale" Term.

Under a term "no arrival, no sale" or terms of like meaning, unless otherwise agreed,

(a) the seller must properly ship conforming goods and if they arrive by any means he must tender them on arrival but he assumes no obligation that the goods will arrive unless he has caused the non-arrival; and

(b) where without fault of the seller the goods are in part lost or have so deteriorated as no longer to conform to the contract or arrive after the contract time, the buyer may proceed as if there had been casualty to identified goods (Section 2–613).

§ 2–325. "Letter of Credit" Term; "Confirmed Credit".

(1) Failure of the buyer seasonably to furnish an agreed letter of credit is a breach of the contract for sale.

(2) The delivery to seller of a proper letter of credit suspends the buyer's obligation to pay. If the letter of credit is dishonored, the seller may on seasonable notification to the buyer require payment directly from him.

(3) Unless otherwise agreed the term "letter of credit" or "banker's credit" in a contract for sale means an irrevocable credit issued by a financing agency of good repute and, where the shipment is overseas, of good international repute. The term "confirmed credit" means that the credit must also carry the direct obligation of such an agency which does business in the seller's financial market.

§ 2–326. Sale on Approval and Sale or Return; Rights of Creditors.

(1) Unless otherwise agreed, if delivered goods may be returned by the buyer even though they conform to the contract, the transaction is

(a) a "sale on approval" if the goods are delivered primarily for use, and

(b) a "sale or return" if the goods are delivered primarily for resale.

(2) Goods held on approval are not subject to the claims of the buyer's creditors until acceptance; goods held on sale or return are subject to such claims while in the buyer's possession.

(3) Any "or return" term of a contract for sale is to be treated as a separate contract for sale within the statute of frauds section of this Article (Section 2–201) and as contradicting the sale aspect of the contract within the provisions of this Article or on parol or extrinsic evidence (Section 2–202).

As amended in 1999.

§ 2–327. Special Incidents of Sale on Approval and Sale or Return.

(1) Under a sale on approval unless otherwise agreed

(a) although the goods are identified to the contract the risk of loss and the title do not pass to the buyer until acceptance; and

(b) use of the goods consistent with the purpose of trial is not acceptance but failure seasonably to notify the seller of election to return the goods is acceptance, and if the goods conform to the contract acceptance of any part is acceptance of the whole; and

(c) after due notification of election to return, the return is at the seller's risk and expense but a merchant buyer must follow any reasonable instructions.

(2) Under a sale or return unless otherwise agreed

(a) the option to return extends to the whole or any commercial unit of the goods while in substantially their original condition, but must be exercised seasonably; and

(b) the return is at the buyer's risk and expense.

§ 2–328. Sale by Auction.

(1) In a sale by auction if goods are put up in lots each lot is the subject of a separate sale.

(2) A sale by auction is complete when the auctioneer so announces by the fall of the hammer or in other customary manner. Where a bid is made while the hammer is falling in acceptance of a prior bid the auctioneer may in his discretion reopen the bidding or declare the goods sold under the bid on which the hammer was falling.

(3) Such a sale is with reserve unless the goods are in explicit terms put up without reserve. In an auction with reserve the auctioneer may withdraw the goods at any time until he announces completion of the sale. In an auction without reserve, after the auctioneer calls for bids on an article or lot, that article or lot cannot be withdrawn unless no bid is made within a reasonable time. In either case a bidder may retract his bid until the auctioneer's announcement of completion of the sale, but a bidder's retraction does not revive any previous bid.

(4) If the auctioneer knowingly receives a bid on the seller's behalf or the seller makes or procures such as bid, and notice has not been given that liberty for such bidding is reserved, the buyer may at his option avoid the sale or take the goods at the price of the last good faith bid prior to the completion of the sale. This subsection shall not apply to any bid at a forced sale.

Part 4 Title, Creditors and Good Faith Purchasers

§ 2–401. Passing of Title; Reservation for Security; Limited Application of This Section.

Each provision of this Article with regard to the rights, obligations and remedies of the seller, the buyer, purchasers or other third parties applies irrespective of title to the goods except where the provision refers to such title. Insofar as situations are not covered by the other provisions of this Article and matters concerning title became material the following rules apply:

(1) Title to goods cannot pass under a contract for sale prior to their identification to the contract (Section 2–501), and unless otherwise explicitly agreed the buyer acquires by their identification a special property as limited by this Act. Any retention or reservation by the seller of the title (property) in goods shipped or delivered to the buyer is limited in effect to a reservation of a security interest. Subject to these provisions and to the provisions of the Article on Secured Transactions (Article 9), title to goods passes from the seller to the buyer in any manner and on any conditions explicitly agreed on by the parties.

(2) Unless otherwise explicitly agreed title passes to the buyer at the time and place at which the seller completes his performance with reference to the physical delivery of the goods, despite any reservation of a security interest and even though a document of title is to be delivered at a different time or place; and in particular and despite any reservation of a security interest by the bill of lading

(a) if the contract requires or authorizes the seller to send the goods to the buyer but does not require him to deliver them at destination, title passes to the buyer at the time and place of shipment; but

(b) if the contract requires delivery at destination, title passes on tender there.

(3) Unless otherwise explicitly agreed where delivery is to be made without moving the goods,

(a) if the seller is to deliver a document of title, title passes at the time when and the place where he delivers such documents; or

(b) if the goods are at the time of contracting already identified and no documents are to be delivered, title passes at the time and place of contracting.

(4) A rejection or other refusal by the buyer to receive or retain the goods, whether or not justified, or a justified revocation of acceptance revests title to the goods in the seller. Such revesting occurs by operation of law and is not a "sale".

§ 2–402. Rights of Seller's Creditors Against Sold Goods.

(1) Except as provided in subsections (2) and (3), rights of unsecured creditors of the seller with respect to goods which have been identified to a contract for sale are subject to the buyer's rights to recover the goods under this Article (Sections 2–502 and 2–716).

(2) A creditor of the seller may treat a sale or an identification of goods to a contract for sale as void if as against him a retention of possession by the seller is fraudulent under any rule of law of the state where the goods are situated, except that retention of possession in good faith and current course of trade by a merchant-seller for a commercially reasonable time after a sale or identification is not fraudulent.

(3) Nothing in this Article shall be deemed to impair the rights of creditors of the seller

(a) under the provisions of the Article on Secured Transactions (Article 9); or

(b) where identification to the contract or delivery is made not in current course of trade but in satisfaction of or as security for a pre-existing claim for money, security or the like and is made under circumstances which under any rule of law of the state where the goods are situated would apart from this Article constitute the transaction a fraudulent transfer or voidable preference.

§ 2–403. Power to Transfer; Good Faith Purchase of Goods; "Entrusting".

(1) A purchaser of goods acquires all title which his transferor had or had power to transfer except that a purchaser of a limited interest acquires rights only to the extent of the interest purchased. A person with voidable title has power to transfer a good title to a good faith purchaser for value. When goods have been delivered under a transaction of purchase the purchaser has such power even though

(a) the transferor was deceived as to the identity of the purchaser, or

(b) the delivery was in exchange for a check which is later dishonored, or

(c) it was agreed that the transaction was to be a "cash sale", or

(d) the delivery was procured through fraud punishable as larcenous under the criminal law.

(2) Any entrusting of possession of goods to a merchant who deals in goods of that kind gives him power to transfer all rights of the entruster to a buyer in ordinary course of business.

(3) "Entrusting" includes any delivery and any acquiescence in retention of possession regardless of any condition expressed between the parties to the delivery or acquiescence and regardless of whether the procurement of the entrusting or the possessor's disposition of the goods have been such as to be larcenous under the criminal law.

(4) The rights of other purchasers of goods and of lien creditors are governed by the Articles on Secured Transactions (Article 9), Bulk Transfers (Article 6) and Documents of Title (Article 7).

As amended in 1988.

Part 5 Performance

§ 2–501. Insurable Interest in Goods; Manner of Identification of Goods.

(1) The buyer obtains a special property and an insurable interest in goods by identification of existing goods as goods to which the contract refers even though the goods so identified are nonconforming and he has an option to return or reject them. Such identification can be made at any time and in any manner explicitly agreed to by the parties. In the absence of explicit agreement identification occurs

(a) when the contract is made if it is for the sale of goods already existing and identified;

(b) if the contract is for the sale of future goods other than those described in paragraph (c), when goods are shipped, marked or otherwise designated by the seller as goods to which the contract refers;

(c) when the crops are planted or otherwise become growing crops or the young are conceived if the contract is for the sale of unborn young to be born within twelve months after contracting or for the sale of crops to be harvested within twelve months or the next normal harvest season after contracting whichever is longer.

(2) The seller retains an insurable interest in goods so long as title to or any security interest in the goods remains in him and where the identification is by the seller alone he may until default or insolvency or notification to the buyer that the identification is final substitute other goods for those identified.

(3) Nothing in this section impairs any insurable interest recognized under any other statute or rule of law.

§ 2–502. Buyer's Right to Goods on Seller's Insolvency.

(1) Subject to subsections (2) and (3) and even though the goods have not been shipped a buyer who has paid a part or all of the price of goods in which he has a special property under the provisions of the immediately preceding section may on making and keeping good a tender of any unpaid portion of their price recover them from the seller if:

(a) in the case of goods bought for personal, family, or household purposes, the seller repudiates or fails to deliver as required by the contract; or

(b) in all cases, the seller becomes insolvent within ten days after receipt of the first installment on their price.

(2) The buyer's right to recover the goods under subsection (1)(a) vests upon acquisition of a special property, even if the seller had not then repudiated or failed to deliver.

(3) If the identification creating his special property has been made by the buyer he acquires the right to recover the goods only if they conform to the contract for sale.

As amended in 1999.

§ 2–503. Manner of Seller's Tender of Delivery.

(1) Tender of delivery requires that the seller put and hold conforming goods at the buyer's disposition and give the buyer any notification reasonably necessary to enable him to take delivery. The manner, time and place for tender are determined by the agreement and this Article, and in particular

(a) tender must be at a reasonable hour, and if it is of goods they must be kept available for the period reasonably necessary to enable the buyer to take possession; but

(b) unless otherwise agreed the buyer must furnish facilities reasonably suited to the receipt of the goods.

(2) Where the case is within the next section respecting shipment tender requires that the seller comply with its provisions.

(3) Where the seller is required to deliver at a particular destination tender requires that he comply with subsection (1) and also in any appropriate case tender documents as described in subsections (4) and (5) of this section.

(4) Where goods are in the possession of a bailee and are to be delivered without being moved

(a) tender requires that the seller either tender a negotiable document of title covering such goods or procure acknowledgment by the bailee of the buyer's right to possession of the goods; but

(b) tender to the buyer of a non-negotiable document of title or of a written direction to the bailee to deliver is sufficient tender unless the buyer seasonably objects, and receipt by the bailee of notification of the buyer's rights fixes those rights as against the bailee and all third persons; but risk of loss of the goods and of any

failure by the bailee to honor the non-negotiable document of title or to obey the direction remains on the seller until the buyer has had a reasonable time to present the document or direction, and a refusal by the bailee to honor the document or to obey the direction defeats the tender.

(5) Where the contract requires the seller to deliver documents

(a) he must tender all such documents in correct form, except as provided in this Article with respect to bills of lading in a set (subsection (2) of Section 2–323); and

(b) tender through customary banking channels is sufficient and dishonor of a draft accompanying the documents constitutes non-acceptance or rejection.

§ 2–504. Shipment by Seller.

Where the seller is required or authorized to send the goods to the buyer and the contract does not require him to deliver them at a particular destination, then unless otherwise agreed he must

(a) put the goods in the possession of such a carrier and make such a contract for their transportation as may be reasonable having regard to the nature of the goods and other circumstances of the case; and

(b) obtain and promptly deliver or tender in due form any document necessary to enable the buyer to obtain possession of the goods or otherwise required by the agreement or by usage of trade; and

(c) promptly notify the buyer of the shipment.

Failure to notify the buyer under paragraph (c) or to make a proper contract under paragraph (a) is a ground for rejection only if material delay or loss ensues.

§ 2–505. Seller's Shipment under Reservation.

(1) Where the seller has identified goods to the contract by or before shipment:

(a) his procurement of a negotiable bill of lading to his own order or otherwise reserves in him a security interest in the goods. His procurement of the bill to the order of a financing agency or of the buyer indicates in addition only the seller's expectation of transferring that interest to the person named.

(b) a non-negotiable bill of lading to himself or his nominee reserves possession of the goods as security but except in a case of conditional delivery (subsection (2) of Section 2–507) a non-negotiable bill of lading naming the buyer as consignee reserves no security interest even though the seller retains possession of the bill of lading.

(2) When shipment by the seller with reservation of a security interest is in violation of the contract for sale it constitutes an improper contract for transportation within the preceding section but impairs neither the rights given to the buyer by shipment and identification of the goods to the contract nor the seller's powers as a holder of a negotiable document.

§ 2–506. Rights of Financing Agency.

(1) A financing agency by paying or purchasing for value a draft which relates to a shipment of goods acquires to the extent of the payment or purchase and in addition to its own rights under the draft and any document of title securing it any rights of the

shipper in the goods including the right to stop delivery and the shipper's right to have the draft honored by the buyer.

(2) The right to reimbursement of a financing agency which has in good faith honored or purchased the draft under commitment to or authority from the buyer is not impaired by subsequent discovery of defects with reference to any relevant document which was apparently regular on its face.

§ 2–507. Effect of Seller's Tender; Delivery on Condition.

(1) Tender of delivery is a condition to the buyer's duty to accept the goods and, unless otherwise agreed, to his duty to pay for them. Tender entitles the seller to acceptance of the goods and to payment according to the contract.

(2) Where payment is due and demanded on the delivery to the buyer of goods or documents of title, his right as against the seller to retain or dispose of them is conditional upon his making the payment due.

§ 2–508. Cure by Seller of Improper Tender or Delivery; Replacement.

(1) Where any tender or delivery by the seller is rejected because non-conforming and the time for performance has not yet expired, the seller may seasonably notify the buyer of his intention to cure and may then within the contract time make a conforming delivery.

(2) Where the buyer rejects a non-conforming tender which the seller had reasonable grounds to believe would be acceptable with or without money allowance the seller may if he seasonably notifies the buyer have a further reasonable time to substitute a conforming tender.

§ 2–509. Risk of Loss in the Absence of Breach.

(1) Where the contract requires or authorizes the seller to ship the goods by carrier

  (a) if it does not require him to deliver them at a particular destination, the risk of loss passes to the buyer when the goods are duly delivered to the carrier even though the shipment is under reservation (Section 2–505); but

  (b) if it does require him to deliver them at a particular destination and the goods are there duly tendered while in the possession of the carrier, the risk of loss passes to the buyer when the goods are there duly so tendered as to enable the buyer to take delivery.

(2) Where the goods are held by a bailee to be delivered without being moved, the risk of loss passes to the buyer

  (a) on his receipt of a negotiable document of title covering the goods; or

  (b) on acknowledgment by the bailee of the buyer's right to possession of the goods; or

  (c) after his receipt of a non-negotiable document of title or other written direction to deliver, as provided in subsection (4)(b) of Section 2–503.

(3) In any case not within subsection (1) or (2), the risk of loss passes to the buyer on his receipt of the goods if the seller is a merchant; otherwise the risk passes to the buyer on tender of delivery.

(4) The provisions of this section are subject to contrary agreement of the parties and to the provisions of this Article on sale on approval (Section 2–327) and on effect of breach on risk of loss (Section 2–510).

§ 2–510. Effect of Breach on Risk of Loss.

(1) Where a tender or delivery of goods so fails to conform to the contract as to give a right of rejection the risk of their loss remains on the seller until cure or acceptance.

(2) Where the buyer rightfully revokes acceptance he may to the extent of any deficiency in his effective insurance coverage treat the risk of loss as having rested on the seller from the beginning.

(3) Where the buyer as to conforming goods already identified to the contract for sale repudiates or is otherwise in breach before risk of their loss has passed to him, the seller may to the extent of any deficiency in his effective insurance coverage treat the risk of loss as resting on the buyer for a commercially reasonable time.

§ 2–511. Tender of Payment by Buyer; Payment by Check.

(1) Unless otherwise agreed tender of payment is a condition to the seller's duty to tender and complete any delivery.

(2) Tender of payment is sufficient when made by any means or in any manner current in the ordinary course of business unless the seller demands payment in legal tender and gives any extension of time reasonably necessary to procure it.

(3) Subject to the provisions of this Act on the effect of an instrument on an obligation (Section 3–310), payment by check is conditional and is defeated as between the parties by dishonor of the check on due presentment.

As amended in 1994.

§ 2–512. Payment by Buyer Before Inspection.

(1) Where the contract requires payment before inspection non-conformity of the goods does not excuse the buyer from so making payment unless

  (a) the non-conformity appears without inspection; or

  (b) despite tender of the required documents the circumstances would justify injunction against honor under this Act (Section 5–109(b)).

(2) Payment pursuant to subsection (1) does not constitute an acceptance of goods or impair the buyer's right to inspect or any of his remedies.

As amended in 1995.

§ 2–513. Buyer's Right to Inspection of Goods.

(1) Unless otherwise agreed and subject to subsection (3), where goods are tendered or delivered or identified to the contract for sale, the buyer has a right before payment or acceptance to inspect them at any reasonable place and time and in any reasonable manner. When the seller is required or authorized to send the goods to the buyer, the inspection may be after their arrival.

(2) Expenses of inspection must be borne by the buyer but may be recovered from the seller if the goods do not conform and are rejected.

(3) Unless otherwise agreed and subject to the provisions of this Article on C.I.F. contracts (subsection (3) of Section 2–321), the buyer is not entitled to inspect the goods before payment of the price when the contract provides

  (a) for delivery "C.O.D." or on other like terms; or

(b) for payment against documents of title, except where such payment is due only after the goods are to become available for inspection.

(4) A place or method of inspection fixed by the parties is presumed to be exclusive but unless otherwise expressly agreed it does not postpone identification or shift the place for delivery or for passing the risk of loss. If compliance becomes impossible, inspection shall be as provided in this section unless the place or method fixed was clearly intended as an indispensable condition failure of which avoids the contract.

§ 2–514. When Documents Deliverable on Acceptance; When on Payment.

Unless otherwise agreed documents against which a draft is drawn are to be delivered to the drawee on acceptance of the draft if it is payable more than three days after presentment; otherwise, only on payment.

§ 2–515. Preserving Evidence of Goods in Dispute.

In furtherance of the adjustment of any claim or dispute

(a) either party on reasonable notification to the other and for the purpose of ascertaining the facts and preserving evidence has the right to inspect, test and sample the goods including such of them as may be in the possession or control of the other; and

(b) the parties may agree to a third party inspection or survey to determine the conformity or condition of the goods and may agree that the findings shall be binding upon them in any subsequent litigation or adjustment.

Part 6 Breach, Repudiation and Excuse

§ 2–601. Buyer's Rights on Improper Delivery.

Subject to the provisions of this Article on breach in installment contracts (Section 2–612) and unless otherwise agreed under the sections on contractual limitations of remedy (Sections 2–718 and 2–719), if the goods or the tender of delivery fail in any respect to conform to the contract, the buyer may

(a) reject the whole; or

(b) accept the whole; or

(c) accept any commercial unit or units and reject the rest.

§ 2–602. Manner and Effect of Rightful Rejection.

(1) Rejection of goods must be within a reasonable time after their delivery or tender. It is ineffective unless the buyer seasonably notifies the seller.

(2) Subject to the provisions of the two following sections on rejected goods (Sections 2–603 and 2–604),

(a) after rejection any exercise of ownership by the buyer with respect to any commercial unit is wrongful as against the seller; and

(b) if the buyer has before rejection taken physical possession of goods in which he does not have a security interest under the provisions of this Article (subsection (3) of Section 2–711), he is under a duty after rejection to hold them with reasonable care at the seller's disposition for a time sufficient to permit the seller to remove them; but

(c) the buyer has no further obligations with regard to goods rightfully rejected.

(3) The seller's rights with respect to goods wrongfully rejected are governed by the provisions of this Article on Seller's remedies in general (Section 2–703).

§ 2–603. Merchant Buyer's Duties as to Rightfully Rejected Goods.

(1) Subject to any security interest in the buyer (subsection (3) of Section 2–711), when the seller has no agent or place of business at the market of rejection a merchant buyer is under a duty after rejection of goods in his possession or control to follow any reasonable instructions received from the seller with respect to the goods and in the absence of such instructions to make reasonable efforts to sell them for the seller's account if they are perishable or threaten to decline in value speedily. Instructions are not reasonable if on demand indemnity for expenses is not forthcoming.

(2) When the buyer sells goods under subsection (1), he is entitled to reimbursement from the seller or out of the proceeds for reasonable expenses of caring for and selling them, and if the expenses include no selling commission then to such commission as is usual in the trade or if there is none to a reasonable sum not exceeding ten per cent on the gross proceeds.

(3) In complying with this section the buyer is held only to good faith and good faith conduct hereunder is neither acceptance nor conversion nor the basis of an action for damages.

§ 2–604. Buyer's Options as to Salvage of Rightfully Rejected Goods.

Subject to the provisions of the immediately preceding section on perishables if the seller gives no instructions within a reasonable time after notification of rejection the buyer may store the rejected goods for the seller's account or reship them to him or resell them for the seller's account with reimbursement as provided in the preceding section. Such action is not acceptance or conversion.

§ 2–605. Waiver of Buyer's Objections by Failure to Particularize.

(1) The buyer's failure to state in connection with rejection a particular defect which is ascertainable by reasonable inspection precludes him from relying on the unstated defect to justify rejection or to establish breach

(a) where the seller could have cured it if stated seasonably; or

(b) between merchants when the seller has after rejection made a request in writing for a full and final written statement of all defects on which the buyer proposes to rely.

(2) Payment against documents made without reservation of rights precludes recovery of the payment for defects apparent on the face of the documents.

§ 2–606. What Constitutes Acceptance of Goods.

(1) Acceptance of goods occurs when the buyer

(a) after a reasonable opportunity to inspect the goods signifies to the seller that the goods are conforming or that he will take or retain them in spite of their nonconformity; or

(b) fails to make an effective rejection (subsection (1) of Section 2–602), but such acceptance does not occur until the buyer has had a reasonable opportunity to inspect them; or

(c) does any act inconsistent with the seller's ownership; but if such act is wrongful as against the seller it is an acceptance only if ratified by him.

(2) Acceptance of a part of any commercial unit is acceptance of that entire unit.

§ 2–607. Effect of Acceptance; Notice of Breach; Burden of Establishing Breach After Acceptance; Notice of Claim or Litigation to Person Answerable Over.

(1) The buyer must pay at the contract rate for any goods accepted.

(2) Acceptance of goods by the buyer precludes rejection of the goods accepted and if made with knowledge of a non-conformity cannot be revoked because of it unless the acceptance was on the reasonable assumption that the non-conformity would be seasonably cured but acceptance does not of itself impair any other remedy provided by this Article for non-conformity.

(3) Where a tender has been accepted

(a) the buyer must within a reasonable time after he discovers or should have discovered any breach notify the seller of breach or be barred from any remedy; and

(b) if the claim is one for infringement or the like (subsection (3) of Section 2–312) and the buyer is sued as a result of such a breach he must so notify the seller within a reasonable time after he receives notice of the litigation or be barred from any remedy over for liability established by the litigation.

(4) The burden is on the buyer to establish any breach with respect to the goods accepted.

(5) Where the buyer is sued for breach of a warranty or other obligation for which his seller is answerable over

(a) he may give his seller written notice of the litigation. If the notice states that the seller may come in and defend and that if the seller does not do so he will be bound in any action against him by his buyer by any determination of fact common to the two litigations, then unless the seller after seasonable receipt of the notice does come in and defend he is so bound.

(b) if the claim is one for infringement or the like (subsection (3) of Section 2–312) the original seller may demand in writing that his buyer turn over to him control of the litigation including settlement or else be barred from any remedy over and if he also agrees to bear all expense and to satisfy any adverse judgment, then unless the buyer after seasonable receipt of the demand does turn over control the buyer is so barred.

(6) The provisions of subsections (3), (4) and (5) apply to any obligation of a buyer to hold the seller harmless against infringement or the like (subsection (3) of Section 2–312).

§ 2–608. Revocation of Acceptance in Whole or in Part.

(1) The buyer may revoke his acceptance of a lot or commercial unit whose non-conformity substantially impairs its value to him if he has accepted it

(a) on the reasonable assumption that its nonconformity would be cured and it has not been seasonably cured; or

(b) without discovery of such non-conformity if his acceptance was reasonably induced either by the difficulty of discovery before acceptance or by the seller's assurances.

(2) Revocation of acceptance must occur within a reasonable time after the buyer discovers or should have discovered the ground for it and before any substantial change in condition of the goods which is not caused by their own defects. It is not effective until the buyer notifies the seller of it.

(3) A buyer who so revokes has the same rights and duties with regard to the goods involved as if he had rejected them.

§ 2–609. Right to Adequate Assurance of Performance.

(1) A contract for sale imposes an obligation on each party that the other's expectation of receiving due performance will not be impaired. When reasonable grounds for insecurity arise with respect to the performance of either party the other may in writing demand adequate assurance of due performance and until he receives such assurance may if commercially reasonable suspend any performance for which he has not already received the agreed return.

(2) Between merchants the reasonableness of grounds for insecurity and the adequacy of any assurance offered shall be determined according to commercial standards.

(3) Acceptance of any improper delivery or payment does not prejudice the party's right to demand adequate assurance of future performance.

(4) After receipt of a justified demand failure to provide within a reasonable time not exceeding thirty days such assurance of due performance as is adequate under the circumstances of the particular case is a repudiation of the contract.

§ 2–610. Anticipatory Repudiation.

When either party repudiates the contract with respect to a performance not yet due the loss of which will substantially impair the value of the contract to the other, the aggrieved party may

(a) for a commercially reasonable time await performance by the repudiating party; or

(b) resort to any remedy for breach (Section 2–703 or Section 2–711), even though he has notified the repudiating party that he would await the latter's performance and has urged retraction; and

(c) in either case suspend his own performance or proceed in accordance with the provisions of this Article on the seller's right to identify goods to the contract notwithstanding breach or to salvage unfinished goods (Section 2–704).

§ 2–611. Retraction of Anticipatory Repudiation.

(1) Until the repudiating party's next performance is due he can retract his repudiation unless the aggrieved party has since the repudiation cancelled or materially changed his position or otherwise indicated that he considers the repudiation final.

(2) Retraction may be by any method which clearly indicates to the aggrieved party that the repudiating party intends to perform, but must include any assurance justifiably demanded under the provisions of this Article (Section 2–609).

(3) Retraction reinstates the repudiating party's rights under the contract with due excuse and allowance to the aggrieved party for any delay occasioned by the repudiation.

§ 2–612. "Installment Contract"; Breach.

(1) An "installment contract" is one which requires or authorizes the delivery of goods in separate lots to be separately accepted, even though the contract contains a clause "each delivery is a separate contract" or its equivalent.

(2) The buyer may reject any installment which is non-conforming if the non-conformity substantially impairs the value of that installment and cannot be cured or if the non-conformity is a defect in the required documents; but if the non-conformity does not fall within subsection (3) and the seller gives adequate assurance of its cure the buyer must accept that installment.

(3) Whenever non-conformity or default with respect to one or more installments substantially impairs the value of the whole contract there is a breach of the whole. But the aggrieved party reinstates the contract if he accepts a non-conforming installment without seasonably notifying of cancellation or if he brings an action with respect only to past installments or demands performance as to future installments.

§ 2–613. Casualty to Identified Goods.

Where the contract requires for its performance goods identified when the contract is made, and the goods suffer casualty without fault of either party before the risk of loss passes to the buyer, or in a proper case under a "no arrival, no sale" term (Section 2–324) then

(a) if the loss is total the contract is avoided; and

(b) if the loss is partial or the goods have so deteriorated as no longer to conform to the contract the buyer may nevertheless demand inspection and at his option either treat the contract as voided or accept the goods with due allowance from the contract price for the deterioration or the deficiency in quantity but without further right against the seller.

§ 2–614. Substituted Performance.

(1) Where without fault of either party the agreed berthing, loading, or unloading facilities fail or an agreed type of carrier becomes unavailable or the agreed manner of delivery otherwise becomes commercially impracticable but a commercially reasonable substitute is available, such substitute performance must be tendered and accepted.

(2) If the agreed means or manner of payment fails because of domestic or foreign governmental regulation, the seller may withhold or stop delivery unless the buyer provides a means or manner of payment which is commercially a substantial equivalent. If delivery has already been taken, payment by the means or in the manner provided by the regulation discharges the buyer's obligation unless the regulation is discriminatory, oppressive or predatory.

§ 2–615. Excuse by Failure of Presupposed Conditions.

Except so far as a seller may have assumed a greater obligation and subject to the preceding section on substituted performance:

(a) Delay in delivery or non-delivery in whole or in part by a seller who complies with paragraphs (b) and (c) is not a breach of his duty under a contract for sale if performance as agreed has been made impracticable by the occurrence of a contingency the nonoccurrence of which was a basic assumption on which the contract was made or by compliance in good faith with any applicable foreign or domestic governmental regulation or order whether or not it later proves to be invalid.

(b) Where the causes mentioned in paragraph (a) affect only a part of the seller's capacity to perform, he must allocate production and deliveries among his customers but may at his option include regular cus-

tomers not then under contract as well as his own requirements for further manufacture. He may so allocate in any manner which is fair and reasonable.

(c) The seller must notify the buyer seasonably that there will be delay or non-delivery and, when allocation is required under paragraph (b), of the estimated quota thus made available for the buyer.

§ 2–616. Procedure on Notice Claiming Excuse.

(1) Where the buyer receives notification of a material or indefinite delay or an allocation justified under the preceding section he may by written notification to the seller as to any delivery concerned, and where the prospective deficiency substantially impairs the value of the whole contract under the provisions of this Article relating to breach of installment contracts (Section 2–612), then also as to the whole,

(a) terminate and thereby discharge any unexecuted portion of the contract; or

(b) modify the contract by agreeing to take his available quota in substitution.

(2) If after receipt of such notification from the seller the buyer fails so to modify the contract within a reasonable time not exceeding thirty days the contract lapses with respect to any deliveries affected.

(3) The provisions of this section may not be negated by agreement except in so far as the seller has assumed a greater obligation under the preceding section.

Part 7 Remedies

§ 2–701. Remedies for Breach of Collateral Contracts Not Impaired.

Remedies for breach of any obligation or promise collateral or ancillary to a contract for sale are not impaired by the provisions of this Article.

§ 2–702. Seller's Remedies on Discovery of Buyer's Insolvency.

(1) Where the seller discovers the buyer to be insolvent he may refuse delivery except for cash including payment for all goods theretofore delivered under the contract, and stop delivery under this Article (Section 2–705).

(2) Where the seller discovers that the buyer has received goods on credit while insolvent he may reclaim the goods upon demand made within ten days after the receipt, but if misrepresentation of solvency has been made to the particular seller in writing within three months before delivery the ten day limitation does not apply. Except as provided in this subsection the seller may not base a right to reclaim goods on the buyer's fraudulent or innocent misrepresentation of solvency or of intent to pay.

(3) The seller's right to reclaim under subsection (2) is subject to the rights of a buyer in ordinary course or other good faith purchaser under this Article (Section 2–403). Successful reclamation of goods excludes all other remedies with respect to them.

§ 2–703. Seller's Remedies in General.

Where the buyer wrongfully rejects or revokes acceptance of goods or fails to make a payment due on or before delivery or repudiates with respect to a part or the whole, then with respect to any goods directly affected and, if the breach is of the whole contract (Section

2–612), then also with respect to the whole undelivered balance, the aggrieved seller may

(a) withhold delivery of such goods;

(b) stop delivery by any bailee as hereafter provided (Section 2–705);

(c) proceed under the next section respecting goods still unidentified to the contract;

(d) resell and recover damages as hereafter provided (Section 2–706);

(e) recover damages for non-acceptance (Section 2–708) or in a proper case the price (Section 2–709);

(f) cancel.

§ 2–704. Seller's Right to Identify Goods to the Contract Notwithstanding Breach or to Salvage Unfinished Goods.

(1) An aggrieved seller under the preceding section may

(a) identify to the contract conforming goods not already identified if at the time he learned of the breach they are in his possession or control;

(b) treat as the subject of resale goods which have demonstrably been intended for the particular contract even though those goods are unfinished.

(2) Where the goods are unfinished an aggrieved seller may in the exercise of reasonable commercial judgment for the purposes of avoiding loss and of effective realization either complete the manufacture and wholly identify the goods to the contract or cease manufacture and resell for scrap or salvage value or proceed in any other reasonable manner.

§ 2–705. Seller's Stoppage of Delivery in Transit or Otherwise.

(1) The seller may stop delivery of goods in the possession of a carrier or other bailee when he discovers the buyer to be insolvent (Section 2–702) and may stop delivery of carload, truckload, planeload or larger shipments of express or freight when the buyer repudiates or fails to make a payment due before delivery or if for any other reason the seller has a right to withhold or reclaim the goods.

(2) As against such buyer the seller may stop delivery until

(a) receipt of the goods by the buyer; or

(b) acknowledgment to the buyer by any bailee of the goods except a carrier that the bailee holds the goods for the buyer; or

(c) such acknowledgment to the buyer by a carrier by reshipment or as warehouseman; or

(d) negotiation to the buyer of any negotiable document of title covering the goods.

(3) (a) To stop delivery the seller must so notify as to enable the bailee by reasonable diligence to prevent delivery of the goods.

(b) After such notification the bailee must hold and deliver the goods according to the directions of the seller but the seller is liable to the bailee for any ensuing charges or damages.

(c) If a negotiable document of title has been issued for goods the bailee is not obliged to obey a notification to stop until surrender of the document.

(d) A carrier who has issued a non-negotiable bill of lading is not obliged to obey a notification to stop received from a person other than the consignor.

§ 2–706. Seller's Resale Including Contract for Resale.

(1) Under the conditions stated in Section 2–703 on seller's remedies, the seller may resell the goods concerned or the undelivered balance thereof. Where the resale is made in good faith and in a commercially reasonable manner the seller may recover the difference between the resale price and the contract price together with any incidental damages allowed under the provisions of this Article (Section 2–710), but less expenses saved in consequence of the buyer's breach.

(2) Except as otherwise provided in subsection (3) or unless otherwise agreed resale may be at public or private sale including sale by way of one or more contracts to sell or of identification to an existing contract of the seller. Sale may be as a unit or in parcels and at any time and place and on any terms but every aspect of the sale including the method, manner, time, place and terms must be commercially reasonable. The resale must be reasonably identified as referring to the broken contract, but it is not necessary that the goods be in existence or that any or all of them have been identified to the contract before the breach.

(3) Where the resale is at private sale the seller must give the buyer reasonable notification of his intention to resell.

(4) Where the resale is at public sale

(a) only identified goods can be sold except where there is a recognized market for a public sale of futures in goods of the kind; and

(b) it must be made at a usual place or market for public sale if one is reasonably available and except in the case of goods which are perishable or threaten to decline in value speedily the seller must give the buyer reasonable notice of the time and place of the resale; and

(c) if the goods are not to be within the view of those attending the sale the notification of sale must state the place where the goods are located and provide for their reasonable inspection by prospective bidders; and

(d) the seller may buy.

(5) A purchaser who buys in good faith at a resale takes the goods free of any rights of the original buyer even though the seller fails to comply with one or more of the requirements of this section.

(6) The seller is not accountable to the buyer for any profit made on any resale. A person in the position of a seller (Section 2–707) or a buyer who has rightfully rejected or justifiably revoked acceptance must account for any excess over the amount of his security interest, as hereinafter defined (subsection (3) of Section 2–711).

§ 2–707. "Person in the Position of a Seller".

(1) A "person in the position of a seller" includes as against a principal an agent who has paid or become responsible for the price of goods on behalf of his principal or anyone who otherwise holds a security interest or other right in goods similar to that of a seller.

(2) A person in the position of a seller may as provided in this Article withhold or stop delivery (Section 2–705) and resell (Section 2–706) and recover incidental damages (Section 2–710).

§ 2–708. Seller's Damages for Non-Acceptance or Repudiation.

(1) Subject to subsection (2) and to the provisions of this Article with respect to proof of market price (Section 2–723), the measure of damages for non-acceptance or repudiation by the buyer is the

difference between the market price at the time and place for tender and the unpaid contract price together with any incidental damages provided in this Article (Section 2–710), but less expenses saved in consequence of the buyer's breach.

(2) If the measure of damages provided in subsection (1) is inadequate to put the seller in as good a position as performance would have done then the measure of damages is the profit (including reasonable overhead) which the seller would have made from full performance by the buyer, together with any incidental damages provided in this Article (Section 2–710), due allowance for costs reasonably incurred and due credit for payments or proceeds of resale.

§ 2–709. Action for the Price.

(1) When the buyer fails to pay the price as it becomes due the seller may recover, together with any incidental damages under the next section, the price

(a) of goods accepted or of conforming goods lost or damaged within a commercially reasonable time after risk of their loss has passed to the buyer; and

(b) of goods identified to the contract if the seller is unable after reasonable effort to resell them at a reasonable price or the circumstances reasonably indicate that such effort will be unavailing.

(2) Where the seller sues for the price he must hold for the buyer any goods which have been identified to the contract and are still in his control except that if resale becomes possible he may resell them at any time prior to the collection of the judgment. The net proceeds of any such resale must be credited to the buyer and payment of the judgment entitles him to any goods not resold.

(3) After the buyer has wrongfully rejected or revoked acceptance of the goods or has failed to make a payment due or has repudiated (Section 2–610), a seller who is held not entitled to the price under this section shall nevertheless be awarded damages for nonacceptance under the preceding section.

§ 2–710. Seller's Incidental Damages.

Incidental damages to an aggrieved seller include any commercially reasonable charges, expenses or commissions incurred in stopping delivery, in the transportation, care and custody of goods after the buyer's breach, in connection with return or resale of the goods or otherwise resulting from the breach.

§ 2–711. Buyer's Remedies in General; Buyer's Security Interest in Rejected Goods.

(1) Where the seller fails to make delivery or repudiates or the buyer rightfully rejects or justifiably revokes acceptance then with respect to any goods involved, and with respect to the whole if the breach goes to the whole contract (Section 2–612), the buyer may cancel and whether or not he has done so may in addition to recovering so much of the price as has been paid

(a) "cover" and have damages under the next section as to all the goods affected whether or not they have been identified to the contract; or

(b) recover damages for non-delivery as provided in this Article (Section 2–713).

(2) Where the seller fails to deliver or repudiates the buyer may also

(a) if the goods have been identified recover them as provided in this Article (Section 2–502); or

(b) in a proper case obtain specific performance or replevy the goods as provided in this Article (Section 2–716).

(3) On rightful rejection or justifiable revocation of acceptance a buyer has a security interest in goods in his possession or control for any payments made on their price and any expenses reasonably incurred in their inspection, receipt, transportation, care and custody and may hold such goods and resell them in like manner as an aggrieved seller (Section 2–706).

§ 2–712. "Cover"; Buyer's Procurement of Substitute Goods.

(1) After a breach within the preceding section the buyer may "cover" by making in good faith and without unreasonable delay any reasonable purchase of or contract to purchase goods in substitution for those due from the seller.

(2) The buyer may recover from the seller as damages the difference between the cost of cover and the contract price together with any incidental or consequential damages as hereinafter defined (Section 2–715), but less expenses saved in consequence of the seller's breach.

(3) Failure of the buyer to effect cover within this section does not bar him from any other remedy.

§ 2–713. Buyer's Damages for Non-Delivery or Repudiation.

(1) Subject to the provisions of this Article with respect to proof of market price (Section 2–723), the measure of damages for non-delivery or repudiation by the seller is the difference between the market price at the time when the buyer learned of the breach and the contract price together with any incidental and consequential damages provided in this Article (Section 2–715), but less expenses saved in consequence of the seller's breach.

(2) Market price is to be determined as of the place for tender or, in cases of rejection after arrival or revocation of acceptance, as of the place of arrival.

§ 2–714. Buyer's Damages for Breach in Regard to Accepted Goods.

(1) Where the buyer has accepted goods and given notification (subsection (3) of Section 2–607) he may recover as damages for any non-conformity of tender the loss resulting in the ordinary course of events from the seller's breach as determined in any manner which is reasonable.

(2) The measure of damages for breach of warranty is the difference at the time and place of acceptance between the value of the goods accepted and the value they would have had if they had been as warranted, unless special circumstances show proximate damages of a different amount.

(3) In a proper case any incidental and consequential damages under the next section may also be recovered.

§ 2–715. Buyer's Incidental and Consequential Damages.

(1) Incidental damages resulting from the seller's breach include expenses reasonably incurred in inspection, receipt, transportation and care and custody of goods rightfully rejected, any commercially reasonable charges, expenses or commissions in connection with

effecting cover and any other reasonable expense incident to the delay or other breach.

(2) Consequential damages resulting from the seller's breach include

(a) any loss resulting from general or particular requirements and needs of which the seller at the time of contracting had reason to know and which could not reasonably be prevented by cover or otherwise; and

(b) injury to person or property proximately resulting from any breach of warranty.

§ 2–716. Buyer's Right to Specific Performance or Replevin.

(1) Specific performance may be decreed where the goods are unique or in other proper circumstances.

(2) The decree for specific performance may include such terms and conditions as to payment of the price, damages, or other relief as the court may deem just.

(3) The buyer has a right of replevin for goods identified to the contract if after reasonable effort he is unable to effect cover for such goods or the circumstances reasonably indicate that such effort will be unavailing or if the goods have been shipped under reservation and satisfaction of the security interest in them has been made or tendered. In the case of goods bought for personal, family, or household purposes, the buyer's right of replevin vests upon acquisition of a special property, even if the seller had not then repudiated or failed to deliver.

As amended in 1999.

§ 2–717. Deduction of Damages From the Price.

The buyer on notifying the seller of his intention to do so may deduct all or any part of the damages resulting from any breach of the contract from any part of the price still due under the same contract.

§ 2–718. Liquidation or Limitation of Damages; Deposits.

(1) Damages for breach by either party may be liquidated in the agreement but only at an amount which is reasonable in the light of the anticipated or actual harm caused by the breach, the difficulties of proof of loss, and the inconvenience or nonfeasibility of otherwise obtaining an adequate remedy. A term fixing unreasonably large liquidated damages is void as a penalty.

(2) Where the seller justifiably withholds delivery of goods because of the buyer's breach, the buyer is entitled to restitution of any amount by which the sum of his payments exceeds

(a) the amount to which the seller is entitled by virtue of terms liquidating the seller's damages in accordance with subsection (1), or

(b) in the absence of such terms, twenty per cent of the value of the total performance for which the buyer is obligated under the contract or $500, whichever is smaller.

(3) The buyer's right to restitution under subsection (2) is subject to offset to the extent that the seller establishes

(a) a right to recover damages under the provisions of this Article other than subsection (1), and

(b) the amount or value of any benefits received by the buyer directly or indirectly by reason of the contract.

(4) Where a seller has received payment in goods their reasonable value or the proceeds of their resale shall be treated as payments for the purposes of subsection (2); but if the seller has notice of the buyer's breach before reselling goods received in part performance, his resale is subject to the conditions laid down in this Article on resale by an aggrieved seller (Section 2–706).

§ 2–719. Contractual Modification or Limitation of Remedy.

(1) Subject to the provisions of subsections (2) and (3) of this section and of the preceding section on liquidation and limitation of damages,

(a) the agreement may provide for remedies in addition to or in substitution for those provided in this Article and may limit or alter the measure of damages recoverable under this Article, as by limiting the buyer's remedies to return of the goods and repayment of the price or to repair and replacement of nonconforming goods or parts; and

(b) resort to a remedy as provided is optional unless the remedy is expressly agreed to be exclusive, in which case it is the sole remedy.

(2) Where circumstances cause an exclusive or limited remedy to fail of its essential purpose, remedy may be had as provided in this Act.

(3) Consequential damages may be limited or excluded unless the limitation or exclusion is unconscionable. Limitation of consequential damages for injury to the person in the case of consumer goods is prima facie unconscionable but limitation of damages where the loss is commercial is not.

§ 2–720. Effect of "Cancellation" or "Rescission" on Claims for Antecedent Breach.

Unless the contrary intention clearly appears, expressions of "cancellation" or "rescission" of the contract or the like shall not be construed as a renunciation or discharge of any claim in damages for an antecedent breach.

§ 2–721. Remedies for Fraud.

Remedies for material misrepresentation or fraud include all remedies available under this Article for non-fraudulent breach. Neither rescission or a claim for rescission of the contract for sale nor rejection or return of the goods shall bar or be deemed inconsistent with a claim for damages or other remedy.

§ 2–722. Who Can Sue Third Parties for Injury to Goods.

Where a third party so deals with goods which have been identified to a contract for sale as to cause actionable injury to a party to that contract

(a) a right of action against the third party is in either party to the contract for sale who has title to or a security interest or a special property or an insurable interest in the goods; and if the goods have been destroyed or converted a right of action is also in the party who either bore the risk of loss under the contract for sale or has since the injury assumed that risk as against the other;

(b) if at the time of the injury the party plaintiff did not bear the risk of loss as against the other party to the contract for sale and there is no arrangement between them for disposition of the recovery, his suit or settlement is, subject to his own interest, as a fiduciary for the other party to the contract;

(c) either party may with the consent of the other sue for the benefit of whom it may concern.

§ 2–723. Proof of Market Price: Time and Place.

(1) If an action based on anticipatory repudiation comes to trial before the time for performance with respect to some or all of the

goods, any damages based on market price (Section 2–708 or Section 2–713) shall be determined according to the price of such goods prevailing at the time when the aggrieved party learned of the repudiation.

(2) If evidence of a price prevailing at the times or places described in this Article is not readily available the price prevailing within any reasonable time before or after the time described or at any other place which in commercial judgment or under usage of trade would serve as a reasonable substitute for the one described may be used, making any proper allowance for the cost of transporting the goods to or from such other place.

(3) Evidence of a relevant price prevailing at a time or place other than the one described in this Article offered by one party is not admissible unless and until he has given the other party such notice as the court finds sufficient to prevent unfair surprise.

§ 2–724. Admissibility of Market Quotations.

Whenever the prevailing price or value of any goods regularly bought and sold in any established commodity market is in issue, reports in official publications or trade journals or in newspapers or periodicals of general circulation published as the reports of such market shall be admissible in evidence. The circumstances of the preparation of such a report may be shown to affect its weight but not its admissibility.

§ 2–725. Statute of Limitations in Contracts for Sale.

(1) An action for breach of any contract for sale must be commenced within four years after the cause of action has accrued. By the original agreement the parties may reduce the period of limitation to not less than one year but may not extend it.

(2) A cause of action accrues when the breach occurs, regardless of the aggrieved party's lack of knowledge of the breach. A breach of warranty occurs when tender of delivery is made, except that where a warranty explicitly extends to future performance of the goods and discovery of the breach must await the time of such performance the cause of action accrues when the breach is or should have been discovered.

(3) Where an action commenced within the time limited by subsection (1) is so terminated as to leave available a remedy by another action for the same breach such other action may be commenced after the expiration of the time limited and within six months after the termination of the first action unless the termination resulted from voluntary discontinuance or from dismissal for failure or neglect to prosecute.

(4) This section does not alter the law on tolling of the statute of limitations nor does it apply to causes of action which have accrued before this Act becomes effective.

Article 2A
LEASES

Part 1 General Provisions

§ 2A–101. Short Title.

This Article shall be known and may be cited as the Uniform Commercial Code — Leases.

§ 2A–102. Scope.

This Article applies to any transaction, regardless of form, that creates a lease.

§ 2A–103. Definitions and Index of Definitions.

(1) In this Article unless the context otherwise requires:

(a) "Buyer in ordinary course of business" means a person who in good faith and without knowledge that the sale to him [or her] is in violation of the ownership rights or security interest or leasehold interest of a third party in the goods buys in ordinary course from a person in the business of selling goods of that kind but does not include a pawnbroker. "Buying" may be for cash or by exchange of other property or on secured or unsecured credit and includes receiving goods or documents of title under a pre-existing contract for sale but does not include a transfer in bulk or as security for or in total or partial satisfaction of a money debt.

(b) "Cancellation" occurs when either party puts an end to the lease contract for default by the other party.

(c) "Commercial unit" means such a unit of goods as by commercial usage is a single whole for purposes of lease and division of which materially impairs its character or value on the market or in use. A commercial unit may be a single article, as a machine, or a set of articles, as a suite of furniture or a line of machinery, or a quantity, as a gross or carload, or any other unit treated in use or in the relevant market as a single whole.

(d) "Conforming" goods or performance under a lease contract means goods or performance that are in accordance with the obligations under the lease contract.

(e) "Consumer lease" means a lease that a lessor regularly engaged in the business of leasing or selling makes to a lessee who is an individual and who takes under the lease primarily for a personal, family, or household purpose [, if the total payments to be made under the lease contract, excluding payments for options to renew or buy, do not exceed $_____].

(f) "Fault" means wrongful act, omission, breach, or default.

(g) "Finance lease" means a lease with respect to which:

(i) the lessor does not select, manufacture or supply the goods;

(ii) the lessor acquires the goods or the right to possession and use of the goods in connection with the lease; and

(iii) one of the following occurs:

(A) the lessee receives a copy of the contract by which the lessor acquired the goods or the right to possession and use of the goods before signing the lease contract;

(B) the lessee's approval of the contract by which the lessor acquired the goods or the right to possession and use of the goods is a condition to effectiveness of the lease contract;

(C) the lessee, before signing the lease contract, receives an accurate and complete statement designating the promises and warranties, and any disclaimers of warranties, limitations or modifications of remedies, or liquidated damages, including those of a third party, such as the manufacturer of the goods, provided to the lessor by the person supplying the goods in connection with or as part of the contract by which the lessor acquired the goods or the right to possession and use of the goods; or

(D) if the lease is not a consumer lease, the lessor, before the lessee signs the lease contract, informs the lessee in writing (a) of the identity of the person supplying the goods to the lessor, unless the lessee has selected that person and directed the lessor to acquire the goods or the right to possession and use of the goods from that person, (b) that the lessee is entitled under this Article to any promises and warranties, including those of any third party, provided to the lessor by the person supplying the goods in connection with or as part of the contract by which the lessor acquired the goods or the right to possession and use of the goods, and (c) that the lessee may communicate with the person supplying the goods to the lessor and receive an accurate and complete statement of those promises and warranties, including any disclaimers and limitations of them or of remedies.

(h) "Goods" means all things that are movable at the time of identification to the lease contract, or are fixtures (Section 2A–309), but the term does not include money, documents, instruments, accounts, chattel paper, general intangibles, or minerals or the like, including oil and gas, before extraction. The term also includes the unborn young of animals.

(i) "Installment lease contract" means a lease contract that authorizes or requires the delivery of goods in separate lots to be separately accepted, even though the lease contract contains a clause "each delivery is a separate lease" or its equivalent.

(j) "Lease" means a transfer of the right to possession and use of goods for a term in return for consideration, but a sale, including a sale on approval or a sale or return, or retention or creation of a security interest is not a lease. Unless the context clearly indicates otherwise, the term includes a sublease.

(k) "Lease agreement" means the bargain, with respect to the lease, of the lessor and the lessee in fact as found in their language or by implication from other circumstances including course of dealing or usage of trade or course of performance as provided in this Article. Unless the context clearly indicates otherwise, the term includes a sublease agreement.

(l) "Lease contract" means the total legal obligation that results from the lease agreement as affected by this Article and any other applicable rules of law. Unless the context clearly indicates otherwise, the term includes a sublease contract.

(m) "Leasehold interest" means the interest of the lessor or the lessee under a lease contract.

(n) "Lessee" means a person who acquires the right to possession and use of goods under a lease. Unless the context clearly indicates otherwise, the term includes a sublessee.

(o) "Lessee in ordinary course of business" means a person who in good faith and without knowledge that the lease to him [or her] is in violation of the ownership rights or security interest or leasehold interest of a third party in the goods, leases in ordinary course from a person in the business of selling or leasing goods of that kind but does not include a pawnbroker. "Leasing" may be for cash or by exchange of other property or

on secured or unsecured credit and includes receiving goods or documents of title under a pre-existing lease contract but does not include a transfer in bulk or as security for or in total or partial satisfaction of a money debt.

(p) "Lessor" means a person who transfers the right to possession and use of goods under a lease. Unless the context clearly indicates otherwise, the term includes a sublessor.

(q) "Lessor's residual interest" means the lessor's interest in the goods after expiration, termination, or cancellation of the lease contract.

(r) "Lien" means a charge against or interest in goods to secure payment of a debt or performance of an obligation, but the term does not include a security interest.

(s) "Lot" means a parcel or a single article that is the subject matter of a separate lease or delivery, whether or not it is sufficient to perform the lease contract.

(t) "Merchant lessee" means a lessee that is a merchant with respect to goods of the kind subject to the lease.

(u) "Present value" means the amount as of a date certain of one or more sums payable in the future, discounted to the date certain. The discount is determined by the interest rate specified by the parties if the rate was not manifestly unreasonable at the time the transaction was entered into; otherwise, the discount is determined by a commercially reasonable rate that takes into account the facts and circumstances of each case at the time the transaction was entered into.

(v) "Purchase" includes taking by sale, lease, mortgage, security interest, pledge, gift, or any other voluntary transaction creating an interest in goods.

(w) "Sublease" means a lease of goods the right to possession and use of which was acquired by the lessor as a lessee under an existing lease.

(x) "Supplier" means a person from whom a lessor buys or leases goods to be leased under a finance lease.

(y) "Supply contract" means a contract under which a lessor buys or leases goods to be leased.

(z) "Termination" occurs when either party pursuant to a power created by agreement or law puts an end to the lease contract otherwise than for default.

(2) Other definitions applying to this Article and the sections in which they appear are:

"Accessions". Section 2A–310(1).
"Construction mortgage". Section 2A–309(1)(d).
"Encumbrance". Section 2A–309(1)(e).
"Fixtures". Section 2A–309(1)(a).
"Fixture filing". Section 2A–309(1)(b).
"Purchase money lease". Section 2A–309(1)(c).

(3) The following definitions in other Articles apply to this Article:

"Accounts". Section 9–106.
"Between merchants". Section 2–104(3).
"Buyer". Section 2–103(1)(a).
"Chattel paper". Section 9–105(1)(b).
"Consumer goods". Section 9–109(1).
"Document". Section 9–105(1)(f).

"Entrusting". Section 2–403(3).
"General intangibles". Section 9–106.
"Good faith". Section 2–103(1)(b).
"Instrument". Section 9–105(1)(i).
"Merchant". Section 2–104(1).
"Mortgage". Section 9–105(1)(j).
"Pursuant to commitment". Section 9–105(1)(k).
"Receipt". Section 2–103(1)(c).
"Sale". Section 2–106(1).
"Sale on approval". Section 2–326.
"Sale or return". Section 2–326.
"Seller". Section 2–103(1)(d).

(4) In addition Article 1 contains general definitions and principles of construction and interpretation applicable throughout this Article.

As amended in 1990 and 1999.

§ 2A–104. Leases Subject to Other Law.

(1) A lease, although subject to this Article, is also subject to any applicable:

(a) certificate of title statute of this State: (list any certificate of title statutes covering automobiles, trailers, mobile homes, boats, farm tractors, and the like);

(b) certificate of title statute of another jurisdiction (Section 2A–105); or

(c) consumer protection statute of this State, or final consumer protection decision of a court of this State existing on the effective date of this Article.

(2) In case of conflict between this Article, other than Sections 2A–105, 2A–304(3), and 2A–305(3), and a statute or decision referred to in subsection (1), the statute or decision controls.

(3) Failure to comply with an applicable law has only the effect specified therein.

As amended in 1990.

§ 2A–105. Territorial Application of Article to Goods Covered by Certificate of Title.

Subject to the provisions of Sections 2A–304(3) and 2A–305(3), with respect to goods covered by a certificate of title issued under a statute of this State or of another jurisdiction, compliance and the effect of compliance or noncompliance with a certificate of title statute are governed by the law (including the conflict of laws rules) of the jurisdiction issuing the certificate until the earlier of (a) surrender of the certificate, or (b) four months after the goods are removed from that jurisdiction and thereafter until a new certificate of title is issued by another jurisdiction.

§ 2A–106. Limitation on Power of Parties to Consumer Lease to Choose Applicable Law and Judicial Forum.

(1) If the law chosen by the parties to a consumer lease is that of a jurisdiction other than a jurisdiction in which the lessee resides at the time the lease agreement becomes enforceable or within 30 days thereafter or in which the goods are to be used, the choice is not enforceable.

(2) If the judicial forum chosen by the parties to a consumer lease is a forum that would not otherwise have jurisdiction over the lessee, the choice is not enforceable.

§ 2A–107. Waiver or Renunciation of Claim or Right After Default.

Any claim or right arising out of an alleged default or breach of warranty may be discharged in whole or in part without consideration by a written waiver or renunciation signed and delivered by the aggrieved party.

§ 2A–108. Unconscionability.

(1) If the court as a matter of law finds a lease contract or any clause of a lease contract to have been unconscionable at the time it was made the court may refuse to enforce the lease contract, or it may enforce the remainder of the lease contract without the unconscionable clause, or it may so limit the application of any unconscionable clause as to avoid any unconscionable result.

(2) With respect to a consumer lease, if the court as a matter of law finds that a lease contract or any clause of a lease contract has been induced by unconscionable conduct or that unconscionable conduct has occurred in the collection of a claim arising from a lease contract, the court may grant appropriate relief.

(3) Before making a finding of unconscionability under subsection (1) or (2), the court, on its own motion or that of a party, shall afford the parties a reasonable opportunity to present evidence as to the setting, purpose, and effect of the lease contract or clause thereof, or of the conduct.

(4) In an action in which the lessee claims unconscionability with respect to a consumer lease:

(a) If the court finds unconscionability under subsection (1) or (2), the court shall award reasonable attorney's fees to the lessee.

(b) If the court does not find unconscionability and the lessee claiming unconscionability has brought or maintained an action he [or she] knew to be groundless, the court shall award reasonable attorney's fees to the party against whom the claim is made.

(c) In determining attorney's fees, the amount of the recovery on behalf of the claimant under subsections (1) and (2) is not controlling.

§ 2A–109. Option to Accelerate at Will.

(1) A term providing that one party or his [or her] successor in interest may accelerate payment or performance or require collateral or additional collateral "at will" or "when he [or she] deems himself [or herself] insecure" or in words of similar import must be construed to mean that he [or she] has power to do so only if he [or she] in good faith believes that the prospect of payment or performance is impaired.

(2) With respect to a consumer lease, the burden of establishing good faith under subsection (1) is on the party who exercised the power; otherwise the burden of establishing lack of good faith is on the party against whom the power has been exercised.

Part 2 Formation and Construction of Lease Contract

§ 2A–201. Statute of Frauds.

(1) A lease contract is not enforceable by way of action or defense unless:

(a) the total payments to be made under the lease contract, excluding payments for options to renew or buy, are less than $1,000; or

(b) there is a writing, signed by the party against whom enforcement is sought or by that party's authorized agent, sufficient to indicate that a lease contract has been made between the parties and to describe the goods leased and the lease term.

(2) Any description of leased goods or of the lease term is sufficient and satisfies subsection (1)(b), whether or not it is specific, if it reasonably identifies what is described.

(3) A writing is not insufficient because it omits or incorrectly states a term agreed upon, but the lease contract is not enforceable under subsection (1)(b) beyond the lease term and the quantity of goods shown in the writing.

(4) A lease contract that does not satisfy the requirements of subsection (1), but which is valid in other respects, is enforceable:

(a) if the goods are to be specially manufactured or obtained for the lessee and are not suitable for lease or sale to others in the ordinary course of the lessor's business, and the lessor, before notice of repudiation is received and under circumstances that reasonably indicate that the goods are for the lessee, has made either a substantial beginning of their manufacture or commitments for their procurement;

(b) if the party against whom enforcement is sought admits in that party's pleading, testimony or otherwise in court that a lease contract was made, but the lease contract is not enforceable under this provision beyond the quantity of goods admitted; or

(c) with respect to goods that have been received and accepted by the lessee.

(5) The lease term under a lease contract referred to in subsection (4) is:

(a) if there is a writing signed by the party against whom enforcement is sought or by that party's authorized agent specifying the lease term, the term so specified;

(b) if the party against whom enforcement is sought admits in that party's pleading, testimony, or otherwise in court a lease term, the term so admitted; or

(c) a reasonable lease term.

§ 2A–202. Final Written Expression: Parol or Extrinsic Evidence.

Terms with respect to which the confirmatory memoranda of the parties agree or which are otherwise set forth in a writing intended by the parties as a final expression of their agreement with respect to such terms as are included therein may not be contradicted by evidence of any prior agreement or of a contemporaneous oral agreement but may be explained or supplemented:

(a) by course of dealing or usage of trade or by course of performance; and

(b) by evidence of consistent additional terms unless the court finds the writing to have been intended also as a complete and exclusive statement of the terms of the agreement.

§ 2A–203. Seals Inoperative.

The affixing of a seal to a writing evidencing a lease contract or an offer to enter into a lease contract does not render the writing a sealed instrument and the law with respect to sealed instruments does not apply to the lease contract or offer.

§ 2A–204. Formation in General.

(1) A lease contract may be made in any manner sufficient to show agreement, including conduct by both parties which recognizes the existence of a lease contract.

(2) An agreement sufficient to constitute a lease contract may be found although the moment of its making is undetermined.

(3) Although one or more terms are left open, a lease contract does not fail for indefiniteness if the parties have intended to make a lease contract and there is a reasonably certain basis for giving an appropriate remedy.

§ 2A–205. Firm Offers.

An offer by a merchant to lease goods to or from another person in a signed writing that by its terms gives assurance it will be held open is not revocable, for lack of consideration, during the time stated or, if no time is stated, for a reasonable time, but in no event may the period of irrevocability exceed 3 months. Any such term of assurance on a form supplied by the offeree must be separately signed by the offeror.

§ 2A–206. Offer and Acceptance in Formation of Lease Contract.

(1) Unless otherwise unambiguously indicated by the language or circumstances, an offer to make a lease contract must be construed as inviting acceptance in any manner and by any medium reasonable in the circumstances.

(2) If the beginning of a requested performance is a reasonable mode of acceptance, an offeror who is not notified of acceptance within a reasonable time may treat the offer as having lapsed before acceptance.

§ 2A–207. Course of Performance or Practical Construction.

(1) If a lease contract involves repeated occasions for performance by either party with knowledge of the nature of the performance and opportunity for objection to it by the other, any course of performance accepted or acquiesced in without objection is relevant to determine the meaning of the lease agreement.

(2) The express terms of a lease agreement and any course of performance, as well as any course of dealing and usage of trade, must be construed whenever reasonable as consistent with each other; but if that construction is unreasonable, express terms control course of performance, course of performance controls both course of dealing and usage of trade, and course of dealing controls usage of trade.

(3) Subject to the provisions of Section 2A–208 on modification and waiver, course of performance is relevant to show a waiver or modification of any term inconsistent with the course of performance.

§ 2A–208. Modification, Rescission and Waiver.

(1) An agreement modifying a lease contract needs no consideration to be binding.

(2) A signed lease agreement that excludes modification or rescission except by a signed writing may not be otherwise modified or rescinded, but, except as between merchants, such a requirement on a form supplied by a merchant must be separately signed by the other party.

(3) Although an attempt at modification or rescission does not satisfy the requirements of subsection (2), it may operate as a waiver.

(4) A party who has made a waiver affecting an executory portion of a lease contract may retract the waiver by reasonable notification received by the other party that strict performance will be required of any term waived, unless the retraction would be unjust in view of a material change of position in reliance on the waiver.

§ 2A–209. Lessee under Finance Lease as Beneficiary of Supply Contract.

(1) The benefit of the supplier's promises to the lessor under the supply contract and of all warranties, whether express or implied, including those of any third party provided in connection with or as part of the supply contract, extends to the lessee to the extent of the lessee's leasehold interest under a finance lease related to the supply contract, but is subject to the terms warranty and of the supply contract and all defenses or claims arising therefrom.

(2) The extension of the benefit of supplier's promises and of warranties to the lessee (Section 2A–209(1)) does not: (i) modify the rights and obligations of the parties to the supply contract, whether arising therefrom or otherwise, or (ii) impose any duty or liability under the supply contract on the lessee.

(3) Any modification or rescission of the supply contract by the supplier and the lessor is effective between the supplier and the lessee unless, before the modification or rescission, the supplier has received notice that the lessee has entered into a finance lease related to the supply contract. If the modification or rescission is effective between the supplier and the lessee, the lessor is deemed to have assumed, in addition to the obligations of the lessor to the lessee under the lease contract, promises of the supplier to the lessor and warranties that were so modified or rescinded as they existed and were available to the lessee before modification or rescission.

(4) In addition to the extension of the benefit of the supplier's promises and of warranties to the lessee under subsection (1), the lessee retains all rights that the lessee may have against the supplier which arise from an agreement between the lessee and the supplier or under other law. As amended in 1990.

§ 2A–210. Express Warranties.

(1) Express warranties by the lessor are created as follows:

(a) Any affirmation of fact or promise made by the lessor to the lessee which relates to the goods and becomes part of the basis of the bargain creates an express warranty that the goods will conform to the affirmation or promise.

(b) Any description of the goods which is made part of the basis of the bargain creates an express warranty that the goods will conform to the description.

(c) Any sample or model that is made part of the basis of the bargain creates an express warranty that the whole of the goods will conform to the sample or model.

(2) It is not necessary to the creation of an express warranty that the lessor use formal words, such as "warrant" or "guarantee," or that the lessor have a specific intention to make a warranty, but an affirmation merely of the value of the goods or a statement purporting to be merely the lessor's opinion or commendation of the goods does not create a warranty.

§ 2A–211. Warranties Against Interference and Against Infringement; Lessee's Obligation Against Infringement.

(1) There is in a lease contract a warranty that for the lease term no person holds a claim to or interest in the goods that arose from an act or omission of the lessor, other than a claim by way of infringement or the like, which will interfere with the lessee's enjoyment of its leasehold interest.

(2) Except in a finance lease there is in a lease contract by a lessor who is a merchant regularly dealing in goods of the kind a warranty that the goods are delivered free of the rightful claim of any person by way of infringement or the like.

(3) A lessee who furnishes specifications to a lessor or a supplier shall hold the lessor and the supplier harmless against any claim by way of infringement or the like that arises out of compliance with the specifications.

§ 2A–212. Implied Warranty of Merchantability.

(1) Except in a finance lease, a warranty that the goods will be merchantable is implied in a lease contract if the lessor is a merchant with respect to goods of that kind.

(2) Goods to be merchantable must be at least such as

(a) pass without objection in the trade under the description in the lease agreement;

(b) in the case of fungible goods, are of fair average quality within the description;

(c) are fit for the ordinary purposes for which goods of that type are used;

(d) run, within the variation permitted by the lease agreement, of even kind, quality, and quantity within each unit and among all units involved;

(e) are adequately contained, packaged, and labeled as the lease agreement may require; and

(f) conform to any promises or affirmations of fact made on the container or label.

(3) Other implied warranties may arise from course of dealing or usage of trade.

§ 2A–213. Implied Warranty of Fitness for Particular Purpose.

Except in a finance of lease, if the lessor at the time the lease contract is made has reason to know of any particular purpose for which the goods are required and that the lessee is relying on the lessor's skill or judgment to select or furnish suitable goods, there is in the lease contract an implied warranty that the goods will be fit for that purpose.

§ 2A–214. Exclusion or Modification of Warranties.

(1) Words or conduct relevant to the creation of an express warranty and words or conduct tending to negate or limit a warranty must be construed wherever reasonable as consistent with each other; but, subject to the provisions of Section 2A–202 on parol or extrinsic evidence, negation or limitation is inoperative to the extent that the construction is unreasonable.

(2) Subject to subsection (3), to exclude or modify the implied warranty of merchantability or any part of it the language must mention "merchantability", be by a writing, and be conspicuous. Subject to subsection (3), to exclude or modify any implied warranty of fitness the exclusion must be by a writing and be conspicuous. Language to exclude all implied warranties of fitness is sufficient if it is in writ-

ing, is conspicuous and states, for example, "There is no warranty that the goods will be fit for a particular purpose".

(3) Notwithstanding subsection (2), but subject to subsection (4),

(a) unless the circumstances indicate otherwise, all implied warranties are excluded by expressions like "as is" or "with all faults" or by other language that in common understanding calls the lessee's attention to the exclusion of warranties and makes plain that there is no implied warranty, if in writing and conspicuous;

(b) if the lessee before entering into the lease contract has examined the goods or the sample or model as fully as desired or has refused to examine the goods, there is no implied warranty with regard to defects that an examination ought in the circumstances to have revealed; and

(c) an implied warranty may also be excluded or modified by course of dealing, course of performance, or usage of trade.

(4) To exclude or modify a warranty against interference or against infringement (Section 2A–211) or any part of it, the language must be specific, be by a writing, and be conspicuous, unless the circumstances, including course of performance, course of dealing, or usage of trade, give the lessee reason to know that the goods are being leased subject to a claim or interest of any person.

§ 2A–215. Cumulation and Conflict of Warranties Express or Implied.

Warranties, whether express or implied, must be construed as consistent with each other and as cumulative, but if that construction is unreasonable, the intention of the parties determines which warranty is dominant. In ascertaining that intention the following rules apply:

(a) Exact or technical specifications displace an inconsistent sample or model or general language of description.

(b) A sample from an existing bulk displaces inconsistent general language of description.

(c) Express warranties displace inconsistent implied warranties other than an implied warranty of fitness for a particular purpose.

§ 2A–216. Third-Party Beneficiaries of Express and Implied Warranties.

Alternative A

A warranty to or for the benefit of a lessee under this Article, whether express or implied, extends to any natural person who is in the family or household of the lessee or who is a guest in the lessee's home if it is reasonable to expect that such person may use, consume, or be affected by the goods and who is injured in person by breach of the warranty. This section does not displace principles of law and equity that extend a warranty to or for the benefit of a lessee to other persons. The operation of this section may not be excluded, modified, or limited, but an exclusion, modification, or limitation of the warranty, including any with respect to rights and remedies, effective against the lessee is also effective against any beneficiary designated under this section.

Alternative B

A warranty to or for the benefit of a lessee under this Article, whether express or implied, extends to any natural person who may reasonably be expected to use, consume, or be affected by the goods and who is injured in person by breach of the warranty. This section

does not displace principles of law and equity that extend a warranty to or for the benefit of a lessee to other persons. The operation of this section may not be excluded, modified, or limited, but an exclusion, modification, or limitation of the warranty, including any with respect to rights and remedies, effective against the lessee is also effective against the beneficiary designated under this section.

Alternative C

A warranty to or for the benefit of a lessee under this Article, whether express or implied, extends to any person who may reasonably be expected to use, consume, or be affected by the goods and who is injured by breach of the warranty. The operation of this section may not be excluded, modified, or limited with respect to injury to the person of an individual to whom the warranty extends, but an exclusion, modification, or limitation of the warranty, including any with respect to rights and remedies, effective against the lessee is also effective against the beneficiary designated under this section.

§ 2A–217. Identification.

Identification of goods as goods to which a lease contract refers may be made at any time and in any manner explicitly agreed to by the parties. In the absence of explicit agreement, identification occurs:

(a) when the lease contract is made if the lease contract is for a lease of goods that are existing and identified;

(b) when the goods are shipped, marked, or otherwise designated by the lessor as goods to which the lease contract refers, if the lease contract is for a lease of goods that are not existing and identified; or

(c) when the young are conceived, if the lease contract is for a lease of unborn young of animals.

§ 2A–218. Insurance and Proceeds.

(1) A lessee obtains an insurable interest when existing goods are identified to the lease contract even though the goods identified are nonconforming and the lessee has an option to reject them.

(2) If a lessee has an insurable interest only by reason of the lessor's identification of the goods, the lessor, until default or insolvency or notification to the lessee that identification is final, may substitute other goods for those identified.

(3) Notwithstanding a lessee's insurable interest under subsections (1) and (2), the lessor retains an insurable interest until an option to buy has been exercised by the lessee and risk of loss has passed to the lessee.

(4) Nothing in this section impairs any insurable interest recognized under any other statute or rule of law.

(5) The parties by agreement may determine that one or more parties have an obligation to obtain and pay for insurance covering the goods and by agreement may determine the beneficiary of the proceeds of the insurance.

§ 2A–219. Risk of Loss.

(1) Except in the case of a finance lease, risk of loss is retained by the lessor and does not pass to the lessee. In the case of a finance lease, risk of loss passes to the lessee.

(2) Subject to the provisions of this Article on the effect of default on risk of loss (Section 2A–220), if risk of loss is to pass to the lessee and the time of passage is not stated, the following rules apply:

(a) If the lease contract requires or authorizes the goods to be shipped by carrier

(i) and it does not require delivery at a particular destination, the risk of loss passes to the lessee when the goods are duly delivered to the carrier; but

(ii) if it does require delivery at a particular destination and the goods are there duly tendered while in the possession of the carrier, the risk of loss passes to the lessee when the goods are there duly so tendered as to enable the lessee to take delivery.

(b) If the goods are held by a bailee to be delivered without being moved, the risk of loss passes to the lessee on acknowledgment by the bailee of the lessee's right to possession of the goods.

(c) In any case not within subsection (a) or (b), the risk of loss passes to the lessee on the lessee's receipt of the goods if the lessor, or, in the case of a finance lease, the supplier, is a merchant; otherwise the risk passes to the lessee on tender of delivery.

§ 2A–220. Effect of Default on Risk of Loss.

(1) Where risk of loss is to pass to the lessee and the time of passage is not stated:

(a) If a tender or delivery of goods so fails to conform to the lease contract as to give a right of rejection, the risk of their loss remains with the lessor, or, in the case of a finance lease, the supplier, until cure or acceptance.

(b) If the lessee rightfully revokes acceptance, he [or she], to the extent of any deficiency in his [or her] effective insurance coverage, may treat the risk of loss as having remained with the lessor from the beginning.

(2) Whether or not risk of loss is to pass to the lessee, if the lessee as to conforming goods already identified to a lease contract repudiates or is otherwise in default under the lease contract, the lessor, or, in the case of a finance lease, the supplier, to the extent of any deficiency in his [or her] effective insurance coverage may treat the risk of loss as resting on the lessee for a commercially reasonable time.

§ 2A–221. Casualty to Identified Goods.

If a lease contract requires goods identified when the lease contract is made, and the goods suffer casualty without fault of the lessee, the lessor or the supplier before delivery, or the goods suffer casualty before risk of loss passes to the lessee pursuant to the lease agreement or Section 2A–219, then:

(a) if the loss is total, the lease contract is avoided; and

(b) if the loss is partial or the goods have so deteriorated as to no longer conform to the lease contract, the lessee may nevertheless demand inspection and at his [or her] option either treat the lease contract as avoided or, except in a finance lease that is not a consumer lease, accept the goods with due allowance from the rent payable for the balance of the lease term for the deterioration or the deficiency in quantity but without further right against the lessor.

Part 3 Effect of Lease Contract

§ 2A–301. Enforceability of Lease Contract.

Except as otherwise provided in this Article, a lease contract is effective and enforceable according to its terms between the parties, against purchasers of the goods and against creditors of the parties.

§ 2A–302. Title to and Possession of Goods.

Except as otherwise provided in this Article, each provision of this Article applies whether the lessor or a third party has title to the goods, and whether the lessor, the lessee, or a third party has possession of the goods, notwithstanding any statute or rule of law that possession or the absence of possession is fraudulent.

§ 2A–303. Alienability of Party's Interest Under Lease Contract or of Lessor's Residual Interest in Goods; Delegation of Performance; Transfer of Rights.

(1) As used in this section, "creation of a security interest" includes the sale of a lease contract that is subject to Article 9, Secured Transactions, by reason of Section 9–109(a)(3).

(2) Except as provided in subsections (3) and Section 9–407, a provision in a lease agreement which (i) prohibits the voluntary or involuntary transfer, including a transfer by sale, sublease, creation or enforcement of a security interest, or attachment, levy, or other judicial process, of an interest of a party under the lease contract or of the lessor's residual interest in the goods, or (ii) makes such a transfer an event of default, gives rise to the rights and remedies provided in subsection (4), but a transfer that is prohibited or is an event of default under the lease agreement is otherwise effective.

(3) A provision in a lease agreement which (i) prohibits a transfer of a right to damages for default with respect to the whole lease contract or of a right to payment arising out of the transferor's due performance of the transferor's entire obligation, or (ii) makes such a transfer an event of default, is not enforceable, and such a transfer is not a transfer that materially impairs the propsect of obtaining return performance by, materially changes the duty of, or materially increases the burden or risk imposed on, the other party to the lease contract within the purview of subsection (4).

(4) Subject to subsection (3) and Section 9–407:

(a) if a transfer is made which is made an event of default under a lease agreement, the party to the lease contract not making the transfer, unless that party waives the default or otherwise agrees, has the rights and remedies described in Section 2A–501(2);

(b) if paragraph (a) is not applicable and if a transfer is made that (i) is prohibited under a lease agreement or (ii) materially impairs the prospect of obtaining return performance by, materially changes the duty of, or materially increases the burden or risk imposed on, the other party to the lease contract, unless the party not making the transfer agrees at any time to the transfer in the lease contract or otherwise, then, except as limited by contract, (i) the transferor is liable to the party not making the transfer for damages caused by the transfer to the extent that the damages could not reasonably be prevented by the party not making the transfer and (ii) a court having jurisdiction may grant other appropriate relief, including cancellation of the lease contract or an injunction against the transfer.

(5) A transfer of "the lease" or of "all my rights under the lease", or a transfer in similar general terms, is a transfer of rights and, unless the language or the circumstances, as in a transfer for security, indicate the contrary, the transfer is a delegation of duties by the transferor to the transferee. Acceptance by the transferee constitutes a promise by the transferee to perform those duties. The promise is enforceable by either the transferor or the other party to the lease contract.

(6) Unless otherwise agreed by the lessor and the lessee, a delegation

of performance does not relieve the transferor as against the other party of any duty to perform or of any liability for default.

(7) In a consumer lease, to prohibit the transfer of an interest of a party under the lease contract or to make a transfer an event of default, the language must be specific, by a writing, and conspicuous.

As amended in 1990 and 1999.

§ 2A–304. Subsequent Lease of Goods by Lessor.

(1) Subject to Section 2A–303, a subsequent lessee from a lessor of goods under an existing lease contract obtains, to the extent of the leasehold interest transferred, the leasehold interest in the goods that the lessor had or had power to transfer, and except as provided in sub-section (2) and Section 2A–527(4), takes subject to the existing lease contract. A lessor with voidable title has power to transfer a good lease-hold interest to a good faith subsequent lessee for value, but only to the extent set forth in the preceding sentence. If goods have been delivered under a transaction of purchase the lessor has that power even though:

(a) the lessor's transferor was deceived as to the identity of the lessor;

(b) the delivery was in exchange for a check which is later dishonored;

(c) it was agreed that the transaction was to be a "cash sale"; or

(d) the delivery was procured through fraud punishable as lar-cenous under the criminal law.

(2) A subsequent lessee in the ordinary course of business from a les-sor who is a merchant dealing in goods of that kind to whom the goods were entrusted by the existing lessee of that lessor before the interest of the subsequent lessee became enforceable against that les-sor obtains, to the extent of the leasehold interest transferred, all of that lessor's and the existing lessee's rights to the goods, and takes free of the existing lease contract.

(3) A subsequent lessee from the lessor of goods that are subject to an existing lease contract and are covered by a certificate of title issued under a statute of this State or of another jurisdiction takes no greater rights than those provided both by this section and by the certificate of title statute.

As amended in 1990.

§ 2A–305. Sale or Sublease of Goods by Lessee.

(1) Subject to the provisions of Section 2A–303, a buyer or sublessee from the lessee of goods under an existing lease contract obtains, to the extent of the interest transferred, the leasehold interest in the goods that the lessee had or had power to transfer, and except as provided in sub-section (2) and Section 2A–511(4), takes subject to the existing lease contract. A lessee with a voidable leasehold interest has power to trans-fer a good leasehold interest to a good faith buyer for value or a good faith sublessee for value, but only to the extent set forth in the preced-ing sentence. When goods have been delivered under a transaction of lease the lessee has that power even though:

(a) the lessor was deceived as to the identity of the lessee;

(b) the delivery was in exchange for a check which is later dis-honored; or

(c) the delivery was procured through fraud punishable as lar-cenous under the criminal law.

(2) A buyer in the ordinary course of business or a sublessee in the ordinary course of business from a lessee who is a merchant dealing

in goods of that kind to whom the goods were entrusted by the les-sor obtains, to the extent of the interest transferred, all of the lessor's and lessee's rights to the goods, and takes free of the existing lease contract.

(3) A buyer or sublessee from the lessee of goods that are subject to an existing lease contract and are covered by a certificate of title issued under a statute of this State or of another jurisdiction takes no greater rights than those provided both by this section and by the cer-tificate of title statute.

§ 2A–306. Priority of Certain Liens Arising by Operation of Law.

If a person in the ordinary course of his [or her] business furnishes services or materials with respect to goods subject to a lease contract, a lien upon those goods in the possession of that person given by statute or rule of law for those materials or services takes priority over any interest of the lessor or lessee under the lease contract or this Article unless the lien is created by statute and the statute pro-vides otherwise or unless the lien is created by rule of law and the rule of law provides otherwise.

§ 2A–307. Priority of Liens Arising by Attachment or Levy on, Security Interests in, and Other Claims to Goods.

(1) Except as otherwise provided in Section 2A–306, a creditor of a lessee takes subject to the lease contract.

(2) Except as otherwise provided in subsection (3) and in Sections 2A–306 and 2A–308, a creditor of a lessor takes subject to the lease contract unless the creditor holds a lien that attached to the goods before the lease contract became enforceable.

(3) Except as otherwise provided in Sections 9–317, 9–321, and 9–323, a lessee takes a leasehold interest subject to a security interest held by a creditor of the lessor.

As amended in 1990 and 1999.

§ 2A–308. Special Rights of Creditors.

(1) A creditor of a lessor in possession of goods subject to a lease contract may treat the lease contract as void if as against the creditor retention of possession by the lessor is fraudulent under any statute or rule of law, but retention of possession in good faith and current course of trade by the lessor for a commercially reasonable time after the lease contract becomes enforceable is not fraudulent.

(2) Nothing in this Article impairs the rights of creditors of a lessor if the lease contract (a) becomes enforceable, not in current course of trade but in satisfaction of or as security for a pre-existing claim for money, security, or the like, and (b) is made under circumstances which under any statute or rule of law apart from this Article would constitute the transaction a fraudulent transfer or voidable preference.

(3) A creditor of a seller may treat a sale or an identification of goods to a contract for sale as void if as against the creditor reten-tion of possession by the seller is fraudulent under any statute or rule of law, but retention of possession of the goods pursuant to a lease contract entered into by the seller as lessee and the buyer as lessor in connection with the sale or identification of the goods is not fraudulent if the buyer bought for value and in good faith.

§ 2A–309. Lessor's and Lessee's Rights When Goods Become Fixtures.

(1) In this section:

(a) goods are "fixtures" when they become so related to particular real estate that an interest in them arises under real estate law;

(b) a "fixture filing" is the filing, in the office where a mortgage on the real estate would be filed or recorded, of a financing statement covering goods that are or are to become fixtures and conforming to the requirements of Section 9–502(a) and (b);

(c) a lease is a "purchase money lease" unless the lessee has possession or use of the goods or the right to possession or use of the goods before the lease agreement is enforceable;

(d) a mortgage is a "construction mortgage" to the extent it secures an obligation incurred for the construction of an improvement on land including the acquisition cost of the land, if the recorded writing so indicates; and

(e) "encumbrance" includes real estate mortgages and other liens on real estate and all other rights in real estate that are not ownership interests.

(2) Under this Article a lease may be of goods that are fixtures or may continue in goods that become fixtures, but no lease exists under this Article of ordinary building materials incorporated into an improvement on land.

(3) This Article does not prevent creation of a lease of fixtures pursuant to real estate law.

(4) The perfected interest of a lessor of fixtures has priority over a conflicting interest of an encumbrancer or owner of the real estate if:

(a) the lease is a purchase money lease, the conflicting interest of the encumbrancer or owner arises before the goods become fixtures, the interest of the lessor is perfected by a fixture filing before the goods become fixtures or within ten days thereafter, and the lessee has an interest of record in the real estate or is in possession of the real estate; or

(b) the interest of the lessor is perfected by a fixture filing before the interest of the encumbrancer or owner is of record, the lessor's interest has priority over any conflicting interest of a predecessor in title of the encumbrancer or owner, and the lessee has an interest of record in the real estate or is in possession of the real estate.

(5) The interest of a lessor of fixtures, whether or not perfected, has priority over the conflicting interest of an encumbrancer or owner of the real estate if:

(a) the fixtures are readily removable factory or office machines, readily removable equipment that is not primarily used or leased for use in the operation of the real estate, or readily removable replacements of domestic appliances that are goods subject to a consumer lease, and before the goods become fixtures the lease contract is enforceable; or

(b) the conflicting interest is a lien on the real estate obtained by legal or equitable proceedings after the lease contract is enforceable; or

(c) the encumbrancer or owner has consented in writing to the lease or has disclaimed an interest in the goods as fixtures; or

(d) the lessee has a right to remove the goods as against the encumbrancer or owner. If the lessee's right to remove terminates, the priority of the interest of the lessor continues for a reasonable time.

(6) Notwithstanding paragraph (4)(a) but otherwise subject to subsections (4) and (5), the interest of a lessor of fixtures, including the lessor's residual interest, is subordinate to the conflicting interest of an encumbrancer of the real estate under a construction mortgage recorded before the goods become fixtures if the goods become fixtures before the completion of the construction. To the extent given to refinance a construction mortgage, the conflicting interest of an encumbrancer of the real estate under a mortgage has this priority to the same extent as the encumbrancer of the real estate under the construction mortgage.

(7) In cases not within the preceding subsections, priority between the interest of a lessor of fixtures, including the lessor's residual interest, and the conflicting interest of an encumbrancer or owner of the real estate who is not the lessee is determined by the priority rules governing conflicting interests in real estate.

(8) If the interest of a lessor of fixtures, including the lessor's residual interest, has priority over all conflicting interests of all owners and encumbrancers of the real estate, the lessor or the lessee may (i) on default, expiration, termination, or cancellation of the lease agreement but subject to the agreement and this Article, or (ii) if necessary to enforce other rights and remedies of the lessor or lessee under this Article, remove the goods from the real estate, free and clear of all conflicting interests of all owners and encumbrancers of the real estate, but the lessor or lessee must reimburse any encumbrancer or owner of the real estate who is not the lessee and who has not otherwise agreed for the cost of repair of any physical injury, but not for any diminution in value of the real estate caused by the absence of the goods removed or by any necessity of replacing them. A person entitled to reimbursement may refuse permission to remove until the party seeking removal gives adequate security for the performance of this obligation.

(9) Even though the lease agreement does not create a security interest, the interest of a lessor of fixtures, including the lessor's residual interest, is perfected by filing a financing statement as a fixture filing for leased goods that are or are to become fixtures in accordance with the relevant provisions of the Article on Secured Transactions (Article 9).

As amended in 1990 and 1999.

§ 2A–310. Lessor's and Lessee's Rights When Goods Become Accessions.

(1) Goods are "accessions" when they are installed in or affixed to other goods.

(2) The interest of a lessor or a lessee under a lease contract entered into before the goods became accessions is superior to all interests in the whole except as stated in subsection (4).

(3) The interest of a lessor or a lessee under a lease contract entered into at the time or after the goods became accessions is superior to all subsequently acquired interests in the whole except as stated in subsection (4) but is subordinate to interests in the whole existing at the time the lease contract was made unless the holders of such interests in the whole have in writing consented to the lease or disclaimed an interest in the goods as part of the whole.

(4) The interest of a lessor or a lessee under a lease contract described in subsection (2) or (3) is subordinate to the interest of

(a) a buyer in the ordinary course of business or a lessee in the ordinary course of business of any interest in the whole acquired after the goods became accessions; or

(b) a creditor with a security interest in the whole perfected before the lease contract was made to the extent that the creditor makes subsequent advances without knowledge of the lease contract.

(5) When under subsections (2) or (3) and (4) a lessor or a lessee of accessions holds an interest that is superior to all interests in the whole, the lessor or the lessee may (a) on default, expiration, termination, or cancellation of the lease contract by the other party but subject to the provisions of the lease contract and this Article, or (b) if necessary to enforce his [or her] other rights and remedies under this Article, remove the goods from the whole, free and clear of all interests in the whole, but he [or she] must reimburse any holder of an interest in the whole who is not the lessee and who has not otherwise agreed for the cost of repair of any physical injury but not for any diminution in value of the whole caused by the absence of the goods removed or by any necessity for replacing them. A person entitled to reimbursement may refuse permission to remove until the party seeking removal gives adequate security for the performance of this obligation.

§ 2A–311. Priority Subject to Subordination.

Nothing in this Article prevents subordination by agreement by any person entitled to priority.

As added in 1990.

Part 4 Performance of Lease Contract: Repudiated, Substituted and Excused

§ 2A–401. Insecurity: Adequate Assurance of Performance.

(1) A lease contract imposes an obligation on each party that the other's expectation of receiving due performance will not be impaired.

(2) If reasonable grounds for insecurity arise with respect to the performance of either party, the insecure party may demand in writing adequate assurance of due performance. Until the insecure party receives that assurance, if commercially reasonable the insecure party may suspend any performance for which he [or she] has not already received the agreed return.

(3) A repudiation of the lease contract occurs if assurance of due performance adequate under the circumstances of the particular case is not provided to the insecure party within a reasonable time, not to exceed 30 days after receipt of a demand by the other party.

(4) Between merchants, the reasonableness of grounds for insecurity and the adequacy of any assurance offered must be determined according to commercial standards.

(5) Acceptance of any nonconforming delivery or payment does not prejudice the aggrieved party's right to demand adequate assurance of future performance.

§ 2A–402. Anticipatory Repudiation.

If either party repudiates a lease contract with respect to a performance not yet due under the lease contract, the loss of which performance will substantially impair the value of the lease contract to the other, the aggrieved party may:

(a) for a commercially reasonable time, await retraction of repudiation and performance by the repudiating party;

(b) make demand pursuant to Section 2A–401 and await assurance of future performance adequate under the circumstances of the particular case; or

(c) resort to any right or remedy upon default under the lease contract or this Article, even though the aggrieved party has notified the repudiating party that the aggrieved party would await the repudiating party's performance and assurance and has urged retraction. In addition, whether or not the aggrieved party is pursuing one of the foregoing remedies, the aggrieved party may suspend performance or, if the aggrieved party is the lessor, proceed in accordance with the provisions of this Article on the lessor's right to identify goods to the lease contract notwithstanding default or to salvage unfinished goods (Section 2A–524).

§ 2A–403. Retraction of Anticipatory Repudiation.

(1) Until the repudiating party's next performance is due, the repudiating party can retract the repudiation unless, since the repudiation, the aggrieved party has cancelled the lease contract or materially changed the aggrieved party's position or otherwise indicated that the aggrieved party considers the repudiation final.

(2) Retraction may be by any method that clearly indicates to the aggrieved party that the repudiating party intends to perform under the lease contract and includes any assurance demanded under Section 2A–401.

(3) Retraction reinstates a repudiating party's rights under a lease contract with due excuse and allowance to the aggrieved party for any delay occasioned by the repudiation.

§ 2A–404. Substituted Performance.

(1) If without fault of the lessee, the lessor and the supplier, the agreed berthing, loading, or unloading facilities fail or the agreed type of carrier becomes unavailable or the agreed manner of delivery otherwise becomes commercially impracticable, but a commercially reasonable substitute is available, the substitute performance must be tendered and accepted.

(2) If the agreed means or manner of payment fails because of domestic or foreign governmental regulation:

(a) the lessor may withhold or stop delivery or cause the supplier to withhold or stop delivery unless the lessee provides a means or manner of payment that is commercially a substantial equivalent; and

(b) if delivery has already been taken, payment by the means or in the manner provided by the regulation discharges the lessee's obligation unless the regulation is discriminatory, oppressive, or predatory.

§ 2A–405. Excused Performance.

Subject to Section 2A–404 on substituted performance, the following rules apply:

(a) Delay in delivery or nondelivery in whole or in part by a lessor or a supplier who complies with paragraphs (b) and (c) is not a default under the lease contract if performance as agreed has been made impracticable by the occurrence of a contingency the nonoccurrence of which was a basic assumption on which the lease contract was made or by compliance in good faith with any applicable foreign or domestic governmental regulation or order, whether or not the regulation or order later proves to be invalid.

(b) If the causes mentioned in paragraph (a) affect only part of the lessor's or the supplier's capacity to perform, he [or she] shall allocate production and deliveries among his [or her] customers but at his [or her] option may include regular customers not then under contract for sale or lease as well as his [or her] own requirements for further manufacture. He [or she] may so allocate in any manner that is fair and reasonable.

(c) The lessor seasonably shall notify the lessee and in the case of a finance lease the supplier seasonably shall notify the lessor and the lessee, if known, that there will be delay or nondelivery and, if allocation is required under paragraph (b), of the estimated quota thus made available for the lessee.

§ 2A–406. Procedure on Excused Performance.

(1) If the lessee receives notification of a material or indefinite delay or an allocation justified under Section 2A–405, the lessee may by written notification to the lessor as to any goods involved, and with respect to all of the goods if under an installment lease contract the value of the whole lease contract is substantially impaired (Section 2A–510):

   (a) terminate the lease contract (Section 2A–505(2)); or

   (b) except in a finance lease that is not a consumer lease, modify the lease contract by accepting the available quota in substitution, with due allowance from the rent payable for the balance of the lease term for the deficiency but without further right against the lessor.

(2) If, after receipt of a notification from the lessor under Section 2A–405, the lessee fails so to modify the lease agreement within a reasonable time not exceeding 30 days, the lease contract lapses with respect to any deliveries affected.

§ 2A–407. Irrevocable Promises: Finance Leases.

(1) In the case of a finance lease that is not a consumer lease the lessee's promises under the lease contract become irrevocable and independent upon the lessee's acceptance of the goods.

(2) A promise that has become irrevocable and independent under subsection (1):

   (a) is effective and enforceable between the parties, and by or against third parties including assignees of the parties, and

   (b) is not subject to cancellation, termination, modification, repudiation, excuse, or substitution without the consent of the party to whom the promise runs.

(3) This section does not affect the validity under any other law of a covenant in any lease contract making the lessee's promises irrevocable and independent upon the lessee's acceptance of the goods.

As amended in 1990.

Part 5 Default
A. In General

§ 2A–501. Default: Procedure.

(1) Whether the lessor or the lessee is in default under a lease contract is determined by the lease agreement and this Article.

(2) If the lessor or the lessee is in default under the lease contract, the party seeking enforcement has rights and remedies as provided in this Article and, except as limited by this Article, as provided in the lease agreement.

(3) If the lessor or the lessee is in default under the lease contract, the party seeking enforcement may reduce the party's claim to judgment, or otherwise enforce the lease contract by self-help or any available judicial procedure or nonjudicial procedure, including administrative proceeding, arbitration, or the like, in accordance with this Article.

(4) Except as otherwise provided in Section 1–106(1) or this Article or the lease agreement, the rights and remedies referred to in subsections (2) and (3) are cumulative.

(5) If the lease agreement covers both real property and goods, the party seeking enforcement may proceed under this Part as to the goods, or under other applicable law as to both the real property and the goods in accordance with that party's rights and remedies in respect of the real property, in which case this Part does not apply.

As amended in 1990.

§ 2A–502. Notice After Default.

Except as otherwise provided in this Article or the lease agreement, the lessor or lessee in default under the lease contract is not entitled to notice of default or notice of enforcement from the other party to the lease agreement.

§ 2A–503. Modification or Impairment of Rights and Remedies.

(1) Except as otherwise provided in this Article, the lease agreement may include rights and remedies for default in addition to or in substitution for those provided in this Article and may limit or alter the measure of damages recoverable under this Article.

(2) Resort to a remedy provided under this Article or in the lease agreement is optional unless the remedy is expressly agreed to be exclusive. If circumstances cause an exclusive or limited remedy to fail of its essential purpose, or provision for an exclusive remedy is unconscionable, remedy may be had as provided in this Article.

(3) Consequential damages may be liquidated under Section 2A–504, or may otherwise be limited, altered, or excluded unless the limitation, alteration, or exclusion is unconscionable. Limitation, alteration, or exclusion of consequential damages for injury to the person in the case of consumer goods is prima facie unconscionable but limitation, alteration, or exclusion of damages where the loss is commercial is not prima facie unconscionable.

(4) Rights and remedies on default by the lessor or the lessee with respect to any obligation or promise collateral or ancillary to the lease contract are not impaired by this Article.

As amended in 1990.

§ 2A–504. Liquidation of Damages.

(1) Damages payable by either party for default, or any other act or omission, including indemnity for loss or diminution of anticipated tax benefits or loss or damage to lessor's residual interest, may be liquidated in the lease agreement but only at an amount or by a formula that is reasonable in light of the then anticipated harm caused by the default or other act or omission.

(2) If the lease agreement provides for liquidation of damages, and such provision does not comply with subsection (1), or such provision is an exclusive or limited remedy that circumstances cause to fail of its essential purpose, remedy may be had as provided in this Article.

(3) If the lessor justifiably withholds or stops delivery of goods because of the lessee's default or insolvency (Section 2A–525 or 2A–526), the lessee is entitled to restitution of any amount by which the sum of his [or her] payments exceeds:

   (a) the amount to which the lessor is entitled by virtue of terms liquidating the lessor's damages in accordance with subsection (1); or

(b) in the absence of those terms, 20 percent of the then present value of the total rent the lessee was obligated to pay for the balance of the lease term, or, in the case of a consumer lease, the lesser of such amount or $500.

(4) A lessee's right to restitution under subsection (3) is subject to offset to the extent the lessor establishes:

(a) a right to recover damages under the provisions of this Article other than subsection (1); and

(b) the amount or value of any benefits received by the lessee directly or indirectly by reason of the lease contract.

§ 2A–505. Cancellation and Termination and Effect of Cancellation, Termination, Rescission, or Fraud on Rights and Remedies.

(1) On cancellation of the lease contract, all obligations that are still executory on both sides are discharged, but any right based on prior default or performance survives, and the cancelling party also retains any remedy for default of the whole lease contract or any unperformed balance.

(2) On termination of the lease contract, all obligations that are still executory on both sides are discharged but any right based on prior default or performance survives.

(3) Unless the contrary intention clearly appears, expressions of "cancellation," "rescission," or the like of the lease contract may not be construed as a renunciation or discharge of any claim in damages for an antecedent default.

(4) Rights and remedies for material misrepresentation or fraud include all rights and remedies available under this Article for default.

(5) Neither rescission nor a claim for rescission of the lease contract nor rejection or return of the goods may bar or be deemed inconsistent with a claim for damages or other right or remedy.

§ 2A–506. Statute of Limitations.

(1) An action for default under a lease contract, including breach of warranty or indemnity, must be commenced within 4 years after the cause of action accrued. By the original lease contract the parties may reduce the period of limitation to not less than one year.

(2) A cause of action for default accrues when the act or omission on which the default or breach of warranty is based is or should have been discovered by the aggrieved party, or when the default occurs, whichever is later. A cause of action for indemnity accrues when the act or omission on which the claim for indemnity is based is or should have been discovered by the indemnified party, whichever is later.

(3) If an action commenced within the time limited by subsection (1) is so terminated as to leave available a remedy by another action for the same default or breach of warranty or indemnity, the other action may be commenced after the expiration of the time limited and within 6 months after the termination of the first action unless the termination resulted from voluntary discontinuance or from dismissal for failure or neglect to prosecute.

(4) This section does not alter the law on tolling of the statute of limitations nor does it apply to causes of action that have accrued before this Article becomes effective.

§ 2A–507. Proof of Market Rent: Time and Place.

(1) Damages based on market rent (Section 2A–519 or 2A–528) are determined according to the rent for the use of the goods concerned for a lease term identical to the remaining lease term of the original lease agreement and prevailing at the times specified in Sections 2A–519 and 2A–528.

(2) If evidence of rent for the use of the goods concerned for a lease term identical to the remaining lease term of the original lease agreement and prevailing at the times or places described in this Article is not readily available, the rent prevailing within any reasonable time before or after the time described or at any other place or for a different lease term which in commercial judgment or under usage of trade would serve as a reasonable substitute for the one described may be used, making any proper allowance for the difference, including the cost of transporting the goods to or from the other place.

(3) Evidence of a relevant rent prevailing at a time or place or for a lease term other than the one described in this Article offered by one party is not admissible unless and until he [or she] has given the other party notice the court finds sufficient to prevent unfair surprise.

(4) If the prevailing rent or value of any goods regularly leased in any established market is in issue, reports in official publications or trade journals or in newspapers or periodicals of general circulation published as the reports of that market are admissible in evidence. The circumstances of the preparation of the report may be shown to affect its weight but not its admissibility.

As amended in 1990.

B. Default by Lessor

§ 2A–508. Lessee's Remedies.

(1) If a lessor fails to deliver the goods in conformity to the lease contract (Section 2A–509) or repudiates the lease contract (Section 2A–402), or a lessee rightfully rejects the goods (Section 2A–509) or justifiably revokes acceptance of the goods (Section 2A–517), then with respect to any goods involved, and with respect to all of the goods if under an installment lease contract the value of the whole lease contract is substantially impaired (Section 2A–510), the lessor is in default under the lease contract and the lessee may:

(a) cancel the lease contract (Section 2A–505(1));

(b) recover so much of the rent and security as has been paid and is just under the circumstances;

(c) cover and recover damages as to all goods affected whether or not they have been identified to the lease contract (Sections 2A–518 and 2A–520), or recover damages for nondelivery (Sections 2A–519 and 2A–520);

(d) exercise any other rights or pursue any other remedies provided in the lease contract.

(2) If a lessor fails to deliver the goods in conformity to the lease contract or repudiates the lease contract, the lessee may also:

(a) if the goods have been identified, recover them (Section 2A–522); or

(b) in a proper case, obtain specific performance or replevy the goods (Section 2A–521).

(3) If a lessor is otherwise in default under a lease contract, the lessee may exercise the rights and pursue the remedies provided in the

lease contract, which may include a right to cancel the lease, and in Section 2A–519(3).

(4) If a lessor has breached a warranty, whether express or implied, the lessee may recover damages (Section 2A–519(4)).

(5) On rightful rejection or justifiable revocation of acceptance, a lessee has a security interest in goods in the lessee's possession or control for any rent and security that has been paid and any expenses reasonably incurred in their inspection, receipt, transportation, and care and custody and may hold those goods and dispose of them in good faith and in a commercially reasonable manner, subject to Section 2A–527(5).

(6) Subject to the provisions of Section 2A–407, a lessee, on notifying the lessor of the lessee's intention to do so, may deduct all or any part of the damages resulting from any default under the lease contract from any part of the rent still due under the same lease contract.

As amended in 1990.

§ 2A–509. Lessee's Rights on Improper Delivery; Rightful Rejection.

(1) Subject to the provisions of Section 2A–510 on default in installment lease contracts, if the goods or the tender or delivery fail in any respect to conform to the lease contract, the lessee may reject or accept the goods or accept any commercial unit or units and reject the rest of the goods.

(2) Rejection of goods is ineffective unless it is within a reasonable time after tender or delivery of the goods and the lessee seasonably notifies the lessor.

§ 2A–510. Installment Lease Contracts: Rejection and Default.

(1) Under an installment lease contract a lessee may reject any delivery that is nonconforming if the nonconformity substantially impairs the value of that delivery and cannot be cured or the nonconformity is a defect in the required documents; but if the nonconformity does not fall within subsection (2) and the lessor or the supplier gives adequate assurance of its cure, the lessee must accept that delivery.

(2) Whenever nonconformity or default with respect to one or more deliveries substantially impairs the value of the installment lease contract as a whole there is a default with respect to the whole. But, the aggrieved party reinstates the installment lease contract as a whole if the aggrieved party accepts a nonconforming delivery without seasonably notifying of cancellation or brings an action with respect only to past deliveries or demands performance as to future deliveries.

§ 2A–511. Merchant Lessee's Duties as to Rightfully Rejected Goods.

(1) Subject to any security interest of a lessee (Section 2A–508(5)), if a lessor or a supplier has no agent or place of business at the market of rejection, a merchant lessee, after rejection of goods in his [or her] possession or control, shall follow any reasonable instructions received from the lessor or the supplier with respect to the goods. In the absence of those instructions, a merchant lessee shall make reasonable efforts to sell, lease, or otherwise dispose of the goods for the lessor's account if they threaten to decline in value speedily. Instructions are not reasonable if on demand indemnity for expenses is not forthcoming.

(2) If a merchant lessee (subsection (1)) or any other lessee (Section 2A–512) disposes of goods, he [or she] is entitled to reimbursement either from the lessor or the supplier or out of the proceeds for reasonable expenses of caring for and disposing of the goods and, if the expenses include no disposition commission, to such commission as is usual in the trade, or if there is none, to a reasonable sum not exceeding 10 percent of the gross proceeds.

(3) In complying with this section or Section 2A–512, the lessee is held only to good faith. Good faith conduct hereunder is neither acceptance or conversion nor the basis of an action for damages.

(4) A purchaser who purchases in good faith from a lessee pursuant to this section or Section 2A–512 takes the goods free of any rights of the lessor and the supplier even though the lessee fails to comply with one or more of the requirements of this Article.

§ 2A–512. Lessee's Duties as to Rightfully Rejected Goods.

(1) Except as otherwise provided with respect to goods that threaten to decline in value speedily (Section 2A–511) and subject to any security interest of a lessee (Section 2A–508(5)):

(a) the lessee, after rejection of goods in the lessee's possession, shall hold them with reasonable care at the lessor's or the supplier's disposition for a reasonable time after the lessee's seasonable notification of rejection;

(b) if the lessor or the supplier gives no instructions within a reasonable time after notification of rejection, the lessee may store the rejected goods for the lessor's or the supplier's account or ship them to the lessor or the supplier or dispose of them for the lessor's or the supplier's account with reimbursement in the manner provided in Section 2A–511; but

(c) the lessee has no further obligations with regard to goods rightfully rejected.

(2) Action by the lessee pursuant to subsection (1) is not acceptance or conversion.

§ 2A–513. Cure by Lessor of Improper Tender or Delivery; Replacement.

(1) If any tender or delivery by the lessor or the supplier is rejected because nonconforming and the time for performance has not yet expired, the lessor or the supplier may seasonably notify the lessee of the lessor's or the supplier's intention to cure and may then make a conforming delivery within the time provided in the lease contract.

(2) If the lessee rejects a nonconforming tender that the lessor or the supplier had reasonable grounds to believe would be acceptable with or without money allowance, the lessor or the supplier may have a further reasonable time to substitute a conforming tender if he [or she] seasonably notifies the lessee.

§ 2A–514. Waiver of Lessee's Objections.

(1) In rejecting goods, a lessee's failure to state a particular defect that is ascertainable by reasonable inspection precludes the lessee from relying on the defect to justify rejection or to establish default:

(a) if, stated seasonably, the lessor or the supplier could have cured it (Section 2A–513); or

(b) between merchants if the lessor or the supplier after rejection has made a request in writing for a full and final written statement of all defects on which the lessee proposes to rely.

(2) A lessee's failure to reserve rights when paying rent or other consideration against documents precludes recovery of the payment for defects apparent on the face of the documents.

§ 2A–515. Acceptance of Goods.

(1) Acceptance of goods occurs after the lessee has had a reasonable opportunity to inspect the goods and

(a) the lessee signifies or acts with respect to the goods in a manner that signifies to the lessor or the supplier that the goods are conforming or that the lessee will take or retain them in spite of their nonconformity; or

(b) the lessee fails to make an effective rejection of the goods (Section 2A–509(2)).

(2) Acceptance of a part of any commercial unit is acceptance of that entire unit.

§ 2A–516. Effect of Acceptance of Goods; Notice of Default; Burden of Establishing Default after Acceptance; Notice of Claim or Litigation to Person Answerable Over.

(1) A lessee must pay rent for any goods accepted in accordance with the lease contract, with due allowance for goods rightfully rejected or not delivered.

(2) A lessee's acceptance of goods precludes rejection of the goods accepted. In the case of a finance lease, if made with knowledge of a nonconformity, acceptance cannot be revoked because of it. In any other case, if made with knowledge of a nonconformity, acceptance cannot be revoked because of it unless the acceptance was on the reasonable assumption that the nonconformity would be seasonably cured. Acceptance does not of itself impair any other remedy provided by this Article or the lease agreement for nonconformity.

(3) If a tender has been accepted:

(a) within a reasonable time after the lessee discovers or should have discovered any default, the lessee shall notify the lessor and the supplier, if any, or be barred from any remedy against the party notified;

(b) except in the case of a consumer lease, within a reasonable time after the lessee receives notice of litigation for infringement or the like (Section 2A–211) the lessee shall notify the lessor or be barred from any remedy over for liability established by the litigation; and

(c) the burden is on the lessee to establish any default.

(4) If a lessee is sued for breach of a warranty or other obligation for which a lessor or a supplier is answerable over the following apply:

(a) The lessee may give the lessor or the supplier, or both, written notice of the litigation. If the notice states that the person notified may come in and defend and that if the person notified does not do so that person will be bound in any action against that person by the lessee by any determination of fact common to the two litigations, then unless the person notified after seasonable receipt of the notice does come in and defend that person is so bound.

(b) The lessor or the supplier may demand in writing that the lessee turn over control of the litigation including settlement if the claim is one for infringement or the like (Section 2A–211) or else be barred from any remedy over. If the demand states that the lessor or the supplier agrees to bear all expense and to satisfy any adverse judgment, then unless the lessee after seasonable receipt of the demand does turn over control the lessee is so barred.

(5) Subsections (3) and (4) apply to any obligation of a lessee to hold the lessor or the supplier harmless against infringement or the like (Section 2A–211).
As amended in 1990.

§ 2A–517. Revocation of Acceptance of Goods.

(1) A lessee may revoke acceptance of a lot or commercial unit whose nonconformity substantially impairs its value to the lessee if the lessee has accepted it:

(a) except in the case of a finance lease, on the reasonable assumption that its nonconformity would be cured and it has not been seasonably cured; or

(b) without discovery of the nonconformity if the lessee's acceptance was reasonably induced either by the lessor's assurances or, except in the case of a finance lease, by the difficulty of discovery before acceptance.

(2) Except in the case of a finance lease that is not a consumer lease, a lessee may revoke acceptance of a lot or commercial unit if the lessor defaults under the lease contract and the default substantially impairs the value of that lot or commercial unit to the lessee.

(3) If the lease agreement so provides, the lessee may revoke acceptance of a lot or commercial unit because of other defaults by the lessor.

(4) Revocation of acceptance must occur within a reasonable time after the lessee discovers or should have discovered the ground for it and before any substantial change in condition of the goods which is not caused by the nonconformity. Revocation is not effective until the lessee notifies the lessor.

(5) A lessee who so revokes has the same rights and duties with regard to the goods involved as if the lessee had rejected them.
As amended in 1990.

§ 2A–518. Cover; Substitute Goods.

(1) After a default by a lessor under the lease contract of the type described in Section 2A–508(1), or, if agreed, after other default by the lessor, the lessee may cover by making any purchase or lease of or contract to purchase or lease goods in substitution for those due from the lessor.

(2) Except as otherwise provided with respect to damages liquidated in the lease agreement (Section 2A–504) or otherwise determined pursuant to agreement of the parties (Sections 1–102(3) and 2A–503), if a lessee's cover is by lease agreement substantially similar to the original lease agreement and the new lease agreement is made in good faith and in a commercially reasonable manner, the lessee may recover from the lessor as damages (i) the present value, as of the date of the commencement of the term of the new lease agreement, of the rent under the new lease agreement applicable to that period of the new lease term which is comparable to the then remaining term of the original lease agreement minus the present value as of the same date of the total rent for the then remaining lease term of the original lease agreement, and (ii) any incidental or consequential damages, less expenses saved in consequence of the lessor's default.

(3) If a lessee's cover is by lease agreement that for any reason does not qualify for treatment under subsection (2), or is by purchase or otherwise, the lessee may recover from the lessor as if the lessee had elected not to cover and Section 2A–519 governs.

As amended in 1990.

§ 2A–519. Lessee's Damages for Non-Delivery, Repudiation, Default, and Breach of Warranty in Regard to Accepted Goods.

(1) Except as otherwise provided with respect to damages liquidated in the lease agreement (Section 2A–504) or otherwise determined pursuant to agreement of the parties (Sections 1–102(3) and 2A–503), if a lessee elects not to cover or a lessee elects to cover and the cover is by lease agreement that for any reason does not qualify for treatment under Section 2A–518(2), or is by purchase or otherwise, the measure of damages for non-delivery or repudiation by the lessor or for rejection or revocation of acceptance by the lessee is the present value, as of the date of the default, of the then market rent minus the present value as of the same date of the original rent, computed for the remaining lease term of the original lease agreement, together with incidental and consequential damages, less expenses saved in consequence of the lessor's default.

(2) Market rent is to be determined as of the place for tender or, in cases of rejection after arrival or revocation of acceptance, as of the place of arrival.

(3) Except as otherwise agreed, if the lessee has accepted goods and given notification (Section 2A–516(3)), the measure of damages for non-conforming tender or delivery or other default by a lessor is the loss resulting in the ordinary course of events from the lessor's default as determined in any manner that is reasonable together with incidental and consequential damages, less expenses saved in consequence of the lessor's default.

(4) Except as otherwise agreed, the measure of damages for breach of warranty is the present value at the time and place of acceptance of the difference between the value of the use of the goods accepted and the value if they had been as warranted for the lease term, unless special circumstances show proximate damages of a different amount, together with incidental and consequential damages, less expenses saved in consequence of the lessor's default or breach of warranty.

As amended in 1990.

§ 2A–520. Lessee's Incidental and Consequential Damages.

(1) Incidental damages resulting from a lessor's default include expenses reasonably incurred in inspection, receipt, transportation, and care and custody of goods rightfully rejected or goods the acceptance of which is justifiably revoked, any commercially reasonable charges, expenses or commissions in connection with effecting cover, and any other reasonable expense incident to the default.

(2) Consequential damages resulting from a lessor's default include:

    (a) any loss resulting from general or particular requirements and needs of which the lessor at the time of contracting had reason to know and which could not reasonably be prevented by cover or otherwise; and

    (b) injury to person or property proximately resulting from any breach of warranty.

§ 2A–521. Lessee's Right to Specific Performance or Replevin.

(1) Specific performance may be decreed if the goods are unique or in other proper circumstances.

(2) A decree for specific performance may include any terms and conditions as to payment of the rent, damages, or other relief that the court deems just.

(3) A lessee has a right of replevin, detinue, sequestration, claim and delivery, or the like for goods identified to the lease contract if after reasonable effort the lessee is unable to effect cover for those goods or the circumstances reasonably indicate that the effort will be unavailing.

§ 2A–522. Lessee's Right to Goods on Lessor's Insolvency.

(1) Subject to subsection (2) and even though the goods have not been shipped, a lessee who has paid a part or all of the rent and security for goods identified to a lease contract (Section 2A–217) on making and keeping good a tender of any unpaid portion of the rent and security due under the lease contract may recover the goods identified from the lessor if the lessor becomes insolvent within 10 days after receipt of the first installment of rent and security.

(2) A lessee acquires the right to recover goods identified to a lease contract only if they conform to the lease contract.

C. Default by Lessee

§ 2A–523. Lessor's Remedies.

(1) If a lessee wrongfully rejects or revokes acceptance of goods or fails to make a payment when due or repudiates with respect to a part or the whole, then, with respect to any goods involved, and with respect to all of the goods if under an installment lease contract the value of the whole lease contract is substantially impaired (Section 2A–510), the lessee is in default under the lease contract and the lessor may:

    (a) cancel the lease contract (Section 2A–505(1));

    (b) proceed respecting goods not identified to the lease contract (Section 2A–524);

    (c) withhold delivery of the goods and take possession of goods previously delivered (Section 2A–525);

    (d) stop delivery of the goods by any bailee (Section 2A–526);

    (e) dispose of the goods and recover damages (Section 2A–527), or retain the goods and recover damages (Section 2A–528), or in a proper case recover rent (Section 2A–529)

    (f) exercise any other rights or pursue any other remedies provided in the lease contract.

(2) If a lessor does not fully exercise a right or obtain a remedy to which the lessor is entitled under subsection (1), the lessor may recover the loss resulting in the ordinary course of events from the lessee's default as determined in any reasonable manner, together with incidental damages, less expenses saved in consequence of the lessee's default.

(3) If a lessee is otherwise in default under a lease contract, the lessor may exercise the rights and pursue the remedies provided in the lease contract, which may include a right to cancel the lease. In addition, unless otherwise provided in the lease contract:

    (a) if the default substantially impairs the value of the lease contract to the lessor, the lessor may exercise the rights and pursue the remedies provided in subsections (1) or (2); or

(b) if the default does not substantially impair the value of the lease contract to the lessor, the lessor may recover as provided in subsection (2).

As amended in 1990.

§ 2A–524. Lessor's Right to Identify Goods to Lease Contract.

(1) After default by the lessee under the lease contract of the type described in Section 2A–523(1) or 2A–523(3)(a) or, if agreed, after other default by the lessee, the lessor may:

(a) identify to the lease contract conforming goods not already identified if at the time the lessor learned of the default they were in the lessor's or the supplier's possession or control; and

(b) dispose of goods (Section 2A–527(1)) that demonstrably have been intended for the particular lease contract even though those goods are unfinished.

(2) If the goods are unfinished, in the exercise of reasonable commercial judgment for the purposes of avoiding loss and of effective realization, an aggrieved lessor or the supplier may either complete manufacture and wholly identify the goods to the lease contract or cease manufacture and lease, sell, or otherwise dispose of the goods for scrap or salvage value or proceed in any other reasonable manner.

As amended in 1990.

§ 2A–525. Lessor's Right to Possession of Goods.

(1) If a lessor discovers the lessee to be insolvent, the lessor may refuse to deliver the goods.

(2) After a default by the lessee under the lease contract of the type described in Section 2A–523(1) or 2A–523(3)(a) or, if agreed, after other default by the lessee, the lessor has the right to take possession of the goods. If the lease contract so provides, the lessor may require the lessee to assemble the goods and make them available to the lessor at a place to be designated by the lessor which is reasonably convenient to both parties. Without removal, the lessor may render unusable any goods employed in trade or business, and may dispose of goods on the lessee's premises (Section 2A–527).

(3) The lessor may proceed under subsection (2) without judicial process if that can be done without breach of the peace or the lessor may proceed by action.

As amended in 1990.

§ 2A–526. Lessor's Stoppage of Delivery in Transit or Otherwise.

(1) A lessor may stop delivery of goods in the possession of a carrier or other bailee if the lessor discovers the lessee to be insolvent and may stop delivery of carload, truckload, planeload, or larger shipments of express or freight if the lessee repudiates or fails to make a payment due before delivery, whether for rent, security or otherwise under the lease contract, or for any other reason the lessor has a right to withhold or take possession of the goods.

(2) In pursuing its remedies under subsection (1), the lessor may stop delivery until

(a) receipt of the goods by the lessee;

(b) acknowledgment to the lessee by any bailee of the goods, except a carrier, that the bailee holds the goods for the lessee; or

(c) such an acknowledgment to the lessee by a carrier via reshipment or as warehouseman.

(3) (a) To stop delivery, a lessor shall so notify as to enable the bailee by reasonable diligence to prevent delivery of the goods.

(b) After notification, the bailee shall hold and deliver the goods according to the directions of the lessor, but the lessor is liable to the bailee for any ensuing charges or damages.

(c) A carrier who has issued a nonnegotiable bill of lading is not obliged to obey a notification to stop received from a person other than the consignor.

§ 2A–527. Lessor's Rights to Dispose of Goods.

(1) After a default by a lessee under the lease contract of the type described in Section 2A–523(1) or 2A–523(3)(a) or after the lessor refuses to deliver or takes possession of goods (Section 2A–525 or 2A–526), or, if agreed, after other default by a lessee, the lessor may dispose of the goods concerned or the undelivered balance thereof by lease, sale, or otherwise.

(2) Except as otherwise provided with respect to damages liquidated in the lease agreement (Section 2A–504) or otherwise determined pursuant to agreement of the parties (Sections 1–102(3) and 2A–503), if the disposition is by lease agreement substantially similar to the original lease agreement and the new lease agreement is made in good faith and in a commercially reasonable manner, the lessor may recover from the lessee as damages (i) accrued and unpaid rent as of the date of the commencement of the term of the new lease agreement, (ii) the present value, as of the same date, of the total rent for the then remaining lease term of the original lease agreement minus the present value, as of the same date, of the rent under the new lease agreement applicable to that period of the new lease term which is comparable to the then remaining term of the original lease agreement, and (iii) any incidental damages allowed under Section 2A–530, less expenses saved in consequence of the lessee's default.

(3) If the lessor's disposition is by lease agreement that for any reason does not qualify for treatment under subsection (2), or is by sale or otherwise, the lessor may recover from the lessee as if the lessor had elected not to dispose of the goods and Section 2A–528 governs.

(4) A subsequent buyer or lessee who buys or leases from the lessor in good faith for value as a result of a disposition under this section takes the goods free of the original lease contract and any rights of the original lessee even though the lessor fails to comply with one or more of the requirements of this Article.

(5) The lessor is not accountable to the lessee for any profit made on any disposition. A lessee who has rightfully rejected or justifiably revoked acceptance shall account to the lessor for any excess over the amount of the lessee's security interest (Section 2A–508(5)).

As amended in 1990.

§ 2A–528. Lessor's Damages for Non-acceptance, Failure to Pay, Repudiation, or Other Default.

(1) Except as otherwise provided with respect to damages liquidated in the lease agreement (Section 2A–504) or otherwise determined pursuant to agreement of the parties (Section 1–102(3) and 2A–503), if a lessor elects to retain the goods or a lessor elects to dispose of the goods and the disposition is by lease agreement that for any reason does not qualify for treatment under Section 2A–527(2), or is by sale or otherwise, the lessor may recover from the lessee as damages for a default of the type described in Section 2A–523(1) or 2A–523(3)(a),

or if agreed, for other default of the lessee, (i) accrued and unpaid rent as of the date of the default if the lessee has never taken possession of the goods, or, if the lessee has taken possession of the goods, as of the date the lessor repossesses the goods or an earlier date on which the lessee makes a tender of the goods to the lessor, (ii) the present value as of the date determined under clause (i) of the total rent for the then remaining lease term of the original lease agreement minus the present value as of the same date of the market rent as the place where the goods are located computed for the same lease term, and (iii) any incidental damages allowed under Section 2A–530, less expenses saved in consequence of the lessee's default.

(2) If the measure of damages provided in subsection (1) is inadequate to put a lessor in as good a position as performance would have, the measure of damages is the present value of the profit, including reasonable overhead, the lessor would have made from full performance by the lessee, together with any incidental damages allowed under Section 2A–530, due allowance for costs reasonably incurred and due credit for payments or proceeds of disposition.

As amended in 1990.

§ 2A–529. **Lessor's Action for the Rent.**

(1) After default by the lessee under the lease contract of the type described in Section 2A–523(1) or 2A–523(3)(a) or, if agreed, after other default by the lessee, if the lessor complies with subsection (2), the lessor may recover from the lessee as damages:

    (a) for goods accepted by the lessee and not repossessed by or tendered to the lessor, and for conforming goods lost or damaged within a commercially reasonable time after risk of loss passes to the lessee (Section 2A–219), (i) accrued and unpaid rent as of the date of entry of judgment in favor of the lessor (ii) the present value as of the same date of the rent for the then remaining lease term of the lease agreement, and (iii) any incidental damages allowed under Section 2A–530, less expenses saved in consequence of the lessee's default; and

    (b) for goods identified to the lease contract if the lessor is unable after reasonable effort to dispose of them at a reasonable price or the circumstances reasonably indicate that effort will be unavailing, (i) accrued and unpaid rent as of the date of entry of judgment in favor of the lessor, (ii) the present value as of the same date of the rent for the then remaining lease term of the lease agreement, and (iii) any incidental damages allowed under Section 2A–530, less expenses saved in consequence of the lessee's default.

(2) Except as provided in subsection (3), the lessor shall hold for the lessee for the remaining lease term of the lease agreement any goods that have been identified to the lease contract and are in the lessor's control.

(3) The lessor may dispose of the goods at any time before collection of the judgment for damages obtained pursuant to subsection (1). If the disposition is before the end of the remaining lease term of the lease agreement, the lessor's recovery against the lessee for damages is governed by Section 2A–527 or Section 2A–528, and the lessor will cause an appropriate credit to be provided against a judgment for damages to the extent that the amount of the judgment exceeds the recovery available pursuant to Section 2A–527 or 2A–528.

(4) Payment of the judgment for damages obtained pursuant to subsection (1) entitles the lessee to the use and possession of the goods not then disposed of for the remaining lease term of and in accordance with the lease agreement.

(5) After default by the lessee under the lease contract of the type described in Section 2A–523(1) or Section 2A–523(3)(a) or, if agreed, after other default by the lessee, a lessor who is held not entitled to rent under this section must nevertheless be awarded damages for non-acceptance under Sections 2A–527 and 2A–528.

As amended in 1990.

§ 2A–530. **Lessor's Incidental Damages.**

Incidental damages to an aggrieved lessor include any commercially reasonable charges, expenses, or commissions incurred in stopping delivery, in the transportation, care and custody of goods after the lessee's default, in connection with return or disposition of the goods, or otherwise resulting from the default.

§ 2A–531. **Standing to Sue Third Parties for Injury to Goods.**

(1) If a third party so deals with goods that have been identified to a lease contract as to cause actionable injury to a party to the lease contract (a) the lessor has a right of action against the third party, and (b) the lessee also has a right of action against the third party if the lessee:

    (i) has a security interest in the goods;

    (ii) has an insurable interest in the goods; or

    (iii) bears the risk of loss under the lease contract or has since the injury assumed that risk as against the lessor and the goods have been converted or destroyed.

(2) If at the time of the injury the party plaintiff did not bear the risk of loss as against the other party to the lease contract and there is no arrangement between them for disposition of the recovery, his [or her] suit or settlement, subject to his [or her] own interest, is as a fiduciary for the other party to the lease contract.

(3) Either party with the consent of the other may sue for the benefit of whom it may concern.

§ 2A–532. **Lessor's Rights to Residual Interest.**

In addition to any other recovery permitted by this Article or other law, the lessor may recover from the lessee an amount that will fully compensate the lessor for any loss of or damage to the lessor's residual interest in the goods caused by the default of the lessee.

As added in 1990.

APPENDIX D
The Sarbanes-Oxley Act of 2002 (Excerpts and Explanatory Comments)

Note: The author's explanatory comments appear in italics following the excerpt from each section.

SECTION 302
Corporate responsibility for financial reports[1]

(a) Regulations required

The Commission shall, by rule, require, for each company filing periodic reports under section 13(a) or 15(d) of the Securities Exchange Act of 1934 (15 U.S.C. 78m, 78o(d)), that the principal executive officer or officers and the principal financial officer or officers, or persons performing similar functions, certify in each annual or quarterly report filed or submitted under either such section of such Act that—

(1) the signing officer has reviewed the report;

(2) based on the officer's knowledge, the report does not contain any untrue statement of a material fact or omit to state a material fact necessary in order to make the statements made, in light of the circumstances under which such statements were made, not misleading;

(3) based on such officer's knowledge, the financial statements, and other financial information included in the report, fairly present in all material respects the financial condition and results of operations of the issuer as of, and for, the periods presented in the report;

(4) the signing officers—

(A) are responsible for establishing and maintaining internal controls;

(B) have designed such internal controls to ensure that material information relating to the issuer and its consolidated subsidiaries is made known to such officers by others within those entities, particularly during the period in which the periodic reports are being prepared;

(C) have evaluated the effectiveness of the issuer's internal controls as of a date within 90 days prior to the report; and

(D) have presented in the report their conclusions about the effectiveness of their internal controls based on their evaluation as of that date;

(5) the signing officers have disclosed to the issuer's auditors and the audit committee of the board of directors (or persons fulfilling the equivalent function)—

(A) all significant deficiencies in the design or operation of internal controls which could adversely affect the issuer's ability to record, process, summarize, and report financial data and have identified for the issuer's auditors any material weaknesses in internal controls; and

(B) any fraud, whether or not material, that involves management or other employees who have a significant role in the issuer's internal controls; and

(6) the signing officers have indicated in the report whether or not there were significant changes in internal controls or in other factors that could significantly affect internal controls subsequent to the date of their evaluation, including any corrective actions with regard to significant deficiencies and material weaknesses.

(b) Foreign reincorporations have no effect

Nothing in this section shall be interpreted or applied in any way to allow any issuer to lessen the legal force of the statement required under this section, by an issuer having reincorporated or having engaged in any other transaction that resulted in the transfer of the corporate domicile or offices of the issuer from inside the United States to outside of the United States.

(c) Deadline

The rules required by subsection (a) of this section shall be effective not later than 30 days after July 30, 2002.

*　　*　　*　　*

EXPLANATORY COMMENTS: *Section 302 requires the chief executive officer (CEO) and chief financial officer (CFO) of each public company to certify that they have reviewed the company's quarterly and annual reports to be filed with the Securities and Exchange Commission (SEC). The CEO and CFO must certify that, based on their knowledge, the reports do not contain any untrue statement of a material fact or any half-truth that would make the report misleading, and that the information contained in the reports fairly presents the company's financial condition.*

In addition, this section also requires the CEO and CFO to certify that they have created and designed an internal control system for their company and have recently evaluated that system to ensure that it is effectively providing them with relevant and accurate financial information. If the signing officers have found any significant deficiencies or weaknesses in the company's system or have discovered any evidence of fraud, they must have reported the situation, and any corrective actions they have taken, to the auditors and the audit committee.

---

1. This section of the Sarbanes-Oxley Act is codified at 15 U.S.C. Section 7241.

SECTION 306

Insider trades during pension fund blackout periods[2]

(a) Prohibition of insider trading during pension fund blackout periods

(1) In general

Except to the extent otherwise provided by rule of the Commission pursuant to paragraph (3), it shall be unlawful for any director or executive officer of an issuer of any equity security (other than an exempted security), directly or indirectly, to purchase, sell, or otherwise acquire or transfer any equity security of the issuer (other than an exempted security) during any blackout period with respect to such equity security if such director or officer acquires such equity security in connection with his or her service or employment as a director or executive officer.

(2) Remedy

(A) In general

Any profit realized by a director or executive officer referred to in paragraph (1) from any purchase, sale, or other acquisition or transfer in violation of this subsection shall inure to and be recoverable by the issuer, irrespective of any intention on the part of such director or executive officer in entering into the transaction.

(B) Actions to recover profits

An action to recover profits in accordance with this subsection may be instituted at law or in equity in any court of competent jurisdiction by the issuer, or by the owner of any security of the issuer in the name and in behalf of the issuer if the issuer fails or refuses to bring such action within 60 days after the date of request, or fails diligently to prosecute the action thereafter, except that no such suit shall be brought more than 2 years after the date on which such profit was realized.

(3) Rulemaking authorized

The Commission shall, in consultation with the Secretary of Labor, issue rules to clarify the application of this subsection and to prevent evasion thereof. Such rules shall provide for the application of the requirements of paragraph (1) with respect to entities treated as a single employer with respect to an issuer under section 414(b), (c), (m), or (o) of Title 26 to the extent necessary to clarify the application of such requirements and to prevent evasion thereof. Such rules may also provide for appropriate exceptions from the requirements of this subsection, including exceptions for purchases pursuant to an automatic dividend reinvestment program or purchases or sales made pursuant to an advance election.

(4) Blackout period

For purposes of this subsection, the term "blackout period", with respect to the equity securities of any issuer—

(A) means any period of more than 3 consecutive business days during which the ability of not fewer than 50 percent of the participants or beneficiaries under all individual account plans maintained by the issuer to purchase, sell, or otherwise acquire

or transfer an interest in any equity of such issuer held in such an individual account plan is temporarily suspended by the issuer or by a fiduciary of the plan; and

(B) does not include, under regulations which shall be prescribed by the Commission—

(i) a regularly scheduled period in which the participants and beneficiaries may not purchase, sell, or otherwise acquire or transfer an interest in any equity of such issuer, if such period is—

(I) incorporated into the individual account plan; and

(II) timely disclosed to employees before becoming participants under the individual account plan or as a subsequent amendment to the plan; or

(ii) any suspension described in subparagraph (A) that is imposed solely in connection with persons becoming participants or beneficiaries, or ceasing to be participants or beneficiaries, in an individual account plan by reason of a corporate merger, acquisition, divestiture, or similar transaction involving the plan or plan sponsor.

(5) Individual account plan

For purposes of this subsection, the term "individual account plan" has the meaning provided in section 1002(34) of Title 29, except that such term shall not include a one-participant retirement plan (within the meaning of section 1021(i)(8)(B) of Title 29).

(6) Notice to directors, executive officers, and the Commission

In any case in which a director or executive officer is subject to the requirements of this subsection in connection with a blackout period (as defined in paragraph (4)) with respect to any equity securities, the issuer of such equity securities shall timely notify such director or officer and the Securities and Exchange Commission of such blackout period.

* * * *

EXPLANATORY COMMENTS: *Corporate pension funds typically prohibit employees from trading shares of the corporation during periods when the pension fund is undergoing significant change. Prior to 2002, however, these blackout periods did not affect the corporation's executives, who frequently received shares of the corporate stock as part of their compensation. During the collapse of Enron, for example, its pension plan was scheduled to change administrators at a time when Enron's stock price was falling. Enron's employees therefore could not sell their shares while the price was dropping, but its executives could and did sell their stock, consequently avoiding some of the losses. Section 306 was Congress's solution to the basic unfairness of this situation. This section of the act required the SEC to issue rules that prohibit any director or executive officer from trading during pension fund blackout periods. (The SEC later issued these rules, entitled Regulation Blackout Trading Restriction, or Reg BTR.) Section 306 also provided shareholders with a right to file a shareholder's derivative suit against officers and directors who have profited from trading during these blackout periods (provided that the corporation has failed to bring a suit). The officer or director can be forced to return to the corporation any profits received, regardless of whether the director or officer acted with bad intent.*

---

2. Codified at 15 U.S.C. Section 7244.

SECTION 402

Periodical and other reports[3]

* * * *

(i) Accuracy of financial reports

Each financial report that contains financial statements, and that is required to be prepared in accordance with (or reconciled to) generally accepted accounting principles under this chapter and filed with the Commission shall reflect all material correcting adjustments that have been identified by a registered public accounting firm in accordance with generally accepted accounting principles and the rules and regulations of the Commission.

(j) Off-balance sheet transactions

Not later than 180 days after July 30, 2002, the Commission shall issue final rules providing that each annual and quarterly financial report required to be filed with the Commission shall disclose all material off-balance sheet transactions, arrangements, obligations (including contingent obligations), and other relationships of the issuer with unconsolidated entities or other persons, that may have a material current or future effect on financial condition, changes in financial condition, results of operations, liquidity, capital expenditures, capital resources, or significant components of revenues or expenses.

(k) Prohibition on personal loans to executives

(1) In general

It shall be unlawful for any issuer (as defined in section 7201 of this title), directly or indirectly, including through any subsidiary, to extend or maintain credit, to arrange for the extension of credit, or to renew an extension of credit, in the form of a personal loan to or for any director or executive officer (or equivalent thereof) of that issuer. An extension of credit maintained by the issuer on July 30, 2002, shall not be subject to the provisions of this subsection, provided that there is no material modification to any term of any such extension of credit or any renewal of any such extension of credit on or after July 30, 2002.

(2) Limitation

Paragraph (1) does not preclude any home improvement and manufactured home loans (as that term is defined in section 1464 of Title 12), consumer credit (as defined in section 1602 of this title), or any extension of credit under an open end credit plan (as defined in section 1602 of this title), or a charge card (as defined in section 1637(c)(4)(e) of this title), or any extension of credit by a broker or dealer registered under section 78o of this title to an employee of that broker or dealer to buy, trade, or carry securities, that is permitted under rules or regulations of the Board of Governors of the Federal Reserve System pursuant to section 78g of this title (other than an extension of credit that would be used to purchase the stock of that issuer), that is—

(A) made or provided in the ordinary course of the consumer credit business of such issuer;

(B) of a type that is generally made available by such issuer to the public; and

(C) made by such issuer on market terms, or terms that are no more favorable than those offered by the issuer to the general public for such extensions of credit.

(3) Rule of construction for certain loans

Paragraph (1) does not apply to any loan made or maintained by an insured depository institution (as defined in section 1813 of Title 12), if the loan is subject to the insider lending restrictions of section 375b of Title 12.

(l) Real time issuer disclosures

Each issuer reporting under subsection (a) of this section or section 78o(d) of this title shall disclose to the public on a rapid and current basis such additional information concerning material changes in the financial condition or operations of the issuer, in plain English, which may include trend and qualitative information and graphic presentations, as the Commission determines, by rule, is necessary or useful for the protection of investors and in the public interest.

EXPLANATORY COMMENTS: *Corporate executives during the Enron era typically received extremely large salaries, significant bonuses, and abundant stock options, even when the companies for which they worked were suffering. Executives were also routinely given personal loans from corporate funds, many of which were never paid back. The average large company during that period loaned almost $1 million a year to top executives, and some companies, including Tyco International and Adelphia Communications Corporation, loaned hundreds of millions of dollars to their executives every year. Section 402 amended the 1934 Securities Exchange Act to prohibit public companies from making personal loans to executive officers and directors. There are a few exceptions to this prohibition, such as home-improvement loans made in the ordinary course of business. Note also that while loans are forbidden, outright gifts are not. A corporation is free to give gifts to its executives, including cash, provided that these gifts are disclosed on its financial reports. The idea is that corporate directors will be deterred from making substantial gifts to their executives by the disclosure requirement—particularly if the corporation's financial condition is questionable—because making such gifts could be perceived as abusing their authority.*

SECTION 403

Directors, officers, and principal stockholders[4]

(a) Disclosures required

(1) Directors, officers, and principal stockholders required to file

Every person who is directly or indirectly the beneficial owner of more than 10 percent of any class of any equity security (other than an exempted security) which is registered pursuant to section 78l of this title, or who is a director or an officer of the issuer of such security, shall file the statements required by this subsection with the Commission (and, if such security is registered on a national securities exchange, also with the exchange).

(2) Time of filing

The statements required by this subsection shall be filed—

---

3. This section of the Sarbanes-Oxley Act amended some of the provisions of the 1934 Securities Exchange Act and added the paragraphs reproduced here at 15 U.S.C. Section 78m.

---

4. This section of the Sarbanes-Oxley Act amended the disclosure provisions of the 1934 Securities Exchange Act, at 15 U.S.C. Section 78p.

(A) at the time of the registration of such security on a national securities exchange or by the effective date of a registration statement filed pursuant to section 78l(g) of this title;

(B) within 10 days after he or she becomes such beneficial owner, director, or officer;

(C) if there has been a change in such ownership, or if such person shall have purchased or sold a security-based swap agreement (as defined in section 206(b) of the Gramm-Leach-Bliley Act (15 U.S.C. 78c note)) involving such equity security, before the end of the second business day following the day on which the subject transaction has been executed, or at such other time as the Commission shall establish, by rule, in any case in which the Commission determines that such 2-day period is not feasible.

(3) Contents of statements

A statement filed—

(A) under subparagraph (A) or (B) of paragraph (2) shall contain a statement of the amount of all equity securities of such issuer of which the filing person is the beneficial owner; and

(B) under subparagraph (C) of such paragraph shall indicate ownership by the filing person at the date of filing, any such changes in such ownership, and such purchases and sales of the security-based swap agreements as have occurred since the most recent such filing under such subparagraph.

(4) Electronic filing and availability

Beginning not later than 1 year after July 30, 2002—

(A) a statement filed under subparagraph (C) of paragraph (2) shall be filed electronically;

(B) the Commission shall provide each such statement on a publicly accessible Internet site not later than the end of the business day following that filing; and

(C) the issuer (if the issuer maintains a corporate website) shall provide that statement on that corporate website, not later than the end of the business day following that filing.

* * * *

EXPLANATORY COMMENTS: *This section dramatically shortens the time period provided in the Securities Exchange Act of 1934 for disclosing transactions by insiders. The prior law stated that most transactions had to be reported within ten days of the beginning of the following month, although certain transactions did not have to be reported until the following fiscal year (within the first forty-five days). Because some of the insider trading that occurred during the Enron fiasco did not have to be disclosed (and was therefore not discovered) until long after the transactions, Congress added this section to reduce the time period for making disclosures. Under Section 403, most transactions by insiders must be electronically filed with the SEC within two business days. Also, any company that maintains a Web site must post these SEC filings on its site by the end of the next business day. Congress enacted this section in the belief that if insiders are required to file reports of their transactions promptly with the SEC, companies will do more to police themselves and prevent insider trading.*

SECTION 404

Management assessment of internal controls[5]

(a) Rules required

The Commission shall prescribe rules requiring each annual report required by section 78m(a) or 78o(d) of this title to contain an internal control report, which shall—

(1) state the responsibility of management for establishing and maintaining an adequate internal control structure and procedures for financial reporting; and

(2) contain an assessment, as of the end of the most recent fiscal year of the issuer, of the effectiveness of the internal control structure and procedures of the issuer for financial reporting.

(b) Internal control evaluation and reporting

With respect to the internal control assessment required by subsection (a) of this section, each registered public accounting firm that prepares or issues the audit report for the issuer shall attest to, and report on, the assessment made by the management of the issuer. An attestation made under this subsection shall be made in accordance with standards for attestation engagements issued or adopted by the Board. Any such attestation shall not be the subject of a separate engagement.

* * * *

EXPLANATORY COMMENTS: *This section was enacted to prevent corporate executives from claiming they were ignorant of significant errors in their companies' financial reports. For instance, several CEOs testified before Congress that they simply had no idea that the corporations' financial statements were off by billions of dollars. Congress therefore passed Section 404, which requires each annual report to contain a description and assessment of the company's internal control structure and financial reporting procedures. The section also requires that an audit be conducted of the internal control assessment, as well as the financial statements contained in the report. This section goes hand in hand with Section 302 (which, as discussed previously, requires various certifications attesting to the accuracy of the information in financial reports).*

Section 404 has been one of the more controversial and expensive provisions in the Sarbanes-Oxley Act because it requires companies to assess their own internal financial controls to make sure that their financial statements are reliable and accurate. A corporation might need to set up a disclosure committee and a coordinator, establish codes of conduct for accounting and financial personnel, create documentation procedures, provide training, and outline the individuals who are responsible for performing each of the procedures. Companies that were already well managed have not experienced substantial difficulty complying with this section. Other companies, however, have spent millions of dollars setting up, documenting, and evaluating their internal financial control systems. Although initially creating the internal financial control system is a one-time-only expense, the costs of maintaining and evaluating it are ongoing. Some corporations that spent considerable sums complying with Section 404 have been able to offset these costs by discovering and correcting inefficiencies or frauds within their systems. Nevertheless, it is unlikely that any corporation will find compliance with this section to be inexpensive.

---

5. Codified at 15 U.S.C. Section 7262.

SECTION 802(a)

Destruction, alteration, or falsification of records in Federal investigations and bankruptcy[6]

Whoever knowingly alters, destroys, mutilates, conceals, covers up, falsifies, or makes a false entry in any record, document, or tangible object with the intent to impede, obstruct, or influence the investigation or proper administration of any matter within the jurisdiction of any department or agency of the United States or any case filed under title 11, or in relation to or contemplation of any such matter or case, shall be fined under this title, imprisoned not more than 20 years, or both.

Destruction of corporate audit records[7]

(a) (1) Any accountant who conducts an audit of an issuer of securities to which section 10A(a) of the Securities Exchange Act of 1934 (15 U.S.C. 78j-1(a)) applies, shall maintain all audit or review workpapers for a period of 5 years from the end of the fiscal period in which the audit or review was concluded.

(2) The Securities and Exchange Commission shall promulgate, within 180 days, after adequate notice and an opportunity for comment, such rules and regulations, as are reasonably necessary, relating to the retention of relevant records such as workpapers, documents that form the basis of an audit or review, memoranda, correspondence, communications, other documents, and records (including electronic records) which are created, sent, or received in connection with an audit or review and contain conclusions, opinions, analyses, or financial data relating to such an audit or review, which is conducted by any accountant who conducts an audit of an issuer of securities to which section 10A(a) of the Securities Exchange Act of 1934 (15 U.S.C. 78j-1(a)) applies. The Commission may, from time to time, amend or supplement the rules and regulations that it is required to promulgate under this section, after adequate notice and an opportunity for comment, in order to ensure that such rules and regulations adequately comport with the purposes of this section.

(b) Whoever knowingly and willfully violates subsection (a)(1), or any rule or regulation promulgated by the Securities and Exchange Commission under subsection (a)(2), shall be fined under this title, imprisoned not more than 10 years, or both.

(c) Nothing in this section shall be deemed to diminish or relieve any person of any other duty or obligation imposed by Federal or State law or regulation to maintain, or refrain from destroying, any document.

*　　*　　*　　*

EXPLANATORY COMMENTS: *Section 802(a) enacted two new statutes that punish those who alter or destroy documents. The first statute is not specifically limited to securities fraud cases. It provides that anyone who alters, destroys, or falsifies records in federal investigations or bankruptcy may be criminally prosecuted and sentenced to a fine or to up to twenty years in prison, or both. The second statute requires auditors of public companies to keep all audit or review working papers for five years but expressly allows the SEC to amend or supplement these requirements as it sees fit. The SEC has, in fact,* amended this section by issuing a rule that requires auditors who audit reporting companies to retain working papers for seven years from the conclusion of the review. Section 802(a) further provides that anyone who knowingly and willfully violates this statute is subject to criminal prosecution and can be sentenced to a fine, imprisoned for up to ten years, or both if convicted.

This portion of the Sarbanes-Oxley Act implicitly recognizes that persons who are under investigation often are tempted to respond by destroying or falsifying documents that might prove their complicity in wrongdoing. The severity of the punishment should provide a strong incentive for these individuals to resist the temptation.

SECTION 804

Time limitations on the commencement of civil actions arising under Acts of Congress[8]

(a) Except as otherwise provided by law, a civil action arising under an Act of Congress enacted after the date of the enactment of this section may not be commenced later than 4 years after the cause of action accrues.

(b) Notwithstanding subsection (a), a private right of action that involves a claim of fraud, deceit, manipulation, or contrivance in contravention of a regulatory requirement concerning the securities laws, as defined in section 3(a)(47) of the Securities Exchange Act of 1934 (15 U.S.C. 78c(a)(47)), may be brought not later than the earlier of—

(1) 2 years after the discovery of the facts constituting the violation; or

(2) 5 years after such violation.

*　　*　　*　　*

EXPLANATORY COMMENTS: *Prior to the enactment of this section, Section 10(b) of the Securities Exchange Act of 1934 had no express statute of limitations. The courts generally required plaintiffs to have filed suit within one year from the date that they should (using due diligence) have discovered that a fraud had been committed but no later than three years after the fraud occurred. Section 804 extends this period by specifying that plaintiffs must file a lawsuit within two years after they discover (or should have discovered) a fraud but no later than five years after the fraud's occurrence. This provision has prevented the courts from dismissing numerous securities fraud lawsuits.*

SECTION 806

Civil action to protect against retaliation in fraud cases[9]

(a) Whistleblower protection for employees of publicly traded companies.—

No company with a class of securities registered under section 12 of the Securities Exchange Act of 1934 (15 U.S.C. 78l), or that is required to file reports under section 15(d) of the Securities Exchange Act of 1934 (15 U.S.C. 78o(d)), or any officer, employee, contractor, subcontractor, or agent of such company, may discharge, demote, suspend, threaten, harass, or in any other manner discriminate against an

---

6. Codified at 15 U.S.C. Section 1519.
7. Codified at 15 U.S.C. Section 1520.

8. Codified at 28 U.S.C. Section 1658.
9. Codified at 18 U.S.C. Section 1514A.

employee in the terms and conditions of employment because of any lawful act done by the employee—

(1) to provide information, cause information to be provided, or otherwise assist in an investigation regarding any conduct which the employee reasonably believes constitutes a violation of section 1341, 1343, 1344, or 1348, any rule or regulation of the Securities and Exchange Commission, or any provision of Federal law relating to fraud against shareholders, when the information or assistance is provided to or the investigation is conducted by—

(A) a Federal regulatory or law enforcement agency;

(B) any Member of Congress or any committee of Congress; or

(C) a person with supervisory authority over the employee (or such other person working for the employer who has the authority to investigate, discover, or terminate misconduct); or

(2) to file, cause to be filed, testify, participate in, or otherwise assist in a proceeding filed or about to be filed (with any knowledge of the employer) relating to an alleged violation of section 1341, 1343, 1344, or 1348, any rule or regulation of the Securities and Exchange Commission, or any provision of Federal law relating to fraud against shareholders.

(b) Enforcement action.—

(1) In general.—A person who alleges discharge or other discrimination by any person in violation of subsection (a) may seek relief under subsection (c), by—

(A) filing a complaint with the Secretary of Labor; or

(B) if the Secretary has not issued a final decision within 180 days of the filing of the complaint and there is no showing that such delay is due to the bad faith of the claimant, bringing an action at law or equity for de novo review in the appropriate district court of the United States, which shall have jurisdiction over such an action without regard to the amount in controversy.

(2) Procedure.—

(A) In general.—An action under paragraph (1)(A) shall be governed under the rules and procedures set forth in section 42121(b) of title 49, United States Code.

(B) Exception.—Notification made under section 42121(b)(1) of title 49, United States Code, shall be made to the person named in the complaint and to the employer.

(C) Burdens of proof.—An action brought under paragraph (1)(B) shall be governed by the legal burdens of proof set forth in section 42121(b) of title 49, United States Code.

(D) Statute of limitations.—An action under paragraph (1) shall be commenced not later than 90 days after the date on which the violation occurs.

(c) Remedies.—

(1) In general.—An employee prevailing in any action under subsection (b)(1) shall be entitled to all relief necessary to make the employee whole.

(2) Compensatory damages.—Relief for any action under paragraph (1) shall include—

(A) reinstatement with the same seniority status that the employee would have had, but for the discrimination;

(B) the amount of back pay, with interest; and

(C) compensation for any special damages sustained as a result of the discrimination, including litigation costs, expert witness fees, and reasonable attorney fees.

(d) Rights retained by employee.—Nothing in this section shall be deemed to diminish the rights, privileges, or remedies of any employee under any Federal or State law, or under any collective bargaining agreement.

EXPLANATORY COMMENTS: *Section 806 is one of several provisions that were included in the Sarbanes-Oxley Act to encourage and protect whistleblowers—that is, employees who report their employer's alleged violations of securities law to the authorities. This section applies to employees, agents, and independent contractors who work for publicly traded companies or testify about such a company during an investigation. It sets up an administrative procedure at the U.S. Department of Labor for individuals who claim that their employer retaliated against them (fired or demoted them, for example) for blowing the whistle on the employer's wrongful conduct. It also allows the award of civil damages—including back pay, reinstatement, special damages, attorneys' fees, and court costs—to employees who prove that they suffered retaliation. Since this provision was enacted, whistleblowers have filed numerous complaints with the U.S. Department of Labor under this section.*

SECTION 807

Securities fraud[10]

Whoever knowingly executes, or attempts to execute, a scheme or artifice—

(1) to defraud any person in connection with any security of an issuer with a class of securities registered under section 12 of the Securities Exchange Act of 1934 (15 U.S.C. 78l) or that is required to file reports under section 15(d) of the Securities Exchange Act of 1934 (15 U.S.C. 78o(d)); or

(2) to obtain, by means of false or fraudulent pretenses, representations, or promises, any money or property in connection with the purchase or sale of any security of an issuer with a class of securities registered under section 12 of the Securities Exchange Act of 1934 (15 U.S.C. 78l) or that is required to file reports under section 15(d) of the Securities Exchange Act of 1934 (15 U.S.C. 78o(d)); shall be fined under this title, or imprisoned not more than 25 years, or both.

*   *   *   *

EXPLANATORY COMMENTS: *Section 807 adds a new provision to the federal criminal code that addresses securities fraud. Prior to 2002, federal securities law had already made it a crime—under Section 10(b) of the Securities Exchange Act of 1934 and SEC Rule 10b-5, both of which are discussed in Chapter 21—to intentionally defraud someone in connection with a purchase or sale of securities, but the offense was not listed in the federal criminal code. Also, paragraph 2 of Section 807 goes beyond what is prohibited under securities law by making it a crime to obtain by means of false or fraudulent pretenses any money or property from the purchase or sale of securities. This new provision allows violators to be punished by up to twenty-five years in prison, a fine, or both.*

---

10. Codified at 18 U.S.C. Section 1348.

SECTION 906

Failure of corporate officers to certify financial reports[11]

(a) Certification of periodic financial reports.—Each periodic report containing financial statements filed by an issuer with the Securities Exchange Commission pursuant to section 13(a) or 15(d) of the Securities Exchange Act of 1934 (15 U.S.C. 78m(a) or 78o(d)) shall be accompanied by a written statement by the chief executive officer and chief financial officer (or equivalent thereof) of the issuer.

(b) Content.—The statement required under subsection (a) shall certify that the periodic report containing the financial statements fully complies with the requirements of section 13(a) or 15(d) of the Securities Exchange Act of 1934 (15 U.S.C. 78m or 78o(d)) and that information contained in the periodic report fairly presents, in all material respects, the financial condition and results of operations of the issuer.

(c) Criminal penalties.—Whoever—

(1) certifies any statement as set forth in subsections (a) and (b) of this section knowing that the periodic report accompanying the statement does not comport with all the requirements set forth in

this section shall be fined not more than $1,000,000 or imprisoned not more than 10 years, or both; or

(2) willfully certifies any statement as set forth in subsections (a) and (b) of this section knowing that the periodic report accompanying the statement does not comport with all the requirements set forth in this section shall be fined not more than $5,000,000, or imprisoned not more than 20 years, or both.

EXPLANATORY COMMENTS: *As previously discussed, under Section 302 a corporation's CEO and CFO are required to certify that they believe the quarterly and annual reports their company files with the SEC are accurate and fairly present the company's financial condition. Section 906 adds "teeth" to these requirements by authorizing criminal penalties for those officers who intentionally certify inaccurate SEC filings. Knowing violations of the requirements are punishable by a fine of up to $1 million, ten years' imprisonment, or both. Willful violators may be fined up to $5 million, sentenced to up to twenty years' imprisonment, or both. Although the difference between a knowing and a willful violation is not entirely clear, the section is obviously intended to remind corporate officers of the serious consequences of certifying inaccurate reports to the SEC.*

---

11. Codified at 18 U.S.C. Section 1350.

APPENDIX E
Answers to Even-Numbered For Review Questions

CHAPTER 1

2A.   Precedent
Judges attempt to be consistent, and when possible, they base their decisions on the principles suggested by earlier cases. They seek to decide similar cases in a similar way and consider new cases with care, because they know that their conflicting decisions make new law. Each interpretation becomes part of the law on the subject and serves as a legal precedent—a decision that furnishes an example or authority for deciding subsequent cases involving similar legal principles or facts. A court will depart from the rule of a precedent when it decides that the rule should no longer be followed. If a court decides that a precedent is simply incorrect or that technological or social changes have rendered the precedent inapplicable, the court might rule contrary to the precedent.

4A.   Commercial activities
To prevent states from establishing laws and regulations that would interfere with trade and commerce among the states, the Constitution expressly delegated to the national government the power to regulate interstate commerce. The commerce clause (Article I, Section 8, of the U.S. Constitution) expressly permits Congress "[t]o regulate Commerce with foreign Nations, and among the several States, and with the Indian Tribes."

CHAPTER 2

2A.   Ensuring legal and ethical behavior
Ethical leadership is important to create and maintain an ethical workplace. Management can set standards, and apply those standards to themselves and their firm's employees.

4A.   Ethical standards
Duty-based ethical standards are derived from religious precepts or philosophical principles. Outcome-based ethics focus on the consequences of an action, not on the nature of the action or on a set of preestablished moral values or religious beliefs.

CHAPTER 3

2A.   Jurisdiction
To hear a case, a court must have jurisdiction over the person against whom the suit is brought or over the property involved in the suit. The court must also have jurisdiction over the subject matter. Generally, courts apply a "sliding-scale" standard to determine when it is proper to exercise jurisdiction over a defendant whose only connection with the jurisdiction is the Internet.

4A.   Pleadings, discovery, and electronic filing
The pleadings include the plaintiff's complaint and the defendant's answer (and the counterclaim and reply). The pleadings inform each party of the other's claims and specify the issues involved in a case. Discovery is the process of obtaining information and evidence about a case from the other party or third parties. Discovery entails gaining access to witnesses, documents, records, and other types of evidence. Electronic discovery differs in its subject (e-media rather than traditional sources of information). Electronic filing involves the filing of court documents in electronic media, typically over the Internet.

CHAPTER 4

2A.   Purpose and categories of torts
Generally, the purpose of tort law is to provide remedies for the invasion of legally recognized and protected interests (personal safety, freedom of movement, property, and some intangibles, including privacy and reputation). The two broad categories of torts are intentional and unintentional.

4A.   Strict liability
Strict liability is liability without fault. Strict liability for damages proximately caused by an abnormally dangerous or exceptional activity, or the keeping of dangerous animals, is an application of this doctrine. Another significant application of strict liability is in the area of product liability.

CHAPTER 5

2A.   Trademarks and patents
As stated in Article I, Section 8, of the Constitution, Congress is authorized "[t]o promote the Progress of Science and useful Arts, by securing for limited Times to Authors and Inventors the exclusive Right to their respective Writings and Discoveries." Laws protecting patents and trademarks, as well copyrights, are designed to protect and reward inventive and artistic creativity.

4A.   Trade secrets
Trade secrets are business processes and information that are not or cannot be patented, copyrighted, or trademarked. Trade secrets consist of generally anything that makes an individual company unique

and that would have value to a competitor. The Uniform Trade Secrets Act, the Economic Espionage Act, and the common law offer trade secrets protection.

CHAPTER 6

2A. *Types of crime and white-collar crime*
Traditionally, crimes have been grouped into the following categories: violent crime (crimes against persons), property crime, public order crime, white-collar crime, and organized crime. White-collar crime is an illegal act or series of acts committed by an individual or business entity using some nonviolent means, usually in the course of a legitimate occupation.

4A. *Constitutional safeguards and criminal process*
Under the Fourth Amendment, before searching or seizing private property, law enforcement officers must obtain a search warrant, which requires probable cause. Under the Fifth Amendment, no one can be deprived of "life, liberty, or property without due process of law." The Fifth Amendment also protects persons against double jeopardy and self-incrimination. The Sixth Amendment guarantees the right to a speedy trial, the right to a jury trial, the right to a public trial, the right to confront witnesses, and the right to counsel. All evidence obtained in violation of the Fourth, Fifth, and Sixth Amendments must be excluded from the trial, as well as all evidence derived from the illegally obtained evidence. Individuals who are arrested must be informed of certain constitutional rights, including their Fifth Amendment right to remain silent and their Sixth Amendment right to counsel. The Eighth Amendment prohibits excessive bails and fines, and cruel and unusual punishment. The basic steps in the criminal process include an arrest, the booking, the initial appearance, a preliminary hearing, a grand jury or magistrate's review, the arraignment, a plea bargain (if any), and the trial or guilty plea.

CHAPTER 7

2A. *Types of contracts*
The various types of contracts include bilateral, unilateral, express, implied, formal, informal, quasi, valid, void, voidable, and unenforceable.

4A. *Acceptance of an offer*
An acceptance is a voluntary act on the part of the offeree that shows assent, or agreement, to the terms of an offer. The acceptance must be unequivocal and must be timely communicated to the offeror.

CHAPTER 8

2A. *Intoxication*
If a person who is sufficiently intoxicated to lack mental capacity enters into a contract, the contract is voidable at the option of that person. It must be proved that the person's reason and judgment were impaired to the extent that he or she did not comprehend the legal consequences of entering into the contract.

4A. *Elements of fraudulent misrepresentation*
Fraudulent misrepresentation has three elements: (1) misrepresentation of a material fact must occur, (2) there must be an intent to deceive, and (3) the innocent party must justifiably rely on the mis-

representation. Also, to collect damages, a party must have been injured as a result of the misrepresentation.

CHAPTER 9

2A. *Intended beneficiary*
A beneficiary will be considered an intended beneficiary if a reasonable person in the position of the beneficiary would believe that the promisee intended to confer on the beneficiary the right to bring suit to enforce the contract. Other factors include whether performance is rendered directly to the third party, whether the third party has the right to control the details of performance, and whether the third party is expressly designated as a beneficiary in the contract.

4A. *Equitable remedies*
When fraud, mistake, duress, or failure of consideration is present, rescission is available. The failure of one party to perform under a contract entitles the other party to rescind the contract. Specific performance might be granted as a remedy when damages is an inadequate remedy and the subject matter of the contract is unique. Reformation allows a contract to be rewritten to reflect the parties' true intentions. It applies most often when fraud or mutual mistake occurs.

CHAPTER 10

2A. *Shrink-wrap and click-on agreements*
A shrink-wrap agreement is an agreement whose terms are expressed inside a box in which the goods are packaged. Generally, courts have enforced the terms of shrink-wrap agreements the same as the terms of other contracts, applying the traditional common law of contracts.

4A. *Partnering agreement*
A partnering agreement is an agreement between a seller and a buyer who often do business on the terms and conditions that apply to all of their transactions conducted electronically. Such an agreement reduces the likelihood of a dispute and provides for the resolution of any dispute that does arise.

CHAPTER 11

2A. *Additional terms*
Under the UCC, a contract can be formed even if the acceptance includes an offeree's additional or different terms. If one of the parties is a nonmerchant, the contract does not include the additional terms. If both parties are merchants, the additional terms automatically become part of the contract unless (1) the original offer expressly limits acceptance to the terms of the offer, (2) the new or changed terms *materially* alter the contract, or (3) the offeror objects to the new or changed terms within a reasonable period of time. (If the additional terms expressly require the offeror's assent, the offeree's expression is not an acceptance, but a counteroffer.) Under some circumstances, a court might strike the additional terms.

4A. *Passage of risk without movement of goods*
If the goods are held by a seller, and the seller is a merchant, the risk of loss passes to the buyer when the buyer actually takes physical possession of the goods. If the seller is not a merchant, the risk of loss to goods held by the seller passes to the buyer on tender of delivery. When a bailee is holding the goods, the risk of loss passes to the buyer when (1) the buyer receives a negotiable document of title for the

goods, (2) the bailee acknowledges the buyer's right to possess the goods, or (3) the buyer receives a nonnegotiable document of title and has had a reasonable time to present the document to the bailee and demand the goods.

CHAPTER 12

2A. *Perfect tender rule*
Under the perfect tender rule, the seller or lessor has an obligation to ship or tender conforming goods, and if goods or tender of delivery fail in any respect, the buyer or lessee has the right to accept the goods, reject the entire shipment, or accept part and reject part. Exceptions to the perfect tender rule may be established by agreement. When tender is rejected because of nonconforming goods and the time for performance has not yet expired, the seller or lessor can notify the buyer or lessee promptly of the intention to cure and can then do so within the contract time for performance. Once the time for performance has expired, the seller or lessor can, for a reasonable time, exercise the right to cure if he or she had, at the time of delivery, reasonable grounds to believe that the nonconforming tender would be acceptable to the buyer or lessee. When an agreed-on manner of delivery becomes impracticable or unavailable through no fault of either party, a seller may choose a commercially reasonable substitute. In an installment contract, a buyer or lessee can reject an installment only if the nonconformity substantially impairs the value of the installment and cannot be cured. Delay in delivery or nondelivery in whole or in part is not a breach when performance is commercially impracticable. If an unexpected event totally destroys goods identified at the time the contract is formed through no fault of either party and before risk passes to the buyer or lessee, the parties are excused from performance. If a party has reasonable grounds to believe that the other party will not perform, he or she may in writing demand assurance of performance from the other party. Until such assurance is received, he or she may suspend further performance. Finally, when required cooperation is not forthcoming, the cooperative party can suspend her or his own performance without liability.

4A. *Remedies for breach*
Depending on the circumstances at the time of a buyer's breach, a seller may have the right to cancel the contract, withhold delivery, resell or dispose of the goods subject to the contract, recover the purchase price (or lease payments), recover damages, stop delivery in transit, or reclaim the goods. Similarly, on a seller's breach, a buyer may have the right to cancel the contract, recover the goods, obtain specific performance, obtain cover, replevy the goods, recover damages, reject the goods, withhold delivery, resell or dispose of the goods, stop delivery, or revoke acceptance.

CHAPTER 13

2A. *Implied warranties*
Implied warranties that arise under the UCC include the implied warranty of merchantability, the implied warranty of fitness for a particular purpose, and implied warranties that may arise from, or be excluded or modified by, course of dealing, course of performance, or usage of trade.

4A. *Defenses*
Defenses to product liability include plaintiff's assumption of risk, product misuse, and comparative negligence, as well as the attribu-

tion of injuries to commonly known dangers. Also, as in any suit, a defendant can avoid liability by showing that the elements of the cause of action have not been properly pleaded or proved.

CHAPTER 14

2A. *Requirements for negotiability*
For an instrument to be negotiable, it must (1) be in writing, (2) be signed by the maker or the drawer, (3) be an unconditional promise or order to pay, (4) state a fixed amount of money, (5) be payable on demand or at a definite time, and (6) be payable to order or to bearer, unless it is a check.

4A. *Liability*
The key to liability on a negotiable instrument is a signature. Every party, except a qualified indorser, who signs a negotiable instrument is primarily or secondarily liable for payment of that instrument when it comes due. Signature liability arises from indorsing an instrument. Warranty liability arises from transferring an instrument, whether or not the transferor also indorses it.

CHAPTER 15

2A. *Dishonor*
A bank may dishonor a customer's check without liability to the customer when the customer's account contains insufficient funds to pay the check, providing the bank did not agree to cover overdrafts. A bank may also properly dishonor a stale check, a timely check subject to a valid stop-payment order, a check drawn after the customer's death, and forged or altered checks. If a bank wrongfully dishonors a customer's check, the bank is liable to the customer for damages for the failure to pay.

4A. *EFTs and consumers*
The four most common types of EFT systems used by bank customers are automated teller machines, point-of-sale systems, systems handling direct deposits and withdrawals of funds, and Internet payment systems. The EFTA provides a basic framework for the rights, liabilities, and responsibilities of users of these EFT systems. For consumers, the terms and conditions of EFTs must be disclosed in readily understandable language, a receipt must be provided at an e-terminal at the time of a transfer, periodic statements must describe transfers for each account through which an EFT system provides access, and some preauthorized payments can be stopped within three days before they are made.

CHAPTER 16

2A. *Attachment and writs of execution*
Attachment is a court-ordered seizure and taking into custody of property prior to the securing of a judgment for a past-due debt. To use attachment as a remedy, a creditor (1) files with a court an affidavit, stating that a debtor is in default and the grounds on which attachment is sought, and (2) posts a bond to cover costs, the value of the loss of use of the good by the debtor, and the value of the property. The court directs the sheriff or other officer to seize nonexempt property, which can be sold to satisfy a judgment. A *writ of execution* is a court order directing a sheriff to seize and sell any of the debtor's nonexempt real or personal property within the court's jurisdiction. This is used when a debtor will not or cannot pay a judgment.

4A. *Debtor's estate in bankruptcy and debtor in possession*

In a bankruptcy proceeding, a *debtor's estate in property* consists of all the debtor's legal and equitable interests in property currently held, wherever located, together with certain jointly owned property, property transferred in transactions voidable by the trustee, proceeds and profits from the property of the estate, and certain after-acquired property. Federal law exempts (1) up to $20,200 in equity in the debtor's residence and burial plot; (2) interest in a motor vehicle up to $3,225; (3) interest in household goods and furnishings, wearing apparel, appliances, books, animals, crops, and musical instruments up to $525 in a particular item but limited to $10,775 in total; (4) interest in jewelry up to $1,350; (5) any other property worth up to $1,075, plus any unused part of the $20,200 homestead exemption up to an amount of $10,775; (6) interest in any tools of the debtor's trade, up to $2,025; (7) certain life insurance contracts owned by the debtor; (8) certain interests in accrued dividends or interests under life insurance contracts owned by the debtor; (9) professionally prescribed health aids; (10) the right to receive Social Security and certain welfare benefits, alimony and support payments, and certain pension benefits; and (11) the right to receive certain personal-injury and other awards, up to $20,200.

CHAPTER 17

2A. *Agency relationships*

Agency relationships normally are consensual: they arise by voluntary consent and agreement between the parties.

4A. *Liability to third parties*

A disclosed or partially disclosed principal is liable to a third party for a contract made by an agent who is acting within the scope of her or his authority. If the agent exceeds the scope of authority and the principal fails to ratify the contract, the agent may be liable (and the principal may not). When neither the fact of agency nor the identity of the principal is disclosed, the agent is liable, and if an agent has acted within the scope of his or her authority, the undisclosed principal is also liable. Each party is liable for his or her own torts and crimes. A principal may also be liable for an agent's torts committed within the course or scope of employment. A principal is liable for an agent's crime if the principal participated by conspiracy or other action.

CHAPTER 18

2A. *Hours and wages*

The Fair Labor Standards Act is the most significant federal statute governing working hours and wages.

4A. *Federal employment discrimination acts*

Title VII of the Civil Rights Act of 1964 and its amendments prohibit job discrimination against employees, applicants, and union members on the basis of race, color, national origin, religion, and gender at any stage of employment. The Age Discrimination in Employment Act of 1967 and the Americans with Disabilities Act of 1990 prohibit discrimination on the basis of age and disability, respectively.

CHAPTER 19

2A. *Advantages and disadvantages of business forms*

Advantages of the sole proprietorship include the proprietor receiving all of the profits and the ease and inexpensiveness to start the business. Disadvantages of the sole proprietorship include the exclusive burden on the owner of any losses or liabilities incurred by the business enterprise and the limitation on capital to personal funds and the funds of those who are willing to make loans. One of the advantages of a partnership is that it can be organized fairly easily and inexpensively. Additionally, the partnership itself files only an informational tax return. The main disadvantage of the partnership form of business is that partners are subject to personal liability for partnership obligations. One of the key advantages of a corporation is that the liability of its owners is limited to their investments. A disadvantage of the corporate form is that profits are taxed twice.

4A. *Joint ventures and other business organizational forms*

A *joint venture* is an enterprise in which two or more persons or business entities combine their efforts or their property for a single transaction or project, or a related series of transactions or projects. Other special business organizational forms include a joint stock company, syndicate, and cooperative. A *joint stock company* has many characteristics of a corporation (its ownership is represented by transferable shares of stock, it is usually managed by directors and officers of the company or association, and it can have a perpetual existence), but most of its other features are more characteristic of a partnership, and it is usually treated like a partnership. A *syndicate* is a group of individuals getting together to finance a particular project, such as the building of a shopping center. A *business trust* is created by a written trust agreement that sets forth the interests of the beneficiaries, who receive the profits, and the obligations and powers of the trustees, with whom legal ownership and management of the property of the business rests. A *cooperative* is an association, which may not or may be incorporated, that is organized to provide an economic service to its members (or shareholders), who have limited liability. Cooperatives that are unincorporated are often treated like partnerships, and the members have joint liability for the cooperative's acts.

CHAPTER 20

2A. *Duties of directors and officers*

Directors and officers are fiduciaries of the corporation. The fiduciary duties of the directors and officers include the duty of care and the duty of loyalty.

4A. *Roles and rights of shareholders*

Shareholders have an equitable interest in the firm. They are ultimately responsible for choosing the board of directors. Shareholders must approve fundamental corporate changes before the changes can be effected. Shareholders possess numerous rights, including preemptive rights in the purchase of new stock, dividends from corporate profits, and the right to inspection of corporate books and records. Shareholders also have the right to act on behalf of the firm by filing a shareholder's derivative suit to compel the directors to act to redress a wrong suffered by the corporation.

CHAPTER 21

2A. *Major statutes and the Securities and Exchange Commission*

The major statutes regulating the securities industry are the Securities Act of 1933 and the Securities Exchange Act of 1934, which created the Securities and Exchange Commission (SEC). The SEC's major functions are to (1) require the disclosure of facts concerning offerings of securities listed on national securities exchanges and of certain securities traded over the counter; (2) regulate the trade in securities on the national and regional securities exchanges and in the over-the-counter markets; (3) investigate securities fraud; (4) regulate the activities of securities brokers, dealers, and investment advisers and require their registration; (5) supervise the activities of mutual funds; and (6) recommend administrative sanctions, injunctive remedies, and criminal prosecution against those who violate securities laws.

4A.   *State securities laws*

Typically, state laws have disclosure requirements and antifraud provisions patterned after Section 10(b) of the Securities Exchange Act of 1934 and SEC Rule 10b-5. State laws provide for the registration or qualification of securities offered or issued for sale within the state with the appropriate state official. Also, most state securities laws regulate securities brokers and dealers.

CHAPTER 22

2A.   *Sherman Act*

Section 1 prohibits agreements that are anticompetitively restrictive—that is, agreements that have the wrongful purpose of restraining competition. Section 2 prohibits the misuse, and attempted misuse, of monopoly power in the marketplace.

4A.   *Enforcing agencies*

The federal agencies that enforce the federal antitrust laws are the U.S. Department of Justice and the Federal Trade Commission.

CHAPTER 23

2A.   *Gifts and other means of acquisition*

To make an effective gift, the donor must intend to make the gift, the gift must be delivered to the donee, and the donee must accept the gift. Property can also be acquired by purchase, possession, production, accession, and confusion.

4A.   *Rights and duties of bailees and bailors*

A bailee has the right to control and possess the property temporarily, which includes the right to recover damages for its loss or damage and to regain possession. A bailee may also have the right to use the property. A bailee has a right to be compensated as provided for in the bailment agreement, a right to be reimbursed for costs and services rendered in the keeping of the bailed property, or both. A bailee may have the right to limit liability as long as the limit is called to the atten-

tion of the bailor and is not against public policy. A bailee has the duty to (1) take reasonable care of the property and (2) surrender to the bailor or dispose of the property in accord with the bailor's instructions at the end of the bailment. The bailor must provide the bailee with goods that are free from known defects that could cause injury to the bailee. In a mutual-benefit bailment, the bailor must notify the bailee of any hidden defects that the bailor could have discovered with reasonable diligence and proper inspection. Also, the implied warranties of merchantability and fitness for a particular purpose apply to a bailment that includes the right to use the bailed goods.

CHAPTER 24

2A.   *Limitations*

Limits on property owners' rights may be imposed for public uses (flights over private land, for example) or to respect others' rights (restrictions on owners' exercise of subsurface rights to protect the surface owners' rights, for example).

4A.   *Environmental impact statements*

An environmental impact statement (EIS) analyzes (1) the impact on the environment that an action will have, (2) any adverse effects on the environment and alternative actions that might be taken, and (3) irreversible effects the action might generate. For every major federal action that significantly affects the quality of the environment, an EIS must be prepared. An action is "major" if it involves a substantial commitment of resources (monetary or otherwise). An action is "federal" if a federal agency has the power to control it.

CHAPTER 25

2A.   *Act of state doctrine*

The *act of state doctrine* is a judicially created doctrine that provides that the judicial branch of one country will not examine the validity of public acts committed by a recognized foreign government within its own territory. This doctrine is often employed in cases involving expropriation or confiscation.

4A.   *Antitrust laws*

U.S. courts will apply U.S. antitrust laws extraterritorially when it is shown that an alleged violation has a substantial effect on U.S. commerce.

APPENDIX F
Sample Answers for End-of-Chapter *Hypothetical Questions with Sample Answer*

1.3A. HYPOTHETICAL QUESTION WITH SAMPLE ANSWER

1. The U.S. Constitution—The U.S. Constitution is the supreme law of the land. A law in violation of the Constitution, no matter what its source, will be declared unconstitutional and will not be enforced.
2. The federal statute—Under the U.S. Constitution, when there is a conflict between federal law and state law, federal law prevails.
3. The state statute—State statutes are enacted by state legislatures. Areas not covered by state statutory law are governed by state case law.
4. The U.S. Constitution—State constitutions are supreme within their respective borders unless they conflict with the U.S. Constitution, which is the supreme law of the land.
5. The federal administrative regulation—Under the U.S. Constitution, when there is a conflict between federal law and state law, federal law prevails.

2.2A. HYPOTHETICAL QUESTION WITH SAMPLE ANSWER

This question essentially asks whether good behavior can ever be unethical. The answer to this question depends on which approach to ethical reasoning you are using. Under the outcome-based approach of utilitarianism, it is simply not possible for selfish motives to be unethical if they result in good conduct. A good outcome is moral regardless of the nature of the action itself or the reason for the action. Under a duty-based approach, motive would be more relevant in assessing whether a firm's conduct was ethical. You would need to analyze the firm's conduct in terms of religious truths or to determine whether human beings were being treated with the inherent dignity that they deserve. Although a good motive would not justify a bad act to a religious ethicist, in this situation the actions were good and the motive was questionable (because the firm was simply seeking to increase its profit). Nevertheless, unless one's religion prohibited making a profit, the firm's actions would likely not be considered unethical. Applying Kantian ethics would require you to evaluate the firm's actions in light of what would happen if everyone in society acted that way (categorical imperative). Here, because the conduct was good, it would be positive for society if every firm acted that way. Hence, the profit-seeking motive would be irrelevant in a Kantian analysis. In a debate between motive and conduct, then, conduct is almost always given greater weight in evaluating ethics.

3.2A. HYPOTHETICAL QUESTION WITH SAMPLE ANSWER

Marya can bring suit in all three courts. The trucking firm did business in Florida, and the accident occurred there. Thus, the state of Florida would have jurisdiction over the defendant. Because the firm was headquartered in Georgia and had its principal place of business in that state, Marya could also sue in a Georgia court. Finally, because the amount in controversy exceeds $75,000, the suit could be brought in federal court on the basis of diversity of citizenship.

4.2A. HYPOTHETICAL QUESTION WITH SAMPLE ANSWER

The correct answer is (2). The *Restatement (Second) of Torts* defines negligence as "conduct that falls below the standard established by law for the protection of others against unreasonable risk of harm." The standard established by law is that of a reasonable person acting with due care in the circumstances. Mary was well aware that the medication she took would make her drowsy, and her failure to observe due care (that is, refrain from driving) under the circumstances was negligent. Answer (1) is incorrect because Mary had no reason to believe the golf club was defective, and she could not have prevented the injury by the exercise of due care.

5.2A. HYPOTHETICAL QUESTION WITH SAMPLE ANSWER

1. Making a photocopy of an article in a scholarly journal "for purposes such as * * * scholarship, or research, is not an infringement of copyright" under Section 107 of the Copyright Act.
2. This is an example of trademark infringement. Whenever a trademark is copied to a substantial degree or used in its entirety by one who is not entitled to its use, the trademark has been infringed.
3. This is the most likely example of copyright infringement. Generally, determining whether the reproduction of copyrighted material constitutes copyright infringement is made on a case-by-case basis under the "fair use" doctrine, as expressed in Section 107 of the Copyright Act. Courts look at such factors as the "purpose and character" of a use, such as whether it is "of a commercial nature;" "the amount and substantiality of the portion used in relation to the copyrighted work as a whole;" and "the effect of the use on the potential market" for the copied work. In this question, the DVD store owner is copying copyright-protected works in their entirety for commercial purposes, thereby affecting the market for the works.
4. Taping a television program "for purposes such as * * * teaching * * * is not an infringement of copyright" under Section 107 of the Copyright Act.

6.2A. HYPOTHETICAL QUESTION WITH SAMPLE ANSWER

1. Sarah has wrongfully taken and carried away the personal property of another with the intent to permanently deprive the owner of such property. She has committed the crime of larceny.

2. Sarah has unlawfully and forcibly taken the personal property of another. She has committed the crime of robbery.

3. Sarah has broken and entered a dwelling with the intent to commit a felony. She has committed the crime of burglary. (Most states have dispensed with the requirement that the act take place at night.)

Note the basic differences: Burglary requires breaking and entering into a building without the use of force against a person. Robbery does not involve any breaking and entering, but force is required. Larceny is the taking of personal property without force and without breaking and entering into a building. Generally, because force is used, robbery is considered the most serious of these crimes and carries the most severe penalties. Larceny involves no force or threat to human life; therefore, it carries the least severe penalty of the three. Burglary, because it involves breaking and entering, frequently where people live, carries a lesser penalty than robbery but a greater penalty than larceny.

7.2A. HYPOTHETICAL QUESTION WITH SAMPLE ANSWER

1. Death of either the offeror or the offeree prior to acceptance automatically terminates a revocable offer. The basic legal reason is that the offer is personal to the parties and cannot be passed on to others, not even to the estate of the deceased. This rule applies even if the other party is unaware of the death. Thus, Cherneck's offer terminates on Cherneck's death, and Bollow's later acceptance does not constitute a contract.

2. An offer is automatically terminated by the destruction of the specific subject matter of the offer prior to acceptance. Thus, Bollow's acceptance after the fire does not constitute a contract.

3. When the offer is irrevocable, under an option contract, death of the offeror does not terminate the option contract, and the offeree can accept the offer to sell the equipment, binding the offeror's estate to performance. Performance is not personal to Cherneck, as the estate can transfer title to the equipment. Knowledge of the death is immaterial to the offeree's right of acceptance. Thus, Bollow can hold Cherneck's estate to a contract for the purchase of the equipment.

4. When the offer is irrevocable, under an option contract, death of the offeree also does not terminate the offer. Because the option is a separate contract, the contract survives and passes to the offeree's estate, which can exercise the option by acceptance within the option period. Thus, acceptance by Bollow's estate binds Cherneck to a contract for the sale of the equipment.

8.2A. HYPOTHETICAL QUESTION WITH SAMPLE ANSWER

Contracts in restraint of trade are usually illegal and unenforceable. An exception to this rule applies to a covenant not to compete that is ancillary to certain types of business contracts in which some fair protection is deemed appropriate (such as in the sale of a business). The covenant, however, must be reasonable in terms of time and area to be legally enforceable. If either term is excessive, the court can declare that the restraint goes beyond what is necessary for reasonable protection. In this event, the court can either declare the covenant illegal, or it can reform the covenant to make the terms of time and area reasonable and then enforce it. Suppose the court declares the covenant illegal and unenforceable. Because the covenant is ancillary and severable from the primary contract,

the primary contract is not affected by such a ruling. In the case of Hotel Lux, the primary contract concerns employment; the covenant is ancillary and desirable for the protection of the hotel. The time period of one year may be considered reasonable for a chef with an international reputation. The reasonableness of the three-state area restriction may be questioned, however. If it is found to be reasonable, the covenant probably will be enforced. If it is not found to be reasonable, the court could declare the entire covenant illegal, allowing Perlee to be employed by any restaurant or hotel, including one in direct competition with Hotel Lux. Alternatively, the court could reform the covenant, making its terms reasonable for protecting Hotel Lux's normal customer market area.

9.3A. HYPOTHETICAL QUESTION WITH SAMPLE ANSWER

As a general rule any right(s) flowing from a contract can be assigned. There are, however, exceptions, such as when the contract expressly and specifically prohibits or limits the right of assignment. Because of the principle of freedom of contract, this type of prohibition is enforced—unless it is deemed contrary to public policy. For example, courts have held that a prohibition clause against assignment that restrains the alienation of property is invalid by virtue of being against public policy. Authorities differ on how a case like Aron's should be decided. Some courts would enforce the prohibition completely, holding that Aron's assignment to Erica is completely ineffective without the landlord's consent. Others would permit the assignment to be effective, with the landlord's remedies limited to the normal contract remedies ensuing from Aron's breach.

10.2A. HYPOTHETICAL QUESTION WITH SAMPLE ANSWER

Anne has entered into an enforceable contract to subscribe to *E-Commerce Weekly*. In this problem, the offer to deliver, via e-mail, the newsletter was presented by the offeror with a statement of how to accept—by clicking on the "SUBSCRIBE" button. Consideration was in the promise to deliver the newsletter and at the price that the subscriber agreed to pay. The offeree had an opportunity to read the terms of the subscription agreement before making the contract. Whether or not she actually read those terms does not matter.

11.2A. HYPOTHETICAL QUESTION WITH SAMPLE ANSWER

1. In a destination contract, the risk of loss passes to the buyer when the goods are tendered to the buyer at the specified destination—in this case, San Francisco.

2. In a shipment contract, if the seller is required or authorized to ship goods by carrier, but the contract specifies no locale, the risk of loss passes to the buyer when the goods are duly delivered to the carrier.

3. If the seller is a merchant, risk of loss to goods held by the seller passes to the buyer when the buyer actually takes physical possession of the goods. If the seller is not a merchant, the risk of loss to goods held by the seller passes to the buyer on tender of delivery.

4. When a bailee is holding goods for a person who has contracted to sell them and the goods are to be delivered without being moved, risk of loss passes to the buyer when (1) the buyer receives a negotiable document of title for the goods, (2) the bailee acknowledges the buyer's right to possess the goods, or (3) the buyer receives a non-negotiable document of title and has had a reasonable time to present the document to the bailee and demand the goods. (If the bailee refuses to honor the document, the risk of loss remains with the seller.) If the goods are to be delivered by being moved, but the contract does not specify whether it is a destination or a shipment contract, it is presumed to be a shipment contract. If no locale is specified in the contract, risk of loss passes to the buyer when the seller delivers the goods to the carrier.

12.2A. HYPOTHETICAL QUESTION WITH SAMPLE ANSWER

No. Cummings had not breached the sales contract because the C.O.D. shipment had deprived him of his absolute right, in the absence of agreement, to inspect the goods before accepting them. Had Cummings requested or agreed to the C.O.D. method of shipment, the result would have been different. Because he had not agreed to the C.O.D. shipment, he was fully within his rights to refuse to accept the goods because he could not inspect them prior to acceptance. In this case, it was the seller who had breached the contract by shipping the goods C.O.D. without Cummings's consent.

13.2A. HYPOTHETICAL QUESTION WITH SAMPLE ANSWER

The Truth-in-Lending Act (TILA) deals specifically with lost or stolen credit cards and their unauthorized use. For credit cards *solicited* by the cardholder and then lost or stolen, the act limits the liability of the cardholder to $50 for unauthorized charges made prior to the time the creditor is notified. There is no liability for any unauthorized charges made after the date of notice. In the case of the Midtown Department Store credit card stolen on May 31, the $500 charge made on June 1, which is prior to Ochoa's notice, causes Ochoa to be liable for the $50 limit. For the June 3 charge of $200 made after the notification, Ochoa has no liability. TILA also deals with unsolicited credit cards. Unless a credit cardholder accepts an unsolicited card (such as by using it), the cardholder is not liable for any unauthorized charges. Moreover, the act prohibits the issuance of unsolicited credit cards. No notice by the cardholder of an unsolicited, unaccepted credit card is required to absolve the cardholder from liability for unauthorized charges. Therefore, Ochoa owes $50 to the Midtown Department Store and nothing to High-Flying Airlines.

14.2A. HYPOTHETICAL QUESTION WITH SAMPLE ANSWER

For an instrument to be negotiable, it must meet the following requirements:

1. Be in writing.
2. Be signed by the maker or the drawer.
3. Be an unconditional promise or order to pay.
4. State a fixed amount of money.
5. Be payable on demand or at a definite time.
6. Be payable to order or to bearer, unless it is a check.

The instrument in this case meets the writing requirement in that it is handwritten and on something with a degree of permanence that is transferable. The instrument meets the requirement of being signed by the maker, as Muriel Evans's signature (her name in her handwriting) appears in the body of the instrument. The instrument's payment is not conditional and contains Muriel Evans's definite promise to pay. In addition, the sum of $100 is both a fixed amount and payable in money (U.S. currency). Because the instru-

ment is payable on demand and to bearer (Karen Marvin or any holder), the instrument is negotiable.

15.2A. HYPOTHETICAL QUESTION WITH SAMPLE ANSWER

Under the Home Mortgage Disclosure Act (HMDA) and the Community Reinvestment Act of 1977, which were passed to prevent discrimination in lending practices, a bank is required to define its market area. This area must be established contiguous to the bank's branch offices. It must be mapped using the existing boundaries of the counties or the standard metropolitan areas (SMAs) in which the offices are located. A bank must delineate the community served, and annually review this delineation. The issue here is how a successful Internet-only bank could delineate its community. Does an Internet bank have a physically limited market area or serve a physically distinct community? Will the Federal Reserve Board, the government agency charged with enforcing this law, allow a bank to describe its market area as a "cybercommunity"?

16.2A. HYPOTHETICAL QUESTION WITH SAMPLE ANSWER

Mendez has a security interest in Arabian Knight and is a perfected secured party. He has met all the necessary criteria listed under UCC 9–203 to be a secured creditor. Mendez has given value of $5,000 and has taken possession of the collateral, Arabian Knight, owned by Marsh (who has rights in the collateral). Thus, he has a security interest even though Marsh did not sign a security agreement. Once a security interest attaches, a transfer of possession of the collateral to the secured party can perfect the party's security interest without a filing [UCC 9–310(b)(6); 9–313]. Thus, a security interest was created and perfected at the time Marsh transferred Arabian Knight to Mendez as security for the loan.

17.2A. HYPOTHETICAL QUESTION WITH SAMPLE ANSWER

Agency is usually a consensual relationship in that the principal and agent agree that the agent will have the authority to act for the principal, binding the principal to any contract with a third party. If no agency in fact exists, the purported agent's contracts with third parties are not binding on the principal. In this case, no agency by agreement was created. Brown may claim that an agency by estoppel was created; however, this argument will fail. Agency by estoppel is applicable only when a *principal* causes a third person to believe that another person is the principal's agent. Then the third party's actions in dealing with the agent are in reliance upon the principal's words or actions and the third party's reasonable belief that the agent has authority. This is said to estop the principal from claiming that in fact no agency existed. Acts and declarations of the *agent*, however, do not in and of themselves create an agency by estoppel, because such actions should not reasonably lead a third person to believe that the purported agent has authority. In this case, Wade's declarations and allegations alone led Brown to believe that Wade was an agent. Gett's actions were not involved. It is not reasonable to believe that someone is an agent solely because he or she is a friend of the principal. Therefore, Brown cannot hold Gett liable unless Gett ratifies Wade's contract—which is unlikely, as Wade has disappeared with the rare coin.

18.2A. HYPOTHETICAL QUESTION WITH SAMPLE ANSWER

The Occupational Safety and Health Act (OSHA) requires employers to provide safe working conditions for employees. The act prohibits employers from discharging or discriminating against any employee who refuses to work when the employee believes in good faith that he or she will risk death or great bodily harm by undertaking the employment activity. Denton and Carlo had sufficient reason to believe that the maintenance job required of them by their employer involved great risk, and therefore, under OSHA, their discharge was wrongful. Denton and Carlo can turn to the Occupational Safety and Health Administration, which is part of the U.S. Department of Labor, for assistance.

19.3A. HYPOTHETICAL QUESTION WITH SAMPLE ANSWER

The court would likely consider the terms of any contracts between the parties and whether or not the parties were acting in good faith. One way to avoid conflicts such as those described in this problem is to institute a Web site in conjunction with a franchisor's franchisees. When a Web site directs interested parties to a franchisee, for example, all parties would seem to benefit. Because territorial conflicts can occur not only between a franchisor and its franchisees but also between competing franchisees, some companies have instituted specific "no compete" pledges.

20.2A. HYPOTHETICAL QUESTION WITH SAMPLE ANSWER

If Artel acquires the stocks and assets of Fox Express, a *merger* will take place. Artel will be the surviving corporation, and Fox Express will disappear as a corporation. If Artel and Fox Express combine so that both corporations cease to exist and a new corporation, A&F Enterprises, is formed, a *consolidation* will take place. In either case, title to the property of the corporation that ceases to exist will pass automatically to the surviving or new corporation without a formal transfer being necessary. In addition, in a merger, the debt liabilities of Fox Express become the liabilities of Artel. Artel's articles of incorporation are deemed to be amended to include the terms stated in the articles of merger. If a consolidation takes place, A&F Enterprises will automatically acquire title to the properties of both Artel and Fox Express without a formal transfer being necessary. A&F Enterprises also will assume liability for the debts and obligations of Artel and Fox Express. The articles of consolidation take the place of the articles of incorporation of Artel and Fox Express, and they will be regarded thereafter as the articles of incorporation of A&F Enterprises.

21.2A. HYPOTHETICAL QUESTION WITH SAMPLE ANSWER

No. Under federal securities law, a stock split is exempt from registration requirements. This is because no *sale* of stock is involved. The existing shares are merely being split, and no consideration is received by the corporation for the additional shares created.

22.2A. HYPOTHETICAL QUESTION WITH SAMPLE ANSWER

Yes. The major antitrust law being violated is the Sherman Act, Section 1. Allitron and Donovan are engaged in interstate commerce, and the agreement to divide marketing territories between them is a contract in restraint of trade. The U.S. Department of Justice could seek fines of up to $1 million for each corporation, and the officers or directors responsible could be imprisoned for up to three years. In addition, the U.S. Department of Justice could institute civil proceedings to restrain this conduct.

23.3A. HYPOTHETICAL QUESTION WITH SAMPLE ANSWER

For Curtis to recover against the hotel, he must first prove that a bailment relationship was created between himself and the hotel as to the car or the fur coat, or both. For a bailment to exist, there must be a delivery of the personal property that gives the bailee exclusive possession of the property, and the bailee must knowingly accept the bailed property. If either element is lacking, there is no bailment relationship and no liability on the part of the bailee hotel. The facts clearly indicate that the bailee hotel took exclusive possession and control of Curtis's car, and it knowingly accepted the car when the attendant took the car from Curtis and parked it in the underground guarded garage, retaining the keys. Thus, a bailment was created as to the car, and, because a mutual-benefit bailment was created, the hotel owes Curtis the duty to exercise reasonable care over the property and to return the bailed car at the end of the bailment. Failure to return the car creates a presumption of negligence (lack of reasonable care), and unless the hotel can rebut this presumption, the hotel is liable to Curtis for the loss of the car. As to the fur coat, the hotel neither knew nor expected that the trunk contained an expensive fur coat. Thus, although the hotel knowingly took exclusive possession of the car, the hotel did not do so with the fur coat. (But for a regular coat and other items likely to be in the car, the hotel would be liable.) Because no bailment of the expensive fur coat was created, the hotel has no liability for its loss.

24.2A. HYPOTHETICAL QUESTION WITH SAMPLE ANSWER

Wiley understandably wants a general warranty deed, as this type of deed will give him the most extensive protection against any defects of title claimed against the property transferred. The general warranty would have Gemma warranting the following covenants, or promises:

1. Covenant to convey—a warranty that the seller has good title and power to convey.
2. Covenant against adverse claims of third parties—a guaranty by the seller that, unless stated, there are no outstanding encumbrances (claims) or liens against the property conveyed.
3. Covenant of quiet enjoyment—a warranty that the grantee's possession will not be disturbed by others claiming a prior legal right. Gemma, however, is conveying only ten feet along a property line that may not even be accurately surveyed. Gemma therefore does not wish to make these warranties. Consequently, she is offering a quitclaim deed, which does not convey any warranties but conveys only whatever interest, if any, the grantor owns. Although title is passed by the quitclaim deed, the quality of the title is not warranted. Because Wiley really needs the property, it appears that he has three choices: (1) he can accept the quitclaim deed; (2) he can increase his offer price to obtain the general warranty deed he wants; or (3) he can offer to have a title search made, which should satisfy both parties.

25.2A. HYPOTHETICAL QUESTION WITH SAMPLE ANSWER

Each system has its advantages and its disadvantages. In a common law system, the courts independently develop the rules governing certain areas of law, such as torts and contracts. This judge-made law exists in addition to the laws passed by a legislature. Judges must follow precedential decisions in their jurisdictions, but courts may modify or even overturn precedents when deemed necessary. Also, if there is no case law to guide a court, the court may create a new rule of law. In a civil law system, the only official source of law is a statutory code. Courts are required to interpret the code and apply the rules to individual cases, but courts may not depart from the code and develop their own laws. In theory, the law code will set forth all the principles needed for the legal system. Common law and civil law systems are not wholly distinct. For example, the United States has a common law system, but crimes are defined by statute as in civil law systems. Civil law systems may allow considerable room for judges to develop law: law codes cannot be so precise as to address every contested issue, so the judiciary must interpret the codes. There are also significant differences among common law countries. The judges of different common law nations have produced differing common law principles. The roles of judges and lawyers under the different systems should be taken into account. Among other factors that should be considered in establishing a business law system and in deciding what regulations to impose are the goals that the system and its regulations are intended to achieve and the expectations of those to whom both will apply, including foreign and domestic investors.

Glossary

A

abandoned property ■ Property with which the owner has voluntarily parted, with no intention of recovering it.

acceptance ■ A voluntary act by the offeree that shows assent, or agreement, to the terms of an offer; may consist of words or conduct. In negotiable instruments law, the drawee's signed agreement to pay a draft when it is presented.

acceptor ■ A drawee who is legally obligated to pay an instrument when the instrument is presented for payment.

accession ■ Occurs when an individual adds value to personal property by the use of either labor or materials. In some situations, a person may acquire ownership rights in another's property through accession.

accord and satisfaction ■ A common means of settling a disputed claim, whereby a debtor offers to pay a lesser amount than the creditor purports is owed. The creditor's acceptance of the offer creates an accord (agreement), and when the accord is executed, satisfaction occurs.

accredited investors ■ In the context of securities offerings, "sophisticated" investors, such as banks, insurance companies, investment companies, the issuer's executive officers and directors, and persons whose income or net worth exceeds certain limits.

act of state doctrine ■ A doctrine providing that the judicial branch of one country will not examine the validity of public acts committed by a recognized foreign government within its own territory.

actionable ■ Capable of serving as the basis of a lawsuit. An actionable claim can be pursued in a lawsuit or other court action.

actual malice ■ The deliberate intent to cause harm, which exists when a person makes a statement either knowing that it is false or showing a reckless disregard for whether it is true. In a defamation suit, a statement made about a public figure normally must be made with actual malice for the plaintiff to recover damages.

actus reus ■ A guilty (prohibited) act. The commission of a prohibited act is one of the two essential elements required for criminal liability, the other element being the intent to commit a crime.

adhesion contract ■ A "standard-form" contract, such as that between a large retailer and a consumer, in which the stronger party dictates the terms.

adjudicate ■ To render a judicial decision. In the administrative process, adjudication is the trial-like proceeding in which an administrative law judge hears and decides issues that arise when an administrative agency charges a person or a firm with violating a law or regulation enforced by the agency.

administrative agency ■ A federal or state government agency established to perform a specific function. Administrative agencies are authorized by legislative acts to make and enforce rules in order to administer and enforce the acts.

administrative law judge (ALJ) ■ One who presides over an administrative agency hearing and has the power to administer oaths, take testimony, rule on questions of evidence, and make determinations of fact.

administrative law ■ The body of law created by administrative agencies (in the form of rules, regulations, orders, and decisions) in order to carry out their duties and responsibilities.

administrative process ■ The procedure used by administrative agencies in the administration of law.

adverse possession ■ The acquisition of title to real property by occupying it openly, without the consent of the owner, for a period of time specified by a state statute. The occupation must be actual, open, notorious, exclusive, and in opposition to all others, including the owner.

after-acquired property ■ Property that is acquired by the debtor after the execution of a security agreement.

agreement ■ A meeting of two or more minds in regard to the terms of a contract; usually broken down into two events—an offer by one party to form a contract and an acceptance of the offer by the person to whom the offer is made.

alien corporation ■ A designation in the United States for a corporation formed in another country but doing business in the United States.

alienation ■ The process of transferring land out of one's possession (thus "alienating" the land from oneself).

alternative dispute resolution (ADR) ■ The resolution of disputes in ways other than those involved in the traditional judicial process. Negotiation, mediation, and arbitration are forms of ADR.

answer ■ Procedurally, a defendant's response to the plaintiff's complaint.

anticipatory repudiation ■ An assertion or action by a party indicating that he or she will not perform an obligation that the party is contractually obligated to perform at a future time.

antitrust law ■ Laws protecting commerce from unlawful restraints.

apparent authority ■ Authority that is only apparent, not real. In agency law, a person may be deemed to have had the power to act as an agent for another party if the other party's manifestations to a third party led the third party to believe that an agency existed when, in fact, it did not.

appraisal right ■ The right of a dissenting shareholder, who objects to an extraordinary transaction of the corporation (such as a merger or a consolidation), to have his or her shares appraised and to be paid the fair value of those shares by the corporation.

appropriation ■ In tort law, the use by one person of another person's name, likeness, or other identifying characteristic without permission and for the benefit of the user.

arbitration ■ The settling of a dispute by submitting it to a disinterested third party (other than a court), who renders a decision that is (most often) legally binding.

arbitration clause ■ A clause in a contract that provides that, in the event of a dispute, the parties will submit the dispute to arbitration rather than litigate the dispute in court.

arson ■ The intentional burning of another's dwelling. Some statutes have expanded this to include any real property regardless of ownership and the destruction of property by other means—for example, by explosion.

articles of incorporation ■ The document filed with the appropriate governmental agency, usually the secretary of state, when a business is incorporated. State statutes usually prescribe what kind of information must be contained in the articles of incorporation.

articles of partnership ■ A written agreement that sets forth each partner's rights and obligations with respect to the partnership.

artisan's lien ■ A possessory lien given to a person who has made improvements and added value to another person's personal property as security for payment for services performed.

assault ■ Any word or action intended to make another person fearful of immediate physical harm; a reasonably believable threat.

assignee ■ A party to whom the rights under a contract are transferred, or assigned.

assignment ■ The act of transferring to another all or part of one's rights arising under a contract.

assignor ■ A party who transfers (assigns) his or her rights under a contract to another party (called the *assignee*).

assumption of risk ■ A doctrine under which a plaintiff may not recover for injuries or damage suffered from risks he or she knows of and has voluntarily assumed.

attachment ■ In a secured transaction, the process by which a secured creditor's interest "attaches" to the property of another (collateral) and the creditor's security interest becomes enforceable.

attempted monopolization ■ Any actions by a firm to eliminate competition and gain monopoly power.

automatic stay ■ In bankruptcy proceedings, the suspension of virtually all litigation and other action by creditors against the debtor or the debtor's property. The stay is effective the moment the debtor files a petition in bankruptcy.

award ■ In litigation, the amount of monetary compensation awarded to a plaintiff in a civil lawsuit as damages. In the context of alternative dispute resolution, the decision rendered by an arbitrator.

B

bailee ■ One to whom goods are entrusted by a bailor. Under the UCC, a party who, by a bill of lading, warehouse receipt, or other document of title, acknowledges possession of goods and/or contracts to deliver them.

bailment ■ A situation in which the personal property of one person (a bailor) is entrusted to another (a bailee), who is obligated to return the bailed property to the bailor or dispose of it as directed.

bailor ■ One who entrusts goods to a bailee.

bait-and-switch advertising ■ Advertising a product at a very attractive price (the "bait") and then, once the consumer is in the store, saying that the advertised product is either not available or is of poor quality. The customer is then urged to purchase ("switched" to) a more expensive item.

bankruptcy court ■ A federal court of limited jurisdiction that handles only bankruptcy proceedings, which are governed by federal bankruptcy law.

battery ■ The unprivileged, intentional touching of another.

bearer instrument ■ Any instrument that is not payable to a specific person, including instruments payable to the "bearer" or to "cash."

beyond a reasonable doubt ■ The standard of proof used in criminal cases. If there is any reasonable doubt that a criminal defendant committed the crime with which she or he has been charged, then the verdict must be "not guilty."

bilateral contract ■ A type of contract that arises when a promise is given in exchange for a return promise.

Bill of Rights ■ The first ten amendments to the U.S. Constitution.

binder ■ A written, temporary insurance policy.

binding authority ■ Any source of law that a court must follow when deciding a case. Binding authorities include constitutions, statutes, and regulations that govern the issue being decided, as well as court decisions that are controlling precedents within the jurisdiction.

blue laws ■ State or local laws that prohibit the performance of certain types of commercial activities on a Sunday.

blue sky laws ■ State laws that regulate the offering and sale of securities for the protection of the public.

bona fide occupational qualification (BFOQ) ■ Identifiable characteristics reasonably necessary to the normal operation of a particular business. These characteristics can include gender, national origin, and religion, but not race.

bond ■ A certificate that evidences a corporate (or government) debt. It is a security that involves no ownership interest in the issuing entity.

bond indenture ■ A contract between the issuer of a bond and the bondholder.

bounty payment ■ A reward (payment) given to a person or persons who perform a certain service, such as informing legal authorities of illegal actions.

breach of contract ■ The failure, without legal excuse, of a promisor to perform the obligations of a contract.

brief ■ A formal legal document prepared by a party's attorney (in answer to the appellant's brief) and submitted to an appellate court when a case is appealed. The appellant's brief outlines the facts and issues of the case, the judge's rulings or jury's findings that should be reversed or modified, the applicable law, and the arguments on the client's behalf.

browse-wrap terms ■ Terms and conditions of use that are presented to an Internet user at the time certain products, such as software, are being downloaded but that need not be agreed to (by clicking "I agree," for example) before the user is able to install or use the product.

burglary ■ The unlawful entry or breaking into a building with the intent to commit a felony. (Some state statutes expand this to include the intent to commit any crime.)

business ethics ■ Ethics in a business context; a consensus as to what constitutes right or wrong behavior in the world of business and the application of moral principles to situations that arise in a business setting.

business invitee ■ A person, such as a customer or a client, who is invited onto business premises by the owner of those premises for business purposes.

business judgment rule ■ A rule that immunizes corporate management from liability for actions that result in corporate losses or damages if the actions are undertaken in good faith and are within both the power of the corporation and the authority of management to make.

business necessity ■ A defense to allegations of employment discrimination in which the employer demonstrates that an employment practice that discriminates against members of a protected class is related to job performance.

business tort ■ Wrongful interference with another's business rights.

business trust ■ A form of business organization in which investors (trust beneficiaries) transfer cash or property to trustees in exchange for trust certificates that represent their investment shares. The certificate holders share in the trust's profits but have limited liability.

bylaws ■ A set of governing rules adopted by a corporation or other association.

C

case law ■ The rules of law announced in court decisions. Case law includes the aggregate of reported cases that interpret judicial precedents, statutes, regulations, and constitutional provisions.

cashier's check ■ A check drawn by a bank on itself.

categorical imperative ■ A concept developed by the philosopher Immanuel Kant as an ethical guideline for behavior. In deciding whether an action is right or wrong, or desirable or undesirable, a person should evaluate the action in terms of what would happen if everybody else in the same situation, or category, acted the same way.

causation in fact ■ An act or omission without which an event would not have occurred.

cease-and-desist order ■ An administrative or judicial order prohibiting a person or business firm from conducting activities that an agency or court has deemed illegal.

certificate of deposit (CD) ■ A note issued by a bank in which the bank acknowledges the receipt of funds from a party and promises to repay that amount, with interest, to the party on a certain date.

certification mark ■ A mark used by one or more persons, other than the owner, to certify the region, materials, mode of manufacture, quality, or other characteristic of specific goods or services.

certified check ■ A check that has been accepted in writing by the bank on which it is drawn. Essentially, the bank, by certifying (accepting) the check, promises to pay the check at the time the check is presented.

chattel ■ All forms of personal property.

check ■ A draft drawn by a drawer ordering the drawee bank or financial institution to pay a certain amount to the holder on demand.

choice-of-language clause ■ A clause in a contract designating the official language by which the contract will be interpreted in the event of a future disagreement over the contract's terms.

choice-of-law clause ■ A clause in a contract designating the law (such as the law of a particular state or nation) that will govern the contract.

citation ■ A reference to a publication in which a legal authority—such as a statute or a court decision—or other source can be found.

civil law ■ The branch of law dealing with the definition and enforcement of all private or public rights, as opposed to criminal matters.

civil law system ■ A system of law derived from that of the Roman Empire and based on a code rather than case law; the predominant system of law in the nations of continental Europe and the nations that were once their colonies. In the United States, Louisiana, because of its historical ties to France, has, in part, a civil law system.

clearinghouse ■ A system or place where banks exchange checks and drafts drawn on each other and settle daily balances.

click-on agreement ■ An agreement that arises when a buyer, engaging in a transaction on a computer, indicates assent to be bound by the terms of an offer by clicking on a button that says, for example, "I agree"; sometimes referred to as a *click-on license* or a *click-wrap agreement.*

close corporation ■ A corporation whose shareholders are limited to a small group of persons, often including only family members.

collateral ■ Under Article 9 of the UCC, the property subject to a security interest, including accounts and chattel paper that have been sold.

collateral promise ■ A secondary promise that is ancillary (subsidiary) to a principal transaction or primary contractual relationship, such as a promise made by one person to pay the debts of another if the latter fails to perform. A collateral promise normally must be in writing to be enforceable.

collecting bank ■ Any bank handling an item for collection, except the payor bank.

collective mark ■ A mark used by members of a cooperative, association, union, or other organization to certify the region, materials, mode of manufacture, quality, or other characteristic of specific goods or services.

comity ■ The principle by which one nation defers to and gives effect to the laws and judicial decrees of another nation. This recognition is based primarily on respect.

commerce clause ■ The provision in Article I, Section 8, of the U.S. Constitution that gives Congress the power to regulate interstate commerce.

commercial impracticability ■ A doctrine under which a seller may be excused from performing a contract when (1) a contingency occurs, (2) the contingency's occurrence makes performance impracticable, and (3) the nonoccurrence of the contingency was a basic assumption on which the contract was made. Despite the fact that UCC Section 2–615 expressly frees only sellers under this doctrine, courts have not distinguished between buyers and sellers in applying it.

common law ■ The body of law developed from custom or judicial decisions in English and U.S. courts, not attributable to a legislature.

common stock ■ Shares of ownership in a corporation that give the owner of the stock a proportionate interest in the corporation with regard to control, earnings, and net assets. Shares of common stock are lowest in priority with respect to payment of dividends and distribution of the corporation's assets on dissolution.

community property ■ A form of concurrent ownership of property in which each spouse technically owns an undivided one-half interest in property acquired during the marriage. This form of joint ownership occurs in only ten states and Puerto Rico.

comparative negligence ■ A rule in tort law that reduces the plaintiff's recovery in proportion to the plaintiff's degree of fault, rather than barring recovery completely; used in the majority of states.

compensatory damages ■ A monetary award equivalent to the actual value of injuries or damage sustained by the aggrieved party.

complaint ■ The pleading made by a plaintiff alleging wrongdoing on the part of the defendant; the document that, when filed with a court, initiates a lawsuit.

computer crime ■ Any act that is directed against computers and computer parts, that uses computers as instruments of crime, or that involves computers and constitutes abuse.

concurrent conditions ■ Conditions that must occur or be performed at the same time; they are mutually dependent. No obligations arise until these conditions are simultaneously performed.

concurrent jurisdiction ■ Jurisdiction that exists when two different courts have the power to hear a case. For example, some cases can be heard in a federal or a state court.

concurrent ownership ■ Joint ownership.

condemnation ■ The process of taking private property for public use through the government's power of eminent domain.

condition precedent ■ In a contractual agreement, a condition that must be met before a party's promise becomes absolute.

condition subsequent ■ A condition in a contract that, if not fulfilled, operates to terminate a party's absolute promise to perform.

condition ■ A qualification, provision, or clause in a contractual agreement, the occurrence or nonoccurrence of which creates, suspends, or terminates the obligations of the contracting parties.

confiscation ■ A government's taking of a privately owned business or personal property without a proper public purpose or an award of just compensation.

confusion ■ The mixing together of goods belonging to two or more owners so that the separately owned goods cannot be identified.

consent ■ Voluntary agreement to a proposition or an act of another; a concurrence of wills.

consequential damages ■ Special damages that compensate for a loss that does not directly or immediately result from the breach (for example, lost profits). For the plaintiff to collect consequential damages, they must have been reasonably foreseeable at the time the breach or injury occurred.

consideration ■ Generally, the value given in return for a promise; involves two elements—the giving of something of legally sufficient value and a bargained-for exchange. The consideration must result in a detriment to the promisee or a benefit to the promisor.

consignment ■ A transaction in which an owner of goods (the consignor) delivers the goods to another (the consignee) for the consignee to sell. The consignee pays the consignor only for the goods that are sold by the consignee.

consolidation ■ A contractual and statutory process in which two or more corporations join to become a completely new corporation. The original corporations cease to exist, and the new corporation acquires all their assets and liabilities.

constitutional law ■ The body of law derived from the U.S. Constitution and the constitutions of the various states.

constructive delivery ■ An act equivalent to the actual, physical delivery of property that cannot be physically delivered because of difficulty or impossibility. For example, the transfer of a key to a safe constructively delivers the contents of the safe.

constructive discharge ■ A termination of employment brought about by making the employee's working conditions so intolerable that the employee reasonably feels compelled to leave.

constructive eviction ■ A form of eviction that occurs when a landlord fails to perform adequately any of the duties (such as providing heat in the winter) required by the lease, thereby making the tenant's further use and enjoyment of the property exceedingly difficult or impossible.

consumer-debtor ■ An individual whose debts are primarily consumer debts (debts for purchases made primarily for personal, family, or household use).

continuation statement ■ A statement that, if filed within six months prior to the expiration date of the original financing statement, continues the perfection of the original security interest for another five years. The perfection of a security interest can be continued in the same manner indefinitely.

contract ■ An agreement that can be enforced in court; formed by two or more competent parties who agree, for consideration, to perform or to refrain from performing some legal act now or in the future.

contractual capacity ■ The threshold mental capacity required by law for a party who enters into a contract to be bound by that contract.

contributory negligence ■ A rule in tort law that completely bars the plaintiff from recovering any damages if the damage suffered is partly the plaintiff's own fault; used in a minority of states.

conversion ■ Wrongfully taking or retaining possession of an individual's personal property and placing it in the service of another.

conveyance ■ The transfer of title to land from one person to another by deed; a document (such as a deed) by which an interest in land is transferred from one person to another.

"cooling-off" laws ■ Laws that allow buyers a period of time, such as three days, in which to cancel door-to-door sales contracts.

cooperative ■ An association, which may or may not be incorporated, that is organized to provide an economic service to its members.

copyright ■ The exclusive right of an author or originator of a literary or artistic production to publish, print, or sell that production for a statutory period of time. A copyright has the same monopolistic nature as a patent or trademark, but it differs in that it applies exclusively to works of art, literature, and other works of authorship (including computer programs).

corporate governance ■ A set of policies or procedures affecting the way a corporation is directed or controlled.

corporate social responsibility ■ The idea that corporations can and should act ethically and be accountable to society for their actions.

corporation ■ A legal entity formed in compliance with statutory requirements. The entity is distinct from its shareholder-owners.

correspondent bank ■ A bank in which another bank has an account (and vice versa) for the purpose of facilitating fund transfers.

cost-benefit analysis ■ A decision-making technique that involves weighing the costs of a given action against the benefits of that action.

counteradvertising ■ New advertising that is undertaken pursuant to a Federal Trade Commission order for the purpose of correcting earlier false claims that were made about a product.

counterclaim ■ A claim made by a defendant in a civil lawsuit against the plaintiff. In effect, the defendant is suing the plaintiff.

counteroffer ■ An offeree's response to an offer in which the offeree rejects the original offer and at the same time makes a new offer.

covenant not to compete ■ A contractual promise of one party to refrain from conducting business similar to that of another party for a certain period of time and within a specified geographic area. Courts commonly enforce such covenants if they are reasonable in terms of time and geographic area and are part of, or supplemental to, a contract for the sale of a business or an employment contract.

covenant not to sue ■ An agreement to substitute a contractual obligation for some other type of legal action based on a valid claim.

cover ■ Under the UCC, a remedy that allows the buyer or lessee, on the seller's or lessor's breach, to purchase the goods, in good faith and within a reasonable time, from another seller or lessor and substitute them for the goods due under the contract. If the cost of cover exceeds the cost of the contract goods, the breaching seller or lessor will be liable to the buyer or lessee for the difference, plus incidental and consequential damages.

cram-down provision ■ A provision of the Bankruptcy Code that allows a court to confirm a debtor's Chapter 11 reorganization plan even though only one class of creditors has accepted it. To exercise the court's right under this provision, the court must demonstrate that the plan does not discriminate unfairly against any creditors and is fair and equitable.

crime ■ A wrong against society proclaimed in a statute and, if committed, punishable by society through fines and/or imprisonment—and, in some cases, death.

criminal law ■ Law that defines and governs actions that constitute crimes. Generally, criminal law has to do with wrongful actions committed against society for which society demands redress.

cure ■ The right of a party who tenders nonconforming performance to correct that performance within the contract period [UCC 2–508(1)].

cyber crime ■ A crime that occurs online, in the virtual community of the Internet, as opposed to the physical world.

cyber mark ■ A trademark in cyberspace.

cyber tort ■ A tort committed in cyberspace.

cyberlaw ■ An informal term used to refer to all laws governing electronic communications and transactions, particularly those conducted via the Internet.

cybernotary ■ A legally recognized authority that can certify the validity of digital signatures.

cybersquatting ■ The act of registering a domain name that is the same as, or confusingly similar to, the trademark of another and then offering to sell that domain name back to the trademark owner.

cyberterrorist ■ A hacker whose purpose is to exploit a target computer for a serious impact, such as corrupting a program to sabotage a business.

D

damages ■ Money sought as a remedy for a breach of contract or a tortious action.

debtor ■ Under Article 9 of the UCC, any party who owes payment or performance of a secured obligation, whether or not the party actually owns or has rights in the collateral.

debtor in possession (DIP) ■ In Chapter 11 bankruptcy proceedings, a debtor who is allowed to continue in possession of the estate in property (the business) and to continue business operations.

deceptive advertising ■ Advertising that misleads consumers, either by making unjustified claims concerning a product's performance or by omitting a material fact concerning the product's composition or performance.

deed ■ A document by which title to property (usually real property) is passed.

defamation ■ Anything published or publicly spoken that causes injury to another's good name, reputation, or character.

default ■ Failure to observe a promise or discharge an obligation; commonly used to refer to failure to pay a debt when it is due.

defendant ■ One against whom a lawsuit is brought; the accused person in a criminal proceeding.

defense ■ A reason offered and alleged by a defendant in an action or suit as to why the plaintiff should not recover or establish what she or he seeks.

deficiency judgment ■ A judgment against a debtor for the amount of a debt remaining unpaid after the collateral has been repossessed and sold.

delegatee ■ A party to whom contractual obligations are transferred, or delegated.

delegation of duties ■ The act of transferring to another all or part of one's duties arising under a contract.

delegator ■ A party who transfers (delegates) her or his obligations under a contract to another party (called the *delegatee*).

depositary bank ■ The first bank to receive a check for payment.

deposition ■ The testimony of a party to a lawsuit or a witness taken under oath before a trial.

destination contract ■ A contract for the sale of goods in which the seller is required or authorized to ship the goods by carrier and tender delivery of the goods at a particular destination. The seller assumes liability for any losses or damage to the goods until they are tendered at the destination specified in the contract.

digital cash ■ Funds contained on computer software, in the form of secure programs stored on microchips and on other computer devices.

disaffirmance ■ The legal avoidance, or setting aside, of a contractual obligation.

discharge ■ The termination of an obligation. In contract law, discharge occurs when the parties have fully performed their contractual obligations or when events, conduct of the parties, or operation of law releases the parties from performance. In bankruptcy proceedings, the extinction of the debtor's dischargeable debts, thereby relieving the debtor of the obligation to pay the debts.

disclosed principal ■ A principal whose identity is known to a third party at the time the agent makes a contract with the third party.

discovery ■ A phase in the litigation process during which the opposing parties may obtain information from each other and from third parties prior to trial.

disparagement of property ■ An economically injurious falsehood made about another's product or property; a general term for torts that are more specifically referred to as *slander of quality* or *slander of title*.

disparate-impact discrimination ■ A form of employment discrimination that results from certain employer practices or procedures that, although not discriminatory on their face, have a discriminatory effect.

disparate-treatment discrimination ■ A form of employment discrimination that results when an employer intentionally discriminates against employees who are members of protected classes.

dissolution ■ The formal disbanding of a partnership or a corporation. Dissolution of a corporation can take place by (1) an act of the state legislature, (2) agreement of the shareholders and the board of directors, (3) the expiration of a time period stated in the certificate of incorporation, or (4) court order.

distributed network ■ A network that can be used by persons located (distributed) around the country or the globe to share computer files.

distribution agreement ■ A contract between a seller and a distributor of the seller's products setting out the terms and conditions of the distributorship.

diversity of citizenship ■ Under Article III, Section 2, of the U.S. Constitution, a basis for federal district court jurisdiction over a lawsuit between (1) citizens of different states, (2) a foreign country and citizens of a state or of different states, or (3) citizens of a state and citizens or subjects of a foreign country. The amount in controversy must be more than $75,000 before a federal district court can take jurisdiction in such cases.

divestiture ■ The act of selling one or more of a company's divisions or parts, such as a subsidiary or plant; often mandated by the courts in merger or monopolization cases.

dividend ■ A distribution to corporate shareholders of corporate profits or income, disbursed in proportion to the number of shares held.

docket ■ The list of cases entered on a court's calendar and thus scheduled to be heard by the court.

document of title ■ A paper exchanged in the regular course of business that evidences the right to possession of goods (for example, a bill of lading or a warehouse receipt).

domain name ■ The last part of an Internet address, such as "westlaw.edu." The top level (the part of the name to the right of the period) indicates the type of entity that operates the site ("edu" is an abbreviation for "educational"). The second level (the part of the name to the left of the period) is chosen by the entity.

domestic corporation ■ In a given state, a corporation that does business in, and is organized under the law of, that state.

dominion ■ Ownership rights in property, including the right to possess and control the property.

double jeopardy ■ A situation occurring when a person is tried twice for the same criminal offense; prohibited by the Fifth Amendment to the U.S. Constitution.

draft ■ Any instrument drawn on a drawee that orders the drawee to pay a certain sum of money, usually to a third party (the payee), on demand or at a definite future time.

dram shop act ■ A state statute that imposes liability on the owners of bars and taverns, as well as those who serve alcoholic drinks to the public, for injuries resulting from accidents caused by intoxicated persons when the sellers or servers of alcoholic drinks contributed to the intoxication.

drawee ■ The party that is ordered to pay a draft or check. With a check, a bank or a financial institution is always the drawee.

drawer ■ The party that initiates a draft (such as a check), thereby ordering the drawee to pay.

due process clause ■ The provisions in the Fifth and Fourteenth Amendments to the Constitution that guarantee that no person shall be deprived of life, liberty, or property without due process of law. Similar clauses are found in most state constitutions.

dumping ■ The selling of goods in a foreign country at a price below the price charged for the same goods in the domestic market.

duress ■ Unlawful pressure brought to bear on a person, causing the person to perform an act that she or he would not otherwise perform.

duty of care ■ The duty of all persons, as established by tort law, to exercise a reasonable amount of care in their dealings with others. Failure to exercise due care, which is normally determined by the reasonable person standard, constitutes the tort of negligence.

E

e-agent ■ A computer program that by electronic or other automated means can independently initiate an action or respond to electronic messages or data without review by an individual.

easement ■ A nonpossessory right to use another's property in a manner established by either express or implied agreement.

e-contract ■ A contract that is formed electronically.

e-evidence ■ Evidence that consists of computer-generated or electronically recorded information, including e-mail, voice mail, spreadsheets, word-processing documents, and other data.

electronic fund transfer (EFT) ■ A transfer of funds with the use of an electronic terminal, a telephone, a computer, or magnetic tape.

emancipation ■ In regard to minors, the act of being freed from parental control; occurs when a child's parent or legal guardian relinquishes the legal right to exercise control over the child. Normally, a minor who leaves home to support himself or herself is considered emancipated.

embezzlement ■ The fraudulent appropriation of funds or other property by a person to whom the funds or property has been entrusted.

eminent domain ■ The power of a government to take land from private citizens for public use on the payment of just compensation.

e-money ■ Prepaid funds recorded on a computer or a card (such as a smart card or a stored-value card).

employment at will ■ A common law doctrine under which either party may terminate an employment relationship at any time for any reason, unless a contract specifies otherwise.

employment contract ■ A contract between an employer and an employee in which the terms and conditions of employment are stated.

employment discrimination ■ Treating employees or job applicants unequally on the basis of race, color, national origin, religion, gender, age, or disability; prohibited by federal statutes.

enabling legislation ■ A statute enacted by Congress that authorizes the creation of an administrative agency and specifies the name, composition, purpose, and powers of the agency being created.

entrapment ■ In criminal law, a defense in which the defendant claims that he or she was induced by a public official—usually an undercover agent or police officer—to commit a crime that he or she would otherwise not have committed.

entrepreneur ■ One who initiates and assumes the financial risk of a new business enterprise and undertakes to provide or control its management.

environmental impact statement (EIS) ■ A statement required by the National Environmental Policy Act for any major federal action that will significantly affect the quality of the environment. The statement must analyze the action's impact on the environment and explore alternative actions that might be taken.

equal dignity rule ■ In most states, a rule stating that express authority given to an agent must be in writing if the contract to be made on behalf of the principal is required to be in writing.

equal protection clause ■ The provision in the Fourteenth Amendment to the Constitution that guarantees that no state will "deny to any person within its jurisdiction the equal protection of the laws." This clause mandates that the state governments must treat similarly situated individuals in a similar manner.

equitable principles and maxims ■ General propositions or principles of law that have to do with fairness (equity).

e-signature ■ As defined by the Uniform Electronic Transactions Act, "an electronic sound, symbol, or process attached to or logically associated with a record and executed or adopted by a person with the intent to sign the record."

establishment clause ■ The provision in the First Amendment to the U.S. Constitution that prohibits the government from establishing any state-sponsored religion or enacting any law that promotes religion or favors one religion over another.

estate in property ■ In bankruptcy proceedings, all of the debtor's interests in property currently held, wherever located, together with certain jointly owned property, property transferred in transactions voidable by the trustee, proceeds and profits from the property of the estate, and certain property interests to which the debtor becomes entitled within 180 days after filing for bankruptcy.

estopped ■ Barred, impeded, or precluded.

estray statute ■ A statute defining finders' rights in property when the true owners are unknown.

ethical reasoning ■ A reasoning process in which an individual links his or her moral convictions or ethical standards to the particular situation at hand.

ethics ■ Moral principles and values applied to social behavior.

eviction ■ A landlord's act of depriving a tenant of possession of the leased premises.

exclusionary rule ■ In criminal procedure, a rule under which any evidence that is obtained in violation of the accused's constitutional rights guaranteed by the Fourth, Fifth, and Sixth Amendments, as well as any evidence derived from illegally obtained evidence, will not be admissible in court.

exclusive distributorship ■ A distributorship in which the seller and the distributor of the seller's products agree that the distributor will distribute only the seller's products.

exclusive jurisdiction ■ Jurisdiction that exists when a case can be heard only in a particular court or type of court.

exclusive-dealing contract ■ An agreement under which a seller forbids a buyer to purchase products from the seller's competitors.

exculpatory clause ■ A clause that releases a contractual party from liability in the event of monetary or physical injury, no matter who is at fault.

executed contract ■ A contract that has been fully performed by both parties.

execution ■ An action to carry into effect the directions in a court decree or judgment.

executive agency ■ An administrative agency within the executive branch of government. At the federal level, executive agencies are those within the cabinet departments.

executory contract ■ A contract that has not as yet been fully performed.

export ■ The sale of goods and services by domestic firms to buyers located in other countries.

express contract ■ A contract in which the terms of the agreement are stated in words, oral or written.

express warranty ■ A seller's or lessor's oral or written promise or affirmation of fact, ancillary to an underlying sales or lease agreement, as to the quality, description, or performance of the goods being sold or leased.

expropriation ■ The seizure by a government of a privately owned business or personal property for a proper public purpose and with just compensation.

F

federal form of government ■ A system of government in which the states form a union and the sovereign power is divided between the central government and the member states.

federal question ■ A question that pertains to the U.S. Constitution, acts of Congress, or treaties. A federal question provides a basis for federal jurisdiction.

federal reserve system ■ A network of twelve district banks and related branches located around the country and headed by the Federal Reserve Board of Governors. Most banks in the United States have Federal Reserve accounts.

fee simple absolute ■ An ownership interest in land in which the owner has the greatest possible aggregation of rights, privileges, and power. Ownership in fee simple absolute is limited absolutely to a person and her or his heirs.

fee simple ■ An absolute form of property ownership entitling the property owner to use, possess, or dispose of the property as he or she chooses during his or her lifetime. On death, the interest in the property descends to the owner's heirs.

felony ■ A crime—such as arson, murder, rape, or robbery—that carries the most severe sanctions, ranging from one year in a state or federal prison to the death penalty.

fictitious payee ■ A payee on a negotiable instrument whom the maker or drawer does not intend to have an interest in the instrument. Indorsements by fictitious payees are treated as authorized indorsements under Article 3 of the UCC.

fiduciary ■ As a noun, a person having a duty created by his or her undertaking to act primarily for another's benefit in matters connected with the undertaking. As an adjective, a relationship founded on trust and confidence.

filtering software ■ A computer program that is designed to block access to certain Web sites based on their content. The software prevents the retrieval of a site whose URL or key words are on a list within the program.

financing statement ■ A document prepared by a secured creditor, and filed with the appropriate state or local official, to give notice to the public that the creditor has a security interest in collateral belonging to the debtor named in the statement. The financing statement must contain the names and addresses of both the debtor and the secured party and must describe the collateral by type or item.

firm offer ■ An offer (by a merchant) that is irrevocable without the necessity of consideration for a stated period of time or, if no definite period is stated, for a reasonable time (neither period to exceed three months). A firm offer by a merchant must be in writing and must be signed by the offeror.

fixed-term tenancy ■ A type of tenancy under which property is leased for a specified period of time, such as a month, a year, or a period of years; also called a *tenancy for years*.

fixture ■ A thing that was once personal property but has become attached to real property in such a way that it takes on the characteristics of real property and becomes part of that real property.

floating lien ■ A security interest in proceeds, after-acquired property, or collateral subject to future advances by the secured party (or all three); a security interest in collateral that is retained even when the collateral changes in character, classification, or location.

forbearance ■ The act of refraining from an action that one has a legal right to undertake.

force majeure **clause** ■ A provision in a contract stipulating that certain unforeseen events—such as war, political upheavals, or acts of God—will excuse a party from liability for nonperformance of contractual obligations.

foreign corporation ■ In a given state, a corporation that does business in the state without being incorporated therein.

foreign exchange market ■ A worldwide system in which foreign currencies are bought and sold.

forgery ■ The fraudulent making or altering of any writing in a way that changes the legal rights and liabilities of another.

formal contract ■ A contract that by law requires a specific form, such as being executed under seal, for its validity.

forum-selection clause ■ A provision in a contract designating the court, jurisdiction, or tribunal that will decide any disputes arising under the contract.

franchise ■ Any arrangement in which the owner of a trademark, trade name, or copyright licenses another to use that trademark, trade name, or copyright in the selling of goods or services.

franchisee ■ One receiving a license to use another's (the franchisor's) trademark, trade name, or copyright in the sale of goods and services.

franchisor ■ One licensing another (the franchisee) to use the owner's trademark, trade name, or copyright in the selling of goods or services.

fraudulent misrepresentation ■ Any misrepresentation, either by misstatement or by omission of a material fact, knowingly made with the intention of deceiving another and on which a reasonable person would and does rely to his or her detriment.

free exercise clause ■ The provision in the First Amendment to the U.S. Constitution that prohibits the government from interfering with people's religious practices or forms of worship.

frustration of purpose ■ A court-created doctrine under which a party to a contract will be relieved of her or his duty to perform when the objective purpose for performance no longer exists (due to reasons beyond that party's control).

G

garnishment ■ A legal process used by a creditor to collect a debt by seizing property of the debtor (such as wages) that is being held by a third party (such as the debtor's employer).

general partner ■ In a limited partnership, a partner who assumes responsibility for the management of the partnership and liability for all partnership debts.

gift ■ Any voluntary transfer of property made without consideration, past or present.

gift *causa mortis* ■ A gift made in contemplation of death. If the donor does not die of that ailment, the gift is revoked.

gift *inter vivos* ■ A gift made during one's lifetime and not in contemplation of imminent death, in contrast to a gift *causa mortis*.

Good Samaritan Statute ■ A state statute stipulating that persons who provide emergency services to, or rescue, someone in peril cannot be sued for negligence, unless they act recklessly, thereby causing further harm.

group boycott ■ The refusal by a group of competitors to deal with a particular person or firm; prohibited by the Sherman Act.

guarantor ■ A person who agrees to satisfy the debt of another (the debtor) only after the principal debtor defaults. Thus, a guarantor's liability is secondary.

H

hacker ■ A person who uses one computer to break into another. Professional computer programmers refer to such persons as "crackers."

holder ■ Any person in possession of an instrument drawn, issued, or indorsed to him or her, to his or her order, to bearer, or in blank.

holder in due course (HDC) ■ A holder who acquires a negotiable instrument for value; in good faith; and without notice that the instrument is overdue, that it has been dishonored, that any person has a defense against it or a claim to it, or that the instrument contains unauthorized signatures, has been altered, or is so irregular or incomplete as to call into question its authenticity.

holding company ■ A company whose business activity is holding shares in another company.

homestead exemption ■ A law permitting a debtor to retain the family home, either in its entirety or up to a specified dollar amount, free from the claims of unsecured creditors or trustees in bankruptcy.

horizontal merger ■ A merger between two firms that are competing in the same marketplace.

horizontal restraint ■ Any agreement that in some way restrains competition between rival firms competing in the same market.

I

identification ■ In a sale of goods, the express designation of the goods provided for in the contract.

implied warranty ■ A warranty that arises by law because of the circumstances of a sale, rather than by the seller's express promise.

implied warranty of fitness for a particular purpose ■ A warranty that goods sold or leased are fit for a particular purpose. The warranty arises when any seller or lessor knows the particular purpose for which a buyer or lessee will use the goods and knows that the buyer or lessee is relying on the skill and judgment of the seller or lessor to select suitable goods.

implied warranty of habitability ■ An implied promise by a landlord that rented residential premises are fit for human habitation—that is, in a condition that is safe and suitable for people to live there.

implied warranty of merchantability ■ A warranty that goods being sold or leased are reasonably fit for the general purpose for which they are sold or leased, are properly packaged and labeled, and are of proper quality. The warranty automatically arises in every sale or lease of goods made by a merchant who deals in goods of the kind sold or leased.

implied-in-fact contract ■ A contract formed in whole or in part from the conduct of the parties (as opposed to an express contract).

impossibility of performance ■ A doctrine under which a party to a contract is relieved of her or his duty to perform when performance becomes objectively impossible or totally impracticable (through no fault of either party).

imposter ■ One who, by use of the mails, Internet, telephone, or personal appearance, induces a maker or drawer to issue an instrument in the name of an impersonated payee. Indorsements by imposters are treated as authorized indorsements under Article 3 of the UCC.

incidental beneficiary ■ A third party who incidentally benefits from a contract but whose benefit was not the reason the contract was formed. An incidental beneficiary has no rights in a contract and cannot sue to have the contract enforced.

incidental damages ■ All costs resulting from a breach of contract, including all reasonable expenses incurred because of the breach.

independent contractor ■ One who works for, and receives payment from, an employer but whose working conditions and methods are not controlled by the employer. An independent contractor is not an employee but may be an agent.

independent regulatory agency ■ An administrative agency that is not considered part of the government's executive branch and is not subject to the authority of the president. Independent agency officials cannot be removed without cause.

indorsement ■ A signature placed on an instrument for the purpose of transferring one's ownership rights in the instrument.

informal contract ■ A contract that does not require a specified form or formality to be valid.

insider trading ■ The purchase or sale of securities on the basis of information that has not been made available to the public.

insurable interest ■ An interest either in a person's life or well-being or in property that is sufficiently substantial that insuring against injury to (or the death of) the person or against damage to the property does not amount to a mere wagering (betting) contract. In regard to the sale or lease of goods, a property interest in the goods that is sufficiently substantial to permit a party to insure against damage to the goods.

insurance ■ A contract in which, for a stipulated consideration, one party agrees to compensate the other for loss on a specific subject by a specified peril.

intangible property ■ Property that cannot be seen or touched but exists only conceptually, such as corporate stocks and bonds, patents and copyrights, and ordinary contract rights. Article 2 of the UCC does not govern intangible property.

intellectual property ■ Property resulting from intellectual, creative processes.

intended beneficiary ■ A third party for whose benefit a contract is formed. An intended beneficiary can sue the promisor if such a contract is breached.

intentional tort ■ A wrongful act knowingly committed.

intermediary bank ■ Any bank to which an item is transferred in the course of collection, except the depositary or payor bank.

international law ■ The law that governs relations among nations. International customs and treaties are important sources of international law.

interrogatories ■ A series of written questions for which written answers are prepared by a party to a lawsuit, usually with the assistance of the party's attorney, and then signed under oath.

investment company ■ A company that acts on behalf of many smaller shareholders/owners by buying a large portfolio of securities and professionally managing that portfolio.

J

joint stock company ■ A hybrid form of business organization that combines characteristics of a corporation and a partnership. Usually, the joint stock company is regarded as a partnership for tax and other legally related purposes.

joint tenancy ■ The joint ownership of property by two or more co-owners in which each co-owner owns an undivided portion of the property. On the death of one of the joint tenants, his or her interest automatically passes to the surviving joint tenant(s).

joint venture ■ A joint undertaking of a specific commercial enterprise by an association of persons. A joint venture is normally not a legal entity and is treated like a partnership for federal income tax purposes.

judicial review ■ The process by which a court decides on the constitutionality of legislative enactments and actions of the executive branch.

jurisdiction ■ The authority of a court to hear and decide a specific case.

jurisprudence ■ The science or philosophy of law.

justiciable controversy ■ A controversy that is not hypothetical or academic but real and substantial; a requirement that must be satisfied before a court will hear a case.

L

larceny ■ The wrongful taking and carrying away of another person's personal property with the intent to permanently deprive the owner of the property. Some states classify larceny as either grand or petit, depending on the property's value.

law ■ A body of enforceable rules governing relationships among individuals and between individuals and their society.

lease ■ Under Article 2A of the UCC, a transfer of the right to possess and use goods for a period of time in exchange for payment.

lease agreement ■ In regard to the lease of goods, an agreement in which one person (the lessor) agrees to transfer the right to the possession and use of property to another person (the lessee) in exchange for rental payments.

leasehold estate ■ An estate in realty held by a tenant under a lease. In every leasehold estate, the tenant has a qualified right to possess and/or use the land.

lessee ■ A person who acquires the right to the possession and use of another's goods in exchange for rental payments.

lessor ■ A person who transfers the right to the possession and use of goods to another in exchange for rental payments.

letter of credit ■ A written instrument, usually issued by a bank on behalf of a customer or other person, in which the issuer promises to honor drafts or other demands for payment by third persons in accordance with the terms of the instrument.

levy ■ The obtaining of funds by legal process through the seizure and sale of nonsecured property, usually done after a writ of execution has been issued.

libel ■ Defamation in writing or other form having the quality of permanence (such as a digital recording).

license ■ In the context of intellectual property law, an agreement permitting the use of a trademark, copyright, patent, or trade secret for certain limited purposes. In regard to property law, a revocable right or privilege of a person to come onto another person's land.

lien ■ An encumbrance on a property to satisfy a debt or protect a claim for payment of a debt.

life estate ■ An interest in land that exists only for the duration of the life of some person, usually the holder of the estate.

limited liability company (LLC) ■ A hybrid form of business enterprise that offers the limited liability of the corporation but the tax advantages of a partnership.

limited liability partnership (LLP) ■ A business organizational form that is similar to the LLC but that is designed more for professionals who normally do business as partners in a partnership. The LLP is a pass-through entity for tax purposes, like the general partnership, but it limits the personal liability of the partners.

limited partner ■ In a limited partnership, a partner who contributes capital to the partnership but has no right to participate in the management and operation of the business. The limited partner assumes no liability for partnership debts beyond the capital contributed.

limited partnership ■ A partnership consisting of one or more general partners (who manage the business and are liable to the full extent of their personal assets for debts of the partnership) and one or more limited partners (who contribute only assets and are liable only up to the amount contributed by them).

liquidated damages ■ An amount, stipulated in a contract, that the parties to the contract believe to be a reasonable estimation of the damages that will occur in the event of a breach.

liquidated debt ■ A debt for which the amount has been ascertained, fixed, agreed on, settled, or exactly determined. If the amount of the debt is in dispute, the debt is considered unliquidated.

liquidation ■ The sale of all of the nonexempt assets of a debtor and the distribution of the proceeds to the debtor's creditors. Chapter 7 of the Bankruptcy Code provides for liquidation bankruptcy proceedings.

litigation ■ The process of resolving a dispute through the court system.

long arm statute ■ A state statute that permits a state to obtain personal jurisdiction over nonresident defendants. A defendant must have certain "minimum contacts" with that state for the statute to apply.

lost property ■ Property with which the owner has involuntarily parted and then cannot find or recover.

M

mailbox rule ■ A rule providing that an acceptance of an offer becomes effective on dispatch (on being placed in an official mailbox), if mail is, expressly or impliedly, an authorized means of communication of acceptance to the offeror.

maker ■ One who promises to pay a fixed amount of money to the holder of a promissory note or a certificate of deposit (CD).

malpractice ■ Professional misconduct or the lack of the requisite degree of skill as a professional. Negligence—the failure to exercise due care—on the part of a professional, such as a physician, is commonly referred to as malpractice.

market concentration ■ The degree to which a small number of firms control a large percentage share of a relevant market; determined by calculating the percentages held by the largest firms in that market.

market power ■ The power of a firm to control the market price of its product. A monopoly has the greatest degree of market power.

market-share liability ■ A theory of sharing liability among all firms that manufactured and distributed a particular product during a certain period of time. This form of liability sharing is used only in some jurisdictions and only when the true source of the harmful product is unidentifiable.

market-share test ■ The primary measure of monopoly power. A firm's market share is the percentage of a market that the firm controls.

mechanic's lien ■ A statutory lien on the real property of another, created to ensure payment for work performed and materials furnished in the repair or improvement of real property, such as a building.

mediation ■ A method of settling disputes outside of court by using the services of a neutral third party, who acts as a communicating agent between the parties and assists them in negotiating a settlement.

mens rea ■ Mental state, or intent. A wrongful mental state is as necessary as a wrongful act to establish criminal liability. What constitutes a mental state varies according to the wrongful action. Thus, for murder, the *mens rea* is the intent to take a life.

merchant ■ A person who is engaged in the purchase and sale of goods. Under the UCC, a person who deals in goods of the kind involved in the sales contract or who holds herself or himself out as having skill or knowledge peculiar to the practices or goods being purchased or sold [UCC 2–104].

merger ■ A contractual and statutory process in which one corporation (the surviving corporation) acquires all of the assets and liabilities of another corporation (the merged corporation). The shareholders of the merged corporation either are paid for their shares or receive shares in the surviving corporation.

minimum wage ■ The lowest wage, either by government regulation or union contract, that an employer may pay an hourly worker.

mirror image rule ■ A common law rule that requires that the terms of the offeree's acceptance adhere exactly to the terms of the offeror's offer for a valid contract to be formed.

misdemeanor ■ A lesser crime than a felony, punishable by a fine or incarceration in jail for up to one year.

mislaid property ■ Property with which the owner has voluntarily parted and then cannot find or recover.

mitigation of damages ■ A rule requiring a plaintiff to do whatever is reasonable to minimize the damages caused by the defendant.

money laundering ■ Falsely reporting income that has been obtained through criminal activity as income obtained through a legitimate business enterprise—in effect, "laundering" the "dirty money."

monopolization ■ The possession of monopoly power in the relevant market and the willful acquisition or maintenance of that power, as distinguished from growth or development as a consequence of a superior product, business acumen, or historic accident.

monopoly ■ A term generally used to describe a market in which there is a single seller or a very limited number of sellers.

monopoly power ■ The ability of a monopoly to dictate what takes place in a given market.

moral minimum ■ The minimum degree of ethical behavior expected of a business firm, which is usually defined as compliance with the law.

mortgage ■ A written instrument giving a creditor an interest in (lien on) the debtor's real property as security for payment of a debt.

mortgagee ■ Under a mortgage agreement, the creditor who takes a security interest in the debtor's property.

mortgagor ■ Under a mortgage agreement, the debtor who gives the creditor a security interest in the debtor's property in return for a mortgage loan.

motion for a directed verdict ■ In a jury trial, a motion for the judge to take the decision out of the hands of the jury and to direct a verdict for the party who filed the motion on the ground that the other party has not produced sufficient evidence to support her or his claim.

motion for a new trial ■ A motion asserting that the trial was so fundamentally flawed (because of error, newly discovered evidence, prejudice, or another reason) that a new trial is necessary to prevent a miscarriage of justice.

motion for judgment N.O.V. ■ A motion requesting the court to grant judgment in favor of the party making the motion on the ground that the jury's verdict against him or her was unreasonable and erroneous.

motion for judgment on the pleadings ■ A motion by either party to a lawsuit at the close of the pleadings requesting the court to decide the issue solely on the pleadings without proceeding to trial. The motion will be granted only if no facts are in dispute.

motion for summary judgment ■ A motion requesting the court to enter a judgment without proceeding to trial. The motion can be based on evidence outside the pleadings and will be granted only if no facts are in dispute.

motion to dismiss ■ A pleading in which a defendant asserts that the plaintiff's claim fails to state a cause of action (that is, has no basis in law) or that there are other grounds on which a suit should be dismissed. Although the defendant normally is the party requesting a dismissal, either the plaintiff or the court can also make a motion to dismiss the case.

mutual fund ■ A specific type of investment company that continually buys or sells to investors shares of ownership in a portfolio.

N

national law ■ Law that pertains to a particular nation (as opposed to international law).

necessaries ■ Necessities required for life, such as food, shelter, clothing, and medical attention; may include whatever is believed to be necessary to maintain a person's standard of living or financial and social status.

negligence ■ The failure to exercise the standard of care that a reasonable person would exercise in similar circumstances.

negligence *per se* ■ An action or failure to act in violation of a statutory requirement.

negotiable instrument ■ A signed writing that contains an unconditional promise or order to pay an exact sum on demand or at a specified future time to a specific person or order, or to bearer.

negotiation ■ The transfer of an instrument in such form that the transferee (the person to whom the instrument is transferred) becomes a holder. As a form of alternative dispute resolution, a process in which parties attempt to settle their dispute informally, with or without attorneys to represent them.

nominal damages ■ A small monetary award (often one dollar) granted to a plaintiff when no actual damage was suffered.

nonpossessory interest ■ In the context of real property, an interest in land that does not include any right to possess the property.

normal trade relations (NTR) status ■ A status granted in an international treaty by a provision stating that the citizens of the contracting nations may enjoy the privileges accorded by either party to citizens of its NTR nations. Generally, this status is designed to establish equality of international treatment.

notary public ■ A public official authorized to attest to the authenticity of signatures.

novation ■ The substitution, by agreement, of a new contract for an old one, with the rights under the old one being terminated. Typically, novation involves the substitution of a new person who is responsible for the contract and the removal of the original partyrights and duties under the contract.

O

obligee ■ One to whom an obligation is owed.

obligor ■ One who owes an obligation to another.

offer ■ A promise or commitment to perform or refrain from performing some specified act in the future.

offeree ■ A person to whom an offer is made.

offeror ■ A person who makes an offer.

online dispute resolution (ODR) ■ The resolution of disputes with the assistance of organizations that offer dispute-resolution services via the Internet.

operating agreement ■ In a limited liability company, an agreement in which the members set forth the details of how the business will be managed and operated. State statutes typically give the members wide latitude in deciding for themselves the rules that will govern their organization.

option contract ■ A contract under which the offeror cannot revoke the offer for a stipulated time period. During this period, the offeree can accept or reject the offer without fear that the offer will be made to another person. The offeree must give consideration for the option (the irrevocable offer) to be enforceable.

order for relief ■ A court's grant of assistance to a debtor. In bankruptcy proceedings, the order relieves the debtor of the immediate obligation to pay the debts listed in the bankruptcy petition.

order instrument ■ A negotiable instrument that is payable "to the order of an identified person" or "to an identified person or order."

ordinance ■ A regulation enacted by a city or county legislative body that becomes part of that state's statutory law.

output contract ■ An agreement in which a seller agrees to sell and a buyer agrees to buy all or up to a stated amount of what the seller produces.

overdraft ■ A check that is paid by the bank when the checking account on which the check is written contains insufficient funds to cover the check.

P

partially disclosed principal ■ A principal whose identity is unknown by a third party, but the third party knows that the agent is or may be acting for a principal at the time the agent and the third party form a contract.

partnering agreement ■ An agreement between a seller and a buyer who frequently do business with each other concerning the terms and conditions that will apply to all subsequently formed electronic contracts.

partnership ■ An agreement by two or more persons to carry on, as co-owners, a business for profit.

past consideration ■ An act that takes place before the contract is made and that ordinarily, by itself, cannot be consideration for a later promise to pay for the act.

patent ■ A government grant that gives an inventor the exclusive right or privilege to make, use, or sell his or her invention for a limited time period.

payee ■ A person to whom an instrument is made payable.

payor bank ■ The bank on which a check is drawn (the drawee bank).

peer-to-peer (P2P) networking ■ The sharing of resources (such as files, hard drives, and processing styles) among multiple computers without necessarily requiring a central network server.

penalty ■ A contractual clause that states that a certain amount of monetary damages will be paid in the event of a future default or breach of contract. The damages are a punishment for a default and not a measure of compensation for the contract's breach. The agreement as to the penalty amount will not be enforced, and recovery will be limited to actual damages.

per se **violation** ■ A type of anticompetitive agreement that is considered to be so injurious to the public that there is no need to determine whether it actually injures market competition. Rather, it is in itself (*per se*) a violation of the Sherman Act.

perfection ■ The legal process by which secured parties protect themselves against the claims of third parties who may wish to have their debts satisfied out of the same collateral; usually accomplished by filing a financing statement with the appropriate government official.

performance ■ In contract law, the fulfillment of one's duties arising under a contract with another; the normal way of discharging one's contractual obligations.

periodic tenancy ■ A lease interest in land for an indefinite period involving payment of rent at fixed intervals, such as week to week, month to month, or year to year.

personal defenses ■ Defenses that can be used to avoid payment to an ordinary holder of a negotiable instrument but not a holder in due course (HDC) or a holder with the rights of an HDC.

personal property ■ Property that is movable; any property that is not real property.

persuasive authority ■ Any legal authority or source of law that a court may look to for guidance but on which it need not rely in making its decision. Persuasive authorities include cases from other jurisdictions and secondary sources of law.

petition in bankruptcy ■ The document that is filed with a bankruptcy court to initiate bankruptcy proceedings. The official forms required for a petition in bankruptcy must be completed accurately, sworn to under oath, and signed by the debtor.

petty offense ■ In criminal law, the least serious kind of criminal offense, such as a traffic or building-code violation.

plaintiff ■ One who initiates a lawsuit.

plea bargaining ■ The process by which a criminal defendant and the prosecutor in a criminal case work out a mutually satisfactory disposition of the case, subject to court approval; usually involves the defendant's pleading guilty to a lesser offense in return for a lighter sentence.

pleadings ■ Statements made by the plaintiff and the defendant in a lawsuit that detail the facts, charges, and defenses involved in the litigation. The complaint and answer are part of the pleadings.

pledge ■ A common law security device (retained in Article 9 of the UCC) in which personal property is transferred into the possession of the creditor as security for the payment of a debt and retained by the creditor until the debt is paid.

police powers ■ Powers possessed by the states as part of their inherent sovereignty. These powers may be exercised to protect or promote the public order, health, safety, morals, and general welfare.

policy ■ In insurance law, a contract between the insurer and the insured in which, for a stipulated consideration, the insurer agrees to compensate the insured for loss on a specific subject by a specified peril.

potentially responsible party (PRP) ■ A party liable for the costs of cleaning up a hazardous waste–disposal site under the Comprehensive Environmental Response, Compensation, and Liability Act (CERCLA). Any person who generated the hazardous waste, transported it, owned or operated the waste site at the time of disposal, or owns or operates the site at the present time may be responsible for some or all of the clean-up costs.

power of attorney ■ A written document, which is usually notarized, authorizing another to act as one's agent; can be special (permitting the agent to do specified acts only) or general (permitting the agent to transact all business for the principal).

precedent ■ A court decision that furnishes an example or authority for deciding subsequent cases involving identical or similar facts.

predatory behavior ■ Business behavior that is undertaken with the intention of unlawfully driving competitors out of the market.

predatory pricing ■ The pricing of a product below cost with the intent to drive competitors out of the market.

predominant-factor test ■ A test courts use to determine whether a contract is primarily for the sale of goods or for the sale of services.

preemption ■ A doctrine under which certain federal laws preempt, or take precedence over, conflicting state or local laws.

preemptive right ■ A right held by shareholders that entitles them to purchase newly issued shares of a corporation's stock, equal in percentage to shares already held, before the stock is offered to any outside buyers. Preemptive rights enable shareholders to maintain their proportionate ownership and voice in the corporation.

preferred stock ■ Classes of stock that have priority over common stock as to both payment of dividends and distribution of assets on the corporation's dissolution.

premium ■ In insurance law, the price paid by the insured for insurance protection for a specified period of time.

prenuptial agreement ■ An agreement made before marriage that defines each partner's ownership rights in the other partner's property. Prenuptial agreements must be in writing to be enforceable.

presentment ■ The act of presenting an instrument to the party liable on the instrument to collect payment. Presentment also occurs when a person presents an instrument to a drawee for a required acceptance.

presentment warranties ■ Implied warranties, made by any person who presents an instrument for payment or acceptance, that (1) the person obtaining payment or acceptance is entitled to enforce the instrument or is authorized to obtain payment or acceptance on behalf of a person who is entitled to enforce the instrument, (2) the instrument has not been altered, and (3) the person obtaining payment or acceptance has no knowledge that the signature of the drawer of the instrument is unauthorized.

price discrimination ■ Setting prices in such a way that two competing buyers pay two different prices for an identical product or service.

price-fixing agreement ■ An agreement between competitors to fix the prices of products or services at a certain level.

prima facie **case** ■ A case in which the plaintiff has produced sufficient evidence of his or her claim that the case can go to a jury; a case in which the evidence compels a decision for the plaintiff if the defendant produces no affirmative defense or evidence to disprove the plaintiff's assertion.

primary source of law ■ A document that establishes the law on a particular issue, such as a constitution, a statute, an administrative rule, or a court decision.

principle of rights ■ The principle that human beings have certain fundamental rights (to life, freedom, and the pursuit of happiness, for example). Those who adhere to this "rights theory" believe that a key factor in determining whether a business decision is ethical is how that decision affects the rights of various groups. These groups include the firm's owners, its employees, the consumers of its products or services, its suppliers, the community in which it does business, and society as a whole.

privilege ■ A legal right, exemption, or immunity granted to a person or a class of persons. In the context of defamation, an absolute privilege immunizes the person making the statements from a lawsuit, regardless of whether the statements were malicious.

privity of contract ■ The relationship that exists between the promisor and the promisee of a contract.

probable cause ■ Reasonable grounds for believing that a person should be arrested or searched.

probate court ■ A state court of limited jurisdiction that conducts proceedings relating to the settlement of a deceased person's estate.

procedural law ■ Law that establishes the methods of enforcing the rights established by substantive law.

proceeds ■ Under Article 9 of the UCC, whatever is received when collateral is sold or otherwise disposed of, such as by exchange.

product liability ■ The legal liability of manufacturers, sellers, and lessors of goods to consumers, users, and bystanders for injuries or damages that are caused by the goods.

profit ■ In real property law, the right to enter onto and remove things from the property of another (for example, the right to enter onto a person's land and remove sand and gravel).

promise ■ An assertion that something either will or will not happen in the future.

promisee ■ A person to whom a promise is made.

promisor ■ A person who makes a promise.

promissory estoppel ■ A doctrine that applies when a promisor makes a clear and definite promise on which the promisee justifiably relies. Such a promise is binding if justice will be better served by the enforcement of the promise.

promissory note ■ A written promise made by one person (the maker) to pay a fixed amount of money to another person (the payee or a subsequent holder) on demand or on a specified date.

property ■ Legally protected rights and interests in anything with an ascertainable value that is subject to ownership.

prospectus ■ A written document, required by securities laws, that describes the security being sold, the financial operations of the issuing corporation, and the investment or risk attaching to the security. It is designed to provide sufficient information to enable investors to evaluate the risk involved in purchasing the security.

protected class ■ A group of persons protected by specific laws because of the group's defining characteristics. Under laws prohibiting employment discrimination, these characteristics include race, color, religion, national origin, gender, age, and disability.

proximate cause ■ Legal cause; exists when the connection between an act and an injury is strong enough to justify imposing liability.

proxy ■ In corporate law, a written agreement between a stockholder and another party in which the stockholder authorizes the other party to vote the stockholder's shares in a certain manner.

puffery ■ A salesperson's often exaggerated claims concerning the quality of property offered for sale. Such claims involve opinions rather than facts and are not considered to be legally binding promises or warranties.

punitive damages ■ Monetary damages that may be awarded to a plaintiff to punish the defendant and deter future similar conduct.

purchase-money security interest (PMSI) ■ A security interest that arises when a seller or lender extends credit for part or all of the purchase price of goods purchased by a buyer.

Q

quasi contract ■ A fictional contract imposed on the parties by a court in the interests of fairness and justice; usually imposed to avoid the unjust enrichment of one party at the expense of another.

question of fact ■ In a lawsuit, an issue that involves only disputed facts, and not what the law is on a given point. Questions of fact are decided by the jury in a jury trial (by the judge if there is no jury).

question of law ■ In a lawsuit, an issue involving the application or interpretation of a law. Only a judge, not a jury, can rule on questions of law.

quitclaim deed ■ A deed intended to pass any title, interest, or claim that the grantor may have in the property without warranting that such title is valid. A quitclaim deed offers the least amount of protection against defects in the title.

quorum ■ The number of members of a decision-making body that must be present before business can be transacted.

quota ■ A set limit on the amount of goods that can be imported.

R

ratification ■ The act of accepting and giving legal force to an obligation that previously was not enforceable.

real property ■ Land and everything attached to it, such as trees and buildings.

reasonable person standard ■ The standard of behavior expected of a hypothetical "reasonable person"; the standard against which negligence is measured and that must be observed to avoid liability for negligence.

receiver ■ In a corporate dissolution, a court-appointed person who winds up corporate affairs and liquidates corporate assets.

record ■ According to the Uniform Electronic Transactions Act, information that is either inscribed on a tangible medium or stored in an electronic or other medium and is retrievable.

recording statutes ■ Statutes that allow deeds, mortgages, and other real property transactions to be recorded so as to provide notice to future purchasers or creditors of an existing claim on the property.

red herring prospectus ■ A preliminary prospectus that can be distributed to potential investors after the registration statement (for a securities offering) has been filed with the Securities and Exchange Commission. The name derives from the red legend printed across the prospectus stating that the registration has been filed but has not become effective.

reformation ■ A court-ordered correction of a written contract so that it reflects the true intentions of the parties.

Regulation E ■ A set of rules issued by the Federal Reserve System's Board of Governors to protect users of elecronic fund transfer systems.

Regulation Z ■ A set of rules promulgated by the Federal Reserve Board of Governors to implement the provisions of the Truth-in-Lending Act.

release ■ A contract in which one party forfeits the right to pursue a legal claim against the other party.

remedy ■ The relief given to an innocent party to enforce a right or compensate for the violation of a right.

replevin ■ An action to recover identified goods in the hands of a party who is wrongfully withholding them from the other party. Under the UCC, this remedy is usually available only if the buyer or lessee is unable to cover.

reply ■ Procedurally, a plaintiff's response to a defendant's answer.

requirements contract ■ An agreement in which a buyer agrees to purchase and the seller agrees to sell all or up to a stated amount of what the buyer needs or requires.

res ipsa loquitur ■ A doctrine under which negligence may be inferred simply because an event occurred, if it is the type of event that would not occur in the absence of negligence. Literally, the term means "the facts speak for themselves."

resale price maintenance agreement ■ An agreement between a manufacturer and a retailer in which the manufacturer specifies what the retail prices of its products must be.

rescission ■ A remedy whereby a contract is canceled and the parties are returned to the positions they occupied before the contract was made; may be effected through the mutual consent of the parties, by the parties' conduct, or by court decree.

respondeat superior ■ Latin for "let the master respond." A doctrine under which a principal or an employer is held liable for the wrongful acts committed by agents or employees while acting within the course and scope of their agency or employment.

restitution ■ An equitable remedy under which a person is restored to his or her original position prior to loss or injury, or placed in the position he or she would have been in had the breach not occurred.

retained earnings ■ The portion of a corporation's profits that has not been paid out as dividends to shareholders.

revocation ■ In contract law, the withdrawal of an offer by an offeror. Unless the offer is irrevocable, it can be revoked at any time prior to acceptance without liability.

right of first refusal ■ The right to purchase personal or real property—such as corporate shares or real estate—before the property is offered for sale to others.

risk ■ A prediction concerning potential loss based on known and unknown factors.

risk management ■ Planning that is undertaken to protect one's interest should some event threaten to undermine its security. In the context of insurance, risk management involves transferring certain risks from the insured to the insurance company.

robbery ■ The act of forcefully and unlawfully taking personal property of any value from another. Force or intimidation is usually necessary for an act of theft to be considered robbery.

rule of four ■ A rule of the United States Supreme Court under which the Court will not issue a writ of *certiorari* unless at least four justices approve of the decision to issue the writ.

rule of reason ■ A test by which a court balances the positive effects (such as economic efficiency) of an agreement against its potentially anticompetitive effects. In antitrust litigation, many practices are analyzed under the rule of reason.

rulemaking ■ The process undertaken by an administrative agency when formally adopting a new regulation or amending an old one. Rulemaking involves notifying the public of a proposed rule or change and receiving and considering the public's comments.

S

S corporation ■ A close business corporation that has met certain requirements set out in the Internal Revenue Code and thus qualifies for special income tax treatment. Essentially, an S corporation is taxed the same as a partnership, but its owners enjoy the privilege of limited liability.

sale ■ The passing of title to property from the seller to the buyer for a price.

sale on approval ■ A type of conditional sale in which the buyer may take the goods on a trial basis. The sale becomes absolute only when the buyer approves of (or is satisfied with) the goods being sold.

sale or return ■ A type of conditional sale in which title and possession pass from the seller to the buyer, but the buyer retains the option to return the goods during a specified period even though the goods conform to the contract.

sales contract ■ A contract for the sale of goods under which the ownership of goods is transferred from a seller to a buyer for a price.

scienter ■ Knowledge by the misrepresenting party that material facts have been falsely represented or omitted with an intent to deceive.

search warrant ■ An order granted by a public authority, such as a judge, that authorizes law enforcement personnel to search a particular premise or property.

seasonably ■ Within a specified time period or, if no period is specified, within a reasonable time.

SEC Rule 10b-5 ■ A rule of the Securities and Exchange Commission that makes it unlawful, in connection with the purchase or sale of any security, to make any untrue statement of a material fact or to omit a material fact if such omission causes the statement to be misleading.

secondary source of law ■ A publication that summarizes or interprets the law, such as a legal encyclopedia, a legal treatise, or an article in a law review.

secured party ■ A lender, seller, or any other person in whose favor there is a security interest, including a person to whom accounts or chattel paper have been sold.

secured transaction ■ Any transaction in which the payment of a debt is guaranteed, or secured, by personal property owned by the debtor or in which the debtor has a legal interest.

securities ■ Generally, stock certificates, bonds, notes, debentures, warrants, or other documents given as evidence of an ownership interest in a corporation or as a promise of repayment by a corporation.

security agreement ■ An agreement that creates or provides for a security interest between the debtor and a secured party.

security interest ■ Any interest in personal property or fixtures that secures payment or performance of an obligation.

security ■ Generally, a stock certificate, bond, note, debenture, warrant, or other document or record evidencing an ownership interest in a corporation or a promise to repay a corporation's debt.

self-defense ■ The legally recognized privilege to protect oneself or one's property against injury by another. The privilege of self-defense usually applies only to acts that are reasonably necessary to protect oneself, one's property, or another person.

self-incrimination ■ The giving of testimony that may subject the testifier to criminal prosecution. The Fifth Amendment to the Constitution protects against self-incrimination by providing that no person "shall be compelled in any criminal case to be a witness against himself."

seniority system ■ In regard to employment relationships, a system in which those who have worked longest for the employer are first in line for promotions, salary increases, and other benefits. They are also the last to be laid off if the workforce must be reduced.

service mark ■ A mark used in the sale or the advertising of services to distinguish the services of one person from those of others. Titles, character names, and other distinctive features of radio and television programs may be registered as service marks.

sexual harassment ■ In the employment context, the demanding of sexual favors in return for job promotions or other benefits, or language or conduct that is so sexually offensive that it creates a hostile working environment.

shareholder's derivative suit ■ A suit brought by a shareholder to enforce a corporate cause of action against a third person.

shelter principle ■ The principle that the holder of a negotiable instrument who cannot qualify as a holder in due course (HDC), but who derives his or her title through an HDC, acquires the rights of an HDC.

shipment contract ■ A contract for the sale of goods in which the seller is required or authorized to ship the goods by carrier. The seller assumes liability for any losses or damage to the goods until they are delivered to the carrier.

short-swing profits ■ Profits earned within six months of a trade. Section 12 of the 1934 Securities Exchange Act requires company insiders to return any profits made from the purchase and sale of company stock if both transactions occur within a six-month period.

shrink-wrap agreement ■ An agreement whose terms are expressed in a document located inside a box in which goods (usually software) are packaged; sometimes called a *shrink-wrap license.*

slander ■ Defamation in oral form.

slander of quality (Trade Libel) ■ The publication of false information about another's product, alleging that it is not what its seller claims.

slander of title ■ The publication of a statement that denies or casts doubt on another's legal ownership of any property, causing financial loss to that property's owner.

small claims court ■ A special court in which parties may litigate small claims (such as $5,000 or less). Attorneys are not required in small claims courts and, in some states, are not allowed to represent the parties.

smart card ■ A card containing a microprocessor that permits storage of funds via security programming, can communicate with other computers, and does not require online authorization for fund transfers.

sole proprietorship ■ The simplest form of business organization, in which the owner is the business. The owner reports business income on his or her personal income tax return and is legally responsible for all debts and obligations incurred by the business.

sovereign immunity ■ A doctrine that immunizes foreign nations from the jurisdiction of U.S. courts when certain conditions are satisfied.

spam ■ Bulk, unsolicited ("junk") e-mail.

special warranty deed ■ A deed in which the grantor warrants only that the grantor or seller held good title during his or her ownership of the property and does not warrant that there were no defects of title when the property was held by previous owners.

specific performance ■ An equitable remedy requiring exactly the performance that was specified; usually granted only when monetary damages would be an inadequate remedy and the subject matter of the contract is unique.

stale check ■ A check, other than a certified check, that is presented for payment more than six months after its date.

standing to sue ■ The requirement that an individual must have a sufficient stake in a controversy before he or she can bring a lawsuit. The plaintiff must demonstrate that he or she has been either injured or threatened with injury.

stare decisis ■ A common law doctrine under which judges are obligated to follow the precedents established in prior decisions.

Statute of Frauds ■ A state statute under which certain types of contracts must be in writing to be enforceable.

statute of limitations ■ A federal or state statute setting the maximum time period during which a certain action can be brought or certain rights enforced.

statute of repose ■ Basically, a statute of limitations that is not dependent on the happening of a cause of action. Statutes of repose generally begin to run at an earlier date and run for a longer period of time than statutes of limitations.

statutory law ■ The body of law enacted by legislative bodies (as opposed to constitutional law, administrative law, or case law).

stock ■ An equity (ownership) interest in a corporation, measured in units of shares.

stock certificate ■ A certificate issued by a corporation evidencing the ownership of a specified number of shares in the corporation.

stock options ■ An agreement that grants the owner the option to buy a given number of shares of stock, usually within a set time period.

stop-payment order ■ An order by a bank customer to his or her bank not to pay or certify a certain check.

stored-value card ■ A card bearing a magnetic strip that holds magnetically encoded data, providing access to stored funds.

strict liability ■ Liability regardless of fault. In tort law, strict liability is imposed on a manufacturer or seller that introduces into commerce a good that is unreasonably dangerous when in a defective condition.

sublease ■ A lease executed by the lessee of real estate to a third person, conveying the same interest that the lessee enjoys but for a shorter term than that held by the lessee.

substantive law ■ Law that defines, describes, regulates, and creates legal rights and obligations.

summary jury trial (SJT) ■ A method of settling disputes, used in many federal courts, in which a trial is held, but the jury's verdict is not binding. The verdict acts only as a guide to both sides in reaching an agreement during the mandatory negotiations that immediately follow the summary jury trial.

summons ■ A document informing a defendant that a legal action has been commenced against him or her and that the defendant must appear in court on a certain date to answer the plaintiff's complaint.

supremacy clause ■ The provision in Article VI of the Constitution that provides that the Constitution, laws, and treaties of the United States are "the supreme Law of the Land." Under this clause, state and local laws that directly conflict with federal law will be rendered invalid.

surety ■ A person, such as a cosigner on a note, who agrees to be primarily responsible for the debt of another.

suretyship ■ An express contract in which a third party to a debtor-creditor relationship (the surety) promises to be primarily responsible for the debtor's obligation.

symbolic speech ■ Nonverbal expressions of beliefs. Symbolic speech, which includes gestures, movements, and articles of clothing, is given substantial protection by the courts.

syndicate ■ An investment group of persons or firms brought together for the purpose of financing a project that they would not or could not undertake ■ independently.

T

takeover ■ The acquisition of control over a corporation through the purchase of a substantial number of the voting shares of the corporation.

taking ■ The taking of private property by the government for public use. The government may not take private property for public use without "just compensation."

tangible property ■ Property that has physical existence and can be distinguished by the senses of touch or sight. A car is tangible property; a patent right is intangible property.

target corporation ■ The corporation to be acquired in a corporate takeover; a corporation whose shareholders receive a tender offer.

tariff ■ A tax on imported goods.

tenancy at sufferance ■ A type of tenancy under which a tenant who, after rightfully being in possession of leased premises, continues (wrongfully) to occupy the property after the lease has terminated. The tenant has no rights to possess the property and occupies it only because the person entitled to evict the tenant has not done so.

tenancy at will ■ A type of tenancy that either party can terminate without notice; usually arises when a tenant who has been under a tenancy for years retains possession, with the landlord's consent, after the tenancy for years has terminated.

tenancy by the entirety ■ The joint ownership of property by a husband and wife. Neither party can transfer her or his interest in the property without the consent of the other.

tenancy in common ■ Co-ownership of property in which each party owns an undivided interest that passes to her or his heirs at death.

tender ■ An unconditional offer to perform an obligation by a person who is ready, willing, and able to do so.

tender offer ■ An offer to purchase made by one company directly to the shareholders of another (target) company; sometimes referred to as a *takeover bid.*

third party beneficiary ■ One for whose benefit a promise is made in a contract but who is not a party to the contract.

tippee ■ A person who receives inside information.

tombstone ad ■ An advertisement, historically in a format resembling a tombstone, of a securities offering. The ad tells potential investors where and how they may obtain a prospectus.

tort ■ A civil wrong not arising from a breach of contract; a breach of a legal duty that proximately causes harm or injury to another.

tortfeasor ■ One who commits a tort.

trade acceptance ■ A draft that is drawn by a seller of goods ordering the buyer to pay a specified sum to the seller, usually at a stated time in the future. The buyer accepts the draft by signing the face of the draft, thus creating an enforceable obligation to pay the draft when it comes due. On a trade acceptance, the seller is both the drawee and the payee.

trade dress ■ The image and overall appearance of a product—for example, the distinctive decor, menu, layout, and style of service of a particular restaurant. Basically, trade dress is subject to the same protection as trademarks.

trade name ■ A term that is used to indicate part or all of a business's name and that is directly related to the business's reputation and goodwill. Trade names are protected under the common law (and under trademark law, if the name is the same as the firm's trademarked product).

trade secrets ■ Information or processes that give a business an advantage over competitors that do not know the information or processes.

trademark ■ A distinctive mark, motto, device, or emblem that a manufacturer stamps, prints, or otherwise affixes to the goods it produces so that they may be identified on the market and their origins made known. Once a trademark is established (under the common law or through registration), the owner is entitled to its exclusive use.

transfer warranties ■ Implied warranties, made by any person who transfers an instrument for consideration to subsequent transferees and holders who take the instrument in good faith, that (1) the transferor is entitled to enforce the instrument; (2) all signatures are authentic and authorized; (3) the instrument has not been altered; (4) the instrument is not subject to a defense or claim of any party that can be asserted against the transferor; and (5) the transferor has no knowledge of any insolvency proceedings against the maker, the acceptor, or the drawer of the instrument.

traveler's check ■ A check that is payable on demand, drawn on or payable through a financial institution (bank), and designated as a traveler's check.

treble damages ■ Damages that, by statute, are three times the amount that the fact finder determines is owed.

trespass to land ■ The entry onto, above, or below the surface of land owned by another without the owner's permission or legal authorization.

trespass to personal property ■ The unlawful taking or harming of another's personal property; interference with another's right to the exclusive possession of his or her personal property.

tying arrangement ■ An agreement between a buyer and a seller in which the buyer of a specific product or service becomes obligated to purchase additional products or services from the seller.

U

U.S. trustee ■ A government official who performs certain administrative tasks that a bankruptcy judge would otherwise have to perform.

unconscionable contract (or unconscionable clause) ■ A contract or clause that is void on the basis of public policy because one party, as a result of disproportionate bargaining power, is forced to accept terms that are unfairly burdensome and that unfairly benefit the dominating party.

underwriter ■ In insurance law, the insurer, or the one assuming a risk in return for the payment of a premium.

undisclosed principal ■ A principal whose identity is unknown by a third person, and the third person has no knowledge that the agent is acting for a principal at the time the agent and the third person form a contract.

unenforceable contract ■ A valid contract rendered unenforceable by some statute or law.

uniform law ■ A model law created by the National Conference of Commissioners on Uniform State Laws and/or the American Law Institute for the states to consider adopting. If the state adopts the law, it becomes statutory law in that state. Each state has the option of adopting or rejecting all or part of a uniform law.

unilateral contract ■ A contract that results when an offer can be accepted only by the offeree's performance.

universal defenses ■ Defenses that are valid against all holders of a negotiable instrument, including holders in due course (HDCs) and holders with the rights of HDCs.

unreasonably dangerous product ■ In product liability law, a product that is defective to the point of threatening a consumer's health and safety. A product will be considered unreasonably dangerous if it is dangerous beyond the expectation of the ordinary consumer or if a less dangerous alternative was economically feasible for the manufacturer, but the manufacturer failed to produce it.

usury ■ Charging an illegal rate of interest.

utilitarianism ■ An approach to ethical reasoning that evaluates behavior in light of the consequences of that behavior for those who will be affected by it, rather than on the basis of any absolute ethical or moral values. In utilitarian reasoning, a "good" decision is one that results in the greatest good for the greatest number of people affected by the decision.

V

valid contract ■ A contract that results when the elements necessary for contract formation (agreement, consideration, legal purpose, and contractual capacity) are present.

venue ■ The geographic district in which a legal action is tried and from which the jury is selected.

vertical merger ■ The acquisition by a company at one level in a marketing chain of a company at a higher or lower level in the chain (such as a company merging with one of its suppliers or retailers).

vertical restraint ■ Any restraint on trade created by agreements between firms at different levels in the manufacturing and distribution process.

vertically integrated firm ■ A firm that carries out two or more functional phases (manufacture, distribution, and retailing, for example) of the chain of production.

vesting ■ The creation of an absolute or unconditional right or power.

vicarious liability ■ Legal responsibility placed on one person for the acts of another; indirect liability imposed on a supervisory party (such as an employer) for the actions of a subordinate (such as an employee) because of the relationship between the two parties.

void contract ■ A contract having no legal force or binding effect.

voidable contract ■ A contract that may be legally avoided (canceled, or annulled) at the option of one or both of the parties.

W

warranty deed ■ A deed in which the grantor assures (warrants to) the grantee that the grantor has title to the property conveyed in the deed, that there are no encumbrances on the property other than what the grantor has represented, and that the grantee will enjoy quiet possession of the property; a deed that provides the greatest amount of protection for the grantee.

wetlands ■ Water-saturated areas of land that are designated by a government agency (such as the Army Corps of Engineers or the Environmental Protection Agency) as protected areas that support wildlife and therefore cannot be filled in or dredged by private contractors or parties without a permit.

whistleblowing ■ An employee's disclosure to government authorities, upper-level managers, or the press that the employer is engaged in unsafe or illegal activities.

white-collar crime ■ Nonviolent crime committed by individuals or corporations to obtain a personal or business advantage.

workers' compensation laws ■ State statutes establishing an administrative procedure for compensating workers' injuries that arise out of—or in the course of—their employment, regardless of fault.

workout ■ An out-of-court agreement between a debtor and creditors in which the parties work out a payment plan or schedule under which the debtor's debts can be discharged.

writ of attachment ■ A court's order, issued prior to a trial to collect a debt, directing the sheriff or other public officer to seize nonexempt property of the debtor. If the creditor prevails at trial, the seized property can be sold to satisfy the judgment.

writ of *certiorari* ■ A writ from a higher court asking the lower court for the record of a case.

writ of execution ■ A court's order, issued after a judgment has been entered against a debtor, directing the sheriff to seize (levy) and sell any of the debtor's nonexempt real or personal property. The proceeds of the sale are used to pay off the judgment, accrued interest, and costs of the sale; any surplus is paid to the debtor.

wrongful discharge ■ An employer's termination of an employee's employment in violation of the law.

Table of Cases

Index

ADAPTING THE LAW TO THE ONLINE ENVIRONMENT

These special features examine cutting-edge cyberlaw issues coming before today's courts.

LANDMARK IN THE LAW

These features discuss seminal cases, statutes, or other legal developments that have had significant effects on business law.